吐鲁番学研究

新疆吐鲁番学研究院◎编

JOURNAL OF THE TURFAN STUDIES
Edited by Academia Turfanica

Essays on The third International Conference on Turfan Studies The Origins and Migrations of Eurasian Nomadic peoples

第三届
吐鲁番学
暨欧亚游牧民族的起源与迁徙
国际学术研讨会论文集

上海古籍出版社

目　录

历史、宗教、语言卷

贺　电

第三届吐鲁番学国际学术研讨会秘书处：

　　今悉第三届吐鲁番学国际学术研讨会在金秋十月的吐鲁番召开，深感欣慰，谨谢大会对我的邀请。我以吐鲁番学学会顾问的名义，热烈祝贺此次国际学术研讨会的隆重召开。

　　吐鲁番学是一门古老而又年轻的学科。说其古老，是因为吐鲁番有人类文明的历史可追溯到三千年以前，宏伟的交河故城和高昌故城那沧桑矗立的残垣断壁，仍旧能想象出当年在丝绸之路上的繁华与昌盛。驼铃声声，商贾穿流。在广袤的吐鲁番盆地留下众多的历史遗迹和文化信息，成为今天我们研究丝路文化有力的佐证。说其年轻，是因为吐鲁番学研究从启蒙至今仅有一百年左右，在历史的长河中，它才初出茅庐。然而，中外学者云集，成果累累，使吐鲁番学一步步走向成熟、走向世界。我深信，此次研讨会必将有益于吐鲁番学学术切磋，互相交流，很好地继承和发扬传统文化。

　　本届盛会，我非常愿意参加，因届时另有活动，难以分身，深感遗憾。

　　我衷心地祝愿，第三届吐鲁番学国际学术研讨会在吐鲁番学的故乡取得圆满成功！

铁木尔·达瓦买提

2008.10.15

贺　词

吐鲁番学研究院：

　　值此第三届吐鲁番学国际学术研讨会隆重召开之际，我谨代表中国敦煌吐鲁番学会及会长季羡林教授，对此次会议的举行表示最热烈的祝贺！

　　前些日子，我们向季老报告：本次会议的举办，在百年吐鲁番学史上应具有里程碑式的重大意义。会议将吐鲁番学真正置于东西方文化交流的大背景之下，涉及诸多学科领域及其交叉、综合、比较研究，进一步开拓了这门学问的深度和广度；会议邀请了为数众多的世界各国著名专家学者与会研讨，并讨论欧亚游牧民族的起源与迁徙，充分展示了举办方的学术眼光与胸怀。季老对此深表赞同并充满了喜悦之情。他期望并坚信此次会议能取得丰硕的成果，大大推进吐鲁番学在世界的发展。他委托我们向与会的新老朋友致以最亲切的问候！祝大会取得圆满成功，祝全体代表在吐鲁番生活愉快、一切顺利！

中国敦煌吐鲁番学会秘书长　柴剑虹

2008 年 10 月 19 日

对吐鲁番学研究的再认识

吴敦夫

新疆维吾尔自治区政协

国人认识吐鲁番,是以其为著名的盆地、火焰山、瓜果葡萄、地处海平面以下,多民族聚居,能歌善舞而入手的。史学界认识吐鲁番,是以其为新疆乃至全国的历史资料的聚宝盆而入手的。由于吐鲁番特殊的地理位置、气候条件、东西方人类的汇聚,留下了大量的历史遗存。随着 20 世纪 80 至 90 年代,《吐鲁番出土文书》的刊布,以及进入 21 世纪后,吐鲁番盆地的巴达木、木纳尔、交河沟西、阿斯塔那及洋海又陆续出土了大量的文物,使国内外的历史学家、考古学家的目光又聚向吐鲁番。无怪乎有人说:"即使比起当年的政治文化中心——长安、洛阳,它在为历史研究者提供珍贵史料方面,也可一争高下。"

历史是研究过去事实的学问,随着时间的逝去,研究者很难掌握全部史实(即使在当代,要掌握某一事件的全部事实,也是很难的),特别是在没有文字记录的情况下,只能根据已掌握的资料,经过整理、研究去接近史实,可以说历史学是一门缺憾的学问。吐鲁番地处西域,远离中原大地,其文物又数遭多国"探险家"的抢掠,至今流散在世界各地。吐鲁番学的故乡在中国,但像敦煌学一样,由于多国"探险队"的考察、盗窃,致使许多珍贵的文物流失异国他乡,使这些学问一开始就带有浓厚的国际性。面对《凉王大沮渠安周造祠功德碑》的拓片,我国史学界先辈们,在震惊之余,纷纷做出努力,利用仅能得到的文物资料对吐鲁番历史进行研究,并取得一定成果。更可喜的是新中国成立以后,中国吐鲁番学的研究,取得了更大的发展。随着 20 世纪下半叶一些国家陆续公布了部分从吐鲁番掠走的古文献,也发表了一些对吐鲁番出土文献的研究成果,丰富了人们对吐鲁番历史的认识,但这毕竟还不是流失文献的全部,尚存一些缺憾。我相信,随着国家以及新疆的综合实力增强,人们对历史学的需求会有新的提高,吐鲁番学的研究也会更加蓬勃地发展。

在新疆广袤的大地上,吐鲁番地区仅仅是一个较小的部分,吐鲁番的历史也只是新疆历史的一个组成部分,也是中国历史的一个组成部分,决不能只站在吐鲁番去研究吐鲁番学,而应该从吐鲁番的实际出发,放在新疆历史、中国历史的大范围中去研究吐鲁番学。在新疆历史研究中,可以称之为"学"的方面还很多,如:龟兹学、于阗学、丝路学等等。所以,在研究吐鲁番学的过程中,应特别注意不能人为地、不适当地缩小或夸大吐鲁番历史地位和作用,使之成为独立的历史单元。因此,吐鲁番学的研究必须在立足吐鲁番的基础上,跳出吐鲁番,站在新疆乃至中国、世界的高度去研究吐鲁番学,则是非常有益的。

对吐鲁番学,在学术界可能有不尽相同的定义。但对吐鲁番学应是古代吐鲁番盆地各种学问的总称,认识则是较为一致的。因此,吐鲁番学内涵的涉及面就应当十分广泛了。吐鲁番学最初之所以有浓厚的国际性,是由于国外列强曾先后组成"探险队"到吐鲁番,对这里的地上、地下的历史文化遗存进行过考察、盗窃,一些人对这些文物进行了整理和研究,发表了专著和论文,取得了一定成果。值得注意的是,在有些文章中,作者站在西方欧洲文化中心论的立场上,歪曲事实,企图在欧洲文化中寻找吐鲁番文化的渊源,或别有所图,为其政治服务。对此,我们在吐鲁番学的研究中,不仅要有专业水平、学术水平较高的专著,还要有一些通俗易懂、雅俗共赏的历史文化普及作品,供广大群众阅读和使用,起到以正视听、潜移默化的作用。

古代的吐鲁番,是一个典型的多民族聚居的地区,也可以看做是一个移民社会。有的专家把吐鲁番的历史分为"四个一千年",是很有道理的。贯穿在"四个一千年"中有一条主线,即不同民族的相互交流和融合。当时的吐鲁番地区,相对其他地区的战乱纷争,保持了较长时间的和平安定,促进了农、牧、商和寺院经济的发展,各民族和睦相处,又进一步促进了各民族的往来和各种外来文明融合交流。正因为如此,才使吐鲁番的文化,既有欧洲、中亚、西亚文化的痕迹,又有中原文化的烙印,形成了五彩缤纷的吐鲁番文化遗产。这恐怕不仅是古代吐鲁番的文化特点,而且也是古丝绸之路重镇的文化特点。

一段时间,人们把敦煌与吐鲁番联系在一起,称之为敦煌吐鲁番学,实际上敦煌学与吐鲁番学有同有异,最大的异处在于敦煌遗存地上的多,吐鲁番遗存地下的多,若不是吐鲁番古堡、古墓的发掘,吐鲁番文书的出土,吐鲁番学恐怕不会有今天的学术地位。因此,如何保护好吐鲁番地上的文物和地下的遗存,以及有计划地发掘一些古堡、古墓,也应是吐鲁番学研究的一个内容。随着发掘的开展,会有更多、更新的东西出现在我们面前。因此,我赞成这样的观点:吐鲁番考古学是吐鲁番学的主要基础。一是,吐鲁番地区有大量的古遗存需要进一步发掘。二是,出土的考古资料需要研究、整理、刊布。三是,考古学专业性很强,原始考古资料并非局外学者都能直接利用。搞好吐鲁番学的研究,必须加强基础工作。对考古资料及吐鲁番学学术史要进一步整理、研究和清理。这里,我想强调一下清理工作,为保证吐鲁番学的研究科学持续地发展,必须对吐鲁番学的学术史进行科学的、全面的系统清理,以防止在研究中走弯路,避免原创性研究减少、重复性研究增多的现象。这在一些学科中是有教训的。

吐鲁番学兴起之初,就带有浓厚的国际性。吐鲁番学发展到现在,取得了如此丰厚的成果,成为20世纪国际显学,其中,不仅包含着我国史学界辛勤的劳动,也有国际史学界的交流的结晶。进入21世纪的今天,可以说,国际性已成为吐鲁番学的特色之一。当然我们不会忘记19世纪下半叶以来的那些抢掠和破坏,但我们是向前看的。我们欢迎对吐鲁番学研究的国际交流和国际合作,这不仅是学术研究发展的需要和规律,而且真诚的国际交流和合作是促进学术研究水平提高、发展的动力之一。今后,吐鲁番学的研究必须进一步加强国际合作与交流,使吐鲁番学不仅是中国的,也是世界的。

吐鲁番学研究院的成立,为吐鲁番学的研究构建了一个学术平台,促进了吐鲁番学研究的发展。特别值得称道的是,吐鲁番文物局暨研究院的同志,克服了许多困难,做了大量工作,取得不少成果,成为名副其实的吐鲁番学研究的组织者和参与者。要使吐鲁番学的研究,不断发展,不断出现新的成果,必须有一支专业知识扎实、学风严谨、甘守寂寞、吃苦耐劳、勇于探索的专家、学者队伍。为使吐鲁番学研究后继有人,必须有目的地大力培养年轻的专家、学者队伍,特别是要让这支队伍能把老一辈的史学家、考古学家的优良作风继承下来,继往开来,为吐鲁番学的研究作出更大的贡献。

以上,仅是个人的一孔之见,不妥之处,请专家、学者和各位同仁批评指正!

吐鲁番盆地青铜时代至初铁器时代与周边地区的文化交流

李 肖

新疆吐鲁番学研究院

一、自然环境简介

吐鲁番地区位于新疆维吾尔自治区东部,地处吐鲁番盆地中间,下辖吐鲁番市、鄯善县、托克逊县。南抵库鲁克山,与巴音郭楞蒙古自治州相邻;北至天山分水岭,与乌鲁木齐、奇台、吉木萨尔等市县毗连。[①]

吐鲁番盆地是新疆东天山中较大的山间盆地。喜马拉雅造山运动以来,这里发生了很大的变动,盆地强烈下沉,大部分降到海平面以下,南部的艾丁湖更低,可达 − 154 米,成为世界上最低的内陆盆地之一。这种地势特殊低降的情况,必然会引起一系列特殊自然现象的发生。首先,这里夏季的气温特别高,全国绝对最高气温(48.1℃)就出现在这里。在吐鲁番县城以西一处沙地上,曾经测得最高温度达82.3℃,这是盆地内最高的地面温度记录。盆地一年的降水量不足 16.6 毫米,而蒸发量却高达 3 003.9 毫米。其次,吐鲁番盆地与天山山地之间的高差很大,引起了气压梯度的增大,加强了北来气流的强度,强烈的风蚀与风积作用造成了盆地里的风蚀地貌。[②]

吐鲁番盆地位于东天山山脉的南坡,降水稀少导致气候干燥,自然环境以戈壁荒漠为主,仅有面积不大的绿洲,夏季不适于放牧牲畜,但由于其紧邻天山北坡的森林——草原地区,冬季却是牲畜和游牧人温暖舒适的越冬地。反之,吐鲁番盆地夏季充裕的光热资源使其成为古代新疆发展绿洲农业和园艺业较早的地区。所以从青铜时代起,吐鲁番盆地的古代文化在与天山以北乃至阿勒泰山周边、南西伯利亚地区的游牧文化有着极为密切的关系,同时,来自西方的大、小麦种植技术和栽培葡萄的园艺技术与来自中原的粟类种植技术在此汇集,产生了极具特色的以游牧业为主、农业和园艺业为辅的混合文化。

虽然吐鲁番盆地位于欧亚草原游牧文化的边缘地区,但由于其特殊的地理位置和极端干燥气候环境,使得在湿润的草原地区难以保存的有机质文物,如尸体、皮革制品、毛织品、食物等得以大量地、完整地保存下来,其种类和数量远远超出了阿勒泰山区和南西伯利亚冰室墓中出土的同类遗物,使这里成为一个巨大的天然博物馆。对近几十年考古发掘成果的整理研究,证明吐鲁番盆地这一时期的考古文化在研究欧亚草原游牧文明和早期东西方文化交流领域占有非常重要的地位。

对吐鲁番盆地青铜时代至初铁器时代的考古研究已持续了近一个世纪,通过对交河故城沟北墓地、[③]

---

① 吐鲁番市地名委员会编:《吐鲁番市地名图志》(内部刊物),1990 年,第 1 页。
② 新疆综合考察队地貌组编著:《新疆地貌》,科学出版社,1978 年,第 106 页。
③ 黄文弼:《吐鲁番考古记》,科学出版社,1954 年。

阿拉沟墓地、①艾丁湖墓地、②喀格恰克墓地、③三个桥墓地、④苏贝希遗址及墓地、⑤洋海墓地、⑥交河沟北墓地、⑦交河沟西墓地、⑧胜金店墓地⑨等发掘资料的研究证明,从公元前1000年中期开始,在吐鲁番盆地居住着的后来以"姑师(车师)"命名的古代民族已进入铁器时代,过着农牧结合的生活。姑师(车师)人世居吐鲁番盆地,交河城及其附近一带是他们活动的中心区域,据史书记载,至迟在公元前126年以前,姑师已经立国。《史记·大宛列传》曰:"楼兰、姑师邑有城郭,临盐泽。"到了公元前108年(汉武帝元封三年),姑师在汉朝军事力量的打击下一分为八,在《汉书·西域传》中则出现"车师前国,王治交河城,河水分流绕城下"的记载,指明交河城为车师前国的都城。

通过对胜金店墓地出土的遗物,特别是汉锦、漆器残片等具有断代意义的中原文物的初步分析,基本上可以认定该墓地的上、下限在战国时期到西汉早期,社会发展处于早期铁器时代,是当地土著文化的墓葬遗存。

二、考古发掘简介

胜金店墓地位于新疆吐鲁番市胜金乡胜金店村南郊、胜金店水库与火焰山之间的坡地上,西距吐鲁番市40公里(图一)。在为配合312国道吐鲁番——鄯善段复线工程建设而进行前期考古调查时墓地始

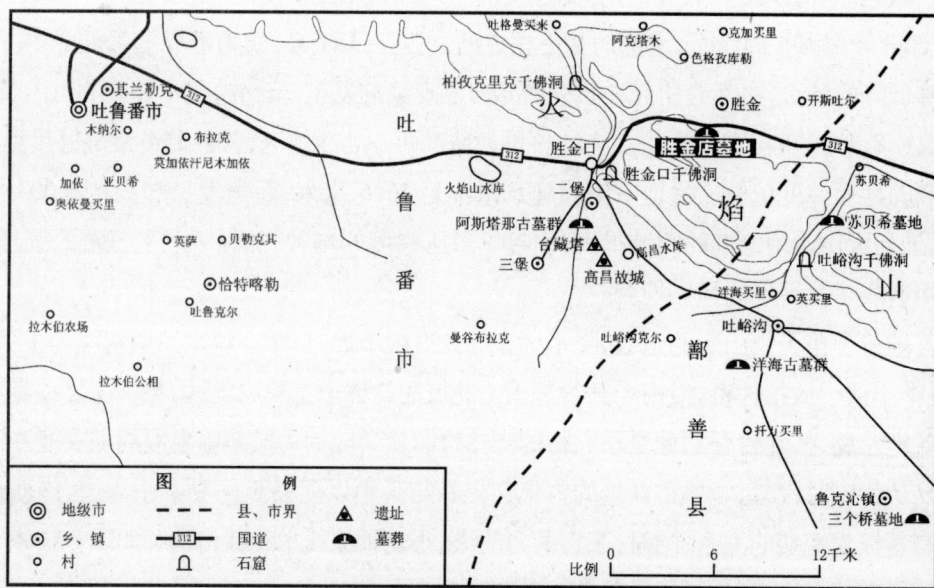

图一　胜金店墓地地理位置示意图

① 新疆社会科学院考古研究所:《阿拉沟竖穴木椁墓发掘简报》,《文物》1981年第1期。
② 新疆维吾尔自治区博物馆、吐鲁番地区文管所:《新疆吐鲁番艾丁湖古墓葬》,《考古》1982年第4期。
③ 吐鲁番地区文管所:《托可逊县喀格恰克古墓群清理简报》,《考古》1987年第7期。
④ 新疆文物考古研究所、吐鲁番地区文管所:《新疆鄯善县三个桥古墓葬抢救清理简报》,《新疆文物》1997年第2期。
⑤ 新疆文物考古研究所、吐鲁番地区文管所:《鄯善苏贝希遗址和墓地发掘简报》,《考古》2002年第6期。
⑥ 新疆文物考古研究所、吐鲁番地区文物局:《鄯善县洋海一号墓地发掘简报》,《鄯善县洋海二号墓地发掘简报》,《鄯善县洋海三号墓地发掘简报》,《新疆文物》2004年第1期。
⑦ 联合国教科文组织驻中国代表处、新疆维吾尔自治区文物局、新疆文物考古研究所等:《交河故城——1993、1994年度考古发掘报告》,第二章,东方出版社,1998年。
⑧ 新疆文物考古研究所:《1996年吐鲁番交河故城沟西墓地汉晋墓葬发掘简报》,《考古》1997年第9期。
⑨ 新疆吐鲁番学研究院考古研究所2007、2008年度对因312国道升级改造而遭破坏的胜金店墓地进行了抢救性清理,共清理墓葬31座,发掘资料正在整理之中。

被发现。2006 年 5 月,由自治区文物考古研究所在公路北侧进行了首次考古发掘,考古资料尚未公布。2007 年修路施工时挖掘机在路边山坡上取土,又挖出了人骨和器物,靠近公路南侧的墓葬又被发现。同时,吐鲁番学研究院的文物考古人员在此又进行了调查。

从 2007 年 10 月至 2008 年 4 月共发掘墓葬 31 座(图二),出土了一批有价值的文物。

1. 墓葬概述

墓地南面为火焰山,北面被旧的 312 国道工程切断,墓地西侧有冲沟,东面有当地村民用于风干葡萄的晾房。由于历年洪水冲刷所夹带的泥沙在墓地上积滞,致使所有的墓葬都埋在淤积层下,墓地地表无任何标志。采用探方法取去 50～80 cm 表土层后,墓口方才露出。由于地面有斜坡,雨水来不及下渗即流开,而且每次雨水过后都会留下新的保护层,所以有些墓葬保存特别好。

现存墓地呈椭圆形,南北长 42 米,东西宽 23 米。墓葬分布均匀,排列有序,间隔 3～8 米。未见打破、叠压现象。少量成人墓旁有儿童祔葬墓。

胜金店墓地的墓葬型制有三种,基本涵盖了吐鲁番盆地史前墓葬的所有型制。第一种为长方形竖穴二层台墓(A 型)。二层台设在长方形的两长边上,距墓口深 0.6～0.8 米,在二层台上横排圆木

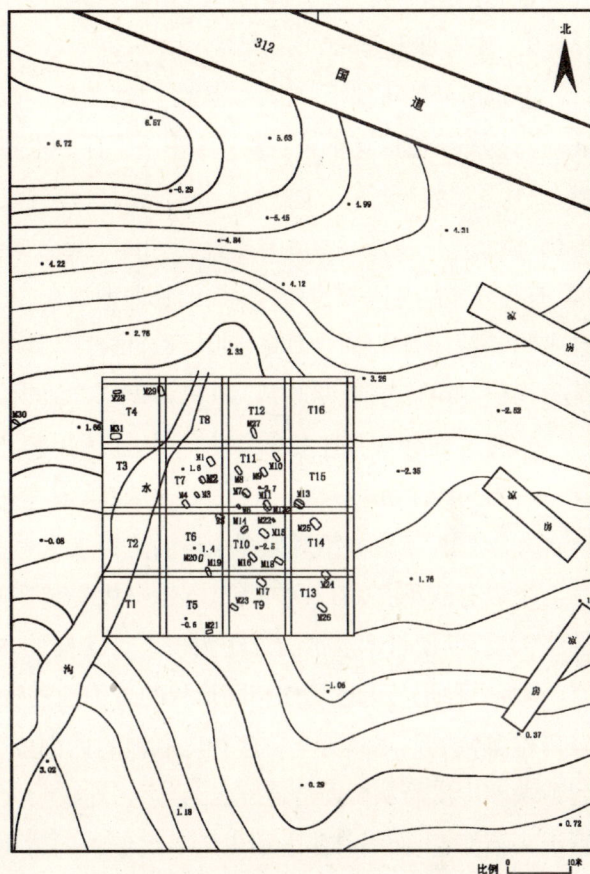

图二　胜金店墓地发掘探方和墓葬分布图

或厚木板,尽可能严密地封堵墓室口,继而在横木上覆盖毛毡或用芦苇编织的帘垫。再在毛毡或帘垫上覆盖植物秸秆,所用植物有黑果枸杞、芦苇、糜子草、香蒲、麦秸等,其上再用黏土压实。第二种数量最多,为长方形竖穴土坑墓(B 型)。直壁,墓口与墓底长、宽相仿。与上一种不同的是篷盖物直接搭建在墓口上。第三种为竖穴偏室墓(C 型),这时的竖穴成为墓道,竖穴上口窄长,正底部顺长边留台阶,再向对面掏进成墓室。横切面呈靴形。在墓室口从台阶下向上斜搭成排的木梁,上面铺毛毡或草席,再覆盖植物秸秆,填土。大多数 C 型墓还用同样的方式在墓道上口即地面上重复搭建棚木,铺芦苇编织的帘子,覆盖植物秸秆,用黏土和成泥后镇压。

葬具主要是长方形四腿木制尸床。长方形边框中有两条横撑,四角各有一只短腿,它们之间都用榫头卯眼接合。上面铺排细木棍或柳树条用皮绳绑紧,有些尸床上还安放一个与其同样大小的长方形拱券顶床罩,床罩用牛皮条和细柳枝捆扎而成,罩上覆盖毛毡。用这样木床的墓在整个墓地群中相对较少,大多数墓葬仅仅在墓底铺细沙和植物茎秆。

该墓地主要为单人葬和双人葬,少有三人以上的合葬。双人合葬大多为夫妻合葬墓,也有少量同性合葬墓。墓葬中除了早期被盗扰的现象外,还有一部分墓葬尸骨凌乱,应是墓室中早期进水使尸骨移位。另外发现用皮质衣服包裹的散乱骨骼,这种现象可能是二次葬。被扰乱的墓葬中还发现两层骨架叠压的现象,这是多次打开墓室葬人所形成。葬式主要有仰身直肢和仰身屈肢,侧身屈肢葬极少。仰身屈肢葬

很有特点,上肢微内曲,双手搭在腹部。下肢上屈,双膝外侧各用一根粗芦苇秆支撑住双腿。

随葬器物中的陶器和木质容器多放于人的顶头位置,而长杆木器如弓箭等都顺放在人体右侧,个别弓袋箭囊还悬吊在墓室盖板上。其余的大多数器物都在其生前携带、穿戴和佩戴位置。

2. 墓地出土器物

墓地所处的火焰山一带,沙质的土层,干燥少雨的气候,以及封闭的墓室空间,使难以保存的木质、毛皮质器物都悉数保存下来。墓葬中出土了许多木器、骨器、皮革制品和毛织物,还有陶器、铜器、铁器、石器、玛瑙珠、玻璃珠等。木器的器类有碗、杯、盘、钵、豆、桶、刀鞘、箸、锥、扣、橛、纺轮、弓箭、镰刀柄、拐杖、冠饰、假肢等。皮质品主要有皮靴、皮扣、扳指、护套、刀鞘、弓袋箭囊、绘有图案的羊皮画等。陶器多为素面,有些外施红色陶衣,打磨光洁,器物造型规整。主要有杯、碗、钵、壶、盆、双耳罐等。金属器物有铁刀、铁带钩、铜刀、铜耳环、金耳环、动物纹金饰件等。在墓道或墓口填充物中,还出土了为数较多的小麦、黍、黑果枸杞、芦苇、香蒲、骆驼刺、稗子、虎尾草等植物。

木质冠饰奇特而且多样,其中一件通体用薄木板加工粘合而成,呈四方长筒状,中空。底口近方形——因为四个面中只有一个面是平直的,其他三个面都略弧,向外先鼓出以后又逐渐细收成尖状体,中间略粗,与直面相对的那个斜面上方安装一个三角形"尾鳍"或"翼"——像船之尾舵状的薄木片。下端有双小孔,插入木销钉,固定一枚安装在筒中的木条。木条为一细长方体,上面有条形孔,并缠绕头发,以便将木冠饰固定在头顶上。这样的木冠饰为成年男性专用。用于成年女性头上的冠饰有两种,一种是与上述男性相同形状的装饰性器物,用整块生牛皮缝制,整体要小一号,比木质冠饰要轻巧得多,销钉、尾鳍具全。这种皮冠饰的后面安装两根起支撑固定作用的柽柳棍,从底部一直延伸到顶端。牛皮筒从后面缝合,至二分之一处收小分开,连尾鳍一起包紧粘牢在两根柽柳棍上。出土时置于头顶部,里面尚有头发和黑色毛线编织的发网残片。还有另一种冠饰,下部呈圆筒形,用薄木板弯曲粘贴而成。顶盖与圆筒组装在一起,口微敞,口沿上有两段突起,薄沿,像一个倒扣的木桶。顶盖中部有两个半圆形或长方形孔,便于发辫从双孔内穿出后打结,好将木桶一样的冠帽稳定在头顶之上。桶顶两侧分别安装一根微曲的圆木棍(冠翅),并向两侧叉开一定角度。木冠冕成型后,通体外包羊皮,并染成黑色,类似于长着动物双角的木冠饰才算做成。上述类似的冠饰都有多件,它们的基本形态和用途、用法也相同。

成套的弓、箭和弓套箭囊(古称韬簸、帐,俗称弓箭袋)是胜金店墓地考古发现中的又一个亮点。弓套箭囊出土时用自带的皮带悬系在墓室口木盖板上。弓套箭囊十分豪华,用皮条缝缀在一起,皮带头上系牛角制成的精致角扣,可与宽皮带联结,因此可背在肩上或系在腰间。弓套用羚羊皮缝制,呈梯形,上宽下窄。箭囊实际上是两个圆筒,也用羚羊皮缝制,一长一短,长者带盖,短者敞口。想必平时不用时,箭保存在带盖的筒内,将要用时把箭放入无盖的短筒中,箭尾向上露出一截,用时方便。弓为反曲的复合弓。这种弓不仅个体大、强劲,而且加工工艺达到了登峰造极的水平。弓箭兼有狩猎工具、作战武器、健身器械等多种功能,应特别注重其性能。弓者制弓一定要按照时令选取六种材料:杆、角、胶、筋、漆、丝,但吐鲁番盆地缺少后两种材料,用鹿皮胶和羊肠衣替代。杆使箭射得远,角使箭射得快,筋使箭射得深,胶使各材聚合为弓身,肠衣使弓身坚固。弓的加工步骤是先制作弓胎(杆),在制弓材料中弓杆最强,所以用韧性最强的绣线菊(俗称兔儿条)木,火烤弯曲成型。牛角是用来支撑弓体的,先将牛角撕开,火烤压平,弯曲成型后两面都划出条纹,以便用胶粘合,粘贴在弓杆的内侧。筋是增加强度的,铺三道在弓杆的外侧。弦反向挂在弓上,烘烤弓体给弓定型。通体再反复缠牛筋、肠衣,刷胶。弓弦用牛筋合成,两端做成固定的环,环上再缠羊皮条,弦的中段也同样要缠皮条,以防过早将弦磨断。

三、相关遗迹的考古发掘成果

1. 棺罩与尸床

众所周知,游牧民族和农业民族在生活上的重要区别是前者逐水草而居,后者是住在固定的房屋之内。对于迁徙于四季牧场之间的游牧民族来说,轻便,易于拆装,制作材料来源便利的毛皮、毛纺织品、羊毛毡质地帐篷的使用贯穿了整个古代游牧文化史。但是,对于游牧民族帐篷源流的演变过程,特别是对早期游牧文化帐篷的研究多依赖于文献记载或岩画及绘画作品,几乎不见实物出土。吐鲁番胜金店墓地的考古发掘为我们了解欧亚草原地区游牧文化青铜时代至早期铁器时代游牧民族帐篷的形制、质地、制作工艺提供了珍贵的实物资料。

根据早期的文献记载,最早的游牧人是住在马车或牛车上的,所以最早的游牧帐篷实际上就是畜力车的车篷。这次胜金店墓地出土的棺罩为拱形顶的长方形,以直径两厘米左右的树条为框架,构成拱顶框架的树条和构成底部长方形框架的树条以榫卯结构相接,框架的结合点用皮条固定,框架外再覆以毛毡,和现在蒙古族、哈萨克族帐篷的基本结构并无二致(图三)。整个棺罩做工细致,虽是葬具,但在结构构成上和实用的帐篷没有差别(图四)。

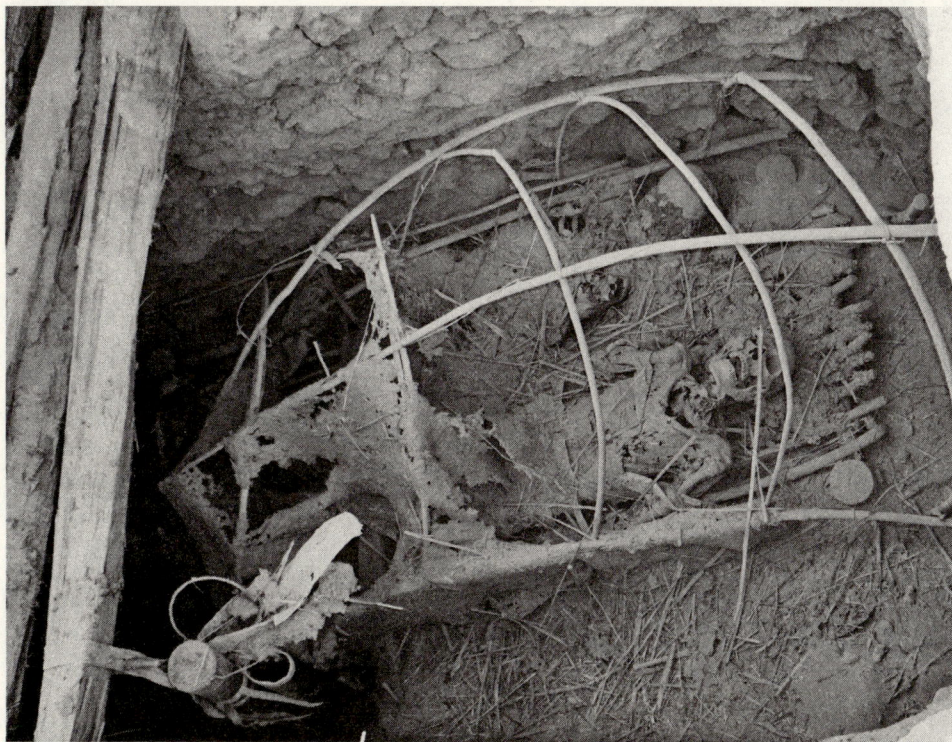

图三　胜金店墓地出土棺罩

图四　实用帐篷

　　这一时期的墓葬中还有一部分带有床形葬具,即尸床,为木材制成的长方形床形葬具(图五)。从洋海、胜金店墓地的发掘来看,它往往和棺罩配套使用,如果推测棺罩是仿自车篷的话,那么尸床则代表了车厢,由棺罩和尸床构成的葬具组合意味着死者在冥界居住的帐篷,是活人世界所居住的帐篷的镜像反映。众所周知,游牧民族不使用床之类的卧具,因为它不便于迁徙和摆放,而是直接在帐篷的地面上铺陈毛毡、地毯或兽皮等柔软、可折叠的物品作为卧具。阿勒泰——南西伯利亚和吐鲁番盆地同时期墓葬中的葬具在形制和使用方式上的一致性,说明了这两个地域在丧葬文化上的密切联系(图六)。

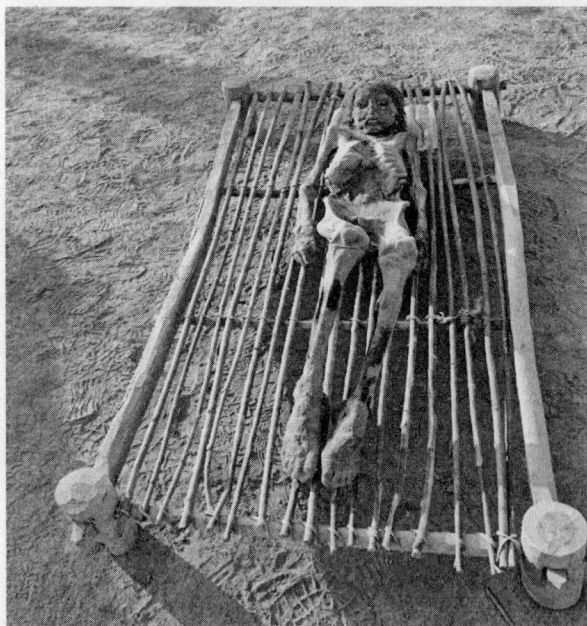

图五　床形葬具

　　2. 面具

　　对于欧亚草原地带的游牧民族来讲,各种现实的及虚幻的动物形象一直是他们的装饰主题,这一点在青铜时代和早期铁器时代更为明显,多为装饰在金器、青铜器、服饰或刻画在岩画上的形象。但似乎只有在南西伯利亚——阿尔泰地区最早将逝者的形象用高浮雕或泥塑的方式记录下来并置于墓地。

　　在洋海墓地出土的泥塑人面相和南西伯利亚塔什提克文化的墓葬中出土的泥塑面罩在用途上非常近似(图七)。①

---

　　① 吉谢列夫:《南西伯利亚古代史》(上册)图一,新疆社会科学院民族研究所,1981年。

图六　阿勒泰——南西伯利亚古墓出土葬具

图七　吐鲁番洋海墓地出土

3. 金项圈

金项圈，形制大同小异，最早出现于西亚两河流域，广泛分布在西起南俄草原，东至阿尔泰山一带的草原地带，在吐鲁番盆地出土的金项圈是迄今为止此类遗物分布的最东南端（图八、九、十）。[①]

1995 年在吐鲁番交河故城沟西墓地的发掘中，在相当于西汉早期的车师人墓葬中就出土有此类金项圈。[②]

4. 铜戈

铜戈，兵器，最早出现于距今 3 800～3 500 年的偃师二里头遗址，下限一直延续到秦汉之际，是出自中原本土的独特兵器。在远离中原的南西伯利亚地区，相当于西周时期的卡拉苏克中也出土有形制接近的同类器物，一般称之为"铜戈形器"。在黑海沿岸的斯基泰文

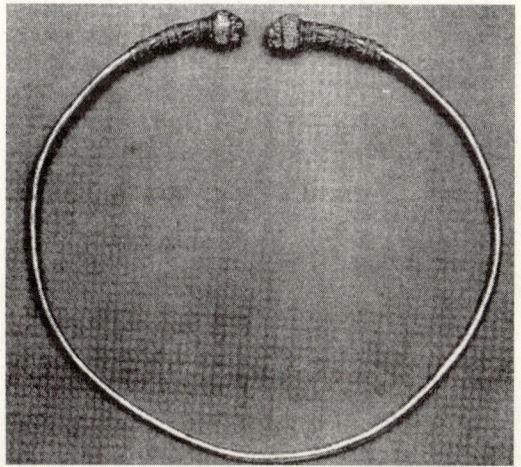

图八　金项圈　库拉埃夫古墓出土
（俄罗斯艾米尔塔什博物馆藏）

化中也有出土。它和中原地区铜戈的最大区别就是没有刃部。[③] 这种由中原地区向南西伯利亚输出的兵器由于文化交流的作用，向南也传入到吐鲁番盆地，最终出现在洋海墓地之中。[④] 洋海墓地虽已发掘约 800 多座墓葬，盗掘的也接近这个数，但仅仅在追回的盗掘文物中发现有两件"铜戈形器"，正式发掘的

①　林俊雄：ヤールホトの「王冠」，（日）島根縣並河萬里寫真財團：季刊「文化遺產」，1997 OCTOBER vol. 4。
②　联合国教科文组织驻中国代表处、新疆维吾尔自治区文物局、新疆文物考古研究所等：《交河故城——1993、1994 年度考古发掘报告》，东方出版社，1998 年。
③　藤川繁彦编：《中央ユーラシアの考古学》，第 3 章，同成社，1999 年 6 月。
④　新疆文物考古研究所：《鄯善县洋海、达浪坎儿古墓群清理简报》，《新疆文物》1989 年第 4 期。

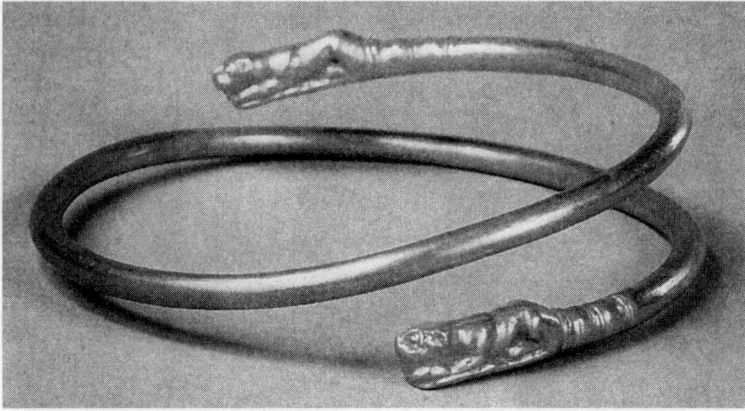

图九　金项圈　切尔托木里克古墓出土
（俄罗斯艾米尔塔什博物馆藏）

图十　金项圈　伊塞克古墓出土
（哈萨克斯坦考古研究所藏）

图十一　吐鲁番洋海墓地出土的铜戈

墓葬中未见一件，说明这两件器物并非是本地模仿铸造的，而是地地道道的由南西伯利亚一带传入的"舶来品"（图十一）。

5. 鱼纹文身

众所周知，吐鲁番盆地极端干旱，严重缺水。境内连一条像样的河流都没有，从古至今，鱼类在这里都不是人类摄取食物的来源。但为什么在吐鲁番早期文化当中却可见到以鱼纹为题材的作品，如在胜金店墓地中就发现有鱼纹的文身（图十二）。当我们再一次把目光投向阿勒泰——南西伯利亚地区青铜时代至早期铁器时代的文化时，这个问题就有了明确的答案。我们在阿勒泰山脉的巴泽雷克古墓中也发现了鱼纹文身（图十三）。① 当时的人们还非常喜欢用鱼形来装饰马匹（图十四）。

图十二　胜金店墓地人手背上的鱼形文身

---

① 史蒂夫·吉尔伯特编介、切拉莉娅·吉尔伯特协助、欧阳昱译：《文身的历史》第一章，百花文艺出版社，2006 年 6 月。

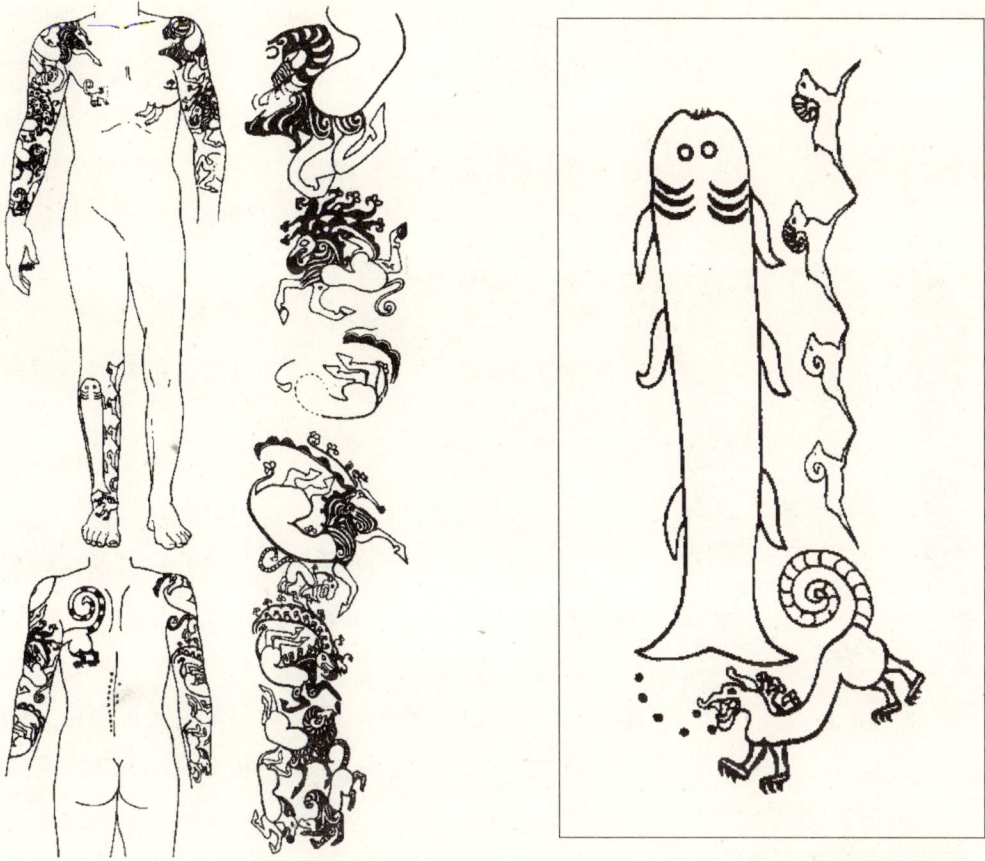

图十三　左图:巴泽雷克2号墓墓主人的文身(右小腿上的鱼形文身);右图:局部放大

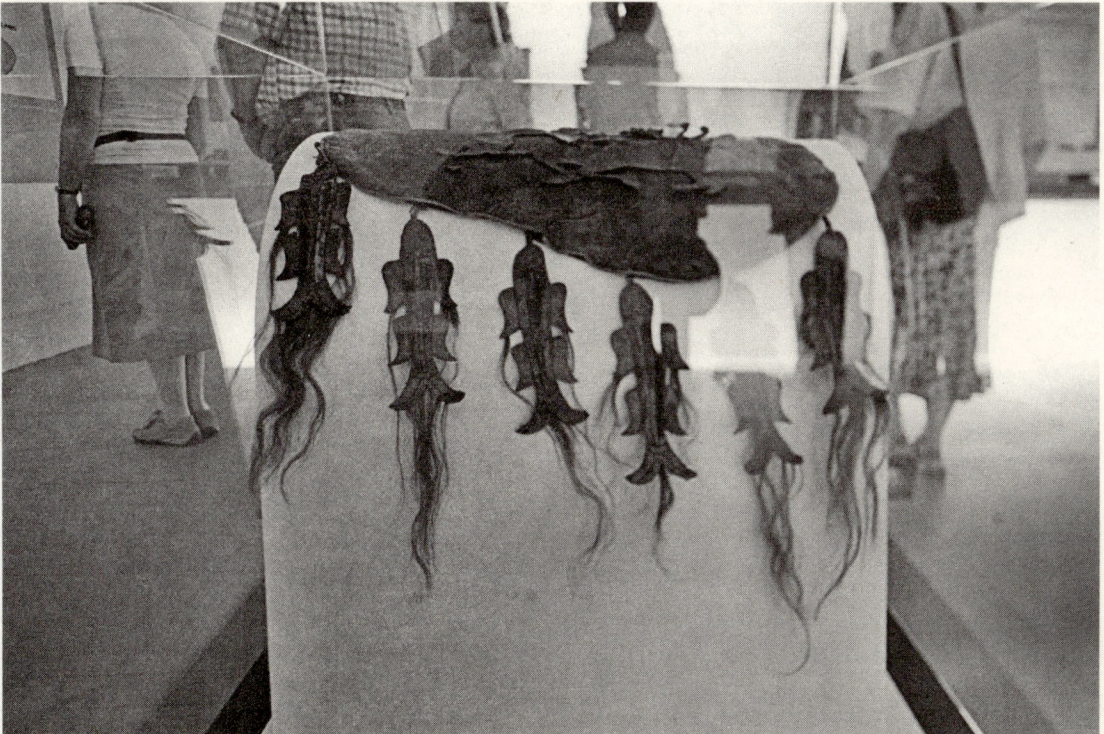

图十四　巴泽雷克古墓出土马鞍垫上的鱼形装饰

6. 冠饰

各种礼仪性的冠饰也是这一时期游牧人在重要祭典活动中,甚至包括其本人葬礼上不可或缺的重要服饰之一。从阿勒泰——南西伯利亚地区到吐鲁番盆地这一时期的冠饰种类繁多,既有硬质的木冠,有鱼背鳍形(图十五)和双角状(图十六),也有软质的毡帽(图十七),复原后的示意图显示出非常高贵、端庄的形象(图十八)。还有插在发髻里的箭杆状装饰(图十九、二十、二十一),甚至是冲天状的发辫(图二十二);但其共同的特征是高耸向上。这和史料上记载的尖帽塞克人的形象是相符的。

7. 马鞭和战斧

对于这一时期的游牧人来说,马鞭既是工具,也是身份地位的象征;战斧既是武器,也是仪仗用具。所以这两件东西常常是组合在一起出土,并且有逐渐朝着非实用化的方向发展。另外一个有意思的现象就是在黄金资源非常丰富的阿勒泰——南西伯利亚地区,这两件东西常常用黄金装饰(图二十三),而在黄金资源缺乏的吐鲁番盆地,只好用铜来装饰(图二十四、二十五)。

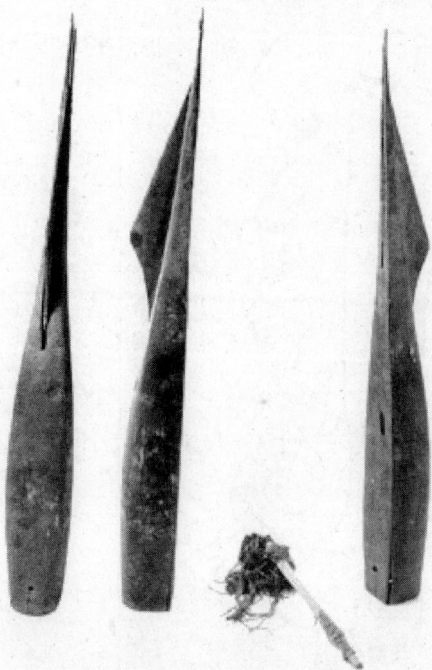

图十五　吐鲁番洋海墓地出土的木冠

图十六　吐鲁番胜金店墓地出土的双角状木冠

图十七　阿勒泰地区青铜时代——早期铁器时代出土的女性毡冠

图十八　毡冠的复原示意图

图十九　哈萨克斯坦伊塞克
　　古墓的金冠饰

图二十　俄罗斯颇罗希马克古墓
　　出土的女性冠饰

图二十一　俄罗斯颇罗希马克古墓群3号
　　　　　墓地1号墓出土的冠饰

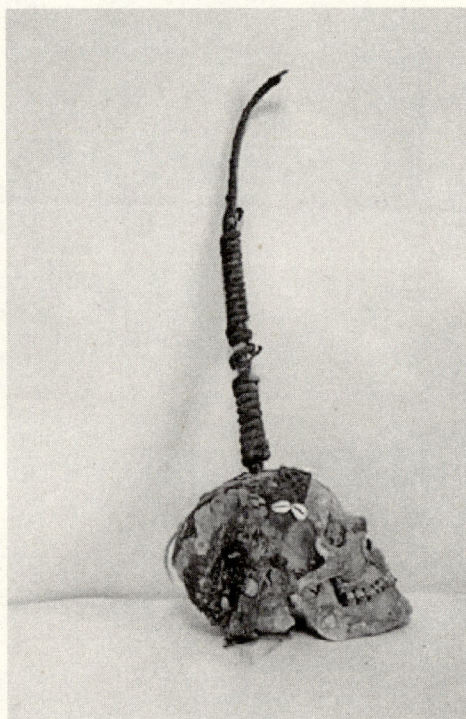

图二十二　洋海墓地出土的头饰

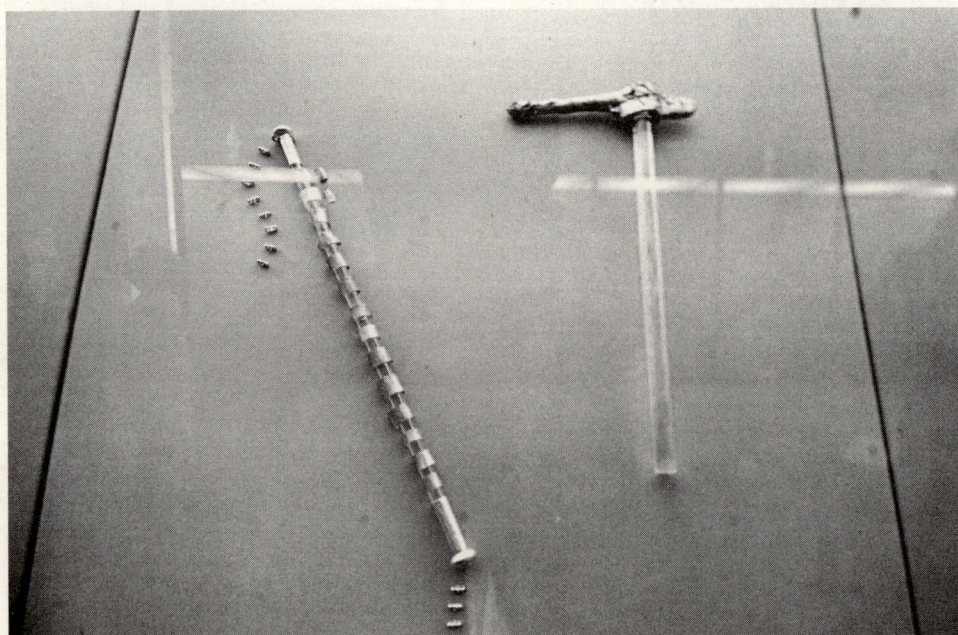

图二十三　阿勒泰——南西伯利亚出土的,包金皮的马鞭和战斧

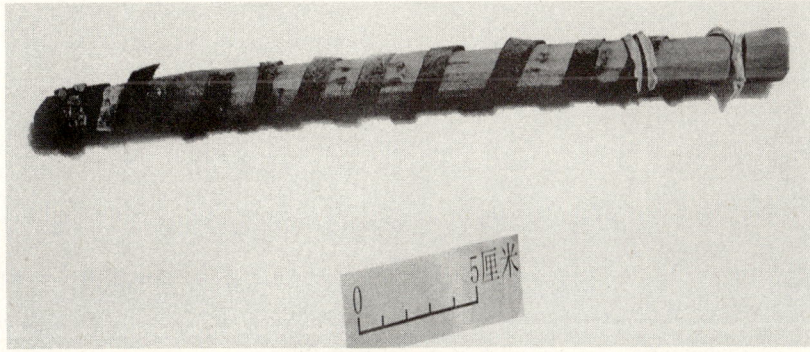

图二十四　吐鲁番洋海古墓出土的缠绕有铜皮的马鞭

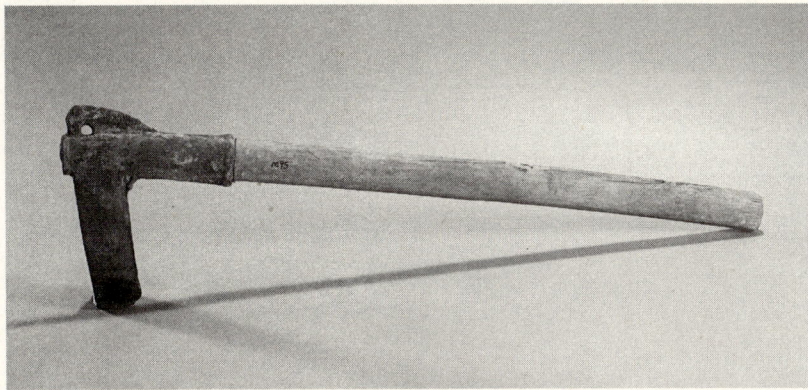

图二十五　吐鲁番洋海古墓出土的铜斧

8. 带柄木瓢

带柄木瓢也是在这两个地区都能找到共性的遗物(图二十六、二十七、二十八、二十九)。除此之外,如单尾翼箭镞(图三十、三十一)、卷曲式动物纹样(图三十二、三十三、三十四、三十五)等都在这两个相距遥远,自然环境差异极大的地区同时存在而且风格一致,足以证明他们之间文化的密切联系,体现着文化的交流和传播。

图二十六　阿勒泰——南西伯利亚出土

图二十七　阿勒泰——南西伯利亚出土

图二十八　罐形勺

车师时期。高 16、口径 12 cm。

托克逊博斯坦乡墓出土。现藏于吐鲁番地区博物馆。

木质，掏挖而成。胎壁较厚，多口，圆腹，圜底，腹部有一曲柄，上钻一孔。器表光滑。

图二十九　吐鲁番洋海墓地出土

9. 单尾翼箭镞

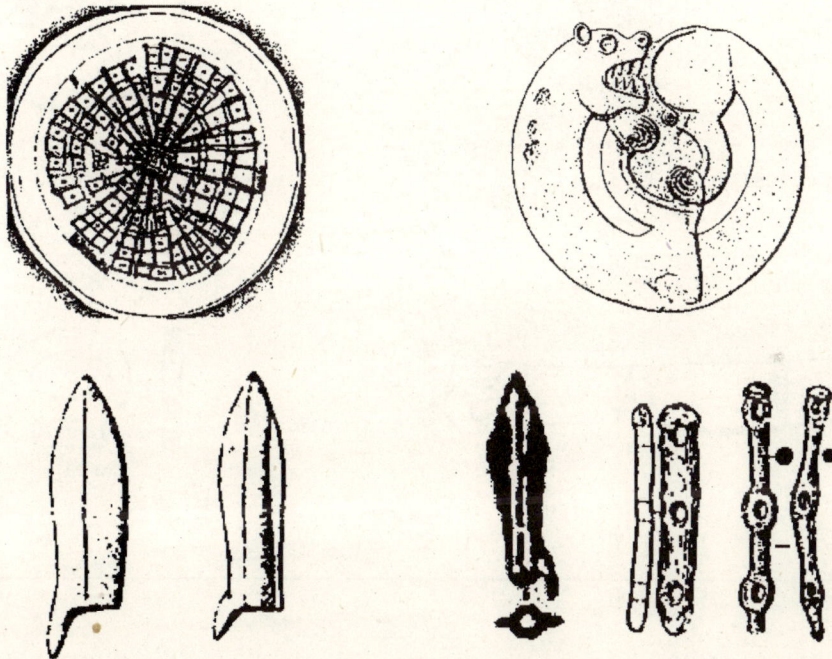

图三十　瓦阿尔赞1号冢及出土器物

0　　　　　　1厘米

图三十一　吐鲁番洋海墓地出土

10. 卷曲式动物纹样

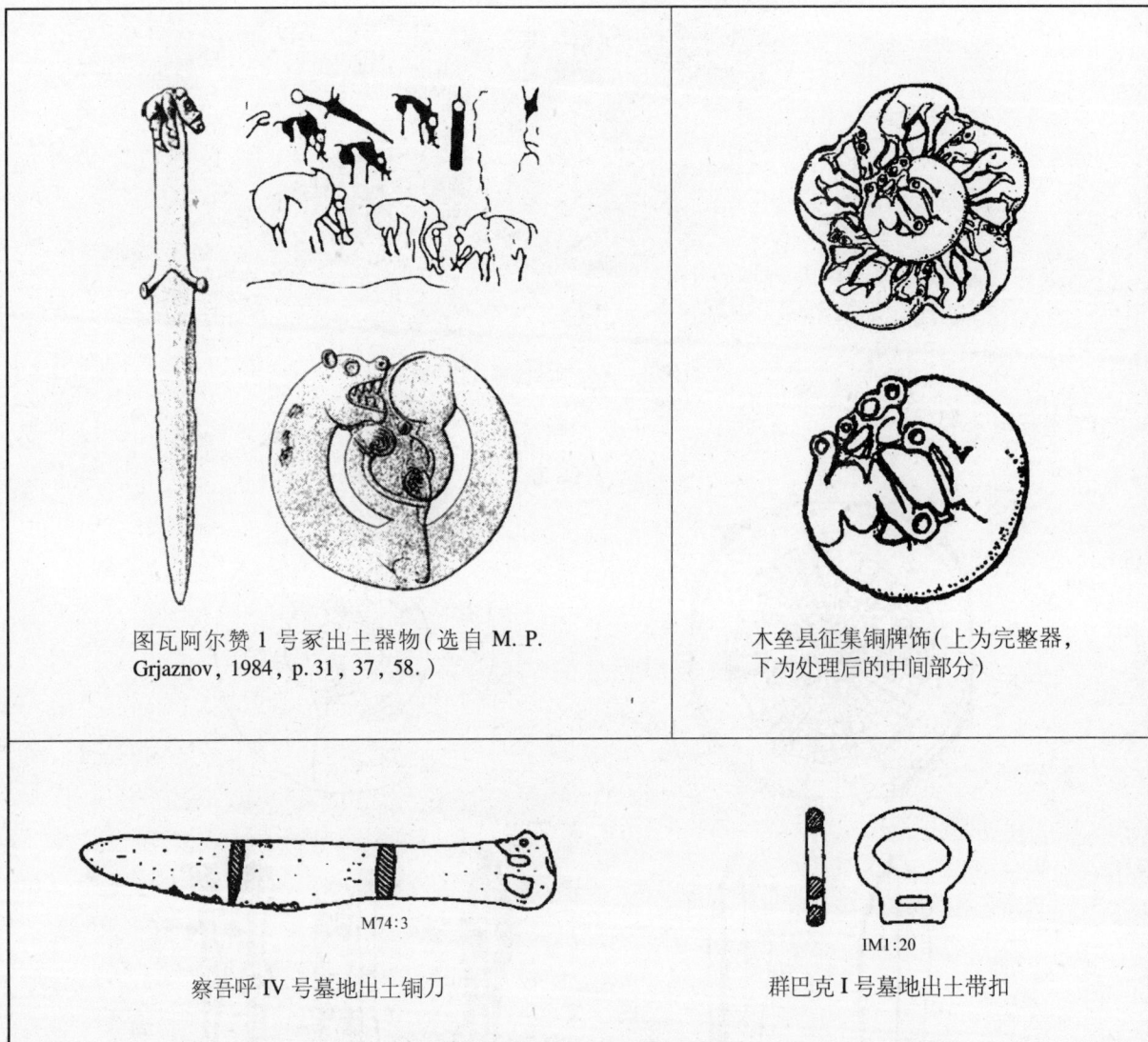

图瓦阿尔赞 1 号冢出土器物（选自 M. P. Grjaznov，1984，p.31，37，58.）

木垒县征集铜牌饰（上为完整器，下为处理后的中间部分）

M74:3

察吾呼 IV 号墓地出土铜刀

IM1:20

群巴克 I 号墓地出土带扣

图三十二　各地出土卷曲式动物纹样

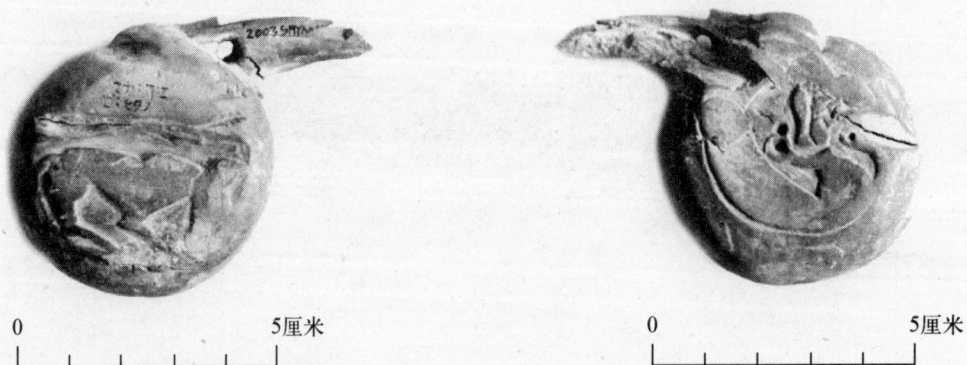

0　　　　　5厘米

0　　　　　5厘米

图三十三　吐鲁番洋海墓地出土

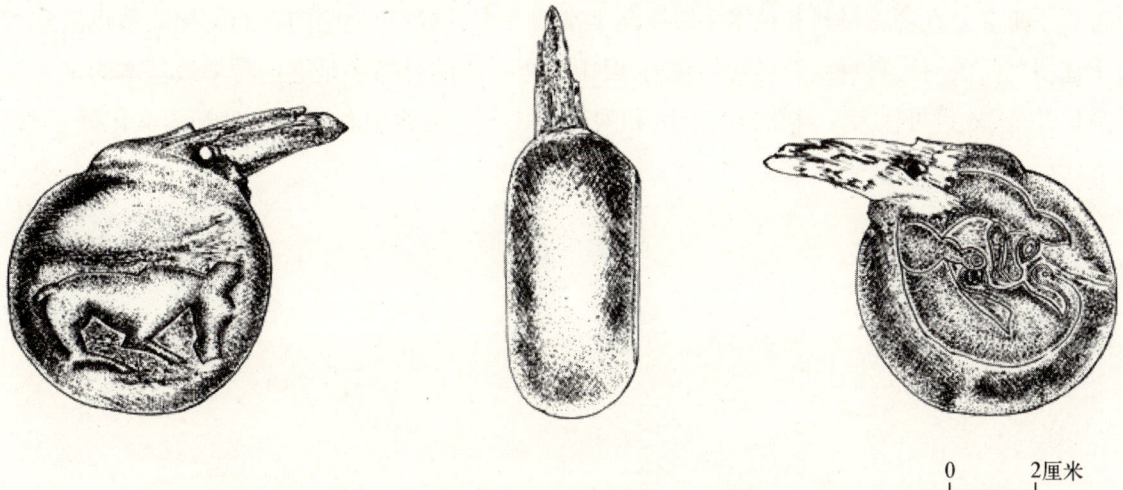

0   2厘米

图三十四　卷曲动物纹样

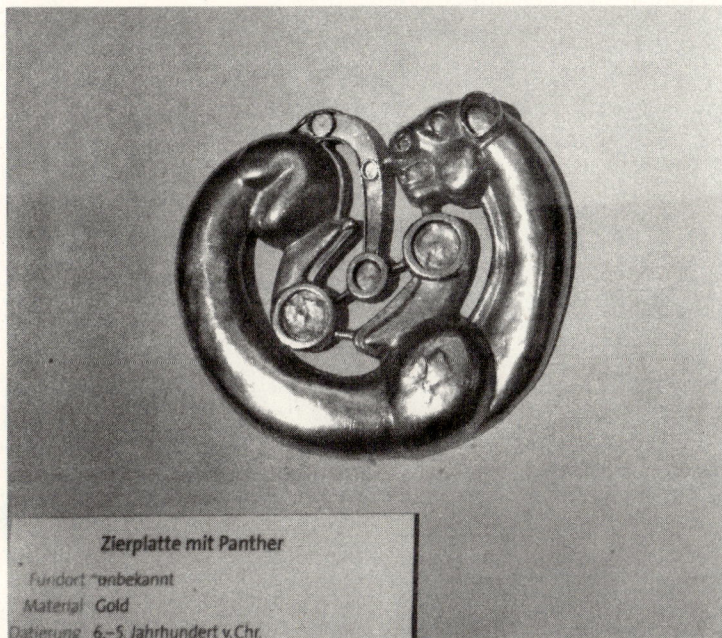

图三十五　阿勒泰——南西伯利亚出土

四、结　语

　　吐鲁番虽然位于欧亚草原地带的边缘,但在青铜时代——早期铁器时代,居住在这里的人们却和中亚地区游牧文化的中心阿勒泰山——南西伯利亚有着非常密切的关系,甚至可以认为这些文化的拥有者其主体是来自上述地区。早在20世纪90年代初,本人在对新疆准噶尔盆地周缘早期文化遗存进行调查时就注意到,这一地区的古代文化最早是受南西伯利亚地区的影响,直到后来才受到东亚及中亚两河流域和南亚地区的影响。[①] 这一观点通过吐鲁番盆地的苏贝希墓地、洋海墓地、胜金店墓地

---

　　① 李肖、党彤:「新疆准噶尔盆地周缘出土铜器初探」,内陆アジア史学会『内陸アジア史研究』,第7・8合併号,1992年10月。

发掘得到了加强。在考古材料和技术手段逐渐丰富的今天,这两个地区内在的文化联系也渐渐明朗,本文上述所列举的对比材料虽然是管中窥豹,但由于所对比的材料多是这一时期最基本的文化要素,极具文化特征,故也可让大家对吐鲁番地区和阿勒泰山——南西伯利亚这一时期的文化联系略见一斑了。

About Cultural Contacts in Altai in Bronze Age

Kubarev Vladimir

Institute of Archaeology and Ethnography Siberian Branch of Russian

Academy of Sciences, Novosibirsk, Russian Federation

Introduction

Two archaeological cultures are known on the territory of Altai in the early Bronze Age: Afanas'evo and Karakol-cultures. Numerous monuments of Afanas'evo culture (Petroglyphs, burials, sacred constructions and settlements) are quite enough investigated. As is well known, the territory of Afanas'evo culture is stretched on Minusinsk basin, Mongolian Altai and Turfan basin in Xinjiang. Monuments of Karakol culture of Altai (Fig. 1) are less known.

Study of monuments of Karakol culture in Altai

The first burial of Karakol culture in Altai has been excavated 30 years ago on river Ten'ga in the village Ozernoe. [1] This discovery remains unnoticed as the cemetery was almost completely destroyed, but in one of burials the stone plate with drawing was found. The image represented the small figure of the woman made by a red paint. In the same village the author found a small series of stele with cap-shaped pricks and drawings in the top of obelisks. [2] The huge megalith was earlier in a kitchen garden of private farm. On its top numerous cap-shaped pricks are represented. Some archaeologists attribute a unique stele (Fig. 2), found in Ozernoe near to the destroyed burials of a Bronze Age, to the Karakol culture. The special publication is devoted to this rare monument. [3] But, probably, stele from Ozernoe belongs to the earlier period and could be modified by Karakol-people for a construction of the tomb. Some steles with cap-shaped pricks have been broken in antiquity and used for funeral constructions in the village Ozernoe. Fragments of plates from four stone

[1] Pogojeva A. P., Kadikov B. H. *Mogil'nik epohi bronzy u poselka Ozernogo na Altae.* In: *Novoe v arheologii Sibiri i Dal'nego Vostoka*, Novosibirsk, 1979; Pogojeva A. P., Rikun M. P., Stepanova N. F., Tur S. S. Epoha eneolita i bronzy Gornogo Altaya, Ch. 1, Barnaul, 2006.

[2] Kubarev V. D. *Chashechnye kamni Altaya.* In: *Materialy po arheologii Gornogo Altaya*, Gorno-Altaysk, 1986; Kubarev V. D. *"Mificheskie" chashechnye kamni Altaya i ih analogii v drevnih kul'turah Evrazii.* In: *Sohranenie i izuchenie kul'turnogo naslediya Altaya*, Barnaul, 2000.

[3] Molodin V. I., Pogojeva A. P. *Plita iz Ozernogo (Gorniy Altay).* In: *Sovetskaja Arheologija*, 1989, № 1.

Fig. 1 Map of Republic Altai.

sarcophagi with remains of the buried people testify this fact. On some plates of tombs cap-shaped pricks and paintings made by dark-crimson ochre have remained. After some year's protective archaeological excavation in the village Ozernoe already on the second funeral complex were continued. It was the latest research of monuments of Karakol culture in Ozernoe to which results some laconic messages have been devoted. [1] In neighborhood with the village Ozernoe during several field seasons, rock drawings of different epochs also were studied and have been published. [2] The most ancient drawing on this petroglyphic site, according to E. M. Miklashevich, is engraved anthropomorphic figure. [3] She interpreted this image as image of Karakol culture of Altai, comparing it with identical personages on plates from burials of Karakol.

Fig. 2   Drawing of images on stele from village Ozernoe.

The second funeral complex of Karakol culture was found accidentally in 1985 in the valley of river Ursul, direct in the centre of the village Karakol, where for the first time undisturbed burials were excavated. [4] This was several burials in stone sarcophagus. During excavation three stone sarcophagi, covered by plates, were discovered. Of great interest is the stepped Karakol burial where under covering of plates the first buried was on the second died. For the teenager the separate tomb has been built. But the most surprising in these burials is perfectly remained paintings on stone plates. They have made not only in the usual for Petroglyphs technique — knock-out and engraving, but also using multi-colored paints. Nothing of the kind till now was not only known in Altai but also in generally in Siberia. The most amazing is the extraordinary brightness of polychromatic paintings. Though their palette is rather poor, at painting only three colors are presented — red, black and white.

Depictions of spirits-ancestors and solar deity

Karakol paintings are surprisingly original. At their close examination it is easy to establish, that all

① Kubarev V. D. O nekotoryh parallelyah v petroglifah Altaya i Gindukusha. In: Problemy sohraneniya, ispol'zovaniya i izucheniya pamyatnikov arheologii, Gorno-Altaysk, 1992a; Kubarev V. D. O proishozzdenii i hronologii karakol'skoy kul'tury Altaya. In: Aborigeny Sibiri: problemy izucheniya ischezayushih yazikov i kul'tur, Tom II, Novosibirsk, 1995; Kubarev V. D. Drevnie rospisi Ozernogo. In: Sibir' v panorame tysyacheletiy (Materialy mezhdunarodnogo simpoziuma), Novosibirsk, 1998; Vdovina T. A. , Trifanova S. V. , Kobzar' M. V. Kollektivnoe pogrebenie epohi bronzy. In: Izuchenie istoriko-kul'turnogo naslediya narodov Yuzhnoy Sibiri, Gorno-Altaysk, 2006, Vyp. 3, 4.

② Martynov A. I. , Elin V. N. , Nekrasov V. A. Svyashennye skaly u s. Ozernogo. In: Sovremennye problemy izucheniya petroglifov, Kemerovo, 1993; Miklashevich E. A. Pamyatniki drevnego iskusstva u sela Ozernogo (Gorniy Altay). In: Arheologiya Yujnoy Sibiri, Vyp. 24, Kemerovo, 2006.

③ Miklashevich E. A. , op. cit. , 2006, tab. VIII, 8.

④ Kubarev V. D. Drevnie rospisi Karakola, Novosibirsk, 1988.

Fig. 3　Personage in spotted animal skin Karakol.

figures surrounding buried person from four sides, are represented in masks. And then there is clear an unusual combination of animal and human features in images of fantastic beings. Taking into account this assumption, some words about clothes of Karakol personages is necessary to tell. Animal masks, gloves and footwear with sharp claws are supplemented with densely fitting a body clothes, sewed, probably, from the whole animal skin. Such clothes with wool on a back and a tail are represented on two figures. On one of them using rare graphic method (white points on a black paint) spottiness of skin is depicted (Fig. 3).

Possibly, on stone plates of Karakol one of the culmination moments of ritual of send-off of died's soul is embodied. It is possible to assume, that the whole group of the people dressed in animal suits and masks, and in such way reincarnated in spirits-ancestors, defenders and patrons, guide in other world, took part in such ritual. Our assumption confirms a simple composition of paintings. To its semantic interpretation we will quite apply a method of classification by system of binary oppositions. It represents a scene of ritual struggle of red spirits with black demons, symbolizing opposition of the kind beginning and malicious forces, struggle between light and darkness, immemorial struggle of a life against death. The scene which is very close to such interpretation was found in another burial excavated on the western outskirts of village Karakol.

In generally more than 70 images are represented on stone plates of Karakol and each of them is unique. Especially frequent in paintings of Karakol the image of "Sun-headed" beings repeats. All of them are shown with a head in the form of a disk or an oval from which radial rays or feathers, sometimes, having an end with round poles. Probably, in such appearance Karakol-people esteemed the solar deity granting to the person warm and a life on the earth. Ancient Indians have imagined it also in the same way. In their sacred book Rig-Veda, solar god Surja is characterized by such epithets like: «the Ruler of rays», «Shining brightly shine», "Radiant". And naturally it is not accidentally that on a head of one of the figure from Karakol 12 rays are represented. This number often appears in the most ancient Asian beliefs and is connected with the sun.

Also unusual are the images of "Bull-headed" beings picked on stone plates (Fig. 4). However, the term "Bull-headed" we are

Fig. 4　"Bull-headed" beings picked on stone plates of Karakol.

using rather conditionally; on similarity to horns of a bull. It could be high headdresses or masks with horns.

Image of syncretic predator and myth about a space pursuit

To the monuments of Karakol culture of Altai belongs also burial from village Besh-Ozek.[1] Protective archaeological excavation has found a tomb built from carefully drafted stone plates. A large skeleton of the man, on a back, a head on the West was laid in this tomb. On stone plates of sarcophagus engraved drawings and color painting were also applied. They are almost identical to the mane scenes and images of Karakol. It is all the same pairs of twins of "Sun-headed" and "Bull-headed" beings, which iconography is practically not different from Karakol images. But in painting of Besh-Ozek the new image, which is unknown in Karakol art, is found. It is the engraved drawing of a predator (Fig. 5) — wolf or a dog. This image doesn't have fantastic features. But, nevertheless, the big sizes of a figure, rather canonical and aggressive pose of an animal allow us to attribute it to a number of known images of syncretic predators of Okunevo type. All depictions of this animal from Altai and especially Khakassia have identical features: wide in shoulders and pared-down croup of trunk; opened large-toothed mouth; thin and long (the bird's?) legs; throwed on a back striped or notched tail. The mythical animal from Besh-Ozek is shown in the same iconographical manner and besides marked by an astral sign in the form of a slanting cross. Identical signs accompany not only almost all images of Okunevo fantastic predators, but also depicted on trunks of bulls.[2] They are presented in Petroglyphs, near to images with masks and also are the central element of tiny masks on Okunevo sculptures and color painted masks of Dzhoiskii type.[3] Becomes clear why the predator from Besh-

Fig. 5   Engraved drawing of syncretic predator in Besh-Ozek.

[1]   Kubarev V. D. *op. cit.*, 1992a; Kubarev V. D. *Dva novyh pamyatnika karakol'skoy kul'tury v Gornom Altae*. In: *Paleoekologiya i rasselenie drevnego cheloveka v Severnoy Azii i Amerike*, Krasnoyarsk, 1992b; Kubarev V. D. *op. cit.*, 1998.

[2]   Leont'ev N. V. *Gravirovannye izobrazheniya zhivotnyh v mogil'nike Chernovaya VIII*. In: *Pamyatniki okunevskoy kul'tury*, Leningrad, 1980, pp. 121 - 122.

[3]   Podol'skiy M. L. *Ovladenie beskonechnost'yu*. In: *Okunevskiy sbornik. Kul'tura. Iskusstvo. Antropologiya*, Sankt-Peterburg, 1997, tab. 7; 8, ж-к; 19 - 21, 26, *a,6* etc.

Ozek is shown in interaction with "Sun-headed" beings (see Fig. 5). Though its pose is static, but all described details underline aggression, an orientation of a mythical animal on the main object of pursuit. Undoubtedly, this laconic scene visually illustrates the most ancient Siberian myth about a space pursuit. At the heart of this myth the monster-animal (wolf-dog) hunts on a light radiant deity, the sun and stars.[①] In Okunevo art the myth about a space pursuit looks as hunt by a fantastic predator of the going west bull identified with the sun. In Besh-Ozek variant of this myth the image of the sun appears already in human image with solar attributes. The predator here is represented, turned to the right, as well as its numerous embodiments in Okunevo art, i. e. it is directed on the West.

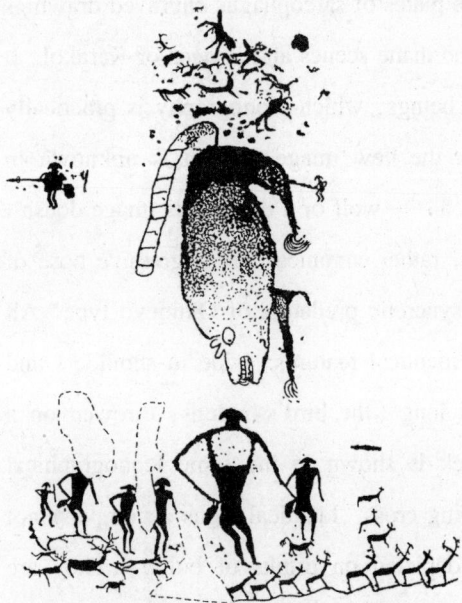

Fig. 6　Fantastic predator attacked a group of human figures. Kalbak-Tash I. Knockout.

The most interesting for comparison drawings of predators are known in Petroglyphs of well-known Kalbak-Tash,[②] which is located in lower course of river Chuja. The most interesting, that the scene from Besh-Ozek is absolutely identical by its sense to Kalbak-Tash scene where the predator is also represented prepared for an attack on group of human figures (Fig. 6). The third, rather laconic scene transferring this myth, similar to Kalbak-Tash and Besh-Ozek scenes, is recently found at foot of mountain Shiveet-Hairhan in Mongolian Altai. Thus, all three Altai images of predators are shown in interaction with anthropomorphic and "Sun-headed" beings that, undoubtedly, is the direct proof of existence of a myth about «space pursuit» in Bronze Age, not only in Siberia, but also in the Central Asia.

Fantastic predators in Petroglyphs

New Besh-Ozek image of Karakol culture gives the chance to synchronies some images of fantastic predators in Petroglyphs of Altai (Fig. 7). The depiction of fantastic animal from Kalbak-Tash II also belongs to such images of predators (Fig. 8, *1*). The main and dating features of this predator are the open mouth and the tongue indicated in it and also two tails: one is thrown on a back, another reaches the earths. It is interesting that the image similar to fantastic beings from Altai is known also in a valley of the river Indus. Depiction of such predator repeats in different petroglyphic sites: Chilas IV, crossing Tal'pan etc. (Fig. 8, *2 - 6*). This well recognized syncretic image forms variety of similar in style depictions. German researchers

---

① Okladnikov A. P. Shishkinskie pisanicy. Pamyatnik drevney kul'tury Pribaykal'ya, Irkutsk, 1959; Chlobistina M. D. *Drevneyshie yuzhno-sibirskie mify v pamyatnikah okunevskogo iskusstva.* In: *Pervobytnoe iskusstvo*, Novosibirsk, 1971.

② Kubarev V. D., Jacobson E. Sibérie du sud 3: Kalbak-Tash I (République de L'Altai). Répertoire des pétroglyphes d'Asie Centrale, T V. 3, Paris, 1996.

Fig. 7　Images of fantastic predators of Karakol culture and their archetypes in Pazyryk art
　　　　of Altai: *1* – Besh-Ozek; *2*, *6* – Kalbak-Tash; *3*, *5* – Elangash; *4* – Bichiktu-Bom;
　　　　7 – Yustyd; *8* – the Kujussky grotto; *9* – Pazyryk; *10* – Tashanta.

are dating them into Scythian period whereas drawing from Petroglyphs of Kalbak-Tash looks more archaically. [1] Probably, it belongs to number of predators of Okunevo-Karakol art, rare for Altai and known on its several drawings in Kalbak-Tash I and to one in Besh-Ozek. At the same time in Okunevo art brutish mythical beings are very well know. [2] They have even more frightening appearance and some images is also

---

　① Bemmann M. Die Felsbildstation Dadam. Die Materialien zur Archäologie der Nordgebiete Pakistans. Band 5, Mainz am Rhein, 2005.
　② Vadeckaya E. B. Izvayaniya okunevskoy kul'tury. In: Pamyatniki okunevskoy kul'tury, Leningrad, 1980, tab. XLIX, *103*; LII, *117*; LIII, *127*, *128*; Leont'ev N. V. , Kapel'ko V. F. , Esin Yu. N. Izvayaniya okunevskoy kul'tury, Abakan, 2006, tab. *117*; *120*; *127*; *140*; *204*; *205* etc.

represented with two tails,[1] as well as by considered above fantastic predators from a valley of the rivers Chuja and Indus. Interesting is also the fact that the most ancient Petroglyphs of a lower reach of river Chuja (the hand image, zebu like bulls with long lyriform horns and another animals) also find direct parallels and exact analogies in rock paintings of Indus. [2]

Iconography, style and even the sizes the considered predators are similar to the same small figures of predators in Petroglyphs of Altai and China and also on deer stones of Mongolia. All of them are made in so-called decorative style. Similar spottiness and "figuration" is characteristic, for example, for images of predators from mountains Inshan in China,[3] for decorative drawings of predators, bulls, maral-cows and fantastic animals in Petroglyphs of Kalbak-Tash in Altai[4] and in recently published rock paintings of Mongolian Altai: Tsagaan-Salaa and Baga-Ojgur.[5] Such graphic tradition has obviously something in common with Karakol images having spotty clothes, probably, sewed from whole skin of leopard or ounce, with a tail and wool on a back.

Depictions of man and woman figures

In the paintings of Karakol culture pair human figures very often are represented. In the absence of obvious sex signs rather difficult is to define where the man and where the woman is represented. But great number of figures of different sexes in Petroglyphs of Central Asia has allowed defining that figures of men were represented in a profile, — female, as a rule, are shown in a full face. Such pair figures are known in Petroglyphs of Kalbak-Tash and Karban, Chuluut in Mongolia and Kantegir in Khakassia.

The human figures which suit is decorated by the bird's feathers are also interesting. Trunk of the person and his feet are also covered with feathers and instead of a foot he has the bird's claws. Identical drawings of women are known in Petroglyphs of Karban on middle reach of river Katun. «Birdlike» figures of women are recently found in Petroglyphs of Green Lake on Altai. Some images in color painting on gravestones and the picked images in Petroglyphs are so similar to each other that existence of special graphic canon, which was distinctive for many primitive "artists" of the Central Asia, could be supposed. For example, amazing similarity is observed between the picked human figures from Karakol and hardly visible engraving of the same image on rocks of Kalbak-Tash. Not accidentally, that near to this human figure the depiction of mask unique for Altai was found. It also can be compared with a mask from Karakol which besides has the bull

---

① Kurochkin G. N. *Izobrazhenie fantasticheskogo hishnika iz Birkanova* (*po materialam raskopok 1989*). In: *Problemy izucheniya okunevskoy kul'tury*, Sankt-Peterburg, 1995, tab. 1; Pyatkin B. N. *Zamechaniya po povodu interpretacii obraza fantasticheskogo hishnika*. In: *Okunevskiy sbornik. Kul'tura. Iskusstvo. Antropologiya*, Sankt-Peterburg, p. 263; Studzickaya S. V. Tema kosmicheskoy ohoty i obraz fantasticheskogo zverya v izobraitel'nyh pamyatnikah okunevskoy kul'tury. In: *Okunevskiy sbornik*, Sankt-Peterburg, 1997, tab. II, 5, 6.

② Kubarev V. D. *op. cit.*, 1992b, p.48; Jettmar K. *Novaya oblast' rasprostraneniya skifskogo zverinogo stilya v Gindukushe*. In: *Itogi izucheniya skifskoy epohi Altaya i sopredel'nyh territoriy*, Barnaul, 1999, pp.64 - 65.

③ Gay Snanlin' In'shan' yan'hua (Petroglify gor In'shan'), Pekin, 1986.

④ Kubarev V. D., Jacobson E. *op. cit.*, 1996.

⑤ Kubarev V. D., Ceveendorzh D., Yakobson E. Petroglify Cagaan-Salaa i Baga-Oygura (Mongol'skiy Altay), Novosibirsk, 2005.

horns. Engravings of Karakol culture are found directly in vicinities of village Karakol: in the place Ustju-Ajry and on the rocks of river Ursul.

Elk-images

As is known the image of a bull was popular among the population of Okunevo culture in Khakassia, — Karakol-people, apparently, preferred an image of an elk (elk-cow) which images are always located in the top part of stele (?), subsequently broken and used for the funeral purposes. In Petroglyphs of Altai and neighboring Mongolia images of elks are often represented but they are different from Karakol-elk in stylistics and technique.[1] Only elks from Turochakskaja petroglyphic site can be included in a circle of graphic monuments of Karakol culture.

Till recently monuments of Karakol culture were known only in the central areas of Altai. But discovery in East Altai, bordering with Mongolia and China, allow us to trace migration ways of Karakol-people in southeast direction. The argument for such conclusion is only one depiction from Petroglyphs on the mountain Kurman-Tau. This is contour figure of elk-cow, made by a red color. The elk-cow from Kurman-Tau is absolutely identical to contour figures of elks from Karakol. Using this analogy, drawing from Kurman-Tau should be dated to an epoch of early Bronze Age.

Conclusions

Graphic materials of Karakol culture make possible dating and definition of a cultural attribution of Petroglyphs of Altai and neighboring regions of Central Asia.

The Petroglyphs of Mongolia, Tuva, Xingjian, Amur, Central Asia and Indus, show that almost unknown Bronze Age culture of Altai, which is known only on several burials and paintings of Karakol, is a small part of a cultural complex, the wide spreading and significance of which we only try to understand.

---

① Kubarev V. D. Analiz petroglifov i kommentarii. In: Mongolie du Nord-Ouest: Tsagaan Salaa/Baga Oigor // Repertoire des Petroglyphes d'Asie centrale, T. V. 6, Paris, 2001.

Discovery of New Cultures of the Bronze Age in Mongolia
(According to the data obtained by the International
Central Asiatic Archaeological Expedition)

Alexey A. Kovalev

St. Petersburg State University, Russia

Organized by Alexey Kovalev in 1998, since 2001 the International Central-Asiatic Archaeological Expedition of St. -Petersburg State University, the Roerich Family Museum-Institute of St. -Petersburg, together with the Institute of History of the Mongolian Academy of Science and the Ulaanbaatar University conduct methodical investigations of Bronze and Early Iron Ages sites on the territory of Outer Mongolia. During seven years of work more than one hundred burial mounds and ritual sites under supervision of **Alexey Kovalev** and Professor, Dean of the Faculty of Human Sciences of Ulaanbaatar State University **Diimaajav Erdenebaatar** were excavated. The investigations were carried out in accordance with the international standards of methodology; the methods of excavation and documentation of stone constructions traditionally used for excavation of such sites at the Russian part of Central Asia was taken as a basic one (According Russian tradition the Central Asia includes 萨彦岭 Sayan, Altay 阿尔泰山, and Khangay 杭爱山 mountain systems and also Gobi 戈壁沙漠 desert).

At the beginning of the expedition working in Mongolia we stated there was a very low level of knowledge of the Bronze Age cultures in Mongolia.

The main problems can be summarized as follows:

- Sites of the Bronze and the Early Iron Ages of Western, Central, and Goby regions excavated by archaeologists were very few.

- The total absence of burial sites of Early and Middle Bronze Age (third and the first half of the second millennium B. C.) (except of several barrows from Altan sandal and Shatar chuluu[①]) among the excavated sites.

- A very poor quality of description of stone burial and ritual constructions, shortage or even absence of reliable drafts (both plans and sections), sometimes no drawings or photographs can be found at all.

- The total absence of reliable radiocarbon dates.

---

① Novgorodova E. Drevnyaya Mongoliya. Moscow. 1989: 81–86 (in Russian)

· 30 ·

The poor knowledge of the Bronze Age in Mongolia at the end of 20th century appears especially obvious in comparison with the neighboring areas of Russia, Kazakhstan and even China. (Many thousands of barrows belonged to cattle-breeding tribes of 3 - 1 millennia B. C. were explored and excavated on those territories up to that time.) This circumstance appeared to be a considerable obstacle for the study of cultural and historical processes in Bronze Age at Central and Inner Asia.

Thus, the principal task of our project was to improve this situation.

The work of our expedition yielded the following main results: [①]

- barrows belonging to Afanasievo 阿凡纳羡沃文化 culture for the first time in the North-West Mongolia (in Bayan-Ulgii 巴彦乌列盖省 aimag) were found; one of them dated back to the first half of the 3rd millennium B. C. had been excavated.

- sites belonging to Chemurchek 切木尔切克文化 culture (2800 - 1800 years B. C.) at the foothills of Mongolian Altai also for the first time were discovered; 6 barrows in Khovd 科布多省 aimag and 4 ones — in Bayan-Ulgi 巴彦乌列盖省 aimag had been excavated.

- a new culture of Middle Bronze Age (about 1700 - 1300 years B. C.) named by us "Munkh-Khairkhan 门海尔汗文化 culture" was discovered; the 13 related barrows in Khovd 科布多省, Zavkhan 扎布汗省-and Hovsgol 库苏古尔省-aimags had been excavated.

- 8 burials dated from the Late Bronze Age (about 12 - 10 centuries B. C.) were excavated in Bulgan 布尔干苏木 sum of Khovd 科布多省 aimag; they belonged to an unknown culture, which was preliminary called a "Baitag 北塔" culture.

- as a result of excavations of burial sites in Gobi Altay 戈壁阿尔泰山 Mountains (Uverkhangai 前杭爱省-, Bayankhongor 巴彦洪戈尔省-and South Gobi 南戈壁省-aimags) a new "Tevsh 特布希文化" culture of Late Bronze Age have been stated (dated from about 13 - 10 centuries B. C.). Several "figured" tombs, which where formerly investigated by Soviet-Mongolian archaeological expedition near Tevsh-uul Mountain in Bogd 博格多苏木 sum of Uverkhangai 前杭爱省-aimag also belong to this culture.

- on the base of excavations, 14 - C dating and cartography of sites the absolute and relative chronologies

① Some results of our work were published in: Erdenebaatar D., Davaatseren B. Shineer oldson zevsgiin dursgaluud // Khar suld (Erdem shinzhilgeenii setguul). Vol. 4 (2004). fasc. 1. pp. 4 - 10. (in Mongolian); Erdenebaatar D., Kovalev A. Munh Khairkhany soyol // Tuukhiin sudlal. Vol. 34 (2003). Fasc. 1. pp. 8 - 12. (in Mongolian); Erdenebaatar D., Kovalev A. Khirigsuur, bugan chuluun khushuug kholbon uzekh n'. In: Ugsaatan sudlal Vol. 15 (2003). Fasc. 16. pp. 150 - 157. (in Mongolian); Erdenebaatar, D., Kovalev A. Mongol Altai dakh' bugan khushuutei khirigsuur. In: Tuukhiin sudlal. Vol. 37 (2007). Fasc. 2. pp. 13 - 25. (in Mongolian); Kovalev A., Erdenebaatar D. Mongol'skii Altai v bronzovom I rannem zheleznom vekakh (po materialam Mezhdunarodnoi Central'no-Aziatskoi Arheologicheskoi Expeditsii Sankt-Peterburgskogo Gosudarstvennogo Universiteta, Instituta Istorii AN Mongolii I Ulan-Batorskogo Universiteta) // Altae-Sayanskaya gornaya strana i istoriya osvoeniya ee kochevnikami. Barnaul. 2007. pp. 80 - 85. (in Russian); Kovalev A., Erdenebaatar D. Dve traditsii ritual'nogo ispol'zovaniya olennykh kamnei Mongolii // Kamennaya skul'ptura I melkaya plastika drevnikh I srednevekovykh narodov Evrazii (= Trudy SAIPI 3), pp. 99 - 105. Barnaul. 2007. (in Russian); Kovalev A., Erdenebaatar D. Discovery of New Cultures of the Bronze Age in Mongolia (According to the data obtained by the International Central Asiatic Archaeological Expedition) // Archeological Investigations in Mongolia: 1997 - 2007. Bonn. 2008 (in print) (in Russian); Kovalev A. Velikaya tangutskaya stena. In: Teoriya i praktika arheologicheskih issledovanii. Vol. 5. Barnaul. 2008 (In print) (in Russian); Varenov A., Kovalev A., Erdenebaatar D. Razvedka pazyrykskikh kurganov v severo-zapadnoi Mongolii // Problemy arheologii, etnografii, antropologii Sibiri i sopredel'nykh territorii. Volume X. Materialy Godovoi sessii Instituta arheologii I etnografii SO RAN 2004 goda. Vol. 1. Novosibirsk. 2004. pp. 211 - 216. (in Russian).

of formerly known types of burial constructions of the Late Bronze and the Early Iron Ages (14 - 3 centuries B. C.) in Mongolian Altai 阿尔泰 have been established. [1]

- for the first time a complete scientific excavations of ritual-burial and ritual sites of "deer stones 鹿石" had been conducted in Khovd 科布多省 aimag (khereksur in Har gov') and Hovsgol 库苏古尔省 aimag (deer stone complex in Surtiin denj) and accordingly two different traditions of deer stones ritual usage — Western-Mongolian one and Central-Mongolian one were discovered, which simultaneously existed at the neighboring territories. [2]

- the area around 200 × 300 km of Pasyryk culture 巴泽雷克文化 monuments distribution over Mongolian Altai 蒙古国阿尔泰山 in 6 - 3 centuries B. C. have been ascertained. [3]

- the Bayan-Bulag 巴彦布拉克 fortress[4] in Nomgon 瑙木冈苏木 sum of South Gobi 南戈壁省 aimag has been attributed: it is Shouxiangcheng 受降城 fortress, which had been built by the order of Wu-di 武帝, the emperor of Chinese Han Dynasty in 105 year B. C.. [5]

- with the aid of the results of 14 - C analysis the exact data of construction of the so called "Chinggis Khan Wall" in South Gobi aimag[6] was ascertained — appearing to be the beginning of 13th century A. C. , this wall probably was build by Tanguts 西夏 as defense against Chingghis-han expansion. [7]

Present paper is devoted only to our discovery of new Bronze Age cultures in Mongolia.

1. Afanasievo 阿凡纳羡沃文化 culture. A barrow belonging to this culture named Khurgak-Govi (Khurai-Gov') #1 was excavated by our expedition in 2004 in Ulankhus 乌兰呼斯苏木 sum of Bayan-Ulgii 巴彦乌列盖省 aimag. The barrow was situated at the first terrace of the left bank of Kara-Dzhamat-Gol River. It looked like a flat round stone pavement, 16 meters in diameter, about 1 meter high limited by a stone fence made of vertical stone slabs (this is characteristic feature of Altai Afanasievo 阿尔泰共和国阿凡纳羡沃文化[8]). (Fig. 1 - 1). One more similar slab stone was erected separately at the eastern side of the mound. In the central part of the construction lay a rectangular tomb pit more than 2 meters deep, in which a man and a child were buried, laid on their backs, with heads eastwards (Fig. 1 - 3). A bottom of a wooden vehicle's body (Fig. 1 - 2) served as a ceiling for the burial goods were laid on it, including a knife and an

① Kovalev A. , Erdenebaatar D. Mongol'skii Altai v bronzovom I rannem zheleznom vekakh (po materialam Mezhdunarodnoi Central'no-Aziatskoi Arheologicheskoi Expeditsii Sankt-Peterburgskogo Gosudarstvennogo Universiteta, Instituta Istorii AN Mongolii I Ulan-Batorskogo Universiteta) // Altae-Sayanskaya gornaya strana i istoriya osvoeniya ee kochevnikami. Barnaul. 2007. pp. 80 - 85. (in Russian).: 83 - 84

② Kovalev A. , Erdenebaatar D. Dve traditsii ritual'nogo ispol'zovaniya olennykh kamnei Mongolii // Kamennaya skul'ptura I melkaya plastika drevnikh I srednevekovykh narodov Evrazii (= Trudy SAIPI 3), pp. 99 - 105. Barnaul. 2007. (in Russian)

③ Varenov A. , Kovalev A. , Erdenebaatar D. Razvedka pazyrykskikh kurganov v severo-zapadnoi Mongolii // Problemy arheologii, etnografii, antropologii Sibiri i sopredel'nykh territorii. Volume X. Materialy Godovoi sessii Instituta arheologii I etnografii SO RAN 2004 goda. Vol. 1. Novosibirsk. 2004. pp. 211 - 216. (in Russian).

④ Batsaikhan, Z. Khunnu. Ulaanbaatar. 2002 (on Mongolian). : 46 - 54.

⑤ 司马迁:《史记》,第1~10页。北京:中华书局,1996: 2915

⑥ This wall was erroneously believed by chinese archaeologists to Early Han period, to so colld "north part of outer Han walls", see 李逸友:《中国北方长城考述》,《内蒙古文物考古》2001 年第1期。第1~51页:23~24。

⑦ Kovalev A. Velikaya tangutskaya stena. In: Teoriya i praktika arheologicheskih issledovanii. Vol. 5. Barnaul. 2008 (In print) (in Russian)

⑧ Pogozheva A. , Rykun M. , Stepanova N. , Tur S. Epokha eneolita I bronzy Gornogo Altaya. Vol. 1. Barnaul. 2006. : 27 - 28

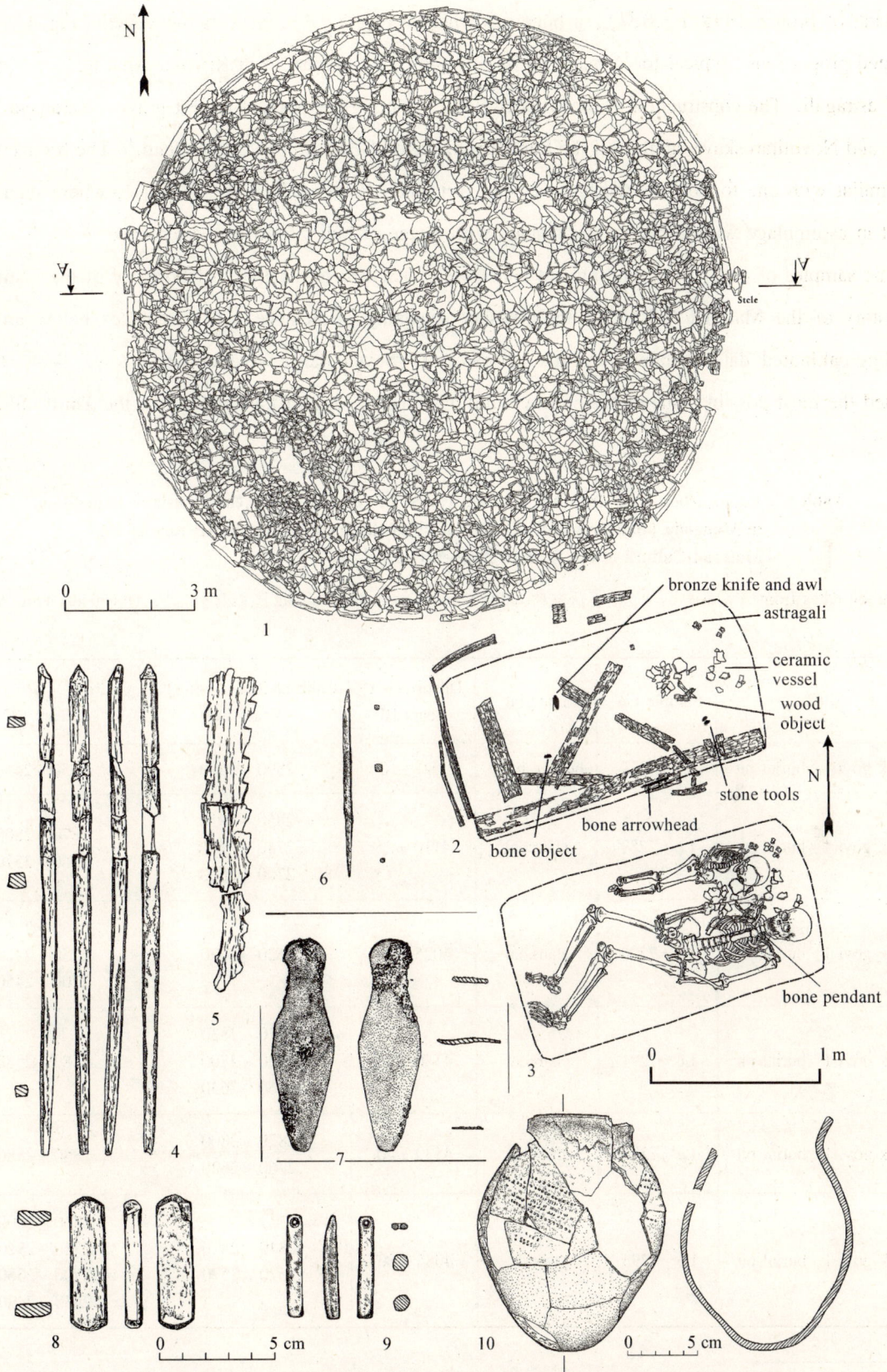

Fig. 1　Afanasievo 阿凡纳羡沃文化 culture. Barrow 1, Kurgak govi (Khuurai gov')
(Ulaanhus sum, Bayan-Ul'gi aimag 巴彦乌列盖省 乌兰呼斯苏木).

1 – plan of barrow　2 – bottom of a wooden wehicle's body with burial goods inside burial pit　3 – plan of the burial　4 – bone arrowhead　5 – wood object　6 – bronze awl　7 – bronze knife　8 – bone tool　9 – bone pendant　10 – ceramic vessel

awl made of bronze (Fig. 1 - 6,7), a bone arrowhead (Fig. 1 - 4), an ceramic vessel (Fig. 1 - 10) of elongated proportions, typical for Afanasievo 阿凡纳羡沃文化 culture from Russian Altai 阿尔泰共和国,[1] sheep' astragali. The construction of the wooden vehicle's body was typical for Pit-grave (Yamnaya 竖穴墓文化) and Novotitaroskaya cultures of the Early Bronze age of East European grassland.[2] The bronze knife is very similar with one found from the barrow near Tarlyshkin River in Tuva 图瓦共和国, where such bronze artifact in assemblage with jasper scepter headed with image of bull's head was discovered.[3]

The samples of coal, wood and human bones were analyzed in the 14 - C laboratory of the Institute for the History of the Material Culture of the Russian Academy of Science (all references below are given according calibrated dates obtained by this laboratory). Seven dates were obtained (see Tabl. 1); all indicated the most possible time of the barrow building to be the end of the first half of the Third millennium B. C.

Table 1   Radiocarbon dates from the sites excavated by International Central-Asiatic Expedition in Mongolia (data from 14 - C laboratory of the Institute for the History of the Material Culture of the Russian Academy of Science)

Radiocarbon dates from Afanasievo 阿凡纳羡沃文化 culture site, Bayan Ulgii aimag 巴彦乌列盖省,Ulaankhus sum 乌兰呼斯苏木

Site	Sample no.	material	Uncorrected, Years BP	Calib 68,2% (1-sig), Years BC	Calib 95,4% (2-sig), Years BC
Kurgak govi 1, burial pit	Le - 7219	human bone	4180 ± 100	2890 ~ 2620	3050 ~ 2459
Kurgak govi 1, burial pit	Le - 7289	charcoal	4110 ± 25	2850 ~ 2810 2740 ~ 2720 2700 ~ 2580	2870 ~ 2800 2760 ~ 2570
Kurgak govi 1, burial pit	Le - 7290	charkoal	4025 ± 50	2620 ~ 2470	2860 ~ 2810 2750 ~ 2720 2700 ~ 2450
Kurgak govi 1, burial pit	Le - 7291	charcoal	4140 ± 35	2870 ~ 2830 2820 ~ 2800 2760 ~ 2630	2880 ~ 2580
Kurgak govi 1. burial pit	Le - 7292	charcoal	4130 ± 40	2870 ~ 2800 2760 ~ 2620	2880 ~ 2580
Kurgak govi 1, burial pit	Le - 7293	wood	4085 ± 30	2840 ~ 2810 2670 ~ 2570	2860 ~ 2800 2760 ~ 2720 2700 ~ 2560 2530 ~ 2490

① Pogozheva A., Rykun M., Stepanova N., Tur S. Epokha eneolita I bronzy Gornogo Altaya. Vol. 1. Barnaul. 2006. (in Russian): Tabl. 28, 37, 40, 48, 57, 62, 64.

② Gei A. Novotitorovskaya kul'tura. Moscow. 2000 (in Russian).: 175 - 191

③ Kyzlasov L. Drevnyaya Tuva (ot paleolita do IX veka). Moscow. 1979 (in Russian). pp. 25 - 26.

Radiocarbon dates from Chemurchek 切木尔切克文化 culture sites，Bayan ulgii aimag 巴彦乌列盖省，Ulaankhus sum 乌兰呼斯苏木

Site	Sample no.	material	Uncorrected, Years BP	Calib 68,2%（1-sig）, Years BC	Calib 95,4%（2-sig）, Years BC
Kurgak govi 2 earliest pit	Le－7294	charcoal	4090 ± 50	2860 ~ 2810 2750 ~ 2720 2700 ~ 2570 2520 ~ 2500	2880 ~ 2800 2780 ~ 2490
Kurgak govi 2 earliest pit	Le－7295	charcoal	4100 ± 30	2850 ~ 2810 2680 ~ 2570	2870 ~ 2800 2760 ~ 2560 2520 ~ 2500
Kurgak govi 2 earliest pit	Le－7296	charcoal	4100 ± 35	2860 ~ 2810 2700 ~ 2570	2870 ~ 2800 2780 ~ 2560 2520 ~ 2490
Kurgak govi 2 secondary burial	Le－7215	human bone	3825 ± 70	2410 ~ 2370 2360 ~ 2190 2180 ~ 2140	2470 ~ 2120 2100 ~ 2030
Kumdi govi earliest pit	Le－7300	charcoal	4050 ± 30	2630 ~ 2550 2540 ~ 2490	2840 ~ 2810 2670 ~ 2640 2630 ~ 2470
Kumdi govi earliest pit	Le－7301	charcoal	4110 ± 20	2680 ~ 2810 2680 ~ 2580	2860 ~ 2810 2750 ~ 2720 2700 ~ 2570
Kumdi govi secondary burial 2	Le－7212	human bone	3900 ± 70	2470 ~ 2280 2250 ~ 2230	2580 ~ 2510 2500 ~ 2190 2170 ~ 2140
Kumdi govi secondary burial 1（the latest）	Le－7221	human bone	3340 ± 70	1690 ~ 1520	1870 ~ 1840 1780 ~ 1440
Kulala ula 1 earliest burial pit	Le－7297	charcoal	4470 ± 90	3340 ~ 3020	3400 ~ 2900
Kulala ula 1 earliest burial pit	Le－7298	charcoal	3950 ± 50	2570 ~ 2520 2500 ~ 2400 2390 ~ 2340	2580 ~ 2290
Kulala ula 1 earliest burial pit	Le－7299	wood	4820 ± 30	3650 ~ 3630 3580 ~ 3570 3560 ~ 3530	3660 ~ 3620 3600 ~ 3520
Kulala ula 1 secondary burial 1	Le－7220	human bone	3725 ± 115	2290 ~ 1950	2500 ~ 1750
Kara tumsik burial pit	Le－7302	charcoal	4025 ± 30	2575 ~ 2545 2540 ~ 2485	2620 ~ 2470
Kara tumsik burial pit	Le－7303	charcoal	4120 ± 20	2860 ~ 2810 2700 ~ 2620 2610 ~ 2600	2870 ~ 2800 2760 ~ 2720 2710 ~ 2580

Radiocarbon dates from Chemurchek 切木尔切克文化 culture sites, Khovd 科布多省 aimag, Bulgan sum 布尔干苏木

Site	Sample no.	material	Uncorrected, Years BP	Calib 68,2% (1-sig), Years BC	Calib 95,4% (2-sig), Years BC
Yagshiin khodoo 1, burial chamber	Le - 6937	human bone	3790 ± 120	2460 ~ 2440 2430 ~ 2420 2410 ~ 2110 2100 ~ 2030	2600 ~ 1850
Yagshiin khodoo 1, burial chamber	Le - 6938	human bone	3720 ± 60	2200 ~ 2030 1990 ~ 1980	2300 ~ 1940
Yagshiin khodoo 1 human bones in situ at the bottom of burial chamber	Le - 7578	human bone	3720 ± 70	2270 ~ 2250 2210 ~ 2020 2000 ~ 1980	2340 ~ 1910
Yagshiin khodoo 2, burial chamber	Le - 6942	human bone	3880 ± 100	2480 ~ 2190	2650 ~ 2000
Yagshiin khodoo 3, human bones in situ at the bottom of burial chamber	Le - 6932	human bone	3770 ± 60	2290 ~ 2130 2090 ~ 2040	2410 ~ 2370 2360 ~ 2020 2000 ~ 1970
Yagshiin khodoo 3, burial chamber	Le - 6933	human bone	4000 ± 80	2830 ~ 2820 2660 ~ 2650 2630 ~ 2400 2380 ~ 2350	2900 ~ 2200
Yagshiin khodoo 3	Le - 6939	human bone	3800 ± 70	2400 ~ 2380 2350 ~ 2130	2470 ~ 2030
Kheviin am 1, burial chamber	Le - 7217	human bone	3560 ± 105	2040 ~ 1740	2200 ~ 1600
Kheviin am 1, burial chamber	Le - 7222	human bone	3440 ± 120	1890 ~ 1600 1560 ~ 1530	2150 ~ 1400
Kheviin am 1, burial chamber	Le - 7224	human bone	3800 ± 200	2550 ~ 1900	2900 ~ 1600
Kheviin am 1 burial 1 (in the fill of stone cist)	Le - 7975	human bone	3520 ± 100	2010 ~ 2000 1980 ~ 1730 1720 ~ 1690	2150 ~ 1500
Kheviin am 1, burial chamber	Le - 7229	charcoal	3770 ± 60	2290 ~ 2130 2090 ~ 2040	2410 ~ 2370 2360 ~ 2020 2000 ~ 1970
Kheviin am 1, burial chamber	Le - 7230	wood	4100 ± 200	2950 ~ 2300	3400 ~ 2000
Kheviin am 2, burial chamber	Le - 7214	human bone	3830 ± 120	2470 ~ 2130 2080 ~ 2070	2650 ~ 1900
Kheviin am 2, burial chamber	Le - 7228	charcoal	3720 ± 30	2200 ~ 2170 2150 ~ 2120 2100 ~ 2030	2200 ~ 2020 1990 ~ 1980
Buural kharyn ar, burial chamber	Le - 7225	human bone	4250 ± 500	3600 ~ 2200	4100 ~ 1500

Radiocarbon dates from Munh-Khairhan 门海尔汗文化 culture sites，Khovd aimag 科布多省，Munh-Khairhan sum 门海尔汗苏木

Site	Sample no.	material	Uncorrected, Years BP	Calib 68,2% (1-sig), Years BC	Calib 95,4% (2-sig), Years BC
Ulaan goviin uzuur 1, burial pit	Le - 6941	human bone	3310 ± 90	1730 ~ 1720 1700 ~ 1490	1880 ~ 1840 1780 ~ 1410
Ulaan goviin uzuur 2, burial pit	Le - 6936	human bone	3150 ± 70	1510 ~ 1370 1340 ~ 1310	1610 ~ 1260
Hotuu davaa 1, burial pit	Le - 6935	human bone	3270 ± 60	1620 ~ 1490 1480 ~ 1430	1690 ~ 1430
Artua, burial pit	Le - 6934	human bone	3480 ± 90	1920 ~ 1680	2040 ~ 1600 1580 ~ 1530

Radiocarbon dates from Tevsh 特布希文化 culture sites，Bayankhongor aimag 巴彦洪戈尔省，Bayanlig sum 巴彦勒格苏木

Site	Sample no.	material	Uncorrected, Years BP	Calib 68,2% (1-sig), Years BC	Calib 95,4% (2-sig), Years BC
Baruun gyalaat 2, burial pit	Le - 7954	human bone	2900 ± 50	1200 ~ 1010	1270 ~ 970 960 ~ 930
Zamyn butz, burial pit	Le - 7971	human bone	2990 ± 70	1380 ~ 1330 1320 ~ 1120	1410 ~ 1010
Zamyn butz, secondary burial	Le - 7966	human bone	2980 ± 110	1380 ~ 1330 1320 ~ 1050	1450 ~ 900

Radiocarbon dates from Baitag 北塔文化 culture site，Hovd 科布多省 aimag，Bulgan sum 布尔干苏木

Site	Sample no.	material	Uncorrected, Years BP	Calib 68,2% (1-sig), Years BC	Calib 95,4% (2-sig), Years BC
Kheviin am, secondary burial	Le - 7223	human bone	2910 ± 90	1260 ~ 1230 1220 ~ 970 960 ~ 940	1400 ~ 850

Two mounds of smaller size also belonging to Afanasievo 阿凡纳羡沃文化 culture with the fences made of vertical slabs were found in the same sum at the first terrace of the left bank of Sogog-Gol river, near another mound, excavated by our expedition, belonged to Chemurchek 切木尔切克文化 culture, named Kumdi-govi (Hundii gov').

2. Chemurchek 切木尔切克文化 culture. As it was ascertained by our expedition, Chemurchek tribes had begun to spread over the territory of Mongolian part of Mongolian Altai from the middle of the third millennium B. C. Formerly the some sites belonging to this culture have been explored only out of the

territory of Mongolia. [1] In 2002 D. Erdenebaatar firstly discovered the Chemurchek 切木尔切克文化 culture site 墓地 on the Mongolian territory in Yagshiin Khodoo. After this we excavated six barrows of Chemurchek 切木尔切克文化 culture near the centre of Bulgan 布尔干苏木 sum of Khovd 科布多省 aimag (burial places Yagshiin Khodoo, Kheviin Am, Buural Kharyn Ar) and also four rectangular burial enclosures in Ulanhus 乌兰呼斯苏木 sum of Bayan-Ulgi 巴彦乌列盖省 aimag (Kulala-Ula (Khul-Uul), barrow 1, Kurgak-Govi (Khuurai Gov'), barrow 2, Kumdi-Govi (Khundii Gov'), Kara-Tumsik (Khar Khoshuu) (one more barrow of such type of Chemurchek 切木尔切克文化 culture have been discovered on the left bank of Tsagaan-Gol River).

The barrows excavated by our expedition in Bayan-Ul'gi 巴彦乌列 looked like rectangular stone enclosures included earth-pits, which were orientated with their longer sides by West-East (Kulala-Ula-by North-South) (see Fig. 2 - 1,2). Two of four stone-fences were joined by stone pillars (stelae), which were established at the Eastern side of the construction: the stele at the barrow of Kulala-Ula had been established at the Southern side and have been worked up to look like a human body (Fig. 2 - 4). At the barrow of Kara-Tumsik one of such stele stood inside the enclosure at the Eastern side of the tomb and had been colored with red ochre (ruddle) (Fig. 2 - 3).

Sites of Chemurchek 切木尔切克文化 type in Bayan-Ul'gi 巴彦乌列 look like those of namely Chinese Altai 阿勒泰地区 Chemurchek burial constructions, [2] which also were rectangular stone enclosures orientated, as the rule, with their longer sides by West-East, and in rare cases — by North-South. At the middle of their Eastern side (or at the Southern side) there was established a stone statue or a stone pillar. Inside the stone fences, along their long sides, there were sepulchers-boxes made of large stone slabs, which contained several burials.

Burial places of Bulgan 布尔干苏木 look like huge stone boxes, oriented by East-West, constructed of massive stone slabs which were situated on the ancient surface or were cut into the soil, and were use as crypt for many burials (till 10 persons). The stone box was reinforced from outside (not covered!) by surrounded stone heaps or by soil cairns covered one another, which were added by rectangular row of light boulders. (see Fig. 3 - 1) At the Eastern side of the barrow Jagshiin Khodoo #3 there was established a typical Chemurchek 切木尔切克文化 statue[3] of a man wearing a helmet, with the face turned to the South, with uncovered chest, and with a "crook" and a bow in his hands (Fig. 3 -3). At the Eastern side of the barrow

---

① Kovalev A. Überlegungen zur Herkunft der Skythen aufgrund archäologischer Daten // Eurasia Antiqua 4 (1998). Berlin. 1999. pp. 247 - 271.; Kovalev A. Die ältesten Stelen am Ertix. Das Kulturphänomen Xemirxek // Eurasia Antiqua 5 (1999): Berlin. 2000. pp. 135 - 178; Kovalev A. Chemurchekskii kul'turnyi fenomen: ego proishozhdeniye I rol' v formirovanii kul'tur epokhi rannei bronzy Altaya I Central'noi Azii // Zapadnaya I Yuzhnaya Sibir' v drevnosti. Sbornik nauchnykh trudov, posvyash'sh'ennyi 60 - letiyu so dnya rozhdeniya Yuriya Fedorovicha Kiryushina. Barnaul. 2005. pp. 178 - 184. (in Russian); Kovalev A. Chemurchekskii kul'turnyi fenomen (statya 1999 goda). // "A. V." Sbornik nauchnykh trudov v chest' 60 - letiya A. V. Vinogradova. Sankt-Petersburg. 2007. pp. 25 - 76. (in Russian)

② 新疆社会科学院考古研究所:《新疆克尔木齐古墓发掘简报》,《文物》1981 年第 1 期,第 23 ~32 页。

③ See 王博、祁小山:《丝绸之路草原石人研究》,乌鲁木齐,1996,石人 Ea 第 1 ~7, 14, 16 ~18, 20, 22, 23, 26 ~28, 30, 31, 34, 38, 41 ~46, 49, 50 号; Kovalev A. Die ältesten Stelen am Ertix. Das Kulturphänomen Xemirxek // Eurasia Antiqua 5 (1999): Berlin. 2000: Tab. 3 - 8.

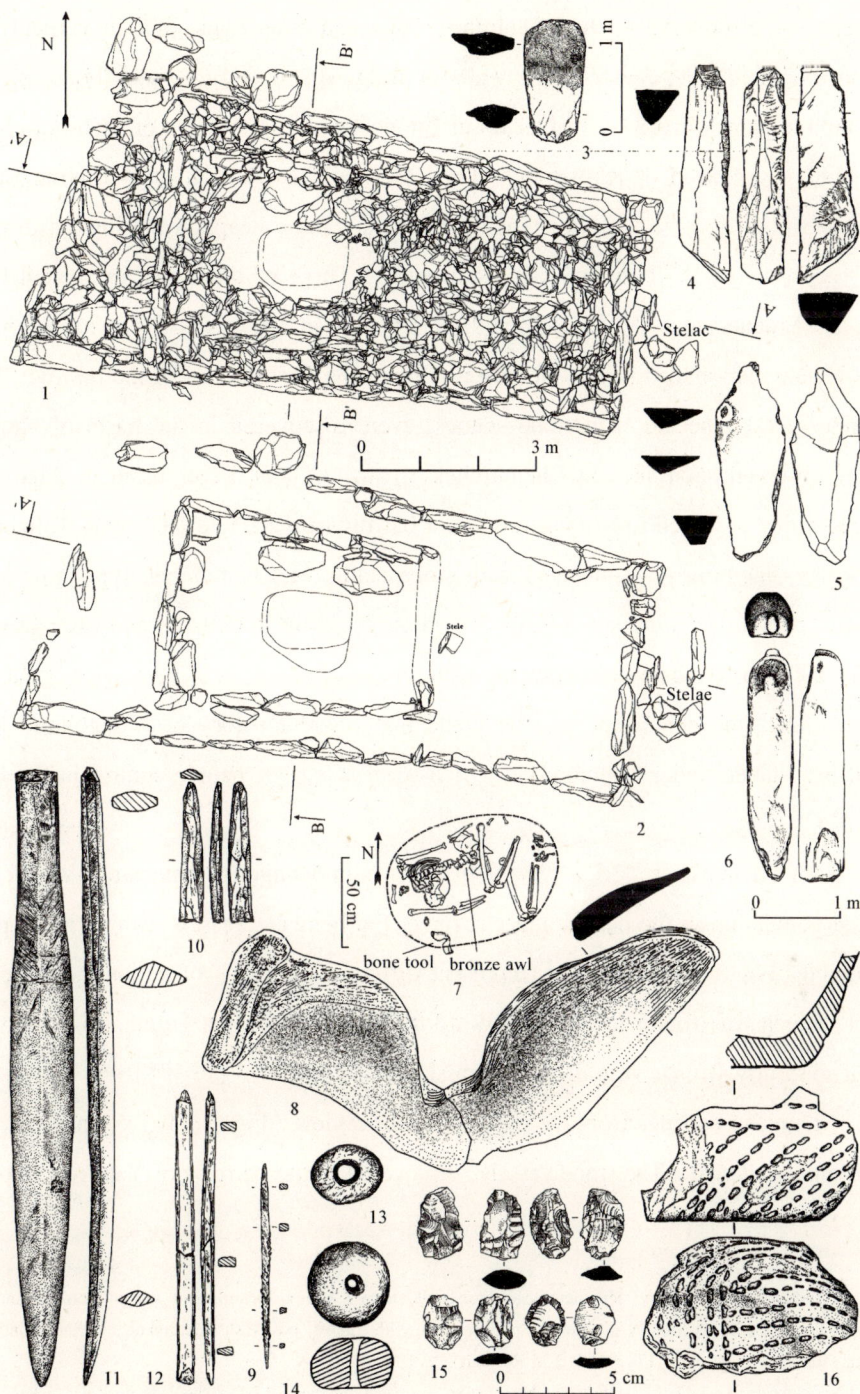

Fig. 2 Chemurchek culture, Ulaanhus sum, Bayan-Ul'gi aimag and analogies.
切木尔切克文化,巴彦乌列盖省乌兰呼斯苏木。

1 – plan of the Kara tumsik (Khar khoshuu) barrow　2 – Kara tumsik (Khar khoshuu) barrow, plan of the stone fence　3 – Kara tumsik (Khar khoshuu) barrow, ochre-covered stele erected on the eastern side of the tomb　4 – Kulala ula (Khul uul) barrow 1, stele erected on the eastern side of the barrow.　5 – Eastern Kazakhstan 东哈萨克斯坦州, Kurchum district, barrow Kopa 2, stele erected on the eastern side of the barrow.　6 – Mongolia, Khovd aimag, Munhkhairkhan sum 科布多省门海尔汗苏木, anthropomorphic stele secondary used in khereksur Har gov'　7 – Kumdi govi (Khundii gov') barrow, plan of the earliest secondary burial　8 – Kumdi govi (Khundii gov') barrow, earliest secondary burial, bone "scutcher"　9 – Kumdi govi (Khundii gov') barrow, earliest secondary burial, bronze awl　10 – Kulala ula (Khul uul) 1 barrow, part of bone arrowhead　11 – Kulala ula (Khul uul) 1 barrow, bone dagger　12 – Kara tumsik (Khar khoshuu) barrow, bone arrowhead　13 – Kulala ula (Khul uul) 1 barrow, limestone ball　14 – Kumdi govi (Khundii gov') barrow, marble ball from the earliest pit　15 – Kurgak govi (Khuurai gov') 2 barrow, secondary burial, stone tools　16 – Kara tumsik (Khar khoshuu) barrow, crock of ceramic vessel

Kheviin-Am 1 there was discovered a ritual "entrance" that had been made of thin vertical stone slabs and pavements made of boulders (Fig 3 - 1). The walls of Bulgan 布尔干苏木 stone boxes were decorated in ancient times by the red paint (Fig. 3 - 2). Our observations show that the area of such burial constructions is wide spread, including low basin of Khovd 科布多河 River and Buyant River.[①] Having took after this in 2006 new Chemurchek 切木尔切克文化 boxes with surronding stone heaps in the low basin of Buyant River near Hovd town 科布多市 by A. Tishkin were discovered.[②] Three of them was excavated by A. Tishkin, Ch. Munhbayar, D. Erdenebaatar, S. Grushin and A. Kovalev in 2007 - 08.[③] The excavations showed that there was a ritual rectangular-shaped pavement with a pillar at the Eastern side of the barrow. The same burial stone boxes, which were connected with stone statues, were discovered in the basin of Ertix 额尔齐斯河 River (A. Kovalev observed such sites in Chemurchek 切木尔切克河 River basin in Altai 新疆阿勒泰县 county,[④] also A. Kovalev observed same construction of barrow near Samute 萨木特 in Tangbaleyuzi village, Qinghe county 青河县唐巴勒玉孜 connected with stone statue of Chemurchek type[⑤]). Even more: the same stone box with two surrounding stone heaps was discovered by S. Grushin and excavated by S. Grushin and A. Kovalev in 2006 in Tretiakovo district of Altai 俄罗斯阿尔泰边疆区 Region (Russia), near the Kazakhstan border. Thus the conclusion can be made that broad territory of Mongolian, Kazakhstan and Russian Altai had been taken under Chemurchek 切木尔切克文化民族 people control in the last centuries of Third millenium B. C.

The findings from Chemurchek 切木尔切克文化 barrows in Mongolia demonstrate wide cultural relations of Mongolian Altai population in the period under review. Earthenware vessels, which in Yagsiin Khodoo 1, 3 barrows were found (Fig. 3 - 9, 10, 11), represent different traditions of ceramic production, including flat-bottom vessel, which was found in the barrow #3 (Fig. 3 - 11), are similar to such vessels of great Elunino culture of the Early Bronze Age of Altai Grassland (Middle Ob' 鄂毕河 River, Altai Region 俄罗斯阿尔泰边疆区).[⑥] The lead earrings from the barrows under review (Fig. 3 - 4,5,6) also are analogous with such earrings of Elunino culture.[⑦] The stone vessels, discovered in the barrows of Yagshiin Khodoo 2, Kheviin

① Kovalev A. Chemurchekskii kul'turnyi fenomen: ego proishozhdeniye I rol' v formirovanii kul'tur epokhi rannei bronzy Altaya I Central'noi Azii // Zapadnaya I Yuzhnaya Sibir' v drevnosti. Sbornik nauchnykh trudov, posvyash'sh'ennyi 60 - letiyu so dnya rozhdeniya Yuriya Fedorovicha Kiryushina. Barnaul. 2005. pp. 178 - 184. (in Russian). : 180

② Tishkin A., Nyamdorzh B., Dashkovskii P., Nyamsuren L., Munhbayar, Ch. Arheologicheskie izyskaniya v Hovd aimake (predvaritel'noye soobsh'sh'eniye) // Ekologo-geograficheskiye, arheologicheskiye I socioetnograficheskiye issledovaniya v Yuzhnoi Sibiri I Zapadnoi Mongolii. Barnaul. 2006. (in Russian). pp. 107 - 114. : 111

③ Tishkin A., Erdenebaatar D. Pervyye rezul'taty Buyantskoi arheologicheskoi expedicii // Altae-Sayanskaya gornaya strana i istoriya osvoeniya ee kochevnikami. Barnaul. 2007. pp. 165 - 168. : 166

④ 王林山、王博:《中国阿勒泰草原文物》,深圳,1996,第 47 页。图:100, 101; Kovalev A. Die ältesten Stelen am Ertix. Das Kulturphänomen Xemirxek // Eurasia Antiqua 5 (1999): Berlin. 2000. pp. 135 - 178. : 145

⑤ Statue from Samute barrow was published in 王林山、王博:《中国阿勒泰草原文物》,深圳,1996,第 37 页。图:65; 王博、祁小山: 《丝绸之路草原石人研究》,乌鲁木齐,1996。石人#161 - Ea - 6 第 163 页.

⑥ Kiryushin Yu. Eneolit I rannyaya bronza yuga Zapadnoi Sibiri. Barnaul. 2002 (in Russian): 48 - 51

⑦ Kiryushin Yu., Tishkin A. Nakhodki svinca pri issledovaniyakh pamyatnikov epokhi rannei bronzy i svidetel'stva ikh proizvodstva v predgorno-ravninnoi chasti Altaiskogo kraya. // 300 let gorno-geologicheskoi sluzhbe Rossii. Istoriya gornorudnogo dela, geologicheskoye stroeniye I poleznyye iskopayemye Altaya. Barnaul. 2000. pp. 8 - 12. (in Russian)

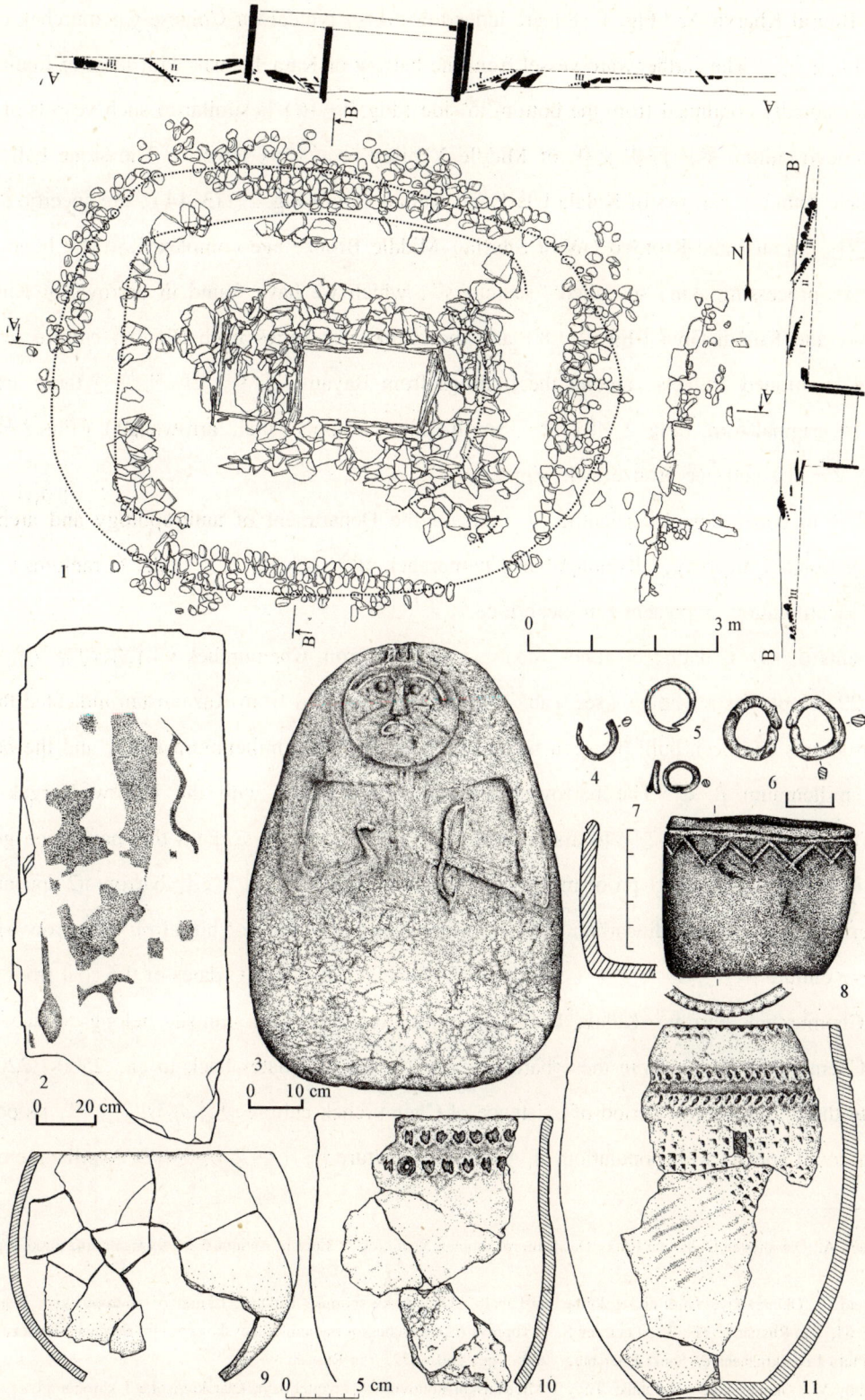

Fig. 3　Chemurchek culture 切木尔切克文化. Khovd aimag 科布多省, Bulgan sum 布尔干苏木.

1 - Kheviin am 1 barrow, plan and sections (I, II, III— soil cairns covering with stones)　2 - Yagshiin khodoo 3 barrow, stone slab with picture (from western wall of the stone box)　3 - Yagshiin khodoo 3 barrow, stone sculpture erected from the eastern side of the barrow　4 - Yagshiin khodoo 1 barrow, lead ring　5 - Yagshiin khodoo 1 barrow, lead ring　6 - Yagshiin khodoo 3 barrow, lead ring　7 - Yagshiin khodoo 1 barrow, bronze ring　8 - Buural kharyn ar barrow, stone vessel　9 - Yagshiin khodoo 1 barrow, ceramic vessel　10 - Yagshiin khodoo 1 barrow, ceramic vessel　11 - Yagshiin khodoo 3 barrow, ceramic vessel

Am 1, and Buural Kharyn Ar (Fig. 3 - 8) are indeed artifacts, typical for Chinese Chemurchek culture 阿勒泰切木尔切克文化. [①] The earthenware vessel from the barrow of Kara Tumsik with lines of impints of stamp which uninterruptedly continued from the bottom to side (Fig. 2 - 16) is similar to such vessels of the earliest stage of Okunevo culture 奥库涅夫文化 of Middle Yenisey 叶尼塞河 River. [②] The stone balls with holes which we have found in barrows of Kulala Ula 1 and Kumdi Govi (Fig. 2 - 13,14), are specific for Okunevo 奥库涅夫文化, Samus' and Krotovo (West Sibiria) Middle Bronze age complexes. [③] The bone artifacts — implements for processing skin, so called "scutchers", which we have found in barrows of Kulala Ula 1, Kurgak Govi, and Kumdi Govi (Fig. 2 - 8) are known in mass series from Elunino culture settlements. [④] Also, above mentioned artifacts, among the findings from Bayan-Ulgi 巴彦乌列盖省 there are two bone arrowheads of original form (Fig. 2 - 10,12), smoll flintstone tools (incl. arrowhead) (Fig. 2 - 15), bone dagger (Fig. 2 - 11) and one bronze awl (Fig. 2 - 14).

According to conclusions of scientific workers of the Department of anthropology and archaeology of Mongolian National University, all mongolian Chemurchek 切木尔切克文化 skulls (craniums), which are suitable for identification, represent European race.

The results of 14 - C dating of bones, coals, and wood from Chemurchek 切木尔切克文化 barrows of Mongolia (29 samples as a whole) (see Tabl. 1) and also 15 items from Kazakhstan indicated that all these burial constructions had been built between second third of the Third millennium B. C. and the beginning of the Second millennium B. C. The barrow Kurgak-Govi 2 coupled with the barrow Kurgak-Govi 1 of Afanasievo culture 阿凡纳羡沃文化 to a separat burial place. Two 14 - C dates that have been got from the coal found in the earliest (ritual) pit of mentioned Chemurchek 切木尔切克文化 barrow #2 appeared to be in the same period that are four radiocarbon dates from the coal from filling of burial pit of barrow #1 belonging to Afanasievo culture 阿凡纳羡沃文化 (ca. 2800 - 2600 BC); also 14 - C dates of the coal from earliest pits of nearest Chemurchek barrows Kulala Ula 1, Kumdi govi and Kara tumsik belong to same period. [⑤] Secondary Chemurchek burials from these barows dated on the 14C dates back to ca. 2500 - 2200 B. C. It may indicate that in the earliest period of existence of Chemurchek culture 切木尔切克文化, its population in Altai region could coexist with population of Afanasievo culture 阿凡纳羡沃文化. A pillar, erected at the

① Kovalev A. Die ältesten Stelen am Ertix. Das Kulturphänomen Xemirxek // Eurasia Antiqua 5 (1999): Berlin. 2000. pp. 135 - 178.: Tab. 13, 15

② Lazaretov I. Okunevskiye mogil'niki v doline reki Uibat // Okunevskii sbornik. Kultura. Iskusstvo. Antropologiya. Sankt-Petersburg. 1997. pp. 19 - 64. (in Russian): 31 - 36; Leont'ev S. K voprosu o keramicheskoi traditsii okunevskoi kul'tury Srednego Eniseya // Okunevskii sbornik 2. Kul'tura I ee okruzhenie. Sankt-Petersburg. 2006. pp. 260 - 272. (in Russian)

③ Semenov Vl. Okunevskiye pamyatniki Tuvy I Minusinskoi kotloviny (sravnitel'naya kharakteristika I khronologiya) // Okunevskii sbornik. Kultura. Iskusstvo. Antropologiya. Sankt-Petersburg. 1997. pp. 152 - 160. (in Russian): 157 - 158

④ Kiryushin Yu., Maloletko A., Tishkin A. Berezovaya Luka — poseleniye epokhi bronzy v Aleiskoi stepi. Vol. 1. Barnaul. 2005. (in Russian): 195 - 199

⑤ Ковалев А. А., Эрдэнэбаатар Д., Зайцева Г. И., Бурова Н. Д. Радиоуглеродное датирование курганов Монгольского Алтая, исследованных Международной Центральноазиатской археологической экспедицией, и его значение для хронологического и типологического упорядочения памятников бронзового века Центральной Азии // Древние и средневековые кочевники Центральной Азии. Барнаул. 2008. С. 172 - 186: 173.

Eastern side of mentioned Afanasievo 阿凡纳羡沃文化 culture barrow #1（Fig. 1 - 1）, as well as finding of bone arrowhead（Fig. 1 - 4）, which is similar to such arrowheads from Kulala Ula 1 and Kara Tumsik barrows（Fig. 2 - 10, 12）, also confirm this proposition. Also as we know to date typical for Afanasievo 阿凡纳羡沃文化 two censers and one egg shaped vessel in Chinese Chemurchek 切木尔切克文化 stone boxes were unearthed.① Just now the paper of Prof. Lin Yun② was published where he also came to conclusion that Chemurchek culture was contemporary with Afanasievo culture, but Prof. Lin Yun erroneously dated Afanasievo and Chemurchek culture to 2200 - 1900 BC based on the old dating of Afanasievo（14 - C dates without calibration, old ideas of Soviet specialists about the dating of Afanasievo typical vessels etc.）. Prof. Lin Yun is perfectly right that Chemurchek culture was the earliest culture of the Bronze Age in China but he unfortunately didn't know that A. Kovalev came to this conclusion ten years ago, which was published in Russia and Germany③ and reported by A. Kovalev on the International Symposium on the Problems of North China Archaeology organized by Institute of Archaeology, CASS in September 2004（Kovalev A. "Qiemuerqieke Culture-the Most Ancient Culture of the Bronze Age in China, Its Origin From the Western Europe and the Cultural Influence on the Neighbouring Cultures of Kazakhstan, Russia and Mongolia".）

Three round ritual pavements, which were explored by our expedition in 2001 at the high-mountain site Khar Gov'（科布多省门海尔汗苏木 Munkh-Hairkhan sum of Khovd aimag）near later khereksur, should be also attributed to Chemurchek culture. Polished stone tools were found there, which appeared to be analogous to discovered in 1999 at Kazakhstan 哈萨克斯坦 Chemurchek 切木尔切克文化 barrow Aina-Bulak 1/2.④ Also a stone pillar with marked out diminutive "head" as it had been done with stone pillars of Chemurchek 切木尔切克文化 barrows Kopa 2（Kazakhstan）（Fig. 2 - 5）and Kulala-Ula（Fig. 2 - 4）had been used for the second time during constructing of this khereksur（Fig. 2 - 6）.

Field research of the Early Bronze Age sites in Dzhungaria 准噶尔盆地 and Mongolian Altai 阿尔泰山 started in the first half of 1960 - s. Chinese archaeologist Li Zheng was the first to reflect different types of burial constructions in Ertix 额尔齐斯河 basin and to connect neighboring stone statues with them. His field report was firstly published in 1962.⑤ After that, in 1963, ten rectangular enclosures with stone boxes in Chemurchek 切木尔切克河（Kermuqi 克尔木齐, Qiemuerqieke）River basin in Altay County 阿勒泰 by Yi Manbai were excavated.⑥ In 1990 - s barrows of this type were subject for investigation of Wang Bo and

① Kovalev A. Die ältesten Stelen am Ertix. Das Kulturphänomen Xemirxek // Eurasia Antiqua 5 (1999): Berlin. 2000. pp. 135 - 178.: 163；张玉忠：《布尔津发现的彩绘石棺墓》,《新疆文物》,2005 年第 1 期, 第 124 ~ 125 页。

② 林沄：《关于新疆北部切尔木切克类型遗存的几个问题——从布尔津县出土的陶器说起》,《庆祝何炳棣先生九十华诞论文集》,《庆祝何炳棣先生九十华诞论文集》编辑委员会编, 西安: 三秦出版社,2008, 第 717 ~ 733 页。

③ Kovalev A. Die ältesten Stelen am Ertix. Das Kulturphänomen Xemirxek // Eurasia Antiqua 5 (1999): Berlin. 2000. pp. 135 - 178: 第 178 页.

④ Ковалев А. А., Дашковский П. К., Самашев З. С., Тишкин А. А., Горбунов В. В., Грушин С. П., Варенов А. В., Омаров Г., Сунгатай С. Изучение археологическихз памятников в Восточном Казахстане // Комплексные исследования древних и традиционных обществ Евразии. Барнаул. 2004. С. 183 - 190:图4。

⑤ 李证：《阿勒泰地区石人墓调查简报》,《文物》1962 年第 7 ~ 8 期, 第 103 ~ 108 页。李证：《阿勒泰地区石人墓调查简报》,《中国考古三十年》,北京,1983。第 128 ~ 133 页。

⑥ 新疆社会科学院考古研究所：《新疆克尔木齐古墓发掘简报》,《文物》1981 年第 1 期, 第 23 ~ 32 页。

Wang Linshan. [1] As result of the exploration Wang Bo undertook an attempt to classify and to date the burial constructions as well as different kinds of stone sculptures. [2] In his article of 1996 Wang Bo used the first time the term "Chemurchek culture 切木尔切克文化" for the Bronze Age sites of Northern Xinjiang 新疆北部. [3] However most of Chinese investigators dated back the "Keermuqi 克尔木齐墓地 burial ground" to Late Bronze Age, not earlier, and most of scholars disclaimed the cultural unity of the stone enclosures and neighboring statues, many researchers are of the opinion that these statues are from the Turk 突厥 time.

In 1998 during exploration in Chemurchek 切木尔切克河 River basin A. Kovalev found remains of stone burial constructions, which had been excavated by Yi Manbai 易漫白, and established unity of stone enclosure #2 excavated by Yi Manbai 易漫白 with stone statue Kaynarl 喀依纳尔 2 #2, which had been published by Wang Linshan and Wang Bo in 1996. [4] This fact confirmed the conclusion of A. Kovalev about synchronism of the most of stone sculptures from Ertix region with the main burials in stone boxes of Chemurchek ("Keermuqi") 切木尔切克 (克尔木齐) 墓地 burial ground, dated to the second half of 3rd millennium-the first half of the 2nd millennium B. C. according analogies in burial goods. [5] In his article published in Germany in 2000 [6] A. Kovalev attributed images of bulls with S-shaped horns and the stone vessel from Uglovo, Altay region 俄罗斯阿尔泰边疆区, Russia as belonging to Chemurchek culture 切木尔切克文化 [7]. Also he attributed the statue from Inya village (Russian Republic of Altay 俄罗斯阿尔泰共和国) [8] as belonging to Chemurchek culture. That gave opportunity to define the area of Chemurchek population spread.

In 1998 – 2000 the International Central-Asian archaeological expedition organized by A. Kovalev (the Russian-Kazakh team of the expedition had been established by St. -Petersburg State University in cooperation with the Institute of Archaeology of National Academy of Science of Kazakhstan and with Altai (Russian) State University 阿尔泰边疆区大学) undertook excavations of 12 rectangular stone enclosures of the Early Bronze Age in Alkabek River basin (Eastern-Kazakh region 东哈萨克斯坦州) (burial places Akhtuma, Aina-Bulak I, II, Kopa, Bulgartaboty) near Chinese border (3 – 5 kilometers on west from 新疆哈巴河县185 团农场). The barrows excavated in Alkabek River basin had rectangular enclosures made of stone slabs; from the middle of eastern side of the enclosure, where an "enrance" marked with huge slabs is placed, to

① 王林山、王博：《中国阿勒泰草原文物》。深圳：1996。

② 王博、祁小山：《丝绸之路草原石人研究》，乌鲁木齐：1996，第153~215 页。

③ 王博：《切木尔切克文化初探》，《考古文物研究》，西北大学考古专业成立四十周年文集(1956~1996)。西安：1996，第274~285 页。

④ Kovalev A. Die ältesten Stelen am Ertix. Das Kulturphänomen Xemirxek // Eurasia Antiqua 5 (1999)：Berlin. 2000. pp. 135 –178. ：140 –141

⑤ Kovalev A. Die ältesten Stelen am Ertix. Das Kulturphänomen Xemirxek // Eurasia Antiqua 5 (1999)：Berlin. 2000. pp. 135 –178. ：160

⑥ Kovalev A. Die ältesten Stelen am Ertix. Das Kulturphänomen Xemirxek // Eurasia Antiqua 5 (1999)：Berlin. 2000. pp. 135 –178. ：150, 152, 157, 167

⑦ Kiryushin Yu. , Simonov E. Kamennyi sosud iz Uglovskogo rayona. In: Sokhraneniye I izucheniye kul'turnogo naslediya Altaiskogo kraya. Materialy nauchno-prakticheskoi konferencii. Vypusk VIII. Barnaul. 1997. pp. 167 – 171. (in Russian)；Kiryushin Yu. Eneolit I rannyaya bronza yuga Zapadnoi Sibiri. Barnaul. 2002 (in Russian)：58 –59

⑧ Kubarev V. Drevniye izvayaniya Altaya. Olennyye kamni. Novosibirsk. 1979 (in Russian)：8 – 10, Kubarev V. Drevniye rospisi Karakola. Novosibirsk. 1988 (in Russian)：88 –90

the burial pit led stone corridor (passage) made from small flat slabs. As the rule, the walls of these corridors surrounded the burial pit. In all barrows, without exceptions, burial pits laid 2 – 5 meters eastwards from the center to the mentioned "entrances". At the burial place Kopa 1 a stone stele that had been worked up to look like a human body at the eastern side of the enclosure was established (Fig. 2 – 5). 14 – C dates that have been got from wood or from human bones prove synchronism of described above sites of Mongolia with those of Kazakhstan.

The results of the described works showed considerable diversity of forms of burial constructions, kinds of burials and of burial goods during this period in Altai 阿尔泰山内外区. At the same time it is possible to assert, that there was definite similarities between material culture of inhabitants of Dzhungaria 准噶尔盆地 and Mongolian Altai 阿尔泰山, which was the result of cultural influence that had been brought to this area by migrants from the Western Europe (France?) not later than the middle of 3rd millennium B. C.

All described kinds of burial constructions did preserve the main features of passage graves of the Western Europe. The "Kazakhstan" enclosures do have corridors, walls of which laid together from some layers of stones, surrounding burial chambers, and asymmetric locations of the sepulchers (the similar construction may be observed at West France[①]). Elongated proportions of "Bayan-Ulgi 巴彦乌列盖省" and Chinese 阿勒泰 Chemurchek 切木尔切克文化 stone enclosures, as well as ritual "entrances", may be considered as derivative of mentioned burial corridor.

The design of burial boxes as well, as of several heaps (cairns) along perimeters of the central stone cist covering one another (see Fig. 3 – 1), is also analogous with this of Neolithic sites of France (for instance: le Petit-Mont (Arzon), Champ-Chalon, Tumulus E of Bougon, Lisquis I, III, La Table des Marchands, Barnenez II, Plouézoc'h, Croix-Saint-Pierre, Dissignac, Larcuste I, Tumulus des Mousseaux, Deux Sévres, La Ciste Des Cous, Ernes, Colombiers-sus-Seulles, Condé-sur-Ifs, Vierville[②]). The Eastern orientation of

---

① L'Helgouac'h J. Les groupes humains du V-e au III-e millénaries. In: Préhistoire de la Bretagne / Giot P. -R, L'Helgouach J., Monnier J. -L.. Rennes. 1979. pp. 157 – 249. ; L'Helgouac'h J. De Barnenez à Colpo. //Allées couvertes et autres monuments funéraires du néolithique dans la France du Nord-Ouest. Allées sans retour/ Masset C., Soulier, Ph. (eds.). Paris. 1995. pp. 67 – 70; Boujot Ch., Leclerc J. Lieux d'orgueil et lieux d'effacement // Allées couvertes et autres monuments funéraires du néolithique dans la France du Nord-Ouest. Allées sans retour / Masset C., Soulier Ph. (eds.). Paris. 1995. pp. 71 – 78.

② L'Helgouac'h J. Les groupes humains du V-e au III-e millénaries. In: Préhistoire de la Bretagne / Giot P. -R, L'Helgouach J., Monnier J. -L.. Rennes. 1979. pp 157 – 249. ; Lecornec J. Arzon, le Petit-Mont. // Allées couvertes et autres monuments funéraires du néolithique dans la France du Nord-Ouest. Allées sans retour / Masset C., Soulier Ph. (eds.). Paris. 1995. pp. 132 – 134; Jossaume R. Benon, Champ-Chalon. // Allées couvertes et autres monuments funéraires du néolithique dans la France du Nord-Ouest. Allées sans retour / Masset C., Soulier Ph. (eds.). Paris. 1995. pp. 139 – 142. ; Ferrer-Joly F. Bougon (Deux-Sevres) // Allées couvertes et autres monuments funéraires du néolithique dans la France du Nord-Ouest. Allées sans retour / Masset C., Soulier Ph. (eds.). Paris. 1995. pp. 143 – 149: 146 – 147; Le Roux Ch. -T. Laniscat, Lisquis (Côtes-d'Armor); Larmor-Baden, Gavrinis (Morbihan) // Allées couvertes et autres monuments funéraires du néolithique dans la France du Nord-Ouest. Allées sans retour / Masset C., Soulier Ph. (eds.). Paris. 1995. pp. 171 – 174. ; L'Helgouac'h J. Locmariaquer, la Table des Marchands et le Grand Menhir (Morbihan). //Allées couvertes et autres monuments funéraires du néolithique dans la France du Nord-Ouest. Allées sans retour / Masset C., Soulier, Ph. (eds.). Paris. 1995. pp. 177 – 180: 177 – 178; Giot P. -R. Plouézoc'h, Barnenez (Finistére). Allées couvertes et autres monuments funéraires du néolithique dans la France du Nord-Ouest. Allées sans retour / Masset C., Soulier Ph. (eds.). Paris. 1995. pp. 196 – 197; Briard J. Saint-Just (Ille-et-Vilaine)//Allées couvertes et autres monuments funéraires du néolithique dans la France du Nord-Ouest. Allées sans retour / Masset C., Soulier, Ph. (eds.). Paris. 1995. pp. 203 – 204; L'Helgouac'h J. Saint-Nazaire, Dissignac (Loire-Atlantique) //Allées couvertes et autres monuments funéraires du néolithique dans la France du Nord-Ouest. Allées sans retour / Masset C., Soulier, Ph. (eds.). Paris. 1995. pp. 206 – 209. ; Le Roux Ch. -T. Quinze ans de recheerches sur les (转下页)

"entrances" and tradition of establishing of statues or pillars at the same side are common for both Altai's and Western European's megalithic sites. The iconography of presently known Chemurchek 切木尔切克文化石人 sculptures (see Fig. 3 – 3) can have origins only in iconography traditions of European Neolithic — Chalcolithic, as it was demonstrated by A. Kovalev already in 1998. The most similar stone statues have been discovered in Languedoq (for instance, Mas de l'Aveugle, Collorgues). [1] Forms and ornamentation of Chemurchek 切木尔切克文化 stone (see Fig. 3 –8) and partly — of earthenware vessels, as well as of stone polished tools probably also have the West European origin. [2] The painting of the walls of stone boxes at 科布多省 Yagshiin hodoo 1, 3 made with red paint has analogies in painting and pictures on walls of megalithic tombs dated to 3th millenium BC of East Europe (Kemi-Oba culture, Nalchik tomb, early Yamnaya 竖穴墓文化 culture of Dnepr region and so on[3]). Painstaking visual exploration of slabs at Yagshiin hodoo 3 gave opportunity to discover an image that may be interpreted as composition of a spear, oval shield with protuberances, and a bow (Fig. 3 –2). If it is actually so, then there is analogous to barrow #28 of burial place Klady of Novosvobodnaya (Maikop 迈科普文化) culture and with the megalithic tomb at Leine-Helich (Germany). [4]

3. Munh-Khairkhan 门海尔汗文化 culture. The Middle Bronze Age at Western and Central Mongolia is represented by Munh-Khairkhan culture 门海尔汗文化. Sites of this culture were firstly discovered by A. Kovalev in 2003 on the territory of Munh-Khairkhan 门海尔汗苏木 sum of Khovd 科布多省 aimag. Barrows of the culture looks from outside like absolutely flat stone heaps round or square in shape, made, as a rule, of one layer of stones. (Fig. 4 –1,2,3) In the center of a barrow lay oval burial pit, 1.3 by 1 meter in size (regular), oriented in latitude direction. The buried human body was placed in extremely curved position on the left side. The head was directed to the East. (Fig. 4 – 6) The burial pit was filled with not processed stone blocks (pieces) and slabs that formed in ancient time something like vault from one or two layers of stones (Fig. 4 –4,5).

(接上页) mégalithes de Bretagne //La France des dolmens et des sépultures collectives (4500 –200 avant J.-C.) / Soulier Ph., Masset, Cl. (eds.). Paris. 1998. pp. 57 –66; L'Helgouac'h J. Mégalithisme dans les pays de la Loire//La France des dolmens et des sépultures collectives (4500 –200 avant J.-C.) / Soulier Ph., Masset, Cl. (eds.). Paris. 1998. pp. 255 –266; Billard C., Chancerel A. Récherches récentes sur les sépultures collectives et les monuments mégalithiques de Normandie (1985 –1995) //La France des dolmens et des sépultures collectives (4500 –200 avant J.-C.) / Soulier Ph., Masset, Cl. (eds.). Paris. 1998. pp. 245 –253; Gutherz X. Le mégalithisme en Poitou-Charente. Aquis, recherches, protection et mise en valeur //La France des dolmens et des sépultures collectives (4500 –200 avant J.-C.) / Soulier Ph., Masset, Cl. (eds.). Paris. 1995. pp. 281 –290.

① Landau J. Les representations anthropomorphes mégalitiques de la region mediterraneenne (3e au 1er millenaire). Paris. 1977: Pl. 1, 4 –6

② Kovalev A. Chemurchekskii kul'turnyi fenomen: ego proishozhdeniye I rol' v formirovanii kul'tur epokhi rannei bronzy Altaya I Central'noi Azii // Zapadnaya I Yuzhnaya Sibir' v drevnosti. Sbornik nauchnykh trudov, posvyash'sh'ennyi 60 –letiyu so dnya rozhdeniya Yuriya Fedorovicha Kiryushina. Barnaul. 2005. pp. 178 –184. (in Russian): 181

③ Chechenov I. Nal'chkskaya podkurgannaya grobnica (III tysyacheletie do nashei ery). Nal'chik. 1973 (in Russian): 12 –16, 23 –28; Formozov A. Ocherki po pervobytnomu iskusstvu. Naskal'nyye izobrazheniya I kamennyye izvayaniya epokhi kamnya I bronzy na territorii SSSR. Moscow. 1969 (in Russian): 150 –172

④ Rezepkin A. K interpretacii rospisi iz grobnicy maikopskoi kul'tury bliz stanicy Novosvobodnaya // Kratkiye soobsh'sh'eniya Instituta arheologii 192. Moscow. 1987. pp. 26 –33. (in Russian): 29; Rezepkin A. Das frühbronzezeitliche Gräberfeld von Klady und die Majkop-Kultur im Nordwestkaukasus. (Archäologie in Eurasien 9). Berlin. 2000: Taf. 83 –85.

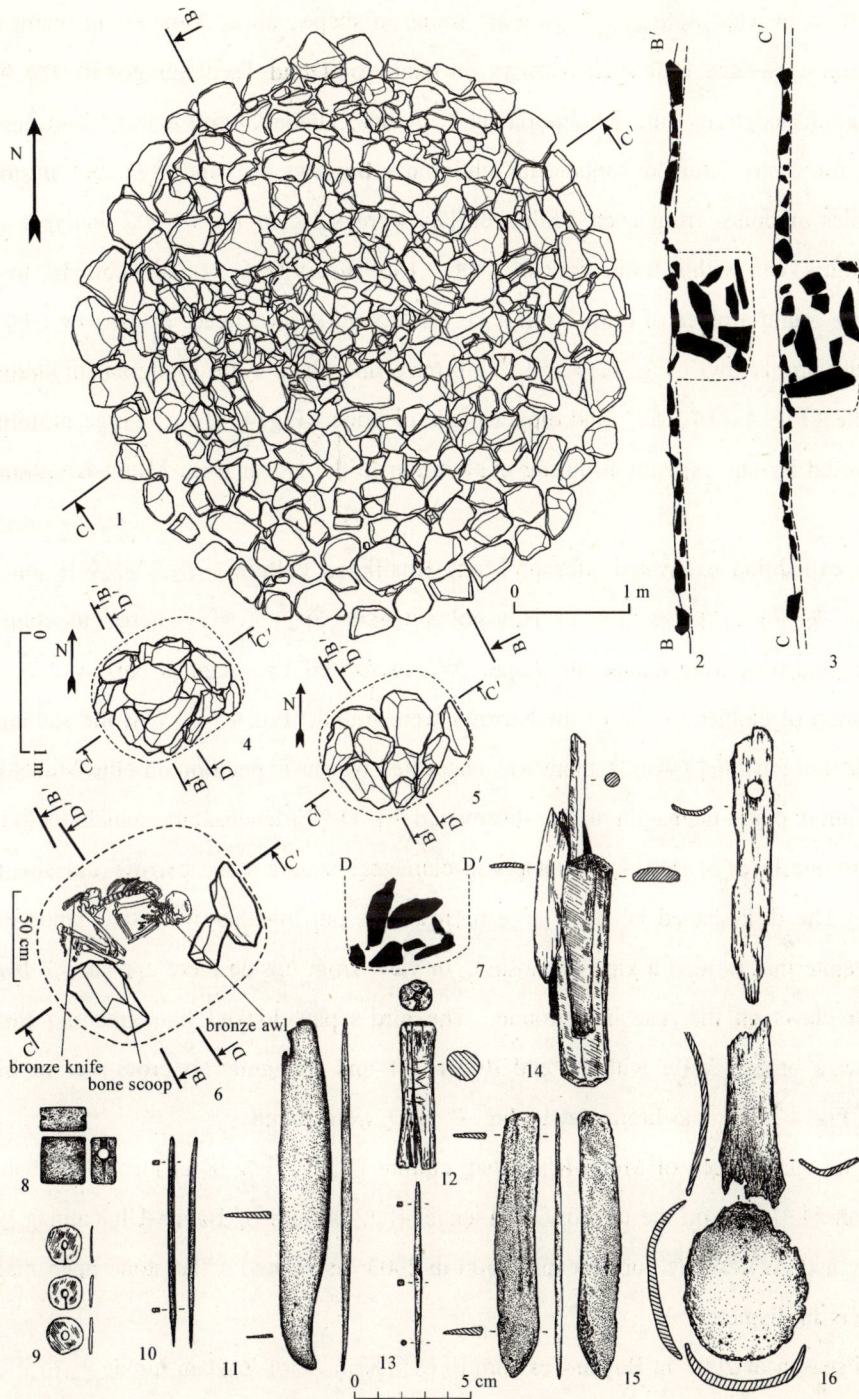

Fig. 4　Munh-Khairkhan culture 门海尔汗文化. Khovd 科布多省, Zavhan and Hovsgol aimags 扎布汗省和库苏古尔省.

1 – Ulaan goviin uzuur 1 barrow (Khovd, Munhkhairkhan sum), plan of barrow　2 – Ulaan goviin uzuur 1 barrow (Khovd, Munhkhairkhan sum), section B-B'　3 – Ulaan goviin uzuur 1 barrow (Khovd, Munhkhairkhan sum), section C-C'　4 – Ulaan goviin uzuur 1 barrow (Khovd, Munhkhairkhan sum), grave, plan of the stone vault (level 1)　5 – Ulaan goviin uzuur 1 barrow (Khovd, Munhkhairkhan sum), grave, plan of the stone vault (level 2)　6 – Ulaan goviin uzuur 1 barrow (Khovd, Munhkhairkhan sum), plan of the burial　7 – Ulaan goviin uzuur 1 barrow (Khovd, Munhkhairkhan sum), grave, section D-D'　8 – Burial ground Khuh-Khushony-Bom I barrow 1, one of bone beads from rectangular "torque"　9 – Tsagan uushig 3 barrow (Burentogtokh sum, Hovsgol aimag), nacre disc-shaped stripes for decoration of clothes　10 – Galbagiin uzuur 2 barrow (Burentogtokh sum, Hovsgol aimag), bronze awl　11 – Galbagiin uzuur 2 barrow (Burentogtokh sum, Hovsgol aimag), bronze knife　12 – Ulaan goviin uzuur 1 barrow (Khovd, Munhkhairkhan sum), wood handle from bronze awl with wood objects　13 – Ulaan goviin uzuur 1 barrow (Khovd, Munhkhairkhan sum), bronze awl　14 – Ulaan goviin uzuur 1 barrow (Khovd, Munhkhairkhan sum), wood handle from bronze knife with wood objects　15 – Ulaan goviin uzuur 1 barrow (Khovd, Munhkhairkhan sum), bone scoop

Regular barrows in Altai 阿尔泰山 region are round in shape, about 3 meters in diameter (see Fig 4 - 1). Our expedition excavated four such barrows on banks of Dund Tsenkher gol River, which preserved bones of buried adult people in situ: Khotuu davaa 1, Artua, Ulaan Goviin uzuur 1 and 2. Near barrow of Ulaan Goviin uzuur 2 are situated supposedly children's barrows #3 and #4, but no bones had been preserved. Samples of bones from each adult's burials were selected for 14 - C analysis. The four dates with high probability keep within framework of 1700 - 1300 years B. C. (See Tabl. 1) In barrow Khotuu davaa 1 there were found a piece of bronze pin (?) with round shaped head. In barrow Ulaan Goviin uzuur 1 there were found bronze awl (Fig. 4 - 12, 13), bronze one-blade knife triangular in cross-section having no separate handle (Fig. 4 - 14,15), and dipper made of bone (Fig. 4 - 16). Three more barrows of such type were discovered by our expedition during exploration to the North from Munh-Khairkhan sum 门海尔汗苏木.

In 2006 our expedition excavated sites of Munh-Khairkhan culture 门海尔汗文化 on the territory of Burentogtokh sum 布拉托戈托赫苏木 of Hovsgol aimag 库苏古尔省. There, in contrast to Western Mongolia, regular barrows were square in shape. We excavated two regular barrows. Nacre disc-shaped stripes for decoration of clothes in one of the barrows were found (Fig. 4 - 9). At the same region (库苏古尔省) in Arbulak sum 阿尔布拉克苏木 there was excavated by our expedition an elite Munh-Khairkhan 门海尔汗文化墓地 burial place Galbagiin uzuur discovered by D. Erdenebaatar, which included a flat stone barrow made from one layer of stones, 30 meters in diameter; square stone barrow and also two rectangular stone pavements. The disk-shaped heap of large barrow was put together from two kinds of stones: black shale and rose granite that formed a kind of mosaic. In view from upside there appeared a black paw of bird of prey with four claws on the rose background. The bird's paw looked like grabbing the burial pit. In rectangular barrow a bronze knife with its end drawn off and triangular in cross-section blade having no separate handle (Fig. 4 - 11) and bronze awl (Fig. 4 - 10) were found.

One more elite burial place of Munh-Khairkhan culture 门海尔汗文化 is located probably at the upper part of Hovd River 科布多河 on the territory of Tsengel 臣格勒 sum of Bayan-Ulgi aimag 巴彦乌列盖省. There A. Kovalev and A. Varenov during exploration in 2003 discovered a flat stone heap made of one layer of stones 30 meters in diameter.

During field season of 2007 in Bayan-Tes sum 巴彦台斯苏木 of Zavhan aimag 扎布汗省 we explored two single barrows of Munh-Khairkhan culture 门海尔汗文化 5 - 7 meters in diameter and burial-ritual place Khuh-Khushony-Bom 1, which included two round barrows, one square barrow, and also two rectangular stone pavements, two vertical stone stelae and a circle made of twelve small stone pillars with semicircular stone pavement inside. Among findings it is necessary to mention two bronze awls, three bone conical-cylindrical arrowheads 15 centimeters in length with splintered haft, and also compound necklace-torque rectangular in shape, which was put together from square bone beads with cuts (Fig. 4 - 8).

The origins and connections of Munh-Khairkhan culture 门海尔汗文化 are still not clear. Probably, the metal industry of this culture had its origins in the Middle Asia or Kazakhstan, where findings of bronze knives looking like mentioned above（Fig. 4 - 11, 15）took place.① The exactly same knife was found on the Qijia 齐家 culture site of Zongzhai 总寨（Qinghai 青海）and very similar item on Qijia site of Linjia 林家（Gansu 甘肃）.② Probably same knives was found in one of the burials from Tianshanbeilu 天山北路墓地（哈密 Hami）③ and in the site Xintala 新塔拉遗址（Heshuo 和硕县）,④ but the published pictures is not clear. Also same knife in Verkhnyaya Mulga hoard（叶尼塞河 Minusinsk basin）was found; this hoard contained also bronze celt and spearhead of Seima-Turbino culture 塞伊马-土尔宾诺文化.⑤ These typical Seima-Turbino 塞伊马-土尔宾诺文化 metal objects dated on first half of second millenium B. C. Forms and material of the nacre ornaments（Fig. 4 - 9）presents continuation of traditions of East Mongolian Neolith,⑥ the same nacre discs recently were found in Russian Altai. Unique bone turque made from rectangular beads with cuts（Fig. 4 - 8）was origin from two tausend years earlier chalkolithic cultures of Ukraina.⑦

4. The Tevsh culture 特布希文化. Our investigations of 2005 - 2007 shows that Southern part of contemporary Mongolia in 13 - 10th centuries B. C. was a part of area of specific archaeological culture of the Late Bronze Age that we proposed to name the Tevsh culture 特布希文化. Barrows of this culture had been already excavated in Bogd 博格多苏木 sum of Uverkhangai 前杭爱省 aimag（not far from Tevsh uul 特布希乌拉山 mountain）by V. Volkov: two barrows were excavated in 1964⑧ and three barrows were excavated in 1971,⑨ nevertheless a most of scholars belong these barrows to the Slab grave culture.⑩

We have excavated four barrows in Bayanlig sum 巴彦勒格苏木 of Bayankhongor aimag 巴彦洪戈尔省（Baruun gyalat 1, 2, 3, Zamyn butz）, four barrows in Bogd sum 博格多苏木 of Uverkhangai aimag 前杭爱省（Khar uzuur I - 1, Khar uzuur II - 1,2, Shar tolgoi）, and also two barrows in Nomgon 瑙木冈苏木 sum of South Gobi aimag 南戈壁省（Khurmen tsagaan uul I - 3, 4）; during explorations a lot of barrows of such type in Gobi Altai 戈壁阿尔泰山 Mountains and in Transaltai Gobi 阿尔泰山南方戈壁沙漠 were discovered. As a result we came to following conclusions.

All excavated barrows were of the similar construction（Fig. 5 - 1,2）. Each of them consists of stone fence enclosing an area filled by stones to make up a flat platform. Eastern and Western walls of fence were

---

① Kuz'mina E. Metallicheskiye izdeliya eneolita I bronzovogo veka v Srednei Azii. （Svod arheologicheskikh istochnikov V4 - 9）. Moscow. 1966（in Russian）: Tab. IX-X

② 白云翔:《中国早期铜器的考古发现与研究》,《21 世纪中国考古学与世界考古学》,中国社会科学院考古研究所编著,北京：中国社会科学出版社,2002,第 180 ~ 203 页.（考古学专刊,甲种第二十八号）: 图3：4, 5

③ 吕恩国、常喜恩、王炳华:《新疆青铜时代考古文化浅论》,《苏秉琦与当代中国考古学》,宿白编著。北京：科学出版社,2001,第 172 ~ 193 页。图16：6

④ Mei Jianjiyn Copper and Bronze Metallurgy in Late Prehistoric Xinjiang: Its cultural context and relationship with neighbuoring regions（BAR S865）. Oxford. 2000: Fig. 2.6: 6.

⑤ Leont'ev S. K voprosu o seiminsko-turbinskoi tradicii na Srednem Eniseye // Stepi Evrazii v drevnosti i srednevekov'e. Kniga 1. Sankt-Petersburg. 2002. pp. 181 - 183

⑥ Novgorodova E. Drevnyaya Mongoliya. Moscow. 1989.（in Russian）: 78 - 81

⑦ Rassamakin Yu. Die nordpontishe Steppe in der Kurferzeit. Gräber aus der Mitte des 5. Jts. bis Ende des 4. Jts. v. Chr. Teil I-II.（Archäologie in Eurasien 17）. Berlin. 2004: 74 - 75, Fig. 59: 1 - 5

⑧ Volkov V. Bronzovyi I rannii zheleznyi vek Severnoi Mongolii. Ulaanbaatar. 1967（in Russian）: 37

⑨ Volkov V. Raskopki v Mongolii // Arheologicheskiye otkrytiya 1971 goda. Moscow. 1972. pp. 554 - 556.（in Russian）: 555 - 556;

⑩ Tsybiktarov A. Kul'tura plitochnykh mogil Mongolii I Zabaikal'ya. Ulan-Ude. 1999（in Russian）: 126 - 128

constructed of vertical stone slabs. Southern and Northern walls were constructed of stone blocks laid in horizontal position in several layers (which is very significant). In the middle of the construction narrow burial pit have been arranged, where a dead body was placed in prone ("face down") position with head directed to the East (Fig. 5 - 1, 3). The pit with the dead body after burial ceremony was filled with ground.

There are two different forms of fences:

- a fence widened to the East having concave sides (looking like "figured" tombs) (see Fig. 5 - 1)

- a fence in almost semicircular shape having convex Northern and Southern sides, and direct Eastern and Western sides: Eastern side is wide, Western is narrow (see Fig. 5 - 2)

Judging by the similarity of construction, of burial rite, and of location of the similar barrows in the same sites, the barrows of both forms are simultaneous and belong to the same culture. As burials in prone position, semicircular fences and fences made of stone blocks lying in horizontal position in several layers were never discovered in Slab graves 石板文化墓 (Slab graves are surrounded with fences made of vertical slabs), we do attribute all mentioned above barrows as belonging to specific Tevsh 特布希文化 culture. Appearance of fences with concave sides among Slab graves 石板文化墓 of Transbaikalia 外贝加尔 and of the Central Mongolia may be explained by cultural influence of the Tevsh culture 特布希文化 on the Northern region.

It is obvious that it was impossible to come to such conclusions before because excavations of "figured" tombs near Tevsh Mountain 特布希乌拉山 were conducted without cleaning of stone constructions, but by excavating of limited squares inside barrows. It became clear after our observation of previously excavated by V. Volkov areas.

All barrows of this culture that was excavated by our expedition were robbed in ancient times, and usually the top parts of skeletons were absent. In barrows Baruun gyalat 2, 3 we found necklace made of cornelian (Fig. 5 - 4, 5), lazurite, and many small limestone beads on the neck of buried person (in barrow Baruun gyalat 3 there was also a golden ring in the necklace), also there were rows of limestone beads in barrow Zamyn Butz (Fig. 5 - 3), which probably were stitched together to clothes of buried person. The only one burial of such type that has not been robbed was excavated by V. Volkov in 1971 near Tevsh Mountain. The assemblage of burial goods included golden hair ornaments, headed with images of sheep heads (Fig. 5 - 6).[1] They were published many times. According their design they are similar to analogous items of North China nomadic culture of Shang-Yin 商殷 period (14 - 12 centuries B. C.); A. Kovalev proposed to name this culture Chaodaogou 抄道沟.[2] Knives, ornaments, daggers and scoops designed in same style have well established dates, as they were found many times in complexes of the Chinese Central Plane. Thus the Tevsh

---

[1] Volkov V. Raskopki v Mongolii // Arheologicheskiye otkrytiya 1971 goda. Moscow. 1972. pp. 554 - 556. (in Russian): 555 - 556; Novgorodova E. Alte Kunst der Mongolei. Leipzig. 1980: 69 - 70, Fig. 40 - 41; Novgorodova E. Drevnyaya Mongoliya. Moscow. 1989: 138

[2] Kovalev A. "Karasuk-Dolche", Hirschsteine und die Nomaden der chinesischen Annalen im Altertum. // Maoqinggou. Ein eisenzeitliches Gräberfeld in der Ordos-Region (Innere Mongolei) / Höllmann T. O., Kossack G. W. (eds.) (Materialien zur Allgemeine und Vergleichende Archäologie 50). Mainz am Rhein. 1992. pp. 46 - 87: 48 - 62; Kovalev, A. Drevneishaya migraciya iz Zagrosa v Kitai I problema prarodiny tokharov. // Archeolog: detektiv i myslitel'. Sankt-Peterburg. 2004. (in Russian)

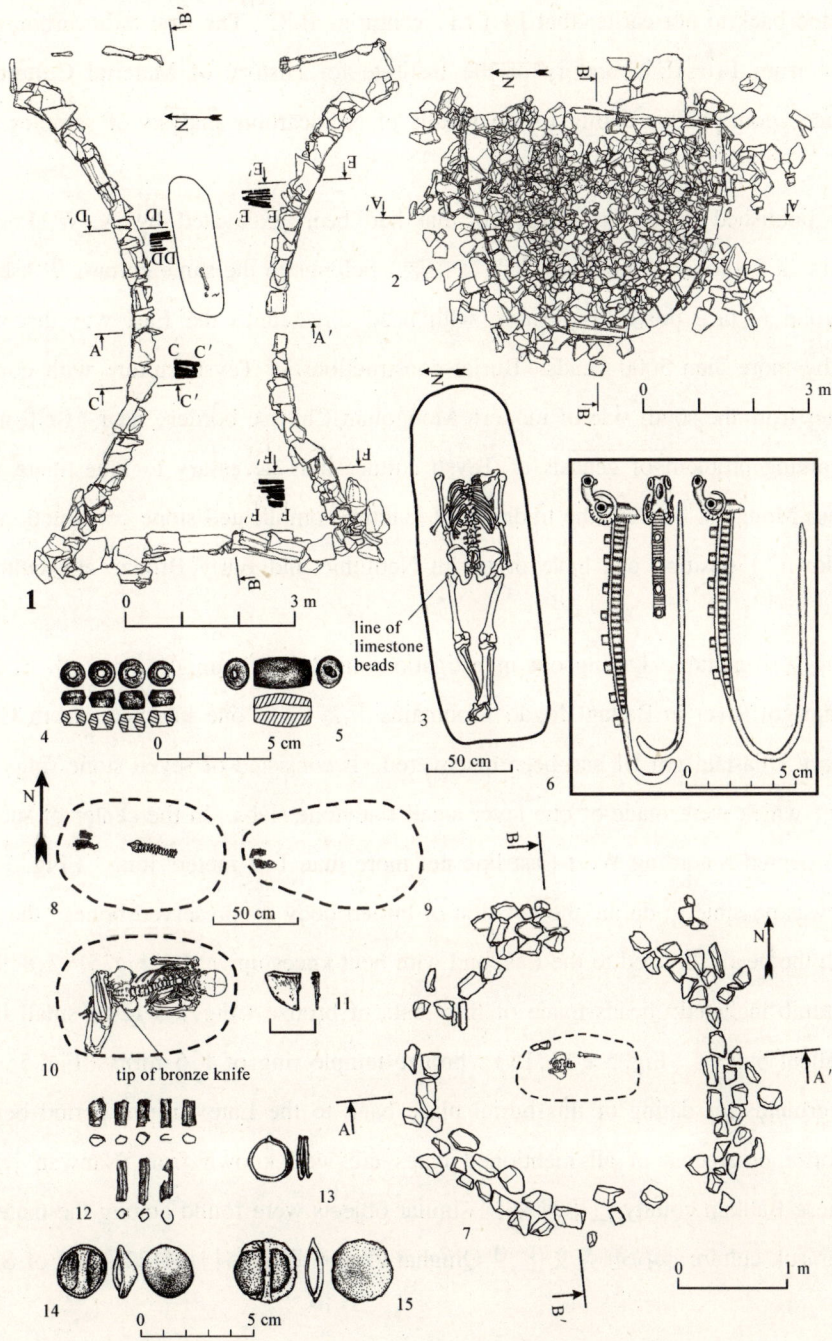

Fig. 5　Tevsh culture 特布希文化 (1 – 6)，Baitag culture 北塔文化 (7 – 15)

1 – Baruun gyalat 2 barrow ("figured tomb") (Bayanlig sum 巴彦勒格苏木, Bayankhongor aimag 巴彦洪戈尔省), plan of the stone fence after disassembling of stone cairn　2 – Baruun gyalat 1 barrow ("semicircular" tomb) (Bayanlig sum, Bayankhongor aimag), plan　3 – Zamyn buts barrow ("semicircular" tomb) (Bayanlig sum, Bayankhongor aimag), plan of the burial　4 – Baruun gyalat 2 barrow (Bayanlig sum, Bayankhongor aimag), cornelian bones　5 – Baruun gyalat 2 barrow (Bayanlig sum, Bayankhongor aimag), cornelian bone　6 – Tevsh uul 特布希乌拉山(Bogd sum 博格多苏木, Uverkhangai aimag 前杭爱省), golg head ornaments excavated by V. Volkov in a "figured tomb" (by Tsybiktarov, 1998, Fig. 55)　7 – Burial ground Uliastain gol III, barrow 2 (Baitag bogdo uul 北塔山, Bulgan sum 布尔干苏木, Khovd aimag 科布多省), plan　8 – Burial ground Uliastain gol III, barrow 7 (Baitag bogdo uul, Bulgan sum, Khovd aimag), plan of the burial pit　9 – Burial ground Uliastain gol III, barrow 4 (Baitag bogdo uul, Bulgan sum, Khovd aimag), plan of the burial pit　10 – Kheviin am 1 (Bulgan sum, Khovd aimag), secondary burial, plan　11 – Kheviin am 1 (Bulgan sum, Khovd aimag), secondary burial, tip of bronze knife　12 – Burial ground Uliastain gol III (Baitag bogdo uul, Bulgan sum, Khovd aimag), bronze beads from barrow 7 (above) and from barrow 3 (below)　13 – Burial ground Uliastain gol III (Baitag bogdo uul, Bulgan sum, Khovd aimag), barrow 7, bronze rong　14 – Burial ground Uliastain gol III (Baitag bogdo uul, Bulgan sum, Khovd aimag), barrow 7, bronze button　15 – Burial ground Uliastain gol III (Baitag bogdo uul, Bulgan sum, Khovd aimag), barrow 7, bronze button

culture may be dated back to not earlier that 14 (13) centuries B. C. The first radiocarbon dates (see Tabl. 1), which we got from 14 - C laboratory of the Institute for History of Material Culture of the Russian Academy of Science, confirm this dating (soon results of radiocarbon analysis of samples from each grave will be ready).

According to published materials, a barrow that had been excavated by A. W. Pond in 1928 near "Tairum Nor" Lake in the Inner Mongolia (乌兰察布盟) belongs to the same culture.[①] A burial of a human being placed in prone ("face down") position with head directed to the East was discovered there; his clothes decorated by more than 5000 beads. Burial constructions of Tevsh culture with concave sides were fixed by J. Maringer from the south side of modern Mongolian-Chinese border, near "Beili-miao"(内蒙古白云鄂博).[②] For solving problem of genesis of Tevsh culture it is necessary to investigate such sites in the central part of Inner Mongolia because the tradition of making complicated stone constructions and of burying in prone ("face down") position can have origin in Neolithic and Early Bronze age cultures of Northern China.

5. Baitag 北塔文化 culture. During our investigations in Bulgan sum 布尔干苏木 of Hovd 科布多省 aimag near Uliastain-gol River in Baitag-Bogdo Mountains 北塔山 in one kilometer from Chinese border in 2005 the burial place Uliastain gol III had been discovered. It consisted of seven stone rings about 1.7 - 2.7 meters in diameter, which were made of one layer small flat stone slabs. In the center of such ring there was an oval burial pit oriented according West-East line not more than 1.2 meters long. (Fig. 5 - 7) In spite of ancient robbing it was possible to define the position of buried body by preserved bones: the bodies were laid on their backs with the heads directed to the East and with bent knees upwards (Fig. 5 - 7,8,9). The artifacts discovered in the tomb included: beads made of thin leafs of bronze (Fig. 5 - 12), small limestone beads, two cast bronze salient buttons (Fig. 5 - 14,15), bronze temple ring of 1.5 turns (Fig. 5 - 13). All these artifacts give backgrounds for dating of this burial place back to the Late Bronze period beginning from 12 century B. C. Bronze ornaments of all mentioned types are well known from Nanwan 南湾 cemetery in neighbouring Chinese Balikun county 巴里坤县,[③] similar objects were found among the materials of the Late Bronze Age of Karasuk culture 卡拉苏克文化,[④] Qinghai Zongri 青海宗日 M122[⑤] and of Siba 四坝 culture

① Fairservis W. A. The Archaeology of the Soutern Gobi — Mongolia. Based on the fieldwork of N. C. Nelson and Alonzo Pond, members of the Central Asiatic Expeditions of the American Museum of Natural History directed by Roy Chapman Andrews. Durham, North Carolina. 1993: 166 - 167

② Maringer J. Contribution to the Prehistory of Mongolia. A Study of the Prehistoric Collection from Inner Mongolia by John Maringer together with the Catalogue prepared by Folke Bergman. Stockholm. 1950. (Reports from the Scientific Expedition to the North-Western Provinces of China under the Leadership of Dr. Sven Hedin. Publication 34. VII. Archaeology 7): 13, Fig. 2a

③ 吕恩国、常喜恩、王炳华:《新疆青铜时代考古文化浅论》,《苏秉琦与当代中国考古学》,宿白编著。北京:科学出版社,2001,第172~193页:图23:3、4、9、13、14。

④ Polyakov A. Periodizaciya "klassicheskogo" etapa karasukskoi kul'tury (po materialam pogrebal'nykh pamyatnikov). Avtoreferat dissertacii. Sankt-Petersburg. 2006.

⑤ 白云翔:《中国早期铜器的考古发现与研究》,《21世纪中国考古学与世界考古学》,中国社会科学院考古研究所编著,北京:中国社会科学出版社,2002,第180~203页(考古学专刊,甲种第二十八号):184,图1:9、10。

in Gansu 甘肃.[1]

Also the same burial traditions were discovered in a secondary burial of a woman in the filling ground of the stone box of earlier Chemurchek 切木尔切克文化 barrow Kheviin am 1 in 200 kilometers to the North from Baitag 北塔山(Fig. 5 – 10). Small part of knife's tip was found there (Fig. 5 – 11), like in Karasuk 卡拉苏克文化 burials. According 14 – C dating of buried bones this grave is dated back (with probability 95.4%) to 1400 – 850 years B. C. (See Tabl. 1) (soon results of radiocarbon analysis of samples from some graves from Baitag 北塔文化 will be ready).

Skulls from the barrow Uliastain gol III-7 and from secondary burial of the barrow Kheviin am have extremely displayed features of European race. The burial traditions of Baitag graves (small stone circles without heaps, position of body, eastern orientation) reflect continuation of Chalkolithic traditions of Ukraine and Russia.[2]

The Southern part of Khovd aimag 科布多省 in Mongolia, where we worked, probably was the Northern periphery of the area of this culture, Nanwan 南湾 cemetery was the site of southern neighbours of this culture. Namely from this culture "Karasuk 卡拉苏克文化" type of artifacts had originated, which by Chinese archaeologists in burial places of agricultural peoples of some oases of Xinjiang were discovered. It is possible to wait for new discoveries, if Chinese archaeologists will pay attention to small stone rings North from Tianshan Mountains 天山, particularly between Barkul Lake 巴里坤湖 and Baitag mountains 北塔山.

① 白云翔:《中国早期铜器的考古发现与研究》,见《21 世纪中国考古学与世界考古学》,中国社会科学院考古研究所编著,北京:中国社会科学出版社,2002,第 180 ~ 203 页:(考古学专刊,甲种第二十八号)184, 图 1: 29, 32

② Rassamakin Yu. Die nordpontishe Steppe in der Kurferzeit. Gräber aus der Mitte des 5. Jts. bis Ende des 4. Jts. v. Chr. Teil I-II. (Archäologie in Eurasien 17). Berlin. 2004: 39 – 52

吐鲁番胜金店墓地考古发现与研究

张永兵

新疆吐鲁番学研究院

胜金店墓地位于吐鲁番市胜金乡胜金店村南郊、胜金店水库与火焰山之间的坡地上。在为了配合312国道吐鲁番——鄯善段复线工程建设而进行的前期考古调查中被发现。2006年5月,自治区文物考古研究所曾在公路北侧进行了考古发掘,考古资料尚未公布。2007年修路施工时挖掘机在路边山坡上取土,挖出了人骨和器物,靠近公路南侧的墓葬始被发现。同时,吐鲁番学研究院的文物考古人员进行了调查。

2007年10月,在请示并得到自治区文物局许可后,吐鲁番学研究院考古研究所组织考古专业人员进行了抢救性清理。发掘工作分两个阶段进行,第一个阶段从2007年10月14日开始至11月30日结束,开10×10米探方9个,发现并发掘墓葬26座。第二个阶段从2008年4月4日开始至4月28日结束,又开10×10米探方4个,发现并发掘墓葬5座。2次共发掘墓葬31座,出土了一批有价值的文物。

一、墓 葬 述 略

墓地南面为火焰山,北面被旧的312国道切断,墓地西侧有冲沟,东面有当地村民用于风干葡萄的晾房。由于历年洪水冲刷所夹带的泥沙在墓地上积滞,致使所有的墓葬都埋在淤积层下,墓地地表无任何标志。采用探方法取去50~80 cm表土层后,墓口方才露出。由于地面有斜坡,雨水来不及下渗即流开,而且每次雨水过后都会留下新的保护层,所以有些墓葬保存特别好。

现存墓地呈椭圆形,南北长42米,东西宽23米。墓葬分布均匀,排列有序,间隔3~8米。未见打破、叠压现象。少量成人墓旁有儿童祔葬墓。

胜金店墓地的墓葬型制有三种,基本涵盖了吐鲁番盆地史前墓葬的所有型制。第一种是长方形竖穴二层台墓(A型),二层台设在长方形的两长边上,距墓口深0.6~0.8米,在二层台上横排圆木或厚木板,尽可能严密地封堵墓室口,继而在横木上覆盖毛毡或用芦苇编织的帘垫。再在毛毡或帘垫上覆盖植物秸秆。所用植物普遍有黑果枸杞、芦苇、糜子草、香蒲、麦秸等,其上再用黏土压实。数量最多的是第二种长方形竖穴土坑墓(B型),直壁,墓口与墓底长、宽相仿。与上一种不同的是篷盖物直接搭建在墓口上。第三种为竖穴偏室墓(C型),这时的竖穴成为墓道,竖穴上口窄长,正底部顺长边留台阶,再向对面掏进成墓室。横切面呈靴形。在墓室口从台阶下向上斜搭成排的木梁,上面铺毛毡或草席,再覆盖植物秸秆,填土。大多数C型墓还用同样的方式在墓道上口即地面上重复搭建棚木,铺芦苇编织的帘子,覆盖植物秸秆,用黏土和成泥后镇压。

葬具主要是长方形四腿木制尸床。长方形边框中有两条横樘,四角各有一只短腿,它们之间都用榫头卯眼接合。上面铺排细木棍或柳树条用皮绳绑紧，个别青年妇女的尸床上还安放一个与其同样大小的长方形拱券顶床罩，床罩是用牛皮条和细柳枝捆扎而成，罩上覆盖毛毡。用这样木床的墓在整个墓地相对比较少，大多数墓葬仅仅在墓底铺细沙和植物茎秆。

该墓地主要为单人葬和双人葬，少有 3 人以上的合葬。双人合葬大多为夫妻合葬墓，也有少量同性合葬墓。墓葬中除了早期被盗扰外，还有一部分墓葬尸骨凌乱，应是墓室中早期进水使尸骨移位。另外发现用皮质衣服包裹的散乱骨骼，这种现象可能是二次葬。被扰乱的墓葬中还发现两层骨架叠压的现象，这是多次打开墓室重新葬人所形成。葬式主要有仰身直肢和仰身屈肢，侧身屈肢葬极少。仰身屈肢葬很有特点，上肢微内曲，双手搭在腹部。下肢上屈，双膝外侧各用一根粗芦苇秆支撑住双腿。9 号墓的情形即如是。墓主女性，未成年，年龄 13～15 岁，裸体，成保存完好的干尸，嘴唇干缩，露上门齿。头顶残留部分棕色毛发，面部有红色彩绘，右眼珠有少许虫蚀，左眼珠保存完好，玻璃体清晰透明。双臂平稳地置于身体两侧，双腿微上屈。其下榻的四腿木床做工考究，四根边框与四只短腿之间用榫头卯眼接合，中间还安装两条横撑，上面整齐地铺排细木棍，并用牛皮条有间距地捆绑住。木床上安放一个与其同样大小的长方形拱券顶床罩，床罩是用牛皮条和细柳枝捆扎而成，罩上覆盖的毛毡已被虫蛀成碎片。13 号墓是男女两人合葬墓，有木床和床罩，女性木冠饰在头前，男性木冠饰在左腿外侧，两人头中间有木纺轮，男性头前脚后都有放陶器，头前有皮画，一对金耳环上都有珊瑚坠饰，身体左侧墓壁边有"长明灯"。所谓灯，是一个"在有座的半球形泥坨上插根棍"的形状。在埋葬习俗和随葬品位置方面，13 号墓很有代表性。

二、出 土 器 物

墓地所处的火焰山一带，沙质的土层，干燥少雨的气候，使难以保存的木质、毛皮质器物都完好无损地悉数保存下来。为进一步的科学研究提供了便利条件。墓葬中随葬了大量木器、皮毛质品、陶器、金属器、骨器、石器、玛瑙珠、玻璃珠等。在墓道或墓口填充物中，还出土了为数较多的小麦、黍、黑果枸杞、芦苇、香蒲、骆驼刺、稗子、虎尾草等植物。木器的器形很多，有碗、杯、盘、钵、豆、桶、刀鞘、簪、锥、扣、橛、纺轮、纺线轴、弓、箭、镰刀柄、拐杖、冠饰、假肢等。

墓地出土的陶器多为素面，彩陶较少。有的陶器外施红色陶衣，打磨光洁，器物造型十分规整，主要有杯、碗、钵、壶、盆、双耳罐等。出土金属器物有铁刀、铁带钩、铜刀、铜耳环、金耳环、金质动物纹饰等。皮质品主要有皮靴、皮扣、扳指、护套、刀鞘、弓袋箭囊等。13 号墓所见绘有图案的羊皮画，呈长方形，四周用黑框将画面分成"回"字形的两部分，在两个框内紧贴框的边线，彩绘有红黑相间的简单的连续图案。女性墓主人身上脸上盖有锦，男性墓主人皮裤的双膝位置刺有镂空精美图案纹饰。木柄铜镜正中镶嵌铜片现已成碎片，背后有钮，上穿有绳子。小木桶口部有蒙皮一直包裹至底部，底涂黑像是木鼓。皮质耳杯制作精湛，通体绘有图案，皮带带面镶红绢，带扣为角质，呈圆角长方形。弓、箭、袋摆放在木床及其罩子的外面，弓和箭都装在皮质弓袋箭囊中。

木质冠饰奇特而且多样，13 号墓的一件通体用薄木板加工黏合而成，呈四方长筒状，中空，高 66 cm。底口近方形——因为四个面中只有一个面是平直的，其他三个面都略弧，向外先鼓出以后又逐渐细收成尖状体，中间略粗，与直面相对的那个斜面上方安装一个三角形"尾鳍"或"翼"——像船之尾舵状的薄木片。下端有双小孔,插入木销钉,固定一枚安装在筒中的木条。木条为一细长方体,上面有条形孔,并缠绕头发,以便将木冠饰固定在头顶上。这样的木冠饰为成年男性专用。用于成年女性头上的冠饰有两种,其一是与上述男性相同形状的装饰性器物,32 号墓的一件是用整块生牛皮缝制,整体要小一号,比木质冠饰要轻巧得多,高 58 cm,销钉、尾鳍具全。这种皮冠饰的后面安装 2 根起支撑固定作用的柽柳棍,从底部一直延伸到顶端。牛皮筒从后面缝合,至二分之一处收小分开,连尾鳍一起包紧粘牢在两根柽柳棍上。出土时置头顶部,里面尚有头发和黑色毛线编织的发网残片。还有另一种冠饰,下部呈圆筒形,用薄木板弯曲粘贴成。顶盖与圆筒组装在一起,口微敞,口沿上有两段突起,薄沿,像一个倒扣的木桶。13 号墓出土的一件顶盖中部有 2 个半圆形或长方形孔,便于发辫从双孔内穿出后打结,好将木桶一样的冠帽稳定在头顶之上。桶顶两侧分别安装一根直径 3 cm、长 40 cm 微曲的圆木棍(冠翅),并向两侧叉开一定角度(中间宽 61 cm)。木冠冕成型后,通体外包羊皮,并染成黑色,这一件的尺寸为口径 16 cm、周长 50 cm,类似于长着动物双角的木冠饰才算做成。上述类似的冠饰都有多件,它们的基本形态和用途、用法也相同。

在 2 号墓中出土的木质假肢是项了不起的发现,因为它是一件稀世珍品。假肢用一块厚榆木板(不确定,疑似桦木)加工而成,通高 90.2 cm。上半部为固定板,长 52 cm,刚好是使用者股骨的长度。板上部宽 8.8 cm、下部 7.2 cm,中间最厚处 2.5 cm,向两边缘渐薄至 1 cm。顶端中间竖排 2 个圆孔,用作皮条伸缩固定贴附在腿上的长短,或固定把手便于左手支撑。两侧各有 7 枚穿孔,孔中还残存皮绳,用以捆绑在大腿上。假肢中间是连杆,圆柱形,直径 3.6 cm。连杆和固定板之间缠三圈用于加固的皮条,并用另一根皮条串联,以避免松动滑脱。底部为支脚,在连杆上套装一个经过加工成形的牛角,牛角套长18 cm,下半截较细,端头呈楔状,利于抓地防滑。在牛角套上穿进一只小马蹄(不确定,疑似驴蹄),用作防陷装置。2 号墓为竖穴偏室墓,二人合葬,竖穴墓道底部埋葬者为女性,偏室内葬一中年男性,二人头朝向相同,都指向西北,从人体陈放位置分析,偏室内所葬男性埋葬在先,随葬的假肢顺放在他的右边,也就是偏室的后壁边。当出土并看清它的形状以后,所有在场的人们都惊诧不已,没有人能知道它的用途和名称。等到检点骨骼做年龄、性别登记时,发现墓主人左腿骨骼有明显的病变,股骨头颜色不同,更为严重的是该男性的左股骨、胫骨、腓骨、髌骨因骨质增生而牢固地长在了一起并形成锐角,即股骨和胫骨呈 70 度夹角,有人惊呼:假肢! 众人才恍然大悟。

成套的弓、箭和弓套箭囊(古称韬箙、帐,俗称弓箭袋)是胜金店墓地考古发现中的又一个亮点,使人叹为观止。24 号墓的弓套箭囊出土时用自带的皮带悬系在墓室口木盖板上。弓套箭囊十分豪华,用皮条缝缀在一起,细皮带头上有牛角制成的 5 cm 长的精致角扣,可与宽皮带联结,因此可背在肩上或系在腰间。弓套用羚羊皮缝制,呈梯形,上宽下窄,长 86 cm,口宽 26 cm、底宽 12 cm,箭囊实际上是两个圆筒,直径 9 cm,也用羚羊皮缝制,一长一短,长者 96 cm,带盖;短者 78 cm,敞口。想必平时不用时,箭保存在带盖的筒内,将要用时把箭放入无盖的短筒中,箭尾向上露出一截,用时极为方便。弓为反曲的复合弓,长 136 cm。这里的弓不仅个体大和强劲,而且加工工艺达到了登峰造极的水平。就算是今天的能工巧匠,加工制作这样的一张弓至少也要一年的时间。弓箭兼有狩猎工具、作战武器、健身器械多种功能,古人特别注重其性能。据成书于春秋战国之际的《考工记》载:弓者制弓,一定要按照时令选取六种材料,也只有六种材料都具备齐全的基础上才能开始制造。这六种材料是杆、角、胶、筋、漆、丝,但吐鲁番盆地缺少后两种材料,用鹿皮胶和羊肠衣替代。杆使箭射得远,角使箭射得快,筋使箭射得深,胶使各材聚合为弓身,肠衣使弓身坚固。选用牛角制弓片,秋季的牛角厚,春季的牛角薄,青色坚韧有力。牛角长二尺五寸,根部发白、中部发青、末端丰满,这是最为理想的材质,其价值足可抵1头牛的价格。鹿胶青白色,牛胶火红色,鱼胶微黄色,时间越久颜色变深且有光泽,黏性越大。小筋要成长条,大筋要连在一起并且有光泽,取做筋的动物要跑得快。在制弓的流程中,冬季制作弓杆,使其细密;春季浸泡牛角,使其润泽;夏季制作弓筋,使其不续结杂乱;秋天合角、丝、漆三材,则坚固致密。初冬微寒时再进一步加固弓体,弓便不会变形。材料备齐后,开始制弓。弓的加工步骤是先制作弓胎(杆),在制弓材料中弓杆最强,所以用韧性最强的绣线菊(俗称兔儿条)木,火烤弯曲成型,调制好后张弓才会像流水一般。牛角是用来支撑弓体的,其要弯曲而不要弯斜,先将牛角撕开,火烤压平,弯曲成型后两面都划出条纹,以利用胶粘合,粘贴在弓杆的内侧。筋是增加强度的,将筋放在水中浸泡变软,用温水洗净后平放在温热的胶锅中浸沾,梳理平整使筋条展开,铺在弓杆的外侧。铺完一道筋等阴干后再铺第二道,最少要铺三道。要制作力量更大的弓,那就多铺几道。弓弰制成三角形,呈倒钩状,弦反向挂在弓上,烘烤弓体给弓定型。通体再反复缠牛筋、肠衣,刷胶。弓弦用牛筋合成,两端做成固定的环,环上再缠羊皮条,弦的中段也同样要缠皮条,以防过早将弦磨断。弦的长短要反复调试松紧度才能合适。箭有3支,其中有1支是三翼带铤的铁镞,至今还锃光发亮,十分锋利。箭是弓箭这一器具的另一部分,因而箭体的选材、制作是又一关键过程。中国周代用楛木,清代用阴山六道木,中亚史前用兴都库什山的树木制作。木质要细腻,轻且直,有韧性。箭杆、箭扣(尾槽)和箭头分开来加工,做成后再组装插粘在一起,打磨光洁后在接头处用肠衣线系紧。箭尾羽用鸟翎的毛,三片同样大小,均分平行的粘在尾部。

三、相关问题探讨

1. 木床罩

出土的床罩中,有2件保存基本完整。床罩为长方拱弧形,用带毛的牛皮条和柳树枝捆扎而成。底座木棍较粗,用榫头卯眼接合成长方形木框,在木框长边上各凿出5个卯眼,插入5根拱弧形的柳树枝,用4根竖向的长木条与拱弧形的柳树枝等距交叉固定,形成正方格。床罩上覆盖着毛毡。由于制作时牛皮条和柳树枝都是湿的,干后整体变形扭曲。这种长方拱弧形床罩,在吐鲁番盆地、新疆乃至中亚地区古墓葬中尚属初次发现,世界上也未见过报道。

长方拱弧形床罩在本墓地5座墓中被发现,这些墓葬也是保存最好的。有竖穴二层台墓、竖穴墓和偏室墓。有床罩的墓葬也一定有木床。从床罩上都覆盖着毛毡来看,床罩的样式有可能代表着墓主人生前所居住毡帐的形式,其不是我们通常所认为的那种圆形穹顶,像现代游牧民族所居住的那样。这不由得让我们想起以前在鄯善县洋海墓地和和静县察吾呼墓地个别保存较好的墓葬中发现的那些弯曲成拱形的木棍,想来也可能是这种床罩的孑遗。同时还有可能这是木棺的雏形,由此导致木棺的流行。阿斯塔那墓葬出土的所谓纸棺,实际上也可能是床罩。另外,使用这种床罩的墓主人,在身份上与众不同,他们有更多的随葬品。如13号墓是夫妻合葬墓,男女各戴不同的木质冠饰。棚木悬挂弓箭袋,袋内装有强弓利箭。二人都戴饰珊瑚坠的金耳环,男性身着皮衣,皮裤上镂刻有精美的图案,腰部系有皮带,脚上穿着皮靴。女性脸上、身上盖织锦,身着丝绸服装。还有红色带盖圆形木盒、绢袋、陶罐、木豆、陶钵、皮革画。木豆内有包金铜扣。另外还有带柄木镜、小皮囊、铁刀等。是该墓地中随葬品最为丰富的一座墓葬。

2. 木冠饰

这次发现了男女不同的冠饰。13号墓女性尸体头顶处,有一木质冠饰,罩头处为桶状,两侧顶装有两根弧形木棍,外部整体涂黑。男性屈肢下有高尖状木质冠饰,呈船形,薄木板粘合而成,底口近方形,在整体四个面仅一面较直,上有二孔,与圆孔对应的另一面亦有一小圆孔。与直面相对的斜面上方安装一个三角形翼,似船舵状的薄木片,通体黑色。这种尖状木质冠饰在鄯善县洋海三号台地、苏贝希墓地均有发现,另外在苏贝希的姑师人墓葬中,还发现个别女子头上戴有一顶高帽,与胜金店冠饰有所不同。鄯善县苏巴希古墓群三号墓地简报载:[①]M8:A,女性,成年,双辫盘在头顶用黑发罩住,头顶中间固定着一个坚硬的皮制圆形帽托连接于发网。当剥开毛毡,发现胸部置一生牛皮缝制的帽饰,粗端圆形,长15 cm,向上分做两根,逐渐变细,顶端固定细木棍。圆形筒与头顶固定的帽托直径相当。M6:B,女性老年,仰身屈肢,仅剩骨架,但服装保存较好,头戴用黑毡绢成的牛角状冠饰,头发盘卷其上,外套圆盘形发网,以黑色毛线制成,头顶中间栽植高帽状毡棒,下端较粗,用毛绳系于头上。外面也套以黑发网,竖立于头顶中央,甚为别致。这种冠饰在胜金店古墓也有发现,看来男女头戴冠饰是姑师人的风俗习惯,并且男女冠饰因地位不同有所差别。头戴冠饰的习俗在远古阿尔泰北部游牧民族也有发现,1993年夏末,俄罗斯的考古工作者在南西伯利亚阿尔泰与中国接壤的乌柯克山区,发掘了一座巴泽雷克人的古墓。[②] 这是一座阿尔泰山区常见的巨型石堆墓,封堆下有竖穴、木椁和木棺。墓主人为中年女性,文身,戴高冠,身高5~6英尺,高冠即达3英尺,为木质。冠上部饰以丝绸,今已腐朽,只见痕迹;冠下部包以贵重毛皮,至今仍有遗留。上面描述的墓葬形制和冠饰情况与胜金店发现的极为相似,如出一辙。俄罗斯南西伯利亚阿尔泰山区的巴泽雷克古墓,其年代在公元前5~3世纪,跟吐鲁番盆地胜金店姑师人墓葬的年代有些区别,但从都戴木质冠饰的风俗看,姑师人与巴泽雷克人似有一定的渊源关系,是不是同一个祖先或部落,还待今后的考古研究证实。

3. 木器

出土木器所占比例很大,个别墓葬出土随葬品均为木器,器型也较丰富,加工制作工艺精湛,并且掌握打磨、钻孔、雕刻、榫头卯眼和拼接等技术。木器种类主要是日常生活用具、劳动生产工具、狩猎工具等。说明当时社会劳动已经有了明显分工,有相当一部分人专门从事手工业木器加工业等劳动。随着木器加工工具的进步和技术的日渐成熟,木器的作用和功能逐渐显现出来。况且木器有比陶器更便于携带,不易破碎,使用时间长等优点,所以在草原地区,无论早期游牧民族或现在生活在草原地区的牧民依然主要是以木器具和皮具为主,这与他们不断迁徙、逐水草而居有关。

4. 小麦

小麦在苏贝希、洋海等墓地个别墓葬中均有发现,但数量较少,微乎其微。这次胜金店墓地发现这么多保存完好的麦秆、麦穗实属罕见,况且充当铺盖墓葬的填充物是用麦秆,说明小麦在当地种植非常多。胜金店周围地下水资源丰富,这里是否当时车师人主要生产农作物小麦的产粮区? 公元前2世纪后期,作为西汉王朝与匈奴王国抗争的一个重要战略步骤,就是西汉王朝在车师前国设置戊己校尉,组织当地居民在交河故城周围屯田以抗击匈奴。胜金店位于火焰山一带,隶属高昌管辖区,高昌地区是当时西汉

---

① 吕恩国、郭建国:《鄯善县苏贝希墓群三号墓地》,《新疆文物》1996年第3期。
② 王樾:《俄南西伯利亚阿尔泰地区出土文物女尸》,《新疆文物》1995年第3期。

王朝经营西域的大后方,所以这一带有可能是西汉王朝在吐鲁番盆地经营的屯田区之一。

5. 丝织品

墓葬中发现很多丝织品,有绢和锦,颜色有黄、绿、蓝等。这是吐鲁番盆地发现的年代最早的丝织品实物之一,由于墓葬潮湿,保存不太好,许多精美的丝织品腐烂成碎片。出土的丝织品反映出汉代的丝绸已经传播到这里,并且得到当地土著人的接受和喜欢。到底丝织品最早何时传到西域,目前史学界仍有分歧,在同时期俄罗斯南西伯利亚阿尔泰地区的巴泽雷克古墓中同样也发现了丝绸,说明了当时丝绸传播距离之遥远。大多数学者认为张骞通西域后,沟通了中原与西域的贸易联系,中原的丝绸才源源不断地传播到西域;也有少数学者认为张骞未通西域之前,中原地区民间就与西域诸国商人有着频繁的贸易往来,丝绸早于张骞通西域之前就已传播到西域,这种说法虽有道理但缺乏实物证据,因为迄今为止新疆地区还未发现张骞通西域之前的丝绸。

四、结　语

此次抢救性清理工作取得重大收获。从墓葬形制和出土文物来分析,与吐鲁番地区发现的姑师文化(车师文化)中的墓葬形制同类器物很相似,有着强烈的共性,说明其文化性质相同。这种文化遗存,在吐鲁番盆地有着广泛的分布:吐鲁番市的艾丁湖古墓葬、①交河沟北墓葬、②托克逊县的英亚依拉克古墓群、③喀格恰克古墓、④阿拉沟古墓、⑤博斯坦乡古墓、⑥鄯善县境内的三个桥古墓、⑦苏巴什古墓、⑧洋海古墓⑨等出土的器物均属于同一文化类型。这些文化遗存的年代距今约在3 000～2 000年之间,晚期已经到了汉代。根据《汉书·西域传》记载,西汉中期以前,在吐鲁番盆地周围居住的是姑师人,姑师人是生活在新疆的土著居民之一,属于秦汉时期所谓"西域三十六国"之一。汉武帝时,赵破奴攻破姑师,"分以为车师前后王及山北六国"。这批墓葬中有碳定年数据,距今2050～2200年,根据其年代推断,胜金店墓葬的墓主人属于姑师人。

随葬品以木器和皮、毛质制品为大宗,说明了此地居民依然以游牧生活为主。出土绢、锦等丝织品,说明当时丝绸之路之畅通和繁荣。内地生产的精美丝织品很快传播到这里并从这里传销到更远的地方。个别墓葬还出土了石磨盘、木镰刀,以及大量的小麦秸秆等,说明小麦已在胜金店周围广泛种植。本地区除大部分居民依然过着游牧生活外,另有一部分人过着半定居生活,只有这样,才有从事农业生产活动的可能性,这一时期有可能是本地区古代民族从游牧向农耕逐渐转型的时期。

长方形竖穴墓多为单人葬、双人葬及多人合葬,但也发现个别有夫妻合葬现象,这说明夫妻合葬墓从最初的长方形竖穴墓向长方形竖穴偏室墓转型。长方形竖穴偏室墓均为夫妻合葬墓。夫妻合葬情况的

① 李遇春、柳洪亮:《吐鲁番艾丁湖古墓葬》,《考古》1982年第4期。
② 《交河故城1993～1994年考古发掘报告》,东方出版社,1997年。
③ 柳洪亮、张永兵:《托克逊县英亚依拉克古墓群调查》,《考古》1985年第5期。
④ 柳洪亮、张永兵、徐新民:《托克逊县哈格恰克古墓群清理简报》,《考古》1987年第7期。
⑤ 王炳华:《阿拉沟竖穴木椁墓发觉简报》,《文物》1981年第1期。
⑥ 侯世新:《托克逊博斯坦墓群清理简报》,《新疆文物》1996年第3期。
⑦ 邢开鼎、张永兵:《新疆鄯善县三个桥古墓葬的抢救清理发掘》,《新疆文物》1997年第2期。
⑧ 柳洪亮、阿不利木:《鄯善苏巴什古墓葬发掘简报》,《考古》1984年第1期。
⑨ 吕恩国、张永兵:《鄯善县洋海墓地考古新收获》,《考古》2004年第5期。

出现,说明当时的姑师人正处于由原始氏族社会向一夫一妻制转移的时期。墓葬中发现戴覆面的葬俗,男、女各戴不同的冠饰,墓葬里还有点燃长明灯的现象,以及制作和安装使用木头假肢来帮助残疾人行走等情形,从更多方面反映了当时姑师人的生活习俗和劳动智慧,当前对姑师文化的研究尚处于探索阶段,这次在胜金店墓地的考古新发现有着极其重要的意义。

以上观点很不成熟,只能作为初步的研究和认识。能为姑师文化的深入探讨和研究添砖加瓦并有所促进,是撰写本文的最大愿望。

New Archaeological Materials of the Stone Age in At-Bashi Rayon

Aida K. Abdykanova

American University of Central Asia, Department of Anthropology,

Bishkek, Kyrgyzstan

The study of sites belonging to Stone Age is of great significance for solving the problem of settling ancient humans in Central Asia. The importance of such study is well demonstrated on the ground of open and studied Paleolithic sites in Batken and Issyk-Kul areas of the Kyrgyz Republic for last years.

Main goal of archaeological survey was the collection of lithic artifacts dated back to the Stone Age in At-Bashi rayon of Naryn region.

The first date of stone tools from Naryn region was received in 1953 as a result of the complex archaeological and ethnographical expedition by A. P. Okladnikov. Professor A. P. Okladnikov had found out some archaic pebble tools on the terrace of On-Archa river .

The rayon including Arpa valley (Burana-Chap, Kochkorok-Zhar), the surroundings of coast Chatyr-Kul lake, the western part of Ak-Saj valley (valley of Terek river) were investigated also in 2007 by an archaeological team, consisting of the students and researchers from American University of Central Asia, Kyrgyz-Turkic University "Manas" and Kyrgyz National University named J. Balasagyn.

The previously investigated rayon was well-known due to the publications of V. A. Ranov, M. B. Yunusaliev and Sh. A. Kadyrov. In 1963, it was the expedition head by the geologist Sh. A. Kadyrov. Later in 1967 and 1968 this territory was investigated by a paleolithic team of archaeological expedition head by V. A. Ranov, an archaeologist of Stone Age.

Burana-Chap location was discovered as a more perspective place of archaeological findings in the Arpa valley, at N 40 47'54. 9 E 74 45'95. 7.

The location of raw materials was found during our preliminary investigations in the form of siliceous rocks that located in Ak-Saj valley nearly to the Tashele Mountain Ridge, at N 40 42'34. 2″ E 75 56'53. 7″.

Description of sites (Arpa valley)

Burana-Chap (Burma-Chap) is located on the left bank terrace of the Arpa river, at N 40° 47'54. 9″, E 74 45'95. 7″. Artifacts were assembled from the first and second terraces. The collection is comprised of 2 artifacts made of pebble and represents debris and retouched flake.

Next location, Kochkorok-Zhar (Kochkor-Adzhol by V. A. Ranov), is located on small ridge draw out of latitude to the east from the Burana-Chap location, which is heavily degraded by the Arpa River, at N 40 45′98,5″, E 74 50′31.4″. The artifacts were assembled from the eastern part of the ridge and at the bottom of the river-bed. The unique feature of this collection is the finding spur. This massive stone tool may be dated from Paleolithic Age. The collection totals 4 specimens, including the product of debitage of primary reduction (n = 1), perforator (n = 1) and notched tools (n = 2) (Fig. 1).

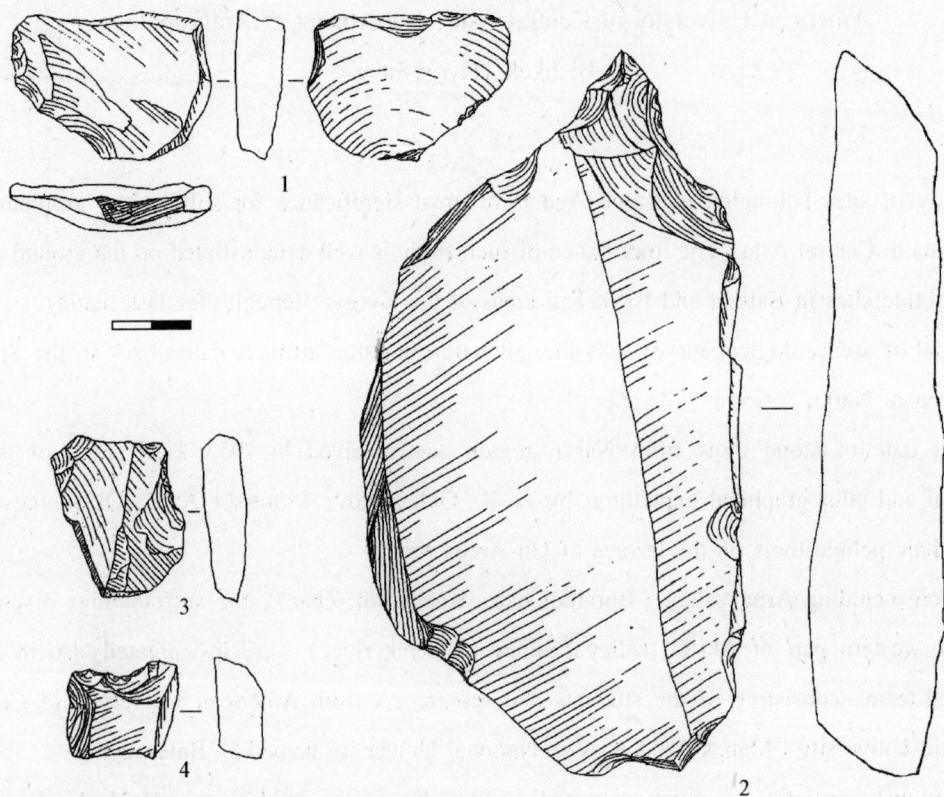

Fig. 1   Artifacts from the Arpa river valley

1 – Burana-Chap   2 – 4 – Kochkorok-Zhar

New discovery was Semetej grotto. The grotto is located in the north-eastern part of the road leading from the Arpa valley to the Tujz-Bel crossing, at N 40 36′19.7″, E 75 03′69.5′. The findings are composed of 2 artifacts: a fragmented microblade and a debris made of dark-blue flint. The grotto is very perspective for further investigations, especially for stationary excavations. The object is preliminary dated from the Middle Stone Age to New Stone Age.

Description of sites (Chatyr-Kul eastern coast)

The Ajgyrzhal location is situated on the western sides of the Ajgyrzhal Ridge, at N 40 41′97.3″, E 75 27′56.3″. The artifacts were manufactured of yellow and red siliceous rock, pebbles and grey-dull chalcedony. The collection represents a mixture of artifacts that can be affiliated with different chronological periods. Some artifacts' surface have been badly preserved. The total collection from the Ajgyrzhal Ridge includes borers (n = 3), a notched tool (n = 1), a spure (n = 1), retouched flakes (n = 2) and retouched debris (n = 8) (Fig. 2).

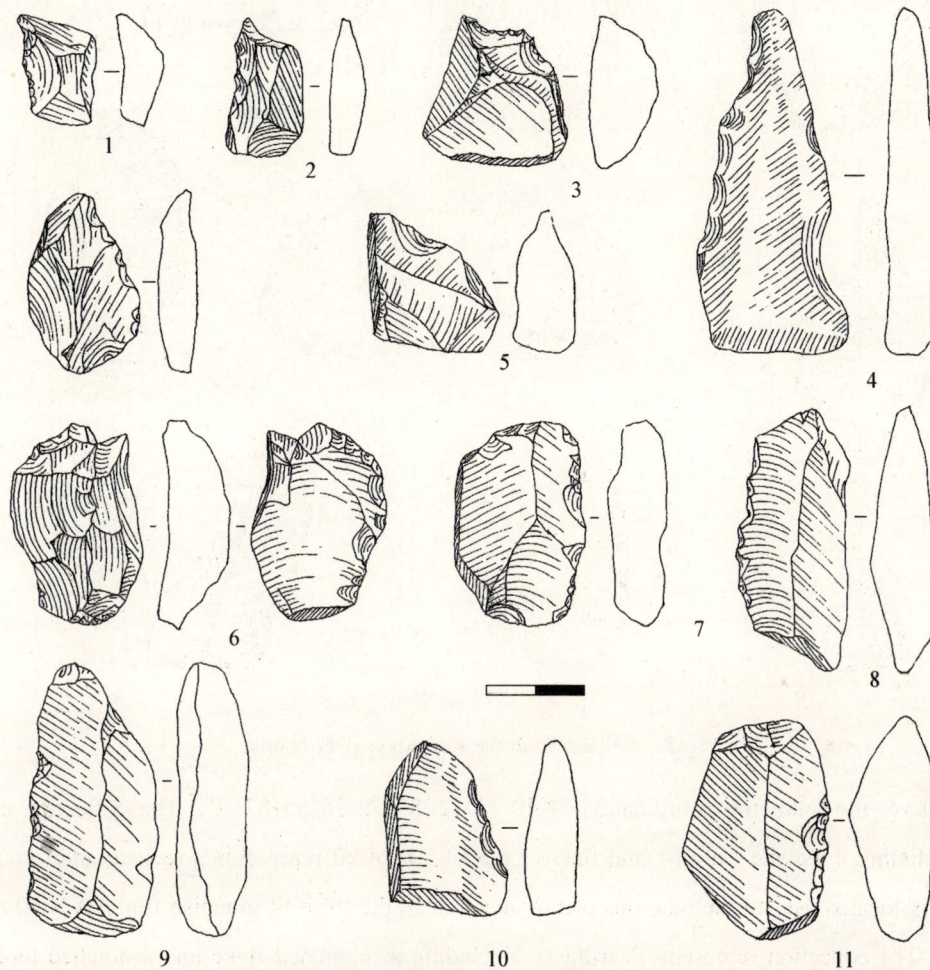

Fig. 2   Artifacts from the Ajgyrzhal location.

The findings were also discovered at the bottom of the Kek-Ajgyr river. All artifacts are tools. This category includes a side scraper (n = 1), borers (n = 3), a notched tool (n = 1), a denticulate-notched tool (n = 1), a spure (n = 1), a perforator (n = 1), retouched flakes (n = 2), and retouched debris (n = 8) (Fig. 3).

Description of sites (Ak-Saj valley)

The complex of open-sites was discovered on the left bank of the Terek river.

Terek-2 is located near the Azhap Sarajy place, at N 40 49′62. 9″, E 75 55′72. 4″. The artifacts totals 4 specimens. The collection includes prismatic cores (n = 2) and massive tools similar to "shaves" (n = 2).

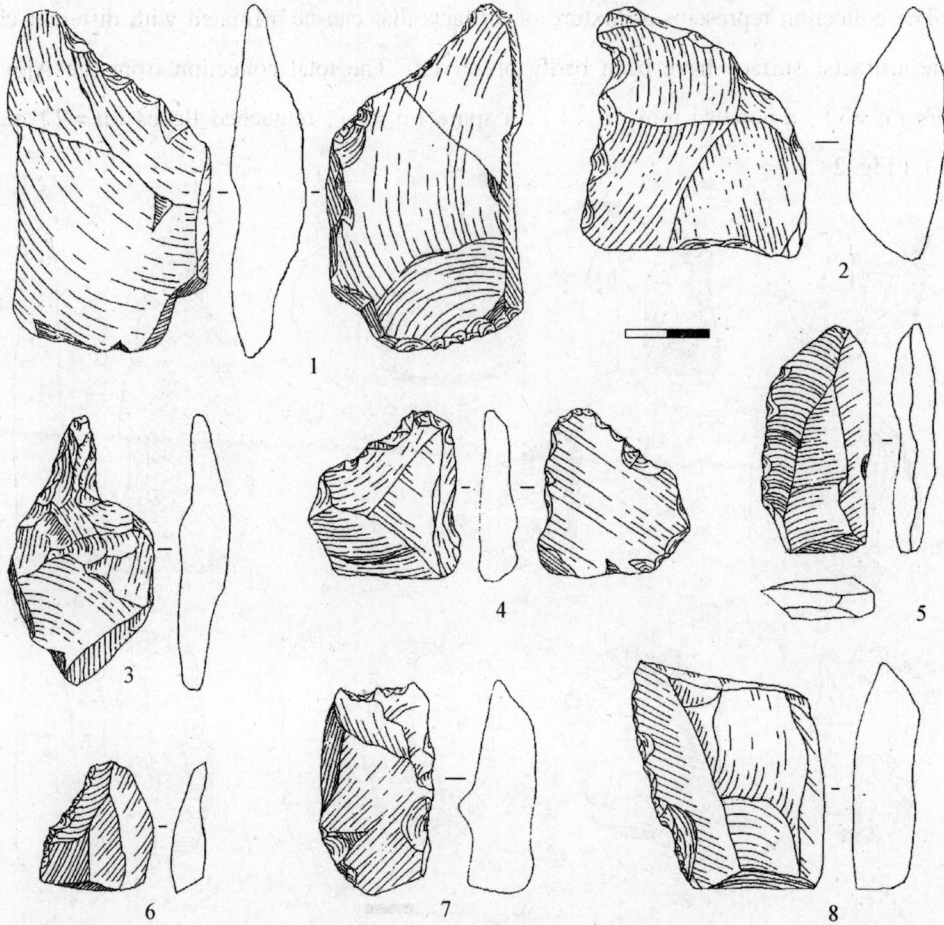

Fig. 3 Artifacts from the Kek-Ajgyr river bottom.

Terek-3 have the following coordinates: N 40 41′12.8″, E 75 55′67.7″. The collection consists of 6 specimens including a reclette (n = 1) and flakes (n = 5). Tool kit represents a reclette and retouched flake.

Terek-5 is located near to the outcrops of raw material in the form of greenish flint, at N 40 42′34.2″, E 75 56′53.7″. The collection represents 2 artifacts, including a retouched flake and a notched tool (Fig. 4).

The findings on the right terrace of Sary-Imek river in the Arpa valley is composed of 3 specimens. It is most probably that this location is Sary-Imek open-site, which was discovered by V. A. Ranov [Ranov, Yunusaliev, 1969]. The collection represents a side-scraper (n = 1) and retouched debris (n = 2).

Conclusion

During the investigation survey in Naryn region a number of archaeological sites including the Semetej rock-shelter was discovered. As a result, the original material collected has broadened our insight about this site and some aspects of prehistory of At-Bashi rayon and Kyrgyzstan on the whole.

All collected materials preliminarily dated from Paleolith, Middle and New Stone Age. Heavily abraded findings from the Kek-Ajgyr site, a perforator from the Arpa valley as well as a pebble tool finding on the terrace of the Zhoon-Aryk river may be dated back to Paleolithic Age.

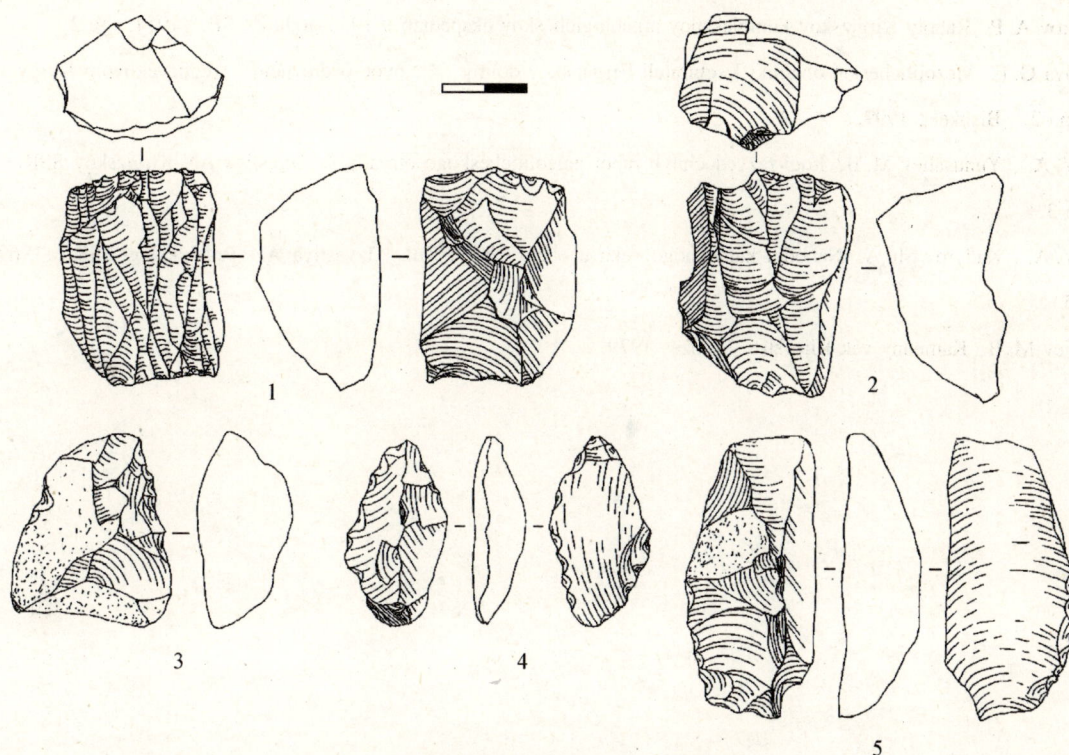

Fig. 4　Artifacts from the Terek river valley.

Considering stone tools, the main source of raw material is most likely located in Ak-Saj valley. The artifacts, especially prismatic cores founded in the Terek river valley date from Middle and New Stone Age. From the point of view of presented data, the hypothesis by V. A. Ranov about the existence of local "ak-saj" culture can have grounds. It is the author's opinion that the "ak-saj" culture has a certain analogy with "markansuj" high mountain culture in Uzbekistan [Ranov, Yunusaliev, 1969; Ranov, Kadyrov, 1969].

The localization of artifacts on the south-western mountainsides of the Ajgyrzhal chine of the Chatyr-Kul lake eastern coast allow outlining the migration ways of ancient peoples from the Ak-Saj valley to eastern coast of the Chatyr-Kul lake and farther along the south coast via Tyuz-Bel pass to Arpa valley. The findings in Torugart pass and the discovery of the Semetej rock-shelter behind the Tyuz-Bel pass confirmed this assumption.

Along with unpublished materials from a number of sites of Kumtor and already discovered first stage of obishir culture in Tash-Kumyr [Korobkova, 1999:], the findings in the Aksaj valley (along Terek river) let us conclude about the existence of a local variant or variants of Stone Age in the high mountains zone of the Central-Asian region within the bounds of Kyrgyzstan.

In general, our research has revealed a large number of archaeological sites, which can be excavated successfully in the future. All archaeological materials deposited in the At-Bashi Museum.

References

Bernshtam A. N. Istoriko-arheologicheskie ocherki Zentralnogo Tyan-Shanya I Pamiro-Alaya. -M., L., 1952. -(MIA №26)

Okladnikov A. P. Raboty Kirgizskoy kompleksnoy arheologicheskoy ekspedizii v 1953 godu // SE. - 1954. -№ 2

Korobkova G. F. Mezoliticheskie ohotniki I sobirateli Ferganskoy doliny // Novoe o drevnem I srednevekovom Kyrgyzstane. -
    Vyp. 2. - Bishkek, 1999.

Ranov V. A. , Yunusaliev M. B. Itogi razvedochnyh rabot paleoliticheskogo otryada // Izvestiya AN Kirgizskoy SSR. - 1969.
    -№ 3.

Ranov V. A. , Kadyrov Sh. A. Nahodki kamennogo veka u ozera Chatyr-Kul. - Izvestiya AN Tadzhikskoy SSR. - 1969. -№1
    (55).

Yunusaliev M. B. Kamenny vek Kirgizii. - Frunze, 1979.

Things of Chinese import in ancient Turkic burials of Altai (To the archaeological evidence of trade and cultural relationship between Ancient Turks and China)

Kubarev Gleb

Institute of Archaeology and Ethnography Siberian Branch of Russian

Academy of Sciences, Novosibirsk, Russian Federation

Introduction

From written Chinese sources we know that between Sui and Tang China and ancient Turks very close diplomatic, cultural and trade relation were existed. Things of Chinese import in archaeological materials from ancient Turkic burials of Altai and neighboring regions can illustrate this cultural and trade relations.

Ancient Turkic antiquities in the Altai include mound burials, stone sculptures and enclosures, rock paintings — graffiti and runic inscriptions, associated with them. These antiquities also include settlements and objects of iron metallurgy. Burials offer the most interesting and informative source for the history of the ancient Turks. At present more than 200 burials have been investigated in the Altai region.

Chinese silk as main import thing

Coins, mirrors and especially Chinese silk are found in ancient Turkic burials of Altai. Unfortunately, things of Chinese import are rather rear finds in the ancient Turkic burials in the Altai. The only exception is the Chinese silk. The inventory of many ancient Turkic burials of Altai contains the remains of clothes in the form of silk, woolen fabric, felt, fragments of leather, and fur. Frequently these are only small fragments; however in several burials significant parts of clothing were found. As a result of laboratory analysis, at least twelve types of silk ornaments were identified. Three represent versions of the same motif: two dragons and a "tree of life" in a medallion (Fig. 1; 4, 1). They differ from each other in the size of the medallions, details in the images and in the colors. Silk with similar ornaments are known to be of Chinese origin, and there are many similar examples from China, Mongolia, Middle Asia, Japan, and so forth. For example, they were

Fig. 1 Chinese silk with ornaments in the form of two dragons and a "tree of life" in a medallion. Yustyd XXIV, kurgan 13.

found in early medieval monuments in Altai-Katanda II, kurgan 1,[①] Tujahta, kurgan 3; Tujahta, kurgan 4; Kurai IV-1,[②] Kurai VI-1,[③] Tuva-Argalykty, Xingjian-cemetery Astana,[④] Mongolia-Nainte-sume.[⑤]

These motifs are reliably dated to the 7th and 8th centuries. In addition to these roundel designs, a few examples of rhomboid, geometrical and floral patterns have also been found. There are also eight or nine kinds of non-ornamented silks of various colors. The overwhelming majority of patterned silks examined are monochromatic textiles; there is only few polychromatic samples known (Fig. 2).

The damask fabric of golden color with rhombuses in which two another rhombuses are entered (Fig. 3, 2) from ancient Turkic burial Barburgazy I, kurgan 20 is of great interest. Silk of the same color with similar but not identical

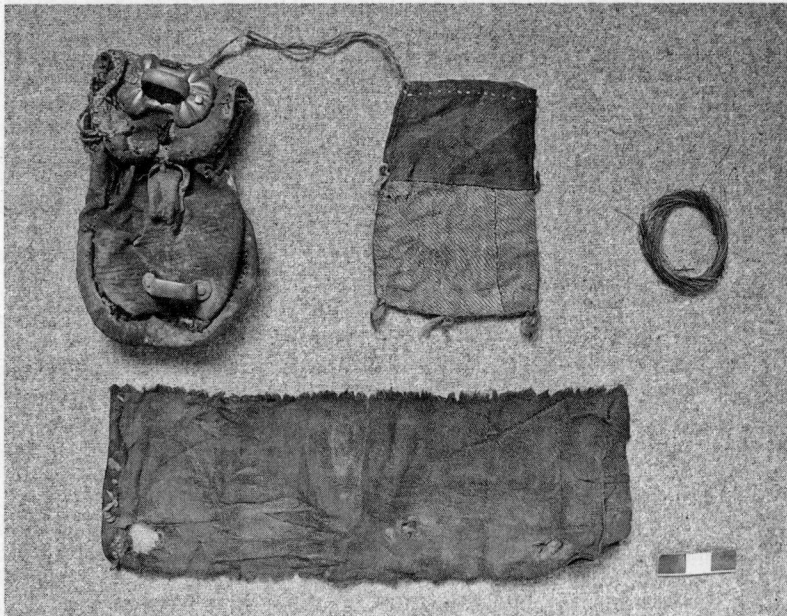

Fig. 2 Leather and silk belt purses. Yustyd XXIV, kurgan 13.

① Zaharov A. A. *Materiali po arheologii Sibiri (raskopki akademika V. V. Radlova v 1865 g.)* In *Trudy Gosudarstvennogo Istoricheskogo Muzeja.* 1926, Vyp. I, p. 100, Fig. VI.

② Kiselev S. V. Drevnyaya istoriya Yuzhnoy Sibiri. Moskva, 1951, pp. 539 – 541.

③ Evtyuhova L. A., Kiselev S. V. *Otchet o rabote Sayano-Altayskoy arheologicheskoy ekspedicii v 1935 g.* In: *Trudy Gosudarstvennogo Istoricheskogo Muzeja*, 1941, Vyp. XVI, p. 110.

④ Sakamoto K., Lubo-Lesnichenko E. I. *Gruppa kamchatnyh tkaney VII-VIII vv. iz Central'noy Azii i Yaponii.* In: *Trudy Gosudarstvennogo Ermitazha*, 1989, Vyp. XXVII, p. 61.

⑤ Borovka G. I. *Arheologicheskoe izuchenie srednego techeniya r. Toly.* In: *Severnaya Mongoliya*, Leningrad, 1927, T. II, p. 74, Fig. 7.

rhombuses is known in ancient Turkic burial in Tuva-Mongun-Taiga-58 – IV. [1] As to other ornaments of silks, such as "flower" (Fig. 3, 1), in the form of simple rhombuses (Fig. 4, 2), two types of a geometrical pattern and also four kinds of a vegetative ornament (Fig. 2) we don't know the direct analogies for it in publications. However, it is necessary to underline, that since the beginning of 8th century in Tang China the Sasanid ornamentation on silk was replaced by vegetative ornaments, and mainly, with flower patterns. [2]

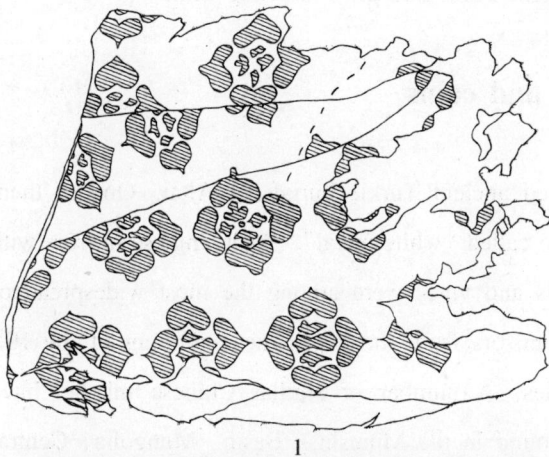

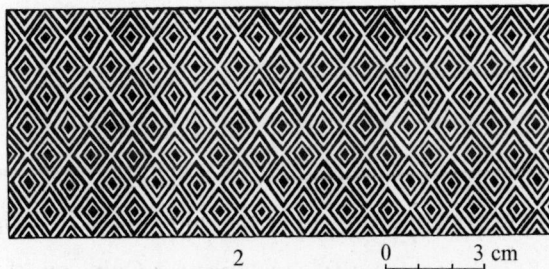

Fig. 3 Drawing of silk ornaments.
Barburgazy I, kurgan 20.

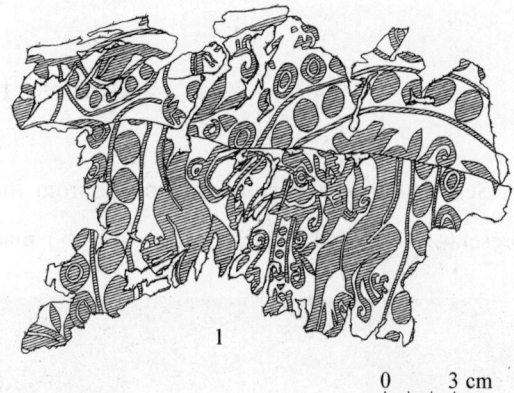

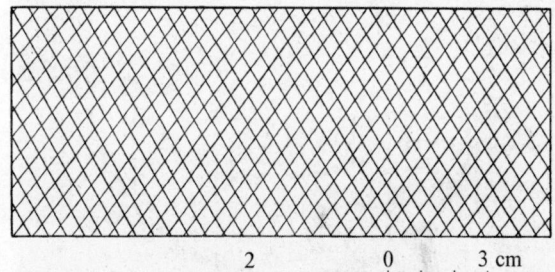

Fig. 4 Drawing of silk ornaments.
Barburgazy I, kurgan 20.

In general, taking into account the few ornamental motifs and textile designs of Sogdian manufacture as well as their geometrical motifs and specific color scales, it is possible to conclude that practically all examined silk textiles are of Chinese origin. It is possible, however, that some of the fabrics were made in Central Asia. Almost all these textile should be dated to the late 7th and the 8th centuries, because many of them came from the complexes where silks with medallions and dragons were also found. Only some of the textiles — in particular those that are non-ornamented — belong, possibly, to the late Tang period (9th– 10th centuries).

At present, the collection of Chinese silks from ancient Turkic burials of the Altai is one of the biggest and can be compared with textile finds from, *inter alia*, Bobrovskiy cemetery in Kazakhstan and Moshevaja Balka in the Caucasus. These finds include ornaments which are absent from other sites. They confirm data in written Chinese records about the quantity of silk sent to the ancient Turks of Central Asia as tribute or

[1] Grach A. D. *Arheologicheskie issledovaniya v Kara-Hole i Mongun-Tayge.* In: *TTKAEE.* 1960, t. 1, p. 136, Fig. 83.

[2] Lubo-Lesnichenko E. I. Kitay na shelkovom puti, Moskva, 1994, p. 208.

payment. Thus, the dating of these silk textiles (7th–8th centuries) coincides with the flourishing of the Silk Road. The distribution areas of Chinese silk in Central Asia could help in the understanding of possible ways of its penetration. The frequency of Chinese silk in ancient Turkic burials allows us to affirm that the wearing of silk clothing was not solely the privilege of rich and noble nomads. These textile finds make it possible to reconstruct the costume of ancient Turks. In addition, they allow us to consider questions of cultural interaction and borrowing between the costumes of the ancient Turks and those of Tang China.

Chinese mirrors and coins

Several Chinese mirrors are known from the excavated ancient Turkic burials of Altai. One of them represents an original Chinese mirror (Fig. 5) made from so called "white metal". Such Chinese mirrors with

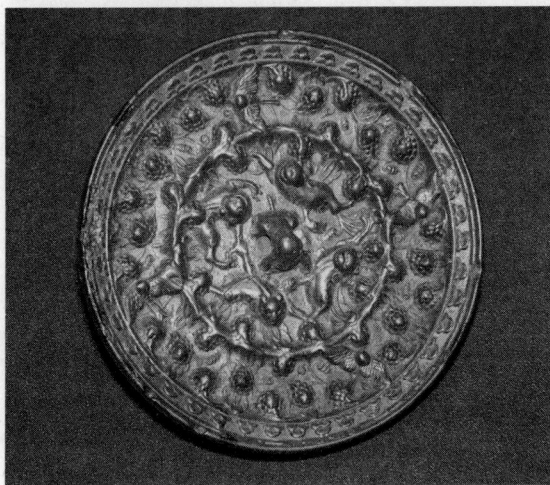

Fig. 5 Chinese mirror with images of animals and vines. Yustyd XIV, kurgan 2.

animals and vines were among the most widespread of Tang mirrors from the 7th to the beginning of the 10th centuries. A number of similar Chinese mirrors have been found in the Minusinsk Basin, Mongolia, Central Asia and Japan. Mirrors with such ornamental motifs have a number of variants.

Such mirrors with images of animals and vines differ in details of the image and the sizes, belong to one of the most widespread types of the mirrors cast in Tang China (7th-beginning 10th centuries). Only on the territory of Minusinsk basin 25 exemplars are known, including local copies. [1] The mirror with animals and vines in fair preservation was found in ancient Turkic burial in Mongolia-Dzhargalanty, kurgan 2. [2] Finds of such mirrors are known in the Middle Asia. [3] The fragment of such mirror has been found in Barabinsk forest-steppe, [4] and one more copy in the Eastern Europe-Upper Posur'e. [5]

Of undoubted interest for dating of mirrors with such ornament is a find of the core-loop in the form of figure of a sitting lion in Pendzhikent in a layer of middle 8th century. [6] The large number of Tang mirrors of

[1] Lubo-Lesnichenko E. I. Privoznye zerkala Minusinskoy kotloviny, Moskva, 1975, p.17.

[2] Evtyuhova L. A. *O plemenah Central'noy Mongolii v IX v.* In: *Sovetskaya arheologiya*, 1957, № 2, Fig.3.

[3] Raspopova V. I. *Zerkala iz Pendzzikenta.* In: *Kratkie Soobshenija Instituta Archeologii*, 1972, Vyp.132, p.69. Usbekistan. Erben der Seidenstraße, Stuttgart-London, 1995, Fig.84.

[4] Molodin V. I. *Drevnee iskusstvo Zapadnoy Sibiri*, Novosibirsk, 1992, Fig.156.

[5] Belorybkin G. N. *Moda na ukrasheniya na territorii Verhnego Posur'ya v IX-XI vv.* In: *Kul'tury evraziyskih stepey vtoroy poloviny I tisyacheletiya n. e. (iz istorii kostyuma)*, Samara, 2001, T. 1, p.217, Fig.6.

[6] Raspopova V. I. *op. cit.*, p.69.

such type is known on the territory of China itself-about 100 copies. Thus, 18 of them, that are especially important, were found in precisely dated Tang burials. [1] Mirrors with the image of animals and vines have wide spread up to Japan where their big number is also known. [2] Distinctive features of the mirror from the river Justyd in Altai allow us to ascribe it to type I E according to Syui Djan'kui. [3] The mirror of this type was found in burial belonging to 10th year of government Kajjuan'. [4] In generally the overwhelming majority of such mirrors are dated in 8th century. The issue of more precise dating of mirrors of such type within Tang period remains open. However using some already proposed criteria the mirror from Yustyd can be dated in bloom period of Tang dynasty (end of 7th-8th centuries).

Several Chinese mirrors were found in ancient Turkic burials of Altai: Kurai III, kurgan 2, [5] Katanda II, kurgan 5, [6] Usuntal, kurgan 5, 6, [7] Bertek, [8] Kor-Koby I, kurgan 46. [9] As a rule, mirrors belong to woman burial inventory but sometimes they are found in mans burials (Mongun-Taiga-57 – XXVI). [10]

A Chinese bronze coin — "kaiuan' tunbao"-(Fig. 6) was found in one of the Turkic burials (Yustyd I, kurgan 8). [11] This coin was the most widespread of Tang China and was cast over a period of more than 300 years (618 – 906). This coin determines the lower chronological horizon of the burial of kurgan 8 cemetery Yustyd I as 620. It is, obviously, so-called cjan'-one of the first issues. Taking into account the diameter, it is a small change coin in one unit. [12] Absence of any signs, legends or hieroglyphs on the back of coins and also the fact that small change «kaiyuan' tunbao» was minted continuously; its exact chronological definition is complicate.

Fig. 6 Chinese bronze coin "kaiuan' tunbao". Yustyd I, kurgan 8.

---

① Syuy Dyan'kuy *Arheologicheskoe izuchenie periodizacii tanskih zerkal*. In: *Kaogu syuebao*, 1994, № 3, p. 305.

② Decorated tombs in Japan. Special Exhibition, Tokyo, 1993, Fig. 132d

③ Syuy Dyan'kuy *op. cit.* , p. 306.

④ Motto of government Kajjuan (713 – 741) of Tan emperor Sjuantszun (712 – 756).

⑤ Evtyuhova L. A. , Kiselev S. V. *op. cit.* , Fig. 34.

⑥ Gavrilova A. A. *Mogil'nik Kudyrge kak istochnik po istorii altayskih plemen*, Moskva-Leningrad, 1965, Fig. 7, 6.

⑦ Savinov D. G. *Drevnetyurkskie kurgany Uzuntala (K voprosu o vydelenii kurayskoy kul'tury)*. In: *Arheologiya Severnoy Azii*, Novosibirsk, 1982, Fig. 5, 9; 11.

⑧ Savinov D. G. *Drevnetyurkskoe vremya*. In: *Drevnie kul'tury Berteskoy doliny*, Novosibirsk, 1994, p. 148.

⑨ Surazakov A. S. *Raskopki pamyatnikov Kurata II i Kor-Koby I*. In: *Problemy izucheniya drevney i srednevekovoy istorii Gornogo Altaya*, Gorno-Altaysk, 1990, Fig. 22, 1.

⑩ Grach A. D. *op. cit.* , Fig. 22.

⑪ Its diameter is 24,5 mm, the sizes of a square aperture-7,1 × 6,7 mm, a thickness on border-1,6 mm, weight-3,66 g.

⑫ Vorob'ev M. V. *K voprosu opredeleniya starinnyh kitayskih monet "kayyuan' tunbao"*. In: *Epigrafika Vostoka*, 1963, t. XV. p. 125.

Nevertheless, diameter of a coin, high quality of minting, regular border testify to its belonging to early Tang period. [1] The peculiarities of the Yustyd coin indicate that it was cast between 621 and 760. Tang coins, thanks to extensive commercial relations of China, have wide spread into the neighboring and remote regions: Central Asia, the Far East, etc. Tang China trade also with nomads what is confirmed by written sources and archaeological materials. However the small number of coins which got to nomads was hardly direct used, i. e. as an instrument of payment. Most likely, the coin was used as an amulet. Coins «kaiyuan' tunbao» are widely known in early medieval burials of Southern Siberia and the Central Asia: in Tuva — Mongun-Taiga-58 – IV,[2] Aimyrlyg 3, k. 1,[3] in Mongolia-Dzhargalanty, kurgan 2,[4] in the Kuznetsk Basin-burial ground Sapogovo,[5] etc.

Conclusions

Period of 7th-first half of 8th centuries can be considered as the period of fullest flower of the Silk way. [6] Moreover "diplomatic" and "exchange" trade ancient Turks with Tang China prospered. So, in written Chinese sources "gifts" by silk of the Chinese emperors or peace treaties with annual payment on some thousand pieces of silk are always mentioned. [7]

Thus, silk represented itself as means of payment. After capture of the central part of the Silk way by Tibetan in the second half of VIII century Chinese silk could reach Altai region using so-called "Kirghiz" way which began in East Turkistan or "Uigur" way, going from Tang empire through Ordos. [8] Thus, into central-Asian nomads hands fall the large amount of Chinese silk, what is traced on materials of ancient Turkic burials.

An important scientific problem is the precise dating of Turkic burials. This question remains the most difficult and debatable in research on ancient Turkic culture. Import articles with firmly established dates of manufacture and "short life" (by textile) are particularly useful for dating Turkic burials. Coins, mirrors and textiles belong to such import articles.

The ancient Turks, who have created even for the short period huge empire, have paved the way for a cultural and trading exchange between the East and the West. [9] Trade of silk was not on the last place in this

---

① Vorob'ev M. V. *op. cit.* , p. 133.

② Grach A. D. *Arheologicheskie raskopki v Mongun-Tayge i issledovaniya v Central'noy Tuve*. In: *TTKAEE*, 1960, t. 1, Fig. 78.

③ Ovchinnikova B. B. *Pogrebenie drevnetyurkskogo voina v Central'noy Tuve*. In: *Sovetskaya arheologiya*, 1982, № 3, Fig. 3 , *1*.

④ Evtyuhova L. A. *op. cit.* , Fig. 8.

⑤ Ilyushin A. M. , Suleymenov M. G. , Guz' V. B. , Starodubcev A. G. Mogil'nik Sapogovo-pamyatnik drevnetyurkskoy epohi v Kuzneckoy kotlovine, Novosibirsk, 1992, Fig. 53, *6*.

⑥ Lubo-Lesnichenko E. I. Kitay na shelkovom puti, Moskva, 1994, p. 256.

⑦ Bichurin N. YA. (Iakinf) Sobranie svedeniy o narodah, obitavshih v Sredney Azii v drevnie vremena, Moskva-Leningrad, 1950, t. 1, pp. 233, 246, 276, 283.

⑧ Lubo-Lesnichenko E. I. *"Uygurski" i "kirgizskii" puti v Zentral'noi Azii*. In: *Trudy Gosudarstvennogo Ermitazha*. 1989, Vyp. XXVII, p. 4.

⑨ Gumilev L. N. Drevnie turki, Moskva, 1993, p. 175.

cultural and trading exchange.

The study of ancient Turkic antiquities in the Altai is of particular significance since this region is considered to have been the native land of the ancient Turks. According to genealogical legends, the Altai is connected to the early history and to the origin of the Turkic community. The Altai period of ancient Turkic history is important, also, as the period during which the Turks developed their own statehood. As a result of the creation of an extended empire, the ancient Turks influenced and transmitted elements of their material culture (e. g., caftan, belt plaque decorations, stirrups) and aspects of their political structure to other nomads of the Eurasian steppe. They also had a significant influence on the settled people of China, Sogd, Sassanian Iran and Byzantium.

Культурные связи Саяно-Алтая и Китая в VIII-IV веках до н. э.

Леонид Марсадолов

Государственный Эрмитаж, Санкт-Петербург, Россия

В I тыс. до н. э. кочевники Евразии неоднократно с разными целями контактировали с народами Китая. Представляется весьма актуальным, начиная с VIII в. до н. э., рассмотреть по векам культурные связи племён Саяно-Алтая и Китая. Пока немногочисленные археологические факты постепенно будут дополняться всё новыми аналогиями, всё глубже раскрывая сложные взаимоотношения этих регионов.

В IX-VII веках до н. э. на юго-востоке Евразии — в Китае и Индии, а также на западе — в Передней Азии и Средиземноморье, уже сложились высокоразвитые рабовладельческие государства. Это один из наиболее ярких периодов в мировой истории — время создания «Книги перемен» в Китае, Ведических текстов в Индии, Библейских текстов в Передней Азии, «Илиады» и «Одиссеи» в Греции.

Но одновременно с этим миром существовал и другой, находившийся на ступени военной демократии, становления раннеклассового общества — мир кочевников степей Евразии. Это время создания, подъема и упадка довольно больших и грозных кочевых союзов — киммерийцев-гимирри, скифов, саков, фракийцев и других племён. Археологами пока исследованы лишь отдельные грандиозные курганы вождей кочевников Евразии — Аржан в Саянах; Чиликта, Бесшатыр, Иссык в Казахстане; Башадар, Туэкта, Пазырык на Алтае; Гумарово, Филипповка в Приуралье; Гордион в Турции; Келермес, Семибратние в Предкавказье; Солоха, Чертомлык, Толстая могила, Огуз в Северном Причерноморье; Птичата могила в Болгарии, а также начинают изучаться большие курганы на северо-западе Китая. Не только в оседлых цивилизациях, но и у кочевников были свои выдающиеся политики, воины, мудрецы, зодчие, мастера-художники и религиозные деятели. Об этом свидетельствуют огромные курганы вождей кочевых объединений и древние святилища на горах и в степях.

Оседлые и кочевые народы довольно часто взаимно обогащали друг друга не только технологическими, социально-экономическими, но также мировоззренческими и этическими идеями. О «не испорченности» кочевников повседневными благами, их близости к Природе, надёжном побратимстве, свободолюбии — свидетельствовали многочисленные сведения, мифы и легенды. Многие народы позаимствовали у кочевников отдельные формы социального устройства, вооружения, средств передвижения, элементы костюма, навыки в управлении и разведении коней, календарные представления и другие элементы духовной и практической жизни. Использование коня в качестве колесничного и верхового животного значительно ускорило и расширило коммуникабельность племён с различным уровнем социальной, политической и экономической организации. Отдельные кочевники или их группы во главе со своими предводителями служили наёмниками и выступали в качестве союзников во многих государствах древнего мира. На территории Евразии в этот период происходило неоднократное проникновение племён и элементов культуры в разных направлениях, хотя археологически уловить реальные неравномерные динамичные процессы на территории Евразии во II-I тыс. до н. э. очень трудно, а сведения о них по письменным источникам часто фрагментарны.

Великий евразийский степной путь, как сумма отдельных, часто независимых от других регионов, участков дорог и троп, проходящих по степному поясу, возникший значительно раньше VIII в. до н. э. и функционировавший позднее, способствовал торговому обмену, широкому распространению жизненно важных мировоззренческих идей, гармоничных художественных образов, передовых изобретений в технике, вооружении, конском снаряжении и т. п. Одна из наиболее длинных трасс Великого степного пути проходила через евразийский «степной коридор»: от Китая — Ордоса по Монголии — Саяно-Алтаю — Казахстану — Приаралью — южной части Урала, вдоль северного и западного берега Каспийского моря (или южнее Арала и Каспия) — в Прикубанье — Предкавказье — через Кавказ — в Переднюю Азию и далее на запад или более прямым путем — от Урала через Поволжье на Украину (будущую Великую Скифию) — Болгарию (Фракию) — Венгрию — Грецию — Францию — до Атлантического океана (Марсадолов, 1999). Позднее по некоторым участкам этого евразийского «степного коридора» проходили боковые трассы знаменитого «Шелкового» пути из Китая. Вероятно, не было единой трассы от Тихого до Атлантического океанов, а были отдельные, контролируемые местным населением участки пути (со своими проводниками и охраной), которые в зависимости от целей и политической обстановки могли быть более или менее длинными и безопасными. Конечно, могли использоваться разные варианты этих путей в зависимости от целей передвижения, удачного окончания военного похода или поражения и многих других факторов. В основном прослеживается близость в изобразительных и вещевых комплексах, находящихся вдоль этих трасс.

Вернувшись из походов, в которых вожди кочевников узнали о преимуществах больших дорог над горными тропами, они часто начинали контролировать участки основных путей и торговых трасс. Как крупные современные посёлки Саяно-Алтая располагаются в наиболее важных узловых точках дорог, ведущих с запада на восток, с юга на север и в другие направления, так и в древности наиболее крупные курганы воздвигались вдоль таких же путей. Они служили в какой-то степени путевыми ориентирами для проводников и свидетельствовали о «праве предков» на занятую территорию.

Разные по происхождению художественные стили через 100 – 200 лет существенно изменяли облик многих евразийских изображений и предметов в I тыс. до н. э. Вероятно, подобные процессы имели место в предшествующие и последующие периоды, только с более или менее продолжительными временными интервалами.

Изображения, доведённые до идеала своей эпохи, как правило, гармоничны по композиционному и конструктивному решению, высокохудожественны по исполнению. Такие образцы для подражания пользовались постоянным большим спросом (модой) и многократно копировались различными мастерами. «Эстафетным» (мирным, военным, торговым...) путём от одного народа к другому идеи, предметы и изображения быстро распространялись на обширной территории независимо от политических границ, от разных идеологических корней искусства, как вне этническое интернациональное явление.

Обычно копировались отдельные образы животных, несложные сюжеты и орнаментальные мотивы. Чем дальше образ (сюжет, композиция) удалены от первоначального «очага», тем труднее сопоставимы изображения в конечных точках. Образ одного животного нередко заменяли в соседнем регионе образом другого наиболее почитаемого животного, но при этом сохраняли характерные черты стиля, независимого также от функции предмета (зеркало, сосуд, поясная пряжка и т. п.) и от материала, на⁄в котором передано то или иное изображение (камень, рог, золото и т. п.). Несомненно, предшествующие стили во многих районах накладывали свой « отпечаток » на изображения последующих периодов. Но как бы ни влияли художественные традиции, изображения в новом стиле почти всегда легко опознаются. Вполне допустимо одновременное сосуществование в одном небольшом районе двух или более стилей, художественных школ и т. п.

При изучении отдельных изображений оленей и других животных важно найти не только центр их возникновения, что часто бывает весьма спорно, но и границы распространения. В качестве примера рассмотрим только один хронологический пласт стилистически близких образов, датируемых IX-VII вв. до н. э. Представляется возможным соединить все эти изображения в одну «цепочку», вытянутую по линии: Ордос — Внутренняя Монголия — Монголия — Тува — Монгольский — Восточный и Западный Алтай — Тянь-Шань — Кавказ — Малая Азия — Греция (рис. 1; Марсадолов, 1999).

Для VIII в. до н. э. образы оленей отмечены на обломке «оленного» камня из насыпи самого большого в Центральной Азии кургана Аржан в Саянах (рис. 1. - 2,3; Грязнов, 1980; Марсадолов, 2008), а также на бронзовом предмете из Ордоса (рис. 1. - 9; Mounted Nomads ..., 1997, pp. 54 (№ 90), 168, VI). Во Внутренней Монголии (Китай) был найден бронзовый кинжал с тремя изображениями оленей на ручке, близкими по стилю к вышеописанным (рис. 1. - 11; Xiang Chunsong, Li Yi, 1995, p. 17).

Близки изображения оленей из кургана Аржан в Саянах, на бронзовом зеркале с р. Бухтармы на Алтае, в петроглифах Монголии, Саяно-Алтая и хребта Каратау. Образы оленя на бронзовой поясной пряжке с Кавказа близки по стилю и времени к многочисленным рисункам на сосудах Ирана периода «Сиалк В», на вазах «геометрического» периода из Анатолии, Греции, Италии и близлежащих к ним

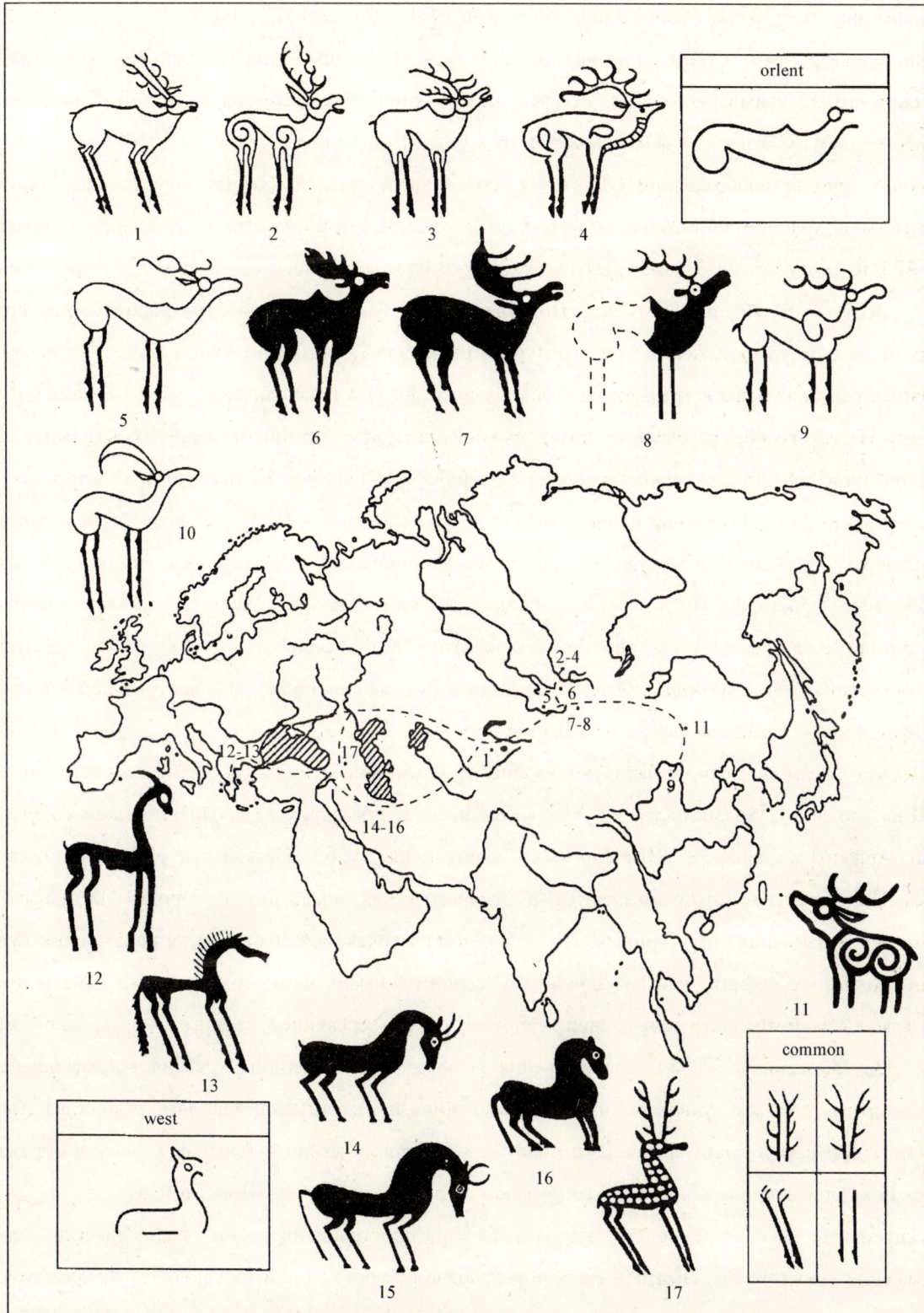

Рис. 1. Распространение близких по стилю образов животных на территории Евразии в VIII-VII вв. до н. э. Штриховой линией обозначен предполагаемый путь, вдоль которого найдены предметы с близкими по стилю изображениями. Местонахождения: 1 – Ур-Марал (Тянь-Шань); 2 – 3 – Аржан (Тува); 4 – Ортаа-Саргол (Тува); 5, 10 – Усть-Бухтарма (Алтай); 6 – Бураты (Алтай); 7 – Монгольский Алтай (Монголия); 8 – Хушотын нур (Монголия); 9 – Ордос (Китай); 11 – Нинчэн (Китай); 12, 13 – Аргос (Греция); 14, 15, 16 – Сиалк B (Иран); 17 – Кобан (Кавказ).

островов（рис. 1.－12－17；Шер, 1980；Ghirshman 1974/1977, Taf. 27, Fig. 8, 9）.

Вполне вероятны открытия подобных по стилю изображений в районах соседних или промежуточных с этими регионами. Все эти изображения объединяет один общий стилистический элемент — четыре тонкие параллельные ноги с выделенными копытцами（№ 8 и 11 －?）. Для восточной группы изображений（1 － 11）более характерна вытянутая вперёд шея, спина с остроугольной холкой, подтянутый живот, подтреугольное ухо позади глаза. Западные изображения（12－17）имеют изогнутую назад шею, «прямую»（или слегка вогнутую）спину и более отвислый живот（особенно в Иране）, ухо поднятое вверх. Чем ближе расположены районы, тем больше общих признаков у изображений（см. контур рогов, головы, глаз, рта, уха, тулова и так далее）. В восточных регионах чаще встречаются образы оленя и лося, а в западных — коня（Греция）и быка（Иран）. Не только образы оленя — козла — коня, но также хищников и других животных имели довольно широкие пределы распространения на территории Евразии в I тыс. до н. э. и позднее.

Границами распространения близких по стилю изображений в I тыс. до н. э. были в основном географические барьеры: на востоке и западе — бескрайние, как тогда казалось, лишь эпизодически пересекаемые просторы Тихого и Атлантического океанов; на севере — малозаселённые и малопригодные для кочевого скотоводства и земледелия лесные районы, а на юге — жаркие пустыни и малоосвоенные высокогорья. Отдельные предметы, характерные для центральной степной и лесостепной зоны, найдены далеко на севере и на юге.

Исследователи по разному датируют китайские, греческие и иранские изображения, в пределах IX-VII вв. до н. э. , большинство — VIII в. до н. э. К последней дате близка и дата сооружения кургана Аржан-1 в Саянах — VIII в. до н. э.（Марсадолов, 1996）. Наскальные рисунки и «оленные» камни, как известно, сами нуждаются в стилистических аналогиях с хорошо датированными предметами и памятниками. Одной из хронологических точек может быть дата сооружения кургана Аржан, точнее его насыпи, так как обломок «оленного» камня из этого памятника найден именно среди камней надмогильного сооружения — под потолком деревянной камеры 34 а（Грязнов, 1980, с. 39 － 43；Марсадолов, 2008）. Изображения на фрагменте «оленного» камня всё же близки по стилю к другим образам животных из этого памятника и каменным изваяниям из посёлка Аржан. Вероятно, при датировании аржанского обломка «оленного» камня и близких к нему изображений следует пока ориентироваться на дату сооружения кургана Аржан — VIII в. до н. э.

Однозначно реконструировать направление распространения этих стилистически единых изображений с востока на запад или наоборот с запада на восток（или из какого-то промежуточного центра）сейчас представляется преждевременным. Например, изображения коней в Греции имеют прототипы на микенских амфорах XIV в. до н. э. В наскальных рисунках, изваяниях и предметах из Азии также можно выделить стилистически предшествующие изображения. Необходимо уточнить датировку памятников, а затем их синхронизировать.

Близкий спиралевидный орнамент на тулове оленей из Аржана и Китая（рис. 1 -2, 9, 11）, как и форма рогов у саяно-алтайских и монгольских образцов, возможно, свидетельствует о каких-то контактах или походе кочевых племён против Китая в первой половине VIII в. до н. э. Не исключено, что это связано с переломными событиями в истории Китая — около 771 года до н. э., когда кочевые племена появились у китайских границ.

Не только высокохудожественные образы, но и передовые идеи широко распространялись вдоль Великого степного пути Евразии. В этом аспекте интересны космологические идеи, в основе которых лежит общая евроазиатская сакральная пространственно-временная концепция, которая может быть рассмотрена на более широком круге источников — на каменных изваяниях, наскальных рисунках, погребальных сооружениях и особенно на зеркалах, которые наряду с другими функциями выполняли и роли своеобразных календарей. Бухтарминское зеркало — это не полный «животный» календарь, а частичный, на диске даны только два основных животных — козёл и олень (Марсадолов, 1982; 2003).

Для VII в. до н. э. можно отметить близкие изображения свернувшегося в кольцо хищника и стоящих кабанов из таких комплексов как курган Чиликта-5 на юго-западе Алтая и Мулей в Китае, а также в Ордосе (Черников, 1965; Ван Бинхуа, 1986).

VI-IV вв. до н. э. — «осевое время» в мировой культуре и истории (по К. Ясперсу, 1994), связанное с такими именами духовных учителей, как Конфуций, Будда, Пифагор, Сократ, Платон, Аристотель — с одной стороны, а также политических деятелей, с другой — Кир, Дарий, Перикл, Филипп и Александр Македонский.

До сих пор еще недостаточно оценена роль климатических влияний на население кочевых и земледельческих культур Северного полушария. Отметим лишь ухудшение природных условий в Северном полушарии в 480 – 400 годах до н. э. Это было время обострения не только межгосударственных отношений типа греко-персидской войны, но и время острой междоусобной борьбы в Греции, Персии (упадок ахеменидской державы), Китае (начало периода «сражающихся княжеств») и в других странах.

Из письменных источников и по археологическим материалам известно, что киммерийцы участвовали в военных событиях Фригийского царства VII в. до н. э. (рис. 2.–2; Дьяконов, 1983; Иванчик, 1996; Марсадолов, 2006). Конец VII — начало VI вв. до н. э. характеризуется становлением в Малой и Передней Азии новых супердержав — Мидии на востоке и Лидии на западе, вместо побеждённой Ассирии и завоёванных ею территорий. В конце VII или начале VI вв. до н. э. царь Лидии Алиатт «изгнал киммерийцев из Азии» (Геродот, I, 16). Слово «изгнал» не свидетельствует о том, что киммерийцы были полностью уничтожены. По мере накопления археологических материалов ныне может быть поставлен вопрос о дальнейшей судьбе киммерийцев после их изгнания. Многочисленные внезапные изменения в культуре на Алтае могут быть объяснены вытеснением киммерийских племён из Передней Азии и их уходом в степи Восточной Европы, в Среднюю и Центральную Азию, на Алтай, по линии ЮЗ-СВ, вдоль горных хребтов или по степному

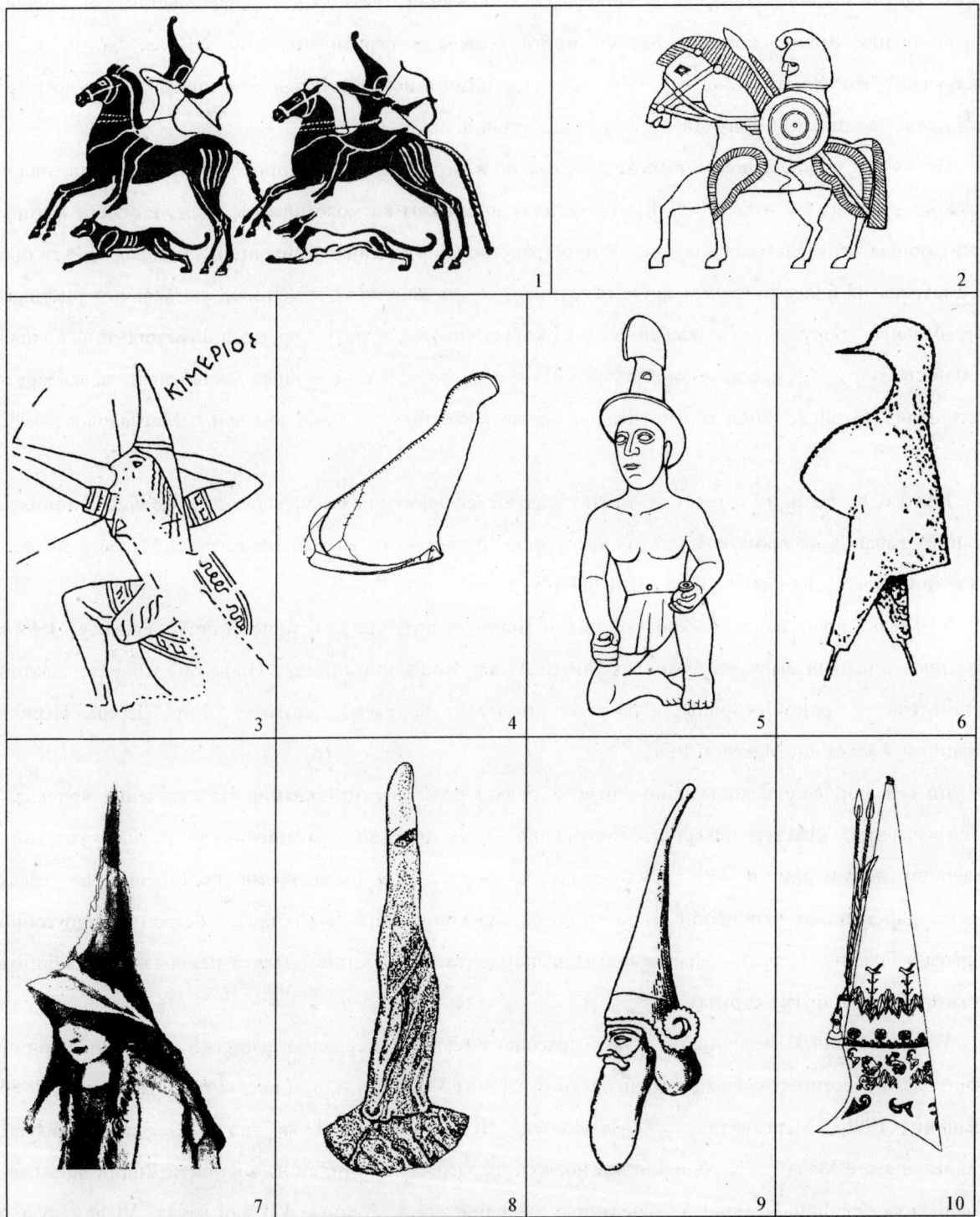

Рис. 2. Остроконечные головные уборы кочевников Евразии VII-III вв. до н. э. : 1 – киммерийцы (?) на этрусской вазе (VI в. до н.э.); 2 – воин из Гордиона в Анатолии (VII в. до н.э.); 3 – киммериец на греческой вазе (VI в. до н.э.); 4 – головной убор из Zugunluke Graveyard, Qiemo, Китай (VIII в. до. н.э.); 5 – бронзовая статуэтка воина из Xinjiang Uigurs Autonomous Region Museum Китай, (V-III вв. до н.э.); 6 – войлочный шлём из Ак-Алахи I, к. 2 (V в. до н.э. -раскопки Н. В. Полосьмак); 7 – реконструкция головного убора из Субаши, Китай (IV-III вв. до н.э. — раскопки Лю Юньго); 8 – войлочный колпак из Ак-Алахи-3, к. 1 (IV в. до н.э. —раскопки Н. В. Полосьмак); 9 – сакский вождь на Бехистунской скале (VI в. до н.э.); 10 – реконструкция головного убора из кургана Иссык (VI-V вв. до н.э. — раскопки К. А. Акишева).

пути. Преодолев большой по расстоянию путь, кочевники могли заимствовать некоторые обряды и формы предметов на территориях, через которые они проходили, в том числе и из северо-западных горных районов Китая.

По времени такой путь они могли преодолеть за 1 — 2 года или несколько лет. Прибывшие кочевники (предки пазырыкцев) принесли с собой на Алтай свои традиционные обряды, такие как восточная ориентировка погребённого человека, «вооруженность», захоронение вместе с конем в одной глубокой яме, деревянные срубы, высокогорлые кувшины, узда с двухдырчатыми псалиями и большими круглыми окончаниями удил, переднеазиатские образы звериного стиля (грифон, лев, сайга и др — см. Марсадолов, 1997).

На Алтае и в Китае известны два типа головных уборов — высокие остроконечные *колпаки* и *шлёмы* с загнутым вперёд или назад окончанием.

Одним из основных признаков костюма киммерийского воина был высокий головной убор, иногда со слегка загнутым вперёд окончанием. На широко известной вазе Франсуа изображён воин в остроконечном шлеме, натягивающий лук, а выше него надпись «ΚΙΜΕΡΙΟΣ» (рис. 2. - 3). На другой этрусской вазе показаны два конных воина, развёрнутых в пол оборота и стреляющих в своих противников (рис. 2 - 1). Обе вазы относятся к первой половине VI в. до н. э., но не исключено, что они лишь копируют более ранние изображения.

При раскопках курганов на плато Укок на Алтае были обнаружены войлочные головные уборы, вытянутой вверх формы со слегка загнутым вперёд окончанием, украшенным изображением головы птицы (рис. 2. - 6; Полосьмак, 1994). В письменных источниках киммерийцы упоминаются совместно с амазонками. В кургане № 1 могильника Ак-Алаха 1 в двух колодах были погребены вооруженные мужчина и женщина-амазонка, в близких шлёмах, что, вероятно, является ещё одним из доказательств возможности прихода киммерийцев на Алтай.

В курганах V в. до н. э. Пазырык-2 и Ак-Алаха-3 на Алтае были найдены высокие войлочные колпаки с небольшими полями, достигающие в высоту 102 и 84 см (рис. 2. - 8; Полосьмак, 2001; Баркова, Чехова, 2006). Такие же войлочные колпаки были надеты на голову женщин из могильника Субаши в Синьцзяне в Китае, имевшие высоту до 60 см и датируемые IV в. до н. э. (рис. 2. - 7; Mallory, Mair, 2000; Полосьмак, 2001).

На голове фигурки воина, сделанной из бронзы и найденной в 1981 г. (Tomb of Kunse River in Xinyuan County, Xinjiang в Китае), относящейся к V-III вв. до н. э., одет головной убор в виде шлёма с загнутым вперёд окончанием и с полями в его нижней части (рис. 2. - 5; Xinjiang Uigurs . . . , 2005, p. 164). Форма этого головного убора объединяет две традиции — высокого *колпака* с небольшими полями и *шлёма* с загнутым вперёд окончанием в виде головы птицы и боковыми «ушами»-завязками. Возможно, одним из прототипов такого шлёма является головной убор с узкими полями внизу и высоким верхом из Zugunluke Graveyard, Qiemo, найденный в 1985 г. (рис. 2. - 4; VIII в. до н. э.; Xinjiang Uigurs . . . , 2005, p. 96).

Саки в «острошапочных» уборах изображены на рельефах Бехистунской скалы (рис. 2. - 9; VI в. до н. э.) и Персеполя (V в. до н. э.). На остроконечном колпаке из кургана Иссык, напоминающим по форме укокские и киммерийске шлемы, наряду со семантически сложной композицией были прикреплены 4 модели символических стрел с листовидными наконечниками, характерными для киммерийского = раннескифского времени (рис. 2. - 10; Акишев А. , 1984, с. 8).

Вышеприведенные факты, возможно, тоже в какой-то мере могут свидетельствовать о дальнейшей судьбе киммерийцев после их ухода из Передней Азии на восток.

На материалах Пазырыкских курганов Алтая можно проследить смену политико-экономических приоритетов в течение 3-х поколений вождей племён. Пять больших курганов в Пазырыке были сооружены за период в 50 лет, начиная с 450-х годов до н. э. Если в ранних курганах Пазырык-2 и 1 заметно сильное ахеменидское влияние, то в поздних 3-м и 5-м курганах начинает преобладать китайский импорт. С начала 440-х годов обострилась политическая обстановка в Китае, началась борьба между различными княжествами. Возможно, кочевники не только нападали на ослабевший Китай в это время, но и сами китайские князья стали искать союзников среди северных кочевых племен. Только в поздних 3-м и 5-м Пазырыкских курганах найдены шёлковые ткани из Китая (рис. 3). Вероятно, китайские ткани из кургана Пазырык-5 (рис. 3. - 1, 3; конец V в. до н. э.), судя по степени стилизации образа феникса и древа, более ранние, чем ткани из могильника Машан в Китае Mashan, Hubei (рис. 3. - 2, 4; IV-III вв. до н. э. ; Jiangling, 1985). В художественно оформленных предметах из 3-м и 5-м Пазырыкских курганов прослеживается китайское влияние — звери с признаками «дракона», птицы с прямыми клювами на тонкой шее и другие.

Как считал С. И. Руденко (1960), один из китайских князей отдал в жёны вождю из Пазырыка-5 «принцессу», которая прибыла на Алтай на деревянной колеснице, запряжённой четвёркой коней (рис. 4). Использование такой колесницы из-за больших колёс, затрудняющих маневрирование на узких горных дорогах Алтая весьма затруднительно (с этим положением согласны многие исследователи). В Китае найдено большое количество разновременных колесниц. В дальнейшем необходимо более детальное сопоставление по разным признакам колесниц Алтая и Китая, что, вероятно, позволит уточнить не только время, но и район Китая, где они могли быть сделаны или находятся прототипы близких колесниц.

Очень интересные связи трёх регионов Алтая, Китая и Передней Азии можно проследить по изображениям «сфинкса» и «птице-дакона?» на войлочном ковре из Пазырыка-5 (рис. 5. - 1). Образ крылатого сфинкса хорошо известен в культурах Передней Азии IX-VI вв. до н. э. и почти неизвестен ранее в степных культурах Евразии. Хотя «сфинкс» из Пазырыка-5 иконографически восходит к переднеазиатским изображениям (рис. 5. - 2, 4), но рядом с ним под явным китайским влиянием изображена «птица-дракон (или феникс ?), имеющая прототипы на бронзовых сосудах V в. до н. э. из Китая (рис. 5. - 5, 6; Полосьмак, 1994) или в образах петухов из Пазырыкских курганов (рис. 5. - 7, 8; Руденко, 1960). Дальнейшее развитие этого сюжета можно найти и на тканях эпохи Хань,

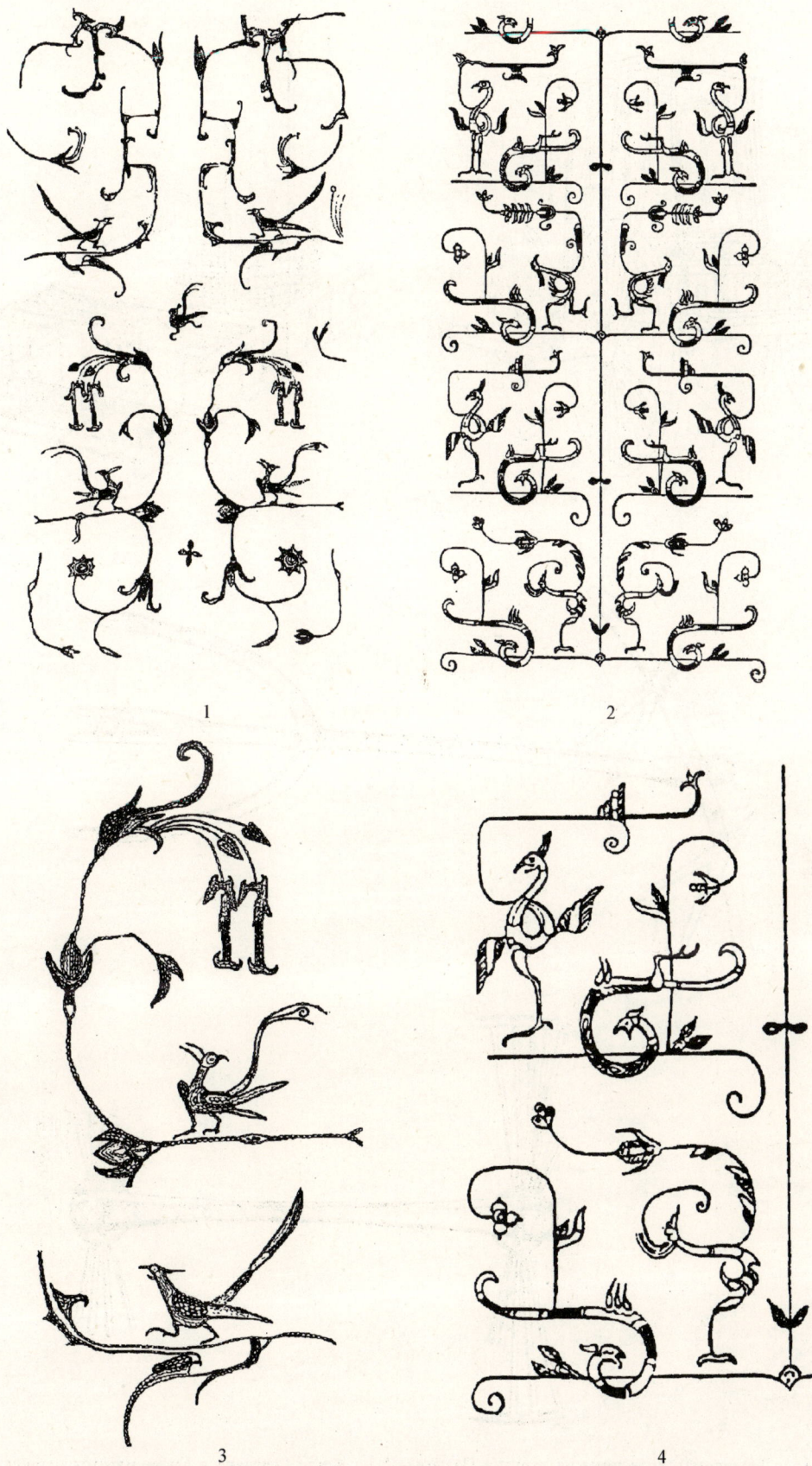

Рис. 3.   Сопоставление изображений на китайских тканях: 1, 3 – Алтай, курган Пазырык-5
(конец V в. до н. э.) ; 2, 4 – Китай, Mashan, Hubei (IV-III вв. до н. э.).

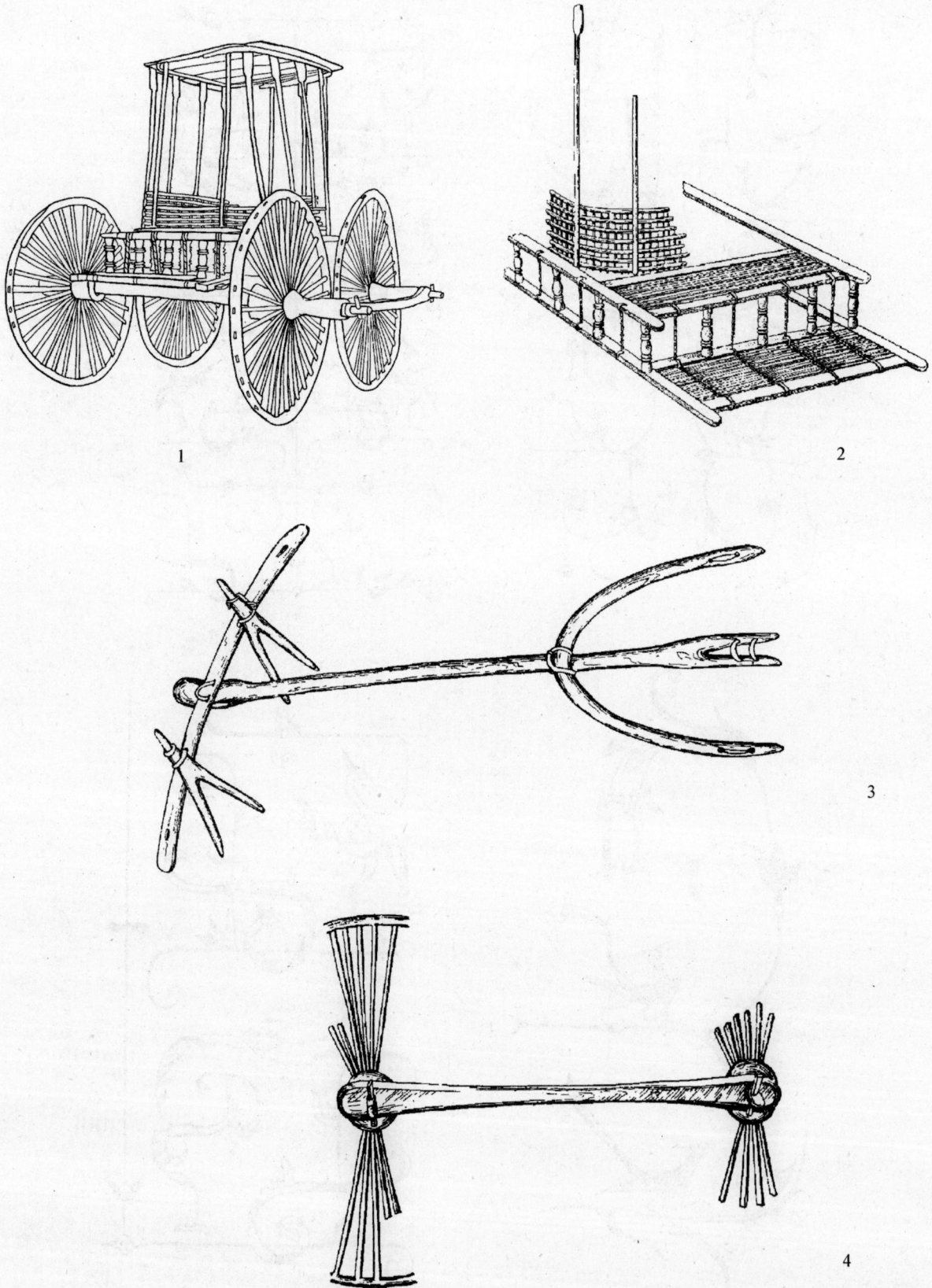

Рис. 4.   Деревянная колесница из кургана Пазырык-5 на Алтае (сделана в Китае или по китайским
образцам): 1 – общий вид колесницы; 2 – 4 – отдельные детали этой колесницы (конец V
в. до н. э., по материалам раскопок С. И. Руденко).

1

2   3   4

5   6   7   8

Рис. 5. Изображения «сфинкса» и «птицы-дракона ?»: 1 – на войлочном ковре из кургана Пазырык-5 на Алтае (конец V в. до н. э.); 2 – рисунок на керамике из Гордиона в Анатолии, Турция (VII в. до н. э.); 3 – на серебряной бляшке-застёжке из могильника Иссык в Казахстане (VI-V вв. до н. э.); 4 – рельеф в Каркамыче, Передняя Азия (VII-VI вв. до н. э.); 5 – 6 – изображения на бронзовых котлах из Китая (V в. до н. э.); 7 – 8 – кожаные аппликации в виде петухов из кургана Пазырык-2 на Алтае (середина V в. до н. э.).

найденных в 1984 г. в гробнице № 1 Shanplula, Luopu в Китае (Xinjiang Uigurs ..., 2005, p. 99).

IV-III вв. до н. э. — время долгой междоусобной борьбы в Китае, период «сражающихся княжеств». Это могло привести к ослаблению торговых связей Алтая с Китаем и алтайские кочевники устремились на юг. Район Пазырыка, расположенный на северо-восточной окраине Алтая и контролирующий один из обходных торговых путей выхода на реки Обь — Енисей и далее, становится «нерентабельным». В это время прекращается сооружение «цепочки» грандиозных курганов в Пазырыке, хотя топографические условия местности позволяли воздвигнуть там ещё несколько больших курганов (Марсадолов, 1984). Центральный алтайский маршрут, около «чуйской дороги», продолжает какое-то время интенсивно функционировать. В это время сооружены большие курганы в Шибе. Китайские изделия стали редкостью на Алтае (обломок зеркала из малого кургана Пазырык-6 и др.). Наступили периоды нестабильности обстановки не только в Китае, но также в ахеменидской державе и других регионах.

О широких межплеменных «эстафетных» обменах от Тихого до Атлантического океанов уже в VIII-IV веках до н. э. свидетельствуют близкие по форме предметы вооружения, конской узды, звериного стиля (так называемая «скифская триада») и многое другое. Корреляция археологических, исторических, антропологических, генетических, этнографических, дендрохронологических и социологических данных позволит по-новому рассмотреть проблемы межплеменных связей в скифское время между Саяно-Алтаем и Китаем, а также с другими регионами Евразии.

Список литературы

Акишев А. К. Искусство и мифология саков. Алма-ата, 1984. - 176 с

Грязнов М. П. Аржан — царский курган раннескифского времени. Ленинград, 1980. - 63 с.

Баркова Л. Л. , Чехова Е. А. Войлочный колпак из Второго Пазырыкского кургана // Сообщения Государственного Эрмитажа. Выпуск LXIV. Санкт-Петербург, 2006, с. 31 - 35.

Дьяконов И. М. К методике исследований по этнической истории («Киммерийцы») // Этнические проблемы истории Центральной Азии в древности. Москва, 1983, с. 90 - 100.

Иванчик А. И. Киммерийцы. Древневосточные цивилизации и степные кочевники в VIII-VII веках до н. э. Москва, 1996. - 323 с.

Марсадолов Л. С. Зеркало из Алтайской коллекции П. К. Фролова // Сообщения Государственного Эрмитажа, выпуск 47. Ленинград, 1982, с. 30 - 33.

Марсадолов Л. С. О последовательности сооружения пяти больших курганов в Пазырыке на Алтае // Археологический сборник Государственного Эрмитажа, выпуск 25. Ленинград, 1984, с. 90 - 98.

Марсадолов Л. С. История и итоги изучения археологических памятников Алтая VIII-IV вв. до н. э. (от истоков до начала 80-х годов XX века). Санкт-Петербург, 1996. - 101 с.

Марсадолов Л. С. Исследования в Центральном Алтае (Башадар, Талда). Саяно-Алтайская экспедиция Государственного Эрмитажа. Выпуск 1. Санкт-Петербург, 1997. - 56 с.

Марсадолов Л. С. Художественные образы и идеи на Великом степном пути Евразии в IX-VII вв. до н. э. // Международная конференция по первобытному искусству. 3 – 8 августа 1998. Труды. Том 1. Кемерово, 1999, с. 152 – 163.

Марсадолов Л. С. Общая «модель мира» и археологические источники // Человек в пространстве древних культур. Материалы всероссийской научной конференции (20 – 25 августа 2003 года, Аркаим). Челябинск, 2003, с. 17 – 19.

Марсадолов Л. С. Гордион в Анатолии (Турция) — военная база кочевников Евразии в VIII-VI веках до н. э. // Современные проблемы археологии России. Материалы Всероссийского археологического съезда (23 – 28 октября 2006 года). Том II. Новосибирск, 2006, с. 40 – 42.

Марсадолов Л. С. Реконструкция «оленного» камня из кургана Аржан-1 // Время и культура в археолого-этнографических исследованиях древних и современных обществ Западной Сибири и сопредельных территорий: проблемы интерпретации и реконструкции. Материалы XIV Западно-Сибирской археолого-этнографической конференции. Томск, 2008, с. 60 – 64.

Полосьмак Н. В. «Стерегущие золото грифы» (ак-алахинские курганы). Новосибирск, 1994. – 124 с.

Полосьмак Н. В. Всадники Укока. Новосибирск, 2001. – 335 с.

Раевский Д. С. Модель мира скифской культуры. Москва, 1985. – 256 с.

Руденко С. И. Культура населения Центрального Алтая в скифское время. Москва-Ленинград, 1960. – 360 с.

Черников С. С. Загадка Золотого кургана. Москва, 1965. – 192 с.

Ясперс К. Смысл и назначение истории. Москва, 1994. – 527 с.

Шер Я. А. Петроглифы Средней и Центральной Азии. Москва, 1980. – 328 с.

Ван Бинхуа. Бронзовые вещи из восточного Синьцзяна // Каогу. № 10. 1986, с. 887 – 890 (на китайском языке).

Jiangling Mashan yihao Chum mu // Wenwu Chubanshe. Beijing,1985, pp. 42 – 43.

Mallory J. P. , Mair V. H. The Tarin Mammies. London, 2000. – 352 p.

Xinjiang Uigurs Autonomous Region Museum // Kataloge. 2005. – 196 p.

Ghirshman R. A propos de la Necropole B de Sialk// Jahrbuch fur prahistorische & kunst, 24 Band, Berlin-New-York-De Gruyter, 1974/1977, pp. 41 – 49.

Mounted Nomads of Asian Steppe. Chinese Northern Bronzes. Tokio, 1997.

Xiang Chunsong, Li Yi. County Excavation of a Stone-chambered Tomb at Xiaoheishigou, Ningcheng Inner Mongolia // Wenwu, № 5, 1995.

Out of the East: Chinese and Eastern Eurasian Components in the Tillya Tepe Assemblage found in northern Afghanistan

Karen S. Rubinson

Department of Anthropology Barnard College, USA

Tillya Tepe, a site located near Shibargan in northern Afghanistan, not far from the Amu Darya River, was excavated by an Afghan-Soviet archaeological team under the direction of Russian archaeologist Victor Sarianidi. In 1978/79, the archaeologists uncovered a small cemetery dug into the remains of a citadel that had existed from the tenth through fifth centuries BCE (Sariandi 1989: 3, 39, 46 – 48). The cemetery contained at least seven burials, of which six at were excavated; the seventh was re-covered but not in fact excavated, because war arrived instead. The burials were extremely rich and contained goods from the length of Eurasia, including glass from the Roman west and mirrors from the Han Chinese east.

Based primarily on the dates of the latest coins found in the burials, the graves date to the middle of the first century CE. This period is a hiatus between the political authority of the Greek kingdoms that were the legacy of Alexander the Great's foray into Central Asia and the establishment of the Kushan Empire sometime in the late first or early second century CE and the burials are seen as a window into the historical development of the area. In the last few centuries BCE and first centuries CE, nomadic groups from the steppe moved into Central Asia from the north and east and those called Yuezhi were recorded in Chinese texts as located just north of the Amu Darya in the period about 130 – 125 BCE (Enoki et al. 1994: 180). The individuals buried at Tillya Tepe have generally been considered to be settled descendants of the nomadic Yuezhi and most scholars have described them as 'proto-Kushans', that is ancestors of the kings who ruled in what is today northwestern India and adjacent areas of Pakistan and Afghanistan from the late first/early second to third centuries CE (Boardman 2003b: 348; Bernar and Abdullaev 1997; Enoki et al. 1994).

The excavated burials were of 5 women and 1 man. Although it cannot be proven on available evidence, some suggest that the women were killed to accompany the man in death based on the fact that in some nomadic complexes of earlier periods such actions did occur, and the facts that the burials were distributed with the male in the center and the women around him and the burials goods appear to be more or less of the same time. In addition, that the burials were inserted into the mound-like formation of a somewhat decayed mud-brick structure might recall the placement of nomadic burials in and under mounds. These characteristics of the burial situation are one element which lead to the identification of these individuals as people with a

· 88 ·

nomadic lifeway or nomadic ancestry.

The most spectacular materials from these burials are the many gold ornaments and jewelry which decorated the clothing, burial wrappings and bodies of the deceased. Artistic influences from the whole of Eurasia are found on these objects, including imagery from the Hellenistic substrate which had existed in Central Asia from the time of Alexander the Great's conquests in the 4th century BCE, elements of decoration associated with the Near East and Southwest Asia, and China. These two temple pendants demonstrate the skill with which the artist, possibly from the region, combined vocabulary from many artistic traditions: the standing male figures in a nomadic tunic but also a plant-like skirt which is more Hellenistic, the crenellated crown easily at home in Central Asia or Iran, the mark on the forehead recalling India, fantastic animals with twisted bodies such as are found on the steppe, but with dragon-like heads that recall China. Hanging from the figures are many cast and hammered elements held together with loop-in-loop chains. The combination is visually sophisticated and one can only imagine what kinds of objects from how many places passed before the eyes of the craftsman who created the pendants.

Other gold objects which most observers have suggested shows Chinese imagery are these two boot buckles from the male burial which have images of a man in a chariot drawn by winged feline creatures. The appearance of the chariot in which the figure stands is interpreted as having a woven body and bamboo supports of the canopied top, which can be compared with Han chariots. Although some have suggested the human figures wear Greek robes, the clothing could be seen as similar to Chinese robes instead. Exceptionally at Tillya Tepe (or so it seems at this time) the buckles have textile impressions on the backs from the casting process, a technique known from China in the latter first millennium BCE (Bunker 1995: 58 - 59,61).

That Chinese artistic influences can be found here is not particularly surprising given the intensity of trans-Asian trade; after all, the Silk Road is named for a commodity sourced in China. But in addition to the imagery there is at least one kind of object obviously from China, the three cosmic mirrors found in burials 2, 3 and 6 (Sariandi 1985: nos. 2.43, 3.70, 6.31). In each case the mirror was placed on the chest of the deceased, a practice which is known from Siberia, (Okladnikov and Sunchugashev 1969: 80, Bokovenko 2006: Fig. 4) and which I have suggested has a symbolic meaning here at Tillya Tepe, especially because other types of mirrors were also found in these graves (Rubinson 2008).

A unique object from Tillya Tepe, a golden crown worn by the woman in burial 6 (Sariandi 1985: no. 6.1), certainly recalls later Korean examples (Nelson 2008: 119; Cambon 2006: 294 and 297). In 1991, Sun Ji had already suggested that the complex of crown and temple pendants shared the same glittering dangles and overall structure of the headdress of a Xiongnu noblewoman buried in tomb 4 at Xigoupan (Sun Ji 1991: Fig. 5, no. 2). The round gold disks that dangle from the Tillya Tepe crown are also found on the ca. 4th century crown from the Tomb of Feng Sufu of the Northern Yan; although the structure of the crowning ornament is closer to one which is part of the head covering of the male from Tillya Tepe burial 4 (Hiebert and Cambon 2008: 277).

Another Tillya Tepe artifact recalling a find from Xiongnu burials are the golden boot/shoe soles from burial 3 (Sarianidi 1985: no. 3. 40); silver ones with curvilinear cut out designs were excavated at Shihuigou (Linduff 1997: 54 and Fig. A68). The practice of placing highly elaborated soles on the bottoms of nomadic boots of the elite is preserved as early as Pazyryk (Rudenko 1970: plate 64A), but these are the only two examples I know from this time in precious metal. However, there are gilded bronze soles from a Silla context (Cambon 2006: 296), just as the crowns have Silla counterparts.

As the decorated soles have connection with the Altai, so does the shape of one dagger sheath of the male in grave 4 (Sarianidi 1985: 247 – 248, no. 4. 8). Designed to be tied to the leg, this form of sheath is found at many Altaian sites, including Ulandrik and Tashanta, dating to the 2nd-1st centuries BCE, where it is made from wood. Highly elaborated, gold and bejeweled variations on this form are found not only at Tillya Tepe, but also in the Sargat culture, Isakovka 1, cemetery, kurgan 3, grave 6 (Korykova 2007: Fig. 12) in western Siberia, and further to west, in middle Sarmatian contexts.

A funerary practice found in all burials except number 1 at Tillya Tepe (Sarianidi 1985: 22, 28, 35, 45, 47) is the use of gold chin straps, presumably used to keep the jaw closed in death. Shing Müller recently completed a thorough study of this practice and noted that although apparently a Greek practice in the second millennium BCE, by the first millennium BCE fabric chin straps were widespread in Xinjiang, while straps of metal and fabric continued to be used in the Greek world (Müller 2006: 45 – 46, 51). So in this case we cannot say whether the Tillya Tepe evidence demonstrates ties to eastern Eurasia or not, but it could be relevant to my discussion.

Amid the splendid, elaborated gold objects at Tillya Tepe, plain gold jewelry of simple annular shape with flared ends are exceptional. Such jewelry was worn on the bodies of all individuals except the woman in grave 1. The women in graves 2, 5, and 6 each wear a pair of anklets, the woman in grave 3 a torque, two bracelets, and two small loops of undetermined function, the male in grave 4 a pair of armlets. Such jewelry is well known beginning in somewhat earlier times further north and east on the steppe, as for example a torque from the cemetery of Besoba in western Kazakhstan, dating to the 6th–5th centuries BCE (Popescu et al. 1998: 146), and the torque dating to about the turn of the BCE/CE millennia from Sidorovka cemetery, kurgan 1, grave 2, of the Sargat culture (Korykova 2007: Fig. 7, 1 and 3). From Xinjiang comes the earrings from burial 325 at Tianshanbeilu Cemetery (Yue 1999: pl. 0258), which I suggest are also related to this tradition. Also perhaps related to this tradition are the earrings with widened end characteristic of Andronovo contexts (Bunker 1998: 611); perhaps the earring shape inspired the distinctive thickened ends of the later gold pieces.

I outlined these several eastern connections without explanation in order to show you as much what may be unfamiliar materials in the short time available. There are of course many reasons why these objects and practices may be found at Tillya Tepe. Some of the objects may have come as the result of trade; the textiles were not well preserved, but silk has been mentioned, for example. Some may occur because they are markers of ethnic or cultural identity, as for example the simple gold circlets worn directly on the body. Alternatively, they could have been adopted by local elites to mark their social positions, for example, perhaps, the distinctive dagger sheath. Another possibility could be that some of these women came from outside the Tillya Tepe area, married into the community for political or military benefit, like perhaps the women with the Chinese mirrors on their chests, or in fact, they could have all come from elsewhere, as the textual references to the travels of the Yuezhi suggest.

Tall Hats: Reaching to the Sky

Karlene Jones-Bley

University of California, Los Angeles

The archaeological evidence gives us a number of examples of people in Eurasia wearing very tall hats or headdresses. Most of this evidence is iconographic or textual. Such conical headgear is found on Hittite reliefs in Anatolia, on seals of Mesopotamian origin, and on Persian monuments. Moreover, a variety of grave sites that range as far east as the Tarim Basin and the Altai mountains preserve the actual hats. This peculiar head gear was referred both to by Herodotus and by official Achaemenian inscriptions that accompany the Old Persian monuments.

The Hittite examples predate Herodotus and the Achaemenian inscriptions by nearly a millennium but nevertheless greatly resemble Herodotus' description of the 6th century BC Saka who wore "tall caps, erect and stiff and tapering to a point" (VII. 64).

In this paper, we will look at examples of these tall headdresses from the Tarim Basin area, Anatolia, and the Eurasian Steppe in an attempt to determine their purpose. Do they have special meaning? Is there a meaning to this headwear that we can ascribe to all of these areas?

To me these headdresses should be considered as 2 separate categories: secular and non-secular, which at some point meld together. It is the non-secular that seems to be the older of the two and the most prevalent. Moreover, it is the non-secular that suggests greater meaning than a simple head covering and it is the type I will concentrate on in this paper.

In addition to the iconography and literary references, we are, in a few cases, fortunate to have, due to exceptional instances of preservation, actual examples of some hats and headdresses. Among these are the hats from the three very similarly dressed female mummies from the Tarim Basin, from Subeshi (Barber 1999; Mallory and Mair 2000: 220). These hats bear a striking resemblance to what in the west, particularly the United States, are thought of as witches' hats and are symbolic of our Halloween festival.

Except for their visual impact, tall hats have no obvious function. Even when they are supplied with brims, these are generally small and do not provide shade for the face or eyes. Moreover, in a warm climate, a pointed crown serves no physical purpose. Most people in hot sunny climates favor either a broad-brimmed flat hat like the Greek *petassos*, the Chinese hat, or the Mexican sombrero which provides sunshade and cooling or they adopt a wrapped headgear, the burnoose or turban which can be adjusted to vary the light exposure and unlike the broader shade hats, will not be blown away by the wind. The conical hat combines the worst of both features. The most important thing such a hat provides is visual identity and could have developed from a softer conical cap. The brim is either entirely absent in the earliest examples and is quite variable in depth even in the later examples with brims. It appears that the brim itself was an afterthought and not the justification for the headgear. It is the elongated, conical crown that is the constant feature, but there is no apparent purpose to such a development aside from its obvious visual impact. If that were in fact the cardinal justification for so unusual a style, it indicates a ritual origin, which, I believe can be shown.

Two examples of this type of tall headdress speaks to this ritual conclusion, and both come from the Steppe: one from a female Pazyryk grave at Ukok in the Altai (Polosmak 1998) and the other is the "gold man" from Issyk, Kazakhstan, which while not so well preserved has been reconstructed. Both of these examples are clearly some sort of ritual wear as both are quite elaborate and without function. While both are distinguished by their height, they are also both decorated with birds, a frequent symbol of the spirit.

If we examine the Hittite examples, the ritual nature of this headwear becomes self-evident in that, with one late exception, the pointed hats are worn only by the gods. Akurgal (1962: 111) says the pointed hats go back to Mesopotamia, and we can see this in the depictions of the goddess Ishtar who was the main goddess of Babylon and known as both the goddess of war and law. She came to the Hittites in Anatolia by way of the Hurrians, and it was under her Hurrian name, Shaushka, that she was known. We can also see the pointed hat on two separate seal impressions where in each case a god is driving a 2-wheeled vehicle, dating from the early 2nd millennium B. C. Although, these earlier Mesopotamian examples are not as exaggerated as the Hittite examples, we can see that the pointed hat has a long history.

Aside from the Mesopotamian evidence, some of the earliest examples are the iconography of the Hittites who because of their ability to assimilate the religions of their conquered peoples, were known as the people "with a thousand gods." The earliest examples of the Hittite deities wearing the pointed hats are found in small (ca. 11 cm) bronze statuettes dating to the 16th – 15th centuries B. C. These statuettes already display characteristics that would long characterize Hittites gods — particular positioning of the arms, short skirts, and pointy hats with horns. Because the Hittites had so many gods, ranking undoubtedly seemed necessary. This ranking is displayed in the number of horns imposed on the tall pointy hats. From the imperial period, Hittite reliefs depict many gods wearing such conical hats. From the relief of the "Meeting of the gods" at Yazılıkaya, Chamber A, the Storm-God (Weather-God), the major Hittite deity, has 6 horns in the front and 6 in the back while the god directly behind him has only 6 horns in the front, and the less esteemed Mountain-gods have but one horn and the peak of the hats are bent over. Moreover, the Weather-god stands on the Mountain-gods. This ranking is further confirmed by the end of the long procession at Yazılıkaya where the gods at the end have only one horn (Akurgal : 110).

In this same meeting of the gods scene, goddesses are also portrayed with tall headdresses which can be pointed or a polos, a flattened cone-shaped cap symbolizing a city. Of the female divinities only Shaushga as Goddess of War at Yazılıkaya wears a horned cap.

While the style and ornamentation of the hat indicates the status of the god involved, there is little evidence that humans are depicted wearing such headgear. It is not until the late period that the somewhat vainglorious Tudhaliyas IV is shown wearing such a pointed crown, an interesting departure for a Hittite emperor, who, according to the Royal Hittite funeral ritual, did not become a deity until his death.

Two sources are offered for the origin of what we may conveniently term the tigraxauda headdress: Mesopotamia or the Eurasian Steppe. A development from Mesopotamia would appear to be supported by chronology, but the route by which it was transmitted to the steppe is unclear; moreover, the later Iranians identify this headdress with steppe people and make no mention of its use among their Mesopotamian subjects which, of course, may simply no longer have been in use. Consequently, a steppe origin better explains the area of attestation. The conical shape is a natural one for felt and points to felt-makers as originators of the style. This suggests that the steppe, where felt has a long history, rather than Mesopotamia was the point of origin although we are not certain of the material of the Mesopotamian cap. But why would such a modest cap evolve into the spectacular elongation seen in Hittite reliefs and in the Tarim mummies? The extended size can most easily be explained in terms of ritual.

Let us now turn to the Tarim mummies, where we have extreme examples.

At least two explanations have been put forth for the Subeshi hats: a priestess, and in the case of the double pointed hat from Subeshi, a women who had two husbands (Mallory and Mair 2000: 25). While the first explanation is more convincing than the second, it requires a fuller explanation.

Barber (1999: 200) relates the pointy hats to the earlier mentioned modern "witches" hats that symbolize Halloween. She connects witches to the word 'magic, magician' which comes from the Iranian word *magué* which "denoted a priest or sage, of the Zoroastrian religion." Huld (1979) looked at the word "witches" itself and found several points that may be pertinent to this discussion. He relates the word to OE *wicca* (m.) and *wicce* (f.) and glosses it as 'waker (of the dead)'. He further quotes from Wulfstan's *Sermo ad Anglos*

> *and hēr syndan wiccan and waelcyrian and hēr*
> *syndan ryperas and rēaperas and worol(d)struderas*

> and here are witches and valkyries and here
> are plunderers and robbers and despoilers.

It is the relationship with the valkyries that I find most interesting. The valkyries were known to choose those warriros who would die on the battlefield and which may confirm Huld's point that witches were necromancers. The modern word necromancy is glossed as "black magic" (*AHD*), but in pre-Christian times one who conversed with the dead may not have had such an "evil" connotation. What I see as important is the intermediary between the Otherworld, or the world of the gods, and the world of the living.

Barber reminds us that the Iranian word *magué* is related to the biblical Magi and the Magi also were known for their high hats. She goes on to say that the Magi professed knowledge of astronomy, astrology, and medicine, of how to control the winds and weather by potent magic, and of how to contact the spirit world" (Barber 1999: 201). In other words, the Magi interpreted to the living world aspects of the Otherworld or the world beyond ordinary understanding. Barber further says that "In the conical hats of Subeshi we have yet more evidence suggesting Iranians in the area. But at this date, late in the first millennium B. C. , their presence is not surprising, since soon afterward we begin to get inscriptions along the south side of the Tarim Basin, some written in a probably Iranian dialect" (Barber 1999: 201). But in order to place the origin of these hats on the steppe, we need to find evidence that is earlier than the Iranian evidence.

In terms of chronology, the Subeshi examples do not seem to come until about 200 B. C. Here the height of the hats/headdresses are extreme (60 cm [2ft]) and would have proved very difficult to wear while walking, particularly without internal support and at least one of the Subeshi hats did have supporting sticks inside (Mallory and Mair 2000). We know little of these women except their very similar dress, and Mallory and Mair say they are thought to be priestesses or royalty or both (Mallory and Mair 2000: 220).

A possibly much older mummy of a woman found by Folke Bergman in the early 20th century, however, may add to our knowledge. Designated as Grave 36 and found near Loulan, she was buried in a hollowed-log. She was wrapped in a "soft brown cloak with red and yellow borders ... and [had] a yellow felt cap... [and] Ephedra twigs had been tied into 3 little bundles formed from the edge of her cloak" (Barber 1998: 107). Another mummy, from Grave 5A, reported by Bergman was that of a young man who "wore a felt headdress with five feathers inserted" (Mallory and Mair 2000: 187). In his grave was a small bag of wheat, a basket of millet porridge, calves ears, grains of wheat, a tamarisk twig, and ephedra strewn on his body; under his body were 4 arrow shafts without points (Mallory and Mair 2000: 187). Ephedra was also found with the Subeshi women as well as nearly every grave of the Loulan/Qöwrighul culture (Barber 1998: 159). We will return to ephedra later.

The woman in Grave 36 was 1.52 m (5ft.) wore an inner and outer cap. The outer cap is pointed and decorated with red cords, ermine fur, and topped with 2 feathers (Barber 1998: 105). No date is given for this mummy, but Barber says the clothing of this woman is much more primitive than the Cherchen clothes and suggests she is much earlier than the 1000 B. C. date for the Cherchen man. Alternatively, the area around Lop Nor may have remained a backwater confirming the lack of sophistication suggested by the early Chinese settlers to this area and repeated by both Aurel Stein and Folke Bergman (Barber 1998: 108). Nevertheless, a mummy from Qäwrighul near Loulan and dating to ca. 1800 B. C. also wears a similar simple garment and a pointed, but by no means extreme, cap. The "Beauty of Krorän" wears only a rounded headdress, but it was topped with a feather and the burial dates to ca. 2000 B. C. Less extreme but still high (32.7 cm [1ft.]) is one of the 10 hats that belonged to the man from Zaglunlug (Chärchän). This is of interest as it seems directly related to some of the hats found on the steppe. I suggest that the use of feathers to produce height on the head is significant and can be related to the example of the Pazyryk woman at Ukuk (5'6") a site only about 600 km NW of the Tarim Basin near the Altai Mountains. Particularly revealing is the decoration of her headdress (which is approximately 61cm.) — 15 birds covered in gold leaf with wings, feet, and tails of leather and a recumbent deer also covered with gold leaf and another deer, this time standing on an orb (Polosmak 1998: 149, Fig. 11), and as I pointed out earlier birds are frequently associated with the spirit or soul. This, however, was not her only head piece. "Outside the sarcophagus — between it and the wall of the burial chamber — a long (84 cm) cap with a narrow brim was found." A similar cap was found in another Pazyryk burial-mound (Polosmak 1998: 150). These hats can be related to the Tarim Basin hats as can the bird decoration and feathers of the much earlier "Beauty of Loulan." Another frozen burial discovered in 1990 contained bodies of an older man (ca. 44) and a younger 17 year old woman. Both are described as wearing pointy felt caps with wooden decoration on them, and much like the burial at Ukok the young woman's cap was adored with a bird's head covered with gold leaf (Polosmak 1994: 351), however, it was not as well preserved.

For a sarcophagus, the Pazyryk woman at Ukok was buried in a larch log. Larch trees were sacred to Siberian people (Polosmak 1998: 130), and the Selkup people "associated larches with the Sun and the Sky. ... It was believed the crowns of larch-trees reached up to the heavens" (Polosmak 1998: 130 – 31). According to Polosmak, burying a noble Pazyryk woman in a larch sarcophagus was a way of returning her to the life source, symbolically returning her to her mother's womb (Polosmak 1998: 131). It is the reaching up to the heavens that I consider the most revealing. As mentioned earlier in the case of the Hittites, and indeed the Mesopotamians, it is only the gods who wear hats that reach upward, perhaps because they are the most connected to the heavens. However, the graves do not contain gods, unless, of course, the death of a person created a god as in the case of the Hittite kings. It is more likely that the occupants of the graves were intermediaries between ordinary people and the heavenly gods. Something like we see in the ceremonial plaque found at Ai Khanum in Afghanistan depicting the goddess Cybele and dating to ca. 200 B. C. Here she stands on a chariot with Nike. Cybele is attended by 2 priests both of whom wear pointed hats — one holding a parasol that shields her from the sun and the other standing on a tall stepped alter making an offering. The placement of the priest on a high alter is much like an event in the much later Anglo-Saxon history when William the Conqueror, around 1070 AD, attempted to drive away Hereward an Anglo-Saxon rebel. William employed the services of a witch who stood on a high platform to perform magical rituals. I suggest there is a need for a high place just as the pointed hats are a reaching up to the heavens. The Afghan plaque itself typifies the melding of traditions. The Cybele cult arose in Anatolia and was later adopted by the Greeks, while the priests are characteristic of Syrian and Persian traditions.

In the Christian world, there are bishops and popes who wear mitres, which, while we may not think of these as tall headdress reaching to the heavens, do distinguish the wearer from ordinary people. But even in the non-Christian world we can find examples of priests or leaders of ritual wearing distinguishing head gear that falls within the our category of pointed hats.

Let us now briefly turn to the secular use of these tall hats and here there is less but later evidence.

Herodotus in his description of the various armies that fought with Xerxes takes note of the pointed hats worn by the Saka, and a Saka king in his pointed hat is seen on the carvings at Bistum. We have clear iconographic examples of these hats on reliefs at Persepolis showing emissaries wearing this distinctive headgear while the accompanying text identify them as Saka, a traditional Persian name for the nomadic people the Greeks called Scythians. Representations of Scythians from the north Pontic steppe agree with this depiction, for they too wear pointed caps. At later times, the Greeks consistently show the Phrygians wearing similar soft pointed caps. But the Parthians and even the Amazons also engaged in this type of headdress.

A link between the Saka and the earlier Tarium mummies may be the ephedra that was so prevelant amongst the mummies. Darius lists two kinds of Saka pointed hats (See Kent 1953: 136a, 186b, 211b): the *tigraxauda*; a phrase is a compound of tigra-'pointed' and xauda 'headdress' and constitutes the Old Persian textual evidence for pointed hats, 'pointy-hatted' and *haumavarka* Haoma(soma)-using. Given the fact that ephedra has been identified as Soma by some Indic traditions, it would appear that at least one and perhaps both of Darius's Sakas were involved in divination.

Conclusions

What then can we conclude about this peculiar headwear? The evidence suggests that the wearers of these tall hats are reaching up to the heavens either as intermediaries between the gods and humans or they are themselves gods. The evidence further suggests the earliest iconographic depictions of the wearers of the tall hats were in fact gods. That is in earlier times only the gods wore the tall hats, pointing to, perhaps, where they resided. As priests and priestesses separated themselves from the rest of society and their relationship with the gods became more intimate, they also took on the headwear of the gods, perhaps to make their position more obvious but certainly to indicate that theirs was a relationship with the gods not afforded to ordinary people. The idea of reaching up to the heavens is not one that was unique to Central Asia and the wearers of tall hats as I have suggested for the Afghan plaque and the Anglo-Saxon incident. This reaching up was even later adopted by the builders of the great cathedrals of Europe. But in this latter case it was not hats but high ceilings and spires that both reached to the heavens and lifted the spirits of the worshipers.

In an earlier paper (Jones-Bley 2006), I pointed out that the psyche or soul which is not animate needed to be represented by something animate, and as we have see has frequently been suggested to be a bird (see Vermeule1979: Figs. 4, 5, 12 – 14). This connects well with the Bronze Age, when there is a great prevalence for the representation of birds, particularly water birds. They appear on ceramics and metal work in great profusion. I have also suggested that smoke might be a means of transport of the soul to the heavens after cremation. Both of these suggestions point to the home of the gods being up — much as Mt. Olympus is home to the Greek gods. With this in mind, it is not a far reach to suggest that gods and particularly their intermediaries need to be as high as possible in order to perform their functions or to be easily recognized by the gods in the heavens. Either way a distinguishing piece of apparel, such as the tall hats would be beneficial.

This melding of the non-secular and secular requires further investigation, but it is evident that the longevity and context of the tall pointy hats indicates a ritual use which may well have religious meaning.

References

Akurgal, Ekrem

 2001 *The Hattian and Hittite Civilizations*. Ankara: Republic of Turkey Ministry of Culture.

 1962 *The Art of the Hittites*. London: Thames and Hudson.

Barber, Elizabeth Wayland

 1999 *The Mummies of Ürümchi*. New York/London: W. W. Norton and Company.

Huld, Martin E.

 1979 English Witch. *Michigan Germanic Studies* 5.1: 36 – 39.

Jones-Bley, Karlene

 2006 Traveling to the Otherworld: Transport in the Grave. In: *Anthropology of the Indo-European World and Material Culture*, Marco V. García Quintela, Francisco J. González García, and Felipe Criado Boado (eds.). Budapest: Archaeolingua, 357 – 368.

Kent, Roland G.

 1953 *Old Persian: Grammar, Texts, Lexicon*. 2nd ed. revised (American Oriental Series 33). New Haven: American Oriental Society.

Mallory, J. P. and Victor M. Mair

 2000 *The Tarim Mummies: Ancient China and the Mystery of the Earliest Peoples from the West*. London: Thames & Hudson.

Polosmak, N. V.

 1994 The Ak-Alakh "Frozen Grave" Barrow. *Ancient Civilizations from Scythia to Siberia* 1(3): 346 – 354.

 1998 The Burial of a Noble Pazyryk Woman. *Ancient Civilizations from Scythia to Siberia* 5(2): 125 – 163.

Vermeule, Emily

 1979 *Aspects of Death in Early Greek Art and Poetry*. Berkeley: UC Press.

试论新疆出土的青铜时代至早期铁器时代的铜镞

田中裕子

早稻田大学博士一年级　北京大学高级进修生

一、前　言

铜镞是草原地带自青铜器时代至早期铁器时代大量出土的文物之一。由于铜镞在各个时代的形态差别很大,铜镞的编年经常成为测定文物年代的线索。尤其在欧亚大陆西部以铜镞为中心的编年和年代研究很盛行。虽然位于欧亚大陆草原地带中央地区的新疆也出土了富有草原地区特色的铜镞,但是专门针对铜镞的研究极其缺乏。本文将整理新疆出土的铜镞的变迁情况。然后,通过与周边遗址出土的铜镞进行比较,阐明新疆遗址在草原地带的年代位置。

研究略史

在欧亚大陆中西部主要进行的是基于铜镞的遗址的年代测定研究,其中有代表性的是 Melyukova《斯基泰的兵器》。[①] Melyukova 先生收集了在黑海沿岸的斯基泰墓出土的武器与兵器并进行分类和编年,其对铜镞也进行了收集与编年,阐明了公元前 7 世纪到公元前 3 世纪的铜镞的变迁。田广金、郭素新两先生在《鄂尔多斯式青铜器》[②]里对自鄂尔多斯地域采集、出土的铜镞进行了研究:镞的造型可分为三大类:A 类为扁铤镞、B 类为有銎镞、C 类为圆铤镞。他们认为 C 类圆铤镞属于中原系统,A、B 两类具有明显的地区特点,这两类是随 C 类的变化而变化的,即由两翼向三翼至三棱式,又向锋利的三翼式发展。此外,北京市文物研究所收集了从延庆玉皇庙墓地出土的铜镞并整理成报告,[③]将春秋早期至晚期的出土铜镞 233 件分为 12 型 11 亚型 18 式。近年来,吉林大学的石岩先生在《中国北方先秦时期青铜镞研究》[④]中,收集和分析了中国出土的铜镞,遗憾的是因资料有限,未能将新疆列为研究对象。总之,新疆周围草原地带出土的铜镞皆已经进行分类研究。

凡例

先定义各部分名称:镞身的基部可以分为"銎"、"铤",镞身的前部为"前锋",末端为"后锋",刃部为"翼",中央的隆起为"脊",铤部中间的段为"关"。

①　Melyukova, A. I. 1964, *Вооружение скифов*. Hayka, Москва.

②　田广金、郭素新编著:《鄂尔多斯式青铜器》,文物出版社,1986 年。

③　北京市文物研究所编著:《军都山墓地》,文物出版社,2007 年。

④　石岩:《中国北方先秦时期青铜镞研究》,吉林大学博士论文,2006 年。

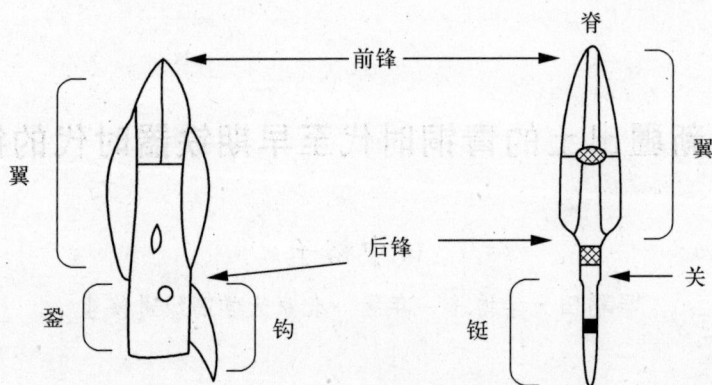

图一　凡例

二、分　类

根据镞的材质及造型进行分类,新疆青铜器时代至早期铁器时代出土的镞有铜镞、铁镞、骨镞等。铜镞和铁镞首先可分为有銎式、有铤式,然后根据镞的剖面可分为以下的型式:

Ⅰ式　有銎　炮弹形

Ⅱ式　有銎　两翼镞　　　　　　　Ⅵ式　有铤　两翼镞

Ⅲ式　有銎　三翼镞　　　　　　　Ⅶ式　有铤　三翼镞

Ⅳ式　有銎　三棱镞　　　　　　　Ⅷ式　有铤　三棱镞

Ⅴ式　有銎　四棱镞　　　　　　　Ⅸ式　有铤　四棱镞

铜镞

Ⅰ式　有銎炮弹形

2件。剖面椭圆形,平面炮弹形。察吾呼Ⅳ号墓第一期212号墓出土2件,[①]M212: 5长3.2 cm,径1.0 cm(图二-1、2)。相同样品从公元前8世纪的图瓦阿尔然1号古坟出土(图二-3至6)。[②]

Ⅱ式　有銎两翼镞

ⅡA式　2件。平面呈三角形,短管銎,圆柱脊。哈密焉不拉克墓地[③]M75: 42长2.4 cm,宽1.5 cm(图二-7)。相同样品从春秋早期至晚期的延庆玉皇庙出土(图二-8、9)。

ⅡB式　2件。平面呈扁椭圆形。长2.8~5.5 cm,宽1.0~1.3 cm。焉不拉克墓地M75: 25、M68: 3(图二-10、11)。

ⅡC式　1件。平面近似三角形。銎呈六棱形。焉不拉克墓地M68: 2长2.5 cm,宽1 cm(图二-12)。

ⅡD式　6件。平面为宽叶形,圆柱脊,后锋内收,长管銎。有的是前锋稍尖。长3.7~5.9 cm。鄯善洋海1号墓地、[④]腐殖酸厂墓地[⑤]等出土(图二-13至16)。这类叶形两翼镞为先斯基泰特文化遗址中

①　新疆文物考古所编:《新疆察吾呼》,东方出版社,1999年。

②　EURASIA ANTIQUA 9,2003年。

③　新疆维吾尔自治区文化厅文物处等:《新疆哈密焉不拉克墓地》,《考古学报》1989年第3期。

④　新疆文物考古所等:《鄯善县洋海一号墓地发掘简报》,《新疆文物》2004年第1期。

⑤　张承安、常喜恩:《哈密腐殖酸厂墓地调查》,《新疆文物》1998年第1期。

的铜镞,早期塞人墓地南塔基斯肯墓地 55 号墓、30 号墓[①]等也有出土(图二-17 至 20),其年代为公元前 8 世纪后期至公元前 7 世纪前期。延庆玉皇庙春秋中晚期也有 1 件 M148 出土。

ⅡE 式 4 件。造型与ⅡD 式同,但銎侧有钩。阜康三工乡墓地出土的 98FSM5: 1 长 3.8 cm,宽 1.4 cm(图二-22)。管銎带钩两翼镞从早期斯基泰期黑海沿岸等地出土,其年代为公元前 7 世纪到公元前 6 世纪(图二-23 至 27)。

ⅡF 式 3 件。平面为叶形,圆柱脊,后锋内收,銎亦内收,长 3.1 ~ 4.0 cm,宽 1.6 cm。焉不拉克墓地 6 号墓、柴窝堡林场Ⅱ号点墓地[②]等出土(图二-28、29)。

ⅡG 式 1 件。平面呈叶形,圆柱脊,后锋有钩。香宝宝墓地[③] M29: 9 长 3.6 cm(图二-30)。

有銎两翼铜镞,出土的年代比较早。

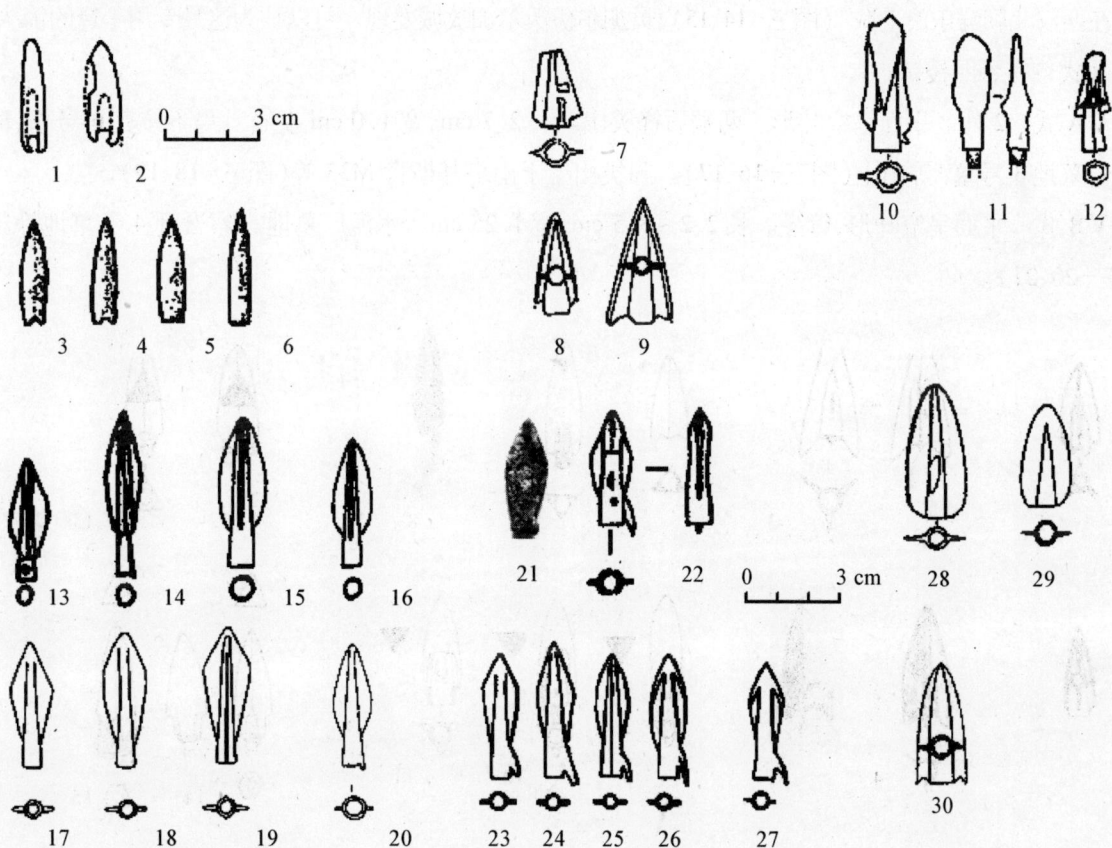

图二 有銎铜镞 两翼镞

Ⅲ式 有銎三翼镞

有关新疆出土的有銎三翼镞的报告不多。

ⅢA 式 1 件。平面呈弧线形的三角,脊圆柱,管銎略长。察吾呼沟口Ⅰ号墓地[④] M16: 3 长 2.6 cm,宽 1 cm(图三-1)。相同样品为从玉皇庙墓地出土的 M174: 17 -3,长 2.3 cm,宽 0.8 cm,管銎长 0.3 cm,

① ITINA, M. A. 1997, *Saka of the Low Syrdarya*, Moscow.
② 新疆文物考古所等:《乌鲁木齐市柴窝堡林场Ⅱ号地点墓葬的发掘》,《考古》2003 年第 3 期。
③ 新疆社会科学院考古研究所:《帕米尔高原古墓发掘报告》,《考古学报》1981 年第 2 期。
④ 中国社会科学院考古所新疆队等:《和静县察吾呼沟口一号墓地发掘简报》,《考古学报》1988 年第 1 期。

属于春秋晚期后段（图三-2）。

ⅢB式　1件。宽三翼，弧形刃，脊侧有三角形血槽。后锋突出，有钩，銎有孔。楼兰古城① C：82②（图三-3）。这类三翼铜镞，从春秋时代毛庆沟墓地、玉皇庙墓地等开始出土，但早期出土的铜镞为直线形翼，翼幅窄。另有弧线形、翼幅宽的铜镞从西汉中期的西岔沟墓地（图三-5）、前1世纪的伊沃尔加城址②等地出土（图三-4）。

Ⅳ式　有銎三棱镞　青铜制有銎三棱镞

ⅣA式　5件。平面呈叶形。后锋略突。长2.5 cm，宽1.1 cm。恰甫其海A区15号墓地M68：31残留有木箭（图三-6）。相同样品自公元前6世纪到公元前5世纪南塔基斯肯63号墓等出土。

ⅣB式　2件。六角形的管銎，长3.0 cm，从楼兰故城佛塔附近采集（图三-12、13）。銎呈六角形的三棱镞在西汉北朝鲜乐浪土城③（图三-14、15）、贝加尔伊沃尔加故城发现。可以认为这是专用于弩的箭头。

Ⅴ式　有銎四棱镞

ⅤA式　2件。平面呈窄叶形。两端后锋突出。长2.7 cm，宽1.0 cm左右。焉不拉克6号墓、群巴克1号墓地3号墓④等出土（图三-16、17）。同类出土于南塔基斯肯M33等（图三-18、19）。

ⅤB式　平面呈窄叶形，管銎。长2.2～3.5 cm，宽1.25 cm。水泥厂墓地、⑤察吾呼4号墓地等出土（图三-20、21）。

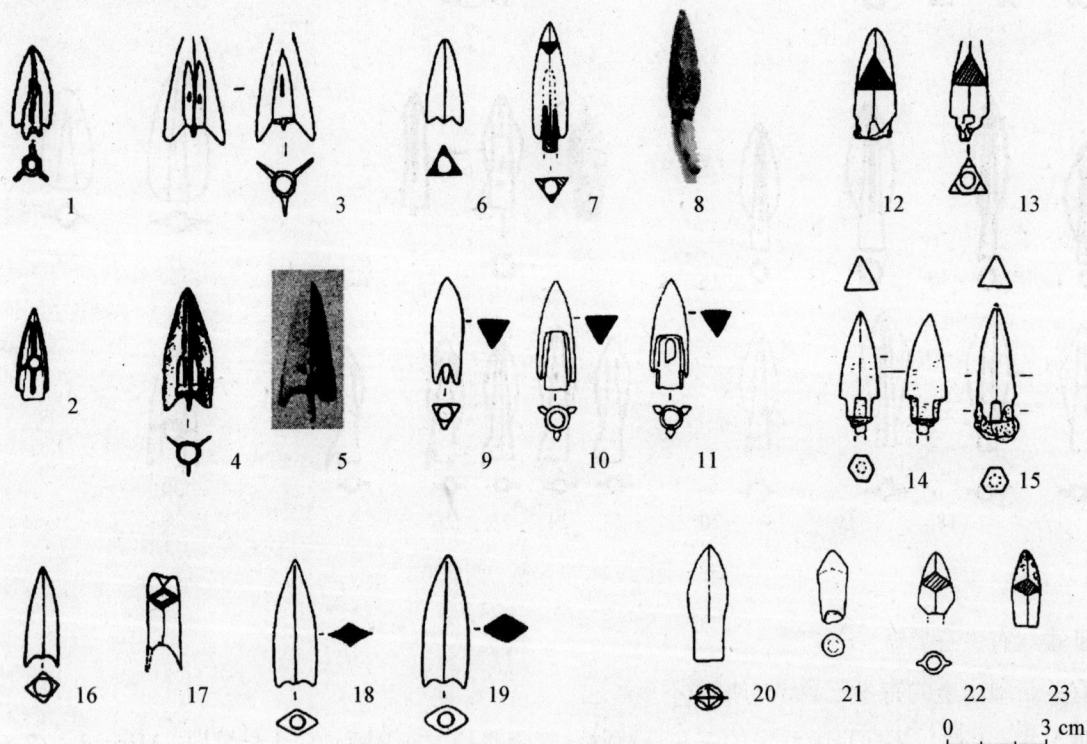

图三　有銎铜镞　三翼、三棱、四棱

① 新疆文物考古所楼兰考古队：《楼兰古城址调查与试掘简报》，《文物》1988年第7期。
② 潘玲：《伊沃尔加城址和墓地及相关匈奴考古问题研究》，科学出版社，2007年。
③ 郑仁盛：《乐浪土城的青铜镞》，《东京大学考古学研究室纪要》17，2002年。
④ 中国社会科学院考古所新疆队等：《新疆轮台群巴克墓葬第二、三次发掘简报》，《考古》1991年第8期。
⑤ 新疆文物考古所等：《石河子市古墓》，《新疆文物》1994年第4期。

Ⅵ式　有铤两翼镞

ⅥA式　1件。平面呈窄叶形。圆脊，有管，圆锥铤，长5.5 cm，香宝宝墓地39号墓出土（图四-1）。

ⅥB式　1件。片面呈宽叶形。扁铤，长6.3 cm，也是香宝宝墓地39号墓出土的（图四-2）。

ⅥC式　1件。平面呈五角形。扁铤，切木尔切克墓地17号[①]墓出土（图四-3）。

Ⅶ式　有铤三翼镞

扁铤为主，基本上没有中原和内蒙古出土的圆铤。

ⅦA式　7件。翼为弧形三角状，后锋略内收，扁铤，长3.0~4.0 cm。群巴克1号墓地等出土（图四-7）。相同样品从春秋早期的玉皇庙 YYM32: 15-4（图四-10）、南塔吉斯肯32号墓等地出土（图四-8、9）。

ⅦB式　1件。翼为直线三角形，翼端刃部剖面呈菱形。柴窝堡林场2号点墓地9号墓出土（图四-19）。南塔吉斯肯31号、32号墓地也出土相同样品（图四-20）。

ⅦC式　2件。平面呈五角形。从柴窝堡林场2号点墓地9号墓出土（图四-25）。

Ⅷ式　有铤三棱镞

长扁铤，平面呈三角，长3.7~5.1 cm，主要从拜勒其尔墓地、察吾呼墓地等察吾呼文化的墓地出土。翼部随时代前进而变大（图四-12~15）。与拜勒其尔 M207: 54（图四-12）类似的铜镞是西周末春秋初期的陕西米脂张坪[②] 84MZM2: 7（图四-16）。与察吾呼ⅡM216: 5（察吾呼文化3期，图四-14）类似的

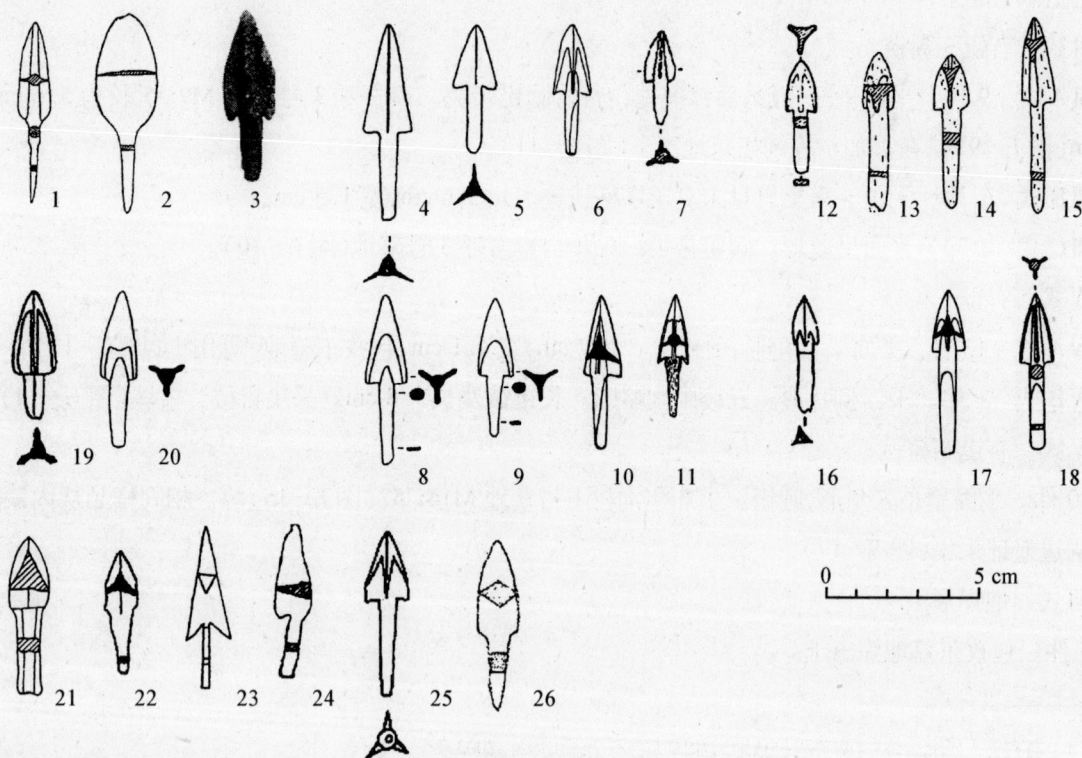

图四　有铤铜镞

①　新疆社会科学院考古研究所：《新疆克尔木齐古墓群发掘简报》，《考古》1981年第1期。

②　陕西省考古研究所商周研究室等：《陕西米脂张坪墓地试掘简报》，《考古与文物》1989年第1期。

铜镞是春秋中期玉皇庙墓地 YYM52: 10 - 2 出土(图四-17)。察吾呼 Ⅱ M305(察吾呼文化四期,图四-15)类似的铜镞是春秋晚期临猗程村① M1059: 9(图四-18)。

Ⅸ式 有铤四棱镞

3件。平面为三角形,翼剖面为菱形。大草滩墓地② M3: 2 长为 5.2 cm(图四-26)。

新疆出土的铜镞分为 9 式 21 类。

铁镞

目前铁镞出土 60 件,主要从哈密上庙尔沟村、③和静察吾呼 3 号墓地等地出土。铁镞大部分为圆铤镞。

Ⅰ式 有銎三棱镞

ⅠA 1件。剖面三角,平面柳叶形,长管銎带圆孔。残长 5.6 cm,宽 1.0 cm。且末夏羊塔格遗址④采集(图五-1)。

ⅠB 1件。平面三角形。管銎。且末夏羊塔格遗址采集(图五-2)。

Ⅱ式 有铤两翼镞

ⅡA 式 3件。平面呈菱形。有的剖梭状。小东沟南口墓地⑤采集的铁镞残长 7.5 cm(图五-3)。相同样品从公元前 1 世纪的伊沃尔加故城、榆树老河深墓地⑥中层等出土(图五-4、5)。

ⅡB 式 3件。平面呈扁菱形,克孜尔千佛洞 K89 - 8F: 09(图五-6)。内蒙古西汉末期的补洞沟墓地等出土同类镞。

Ⅲ式 有铤三翼镞

ⅢA 式 9件。平面呈三角形,后锋突处,有钩,圆铤带关。察吾呼 3 号墓地 M9: 5 长为 5.6 cm,宽 2.1 cm(图五-9)。在贝加尔等匈奴墓地出土(图五-11)。

ⅢB 式 1件。无铤。采集自且末夏羊塔格遗迹。长 5.6 cm,宽 1.5 cm。

ⅢC 式 1件。平面呈菱形。圆铤带关。采集自察吾呼 3 号墓地(图五-10)。

Ⅳ式 有铤三棱镞

ⅣA 式 13件。平面呈三角形,前锋尖。长 7 cm,宽 4.1 cm,包孜东墓地⑦等出土(图五-13)。

ⅣB 式 1件。平面柳叶形。三棱中间略凹。长铤镞残长 9.8 cm。采集自楼兰古城(图五-14)。

Ⅴ式 有铤四棱镞

10件。平面呈长三角形,圆铤。上庙尔沟村 1 号墓地 M14: 57(图五-15)等。相同样品从内蒙古西沟畔周边遗址采集(图五-17)。

Ⅵ式 炮弹形

5件。包孜东墓地等出土。

---

① 山西省考古研究所等:《临猗程村墓地》,中国大百科全书出版社,2003 年。
② 新疆社会科学院考古研究所:《米泉大草滩发现石堆墓》,《考古与文物》1986 年第 1 期。
③ 新疆文物考古所等:《1996 年哈密黄田上庙尔沟村 I 号墓地发掘简报》,《新疆文物》2004 年第 2 期。
④ 塔克拉玛干综考队:《安迪尔遗址考察》,《新疆文物》1990 年第 4 期。
⑤ 新疆考古研究所:《哈密——巴里坤公路改线考古调查》,《新疆文物》1994 年第 1 期。
⑥ 吉林省文物考古研究所编:《榆树老河深》,文物出版社,1987 年。
⑦ 新疆维吾尔自治区博物馆等:《温宿县包孜东墓葬群的调查和发掘》,《新疆文物》1986 年第 2 期。

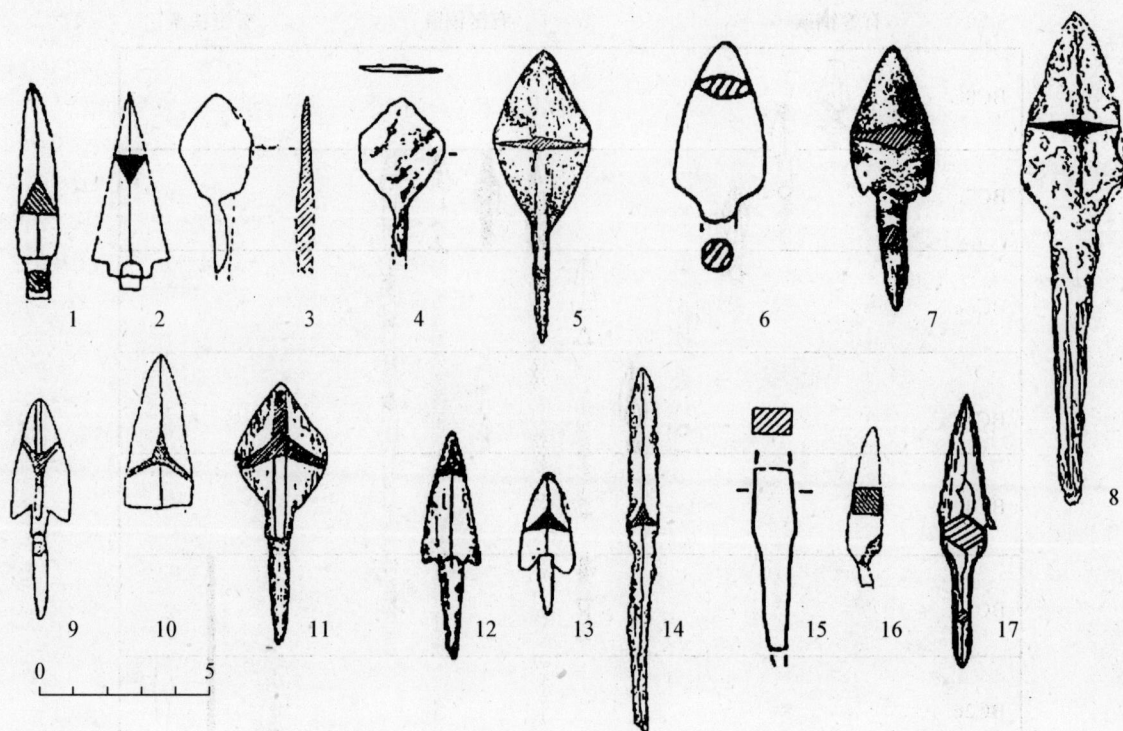

图五　铁镞

铁镞,最早从洋海2号墓地、柴窝堡1期墓出土。

三、铜镞的演变

根据分类结果,可以将新疆出土的铜镞的演变和各个时期的特征整理如下(图六)。

第一段　公元前9世纪之前。

南湾墓地也有铜镞,但未知其详。

第二段　公元前8世纪~公元前7世纪。

有鋬铜镞增多,Ⅰ式、ⅡA~D式为主。

第三段　公元前7世纪~公元前5世纪。

开始出土扁铤三棱铜镞。铜镞的种类增多。

第四段　公元前4世纪~公元前3世纪。

开始出土铁镞。扁铤铜镞减少。

第五段　公元前2世纪~公元前1世纪。

圆铤铁镞为主。

总的来说,以有鋬两翼铜镞、扁铤铜镞、圆铤铁镞为顺序演变。以铜镞ⅧA式(长扁铤三棱镞)为主。出土于新疆的镞,并非集中埋葬于一个墓葬中,而是每个墓葬中仅仅埋葬少量,木镞则经常大量埋葬。新疆各个时代跟欧亚草原地带交流密切,特别是早期跟西边斯基泰文化和早期塞人文化交流频繁,然后到

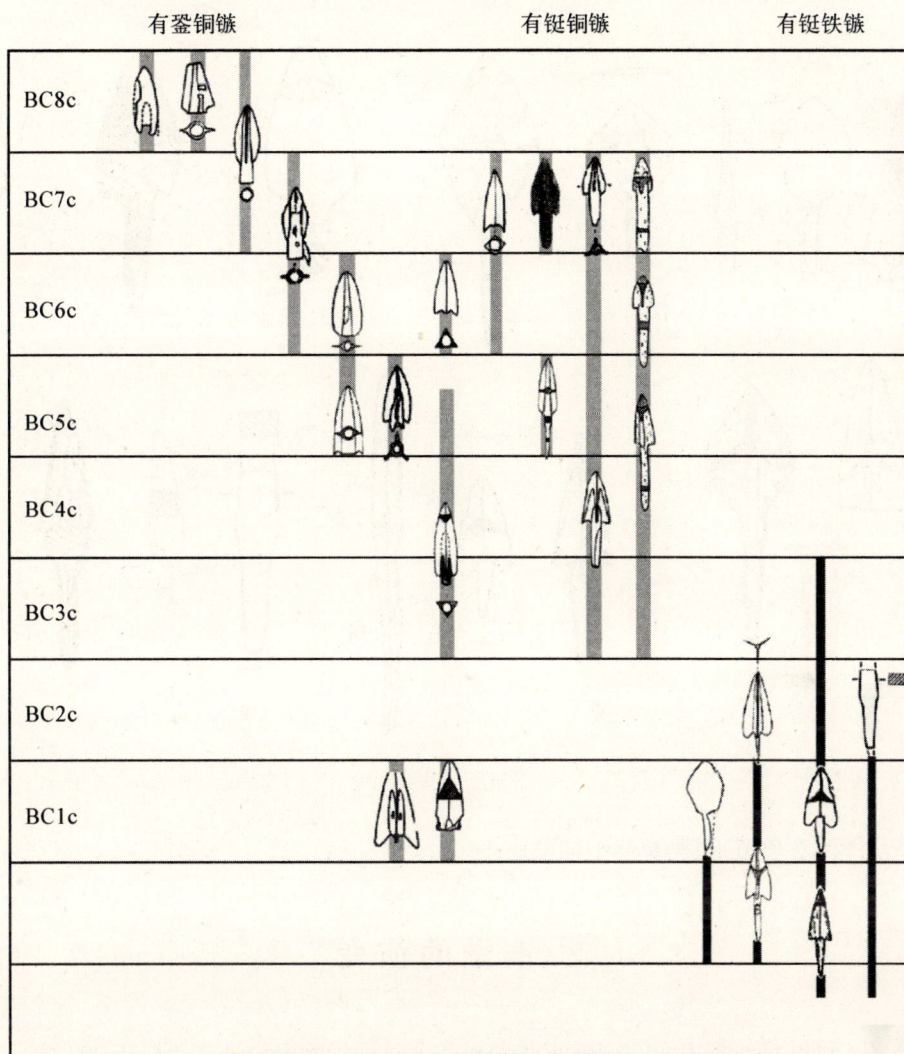

图六　新疆出土铜镞和铁镞的演变

第四、五期，圆铤铁镞的出土可证明跟中国东部交流增加。

四、结　论

　　将新疆青铜时代至早期铁器时代出土的铜镞进行分类。根据铜镞的出土情况，可以阐明新疆和欧亚大陆草原地带的频繁交流关系。笔者希望今后能增加比较资料，以提供判断新疆遗址年代的材料。

The Culture of Central Tien-Shan Nomads, Semirechie and Future Trends of Comparative Research

Kubatbek Tabaldiev

Kyrgyzstan-Turkey "Manas" University, Kyrgyz Republic

The invitation to "Turfan Studies" conference gives us opportunity to exchange knowledge of many researches from different countries. We, the delegation of Kyrgyz Republic, want to thank organizers of the conference.

In my speech I want to show the cultural aspect of nomads in Central Asia and Semirechie.

The research of monuments of nomadic people is one of the main trends in archaeology of Central Asia. The main part of materials, in the culture research, are kurgans. Across with kurgans, burial monuments are examined — "eight-stone" funeral monuments, "olenn stones", sculptures, balbals. Except the kurgans and burial monuments, we investigate their lodgings and settlements. During the archaeological excavations in specified field, we find objects of domestic life, horse outfit, arming and dornments. Near the settlement of nomads, rock arts are located. A places of rock arts concentration were used for ritual ceremonies. We can see the high level of spiritual culture through the written sources. So, archaeologists got real chance to recostrct the lifestyle of ancient and medieval nomads.

Nowadays, the most important problems are those, which are linked with the origin and development of ancient nomads(I millenium B. C.).

Except the burial monumnets, the problems of origin of the early nomadic cultures are solved with funeral monuments: "olenn stones" and "eight-stone" fences. "Eight-stone" fences of Tien-Shan were known in scientific literature since the beginning of XX century. Both types of monuments got their origin from East regions of Central Asia: North-West Mongolia, North China. They are monumets of culture of hereksuurs and ollen stones. They were not known earlier, at the age Bronze, on the territory of Central Tien-Shan and Semirechie. This type of monuments was brought by the tribes from eastern regions of Central Asia, and show the connections between ancient people of Kyrgyzstan with that territories.

The found things show that, people of Tien-Shan, who left "ollen stones" and "eight-stone" fences, were genetically close to the people of Central Asia. The got point-to-point connection to the formation of Sak culture in Tien-Shan. This conclusion fits with the results of physiological researches in antropolgy.

In the period of Great Migration the nomads of Tien-Shan and their neighbors greatly changed. It was related to the appearance of new wave of namds. They brought new elements to burial ceremony and material culture. The changes, brought by new nomads, are prooved by the kraniological materials. The elements of burial ceremony, of Tien-Shan namds, are similar to the culture of Central Asian nomads; some are similar to cultural elements of territories located on the west of Tien-Shan. Because of it, researches of archaeological monuments are important for Eurasia. During two years of our research of one nomads group, whose culture is close to kenkols, usun and also similar to Mongolian and tesin stage fo Tagr culture in Syberia.

During several years, we were looking for and investigating kurgans of early medieval — Turk period. Typacal for them are, burials with horses, constraction of funeral fences and stone statues. Their main achievement was the kind of runic writing. The found and interpreted writings; some were dedicated to dead and other were visitors; inscriptions. By the complex research, we could emphesize the rock arts of turk period, with warrior carved on it. The number of rock arts increases from year to year.

The most interesting is kurgans of Mongol period XIII-XIV centuries A. D. They are similar to the material culture of turk and mongol people. These burial monuments are important in the investigation of formation basis of late turk and mongol people. During the Mongol invasion and migration of turk and mongol people, they were got interdependence. Often, it's difficult to distinguish their features. Mongol got some elements from the culture of eastern turks. By the political and cultural events later, the part of ethno-differential features were not same. Because of it, some kurgans are named mongol, kypchak or kyrgyz. But they can be concretisized by further resaerches of specific features.

The important role in life of nomads, was migrational processes. Because of it, we find similarities in the culture of Eurasian nomads. The comparative research can help to distinguish the migrations. The each migration takes some culture elements from one to another region. The interdependence between cultures, of nomads and settled people, brought to the development and formation of new features.

The culture of Central Tien-Shan nomads and Semirechie is similar to Syberian, Altain, Mongolian and North Chenese. So the ancient and medieval history is more wide, than modern. They greatly influenced to the culture of neighbour territories. This could be seen on stages of evolution of early nomadic cultures. So the comparative research, of archeaological materialsof Central Asian and Semirechie with territories of Kazakstan, Uzbekistan, and North China, is important. The comparetive research can help to know more about the material aspect of early nomadic culture of this region.

For example, on the territory of Szinszan olenn stones were found. Same stones were found in Western Mongolia, Altai, Tuva, Central Tien-Shan and near Issyk-Kul. By published information, we know about the similar monuments of hereksur.

The formation of stone monuments, of Early Iorn Age, is a problem for the Eurasian archeaology. One of versions is, that tradition of stone monuments came from the culture of early Szinszan nomads. The evidence for that, are stone monuments from Szinszan. Also we are interested in result of chinese archeaological research on medieval turk stone monuments.

Judging by the finds at the territory of Xinjiang it is possible to think that Tine Shan nomads of the developed bronze age wore felt caps and leather boots typical for ancient nomads of Eurasia steppe belt. [1]

During late bronze period Tien Shan region was invaded by separate groups of ancient nomads, who used military chariots and to honor their chariot-riders built khereksury (kurgans with stone mound and ring fence) and built in memory of their perished heroes monumental stone steles with images of arms and decorations which are called in scientific literature "olenn stones". [2]

A few of such monuments were found in Kyrgyzstan. [3] Probably these were small groups of nomads who migrated from Eastern Turkestan and western regions to Mongolia. Beyond their main area of residence in mountains and valleys of Tien Shan they gradually assimilated among local nomads, descendants of Andronovskaya culture. Descendants of the nomads became the main ethnic substratum of the saks tribes, who settled at the territory of Kyrgyzstan during early iron age.

So on this conference I want to collect opinions of researchers on this problem. We are going to cooperate with interested ones.

Thanks for your attention.

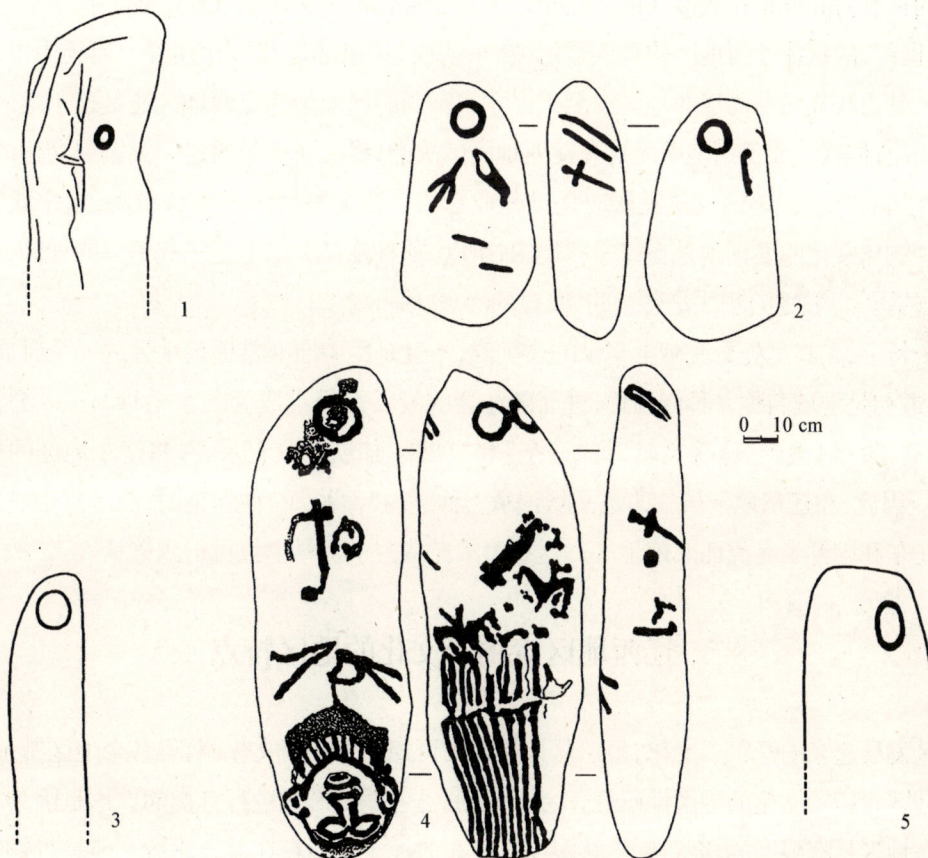

"Olenn stones" (Kyrgyzstan)

① Yu. S. Hudyakov, S. A. Komissarov. "Nomadic civilization of Xinjiang". Novosibirsk, 2002. page. 32..

② Yu. S. Hudyakov. "Hereksury and olenn stones". (Археология, этнография и антропология Монголии.) Novosibirsk, 1987. pages. 156－158.

③ V. P. Mokrynin. "Following traces of the past". pages. 24－25.

中国东北地方青铜器文化和朝鲜、涉貊

宋镐晸

韩国教员大学

一、概　观

历来,人们对中国辽河以西地区,包括辽宁省辽西地区及内蒙中南部地区考古学资料的讨论,均围绕辽宁式铜剑文化如何解释来展开的。在讨论过程中,针对古朝鲜问题涉及最多的话题是关于辽西地区的青铜器文化的拥有者和分布在大凌河以东辽东地区的辽宁式铜剑文化的族属问题。在中国先秦文献上,公元前8~7世纪,活跃在辽西地区的种族是山戎、东胡族,其东部是涉貊和朝鲜。但集中出现辽宁式铜剑文化的地区是山戎族活动的辽西地区。至于辽宁式铜剑的起源地为辽西地区还是辽东地区,是有待进一步探讨的问题,但其主要使用地区无疑是辽西地区。故此,将辽西一带的辽宁式铜剑文化的民族,视为居住在辽西地区的"山戎"等诸戎狄民族应是顺理成章的。在辽东地区和朝鲜半岛,辽宁式铜剑出土相对较少。这种铜剑文化的发祥地是在辽宁省境内,所以,那种凡是将出土辽宁式铜剑的地区,理解为古朝鲜(朝鲜最早的国家)领地的想法是恣意的、浅显的历史认识。

在文献资料上,尤其是先秦文献上记录的古朝鲜,不过是距中原非常遥远地区的一个种族集团而已。所谓古朝鲜,最初是地域名称兼种族名称,进而随社会的发展而固定成为国家名称。记录公元前4世纪以前事迹的《管子》或《战国策》等文献,将"辽东"和"朝鲜"加以区分记录,并将辽东地区的居民集团标记为"涉貊"。因此,在辽东地区居住的是文献记录上称之为"涉貊"的种族集团;而区别于它的古朝鲜民族则居住在辽东和朝鲜半岛的西北部地区。这种事实在考古学资料上也可得到确认。

二、辽西地区青铜器文化的地区特点

辽西地区发展起来的青铜器文化,虽然从大的方面可规定为一个文化圈,但各个地区都呈现独特性。从来对辽宁地区青铜器文化的地区性研究,大致都是通过青铜剑形式进行分类的。这是因为有特点的青铜短剑的分布地区是有限度的,而可以承认跟没有分布的地区之间存在差异之故。但是青铜短剑的分布地区区分,并不是有那么明显。虽然有些地方出土相同形式的铜剑,但是有些则出土各种种类的铜剑。尽管如此,如果通过探讨铜剑的各种属性或者一起出土之遗物,那么在一定程度上还可以细致地弄清其地区特点。

以公元前10世纪至公元前6世纪使用的典型的辽宁式铜剑(林沄的A式铜剑)为例探讨地区特点,如果首先考察青铜短剑、陶器以及其他青铜遗物,那么大致可以证实在辽西地区内的冀北地区、滦河地区、老哈河流域,都具有地区特点文化。

1)直刃剑母胎地(发祥地),冀北地区

冀北地区(河北平原东北部地区)。在周代燕国的中心地区冀北出土多种形式的铜剑。短剑的制造年代被推定为西周初期公元前 10 世纪前后。在北京市白浮村两座木椁墓中出土 6 件卡拉苏克系短剑,在董家林村遗址第 52、53 号墓中各出土同样的有柄铜剑 1~2 件,延庆军都山一带玉皇庙等出土鄂尔多斯式铜剑 10 余件,除此之外,在北辛堡、小白杨等地发现有柄直刃剑,而且在这些有柄铜剑中发现了许多初期形态的銎柄式直刃剑。这些事实说明冀北地区是銎柄式直刃剑发祥地。

冀北地区铜剑形制跟燕的周边地区不同,呈现中原形制,因此冀北地区出土的铜剑属于"东周式铜剑"系统的可能性很大。另外在这一地区出土的有柄式铜剑跟鄂尔多斯式铜剑有很深的关系,对后来形成的西拉木伦河流域銎柄式青铜短剑文化有强烈影响。若是做总结,那么可以说冀北地区不但接受了许多中原文化影响,而且对西拉木伦河等辽西地区青铜器文化形成予以许多影响。

2)滦河流域辽宁式铜剑和鄂尔多斯式铜剑

与冀北地区不同,河北平原东北地区南部,即七老图山南麓及在燕山附近的滦河流域,则出土更为复杂形制的铜剑。在这一地区,可见到许多辽宁式铜剑剑身,也出现了鄂尔多斯式铜剑。另外还出土剑身与辽宁式铜剑相同;刃为曲刃、剑把则是鄂尔多斯剑把的剑和有銎部、直刃、在剑格上有耳的剑。

依据滦河流域出土的三足器(鼎、鬲、甗等)和红褐色磨光陶器情况看,可以把它视为广义的夏家店下层文化区域。但是依据与青铜短剑一起出土的遗物来看,它又反映出不同的地区性。恐怕,这很可能是辽西土著集团"戎狄"系统居民集团在接触冀北地区文化过程中产生的差别。

3)老哈河流域独特的铜剑

努鲁儿虎山北老哈河流域,是所谓的夏家店上层文化中心地区。夏家店上层文化是以饲养家畜,定居农业为基础。这一点通过已发现的石斧已得到证实。特别是在这一地区出土了许多在中国青铜器影响下又反映地方形式的青铜器。其中有只在中国东北地方辽西地区出土的用青铜制造的鼎、簋(盛高粱或黍的盛器)、鬲、尊、卣(盛酒的祭器)、盘、簠(盛粮谷的祭器)等。这一情况应认为是这一文化经过北京昌平或唐山琉璃河接触商代中原文化而产生的结果。

在老哈河流域代表性遗址南山根遗址中,共出土了 7 件青铜短剑,其中的一件剑身为典型的辽宁式青铜短剑剑身,不见剑把及剑把装饰件。除此之外,还出土了盛行在米努辛斯科盆地卡拉苏克文化系统的铜剑 5 把。特别是在这一地区出土了辽宁式铜剑剑身和不属于任何卡拉苏克短剑形制的只是在这一地区独有的铜剑,这种剑是把剑把、剑身合铸为一体,刃既有曲刃,又有直刃,有的还在把上饰有锯齿形。

在位于老哈河上游黑离河川南岸小黑石沟遗迹长方形石棺墓中,出土了跟南山根铜剑一样的铜剑等超过 400 件的青铜器和少量的石器、金器、骨器等。小黑石沟遗迹面积很大,遗迹密集,可认为对它的调查对重新了解辽西地区青铜文化将具有很重要的意义。如上所述,在以小黑石沟遗迹和南山根遗迹为代表的老哈河流域夏家店上层文化地区,跟辽宁式铜剑一起集中出土有銎柄的曲刃短剑和直刃匕首式短剑,特别是大量的出土铜镞、铜戈、青铜矛、青铜头盔等武器类,说明此地已存在带有军事性质的居民集团的征服战争,并很活跃。

考察这一地区出土的全部青铜器遗物,可以认为其虽然接受了鄂尔多斯地区和冀北地区文化的一定影响,但根据青铜短剑剑刃曲刃的情况看,更多的接受了辽宁式铜剑文化影响。另外,出土了商代有銎柄的青铜短剑,则是更多的反映了卡拉苏克系统的铜剑因素的影响,其主要原因一般认为是中国的影响,但是最近却有从卡拉苏克地方寻找其起源的见解,并成了主流。从这一点看,可以认为在把上有鋬柄的铜剑,是中国北方地区的遗物。

4)喀左县~凌源地区曲刃短剑

由河北省东北部至滦河流域的喀左南洞沟、凌源三关甸子等地区是商朝系统居民进入东北的据点。在这里建造有受中原和内蒙古土坑墓影响很深的土圹竖穴墓。这里发现很多商、周时代青铜器储藏坑,但是越过七老图山地到夏家店上层文化中心地区后,这些遗迹就减少。另外在夏家沟、喀左南洞沟等地发现的公元前5世纪以后(战国时代)遗迹中出土了前一阶段见不到的铸造的剑把。这一地区虽然属于老哈河流域夏家店上层文化地区,但因其位于由北京一带至辽东地区的辽西走廊中心地这一地理上的特点,而使其受到了商周文化和中国北方文化的双重文化影响。只要一看青铜短剑的形制,发现典型曲刃短剑跟丁字形剑把一起出土,由此可知这一地区是在辽宁式铜剑文化圈内许多种族集团的核心居住地区。

5)大凌河流域~朝阳地区的典型辽宁式铜剑

夏家店上层文化,不但在赤峰夏家店或宁城南山根等中心地区,而且在向东略有距离的大凌河流域的朝阳、锦西和辽河平原也有发展。这一地区以朝阳十二台营子、锦西乌金塘、北票市一带为中心出土了典型的辽宁式铜剑,特别是出土了带有装饰性的青铜制品。

这一地区地势较低,在以如此平坦的地区夏家店文化和辽东地区农业文化有了复合,在青铜器和其他遗迹、遗物中,也有中原文化和北方游牧文化以及辽宁地区农耕文化等各种因素及多种形式混合在一起。通过这一情况看,这一地区很可能是位于戎族居住区东部,山戎族好像以大凌河、医巫闾山为界与其东部的涉貊族接触。

另外,以大凌河东部医巫闾山脉为起点直到辽河流域,则是一个文化接触地区,在这里辽西地区游牧性质很强的文化和辽东地区农业文化互相结合,并有了发展。

三、辽东地区青铜器文化的特征

辽东地区,由于自然地理位置上的原因,容易输入辽西地区和中国北方草原文化,而且又可以传授给东部的吉林一带或朝鲜半岛。正因为这种原因,辽东地区青铜器文化呈现复杂形态,而变化也很快。因此,区分其文化因素特征并不那么容易。

辽东地区青铜器文化的代表性遗物是辽宁式铜剑,它跟辽西地区出土的铜剑相比,剑身略短,中间突起下半部略宽,属于初期形式。在当时青铜器制作和文化方面,总起来看辽西地区处于领先地位。另外有人还提出了把被北朝鲜学界划入初期形式的铜剑,看成是跟使用器有距离的"宝器化"、"仪器化"装饰品的主张。

1)高台山文化

高台山文化是辽河中流的早期青铜器文化,依靠向辽河北部移动的居民集团而发展,在铁岭地区变成顺山屯文化,然后这一顺山屯文化由使用辽宁式铜剑文化的新乐上层文化继承,从此辽河流域进入新时代。享受高台山文化的一部分居民集团从辽河以西阜新、库伦一带越过医巫闾山定居大凌河流域,然后受夏家店下层文化影响,与当地土著文化融合创造了魏营子文化。在辽东地区青铜器的出现相对晚于夏家店上层文化。作为它的代表性遗物就是在新乐上层文化遗迹中出土的公元前 12～8 世纪周代制造的青铜斧和刀。

新乐上层文化阶段,是青铜器文化在辽东地区正式发展时期,到了这一时期在辽东全区内已经有支石墓和石棺墓地普及,并使用了辽宁式铜剑。而且,还可以见到这一阶段开始带着区域性而发展起来的各类型文化集团都被包括在辽宁式铜剑文化之中。

2)庙后山文化

辽东地区最早的青铜器文化是辽河中流流域的庙后山文化类型。庙后山类型以太子河流域本溪地区为中心,跟辽河两岸青铜器文化进行各层次的接触和交流,并在影响东北部吉林省地区、南部的辽东半岛和浑江、鸭绿江流域的过程中有了发展。

3)美松里型陶器文化

自公元前 8～7 世纪至公元前 5～4 世纪间,以辽阳二道河子支石墓为代表的青铜器文化,即所谓的辽宁式铜剑社会,因为青铜斧、青铜凿的出现而发生了很大变化。这是在下一章中还要详细探讨的问题。自公元前 8～7 世纪以后,辽东地区就进入这一阶段,跟辽宁式铜剑一起出现了美松里型陶器文化。可以说这一青铜器文化正是成为古朝鲜和扶余等古代韩民族源流的居民集团的文化,即涉貊系统的文化。

4)辽东地区青铜文化编年和特性

依据至今为止的资料编制的辽东地区青铜文化编年表,可以认为在下辽河平原地区文化发展曾经过了三个阶段,即高台山文化、新乐上层文化、郑家洼子文化。对这种文化继承关系,学界已有了明确认识。特别是相当于第二阶段(新乐上层文化)时期的公元前 1 000 年前后商、周时期,开始出现支石墓、石盖石棺墓、积石墓、辽宁式铜剑。所以这一时期是进行编年,认识继承关系的很重要的时期。然而,由于可以决定具体年代的明确资料的不足,因而想要认识其系统并不那么容易。

与古朝鲜及涉貊势力圈或领地有关的是辽东地区,其标志性代表遗物是支石墓(即石棚)和美松里型土器,而非辽宁式铜剑。尤其当时北方式支石墓文化(即桌子式支石墓文化)形成了一定的势力圈,并密集分布于辽东地区和朝鲜西北部地区。

通过综合分析有关文献记录和相关考古资料,笔者得出了唯有以北方式支石墓为特性所形成的文化圈才是真正古朝鲜势力圈的结论,尤其是提出了将分布于朝鲜西北部地区的陀螺形土器文化是区别于辽东地区美松里型土器文化的古朝鲜青铜器文化的核心地区的主张凸显出来,并指出将迄今为止视为古朝鲜文化的以辽东地区为中心的美松里型土器文化归属为涉貊族文化,但与陀螺形土器文化有着密切联系的观点。

到了公元前 5～4 世纪,辽东地区受中原文化影响出现土圹墓(即土坑竖穴墓),在这些墓葬当中,除个例外,均出土有青铜短剑。但这一时期的青铜短剑,已摆脱辽宁式铜剑的曲刃形态,而步入初期细型铜剑形状阶段。拥有这种初期细型铜剑文化的集团,在辽东——朝鲜西北部地区可划分为三个区域。后来,辽东地区和吉林省一带的这种青铜短剑文化首先退出历史舞台,只有朝鲜半岛地区的此类文化受到辽东地区的影响而发展成为新的真正意义上的韩国式铜剑文化。这一现象也恰好反映了公元前 5～4 世纪阶段在辽东——朝鲜西北部地区存在着很广范围的联盟的史实。

辽宁式铜剑文化是青铜器时代初期古朝鲜社会面貌的标志,并说明了当时古朝鲜社会是由土著族长们在各地区引导部族形成国家的一个阶段。此后,古朝鲜社会以青铜器阶段的发展为基础,以铁器为代表的金属文化得到了普及,农业生产力也得到了更高一层的发展,在以此所带来的社会分化发生过程中形成了国家。再有,在受到拥有先进铁器文化的中国势力的压迫等诸多复合因素的作用下,约于公元前4~3世纪时,逐渐形成了中央集权制。

四、结　论

古朝鲜自公元前4世纪以来,在燕国的势力向辽西地区扩张后,吸收了中国的先进铁器文化而成长为初期国家,它的势力范围当中应包含了一部分生活在辽东地区的涉貊族地区,因而形成了联盟制的国家体系。此时代表古朝鲜文化的支石墓文化,被土圹墓、韩国式细形铜剑、各种铁制武器等文化要素所替代。此时,韩国的初期国家——古朝鲜,以最初青铜器文化为基础成长后,汲取铁器文化取得了实质意义上的发展。因此,我们不能一提起古朝鲜文化就联想到辽宁式铜剑文化,而实际上进入铁器阶段后的韩国式铜剑文化才是真正的古朝鲜文化。

トルファン五銖銭と中原五銖銭

岡内三眞

早稲田大学文学部考古学研究室

は じ め に

新疆のトルファンは、シルクロードの要衝であり、古来、東西南北の文物が交易された都市・文明の十字路として名高い。現在も観光都市・世界遺産の史跡の街として繁栄をほこっている。新石器時代からトルファンオアシスに住み着いた人々が、集落からしだいに展開して都邑を形成し、やがてまとまったひとつの国家・車師前国を築いたのは、遅くとも紀元前3世紀のごろのことである。

ユーラシア大陸の東には、中国を統一した秦の後をうけて前漢帝国が成立し、西には、ギリシャ文明の系譜をひくローマ帝国が存在していた。この両帝国に導かれるように、東西南北の各地から文物や文化を携えた人々が、東西に移動しつぎつぎと中継して手渡しながら交流したのである。紀元前3世紀～紀元前2世紀ころになると、商品相互の物々交換のほかに、貨幣による取引や決済もすでに始まっていた可能性が高い。

その物証としては、新疆域内のシルクロード沿線各地で出土する前漢時代の半両銭や五銖銭などの貨幣、星雲紋鏡や銘帯鏡などの銅鏡、錦や羅の絹織物などを挙げることができる。西からの交易品としては、手の込んだ装飾のある金銀器やローマングラス、ローマ金貨などが東にもたらされている。

この論文は、紀元前2世紀前後のトルファン地域を取り上げ、トルファンと中原とで出土した五銖銭の型式分類と編年とをおこなった上で比較研究し、トルファン出土五銖銭の特徴と用途、当時の社会経済に占める位置などを明らかにすることを目的としている。

I　五銖銭出土の遺跡

トルファンでは、交河故城の都市遺跡を中心にして、西北の交河故城溝北区1号台地墓(A)と、東南の交河故城城南区墓地(B)から五銖銭がそれぞれ出土している。いずれも埋葬址の竪穴土壙墓から他の副葬品や土器と共に発見されているが、銅銭は五銖銭のみであり、他の貨幣を伴っていない。以下に出土遺構と伴出遺物について記述する。

1　交河故城溝北区1号台地墓『交河故城』

溝北区1号台地には、数基の大型竪穴土壙墓が存在する。そのうち3基が1994年に発掘調査され、そのなかの1号墓の陪塚であるmj1号墓から1枚の五銖銭が検出された。この墓は盗掘を受けていたために、出土した副葬品は少なく遺物相互の関係も不明である。1体の埋葬に伴った遺物には、ふた瘤ラクダの金製飾り、グリフィンと虎の闘争文金製飾り、木製容器や土器、骨角製品、鉄器などがある。さらに骨でかたどった仿製の子安貝製品が1点伴っている。代用貨幣としての子安貝がすでに存在していたのであろう。動物の犠牲壙や殉葬壙をもつ直径10m前後を計る巨大な竪穴土壙墓は、王侯の墓であろう。わずかに遺存している遺物によっても王侯墓の多様な品物の副葬を想像できるが、盗掘に遭って原位置や伴出状況、組み合わせなどを探る手がかりが失われた点が惜しまれる。

　この墓で遺存していた五銖銭は、1枚だけである。五の字は丸みを帯びて交叉し、銖の字の金偏は三角頭が小さく、朱の上部は角張っている。穿の上に横文があり、周郭は一定の幅がある。3.1gの重さや直径2.5cmの規格からみても、前漢代の五銖銭である。

　2　交河故城城南区墓地『交河溝西』

　城南区墓地では、3基の墓から合計10枚の五銖銭が出土している。五銖銭のみで他の貨幣を伴わない状況は、前に述べた溝北墓と一致している。これらの五銖銭を発掘するきっかけになったのは、5号墓における五銖銭の発見であった。当時の記録をたどりながら述べてみよう。

　a）最初に発見されたのは、城南区JⅥ区5号墓地の五銖銭である。1996年9月6日、新たに車師前国時代の墓を調査するために、ヤールホトの遺跡を調べて歩いていた私の目に、とある窪みの底で青緑色に光っている丸い物が目にとまった。近寄って確かめると五の字がくっきりと読み取れる。字体や大きさから見て、まぎれもない前漢時代の五銖銭と判定できた。はやる心をおさえて周りを観察すると、30cmほど南にも五銖銭が砂の中から顔を出している。これは墓だとおもって窪み全体を見渡すと、銅製の指輪や鉄片、土器片がむき出しになって窪みの底に点在している。車師の墓がおよそ2000年の間に風雪に削られ曝らされて地上に露出し、墓壙の床面と遺物とがわずかに残っていたのである。合計3枚の五銖銭と銅指輪、鉄環、鉄器片などを墓壙の底から検出することができた。

　墓壙は長さ2.46m、幅1mの長方形で、深さはわずか数cmにすぎない。

　五銖銭は3枚出土している。No1の五銖銭は、直径2.45cm、穿長1.0cm、重さ2.99gである。No2は、直径2.5cm、穿長1.0cm、重さ3.48gである。No3は、直径2.5cm、穿長0.9cm、重さ3.61gである。出土状態や位置関係は、を参照していただきたいが、東側にかたよって五銖銭が出土している。おそらく墓壙の東寄りに頭部があり、その付近に五銖銭を副葬したのであろう。

　b）城南区Ⅵ区16号墓は，墓泥棒に荒らされることもなく埋葬された当時のままの配置状態で発掘されたトルファン地域の墓では稀有な未盗掘墓である。墓は台地の縁辺に築かれ、固い地山に掘りこまれた長方形の竪穴土壙墓である。長さ2.76m、幅1.40m、深さ1.70mの規模である。墓の深さが幸いしたようである。

　最初に頭部付近から黄金製頭飾りが出土し、続いて頸の部分から緑松石（トルコ石）製の首飾り玉を検出した。そして腹部中央からは、牡牛をかたどった黄金製のバックルが埋葬当時の原位置のままで出土した。さらに右の足首付近から黄金製のブーツ留め飾りが出土したので、注意深く掘り進めると、左足首付近からも原位置を保って黄金製のブーツ留め飾りが出土した。この留め飾りは、左右の足首に1個ずつペアーで着装されていた同形、同大の金製留め飾りである。今までエルミタージュ美術館などで知られている小型の金製や青銅製帯鉤は、原位置を保った本例の検出によって、ブーツの留め飾りまたは足首金具の可能性を指摘できるようになった。

　その他に、身体の右側からは鉄鏃や五銖銭がまとまって出土した。頭部付近からは、飲食物をいれたと想定できる壺、浅鉢、盤が並んで出土している。足元からは犠牲にされた馬の頭骸骨と大腿骨とが重なって隅に寄せられた状態で出土した。そのほか鉄ナイフや鋲留め金具、鉄片などが墓壙内から出土している。

　出土した五銖銭は3枚である。No1は、直径2.5 cm、穿長1.0 cm、重さ5.24 gである。No2は、直径2.5 cm、穿長1.0 cm、重さ4.01 g。No3は、直径2.5 cm、穿長1.0 cm、重さ3.68 gである。No3は、穿の下に半月があらわされた記号銭である。

　c）城南区JⅥ区12号墓からも、土器と五銖銭とが出土している。竪穴土壙墓は長方形で、規模は長さ2.80 m、深さ1.26 m、幅は頭部で1.50 m、脚部側で1.16 mと狭くなっている。

　墓は撹乱をうけており、遺物は原位置が不明で、墓壙内の埋土の中から検出されている。それでも浅鉢3点と五銖銭4枚が遺存していた。五銖銭のNo1は、直径2.5 cm、穿長1 cm、穿上横文のついた記号銭である。No2は、直径2.4 cm、穿長1 cm。No3は、直径2.5 cm、穿長1 cm。No4は、直径2.4 cm、穿長1 cmである。盗掘を受けたため、埋葬当時の配置が明らかでない点が残念である。

　以上でトルファン出土五銖銭の遺構と出土状態を紹介した。

　つづいてトルファン出土五銖銭の編年を試みる。そのために中国中原の五銖銭を分類し、編年案を検討する必要がある。

Ⅱ　五銖銭の分類と編年

1　前漢の五銖銭

　五銖銭は、漢の武帝が元狩五（BC118）年に各郡や国ごとにまかせて鋳銭させたのが始まりである。『史記』と『漢書』によると、武帝は御史大夫・張湯の意見を入れて、元狩五年に半両銭をやめ、銀と錫の合金である白金と、銅、錫、鉛の青銅合金で作った五銖銭とを通行させたという。ところが郡国ごとに五銖銭には差異があり、私鋳銭も横行して重量、規模、字体などに違いが著しく、貨幣経済に混乱が生じた。そのために元鼎二（BC115）年に官営工房で赤仄五銖銭を鋳造して発行させた。赤仄五銖銭1枚は、従来の五銖銭5枚に相当するとした。そして貴族や公的機関での納税に赤側五銖銭の使用を義務づけたという。

　文献によると「郡国銭賎、民多奸鋳、銭多軽、而公卿請令京師鋳鍾官赤仄、一当五、賦官用非赤仄不得行。…是歳也、張湯死、而民不思」、「赤仄五銖只用于官府和貴族、為納賦与官府用銭、併不流通于民間」と記されている。

　ところが翌々年の元鼎四（BC113）年には、「其后二歳、赤仄銭賎、民巧法用之、不便、又廃、」という結果になり「于是悉郡国母鋳銭、専令上林三官鋳」という。赤仄銭は、質が悪くなり、民間で巧みに私鋳して用いるため官府用としては不便になったので、郡国の五銖銭と赤仄五銖銭とを全面的に廃止し、上林三官を設けて官営工房で五銖銭を専門に鋳造させることになった。ここに貨幣の規格統一と国家による統制、独占鋳造を開始したのである。武帝が死去した後元二（BC87）年まで、この上林三官での鋳銭制度は維持され、後の昭帝、宣帝などにも国家による鋳銭制度は引き継がれた。ただし昭帝や宣帝の五銖銭と武帝の五銖銭とでは、字体や重さなどで相違が認められ、比較的に区別が容易である。

かつて1957年に発掘された『洛陽焼溝漢墓』出土の五銖銭を基準に編年が組まれ、1959年に報告書が出版された。これが漢代遺構、遺物編年の基準となり、墓の構造、銅器、銅鏡、土器などに適用され、長く使われ続けてきた。

しかし1968年に発掘された武帝の異母兄・劉勝墓から五銖銭の新資料2317枚が出土して、『洛陽焼溝漢墓』の武帝時期の編年に限界があると認識されるようになった。1980年に公表された『満城漢墓発掘報告』では、五銖銭をⅠ、Ⅱ、Ⅲの3型式に分けている。

筆者は『満城漢墓』の資料によって、五銖銭を論じたことがある（岡内1984）。しかし朝鮮出土の五銖銭の編年を目標としたため、赤仄銭や上林三官銭の細分までは論じるゆとりがなかった。

2　満城漢墓の五銖銭

『史記』と『漢書』によれば、劉勝は元鼎四（BC113）年春二月に死去している。これは、郡国五銖銭と赤仄銭とが廃止され、上林三官で五銖銭が鋳造された年にあたっている。

呉栄曽（呉1986 - 12）は、中室の五銖銭を郡国銭、後室の五銖銭を三官五銖とみなしている。

かつて『洛陽焼溝漢墓』の五銖銭を報告書で記述した蒋若是（蒋1989 - 4）は、『満城漢墓発掘報告』と河北省博物館から提供された拓本とによって、満城漢墓の中室出土の五銖銭は郡国銭、後室出土の五銖銭は赤仄五銖銭と認定した。

日本の関道夫（関1990 - 3）は、Ⅰ型式は郡国五銖銭、Ⅱ型式には郡国五銖銭と赤仄銭とが混在し、Ⅲ型式は赤仄五銖銭、後室出土銭は初鋳三官五銖銭に比定している。

また戴志強・周衛栄・樊祥繍（戴ほか1991 - 2）とは、満城漢墓出土の五銖銭10枚についての成分分析をおこなっている。

そのご李建麗・趙衛平・陳麗鳳（李ほか1991 - 2）たちは、劉勝墓の五銖銭を再検討して従来のⅡ式をⅡ式とⅣ式に分割して4型式に分けた。そしてⅠ、Ⅱ、Ⅲ型式を郡国五銖銭、Ⅳ型式を上林三官五銖銭としている。

これに対して方成軍（方2000 - 2）は、Ⅰ、Ⅱ、Ⅲ型式を郡国五銖銭にあて、Ⅳ型五銖銭は赤仄銭だとして、蒋若是と同じ結論に達している。

現在は4型式の分類をどの時期の貨幣にあてるかに、論議の争点が移っている。

ところが武帝の御史大夫であった張湯の墓が2002年に西安で発掘され、「張湯」の印とともに8枚の五銖銭を検出した。2004年に張湯墓の「簡報」が『文物2004 - 6』に公表されている。張湯は、元狩五年に白金と五銖銭とをはじめて鋳造させた人物である。当時は御史大夫の職にあったので、元鼎二年の赤仄銭の鋳造にも関係したと想定できる。讒言によって罪を着せられ、元鼎二年冬に自殺しているので、張湯墓出土の五銖銭は、年代判定について重要な鍵をにぎっている。

3　張湯墓出土の五銖銭

張湯は、『漢書』によると、元鼎二（BC115）年冬十一月、『史記』によると元鼎三（BC114）年に罪をえて自殺したという。詳細を省くが、帝紀や食貨志から解釈して、漢書の元鼎二年説が妥当である。

『漢書』張湯伝によると、「張湯は杜の人也」と記されている。張湯は父の死後に長安の官吏となって身を起こし、のちに内吏につかえて給事となり、茂陵の尉となった。このとき武帝の寿陵を建設する責任者となり、截頭方錐形の墓を造る工事を監督したという。武安侯の田蚡が丞相になるとその属官となり、さらに推薦されて侍御史となり皇帝の庶務を補任した。陳皇后が衛夫人を呪詛した「巫蠱の獄」を取り調べて才能を認められ、太中大夫となり、法令を執行する役についた。のちに廷尉となり裁判を担当したが、法の適用が厳しく、皇帝の意に添うようにして必ずしも公平ではなかった。張湯は皇帝にますます信任されて御史大夫となり、位は三公に列した。湯は皇帝の意をうけ、白金と五銖銭とを鋳造し、天下の塩鉄を専売制に替え、富商・大商を排除し、「告緡令」を施行した。湯が参内して国家の財政について語るとき、天子は日が暮れるまで食事も忘れて傾聴したという。当時の丞相・庄青霍は、ただその地位を占めているに過ぎず、天下の大事は皆、張湯の進言によって裁可されたという。かつて湯が病気になると、皇帝が親しく自ら湯の家まで出かけて見舞ったほどで、信任があつく寵愛されていた。しかし讒言と告発とによって、御史太夫にあること七年で失脚した。書をしたため「湯はいささかの功もなく小役人の刀筆の吏から身を起こし、幸いにも陛下のお陰で三公の位に至りましたが、その責任をまっとうすることができませんでした」と詫びると共に感謝し、「しかしながら湯を罪に陥しいれようと謀った者は、丞相の3人の長吏です」と記し終えると、ついに自殺して果てた。

湯が死んで調べてみると、その遺産はわずか五百金にすぎず、みな俸禄や天子からの賞賜品であり、他に余財はなかった。兄弟や子供たちが手厚く葬ろうとすると、湯の母は「湯は天子の大臣となりながら悪評を蒙って死んだ。どうして手厚く葬れようか」と言い、遺骸を牛車に載せて運び、木棺に入れるだけで木槨を築かせなかった。皇帝はこれを聞いて「この母にしてこの子あり、この母あらずんばこの子生ぜず」と言って嘆息したという。そして一切の事情を取り調べなおし、讒言した長吏の三人を誅殺し、上奏した丞相の青翟を自殺させた。皇帝は湯を惜しみ、その子である長安世を引き立てたという。

張湯の息子であった張安世は、武帝、昭帝、宣帝の三帝に仕え、大司馬将軍となり富平侯に封じられ、その子である千秋、延壽、彭祖はいずれも高官となり、みな天寿をまっとうした。

元康四年春、安世は病にかかり、秋に薨じた。天子は印綬を贈り、軽車と甲士を送って葬り、諡名して敬侯といった。墓地を杜の東に賜り、将作が覆土を掘って墓と祠堂を起こした。子の延壽があとを継ぎ、孫の勃や曾孫の臨、その後を継いだ放、純など子々孫々まで栄え、功臣の名をほしいままにしたという。

贊に言う。湯は酷烈で、身に咎を蒙るに至ったとはいえ、その賢士を推挙し人の善を称揚した。もとより後継の子孫があってしかるべきである。安世は正道をふみ行ない、満ちて溢れなかった。安世の兄である賀が陰徳を積んだことも、また張家一族を助けたというべきであろう。

張湯の墓

張湯は、杜県の出身であった。息子の安世は、元康四年春に病気となり、秋に薨じている。墓地の塋を杜の東に賜り、将作監が土を穿って塚を覆い、祠堂を起こしたと記述している。西安市東南方の宣帝杜陵の東に、張家一族の墓地があったことが知られる。

　　2002 年の4 月から10 月にかけて、西安市文物保護考古所は、西安市長安区郭杜鎮西北政法学院南校区で発掘調査をおこなった。体育弁公楼の基礎工事現場で、88 基の墳墓を発掘調査した。その中に、東西方向に長軸をもち、墓道、羨道、玄室をもつ斜墓道の土洞墓を発掘した。玄室の東端には麻織物と漆皮の痕跡が残っていた。北壁寄りに木箱の腐った痕跡があり、こまごまとした車馬具や武器、容器などを副葬している。南壁寄りに帯鉤、銅印、鉄剣を身におび、銅鏡、鐸、鉄刀を頭寄りに随葬した男性ひとりの埋葬を復原できる。被葬者と副葬品の位置関係については、報告者と異なる意見である。

　　前に述べたように「湯死、家産直不過五百金、皆所得奉賜、無它赢。昆弟諸子欲厚葬湯、湯母曰『湯為天子大臣被悪言而死、何厚葬為』載以牛車、有棺而無槨」という記載が漢書列伝にある。

　　この墓は、素掘りの土洞墓で、木槨がなく木棺のみの簡素な構造である。また盗掘孔が羨道と奥壁の2 箇所に穿たれているが、遺物の撹乱は少なく、副葬品もほぼ原位置を保っているように筆者にはみえる。幸いにも銅印 2 顆が玄室内で検出された。銅印 2 点は、いずれも長さ1. 8 cm 四方、厚さ0. 7 cm で、前漢時代の方寸印にあたる。両面に文字を陰刻し、ひとつには「張湯」「張君信印」の文字、他のひとつには「張湯」「臣湯」と彫り込まれている。この銅印や後述する武器、車馬具、銅帯鉤、石料などによって、罪をえて埋葬された張湯の墓と認定できる。

　　北壁寄りには、鉄鋪首、青銅製四葉座金具などの棺金具、銅洗、銅容器残欠、青銅製の衡や馬面、車軸頭、蓋弓帽などの車馬具、弩などの武器が置かれている。これらの副葬品は、木箱の中に納められていたのであろう。

　　南壁寄りには、鉄剣、銅鏃、銅弩、銅帯鉤、銅印、石料、五銖銭などが長さ3m、幅 1mほどの範囲内に置かれていた。頭寄りの東壁側1m 四方の範囲内に、鉄刀、銅鏡、銅鈴などを、配置している。銅鏡は、連峰鈕の星雲紋鏡で、外縁に16 個の連弧紋を巡らしている。前漢武帝代に流行したモデルの鏡である。

　　五銖銭は、副葬の木箱東寄りで4 枚、木棺の副葬区画の東よりで2 枚、木棺内の西寄りで2 枚、合計8 枚が出土した。その内の1 枚は銅銭に鍍金し、他の7 枚は鋳造銅銭である。

張湯墓出土の五銖銭

　　鍍金五銖銭は、方穿の下に半月の突起がある記号銭である。他の7 枚は、満城漢墓出土のⅣ型五銖銭と同じタイプに属している。上林三官での五銖銭の鋳造は、元鼎四（BC113）年に始まるため、張湯墓に上林三官五銖銭が副葬される余地はない。郡国五銖銭か赤仄五銖銭かのどちらかであるが、赤仄五銖銭の可能性が高い。

　　后曉栄によると、赤銅製で外郭を磨き端正な作りで漆黒色を呈すという。郭の幅は厚く広く均一で、文字は明確である。五字はゆるく曲がって交叉している。銭面には記号がなく、銭は軽いとしている。

　　いずれにしろ『龍首原漢墓』や『長安漢墓』、張湯墓など墓の出土資料、鋳銭址から出土する鋳型や笵模の紀年銘遺物、『鍾官鋳銭址』など、新出資料によって五銖銭の編年が再検討され、見直しが加えられつつある。

　　筆者は前述したように、かつて漢代の五銖銭を分類した論文「漢代五銖銭の研究」を発表したことがある。朝鮮半島出土の五銖銭を比定することに主眼があり、前漢から後漢までを含む長い時期の五銖銭を対象にした。しかし今となっては20年以上も古い資料に依拠しているため、改訂の必要が生じている。このため最近の出土資料を加えて再度五銖銭の分類と編年とを試みよう。

　　まだ成案を得るには至っていないが、郡国五銖銭と赤側五銖銭、三官五銖銭、昭帝五銖銭、宣帝五銖銭をそれぞれ分類した。郡国銭、三官銭、昭帝、宣帝の五銖銭は、いくつかの型式に細分できる可能性が高い。

　　張湯が関係して鋳造し始めた郡国五銖銭は、各国や郡で製造したためにバラエテイが多くばらつきがあり、型式にまとめるのが困難なほど多様性に富んでいる。これを改めて統一をはかる目的で創始されたのが赤側五銖銭なのであろう。このため赤側五銖銭は、先行する郡国五銖銭よりも形態が均一で重量も重く、字体も整一性が高い。

　　武帝の三官五銖銭は、赤側五銖銭を受け継いだタイプと、それとは異なる新しい字体をとったタイプに大きく分かれる。おそらく三官の官営工房ごとに特色をもたせながら、多量の五銖銭を鋳造させたと考えられる。

　　これをうけた昭帝の五銖銭は、両者をミックスして整った長く流麗な字体となっている点に特色がある。

　　宣帝の五銖銭は、ふたたび武帝代の三官五銖銭にちかいタイプが造られ、多様な型式を示している。

　　かつての論文で筆者が紀年銘のある鋳型から宣帝の神爵年間に鋳造されたと想定した穿上横文五銖銭は、そのご紀年銘のある五銖銭鋳型が出土して、もっと遡る事実が明らかになった。このため穿上横文五銖銭でもって宣帝の年代に当てることはできなくなった。

　　トルファン出土の五銖銭にも穿上横文五銖銭が存在するが、穿上横文のみで宣帝の年代に比定することは今や適切ではない。そこで本論のために五銖銭の再検討を始めたのだが、「日暮れて道遠し」の感をぬぐえず遅々として進まない。ともあれ現在の到達点である分類試案を提示して、批判を仰ぎたい。

Ⅲ　トルファン出土五銖銭の特徴と用途

　　交河故城溝北区1号台地1号墓陪塚mj1号墓出土の五銖銭は、五や銖の字体からみて郡国五銖銭に相当する。伴出した金製品や骨角器なども紀元前2～3世紀ごろの特徴を備えている。

　　交河故城城南区JVI　5号墓出土の五銖銭は、五銖の文字が直線的で生硬な印象が強く、郡国五銖銭の特徴を備えている。1枚が穿上横文五銖の記号銭で、他の2枚は特に記号や特色のない五銖銭でいずれも郡国銭であろう。

　　交河故城城南区JVI　16号墓出土の五銖銭は、1枚が五の文字が直線的で、1枚が長く、1枚が五銖の文字が流麗である。2枚の郡国五銖銭と昭帝の三官五銖銭とにあたるのであろうと今は想定している。

　　交河故城城南区JVI　12号墓出土の五銖銭は、トルファン出土五銖銭の中で特徴のある一群である。五銖の字体は3枚が直線的かつ生硬で、のこる1枚は穿上横文五銖銭で流麗な感じをうける。3枚の郡国五銖銭と1枚の宣帝以降の五銖銭である可能性を捨てきれない。3枚の郡国五銖銭の穿には切込みがあり、六角形を呈している。こうした貨幣は花銭と呼ばれ、今まで後漢時代に下がる例が知られている。しかしこの遺構は、伴出した土器や竪穴土擴墓などの特色から、後漢時代まで年代が下降するとは考えにくい。やはり前漢時代に属する資料で、花銭の出現年代を遡らせ得る資料なのであろう。

このようにトルファン出土の五銖銭は、郡国五銖銭から昭帝の三官五銖銭（可能性としては宣帝代）までに該当するタイプで、多くは郡国五銖銭である。しかし前時期の半両銭を伴わず、次代の王莽銭を伴わない前漢時代の貨幣である点に間違いはない。

年代は郡国銭の上限である紀元前118年を遡ることなく、下限は王莽の新時代に下ることはない。多くは武帝時代の貨幣とみなし得よう。

上述のように時期を設定してよければ、武帝の対匈奴戦や西域開発にともなって齎された可能性が高いといえよう。伝来ルートは、長安から河西回廊を通じる基幹ルートで、時にはより北方の沙漠、オアシスルートや草原ルートを通じて、トルファンなど西域各地に運ばれたのであろう。

新疆出土の貨幣は、墓からの出土が多く、鏡や絹織物を伴っている。鏡や絹織物は当時の中国を代表する交易商品であり、東から西へと運ばれて行った。なかでも絹織物は西アジアをへて遠くギリシャ、ローマにまで運ばれた事実はよく知られている。また中国製の銅鏡もシベリアから中央アジアや西アジアにまで到達している。やはり交易商品としての広い販路を示している。それに比べると前漢時代の貨幣である五銖銭は、その分布圏は意外と狭く西は新疆域内に限定されている。この事実は、五銖銭が交易品ではなく貨幣として用いられ、その流通範囲は前漢勢力の及ぶ範囲内であった状況を明白に示すものであろう。

トルファン出土の五銖銭から、紀元前2世紀から紀元前1世紀の時代における車師前国と前漢王朝との交渉を垣間見ることが可能である。これら五銖銭の多くは、前漢武帝の西域開発によって齎され、現地の車師の人々によって使われたものであろう。

謝　辞　本稿作成にあたって、中国社会科学院考古研究所の王巍所長ほか研究員の方々、西安市文物保護考古所の皆様、共同研究チームの新疆文物考古研究所の皆さんに資料調査等で大変お世話になりました。また早稲田大学シルクロード調査研究所の皆さんには、つね日頃ご協力を戴いています。とくに今回の図版作成では、持田大輔COE助手の助力を得ました。皆様のご助力、ご協力に対して心から感謝いたします。

引 用 文 献

新疆文物考古研究所 1999年『交河故城』東方出版社。

新疆文物考古研究所 2001年『交河溝西』新疆人民出版社。

洛陽区考古発掘隊 1959年『洛陽焼溝漢墓』科学出版社。

中国社会科学院考古研究所 1980 年『満城漢墓発掘報告』文物出版社。

岡内三眞 1982 年「漢代五銖銭の研究」『朝鮮学報』102 輯、朝鮮学会。

丁福保『古銭大辞典』下巻、1982 年、中華書局。

呉栄曽 1990 年「対漢武帝早期五銖銭的探討」『中国文物報』1990－3。

蒋若是 1989 年「郡国、赤仄与三官五銖銭之考古学験証」『文物』1989－4。

関道夫 1990 年「中山国劉勝墓五銖─郡国，赤仄，三官五銖諸問題」『中国銭幣』1990－3。

戴志強，周衛栄，欒祥繻 1991 年「満城漢墓出土五銖銭的成分検測」『中国銭幣』1991－2。

李建麗、趙衛平、陳麗鳳 1991 年「満城漢墓銭幣新探」『中国銭幣』1991－2。

蒋若是 1997 年『秦漢銭幣研究』中華書局。

方成軍 2000 年「従満城漢墓探尋赤仄五銖銭」『華夏考古』2001－2。

后暁栄 2004 年「赤仄五銖銭五銖銭的考古新験証」『中国銭幣』2004－2。

西安市文物保護考古所 2004 年「西安市長安区西北政法学院西漢 張湯墓発掘簡報」『文物』2004－6。

西安市文物保護考古研究所 1999 年『西安龍首原漢墓』西北大学出版社。

西安市文物保護考古所ほか 2004 年『長安漢墓』陝西人民出版社。

西安文物保護修復センター 2004 年『漢鍾官鋳銭遺址』科学出版社。

中国銭幣雑誌編集部 2005 年『中国銭幣 1983～2003』新華音像中心。

Tsaraam-Xiongnu Royal Complex in the Trans-Baikal area

Sergei S. Miniaev

Institute of the History of Material Culture (Russian

Academy of Sciences), St. Petersburg

During the 1997 – 2005 field seasons the Trans-Baikal Archaeological Expedition of the Institute of the History of Material Culture, Russian Academy of Sciences, St. Petersburg, investigated a Xiongnu Royal burial complex in the Tsaraam Valley, situated 1.5 km to the south of Naushki village (Buriat Republic, Russian Federation). The royal complex is first which one was systematically excavated using modern archaeological methods.

The Tsaraam Cemetery was discovered by the pioneer of Xiongnu archaeology, Iu. D. Tal'ko-Gryntsevich in June of 1896. He drew a schematic map with an approximate location of the burial site; however, over time a place of the cemetery was forgotten. In September 1996, the cemetery was rediscovered by the Trans-Baikal Expedition, which made an accurate map marking the location of all barrows. The survey showed that in the valley were concentrated the largest burial structures of the Xiongnu now known in Russia, and these are among the largest anywhere. Around several of the large barrows are located smaller barrows, which, according to both the historical sources and recent archaeological evidence, are likely to have been sacrificial interments. The combination of a central large barrow ringed by several smaller barrows can be considered a single mortuary complex.

The central barrow of the cemetery No. 7 was a main object of the excavation. This is the largest Xiongnu barrow in Russia and one of the largest known at present anywhere. The surface construction of the central barrow consists of a quadrangle-shaped platform surfaced with clay. It measures approximately 29 × 28 m with a height of approximately 1.5 m above the present surface. The entrance chamber is 20 m long and extends to the south of the central platform. The walls of the platform are sided with stone slabs marking the perimeter of the walls. Several stone stelae were discovered, some of which were intact and others of which had fallen away from the platform.

A single longitudinal and seven perpendicular partitions divided the upper section of the burial pit into nine distinct compartments. Each partition was constructed from wooden logs stacked one upon another, sometimes having a thickness of two to three logs. Four covers of the burial chamber were excavated under the partitions. The uppermost cover of the burial chamber consisted of stone plates and wood; under the logs was a reed stratum. The second cover of the burial chamber was situated in 1.5 – 1.7 m below the upper one and covered the entire area of the burial pit. This second cover consisted of large stone plates, stacked in close proximity to each other. There was also a thin stratum of reed 0.7 m below the second cover. In both the upper and second covers, there was some difference between the eastern and western parts. The eastern part of the second cover consisted of large plates and boulders approximately 100×70 cm in area and with a thickness of $40 - 50$ cm. The stone plates of the western half of the cover were of smaller size, approximately 40×50 cm and with a thickness of only $10 - 15$ cm. At each corner of the burial pit on the level of the second cover there were small-sized stones lying on top of the large ones. The third cover was 11 m below the modern surface. This third cover consisted of large stone plates; under the stones there was a stratum of pebble, charcoal, birch cortex and small-sized stones. Bones of domesticated animals were found along northern edge of the third cover, among them skulls of horses, cows, sheep and goats which were placed in line with each other. Near the skulls were tail and leg bones. The fourth cover, located one meter below the third one, consisted of large stone plates, birch cortex, a stratum of pebble mixed with small-sized stones and a stratum of charcoal. In fact this fourth cover was a roof of a stone sarcophagus, walls witch one were constructed from large stones placed by some rows between walls of the burial pit and an intraburial construction. A common deep of the burial pit is 17th meters.

The intraburial construction itself consisted of three chambers: an external framework, an internal framework, and the coffin. The external chamber consisted of seven rows of squared beams; the overall height of the chamber was ca. $170 - 180$ cm. The internal frame consisted of five rows of squared beams each measuring 20×20 cm. The construction of the rows of the frame was analogous to the construction of the rows of the external chamber. As in the case of the external chamber, the frame had a covering of transverse boards and a floor similarly constructed of transverse boards.

The coffin inside the frame had been to a considerable degree destroyed by the robbery from the south end and by the subsequent collapse of the chamber. One may suppose that its floor and roof consisted of two boards laid lengthwise; the side walls of the coffin were made of wide boards, one-two to each wall.

Objects Found Inside the Burial Pit: The Chinese Mirror

Fragments of a Chinese bronze mirror were found under the logs at the second level of the longitudinal partition in the center of the burial pit, 218 cm below the surface. The ten fragments of the mirror were in the following positions: six lay one above the other and the remaining four alongside of them. Taken together they do not form a complete mirror — its center is only partially preserved — although they suffice to reconstruct its size and decoration. The diameter is 13 cm; around its edge is a rim 2.1 cm wide and 3 cm thick. The characteristic elements of the decoration make it possible to identify a wide range of analogies and reconstruct the entire decorative scheme.

Apart from the smooth rim, on the reverse surface of a mirror of that type are several concentric ornamental bands. Directly adjoining the rim is a narrow (3 mm) band with a comb-tooth pattern, inside of which is the main ornamental band with images which were separated from the center of the mirror also by a narrow band with a comb-tooth pattern. A smooth protruding band 3 mm wide separated the outer bands from the center, where there was a pierced knob for hanging the mirror. Narrow protruding lines divided into four sectors the area around the knob and inner smooth band. In each sector in turn were three round knobs or nipples, the central one of which was connected with the protruding smooth band by three short lines.

The main ornamental band situated between the two narrow bands with the comb-tooth pattern was divided into four sectors by means of small rounded projecting knobs. The area between the knobs was covered by virtually identical compositions, the center of which was a large scroll in the shape of a comma. It is possible that initially this was the depiction of the body of an animal which with time had been transformed into a geometric composition. Above and below this scroll were figures of birds, or, more rarely, other animals.

Mirrors of this type are not uncommon. They are known in museum collections; some examples of such mirrors have been found in archaeological excavations both of the Han Dynasty itself and in Xiongnu excavations of that same period on the territory of Mongolia and Russia. (See, e. g., Tal'ko-Gryntsevich 1999, p. 50, Fig. 3c; Chou 2000, p. 39, Fig. 20, Cheng and Han 2002, Fig. 25: 1,2 and Fig. 26: 1,2; Wenwu 1977, Fig. 27: 2) According to the standard classification (Zhongguo tongjing 1997, p. 247) they belong to the group of mirrors "with four nipples and four S-shaped figures" (or dragons). The given group is dated normally between the 1st century BCE and 1st century CE.

An important characteristic of the mirrors from Xiongnu sites is their fragmentary state. Unlike those in Han burials (and in a rare instance such as the Xiongnu burial at the Tamir site excavated in 2005), the mirrors in most Xiongnu burials are found either in separate fragments or in several pieces of a mirror that had been intentionally broken. Evidence of the intentional breaking of mirrors is seen, for example, in the mirror discovered in a residence in the fortress of Bayan-Under, where it was unearthed along with the iron knife which broke it (Huns 2005, p. 46, Fig. 63).

It is very likely that the Tsaraam mirror, initially intact, likewise had been intentionally broken. Traces of scale clearly visible on its surface indicate that the mirror had been broken by means of heating it to a high temperature and then abruptly cooling it, possibly in cold water. After that, some of the fragments were removed and the rest placed under the beams of the longitudinal partition. Removed as a result of this process were the central knob of the mirror, the three nipples dividing the main ornamental zone into parts, and two segments with ornament in the form of a central "comma" and adjoining birds. The depiction of a bird above the "comma" in the third section also has been damaged. In essence then, the only remaining complete segment is the fourth one. We note in particular that although the third and fourth segments had been broken into several parts during the ritual, these parts were not removed but placed in the grave pit along with other fragments. At the same time, a small fragment of the mirror with the dividing knob between the third and fourth segments was removed along with two other fragments with nipples. The fragment with a nipple which was placed in the grave pit had first been subjected to strong secondary heating, the result of which was that the knob had melted. The melting of the nipple was a result specifically of that second heating of a separate fragment, since otherwise the adjoining more delicate parts of the mirror also would have melted.

Thus one can hypothesize that during the burial ceremony a special ritual was performed over the mirror, a ritual which possibly was the norm for the burial practices of the Xiongnu more generally. The ritual involved subjecting the mirror to mechanical or heat treatment and breaking it into several fragments. One or several of such fragments accompanied the dead, while other parts of the mirror were removed and possibly preserved by the family or relatives of the deceased in order subsequently to accompany other burials and serve as a kind of sign of recognition upon meeting in the other world. The burial of some parts of the mirror in the grave pit and the removal of others (of analogous design) suggests that such mirrors and the ritual actions performed over them served as a kind of connecting link between the world of the living and the world of the dead, symbolizing in both worlds the unity of the collective which the deceased had left behind.

Objects Found Inside the Burial Pit: The Chinese Chariot

A Chinese chariot was found in the center of the barrow at a depth of 10.5 – 11 m (Miniaev and Sakharovskaia 2007). To its north, at the wall of the pit about a meter from the incline of the fifth step at a depth of 10 m were the skull, two neck vertebrae and the metapodials of a horse. The arrangement of the chariot's parts suggests that its body had been placed beneath the third cover when the pit was being filled, while the canopy and wheels were found above the stones of the third cover in the center of the barrow and thus must have been located above the level of that ceiling. Probably the chariot had been set onto the stones of the fourth cover where it was buried by the filling of the pit as well as by gravel, pebbles, charcoal and slabs of the third ceiling (the canopy and the wheels of the chariot having remained above the latter). When the fill of the pit sank, the parts of the chariot were displaced: in the process, the movement of stone slabs, gravel, and pebbles — acting like millstones — inflicted serious damage. Some time later, the chariot was yet further disturbed by robber passages: the northern passage damaged part of the harness and frame, while the southern one crossed the presumed location of the seat, in the process demolishing a considerable part of the canopy. Altogether, the parts of the chariot were very poorly preserved: the wooden parts and organic material of the canopy had decayed almost completely, the bronze and iron fastenings of the harness had been severely oxidized and lost their original structure. Here is a description of the preserved parts of the chariot:

The remains of *the canopy* were in the center of the pit 4 m from its northern edge above the stones of the third cover. The canopy consisted of a wooden frame, over which some organic material had been stretched. The base of the frame was composed of thin wooden strips about 4 cm wide set crosswise, to which were attached a number of thick arched twigs. The base included as well thinner twigs 1 – 1.5 cm in diameter, arrayed radially from the center of the frame. The organic cover of the frame was duofold, its upper layer consisting of a dark organic material (leather or felt), below which there was a thin layer of cloth. This canopy covering was fixed to the strips and twigs of the frame with thin, iron L-shaped nails. The inside of the canopy was coated with red lacquer, which preserved traces of geometric ornament rendered in white, brown and dark-red paints. A robber trench had destroyed the southern part of the canopy.

The *front yoke-pole* of the chariot was found on the layer of pebbles and charcoal under the stones of the third cover of the pit, 2.5 m north of the canopy. Its western edge had been completely destroyed during the collapse of the third cover. The preserved length of the pole was 2.5 m; its diameter was 18 – 20 cm. A bronze ferrule 10 cm long and 7 cm in diameter was attached to the eastern tip of the pole. The ferrule had completely oxidized and been crushed by the pressure of the fill. Probably a similar ferrule had been attached to the western, destroyed end of the pole. Five pairs of square mortises measuring 3 × 1.5 cm for attaching parts of the harness were discernible. They began 12 cm from the eastern tip of the yoke-pole and ran along its entire length at intervals of 40 – 45 cm (the mortises in each pair were spaced 4 cm apart). Near the mortises were fragments of bronze — probably traces of arc-shaped harness rings which had been set into the mortises.

Remains of yoke-heads were uncovered at the western and eastern sides of the yoke-pole, as well as in its center. These consisted of boards 4 cm thick, 8 cm wide, and with the preserved length of 25 – 30 cm. The position of the western yoke-head *in situ* suggests that the heads were attached to the yoke-pole by means of special incisions. The lower parts of the yoke-heads were not preserved. In the upper part of the western and central yoke-heads there was a cylindrical projection on which a bronze ferrule had been placed. On the eastern head, this projection had been broken off in antiquity but its traces were discernible in the upper part of the head. The entire surface of the yoke-pole and yoke-heads was coated with black lacquer, over which a geometrical pattern was drawn in white and red paint. Stylistically, fragments of this pattern are similar to that on the inside of the canopy of the chariot.

The two *wooden shafts* of the chariot were beneath the front yoke-pole lying parallel to each other in the N-S direction and 60 cm apart. They were very poorly preserved: their southern parts had been cut off by the robber trench; the preserved length was 95 – 100 cm. Traces of lacquer and a pattern rendered in red and white paints were visible on the surface of the shafts. Near the eastern shaft at a distance of 10 cm from it was a line of iron oval plates with holes on the shorter sides. Probably these had once been sewn onto the leather straps of the harness or the reins. Below this line of plates, 30 cm to the east, was an iron ring 6.5 cm in diameter.

The remains of the *wooden wheels* were located 1 m south of the shafts, on the stones of the third ceiling. The lower part of the western wheel was in the layer of pebbles and gravel underlying that ceiling. The wheels were spaced 2 m from one another, each consisting of a felloe, spokes and, possibly, a central disc into which the ends of the spokes had been inserted and in the center of which the iron hub of the axle had been placed. The wheels were considerably damaged by the pressure of the filling of the pit and ceilings. The wheels were 120 cm in diameter and had 22 spokes whose thickness was 3 – 4 cm. Remains of a number of iron shackles were traceable around the felloe of the western wheel. Tiny fragments of red and white paint were preserved on the felloe and spokes. The felloe and the adjoining parts of the spokes were painted red to a length of 10 – 12 cm, whereas the rest of the spokes was painted white. Practically nothing of the central parts of the wheels survives; nevertheless traces of red paint detected there suggest that the central disc of the wheel into which the spokes had been inserted was painted red.

Small iron hubs with two projections were uncovered directly outside of the wheels in the pebble layer which underlay the third ceiling. There were traces of wood on the outer side of the hubs. Large iron hubs with three projections on the outside of each were found under the wheels in the pebble layer of the third ceiling. These also bore traces of wood on the outer side, whereas in the center of the large and small hubs no traces of wood have been detected. The iron nails with which the hubs were fixed to the wooden cores of the wheels were preserved on the outer side of the larger hubs.

The rear yoke-pole. This is an arbitrary designation for this part of the chariot, since its real purpose still is not clear. A number of facts suggest, however, that it is not the axle of the chariot, viz. :

— the difference between the diameter of the pole and the inner diameter of the large iron hubs into which the axle must have been inserted;

— the separate position of the bronze axle-caps (as described below), which were usually put onto the ends of the axle and whose diameter differs from that of the rear pole (which furthermore had its own bronze caps).

In its shape and dimensions (7 cm in diameter and about 3 m long) the "rear yoke-pole" resembled the front pole. The largest part of the pole had been cut off by the northern robber trench; only its eastern and western ends were preserved. Bronze caps 5.5 cm in diameter and 7 cm long were placed on the tips of the pole. On the surface of the caps was a small cylindrical flange. Two arc-shaped iron fastenings were driven into the yoke-pole 3 − 4 cm from these caps. Possibly some elements of the harness (straps or ropes) once passed through these fastenings. The surface of the rear yoke-pole showed traces of lacquer and a pattern rendered in white paint.

Wooden elbow-rests of the seat. After the wheels had been removed, directly below them were found remains of some pinewood blocks which possibly were once the elbow-rests of the seat. These consisted of boards 3 − 4 cm thick, decayed and compressed by the powerful pressure of the filling of the pit. The elbow-rests presumably measured 25 × 50 cm. A painted geometrical design could be made out on their lacquered surface.

The body of the chariot. After the wheels had been cleared and removed, remains of a trellised frame of the chariot and bronze axle-terminals were uncovered in the space between the wheels and the remains of the chariot shafts. The remains of the frame consisted of several wooden laths, 2 − 3 cm thick, from which the trellised part of the body had been constructed. The laths were attached to each other with iron nails where they crossed. The northern and southern parts of the trellised frame of the chariot, as well as, perhaps, the entire seat had been destroyed by the robber trenches. North of the trellised frame, under its wooden laths, were two cylindrical bronze axle-caps at whose bases were circular flanges. The axle-caps were 10 cm long and 12 cm in diameter in their base and 5 cm in diameter on the top. In the lower part of the caps there were rectangular holes measuring 3 × 1.5 cm for insertion of the pins. In their upper part they had L-shaped projections probably to fix the straps of the harness. The iron pins, found lying between the caps, were 10 cm long with a rectangular section and a ring or eye on one end.

The absence of the wheel axle and the unusual position of the pair of axle-caps (beneath the trellised body) suggest that the chariot had been placed in the tomb in a disassembled and possibly incomplete state. It is also noteworthy that the presence of three yoke-heads implies the use of three horses in the team. However, as mentioned above, only the skull, two cervical vertebra and metapodials of a single horse were discovered. This horse was evidently laid into the tomb according to the principle "a part instead of the whole".

The construction of this chariot and its decorations have very close parallels among Chinese chariots of the Han period. The most comprehensive recent study of these chariots distinguishes a number features very similar to those of the chariot from Tsaraam (Wang and Li 1997). Like the Han examples, the Tsaraam chariot has a canopy consisting of a wooden framework covered by some organic material, four wooden posts supporting the canopy, a trellised seat and wooden "elbow-rests". The body of the chariot and the painting of the wheels are remarkably closely paralleled in a recently restored chariot from the burial of the famous Han general Huoqübing who fought against Xiongnu (Cooke 2000). The use of two yoke-shafts on the Tsaraam chariot suggests it was originally intended for a team of three horses, whereas the single central shaft typical of the Han chariots implies an even number of horses on the team.

Written sources often attest that chariots were among the gifts offered by the Han court to the first-rank Xiongnu nobility. Thus in 51 BCE *shanyü* Huhanye received along with other gifts a "chariot with a seat" (Taskin 1968 – 1973, Vol. 2, p. 35). Subsequently, as mentioned in the *Hanshu*, on more than one occasion the shanyü was given presents similar to those he received the first time (Ibid., pp. 36, 37, 51). During the epoch of Wang Mang (9 – 24 CE), who intended to divide the Xiongnu into separate nomadic bands and to set his own chief at the head of each, one of the Xiongnu deserters, the right *liyü-wang* Xian was awarded the title of *Xiao-shanyü* and, among other presents, given a "chariot with a seat and a chariot with a drum" (Ibid., p. 57). In 50 CE the shanyü of the southern Xiongnu, Bee (grandson of Huhanye ruling under the same name as his grandfather) was granted "a carriage with a seat and an umbrella of feathers and a team of four richly harnessed horses" (Ibid., p. 72). In 143 CE the southern shanyü Hulanzhuo in the throne hall of the imperial palace was granted along with other gifts "a chariot with a black top harnessed to a team of four horses, a chariot with a drum, a chariot with a seat"; the shanyü's wives were granted "two carriages decorated with gold and brocade and draught horses" (Ibid., p. 94).

It is thus quite possible that the chariot found in Tsaraam was also a gift from the Han court to one of the representatives of the Xiongnu elite. However, judging by the evidence from the *Hanshu* we might connect the chariot with a different event. In Wang Mang's reign, the above-mentioned Xiao-shanyü's son, Deng, who was then at the imperial court as a hostage, was executed because of his father's desertion to the northern Xiongnu and his brother's frequent raids on the borderlands. At the demand of the Xiongnu the corpses of Deng and some other noblemen executed together with him were returned to their homeland for burial. The bodies they were "laid into chariots" for transport (Ibid, p. 62). We may not rule out that later these chariots were buried in the tombs together with other funerary offerings.

It should be emphasized that in any case the records of chariots either as gifts or in connection with funerary ceremonies concern only the first-rank Xiongnu nobility, i. e. shanyüs, their wives, or sons. This fact is a further confirmation of the probability that Barrow No. 7 at Tsaraam is a burial of a representative of the Xiongnu elite, possibly a shanyü. Parts of chariots were found also in the Xiongnu royal tombs at Noin-Ula, but unfortunately the archaeological record from that site is insufficiently precise to permit reconstructing their details.

Objects Found in the Burial Chamber

The bulk of the burial goods were located in the corridors between the walls of the chamber, the frame, and the coffin. Several sets of harness (iron bits, cheek-pieces, harness buckles) and two burial dolls were found in the western external corridor. Iron hooks, found in the walls of the external chamber suggest that originally the bridle arrays had hung on such hooks and ended up on the floor of the chamber only after its deformation.

The doll found in the center of the western corridor (the northern of the two, to which we have given the provisional designation "Doll No. 1") was formed in the following fashion. The head of the doll was made of a human skull, which, judging by the baby teeth, was that of a 2 –4-year-old child. On the skull of the doll were six braids of black stiff hair, which probably had been attached to the skull using some kind of glue. Along with the braids on the skull were several turquoise beads. Two more braids were in front and in back of the skull and two braids in the waist region along with iron plaques. Wooden sticks covered with red lacquer formed the extremities of the doll.

The burial inventory of Doll No. 1 consisted of two separate iron belt plaques measuring 15×6 cm (the leather strap of the belt was preserved along with the plaques) and a wooden lacquered box placed behind the head of the doll next to which were four birchbark containers (possibly they were originally inside the box). The box was covered in red lacquer and along the edges decorated with a red lacquer design along a band of yellow lacquer. Under the box was a hair pin of some kind of organic material (possibly tortoise shell). Under the birchbark containers was a birch bark circle, on which was found a fragment of a Chinese bronze mirror. On one of the birchbark containers were unique drawings, showing the Xiongnu camp with carts and yurts placed on carriers and the profile of a person in a helmet — possibly a copy of a depiction on some coin.

In front and behind the skull of the doll were several iron buckles, a bit, cheek pieces and fragments of iron objects. Probably they were not connected to the inventory of the doll but originally had hung on the wall of the chamber and ended up on the floor after its deformation.

The other doll found in the western corridor, given the provisional designation "Doll No. 2", was formed in an analogous fashion. It lay one meter to the south of Doll No. 1. The core of Doll No. 2 was also a human skull which had completely disintegrated. Only small baby teeth were preserved, on the basis of which it was determined that the skull might have belonged to a child only a few months old. In the vicinity of the skull was a short braid of stiff black hair. The modeling of the upper extremities could not be determined. The lower extremities were made of thin iron plates, placed in a wooden sheath and covered with red lacquer.

In the vicinity of the neck of Doll No. 2 was a necklace of glass, turquoise, fluorite and large crystal beads. In the vicinity of the waist of the doll were two corroded iron plates measuring 20×11 cm lying on the leather strap of a belt, which was preserved only in fragments and in places had been covered with red lacquer. A loop of beads, consisting of now almost completely scattered glass beads, had been suspended from the belt. There were as well some heart-shaped fluorite and amber beads.

Below the waist of Doll No. 2 under the bottom beam of the outer chamber were remains of a crushed wooden lacquered vessel with geometric ornament. Inside the vessel were fragments of a bronze mirror, a piece of mica, two wooden combs and a collection of iron needles in a wooden holster. On the exterior of the vessel was a chinese inscription, which one Prof. Michèle Pirazzoli-t'Serstevens has reconstructed (see below).

The finds in the eastern external corridor were practically the same as those in the western one. Here there were also sets of bridles (consisting of iron bits, cheekpieces and buckles) and burial dolls. The burial doll which lay in the center of the eastern corridor to the south of the pieces of harness and which was given the provisional designation "Doll No. 3" was formed in the same way as the dolls in the western corridor. The skull of the doll had practically completely disintegrated. In the vicinity of the skull lay several braids of stiff black hair, on the ends of which were little turquoise, glass and amber beads. Lacquered wooden sticks formed the extremities. Near the neck on both right and left in the vicinity of the skull were remains of two round pendants of wood covered with lacquer which possibly had been formed from the walls of wooden lacquered cups.

At the waist of the doll were also two wide corroded iron buckles measuring 19×12 cm. Behind the head of the doll were remains of a wooden object (possibly a box), on which was a small birchbark container and a large fragment of a Chinese mirror.

The fourth doll apparently had been removed by the robbers; only its feet remained.

But for two bronze coffin handles, found near its southwestern and southeastern corners, there were practically no artifacts in the western internal corridor:

The finds in the eastern internal corridor were confined to its southern part, since robbers had destroyed the northern part. These finds included sets of harnesses — iron bits, cheekplates, bronze harness-plates, bronze plaques with depictions of a running goat; silver chest medallions with images of mountain goats — arrowheads, a lacquered wooden staff, a lacquered wooden cup and a lacquered wooden quiver with iron arrowheads.

To a substantial degree, the entrance of a looter had destroyed the northern external corridor, but fragments of ceramics and lacquered wooden objects were found there. Nothing was found in the southern external corridor, but in that corridor, attached to the interior wall of the external chamber, were remains of a woolen carpet which had been destroyed by the shifting of the beams of the chamber. In the southern internal corridor were a flat iron ring and two iron fasteners.

The northern section of the coffin had been destroyed by robbers, but jade plaques of armor and a jade diadem were found there. In the preserved southern section of the coffin were the remains of a covering of some organic material (felt or compressed fur), two iron buckles covered in gold foil and depicting a satyr, and two gold necklaces. Next to the remains of a ritual sword were three gold objects decorated with turquoise inlay. Two of them may be finials; the third, with the image of a mountain goat is a small flask.

The Date of the Complex

We consider the central barrow and sacrificial burials as a unique burial complex, put in place during one funerary ceremony, in one day or a maximum of several days. The basis for determining the chronology of the complex is follow.

The inscription on the lacquered box found near Doll No. 2. Prof. Michèle Pirazzoli-t'Serstevens has reconstructed this inscription like this:

"〔乘輿〕〔…〕〔…〕〔…〕年考工工賞造畬夫臣康掾臣安主右丞臣〔…〕〔…〕令臣〔…〕護工卒史臣尊省。"

The translation:

"〔Fit for use by the emperor〕made in the〔?〕year of the〔? era〕by the master artisan of the Kaogong imperial workshop Shang. Managed by the workshop overseer your servant Kang, the lacquer bureau head your servant An. Inspected by the Assistant Director of the Right your servant〔?〕, the Director your servant〔?〕and the Commandery Clerk for Workshop Inspection your servant Zun."

She concluded that the inscription dates no earlier than 36 – 27 BCE and might date between 8 BCE and 4 CE (that is, immediately before the Wang Mang period). However, she cautions that these dates are at best a *terminus ante quem*, since the box with the inscription might have been placed in the grave long after it had been manufactured (Pirazzoli-t'Serstevens, 2007). We can add that fragments of a lacquered cup with the same design as in Noin-Ula were found in the northern corridor in the central Barrow No. 7 and in the Sacrificial Burial No. 16. It is very probable that the fragments can be dated from the same period — from the end of the 1st century BCE to the beginning of the 1st century CE (cf. Louis 2007).

Chinese mirrors. On the basis of modern classification (Zhongguo tongjing 1997) all four mirrors whose

吐鲁番学研究——第三届吐鲁番学暨欧亚游牧民族的起源与迁徙国际学术研讨会论文集

fragments were found in the central barrow in the burial pit and amid grave goods of the dolls can be dated between the end of the Western Han and early Eastern Han periods, that is not earlier than the 1st century BCE.

14C dates

Burial	Sample number	Original data, BP	1 sigma	2 sigma
Barrow No. 7 Logs of the fence in entry to the burial pit	Le – 5930	2120 ± 30	182BCE – 74BCE	192BCE – 52BCE
Barrow No. 7 Charcoal between outside chamber and a wall of the burial pit	Le – 7510	2130 ± 20	200BCE – 135BCE	350BCE – 50 BCE
Barrow No. 7 The chariot	Le – 7680	1925 ± 40	50CE – 130CE	40BCE – 180CE
Sacrificial Burial No. 12, the coffin	Le – 5917	2050 ± 25	56BCE – 2CE	110BCE – 14CE
No. 13, the coffin	Le – 5918	1945 ± 25	24CE – 116CE	18CE – 122CE
No. 14, the coffin	Le – 5919	1900 ± 25	82CE – 130CE	70CE – 210CE
No. 10. the coffin	Le – 5920	2070 ± 40	97BCE – 41BCE	153BCE – 3BCE
No. 15. the coffin	Le – 5921	1990 ± 30	2CE – 66CE	38BCE – 66CE

Eight ^{14}C dates were obtained in laboratory of the Institute of the History of Material Culture. While the dates fall within a broad range, calibration of values by the program OxCal suggests (with a probability 95.4%) that the burials were made in approximately the period period 30 – 120 CE.

In sum then, we know that the complex is no earlier than about the last third of the first century BCE and very likely is to be dated in the first half of the first century CE.

Conclusion

The application of modern archaeological techniques to the excavation of Complex No. 7 in the Tsaraam Valley has yielded entirely new information about Xiongnu mortuary practice, the construction of such barrows, and Xiongnu social structure. New examples of Xiongnu art and material culture were discovered. Yet much needs to be done to complete the study. Conservation of the finds is the first priority. Study of the material must include DNA and morphological analysis of the skeletal remains and faunal and botanical samples and component analysis of ceramic and metal objects and organic materials such as the birchbark containers, lacquerware, and textiles. The result should provide impressive new archaeological evidence concerning the organization, chronology, and regional interaction of the Xiongnu nomadic polity. This research will complement on-going projects in Kazakhstan, Mongolia, Inner Mongolia and Xinjiang and will

· 134 ·

contribute to the developing theories on complex organization among nomadic groups.

Acknowledgements

The authors are especially grateful to Dr. Maria Kolosova of the State Hermitage Museum for her classification of the wood samples and to Prof. Michèle Pirazzoli-t'Serstevens of The Sorbonne for her important observations regarding the Chinese inscription.

Material in this article has appeared in various forms both in Russian and in English on Dr. Miniaev's website: http://xiongnu.atspace.com.

References

Chou 2000

Chou Ju-hsi. *Circles of Reflection: The Carter Collection of Chinese Bronze Mirrors.* Cleveland: The Cleveland Museum of Art, 2000.

Cheng and Han 2002

Cheng Linquan and Han Guohe. *Chang'an Han jing* (Chang'an Han Mirrors). Xi'an: Shaanxi renming chubanshe, 2002.

Cooke 2000

Bill Cooke. *Imperial China: The Art of the Horse in Chinese History.* Louisville, Ky. : Harmony House, 2000.

Huns 2005

Les Huns. Bruxelles: Europalia International, 2005.

Lai 2006

Guolong Lai. "The Date of the TLV Mirrors from the Xiongnu Tombs." *The Silk Road* 4/1 (2006): 36 – 44.

Louis 2007

François Louis. "Han Lacquerware and the Wine Cups of Noin Ula." *The Silk Road* 4/2 (2007): 48 – 53.

Miniaev 1998

Sergei S. Miniaev. *Dyrestuiskii mogil'nik* (Derestui cemetery). Arkheologicheskie pamiatniki siunnu, vyp. 3. Saint-Petersburg, Evropeiskii dom, 1998.

Miniaev and Sakharovskaia 2002

Sergei S. Miniaev and Lidiia M. Sakharovskaia. "Soprovoditel'nye zakhoroneniia 'tsarskogo' kompleksa No. 7 v mogol'nike Tsaram." *Arkheologicheskie vesti* (St. Petersburg) 9 (2002): 86 – 118.

In English as: "Sacrifice burials of the royal complex no. 7 at the Tsaraam cemetery" < http://xiongnu.atspace.com/Sacrif. htm, 2006 > , accessed October 23, 2007.

Miniaev and Sakharovskaia 2006a

Sergei S. Miniaev and Lidiia M. Sakharovskaia. "Investigation of a Xiongnu Royal Complex in the Tsaraam Valley." *The Silk Road* 4/1 (2006): 47 – 51.

Miniaev and Sakharovskaia 2006b

Sergei S. Miniaev and Lidiia M. Sakharovskaia. "Khan'skoe zerkalo iz mogil'nika Tsaram" (A Han Mirror from the Tsaraam Cemetery). *Papers of the Institute of the History of Material Culture* (St. Petersburg) 1 (2006).

Minyaev and Sakharovskaia 2007

Sergei S. Minyaev and Lidiia M. Sakharovskaia. "Khan'skaia kolesnitsa iz mogil'nika Tsaram" (A Han Chariot from the Tsaraam Cemetery). *Arkheologicheskie vesti* (St. Petersburg) 13(2007).

Pirazzoli-t'Serstevens 2007.

M. Pirazzoli-t'Serstevens. CHINESE INSCRIPTION FROM XIONGNU ELITE BARROW IN TSARAAM CEMETERY. The Silk Road, Vol.5, No. 1, summer 2007.

Tal'ko-Gryntsevich 1999

Iurii D. Tal'ko-Gryntsevich. *Materialy k paleoetnologii Zabaikal'ia.* (Materials on the Paleoethnography of the Trans-Baikal.) Arkheologicheskie pamiatniki siunnu, vyp. 4. St. Petersburg: Fond Aziatika, 1999)

Taskin 1968－1973

V. S. Taskin, tr. and ed. *Materialy po istorii siunnu.* (*Po kitaiskim istochnikam*), 2 Vols. Moscow: Nauka, 1968－1973.

Wang and Li 1997

Wang Zhenduo and Li Qiang. *Dong Han che zhi fu yuan yan jiu* (Reconstruction and study of the Eastern Han vehicle). Beijing: Kexue chubanshe, 1997.

Zhongguo tongjing 1997

Zhongguo tongjing tu dian (Encyclopaedia of Chinese Mirrors). Comp. by Kong Xiangxing and Liu Yiman. Beijing: Wenwu chubanshe, 1992 (reprinted 1997).

秦汉时期中原与中亚地区单兵制式化装备比较研究试析

李　韬

意大利那不勒斯东方大学硕士研究生

一、历史背景与释题

公元前4世纪始,地中海东岸地区进入希腊化时代(Hellenistic Period)。[①] 色诺芬长征[②]以后,以希腊城邦为代表的古典文明与阿契美尼德王朝为代表的两河文明之间的军事接触日趋频繁。尤其是随后的亚历山大东征,有史以来第一次彻底地打破了东地中海与中东地区的军事平衡,使历史的天平向西方倾斜,[③]让西方的军事存在,如此深入的进入到亚洲腹地。[④]

在东亚,几乎与此同时,秦惠文王继承商鞅的政策,进一步深化改革,正式确立了以"农战"[⑤]为基础,远交近攻为方略的一统东亚的军政方针。[⑥]

东西方的势力角逐此起彼伏,中间的政治真空地带,不断被填补;[⑦]军事接触成为有史以来联系东西方最直接、最迅速的传播方式。战争在一系列交流中拔得了头筹。

公元前2世纪,环地中海地带的罗马异军突起,通过两百多年的兼并战争,横扫中东希腊化王国的残余,在美索不达米亚平原与波斯帝国的第二任继承者——帕提亚王朝展开了旷日持久的拉锯战。[⑧]

与此同时,蒙古高原集游牧势力于一身的匈奴,首次使土著农耕的中原王朝——汉帝国宿夜枕戈待旦。出于地缘战略的原因,向西寻找联盟,壮大自己,牵制敌方,成为汉匈战争中的基本信条。作为矛盾双方——远东地区的游牧和土著政权,开始多次翻越帕米尔高原,进入希腊化文明早已滥觞的中亚腹地。由此蔓延的兵燹,引起了敌对方军事技术的竞争,使兵器装备技术得以迅速发展。当然,随着岁月的流

[①] 西方古典学界对于希腊化的下限,有着不同的看法。他们以环地中海文明演进的谱系为基准,确定至亚历山大东征结束,希腊化进程基本完成。之后的文化主流,应该从亚平宁半岛的罗马文明说起。至于希腊化波及的东方地区(近东、中东和远东),则是东方学研究的议题。这类学说确有相当的客观性,因为从地中海沿岸乃至中亚腹地的希腊化过程相当复杂,学者很难仅仅通过出土的艺术品,就断定土著文化受到希腊化的洗礼。即使有所浸淫,其尺度也很难把握。更何况在年代学上,帕米尔以东的诸多典型发现早已进入东汉纪年,而古大陆另一端的环地中海地区,罗马文明则占有统治地位。因此,本文所指的"希腊化",是东方学范畴内的希腊化,而非古典学意义上的。

[②] 色诺芬著,刘家和译:《长征记》,《汉译世界学术名著丛书》,商务印书馆,1983年。

[③] 阿利安著,李活译:《亚历山大远征记》,《汉译世界学术名著丛书》,商务印书馆,1985年。

[④] *From Samarkhand to Sardis, a new approach to the Seleucid Empire*, written by Susan Sherwin-White & Amélie Kurht, 1993, published by Duckworth.

[⑤] "国之所以兴者,农战也",参见《商君书·农战第三》,《商君书/韩非子》,张觉注释、点校,巴蜀书社,1990年。

[⑥] "……变法修行,内务耕稼,外劝死战之赏罚……"《史记·秦本纪》,又见《史记·商君列传》,司马迁著,中华书局,1982年。

[⑦] 匈奴—乌孙集团西逐月氏—塞种集团;大月氏入主河中,南斥大夏,西拒安息,草创贵霜等一系列民族迁徙运动,就是这一例证的最好说明。语见《史记·大宛列传》、《史记·匈奴列传》等,出处同上。

[⑧] 阿庇安著,谢德风译:《罗马史》,《汉译世界学术名著丛书》,商务印书馆,1979年。

逝,只有极少数以出土物和二维或三维图像的形式得以保存。如何系统的归纳、认识、比较公元前后共六百年内的冷兵器,是本文论述的核心。

首先,可以肯定的是,秦汉时期,[①]即公元前 3 世纪至公元 3 世纪,[②]中原与中亚的交流逐步进入以官方交流为主的纪年时代。这为跨区域横向比较,提供了基本的前提。

其次,本文所指的中原,从资料来源上看,以中原王朝关陇腹地为中心,涉及黄河、长江下游地区。而中亚的概念,是中原王朝西部塞防工事以西,包括政治势力相重叠的新疆地区,直至帕提亚(安息)王朝的传统东境与希腊化王国及游牧政权势力胶着的地带。在现代地理学上,主要包括东起关中,西至河中,北及南西伯利亚,南达印度河上游地区。

在以上的时空框架下,论述的核心议题是这一时期和区域内的古代兵器。笔者结合以往研究成果认为,以考古器物类型学为基础方法论,从单兵制式化装备入手,可以提纲挈领的将古代兵器研究的基本框架局部的构建起来。再辅以实物资料,进行纵向梳理;待形成谱系后,与同期同材质的进行横向比较,大致可以摸清兵器——这一东西交流最快最直接的文化因素的演进与流变。

这里有必要先澄清“单兵制式化装备”这一复合概念。“单兵”顾名思义,一名普通的战士或士兵。根据冷兵器时代战争的需求和年代序列,陆路只有步兵、车兵和骑兵。车兵由于必须多人协同操作作为武器运载工具的马车,才能发挥集体战术效应,因此不在本文论述之列。此外,对于必须多人协力使用重型攻防器械的围城工程步兵群,也不符合笔者论述的标准。可知,本文主要论述的是农业和游牧背景下的步兵和骑兵。[③] 这两者,不论任何一方中的一员都能在一般情况下,独立作战、产生基本战术效应;更能通过协同训练,产生战役效能。当然,前者中还能细化出专业的投射部队,后文将详述。

“制式化装备”一词出现的比较晚,起码在工业革命以后。根据制式化标准的“权威”——北大西洋公约组织的解释,[④]制式化装备是按照一定标准,系统化生产的武器装备。其概念、学说、程序与构想的发展与执行,在运作、程序化、材料、技术和管理领域,需实现必要的兼容性、交互性、共属性、度量性和标志性的标准,最终达到协同作战的目标。因此,“单兵制式化装备”是为一名普通士兵所列装的,按照一定标准、系统化生产的武器装备,包括攻防与基本后勤保障在内的装备;在技术、材料的工业化生产、管理中,它们具有兼容性、交互性、共属性和标志性的特点;可为一名普通士兵独立使用,并产生相关的军事效能,而非多人合作或集团共用的攻防、后勤保障装备。其实戚继光[⑤]在明中叶已做了总结:他认为制式化装备的终极目标,是要通过协同作战,实现最佳的战役效能。[⑥] 因此,兵器装备一定得实现以上北约遵循

---

① 本文所指的秦,上溯至战国晚期的秦国。

② 公元 3 世纪,随着东方汉帝国以及西方罗马帝国的分崩离析,欧亚大陆开始进入新一轮的民族迁徙与融合,军事的竞争导致了新型单兵装备、军工体系的巨变,与此前完全不同。限于篇幅与经历,暂不列入本文讨论内容。本文的下限选择在公元 3 世纪。宏观上,东西方——汉与罗马帝国的分崩离析,以及新一轮的民族大迁徙,在客观上,一则破坏了原有的军工体系;二来,由于敌对方的转化(蛮族入主欧陆,五胡逐鹿中原,骑兵在战争中的地位得到第二次提升),使单兵制式化装备发生了质的转变。所以,此后的中古或中世纪时代的单兵制式化装备不在本文的讨论范围内。

③ 不包括受南亚传统影响的战象及象兵。

④ 详见《北大西洋公约组织制式标准协议》,网页链接:http://www.nato.int/docu/standard.htm。

⑤ 戚继光(1528~1588 年),字元敬,号南塘,晚号孟诸,登州人。他总结冷兵器时代经验,结合实战,吸取火器之长,改革了日渐凋敝的明军工、军事系统。从军事史,特别是军事装备发展史角度看,他是东亚冷兵器时代制式化装备研究的集大成者。其指导思想,直至二战时期仍为广大抗日武装所继承、运用。

⑥ 戚子云:“夫天有五行,以应五兵,长短相救,势所必至。但五兵种类既繁,人力有限,第适于用足矣,不必求奇。”参见《纪效新书》(十四卷本),第 47 页,戚继光著,高扬文、陶琦主编,范中义、张德信副主编,范中义校释,中华书局,2001 年。

的标准,而"独门"兵器,不能用于部队的列装和训练。①

从考古器物类型学角度看,单兵制式化装备亦是一种器物组合。这是符合考古发掘的基本情况的。上迄青铜时代,兵器就大量埋藏于中原和中亚的墓葬之中。更有甚者如秦始皇陵、汉景帝阳陵、徐州汉楚王陵等,还有大量战役规模的列俑出土。在中亚的城邦中,兵器装备的二维或三维图像,是纪念性建筑雕塑中的主要题材之一。因此使古代单兵制式化装备的考古类型学研究成为可能。

二、中原地区秦汉时期的单兵制式化装备

古代兵器的分类往往主旨类似,但研究的视角不同。如上所述,本文研究的兵器所属的兵种,只是陆军的步兵和骑兵。

其次,按照正战②的一般序列或对垒接战顺序,每一兵种下,又可分为投射部队和格斗部队。其中每一种部队所列装的单兵制式化装备,又可分为被动防御型和主动攻击型。

这里有必要先说明一下兵器的"短长"的问题。"短长"必须结合特殊的语境。比如《国殇》中描述战国晚期诸侯兼并战中"矢交坠兮士争先,车错毂兮短兵接"。杨泓先生认为根据接战顺序,"矢交坠"说明敌对一方先使用投射兵器进行集群火力压制,这是所谓"长兵",即长远距离投射的兵器;紧接着,敌对双方战车错毂,作为车战格斗用的戈、戟,首先进出火花——此所谓"短兵"。又如,戚继光兵书强调"短长相救",根据上下文,有三种解释:③一种语境下,"长"是投射兵器,"短"是格斗兵器;此外,"长"或专指长杆兵器,"短"即短柄兵器;还有,从技战术运用上,"长"又可作"短兵长用","短"又可作"长兵短用"。

以上观点都有特定的语境,由此产生的分类自然不同。因此,兵器"短长"分类的争论,似不必再做纠缠。

(一)步兵单兵制式化装备

1. 投射部队单兵制式化装备

1)防御型:铠甲

铠甲的分类以材质为准。据文献和考古发现可知,甲本来是动物皮革材质制成的。④ 虽然,秦汉之际皮革制和金属制甲胄有相当长的交错并用时期,但总趋势是随着钢铁攻击型兵器的列装、普及,皮甲不得不迅速退出疆场,取而代之的是铁铠。

秦陵兵马俑坑的跪射俑,为我们提供了公元前3世纪中原青铜时代末期模型皮甲的基本形态。

根据以往的研究,跪射俑所着甲衣,属"第二类二型"(图一)。⑤ 其特点是,甲衣"由甲片编缀而成,身

---

① 戚子云:"马上为力轻捷锋芒,他如斧、钺、锤、挝、大刀、钩镰之类,胆大艺精,能独马入阵者,间或有之,不可以教队兵,不可以当堂堂大敌。"又曰:"以上(制式化兵器)之外,又有飞标、毒弩、枪、刀、戈、戟等名不一,皆可俾素习精熟者间或用之,不可以齐大队,为堂堂阵也。"这两段话的宗旨,都是在教导将士,战争不是武打群殴,狭义上就是敌对集团间的战役决斗。非制式化装备,只能由个别"艺高人胆大"的将官使用,普通部队必须使用制式化装备,发挥协同作战效能。后者才是决定胜负的关键!参见《练兵实纪》,第305、309页,戚继光著、高扬文、陶琦主编,范中义、张德信副主编,邱心田校释,中华书局,2001年。
② 正战一词来源于《孙子兵法》的"奇正",本文指战役中,两军对垒集团野战。有关"奇正"的阐释,详见《兵以诈立——我读〈孙子〉》,第177~191页,李零著,中华书局,2006年。
③ 参见《手足篇第三》:"长器短用解"和《手足篇第四》:"短器长用解",《纪效新书》(十四卷本),第48、50、75页。
④ "函人为甲",参见《周礼正义》,第3285~3291页,孙诒让撰,中华书局,1987年。
⑤ 参见《中国古代的甲胄》,《中国古兵器论丛》,杨泓著,第25页,中国社会科学出版社,2007年。

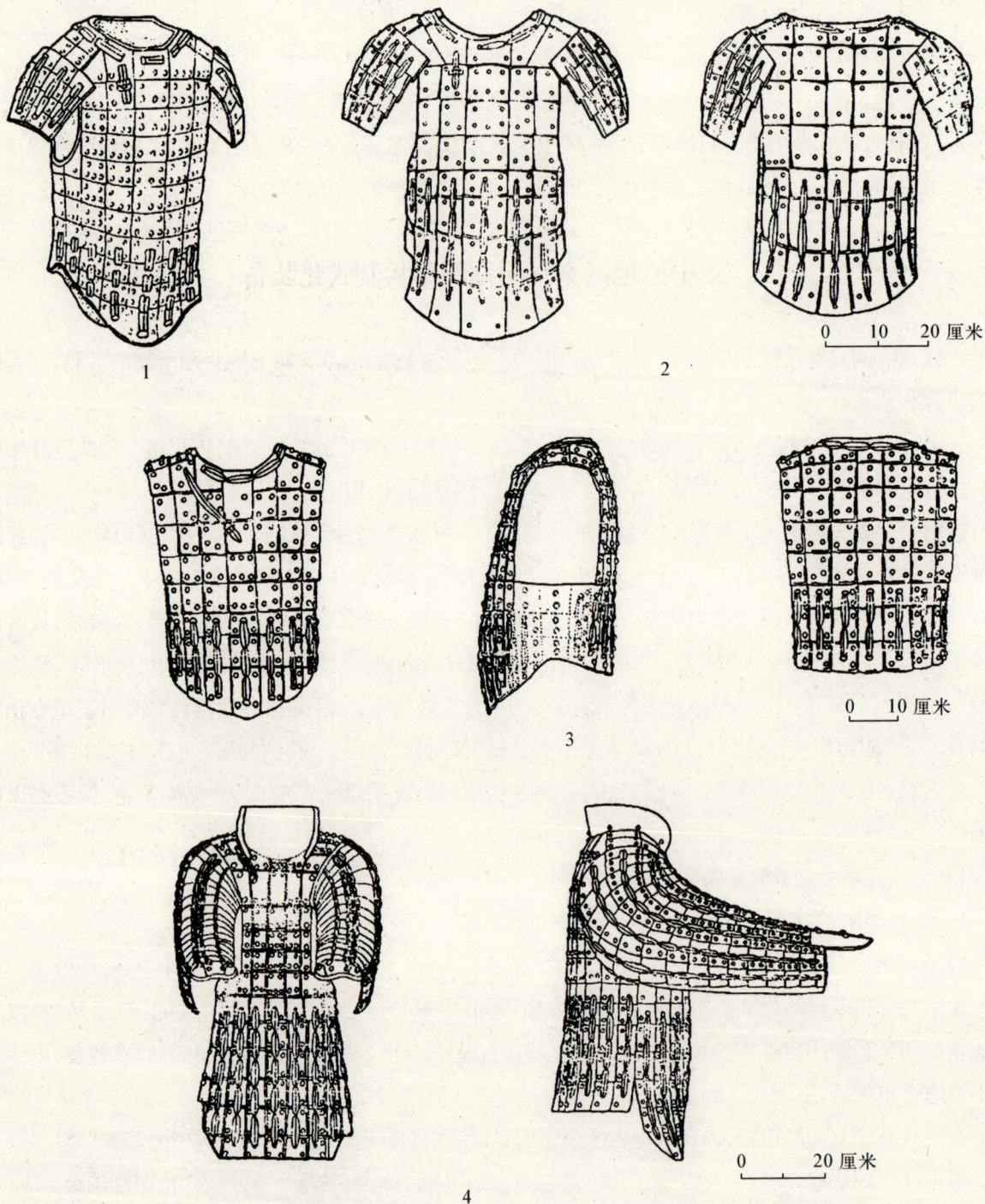

图一　1为秦俑甲胄"第二类第一型";2为"第二类第二型"(摘自《秦始皇陵兵马俑一号坑》)

甲较'一型'稍长,两肩有披膊,披膊也是由甲片遍缀而成"。这种穿甲衣的跪射俑使用的攻击型兵器,很可能是弩。

汉祚以降的发现,主要来自汉景帝阳陵的从葬坑兵俑群。从葬坑中出土的荷弩兵俑与咸阳杨家湾出土的基本一致。由于形制与格斗部队的铠甲类似,所以详见后文。

2)攻击型:弓、箭、弩、韬、箙及附属装备

由于埋藏条件的限制,中原秦汉时期弓的实物并不多见。不过,根据《考工记》记载,弓的制作是非

常复杂的,需要一整套分工细密、流程繁复、协同组装的工业化生产系统。① 从秦俑坑、汉汝阴侯墓、马王堆三号墓(图二)、胡常五号墓及甲渠候官遗址的弓箭出土情况看,②复合反曲是东亚地区弓的一大特点。复合,是指整张弓分别由弣、渊(肩)、萧、弭、弰、弦等三大部分组成;反曲是指松弛状态下,整张弓会向射击方向反向弯曲。这主要与渊、萧反面粘附的角、筋有关。弭、弰部分另行制作,再插附于弓体——萧的末段。从长度上看,基本在 130 ~ 140 cm 左右。弓弦几乎从未在中原地区发现过,但结合文献与东南、西北地区的发现,我们知道它既可由动植物纤维,也可由动物的皮革编织而成。后者在干燥的环境下,弹性极强。

箭包括镞(刃、箭头)、葛(箭杆)、羽、栝(叉、比)四部分。镞的材质按时代顺序,主要有青铜、铜铁和铁制三种。青铜镞在秦汉时期广泛使用,铁镞发展势头迅猛。不过根据考古发现,前者可能多为弩箭镞。中原地区青铜镞的形制主要为双翼、三翼、三棱三种。这三种镞都带铤,然后再插入箭杆端部,最后用纤维缠绕、鬃胶。前两者的后锋相当尖锐,一旦射入体内,很难拔除。如果前锋夹角偏大,从创伤学角度上看,会造成致命一击。至于三棱锥体型,出现在东周,汉代一直沿用。古称"三镰"、"羊头"(图三)。其正截面是等边三角形,三棱刃弧聚而向前成为锐锋。有的后部为铁铤,装配方式与前两者相同。这种类型,在汉代也有铁制。此外,汉代还有圆柱型四棱铁镞和三叉状铁镞。以前者数量居多,其箭镞长度在 1.4 ~ 3 cm 左右,后附铤部残长可至 37 cm。这种铤长于镞的定制,为历代军工系统所恪守,其作用在于提高穿透力。③ 此外,还有一些异形箭镞,如秦铜车马上的蘑菇形镞。以往的研究中,学者认为它是一种"教练弹"。但这一推测又无法与铜车马的性质相符。皇帝巡行,一级警备,驭手为何装备"教练弹"? 同样的形制的骨箭镞,其实一直沿用至清代。杨福喜先生曾提醒笔者,根据满清文献记载,这种冬菇形箭镞叫"墩子",一般是皇帝出行时所用,目的是对那些冒犯仪轨,擅自瞻观的个别百姓以非杀伤性惩戒,作用好似当今的防暴橡皮子弹。④

至于箭杆,其长度多在 57 ~ 87 cm 之间。但笔者以为,杆的长度是与弓弩的长度及拉力有关的。一

图二 马王堆三号墓竹木弓
(摘自《古代兵器通论》)

---

① "弓人为弓"、"矢人为矢",参见《周礼正义》第3531、3357 ~ 3367 页。
② 参见《古代兵器通论》,杨泓著,第 154 ~ 158 页,紫禁城出版社,2005 年。长江下游地区弓的统计表(包括单体和复合弓),参见《弓和弩》,《中国古兵器论丛》,杨泓著,第 278 页。
③ 《周礼·考工记·冶氏》:"冶氏为杀氏,刃寸长,铤十之。"戚继光根据治军经验,认为"矢必镞重……镞必用透甲锤点钢,射则不卷,中入最深,若凿头(刃口呈平线形)、燕尾(分叉形)、牛奶(呈圆头形)之类,皆不能入坚,又入不深也";"倭虏之箭,射皆不远,盖箭重故也。箭重故中人深重。倭箭镞后铁信长七八寸、一尺者,所以入人深也"(《纪效新书》(十四卷本),第 60、134 页)。又认为"镞干长,深入竹木三寸、五寸尤佳";"镞信要长,射入则深"(参见《练兵实纪》,第 302 页)。据承袭弓箭制作传统的"聚元号"杨福喜先生说,工匠不循此制,按清律当斩!
④ 无独有偶,长沙浏城桥一号墓中与车马器同出的还有十三枚平头圆柱状铜镞。杨泓先生认为是猎镞,笔者以为亦不排除警示的作用。具体结论,有待新发现验证。参见湖北省博物馆《长沙浏城桥一号墓》,《考古学报》1972 年第 1 期;又见《弓和弩》,《中国古兵器论丛》,第 276 页。

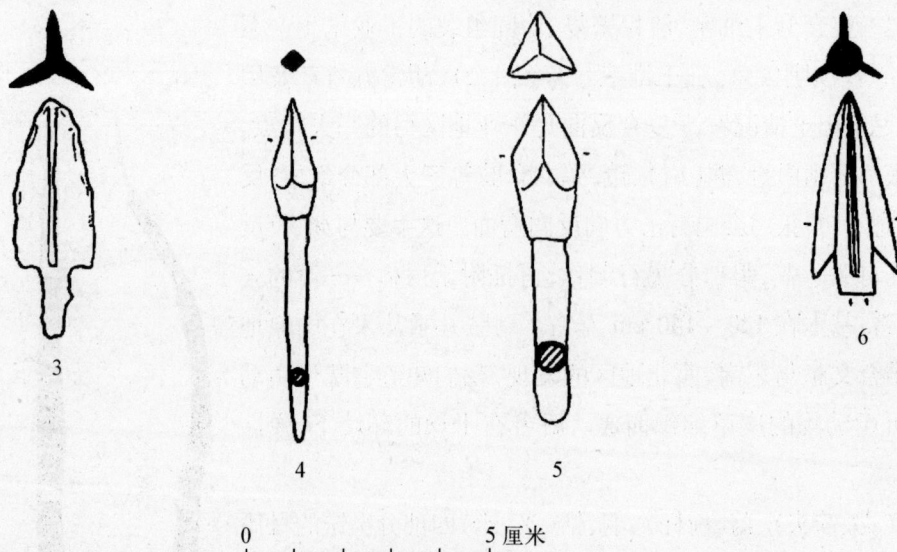

图三　汉镞(摘自《汉长安城武库》)

般情况下,弓长而弦劲者,当然得配长箭。至于箭杆的材质,目前尚未有学者公布这方面的理化分析结果。不过,根据杨福喜先生的经验,箭杆的原材料一般得是纤维笔直成束的植物茎部。满清兵部曾通令使用一种叫"六墩木"的植物茎部做箭杆。据说,这种植物多生于燕山北麓半干旱的山前地带。笔者以为,从形制上看,很可能是柽柳一类。①

接下来谈谈中国特色的弩。这么说,是因为弩作为人类重要发明之一,并非为中国人独有,同期地中海地区的希腊先民也有类似的单兵——腹弓。②

中国弩主要由弩弓、弩臂两大部分组成。前者的结构与复合反曲弓相似,后者的核心技术则是由牙、望山、枢、悬刀组成的弩机(图四)。

有意思的是,东周弩机一出现,形制就相当完善,至汉末都未发生本质上的变化。其工作原理均是发射前张弓,将弦钩在牙上;然后再将箭放入矢道;通过望山瞄准目标;抠动悬刀,松开钩心,望山前倾、牙下落,弩弦释放,绷出弩箭。

弩机多为青铜制,长度一般在 9.5~14.4 cm 间。汉代的弩机增加了郭和望山刻度。

与其他部分相较,汉弩的弩臂与弓的长度比例为 1:2.4,郭与弩臂的长度比例为 1:4.5~5.8。

汉弩的强度单位是"石"。据居延汉简的记载,戍卒弩的强力以三、五、六石居多,也有四、七、八石的。至于京畿卫戍部队的强力更大,从八石直至卅石。弩的强力是以射程为目标的,三到六石的弩,射程约 167~278 米。

弩的优势在于易普及、潜伏久、精度高、射程远、范围广、威力大。在团队协同的前提下,"弦无绝响,

---

① 箭杆的粗细有一定原则,戚继光认为应是"……粗木杆,有力"(参见《练兵实纪》,第 302 页);"但杆粗体重,发去不远。长兵短用,原不在远;远则不中,中亦不深,所谓强弩之末,不能穿鲁缟是已。大端倭虏矢皆重,弓皆劲,发皆不远,不轻发,发必中人,中者必毙,故人畏之"(《纪效新书》(十四卷本),第 60 页)。又汉代工官亦监造箭杆,参见甘肃居延考古队《居延汉代遗址的发掘和新出土的简册文物》,《文物》1978 年第 1 期。

② 参见 Les Armes des Romains, Michel FEUGERE, Editions Enrrance,1993. 二者主要原理都是通过机械反弹力发射弩箭。前者是通过手拉脚踹上弦,用弓弦弹弩箭;后者是通过腹部向下挤压机槽,用弓弦推动机槽,机槽甩出弩箭。笔者揣测,后者与欧洲旧石器时代的标枪投掷助推器传统,在物理学上有一定联系。不过,这一特例独行的投射兵器并未被推广且继承下来。也许与中西方不同的兵制和军工体系有关。

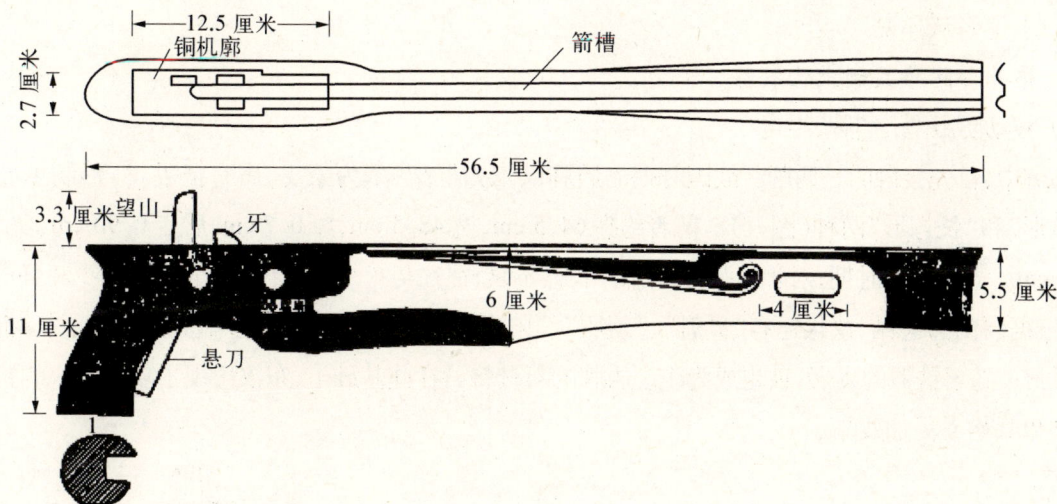

图四　汉弩结构示意图(摘自《中国古兵器论丛》)

弩无绝发",可以给敌方集团以持续性毁灭打击。

但弩的生产具有工艺相对复杂的特点,没有完善的国家军工监造系统,弩不可能大批生产、列装部队,并最终形成战斗力。汉、匈征战数百年,游牧民族一直没有掌握、推广这一技术。① 这也是匈奴往往不愿意和汉军正面交锋的原因。

弓弩要形成持续杀伤力,与单兵箭支携带的数量有关。所以,就离不开箙——箭囊。箭箙的材料主要为轻便的木制或皮制。前者精美的,还常常髹漆,但这主要还是礼仪、冥葬所用。部队列装的,估计主要还是后者。② 战国时期魏国的"特种兵"——武卒,据说每人要求携带五十支弩箭,③想必这是极限。

至于承弓的韬(又称韝),至今尚未在中原地区发现秦汉时期的遗物,只有个别图像遗存,④有待进一步发现。

最后一提的是套在拇指上开弓的扳指,即古文献中所说"韘"。这种器物早在《诗经》⑤时代就已出现,形态最简单的就是内径、宽度与拇指下半截相同的大号戒指。复杂的,还会在一边做出一个回钩,帮助控弦。韘的材质主要有骨制和玉石制两种。根据满清仪轨,后者是所谓"文扳指",礼仪、玩赏用的;前者才是开弓拉箭的"兵器"。不过,根据笔者的经验,不论"文武",这种戒指型扳指,用起来都不太舒服。⑥而传统的日式拇指开弓皮套却十分舒适耐用。吐鲁番胜金店出土的韘,充分的证明了其原形为皮质的特征。⑦ 还有一个特例是《仪礼·大射礼》中的"极",注家因文中作"朱极三",认为它是红色的套三指(可能是食指、中指和无名指)的引弓指套。但"极"字从"木",似不是皮革制品。孙机先生认为有待进一步

---

① 中国北方和蒙古的匈奴墓葬中曾零星出土过弩机,但学者认为其性质为收藏品。

② 参见《汉代物质文化资料图说》,第139页,孙机著,文物出版社,1991年。

③ 《荀子集解·议兵》,中华书局,2007年。

④ 参见《汉代物质文化资料图说》,第213页。又见于西安理工大学西汉壁画墓。该壁画墓中有一射手,左手执弓,右手持猎获的飞禽,左胯有黑色矩形物,笔者怀疑不是箙,便是韬。参见《西安理工大学西汉壁画墓发掘简报》,《文物》2006年5期,第7~44页。

⑤ 《诗经·卫风·芄兰》中有"童子配韘"。

⑥ 扳指明代称"指机"。戚子云:"……近世做者无式,眼孔皆圆,人指却扁,孔圆必塞以楮布,外则杜血指黑,里则兜弦致扫食指根之皮。宜将孔做前后稍长,横入指中转正,则骨扁机长,不复打落,而眼中圆活,不磨指节,不逼矢扫皮"(参见《练兵实纪》,第302页)。

⑦ 胜金店墓葬出土的"韘",为皮革鞣制而成,长度与粗细刚好与拇指匹配,背面开有一隙,两侧各有一排孔眼,内穿一根皮条,用于绑缚固定。

发现证明,笔者从孙说。

2. 格斗部队单兵制式化装备

1) 被动防卫型:盾牌、甲胄

防御中,首先接触的是盾牌。战国时期的盾牌以木为框架、革为蒙皮,后有把手。[①] 形制主要有"对称双弧形"和"长方形"两种(图五)。前者约高 64.5 cm,宽 48.5 cm,厚 0.7 cm,后者高 90 cm,宽 50 cm,厚 1.5 cm。进入秦汉时期,对称双弧形"子盾"长盛不衰,往往与车马器同出,亦是杨家湾步骑俑的装备。此外,根据《释名》总结,汉代还有"吴魁"、"须盾"、"陷虏"、"步盾"等种类。形制上新出现了长椭圆和对称单弧形。随着铁器的发展,铁也成为生产盾牌的新材料。在此基础上,东汉出现了攻防合一的钩镶(图六),使单兵格斗更加残酷。

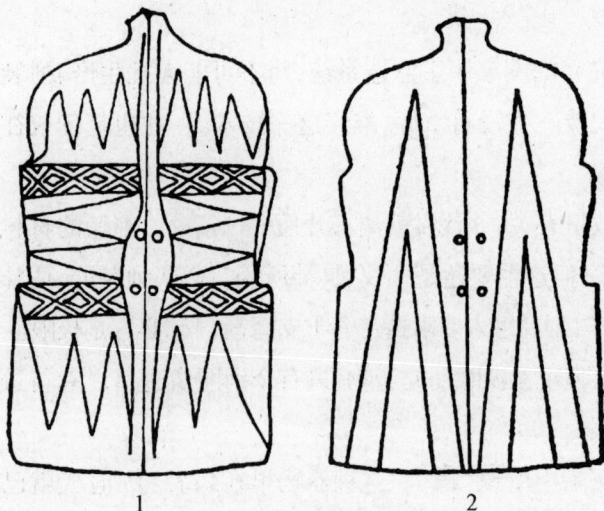

图五 咸阳杨家湾出土汉盾(摘自《中国古代兵器》)

图六 执钩镶的汉兵(复原图作者不详)

(引自:http://hfsword.com/bbs/attachments/X42N_urqzr7K9sfizpA==.jpg)

甲胄一直是单兵制式化装备研究的重点。因为,它是生命的最后一道防线,自然需费时费工。所以也能直接体现军工系统的面貌和水平。

战国晚期至秦代,皮质甲胄依然使用,从考古发现上看,其主体地位并未变化。史载燕国男子大都会做皮甲,但有趣的是,燕地却有不少铁甲胄的出土。比如,燕下都的铁兜鍪,用八十九片铁甲片合缀而成。全高 26 cm,顶部圆平,往下由圆角长方形甲片合缀,共七层。编法都是上压下、前压后。另有护领、护额等部分。铁兜鍪所用甲片形制与周围其他遗址的发现一致,说明当时铁甲胄制造精良,开始普及。[②]

秦国的发现,还是主要以皮甲胄模型为主。其中秦俑坑中的第二类第二型,被推测是秦军普通步兵的

---

① 所谓"盾鼻",一则从背面上下固定盾体,二来中部凸起用于把持("盾圭")。参见《汉代物质文化资料图说》,第 139 页,图 35-14。
② 参见《中国古代的甲胄》,《中国古兵器论丛》,第 20 页。

主要防护甲胄。又根据秦陵石铠甲坑的发现，学者推测铠甲中第一类的以长方形或方形石甲片编缀成的扎甲的祖形，可能是皮甲，这种甲胄，兜鍪与燕下都的十分类似（图七）。所不同的是兜鍪下沿进一步向下延伸并外翘，有效地保护了士兵的颈部。而铠甲裙摆更长，正面下沿弧形内收，前长后短，两侧开岔。披膊及上部与秦俑坑第二类第二型雷同。此外，有学者推测石甲坑内第二类鱼鳞甲，模仿铁铠甲的可能性很大。[①]

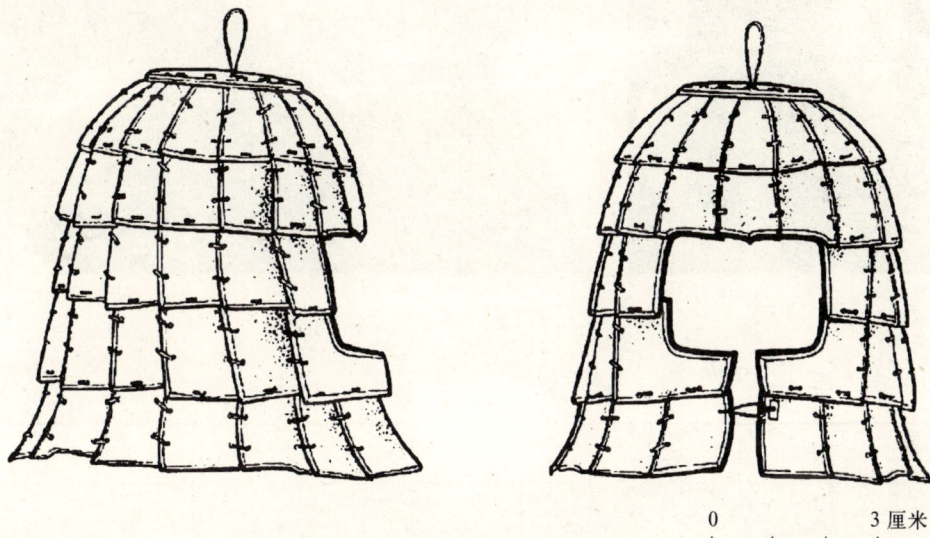

图七　秦石兜鍪（摘自《古代兵器通论》）

汉承秦制，继续在秦铠甲的基础上，发展自己的单兵卫体装备。这一时期，包括长城塞防地区在内，铁兜鍪、铠甲屡有发现，完整者亦不在少见。

兜鍪主要有两类（图八），一类如西安北郊汉墓出土的，形如覆扣的鍪，下沿连缀护耳和护颈。另一类如齐王墓出土的，兜鍪前高后低，顶部透空，下沿有左右连缀的护耳。这种兜鍪不排除与武弁等帽子合用的可能。[②]

图八　西汉铁兜鍪（摘自《古代兵器通论》）

① 参见《古代兵器通论》，第119～121页。
② 注同上，第170～171页。又，根据实战的需要，防止滑脱，头盔下一般还有陌额和纱弁（帻）等。剑道的头盔——"门"下，也必须绑缚用于固定和吸汗的头巾，否则即使有绳索扎紧，亦至脱落（图九）。

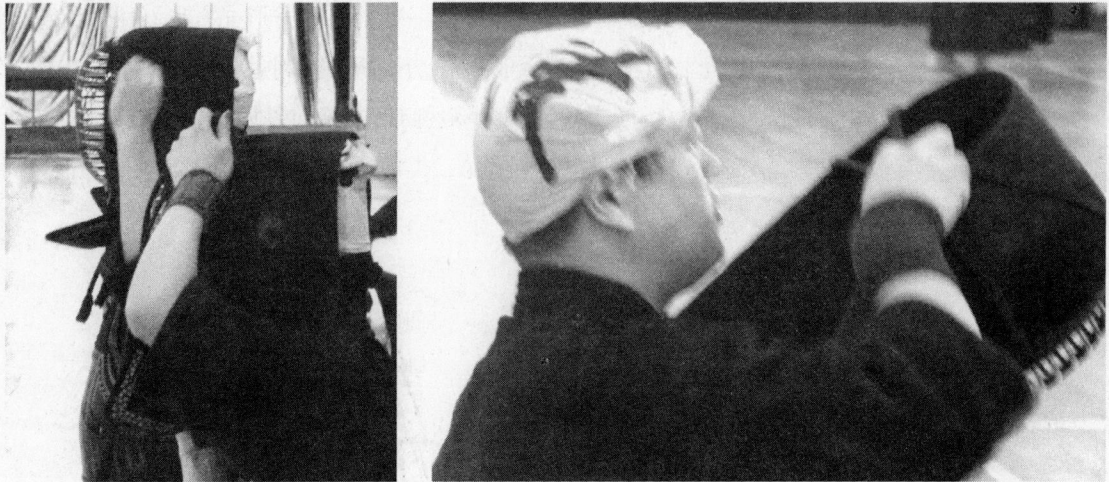

图九　剑道的"面"与头巾(摄影/李韬)

汉代身甲总体形态上分为两类：①扎甲、鱼鳞甲(图十)。

类　型	一		
型	一	二	三
铠甲			
出土地点	咸阳杨家湾陶俑	咸阳杨家湾陶俑	呼市二十家子汉城实物
类　型	二		
型	一	二	三
铠甲	（残）		（残）
出土地点	呼市二十家子汉城实物	咸阳杨家湾陶俑	洛阳西郊 M3023 实物

图十　西汉铁铠甲(摘自《中国古兵器论丛》)

---

① 参见《中国古代的甲胄》,《中国古兵器论丛》,第34～40页。

扎甲第一型前后只护住胸背,前后由肩部的系带相连。甲叶较大,多为长方形。

扎甲第二型除保持第一类基本形态外,另有披膊,与秦俑第二类第二型貌似。

扎甲第三型以内蒙二十家子出土的实物最为典型。该甲正面中部开襟,以铁扣相连。颈部有盆甲,披膊似以上第二型,下不封口。

鱼鳞甲也有三型:

鱼鳞甲一型也出土于内蒙二十家子,用圆角长方形甲叶编缀而成,形似鱼鳞。

鱼鳞甲二型甲叶形态更小,编缀更密,典型者如咸阳杨家湾陶俑(图十一)。值得注意的是,这尊陶俑缺少左护膊。这种情况,在希腊化时代也有。研究者发现,由于大型铜皮圆盾的广泛应用,以及长途奔袭机动性的需要,轻装步兵取掉了左肩头的披膊,因为圆盾完全可以遮护那个部分。[①]

鱼鳞甲三型实物残损严重,无法料知全貌。

2)主动攻击型:戈、矛(包括铍、铤)、戟、剑、刀

戈是东亚传统的古代兵器,分布广泛、列装普及、形态多样。戈的来源尚不清楚,但祖型确为石制。客观地说,戈形兵器,并非为东亚民族所独有。早在公元前22世纪中欧多瑙河流域的青铜时代文化就拥有大量制造精良的戈形兵器,其规格、工艺都在我之上。

战国时期的铜戈可以分为五种:长胡三穿型、短援长胡型、前内长阑型、狭援内刃型和狭援胡刺型。[②]战国晚期,戈早已丧失了作为徒戈的单兵性质,而是与矛联装成戟。秦代短祚,戈的形态没

图十一　咸阳杨家湾汉俑
(摘自《中国古兵器论丛》)

有什么太大变化。而汉代的有銎长胡三穿戈和长胡四穿鸡鸣戈,基本已沦为仪仗用具。戈秘部的横截面,基本是卵形。尖头与援的方向一致,使士兵随时都能感知到把持兵器的攻击方向。

戈的功用主要有四:推、啄、钩和横击。这些功能也为戟所继承。

矛是最典型的进攻型长杆兵器。战国时期的铜矛根据形制,主要分为四种:菱形尖刃矛、锥体形铜矛、宽体窄刃粗骹矛、宽体细骹矛。[③]前者主要是战国初期器,后者流行于百越地区。

战国时期亦是青铜兵器向钢铁兵器的过渡阶段,燕下都墓葬曾出土一定数量的铁矛(图十二)。它们的刃、叶、骹部较长,銎部截面为圆形,刃部截面为菱形。

秦代铜矛基本类似于战国宽体窄刃粗骹矛,根据秦俑坑的发现,可分为二型:[④]前者刃体扁宽而直,中部起脊,两侧有血槽断面为菱形,骹部椭圆,上有钉孔;后者通体中空,中脊无血槽。二者均可单一或与戈和而为戟。至于铁矛,在秦俑坑和石甲坑有所发现。前者与燕下都出土的较为相似。

① *The Persian and Peloponnesian Wars, Warfare in Ancient Greece: Arms and Armor from the Heroes of Homer to Alexander the Great*, written by Tim Everson, published by Sutton Publishing 2004.

② 参见《中国古代兵器》,第120页,陕西人民出版社,1995年。

③ 注同上,第125页。

④ 注同上。

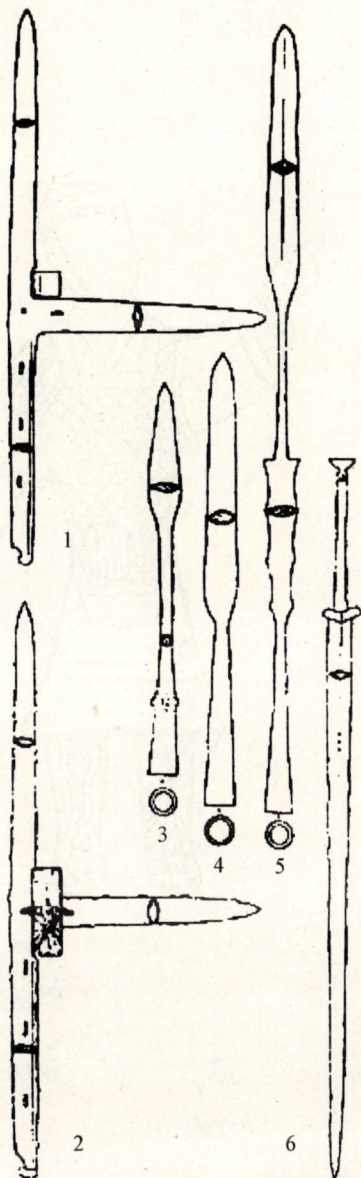

图十二　河北易县燕下都遗址44号墓出土铁兵器
（摘自《古代兵器通论》）

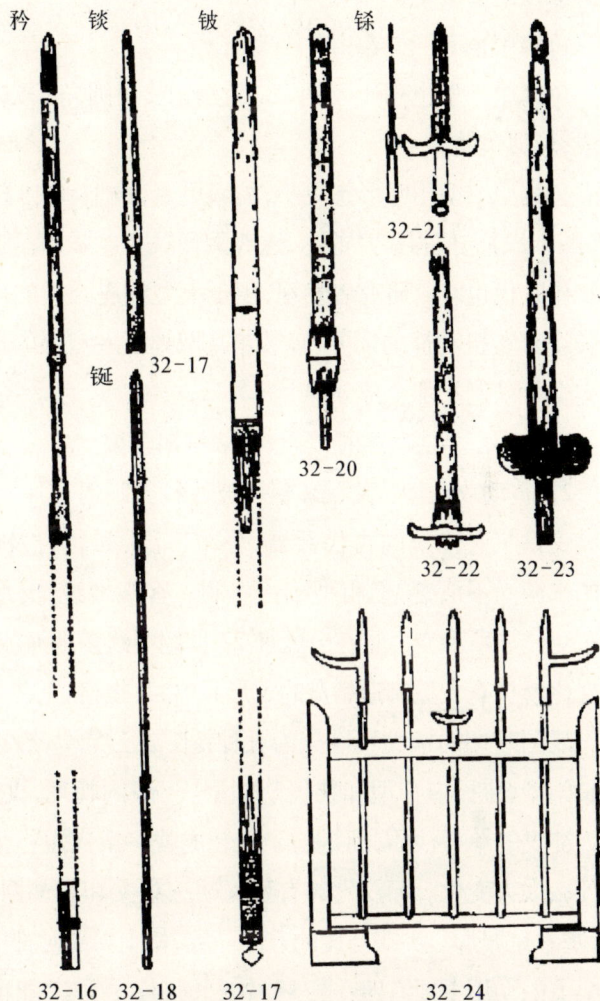

图十三　汉代铁制长兵
（摘自《汉代物质文化资料图说》）

汉代初期，铜矛依然沿用。矛叶与骹部比例相当，断面为菱形，有中空和实心两种。汉代铁矛早已普及，形制为柳叶形扁体，长骹，圆銎。

以上各型矛，如装上矜、鐏，全长都在190 cm以上。

铍是一种始于东周的阔刃铜矛，矛头似短剑，中部有格，后段有与剑柄类似的短茎，用以插入长柄内。秦汉两代的铜铍，依然继承战国风格，铍身长度以50 cm左右的较多。同时钢铁在西汉时期也运用到了铍的制造上。这种铁铍与矜、鐏相连，长度均在250 cm以上。还有更特殊者，铜籱上下装有三尖齿牙，增加杀伤力。将铍的格换为两头上翘的鐔，就成为了铢。根据作战任务不同，[1]铢可以装上长矜或短矜（图十三）。

————

① 德川时代"忠臣藏"的家臣复仇时，也考虑到在居室中，长矜无用武之地，必须换上短矜。笔者认为铢是明代锐钯的祖形，"可击可御，兼矛盾二用"，参见《纪效新书》（十四卷本），第86页。

以矛为基本形态,如果换成铁矜,汉代叫铤。① 目前发现的长度在 130～157 cm。《史记·匈奴列传》中说匈奴人善使铁铤,但不知这种兵器是否为骑兵所用。

将戈与矛联装,就是联装戟。这种联装戟为铜铸,战国晚期的更有在柲上联装两三个长胡戈的情况。不过,这应是车战兵器,本文不做详述。

战国晚期,随着冶铁术的发展,"卜"字戟在燕国和秦国均有发现,从此第一次被插在历史的兵栏上。"卜"字戟的基本形制,就是将 T 顺时针旋转 90 度,在夹角处安置底部中空的铜帽。上下部叫刺胡,横出的叫枝。胡刺下部内侧依然有穿,经过绑缚,与长柲相连。公元以前的"卜"字铁戟,刺弧不超过 50 cm,装柲均在 200 cm 以上。公元后,胡刺尺寸加长,几近 70 cm。关于"卜"字戟 T 型九十度夹角的形态,有学者认为,这与当时中国尚不发达的冶铁术有关。笔者认为可备一说。当然,这种情况"笔直不曲"的形态,也在刀剑上长期存在。笔者以为,从秦汉的兵制与军工体系角度考虑,也许还能找到更多的答案。

剑是徒手肉搏前的最后一道防线。与欧洲相比,中原地区剑的起源较晚,形制较为简单落后。但由于我国青铜铸造业的高超技术,自东周开始,我国青铜剑的制造,迅速达到了登峰造极地步,并广泛普及,成为士兵的最基本进攻装备。

战国晚期流行的铜剑,主要是柱茎剑:茎为实心圆柱形,茎上一般有两周或三周圆箍(极少数没有),上缠织物,首呈圆盘形,剑格宽而厚。高品级剑脊、刃复合铸成,上有菱形花纹,剑锷前部往往内收,②刃锋异常锋利。这种剑长度一般在 70 cm 以内。同时,铁剑也开始在各地推广。战国的铁剑,以燕下都的为准,形体修长(90 cm 左右),两侧直刃,前聚成锋。格部较短小,另行装配。剑柄细长,可双手握持,截面为扁茎,得夹木绕丝形成缑,方可使用。剑首圆平,截面似凤尾菇,与剑柄铆合。另外,甘肃秦安上袁家秦墓中亦有长铁剑出土,形制与燕国的类似,腊窄,不见格、首,柄为方棱扁茎。同墓出土的还有一柄铁匕首。

秦代的铜剑与燕下都出土的铁剑形制基本相同,高级品表面有防锈铬盐氧化处理。

汉代铜剑基本继承秦代风格。少数短青铜剑装饰豪华,并非实战用品。汉代铁剑基本继承战国晚期以来的风格,只是在质地上广泛出现了钢剑。随着环首刀的普及,汉代铁剑逐步成为礼仪用具。

剑的附件还有剑鞘、玉彘和摽。剑鞘多为木制,上髹胶漆。剑鞘的内侧有玉彘,其空挡中插入腰带,可佩带于士兵腰部左侧。摽位于剑鞘末段,用于保持剑体平衡。

刀的形制并不晚出,商周时期拱背、直背的青铜短刀很常见。从战国晚期开始,随着冶铁技术和锻造技术的提高,钢铁刀迅速增长,以甘肃秦安上袁家秦墓的铁刀为例。该刀刀体通直,单刃双面开锋,截面为锐角三角形。刀尖不似剑尖对称,一边有弧。刀柄较短,为方棱扁茎。至西汉,钢铁制成的环首长刀出现,③这首先与骑战有关,后文另作详述。

---

① 关于铤的优势,《汉书·晁错传》有"蕇苇竹萧,屮木蒙茏,枝叶茂接,此矛铤之地也,长戟二不当一"。

② 杨泓先生认为这"更说明剑在使用时注意的它的直刺的功能,而不是以斫击为主"(参见《中国古代的甲胄》,《中国古兵器论丛》,第 165 页)。此外,笔者认为内收的部分,也是剑的有效攻击部位。剑道的竹刀前部从"剑尖"至"中节皮",是比赛中打击的有效得分部位。而以下至 tsuba(相当于剑格),则用于封护、防御。由此反推战国铜剑内收和宽腊的部位,其功效可见一斑。当然,即使没有内收,剑、刀的攻击部位也是在前端。这是武家根据长期血腥的搏斗,总结的实战经验,付诸于铜剑的改进。

③ 西汉还有不少与环首刀并用的钢铁短刀。其尺寸只有环首刀的一半,甚至更短。根据馘首立功的传统,割取敌人的首级,用环首刀太长,且其主要作用是攻坚格斗,所以必须用"拍髀"、"解首"类的短刀。这在古代东亚的军事传统中很普遍。有关钢铁制短刀的出土情况,参见《洛阳西郊汉墓发掘报告》,《考古学报》1963 年第 2 期,第 55～56 页。

最后说说"钺"、"斧"。其虽然在考古中偶有发现,但史籍中并不见被大规模列装部队。前者在新石器时代的高等级墓葬中就有出土,一般被阐释为权力的象征。进入三代,进一步升华为王权和刑罚的象征。后者除作为工具外,在野战工事及相关简册中偶有发现。从战术角度看,似为要塞守备兵器。至于武威雷台"汉墓"出的骑俑手执的长柯斧,似为军法刑具。秦陵的司寇衙属遗址及汉阳陵丛葬坑,亦有实证,似可与古罗马法西斯笞棒做以比较。①

(二)骑兵用单兵制式化装备

亚洲骑兵的一大特点是既善骑战,更善骑射。从赵武灵王胡服骑射开始,中原的农业民族,不得不强迫自己在技战术上,逐步向毗邻敌对的游牧民族靠拢。② 因此,似不应在骑兵中再划分出投射、格斗部队。

骑兵的优势在于胯下的战马。③ 战国晚期战马及马具的形象,从塔尔坡秦墓④的陶马俑能看个大概(图十四)。马俑辔头缰绳虽然过于简单,描绘还算清晰。马身上并无鞍蹬痕迹,甚至连秦俑坑陶马背上的垫子也没有。从整体比例上看,这种马身材较矮小,与秦俑坑陶马体形比例相似。

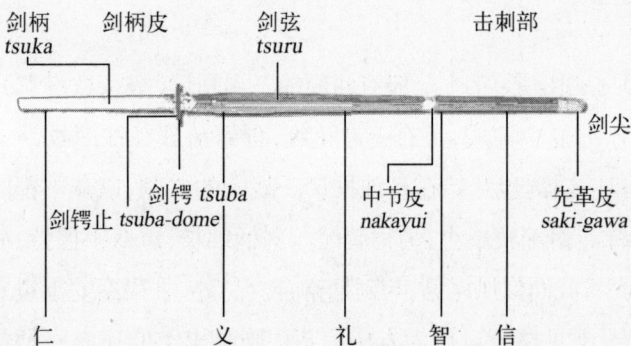

图十四　左图为竹刀各部位一览(引自http://www.kendocn.com/kendo_do/01 - shinai.htm);
右图为日本剑道三段闫睿女士"打面"示范(摄影/李韬)

骑手头戴翻沿护耳风帽,其形制与哈萨克斯坦出土的青铜盘上的踞坐骑士像(公元前5世纪至前3世纪)⑤的风帽一模一样。更有意思的是,他身旁的坐骑也仅能看到辔头的痕迹。笔者不愿过多的讨论中原与中亚的民族文化交流,这是后面的议题。此处姑且将舆服上的相似点,看作是游牧文化因素的共通性。

秦俑坑的骑兵、马俑,为我们提供了东亚骑兵的最早的、最清晰的形象:

陶马高约1.72米,长2.03米。马背铺鞯,鞯上放有鞍垫。鞍垫中间微凹,有排列整齐的钉泡,周围缀饰垂缨和短带。肚带设在鞍垫下缘中部,勒过马腹后,用带扣在左侧拉紧,使鞍垫固定在马背上。又在鞍垫后置鞘带套结马臀,使鞍鞯更加牢固。马头上有衔镳,马衔是铜质的,衔端装有"S"形的铜镳。镳和缰绳都配有青铜饰件。

---

① 有关"钺"、"斧"的研究,见《汉代物质资料文化图说》,第128页。又,戚继光总结实战,"斧、钺则短柄细,一击过首,多自摧折"。参见《练兵实纪》,第309页。

② 至西汉,情况更为普遍,已成风俗。居延汉简中,骑士多为边郡人,"大约边地产马,人多善骑乘"。参见《关于居延汉简的发现和研究》,《考古》1960年第1期,第51页。

③ 戚子云:"夫国之大事在戎,兵之驰骋在马。"参见《纪效新书》(十四卷本),第127页。

④ 《塔尔坡秦墓》,三秦出版社,1998年。

⑤ 但文物画册中的年代是前4世纪至前2世纪。不过,确定在前3世纪至4世纪,应该问题不大。

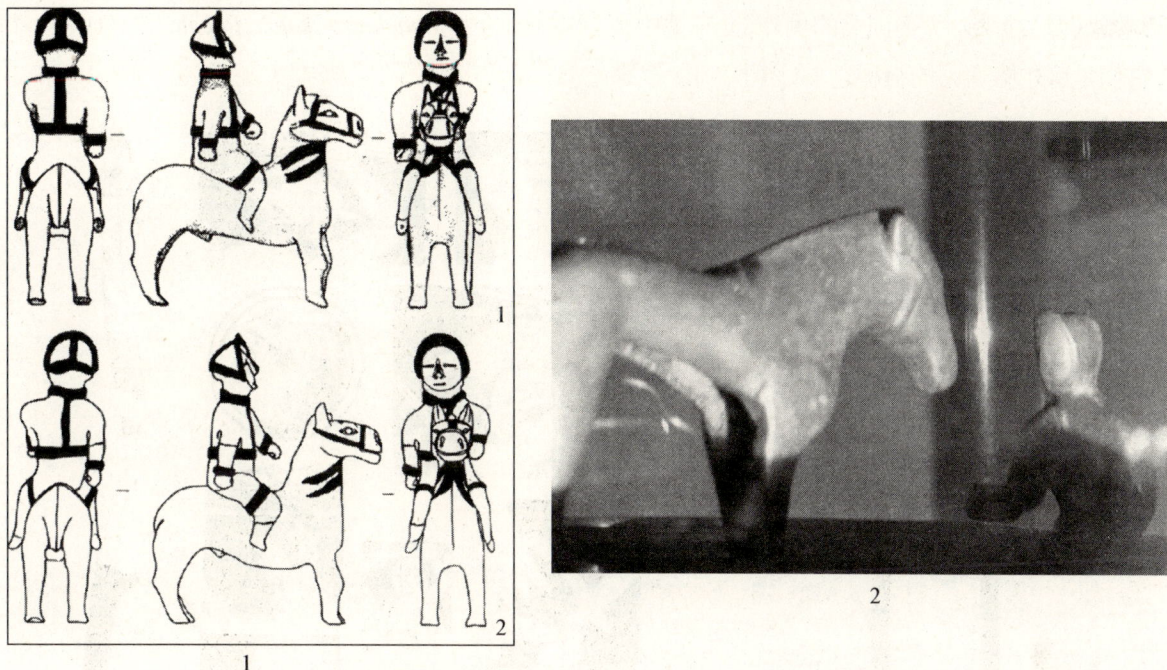

图十五　1.塔尔坡秦墓骑俑;2.哈萨克斯坦骑士铜盘
(1,摘自《古代兵器通论》;2,摄影/李韬)

骑俑头戴武弁,系于颌部。身着无披膊较短小的二类一型甲,足上蹬靴。与骑俑同出的,还有铜剑、铜弩机和残木弓。形制详见前文。

汉初骑兵的装束与秦代略同,也是头戴武弁,身着无披膊的扎甲第一型,不过材质换成了铁,因为色黑,又称"玄甲"。汉初马具与秦代同,在称谓上,将鞍垫称为"鞍"。西汉后期鞍鞯垂长,遮住马腹,鞭长莫及。这方面最形象、清晰的例证,要属西安理工大西汉壁画墓。[①] 壁画中,猎手们多骑乘变种的高大肥马,马背上披有长鞍鞯,下无马镫。猎手们使用的兵器主要是弓箭和 V 型二股叉。前者形体非常清晰,可见弓弦。整张弓的尺寸,按比例约在 150 cm 左右,与传世满洲弓的大小差不多。猎手小臂上都绑缚着束袖的护臂[②](防弓弦绷伤),其中一位提飞禽者,左右膊服色不一,左袖为红色,笔者怀疑可能是射箭专用的护膊。这一射箭装备一直流传至今,东西通用。另外,仔细观察提飞禽猎手的左胯部还有一件平口深褐色的囊,作者推测可能是韬或箙。至于 V 型二股叉,应该属于猎具。[③]

此外,剑、刀也是秦汉骑兵的标准制式化装备。后者,在西汉广泛列装普及,形态为钢铁制环首、短柄、直体单刃的长刀,刃部双面打磨,截面承锐角三角形;锋部为不对称优弧;无格或窄格,刀柄为方棱宽扁茎,与首部大环均缠绕缑。现今发现的汉代环首刀,长度在 80 ~ 118 cm 间,非常适合骑兵冲锋劈砍。大部分环首刀刀身笔直,流传到唐代,也没有太大变化。环首刀的强度比剑更高,不过这是相对的。直刃的形态,还是先天就容易折断的。因为刀刃窄,若见血多、使用不正确或与其他硬物碰撞,都会迅速造成

---

① 参见《西安理工大学西汉壁画墓发掘简报》,《文物》2006 年 5 期,第 7 ~ 44 页。

② 仅从图像上,无法判断护臂的材质。又《史记·苏秦列传》云"坚甲铁幕",司马贞:《索隐》引刘云"谓以铁为臂胫之衣"。云南李家川的护臂为铜制,这一传统似非来自中原,参见《云南江川李家山古墓群发掘报告》,《考古学报》1975 年 2 期,第 120 ~ 121 页。

③ 但就是这一猎具的使用,充分说明了雷同的长杆格斗兵器(如矛、戟)和马镫的使用,没有必然的联系。下文中,中亚以及现实中环地中海地区广泛出土的早期无镫、执长兵的重装骑士形象的文物,进一步证实了这一观点。所谓"马镫革命",具有相当的时空局限性。

刀刃卷缺、刀身折断。[①] 而同类的例外,惟有地中海至中亚地区的 *máchaira*、*kopís*、*falcata*。[②] 有些学者认为,它们是廓尔喀弯刀的祖型之一(图十六)。

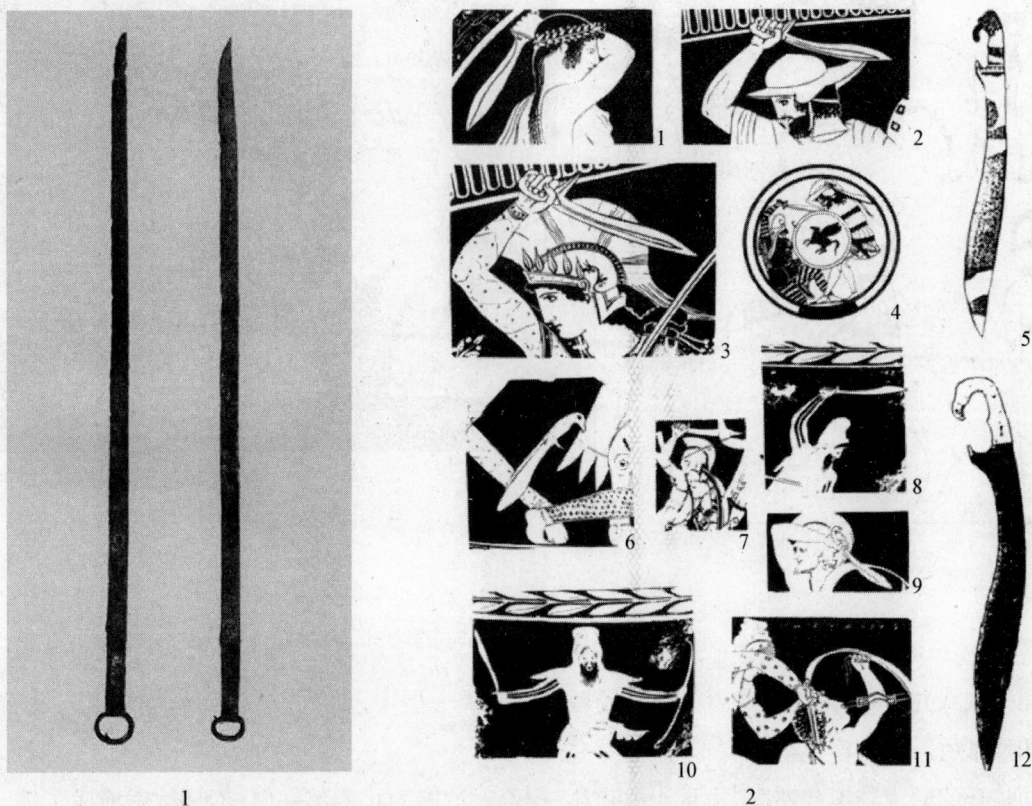

图十六　1. 徐州狮子山楚王陵出土环首铁刀;2. *kopis* 的图像及实物

(1 摘自《大汉楚王》;2 摘自 *In the Land of the Gryphones Papers on Central Asian archaeology in antiquity*)

至于防护用的盾,汉代依然使用"对称双弧盾",从杨家湾兵马俑可见一斑。

(三)总结:步骑单兵组合的协同作战

诚如戚继光所言,战役的胜负在根本上,取决于步骑单兵组合的协同作战。换句话说,只有合理的"短长相卫",才有取胜的资本。

从接战序列上,投射部队一般是最早投入战斗。但按照战史的记载,投射部队并不一定被安置在前排,相反是起到保护战阵的橹楯放在最前。《汉书·陈汤传》记载,汉军在攻击时"橹楯在前,戟弩为后"。可见,投射部队被安排在橹楯防护墙之后。[③]

---

① 环首刀的直刃,并非是中原锻造技术落后所致。比如汉阳陵的环首刀是拱背,而徐州狮子山楚墓出土的环首刀的刺击部,也是拱背而刀锋上翘。但制作这样的刀,工序势必较为繁复。可见,环首刀直体的问题,似应从当时装备列装、军工体系和军队规模的关系考虑。杨泓先生说,"……军种主要的格斗兵器,既要求质精,又要求量足,因此工艺简便易造……更合于战争的需要"。参见《中国古代的甲胄》,《中国古兵器论丛》,第 255 页。

② 这些兵器的来源,依然是个谜。不过早期的希腊瓶画中,一般都是黑海的斯基泰人或波斯人使用这种兵器。罗马共和时期,伊比利亚半岛土著居民亦大量装备,而且增添护手,做工更加精良,常令罗马部队望而生畏。kopis 向东方的最远分布,可及撒玛尔罕。那里曾出土 kopis 典型勾喙短柄(也不能排除是剑柄),相信和希腊化有一定的关系。另外,著名将领色诺芬曾亲自使用这种兵器骑马征战,并将其作为军制,写入 *Horsemanship*(《骑士之道》)。

③ 又"敌已附,鹿角裹兵但得进踞,以矛戟刺之,不得起住,起住妨弩",参见《太平御览》卷三三七、三三九引诸葛亮军令,第 1548、1554 页。

如果单人操弩,射速当然不如弓箭;要形成持续性集群杀伤力,一般由三人协同:前排射击,中排待命,后排填装,"游弩往来"。① 如此,便形成了"弩无绝发,弦无绝响"的毁灭性攻势(图十七)。

图十七 "弩无绝发,弦无绝响"(摘自《古今图书集成》)

根据古代兵法和军事家的经验,我方的弓箭一般在齐射三次后,敌军的骑兵部队基本就迫近或即将冲破第一道防线。② 这时,橹楯人墙或坚守岗位,或与投射部队撤下,换持矛戟、拥盾牌的格斗战阵(或其他战斗队形)——格斗部队发挥决胜性作用了。不论握"长兵"的格斗战队能否取胜,最后都是剑、刀、盾组合的肉搏。

这里值得注意的是,战国晚期至两汉流行的长柄剑,很可能是双手握持。这在中世纪东西方的技击中,早已司空见惯。根据笔者练习剑道的经验,双手握持,不论攻守都强而有力,能将技战术发挥到极致。相反,单手短柄剑,若无宽厚的腊部,又不与盾牌结合,同样技击水平的情况下,很难抵挡住前者的进攻。刀也同理,这也是为什么戚继光痛定思痛,借鉴双手持倭刀,发明苗刀的原因之一。③

另外,古人总结刀剑的使用,还有两大区别和特点,归纳起来就是:"刀行龙虎,剑走轻盈";"刀行

① "坚甲利刃,长短相杂,游弩往来,什伍俱前,则匈奴之兵弗能当也",参看《汉书·晁错传》,第2281页。又"阵中张,阵外射,番火轮回,张而复出,射而复入,则弩不绝",参见《通典》卷一四九。
② 强弓的有效射程在八十步(约110米);三、六石弩的有效射程在一百二十步到二百步(约160~278米),而"超足"的大黄劲弩的有效射程有六百步(约828米)。马的平均时速约16~22米/秒,如果取中间值19米/秒的话,敌骑兵群从进入有效射程到短兵相接,我方最多约有44秒的投射火力压制时间。若投射部队错落有致、搭配得当,弓箭手在6秒内,约齐射三次,平均2秒/次;而成排的弩弓手可在44秒内,大约连续射击20次,平均2秒/次。难怪汉军围攻郅支城时,尽管腹背受敌,但依仗营、盾、戟、弩,摆出一副"其奈我何"的架势,游牧敌兵只得望城兴叹,自将散去。
③ "(长刀解)此自倭犯中国始有之。彼以此跳舞,光闪而前,我兵已夺气矣。倭善跃,一进足则丈余,刀长五尺,则丈五尺矣。我兵短器难接长器,不捷,遭之者身多两断,缘器利而双手使,用力重故也",参见《纪效新书》(十四卷本),第82页。

中宫,剑走偏锋"。前者的优势是砍劈,所以要么劈脑袋(剑道称"打面"),要么砍肚腹(剑道称"打胴")。如此才能一招置敌,速战速决。剑的优势在于刺击,要么刺喉(剑道称"突刺"),要么击手腕(剑道称"小手"),让对手丧失战斗力。剑在刺击要害部位时,最好剑刃与肋骨平行,这样可以在轻易插入敌体内,同时保护剑锋刃部的锐利。《三国志》中记载,曹丕就是击剑高手,他能常胜的要素,基本如此。

此外,"折戟沉沙"之后的肉搏中,还得用短剑(匕首)和短刀。战国文献中,多将前者称为短铗,为刺客所用。史载的"正战"中,尚未见闻。当然,从实战角度出发,这些"卫体短兵",在生死攸关之际,还是经常能发挥保命的作用。

不论兵器多锋利耐用,起关键作用的还是人。[①] 史书上夸张的"百人斩"、"万人敌",对于普通士兵来说,是很难企及的。从使用竹木装备的竞技剑道看,一个人想要在与二三名敌手同时对抗中取胜,没有三年坚持不懈的艰苦训练,只能被动挨打。所以,必须平时多流汗,战时才能少出血。在指挥和技战术运动得当的前提下,每人只要发挥平时实力的两成,再将所有的"两成"集合并有机协同,就能在战役中产生制胜的基本效能。

骑兵在中原地区的运用,肇始于赵武灵王。但这并不表明,边胡的秦燕就不使用游牧雇佣兵。[②] 在战国晚期的长平之战中,虽然骑兵不是主力,但由于秦骑兵迅速将赵军与后方分割,在会战中起到了关键作用,故在后世备受青睐。此外,史载汉代以前的著名的骑战战例,还有李牧指挥的赵匈战争和楚汉垓下之战。这两者都是骑兵对骑兵的范例,前者规模相当大,后者主要体现在突围和追逐。

西汉初年,内地兵燹尚未熄灭,边塞早已烽烟不绝。在遭到多次惨败之后,汉武帝不得不调整军政策略,迅速扩充、集训骑兵,军备竞赛逐日升级。值得注意的是,武帝时的骑兵部队之所以强盛,是因为汉军注意发挥骑兵之长,并以步兵和辎重车兵护骑兵之短,如此有机协同,方令几十万草原控弦之士,不敢对阵争风。[③]

由于汉军骑兵的基本战法继承自北方游牧民族,所有两军对垒时,骑兵战术雷同,故放在以"骑战"为主的中亚篇里讨论。

三、中亚地区单兵制式化装备

本文所指的中亚地区,东起河西走廊西端,西达河中地区,北及南西伯利亚,南至印度河上游及昆仑山一线。这一地区,从地理环境看,纬度偏高的北部地区,以草原游牧文化为主;纬度偏低的南部地区,以沙漠绿洲文明为主;天山山脉是二者间的地理、人文界线;又因为南北向的帕米尔——喀喇昆仑的阻隔,东西方形成两种独立的地理单位。东边的新疆地区,历史时期受到来自蒙古高原和中原地区的强烈影

---

① 戚子云:"彼有精器而无精兵以用之,是谓徒费;有精兵而无精器以助之,是谓徒强;须兵士立得脚根定,则曳柴可以败荆,况精器乎!"又,"临敌之时,若使仍是照前从容酬应,如教场比试之一般,不必十分武艺,只学得三分亦可无敌。奈每见贼时,死生呼吸所系,面黄口干,手忙脚乱,平日所学射法、打法尽都忘了,只有互相乱打,已为好汉,如用得平时一分武艺出,无有不胜;用得二分出,一可敌五;用得五分出,则无敌矣。"参见《练兵实纪杂集》卷二《储练通论·原火器》。

② 塔尔坡秦兵马俑就有这种可能,西汉更是如此。如果尚无资料确认高祖麾下善骑射者——楼烦乃胡人的话(参见《史记·项羽本纪》,第323页),那么晁错建议招募、武装边胡以备匈奴,就是再明白不过了(语出《汉书·晁错传》,第2282~2283页)。

③ 西汉出塞骑兵往往环营以阵,埋伏在辎重车墙以内,以逸待劳,用弓弩大量杀伤游牧骑兵的有生力量。

响,处于被支配地位;西边狭义上的中亚地区,受到西方环地中海——两河文明、北部欧亚草原文明和南亚次大陆文明的多重熏陶,是名副其实的"十字路口"。

不过,因为地理环境的相似性,在大规模持续的民族迁徙下,帕米尔从未真正成为阻碍强权征服的天堑。同时,北部草原地区,平坦开阔,游骑纵横驰骋,本来就没有什么障碍。

为便于和前文中原部分联系,本篇将遵循由东向西,由北至南的论述顺序。

此外,与中原地区相比,中亚地区兵器的发现,相对不平衡。在帕米尔以东地区,游牧文化浓厚的骑兵装备广泛出土,而明确的步兵装备发现较少;完整实用非金属兵器较多见,清晰的二维、三维图像较少。帕米尔以西地区不论步骑,发现较为丰富,特别是有不少清晰的壁画和雕塑资料。不过,由于保存条件所限,出土的非金属完整实用兵器较少。

有鉴于此,本篇暂不刻意划分步兵与骑兵装备。

(一)防卫型单兵装备:甲胄、盾牌

帕米尔以东地区的甲胄实物资料很罕见,据说阿尔泰山地区曾出土匈奴铠甲。[①] 至于新疆境内的,目前笔者只听说过吐鲁番洋海二号墓地出土的皮甲。据发掘人员介绍,该皮甲长约 100 cm,宽 60 cm,外层甲片通过编缀,附着在内层整张皮革上,甲片排列与长轴方向同。研究小组目前有两种意见:一种认为是马(人)甲,另一种认为是鞍垫。笔者经过仔细观察,根据其形制、痕迹推测,其前身可能是某种皮甲,破损后可能经过再加工,制作成了一种特殊的"鞍垫"。但不管怎样,这一发现在整个新疆地区,都是具有划时代意义的,因为洋海二号墓地的年代被定在距今 2 300 年,即公元前 3 世纪左右。

此外,疑似身甲的资料,仅出现在阿尔泰山麓地区岩画上。这一地区早期人物岩画的特征是瘦长,而有一些手持长矛的战士,上身却呈宽大的矩形。笔者认为,不排除这一矩形形象代表甲胄的可能(图十八)。

新疆地区秦汉时期的头盔实物资料,尚未见著于出版物。不过有理由推测,新疆地区早期头盔的形制,可能受到来自蒙古高原[②]和中原地区的影响。

另外,伊犁青铜武士像也证明,希腊式的圆边宽沿鸡冠顶头盔,也曾为新疆地区的先民所知。至于这种头盔的材料和工艺,目前还不得而知。根据希腊头盔的传统,如果这种头盔的实物是金属制的话,其工艺很可能是锻造铆铸的,而时代一定晚于马其顿崛起。

岩画方面的头盔形象也普遍出现,最典型的就是菌形帽盔。定名为"帽盔",是因为仅通过岩画,很难料知其材质,所以不排除由皮革或毛毡制成。顾名思义,这种帽盔的基本形态似蘑菇,有人类学家推测跟北亚萨满教服用毒菌的灵异习俗有关。[③] 特殊的菌形帽盔上,左右对称还有两至四根小枝,具体寓意不太清楚。这种菌形帽盔的分布很广,基本呈"凸"字形。最北边翻越阿尔泰——萨颜岭,进入叶尼塞河的泰加林地区;东边,在阴山岩画中也偶有发现;西边不论天山东西,都有发现,其中巴里坤的发现,在新

---

① 参见《阿尔泰山区匈奴的萨尔马泰时代的铠甲》,《苏联考古学》1997 年第 4 期。中文索引由孙危博士翻译、提供,链接: http://www.eurasianhistory.com/data/articles/e02/1716.html。

② 从青铜时代到匈奴时代的发现证明,青铜模铸的一体式半球形头盔是主流。其形制与白浮西周墓和高加索库班墓出土的基本一致。

③ *Myths in Stone*, *World of Rock Art in Russia*, written by E. G. Devlet & M. A. Devlet, published by Moscow <ALETHEIA>, 2005.

图十八 天山——阿尔泰山地区战士岩画

(1、2、3,摘自 *Archaeology Ethnology & Anthropology of Eurasia*, *Vol. 19*;4,巴里坤东黑沟遗址群岩画,摄影/马健)

疆地区尚属首次。

　　还有一种尖顶毡帽,也为中亚游牧战士普遍使用。这也是所谓"斯基泰——塞种"的一大服饰文化特色(图十九)。这种尖顶帽,一般有两式:一式冠部似禽首(也往往装饰成禽鸟的头部),后部和鬓角部下沿较长,基本遮住颈部左右后三面;第二式完全是圆锥型高冠,根据图像和实物分析,后者佩戴的身份多为高级贵族和萨满巫师,因此,不在本文讨论之列。①

　　① *Zur Kleidung der Pazyryk-Bevolkerung aus Ukok, Sudaltaj, Die archaologischen Spuren der Kimmerier im Vorderen Orient und das Problem der Datierung der vor- und fruhskythischen Kulturen*, written by Natalija V. Polos'mak, Dr. Rudolf Habelt GmbH. Bonn 2001.

图十九　中亚尖顶高冠一览

(摘自 *Die archaologischen Spuren der Kimmerier im Vorderen Orient und das Problem der Datierung der vor- und fruhskythischen Kulturen*)

帕米尔以西的中亚地区的甲胄,种类丰富、来源复杂(图二十)。

除了前文所述的翻沿风帽和上文的尖顶帽二型外,源自北方欧亚草原地区的头盔,主要是第三型"库班式",撒玛尔罕曾有出土。

其次数量最多的是希腊化风格的各式帽盔,最常见的是第四型"皮奥夏式"头盔。这种头盔的祖型来自于马其顿骑士佩戴的草编阔沿遮阳帽,后由青铜锻造而成:帽檐尖直前出,顶部浑圆有枝或矮脊,上或有盔缨,耳部对称起一二折或平直(平直者,整体侧面似维多利亚式头盔,中国俗称"吕宋帽"),后脑浑圆,下沿外翻。

还有较普遍的是第五型"雅典式":短帽檐微前出,顶部浑圆有矮脊,双耳为活叶护住面颊,后脑浑圆,下沿短而外翻。

希腊化的最后一种是第六型"兽首式"。其材质主要是金属,但祖型的确是兽头。其承袭自古希腊神话英雄赫拉克利斯的狮头冠,具有一定的神化色彩。在中亚发现的,还有狮、羊、象首之分。前两者是地中海传统,后者是南亚风格,它们往往用来表现亚历山大大帝及其中亚继承者的神圣性和对属地统治的合法性。

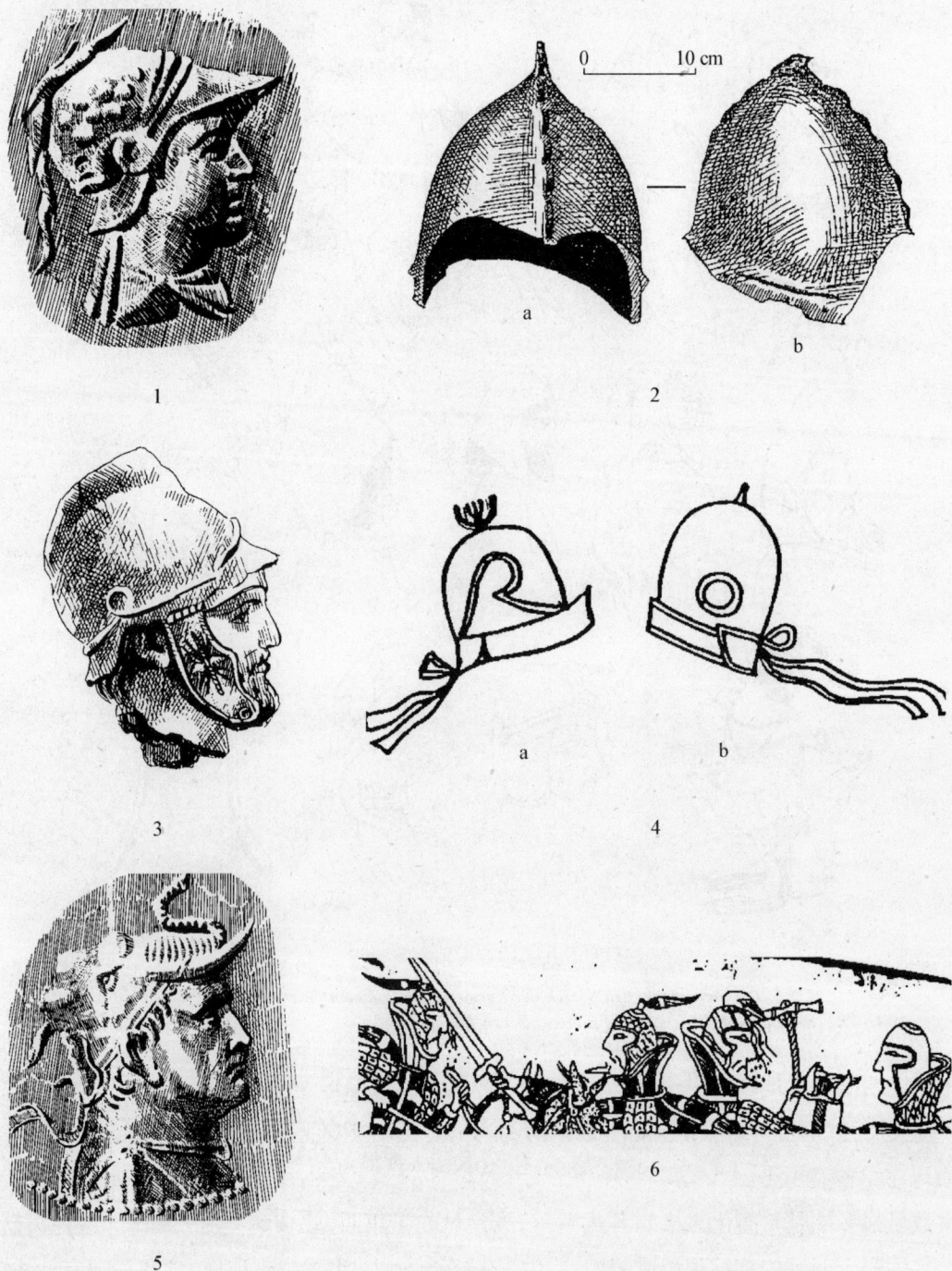

图二十 1. 皮奥夏式盔;2. 库班式盔;3. 雅典式盔;4. 半橄榄珠宝冠盔;
　　　　　5. 兽首式盔;6. 奥拉特复合式盔

（1、4、6,皆为中亚出土希腊化钱币头盔形象;2,为撒玛尔罕发掘品;3,为中亚出土塑像;
6,为奥拉特骨板画。均摘自 *The Armies of Bactria*）

　　第七型头盔为半截橄榄形,上饰珠宝冠,后有飘带。以上所述后两者头盔的图像可知,它们均为统治者所佩戴,应该不是普通士兵列装的装备。[1]

　　① *The Armies of Bactria*, Valerii P Nikonorov, published by Montvert Publications, 1997; *Greek hoplite 480－323 BC*, written by Nicolas Sekunda & Adam Hook, published by Osprey Military.

最后第八型仅出现在奥拉特墓地的骨板画上。① 该头盔顶部浑圆,似由纵向排列的鱼鳞形或长方形甲片编缀而成,顶部有絮状盔缨;有对称双劣弧面颊,并无分铸痕迹;头盔下沿较长,可完全护住脖颈。此外,还有一种亚式,基本形制没有太大区别,只是头盔上并无用以表现甲片的纹饰,顶部亦无盔缨。因此,笔者推测这种头盔似一体化铸造而成,而非甲片编缀。

帕米尔以西中亚地区的铠甲类型较为丰富,主要有三大型:第一型是本土游牧风格型,第二型是希腊化风格型,第三型是复合风格型。

准确地说,第一型游牧风格的不是铠甲,而是一种具有强烈草原地域风格的服装。它主要由短襟上衣、长大衣、长裤和长筒毡靴组成(图二十一)。短襟上衣无领,前开襟,左衽,窄长袖筒,或与护臂搭配。上衣腰部一般系有带钩或带扣的皮带,皮带上又有多件金属或皮革带环,带环下部延伸出的部分领有挂钩,用于悬挂各种装备和饰件。

长大衣多为皮毛制,毛里皮外;窄长袖筒;大衣长可过膝,前开襟,后部有半圆形延长部分,骑乘时可护住鞍垫后部甚至马臀上部。

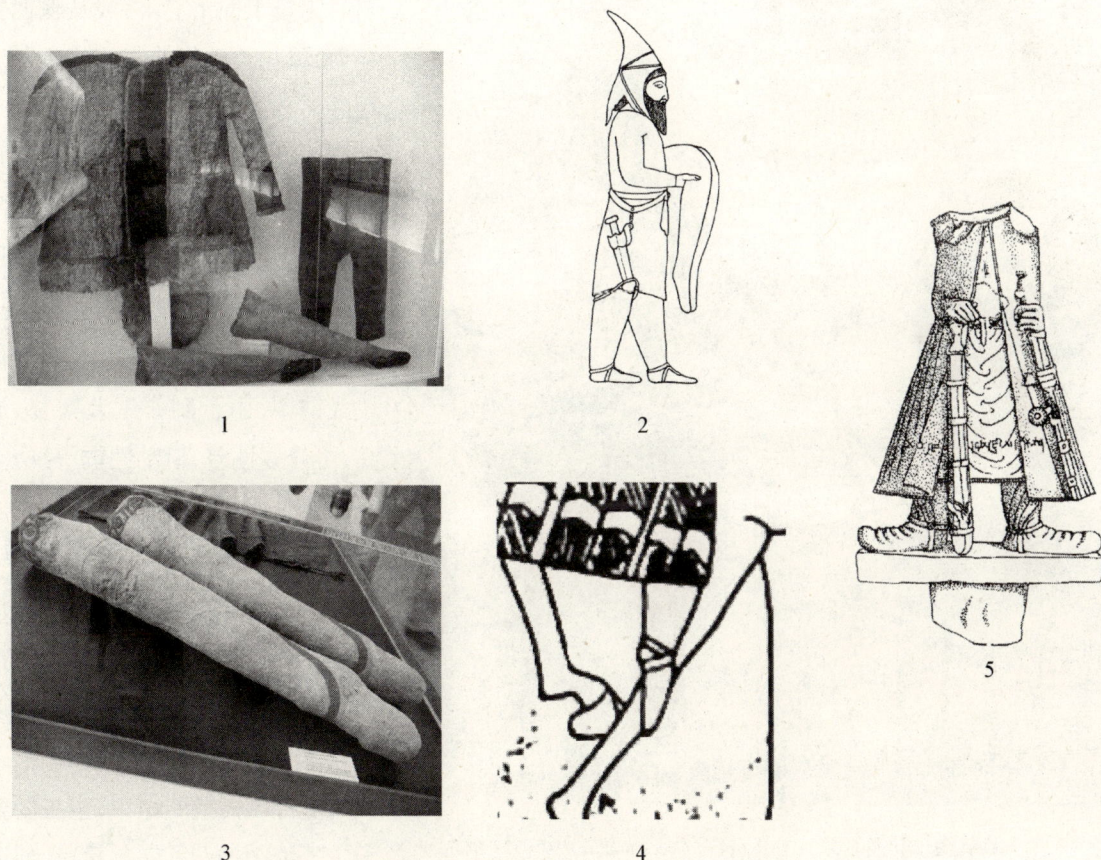

图二十一　1、3. 为萨颜岭——阿尔泰山地区出土早期铁器时代游牧服饰;
2、4. 为伊朗、中亚地区长毡筒靴;5. 为贵霜时期石雕服饰

(1、3,摄影/李韬;其余摘自 *The Armies of Bactria*)

① *A Study on the Bones from Orlat*, Silk Road Art and Archaeology, Vol. 7, written by Jangar Ya. ILYASOV & Dmitriy V. RUSANOV, published by The Institute of Silk Road Studies, 2001; *Armour of Ancient Bactria*, In the Land of the Gryphones Papers on Central Asian *archaeology in antiquity*, written by K. Abdullaev, published by Casa Editrice Le Lettere, 1995; Nomadism in Central Asia — The Archaeological Evidence, $2^{nd}-1^{st}$ c. BC, written by K. Abdullaev, published by Casa Editrice Le Lettere, 1995.

长裤腰部、胯部肥大,裤管并不及踝。裤内双腿蹬长筒毛毡马靴。这种马靴在穿着时,足部紧绷,几乎与腿部成一条直线,因此站立时,足面会有多重褶皱。足部由深色毛毡制成,形态似中国传统圆口布鞋,但与腿部毡筒实为一体。高级品足面有花纹,足底有矩形小块排列的铁矿石;普通者则以绳子系绕足弓,以此防止行走时打滑。与中原地区山民,冬季爬山足弓系的防滑草绳的功用一样。

此外,伊塞克"金人"的胫部还有类似绑腿作用的护胫。这在中亚北部及以东的游牧地区,并不常见。因此,不排除是一种希腊化的结果。

希腊风格型的铠甲的实物,并未在中亚大量出土,而往往以二维、三维图像的形式展现。最具希腊风格的是整体模块式锻造的身甲(图二十二),将图像与地中海实物对照可知,这种铠甲的材质是青铜,分前后两部分,上无领,下长及小腹。前后并无开襟,有的侧面、肩部有开襟,穿着时需自上而下套上,或从侧面打开穿着,再扣合。统治者或将领所穿铠甲的前部,往往锻造出肌肉的形状,煞是威猛。肩部有的有皮条作护膊。腰部至膝盖以上有皮条短裙,有的皮条上亦上下排列编缀有大块矩形甲片。胫部有青铜护胫,下可及足踝、脚面。其实这种传统的重型整体模块式铠甲,由于制作工艺繁复、成本高、可修复性差、机动性弱等缺点,早在古典时代就已逐渐退出战场。取而代之的是锁子甲、鱼鳞甲、皮铠甲和可以保护全身主要部位的圆形大铜盾,而更多的士兵愿意足蹬色雷斯式高腰系带长靴。虽然,后者主要是马其顿骑兵装备。

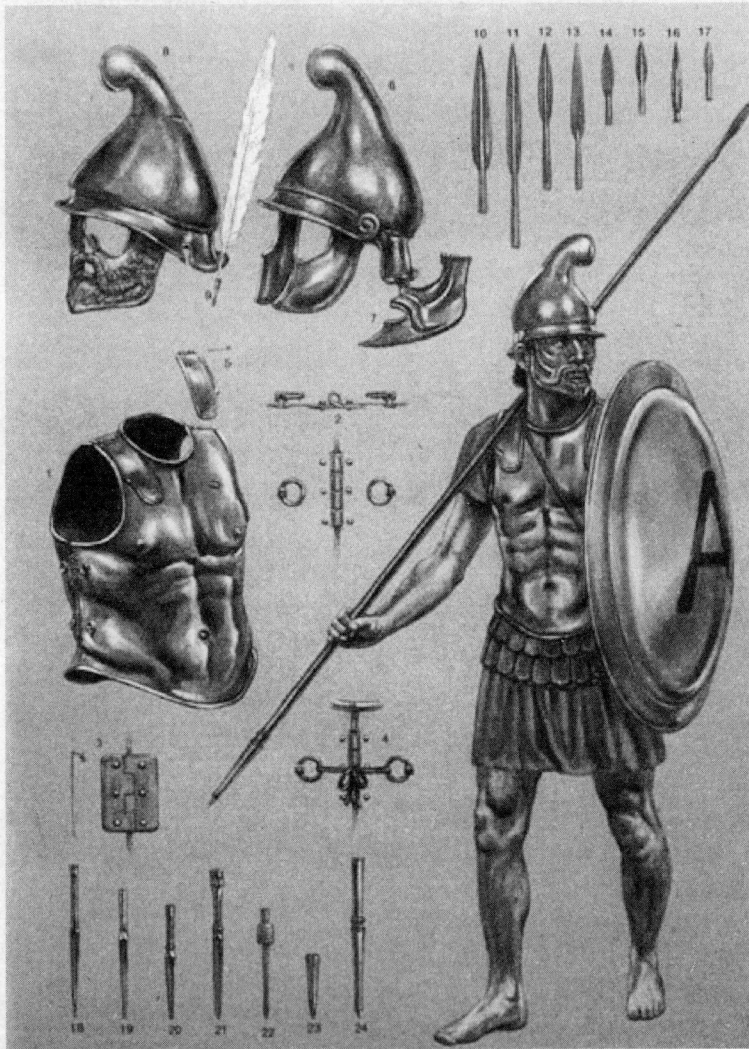

图二十二　马其顿步兵及其单兵装备(摘自 *Greek hoplite 480 – 323 BC*)

复合风格型的铠甲,也主要来自于二三维图像(图二十三)。与这种铠甲搭配的头盔,要么是"雅典式"的,要么是半橄榄形高冠式,要么是具有"库班式"风格的"奥拉特式"。复合风格铠甲拥有高耸的盆甲,可以保护颈部。从侧面观察,盆甲前低后高,以弧形过度。盆甲由长方形大块甲片纵向排列而成。铠甲的臂膀有两种亚式,一种是环形甲叶,自上而下编缀成袖筒,长及手腕。这种铠甲的祖型,最早发现在地中海东岸的希腊化王国,以帕迦玛遗址的浮雕最为典型。另一种紧束,从图形判断,很可能上下由多片长方形大块甲叶编缀而成。战裙或已过膝盖,为一整体,但前后开襟,利于骑乘。战裙上的甲叶形状、排列编缀顺序和上述紧束袖筒的基本一致。

1

2

3

4

5

图二十三　1.奥拉特骨板画;2、4、5."奥克斯河神庙"浮雕及复原图;3. 帕迦玛祭坛浮雕

(1、2、4、5 摘自 *The Sculpture of Khalchayan*;3,摄影/李韬)

　　新疆至中亚地区的盾牌,主要有两类(图二十四),一类是本土风格的,一类是希腊化风格的。前者主要以实物的形式在阿尔泰至天山南麓地区出土,因为那里具有得天独厚的保存环境。本土风格的盾牌,又分两型:一型是长方形平面藤牌,一型是长方形弧面木牌。前者主要材料是半干旱地带成长的类似柽柳的植物的茎部。从表面观察,首先是木条制作成长方形木框;再将尺寸一样的小指般粗细的藤棍横向排列,中间用皮条编缀,并在正面形成一定的图案;最后将藤排与长方形木框用皮条编缀、绑缚。这种藤牌的分布范围很广,西起黑海,东至哈密。根据前一地区的大量发现可知,这种藤牌在不使用时,会横向绑在后背上部,起到铠甲的作用。第二型长方形弧面木盾,只在阿尔泰墓葬中有发现。它由整块原木为材料,被截成长方形。盾的内侧,随原木的外形刨成弧形;外侧则纵向雕出排列的线条。因为出土物正中间有一条纵贯的裂缝,可知其坚固程度并不尽如人意。

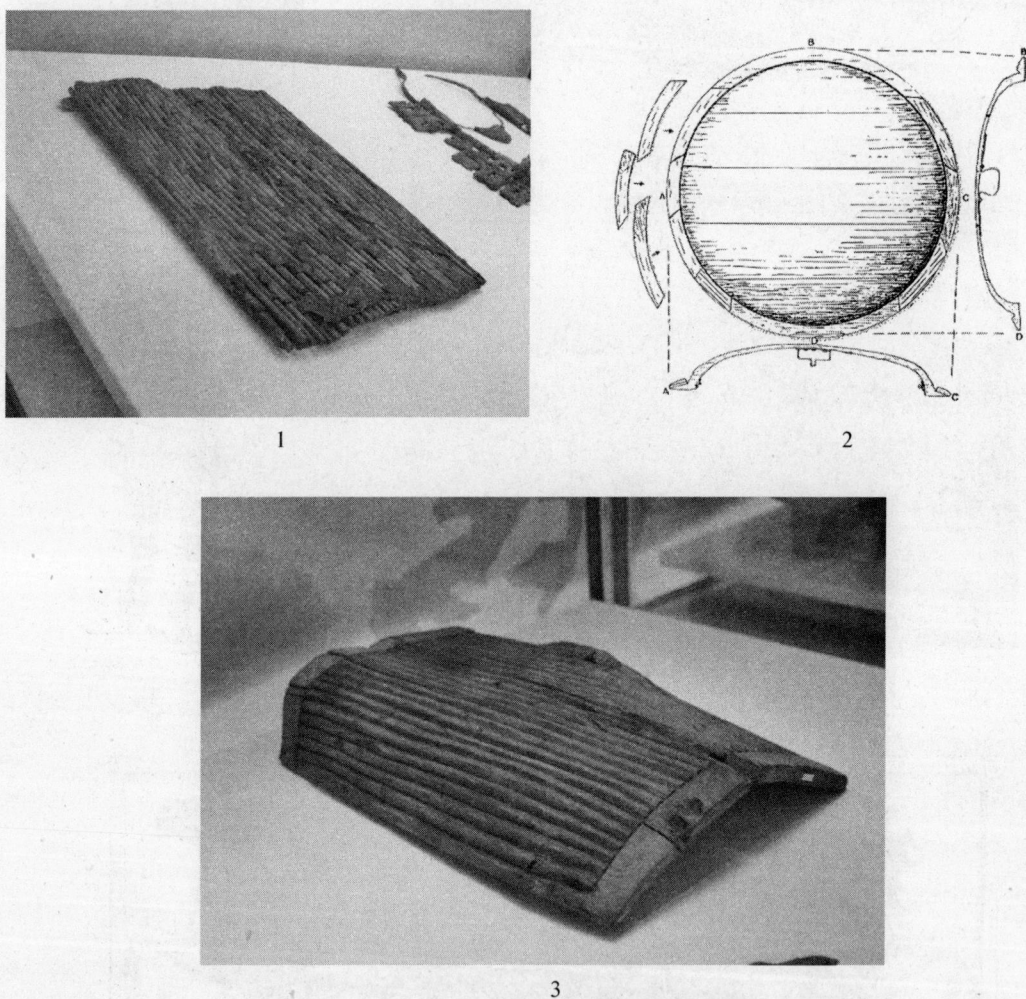

图二十四　1、3. 巴泽雷克墓藤牌;2. 希腊圆盾。

(1、3,摄影/李韬;2,摘自 *Greek hoplite 480－323 BC*)

　　至于希腊化的盾牌,主要是凸面大圆盾,亦有椭圆形盾牌发现。与其地中海地区的祖型——凸面大圆盾本质没有改进和变化。内侧中央有一套换,盾沿内侧有把手。盾体为藤木制,盾面包有皮革和青铜。这种盾主要以图像的形式,在中亚地区出现。

　　这一时期的马具,最值得注意的是无镫的甲骑具装的出现。首先,本地区所有的实物和图像资料都证明,秦汉时期中亚并没有出现马镫。但这并不能阻止重装骑士驾驭着甲骑具装驰骋疆场。"奥克斯河神庙"的浮雕,为我们证实,头顶"雅典式"头盔,身着复合式铠甲,手持长矛的骑士,胯下的坐骑颈部和前胸有由长方形甲叶编缀成的铠甲,身上披附的是鱼鳞甲。[①] 与萨珊波斯早期的重装无镫骑士石雕相结合,[②]再次说明甲骑具装与长杆兵器的组合早于马镫的出现,"马镫革命"具有狭隘的时空局限性。

（二）攻击型单兵装备

战斗序列中,投射兵器往往最先接战,中亚地区也不例外,而且更具特点,因为那里是骑射的发祥地之一。

中亚地区出土的较完整的弓箭资料,基本在帕米尔以东的地区。这一地区的弓,主要分五型(图二十五):第一型是洋海一型弓,第二型是洋海二型弓,第三型是洋海三型弓,第四型是洋海四型弓,第五型是巴泽雷克弓。

第一至四型弓,主要出土地点在吐哈盆地及塔里木盆地南缘。由于大部分资料尚未发表,笔者仅根据观察记忆作以略述。

据主持和参与吐鲁番田野考古工作的师长介绍,吐鲁番出土的弓形态最原始,时代最早的是单体木弓,弓体由单根木棍制成。这是第一型,在洋海墓地有出土。

第二型弓体由两片长条木片胶黏、绑缚而成,弓弣有折角,整体呈反曲,与两河流域浮雕上的"亚述弓"相似。

第三型,即洋海三型弓,出土在洋海二号台地的"萨满巫师墓"中,年代约2 800 BP。这种弓的渊、萧宽阔,内侧并排纵向贴数块筋角,而正面观察,弰、弭部则窄长。从力学角度上看,这样的设计可以使射手使用强度很大的劲弓和长度更长的长箭。本型弓在和田和尼雅的墓地中均有出土,两者约在公元1世纪至3世纪。有学者根据历史叙述及图像资料将第三型弓误称为"匈奴弓",这是不符合考古学标准的。

第四型弓在洋海墓地、苏贝希墓地和胜金店墓地广泛出土。由于洋海墓地出土数量最多,样式典型,时代最早,因此笔者将其命名为洋海四型弓。本型弓为复合反曲弓:弭部卷曲向前,渊部侧面为隆起两个对称的钝角。通过观察,很难判断弓的弭部是否是独立制作后再与萧部组装的。但可以看清楚的是,萧、渊的背面的确有筋角的黏附和纤维绑缚的痕迹。其尺寸在80～150 cm左右,80 cm的从儿童墓出土,渊上部比下部折角更大。充分体现了控弦游骑的剽悍——"儿能骑羊,引弓射鸟鼠;少长则射狐兔,用为食;力士能贯弓,尽为甲骑"。本型弓所属墓葬的年代约2 400 BP。同样形制的弓,在环地中海地区的希腊古风时代以降的瓶画中大量出现,多为斯基泰、波斯射手使用,故古典学界称其为"斯基泰弓"。可惜,环地中海地区的墓葬中,从未出土过这种弓的实物。而在考古和历史学上,斯基泰文化的来源与中亚息息相关。因此,笔者认为,将这种弓命名为"洋海四型弓",是符合考古学标准的。

第五型是巴泽雷克弓,分布范围与巴泽雷克文化一致。这种弓为木制,渊部不像前者那么有棱有角,相对呈弧形。其次,单独出土的弭证明,其与弓萧是复合组装的。弭的形态,上部为一小指大小,扁平的弧;下部延伸的部分开长叉,与弓萧组装。根据复原形态看,它也是复合反曲弓。

---

① *The Sculpture of Khalchayan* (Russian Version), written by Pugachenkova, published in 1971.
② *Das Reiterkampfbild in der Iranischen und Iranisch Beeinflussten Kunst Parthischer und Sasnidischer Zeit*, written by Hubertus von Gall, published by Gebr. Mann Verlag. Berlin, 1990.

　　中亚地区的箭与中原相比没有什么特别之处,只是在箭镞上不见三棱锥体的"三廉羊头镞"。这与中世纪以前,中亚部队并不装备弩有关。至于具有地方特色的箭镞,要属小型三翼空腔镞。这种三翼镞多为青铜铸造,中空,双翼间有单镂孔。箭杆的头部往往削成带倒刺锥形,插入箭镞腔体内,倒钩与镂孔铆合。由于这种箭镞尺寸小,形态原始,从力学角度看,不太具备穿甲功能,很可能是狩猎用的箭镞。①

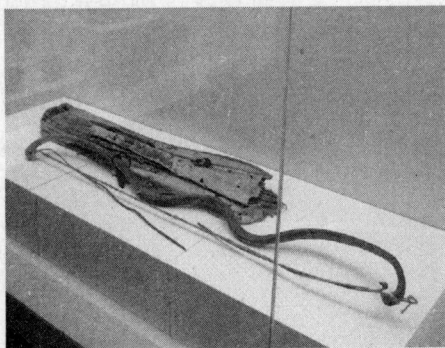

1

2

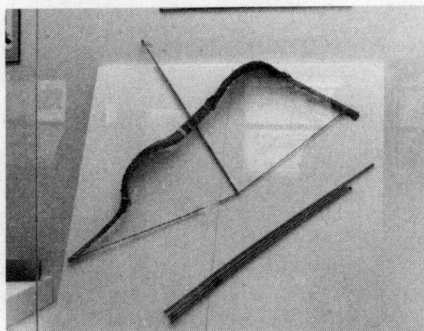

3

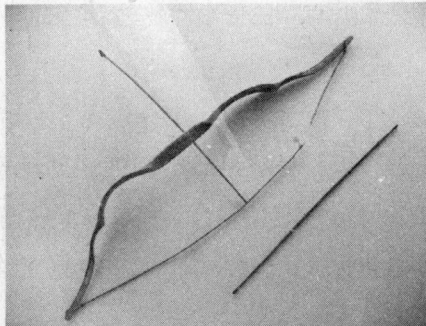

4

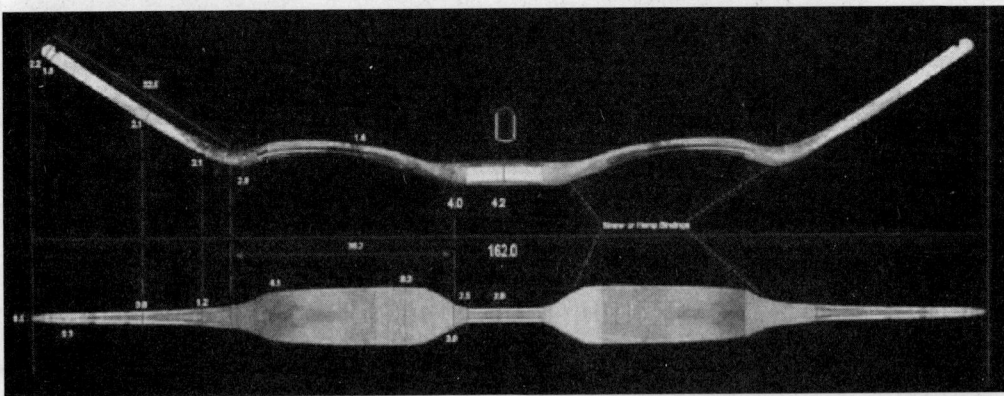

5

图二十五　1. 第四型弓,鄯善出土;2. 希腊瓶画中的"斯基泰弓";3、4、5. 第三型弓,和田、民丰出土

(1、2、3、4,摄影/李韬;5,摘自http://www.atarn.org)

---

　　① 众所周知,为了不破损昂贵的皮毛,猎人往往选择创伤面积小,但流血多的箭镞,这与现代弹头同理。猎杀野兔多用霰弹,对付野猪用大口径独头弹,但不管怎样猎取这两种动物,都是为了肉食;而对于鹿、狐狸、紫貂等皮毛贵重的动物,往往得使用小口径弹头,这样不至于使皮毛过分破损,保护其经济价值。笔者以为小型三翼空腔镞,也是同理。

其他射箭装备还有"韬"、"箙"。中国古籍称二合一的为"韇丸",[1]古典学叫 *gorytus*（Gorits）：它兼具"韬"、"箙"形态和功能（图二十六）。

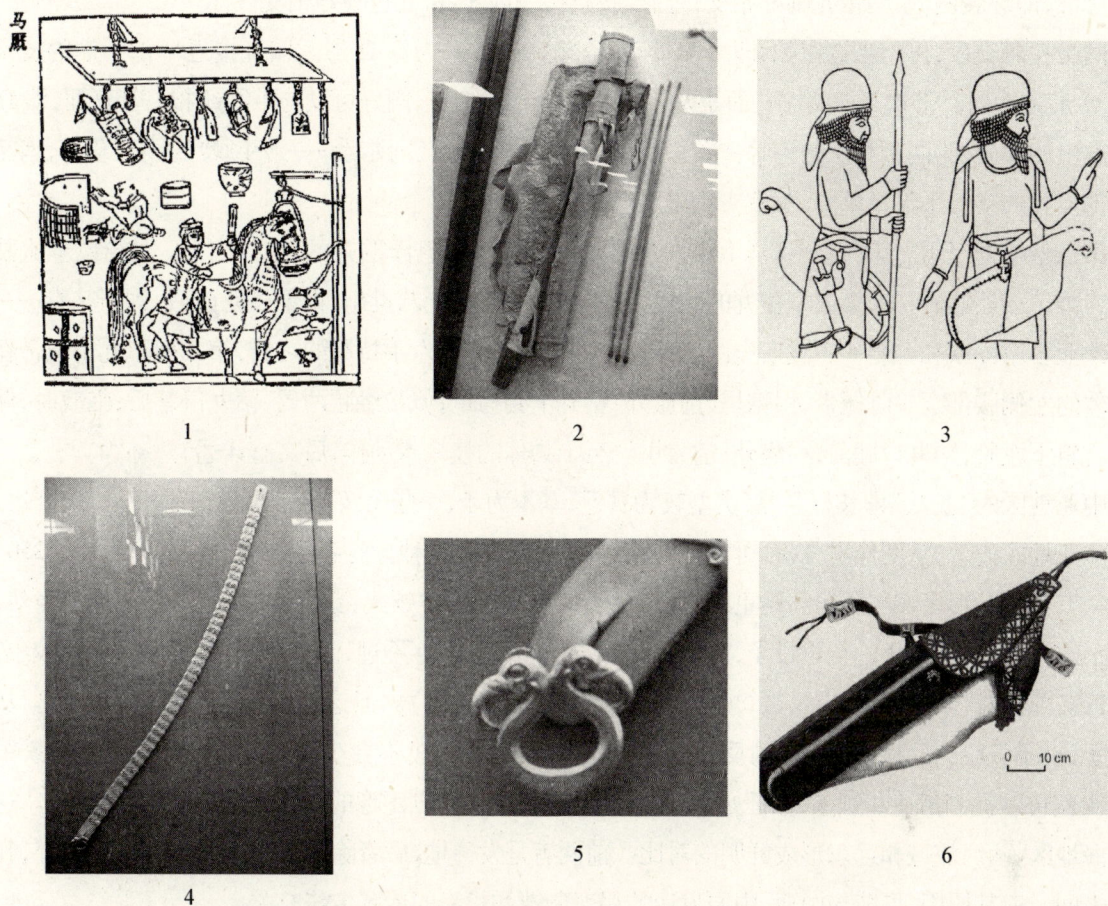

图二十六　1. 汉代画像中的韇丸;2. 第一型韇丸,和田出土;3、6. 第二型韇丸与平时的佩带方式;4、5. 第二型韇丸的佩带与 Ω 型带钩

（1,摘自《汉代物质文化资料图说》;2、4、5,摄影/李韬;3,摘自 *The Armies of Bactria*;
6,摘自 *Archaeology Ethnology & Anthropology of Eurasia*, *Vol. 3*）

韇丸有两型：第一型韇丸的韬、箙分化明显。韬的部分由毡制成,呈半截张弓形;箙则是长圆柱皮筒（晚期有盖）,并缝制在韬的长边一侧。这种韇丸的实物出土在塔里木盆地南北缘,早期的出土于洋海二号台地的"萨满"墓中,时代约 2 800 BP,与第三型弓（洋海三型弓）搭配。从图像学角度看,其形象亦流行于萨珊——贵霜时期的中亚和伊朗地区。

第二型韇丸由三部分组成：皮囊、佩带和带钩。皮囊分两层,内层是韬,口大囊深,用于承弓。为了固定,一侧还有木条固定,与皮囊缝合在一起,上面往往雕刻有精美的动植物纹饰。有的木条底端,与皮囊底部相连的部分,还有一个水滴形底座,大头与木条相连,整体形成支撑韇丸的框架。韇丸外侧箙口较浅,有的更有褶皱隔层,可以分类排放不同箭镞和功用的箭矢。根据出土的情况看,箭头都朝下,向着皮囊

---

① 孙机先生怀疑东汉郑玄的注释,认为韇丸不能装弓。但新疆的发现说明,"韇丸"的确是秦汉时期胡汉皆用的,兼具韬、箙形态与功用的标准装备。参见《汉代物质文化资料图说》,第 139 页。

底部。鞲丸的顶部,往往还有一块为了防止筋角、弓弦受潮的毡套,形制似半截弓,刚好将露出韬的弓遮住。

鞲丸的佩带为皮制,两端有孔。佩带上又有环佩、挂钩等,用于配搭各种饰物和兵器。佩带的长度有一定标准,即环腰两周,两带孔刚好相交;过肩、腰斜挎一周,两带孔也刚好相交。

两带孔相交后,再与带钩纽扣,即可佩带鞲丸。这种挂钩,为倒 Ω 形。鞲丸接近口部一端的皮环可套入 Ω 形带钩内。带钩开口两端背面是两枚截面为 T 形的钮钉,刚好可以与带孔纽扣。其正面,即 Ω 下端翻卷出的部分,为两颗相反的勾喙禽首。[1] 这种 Ω 形带钩北至阿尔泰——萨颜岭的图瓦墓葬,南至天山中部南麓的察乌乎沟口墓葬,都有实物出土。

第二型鞲丸经常与第四型弓(洋海第四型弓)和第五型弓(巴泽雷克弓)相伴出土。结合欧亚大陆古代的二维、三维图像可知,第二型鞲丸的时代,基本始于公元前七八世纪,止于公元前后,为斯基泰——塞种等欧亚草原民族和希腊——波斯先民广泛使用。按一般人类左手持弓的习惯,第二型鞲丸也佩带在射手身体的左侧腰部。平时佩带,弓韬里、箭箙外,鞲丸上套弓罩,佩带绕腰两周,鞲丸口朝后;临战时,佩带自右肩斜下左胯,鞲丸口朝前,弓囊外、箭囊里。至于具体的技战术动作,后文有详述。

中亚地区的“长兵”即长杆兵器,类型较为贫乏,基本为矛,一些图像上也显示有三股叉。

中亚地区的矛,从图像上分析,可能存在格斗用矛和投矛二种。前者矜部较长,按比例也在 250 cm 以上。有鋬扁叶形矛头与长矜和厚重的三棱有尖鐏组合,是马其顿式希腊化方阵的中坚装备。当然,鐏部较小的,多为马上使用。至于投矛,则很难在形态上进行区分。不过,为了追求射程,矛头一般较小,有的銎管骹部特长,矛底端没有鐏、镦,短矜部呈流线型(头粗尾细)。但这种实物在中亚很少发现。从图像判断,投矛一般为反持(即虎口的反方向);投掷手装备的一般不会少于两根(罗马军团和戚家军例外),由此可以提高射速和频率,保证必杀。当然,中亚投矛主要以图像的形式出现,实物出土不多。这与地中海地区、两河流域和远东形成鲜明的对比。前两者是发祥地,后者除羌人及晚期的个别例证外,几乎闻所未闻。究其原因,可能与中亚、中原发达的弓弩制造和精湛的射艺传统有关。

至于“长兵”中的三股叉,它往往是王权神化的标志之一。当然,其形象也出现在希腊化之后,是希腊海神波士顿的象征,故应属于仪仗用具。

“短兵”中的基本组合是长剑、短剑、阔头拱背砍刀、鹤嘴稿、棒(鞭或锏)和大槌。

中亚地区的长剑大致可分为短柄和长柄两型。

短柄长剑身长度超过 100 cm,双刃而锋尖锐利。由于多为铁制,腊部横截面为扁菱形,出土时锈蚀严重,很难判断出脊部的形态。同样,剑格是否为合铸或组装,很难判断;不过形制较大,扁平似 B。剑柄宽扁平而短,首部为扁平椭圆形。

长柄长剑不论是剑身还是剑鞘及附件的形制与佩带方式,都和战国至汉的长柄长剑形制基本一致,只是在首部平面中心又有一小块圆形凸起。[2]

中亚地区秦汉时期是否有刀的存在,一直是一个有争议的话题。因为,那里不论是实物还是图像都没有类似中原那样的短柄环首直刃长刀。但从历史资料和个别部件上分析推测,中亚的确存在过希腊式

---

① 这一实验考古成果,笔者发现于柏林“斯基泰文物展”的展板中。影印内容好像是复原笔记。由于文字潦草、图像模糊,无法得知研究者的姓名。但可以肯定,这一成果属于阿尔赞二号冢项目组。

② *A Study on the Bones from Orlat*, Silk Road Art and Archaeology, Vol. 7, written by Jangar Ya. ILYASOV & Dmitriy V. RUSANOV, published by The Institute of Silk Road Studies, 2001.

的阔头拱背短柄砍刀——kopis。历史上的佐证，自不必说，因为中亚曾经惨遭马其顿铁蹄的蹂躏。实物上，撒玛尔罕曾经出土过骨制鸷首的短柄。有学者推测，其为 kopis 刀柄的可能性较大。笔者认为可备一说，但还不够充分。因为鸷首短柄也可能是剑柄，不论是帕加玛，还是伊朗的浮雕都能充分说明这一点。因此，kopis 是否长期存在于中亚，还有待于考古发现的进一步证明。但可以肯定的是，在帕米尔以东地区闻所未闻。①

汉文古籍对中亚的短剑，没有明确的称谓。相反，古典文献中，称这种同样流行于波斯的短剑为"Acinaces"。在时空上，它分布极广：东起黑海——地中海，西到中原，亦铜亦铁；时代跨度从西周晚期直至公元二三世纪。其基本形制为长叶形剑身，腊部较窄，青铜制的往往全身合铸，有剑脊或血槽。剑柄较短，仅容一手把持，中间或镂空。首部形态多样，有圆形、半圆形、菌形等等，是传统类型学研究的一个基本要素。短剑的剑鞘是一个文化分野上的标志。以中原为中心的东亚地区和以西的中亚乃至西方地区完全不同。后者剑鞘多为木制，剑鞘一面扁圆，一面平整。两侧对称有时各有两个系；或鞘口布内侧有系带，可以与右腰的皮带相连，剑鞘下端亦有系带，可绑缚在右股外侧。另外，中东及以西地区的剑鞘底端还有保持剑身竖直平衡的摽（图二十七）。

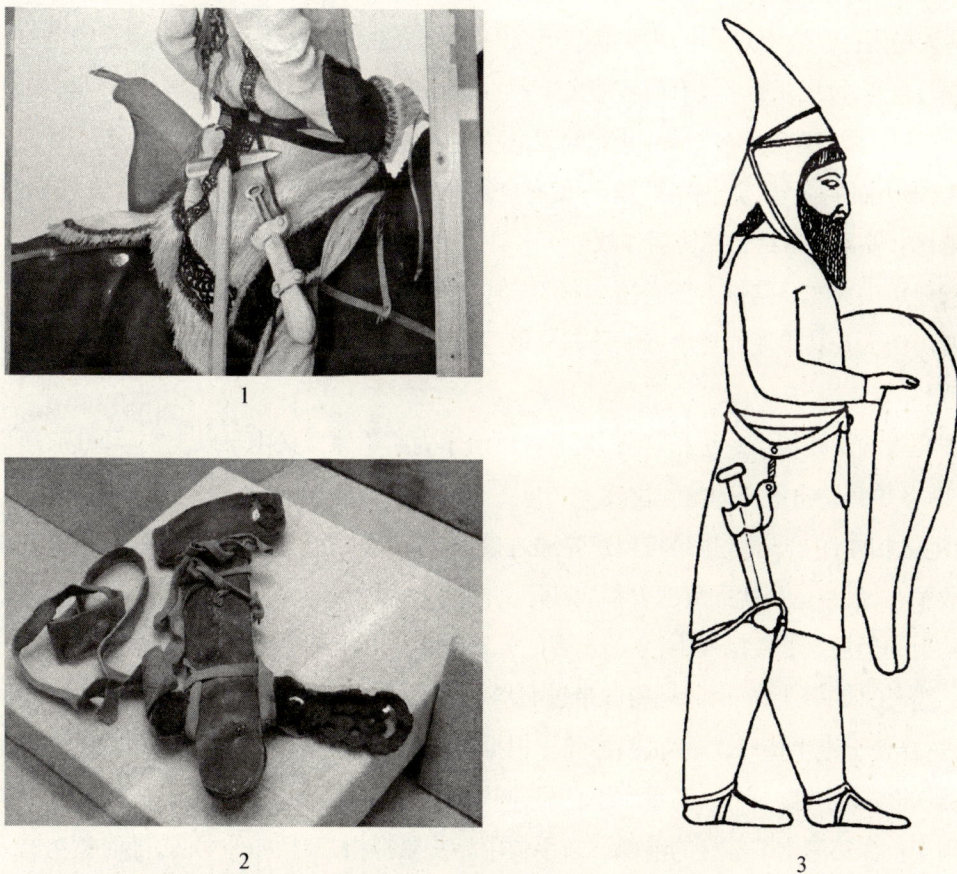

图二十七　1、3. 中亚短剑的佩带方式；2. 短剑鞘，民丰出土

（1、2，摄影/李韬；3，摘自 The Armies of Bactria）

---

① An Achaemenian Griffin Handle from the Temple of the Oxus, the Makharia in Northern Bactria, In the Land of the Gryphones Papers on Central Asian archaeology in antiquity, written by B. A. Litvinskij & I. R. Pičikian, published by Casa Editrice Le Lettere, 1995.

鹤嘴镐是一种极具草原风格的兵器,在中亚地区广泛出土且特别流行。鹤嘴镐由青铜制成,分三部分:镐头、柲和鐏。由于鹤嘴镐的形态类似无胡直援戈,所以笔者暂且借用戈的各部位名称来描述鹤嘴镐。镐援一般为长圆锥形、尖头圆柱形或无刃尖头扁窄长条形。后者如是优弧头,那就是战斧。镐都有圆形或椭圆形銎孔或管銎。镐内的部分,或为窄扁长条形战斧,或为镂空装饰的窄扁长条,或为冬菇头形的榔头。镐柲横截面或通体椭圆形;或头部圆形,尾部和鐏部椭圆形。柲的尾端一般削成鐏的圆锥帽形态与鐏通过铆钉、铆孔榫合。

最后一类“短兵”是棒(鞭或锏)和大槌,均属钝器。棒在中亚出现较晚,已进入贵霜帝国时期。从形态上看,棒身是一根或几根直竖木,头部削得浑圆,个头较尾端为大,上包金属。棒身由几个排列的金属箍束紧。棒柄较短,首部为一金属圆球,以保持整体平衡。棒在中亚地区的起源很难说,但作为殖民者——希腊人的棒,时代久远,起码古风时代的英雄、诸神就已使用,特别《奥德塞》中的赫拉克利特。中原地区则很难找到这种短柄大头棒的原形。又根据萨珊波斯的石雕可知,这种棒往往悬挂在右腿前马鞍一侧。因此,笔者推测,它是公元后中亚重装骑兵的装备之一。对于中原,不排除它是唐宋时期鞭、锏的祖型。

与棒的功效相同的还有大槌。[①] 大槌的形态,多为圆形球体,下加一短柄,有的短柄后还系有绳索。大槌的形象主要出现在阿尔泰、天山地区的岩画上。有的大槌拴在腰后,起先让学者匪夷所思。经过横向比较,发现有些大槌则握在战士的手中,力大者甚至双手各抢一槌。笔者以为,这也许就是中世纪锤(骨朵)和流行锤的祖型,当然,按尺寸后者没有前者那么夸张的大。根据蒙古博物馆的民族学资料可知,这种圆形大槌为坚木所制,尺寸跟篮球差不多。而中世纪的锤,多为金属制,所以锤头也就拳头那么大。可见,后世小说演义中,各路英雄使用的特大号“金银铜铁”锤,即使有金属的部分,也只是表皮和把柄,锤的核心应该还是坚木。

(三) 总结:单兵装备组合的协同作战

在中亚,亚历山大的马其顿方阵曾所向披靡,但依然不能改变这一地区以骑战为主力的草原特色。而事实上,亚历山大及其中亚的继承者就是充分地运用了骑兵的优势,并以坚强步兵方阵为后盾,才在中亚站稳了脚跟。

希腊、罗马人的步战相当系统和复杂,为笔者目前学力所不逮。又由于以上实际原因,所以此处主要论述骑兵部队各单兵装备组合的协同作战。

与中原地区相同,中亚部队也是希望首先通过投射兵器持续性集群攻击,大规模杀伤敌有生力量,挫敌锐气,撼敌军心,最终达到扰乱敌部署和战斗序列的战术战役目的。

因此,骑射的运用是非接触战中,至关重要的先锋。根据出土图像资料显示,配备第四型弓(洋海四型弓)和第二型鞬丸的骑士,战时将韬箙佩带过肩斜挎,韬箙置于左腰,箭箙在内侧,弓韬在外侧,韬箙口朝前上方。这样便于左手持弓,右手拔箭控弦。根据民族学资料和历代军事家总结,冲锋骑射时,一般有三个名称不同的攻击步骤。首先,骑手左手持弓,同时用除拇指外的四指和弓弣一起握紧两支镞头朝下的箭;拇指则架控住第三支箭箭杆的前部。右手食中指扣紧拇指,箭栝扣住弓弦,随时蓄势待发。骑士双腿策动马匹向前方或右前方冲刺,待战马四蹄飞腾,身体重心平稳后,迅速接近目标,在11点、9点和7点三个方向开弓放箭,对目标发起连续攻击。所谓“11点”射击,兵书中称“分鬃射”;“9点”射击,称“对镫

① *The Weaponry of Early Nomads in Altai Rock Art*, *Archaeology Ethnology & Anthropology of Eurasia*, Vol. 19, written by V. D. Kubarev, published by Siberian Branch of RAS, 2004.

射";"7 点"射击,称"抹秋射"。根据阵形,一般右手开弓的骑士,可排一字长蛇阵,鱼贯而入,进入适合攻击夹角后,纷纷齐射。如敌军派兵尾随追击,骑士可以伏鞍低头,右手暗中从左侧抽箭、搭弦,待进入攻击范围内,迅速回身以"抹秋射"射杀追兵。[①] 这种"托刀计"、"回马枪"是"飞将军"李广和追击色诺芬兵团的波斯骑兵的拿手绝活。它屡试不爽,令敌手——特别是步兵,防不胜防、心惊胆寒(图二十八)!

1

2

3

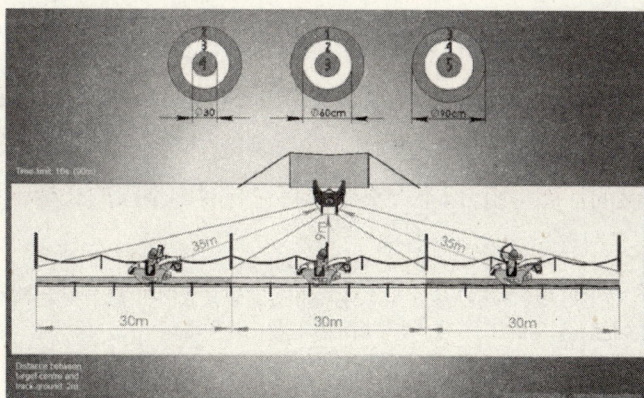

4

图二十八　骑射诸法

(1,摄影/李韬;2,摘自 *The Armies of Bactria*;3,摘自 *Das Reiterkampfbild in der Iranischen und Iranisch Beeinflussten Kunst Parthischer und Sasnidischer Zeit*;4,摘自 http://www.diesteppenreiter.de)

---

① 《射经》,[明] 李呈芬,明德出版社,东京,1990 年。

如果敌人是相对而来的骑兵,且在我的右侧,按基本战术,骑士得旋马将对手让至左侧再射杀。若时空不够,就应迅速接近,用格斗兵器瞬间将其解决。

骑兵格斗首先碰出火花的是长矛。不过按中东和黑海——地中海地区骑兵的传统,他们也会在错镫之前,投掷两根投矛或标枪,以期先干掉敌酋。作为正手把握(矛头与虎口方向一致)的长矛,其攻击方向更为自由,几乎是 360 度的。同时为了防御,草原骑士也许会用左手的藤牌,巧妙的架开对方的锋刃。如敌骑从左侧相对而来,刚一错镫,技术高超的骑士也许有机会迅速用左手从马鞍右前侧抽棒,反手狠砸敌兵后脑背("撒手锏"就是对这一战术动作的形象说明)。此时,如戚继光所说,对手纵使铠坚甲厚,挨上这一砸,不脑浆迸裂,也得骨断筋折,吐血败走。可见,根据辩证原理,大棒的出现,也表明重装甲胄早已普及。[①]

一旦双方落马,接下来就是长短剑或鹤嘴镐的对决。中亚地区的战士普遍同时装备长剑和短剑,在战术技击上,与剑道中"二刀流"或"二天一流"的道理一样。即一手实,一手虚;一手正,一手奇;一手攻,一手防;一手远,一手近;虚实相卫,攻防自如。当然,这主要是落马后的步战。不过,应当指出的是,练"双剑"的功夫可非一般。以剑道为例,没有强健的体魄,五年刻苦的训练,外加二段以上的资历,对决时"要双刀",只能破绽百出,命丧黄泉。

鹤嘴镐其实是一种十分原始的兵器,它只能从上往下,从一侧向另一侧发起攻击,而且还得先蓄势。这会给对手以可乘之机,架或绕开鹤嘴镐,然后就势用锋刃迅速有效的杀伤。因此,这种兵器在贵霜王朝以后,就迅速地退出了历史的疆场,而成为中世纪中东的肉搏战中步兵的装备,其形制也变成了用于凿开头盔的短柄"羊角榔头"。

四、结论:中原与中亚地区单兵制式化装备的交流与比较

(一) 文化因素的比较与交流

在单兵制式化装备的文化因素方面,中原与中亚地区有很多共通性。在一定历史军事冲突背景的条件下,可以推断为交流的结果。

这一交流的集中突出体现,就是奥拉特墓葬中出土的战斗骨板画。

首先是甲胄。中原地区甲胄最突出的特色,就是盆领。从曾候乙墓和秦俑皮甲盆领,到二十家子的汉"锻鎧",这些例证的时代都在公元前。而骨板画上的重装铠甲的项后,也有盆领高高耸起。[②] 此外,画中长柄长剑及其剑鞘和玉彘的形态与组合,不得不令人将它与战国秦汉的长柄剑相联系(图二十九)。[③]

---

① 戚子云:"西北原野之战,旧传俱用大棒,……大棒亦无式,不知用法,缘以虏人盔甲坚固,射之不入,戳之不伤,遂用棒一击,则勿问甲胄之坚,皆靡。"戚继光说的大棒是长棍,即《吕氏春秋·贵卒篇》说的"赵氏攻中山,中山之人多力者曰吾丘鸠,衣铁甲操铁杖以战"的"杖"。孟子把它叫梃,又说:"执梃可以挞秦楚之坚甲利兵。"虽然中西的棒:"一长一短,一步一骑",但重击破甲的作用是一样的。参见《练兵实纪》,第 308 页。

② 有关盆领和钩兵的辩证关系,最早是林巳奈夫先生告知杨泓先生的,语在《中国古代的戟》,《中国古兵器论丛》,第 234 页。笔者沿着这一思路,再补充几点:一,云南滇国青铜一体式盆领与中原铠甲合缀式盆领并非同出一门。因为其与公元前 13 世纪迈锡尼文明的青铜铠甲盆领,结构几乎完全一致。但目前尚无法将二者直接联系,毕竟时空跨度太大,而且克里特岛出土的那副铠甲是车战用的孤品,后世罕见。二,不论原出如何,早期盆领与钩兵的辩证关系,是可以肯定的。因为在欧洲的青铜时代,戈形兵器大量出现并被使用。所以,克里特岛出现盆领,也就不足为奇。而中原、云南地区的早期盆领,本来就是和钩兵伴出的。三,中原地区进入铁器时代后,钩兵渐渐退出战场,而盆领作为一种兵器传统被保留下来,甚至传播到中亚地区。因此,河中地区出现合缀式盆领,很大程度上是对中原盆领传统的承袭,而与钩兵无关。

③ 参见《玉具剑与玉彘式佩剑法》,《中国圣火》,第 15~43 页,孙机著,辽宁教育出版社,1996 年。

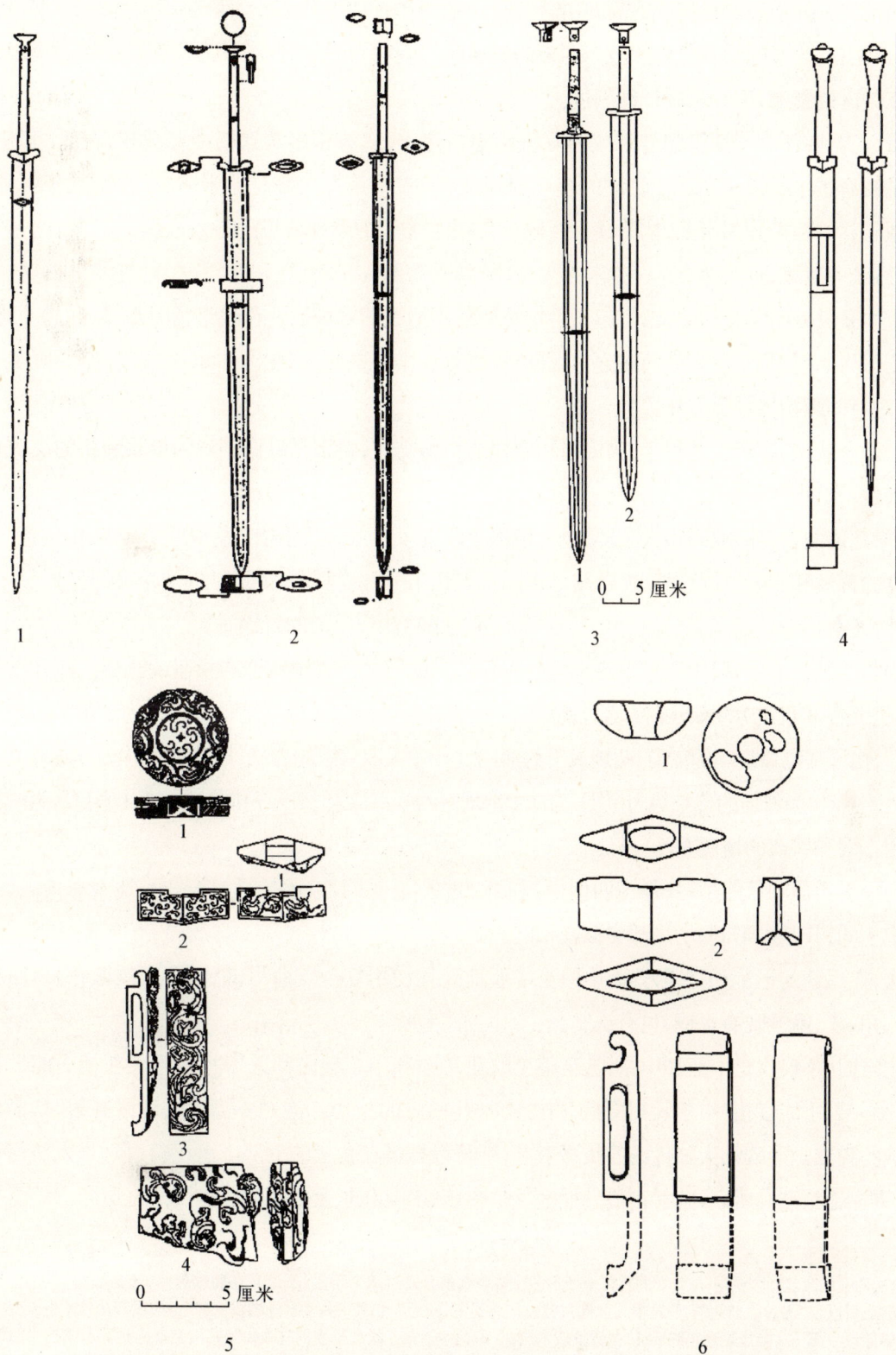

图二十九　1. 燕剑;2. 秦剑;3. 汉剑;4. 奥拉特剑;5. 汉剑饰;6. 奥拉特剑饰

（1、3、5,摘自《古代兵器通论》;2,摘自《中国古代兵器》;6,摘自 *Silk Road Art and Archaeology, Vol. 7*）

学界对奥拉特出土骨板画墓的断代,有着不同的看法。以普卡琼克瓦为首的发掘者于上世纪70年代提出可能在公元前一二世纪。之后80年代,有一部分学者认为其已进入萨珊——贵霜时期。从90年代到21世纪初,更多的学者分析比较东西方的资料,认为在公元一二世纪较为妥善。后者虽提出有自帕米尔以东地区的影响,但并未做详细阐述。

笔者以为,西汉中晚期汉朝与匈奴的斗争日趋白热化,双方都多次连横中亚政权,在战略上牵制对手。于是就有了中原汉王朝武帝时期的李广利西征。①汉军第二次翻越帕米尔,在宣帝初年。当时,战略上气数已尽的西遁匈奴余部,依然横行西域。汉朝西域都护乘郅支单于自毁联盟之机,迅速邀集西域诸部,建立统一战线,进兵两支:一支南入大宛,断郅支后路;一支西出伊犁,稳扎稳打地进抵塔拉斯,迫使战略上本来就处于劣势的郅支,打起了游牧民族最不擅长的守城战。在战略意图明确,后勤补给充足,战术运用得当的前提下,汉军借西域之力,歼灭了匈奴在中亚的势力,帕米尔东西"咸震怖",直至王莽篡权,南北对峙的政治格局暂时作罢!

以上两个战例,在历史背景上,为中原和中亚的军事交流,特别是针锋相对的单兵装备的交流创造了基本的条件。

同样,此前两百年的亚历山大东征,也在根本上改变了中亚的政治格局。从单兵制式化装备角度看,重装甲胄的普及和步骑协同作战,使希腊化王国不仅在中亚站稳脚跟,更延续近两个世纪。

当然,还有不少共通点。②这些共通点,可上溯至张骞凿空之前的青铜时代。

作为防卫装备的甲胄,中亚和中原都拥有时代较早的整体式青铜铸造的头盔或兜鍪。前者以早期铁器时代(公元前8世纪)的库班式为著,后者则以北京白浮青铜时代西周墓地出土的为典型。

此后,由于提高修复率的需要,两地又不约而同地开始采取编缀的方式,制造以甲片为基本的复合式头盔。当然,中亚作为波斯的传统势力范围,与地中海地区的联系从未中断,不排除这一变化来自后者的影响。

铠甲方面和头盔的情况基本一样。

作为投射兵器的第四型弓(洋海四型弓)和第二型镝丸其附件,不论是黑海——地中海地区,还是吐哈盆地出土的,其基本形制、功用都类似或相同。③

其次,在弓箭的形制和材质方面,中原至中亚地区均使用复合反曲弓,箭镞多三翼镞;弓体原料主要为木、筋、角、皮,箭镞既有青铜,也有铁制。

射艺方面,不仅仅是中亚和中原,甚至整个欧亚草原和中东地区都采取将箭杆架在持弓的拇指内侧虎口上,另一只手的食指、中指紧扣拇指,用拇指张开弓弦的技巧。这一姿势可以确保骑射时,箭杆的稳定和准确的瞄准。而欧洲大陆传统的长弓射艺,则将箭杆搭在食指的上部。这在骑射时是无法保证箭杆稳定的,更遑论精准。所以,骑射在很大程度上是中东、中亚和东亚共有的非物质文化遗产。④

---

① 这次西征的政治意图模糊,与匈奴的直接牵涉不多。整个战争分前后两个阶段,不论是在后勤保障,还是战略决策上,都犯了几乎致命的错误,可以说"去时强弩之末,归时损兵折将",劳民伤财不说,政治上来去如潮水的游牧铁骑一样,没有从根本上改变中亚的现状。不过,中原政权第一次翻越帕米尔的远征,在战役战术层面,却让中亚第一次感受到拥有强大制式化装备的训练有素的中原军队的威力和剽悍。因此也逼得守城的大宛被迫雇佣"秦人"凿井,以解决水源补给问题。

② 目前还找不到支持交流说的直接证据,因此暂时推断是人类社会演进造就的共通点。

③ 根据希腊瓶画图像和洋海墓地的实物判断,其年代均在公元前3世纪之前。但由于缺乏长距离间的连续证据,使学者不得不将其作为欧亚草原文化因素内部趋同性的例证来考虑。

④ 在欧洲大陆,长弓一直为步兵使用和继承,而骑射也从未得以推广和普及。

（二）中原与中亚地区单兵制式化装备的标准

除民族传统外，兵器的形态与其所处的人文地理环境、社会生产模式、社会生产力水平、战略指导思想、技战术的运用和政治格局有着紧密的联系。

所谓人文地理环境，中国传统称"风水"。即什么样的环境，决定什么样的战场，决定适应战场环境的装备。好比江南吴越，湖沼河渠密布，古人多步战或水战，与马有关的车战、骑战仅占很次要的地位。因此，古人必须发明适用于步战、水战和潮湿环境下的单兵装备。相反，东亚干旱的北方和西北方，疆域广袤，适合大兵团，特别是骑兵迅速的展开。因此，骑兵装备就应运而生。

社会生产模式与生产力水平是相辅相成的。生产力水平低下，包括管理和系统运作在内的生产模式自然落后；反之，则能产生强大的军工生产系统，生产出具有一定标准的制式化装备。

战略指导思想也和单兵制式化装备密不可分。比如北方游牧民族因经济、环境条件所限，经常对南部农耕地区发动侵袭。但其早期的目的，主要是以劫掠补充不足，并非在于长期占领统治。所以，战略上自然没有相应跟进的政治措施。这就要求战争速战速决，尽量避免持久扩大。而游牧骑兵的装备，基本是遵循这一指导思想而制造的。相反，农耕政权以守土为准则，纵然有战略进攻，也是反击性的。而对付游骑的速战速决，必须采取大规模持久性的战争模式和一系列的配套统治措施。这势必要求军队稳扎稳打，步步为营：在有条件的地方，建立一系列有城防设施的军事要塞；在条件不具备的地方，步、骑、车连环相卫、协同作战，最终置游牧敌手于死地。这更要求单兵必须拥有工业化生产的制式化装备，各兵种间装备必须适合各种环境下的协同作战。由此，方能长期保持一定的军事优势。

技战术的运用和单兵制式化装备有直接的联系。为了实现一定的集团杀伤功效，军队必须使用符合技战术要求的单兵制式化装备。[①] 这必须要求上兵手中的兵器符合相应技战术的标准，方能将单兵和单兵装备组合的威力发挥得淋漓尽致、恰到好处。

因此，笔者以为，秦汉时期中原和中亚地区存在着两种标准的单兵制式化装备生产系统：

第一标准，即国家化军工生产系统。这一类单兵制式化装备和其所属的社会一样，处于古代社会演化的顶层。这种单兵制式化装备在生产上，采取统一采购、定制定量生产，产品具有一定的兼容性、交互性、共属性，并有明显的标志性，从形态和功用上，其完全符合北约现代理念标准。充分体现这一标准的例证，就是中原的以秦为首的战国七雄、统一的秦帝国和武帝以后的汉帝国，它们的装备往往以铭文的形式，在兵器上标注出生产兵器的工匠、单位、监造者及生产年代。

第二标准，即社会化军工生产系统。它拥有发达的生产力，先进的生产技术。表现在单兵制式化装备上，与国家化军工系统生产的没有本质区别。其最大的不同在于生产的组织、管理方式。即社会中存在特定的工匠阶层和商业组织，他们根据敌对双方的需要，系统的生产符合战役战斗标准的单兵制式化装备。能充分体现这一特色的例证，就是中亚的希腊化王国和战国、汉初、汉末的地方诸侯或豪强武装。

在考古发掘中，兵器往往以固定形式的组合出现，不同地区的兵器组合中单兵装备的形制，也经常类似或相同。根据这些客观的存在，我们有理由推测，其所属的社会中，存在一定的社会化分工和系统的生产。连接中亚和中原的欧亚草原地区的单兵制式化装备，基本属于这一系统的产物。从现代军事术语上区分，第一标准是系统化列装，而第二标准则是系统化选装。

---

① 比如，陈汤西征围攻郅支城时，为了对付城内的反攻和营外游骑的袭扰和反包围，于是采取"橹楯在前，戟弩为后"的战役战术。

　　这两种标准生产出的单兵制式化装备,很难判断孰优孰劣。关键得与特定的人文地理环境、历史背景、战略思想和战役指挥相结合。事实上,没有一种单兵制式化装备组合适应所有的战斗环境和战斗人员。标准化生产的单兵制式化装备,意味着仅适应大部分战斗人员和基本的战斗环境。在战斗环境和敌情变化后,已生产的单兵制式化装备必须尽快改进,以适应变化,否则只能惨遭血腥的淘汰。这也是赵武灵王胡服骑射改革的主旨所在,"兵无常势,水无常形"可谓一语道破天机。而单兵制式化装备的不断改进、革新,需要先进技术和管理理念的运用,这在客观上推动了社会生产力的发展,最终不断打破势力平衡,社会形态逐步演进,文化交流涤荡千年,绵绵不断!

腰 刀 与 发 辫

——唐陵陵园石刻蕃酋像中的突厥人形象

张建林

陕西省考古研究院

一、唐陵蕃酋像石刻的发现与定名

蕃酋像是唐代帝陵石刻中特殊的一类雕像,宋至明清,学人踏查唐陵者多有记述。20 世纪初,日本学者足立喜六、桑原隲藏在踏查唐陵时均已经注意到乾陵石刻中极为特殊的一类石人——"蕃酋像"。

王子云 1940 年上半年至 1942 年末调查了关中西汉十一陵和唐十八陵,其中乾陵的蕃酋像被称之为"客使像"。[①]

20 世纪 50 年代陕西省文物管理委员会先后对唐十八陵进行多次调查,80 年代初,贺梓城以调查记的形式简单做了介绍,注意到一些石像的"服饰和汉族不同"。[②]

刘庆柱、李毓芳曾在 1980 年代调查唐十八陵,所发表的调查报告中提及有蕃酋像的唐陵有昭陵、乾陵、定陵、泰陵、崇陵、庄陵、简陵等 7 座,并对部分作了简略描述。将昭陵蕃酋像称为"蕃君长像"、乾陵称为"蕃臣曾侍轩禁者群像"、其余 5 陵称为"蕃民像"。

近年,随着"唐代帝陵大遗址保护项目考古调查"的逐步展开,又分别在桥陵、建陵、光陵、贞陵、简陵、靖陵发现有蕃酋像石刻,原曾经发现蕃酋像的昭陵、泰陵、崇陵又新发现数量不等的蕃酋像,极大丰富了对于蕃酋像的认识。除了蕃酋像石人,还分别在昭陵、乾陵、桥陵、贞陵、崇陵发现当时安放蕃酋像的建筑遗址。

关于这类石人至今学术界没有一个统一的名称,可以说相当混乱,有"蕃酋"、"蕃君长"、"蕃臣"、"蕃民"、"王宾"、"客使"诸称。根据唐宋文献,对于少数民族首领或外国君长通常称之为"蕃酋"、"蕃君长"或"蕃夷君长",《唐会要》将昭陵北司马门的此类石人明确称为"蕃君长",《封氏闻见记》则称为"蕃酋"。我们认为,应当将这类石人像称为"蕃酋像"。

二、唐陵蕃酋像的识别

蕃酋像族属的识别难度极大,故学者很少涉及。昭陵"十四国蕃君长像"史载明确,且有残存的刻铭

---

① 王子云:《从长安到雅典——中外美术考古游记》,陕西人民美术出版社,1992 年,第 26 页。
② 贺梓城:《"关中唐十八陵"调查记》,《文物资料丛刊》3,文物出版社,1980 年,第 143 页。

像座印证,但像与座早年分离,现已无法一一对应。乾陵蕃酋像尚有7尊背后残存刻铭,使得个别雕像身份得以确认。此后诸陵蕃酋像,均未发现像座或雕像背后有刻铭,族属、身份认定缺乏依据。因此,大部分蕃酋像身份与族属主要还须根据其服饰、形象作推测。

迄今唐陵发现的百余座蕃酋像几乎都已身首分离,只有乾陵西侧一座雕像残存有头部下半截,作为形象特征最为显著的面部缺失,已经使我们无法根据形象来判别人种族属,服饰和个别保留于肩背的长发成为我们唯一可以进行分析和推测的依据。唐陵蕃酋石像的服饰大体可以分为三大类:一为圆领或翻领的窄袖袍服,脚穿靴;二为袒右跣足或穿着凉鞋;三为褒衣博带,脚穿高头履。前者数量最多,可能为北方和西域、中亚少数民族或国家的人;第二类可以被认为是南亚、东南亚少数民族或国家的人;第三类很有可能是新罗或日本人。

在着圆领或翻领袍服的石人中,有一些腰前佩戴有短弯刀,还有个别石人背后有下垂的长辫。这类石人与北方草原广泛分布的突厥石人有较多相似的特点。

三、北方草原石人中的突厥石人

在我国的新疆、内蒙以及蒙古共和国、南西伯利亚地区、中亚地区、南俄地区的广大草原地带,分布着众多被称为"草原石人"的石雕人像。这些石人多位于墓葬附近或祭祀遗址附近,年代从公元前3000年至公元13世纪。其中有不少被认为是6~8世纪的突厥民族石人。王博、祁小山对突厥石人有专门分析:"突厥时期的墓地石人在蒙古各省区境内都有发现,……许多石人都保留了与墓葬的组合关系。"蒙古地区和新疆地区的突厥石人主要有五种类型,其中有一种石人长发披肩或长发披后,有些腰间还佩戴有短腰刀,这类石人在新疆发现较多。[①]新疆阿勒泰地区清河县乔夏墓地石人、富蕴县水泥厂石人、布尔津县海流滩墓地石人、博尔塔拉州温泉县阿尔卡特墓地石人、博乐市加勒赛沟口墓地石人、伊犁地区新源县野果林改良场墓地石人均在腰前佩戴短弯刀;伊犁地区昭苏县种马场墓地石人则在背后垂有7根长辫。

日本学者林俊雄曾对欧亚大陆石人做过综合研究,他特别注意石人的细部表现,分别就发型、帽子、衣服的衣襟、手持容器、手指、佩戴的火镰等进行了观察和分析。他注意到天山北部至哈萨克斯坦分布的石人,有将头发编成7~8根或更多根辫子垂于后腰者。束有这种发辫的人物形象在乌兹别克斯坦撒马尔罕市的阿芙拉希阿仆遗址王宫壁画上(7世纪中叶粟特人统治者的王宫)可以见到,在宫殿西壁描绘有数位背向而坐的人物,后背有数根辫子垂下,被认为是西突厥人。像这样的人物形象还有几例:俄罗斯阿尔泰共和国的库德尔格(Kudyrge)古墓群9号墓(6~7世纪)出土马鞍的前桥,饰板上雕刻的骑马狩猎人背后垂有数根发辫。同样在乌兹别克斯坦秀丢布拉克(Sütüü-Bulak)Ⅰ-54号墓(7~8世纪)出土的一件骨饰板上,所刻的骑马人背后拖着7根辫子。塔吉克斯坦的威尔夫尼奇尔尤特(Verkhnii-Chiryurt)古墓群17号墓出土马鞍的鞍桥饰板所雕刻的骑马人更为清晰,7根长辫垂在身后。更为典型的是吉尔吉斯斯坦伊塞克湖北岸的科尔穆德(Korumdy)石人,这件高2.8米的石人身穿翻领袍服,一手持高脚杯,一手按腰刀,身后垂下7根长辫。[②]

---

①　王博、祁小山:《丝绸之路草原石人研究》,新疆人民出版社,1995年。
②　林俊雄:《ユーラシアの石人》,雄山阁(日本东京),2005年。

四、文献中有关突厥人形象与服饰的资料

文献中关于突厥人服饰与形象的记载多流于简略,较早见诸史书者为《北史》、《周书》,仅寥寥数字:"其俗被发左衽,穹庐毡帐,……身衣裘褐。"①南北朝至隋唐文献中记述周边民族风俗最详者莫过于《隋书》,所记突厥风俗也仅"穹庐毡帐,被发左衽,食肉饮酪,身衣裘褐,……有角弓、鸣镝、甲、矟、刀、剑"。②所谓"被发"应当是长发披下直至肩背,可以是散发披下,也可以是辫发下垂。两唐书中关于突厥风俗服饰记载极少。唐高宗时兰台舍人徐齐聃《谏突厥酋长子弟给事东宫疏》有"今乃使毡裘之衣,解辫而侍春闱;冒顿之苗,削衽而陪望苑"句,③可知突厥人是有辫发习俗。还有一则史料也可证明突厥人为辫发:"常山愍王承乾……又好突厥言及所服,选貌类胡者,被以羊裘,辫发,五人建一落,张毡舍……"。

五、唐陵蕃酋像中的突厥人形象

在昭陵、乾陵、崇陵的蕃酋像石人中有数例腰带悬挂短腰刀或背后有长辫垂下。昭陵北司马门发现的蕃酋像中有3件,其一身穿翻领袍服,腰系带,腰前右侧有短腰刀悬挂在腰带下,刀鞘有两根系带与腰带连接;左手按腰带,右手置胸前;背后垂5根长辫,发辫下部用长方形饰片夹住发辫,辫梢从5个圆孔中穿出。其二仅存上半身,肩部以上残缺,身穿袍服,双手拢于袖中,腰带以下残缺;背后垂有7根长辫,每根辫子近辫梢处分别箍有管状物,辫梢垂于腰带下。其三仅存下半身,腹前的腰带下悬挂有短腰刀,刀鞘以两根系带与腰带连接,左侧还佩戴有囊袋。

乾陵有两件腰悬短弯刀的蕃酋像,一件为西侧20号石人,一件为东侧7号石人。两件石人大同小异,均身穿圆领袍服,双手拱于胸前,从手中残存的长方形孔窝观察,原应持笏。石人腰带下方悬有短腰刀,刀鞘用两根系带与腰带连接。因风化严重,腰刀细部模糊不清。这两件石人均未见到有披发或发辫。

2007年,在崇陵南门门阙以南发掘出土14件蕃酋像石人,其中有两件腰悬短弯刀的蕃酋像。其一肩部及头部残缺,身穿袍服,双手在胸前施"叉手礼";其二头部残缺,肩搭披肩,双手拢于袖中。两件石人腹前的腰带下均悬挂短腰刀,由于石人长期埋在地下,石刻保存状况较好,腰刀各部位清晰可见。

以上蕃酋像或腰悬短腰刀,或辫发后垂,与北方草原石人中的突厥人石像相似。

六、相关问题

1. 蕃酋像石刻是唐代帝陵陵园石刻的重要组成部分,自昭陵开始出现,一直延续至唐末。对后代的帝陵石刻制度也有影响,如北宋皇陵就有蕃酋像。

2. 唐陵蕃酋像中一些佩戴短腰刀或背后有长辫的石人应当是突厥民族的酋长形象。

3. 唐陵蕃酋像的创立,很可能受到北方草原地带墓葬石人影响。

---

① 《北史》卷九九《突厥传》,《周书》卷五〇《突厥传》。
② 《隋书》卷八四《突厥传》。
③ 《全唐文》卷一百六十八。

Costume of the Early Turks in Chinese Art of the 6th – 7th CC.

Sergey A. Yatsenko

Russian State University for the Humanities Moscow, Russia

Introduction

I have been studying the costume of ancient Eurasian peoples (clothing and hairstyle, rather large costume accessories) since my student years. One of the main tasks was the *comparative and complex analysis* of the costume of 13 well documented related ancient and early medieval Iranian-speaking nations — the biggest ethno-cultural unity of ancient Eurasia (among them were the Sakas of Khotan in Xinjiang). It became possible after reconstruction of the series of certain ethnic costume complexes in texts and drawings (based on all types of sources) and unification of terminology and descriptive principles. These problems were analyzed in my last book published in Moscow in 2006. [1]

The results of such analysis made it possible *to find out the motherland areas for a number of largest nomadic tribe groups* in Eurasia. For example, the costume of "*classic*" European Scythians of the 5th– 4th cc. BC has the biggest number of costume similarities to the "Sakas" of South Siberia, including the Pazyrykians and also to Tokharian-speaking peoples of Xinjiang. Their predecessors, the *Early* Scythians of the 7th– 6th cc. BC, have similarities in the costume analogous first of all to the nomadic ethnic groups in Transoxiana. As far as their costume is concerned, the Pazyryk culture peoples of South Siberia are very close to their southern neighbors in above-mentioned Xinjiang. In clothes of the European Early Sarmatians, beginning from the 2nd– 1st cc. BC and the Late Sarmatians in the 2nd– 3rd cc. AD, a large number of analogies with the Yuech-chihs/the Kushans is quite evident. [2]

Another complicated problem in my research is the problem of *ethnic identification of foreigners' images* in high-developed art traditions of some ancient countries (first of all, in the art of ancient Greece, the Roman and Persian Empires, Sogd, North-West India and China). Local art stereotypes and stereotypes in general perception of foreigners (considering the social rank of those who migrated) resulted in the degree of

---

① S. A. Yatsenko. *Costume of the Ancient Eurasia (the Iranian-Speaking Peoples)* (*Kostyum drevney Evrazii* [*iranoyazychniye narody*]). Moscow, 2006.

② S. A. Yatsenko. Op. cit., pp. 306 – 312.

costume stylization. [1] Such ethnic identification conclusions are important for dating and other attribution of misunderstood artifacts from many private and museum collections in the whole world.

Another big ethno-cultural group for my analysis is Early Medieval Turkic peoples. 21 years ago, in 1987 I wrote a big chapter on the costume of Xinjiang region before Chengis-khan invasion. It was devoted not only to Pre-Uygurian ancient peoples of Khotan and Kutcha, but also Uygurs of the late 9th – 12th cc. [2]

The next step in my Early Turkic costume studies was a special research of Turkic officials' images in Sogdian wall-paintings (the mid. of the 7th c.) in Samarkand/Afrasiab. [3] It was based on more correct Galina V. Shishkina expedition copies of 1978, still unpublished. My text of 1985 was published in English only 10 years later. [4]

During the last two years some of my colleagues and friends said to me: "You have studied the costume of ancient Iranian peoples. And what about Turkic ones?" I answered: "I have been analyzing the costume of Iranians during 31 years. But my life is so short for such studies of Turks!" But in reality I was very interested in the new materials which were sent to me by two of my American colleagues. Dr. Judith Lerner (New York) sent some most interesting images of Turks on some *funerary couches and sarcophaguses of the late 6th-early 7th cc. from Northern China* where Sogdian "sabao"-officials present their trips to Nomadic Eastern Turks. [5] This spring Prof. Mike Sanders from California asked me many questions on ethnic identification of the *Early Tang clay tomb figurines* from Ezekeil Schloss catalogue of the exhibition in China House Gallery, New York, March-May 1969 (the biggest collection in the West) and some analogous figurines from private collections in Sotheby's and other catalogues.

The political might of the Early Turks and the big area of their migrations beginning from the Great Turkic Qaghanat foundation in 551 AD, their functional military equipment and costume are well-known. The costume of early Turkic tribes was comfortable for warriors and hunters; the symbolic of its details (first of all, the belt) was attractive for other nations. Unfortunately, the relics of real early Turkic clothes elements are rare and fragmentary. Some interesting details we can see on Turkic stone tomb statues of the late 6th – 8th cc. from some regions of Central Asia (for example, in the Tuva Republic Museum, Kyzyl). In the past

---

① See, first of all: S. A. Yatsenko. Op. cit., pp. 31 –33, 47, 55 –57, 61, 65 –67, 113 –115, 129 –130, 134, 166 –169, 229 –230, 245 –247, 261 –262, 273 –274.

② S. A. Yatsenko. *Chapter 3 "Costume"* (*Kostyum*). In: The Eastern Turkestan in Antiquity and Early Middle Ages. /Vol. 4/. Architecture. Fine Art. Costume (Vostochnii Turkestan v drevnosti i rannem srednevekov'e). (T. 4). Arkhitektura. Iskusstvo. Kostyum. B. A. Litvinskii (ed.). Moscow, 2000, pp. 296 –384, see on Uygurs — pp. 367 –382, Figs. 64 –69.

③ L. I. Al'baum. *Wall-Painting of Afrasiab* (*Zhivopis' Afrasiaba*). Tashkent, 1975.

④ S. A. Yatsenko. *The Costume of Foreign Embassies and Inhabitants of Samarkand on Wall Painting of the 7th c. in the Hall of Ambassadors from Afrasiab as a Historical Source.* In: Transoxiana. Número 8. P. Raffetta (ed.). — http://www.transoxiana.org/8/yatsenko. Rome, 2004.

⑤ See the first results: S. A. Yatsenko. *Ancient Turks: Costume in a Color Images* (*Drevnie Tyurki: kostyum na raznotsvetnykh izobrazheniyakh*). In: Museum, November 2007 Internet-Conference "Antiquities in Museums Collections" (Internet-konferentsiya "Drevnosti v muzeinykh kollektsiyakh") T. N. Krupa (ed.). — http://www.formuseum.info/2007/11/25/jacenko_sa_drevnie_tjurki_kostjum_na_raznocvetnykh_izobrazhenijakh.htm. Kharkov, 2007.

some colors were painted on many details of these statues, [①] but now their relics are not preserved. Ancient Turks also put wooden statues with real fabric and felt clothing and natural plaits into barrows graves, but we know only one or two later samples of such statues in the later barrow of European Kypchaks (Polovtsy). [②]

Chinese images of Early Turks are very important due to their *colors* (in my opinion — authentic for Turkic cultural reality) and *realistic* type of depiction. In some cases there are compositions of *many anthropomorphic figures* (funerary couches and sarcophaguses). They are the *earliest detailed images* of Early Turks in the world art. But specialists on ancient costume still do not use these images actively in their research work.

Early Turkic (Eastern Turkic) clay figurines
from tombs of the Early Tang dynasty time

There are not numerous supposedly. Ethnic identification is possible now only for *some of* such figurines due to some reasons. *First*, in the native art of these nations in their motherland we usually see kings or aristocrats. But people who usually traveled to China belonged to other social ranks (merchants, actors and dancers, painters etc.). We may see their images in their *native* art (in comparison with Chinese objects) very seldom. That is why we may identify only some elements of costume, probably common for some social groups. Identification of such figurines is usually only approximate. *Second*, in these detailed figurines we see "stylized Barbarians" with the standard color range (the craftsmen usually use only three colors for glaze and unglazed details were covered with red and black pigments). *Third*, we must take into account the Chinization of "Barbarian" costume (of those who lived and worked in China). **1.** Short sleeved coats had not deep wrap to the right in a Chinese way, not to the left (this way was traditional for early Eurasian nomads). Clothes wrapped to the right were a Chinese innovation for Central Asian "barbarians" since the 4th cc. AD., after nomadic invasion to the north part of China; we know several analogous personages in art of Kutcha, Khotan and Tumshouq in Xinjiang, the 5th–6th cc. [③] **2.** Chinese male headdress "putou" in some variants. All these variants are dated back to the mid. of the 7th— beg. of the 8th cc. AD. It should be mentioned that Uygur common people of Xinjiang used it from the end of the 9th c. AD. [④] Men who used

---

① See, for example, L. N. Ermolenko. *May be the Ancient Turkic Statues Colored?* (*Mogli li raskrashivat'sya drevnetyurkskie izvayaniya?*). In: Steppes of Eurasia in Antiquity and in the Middle Ages (Stepi Evrazii v drevnosti i srednevekov'e). Part II. Yu. Yu. Piotrovsky (ed.). St-Petersburg, 2003, p.238.

② L. N. Ermolenko. *Once More on the Problem of Original View of the Stone Nomadic Statues* (*Eshche raz k voprosu o pervonachal'nom vide kamennykh kochevnicheskikh izvayanii*). In: Stone Sculpture and Small Art Plastic Wares of the Ancient and Medieval Peoples of Eurasia (Kamennaya skul'ptura i melkaya plastika drevnikh i sresnevekovykh norodov Evrazii) (Proceedings of Siberian Association of Primitive Art. Vol. 3). A. A. Tishkin (ed). Barnaul, 2007, pp.126–127.

③ S. A. Yatsenko. *Chapter 3 "Costume"* (*Kostyum*). In: The Eastern Turkestan in Antiquity and Early Middle Ages. /Vol. 4/. Architecture. Fine Art. Costume (Vostochnii Turkestan v drevnosti i rannem srednevekov'e). (T. 4). Arkhitektura. Iskusstvo. Kostyum. B. A. Litvinskii (ed.). Moscow, 2000, pp.360–361. See also: S. A. Yatsenko. *Costume of the Ancient Eurasia* (*the Iranian-Speaking Peoples*) (*Kostyum drevney Evrazii* [*iranoyazychniye narody*]). Moscow, 2006, p.247.

④ S. A. Yatsenko. *Chapter.3 "Costume"* (*Kostyum*). In: The Eastern Turkestan in Antiquity and Early Middle Ages. /Vol. 4/. Architecture. Fine Art. Costume (Vostochnii Turkestan v drevnosti i rannem srednevekov'e). (T. 4). Arkhitektura. Iskusstvo. Kostyum. B. A. Litvinskii (ed.). Moscow, 2000, p.367.

putou were not young. **3**. In some situations there are very wide sleeves of a sleeved coat. **4**. A handkerchief attached to the belt worn in a specific manner. Chinese costume elements were, first of all, the result of these common people living in China for a long time.

Ethnic identification of foreigners on such terracotta is still non-correct. The reason is very simple: the authors are not specialists on the ancient costume of various regions, they do not know the most part of material on each ancient national costume complex (especially unpublished) and as a result they cannot use analogies and costume classifications correctly and they cannot make a correct comparative analysis.

Some words about Tang figurines from Ezekeil Schloss exhibition catalogue in 1969. Ethnic identification based on correlation of *several* types of clothing, hairstyle, shoe and belt elements, specific for certain Iranian, Turkic or Tokharian nations. In my opinion "Barbarian" images of this catalogue are usually Sogdians and Tokharistanians from Transoxiana, more seldom — Eastern Turks, peoples from Khotan and Kutcha in Xinjiang. This conclusion is well correlated with Chinese written sources on foreigners in Sui and the Early Tang China. There are only two real Turkic personages.[1] For these images the ethnic identification is possible due to some specific types of headdresses and hairstyle. Many personages were not identified because there hairstyle and clothes are typical for *some* regions of Central Asia. Many figurines are schematic, some details are absent and the information on the costume in not sufficient. Sleeved coats with two lapels (there were also sleeved coats with one right lapel) originated from Western Xinjiang (Khotan) in the 2nd–4th cc. AD. They became popular in some regions, and due to the Early Turks spread to many regions of Central Asia in the 7th – 8th cc.[2] Some still mysterious personages will be identified in future as Turks (Ns. 2, 55, 56).

No 39 (Fig. 1). These noble Mongoloid ladies have narrow long sleeved coats of a Turkic type with two lapels and high (?) boots. Their belts with additional straps are also of a Turkic type. The *headdresses* are unique, without analogies. They are not Chinese women-attendants in the costume of a Turkic type (in such case they use some Chinese costume elements which are absent here). They are women from one unknown Eastern Turkic tribe (probably dated back to the 7th c., earlier than Uighurs or Kyrgyzs). These figurines are very interesting and important for the history of Early Turkic female costume.

No 42 (Fig. 2). The costume of this horseman is typical for

Fig. 1

---

[1] Schloss E., 1969. *Foreigners in Ancient Chinese Art from Private and Museum Collections* [*Cataloque*]. *March 27 through May 25, 1969. New York, 1969*, Ns. 39, 42.

[2] S. A. Yatsenko. *Costume of the Ancient Eurasia (the Iranian-Speaking Peoples)* (*Kostyum drevney Evrazii* [*iranoyazychniye narody*]). Moscow, 2006, p. 204, 206, 269.

the "Turkic complex": a long sleeved coat with two lapels, high boots. His *headdress* is very interesting. I know only one image of this headdress in Eastern Turkic regions of Mongolia. ①

There are also some Early Turkic personages from Sotheby's and other catalogues.

Fig. 3. This personage is typical Eastern Turkic. But the headdress of such type with a big figure of eagle is known only for Turkic *nobility*: a statue of Kül-Tegin qaghan (the beginning of the 8th c.) in his palace in Mongolia. ② This type of headdress we also see on sarcophagus from Aschat in Mongolia. ③

Fig. 2

Fig. 4. ④ There are also Turkic personages. Such type of headdress was used by Early Turks. ⑤ We also know such rare very long sleeved Turkic coats (up to heels), which are thrown on shoulders. ⑥ But dark blue color of their long sleeved coats was not popular with Early Turkic tribes; the color could be dark green or black in reality (the green upper body garment was seen by Huen Tsiang in 630 on the Western Turkic qaghan). ⑦ And such very long sleeves (much longer than hands) are not typical for them. I think they were real Turks with some Chinese costume elements (very long sleeves). And, of course, they were not "attendants" (the Cataloque author attribution) but nobles in the attractive aristocratic costume (with very long elements of long sleeved coats and shirts uncomfortable in everyday life).

---

① See sarcophagus from Aschat: E. Nowgorodowa. *Alte Kunst der Mongolei.* Leipzig, 1980, Fig. 204.

② E. Nowgorodowa. Op. cit. , Fig. 184.

③ E. Nowgorodowa. Op. cit. , Fig. 204.

④ Figs. 3 - 6: courtesy, M. Sanders, spring 2008.

⑤ See, for example: L. N. Ermolenko. *The Medieval Stone Statues of Kazakhstan Steppes* (*Srednevekovye kamennye izvayaniya Kazakhstanskih stepei*). Novosibirsk, 2004, pl. 14, 8.

⑥ For example, on the Tien-Shan mountains' stone statues: G. Sh. Eleukenova. *Essay on History of the Medieval Sculpture of Kazakhstan* (*Ocherk istorii srednevekovoy skul'ptury Kazakhstana*). Almaty, 1999, Fig. 70.

⑦ E. Chavannes. *Documents sur les Tou-kiue* (*Turcs*) *Occidentaux.* In: Proceedings of Orkhon Expedition (Sbornik trudov Orkhonskoy expeditsii). Vol. VI. St. -Petersburg, 1903, p. 194.

Fig.5. Some main details in the upper garment of this man we know in Tokharistan. But his (felt?) headdress is typically nomadic. Such garments with big buttons on each lapel were used that time by Early Turkic peoples. Other costume details do not contradict this version. Only big eyes and a long beard are rare for Early Turks. He is not a common man (not a servant etc.).

Fig.6. This personage is also Early Turkic. His upper body garment (with two lapels) is made from sheep skin; we see the summer type of its wearing (it is usual in real everyday life but unique for art!). This is a rare image common man (herdsman?).

  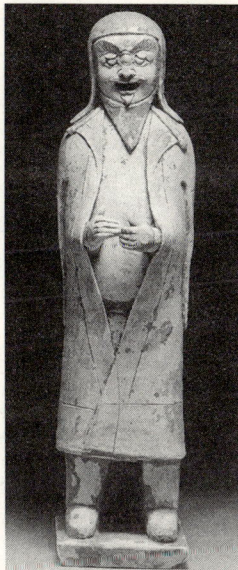 

Fig. 3   Fig. 4   Fig. 5   Fig. 6

Marble and granite funerary couches and sarcophaguses of Sogdian "sabao" and other titled officials of the Northern Dynasties and Sui periods of the 2nd half of the 6th c. — the beginning of the 7th c. AD from Xi'an, Taiyuan and some other cities

Their painted panels present biographical details of the dead and, among them, their travels to Turkic steppes and reciprocal visits of Turkic nobles to Chinese cities[1](*Fig. 7*[2]). The costume of Turkic personages

① *Short Report on the Tomb of Yu Hong, Sui Dynasty, excavated in Taiyuan, Shaanxi* (in Chinese). In: Wenwu. 2001, No 1, pp. 27 –52; *Northern Zhou tomb of An Qie excavated in Xi'an* (In Chinese). In: Wenwu. 2001, No 1, pp. 4 – 26, Fig. 12; B. I. Marhak. *La thematique sogdienne dans l'art de la Chine de la seconde moitie du VIe siecle.* In: Academie des Inscriptions et Belles-Lettres. Compur rendus des séances de l'annee 2001 janvier-mars. Paris, 2001, pp. 228 – 264; J. A. Lerner. *Anjia [An Qie] Tomb of Northern Zhou at Xi'an.* In: Shaanxi Provincial Institute of Archaeology (in Chinese). Beijing, 2003; J. A. Lerner. *Aspects of Assimilation. The Funerary Practices and Furnishings of Central Asians in China* (Sino-Platonic Papers. Vol. 168, December 2005). Philadelphia, 2005; A. L. Juliano. *Converging Traditions in the Imagery of Yu Hong's Sarcophagus: Possible Buddhist Sources.* In: Journal of Inner Asian Art and Archaeology. Vol. 1. Turnhout, 2006, pp. 293 – 316.

② 1 — sarcophagus of Yu Hong and his wife from Taiyuan, Sui dynasty (after Wenwu. 2001, No 1, p. 34, Fig. 14); 2 — funeral couch of An Qie from Xi'an, Northern Zhou dynasty (after A. L. Juliano, J. A. Lerner. *Monks and Merchants. Silk Road Treasures from Northern China. Gansu and Ninxia*, 4th – 7th Century. New York, 2001, p. 226, Fig. 4).

on some panels is usually painted on the white marble background only with several colors — red (two tints), black and brown, more seldom also gray and yellow. The comparison with a later series of Turkic images in other regions demonstrates that the colors of details are of the same importance as the white background. These colors were sufficient in depicting authentic prevalence of bright one tint coloring in the Early Turkic costume. A very important specificity of these reliefs is the variety of poses of one and the same personage, which makes it possible to represent the costume more completely. The specific marker of Turkic men was, first of all, a *hairstyle with several long, fixed together plaits.*

1

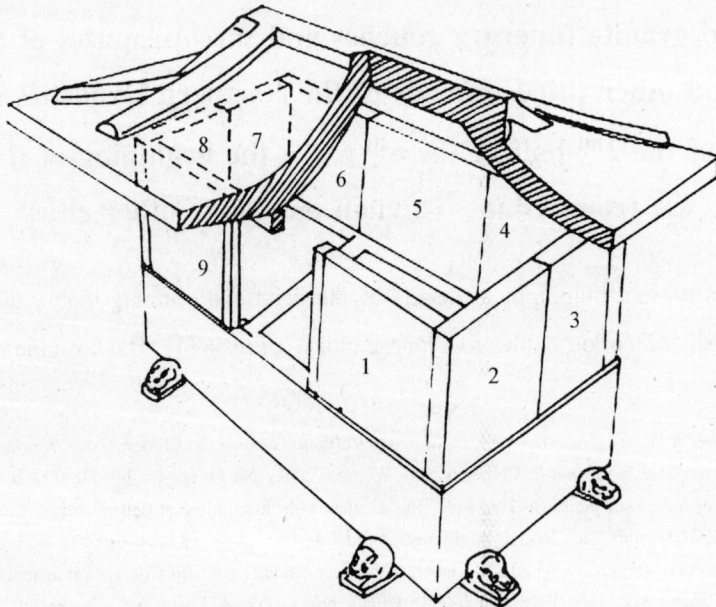

2

Fig. 7

*The **granite** funerary couch of Sogdian official An Qie* (first, non-correct Western transcription — An Jia) and his wife is the most interesting sample for Early Turkic costume studies. An Oie died in 579 in Xi'an. This official contacted Nomadic Turks during the period of their most powerful ruler — Mugan-qaghan (553 – 572 AD). There are only 4 panels presenting Turks. Probably, in all these panels we can the same two Turkic men: the aristocrat from the high "*beq*" estate — the ruler of one of the Qaghanat' provinces neighboring with China (Tabgach) with "*irkin*" or "*chor*" title and also his favorite young servant (or his son? or his private secretary?). Boris Marshak's identification of this personage as Turkic qaghan (!)[1] is not correct: it contradicts the information of Huen Tsiang on Turkic qaghan costume and attributes.[2] And, of course, the Great Qaghan cannot visit the residence of a small Sogdian official in a Chinese city. It is interesting that in scenes where Turks and Sogdians are sitting together, the Sogdians occupy *the most prestigious right hand side* (except the episode in the "yurt" — a nomadic building where the guest — a Sogdian diplomat from China is sitting to the right from the noble Turk) and Turks always raise the left hand.

On the most important panel in the *upper level* we see the meeting of An Qie and his two servants with two Turks while hunting (*Fig. 8*).[3] In this scene the craftsman accentuated the belt details: the Turks had no more than 12 metal plaques (may be silver, as the craftsman depicted gold with the yellow color in some panels of this couch) and a rectangular buckle. The silver plaques mean not a high rank. On the *lower level* with a banquet scene the Turks have several long plaits, small beards and short moustaches. Their long sleeved coats are white, without two "classic" lapels but with a red line of décor on the hem and coat beasts and also high red cuffs. This type of décor is typical *for Sogdians at that time*[4] but very rare for Early Turks (see only the

Fig. 8

① B. I. Marhak. *La thematique sogdienne dans l'art de la Chine de la seconde moitie du VIe siecle.* In: Academie des Inscriptions et Belles-Lettres. Compur rendus des séances de l'annee 2001 janvier-mars. Paris, 2001, p. 25.

② See, for example: E. Chavannes. *Documents sur les Tou-kiue (Turcs) Occidentaux.* In: Proceedings of Orkhon Expedition (Sbornik trudov Orkhonskoy expeditsii). Vol. VI. St.-Petersburg, 1903, p. 194.

③ Figs. 8 – 10: J. A. Lerner. *Anjia [An Qie] Tomb of Northern Zhou at Xi'an'.* In: Shaanxi Provincial Institute of Archaeology (in Chinese). Beijing, 2003, pl. 54, 63, 57.

④ S. A. Yatsenko S. A. *The Late Sogdian Costume (5th – 8th cc. AD).* In: Eran ud Anērān. Studies Presented to Boris I. Marshak in Occation of His 70th Birthday. M. Compareti, P. Raffetta, G. Scarcia (ed.). Venice, 2006 (Internet-version, 2003: http://www.transoxiana. org/Eran/yatsenko); S. A. Yatsenko. *Costume of the Ancient Eurasia (the Iranian-Speaking Peoples) (Kostyum drevney Evrazii [iranoyazychniye narody]).* Moscow, 2006, Figs. 181/40; 184.

strange costume of the Turk in Hall 3 in Samarkand, neighboring with the famous "Hall of Ambassadors"). [1] His shirt is also red. The black belt (without metal plaques) girds him two times. Another interesting and rare detail is low black shoes. The second Turkic personage (the servant?) usually stays behind his superior. His clothing is a "simple" long sleeved coat without red decorative borders. It is also buttoned up though, it is shorter. His belt is also shorter and narrower, but (traditionally for Turks) with some additional straps. He also uses traditional high black boots with triangle projections.

Another panel demonstrates the banquette with Turks in An Qie apartments (*Fig. 9*). There the main Turkic personage is wearing a long sleeved coat of another type: it is made from black textile and has a narrow turn down collar; [2] its lapels and cuffs are not accentuated by color. Under the upper body garment he is wearing the same red shirt. His belt is also without metal plaques.

In the third panel we see only one Turkic personage — an aristocrat in his own "yurt" building (*Fig. 10*) who is meeting a Sogdian delegation from China. The Turk has a dagger. His long sleeved coat, trousers and shoes are the same as in the first panel, but the belt does not have metal plaques. On the forth panel (a banquet scene) in the upper level we see two sitting Turks: a nobleman and to the left — a musician with a lute. Both of them are wearing low boots. The upper body garment of the aristocrat has a wrap to the left, and he loosened his left sleeve. The ends of several plaits of the Turkic musician are fixed together with a small metal case.

The panels of another *marble funerary couch are preserved in Miho Museum* in Shigaraki, Japan. The place of their origin is unknown [3] (*Fig. 11*). They demonstrate the life of Chinese Sogdians with their servants and Chinese wives. One panel demonstrates the travel of the person buried there to nomadic Turks. There we see a noble Turk in the "yurt"-building. His courtiers (?) are sitting on the red carpet near this nomadic building. There are also two servants who are bringing presents of

Fig. 9

---

① L. I. Al'baum. *Wall-Painting of Afrasiab* (*Zhivopis' Afrasiaba*). Tashkent, 1975, pl. IV.

② See the same on the Turkic statue from Saryg-Bulun in Tuva: *Steppes of Eurasia in the Middle Ages Epoch* (*Stepi Evrazii v epokhu srednevekov'ya*). S. A. Pletneva (ed.). Moscow, 1981, Fig. 17, 1.

③ *Miho Museum. South Wing*, Shigaraki, 1997, p. 250, Fig. C; A. L. Juliano, J. A. Lerner. *Monks and Merchants. Silk Road Treasures from Northern China. Gansu and Ninxia, 4th–7th Century*. New York, 2001, p. 309, Fig. K.

Chinese administration. Unfortunately, the Turks (except the aristocrat in the yurt) are turned back. In the lower level we see hunting of riding Turks in the mountains; there are some unique elements of the Early Turkic costume.

Fig. 10

Fig. 11

The long sleeved coat of the noble Turk in the yurt has a wide decorative border on the beasts and it has a wrap to the right — in a Chinese manner! (it is, probably, the earliest depiction of this element of the Chinese costume influence): other participants are wearing coats with a wrap to the left, traditional for ancient nomads (compare the Early Turkic statues and "Zhoushu" chronicles data). This image demonstrates us that the anxiety of the Great Turkic Qaghan in 590 AD about this problem was not groundless. That year, according to "Tangshu", the Qaghan tried to force the population of Turfan oasis (at that time most of them were Chinese) to return to ancient Turkic clothing (long sleeved coats with a wrap to the left) and hairstyle with several plaits. ① It was the reply to the spread of Chinezetion in Turfan region, which was, according to "Suishu", the native land of the Early Turks. The long sleeved coat of the nobleman is white (with lines of red arcs), the shirt and trousers are of the same color.

All the Turks do not have beards but have long horizontal moustaches (using special pomade). Their coats are very long. The personages of higher ranks are wearing five plaits, but the servants on the back with horses are wearing their long hair loose with hair ends fixed together. The more important persons are wearing traditional high boots with triangle projections, but the back hunter has low red boots. The main colors of long sleeved coats are white or red; *all personages of higher ranks are in white* (the noblemen in the yurt, the two front servants with Sogdian presents, the front riding hunter). It is unusual for other Early Turkic images. The second interesting detail is the light color of belts on all the Turks (made of textile?). Other specific details are long horizontal moustaches with pomade and the hierarchy in the male hairstyle and shoes.

Fig. 12

The *sarcophagus of Yu Hong*, who died in 592 AD, was discovered in Taiyuan. This Sogdian man firstly was a "sabao"-official but later he became the Chinese ambassador to several countries (for example, in Sasanid Iran). The most of scenes on this sarcophagus are Zoroastrian (or, more correctly, Mazdeist Sogdian). Only one Turkic personage is depicted on eastern panel No 4 (*Fig. 12*②). He is the rider on the camel, and he is the only one, who is hunting (two lions) without success. ③ The man is turned back.

The costume of this Turk is very strange. His long hair, fixed at the end, and the belt with additional straps are the only really Turkic elements of this personage. He is wearing low shoes. The upper body garment is shorter but has short widened sleeves, the underwear is longer and has "usual" sleeves. The borders of sleeves are decorated with scallop projections. Such specific correlation of two body garments at that time is very

---

① E. Chavannes. *Documents sur les Tou-kiue (Turcs) Occidentaux.* In: Proceedings of Orkhon Expedition (Sbornik trudov Orkhonskoy expeditsii). Vol. VI. St.-Petersburg, 1903, p. 103; see also: S. A. Yatsenko. *Chapter 3 "Costume" (Kostyum).* In: The Eastern Turkestan in Antiquity and Early Middle Ages. /Vol. 4/. Architecture. Fine Art. Costume (Vostochnii Turkestan v drevnosti i rannem srednevekov'e). (T. 4). Arkhitektura. Iskusstvo. Kostyum. B. A. Litvinskii (ed.). Moscow, 2000, p. 361, 363, 367.

② *Short Report on the Tomb of Yu Hong, Sui Dynasty, excavated in Taiyuan, Shaanxi* (in Chinese). In: Wenwu. 2001, No 1, p. 36, Fig. 19.

③ Compare with other personages, hunting lions: *Short Report on the Tomb of Yu Hong, Sui Dynasty, excavated in Taiyuan, Shaanxi* (in Chinese). In: Op. cit. p. 38, Fig. 20; p. 36, Fig. 17.

rarely used by Sogdians[1] but *it is typical, first of all for Tokharian-speaking population of Kutcha oasis.* [2] Peoples from Kutcha were well-known in China as talented musicians, dancers and composers. Another specific costume element is a bundle of 5 short ribbons on the shoulders, which is typical only for Kutcha' aristocratic men either[3] common officers wore it only on one shoulder. [4] The breast decorative ribbon[5] and the types of trousers and low shoes are also usual for the Kutcha costume. It is a very interesting example of strong costume influence of a small, not powerful oasis region on Turks. What was the reason of this influence on a small Tuirkic group or on one man only? political migrants? military brotherhood? costume gifts which were presented in specific situations? We do not know now, and this image is still mysterious.

① S. A. Yatsenko. *Costume of the Ancient Eurasia* (*the Iranian-Speaking Peoples*) (*Kostyum drevney Evrazii* [*iranoyazychniye narody*]). Moscow, 2006, Figs. 181, 49 –50; 182, 19.

② S. A. Yatsenko. *Chapter 3 "Costume"* (*Kostyum*). In: The Eastern Turkestan in Antiquity and Early Middle Ages. /Vol. 4/. Architecture. Fine Art. Costume (Vostochnii Turkestan v drevnosti i rannem srednevekov'e). (T. 4). Arkhitektura. Iskusstvo. Kostyum. B. A. Litvinskii (ed.). Moscow, 2000, pl. 75, 2; 58, 9; 60, 5; 62, 3.

③ S. A. Yatsenko. Op. cit. , pl. 59, 2 –3.

④ S. A. Yatsenko. Op. cit. , pl. 60, 1 –2.

⑤ S. A. Yatsenko. Op. cit. , pl. 59, 1, 3 –4.

吐鲁番交河沟西墓地突厥因素略论

陈 凌

中国社会科学院考古研究所

一

吐鲁番地区位于天山东部山间盆地,其北部天山与博格达山之间的大通道是天山南北往来重要的通路之一。吐鲁番作为西域重镇,自两汉以来此地一直是中原王朝与草原游牧民族争夺的重点。在这里留下了许多反映各民族文化交流重要实物见证。我们草成此文,旨在说明沟西有一类墓葬可能在一定程度上受到突厥葬俗的影响。无知妄说之处,敬祈学界君子不吝赐正。

在吐鲁番众多的遗存中,交河沟西墓地有非常重要的价值。1928 年,中瑞西北考察团成员的黄文弼先生最先对交河沟西地区进行调查和发掘,发表了《高昌砖集》、《高昌陶集》两部重要的著作。1956 年新疆首届考古专业人员训练班在沟西地区发掘了 24 座墓葬,但只有简单的简报,完整报告迄今尚未面世。1994～1996 年,新疆考古所对交河沟西台地进行了全面的调查,并发掘其中一批墓葬。经调查发现,沟西台地上主要有两种类型的墓葬,一类为竖穴土坑墓,一类为斜坡墓道洞室墓。其中第一类墓葬的年代较早,时间范围大体在公元前 1 世纪至公元 3 世纪左右。第二类墓葬的年代相对较晚,属高昌王国至唐代这个时间段。[①]

沟西第二类斜坡墓道洞室墓中出土三方墓志。

一方出自 95TYGXM7：

1. 延昌廿六年丙午歲十
2. 月戊申朔,寢疾卒。
3. 春秋七十七,張元尊
4. 之墓表。

一方墓志出自 96TYGXM1,录文如下:

1. 延昌廿六年丙午

---

① 新疆文物考古研究所:《交河沟西 1994～1996 年度考古发掘报告》,新疆人民出版社,2001 年。90 年代交河沟西地区几次发掘都有相应的简报发表,这些简报后来汇总为《交河沟西 1994～1996 年度考古发掘报告》。简报与正式报告不尽相同之处,以正式报告为准。本文所用的沟西墓地资料全部出自该报告,为免烦琐,不一一出注。

2. 歲十一月朔丁丑

3. 卅日丙午初,鎮西

4. 府省事,後遷中兵

5. 參軍,於交河岸遇

6. 患殂喪,春秋五十有

7. 五。辛氏之墓表。

另一方出自95TYGXM2,墓志内容如下:

1. 維大唐咸亨五年歲次甲

2. 戌朔,五月庚戌,四日癸丑,

3. 西州交河縣人前錄事張歡

4. 睿? 妻唐氏早稟生知,託於人①

5. 世,為四蛇葬逐,二鼠相摧,一旦

6. 無常,生於淨國,何其竹柏

7. 與蒲柳而先彫。嗚呼哀哉,

8. 伏惟尚饗!

9. 咸亨五年五月四日記

延昌为高昌麴乾固年号(560~601)。因此,根据上述三方墓志,可知这类斜坡墓道洞室墓的年代在6世纪80年代至7世纪80年代这百年间。

从发表的材料看,这类斜坡墓道洞室墓大致有两种形制。一种为单人墓,第二种为坟院式家族墓。两种类型墓葬均为东北—西南向。

单人墓 以95TYGXM5、95TYGXM2为例。(图一:2、4)这种类型的墓葬一般开挖一段长斜坡墓道,在墓道尽头再开洞室作为墓穴。墓穴正上方地表有封土,封土上再堆石。石堆呈方形。墓道上方也有零星堆石。

坟院式家族墓 以94TYGXM1、95TYGXM1为例。这种类型墓葬由多个上述单人斜坡墓道洞室墓组合而成。不同的是,在地表有石堆围成方形坟院将这些墓围在其中。坟院前方正中有开口,用石堆出一条通道。(图一:1、3)

二

突厥墓葬依其等级可粗略地分为大型陵园和普通墓葬两类。其中,大型陵园的墓主人多系可汗或汗国的高级贵族。

---

① "睿"字原报告未释,此据图版补入。

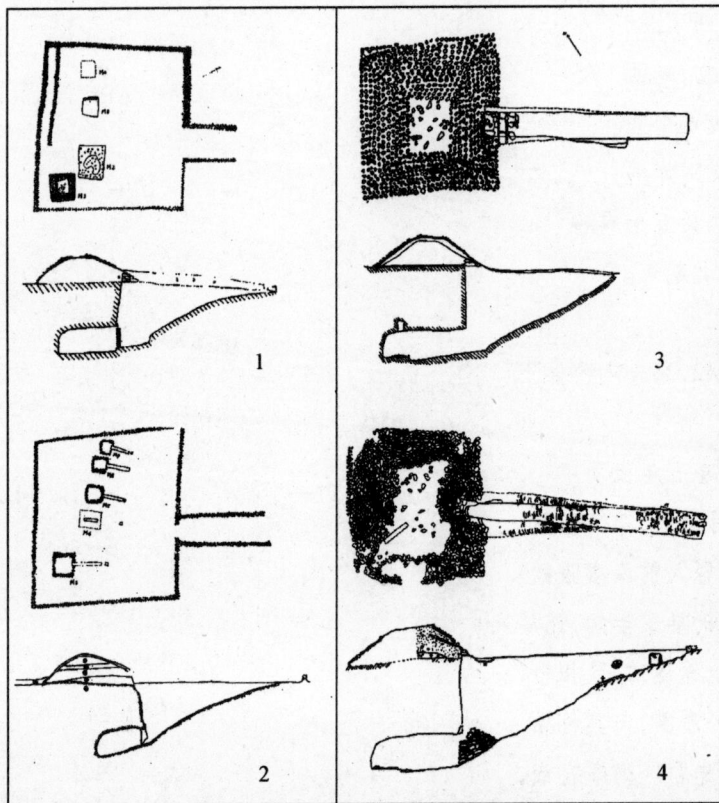

图一 交河沟西晚期墓葬

1 94TYGXM1 平剖面图　2 95TYGXM5 平剖面图　3 95TYGXM1 平剖面图　4 95TYGXM2 平剖面图

突厥大型陵园按时代先后可以分为前后两期。前期为第一突厥汗国时代,后期为第二突厥汗国时代。

前期的突厥大型贵族陵园目前已知有两座,一座是位于蒙古国中部车车尔格勒呼尼河畔布古特的佗钵可汗陵园,另一座是位于中国新疆伊犁自治州昭苏县的泥利可汗陵园。这两座陵园分别代表了第一汗国时代东、西两部突厥贵族墓葬的情况。

布古特佗钵可汗陵园建于一土丘(长 35 米,宽 16 米,高 0.5 米)之上。石堆冢直径 10 米,高 0.7 米。土丘前面有一排 270 余块立石(按即杀人石)。石堆冢东南处有一石碑,立于龟趺之上。发现时碑和龟趺几乎全部埋入地表下,只有石碑上方还有部分暴露在地表上。该碑高 198 cm,厚 20 cm,底部基座宽 70 cm。石碑的四侧都刻有铭文。[1] 据研究,布古特碑文中的 kwts't 即突厥佗钵可汗。[2] 佗钵可汗陵园基本上呈东南—西北方向,朝向东南。夯土台基分三层,东南一侧中部有一缺口,应该是表示陵园的入口。石围石堆墓位于台基中后部。石围石堆的结构是:先以石板围砌成一长方形石框,其中再堆石。(图二)佗钵可汗陵园布局呈长方形,陵园开口到石围墓之间已经开始具有出现神道的倾向。

小洪那海泥利可汗陵园发现于 20 世纪 50 年代。1953 年,伊犁考古队在新疆昭苏县特克斯河支流小

---

① 克里雅什托内:《布古特粟特文碑铭补正》,龚方震译,《中外关系史译丛》第 3 辑,上海译文出版社,1986 年,第 35～36 页。关于布古特碑及陵园的调查和研究情况,见陈凌《突厥汗国考古与欧亚文化交流》第二章相关讨论,北京大学博士论文,2006 年。

② 克利亚什托尔内上揭文,第 38 页。森安孝夫:《モンゴル国现存遗迹·碑文调查研究报告》,ェーランァ中央学研究会,1999 年,第 123 页。林梅村:《西域文明》,东方出版社,1995 年,第 344～358 页。

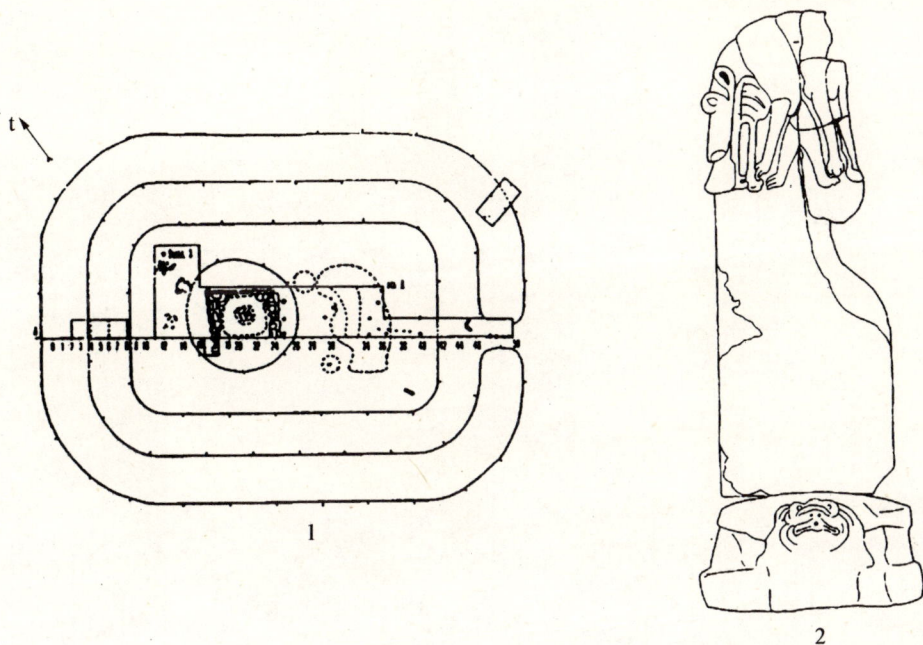

图二　佗钵可汗陵园

1　佗钵可汗陵园平面图　2　布古特碑正面线图

洪那海(Khonakhai)发现刻有文字的突厥石人。根据对其中粟特文的释读,表明这是隋文帝仁寿四年(604年)处罗可汗为其父泥利可汗建造的陵园。[①] 1993年,林俊雄勘测了小洪那海突厥陵园的布局。据他调查,小洪那海石人下的土台,呈正东西向,朝东。南北宽30.5米,东西长31米。土台四周还环绕一条深1米、宽5~6米的围墓沟。尽管林俊雄言之凿凿,但我们对实地做了相当细致的勘查过后,发现实际情况和他所说的并不完全一致。我们在调查中发现,与佗钵可汗陵园不同的是,泥利可汗陵园基本成方形。石人南侧的数十米外(在沟外)的地表显然要比石人所在处还高得多。这就说明小洪那海泥利可汗陵园的土台并不是特意夯筑的,而就是原来实际的地表。只不过建陵园时或许曾经开挖过围墓沟,将墓葬和周围分隔开来,才出现了目前这种状况。不过,迄今为止还没有在石人附近发现过石围、石堆墓一类的遗迹。

后期大型贵族墓葬以第二汗国几位重要人物的陵园为代表。与第一汗国时期相比,第二汗国贵族陵园汉化的程度进一步加深。

毗伽可汗陵园位于蒙古国后杭爱省鄂尔浑河左侧的和硕柴达木盆地(Khusho-Tsaidam)西南,是目前所知最大的古代突厥墓葬遗址。在和硕柴达木盆地,还有其他几处重要的墓葬遗址。阙特勤碑在毗伽可汗陵园北部,其周围还有两处规模相对较小的陵墓。这四处分别被编号为和硕柴达木1、2、3、4号墓葬。

---

① 参吉田丰《ソグドカら见たソグドのユーラッアの统合》,东京:岩波书店,1997年,第227~248页。据小洪那海石人铭文,泥利可汗卒于604年(仁寿四年,鼠年)。如果释读无误的话,那么这一记载应该要比汉文史料更为可靠。《隋书·西突厥传》:"(泥利)卒,子达漫立,号泥撅处罗可汗。其母向氏,本中国人,生达漫而泥利卒,向氏又嫁其弟婆实勤。开皇末(600),婆实共向氏入朝,遇达头乱,遂留京师,每舍之鸿胪寺。"《通典》略同。《通鉴》记此事时,删去"生达漫而泥利卒"一句。《通鉴》之所以作这样的改动,可能是觉察到其间有问题,因为如果真如《隋书》所记载的那样,则达漫继立时还是刚出生的婴儿。婆实、向氏两人入朝之年诸书都系于开皇末,则泥利的卒年当在开皇末年(600)或稍早。但开皇二十年(600)是庚申年(猴年),与小洪那海铭文所说相差四年。我们认为《隋书》"开皇末"的说法可能是"仁寿末"之误。达头部大乱是仁寿三年(603)以后的事,因此如果向氏与婆实是开皇末入朝的话,那么至少要在中国停留三年的时间。这恐怕不太合情理。我们推想,泥利死于仁寿末年西突厥之乱,故而向氏与婆实在此时来朝。

图三　泥利可汗陵园及部分遗物

1 陵园平剖面图　2、3 陵园出土板瓦、筒瓦　4~6 陵园出土陶器残片　7 泥利可汗石人

但两处规模较小的陵墓至今还未能确定其主人。最近几年的调查又在和硕柴达木盆地找到了其他 5 处新的遗迹，编号为和硕柴达木 3~7 号墓，但同样不能确定墓葬的主人。其中有两处只有由四块雕花石板拼成的石棺，没有立石碑。由于在毗伽可汗陵园的祭坛附近发现的类似雕花石棺也没有立碑，有学者怀疑这两处没有石碑的石棺应当也属于毗伽可汗陵园的组成部分。

毗伽可汗陵园呈长方形，长 90 米，宽 60 米，正东西向，面东。毗伽可汗陵园四周垒筑方形土围墙，外面还环以濠沟。陵园正东立着用突厥文和汉语书写的双语碑铭。石碑附近有毗伽可汗本人和其可敦的大理石像，以及一尊已经残损的青大理石坐像和石狮。在不远处另有一尊立像（现已经仆倒），身侧佩有长刀。新近的发掘显示，陵园中包括神道、陵庙、祭坛等等几个部分。陵庙遗迹位于整个陵园的中部。

阙特勤陵园呈东西向长方形，台基长 67.25 米，宽 28.85 米，上铺四方形砖坯（33×33 cm）。陵园外围以濠沟，深 2 米，开口宽大约 6 米，底宽 1.2 米。陵园有砖砌围墙。陵园开口于东面，开口处无濠沟。在陵园开口处两排共计 169 块杀人石。杀人石面向东排列，最前面的两尊略做雕饰。陵园入口处还有两尊大理石羊。入口处以西 8 米处有一大理石龟趺，长 2.25 米。[①] 陵园内部中轴线为神道，两侧排列大理石石人像。现在仅存一尊手持巾帕女人立像，一尊手持剑的男子立像，还有两尊男跪像。陵庙位于陵园中部，地面为烧砖地基（13×13）。从地面残存情况看，原来陵庙呈方形，边长 10.25 米。陵庙外墙抹灰泥，向外一面绘有红色花纹，并有龙纹泥塑。有 16 根木柱立于石础上。陵庙内还有一间神殿，也是东向

---

① 诺芙哥罗多娃：《蒙古的考古发现与古代史问题》，乌恩、莫润先译，载中国社会科学院考古研究所编：《考古学参考资料》（一），文物出版社，1978 年，第 56 页。克里亚什托尔内：《古代突厥鲁尼文碑铭——中亚细亚史原始文献》，李佩娟译，黑龙江教育出版社，1991 年，第 59~61 页。

开口。在神殿内有两尊坐像,一男一女,分别为阙特勤和其妻子的塑像。在坐像前有一洼坑,内埋有一些祭祀品和瓦罐,其中还有阙特勤头像。神殿后面有一方形花岗岩巨石,上部中间开一圆孔。一般认为这是祭坛。同样的巨石也见于毗伽可汗陵园中。祭坛西面有一大型的石椁。石椁由四块大型雕花石板围成。关于这种石椁的意义,国外学者有过一些争论。我们认为,这种石椁是真正埋藏尸骨地方,神殿之内只是用于供奉死者的塑像而已。阙特勤的尸骨应该在此石椁之内。

图四　阙特勤陵园及遗物

　　暾欲谷(Tonyuquq)陵园位于乌兰巴托东南 66 公里巴音朝克图(Bayin-tsokto)。陵园整体布局近似于毗伽可汗陵园和阙特勤陵园。陵园呈长方形,东西向,面东。陵园建于一夯土台上,土台四周围开濠沟。陵园入口在东面,濠沟在入口处断开。陵园内地面铺以方形砖坯。有八尊石人东西向排列,从陵园入口处一直排到祠庙前。祠庙位于土台中央,庙墙由灰泥砌成,还有一些泥塑饰品。祠庙后有两具方形石椁。大的一件位于中轴线上,由四块雕花石板围成,石板长 2.60 米,高 1.50 米。小石椁位于大石椁以北,也是四块石板围成,石板边长 1.50 米。①

①　克里亚什托尔内:《古代突厥鲁尼文碑铭——中亚细亚史原始文献》,第67页。

阙利啜陵园位于蒙古人民共和国乌兰巴托以南的伊格阔硕图（Ikhe-Khoshootu）。陵园外有一圈夯土围墙。围墙呈长方形，东西向，面东。东西长 40 米，南北宽 30 米，厚 5 米。围墙未发现明显开口。但从种种迹象看，开口处应在东面围墙正中。这里南北各有一只石羊。石羊以西两边分列石人。阙利啜碑位于东面土围以西 8 米处的中轴线位置上。祠庙位于陵园中部，呈方形，东西边长 5 米，南北长 6 米。祠庙位置上发现有大量残瓦。石椁位于祠庙以西，也在中轴线上。石椁下为一直径约 7 米的圆台。石椁由四块雕花大型石板围成。其中一面石板上刻有展翅对鸟图案。

翁金陵园位于蒙古和硕柴达木盆地以南 180 公里处的翁金河畔，呈东西正向的长方形，面东，东西长约 45 米，南北宽约 30 米。陵园外有一道濠沟，上端开口最宽处 10 米左右，底径 2 米左右。该陵园破坏较严重，石椁残片位于陵园中部偏南，附近还有龟趺、石羊、石人像等。[①]

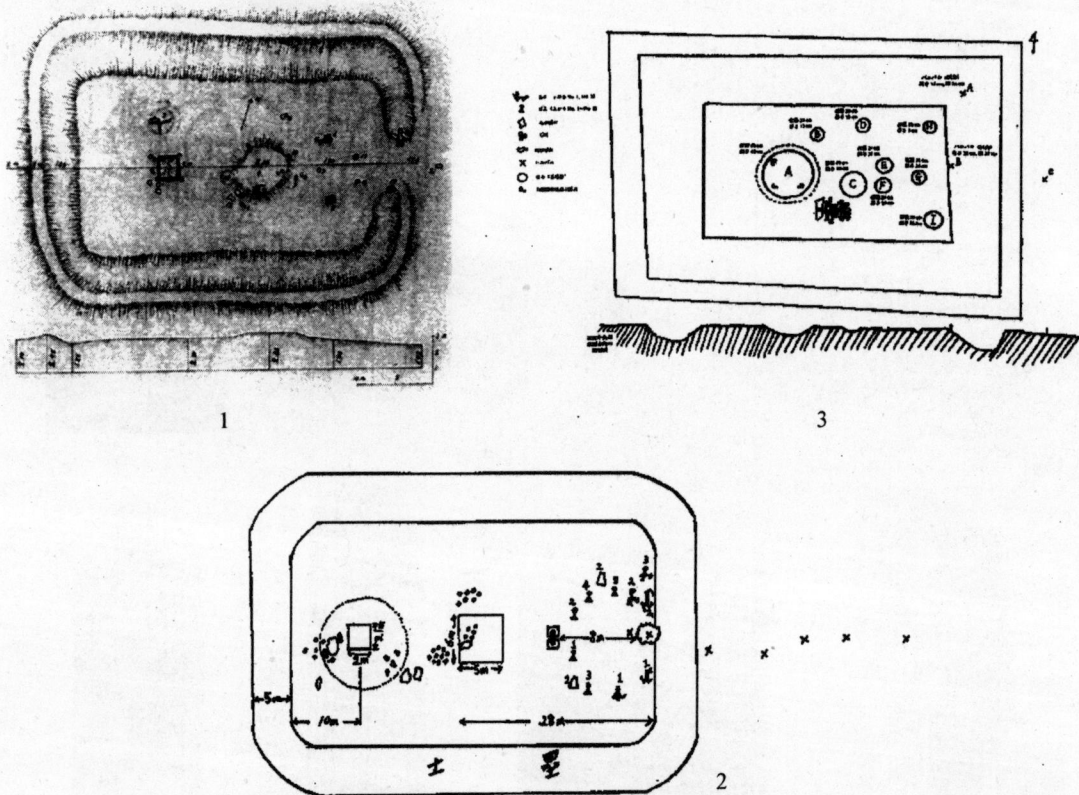

图五　第二汗国其他贵族陵园平面图
1 暾欲谷陵园平面图　2 阙利啜陵园平面图　3 翁金陵园平面图

从现有材料来看，属于突厥民族的墓葬大体可以分为四种类型。（图六）前三种不同类型可能分别属于突厥民族内部不同部落的墓葬形态。[②]

1. 石人石围墓。这种类型的墓葬通常在地面竖栽石板围成方形石围，墓穴位于石围中部，墓东西向。墓穴中往往没有尸骨，应与突厥人实行火葬有关。石围之内有时还堆石块。这种类型的墓葬又可以分为单人墓（图六：2）和家族墓两种。家族通常由几个石围墓共用一面石围组合而成。（图六：3）

---

① 森安孝夫上揭文，第 126~128 页。
② 关于突厥墓葬的详细研究，请参见上引陈凌《突厥汗国考古与欧亚文化交流》有关章节。

早期的石围墓通常不立石人,也没有杀人石。突厥汗国时期的石围墓有一些立有代表墓主的石人。石人的位置或者位于石围墓正前方(东面),或者立于石围墓中央。(图六:5)我们怀疑,石围墓立石人可能是在突厥汗国兴起之后才开始的。突厥汗国时期的石围墓有些还列立杀人石,(图六:6)这种做法也不见于前代。

这种类型的墓葬在图瓦西部墓地、库迪尔格墓地、阿尔泰山西北麓墓地都有发现。中国境内的内蒙古、新疆以及中亚其他一些地方也有发现。这类的石围墓有相当大比重都立有突厥石人,因此我们认为石人石围墓属于突厥(狭义上的)典型的墓葬形式。

2. 石圹墓。石圹墓通常是在地表开挖一竖穴土坑,再以石块填围墓坑四周。墓东西向,头向东,仰身直肢,通常殉一至二匹马。人、马大多同向,不过也有部分反向。随葬品多为马具、带具、箭头等等。有部分石圹墓还出土木制葬具。(图六:4)

石圹墓的形式比较简单,分布也较广。这种类型的墓葬非常早就出现,米努辛斯克盆地卡拉苏克时期就流行这种墓葬形制。乌科克地区这种类型的墓葬中曾经出土过金代典型的"柳毅传书镜",可知这种类型的墓葬还沿用到13世纪左右。因此,如果缺乏有明显时代特征的随葬品的话,其年代往往不易判别。

这类墓葬主要见于库迪尔格墓地,阿尔泰山西北麓墓地也有零星几座,在中国境内的内蒙古、新疆等地,以及外蒙古、中亚都有发现。

我们认为,某一些突厥部族采用这种类型的墓葬。但具体是哪些部族,史料不足征,目前还不能做出判断。

3. 石堆墓。突厥时代另一种常见的墓葬形制是石堆墓。(图六:1)石堆墓出现的时代非常早,天山南北、阿尔泰山地区有大量公元前一千年的石堆墓,一般认为是塞种人墓葬。

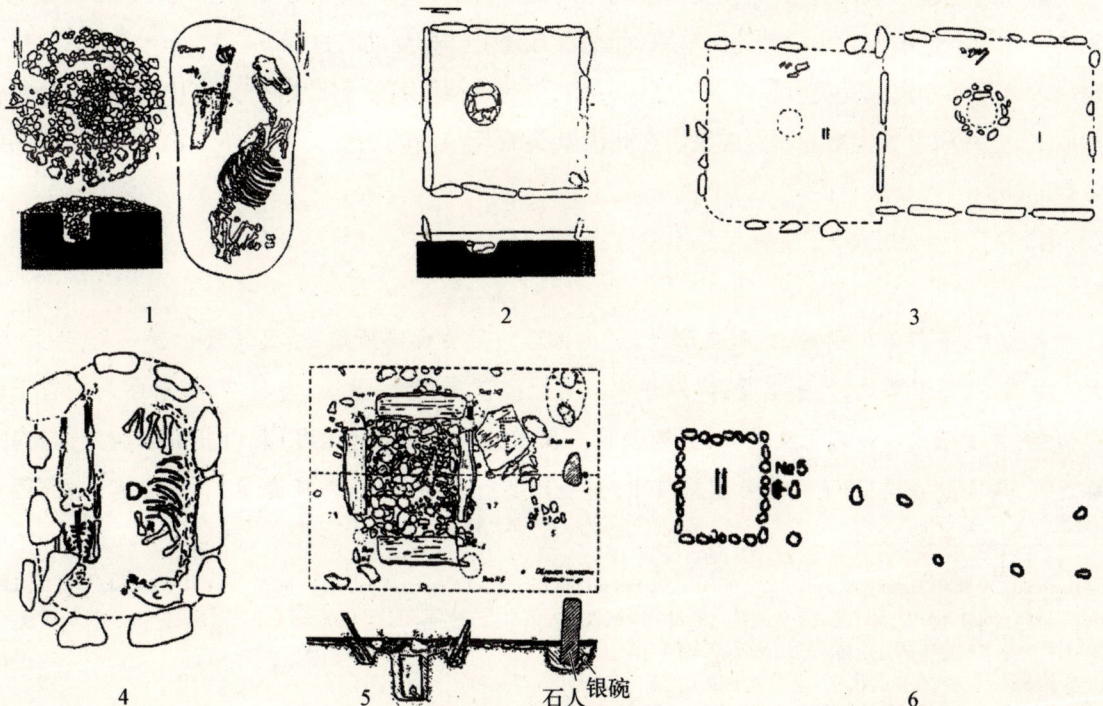

图六 突厥普通墓葬类型

石堆墓通常在地表往下开挖竖穴土坑,再在地表大量堆石。堆石多呈圆盘状。不过,大量石堆常因后人取石而遭破坏,不复保存原有形状。也正是由于这个原因,按地面堆石的外观形状对石堆墓分型式意义不大。

突厥时代这种石堆墓主要见于阿尔泰山西北麓地区、图瓦西北部墓地。库迪尔格墓地不见这种形制的墓葬。

从时间和地域分布上看,突厥民族中一些部族使用这种类型的墓葬。

4. 纳骨器。巴托尔德(V. V. Barthold)曾经指出,中亚地区火祆教徒与波斯不同是一点是流行使用纳骨器(Ossuary)。[①] 值得注意的是,在中亚和新疆地区都发现过一些帐篷式的纳骨器,一般认为这种形制的纳骨器是突厥火祆徒所有。[②] 有苏联学者认为,使用纳骨器是由东伊朗部落天葬和火葬两种方式合流而产生的。[③]

三

交河沟西两种类型的墓葬此前、此后似不见于吐鲁番地区。通过对比突厥的墓葬形制,我们认为,交河沟西两种类型墓葬的出现或与突厥在高昌地区活动有关。这两种类型墓葬地表的形制与突厥普通墓葬的第一种类型石人石围墓完全相同,也与前期突厥大型贵族陵园的地表形制近似(但没有夯土台基)。我们怀疑,两者之间或当存在关联,沟西墓葬的这种地表形态,很可能渊源自突厥,是将突厥石围墓地表形式与中原斜坡墓道有机地组合在一起。与中原斜坡墓道墓的关系,姑置不论,但方形石堆和石坟院的出现则反映了当地文化受突厥影响的事实。

突厥统治欧亚草原百余年之久,其与西域地区的关系尤为密切。其间政治往来,人物迁移、姻娅婚媾种种不一。在这些过程中,既有突厥接受西域文化的薰习,同时其部分文化习俗也对西域深有影响。文化因素的流动绝不是单向的由绿洲流向草原,而是双方处于一种互动的过程。

高昌地区墓葬方式深受突厥影响这一事实,从未引起学界注意。自吐鲁番文书出土以后,吐鲁番研究蔚然成风,已经积累了大量的研究成果。在此仅就突厥与高昌的历史关系略作申论,以说明沟西两种类型墓葬的突厥因素其来有自。

《周书》卷五十《突厥传》记突厥起源传说称:[④]

> 突厥者,盖匈奴之别种,姓阿史那氏,别为部落。后为邻国所破,尽灭其族。有一儿,年且十岁,兵人见其小,不忍杀之,乃刖其足,弃草泽中。有牝狼以肉饲之,及长,与狼合,遂有孕焉。彼王闻此儿尚在,重遣杀之。使者见狼在侧,并欲杀狼。狼遂逃于高昌国之〔西〕北山。山有洞穴,穴内有平壤茂草,周回数百里,四面俱山。狼匿其中,遂生十男。十男长大,外托妻孕,其后各有一姓,阿史那

---

① Barthold: A Short History of Turkestan, in Four Studies on the History of Central Asia, tran. by V. and T. Minorsky, vol. 1, Leiden: E. J. Brill, 1956, vol. 1, pp. 9 – 10. 笔者新近对纳骨器及中国祆教徒葬俗有进一步的讨论,见陈凌:《中古时期中国境内祆教遗迹考古学研究》,中国社会科学院考古研究所博士后出站报告,2008 年。

② 参考滕磊:《祆教在华遗存考》,北京大学硕士论文,2001 年,第 25 ~ 26 页。

③ 参考蔡鸿生:《唐代九姓胡与突厥文化》,中华书局,1998 年,第 135 页。

④ 《周书》,中华书局点校本,第 3 册,第 907 ~ 908 页。

即一也。子孙蕃育,渐至数百家。经数世,相与出穴,臣于茹茹。居金山之阳,为茹茹铁工。金山形似兜鍪,其俗谓兜鍪为"突厥",遂因以为号焉。

高昌国西北山就是吐鲁番盆地以北的博格达山。这一传说说明突厥初起之地与高昌地壤相接。因此,突厥勃兴之初就与邻近的高昌有颇多纠葛。

1911 年吐鲁番阿斯塔那发现的《麹斌造寺碑》提供了突厥与高昌早期交往的重要史料。1944 年,盛世才在乌鲁木齐盖房时将该碑移做奠基,至今尚重未见天日。《麹斌造寺碑》的图版和录文见于黄文弼先生《吐鲁番考古记》一书。[①] 该碑建于麹乾固延昌十五年(575),其中一段内容如下:[②]

(前略)宁朔将军绾曹郎中麹斌者,河州金城郡□□□□(之)从叔也……天姿秀发,英略□□,□□瑚琏,操刀斯任。年十九,擢拜威远将军、横截令……寻转折冲将军、新兴令……其后属突厥雄强,威振朔方,治兵练卒,侵我北鄙。□□□□军之委,承庙胜之策,鹰扬阃外,虎步敌境,兵锋暂交,应机退散。□□□□数之期,深知□□□□,□安虑危,见机而作,乃欲与之交好,永固拜疆。以专对之才,非人莫□,□□君厥庭,远和□□。□□□之以机辨,陈之以祸福。厥主钦其英规,□众畏其雄略,遂同盟结姻,□□而归。自是边□□□,□□无虞,干戈载戢,弓矢斯韬,皆君之力也。以功进爵,乃迁振武将军、□□□史。寔乃柱石□□□□,□□社稷之器。苞刚柔于胸衿,备文武于怀抱,名不虚称,斯其膺矣(后略)

碑文称突厥在初兴之时即开始侵扰高昌北境,由于双方力量悬殊,麹斌才出使突厥,以结盟好。经由这次出使,突厥与高昌开始联姻。据马雍先生考证,麹斌出使时间在 554 年 3 月至 555 年 2 月之间,高昌王麹宝茂娶突厥可汗女的时间为 555 年。[③] 自此之后,高昌与突厥世代联姻。

阿斯塔那 307 号墓出土《高昌□善等传供食帐》之一:[④]

1. (前阙)陁中十人下十人尽世日(后阙)
2. (前阙)斗供外生儿提勲珂都虞卅五人(后阙)
3. (前阙)善传麦五斗,供阿博珂寒铁师居(后阙)
4. (前阙)七斛五斗,次畦少何传麦五斗供栈头大官(后阙)
5. (前阙)下三人,尽世日。合用麦□斛五斗,将康师得(后阙)
6. (前阙)珂寒使陁钵大官□□上六人中四人,尽卅(后阙)
7. (前阙)次虎牙都子传麦(中阙)粟米二斗供南厢珂寒(后阙)[⑤]

① 黄文弼:《吐鲁番考古记》,中国科学院,1954 年,第 54 页后附录文及图版 59。
② 录文参考马雍《西域史地文物丛考》,文物出版社,1990 年,第 146～153 页。
③ 马雍上揭文。
④ 《吐鲁番出土文书》(图版本),第 1 册,文物出版社,1992～1996 年,第 415 页。
⑤ 厢、寒二字原录文阙,此据同墓所出《高昌虎牙都子等传供食帐》、《高昌□善等传供食帐》二、三等均见有"南厢珂寒",此据以补入。见《吐鲁番出土文书》第 1 册,第 414、416、417 页。

文书中阿博可汗即西突厥之阿波可汗,[①]其统治时间为581至587年,从而可知该文件文书属麹乾固时代。《通典》卷一九七《边防典十三·突厥传上》载突厥制度称"其子弟谓之特勤"。该文书称提勤珂都虔为外生儿(外甥),那么他的母亲就是麹乾固的姊妹(也即麹宝茂之女)嫁给突厥可汗为可敦者。玄奘西行求法行经活国(Warwālīz,今昆都士附近),遇统叶护长子咥度设。咥度设为高昌王妹婿,[②]其妻为麹文泰之妹,麹伯雅之女。

高昌不仅与突厥世代联姻,而且还受突厥的官号。《麹斌造寺碑》碑阴麹宝茂署衔"使持节、骠骑大将军、开府仪同三司、都督瓜州诸军事、侍中、瓜州刺史、西平郡开国公、希董、时多浮跌、无亥、希利发、高昌王"。其中希董即俟斤,希利发即俟利发。麹乾固署衔"卫将军、波多旱、输屯发、高昌令尹",其中输屯发即吐屯发。

在吐鲁番出土文书有多份传供食帐,里面数处见载突厥人名,由此可以推知往来于高昌的突厥人不在少数。[③]

唐初,高昌还与西突厥联合攻略附近小国。《旧唐书》卷一九八《高昌传》:"时西戎诸国来朝贡者,皆涂经高昌,文泰后稍壅绝之。伊吾先臣西突厥,至是内属,文泰又与叶护连结,将击伊吾。太宗以其反覆,下书切让,征其大臣冠军阿史那矩入朝,将与议事。文泰竟不遣,乃遣其长史麹雍来谢罪。"[④]阿史那矩很可能是突厥派驻监控高昌国政的人。高昌又曾经"与西突厥乙毗设击破焉耆者三城"。[⑤] 为了保证在西域的地位,"(麹)文泰与西突厥欲谷设通和,遗其金帛,约有急相为表里"。[⑥]

自554/555年起高昌就与突厥有密切的往来,双方又联姻结盟,因此必然有突厥文化因素渗入高昌。沟西墓地堆石、坟院式斜坡墓道洞室墓的出现在6世纪中叶之后,恰是高昌与突厥建交后不久,其消失又是在第一汗国灭亡后不久。也就是说,这种形制的墓葬的使用时间正好与突厥活跃的时间相一致。因此,我们有理由推断高昌方形石堆和石坟院墓葬形式是在突厥影响下产生的。

① 姜伯勤:《敦煌吐鲁番文书与丝绸之路》,文物出版社,1994年,第91页。
② 慧立、彦悰:《大慈恩寺三藏法师传》,孙毓棠等点校,中华书局,1983年,第31页。
③ 《吐鲁番出土文书》,第1册,第414~418、455、461页。
④ 《旧唐书》,中华书局点校本,第16册,第5294页。
⑤ 《旧唐书》,第16册,第5294页。
⑥ 《旧唐书》,第16册,第5296页。

新和县克孜勒协海尔古城调查与研究

张 平

新疆文物考古研究所

新和县境保存的唐代古城、戍堡等各类遗址众多,其中克孜勒协海尔古城的建筑形制和周邻分布的相关遗迹,以及所曾出土的历史遗物都很有特点,值得做进一步的探讨,并加以保护。

一、黄文弼开考古调查之先河

我国考古学者黄文弼曾于1928年9月初来库车、新和、沙雅、拜城做考古调查,历经艰苦,有古必访,其《考察日记》、《塔里木盆地考古记》等著作,为我们今天的文物考古工作奠定了基础,提供了宝贵的借鉴。克孜勒协海尔古城即是当年黄文弼所考察到的一座古城遗址。在《黄文弼蒙新考察日记》中,1928年9月24日记载:"饭后带三人查看'克子西耳',在此地之南约五六里地(克子尔庄)。4点50分向南出发,走白泥滩中大道。5点40分即抵旧城。为二城相连,迤北之城,周250步。北有土墩3,中高大,为红土所筑,中有一沙窝,城墙高数尺。隔数步,又有一城,较大,周500步,青草丛生,城墙略高,审视无他物,瓦片为红色,与大望库木同,疑亦为唐代之城。余绘一形势图,归已7时矣。"[1]

在《塔里木盆地考古记》中曾载:"九月二十四日由伯勒克斯(庄)出发,庄南有一古城名克子尔沁,两城相连,迤北一城周三百三十米。有墙基,高约二米不等,红土所筑。北有土墩三。此城南又有一城毗连,相隔不过十余步,稍大,周约六百米。满生青草,墙基稍高,除散布红陶片外,无其他遗物。"[2]从上述黄文弼先生的记载中可得知克孜勒协海尔城是由南、北两座土城组合的遗址,疑为唐代之城,北城墙周长约330米,南城墙周长约600米,但是所绘平面图失误甚多。

二、我们历次的调查与发现

20世纪的80年代起,笔者和同事及县文化馆的同志曾几次到此调查。岁月流逝,沧桑巨变,古城曾有"克子西耳"、"克子尔沁"、"克孜里下城",到今日的"克孜勒协海尔"古城的标准称谓。如今的遗址四周均被农田、道路、林带和水渠所蚕食和包围。南北相依的两座古城东侧有条南北流向的水渠和通往大尤都斯乡(玉奇喀特乡)的大道,水渠和道路穿过城址的东部,其南城的东城墙均置于道路和林带之外。[3]

---

① 黄文弼遗著,黄烈整理:《黄文弼蒙新考察日记》(1927～1930),文物出版社,1990年,第275页。
② 黄文弼:《塔里木盆地考古记》,科学出版社,1958年,第21页。
③ 自治区文物普查办公室阿克苏地区文物普查队:《阿克苏地区文物普查报告》,《新疆文物》1995年第4期,第36～37页。

南城址：基本上呈正方形，边长 161×151 米。城址的西北角有向外斜向伸出的垛墙，此类古城的另外三个角也应有斜向伸出的垛墙，其古城的形状应该呈"◇"状。南城现只有西墙垣保存较好，北墙一段还保存有距现地表 2～4 米高的城墙基。东、南墙垣存仅存有低矮的墙基痕，并被利用为现在农田的田埂。从目前保存的墙垣较好的两墙垣来看，现长约 161 米，靠南的 3 米墙垣已破坏。北墙垣保存长约 80 米。现墙垣最高约 6 米，上宽约 3 米，基部宽约 5 米，横剖面呈梯形。墙垣外观可以观察到有三个马面，均长 7～7.5 米，宽 7～7.5 米，高 6 米。西墙垣与北墙垣衔接处有一向外斜向伸出的垛墙，长 9 米，基宽 6 米，上宽 3 米，高约 6 米。

从保存较好的西墙垣观察，墙垣为夯筑，夯层之间保存有夯洞，一层层一排排的夯洞清晰可见，有些夯洞现已成为鸟巢。每排夯洞的间距为 57 cm 左右，洞径为 3.5～15 cm 之间，夯洞为东西向。夯洞层与层的距离不等。夯层厚度在 11～19 cm 之间，夯土很硬。

南墙垣与东墙垣现仅存一部分低矮的墙基，大部分墙垣已被开辟为农田。北墙垣保存情况较东、南墙垣要稍好一些。墙垣长约 151 米，高约 2.4 米，宽约 4 米。北墙垣西段保存有一个马面，长 7 米，宽 7 米，高 3 米。在北墙垣的近中部地段的基部和现地表齐平的地方，发现一个圆形的呈南北走向的洞穴，洞穴四周散露有被老乡挖出并打碎的许多夹砂红陶片。其次，在北部墙垣的下部见有土坯，土坯长度不明，宽 15 cm、厚 8 cm。

北城址：北城与南城间隔约 115 米。城址呈方形，东西墙垣长约 100 米，南北长约 97 米。现仅存 2～6 米高的墙垣。墙垣上长有甘草、芦苇、骆驼刺等植物。大部分墙垣高约 2 米。墙垣为夯筑，因坍塌堆积，夯层情况不明。古城北墙垣外，中段有一缺口，宽约 10 米，缺口外为一向北突出的梯形状瓮城遗迹。瓮城外墙垣东西墙边长 30 米，北墙现为一土台，高约 1 米，长约 15 米。瓮城内东西长约 19 米、南北宽约 7 米。城内已开辟为农田，在沟渠内散见陶片。陶器形为罐、缸之类，皆为夹砂的红陶、红褐陶、灰陶、少量的绿釉陶和铺地方砖，以及残铜钱、铜器等。

随着古城内外开辟为农田之后不断有文物出土，如 1983 年 8 月县文管所收藏的三耳釉陶罐、大陶瓮，1978 年收藏的铜肖像形花押（人骑毛驴），1989 年 10 月的自治区文物普查中发现的 2 件陶水管等文物，对古城的时代、定性定位等研究都是重要的实物例证。

三、陶水管的相关问题

陶水管出土于南城内的北城墙中段墙基底部，曾被老乡挖出后打碎而弃之。粘接完整的陶水管有二件。一长一短的形制和作用不同，可分二式：

Ⅰ式：夹砂红陶，表面饰土黄色陶衣，泥条盘筑成型加工，呈圆柱状，两端有子母接口，长 72 cm，直径 20 cm，壁厚 1～3 cm。

Ⅱ式：夹砂红陶，表面饰土黄色陶衣，泥条盘筑成型加工，呈短柱状，两端亦有子母接口，长 20.8 cm，壁厚 1～3 cm，短径约 15.2 cm，长径约 19.2 cm。

根据两节陶管形体特点比较研究，这是一套管的两件，长形的为管子，短形的为两长水管相通的接头，称之为"管箍"。两种陶管均为一端径大，另一端径小。如将各节陶水管连接在一起组成排水管道时，即将长陶管的小头插入短陶管的大头内（管箍），短陶管的小头再插入长陶管的大头，依此类推。这种组合的陶制排水管道的发现,对于提升克孜勒协海尔古城在新和县唐代古城中的历史地位提供了实物例证,具有珍贵的史料和文物价值。遗憾的是这两件文物如今各分东西,长陶管留在了库车博物馆,而短的陶管箍却为地区博物馆收藏。[①]

新疆古城建筑中发现地下有陶水管遗物的尚有先例:一个是库车县的皮朗古城。1972 年和 1986 年都曾在皮朗古城遗址内出土过陶水道管,为唐代遗物,残长 34.5 cm、直径 15 cm。加砂红陶,表面饰土黄色陶衣,泥条盘筑工艺,呈圆柱形,一端口部束唇作榫,管道串联时榫口结合,是专用地下的排水或输水管道。[②] 另一个发现地点是吐鲁番的高昌故城,1986 年曾出土两节陶管。其中 86TG:1,长 47.5 cm,前端口径 13.5 cm,后端口径 16 cm,前端壁厚 0.8 cm,后端壁厚 2.5 cm。其形如烟囱,后端粗,前端细,腹部略鼓。泥条盘筑成型,由后端开始,泥条凸棱明显。后端制作粗糙厚重,在表面随意按捺一些洼坑,前端制作细致轻薄,直口圆唇,为泥质灰陶。86TG:2,长 40.5 cm,前端口径 11.5 cm,后端口径 16.5 cm,前端壁厚 0.8 cm,后端壁厚 1.6 cm。其形制特征同前,两件均出土于高昌城东北部附廓约 200 米处的一夯筑的方形土台基的殿堂遗址内,属高昌国中叶以后的遗物。依陶管形体特征并结合出土情况分析,这两节陶水管,很可能是供排除污水使用的,用法犹如现在建筑物上的排水斗,对台基起保护作用。[③]

综上所述,根据迄今为止的新和县克孜勒协海尔古城的唐代排水陶管规格均比库车皮朗城和高昌城的长度及口径的尺寸要大得多,而且有串联陶管的管箍(接头),其形制的粗大特征,以及出土情况的综合分析,其形制和用途很可能是一节节串联起来,铺设在地下的供水或排水的陶管道。而高昌城发现的两节陶水管则是殿堂建筑物上的排水设施,其目的和作用是对台基起保护作用。而库车皮朗古城所发现的残陶水管,因形体特征不完整,且出土情况不明,很难做出用途和作用的判断,有待新的陶水管的发现。不言而喻,克孜勒协海尔古城能和高昌故城、库车皮朗古城都发现了排水或供水的陶水管建筑构件,给人以深深的历史悬念。

四、三耳绿釉陶罐及相关问题

克孜勒协海尔古城出土的三耳绿釉陶罐,1996 年国家文物局委派国家级的专家组来新疆做一级文物鉴定,当时专家组将三耳绿釉陶罐定为一级文物,称为"波斯绿釉陶盘口瓶"。

根据三耳绿釉陶罐的时代,以及其造型、贴塑的装饰、玻璃釉色工艺等堪为上品,定为一级文物当之无愧。但是,"波斯釉"和"盘口瓶"的定性称谓仍值得商榷。事后我曾请教过专家组中的张朋川馆长(甘肃省博物馆),询问"波斯釉"的来龙去脉的相关问题,他们也解释不清楚。其次,"盘口瓶"的叫法也不妥当。观察克孜勒协海尔古城出土的这件三耳绿釉陶罐的口沿部位为敞开式的喇叭口形状,沿内并没有一圈规范的"盘口"。所谓的盘口应类似今天仍生产的"泡菜坛子"式的口沿。类似克孜勒协海尔古城出土的这件三耳绿釉陶罐造型器物,曾在喀什地区、阿克苏地区和焉耆盆地多有发现。有素面的,也有施深绿、蓝绿,或绿中泛黄的黄绿色釉的。有刻划、贴塑或模压和贴塑相结合的装饰纹样,均位于陶罐的肩至上腹部位置。陶罐上的三个把手有呈条带状的、圆柱状的,三个把手的装饰纹样有素面的,刻划纹样的,

---

① 自治区博物馆编:《新疆出土文物》,文物出版社,1975 年;刘松柏:《龟兹二体钱的发现及其认识》,《中国钱币》1987 年第 1 期。
② 《阿克苏地区文物普查报告》,《新疆文物》1995 年第 4 期,第 36～38 页。
③ 柳洪亮:《古代高昌城市建设中使用的陶管道》,《新疆文物》1991 年第 3 期,第 36～37 页。

或捏塑动物的兽头等装饰。然而,迄今为止,考古发现的以三耳绿釉陶罐为代表的低温色釉的陶土制品却都出自龟兹地区的遗址中,这一历史文化现象不得不引起我们关注的视野。

克孜勒协海尔古城出土的三耳绿釉陶罐,喇叭口、高束颈、溜肩、鼓腹、小平底,三耳自沿部通达肩上,通高42 cm、口径19 cm、底径15 cm。在装饰上采用了堆贴图案的技法,亦即由浅浮雕式的葡萄叶和人面装饰纹组合的方连图案,堆贴在肩腹部。表面挂的绿中透黄的绿釉色彩与堆贴的装饰图案浑然一体。其绿色玻璃釉色泽绚丽,造型精美,代表了唐代龟兹低温釉陶的自身格调和时代特征。绿釉陶的制品在新和县境内的唐代遗址中均有发现,如来合曼戍堡出土的细砂泥质绿釉陶猪、绿釉陶狗、绿釉陶羊等动物小摆件,形象生动。托帕墩古城出土的三耳绿釉陶罐,细砂红陶,通高7 cm、口径和底径均2.3 cm。通古斯巴什古城、托克拉克艾肯千佛洞、夏合吐尔、吐孜吐尔、吐尔拉、且热克协海尔等遗址都发现一些绿色釉的陶器制品残片。

低温绿釉陶器制品,建筑装饰和摆件等在邻近各县也有发现。如库车县博物馆收藏的三耳釉陶罐,敞口、直颈、溜肩、鼓腹、小平底,三耳自沿部通达肩上,细砂红陶,表面饰通体的绿色玻璃质的釉。其通高15.1 cm、口径8 cm、底径4.5 cm。[1] 绿釉陶灯,泥质红陶,表面挂绿色玻璃釉。灯具造型新颖,灯壁作莲瓣纹,条带状的横把柄,平底。高4.5 cm、口径8.4 cm、底径4 cm。我们在库车县境文物考古调查中发现唐王城、库木吐拉遗址、玉奇吐尔戍堡、苏巴什佛寺、博其罕那佛寺等遗址中都有深绿色、翠绿色、蓝色、黄绿色釉的釉陶罐、釉陶杯、釉陶钵和釉陶方砖等。[2]

1980年至1981年,笔者和同事在轮台县做考古调查,曾在拉伊苏清理了一座曾被扰乱过的唐代洞室墓,出土的5件陶器中就有3件低温绿釉陶器:三耳绿釉陶罐一件,细砂红陶,轮制、喇叭口、卷唇、高束颈、溜肩、小平底,三耳自口沿通达肩部。表面饰深绿色玻璃釉,口沿上并饰乳钉状釉斑。通高16.5 cm、口径10 cm、底径6.5 cm。釉陶碗一件,细砂红陶,轮制、敞口、小圈足,表面饰绿色玻璃釉,[3]通高5.5 cm、口径9.5 cm、底足径3.9 cm。釉陶壶一件,细砂红陶,轮制、敞口、长颈、溜肩、鼓腹、小平底,表面饰绿色玻璃釉。[4] 同时,唐代的拉伊苏烽戍、乌垒州城、阿克墩戍堡也发现一些绿釉陶器残片。

拜城县的克孜尔石窟寺遗址曾出土了丰富的低温绿釉制品。主要有釉陶罐、釉陶钵、釉陶碗、釉陶杯、釉陶豆、釉陶盘、釉陶香炉等,均为龟兹石窟研究所收藏。1977年修建通往克孜尔石窟的土路工程过程中,在克孜尔墓葬区内出土一件三耳绿釉陶罐,盘口、高颈、溜肩、斜腹、小平底。通高16 cm、口径10.5 cm、底径6 cm。三耳自沿通达肩部,绿色釉斑驳。1989年至1990年,克孜尔石窟西区的维修保护工程中清理出二件三耳绿釉陶罐:一件编号K89-6F:13,三耳绿釉陶罐,泥质红陶,敞口、短颈、溜肩、鼓腹、小平底。通高3.4 cm、口径2 cm、底径1.4 cm。其玻璃质绿釉斑驳,杂有气泡。另一件编号K90-23,形制同上,通高7.6 cm、口径2.4 cm、底径2.2 cm。单耳绿釉杯一件,泥质红陶,模制。敞口、尖唇、弧形腹、平底。腹至器底部有一平头柱状的单耳,耳部呈梯形状。杯的腹内壁有模制呈凸起的纹饰,主体图案为莲花、叶蔓和联珠纹。通高4.2 cm、口径12.5 cm、底径12.5 cm。另外还有:绿釉陶豆一件,细砂红陶,

① 新疆文物局、自治区博物馆等主编:《新疆文物大观》,新疆美术摄影出版社,1999年,第217页。
② 《阿克苏地区文物普查报告》,《新疆文物》1995年第4期,第10~48页;拙文:《库车唐王城调查》,《新疆文物》2003年第1期,第28页。
③ 《轮台县文物调查》,《新疆文物》1991年第2期,第1页。
④ 《轮台县文物调查》,《新疆文物》1991年第2期,第1页。

手制。豆柄部残缺，侈口、平沿、弧腹、高圈足，已残。豆腹外壁饰以附加卷草纹和连续的变形 S 纹。通体饰深绿色釉彩，釉彩与附加卷草纹饰浑然一体。口径 12 cm。绿釉陶香炉一件，细砂红陶，轮制。香炉由内外两部分组成。外部型为敞口、平岩、直斜腹，呈斗形，小平底。通高 26 cm、口径 44 cm、底径 12 cm。内部形状为侈口，径 9 cm，方唇略卷，外饰一周凹入的弦纹。短束颈、溜肩、鼓腹、腹部均匀分布有 5 个椭圆形熏孔，孔径 5~6 cm，内部表面饰土黄色陶衣不挂绿釉。克孜尔石窟群发现最多者为绿釉陶钵和绿釉方砖的残块，均为泥质和细砂红陶，表面挂厚薄不同的深绿色或浅绿色釉彩，釉层内含有小气泡，新出土时釉色晶莹光泽。①

从已知釉陶的类型划分，除作为铺地装饰的琉璃砖属建筑材料之外，其余皆为罐、盆、壶、碗、钵、豆之类的实用生活器皿和摆饰物品。其制作工艺有手制、轮制和模制，均以陶土作胎，普遍施以绿色的玻璃釉。装饰纹样有刻划、堆贴和模制的几何纹、莲花、卷枝（忍冬）、葡萄叶和人面图案等。值得注意的是，在上述类型的釉陶器皿中出现一些显然是中原汉文化饮食习俗的生活器具，如圈足的釉陶碗、釉陶豆、釉陶盆和釉陶甑（箅子、蒸锅）等，这些新型的汉化类型的釉陶制品的出现，深刻地反映出唐代龟兹饮食习俗增加了新的文化内容，构成了龟兹釉陶具有造型古朴实用的自身特点。

五、龟兹低温色釉的初步分析

我国陶器工艺美术史表明，颜色釉陶在我国陶瓷史上占据十分重要的地位。颜色釉陶又可分为高温色釉和低温色釉两大类。其中高温色釉的出现，可追溯到公元前一千多年前的殷周时期。最早发现的高温色釉是以铁的氧化物为着色剂，以氧化钙为熔剂的青釉。而低温色釉的出现要比青釉晚得多，其釉是以氧化铅为主要熔剂，故有"铅釉"之称。其胎质为普通陶土，胎多为红色，常施深绿、翠绿、茶黄、赭黄、粟黄、蓝等色铅釉，烧成温度在 700~900 度左右。低温色釉陶表面平整光滑、釉层清澈、光泽强、色彩丰富。但是硬度较低，易出现划痕，其化学稳定性也较差。汉代已相当普遍出现低温色釉工艺，但质料不纯。经南北朝和隋的发展，低温色釉工艺取得了卓越成就，出现了高质量的"琉璃工艺品"和"唐三彩"。②

唐代龟兹低温色釉陶的釉色，主要是一种单色釉陶。釉色以绿色、翠绿色为主，少数为蓝色釉或黄绿色釉。为了分析龟兹低温色釉的化学成分，我们选择了部分遗址中的残破标本做了定性、定量的化学分析。各类标本观察分析表明：龟兹低温色釉主要是单色的绿釉。色釉的主要着色是铜和铁。该釉以氧化铅为主要熔剂。就其化学组成而言，应属于我国传统的 $PbO—SiO_2$ 二元系统。从低温釉陶的制造工艺观察，其工艺显然是受到中原地区传统的绿色铅釉制陶技术的影响，另一方面则表现具有自身传统文化的特点，表现出传统文化和外来文化相互交流和融合。

含铅矿物是地球上一种分布甚广的矿物，我国很早就已掌握了铅的冶炼技术。据考古发现，殷商时就已出现铅的冶炼，曾出土有铅卤、铅爵、铅瓿等器皿。据已有的研究，我国古代玻璃即是以铅（方铅矿、白铅矿）为主要助熔剂的铅玻璃。我国劳动人民在冶炼和使用铅金属的长期实践中，不断提高对这种铅

---

① 自治区文化厅文物保护维修办公室：《1989 年克孜尔千佛洞窟前清理简报》，《新疆文物》1991 年第 3 期，第 6~34 页；新疆文物考古研究所：《1990 年克孜尔石窟库前清理报告》，《新疆文物》1992 年第 3 期，第 17~58 页。
② 张福康、张志刚：《中国历代低温色釉的研究》，《硅酸盐学报》1980 年第 8 卷第一期；余谱保、余家栋：《颜色釉的产生与发展》，《景德镇陶瓷》第二辑，1984 年。

玻璃物质的形成规律及其性质的认识,并应用到陶器的制作生产中,这就导致铅釉的出现。铅质的低温色釉有着自身的特点,如釉面光泽强,表面平整光滑,有玻璃质感。但其硬度比较低,化学稳定性差,易受水分和大气中碳酸气一类气体的侵蚀。但在铅釉中加入少量含铜、含铁、含钴的矿物煅烧后,便会出现绿、黄、蓝色调的低温色釉,使陶器表面平整光泽,便于拭洗,成为新型的既美观又耐用的生活器具。

六、龟兹低温釉陶产生的历史背景

考古发现我国中原地区所出土的低温色釉陶系列产品,是以三彩釉陶器和各类俑的出土而著名于世。[①] 为什么唐代能够出现这类雍容华贵、色彩清新、造型生动的低温釉陶制品?这是有着极深刻的历史背景与文化前提的。丝绸之路上的东西文化交流源远流长。自两汉以来,其盛世当推唐代。尤其是天宝年间的唐王朝,国内政治统一,经济繁荣使得李氏王朝有足够的力量实行经济文化的开放政策。[②] 在科技文化方面也有足够的"吞吐"能量,对外来文化进行兼收并蓄的吸收和融会,使传入的任何一种外来文化科技都能作为养料吸收到自己的体内,推陈出新,并成为自身的一个组成部分。唐代低温釉陶新科技产品的出现,亦即三彩釉陶的产生,是在我国传统的铅釉陶、铅玻璃等生产实践积累之下,吸收并融汇了古代西方玻璃制造技术和化学知识,并有抉择地损益取舍,使传统的低温釉陶工艺产品在唐代达到炉火纯青,取得卓越成就。考古发现表明,我国所生产的唐三彩陶器,在陆路的丝绸之路沿线的中亚、西亚地区都有出土。如伊朗内沙尔布和德黑兰,伊拉克的巴格达,叙利亚的腊卡和阿勒颇,以及中亚的撒马尔罕等。[③]

值得注意的是,迄今新疆考古发现的低温釉陶主要是在龟兹,这是耐人深思的问题。这正是我们还要考察和研究龟兹低温釉陶的重要原因。深入研究龟兹低温釉陶,对于丰富我国的玻璃制造史,以及研究东西文化科技交流的轨迹也是十分重要的课题。龟兹是新疆古代丝绸之路上的城邦大国,地处天山南麓,塔里木河流域。"东西千余里,南北六百余里。"其中心在今库车、新和等县。史籍所载,龟兹盛产煤、铁、铜、锡、铅、金。公元前2世纪即能冶铸。4世纪时,其铁器的生产就能"恒充三十六国"之用,5世纪之时,已开用煤记载之先河。近年的考古资料则证明,龟兹在先秦时期已有相当辉煌的青铜文化。早自汉武帝时代(公元前141~前87)起,龟兹就与内地政权有了直接交往。在漫长的历史岁月中,这种交往始终未曾中断。汉唐两代的西域都护府和安西都护府的治所设置在龟兹决非偶然。由于特定的地理位置,丰富的物质资源,众多的人口,以及适当丝路贸易的重镇,极大地促进了龟兹社会经济的长足发展。[④] 在吸收和融汇外来文化因素的基础上,产生出灿烂的龟兹物质文明。如4世纪时,素享盛誉的龟兹佛教艺术和龟兹乐舞已脱颖而出;5世纪已产生本土的文字;六七世纪之际又出现具有自身特点的地方铸币。[⑤] 不言而喻,上述所列举的龟兹文化的内涵,丰富了我国多民族的历史文化遗产,在我国民族史和中外关系史的

---

① 洛阳市博物馆:《洛阳唐三彩》,文物出版社,1980年;杨正兴:《唐三彩的造型工艺》,载《咸阳文物考古丛》,1982年。
② 张广达:《论隋唐时期中原与西域文化交流的几个特点》,载《西域史地丛稿初编》,上海古籍出版社,1995年。
③ 宋龙华:《伊拉克共和国古代文物》,文物出版社,1958年;[苏] 米·谢·伊凡著,李希泌、孙伟、汪德全译:《伊朗史纲》,生活·读书·新知三联书店,1973年。
④ 拙文:《汉龟二体五铢钱及其有关问题》,《中国钱币》1987年第一期;《龟兹小铜钱范的发现及其研究》,《新疆钱币通讯》第三十六期,1993年。
⑤ 同④。

研究中都具有重要的地位。

唐代是我国封建社会经济繁荣的一个重要历史时期。从唐代西北边政史的宏观考察,龟兹为当时安西大都护府驻节之地。① 统辖龟兹、疏勒、于阗、碎叶(焉耆)四镇,其辖地"西尽波斯"。大量的中原士兵在龟兹驻防,进行屯田、屯牧、开矿等经营建设,推动了龟兹社会经济的发展,保证了中西丝路贸易的畅通。内地汉族士兵、工匠移驻龟兹,促进了汉民族和西部边陲各少数民族文化的融合。唐代的低温釉陶工艺能在龟兹产生,正是内地先进的生产科技在祖国西北边陲开花结果的缩影。我们认为:龟兹低温色釉陶器制品,其色釉的主要着色素是铜和铁;就其化学组成而言,应属于我国传统的 PbO—SiO_2 二元系统;其生产工艺,明显是受到唐代中原地区传统低温釉陶工艺的影响。

结　语

克孜勒协海古城内出土的地下排水或供水的陶水管和三耳绿釉陶罐等高等级的文物已引起学者关注的目光。目前,该城遗址自身文化的面貌和内涵仍不十分清楚,如究竟是相近的两座城址,还是同属于一座古城址内的建筑形制? 古城周邻的原野中分布的唐代古城、戍堡、烽燧、居住遗址和遗迹数量众多,迄今为止,田野考古的调查十分薄弱,很难就克孜勒协海古城的定性和定位等相关问题提出探讨性的结论。

笔者通过这一地区唐代古城考古调查的感知并结合唐代史籍文献提出如下认识,以作抛砖引玉。

轮台、库车、新和、沙雅、拜城等五县之地,曾是唐代安西大都护府治下的重心地区,在这一地区考古调查所发现的唐代古城中,建筑规模较大者只有五座。其中,首先就是龟兹城,遗址位于今库车镇的新城与老城之间,俗称"皮朗古城"或"麻扎布坦古城"。初唐的玄奘曾记载"国大,都城周十七、八里"。安西大都护府驻节于此后,该城又在原基础上曾做过改建和扩建,黄文弼的《龟兹城的查勘》一文中,认为龟兹城的周长为 7 公里左右。② 1989 年,我们调查认为龟兹国城的周长约 6 600 米左右。③ 其次,占地面积排行第二者,即是新和县克孜勒协海尔的南北两城,其周长加在一起约 1 018 米,④第三位是新和县通古孜巴什古城,周长约 960 米,⑤第四位是库车县的唐王诚,周长约 840 米,⑥第五位是轮台县的阔那协海尔古城,周长约 700 米。⑦ 龟兹唐代古城的考古调查与研究已经历了半个世纪,目前学者普遍认可库车县的皮朗古城就是安西大都护府的府治城,轮台县的阔那协海尔古城为唐龟兹乌垒州的治所,库车县唐王城与新和县通古孜巴什古城则是唐安西驻屯的中心城址。

《旧唐书》卷四十《地理三》所载安西大都护所统四镇条中曾记有"龟兹都督府,本龟兹国……领蕃州之九"。⑧ 然而《旧唐书》中缺载九州的名字。《新唐书》卷四十三下《地理七》所载四镇都督府条中记"龟

① 张广达:《唐灭高昌后的西州形势》,载《西域史地丛稿初编》,上海古籍出版社,1995 年。
② 黄文弼:《龟兹城的勘查》,载《新疆考古发掘报告》,文物出版社,1983 年,第 55 页。
③ 《阿克苏地区文物普查报告》,《新疆文物》1995 年第 4 期,第 22 页。
④ 《阿克苏地区文物普查报告》,《新疆文物》1995 年第 4 期,第 36 页。
⑤ 拙文:《新和通古孜巴什古城遗址的调查与研究》,《吐鲁番学研究》2003 年,第 37 ~ 43 页。
⑥ 拙文:《库车唐王城调查》,《新疆文物》2003 年第 1 期,第 28 ~ 35 页。
⑦ 拙文:《龟兹考古中所见唐代重要驻屯史迹》,《新疆文物》2006 年第 3、4 合期,第 35 ~ 48 页;《唐乌垒州及其有关问题》,《新疆社会科学》1990 年第 2 期。
⑧ 《旧唐书》卷四《地理三》,中华书局 1975 年,第 148 页。

兹都督府,领州九"。在同书"河西内属"十二个胡州中搜捡出有龟兹都督府所属的乌垒州、和(姑)墨州、温府(宿)州、蔚头州。这四州均为汉魏时龟兹属国,即汉魏的乌垒国(今轮台)、姑墨国(今温宿和阿克苏之地)、温宿国(今乌什、阿合奇之地)、蔚头国(今巴楚、图木舒克之地)。[①] 但是,《新唐书》记载中所剩的遍城州、耀建州、寅度州、猪拨州、达满州、蒲顺州、郖及满州、乞乍州中是否包含着龟兹所失载的五州? 目前仍是一个历史的悬案。汉时龟兹王国疆域范围大体包括今库车、新和、沙雅、拜城四县之地,唐代移安西大都护府于龟兹国城后,考虑到人口的增加,地广和胡汉杂居等情况,新旧两唐书所失载的五个州的设置可能就分布在上述四县之地,而这种推测同这四县都发现有一定数量和规模的唐代古城遗址的分布状况是相符合的。而克孜勒协海尔古城的建筑形制和规模,以及所发现的排水或供水的地下陶水管道等综合因素表明,古城很有可能就是两唐书所失载的五个州城之一。这一判断正确与否? 有待于今后新的考古发现所印证。

---

① 《新唐书》卷四十《地理七》,中华书局1975年,第1134~1135页;《中国历史地图集》第五册"唐陇右道西部",中华地图学出版社,1975年,第41~42页。

Khotanese Collection of the State Hermitage

Elikhina Julia

The State Hermitage Museum St. Petersburg, Russia

The Khotan collection of the State Hermitage Museum includes more than three thousand objects. At its core is the collection of Nikolai F. Petrovsky (1837 – 1908), who, beginning in 1874, served as an official of the Russian Ministry of Finance in Xinjiang and then Russian Consul in Kashgar from 1882 – 1902. Petrovsky knew the local languages well and was interested in the history and culture of the region. The objects of N. F. Petrovsky's collection represent surface finds. He published a good many articles and notes[1] and maintained close scholarly contacts with the leading orientalists of his time such as Sergei F. Ol'denburg and Vasiliy V. Bartol'd. As Ol'denburg wrote, it was Petrovsky "who first encouraged scholars to devote detailed attention to the scholarly treasures of Xinjiang; he was a man of whom Russia rightly was proud". [2] In a letter to Academician Viktor R. Rozen, Petrovsky wrote: "the archaeological objects in the collection were obtained through agents from the local inhabitants. The objects come from the territory of the town of Borazan, where they were discovered mainly in the channel of the irrigation canal which watered the soil of the ancient settlement". [3] The objects in the collection of Petrovsky were obtained by the Imperial Hermitage in 1897. In addition, the collection contains a significant number of finds obtained by S. A. Kolokolov, Sobolevsky and the engineers L. Ia. Liutsh and Belinko. A relatively small number of the objects were acquired from the scholars Nikolai I. Veselovsky and Sergei E. Malov.

A significant part of the collection is objects made of terracotta, numbering more than 2500. They were found in Yotkan, the location which Petrovsky referred to as Borazan. Similar objects are also in collections outside of Russia. The collection contains some forty intact dishes and more than 800 fragments. Scholars generally date the Yotkan ceramics to the second-fourth centuries CE. The collection includes as well coins, statuettes carved from stone, small bronze sculptures and relieves, bronze seals and intaglios, painting and written documents on wood.

---

[1] N. F. Petrovskii. "Buddiiskii pamiatnik bliz Kashgara" (A Buddhist monument near Kashgar). ZVORAO 7 (1892) ZVORAO (Zapiski Vostochnogo otdeleniia Russkogo arkheologicheskogo obshchestva).

N. F. Petrovskii. "Otvet konsula v Kashgare N. F. Petrovskogo na zaiavlenie S. F. Ol'denburga" (The response of the Consul in Kashgar N. F. Petrovskii to the statement by S. F. Ol'denburg). ZVORAO 7 (1893).

N. F. Petrovskii. "Zametka po povodu soobshcheniia A. Krigofa o nakhodke kamennykh orudii" (A note on the communcation by A. Krigof concerning the discovery of stone implements). Turkestanskie vedomosti 24 November 1906 etc.

[2] S. F. Ol'denburg. "Pamiati N. F. Petrovskogo 1837 – 1908" (In memory of N. F. Petrovskii 1837 – 1908). ZVORAO 20 (1911): pp. 1 – 8, p. 3.

[3] IRAO 1882, protocols of 27 March; 1893, protocols of 20 June.

The question of the history of Yotkan remains open, pending archaeological investigation of the site. Some scholars are of the opinion that it was the capital of the oasis; others consider that it was the location of a cemetery. There were other centers in Khotan besides Yotkan, some of them better documented from the archaeological standpoint: Ak-Terek, Ak-Sipil, Dandan-oilik and Rawak. We do know that the Kingdom of Khotan maintained contacts with China, the West and the states of Central Asia. This explains why Khotan ceramics have much in common with Central Asian late Kushan and especially Bactrian ceramics. [1] There are some parallels with Chinese bronze dishes and with Classical vases. The figured dishes resemble Classical ones only in their shape. According to Gösta Montell, the dishes with human representations derive from Classical prototypes. [2] Classical and Persian influences were reflected in the intaglios carved from semiprecious stones, in the bronze seals and in small terracottas.

Fig. 1

The distinctiveness of Khotan ceramics consists above all in their ornamental compositions. Characteristic is the combination of applied and stamped relief, sculpture, and flat ornament, which is also common in Kushan Bactrian ceramics. Probably the Khotan vases were imitations of metal ones (gold or silver). [3] In Khotan vases were made of thin clay mixed with loess and after firing took on a bright red or yellowish-red color. The purpose of the vases remains unclear, whereas the dishes were used in daily life.

Russian scholars usually date the ceramics from Yotkan II – VI centuries AD. Vases often are decorated numerous appliqué ornamentations and have figured handles. The most valuable exhibit of a collection is the vase (Fig. 1) with the Khotanese inscription which scientists cannot translate till now. This vase has three handles as stylized figures predatory animals. Appliqué ornamentations as female heads are placed on the basis of handles. They were made in one matrix. Three female heads of the smaller sizes are placed in intervals between handles, and hardly below — monkey's heads. Appliqué ornamentations might have fulfilled some amuletic purpose.

① B. A. Litvinskii, ed. Vostochnyi Turkestan v drevnosti i rannem srednevekove. Khoziaistvo, material'naia kul'tura (Xinjiang in antiquity and the early Middle Ages. Economy, material culture). Moscow: Vostochnaia literatura, 1995, p. 123.

② Gösta Montell. "Sven Hedin's Archaeological Collections from Khotan: Terra-cottas from Yotkan and Dandan-Uiliq." The Bulletin of the Museum of Far Eastern Antiquities 7 (1935): pp. 145 – 221, pp. 158 – 159.

③ Nataliia V. D'iakonova and Sergei S. Sorokin. Khotanskie drevnosti. Katalog khotanskikh drevnostei, khraniashchikhsia v Otdele Vostoka Gosudarstvennogo Ermitazha: terrakota i shtuk (Khotan antiquities. A catalogue of the Khotan antiquities in the Oriental Section of the State Hermitage: terracotta and stucco). Leningrad: Izd-vo. Gos. Ermitazha, 1960, pls. 1 – 5.

Vases from Khotan have handles of different types such as smooth, decorated with figurines of birds, ornamented ones and in the shape of animals, monkeys and griffins. The most interesting is two-faced vase (h. 7 cm.) and the dish in the shape of elephant (h. 8 cm.).

The special attention is attracted with the terracotta figurines representing men and women in secular clothes, received spreading in Eastern Turkestan in IV–V centuries. There is not clear the purpose till now: they could be toys, votive or funeral figurines. They were duplicated in huge amount with the help of stamps.[1]

Fauna of Khotan is represented in the collection rather full. The first place here belongs to a two-humped Bactrian camel. It played a significant role in life of Khotan, as one of reloading points on a caravan's roads of the ancient and medieval East. Similar figurines were made in matrix in big quantity.

The image of the monkeys estimated in hundreds among Khotanese finds. During historical time severe continental climate of Khotan excluded an opportunity of existence this animal here in a wild condition. Khotanese terracotta monkeys are represented with fine knowledge of a nature, realistic, sometimes with the big humor. Purpose of these figurines also remains not clear.

In Khotan besides Yotkan, there were also other centers: Ak-Sipil, Aκ-Terek, Dandan-Uiliq and Rawak.

Clay and stucco relief images of Buddhas and bodhisattvas were wide-spread in art of Khotan, starting from tiny and finishing a large sculpture. Buddhism penetrated to Khotan from India. From first centuries A. D. Khotan became one of the largest centers of the Buddhism. A lot of monasteries were constructed there. The most typical were images of Buddha for early Buddhism. Iconography of Buddhas is demonstrated by two types generated under influence of Gandharian school: the Buddha standing and the Buddha sitting. Each of these types included a range of iconography. A standing Buddha holds the right hand before the chest in the gesture of reassurance (fearlessness) (*abhaya mudra*). The left hand, extended along the body, grasps the end of the robe. The seated Buddha is in the lotus pose (*padmasana*), the hands held in the gesture of meditation (*dhyana mudra*). Such images are of small size and could have been placed around large statues in temples. In addition to stucco and clay, the depictions of the Buddha were made of carved stone and bronze. There is a bronze Buddha (Fig. 2) seated against the backdrop of a mandorla and with a robe sculpted in

Fig. 2

---

① N. V. D'iakonova. "Izobrazitel'noe iskusstvo" (Representational art), pp. 218–251. In: A. B. Litvinskii, ed. Vostochnyi Turkestan v drevnosti i rannem srednevekove. Arkhitektura, iskusstvo, kostium (Xinjiang in antiquity and the early Middle Ages. Architecture, art, costume). Moscow: Vostochnaia literatura RAN, 2000, pp. 229–230.

Fig. 3

flowing folds.

Among bronze relieves and a fine Buddhist sculptures it is possible to allocate the images of different Buddhist deities. Image of Avalokitesvara represents the relief of standing bodhisattva. His body has S-shaped bend. The right hand is lifted to a breast, he holds a stalk of a lotus in it, in the left, lowered along a body there is a vessel (kamandalu). It is dated IX century. The wide-spreading of the cult of Avalokitesvara, bodhisattva of compassion, has testified by archeological finds in Xinjiang, frescos and written documents. Bronze relieves of Avalokitesvara-Padmapani were used as ornaments for Buddhist temples. Avalokitesvara was esteemed as one of eight bodhisattvas, having a residence in Khotan. Avalokitesvara has mentioned in the list of eight bodhisattvas in the Tibetan text 《The Prophecy of Li country》(Khotan).

Maitreya (Fig. 3) represents the relief image directly worth bodhisattva. He holds a vessel in the right hand which lowered downwards along his body, the left is lifted to a breast. The vessel is characteristic attribute for Maitreya. The cult of Maitreya was rather popular in Khotan. One of Khotan's king by name Vijaya Sambhava it was esteemed as reincarnation of Maitreya. He ruled within five years after hundred sixty five years since the time of formation the state of Khotan. Second reincarnation of Maitreya was Vijaya Virya, both they have become famous for construction of Buddhist temples.

Architecture constructions have not preserved to nowadays. All of them were constructed by wood. A. Stein's expedition has found out only the bases of temples in the oasis in 1900 – 1901. There are three painted wooden beams, decorating Buddhist temples in the collection of the Hermitage. Images of Buddhas and traces of gilding and painting were kept on them.

The group testifies to connections with Indian Gandharian monuments made of a carved stone. They are totaled more than twenty pieces. In the first centuries of our era fine Buddhist Gandharian plastics have got a wide-spreading in the territory of Eastern Turkestan and Central Asia. As acknowledgement this is confirmed with finds of various archeological expeditions and numerous scientific publications.

A particularly interesting example of such sculpture is the statuettes from a small (h. 13 cm) wooden diptych (Fig. 4) in the collection of Petrovsky. The diptych is in the shape of a lotus bud, carved from rosewood (Palisandra [Dalbergia]). The lotus in Buddhism symbolizes sanctity and purity. Carved in each

of the halves is a special niche in which is placed a miniature (h. 5.5 cm) sculpted image of a Buddhist divinity. The diptych is held together by a metal strap on the outside and closes with a hook on the face. Judging from the condition of the metal, one can surmise that the closures are of later origin. An unusual feature of this reliquary is the fact that the statuettes were crafted from a non-traditional material — juniper resin. Normally Gandharan sculptures were fashioned from schist or agalmatolite (pagodite), less commonly of soapstone and elephant ivory.

Fig. 4

In one half of the diptych is an image of a Bodhisattva seated on a lion throne. A nimbus surrounds his head, the body is extensively decorated, the right hand is broken off to the elbow, the left lies on the knees in the gesture of meditation (*dhyana mudra*). Due to the considerable losses, it is impossible to establish which Bodhisattva is represented here. From the form of the decorations, the pose, and the overall treatment of the image there can be no doubt that this is a Gandharan work of the 3rd– 4th centuries. [1]

In the other half of the diptych is a Maitreya under a triple arch. He is depicted as the future Buddha, without decoration. On the head is the *usnisha*, one of the marks of the Buddha. He is seated in the so-called "European" pose with the legs, somewhat broken off, extending pendent to a semicircular lotus footstool. This is the pose of *bhadrasana*, typical only for Maitreya. For the majority of the images of Maitreya in Khotan the characteristic pose is that of *bhadrasana*, in which the legs of the divinity cross at the bottom. Such an iconography of Maitreya was widespread in China in the 4th– 6th centuries. [2] In all probability, the right hand formed the gesture of reassurance (*abhaya mudra*) or possibly the gesture of reasoning, *vitarka mudra*. According to the iconographic canon both gestures are characteristic for Maitreya. The left hand of

① W. Zwalf. Catalogue of the Gandhara Sculpture in the British Museum. 2 vols. London: British Museum Press, 1996, pp. 37 – 55.
② China: Dawn of a Golden Age 250 – 750. The Metropolitan Museum of Art, NY., 2004, p. 165.

the divinity has been broken off. Possibly it held a water-bottle (*kamandalu*), known from Ghandaran sculptures to be an attribute of Maitreya.

The iconography of Maitreya in the monuments found in Xinjiang is quite varied. He can be depicted both as a Buddha and as a Bodhisattva, standing and seated in various poses: in the lotus position (*padmasana*) and with pendent legs (*bhadrasana*). Similar representations of Maitreya are found in Khotan. The mudras also may be quite varied. [①] Ol'denburg published two images of Maitreya from Khotan. [②]

The diptych has good state of preservation and the distinctive nature of the materials used make this one unique among the works from Xinjiang preserved today in the Hermitage.

Khotan it was glorified by the jade. The jade served as object of export, therefore the finds executed from a jade meet a little and they concern to different time. In a collection there is one monkey made of jade. It is shown in a sitting position, having clasped forepaws back. The head of it is involved in shoulders. A piece of jade is grey, with brown spots. In a collection of the Hermitage are submitted jade figurines animals and seals.

There are three objects made of gold in a collection.

The structure of a collection includes coins (about two hundred), figurines from a carved stone, a fine bronze miniature sculptures and reliefs, bronze seals and intaglio seals (about hundred fifty), painting and written documents on wooden tablets. There is an interesting group of objects of soap stone, more than thirty finds. The part from them represents Buddhas and bodhisattvas, other part consists of anthropomorphous figurines with unnatural big trunks. The purpose of such figurines also is not clear. Antique and Persian influences have found the reflection on carved intaglio seals from semiprecious stones, bronze seals and in fine small objects. From local cults the greatest distribution has received reverence of a deity of weaving, its painting images are represened on two wooden icons. They occur from Dandan-Uiliq and are dated of Ⅵ-Ⅷ centuries.

Thus, objects from Khotan is possible to allocate some groups: 1. terracotta vases, vessels and their fragments; 2. tiny images of people and animals; 3. subjects of a Buddhist cult (as local, and Gandharian import); 4. finds representing local deities, 5. seals and intaglio seals, 6. coins; 7. written documents; 8. items of everyday life; 9. architectural fragments.

For Khotanese finds there is a problem of dating. There is no uniform for experts all over the world a system of dating of finds till now. Written documents can be dated on epigraphy. Dating of English, Germans, Americans, Koreans and the Russian experts considerably differs. This question also demands all-round consideration.

Objects of terracotta and stucco has been published by N. V. Djakonov and S. S. Sorokin. Other finds, except several, were not published and demand the further studying and input in a scientific publication.

---

① Joanna Williams. "The Iconography of Khotanese Painting." East and West, N. S., 23/1-2 (1973): pp. 109-154, pp. 129-130.

② S. F. Ol'denburg. "Dva khotanskikh izobrazheniia Maitrei" (Two Khotanese images of Maitreya). Zapiski Vostochnogo otdeleniia Russkogo arkheologicheskogo obshchestva 12 (1898): pp. 0106-0108, pp. 0106-0107.

Chinese Seals in the Mongol Official Documents in Iran:
Re-examination of the Sphragistic System in the
Il-khanid and Yuan Dynasties

Yokkaichi Yasuhiro

Tokyo University, Japan

Introduction

In the thirteenth and fourteenth centuries, the official documents of the Mongol regime in Eurasia shared certain common aspects, despite the influence of traditional documents in cultural regions like China and Iran. The Mongolian, Turkic, Chinese, Tibetan, and Persian documents of the Mongol period exhibited similar phrases and sentence constructions. The official documents of the Il-khanid dynasty also exhibited a style similar to that of the Mongol regime. While Mongolian language was used at the upper level of the command structure of the Il-khanid administration, in which the Mongol royal families were at the central, both Mongolian and Turkic were used at the level of *amīr*s or *noyan*s. On the other hand, *vazir*s and government officials from the local societies in Iran and Central Asia acquired traditional writing skills in Arabic and Persian, with some of them even mastering Mongolian and Turkic. [1] When an order was issued in the local society of Iran, although the content was written in the local language, i. e., Persian, at the top of each document, formulaic phrases were written in Turkic or Arabic as a status symbol, [2] depending on the rank of the issuer and the aim of the issue.

Some Il-khanid official documents have the Chinese *tamγa*s (seals). Such seals are called *al tamγa* ("red seals") or *altan tamγa* ("golden seals"). There exist, for example, the *altan tamγa* of "*fuguo anmin zhi bao*" 辅国安民之宝 in the Arγun *üge* document in *üker jil* (year of the rabbit) at the Archivio Segreto Vaticano[3] and the *al-tamγa* of "*zongguan yinyuan zhi yin*" 总管隐院之印 in the Husein *söz* document in 704

---

[1] The epistolary art for the official and private correspondence in the Persian cultural background is called *Inshā'*. From the Saljūqid period to the Safavid period, especially in the Mongol period, many *Inshā'* manuals were compiled in Iran. See Paul, Jürgen 1995, pp. 535 – 540; Paul, Jürgen 1999, pp. 277 – 285; Watabe Ryōko 2002, pp. 1 – 23; Watabe Ryōko 2003, pp. 200 – 208, and Qāe'm Maqāmī 1350.

[2] This formulaic expression at the top of a document corresponds to "*shangtian juanming, huangdi shengzhi*" 上天眷命，皇帝圣旨 or "*changsheng tian qili li, da fuyin huzhu li, huangdi shengzhi li*" 长生天气力里，大福廕护助里，皇帝圣旨里 in Chinese.

[3] See Mostaert, A. et Cleaves, F. W. 1952, pp. 445 – 467.

A. H. of the Ardabil archives. [①] The *Il-khan* emperors strengthened his political power in Iran by using the authority of the Mongol *Qayan*. Therefore, it can be said that the use of Chinese *tamyas* that symbolized the authorities of the Mongol Empire or the Yüan dynasty proved to be highly advantageous for the *Il-khan* emperors.

These seals help us understand the Mongol ruling system in Iran and Central Asia, multiethnic social conditions, and interaction between east and west Eurasia under the rule of the Mongol empire. This paper focuses on the Chinese seals of the Il-khanid dynasty in Iran and overviews the relevant issues in the Mongolian sphragistic system.

What are the Mongol official document style?

We can observe similar styles in the existing official documents of the Mongol empire, the Yuan dynasty, and the Il-khanid dynasty. In this paper, we refer to such documents as "the Mongol official documents." Of these documents, the *jarliy*, which originally meant "noble words" spoken by an honorable person, implies only "imperial decrees" in the Mongol empire's documentation system. [②] Such documents were issued in the Il-khanid dynasty too. The decree issued by the Il-khan was called *yarligh* in Persian historical material.

In east and west Eurasia, which were ruled by the Mongol empire and its succession regimes, Mongolian, Turkic, Chinese, Tibetan, Persian, and multilinguistic documents, which share certain common characteristics and expressions, were issued officially. Some scholars studied such documents from the standpoint of each language, including Mongolian, Tibetan, and Chinese. In particular, the opening and ending phrases with a typical feature of the Mongol official documents were examined by Kotwicz, W. 1934, Григорьев, А. П. 1978, Ono Hiroshi 1993 and others. According to Schuh, D. 1977 and Čenggel 1994 and Matsukawa 1995, we can observe a common ground in the sentence structures in Mongolian and other linguistic documents. [③] Čenggel pointed out the internal structure of a Mongolian edict as follows:

1. Opening phrases

(1) praying words (*dayadqalun üge*), (2) Indication of the issuer of an edict (*jarliy bayukyayči*)

2. Recipient of an edict (*jarluy dayulyaqui eteged*)

3. Contents of an edict

(1) quotation of previous edicts (*uridaqi qayad-un jarliy-un duradqal*), (2) display allegiance to

---

[①] See Herrmann, G. 2004, pp. 84 – 89, Abb. 25 – 35.

[②] *Jarliy* in Mongolian corresponds to *yarliy* in Turkic, *yarlīgh* in Persian/Arabic, and *shengzhi* 圣旨 in Chinese, under the Mongol empire.

[③] Schuh, D. 1977 dealt with Tibetan documents and Čenggel 1994 and Matsukawa Takashi 1995 mainly discussed Mongol official documents during the Mongol empire and the Yuan periods.

previous edicts by the successive Qaɣans (*uridaqi qaɣad-un jarliɣ-i daɣaqu čiqulčilaɣ_a*) , (3) objects of an edict (*jarliɣ küliyegči*) , (4) contents of an order (*jorbuslaɣsan čaɣaja*) , (5) intimidating words (*sürdegülülge üge*)

    4. Ending phrases

    (1) confirmation of an edict (*batulaburi*) , (2) year of issue (*jarliɣ bayulɣaɣsan on*) , (3) month of issue (*jarliɣ bayulɣaɣsan sar_a*) , (4) day of issue (*jarliɣ bayulɣaɣsan edür*) , (5) place of issue (*jarliɣ bayulɣaɣsan ɣajar orun*)

    5. Impress (*tamaɣ_a*) [1]

In a similar way, Matsukawa Takashi who modified the Schuh's view partially also showed the internal structure of a document as follows:

    1. Grounds for empowerment

    2. Indication of the issuer and style of an edict

    3. Recipient of an edict

    4. Contents of an edict

    (1) indication of legality, (2) explanation of the situation, (3) command 1 (to the recipient of an edict), (4) object of an edict, (5) command 2 (to the object of an edict), (6) provision for commination and sanction

    5. Formulaic phrase at the end

    (1) date of issue, (2) place of issue, (3) indication of an edict style [2]

Compared with such views, although some parts of the structure are sometimes omitted, we observe same structure in the official documents of the Il-khanid, too. There existed, in general, two types of the Mongol official documents in the Il-khanid dynasty. One is the *jarliɣ* document issued by the Mongol *Qaɣan* and the other is a general edict issued by other issuers like the *amīr*s and *vazīr*s of the *Qaɣan* or *Qan*. The former is often completely written in Mongolian and the latter is written in multiple languages like Turkic and Persian. [3] In fact, in most of the Ardabil archives, the opening formulaic phrases are written in Turkic or Arabic, while

---

    [1] Čenggel 1994, pp. 31 – 37. The items above mentioned are numbered serially from 1 to 13 in his original article. I renumbered them for descriptive purposes. The last item (Impress (*tamaɣ_a*)) was added in his paper "A comparative study of diplomatic and general documents in the Mongol empire" at the symposium: *War and diplomacy in East Asia from a paleographical point of view* at Kyushu University, Fukuoka in December 2007.

    [2] Matsukawa Takashi 1995, pp. 36 – 44. Those items are not numbered in his original article. For descriptive purposes, I added numbers to categorized items.

    [3] Although the actual *jarliɣ / yarligh* document issued by the Il-khanid emperors in Persian language has not been found at present, it is highly possible that a copy of the *jarliɣ / yarligh* document in Persian or another language was drafted in addition to the Mongolian original copy. This is because the Turkic and Persian copy issued by Güyük Qan is present at the Segreto Archivio Vaticano.

the remaining text is written in Persian. [1]

Seals with Chinese characters in the official documents of the Il-khanid

Some official documents of the Il-khanid dynasty have a square-shaped red seal impression of a fixed size. Such red seals are called *al tamya* in Persian historical sources. [2] Most of these seals, especially before the era of Öljeitü Sultān, were inscribed in Chinese characters. Why were Chinese characters, which were hardly used in the Il-khanid court and Iranian-Islamic societies, adopted as official seals? This might be because the Il-khanid dynasty considered the Yuan as a suzerain power, in principle at least, and Chinese *tamyas* symbolized the authoritative power of the *Qaγan*. This indicates the solidarity between the Yuan and the Il-khanid dynasties. The existing Chinese *tamyas* in the Il-khanid official documents at present are as follows:

(a) ***Xing-hubu Shangshu Yin*** 行户部尚书印 (seal of the Minister of the Branch Office of the Ministry of Revenue) Gaihatu period

(b) ***Wangfu zhi Yin*** 王府之印 (seal of the Secretarial Council of a Prince) Öljeitü period

(c) ***You-shumishi zhi Yin*** 右枢密使之印 (seal of the Minister of the Right of the Military Council) Öljeitü period

(d) ***Zongguan Yinyuan zhi Yin*** 总管隐院之印 (seal of the Superintendent of the Hermitage Bureau) Öljeitü and Abū Saīd periods

(e) ***Fuguo Anmin zhi Bao*** 辅国安民之宝 (Great seal of assisting governances and pacifying people) Abaγa and Arγun periods

(f) ***Wangfu Dingguo Limin zhi Bao*** 王府定国理民之宝 (Great seal of stabilizing the realm and ruling the people by the Secretarial Council of Prince) Gazan period

(g) ***Zhenming-Huangdi Tianshun-Wanshi zhi Bao*** 真命皇帝天顺万事之宝 (Great seal of the true emperor with whom the Heaven makes everything go along) Öljeitü and Abū Sa'īd periods

Of the above, seals (a) - (d) were bestowed upon bureaus or administrators and were called *al tamghā* (Tur. *al tamya*) or red seals in Persian sources. [3] Although (e) - (g) are similar red-colored Chinese seals, they cannot be called *al tamgha*, because they were not government seals or *guanyin* 官印; rather, they were the great seals or *baoxi* 宝玺, which were stamped on the imperial edicts by *Il-khanid* emperors. From the viewpoint of the exergue of these seals, on the one hand, (a) - (d) are inscribed with "... *zhi yin*" 之印 ("seal of ...") and on the other hand, (e) - (g) have "... *zhi bao*" 之宝 ("great seal of ..."), which

---

[1] See Urkunde 1 - 9,13 - 15,21 - 24,27 in Herrmann, G. 2004.

[2] See Doerfer, G. 1982 - 1985, pp. 766 - 768.

[3] With respect to the outline of *al tamya*, see Doerfer, G. 1982 - 1985 (a), pp. 766 - 768.

could be used only by the imperial family of the Yuan.[1] In my view, they correspond to *altan tamɣa / altūn tamgha* or golden seals rather than *al tamɣa* or red seals.[2]

Since these seals were standardized to befit the Yuan dynasty, it appears that they were originally bestowed by the *Qaɣan* of the Yuan. In the government seals (a) - (d), "*xing-hubu*"行户部, "*wangfu*"王府, "*shumiyuan*"枢密院, and "*zongguanfu*"总管府 were the original administrative agencies of the Yuan. When it comes to the *altan tamɣa* (e) - (g), however, the Yuan court could never have permitted the use of the great seals with the inscription "... *zhi bao*"之宝 by anyone apart from the *Qaɣan*, the *Qatun* (Empress), and the Crown Prince. Even a blood royal with the exception of them had to use a regular government seal for the princes or *zhuwang guanyin* 诸王官印.[3] Therefore, at least the *altan tamɣa* (e) - (g) were not the seals bestowed by the Yuan court, but were prepared by the Il-khanid court.

In respect of locus sigilli of the official seals, the seals of the *al tamɣa* or *altan tamɣa* were basically appended to an adhesively bonded paper joint and to an ending of the document in which formulaic phrases including the date and place were mentioned. In the case of an edict of the Yuan, the great seal or *baoxi* 宝玺 was appended on the names as the recipient of an edict, following an opening formulaic phrases;[4] however, in Il-khanid official documents, the seals were not appended there.

---

① The Yuan emperor (*Qaɣan*) had eight great seals, i.e. *babao* 八宝, namely, the *Shouming bao* 受命宝 (great seal of bestowing the Heaven's will), *Chuanguo bao* 传国宝 (great seal of the imperial regacy), *Tianzi zhi bao* 天子之宝 (great seal of the Heaven's son), *Huangdi zhi bao* 皇帝之宝 (great seal of the emperor), *Tianzi xing bao* 天子行宝 (great seal of issue by the Heaven's son), *Huangdi xing bao* 皇帝行宝 (great seal of issue by the emperor), *Tianzi xin bao* 天子信宝 (great seal of approval by the Heaven's son), *Huangdi xing bao* 皇帝信宝 (great seal of approval by the emperor) (*Yuanshi*《元史》j. 79, yufuzhi 舆服志二, chongtianlubu 崇天卤簿 (YS/Jiao, p. 1980)). See also Xie Qifeng 2003, pp. 246 - 247. Farquhar, D. M. classfied the seals of the Yuan period into princely seals and official seals (Farquhar 1966, pp. 362 - 368). Strictly speaking, princely seals other than the crown prince's is also categorized as official seals based on *Yuandianzheng* (See note 15).

② Gerhard Doerfer supposed that *altan tamɣa* was used almost exclusively for financial or fiscal edicts (Doerfer, G. 1982 - 1985 (a), p. 768; Doerfer 1982 - 1985 (b), p. 913) and Herrmann shared his view (Herrmann, G. 1997, pp. 324 - 327). In fact, as Herrmann and Doerfer showed the actual documents of the *altan tamɣa*, we can see some seal impressions of the small *altan tamɣa* of Arabic script in the Il-khanid and post Il-khanid documents (See Herrmann, G. und Doerfer, G. 1975(a), p. 321, p. 331; Herrmann, G. und Doerfer, G. 1975(b), pp. 38 - 44). Doerfer's a view is, in addition, supported by the accounts of *Jāmi*, *al-Tavārīkh*, in which Rashīd al-Dīn Faḍlallāh Hamadānī discribed that the small *altan tamɣa* (*altūn tamghā-ye kūchek*) was used for financial affairs (*Jāmi*,/Roushan, pp. 1468 - 1469). Although, in the said description, Rashīd al-Dīn refered to several great seals including a great seal made of jasper (*tamghā-ye bozorg-e yashm*), smaller sized great seal (*yekī-ye dīgar az yashm-e andakī-ye kūchektar*), small sized great seal made of gold (*tamghā-ye bozorg az zar*), and special seal made of gold (*tamghā-ye makhṣūs az zar*), only the small *altan tamɣa* and no other *altan tamɣa* was refered to. Were such jusper and gold sealscategorized into *al tamɣa* or *altan tamɣa*? Judgeing from the order of the Rashīd al-Dīn's account, the great seals made of jusper and gold were the higher ranked seals than the small *altan tamɣa*. If *altan tamɣa* were prepared other than small one in the Il-khanid court, the great and special seals should be also included the category of *altan tamɣa*. Doerfer assumed that *altan tamɣa* means the seal made of gold and the seals (e)-(g) are *al tamɣa* (Doerfer 1982 - 1985 (a), p. 767; Doerfer 1982 - 1985 (b), p. 913), but I do not share this opinion. We have to distinguish "*altan tamɣa*" (*altūn tamghā*) from "seal made of gold" (*tamghā az zar*) in the context of Persian historical sources. Because, strictly speaking, "*altan*" does not only mean "gold" in the etymological sense but also "imperial", i. e. "the Chingisid legitimate" or "the golden clan of Borjigin" in the historical sense. Thus, we see that all of those includng the great seals were categolized into the *altan tamɣa*s. On the other hand, the seals (e)-(g) have the script of "... *zhi bao*" 之宝, which derived from the great seal script with the highest rank in the Yuan's sphragistic system. Thus, those seals corresponds to the great seals (*tamghā-ye bozorg*) in the Il-khanid sphragistic order. Viewed in this light, we may reasonably conclude that the seals (e)-(g) are not *al tamɣa* but *altan tamɣa*. I would like to present a detailed discussion of the function of *altan tamɣa* and its distinction from *al tamɣa* in another paper.

③ *Yuandianzheng*《元典章》dianzheng 典章 29, libu 礼部 2, yinzheng 印章 (YDZ/Chen, p. 454).

④ See, for example, *jarliɣs* by the Yuan Qaɣan in Xizongzizhiqu Dang'anguan 1995, n. 1 - 6.

In the Il-khanid court, only a limited number of people, for example, missionary subjects from the Yuan, could read Chinese characters. However, the top and bottom of each Chinese seal always takes the same direction. In the Mongol official documents, in which Uighur letters were written in a longitudinal fashion, Chinese seals were also inserted in the same direction (see Fig. 1). On the other hand, in Persian documents, in which Arabic letters were written from right to left, Chinese seals were inserted with their top to the right and their bottom to the left, alongside the Persian lines (see Fig. 2). On the contrary, the seal inscribed in Arabic characters that appeared after the Sultān Öljeitü reign was inserted with their top upward and their bottom downward in the same direction as that of the Persian letters (see Fig. 3). Thus, there exists a strong possibility that the manner in which the Chinese seals in Persian documents were inserted on the right side unexceptionally followed from the style of Mongolian documents.

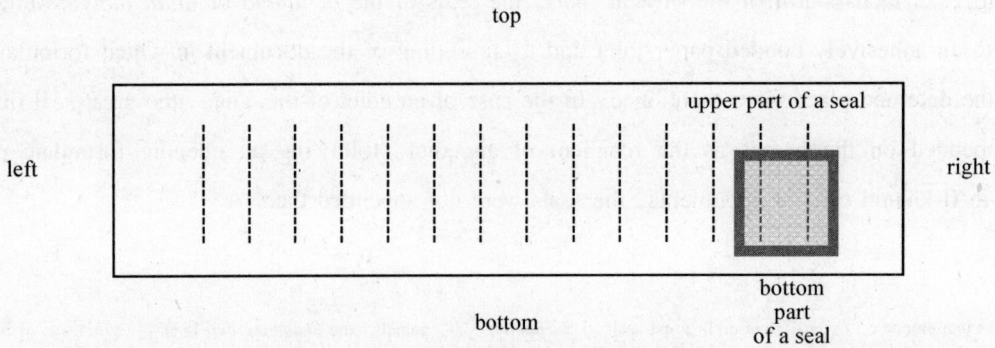

Fig. 1　Chinese seal in a Mongolian document

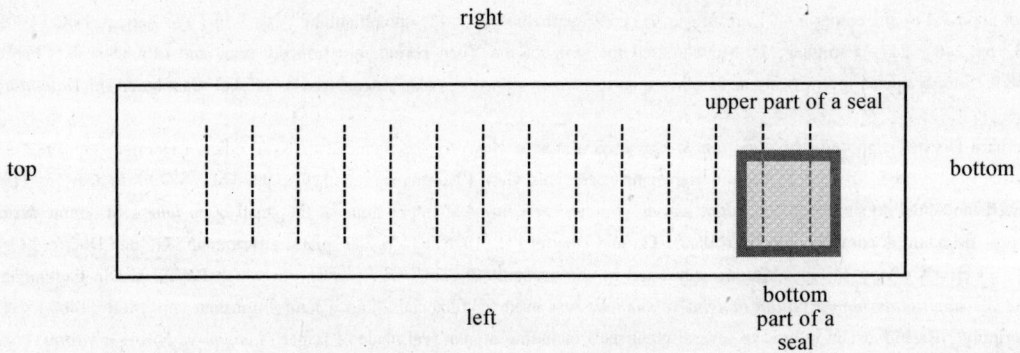

Fig. 2　Chinese seal in a Persian document

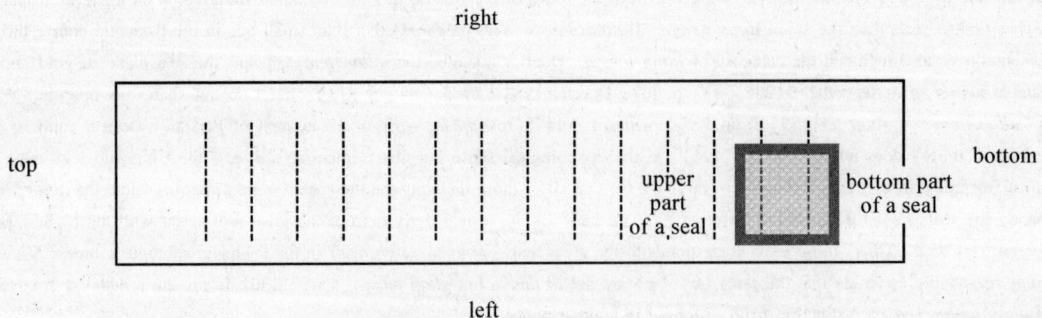

Fig. 3　Arabic seal in a Persian document

Nonetheless, in Iran, Chinese seals were prepared based on the understanding of Chinese language, and the official post names inscribed on the seals were actually based on the administrative organization of the Yuan dynasty. In addition, the inscription of the Chinese seals was related to the content of each document in some measure. Thus, we can comprehend the Il-khanid administrative structure, which is poorly understood heretofore, from the inscriptions of the seals and content of the documents.

Judging from the use of Chinese seals, this documentation system of the Il-khanid dynasty, at least before the reign of Gazan Qan, had a stronger influence on Chinese-Mongolian chancellery practices than on Iran-Islamic practices. An analysis of the sphragistic system explains the documentation system of the Il-khanid dynasty as well as that of the Mongol empire and the Yuan dynasty.

the Il-khanid Official Documents with the Chinese Seals

Al Tamγa Documents (Persian Documents with the Chinese *guanyin* 官印 Seal)

(a) *Xing-hubu Shangshu Yin* 行户部尚书印

(a) −1. Ardabīl- AH 692 Sāheb-e Dīvān Ahmad *söz* (Mūse-ye Mellī Īrān)

Size: 118 × 18.5 cm

Date Issued: Latter part of Rabī al-Awwal 692A. H. (1293 A. D.), in the Irinčin Dorji (Gaikhatu) period

Place Issued: Pol-e Čaγan (White Bridge)

Issuer: Sāheb-e Dīvān Ahmad

Objects of the Decree: Nothing

Style of the Decree: (*l.*03) *söz* "Ahmad Sāheb-e Dīvān sūzī" (Ahmad the Chief of Dīvān, his word)

Given Authority: (*ll.*01 − 02) *yarliγ* "az hokm-e / yarligh"

Languages of the Opening Phrases: (*l.*01) Persian-Turkic (*l.*02) Persian-Turkic (*l.*03) Turkic

Language of the Main Sentence: Persian

Written Characters: Arabic

Seal: (*ll.*08 − 10) Square-shaped Red Seal in the Chinese language -Chinese characters "*Xing-hubu Shangshu Yin*" 行户部尚书印

Size of the Seal: 9 × 9 cm

Location of the Document: Mūse-ye Mellī Īrān (Iran National Museum)

Facsimile: Herrmann 2004 (U. 3)

Text: Herrmann 2004 (U. 3)

Notes: There is the Arabic-Persian script on the reverse.

(a) −2. AH 692 Sāheb-e Dīvān Ahmad *söz* (Smithsonian Institution)

Size: 134 × 27.5 cm

Date Issued: Early part of Jumādā al-Ākhīr 692 A. H. (1293 A. D.) in the Irinčin Dorji (Gaikhatu) period

Place Issued: Kārīz

Issuer: Sāheb-e Dīvān Ahmad

Objects of the Decree: *bāsqāq* (viceroy), *nā'ib*s (vicegerents) and *motasarref*s (landlords) of Ardabīl

Style of the Decree：(*l*. 03) *söz* "Ahmad Sāheb-e Dīvān sūzī" (Ahmad the Chief of Dīvān, his word)

Given Authorities：(*l*. 01) *yarliɤ* of Irinčin Dorji　(*l*. 02) *söz* of Sikütür, Aq Buqa and Taɤačar

Languages of the Opening Phrases：(*l*. 01) Turkic　(*l*. 02) Turkic　(*l*. 03) Turkic

Language of the Main Sentence：Persian

Written Characters：Arabic

Seal：(*ll*. 05 – 06)(*ll*. 11 – 12) Square-shaped Red Seals in the Chinese language -Chinese characters "*Xing-hubu Shangshu Yin*" 行戶部尚書印

Size of the Seal：Unknown

Location of the Document：the Freer Gallery of Art of the Smithsonian Institution

Facsimile：Soudavar 1992

Text：Mohsen Ja'farī 2000

(b) *Wangfu zhi Yin* 王府之印

(b) – 1. Ardabil- AH 704 Sa'd al-Dīn *söz* (Mūse-ye Mellī Īrān)

Size：76 × 20 cm

Date Issued：13th of Dhū al-Qādah 704 A. H. (1305 A. D.) in the Öljeitü Sultān period

Place Issued：Islamic Town (shahr-e Eslām) in ūjān

Issuer：[Vazīr] Sa'd al-Dīn

Objects of the Decree：Nothing

Style of the Decree：(*l*. 04) *söz* "Sa'd al-Dīn sūzī" (Sa'd al-Dīn, his word)

Given Authorities：(*l*. 01) the name of Allāh　(*l*. 02) *yarliɤ* of Öljeitü Sultān　(*l*. 03) *söz* of Qutluɤ Shā, Čoban, Bolad, Hosein and Sevinč

Languages of the Opening Phrases：(*l*. 01) Arabic　(*l*. 02) Turkic　(*l*. 03) Turkic　(*l*. 04) Turkic

Language of the Main Sentence：Persian

Written Characters：Arabic

Seal：(*ll*. 06 – 07) Square-shaped Red Seal in the Chinese language -Chinese characters "*Wangfu zhi Yin*" 王府之印

Size of the Seal：9. 5 × 9. 5 cm

Location of the Document：Mūse-ye Mellī Īrān (Iran National Museum)

Facsimile：Herrmann 2004 (U. 6)

Text：Herrmann 2004 (U. 6)

Notes：This document is the reverse side of the document (c) – 1.

(c) *You-shumishi zhi Yin* 右樞密使之印

(c) – 1. Ardabil-AH704 Qutluɤ Shā *söz* (Mūse-ye Mellī Īrān)

Size：76 × 20 cm

Date Issued：Middle of Dhū al-Qādah 704 A. H. (1305 A. D.) in the Öljeitü Sultān period

Place Issued：cloister of Qūdūgh

Issuer：[Amīr] Qutluɤ Shāh

Objects of the Decree：*bāsqāq* (viceroy), *malek* (local lord), *qādhī* (judge), *nā'ibs* (vicegerents) and *motasarref*s (landlords) of Ardabīl

Style of the Decree: (*l.*03) *söz* "Qutlugh S͟hāh sūzī" (Qutluγ S͟hāh, his word)

Givan Authorities: (*l.*01) Allāh   (*l.*02) *yarliγ* of Öljeitü Sultān

Languages of the Opening Phrases: (*l.*01) Arabic   (*l.*02) Turkic   (*l.*03) Turkic

Language of the Main Sentence: Persian

Written Characters: Arabic

Seals: (*ll.*07 − 08) (*ll.*11 − 12) Square-shaped Red Seals in the Chinese language -Chinese characters "*You-shumishi zhi Yin*" 右枢密使之印

     (*l.*12) Square-shaped Black Seal in the Mongolian language -Phagspa characters "*Qutluγ Ša-yin belge*" (the Seal of Qutluγ S͟hāh)

Size of the Seals: "*You-shumishi zhi Yin*" 9 × 9 cm; "*Qutluγ Ša-yin belge*" 3. 8 × 3. 8 cm

Location of the Document: Mūse-ye Mellī Īrān (Iran National Museum)

Facsimile: Herrmann 2004 (U. 5)

Text: Herrmann 2004 (U. 5)

Notes: This document is the reverse side of the document (b) − 1.

(d) Zongguan Yinyuan zhi Yin 总管隐院之印

<u>(d) − 1. Ardabil-AH704 Hosein *söz* (Mūse-ye Mellī Īrān)</u>

Size: 220 × 16. 5 cm

Date Issued: 25th of D͟hū al-Hijjah 704 A. H. (1305 A. D.) in the Öljeitü Sultān period

Place Issued: the Royal City Tabrīz

Issuer: [Amīr] Hosein

Objects of the Decree: *bāsqāqs* (viceroies), *maleks* (local lords), *nā'ib*s (vicegerents), *motasarref*s (landlords), *bitikchi*s (secretaries) and officials in Tabrīz and Ardabīl

Style of the Decree: (*l.*01) *söz* "<u>H</u>osein sūzī" (Hosein, his word)

Given Authority: Nothing

Language of the Opening Phrases: (*l.*01) Turkic

Language of the Main Sentence: Persian

Written Characters: Arabic

Seals: (*ll.*04 − 05) (*ll.*10 − 11) (*ll.*17 − 18) (*ll.*23 − 26) Square-shaped Red Seals in the Chinese language -Chinese characters "*Zongguan Yinyuan zhi Yin*" 总管隐院之印

     (*ll.*25 − 26) Square-shaped Black Seal in the Mongolian language -Uighur characters "*Üseyin-ü Varman_a Belge*" (the seal of approval by Hosein)

Size of the Seals: "*Zongguan Yinyuan zhi Yin*" 8 × 8 cm; "*Üseyin-ü Varman_a Belge*" 2. 8 × 3. 8 cm

Location of the Document: Mūse-ye Mellī Īrān (Iran National Museum)

Facsimile: Herrmann 2004 (U. 7)

Text: Herrmann 2004 (U. 7)

Notes: There is the Uighur-Mongolian script on the reverse.

(d) -2. AH 730 Shaykh Hosein *söz*（Matenadaran）

Size：113 × 21 cm

Date Issued：Dhū al-Qādah 730 A. H.（1330 A. D.），in the Abū Saʿīd period

Place Issued：Ūjān

Issuer：Shaykh Hosein①

Object of the Decree：*ḥākem*s（governor generals），*nāeʾb*s（vicegerents），*motasarref*s（landlords）and *bitikchi*s（secretaries）
of Nakhchevān

Style of the Decree：（*l.*03）*söz* "Shaykh Hosein *sūzī*"（Shaykh Hosein, his word）"

Given Authorities：（*l.*01）Allāh　（*l.*02）*yarliγ* of Abū Saʿīd Bahādur Khan

Languages of the Opening Phrases：（*l.*01）Arabic　（*l.*02）Turkic　（*l.*03）Turkic

Language of the Main Sentence：Persian

Written Characters：Arabic

Seals：（*ll.*11 - 12）（*ll.*14 - 16）　Square-shaped Red Seals in the Chinese language -Chinese characters "*Zongguan Yinyuan zhi
Yin*" 总管隐院之印；

　　（*ll.*15 - 16）　Square-shaped Black Seal in Arabic characters, Unreadable

Size of the Seal：8 × 8 cm

Location of the Document：Matenadaran（Mashtots Institute of Ancient Manuscripts）

Facsimile：Papazian, H. D. 1961

Text：Papazian, H. D. 1961

Altan Tamγa Documents（Mongolian Documents with the Chinese *baoxi* 宝玺 Seal）②

(e) *Fuguo Anmin zhi Bao* 辅国安民之宝

(e) -1. *taulai jil* Abaγa *üge*（Archivio Segreto Vaticano）

Size：68.6 × 27.8 cm

Date Issued：16th of the first month of winter, the year of the Rabbit（1267 A. D.）in the Abaγa period

Place Issued：Aras

Issuer：Abaγa [Qan]

Objects of the Decree：*darγa*s（viceroies），*noyad*（*amīr*s），*todqaγul*（guardee），*qaraγul*（sentinel），*jamčin*（postal station
keepers），and *ongγačačin*（boatmen）of cities in Samaγar

Style of the Decree：（*l.*01）*üge* "Abaγ_a üge manu"（Abaγa, our word）

Given Authorities：Nothing

Languages of the Opening Phrases：（*l.*01）Mongolian

Language of the Main Sentence：Mongolian

---

　　① My special thanks are due to Dr. ʿEmād al-Dīn Shaykh al-Hokamāī for valuable advice on the decipherment of this personal name-
toghrā.

　　② An *Altan Tamγa* document is refered to merely as "*yarligh*" or "*yarligh va altūn tamghā*" in Persian historical sources like *Jāmiʾ al-
Tawārīkh*, *Tārīkh-e Vassāf*, and *Dastūr al-Kātib fī Taʿayīn al-Marātib*. We can, for example, see the standard expression in *Dastūr al-Kātib fī
Taʿayīn al-Marātib* as follows: "For these reasons, this edict of *yarligh* with blessed（imperial）*altūn tamghā* has been issued." See also *Laṭāʾif
al-Inshā*ʾ/*Majres* fol. 115b and Watabe Ryōko 2003, pp. 204 - 205.

Written Characters: Uighur

Seal: (*ll*. 13 - 16) Square-shaped Red Seal in the Chinese language -Chinese characters"*Fuguo Anmin zhi Bao*"辅国安民之宝

Size of the Seal: 14.5 × 14.9 cm

Location of the Document: Archivio Segreto Vaticano (A. A., Arm, I -XVIII, 1801(1))

Facsimile: Mostaert, A. et Cleaves, F. W. 1952 (Doc. A); Dobu 1983; Tumurtogoo 2006 (Abaγa II)

Text: Mostaert, A. et Cleaves, F. W. 1952 (Doc. A); Dobu 1983; Tumurtogoo 2006 (Abaγa II)

(e) -2. *üker jil* Arγun *üge* (Archives nationales)

Size: 183 × 25 cm

Date Issued: 6th of the latter part of the first month of summer, the yaer of the Cattle (1289 A. D.) in the Arγun period

Place Issued: Köndelen

Issuer: Arγun [Qan]

Objects of the Decree: Ired Barans (Roi de France)

Style of the Decree: (*l*. 03) *üge* "Arγun üge manu" (Arγun, our word)

Given Authorities: (*l*. 01) Power of the *tengri* (Heaven) "möngke tngri-yin kücün" (*l*. 02) Energy of the *Qayan* "Qayan-u süü"

Language of the Opening Phrases: (*l*. 01) Mongolian (*l*. 02) Mongolian (*l*. 03) Mongolian

Written Characters: Uighur

Language of the Main Sentence: Mongolian

Seals: (*ll*. 10 - 13) (*ll*. 24 - 27) (*ll*. 31 - 34) Square-shaped Red Seal in the Chinese language -Chinese characters" *Fuguo Anmin zhi Bao*"辅国安民之宝

Size of the Seal: 15 × 15 cm

Location of the Document: Archives nationales de France, Paris

Facsimile: Bonaparte, R. N. 1895; Mostaert, A. et Cleaves, F. W. 1962 (Doc. A); Dobu 1983

Text: Abel-Rémusat 1824; Meadows 1850; Mostaert, A. et Cleaves, F. W. 1962 (Doc. A); Dobu 1983; Tumurtogoo 2006 (Ar. II)

(e) -3. *bars jil* Arγun *üge* (Archivio Segreto Vaticano)

Size: 110. 2 × 26. 4 cm

Date Issued: 5th of the early part of the first month of summer, the yaer of Tigar (1290 A. D.) in the Arγun period

Place Issued: Urumi (Urmiye)

Issuer: Arγun [Qan]

Objects of the Decree: (Nicolaus IV)

Style of the Decree: Unknown (*üge*?)

Given Authorities: Unknown

Languages of the Opening Phrases: Unknown (Mongolian?)

Language of the Main Sentence: Mongolian

Written Characters: Uighur

Seals: (*ll*. 13 - 18) (*ll*. 30 - 34) Square-shaped Red Seal in the Chinese language -Chinese characters " *Fuguo Anmin zhi Bao*" 辅国安民之宝

Size of the Seal：15.3 × 14.9 cm & 13 × 14.8 cm

Location of the Document：Archivio Segreto Vaticano（A. A. , Arm, I-XVIII , 1801（3））

Facsimile：Mostaert, A. et Cleaves, F. W. 1952（Doc. B）；Dobu 1983；Staatliches Museum für Völkerkunde München 2005（312）；Tumurtogoo 2006（Ar. Ⅱ）

Text：Mostaert, A. et Cleaves, F. W. 1952（Doc. B）；Dobu 1983；Tumurtogoo 2006（Ar. Ⅲ）

Notes：The beginning of the document is lost.

（e）-4. anonymous *bičig*（Mūse-ye Mellī Īrān）

Date Issued：Unknown（After Arγun Qan）

Place Issued：Unknown

Issuer：Unknown（Arγun?）

Objects of the Decree：Unknown

Style of the Decree：Unknown

Given Authorities：Unknown

Languages of the Opening Phrases：Unknown（Mongolian?）

Language of the Main Sentence：Mongolian

Written Characters：Uighur

Seals：（*ll.*01 - 02）（*l.*05）Square-shaped Red Seal in the Chinese language -Chinese characters "*Fuguo Anmin zhi Bao*"辅国安民之宝

Size of the Seal：Unknown

Location of the Document：Mūse-ye Mellī Īrān（Iran National Museum）

Facsimile：Pelliot, P. 1936；Mostaert, A. et Cleaves, F. W. 1952（Doc. Ⅱ）

Text：Pelliot, P. 1936；Mostaert, A. et Cleaves, F. W. 1952（Doc. Ⅱ）

Notes：The beginning of the document is lost.

（f）*Wangfu Dingguo Limin zhi Bao* 王府定国理民之宝

（f）-1. *bars jil* Γasan *üge*（Archivio Segreto Vaticano）

Size：88.1 × 42（42.4）cm

Date Issued：14th of the last month of spring, the yaer of Tigar（1302 A. D. ）in the Γasan period

Place Issued：Qos Qabuq

Issuer：［Mahmud Sultan］Γasan Qan

Objects of the Decree：Bab（Papa［catholicus Bonifacius Ⅷ］）

Style of the Decree：（*l.*01）*üge* "Γasan *üge* manu"（Γasan, our word）

Given Authorities：Nothing

Language of the Opening Phrases：（*l.*01）Mongolian

Language of the Main Sentence：Mongolian

Written Characters：Uighur

Seals：（*ll.*08 - 10）（*ll.*12 - 14）Square-shaped Red Seal in the Chinese language -Chinese characters "*Wangfu Dingguo Limin zhi Bao*"王府定国理民之宝

（verso）Square-shaped Black Seal in the Chinese language -Chinese characters "*Bao*"宝

Size of the Seal: "*Wangfu Dingguo Limin zhi Bao*"9.5 × 9 cm & 9.5 × 9.4 cm; "*Bao*" 3.2 × 3.2 cm

Location of the Document: Archivio Segreto Vaticano (A. A., Arm, I-ⅩⅧ, 1801(2))

Facsimile: Mostaert, A. et Cleaves, F. W. 1952 (Doc. C); Dobu 1983; Tumurtogoo 2006 (Гas)

Text: Mostaert, A. et Cleaves, F. W. 1952 (Doc. C); Dobu 1983; Tumurtogoo 2006 (Гas)

Notes: There are the Uighur-Mongolian script and square-shaped black seal in Chinese "Bao"宝 on the reverse.

(g) *Zhenming-Huangdi Tianshun-Wanshi zhi Bao* 真命皇帝天顺万事之宝

(g) −1. *moγai jil* Öljeitü *üge* (Archives nationales)

Size: 300 × 50 cm

Date Issued: 8th of the latter part of the first month of summer, the year of the Serpent (A. D. 1305) in the Öljeitü Sultān period

Place Issued: Aliwan

Issuer: Öljeitü Sultān

Objects of the Decree: Iridiwarans Sultan (Roi de France, l'emperor)

Style of the Decree: (*l*. 01) *üge* "Öljeitü Sultan üge manu" (Öljeitü Sultān, our word)

Given Authorities: Nothing

Language of the Opening Phrases: (*l*. 01) Mongolian

Language of the Main Sentence: Mongolian

Written Characters: Uighur

Seals: (*ll*. 06 − 08) (*ll*. 15 − 17) (*ll*. 25 − 27) (*ll*. 36 − 38) (*ll*. 40 − 42) Square-shaped Red Seals in the Chinese language - Chinese characters "*Zhenming-Huangdi Tianshun-Wanshi zhi Bao*"真命皇帝天顺万事之宝

Size of the Seal: 13 × 13 cm

Location of the Document: Archives nationales de France (Nr. 96 − 9 − 13)

Facsimile: Bonaparte, R. N. 1895; Mostaert, A. et Cleaves, F. W. 1962 (Doc. B); Dobu 1983; Staatliches Museum für Völkerkunde München 2005 (313)

Text: Abel-Rémusat 1824; Meadows 1850; Mostaert, A. et Cleaves, F. W. 1962 (Doc. B); Dobu 1983; Tumurtogoo 2006 (Ölj)

Notes: There are the Uighur-Mongolian script and square-shaped black seal in Uighur-Mongolian "... belge bičig" on the reverse.

(g) −2. *bičin jil* Abū Sa'īd *üge* (Mūse-ye Mellī Īrān)

Date Issued: 8th of the latter part of the second month of autumn, the year of the Monkey (1320 A. D.) in the Sultān Abū Sa'īd period

Place Issued: Soltaniya (Sultāniyeh)

Issuer: Busayid (Abū Sa'īd) Baγatur Qan

Objects of the Decree: *Noyad* (*Amīr*s) of centurions in Gilan

Style of the Decree: (*l*. 01) *üge* "Busayid Baγatur Qan üge manu" (Abū Sa'īd Baγatur Qan, our word)

Given Authorities: Nothing

Language of the Opening Phrases: (*l*. 01) Mongolian

Language of the Main Sentence: Mongolian

Written Characters: Uighur

Seals：Square-shaped Red Seal in Chinese language -Chinese characters "*Zhenming-Huangdi Tianshun-Wanshi zhi Bao*" 真命皇帝天顺万事之宝

Size of the Seal：Unknown

Location of the Document：Mūse-ye Mellī Īrān（Iran National Museum）

Facsimile：Pelliot, P. 1936；Cleaves, F. W. 1953（Doc. Ⅲ）；Tumurtogoo 2006（Bus. 1）

Text：Pelliot, P. 1936；Cleaves, F. W. 1953（Doc. Ⅲ）；Tumurtogoo 2006（Bus. 1）

Notes：There is the Uighur-Mongolian script on the reverse.

Reference

Primary Sources

Anonymous. *Yuandianzhang*《元典章》

［YDZ/Yuan］*Dayuan Shengzhengguozhaodianzhang*《大元圣政国朝典章》60 vols. + xinji 新集，Yuan kanben 元刊本. Taibei：Guoli Gugong Bowuyuan 故宫博物院，1976.

［YDZ/Chen］（ed.）Chenyuan 陈垣. *Yuandianzhang Chenke Yuandianzhang Jiaobu*《沈刻元典章校补》60 vols. + xinji. Beijing：Zhongguo Shudian 中国书店，1990.

Muhammad ibn Hindūshāh Nakh chiwānī. *Dastūr al-Kātib fī-Taʿyīn al-Marātib*.

［*Dastūr*/Али］А. А. Али-заде（ed.）. *Дастур ал-катиь фи таʿйин ал-маратиь*. том. II. москва. 1976

Rashīd al-Dīn Fadhl-Allāh Hamadānī. *Jāmiʿ al-Tavārīkh*.

［Jāmiʿ/Roushan］（ed.）M. Roushan & M. Musavī, *Jāmiʿ al-Tavārīkh*., Tehran, 1373/1995

［Jāmiʿ/TS1518］*Jāmiʿ al-Tavārīkh*, MSS. Topkapı Sarayı Muzesi Kutuphanesi, Reven 1518

Shihāb al-Dīn ʿAbd-Allāh Sharāf Shīrāzī. *Tajziyat al-Amsār wa Tazjiyat al-Aʿsār*. (*Tārīkh-e Vassāf*)

［Vassāf/Bonbay］*Tārīkh-e Vassāf al-Hadrah dar Ahvāl-e Salatīn-e Moghūl*. Tehran. 1338/1960.

［Vassāf/Malek］*Tārīkh-e Vassāf*. MSS. Ketābkhāneh-ye Mellī Malek. sh. 3900.

Sung Lien 宋廉 et al. *Yuan Shi*《元史》(*Yuan dynastic history.*)

［YS/Jiao］*Yuan Shi*. Beijing：Zhonghuashuchu, 1976.（《元史》北京：中华书局）（校点本）

［YS/Bai］*Yuan Shi*. sibucongkan.（Mingkanben）.（《元史》四部丛刊（明刊本））（百纳本）

Secondary Sources

Abel-Rémusat, M. 1822-1824. "Mémoires sur les relations politiques des Princes chrétiens, et particulièrement des Rois de France, avec les empereurs Mongols." *Histoire et mémoires de l'institut royal de France, académie des inscriptions et belles-lettres* 6-7.

Bonaparte, R. N. 1895. *Documents de l'époque mongole des XIIIᵉ et XIVᵉ siècles*. Paris：Grave et imprimé pour l'auteur.

Čenggel, Qošud 1994. "13-14 düger jaɣun-u šasintan-du baɣulɣaqsan jarliɣ-un bičig-ün keb kelberi-yin sinjilel." *Juu uda-yin Mongɣol ündüsüten-ü baɣsi-yin tusqai mergejil -ün erdem sinjilegen-ü sedkül* 1994/3.（Mongolian）

Cleaves, F. W. 1948. "A Chancellery Practice of the Mongols in the Thirteenth anf Fourteenth Centuries." *Harvard Journal of Asian Studies* 11.

Cleaves, F. W. 1953. "The Mongolian Documents in the Musee de Teheran." *Harvard Journal of Asiatic Studies* 16/1-2.

Dobu 1983. *Uyiyurjin mongyul üsüg-ün durasqaltu bičig-üd*. Begejing: ündüsüten-ü keblel-ün qoriy_a. (Mongolian)

Doerfer-TMEN: Doerfer, G. 1963 - 1975. *Türkische und mongolische Elemente in Neupersischen*. 4Bde. Wiesbaden: Franz Steiner Verlag GMBH.

Doerfer, G. 1975. "Mongolica aus Ardabīl." *Zentralasiatische Studien* 9.

Doerfer, G. 1982 - 1985 (a). "Āl-tamĝā." *Encyclopaedia Iranica*. vol. 1. London: Routledge & Kegan Paul.

Doerfer, G. 1982 - 1985 (b). "Altūn-tamĝā." *Encyclopaedia Iranica*. vol. 1. London: Routledge & Kegan Paul.

Emad al-Din 2005: see ۱۳۸۳ عماد الدين شيخ الحكمايى

Emad al-Din 2002: see ۱۳۸۰ عماد الدين شيخ الحكمايى

Farquhar, D. M. 1966. "The Official Seals and Ciphers of the Yuan Period." *Monumenta Serica. Journal of Oriental Studies* 25.

Григорьев, А. П. 1978. *Монгольская Дипломатика XIII - XV вв*. Ленинград: Издательство Ленинградского Университета.

Herrmann, Gottfried 2004. *Persische Urkunden der Mongolenzeit*. Wiesbaden: Harrassowitz Verlag.

Herrmann, G. 1997. "zum persischen urkundenwesen in der Mongolzeit Erlasse von Emiren und Wesiren." Denise Aigle (ed.). *L'Iran face à la domination Mongole*. Téhéran: IFRI.

Herrmann, G. und Doerfer, G. 1975 (a). "Ein persisch-mongolischer Erlaß aus dem Jahr 725/1325." *Zeitschrift der Deutschen Morgenländischen Gesellschaft* 125.

Herrmann, G und Doerfer, G. 1975 (b). "Ein persisch-mongolischer Erlass des Ğalāyeriden Šeyh Oveys." *Central Asuatic Journal* 19/1 - 2.

Huang Dun 1999: 黄惇《元代印风》重庆出版社

Jacomet, Daniel & C^le. *Firman de Soltan Ahmad Djalaïr, Prince Ilkhanien* (MS Bibliothèque Nationale de Paris, supplément persan N°1630; E. Blochet, Cat. Mss. persans, N°2334), La Fondation Nationale pour la reproduction des manuscrits précieux et pièces rares d'archives. Paris.

Kotwicz, W. 1934. "Formules initiales des documents mongols aux XIIIe et XIVe ss." *Rocznik oryentalistyczny* 10.

Luo Zhenyu 1916: 罗振玉《隋唐以来官印集存》罗雪堂先生全集三编, 册三

Matsukawa Takashi 1995. "*Dai-Gen Ulus* Meireibun no Shoshiki. (On the *Daiyuan-Ulus* Style in the Mongolian Edicts of the 13th and 14th Centuries)" *Machikaneyama Ronsō: Shigakuhen* 29 (松川節「大元ウルス命令文の書式」《待兼山论丛・史学篇》).

Meadows 1850. "Translations and Notice of two Mongolian Letters to Philip the Fair, king of France, 1305." *The Chinese Repository* 19.

Mohsen Ja'fari 2000: see محسن جعفرى مذهب

Mostaert, A. et Cleaves, F. W. 1952. "Trois documents mongols des Archives secretes vaticanes." *Harvard Journal of Asiatic Studies* 15/3 - 4

Mostaert, A. et Cleaves, F. W. 1962. *Les Lettres de 1289 et 1305 des ilkhan Aryun et Öljeitü à Philippe le Bel*. Cambridge, Massachusetts: Harvard U. P.

Ono Hiroshi 1993. "Tokoshie no Ten no Chikara no Moto ni: Mongol-jidai Hatsureibun no Bōtō-Teikeiku wo Megutte ("With the Might of Everlasting Heaven": Some Expression Parallel to the Initial Formulae of Mongolian Edicts)." *Kyōto Tachibana Joshi Daigaku Kiyō* (*Memoirs of Kyoto Tachibana Women's University*) 20 (小野浩「「とこしえの天の力のもとに」: モンゴル時代発令文の冒頭定型句をめぐって」《京都橘女子大学研究纪要》).

Paul, Jürgen 1995. "*Inshā'* Collections as a Source on Iranian History." Bert G. Fragner et al. [eds.] *Proceedings of the Second European Conference of Iranian Studies*. Roma: Istituto Italiano per il Medio ed Estremo Oriente.

Paul, Jürgen 1999. "Some Mongol *Inshā'* - Collections: the Juvaini Letters." Charles Melville [ed.] *Proceedings of the Third European Conference of Iranian Studies. Part 2: Mediaeval and Modern Persian Studies*. Wiesbaden: Dr. Ludwig Reichert Verlag.

Pelliot, Paul 1936. "Les documents mongols du Musée de Teheran." *Athār-e Īrān, Annales du Service Archéologique de l'Iran* 1.

Qāe'm Maqāmī 1350: see ۱۳۵۰. جهانگیر قائم مقامی

Soudavar, A. [ed.] 1981. *Persian Courts: Selections from Art and History Trust Collection*. New York: Rizzoli.

Soudavar, A. 2006. "The Mongol Legacy of Persian *Farmāns*." Linda Komaroff (ed.), *Beyond the Legacy of Genghis Khan*. Leiden-Boston: Brill.

Seiyed Husein 1381: see سید حسین شهرستانی

Staatliches Museum für Völkerkunde München 2005. *Dschingis Khan und seine Erben: Das Weltreich der Mongolen*. München: Kunst- und Ausstellungshalle der Bundesrepublik Deutschland, Hirmer Verlag GmbH.

Schuh, D. 1977. *Erlasse und Sendschreiben mongolischer Herrscher für tibetische Geistliche: Ein Beitrag zur Kenntnis der Urkunden des tibetischen Mittelalters und ihrer Diplomatik*. St. Augustin: Wissenschafts- verlag.

Tumurtogoo [ed.] 2006. *Mongolian Monuments in Uighur-Mongolian Script (XIII-XVI Centuries): Introduction, Transcription and Bibliography*. Taipei: Institute of Linguistics, Academia Sinica.

Watabe Ryōko 2002. "*Shoki Tenpan no Seiritsu Haikei*: 14 - seiki ni okeru Persia-go *Inshā'* Tebikisho Hensan to Mongol Monjo-gyōsei. (The Historical Background to the Compilation of *Dastūr al-Kātib*: Persian *inshā'* Tradition and the Mongol Chancellery System in the 14th Century)" *Shigaku Zasshi* 111 - 117（渡部良子「《書記典範》の成立背景———一四世紀におけるペルシア語インシャー手引書編纂とモンゴル文書行政」《史学杂志》）.

Watabe Ryōko 2003. "Mongol-jidai ni okeru Persia-go *Inshā*-Jutsu Shil-Kanansho. (Persian *Inshā'* Manuals in the Mongol Period)" *Orient* 46 - 42（渡部良子「モンゴル時代におけるペルシア語インシャー術指南書」《オリエント》）.

Xizongzizhiqu Dang'anguan 1995: 西藏自治区档案馆（编）《西藏历史档案荟粹》北京: 文物出版社.

Xie Qifeng 2003: 叶其峰《元官印》(《古玺印通论》北京: 紫禁城出版社.)

سید حسین شهرستانی(پژوهش) ۱۳۸۱. جلوه های هنر ایرانی در اسناد ملی. تهران: سازمان اسناد ملی ایران.

عماد الدین شیخ الحکمایی ۱۳۸۳. بررسی یک پاره سند ایلخانی(مورّخ ۷۲۶ق). نامهء بهارستان ۱۰-۹.

عماد الدین شیخ الحکمایی ۱۳۸۰. کاتبان و قضیان اسناد بقعهء شیخ صفی الدین اردبیلی (اسناد قرن ۶ تا ۱۰ هجری). نامهء بهارستان ۴.

محسن جعفری مذهب (ترجمه)، ابو العلا سودآور ۱۳۷۹. نخستین فرمان فارسی ایلهانان. وقف: میراث جاویدان ۲۹.

جهانگیر قائم مقامی ۱۳۵۰. مقّدمه یی بر شناخت اسناد تارخی. تهران: شهریورماه.

鄯善洋海墓地出土毛织衣物的特点

贾应逸　李媛　玛丽亚木·依不拉音木

新疆博物馆　吐鲁番地区文物局

　　洋海墓地，位于新疆吐鲁番地区鄯善县吐峪沟乡，是近几年来新疆发掘规模较大的古墓群，根据墓葬分布可分为Ⅰ号、Ⅱ号、Ⅲ号3个墓地，发掘者研究认为，其时代分别为春秋、战国至西汉和东汉时期。该墓葬群出土了大约400多件用毛纺织物缝缀的衣服和毛织物残片。我们经过近两年的清洗、整理、拼对，共整理出毛纺织衣物167件，不少织物腐蚀严重，难以测量分析；其中可供分析的有126件，衣服40件，毛纺织物残片48件，栽绒毯6件，毛编织带32条。这些毛织物向我们展示了洋海人的物质生活及其毛纺织手工技艺；而且，由于洋海墓地延续时间较长，虽然Ⅱ、Ⅲ号墓地出土毛织物较少，却为我们了解其发展演变提供了佐证。这些毛织衣物对了解和研究新疆早期的物质文化生活、毛纺织手工业的发展、东西方文化交流和古代人们的活动具有重要的意义。

　　洋海墓地的这些毛织物与新疆其他地区出土毛织物有许多共同点，如衣服大多用"织成"缝缀；织物的组织法主要有平纹、斜纹、绵毛、栽绒毯；经线加捻较紧，纬线相对较蓬松等表现了毛纺织物的规律等。但也存在一些与新疆其他地区不完全相同的现象，有着自己的特点，如毛纱加捻及其在织物中的配置，毛织物的幅宽和幅边的处理，斜纹变化组织的大量运用，绵毛织物基础组织的多样性及其图案的表现；栽绒组织较早出现等。现分别叙述于后。[①]

一、衣　　物

　　洋海墓地出土毛织衣服的种类比较单一，仅有衣服、裤子、披风、披巾等。

　　（一）上衣

　　衣服有长衣、短衣、披风。其中长衣较多，尤以Ⅰ号墓地为最，发现16件，可供分析的14件；Ⅱ号墓地出土2件，可供分析的1件；Ⅲ号墓地1件。

　　Ⅰ号墓地以长衣为主。长衣基本形式是长及膝下，前身正中开襟，通体肥大。在衣服下摆、袖口处绵织边饰；领口、两前襟、腋下前后身接缝、袖头处都装饰有编织带或彩色压缘，少数后身接缝处也缝缀有压缘。

　　这种长衣均为根据需要专门织制出的织物，即"织成"缝缀而成。如缝制长外衣，有的是分别织出两幅等长的毛织物，将两幅布的部分对折缝合成后身，其余的一半是前身，两幅敞开作为开襟式；然后，分别

　　① 对于毛织物组织法的命名，主要参考沈兰萍主编：《织物结构与设计》，中国纺织出版社，2005年第一版。需要说明的是，洋海墓地出土的毛织物大多为死者身穿的衣服，有的生前已多年穿着，遭到磨损，甚至已经缝补；死后埋入墓葬，经几千年迭压、腐蚀；……多已严重残破，因而，文中所说毛织物的资料多为大约数，特别是织物的厚度，经、纬线粗细度也已变为宽度。

缝缀两只预先织成的袖子,如03SYIM149:1黄地几何纹缂毛开襟长外衣。有的后身织成整幅,在上端脖际处再分成两幅,分别织成两前襟,然后,再缝缀两袖,如03SY1M26:9黄棕色条纹斜褐开襟长外衣(图版一)。

图版一　03SY1M26:9 黄棕色条纹斜褐开襟长外衣

Ⅱ号墓地仅有一件黄棕色斜褐残长衣,其基本形式与Ⅰ号墓地长衣类似,也是开襟式。但在下摆处缂饰一条红绿色勾连纹饰的图案色泽鲜艳,纹样面积大,显得较为突出。与扎滚鲁克墓葬出土的长衣相似。[①]

Ⅲ号墓地出土了一件短上衣,为套头式。人工挖出领口,其周围缝缀红色绦带,且前身正中和肩上压饰红色绦带。衣身两侧,即腋下接缝梯形织物,下摆处裁剪成弧形,衣服整体随身,显出细腰、丰臀,增加了美感。

看来,洋海墓地毛纺织长衣形式演变进程是,由缝缀"织成"发展到使用部分裁剪法缝制,使衣服显得更合身美观。

(二)裤子

裤子有长裤、短裤。大多在腰两侧开口,接带;裤裆有"十"字形和梯形。Ⅰ号出土11条,可供分析的有8条;Ⅱ号墓地1件。

这些裤子形式基本相似:裤腰和裤腿均由"织成"对折缝缀而成。先将两幅织物的上端相对缝合,构成腰围和臀围。再分别将左面和右面的前后两片合在一起,变成两幅,分别织制成裤腿,如03SYIM26:10红蓝色锯齿纹缂毛短裤(图版二)。

---

① 有关扎滚鲁克墓地的材料,请参看新疆博物馆文物队《且末县扎滚鲁克五座墓葬发掘报告》,《新疆文物》1998 年第 3 期。

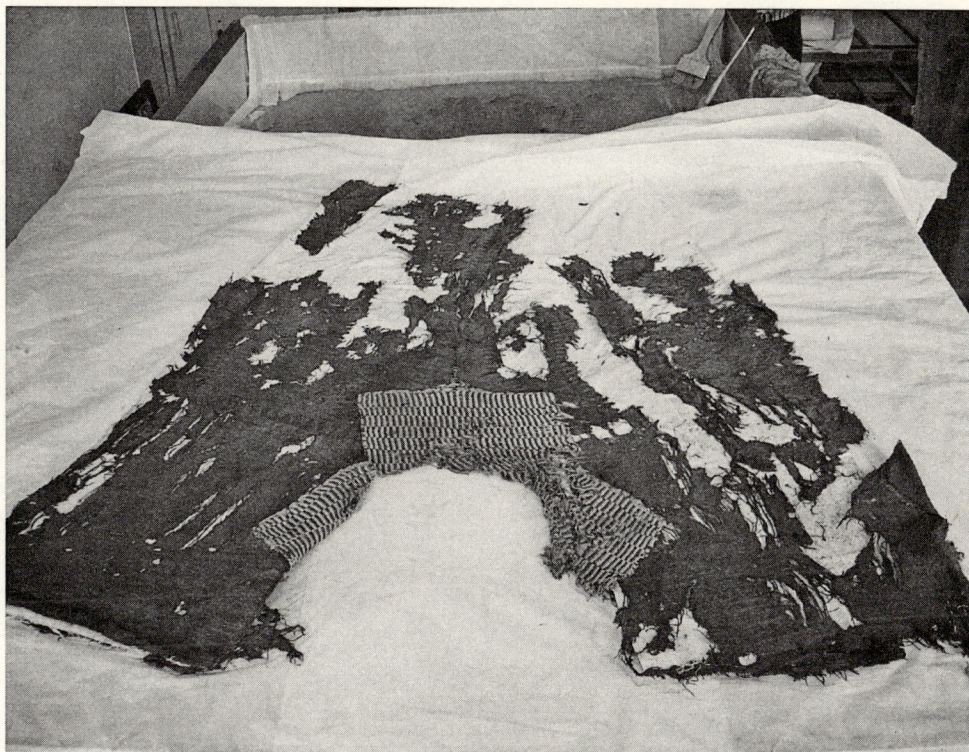

图版二　03SYIM26：10 红蓝色锯齿纹缂毛短裤

有的腰围和臀围分四幅织制,先两幅相对缝合成前后两片,再将这两片相对缝合;然后再分别将左面和右面的前后两片合在一起,变成两幅分别织制;每幅织物再各自对折相缝合成裤腿,如03SYIM67：3 蓝地黄色几何缂毛长裤。

Ⅰ号墓地出土裤子在腰的两侧开口,并缝缀编织带,以供系结。其中3件还保存有裤裆,分别为"十"字形和"阶梯形"两种,使用前者的有2条,使用后者为1条。Ⅱ号墓地出土裤子的裤裆为方形裆,以对折三角形缝合,明显比Ⅰ号墓地出土的简便易织,穿用又方便。

（三）裙子

Ⅰ号墓地没有发现裙子,最早出土于Ⅱ号墓地中时代较晚的竖穴土坑直壁墓,共5条,Ⅲ号墓地发现2条。

裙子有两种:一种是用编织带缝缀,另一种彩色毛织物缝缀。Ⅱ号墓地中有3条是将一条条毛编织带纵向相接,缝缀而成呈横向循环的彩色条纹裙,如03SYIIM223 毛编织带接裙（图版三）。另有2条为用彩色斜纹的毛织物纵向接缝而成。裙子呈横向的彩色条纹。色彩方面多以红色为主,配以黄、蓝、绿、棕色,大多形成红色地的彩色裙,色泽绚丽。Ⅲ号墓地出土的分别为红、黄色和红、蓝色毛织物接裙,前者03SYIIIM318 为平纹组织（图版四）,后者是斜纹织物。

（四）披巾

洋海Ⅰ号墓地出土5件披巾。披巾均为长方形,但残损较为严重,仅可辨出两端饰有流苏,多数饰有条纹图案,如03SYIM76。同样是根据需要而专门织制的。

此外,洋海Ⅰ号墓地出土了过去其他墓地从来了没有发现过的"法衣"和披风。出土的两件"法衣"都是用斜纹基础组织的缂毛织物缝缀而成,两件披风则是用斜纹条纹或格纹毛织物缝缀的。

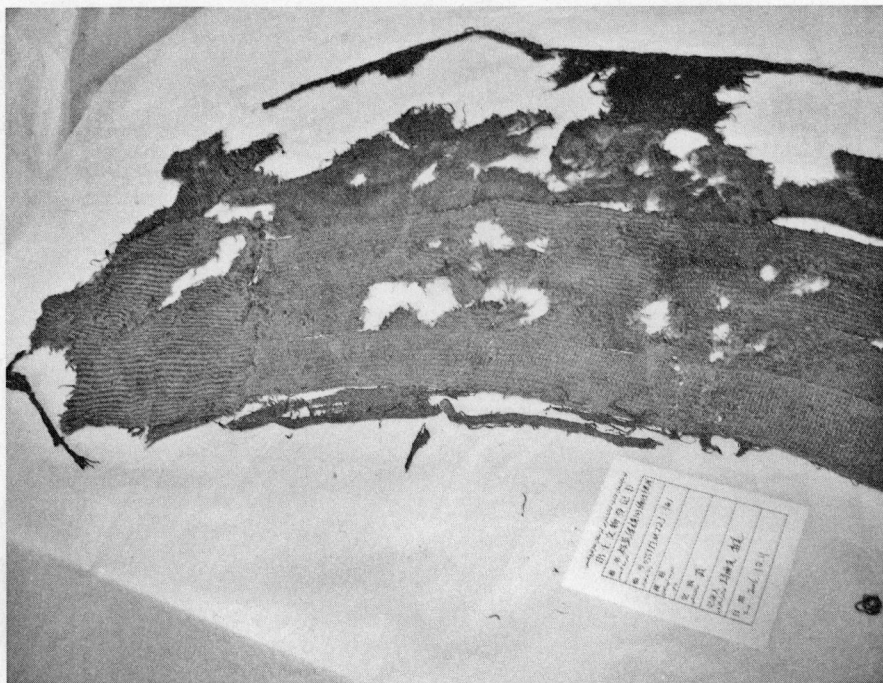

图版三　03SYIIM223 毛编织带接裙

图版四　03YIIIM318 为平纹组织

二、毛纺织物

洋海墓地出土的这些衣物都是用毛纺织物缝缀的,同时还残存许多毛纺织物。我们分析了他们的毛纱、组织结构、图案纹样等。

(一) 毛纱的纺捻及其在织物中的配置

洋海Ⅰ号墓地出土毛织物的经、纬线,都是使用木制的纺塼加捻而成的。

1　关于毛织品的捻向　这些毛织品的经、纬线,捻向有"Z"向和"S"向两种(图一)。

Ⅰ号墓地的毛织物中毛纱的捻向有"Z"向和"S"向,两者的比例几乎相等,且两种捻向的毛织物在墓葬中的分布比较集中。如03SYIM76出土6件毛织物,均为"Z"向加捻,且都为平纹组织。而03SYIM67出土的3件和03SYIM146出土的2件毛织物均为"S"向加捻,且都是缂毛织物。少量墓葬出土毛织物中两种捻向的都有,如03SYIM164出土5件,均为平纹组织织物,其中3件为"Z"向加捻,2件是"S"向加捻。

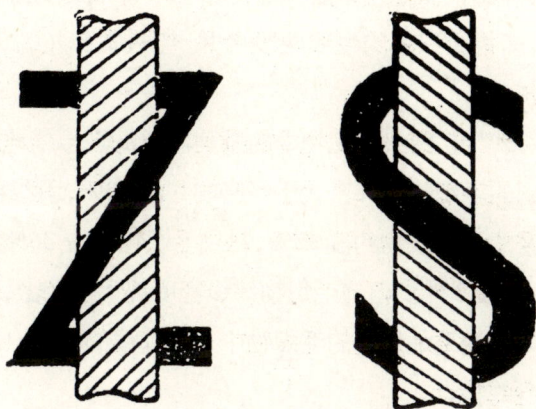

图一　Z捻向和S捻向

以"Z"向加捻的毛织物中,平纹组织的织物较多,其中5件披巾均为"Z"向加捻;6件栽绒组织的毯类全用"Z"向加捻的毛纱织制。斜纹组织织物的数量仅次于平纹织物,现知的2件披风均为"Z"向加捻;以斜纹为基础组织的缂毛织物中只有2件为"Z"捻。以"S"向加捻的毛织物中,以通经断纬的缂毛织物最多。

有4件毛织物的经线为"Z"向,纬线为"S"向,其中3件是斜纹组织,仅有1件是平纹毛织物。经、纬纱捻向对织物有着明显的影响,在斜纹组织的毛织物中,经、纬线的捻向相反,织物表面明暗分明,斜路清晰。在平纹织物中,则使表面反光一致,光泽较好。

虽然Ⅰ号墓地出土的毛织物两种捻向的都有,但Ⅱ、Ⅲ号墓地的毛织物则都是以"Z"向加捻的。

2　关于经、纬线的捻度

由于这些出土毛织物的牢固性很差,我们无法用仪器测量其捻度,仅能用肉眼进行观察分析:发现织物经线的捻度一般大于纬线捻度,如03SYIM8:21深红色褐长衣残片中的经线每厘米约加捻10圈,纬线每厘米约8圈。03SYIM157:11绿地红黄格纹斜褐裤,经线加捻8圈/厘米,纬线加捻6圈/厘米。03SYIM67:1绯地蓝色菱形涡旋纹缂毛长衣残片,其经线约8圈/厘米,纬线为5圈/厘米。

3　关于经、纬线的直径

用纺塼纺捻成的经、纬线基本是圆柱式,一般用支数计算。但作为古代毛织物,不仅经过长期穿用,而且又在墓葬中沉睡两千多年,已改变了原来的形状,变成扁平状,所以我们以投影宽度来计算。洋海墓地出土毛纱的宽度大多在0.005~0.029 cm之间,个别的最宽可达0.065 cm。一般情况下,平纹织物的经、纬线宽度较小些;供铺垫用毯类织物的经、纬线都较宽,如03SY1M133:9-6原黄色铺垫毯的经、纬线分别宽0.038、0.020 cm。

经、纬线宽度在毛织物中的配置,一般是经线宽于纬线,无论是平纹或斜纹组织的织物,特别是缂毛织物,所有的经线宽度都大于纬宽。仅有4件平纹和4件斜纹毛织物的纬线大于经线,一件斜纹毛织物的经、纬线宽度相同。

4　这些毛织物的经、纬线一般是以单股进行交织。仅在某些衣物的边缘,将原织物中的经线合并为双股,再与两股合并的纬线缂织出装饰图案,如03SY1M26:9黄棕色条纹斜褐开襟长外衣,是使用斜纹组织法织成的棕黄色条纹毛织物缝制的。在长衣下摆及袖口处装饰一圈宽6~7.5 cm的蓝色边饰,上面缂织黄色的变体三角形图案,就是将原长衣的棕黄色经线,两根合并,与双股的黄、蓝色纬线交织成方重平组织基础组织,再以通经断纬法,缂织出一排蓝、黄色相错三角形图案。而03SY1M67:3蓝地黄色缂毛长裤,整体是用单股经、纬线,以2/2斜纹组织法织制的毛织物缝缀的。而在裤腿上缂织横向图案时,却将原织物的经线两股合并,与两股合并的黄、蓝色纬线交织成重平组织,并运用通经断纬技法缂织图案。

　　5　经、纬线在织物中的排列。洋海Ⅰ号墓地出土毛织物中,经、纬线排列密度的规律不太明显,平纹组织的毛织物中纬密大于经密的约占60%,斜纹毛织物中经密小于纬密的占近55%。而经线密度大于纬密的平纹织物约占32%,斜纹毛织物约占36%。另外,有3件毛织物的经纬线密度相同,其中平纹1件,斜纹2件。但缂毛织物纬线密度都大于经密,仅有2件的经纬线密度相等。

　　洋海墓地发现的毛织物中,经、纬线的捻向、捻度、投影宽度及其在织物中的交织和排列等都显示出自身的特点。

　　首先,洋海Ⅰ号墓地发现毛织物经、纬线有"Z"向和"S"向两种,而新疆其他地区,如且末扎滚鲁克、洛浦山普拉、尉犁营盘等墓地出土毛织物的经、纬线大多是以"Z"向加捻。但洋海Ⅱ、Ⅲ号墓地的毛织物则都是以"Z"向加捻,表明了洋海毛纺织物发展的过程。

　　其次,洋海Ⅰ号墓地出土的毛织物中,没有一件的经、纬线是并股后进行交织的。这点与扎滚鲁克墓地出土毛织物比较接近,扎滚鲁克仅有个别织物是并股的,且主要在织物的显花处,与洋海相同。而在山普拉墓地出土毛织物中,并股现象较多,主要用在斜纹组织的毛织物中。

　　再次,新疆其他墓葬和遗址出土的毛织物,平纹织物的经线排列较密,纬线较疏松;斜纹织物的纬线排列紧密,而经线排列比较疏松。而洋海Ⅰ号墓地的毛织物中,经线密度小于纬线密度的占较大的比例,规律不够明显。但缂毛织物的纬线密度都大于经密,或两者密度相等。

　　至于形成这些不同的原因仍待今后进一步探索。

　　(二)织物的幅宽与幅边

　　洋海Ⅰ号墓地出土的这些毛织衣物,无论是长外衣、法衣,或是裤子、披风、披巾,或铺垫毯等物,其织物都是根据缝制物的需要而确定其幅宽的,所以,从某种意义上来讲,均可以称为"织成"。这一点与扎滚鲁克、山普拉墓地出土的毛织衣物相同。

　　缝制长外衣织物的幅宽:将两幅布的部分对折缝合成后身,其余的一半是前身,前面呈开襟式的衣料,幅宽一般在42～49 cm之间。如03SYIM149:1黄地几何纹缂毛开襟长外衣的衣料幅宽为44.5 cm。后身织成整幅,在上端脖际处再分成两幅形成前襟的,幅宽一般为80多厘米,如03SYIM26:9/1黄棕色条纹斜褐开襟长外衣的织物幅宽82 cm,在脖际处分成两幅,分别织制成前身的左、右两襟,每幅宽39 cm。袖子的幅宽约均在38～40 cm,上述两件长衣,前者幅宽40 cm,后者宽38 cm。

　　至于缝缀裤子使用的织物幅宽:一般腰围处为45～49 cm间,裤腿处为27～30 cm。如前述03SYIM26:10红蓝色锯齿纹缂毛短裤的织物,腰围处为49 cm,两条裤腿分别分前、后两片分别织制,幅宽28 cm。03SYIM67:3蓝地黄色几何缂毛长裤,从腰围至裤裆处的四幅织物幅宽27 cm;左、右面的前后两片合在一起织成的裤腿幅宽48 cm。

　　此外,仅存可供统计数据的几件衣物:法衣03SYIM21:4毛织物的幅宽为66 cm。缝制披风03SYIM87:22的幅宽为74 cm。披巾03SYIM76:3的幅宽45 cm。残存的一件毛织物03SYIM183:1原黄色斜褐残片的幅宽最大,达87 cm,也可能是一件长外衣的残片。当时的洋海人可以织制幅宽达80多厘米以上的毛织物,现知最大幅宽是 87 cm。

关于幅边的处理方法,洋海墓地出土的毛织物是由几股经线合并,或几根经线加捻两种方式与纬线相交织形成幅边,以增加织物的张力,增强坚固性。经线为并股或加捻的股数也不完全相同,一般是 2~5 根,其中 3 根和 4 根的较多,2 根和 5 根的较少。织物比较轻薄的多用并股,现保存幅边、可供统计的幅边为并股的毛织物中有 9 件是平纹织物、7 件斜纹、4 件缂毛。如 03SYIM76:1 蓝色褐长衣残片的幅边由 4 根经线合并。比较厚重的织物幅边多用加捻经线,在现存 18 件幅边为加捻经线的织物中,就有 10 件为缂毛织物。如 03SYIM26:12 红蓝色锯齿纹缂毛裤,斜纹基础组织,厚 0.096 cm,幅边由 4 根经线合捻。

看来,洋海Ⅰ号墓地出土毛织物地幅边还没有形成一个固定的模式。

（三）斜纹及其变化组织的毛织物

洋海Ⅰ号墓地出土的毛织物中,斜纹与平纹组织织物的比例相差无几,但斜纹织物比较复杂,有 2/1、1/2 和 3/1 的原组织织物,更多的是斜纹变化组织,斜纹变化组织中,尤以 2/2,即双面加强斜纹组织最多,共有 11 件,其中有 6 件为缂毛织物的基础组织。此外有破斜纹 1 件,山形斜纹 1 件。

这些织物的斜向大多为左向,可供统计的 13 件中,有 10 件左斜纹,斜度以 35°和 40°为最多,最小的 20°,最大的 55°。03SYIM1014:5 棕地黄色横条纹斜褐裤,以 S 向加捻、单股的棕色经线和棕、黄色纬线相交为 2/1 斜纹原组织（图二）,左斜,35°。03SY1M87:20 黄色斜褐,黄色经、纬线均为单股,经线 Z 向加捻,纬线以 S 向加捻。经纬线以二上二下的斜纹组织法相交成 2/2 双面加强斜纹组织,左向 40°（图二）。仅有 1 件右向斜纹,即 03SYIM31:1 红地蓝条纹斜褐披风。

图二　2/1 左斜纹组织图

图三　2/2 左斜纹组织图

洋海墓葬出土了现知新疆最早的山形斜纹和破斜纹组织织物。03SY1M157:11 绿地红黄格纹斜褐,由黄、棕两色经线和绿、红色纬线相交织而成;以 2/2 为基础组织相交,每织入一定根数纬线后,改变织物斜向的方向,织入同样根数纬线,使织物表面的纹路一半向右斜,一半向左斜,组成山形斜纹（图四）。

03SY1M149:2 黄地横向蓝色条纹斜褐,经线为黄色毛纱,纬线有蓝、黄两组,主体部分是在蓝色地上,显出黄色条纹。组织法为 2/1 斜纹为基础组织,与上述山形斜纹的织法相同,使织物的斜纹方向一半向左,另一半向右;但在左、右斜纹的交接处有一条明显的分界线,称为断界（图五）。这种组织法的毛织

图四　2/2 山形斜纹

图五　2/1 破斜纹

物,1995 年曾在营盘墓地发现一件,即 95BYYM30:6 彩条纹斜褐,时代为汉～晋,比这件晚了几百年。①

织物中经、纬线捻向的配合对织物的手感、厚度、表面纹路等都有一定的影响。洋海墓地出土了几件经纬、线捻向不同的织物,其中 3 件是斜纹变化组织,2 件为 2/2 双面加强斜纹,1 件为破斜纹。

这些斜纹织物的厚度较多在 0.09 cm 左右,比较厚重,大多织成裤料、披风、法衣、长外衣和铺垫毯等。

这种斜纹变化组织毛织物的出现,显示了洋海人毛纺织技术的发展水平,不仅能操作织制,而且了解斜纹组织的性能,能熟练地掌握斜纹织物织制技术。

(四)缂毛织物的多样性及其图案

洋海 1 号墓地出土的这些织物中,最精美的要算是缂毛织物了,共有 18 件。在 14 件可供统计的缂毛织物中,有 6 件的基础组织为平纹,8 件使用斜纹组织法织制,其中 2 件是 2/1 斜纹原组织,6 件以 2/2 双面加强斜纹作基础组织。

在平纹为基础组织的缂毛织物中,有通体缂织图案:如 03SYIM67:1 绯地蓝色变体涡旋纹缂毛开襟长衣,原棕色经线和绯、蓝色纬线均为单股,以 S 向加捻。经、纬线以一上一下的平纹织组织法相交织,纬

---

① 赵丰主编:《纺织品考古新发现》,图版 14,香港艺纱堂出版,2002 年。

线紧紧地缚住了经线,织物表面呈经向凸起,并由纬线显出绯色和蓝色图案。当两组不同色彩的纬线在织物上相遇时,相错与经线交织,表面呈现梳齿状。因而,整个织物不存在裂缝,显得结实厚重。织物背面的纬线交叉不零乱,显得较有规律。

03SY1M149:1 黄地几何纹缂毛开襟长外衣,左半身是黄地红蓝色长方格和折线纹缂毛,右半部为黄地蓝色宽条和折线纹缂毛。衣服仅在上部和袖子上缂织出图案,其余部分如衣服下部仍是黄色平纹织物。且两侧图案的色泽不同,但组织法是一致的。其图案纹样的缂织方法与上述相同,缂织图案部分厚于织物本身。

以斜纹为基础组织的缂毛织物8件中,有2件为2/1原斜纹组织,6件是2/2双面加强斜纹组织,03SYIM26:12红蓝色锯齿纹缂毛裤,棕色经线与红、蓝色纬线以2/1的斜纹原组织法相交织。当两组不同颜色的纬线相遇时,分别与相邻的两根经线相交;下次再相遇时,再相错与经线交织,如此循环。因为这件织物的组织法是斜纹,因而织物表面呈现出斜向的一个个豁口。03SY1M67:2绯地蓝色变体涡旋纹缂毛法衣,原棕色经线和绯、蓝色纬线,以2/2基础组织相交织成左斜25°的双面加强斜纹。与上件织制法相同,在绯色地上,显出斜向的蓝色变体四方连续涡旋纹。

新疆境内发现的缂毛织物中,以平纹为基础组织的最早见于且末扎滚鲁克墓地,与洋海墓地时代相近的85QZM1—5中的红地羊角纹缂毛饰带,但到汉代及以后的山普拉墓地及尼雅、楼兰、营盘等处,平纹组织是其缂织物的主要组织法。以斜纹为基础组织地缂毛织物,新疆其他地区少有发现,仅且末扎滚鲁克墓地发现较多。

洋海墓地出土的这些缂毛织物不论是以平纹为基础组织,还是斜纹为基础组织都有个共同的特点:在图案的边缘处,两种不同颜色的纬线总是斜向显花。因而,这些缂毛织物的图案多呈菱格、锯齿和斜线构成的变体涡旋纹。其实,斜纹组织法最适合于缂织斜向的几何图案。这是因为两组不同色泽的纬线总是斜向相遇,然后,再向下或向上倾斜而成斜线状。织物表面形成一个个斜向的豁口,而不是裂缝,因而,图案的轮廓也现斜向。织物背面的色泽、图案与正面相同。

运用缂毛技法显出图案是洋海人美化织物的重要手段,也是新疆毛纺织业较早使用的一种技法,早在距今3 800年以前的小河墓地就有发现。这种技法传入中原,后来运用于丝织业中,出现了缂丝。这是聚居在新疆地区古代各族人民对祖国物质文化的重要贡献。新疆吐鲁番阿斯塔那出土了7世纪时期的缂丝带,是我国现知最早的缂丝实物。

(五)现知新疆最早的栽绒毯

洋海Ⅰ号墓地出土了6条栽绒组织的毯类,大多是作为鞍毯使用,其中03SY1M87:23红蓝色菱格纹鞍毯保存较完整,下面缝缀4层原白色毡。

这些栽绒组织的鞍毯均是由经线、地纬线交织成基础组织,再在经线上拴结绒头(绒纬)而成的栽绒织物。洋海出土栽绒毯的经线、地纬和绒纬均以Z向加捻;经线由两股合并,地纬和绒纬为单股。经线与地纬以1/1的平纹组织法相交织,再用彩色绒纬拴结一排绒头。由彩色绒头(纬)显出图案。绒头的结扣法用"马蹄扣"法,或称"剪刀扣"法。每两排绒头之间的地纬根数不等,最少的4~6根,最多的有12~15排,规律性不强;但每10 cm内平均栽绒10~11道,基本为100道地毯却是差距不大的。洋海栽绒毯的图案多为几何形,其中尤以三角和菱格为最。

洋海墓地出土的栽绒毯虽然面积不大,均为鞍毯,图案简单,但它却已具备了新疆地毯的一些特点:

首先从栽绒毯的结扣法看,已经形成绒头缠绕在相邻的两根经线上的双经扣,即马蹄扣法,或称剪刀扣。这种结扣法一直沿用到公元 17 世纪或以后。再从图案纹样上看,洋海出土的栽绒毯多为几何纹饰,尤其三角、菱格,这也是后来新疆地毯中最为流行的图案(图版五)。但它毕竟是新疆现知最早的栽绒毯,没有形成装饰多层边框的特点。再从绒纬的色彩看,红、蓝、黄等彩色配置的浓艳悦目,对比强烈。这些特点在后来几千年的演变发展中,更加丰富多彩。

03SYM149:2　2/1 破斜纹

图版五　地毯

　　通过对洋海墓地发现毛织物的探讨,我们可以了解当时人们的物质生活水平,毛纺织手工业发展状况,及其文化内涵和科学知识的掌握等等。但是由于我们对其纺车、织机、染料及其加工过程等一系列的问题了解得非常不够,故仍待进一步的发现和研究。

TAM170 出土丝织品的分析与研究[*]

赵丰　万芳　王乐　王博

东华大学　新疆维吾尔自治区博物馆

TAM170 位于吐鲁番阿斯塔那墓地北区中部,与 TAM 169、TAM 171 及 TAM 186 三墓相邻。1972 年末,由新疆博物馆考古队和吐鲁番县文物保管所共同组成的考古工作队对其进行了清理发掘,李征、岑云飞、林福才、吴震、阿吉、王明哲和梁礼波等考古学家参加了此次发掘,最后由李征整理了出土文物。2005 年,在新疆博物馆王博的帮助下,对 TAM170 墓中出土的部分丝织品和服饰进行了整理和研究。由于我们的工作距发掘已有三十多年,部分资料无法一一对应,当年的发掘人员也无法追忆,甚为可惜。

一、TAM170 丝织品的出土情况

1. TAM170 的墓葬情况

鲁礼鹏在《吐鲁番阿斯塔那古墓群发掘墓葬登记表》中,[①]对 TAM170 的墓葬型制略有提及。该墓为麹氏高昌时期斜坡墓道洞室墓,墓室平面为方形,长 3.5 米、宽 3 米,墓底距地面深 1.5 米。墓室中葬有一男二女,三人皆仰身直肢。

TAM170 虽遭严重盗扰,仍出土了一批颇具研究价值的文物,包括墓表、文书、丝织品及少量日用器物等。其中,两方墓表及三份衣物疏保存较完好,为我们提供了墓葬纪年及墓主身份的准确信息。

据墓表及相应衣物疏,TAM170 最早入葬者为张洪妻焦氏,死于高昌章和十三年(543 年)。焦氏墓表为灰砖,黑地刻格刻字填朱,五行,长 36 cm、宽 36 cm、厚 4.5 cm。对照伴出的《高昌章和十三年孝姿随葬衣物疏》,知张洪妻焦氏身前信佛,法名孝姿。焦氏死后五年,即高昌章和十八年(548 年),张洪的第二任妻子光妃亦同葬此墓。而最后入葬者为张洪,死于高昌延昌二年(562 年),后追赠振武将军。其墓表为灰砖蓝地朱书,八行,长 42 cm、宽 42 cm、厚 4 cm。对照《高昌延昌二年长史孝寅随葬衣物疏》,知张洪身前亦信佛,并有佛名孝寅。

2. 出土丝织品和文书材料的刊布

虽然吐鲁番的考古报告一直没有正式出版,但 TAM170 墓中的部分文物已见于不同的出版物,并在不同的场合进行展出,包括天青色幡纹绮(TAM170:20)、[②]树叶纹锦(TAM170:38)[③]以及对羊纹锦覆面

---

[*]　本研究为上海市重点学科建设项目资助,项目编号:B601。

①　新疆文物考古研究所:《吐鲁番阿斯塔那古墓群发掘墓葬登记表》,《新疆文物》2000 第 3、4 期。

②　最早的《新疆出土文物》中名为几何纹填花绮,见新疆维吾尔自治区博物馆:《新疆出土文物》,文物出版社,1975 年,第 48 页。后来武敏的《织绣》和《吐鲁番地域与出土绢织物》中称为天青色幡纹绮,见《织绣》,幼狮文化事业公司,1992 年,第 108 页;新疆维吾尔自治区博物馆、日本奈良丝绸之路学研究中心,《吐鲁番地域与出土绢织物》,2000 年,图版 104。

③　树叶纹锦原称为树纹锦,见《丝绸之路——汉唐织物》,文物出版社,1973 年,图 23。但到后来逐渐被改成树叶纹锦,见武敏:《织绣》,第 104 页;《吐鲁番地域与出土绢织物》,图版 79、81。

（TAM170：66）三件文物，[①]但定名略有不同。其中的对羊纹锦覆面还参加了美国大都会博物馆举办的《走向盛唐》展览。

除了出土丝织品之外，非常重要的是 TAM170 墓中还出土了三件衣物疏，均已全文刊布，[②]并已有部分学者对此进行了研究。[③]

较为全面的 TAM170 墓考古发掘材料发表于《阿斯塔那古墓群第十次发掘简报（1972～1973）》中。[④]《简报》正文重点介绍了绿地对羊纹锦覆面（TAM170：66）、红地人面鸟兽纹锦裤（TAM170：60）、树叶纹锦覆面（包括其中的吹奏人物纹锦残片 TAM170：11）、鸡鸣锦枕（TAM170：25）、绛紫色幡纹嵌对凤立人兽面纹绮（TAM170：59）、绛色大联珠对狮纹绮（TAM170：59）和黄色龟甲填花绮（TAM170：A）。此外，《简报》的附表二中刊布了同墓出土的更多的丝织品信息。

3. 出土丝织品的记录材料

为了更好地整理 TAM170 出土的丝织品，我们查阅了当年考古学家的原始登记表和墓葬平面图记录（登记表中有部分编号为空格，但在墓葬平面图上有出土实物的名称，我们将其合并成为一表，本文中称为 A），并对照了《简报》中正文以及附录中的报道（本文中总称为 B），[⑤]将它们与我们所看到的出土实物核对，重新整理 TAM170 出土丝织品的总体情况如下：（需要指出的是，我们并没有看到原始登记表上的所有丝织品。）

表一　TAM170 出土丝织品的相关记录

文物号	A 原始登录	B《简报》报道	相关形态描述（备注）	本文采用命名
TAM170：11	树叶纹锦覆面	树叶纹锦覆面	AB 相同：单层白细罗边	树叶纹锦覆面
TAM170：12	树叶纹锦覆面	树叶纹锦覆面	AB 同：上紫荷叶边，下本色白细罗紫荷叶边，内有丝絮	树叶纹锦覆面
TAM170：14	绿地宝塔纹锦	绿地对鸟对羊灯树纹锦	AB 相同：8×36 cm（B 名有误）	未见
TAM170：15	白绢	无记录		未见
TAM170：16	白纱	无记录		未见
TAM170：20	天青绮	天青绮	AB 相同：70×51.6 cm（A 原名"绿绢"）	天青色楼堞纹绮

① 《新疆出土文物》称对羊纹锦覆面；《吐鲁番地域与出土绢织物》称对羊树锦覆面；上海博物馆、新疆维吾尔自治区文物局《丝路考古珍品》称对羊树锦覆面。

② 唐长孺主编：《吐鲁番出土文书（壹）》，文物出版社，1992 年；侯灿：《吐鲁番晋—唐古墓出土随葬衣物疏》，《吐鲁番出土砖志集注》，巴蜀书社，2003 年。

③ 《吐鲁番出土魏晋南北朝时期的随葬衣物疏研究》一文，论述了 TAM170 出《高昌章和十三年（543 年）孝姿随葬衣物疏》中所见"面衣"、"绣罗当"、"少衫"、"中衣"、"脚靡"、"绣鞾"、"丑衣"等名物。《吐鲁番出土文书中的丝织品考辨》一文，对"魏锦"、"钵（波）斯锦"、"丘慈（龟兹）锦"的风格及产地进行了推测，又就"树叶锦"、"合蠡纹锦"、"阳（羊）树锦"的名称及纹样进行了考证。此外，《吐鲁番出土文书词语考释》、《敦煌吐鲁番所出随葬衣物疏中"脚靡（足靡）"新探》等文亦涉及有 TAM170 衣物疏的名物考证。

④ 新疆文物考古研究所：《吐鲁番阿斯塔那第十次发掘简报（1972～1973）》，《新疆文物》2000 第 3、4 期。以下简称《简报》。

⑤ 本文所指"原始记录"，为李征先生于发掘时所绘制、登记原稿。

文物号	A 原始登录	B《简报》报道	相关形态描述（备注）	本文采用命名
TAM170:22	绢褥	绢褥	A 多 B 少：长 164 cm，幅宽 46.5 cm；麻布里，深天青色绢面，用麻线缝制	未见
TAM170:23	白绢	无记录		未见
TAM170:24	鸡鸣锦枕	表无,正文有,彩版有照	A 原记录为黄绮	彩条花卉纹锦鸡鸣枕
TAM170:25	黄绮	无记录	A 原记录为锦枕	黄色联珠石柱纹绮
TAM170:30	树纹锦	无记录		未见
TAM170:31	绛绢	无记录		未见
TAM170:34	握木	无记录	A：上有树叶纹锦	未见
TAM170:35	白纱	无记录		未见
TAM170:36	白绢	无记录		未见
TAM170:38	树叶纹锦覆面	树叶纹锦覆面	AB 同：19.5×22.4 cm，有白绢边	未见
TAM170:39	手套	无记录		未见
TAM170:40	手套	无记录		未见
TAM170:41	兽纹锦领口	兽纹锦领口		对波云珠龙凤纹锦领口
TAM170:42	握木	无记录	A：上缠树叶纹锦紫绢边	未见
TAM170:45	树叶纹锦手套	树叶纹锦手套	A：1 只；B：18×11 cm	树叶纹锦手套
TAM170:50	树叶纹锦手套	树叶纹锦手套	A：1 只	树叶纹锦手套
TAM170:51	握木	无记录	A：有花纹对兽纹	未见
TAM170:56	宝塔纹锦	宝塔纹锦	AB 同：36×7.5 cm，麻布里	绿地几何花卉纹锦腰带
TAM170:58	树叶纹锦裙	树叶纹锦裙		树叶纹锦裤
TAM170:59	绛色绮	绛色绮		褐色大窠联珠狮纹绮
TAM170:60	朱红地对鸟对兽纹锦裤	朱红地对鸟对兽纹锦裤		红地人面鸟兽纹锦裤
TAM170:61	绛绮衣	绛绮衣	AB 同：白纱里	紫色楼堞立人对龙纹绮上衣
TAM170:66	绿地对羊纹锦覆面	绿地对羊纹锦覆面	B 多 A 少：26×34 cm；13×22 cm；绢荷叶边 6.5 cm	绿地对羊纹锦覆面
TAM170:68	绢衣	无记录		未见
TAM170:69	树叶纹锦覆面	树叶纹锦覆面	A 多 B 少：锦心 20×15.5 cm；紫绢边 5.5 cm；紫荷叶边，里白绢，荷叶边中夹丝絮	未见

续　表

文物号	A 原始登录	B《简报》报道	相关形态描述(备注)	本文采用命名
TAM170: 74	锦针囊	锦囊	B: 12.5×11 cm	未见
TAM170: 76	绢	无记录		未见
TAM170: 81	麻布	无记录		未见
TAM170: 82	绿鸡鸣枕	鸡鸣枕	AB 同: 麻布里,内充草灰	未见
TAM170: 83	绢枕	绢枕	AB 同: 长方形麻布里	未见
TAM170: 85	树叶纹锦边绢褥	树叶纹锦边褥	AB 同: 104×36 cm;麻布里,蓝绢面,锦边宽下 7.5 cm(B 漏绢字)	树叶纹锦缘蓝绢褥
TAM170: 87	握木	无记录	A: 缠有树叶纹锦	未见
TAM170: 98	蓝绢	无记录		未见
TAM170: 99	黄绫	黄绮	AB 同: 幅宽 51 cm;白纱里(A 原作"黄绮")	黄色龟背纹绮裙
TAM170: 104	绛纱被单	绛纱被单	AB 同: 长 130 cm,幅宽 52 cm,由三幅缝成	未见
TAM170: 105	白绢衣	无记录		未见
TAM170: 106	镶锦边麻布	镶锦边麻布		绿地几何花卉纹锦腰带
TAM170: 107	红绢衣	无记录		未见

表注: 件数均为一,其中手套为一只;材质如不注明,即为丝质。B 少意为内容与 A 同,但字数较少。

原始登记表与《简报》附录二中均有部分与文物不完全相符,部分文物卡片上没有编号。但通过核对,我们基本判定了其原来的编号,并最后校正、总结如下:

1) 实物中有一件带紫色绢裙腰、黄色龟背纹绮作面、白纱作里的裙残件,卡片上没有编号,只写(TAM170:),似有待编号,但写明为黄绫裙。另有一片黄色龟背填花绮残片,编号特殊(TAM170: A)。经比对研究,应为原登记表 A 中的 TAM170: 99,原记作"黄绮",后改为"黄绫",与卡片上的"黄绫裙"相合。而且,当时登记表 A 中的描述为:"幅宽 51 cm,白纱里",也与此相吻合。

2) 原 TAM170: 99 的卡片上依然写着"黄绮",目前与 TAM170: 25 的卡片放在一起,这也是一件写着"黄绮"的卡片,实为联珠石柱纹绮,风格外貌与龟背纹绮非常相似。推测当时刚发掘时不易分辨而混淆。

3) 登记表 A 中的 TAM170: 59 为绛色绮,经核对应为联珠纹团窠对狮纹绮,此件原无相应卡片,目前的色彩已褪为褐色。

4) 登记表 A 中的 TAM170: 61 为绛绮衣,其面料经核对应为紫色楼堞立人对龙纹绮。此件在卡片上称为"紫绫衣",亦无编号(TAM170:)。另有一件相同残片编号为 TAM170: 59,原定名为绛紫色幡纹嵌对凤立人对兽纹绮,现将它们编在一起,统一用 TAM170: 61 的编号。

这样,虽然我们没有看到在登记表 A 中出现的所有纺织品实物,但凡是我们所看到的实物均与登记表 A 中的编号及载录一一对应起来了。

4. 死者与丝织品的出土位置

以上,我们整理了 TAM170 出土丝织品的相关记录,核对了所有编号,了解了丝织品的整体保存情况。在此基础上,我们有必要比对丝织品出土位置及衣物疏中相关信息,借此确定疏主与墓主的关系,这也有助于我们后面的丝织服饰品的描述与分析。

据原发掘者记录,此墓曾遭盗扰。有一女尸身首异处,男尸口中有木棍撬断,部分丝织品已移位,不再覆于身上,而所出衣物疏三件,也多移位。凡此种种,均是盗扰的证据。其中,《高昌章和十三年孝姿衣物疏》,基本完整,共 17 行,出土时位于墓室中部;《高昌章和十八年光妃衣物疏》,残存 14 行,出土时位于男尸左侧;《高昌延昌二年长史孝寅随葬衣物疏》,共 16 行,出土时位于男尸头部右侧。[①]

三件衣物疏中,较易与墓中尸体对应的是《高昌延昌二年衣物疏》。对照同为延昌二年的墓表,可知 TAM170 的男尸即高昌国长史令、振武将军张洪,孝寅可能是他的法名。

孝姿及光妃衣物疏均未置于尸身上,其对应关系需要名物的比对。最为直接的资料是墓中发现的相对好的红地人面鸟兽纹锦裤(TAM170:60),这条锦裤出土时位于尸体较为完好的女尸的腿部。对照两封衣物疏中与裤相关的载录仅有两条,一为孝姿衣物疏上的"合蠡文锦袴一枚",二是光妃衣物疏上所列"树叶锦袴一枚"。由于树叶纹锦在同墓出土甚多,其外观十分明确,因此,我们可以认定红地人面鸟兽纹锦裤就是孝姿衣物疏上载录的合蠡文锦袴,同时,我们也可以认定,这一女尸即为死于543 年的孝姿,而另一个身首异处的女尸应为死于 548 年的光妃。由此,我们可以画出三具尸体与出土丝织品的位置(图一),[②]也可以初步判定出土丝织品与其所属者之间的关系。图中所标的 11～31,99～104 不能判定,34～35,45～56 应属光妃,38～42,58～61 应属孝姿,66～98 应属孝寅。

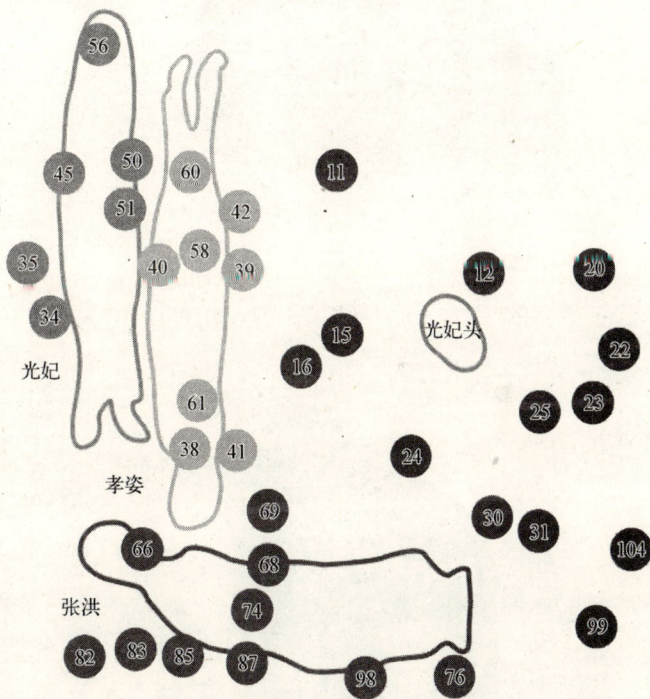

图一　TAM170 丝织品出土位置

二、TAM170 出土的丝织品服饰

墓中出土的丝织品原均应该有形状,部分体形较小的包括覆面、褥、手套、握木等保存比较完好,但体形较大的除合蠡文锦裤之外均十分破残,大部分需待修复整理之后才能辨认款式和量得较为准确的尺

---

① 三件衣物疏录文均参见唐长孺主编:《吐鲁番出土文书(壹)》,文物出版社,1992 年。
② 据李征原始平面图绘,图中编号为原始编号。

寸。本文只描述经我们重新核对、并进行简单测绘的丝织品服饰共 15 件,以下按其款式类型加以分述。①

1. 覆面

(1) 红地树叶纹锦覆面(TAM170:11)

该覆面由绢边和锦芯组成,出土时散落于墓室中部,靠近光妃头侧。整体残长 24 cm,宽 27.3 cm。其中,白绢边宽 8.5 cm,残损严重。锦芯总长 23 cm,宽 24 cm,由两种面料拼合而成,主要是红地树叶纹锦,长 21 cm、宽 17.5 cm。与此相拼缝的是一块吹奏人物纹锦,长 23 cm、宽 6.5 cm(图二)。

图二　红地树叶纹锦覆面(TAM170:11)

图三　红地树叶纹锦覆面(TAM170:12)

图四　绿地对羊纹锦覆面

(2) 红地树叶纹锦覆面(TAM170:12)

该覆面出土时,散落于墓室中部,光妃头侧。整体残长 25 cm,宽 35 cm。覆面以红地树叶纹锦为芯,锦芯长 17 cm、宽 20.3 cm,背衬相同大小的白色纱,中填绵絮,尚未测试是棉絮或是丝绵。锦芯四周缘宽约 6.5 cm 的紫色绮边,绢边压褶缝,呈荷叶状。背后衬白色纱,亦作荷叶边,宽约 7.8 cm(图三)。

(3) 绿地对羊纹锦覆面(TAM170:66)

覆面出土时居张洪头部,保存相对较好,应即其衣物疏中所指"右面衣一颜"。覆面以绿地对羊纹锦为芯,长 35 cm、宽 27 cm。四周以白绢作荷叶边,部分已残,边宽 11～13 cm(图四)。

TAM170 共出覆面 5 件,除上述三件外,我们未见编号为 TAM170:38、69 的另外两件。但其原始记载中对它们

---

① 部分内容在《简报》中已有所述,本文则不避繁琐,重新合成综述。

有着较为明确的描述。

树叶纹锦覆面(TAM170:38)出土时覆于孝姿面部,该覆面残长 19.5 cm、宽 22.4 cm,以树叶纹锦为锦芯,四周以白绢作边。此件树叶纹锦覆面的出土位置、基本特征均可与孝姿衣物疏中所列"树叶面衣"相对应。

树叶纹锦覆面(TAM170:69)亦出自孝姿头侧,其锦心长 20 cm、宽 15.5 cm,紫绢作荷叶边,边宽 5.5 cm,衬里白绢,荷叶边中夹有丝絮。

2. 上衣

(1)对波云珠龙凤纹锦领口(TAM170:41)

原始记录中的原名为"兽纹锦领口"。出土时居孝姿脖颈处,残作三片。领口制为双层,内外缘仍见缝头折边。净宽 2.8 cm,内有白绢里,内缘残长 17 cm。内外领口线为圆顺弧线,弧度较大,基本可排除原为交领的可能性。孝姿衣物疏中明确以锦制作的衣类名目有"锦襦"、"锦褶",两条均无纹样描述。参照花海毕家滩 M26 墓的衣物疏及出土实物,当知"襦"的基本形制为长袖交领短衣。[①] 而褶也是一种外衣,其形如袍。由此推测,这件对波云珠龙凤纹锦领口原为一件"锦褶"的领口,同时也可以说明,当时的褶已采用了圆领(图五)。

图五 对波云珠龙凤纹锦领口(TAM170:41)　　　　图六 紫色楼堞立人对龙纹绮上衣(TAM170:61)

(2)紫色楼堞立人对龙纹绮上衣(TAM170:61)

此衣在原始记录和《简报》附表中均称为"绛绮衣,白纱里",未提及尺寸。核对实物,该衣存有大量残片,有些残片可以看到缝线,有些残片尚存完整幅宽。出土时位于孝姿上身,查孝姿衣物疏中有"紫 绫 褶二枚",此外没有紫色织物的名称,所以,紫色楼堞立人对龙纹绮上衣应该就是衣物疏中的紫绫褶(图六)。

3. 裙、裤

(1)黄色龟背纹绮裙(TAM170:99)

此件在原始登记表和卡片中曾被写作"黄绮"、"黄绫"和"黄绫裙"之名,残作数片。其中一片较大的

---

① 赵丰等:《甘肃花海毕家滩 26 号墓出土的丝绸服饰》,《西北风格——汉晋织物》,艺纱堂/服饰出版(香港),2008 年。

保留有宽约为 5 cm 的紫绢裙腰,与裙腰缝合的黄色龟背纹绮裙面,残长 37 cm,残宽 30 cm。裙面背衬有白纱作里,现其残存大小与裙面相当(图七)。此外,另有一片黄色龟背纹绮残长 30 cm 左右,保存有完整的幅边,幅宽 48.5 cm,此片也应是裙残片(图八)。TAM170:99 出土时散落于墓室一隅,而孝姿及光妃衣物疏均列有"黄绫裙"条目,故此裙原属人难以确定。

图七 黄色龟背纹绮裙(TAM170:99)(背面)　　　　图八 黄色龟背纹绮裙裙片(TAM170:99)局部

(2)树叶纹锦裤(TAM170:58)

此件出土时位于孝姿腰臀处,原始记录中定名为"树叶纹锦裙"。现残作数条,裙型难辨,且触手即碎,尺寸无法测量。从孝姿和光妃的衣物疏来看,仅有光妃的衣物疏中提到有"树叶锦袴一枚",由于孝姿与光妃两具尸体紧紧相邻,而且裤、裙在此状态下很难区分,因此,我们推测此件很有可能是原属光妃的树叶纹锦裤(图九)。

图九 树叶纹锦裤(TAM170:58)

（3）红地人面鸟兽纹锦裤（TAM170:60）

红地人面鸟兽纹锦裤是墓中保存最为完好的一件大型服装，此裤出土时位于孝姿腿部，无疑即是孝姿衣物疏中所录的"合蠡文锦袴"（图十）。因为衣物疏中关于裤的记载仅有两条，一为孝姿衣物疏中的"合蠡文锦袴一枚"，二是光妃衣物疏中的"树叶锦袴一枚"。[①] 红地人面鸟兽纹锦的纹样题材为人面（或兽面）、对鸟、对狮、对鹿、花瓶等，[②] 显然与树叶纹锦的描述相去甚远，而且吴震认为"合蠡"即"合离"，与红地人面鸟兽纹锦中鸟兽对称出现的形式较为相关。[③] 对于此裤的款式，王乐已进行过较为详细的复原研究。[④] 其裤长 104 cm，裤腰高 5.7 cm，残长 38 cm，直裆长约 36 cm，开裆。裤腿宽约 32 cm，下部收口，宽约 24 cm。裤的主要面料是红地人面鸟兽纹锦（即合蠡纹锦），裤裆处由蓝绢、绿色几何纹绮以及团窠卷云对兽对凤纹锦相间形成褶裥。裤腰外层用团窠卷云对兽对凤纹锦和绿地几何花卉纹锦拼缝，中夹白色麻布作衬。整条裤子内衬白纱。

图十　红地人面鸟兽纹锦裤（TAM170:60）

需要指出的是原始记录中有三件狭长织物残片。一件 TAM170:14 称为"宝塔纹锦"，记录中尺寸为宽 8 cm、长 36 cm，此件我们未见。第二件 TAM170:56 亦称为"宝塔纹锦"，残宽 7.5 cm、长 36 cm，麻布作里（图十一 a、b）。第三件 TAM170:106 称为"镶锦边麻

图十一 a　TAM170:56 正面

图十一 b　TAM170:56 反面

① 随葬衣物疏的记载中用的是"袴"字。袴，本意指无裆的套裤，即古人套在有裆裤的外面的下裳，现通"裤"。本文按照今人的阅读习惯，将"袴"作"裤"。

② 新疆文物考古研究所：《阿斯塔那古墓群第十次发掘简报》，《新疆文物》2000 年 3、4 期。

③ 吴震：《吐鲁番出土文书中的丝织品考辨》，《吐鲁番地域与出土绢织物》，中国新疆维吾尔自治区博物馆、日本奈良丝绸之路学研究中心，2000 年。

④ 王乐：《合蠡纹锦袴复原报告》，《西域异服——丝绸之路出土古代服饰复原研究》，东华大学出版社，2007 年。

布", 实测宽度亦在 7.5 cm, 但上面的织锦基本不存(图十二)。这两件残片上的织锦纹样均与红地人面鸟兽纹锦裤腰部的绿地几何花卉纹锦相同, 其残片的宽度及制作方法亦与裤子腰部相同, 因此, 我们推测知这两件残片很有可能原属于这件锦裤的裤腰, 或者可能是另一条裤子的裤腰。

图十二　TAM170:106 背面

4. 手套

树叶纹锦手套(TAM170:45、TAM170:50)出土时分别位于光妃左、右手处。其中 TAM170:45 制为筒形, 高 19 cm、宽 11.5 cm(图十三); TAM170:50, 残损严重, 残高 20 cm、宽 25 cm, 存有部分白绢里(图十四)。原始记录中标明为"手套"的文物还有两件, 其编号为 TAM170:39、40, 出土时位于孝姿右手、左手处, 但没有说明手套所用的织锦。

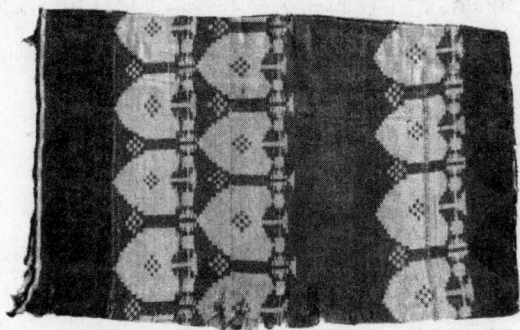

图十三　树叶纹锦手套(TAM170:45)

图十四　树叶纹锦手套(TAM170:50)

有学者认为, 吐鲁番衣物疏中常见词条"手爪囊", 即手套。① TAM170 墓中虽出有手套实物, 但伴出衣物疏中未列"手爪囊"一条。而孝姿及光妃衣物疏中, 成双出现的名目仅有"绣鞾"、"丑衣"、"金钏"、"金钗"、"履"五种, 排除非纺织品的"钏"、"钗"以及明显为足服的"鞾"、"履"四个名目后, 仅剩"丑衣"一条与手套相吻。孝姿衣物疏中是"故树叶锦丑衣二枚", 光妃衣物疏中是"丑衣(两)双", 前者明确指出了所用的织锦是树叶纹锦, 起码与光妃的树叶纹锦手套相吻合。

《说文·丑》:"纽也。十二月, 万物动, 用事。象手之形。时加丑, 亦举手时也。"《后汉书·陈宠传》:"十二月阳气上通, 雉雊、鸡乳, 地以为正, 殷以为春。其字象人举手有为, 又者手也"。又, 《六书正讹》丑:"手械也。从又, 手也, 有物以絷之。象形。因声借为子丑字, 十二月之象也。又丑象子初生举手。"

---

① 王启涛:《吐鲁番出土文书词语考释》, 巴蜀书社, 2005 年。

因"丑"字象手之形,"丑衣"即为手套名的可能性是存在的。① 但查 3～7 世纪吐鲁番及河西出土衣物疏,均未见"丑衣"一词。

5. 枕

橙地彩条花卉大王锦枕(TAM170:24)仅存锦面。枕长 50 cm(两端鸡咀间距离),高 14.5 cm。锦地色分区为黄、红色,显花色为绿、绛、白。纹样沿经向呈条状排列,纹样细小,在小方框中填织"大"、"王"字样,除整片锦面外,另有一直径约 2 cm 的圆形紫绢片,原贴于鸡鸣枕鸡眼处(图十五)。出土时散落于墓室中部,光妃头侧。孝姿、光妃衣物疏中均列有鸡鸣枕条目,而 TAM170:24 形态相似者为孝姿衣物疏中"故绯红锦鸡鸣枕一枚"。

图十五　橙地彩条花卉大王锦枕(TAM170:24)

6. 褥

树叶纹锦缘蓝绢褥(TAM170:85)的褥芯面料为蓝色绢,四周缘以红地树叶纹锦,底衬白色棉布。绢褥残长 127 cm、宽 33 cm,其中锦缘宽约 5 cm(图十六)。出土时居男尸张洪腿部右侧,应该就是孝寅衣物疏中"右被辱(褥)一具"所指。

图十六　树叶纹锦缘蓝绢褥(TAM170:85)

此外,原始登记表上还载录了一件绢褥(TAM170:22),长 164 cm、幅宽 46.5 cm,麻布里,深天青色绢面,用麻线缝制。表上另有一件原登为绿绢、后改为天青绮的天青色楼堞纹绮(TAM170:20),与此紧邻

---

① 有学者认为"丑衣"是一种裹衣,或称(袒)衣,缺佐证。参见钱伯泉《吐鲁番出土魏晋南北朝时期的随葬衣物疏研究》,《吐鲁番学研究》2001 年第 1 期;又王启涛:《吐鲁番出土文书词语考释》,巴蜀书社,2005 年。

出土,而此绮残存较大,基本作平面状,整幅不裁,幅宽约为 51 cm,很有可能正是此件被褥的表面。如是,此件应称天青色楼堞纹绮褥。

三、TAM170 出土丝织品分析

1. 平纹经锦

（1）树叶纹锦

树叶纹锦在此墓中出土最多,目前所见有覆面锦心（TAM170：11、TAM170：12、TAM170：30、TAM170：38、TAM170：69）、缠绕握木（TAM170：34、TAM170：42、TAM170：87）、手套（TAM170：45，TAM170：50）、裙（TAM170：58）；绢褥缘边（TAM170：85）。这件织锦采用的是平纹经二重组织,一组经线为红色,另一组使用蓝、绿、白、黄四色进行交替织造。所以在正面来看,它通常是在红地上作蓝、绿、白、黄色的树叶排列。但在反面,则可以看到是在蓝、绿、白、黄的彩条上排列红色的树叶纹,十分漂亮（图十七）。

图十七　红地树叶纹纹样复原

树叶纹是西域地区以及西方较为常见的装饰题材,在埃及安丁诺曾发现属于 4 至 6 世纪的波斯织物,其中有不少选用植物叶子作主题纹样的情况,它们的造型有点类似扑克牌中的花式造型。[1] 在新疆洛浦县山普拉汉墓群中,也曾发现缂毛的树叶纹坐垫,叶形有些类似葡萄叶。[2] 吐鲁番文书中也屡屡出现树叶锦的记载,其中还有特指明为"柏叶锦"或"大树叶（锦）"者,说明此类织锦甚多。而且,此处的树叶明显受到了西域风格的影响,尤其是叶柄上的绶带更是证据。

锦纹为红地上蓝、米白、米黄及绿色树叶纹。经向循环约为 1.5 cm,纬向循环约为 3.5 cm。其一侧保存有幅边,幅边宽 0.3 cm。

---

[1]　Geijer, A, AHistory Of Textile Art, Pasold Resarch Fund, 1979.

[2]　黄能馥：《中国美术全集·印染织绣》,文物出版社,1986 年。

（2）吹奏人物纹锦

此锦原属于树叶纹锦覆面（TAM170:11）中间的一部分，虽然是一片残片，纹样却十分清晰。左侧部分显示出一幢建筑，屋内有三人席地而坐，左侧一人吹箫，中间一人弹奏琵琶，右侧一人拱手而听（图十八）。

图十八　吹奏人物纹锦

目前同类的织锦在吐鲁番尚未发现，但在国外私人收藏中却有不少保存。伦敦的一件私人收藏保存了更为完整的织物，从中可以知道这一图案的原貌。织物由许多方块间隔出横向的空间，从幅边到幅边。织物中的人物通常都是向右，这样，纹样从右到左的排列为：忍冬纹起头，一人挑拨浪鼓状物，一人吹笙状乐器，一个举旗，此后是一骑马人物，马后还有一人扛一杆，此后为一众兽拉车纹样。车后有一建筑，即与吐鲁番出土者相似，建筑内也有三人，两人右向，一人左向，均作吹、弹乐状。建筑后还有四人，一人行走，一人摇鼓，一人举旗，一人似为牵马，此人后面有一骑马人物正回身引弓射兽，兽后是一树。这样，整个图案就完成了。从那些较为完整的织锦来看，它们的题材总体是宴乐和车马出行，场面气势宏大，早期应多见于汉代画像石及壁画等艺术品中。但在丝织品上的出现已是在北朝时期。

（3）彩条花卉大王锦

彩条纹大王锦（TAM170:24）属于一类纹样极细小、表观呈现彩条的织锦。它采用 1:2 的平纹经重组织，从局部保存较好的色彩及复原的图案来看，它以橙色作地，白色勾边，其纹样主体以蓝和褐色交替出现。纹样的题材总体是花卉，有的是正面的朵花，有的是侧面的小花，类似于忍冬纹。由于纹样的个体较小，整个图案循环在经向很小，在纬向则是呈左右对称排列，循环约为织幅的一半，同时还有主题纹样上的蓝、褐色交替，所以图案呈现彩条状。同时，图案中还有四个小方框，里面分别两次出现大、王两字。因此，我们称此锦为彩条花卉大王锦（图十九）。

图十九　彩条花卉大王锦纹样复原

这类彩条效果的织锦在北朝晚期到隋代之间出现非常频繁,要区分这类织锦的纹样也确实不易。新疆吐鲁番阿斯塔那曾出土过一件天王化生纹锦,锦中织出佛教中的化生形象并有天、王两字。[①] 另一件保存极为完好的藏于伦敦私人手中的吉祥天王锦则有完整的幅边,整个幅宽之中的图案无法完全看清,但已知的内容中包括正面而坐的化生、飞天、凤凰、飞鸟、走兽及各种花卉等。在其经向对称轴上,还间隔织有吉、祥、天、王四字。由此来看,这类彩条纹锦的图案应该与佛教在中国的流行相关,吉祥天王就是最好的例子。而且,TAM170 的这件彩条花卉大王锦中的大王两字,也很有可能就是天王的讹误。

不过,从文书来比较,用这件织锦制成的锦枕应该就是孝姿衣物疏中所提到的"绯红锦枕",因此,这件织锦在当时应该称作绯红锦。绯色一般由红花染成,较易褪色,因此这件织锦的大部分区域都已褪成橙色,但在枕角一端,还可以看到较为鲜艳的红色。由于这类织锦图案很细,而红色的地很大,因此称为绯红锦还是很合适的。

(4)绿地几何花卉纹锦

这件织锦用于红色织锦裤的裤腰(TAM170: 60),另一件是原名为"宝塔纹锦"的一小段腰带(TAM170: 56)和一件名为锦缘麻布条的残片(TAM170: 106),都很有可能来自同一件裤腰。此件织锦采用的也是平纹经重组织,但在不同的区域分别采用1∶1 和1∶2 经线比。总体以绿色作地,白色勾边,褐和黄色作纹样主题。但由于在黄色显花的区域内只是1∶1 的组织结构(好像是勾边的白线也换作了黄线),整个图案就变得很难释读。但总体依然可以判断为变形的花卉纹,更多地带有几何形装饰风格,因此暂称其为绿地几何花卉纹锦(图二十)。

图二十　绿地几何花卉纹锦局部

(5)对波云珠龙凤纹锦

这件织锦原名兽纹锦,出土时发现于一件残存的锦缘领口(TAM170: 41)。此锦采用的是1∶2 的平纹经重组织,总体在深蓝色作地,但在不同的区域分别采用红花白勾、白花黄勾、绿花黄勾等色彩组成(图二十一)。整个以卷云纹和联珠纹构成对波形的骨架,主题纹样目前只能复原出对凤和对龙,凤的形象更

① 新疆博物馆出土文物展览小组:《丝绸之路——汉唐织物》,文物出版社,1972 年。

像站立的朱雀,龙的形象则作行走状,龙凤之下均有忍冬纹构成的平台。与此风格相近的纹样在当时非常多见。同样出土于吐鲁番阿斯塔那墓地的一件对龙对凤纹绮虽然骨架为圆形,但龙凤的造型基本与此相同。敦煌藏经洞发现的楼堞龙凤虎纹锦、都兰吐蕃墓出土的织物中也有大量的联珠对波骨架中的对龙对凤对狮纹样,均可看作是与此相同的题材和风格。

图二十一　对波云珠龙凤纹锦纹样复原

图二十二　绿地对羊纹

2. 平纹纬锦

(1) 绿地对羊纹锦

绿地对羊纹锦(TAM170:66)采用的是平纹纬锦的组织结构,绿色为地,对羊的图案以白色显花,其羊身形矫健,四腿修长,头部长有两只弯曲的角,颈部则系有绶带,随风向后飘成三角形。但在羊体上和羊腿上各有三条红色的色带,其中羊体上的红色色带使得这件织锦在局部必须采用纬线1∶2纬重组织。不过,这种红色的点缀色泽对比强烈,增加了织物的艳丽感(图二十二)。

这类平纹纬重组织是典型的西域本地技术,其无骨架的对称排列也被看成是西域一带的织锦图案排列方法,直到在唐代中期,大量被认为是中亚织物的斜纹纬锦如对鹰、对饮水马等织锦大多是沿纬向方向展开,左右对称。可以说,这是西方特有的图案循环方式,可能是新疆当地的丝织产品。[1]

(2) 红地人面鸟兽纹锦

红地人面鸟兽纹锦是一条同名锦裤(TAM170:60)的主要面料。它采用1∶1和1∶2的平纹纬重组织,经纬丝线均较粗,夹经双根,加有较强的Z捻,其余丝线亦紧,但其捻度与捻向不很明显。织锦通体在红地上以黄色或白色、有时还有紫色显示纹样。其基本图案在用约5 cm的圆角方形线条构成的方格骨架中填以各种纹样,其中主要是人面和鸟兽纹,也有部分其他纹样。从王乐进行的研究来看,本件红地人面鸟兽纹锦的原织物的宽度约在65 cm,为幅宽,长度约170 cm。一幅中应有方格12列,一列方格就是一个纬向图案循环,经向的长度上约有方格29行,各行之间的方格中填入不同的图案,其基本规律是

---

[1]　赵丰:《中国丝绸艺术史》,文物出版社,2005年。

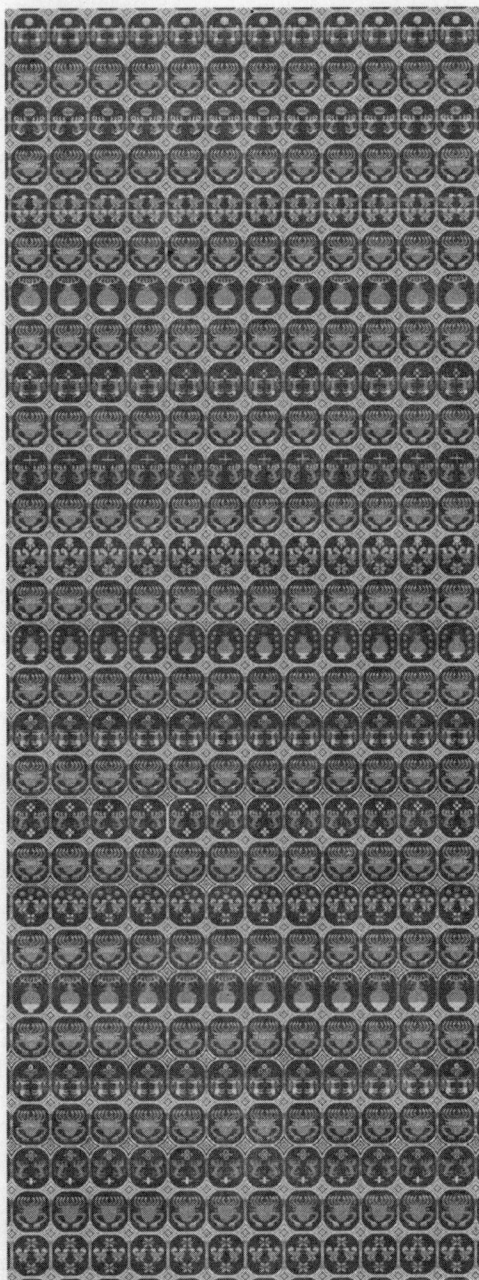

图二十三　红地人面鸟兽纹锦纹样复原

每隔一行就有一行人面（或兽面）的纹样，其余是四行为一个单元，由上至下分别可能是对鹿、对狮、对孔雀和花瓶。但每一对鹿、狮、孔雀和花瓶的造型也各不相同，因此这一图案在经向还是没有循环（图二十三）。①

（3）团窠卷云对兽对凤纹锦

红地人面鸟兽纹锦裤（TAM170:60）的腰部的正面以及锦裤上部折褶处由一种团窠卷云纹锦作为面料。由于织物较为残破，只能看清其作卷云纹作环形成互不相连的团窠进行排列，团窠之外是四片小叶的十样花纹，团窠之内的纹样不清，较为明显的有对兽纹样和一对残了的对凤纹样。织锦采用1∶1的平纹纬重组织，红、白两色纬线互为花地，但在正面看是白地红花（图二十四）。经纬丝线均无捻，与绿地对羊纹锦的技术特点较为相似。

图二十四　团窠卷云对兽对凤纹锦纹样复原

3. 平纹地显花的绮

（1）黄色龟背纹绮

黄色龟背纹绮是一件紫绢作腰、黄绮为面、白纱为里的裙子的主要面料（TAM170:99），它以平纹为地，以并丝织法织成的变化斜纹显花。织物以正六边形的联珠或直线作骨架，在六边形的骨架中置以龟背、朵花等其他几何花纹（图二十五），其中的龟纹据说可能是受了印度文化的影响。这类织物一直到青海都兰热水墓中仍有出土，在日本正仓院中也见保存。

（2）紫色楼墱立人对龙纹绮

紫色楼墱立人对凤纹绮应是出土紫绫衣（TAM170:61）的面料，它也是以平纹作地、并丝织法织成的

---

① 新疆文物考古研究所：《吐鲁番阿斯塔那第十次发掘简报（1972～1973）》，《新疆文物》2000第3、4期。

图二十五　黄色龟背纹绮纹样复原

变化斜纹显花。图案的主要骨架是两排对称的以三层卷云纹叠成的 S 形楼堞纹,在楼堞之外是对龙纹,楼堞之内各站立有一个立人。而在两立人之间还有一处近似于人面纹的纹样,但不知其原意(图二十六)。

图二十六　紫色楼堞立人对龙纹绮纹样复原

楼堞锦一名最早见于《大业拾遗记》,书中曾说周成王时就已有"楼堞锦",说其为周成王时代就已存在显然有误,但此书成于隋代,十分有可能就是涡云式云气动物纹锦的反映。而楼堞或层楼的结构设计则可能是受了西方柱式和圈拱建筑造型的影响,这从罗马斗兽场的造型和楼堞纹之间的相似性中就可以看出。

(3) 天青色楼堞纹绮

可能是某件被褥的面料(TAM170:22)。但事实上,这件织绮的图案骨架也是两排同向的卷云楼堞纹,但这楼堞纹上的卷云只有两层,较上件紫色绮来自较为简单些,骨架里面看不清有具体种类的动物或植物(图二十七)。

图二十七　天青色楼堞纹绮纹样复原

（4）褐色大窠联珠狮纹绮

褐色大窠联珠狮纹绮（TAM170:59）是北朝时期十分难得一见的大窠图案，它用平纹作地，也是变化斜纹起花。织物的幅宽约为50 cm，其团窠图案的直径也应该在50 cm左右。团窠环分为内外两层，里环由莲花瓣组成，外层环是联珠纹。与一般团窠不同的是，这一图案在团窠内还有联珠柱将其分为四个区域。在靠近幅边的两个区域中，布置的是两个对狮纹样（图二十八）。这狮子的纹样不是很清楚，较难复原。其他的地方也存在着同样的问题。

图二十八　褐色大窠联珠狮纹绮纹样复原

（5）黄色联珠石柱纹绮

此绮原来未被重视（TAM170:25），直到后来才从龟背纹绮中区别开来。虽然简单，但很有研究价值。此绮的图案在长方形的框架内连续排列多处联珠，与楼堞图案中作为柱子的部分十分接近，也与唐代初期团窠双珠对龙纹绮中间的石柱十分接近，因此，我们推测这很有可能就是孝姿衣物疏中提到的"石柱小绫"（图二十九）。

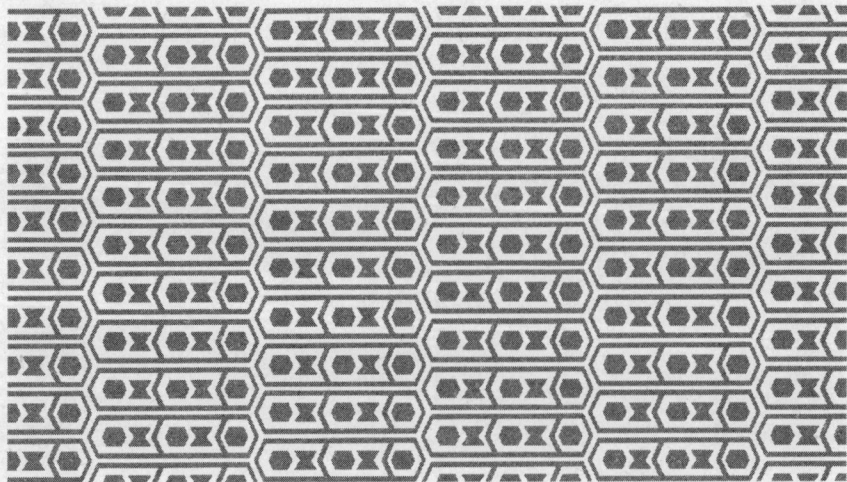

图二十九　黄色联珠石柱纹绮纹样复原

（6）绿色几何纹绮

是属于锦裤（TAM170:60）腰部上面侧部的一种绿色面料，只有几何格子纹出现。

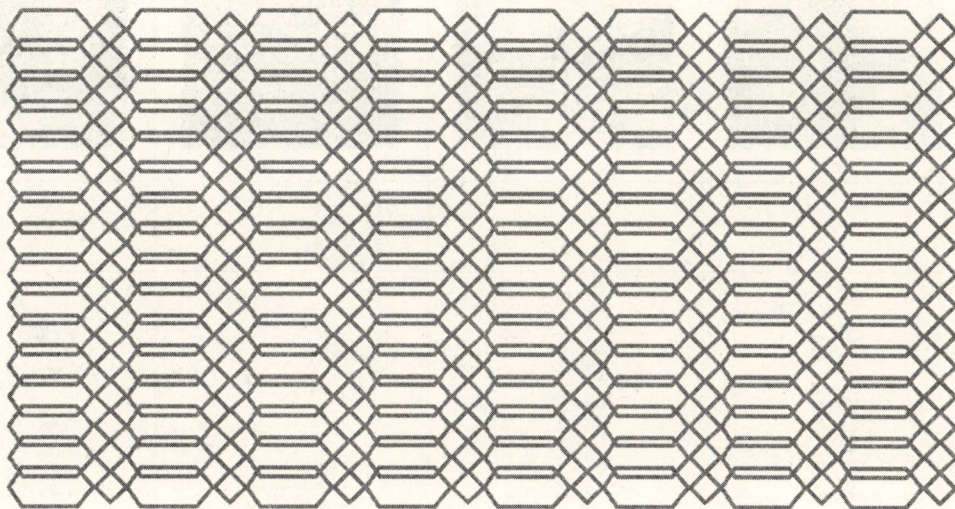

图三十　绿色几何纹绮纹样复原

下面将 TAM170 中所有的丝织品（包括其他纺织品）的分析均列表如表二。

四、小　　结

经过以上我们对吐鲁番阿斯塔那 TAM170 墓出土丝织品考古发掘原始档案的整理、对目前我们所能见到出土丝织品的分析研究以及对于同出衣物疏的比较研究，我们得出以下结论：

1. TAM170 的原始发掘记录还是比较完整，可以作为将来整理吐鲁番阿斯塔那墓地出土报告的主要依据。但与实物之间的比较核对，还需要较大的工作量才能完成。我们通过比对形成了一份与原始记录基本吻合的清单，并纠正了其中的一些笔误，标明了我们看到的实物，并对进行了重新定名。

2. TAM170 中出土的丝织品原状好于我们的预测，其中大部分可以判断其原来的款式，如覆面、褥、手套、握木、上衣、裤、裙、枕、褥等等，其中大部分可以通过保护修复后得到较为完整的形状与尺寸。这对吐鲁番出土丝织品的修复保护具有很大的指导意义。

3. TAM170 中出土的丝织品种类也十分丰富，其中包括平纹经锦、平纹纬锦、绮、纱、绢等。特别是锦绮的图案相当复杂，其中不仅可以发现大量的树叶纹锦，同时还有吹奏人物纹锦、彩条纹花卉大王锦、几何花卉纹锦、对波云珠龙凤纹锦、红地人面鸟兽纹锦、团窠卷云对兽对凤纹锦、绿地对羊纹锦等平时出现不多的织锦，此外还有一些平时连图案也不很清楚的黄色石柱联珠纹绮、天青色楼堞纹绮、褐色大窠联珠狮纹绮、紫色楼堞立人对龙纹绮和黄色龟背纹绮等图案。

4. 通过 TAM170 出土丝织品与同墓出土衣物的疏的对比研究，我们发现其中有不少名物可以对照起来。如丑衣就是手套、合蠡纹锦裤就是红地人面对鸟兽纹锦裤、绯红锦就是彩条花卉大王锦、石柱小绫就是石柱联珠纹绮等。从出土实物与文书的比对，常常可以获得最为真实的文书研究结果。

表二　主要出土丝织品的组织结构

文物号	织物名称	用途	经线	纬线	组织结构	图案	幅宽	组织结构图
72TAM170:11a	树叶纹锦	覆面锦芯	丝，无捻，红、白、蓝、绿、黄色，62套/cm	明纬：丝，无捻，红色，双根排列，14×2根/cm；夹纬：丝，无捻，双根排列，14×2根/cm	1:1平纹经重	树叶纹。循环：经向：3cm；纬向：7cm。		
72TAM170:11b	吹奏人物纹锦	覆面锦芯之一部分	丝，无捻，红、白、绿、浅褐色，42套/cm	明纬：丝，无捻，红色，双根排列，14×2根/cm；夹纬：丝，无捻，双根排列，14×2根/cm	平纹经锦	建筑、吹奏人物、忍冬纹。循环：经向：约7cm。		
72TAM170:11c	白纱	覆面荷叶边	丝，无捻，单根排列，白色，46根/cm	丝，无捻，双根排列，24×2根/cm	1/1平纹			
72TAM170:12a	树叶纹锦	覆面锦芯	丝，无捻，红、白、蓝、绿、黄色，62套/cm	明纬：丝，无捻，红色，双根排列，14×2根/cm；夹纬：丝，无捻，双根排列，14×2根/cm	平纹经锦	树叶纹。循环：经向：3cm；纬向：每叶约长7cm。		

续 表

文物号	织物名称	用途	经线	纬线	组织结构	图案	幅宽	组织结构图
72TAM170:12b	紫色绮	覆面荷叶边	丝，无捻，单根排列，紫红色，50根/cm	丝，无捻，单根排列，紫红色，28根/cm	1/1 平纹地上以 1/3Z 斜纹显花			
72TAM170:12c	白纱	覆面荷叶边衬	丝，无捻，白色，48根/cm	丝，无捻，双根排列，白色，18×2根/cm	1/1 平纹			
72TAM170:20	天青色楼蝶纹绮	裤子面料	丝，无捻，单根排列，天青色，52根/cm	丝，无捻，单根排列，天青色，33根/cm	1/1 平纹地上以 1/3Z 斜纹显花	几何纹，植物涡卷。循环：经向：4 cm；纬向：50 cm。	51 cm	
72TAM170:24a	彩条花卉大王锦	鸡鸣枕面料	丝，无捻，橙、白、绿、褐色，62套/cm	明纬：丝，无捻，红色，双根排列，18×2根/cm；夹纬：丝，无捻，红色，双根排列，18×2根/cm	平纹经锦	植物，花卉，"大，王"。循环：经向：1.5 cm；纬向：55 cm，左右对称。	55 cm	

续表

文物号	织物名称	用途	经线	纬线	组织结构	图案	幅宽	组织结构图
72TAM170:24b	紫红绮	鸡鸣枕上作鸡眼	丝，无捻，单根排列，紫红色，48根/cm	丝，无捻，单根排列，紫红色，41根/cm	1/1平纹地1/3S斜纹显花			
72TAM170:25	黄色联珠石柱纹绮	用途不明	丝，无捻，单根排列，黄色，53根/cm	丝，无捻，单根排列，黄色，34根/cm	1/1平纹地3/1SZ斜纹显花	长六边形，中有联珠等纹样。循环：经向：0.7cm；纬向：六边形长约3.5cm。		
72TAM170:41	对波云珠龙凤纹锦	锦褶领口	丝，无捻，红、蓝、黄色，44套/cm	明纬：丝，无捻，红色，单根排列，13根/cm；夹纬：丝，无捻，红色，单根排列，13根/cm	平纹经锦	联珠和涡云构成对波纹骨架，内填对兽纹和对凤纹。循环：经向：约8cm。		
72TAM170:45	树叶纹锦	手套面料	丝，无捻，红、白、蓝、绿、黄色，62套/cm	明纬：丝，无捻，红色，双根排列，14×2根/cm；夹纬：丝，无捻，红色，双根排列，14×2根/cm	平纹经锦	树叶纹。循环：经向：3cm；纬向：7cm。		

续表

文物号	织物名称	用途	经线	纬线	组织结构	图案	幅宽	组织结构图
72TAM170:50	树叶纹锦	手套面料	丝、无捻、红、白、蓝、绿、黄色，62套/cm	明纬：丝，无捻，红色，双根排列，14×2根/cm；夹纬：丝，无捻，红色，双根排列，14×2根/cm	平纹经锦	树叶纹。循环：经向：3 cm；纬向：7 cm。		
72TAM170:56	绿地几何花卉纹锦	腰带	丝，无捻，红、白、黄、绿色，42套/cm	明纬：丝，无捻，暗红色，14×2根/cm；夹纬：丝，无捻，双根排列，14×2根/cm	平纹经锦	几何花卉纹。循环：经向：5.5 cm。		
72TAM170:58	树叶纹锦	锦裤面料	丝，无捻，红、白、蓝、绿、黄色，62套/cm	明纬：丝，无捻，红色，双根排列，14×2根/cm；夹纬：丝，无捻，红色，双根排列，14×2根/cm	平纹经锦	树叶纹。循环：经向：3 cm；纬向：7 cm。		
72TAM170:59	褐色大窠联珠狮纹绮	用途不明	丝，无捻，单根排列，绛色，44根/cm	丝，无捻，单根排列，绛色，24根/cm	1/1平纹地上以2～4并丝织法显花	联珠和花瓣构成团窠环，环内两两对狮。循环：经向：45 cm；纬向：50 cm。	50 cm	

续 表

文物号	织物名称	用途	经 线	纬 线	组织结构	图 案	幅宽	组织结构图
72TAM170:60a	红地人面鸟兽纹锦	锦裤面料	明经:丝,Z捻,单根排列,浅褐色,10根/cm;夹经:丝,Z捻,双根排列,浅褐色,10×2根/cm	丝,无捻,红、土黄、白、蓝色,22副/cm	平纹纬锦	人面、鸟、兽、花瓶等。循环:纬向:5.3 cm。	65 cm	
72TAM170:60b	蓝色绢	锦裤胯裆处	丝,无捻,单根排列,蓝色,55根/cm	丝,无捻,单根排列,蓝色,28副/cm	1/1平纹			
72TAM170:60c	绿色几何纹绮	锦裤胯裆处	丝,无捻,单根排列,黄绿色,58根/cm	丝,无捻,单根排列,黄绿色,34根/cm	1/1平纹地上以3/1S斜纹显花	六边形菱格。循环:经向:0.6 cm;纬向:2.3 cm。		
72TAM170:60d	团窠卷云对兽对凤纹锦	锦裤胯裆处和腰部	明经:丝,无捻,单根排列,暗红色,18根/cm;夹经:丝,无捻,单根排列,暗红色,18根/cm	丝,无捻,红、白色,28副/cm	平纹纬锦	卷云环、对兽、对凤等。循环:纬向:3.2 cm。		

续 表

文 物 号	织物名称	用途	经 线	纬 线	组织结构	图 案	幅宽	组织结构图
72TAM170:60e	绿地几何花卉纹锦	腰带	丝,无捻,红、白、黄、绿色,42套/cm	明纬:丝,无捻,双根排列,暗红色,14×2根/cm;夹纬:丝,无捻,双根排列,暗红色,14×2根/cm	平纹经锦	几何花卉纹。循环:经向:5.5cm。		
72TAM170:61a	紫色楼堞立人对龙纹绮	上衣面料	丝,无捻,单根排列,绛色,56根/cm	丝,无捻,单根排列,绛色,42根/cm	1/1平纹地1/3SZ斜纹显花	楼堞、立人、对龙纹。循环:经向:3.5cm;纬向:50cm。	50cm	
72TAM170:61b	白纱	上衣衬里	丝,无捻,单根排列,白色,34根/cm	丝,无捻,双根排列,白色,34×2根/cm	1/1平纹			
72TAM170:66	绿地对羊纹锦	覆面锦芯	明经:丝,无捻,双根排列,暗红色,13×2根/cm;夹经:丝,无捻,四根排列,暗红色,13×2根/cm	丝,无捻,红、白、绿色,23副/cm	平纹纬锦	对羊。循环:经向:12.3cm;纬向:9.2cm。		

续表

文物号	织物名称	用途	经线	纬线	组织结构	图案	幅宽	组织结构图
72TAM170:85a	树叶纹锦	绢裤缘边	丝、无捻、红、白、蓝、绿、黄色,62套/cm	明纬：丝，无捻，红色，双根排列，14×2根/cm；夹纬：丝，无捻，红色，双根排列，14×2根/cm	平纹经锦	树叶纹。循环：经向：3cm;纬向：7cm。		
72TAM170:85b	蓝绢	绢裤面料	丝、无捻、单根排列，蓝色,56根/cm	丝，无捻，单根排列，蓝色,30根/cm	1/1平纹			
72TAM170:85c	白麻布	绢裤衬底	麻，S捻，单根排列，白色,13根/cm	麻，S捻，单根排列，白色,10根/cm	1/1平纹			
72TAM170:99a	黄色龟背纹绮	裙面料	丝，无捻，单根排列，黄色,49根/cm	丝，无捻，单根排列，黄色,33根/cm	1/1平纹地3/1SZ斜纹显花	龟背骨架中填以小花、龟纹。循环：经向：3cm;纬向：龟背循环6cm。		

续 表

文物号	织物名称	用途	经线	纬线	组织结构	图案	幅宽	组织结构图
72TAM170:99b	紫色绢	裙腰	丝,无捻,单根排列,紫红色,46根/cm	丝,无捻,单根排列,黄色,29根/cm	1/1 平纹			
72TAM170:99c	白纱	裙衬里	丝,无捻,白色,42根/cm	丝,无捻,双根排列,白色,13×2根/cm	1/1 平纹			
72TAM170:106a	绿地几何花卉纹锦	腰带	丝,无捻,红、白、黄、绿色,42套/cm	明纬:丝,无捻,暗红色,14×2根/cm;夹纬:丝,无捻,双根排列,暗红色,14×2根/cm	平纹经锦	几何花卉纹。循环:经向:5.5 cm。		
72TAM170:106b	白麻布	腰带里	麻,S捻,单根排列,白色,10根/cm	麻,S捻,单根排列,白色,9根/cm	1/1 平纹			

The Wither Away of Aiding Kol and Taite-Mar Lake

梁匡一

中国科学院新疆生态与地理研究所遥感技术研究室

Xinjiang is an inner most continental arid region. Its orientation is 42°40′– 42°35′; 89°12′– 89°35′. It was formed in geological era when there had been plenty of rain and snow, that formed big rivers and thick snow, especially in the Kun-lun mountain, with the orogenic movement, the Kun-lun was greatly uplifted and it gained more snow. Many big rivers flow grand flood, that fed many oases. But before these several hundred years there had been very slight human activities compared with the great territory.

Begin with with this several era, the snow line retreated, rainfall decreased because of the environmental change, the whole Xinjiang became drier and drier.

In Xinjiang, either in intermountain or in the plain, the relief of the earth surface caused some depressions and many of them formed lakes.

Turpan Basin is a very deep depression. It was formed by geoneotectonics in early stage of Quaternery epoch. It is famous of its depth — the second deepest depression in the world – 154 m. (i.e. under the sea level). It collects all the waters that run down from the northern mountain Tianshan (they are the melted water), but passed through the Flamming Mountain (Cenozoic strata) — through 3 streams (ground water returned to ground surface).

After the using for agriculture by a kind of hydraulic measure — karez, it irrigated all the farming land. In the winter time the irrigation mostly stopped so the rest of karez water and Bai-yang-gou river water flowed into the basin, thus formed the Aiding Kol.

The Aiding Kol lake, in fact, is exactly occupied the depression, no water can flow out of this basin; the exhaustion of the basin water is by evaporation, very little part of the exhaustion is to sink down to the very depth of the basin.

No exact research on the formation of the Aiding Kol lake. We know only the size of Aiding Kol had a length of 24$^+$ km. in E-W direction and 2.5 – 3 km in S-N direction, its area was 469 km^2, but by Landsat image of 1976, it decreased to 307 km^2 before when it withered out.

The total amount of karez water and river water until now it is impossible to be measured — nobody can measure each of these karez has how much residual water flowed into the lake, nor the river water from Bai-Yang-Gou, they vary greatly in different seasons. Hundred years before, the farmers have no idea of winter irrigation, so there had been a lots of water flowed into the lake, but begin from 1960, the farmers recognized the benefits of winter irrigation, since then there have less or even no water flowed in. The lake

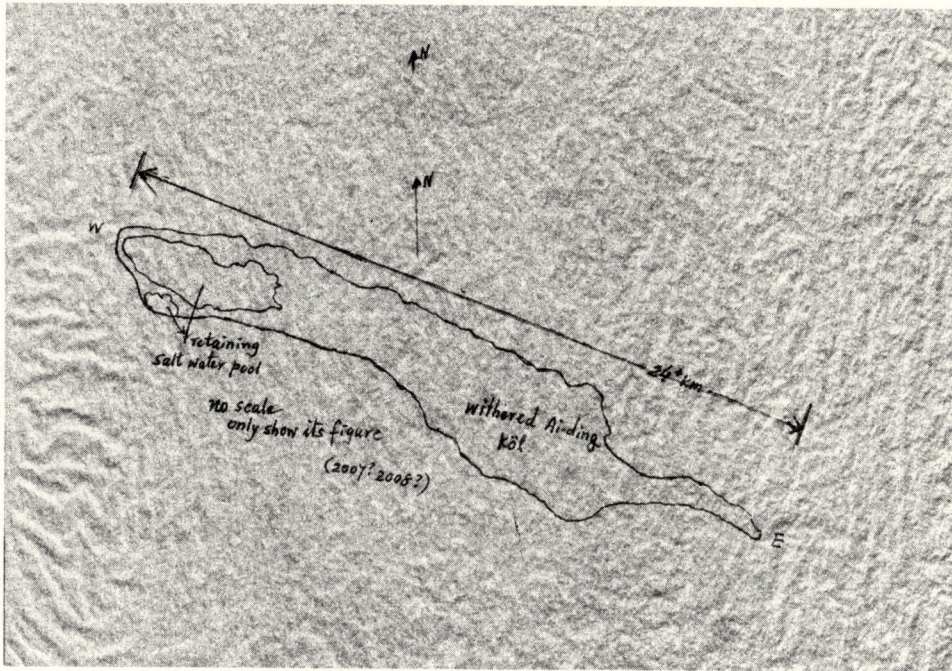

The Aiding Kol Lake — a sketch map

water under the furious evaporation became gradually less and less water left, lastly it became withered out.

In December 1, 1959 I once got the chance dropped in the center of the lake to make an investigation, the depth of the lake water was 18 cm. I discovered the mirabolite crystals on the bottom in needle form but the bottom was not sinkable. I took the lake water sample, its mineralizatioin was 316–326 g/l, cl-na typed water. In year 1988, I had other chances to investigate the natural conditions of the Aiding Kol at the most NE corner, I found it had already withered up — may be several years before it was already dried out, and I doubted the lake mud must be sinkable, I didn't stepped in.

On the north bank of the Aiding Kol there was a salt crystal belt about 2 km wide and nearly 25 km long, because the karez lake water formed groundwater and it suffered furious evaporation, and it became concentrated during a long period thus constructed an undulated salt crystal belt around the north bank; but strange enough, there are none salt crystal belt on the south lake bank.

Taite-mar (Kol) Lake

On the southern slope of Kun-lun Mountain Range, and on its terminus of diluvial fans, there existed a lake in the historical period, it had a long history but failed to extend its life due to the bitter arid weather. On its east side, there had been another near distant neighbor lake called Kara-kushun it died earlier than this lake.

This lake is called Taite-mar kol (lake), it was on the terminus of Tarim River, in fact, this lake was fed not only by Tarim River water but also by the older Kun-que Daria (River) from the north and the Cherchen River from west. Its most prosperous period was the same period with the Tarim River — several thousand years ago, when there had been very slight or none human activities. It had an area nearly 10×10 km². (see attached figure) September 25 1964, I, together with Prof. PENG jia mu, we stood on the western bank of the lake and saw the lake was full of water, we looked far distant east but can't see the terminus, that meant it was a big lake, the water was fresh water; on the southern bank there was dense reeds; the feeding water from Cherchen River continues flowed in, and we also saw the footprint of a wild boar, all these showed a vivid life. I also investigated the inlet of the lake, the Tarim River cut deep river bed in 6. 2 m, and still it formed a small waterfall. The inlet has an altitude of 811 m. in the center of the lake is 805 m. But in the summer of 1983, our Tarim Expedition again came and investigated the lake, the lake water disappeared and left a bare bottom with several gastropoda crusts, and everywhere the cracks.

Interesting to know that the flowed-in water was from the Tarim River, but in the historical period it was both from Tarim River and Kun-que Daria, because the river bed belong to the Kun-que Daria (daria means river), the geological history showed that the Tarim River snatched the river bed of Kun-que daria at Aragan, because of the uplift of Tiliyati mountain (a neotectonic movement in early Quaternery epoch), this new uplift of the mountain obstructed the flow direction of Tarim River to the south.

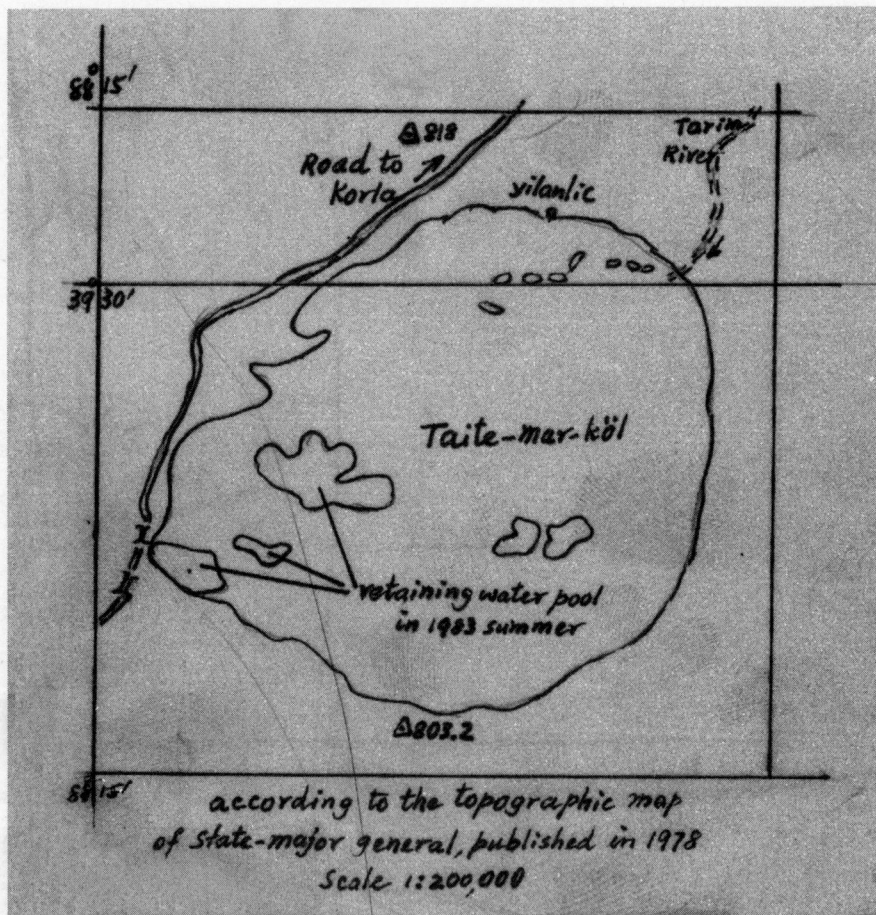

The old Kun-que Daria also fed the Taite-mar lake, at Aragan (in Svin-Hedin's literature) it was called as "Alelgan" the Kun-que Daria in this river section was called Na-sheng River, when we did the research work with Russian researcher Prof. KUNIN, we saw the river was 6 m. deep, and flowed full of water in August 1958, and in September 1964 it was still full of water, but in August of 1983 the river was dried out because the water reservoir was constructed and sealed the Tarim river water out.

Another peculiarity of Taite-mar kol (lake), was that it played a role of a regulatary water reservoir — the Tarim River water flowed in, it accepted and stored, but at the same time it flowed out to the east to feed old Kara-kushun kol, (this was the old lake that Svin-hedin mistook as the Lop-nor lake that had migrated to this place in every 15 years, but because he had not a precise topographic map, nor aerophotos and Landsat images, in fact, Lop-nor never had migrated). And in the east border, it had also an outlet, its water flowed out and fed into Lop-nor; this Kara-Kushun was also mentioned by Pridgevalski in 1887, but he didn't know this lake had relation with Taite-mar Kol and Lop-nor Lake.

Unexpectedly with the shallow water depth, very rare precipitation, (in Ruo-qiang county the annual precipitation is 9 mm) furious evaporation is 2500^+ mm, and the most important cause was the block up of Tarim River by the Da-xi-hai-zi water reservoir dam in 1964, since then no more water flow into Taite-mar Kol, thus the impact from both the natural and artificial calamities, such an ecologic and useful and valuable lake withered away forever.

用地理信息系统看新疆史前时代遗址的分布

后藤　健（Goto Ken）

早稻田大学

对考古学研究而言,空间分析是一项重要方法。近年来,相当一部分学者注意到考古资料的空间和地理分布,开始考虑其与人类的社会、文化的密切联系。目前有许多借助考古资料的空间布局关系分析探讨人类文化和社会组织模式的研究,但所需处理的数据十分复杂,处理时间和空间系统中的考古信息对理论的验证较困难。因此,有必要寻求新的考古学空间分析技术方法。地理信息系统（Geographic Information Systems）是基于空间信息的采集、管理、分析与综合应用系统。特别是对处理大规模空间信息具有独特的优势,受到了考古专家的重视,被利用到聚落考古的研究。① 目前已经有了许多应用 GIS 的区域考古研究,在考古学上的应用在 1990 年代以后也增加了,考古学上的地理信息系统的方法和理论还不够成熟,对分析人地的关系,有关资料也比较少,但为了处理此后增加的考古资料,地理信息系统的方法仍然具有重要作用。本文以现有的调查资料为基础,尝试应用 GIS 分析对新疆史前时代遗址的空间布置做些初步的分析,提出几点认识。

一、新疆史前时代考古遗址的分布

随着近年来考古调查的增加,已发掘的新疆史前时代的遗址已经超过一千多处。目前新疆境内正在开展考古学文化的分组、分期等分析工作。东部哈密地区的焉不拉克文化、吐鲁番盆地的苏贝希文化、和静的察吾呼文化、西部伊犁地区的伊犁流域文化等具有地域性特征的考古学文化的面貌,越来越凸显出来。韩建业对新疆史前文化进行分成小区和三段五期的分期。②

他将整个新疆分成塔里木盆地北缘小区、吐鲁番盆地——中部天山北麓小区、哈密盆地——巴里坤草原小区、伊犁河流域小区、塔里木盆地南缘小区、石河子——乌苏小区、帕米尔小区、阿尔泰小区、罗布泊小区、塔城小区等十个小区,以及以公元前 1900～1300 年（第一阶段一期）为青铜时代,早期铁器时代分为公元前 1300～1100 年（第二阶段二期）,公元前 1100～800 年（第二阶段三期）,公元前 800～500 年（第二阶段四期）,公元前 500～100 年（第三阶段五期）。这些地区内,哈密盆地——巴里坤草原小区,吐鲁番盆地——中部天山北麓地域,塔里木盆地北缘,伊犁河流域发现了较丰富的考古资料。但大部分是由普查获得的表采资料,详细的面貌还不清楚。

许多报告中记载有遗址所在地方的经纬度信息,因此我们可以把握遗址的大概位置。同时,在新疆

---

① 地理信息系统的概要参见刘建国《考古与地理信息系统》,科学出版社,2007 年。
② 韩建业:《新疆的青铜器时代和早期铁器时代文化》,文物出版社,2007 年。

的墓葬大多地上有土堆和石堆等,如不经过发掘调查也能确认墓葬的所在。目前利用 Google Earth 等免费的软件,可以较简单地便能参照高分辨率的卫星照片。至今为止,尚未开展利用卫星照片和航空照片进行确认遗址的工作。现在的最高分辨率卫星照片上,可以明确辨认较大规模的遗址,如伊犁地区夏塔墓地,从墓葬的排列等就能明显看出。利用这样的照片可确认没有报告的墓葬,记录其位置和范围。本文按照已经报告的遗址和卫星照片上确认的遗址位置信息,进行遗址位置信息的数据化。然后,应用地理信息系统的方法,对遗址的分布进行初步的分析。

本文有关遗址的信息数据主要采自新疆各个地区的普查报告,部分采自发表于各类刊物的考古调查和发掘简报,同时参考卫星照片上确认的未报告遗址。底图使用的是美国 NASA 公开的 SRTM 数字高程模型(DEM)。

二、地势和遗址分布的倾向

新疆史前时代的遗址大部分分布于塔克拉玛干沙漠和准噶尔盆地内外,特别是在天山山脉的南麓和北麓。遗址大都是墓葬,但当时的聚落也有发现。如巴里坤岳公台遗址——西黑沟遗址群[1]和东黑沟遗址,[2]其祭祀遗迹、石围基址、墓葬和岩画等分布于一定的范围内。有的地区也发现许多岩画。这些遗址具有哪些特征?遗址的分布有什么规律性?

首先用 SRTM 数字地形模型对所在遗址地方的地势进行分析。新疆境内大概海拔约 –170 至 6 000 米。遗址分布于海拔 –150 至 4 000 米之间,特别是 1 000 至 2 000 米之间的地带很多。地面坡度是 0 至 20 度之间,遗址多存在小于 17 度的地点,最多的是 5 度左右的缓慢倾斜地。

遗址最多分布于朝南坡面,朝西、东的方向相当少。古代人居住时选择朝南的坡向可以接受更多的日照,较少经受寒冷的风。因此选择朝南向坡面是合理的。这是整个新疆的倾向。

三、哈密盆地——巴里坤草原小区的倾向

哈密盆地——巴里坤草原小区,天山山脉穿过中间,包括多种多样的环境。石围基址、岩画、墓葬等发现较多,分布较密集。

墓葬主要分布于东天山山脉的南北麓,这个地区哈密盆地南部以外,墓葬、石围基址以及岩画都在同一遗址之内,或者非常接近的地点。这类的遗址目前超过 40 个。[3]

石围基址,在甘肃、乌鲁木齐、温泉以及中亚的哈萨克斯坦等地方也有发现。目前哈密地区的发现最多。这样的遗址有作为季节性的聚落的可能性。

西北部的巴里坤地区的墓葬集中于天山北麓,基本上位于从急斜面向稍平坦过渡的山麓,平原几乎没有遗址存在。在高山也基本没有发现,北部遗址也少。已发掘的遗址有岳公台——西黑沟遗迹群,东黑沟遗迹和南湾墓地。基本上属于一期,平坦地的遗址稍晚,但无法做出准确判断。东北的伊吾地区的

① 西北大学考古专业、哈密地区文管会:《新疆巴里坤岳公台——西黑沟遗址群调查》,《考古与文物》2005 年 2 期。
② 西北大学考古专业、哈密地区文管会:《2006 年巴里坤东黑沟遗址调查》,《新疆文物》2007 年 2 期。
③ 《哈密文物志》编撰组:《哈密文物志》,新疆人民出版社,1993 年。

墓葬集中于伊吾沟的流域,分布于丘陵和台地上,平坦地上非常少。一期的遗址较多。哈密地区南部,遗址分布于天山南麓和远离山脉的盆地内部。在天山南麓,西部与巴里坤同样,墓葬位于山麓、沟谷附近为多;东部的一部分遗址分布于山腰。南方的盆地基本沿着水系分布于远离山脉的平坦地。在盆地没发现石围基址和岩画,布局和遗迹的种类上是与山麓地带区别的一个独立区。

石围基址集中于海拔1 000～2 200米,墓葬在200～2 200米,岩画在1 100～2 500米的地方。遗址之间有时期的差别,较晚的遗址有从低地向高地移动的倾向。

(一) 水文的分析

有了地形数据复原水流路径的方法,现在没有水的旧河川也可能复原。哈密地区的遗址基本上是在复原水流路径约300米的范围内,遗址的选择很可能是与靠近水源的需要有关,或者说水源是当时选择居住地点的重要条件。

(二) 最短路径

对遗址布局的研究而言,人们的移动是重要的因素。当然,当时的居民不是孤立活动的,应该有些交流。那么,他们在怎样的途径移动? 路径和遗址的关系怎样? 作为复原史前交通的一个要素,要分析最短路径。所谓最短路径,是指以地形的坡度为主,算出人的步行速度,决定耗费最短时间的途径的方法。[①] 这个办法以地形的坡度为主要的因素,当然由于步行或者骑马,或者使用其他的方法,路径也会变化。但除此以外现在没有适合的分析方法为一个例子进行分析。

我们可以以人们活动规模较大的岳公台——西黑沟(兰州湾子)遗址和乌拉台遗址为基点算出最短路径。这两个遗址之间,越过东天山山脉中央附近是最短的路径。可是,如果考虑到其他遗址的路径,越过山岭的地点也还有几个。当然,由于是去那个遗址,选择别的路径的可能性不高。

(三) 可视域分析

可视域是从一点或几点上能够观察到的范围。遗址间的可视与相互通视的观点在考古学分析中有十分重要的意义。古代人在选择居住地、墓葬的位置时,往往会考虑可视性。但是现有考古的材料尚不够完备,可视性研究还不能很好地开展。这次分析从各个岩画能看到的范围。哈密地区的岩画分布于山脚和山腰。山脚的岩画靠近石构件建筑和墓葬,但山腰的岩画是较孤立的。相互通视的岩画非常少,能看到墓葬等的岩画地点也少。山腰的岩画和其他遗址的关系不密切。选择那样地方的原因现在不清楚(图一)。

四、伊犁河流域地区的分布

伊犁河流域地区位于新疆的西北部,上流是植被很好的高山,中下流是河川两岸开阔的地势,周围围绕山脉,中部形成伊犁河谷。水系有伊犁河、喀什河、巩乃斯河和特克斯河等。

在伊犁地区的穷科克遗址[②]和七十一团遗址[③]发现居住遗迹。在穷科克遗址,房址分布于墓地的周

---

① Kantner, John 1996 *An Evaluation of Chaco Anasazi Roadways*. Current Technology Applied to Archaeology Poster Session, 61st Society for American Archaeology Annual Meeting, pp. 1 – 22.

② 新疆文物考古研究所:《尼勒克县穷科克一号墓地考古发掘调查》,《新疆文物》2000 年 3、4 期。

③ 新疆博物馆文物队:《新源县七十一团一连渔场遗址》,《新疆文物》1987 年 3 期。

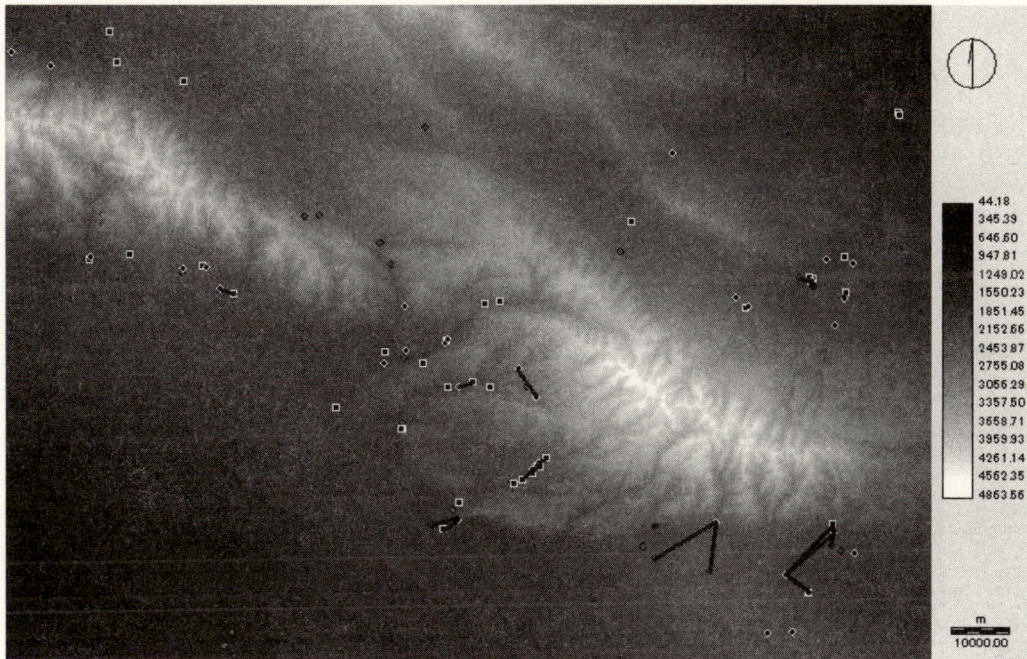

图一　遗址之间的可视关系（黑线：互相通视的遗址）

围,有石围基址。在七十一团遗址发现房址、灰坑、墓葬,居住区和墓区明显接近。因资料较少,因此整体倾向的把握较困难,不过,一些主要的遗址有沿河分布的趋势。

墓葬遍地分布。基本上分布于山脚,一部分的墓地在远离山麓的平原,多数位于沟谷,也有沿着喀什河、特克斯河等的大水系分布者。

岩画较少存在于穷科克遗址的附近。但也可以推测出在这个地区墓地和岩画的关系较密切,其他的情况不清楚。因此不能判断出是否是整个地域的倾向。

最近进行了许多调查,发现的墓地也很多。根据卫星照片,能确认更多的墓地。由于许多地区不能免费利用高分辨率卫星照片进行调查,因此肯定还有很多的墓地尚未被发现。目前伊犁地区发现的遗址大部分是墓葬,几乎没有聚落、岩画等。从卫星照片上确认墓葬以外的遗址非常困难,因此在这个地区只进行对墓葬的分布进行确认。在伊犁地区,特别在尼勒克地区确认了较多墓地。我们可对这个地区进行一下分析。

（一）尼勒克地区的遗址分布

在伊犁河的北部,喀什河的流域,墓地相当密集。一个墓地的范围比较大。不清楚墓地里有多少墓葬,但各个墓地至少有10座以上的墓葬。

由地形数据制作的等高线上叠加复原的水流路径,来看墓地的分布:墓地的大小各样,在靠近喀什河的河岸台地和山麓比较多,在远离平原的山腰也有较多的墓地,不一定靠近河谷的周围。分析标高、地面坡度、地面方向,可以看到尼勒克地区的墓地是在标高550～2 200米,坡度0～13度的地方,地面方向可以说南方和北方较多,西方非常少。与哈密地区比较的话,遗址布局上有较大的区别。

（二）时间距离的分析

在这个地区,几乎没有确认为人们日常活动的遗址,以重要遗址之一的尼勒克铜矿为对象,从那里进行时间性分析。这样的分析,考虑自然资源的便利性是一个重要的因素。在这个地区,距尼勒克铜矿约

5~7个小时和9个小时左右路程的墓葬分布较多(图二)。因此墓葬不一定是选择靠近铜矿山地方。当然,墓地和人们日常活动的据点有所不同,可以说墓葬的布局和铜矿的距离之间的关系不太大。分析一下到达各个墓地的时间,每个墓地之间好像有30分钟到一个小时左右的距离。

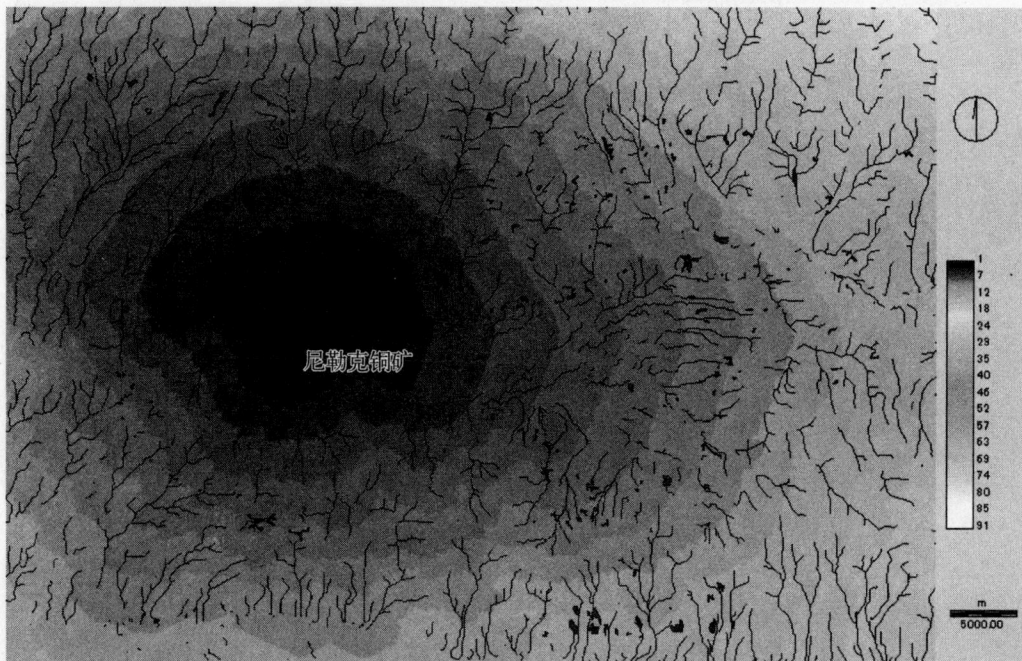

图二　尼勒克铜矿为基点的时间距离(黑色:墓地　凡例:小时)

五、结　语

　　本文只是对新疆的部分地区进行了分析。由于资料的限制,还只能简单地勾画出各个小区的遗址分布的趋势以及哈密地区和伊犁地区之间的区别等,但是问题也很多,特别是伊犁尼勒克地区。我认为,卫星照片上确认的墓葬时期多属于汉前后,由于许多信息不清楚,因此不能分析其时期的演变。

　　遗址分布的原因有各种各样:地形、水系、动物植物等遗址周围的古环境、遗址的面貌和时期等。要把各种的因素结合在一起,进行综合分析,相信能推进把史前人们的活动内容和变化过程等进行复原的工作。如果把这样分析的结果在遗址进行实地确认,能得到更成熟的认识。

对回鹘文印刷文献进行图像分析的初步结果：
断代和印刷方法的新探索

孙飞鹏　　阿不都热西提·亚库甫

中国西安交通大学考古工程和文物保护研究中心

德国柏林国家博物院拉特根研究所

德国柏林-勃兰登堡科学院吐鲁番学研究中心

回鹘文印刷文献在敦煌和吐鲁番出土文献中占有一定的比例。在德国的柏林-勃兰登堡科学院的吐鲁番学研究中心和亚洲博物馆，法国的国立博物馆和吉美亚洲艺术博物馆，俄罗斯的俄罗斯科学院圣彼得堡东方学研究所，英国大英图书馆，日本龙谷大学图书馆、天理图书馆、京都藤井有邻馆以及中国的国家图书馆、敦煌研究院、甘肃博物馆、吐鲁番博物馆等藏有约一千四百多件回鹘文印刷文献。其中，密宗文献最多，占回鹘文印本的三分之一。大乘佛教经典的数量也不少，仅藏在柏林-勃兰登堡科学院吐鲁番学研究中心的就有一百九十件。此外，还有一些汉文疑伪经的回鹘语译文〔共一百七十七件〕、小乘佛教故事残片〔共四十七件〕、跋文〔共二十五件〕以及少量的佛经注释残片〔共三件〕、木刻画〔八件〕和历书残片〔仅一件〕。[①] 这些文献不仅在回鹘佛教、古代维吾尔语言文学、西域翻译史研究方面具有重要价值，也为回鹘印刷技术和回鹘科技史的探索以及东西文化交流史的研究提供可贵依据。

虽然相当数量的印刷文献已经得以刊布，但对其印刷方法、断代等至今缺乏系统研究。本文采用图像处理方法，拟就回鹘文印刷文献的断代、印刷方法的鉴别等两个焦点问题进行新的探索并对通过采用多种科学分析方法全面考察古代印刷技术有关的一些基本问题进行展望。

一、回鹘文印刷文献的年代和字符特征

回鹘文印刷文献中能够确定印刷年代和印刷地点的屈指可数。表一是已确定年代的回鹘文印刷文献的基本情况。[②]

由表一看见，回鹘文印刷品的印刷地点有中都（元大都）、甘州、杭州等三地。据我们初步研究，早期印本边框似多为单线框，双线框较晚出现。页边单双线框与印刷年代的相关性同汉文印刷文献相似。[③] 回鹘文文献的印刷地点和年代一般是根据跋文和文献本身所提供的其他一些信息来确定的。

---

① 细见 Yakup et al. 2007, Yakup 2008 和 Yakup 2009。
② 细见 Zieme 1981；Zieme/Kudara 1985，第 29～34 页。
③ 竺沙雅章教授曾提出汉文印刷文献页边单双线框与印刷年代之间存在相关性，见竺沙 2006，第 120 页。

表一　具有确定印刷年代的回鹘文印本

印刷年代	收　藏　号	原编号	印刷地点	其他信息
1248	U 4791	T M 36	中都弘法寺	单线框
1296	U 4688	T II S 63	不详	单线框
1300〔?〕	Tulufan Kaoguji 图版 106，107	无	杭州〔陈宁刊〕	双线框
1302	U 4759	T M 14	大都白塔寺	双线框
1313	U 4829〔抄本?〕	T III M 108	不详	单线框
14 世纪初期	U 4711	T III M 195	不详	单线框
	B 464:13〔敦煌北区出土〕	无	不详	双线框
1330	U 4707	T III M 187	不详	双线框
1333	U 4124	T I μ 21	大都普庆寺	双线框
1347	U 4753	T III M 10	不详	双线框
	U 4758	T M 13	不详	单线框
1348	U 497	T I a 561	不详	单线框
1361	Fujii Yūrinkan Uigur No. 24	无	甘州	单线框

　　采用图像处理软件进行比例矫正后,对上述部分印本字符的长度、宽度和面积进行处理。图一显示字符长度分布与印本年代的关系。如图所示,在所选样品当中,早期印本字符长度分布区间较广,有许多长字符;晚期印本字符长度则几乎都在 30 毫米以内。图二显示的是字符宽度与印本年代的关系。除早期个别字符较宽外,所有印本绝大多数字符宽度小于 15 毫米。

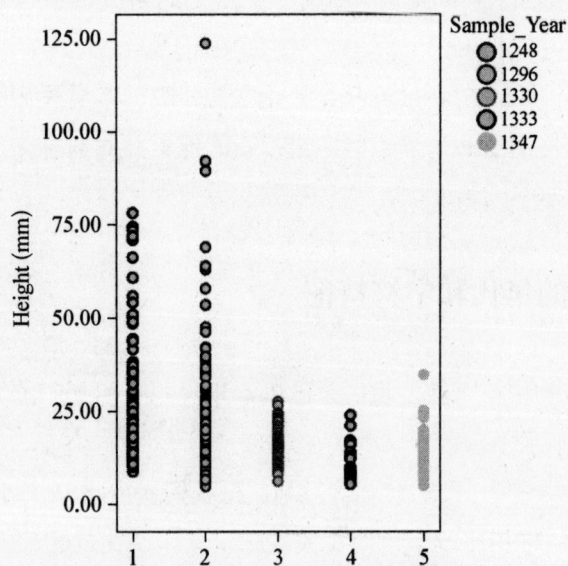

图一　回鹘文印本字符长度分布图

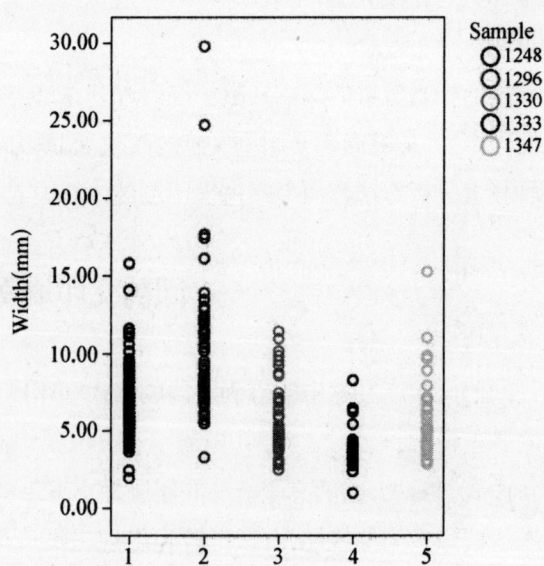

图二　回鹘文印本字符宽度分布图

　　鉴于回鹘文字符的特征,可以大致由其面积对长宽和的比值来反映字符笔画的粗细。以字符长宽和为横坐标,面积为纵坐标作图。这可用图三来标示:

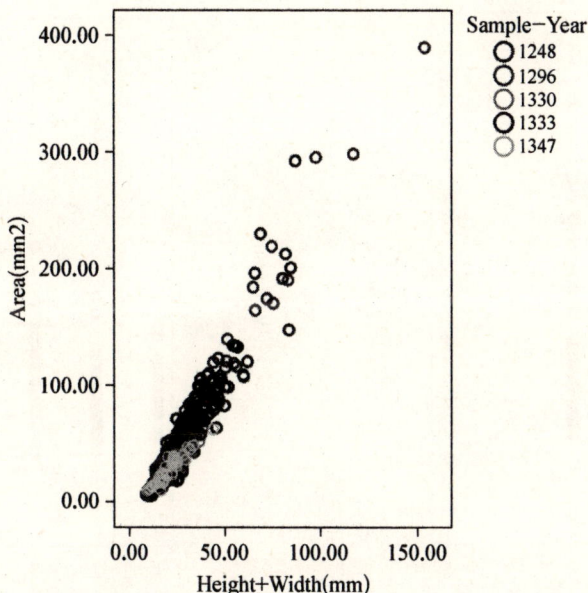

图三　回鹘文不同时代印本字符面积与长宽和的关系

由图三可看出,对每一确定的印本,其字符面积与长宽和大致成正比关系,相应的斜率大小反映字符笔画的粗细。所选的样品中,早期印本字符基本上处于图像的左上方,即斜率较大,字符笔画较粗;晚期印本笔画变细。

二、对回鹘文《华严经》〔四十华严〕不同版本年代早晚的判断

下面我们按同样的处理程序对柏林科学院吐鲁番学研究中心藏回鹘文《华严经》〔《四十华严》〕印本不同版本(表二)的字符进行图像分析。回鹘文《华严经》各版本的字符长度及宽度分布分别如图四、图五所示。

表二　柏林吐鲁番学研究所藏《四十华严》①

收　藏　号	尺　　　寸	其 他 信 息
U 4364	20.7 cm（h）× 8.7（w）	双线框
U 4480	21 cm（h）× 9 cm（w）	双线框
U 4667	20.7 cm（h）× 11 cm（w）	双线框
U 4668	20.4 cm（h）× 8 cm（w）	双线框（连接紧密）
U 4669	20.8 cm（h）× 9.7 cm（w）	单线框
U 4687	22.4 cm（h）× 10.3 cm（w）	单线框

各版本的字符长度分布没有显著差异。除 U 4667 和 U 4669 个别字符较宽外,其余字符宽度均小于15 毫米。

---

① 该印本的详细描写见 Yakup, 2008;《四十华严》印本残片的研究见 Yakup, 2008a。

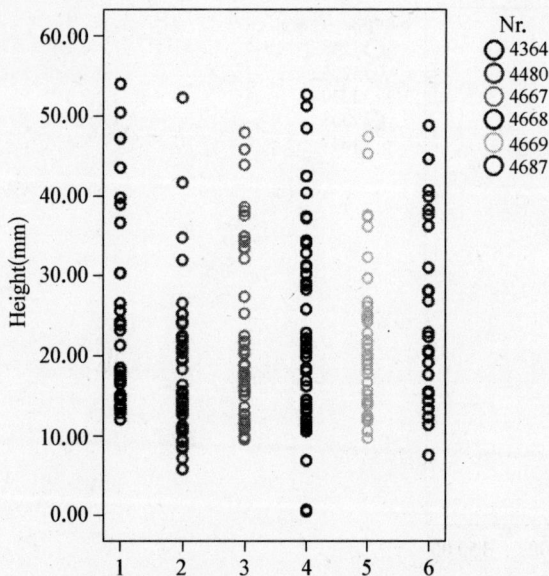

图四　回鹘文《华严经》字符长度分布图

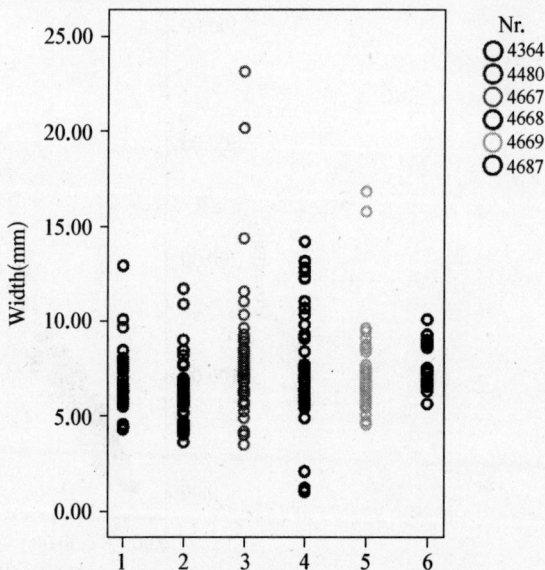

图五　回鹘文《华严经》各版本字符宽度分布图

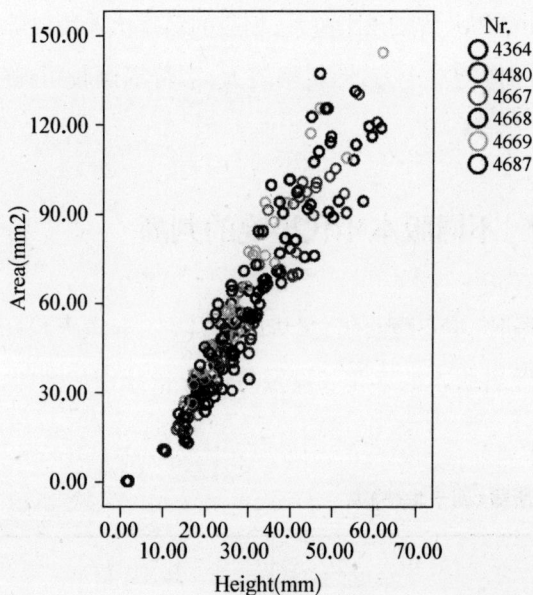

图六　回鹘文《华严经》各版本字符面积与长宽和的关系

回鹘文《华严经》各版本字符面积与长宽和的关系如图六所示。由图六,各版本字符从粗到细依次为:U 4687 和 U 4669、U 4668 与 U 4667、U 4480 和 U 4364。

回鹘文《华严经》各版本与上述已确定年代的印本字符图像特征的分析结果可归纳为以下几点:

〔一〕与双线框印本字符相比,单线框印本字符笔画较粗;

〔二〕线框与字符长宽分布无明显相关性,或许字符长宽取决于印本的文字内容。

由此,我们大致可以推测,随着回鹘文刻版技术的提高,印本字符逐渐变细,印边由单线框渐变为双线框。

三、关于活字印刷的判别和活字技术的鉴别方法

学术界对活字印刷术的发明与传播路线历来存在一些争论。印刷品年代的确切断定、其印刷方法(为雕版印刷或活字印刷)的正确辨别以及所采用活字技术的科学鉴别,无疑为讨论这些争论问题提供有益证据。然而,确认某一印刷品是否活字印刷不是一件容易的事情,要进一步确认是其采用的是泥活字或是木活字等活字技术更是一件难度很大的工作。目前判断印本是否采用活字印刷技术主要采用如下方法:[1]

---

[1]　主要根据史金波和雅森吾守尔, 2000, 第 54 ~ 60 页的内容整理而成。

1. 根据文献记载和印刷品的题跋。

2. 根据目视观察字符形体、笔画粗细是否均一。

3. 根据目视观察字符之间距离是否规整，是否有字符显著接触。

4. 根据目视观察字符是否有歪斜倒置现象。

5. 根据目视观察字符墨迹浓淡是否均一，边缘是否有墨迹。

6. 根据目视观察四周栏线交角是否有空缺不接。

7. 根据目视观察同一印本各页之间是否有异常。

史金波先生根据以上方法已鉴别出十数种西夏活字印品，为西夏印刷技术的研究作出很大贡献。但是，以上方法都是间接的确认方法。我们认为，在缺乏活字实物的条件下也可以采取直接的判别方法，如通过图像分析、比对字符本身来寻找活字。下面以中国国家图书馆藏西夏文《大方广佛华严经》卷第八十（馆藏号 XiX6.16）为例，对此方法进行说明。

我们从西夏文《大方广佛华严经》第八十卷中选取一些字符对它们进行了初步图像分析。图七显示的是该文献前四叶（排版印刷页）中所出现的字符"𢁬"的全体。此字符在前四叶共出现二十八次，其中在第二叶中频率最高，共出现了十二次。我们初步确认，该字符在二十八处的形式分别构成三组甚为类似的小类，即第一和第三叶的形式构成一类，第二和第四叶的形式构成两个小类（图七中以椭圆和线条所示）。由此可判定，这三小类的六个字符形式是分别采用三个不同的活字来进行印刷的；其余二十二处的形式则可能采用了二十二个不同的活字。

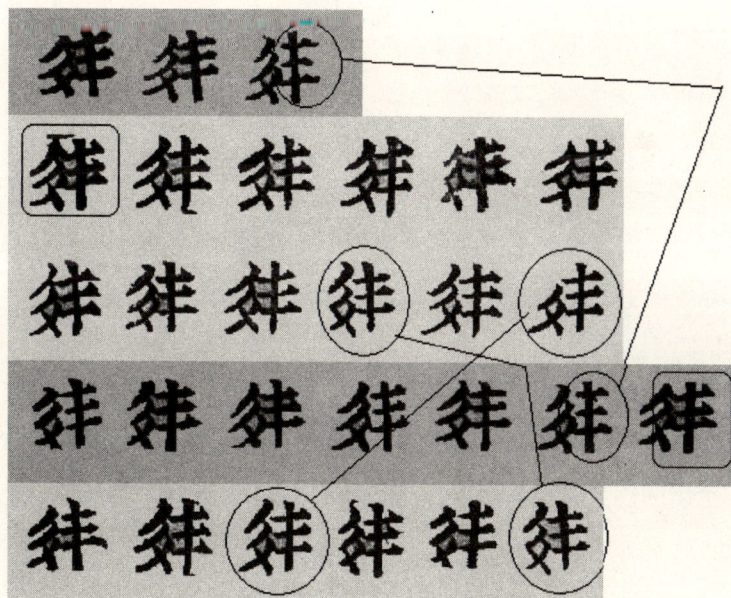

图七　西夏文《华严经》的字符"𢁬"

通过图像处理找出活字并以此确认活字印刷品后，可以进一步通过统计某字符活字出现的频率以及分析其分布关系来研究排版印刷的规程。仍以西夏文《华严经》的前四叶为例来看，字符"𢁬"的活字总数目（3+22 个）远多于其在每叶中出现的数目（四叶分别为 3、12、7 及 6 个）。理论上，可以同时排好数叶，再行印刷。但是，活字的重复使用说明，实际上在该文献的排版中并未同时排好数叶,至多也不会同时排好三叶。相邻叶中,一、二叶该字符无重复使用的活字;三、四叶也没有同样的活字。第二和第三叶出现了十分相似的字符(图七中方框内所示),但它们有一些细微的差别。这是由于同一活字在印刷中造成的还是来自相似的不同活字,尚不能十分确定。如果不是同一活字,那么该经卷的印刷很有可能与《梦溪笔谈》所载排版印刷程式类同:一叶印刷的同时,下一叶排版。①

假若第二、第三叶的"**犇**"字符是同一活字,这表明该文献的排版不全是一板印刷的同时布排下一叶,而是有可能排好一叶,印刷好撤版后,再排另一板。如果采用的是单叶排版印刷程式,那为什么同一字符活字数目能有这么多? 其重复出现的几率为何不高? 这是否因为其寿命有限,很容易在印刷过程中毁坏或者发生变化而需要重新修整所造成的呢? 这些问题有待通过更多的统计分析和模拟试验加以回答。

以上仅以单个字符为例,对判定活字印刷以及研究排版印刷规程的方法进行了初步探索,详细的图像处理和系统统计分析有待进行。我们认为,通过对多种文献中更多字符活字出现频率以及分布关系的系统统计,可以综合考察排版印刷规程。如辅以简单的仿制活字、模拟印刷等试验,可进一步推断印本所用活字的寿命和可能采用的活字种类。

四、采用图像分析方法考察回鹘文文献的印刷技术

西夏印刷文献虽然发现有活字印本,但缺少活字实物。回鹘文印刷文献则不同,目前已经发现有一千一百余枚"木活字",②其规格宽度约为 13 mm,长度依内容而不等。其内容说是包括字母、单词、动词词干、词缀、语音组合、版框线、标点等。③ 但是尚未有经确认的回鹘活字印本见诸报导。这些"木活字"是否真正曾用于活字印刷,目前还难以证明。④

我们除通过目视观察回鹘文印本行间距离以及图像处理统计字符宽度分布来粗略筛选是否有采用活字印刷的可能外,还通过比对多叶印本中同一字符的相似程度来寻找活字。遗憾的是,回鹘印刷文献缺完整的整本,多叶印本文献的数量也不太多。根据目前对一些多叶印本所进行的分析与统计,我们未能确认有回鹘文活字印本,但发现一些应引起注意的现象。下面分别以有单线框的 U 4711 和有双线框的 U 4739 为例,对这些现象加以说明。

柏林所藏回鹘文印本残片 U 4711 有三印页,印刷精美。印本中的汉字数字符号似乎是表示刻写、刊印、装订工序中有人不认识回鹘文。下面,图八是 U 4711 中重复出现的一些字符;表三是其中具有全部、所有等意义的 *alku* 一词的字符所出现的页数和相应的长度、宽度和面积数据。

---

① 沈括:《梦溪笔谈》载:"常作二铁板,一板印刷,一板已自布字,此印者才毕,则第二板已具,更互用之,瞬息可就。每一字皆有数印,如'之''也'等字,每字有二十余印,以备一板内有重复者。"
② 见森安1985,第95~96页;百济1988,杨富学1990,雅森·吾守尔1998,史金波和雅森·吾守尔2000,第87~110页;彭金章等2000,第156~158页。
③ 参见史金波和雅森2000,第91~105页。
④ 冯佳班(Annemarie von Gabain)教授曾提到这些活字并质疑其实用性,见 Gabain 1967,第29~31页。最近庄垣内正教授经对"木活字"进行较详细的分析,也否定回鹘人曾用木活字印刷回鹘语文献,见 Shōgaito 2005,第413~414页。

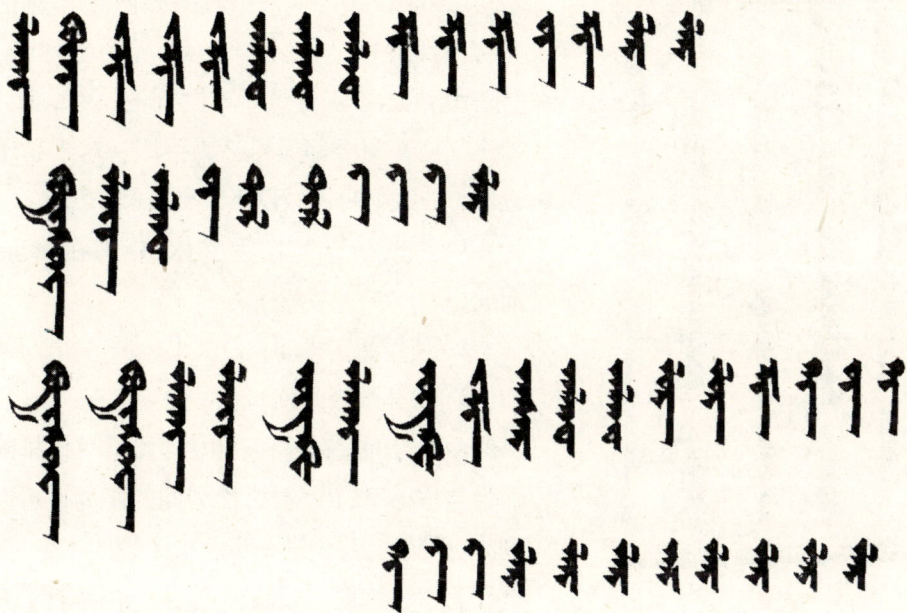

图八　回鹘文 U 4711 印文中的一些字符

表三　柏林所藏回鹘文印本残片 U 4711 中字符"*****"（*alku*）的特征数据

出 现 的 位 置	宽/(mm)	长/(mm)	面积/(mm^2)
第 1 叶	7.75	24.52	77.10
第 1 叶	7.96	24.31	78.35
第 1 叶	7.96	23.89	69.14
第 2 叶	8.17	25.15	65.27
第 2 叶	8.17	23.26	69.33
第 3 叶	8.17	24.10	79.69
平均值	8.03	24.21	73.14
标准方差	0.17	0.63	5.96
相对标准差 /%	2.12	2.61	8.16

　　由图八和表三，虽然未能确认活字的存在，但我们发现，无论在同一叶还是不同叶中出现的同一字都具有很大的相似性。这种相似性超越了按照单纯书写而后雕刻印刷形成的字符的相似性。[①] 据此我们认为，应该存在过一种介于完全书写整版刻版与活字版之间的整版技术，即"活字模范字整版刻版印刷术"。刻版者依据书写文献，以"活字模范字"或其组合在纸上拓印出组成所需印刷文献内容的字符，将其反贴在选好的木板上，依照拓样逐字符刻出整版。

　　另以具有双线边框的回鹘文印本 U 4739 为例，它有三印刷叶，每叶包含 6 折页，每折页布排 5 列

---

　　① 对该字符在 U4829〔手抄本?〕中出现的 4 处进行比较，其差异可用肉眼明显区分，字符宽与长的相对标准差分别为 6.57% 和 4.23%。

图九　柏林所藏回鹘文印本残片 U 4739
中多次出现的两行经文

字符。如图九所示，其中有两列内容分别在同叶与邻叶多次出现。

看上去，不仅是该印本同样的字符，而且是左侧的婆罗迷文注音图像都显得甚为雷同。对于其印刷可能采用过的方法我们可以做以下几种推测：

1. 以两列内容作为整体，分别在出现的三处拓印而成；

2. 使用活字排印；

3. 整体雕版印刷。

由字符间存在的相对位置差异，可以排除该两列经文作为整体拓印的可能性；由列间的距离也可以排除活字印刷的可能性。我们进一步分析了该印本各字符的长度、宽度和面积等特征。表四列出了其中两个字符在印文中数处出现的长、宽和面积数据。

表四　U 4739 中两字符的特征数据

字　符	宽/(mm)	长/(mm)	面积/(mm²)
	8.00	36.84	114.19
	8.63	38.94	110.32
	7.79	39.16	121.82
	8.00	37.89	110.31
	8.42	40.42	124.80
	8.21	34.10	108.51
	8.84	32.84	103.03
	8.21	32.42	98.87
	8.42	32.84	104.06
	8.00	28.42	82.44

由表四可以看出，除个别有一定偏差外，同一字符出现的数处其特征数据基本上较为接近，即具有很大的相似性。据此我们认为，该印本仍是采用"活字模范字整版刻版"印刷而成。

不管是在带有单线框的早期回鹘文印本还是带有双线框的晚期印本中，都没有发现存在活字印刷品。是否存在回鹘文的活字印刷，尚待研究。研究的出发点应是在尽可能多的多页印刷文献中寻找"活字"并对它进行统计分析。根据目前的初步研究结果，我们推测，所发现的所谓"木活字"当中起码一部分实际上作为"活字模范字"用于整版刻版的可能性较大。[①]　至于"木活字"的制作方法，我们认为主要是

---

① 史金波和雅森·吾守尔 2000，第 110 页所展示的实际上也是这方面类似的尝试。庄垣内正弘教授也曾发表同样的评论。见 Shōgaito 2005，第 414 页。

截取旧雕版所得。[①] 此外，据学者们研究，在回鹘文"木活字"当中，存在一些多余的字符。[②] 如果这些多余字符用于活字印刷，必将造成印刷错误。然而，多余字符不妨碍以其为"活字模范字"来拓印刻版。因为，多余的部分可以有意不予刻出。此外，在回鹘文"木活字"当中，还存在一些表示页面版框线的"木活字"。这似乎在印刷中很难能用得着，它们很可能是旧雕版中截取"活字规范字"后的剩余成分。

五、结论与展望

通过对一些西夏文和回鹘文印刷文献的图像处理，我们初步得出以下结果：

1. 字符特征和印刷年代之间存在一定的相关性。可以由单线框、双线框以及字符笔画粗细来大致对回鹘文印刷品相对年代进行判断。

2. 在缺少活字实物的情况下，可以通过字符图像比对作为直接依据来判断印刷技术和程序。

3. 在目前研究的回鹘文印本中没有发现回鹘文活字印刷品，已知回鹘文"木活字"，起码是其中一部分很有可能作为"活字模范字"用于整版刻版。

图像分析只是取得了初步结果，期待深入研究，希望在如下方面取得更大进展：

1. 决定字符特征的应是书写者，而书写者的不同又反映在时代、印刷地点以及刻工方面。我们期待能够有更多的、具有明确印刷年代和地点的回鹘文印本出现，以其作为标准样品，建立字符特征标准数据库。之后，以标准样品为参照点，对众多的印刷文献进行印刷年代、印刷地点等的判断。

2. 对更多的多页印刷品进行图像分析统计，从其中寻找回鹘文"活字"，以此判断是否存在回鹘文活字印刷，同时对"活字规范字"整版刻版印刷进行系统验证。

3. 对西夏文活字印本中同一字符出现的数量、同一字符的活字个数、活字出现的频率以及其分布关系等全面系统的统计，并依此探讨排版印刷规程。

4. 对比不同印本中同一字符的相似性，可以依照现能明确断代的印本为其他印本提供断代参考。

5. 辅以简单的仿制活字、模拟印刷等进一步推断印本所用活字的寿命和可能采用的活字种类。

6. 综合采用多种现代科技手段，系统分析比对印本纸张和字墨的成分、结构，同时采用 C14 对纸、墨、"木活字"等进行绝对年代测定。与字符特征处理结果相结合，综合研究印本的印刷地点和年代。

参 考 文 献

竺沙雅章 2006．"西域出土の印刷佛典"，载《日本敦煌學論叢》，第一卷，東京：比較文化研究所，第 118～134 页。

Von Gabain, Annemarie 1967: *Die Drucke der Turfan-Sammlung*. Berlin 1967. (SDAW. Klasse für Sprachen, Literatur und Kunst. 1967, 1.)

彭金章、王建军 2000：《敦煌莫高窟北区石窟》，第 1～3 卷，北京：文物出版社，2000～2004 年。

彭金章、王建军 2000："敦煌莫高窟北区洞窟所出多种民族文字文献和回鹘文木活字综述"，载《敦煌研究》2000 年 2 期，第 154～159 页。

---

① 庄垣内正弘也曾提出类似的观点，见 Shōgaito 2005，第 413 页。
② 见史金波和雅森 2000，第 92 页。

森安孝夫 1985:"ウイグル语文献",载山口瑞风编:《敦煌胡语文献》(=《讲座敦煌》第6卷),东京:大东出版社,1985年,第1~98页。

史金波、雅森·吾守尔 2000:《中国活字印刷术的发明和早期传播——西夏和回鹘活字印刷术研究》,北京:社会科学文献出版社,2000年。

Shōgaito, Masahiro 2005. Uighur movable wooden type and its practicality. In: Ewa Sieineniec-Golaś and Marzanna Pomorska (edd.) *Turks and Non-Turks. Studies on the history of linguistic and cultural contacts.* (Studia Turkologica Cracoviensia 10.) Kraków, 第405~415页。

Yakup, Abdurishid 2008. *Alttürkische Handschriften Teil 12: Die uigurischen Blockdrucke der Berliner Turfansammlung. Teil 2: Apokryphen, Mahāyāna-Sūtren, Erzählungen, Magische Texte, Kommentare und Kolophone.* (Verzeichnis der Orientalischen Handschriften in Deutschland, Bd. XIII 20.) Stuttgart: Franz Steiner Verlag.

Yakup, Abdurishid 2008a. Berlin fragments of the block-printed Uyghur edition of the *Buddhāvataṃsaka-sūtra* in fourty volumes. In Peter Zieme (ed.) *Aspects of research into Central Asian Buddhism. In memoriam Kogi Kudara*, 第435~459页。

Yakup, Abdurishid 2009. *Alttürkische Handschriften* Teil 15: *Die Uigurischen Blockdrucke der Berliner Turfansammlung. Teil 3: Stabreimdichtungen, Kalenderstücke, Bilder, Unbestimmte Fragmente und Nachträge.* (Verzeichnis der Orientalischen Handschriften in Deutschland, Bd. XIII 23.) Stuttgart: Franz Steiner Verlag.〔即出〕

Yakup, Abdurishid und M. Knüppel 2007. *Alttürkische Handschriften.* Teil 11: *Die Uigurischen Blockdrucke der Berliner Turfansammlung. Teil 1: Tantrische Texte* (VOHD XIII,19.). Stuttgart: Franz Steiner Verlag, 2007.

杨富学 1990:《敦煌研究院藏回鹘文木活字》,《敦煌研究》1990年第2期,第34~37页。

Yang Fuxue 2001: Uighur Wooden Movable-Types from Dunhuang and Related Problems. 见《敦煌学与中国史研究论集——纪念孙修身先生逝世一周年》,兰州:甘肃人民出版社,2001年。

雅森·吾守尔 1998:《敦煌出土回鹘文木活字及其在印刷术西传中的意义》,载《出版史研究》,第6辑,北京:中国书籍出版社,1998年。

Zieme, Peter 1981. Bemerkungen zur Datierung uigurischer Blockdrucke. In: *Journal Asiatique* 269, 第385~399页。

Zieme, Peter / Kōgi Kudara 1985. *Guanwuliangshoujing in Uigur.* Kyoto: Nagata Bunshōdō.

利用 Google Earth 分析与评价斯坦因地图

西村阳子　　大西磨希子　　北本朝展

日本国立信息学研究所

一、序　言

本文基于古地图的数字化及其应用,主要讨论了使用 Google Earth 评价古地图精密度,并与作者所写地图绘制记录互相比较的方法。本文的讨论对象是约 100 年前进行丝绸之路考察的 M. A. Stein (以下略称斯坦因)制作的两种古地图。这两种地图在当前研究中主要作为纸本地图被利用,为了提高学术研究的便利,现在除了将其数字化外,还将其与地理信息平台相结合。

因此,我们首先讨论把这两种地图导入 Google Earth (以下略称 GE),以提高古地图使用便利性的方法(第三章)。然而,通过 Google Earth 卫星照片与古地图的比较,我们发现古地图存在误差。因此,我们在第四章到第七章中,通过分析古地图误差的详细特征,试图明确利用数字版斯坦囚地图时所应注意的问题。由于我们所讨论的地图,保存有作者斯坦因自己的关于地图精密度的记录,所以我们可以参考斯坦因留下的记录,来追究地图中误差发生的原因。这样,我们利用了两种古地图及其绘制记录是本文的最大特征。最后,我们讨论了将研究成果发展为今后丝绸之路研究的学术平台,还需要解决的问题。

二、斯坦因地图是什么?

斯坦因是 20 世纪初丝绸之路探险的代表性人物。以 1900 年的中亚探险为开始,一共四次前往中亚进行探险。后来,出版了第一次探险(1900～1901)的报告书,即 Ancient Khotan (共 2 卷),作为第二次探险(1906～1908)的报告书出版了 Serindia (共 5 卷),此外还有作为第三次探险报告书的 Innermost Asia (共 4 卷)。

尤其是在第二次与第三次探险的时候,斯坦因考察了丝绸之路的中心塔里木盆地(现在的新疆维吾尔自治区),在其报告书 Serindia 以及 Innermost Asia 的卷末,附上了带经纬度的很详细的地图。现在,这种地图作为研究丝绸之路的基本学术资料被利用。据此,在国立信息学研究所的数字丝绸之路项目(以

图一　Google Earth 上的斯坦因地图

下略称 DSR 项目)中,对这两种地图进行了数字化,现已完成。

但是,这两种地图中存在着较大问题。第一,因为地图数量特别多,比如 Serindia 地图达到 94 张,Innermost Asia 也达到 47 张之多,所以丝绸之路被切割成很多部分,难以把握全貌。第二,因为被分割为图幅巨大、数量众多的纸张,阅览也很不方便,所以从来没有进行过评价斯坦因地图整体精密度的尝试。为了今后作为学术平台来利用斯坦因地图,在提高阅览方便性的同时,也需要评价其精密度,作为利用地图时所应注意的问题。

三、将古地图导入 Google Earth 的方法

我们为了提高地图阅览的方便性,首先利用 GE 配置阅览环境。我们选择 GE 的原因是:GE 具有网络免费下载,操作以及公开数据方法简单等优点。考虑到上述优点,我们利用 GE 地理信息平台进行阅览环境的配置。把古地图导入 GE 的方法如下:

1. 将斯坦因地图的每一幅分图,以经纬度为标准,进行几何校正。

2. 汇集全部古地图的经纬度信息,并转换为导入 GE 所必须的 KML(Keyhole Markup Language)格式的数据。

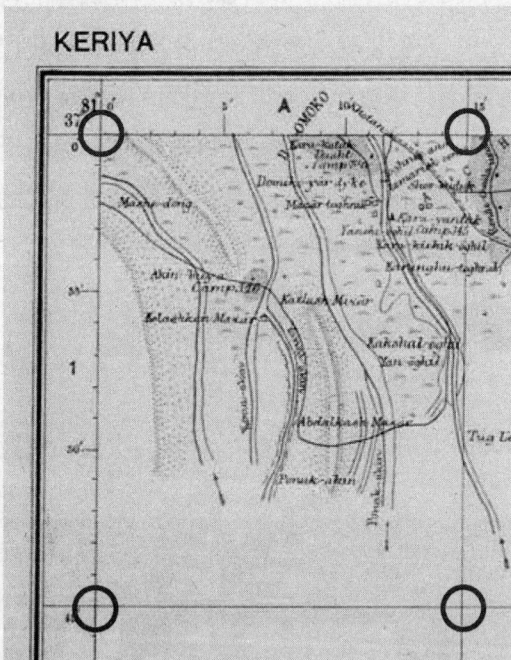

图二　Serindia 地图纸张的例子

斯坦因地图根据经纬度分割为多幅分图,像图二表示的那样,在每幅分图中有几条直交的纬度线与经度线。据此,以这些经纬度线的交点为标准点,使之与 Google Earth 中相对的点重叠起来,获得校正图片。在每一张地图中,各有三四条纬度线与经度线,所以在一张地图中,可以汇集三四十个标准点。据此,搜集各个交点的经纬度,再利用共一次内插法计算校正图片。然后,对所有地图进行这样的再排列计算,由此可以完成斯坦因地图的调整。

最后,利用计算结果制作 KML 格式的数据。然而,因为连接后的地图文件很大,所以利用了复数清晰度的存取方法(Super-Overlay)。完成后的地图已经在我们网页(http：//dsr. nii. ac. jp/geography/)上对外公开。

因此,与 GE 结合的斯坦因地图比纸本地图更易于阅读。除了在地球上能够连续地表示全部地图以外,利用变焦放大、缩小功能,可以放大任意局部的地图。此外,通过 GE,我们可以重叠比较古地图与现在的卫星照片。由此,可以免费利用高清晰度的卫星照片也是 GE 的另外一个优点。

于是,我们在斯坦因的地图中搜集几个遗址地点,与现在的卫星照片比较位置。结果,我们发现古地图与现在卫星照片之间的位置并不一致。

四、古地图与卫星照片不一致的原因

古地图与卫星照片的遗址位置不一致,我们可以设想出以下几点原因:

1. 将地图导入 Google Earth 时,数据处理中存在误差。

2. Google Earth 卫星照片的误差。

3. 斯坦因地图的误差。

首先探讨第一点的可能性。斯坦因地图上的纬度线与经度线的交点可以确定准确的位置,交点以外的地点通过内插法计算位置,所以存在发生若干误差的可能。可是,因为斯坦因地图的歪斜很小,所以通过这种处理发生的误差也极小,不可能发生达到几公里以上的误差。所以,第一点原因的可能性很小。对于这一点,我们以后再详细讨论。

接着讨论第二种原因的可能性。到现在,因为 Google 没有公开有关 GE 卫星照片的精密度信息,所以很难评价。但是现代卫星照片的测绘技术已经非常准确,所以没有发生误差的可能。

通过以上论述,斯坦因地图与 GE 卫星照片之间不一致的原因,最大的可能是由于斯坦因地图本身的误差。如果考虑到一百年前斯坦因制作地图时技术上的限制,在地图上发生误差也不是不可思议的事情。于是,本文关注斯坦因地图所具有的精密度及其特征,下面从多个角度对这一问题进行讨论。

五、斯坦因地图精密度的整体特征

5.1 标准点的选择

为了评价斯坦因地图的精密度,我们应当将古地图中和现在照片中位置没有发生变化的地点作为标准点,比较古地图与现在卫星照片之间的位置。比如说,因为干燥地带的变动,我们不能选择河道等地理要素。于是我们首先关注遗址。因为遗址的形态较有特色,可以很容易确定一百年前地图上的地点和当前地点是同一地点。

斯坦因地图中绘有很多遗址,而且我们在 GE 的卫星照片上也可以分辨出一些对应的遗址地点。图三、图四显示了几个可以确定是相同遗址的例子。

图三　庙儿沟遗址(Ara-tam temple ruins)

　　图三是以庙儿沟遗址为例子,同时表示了 GE 上的遗址地点和 Serindia 以及 Innermost Asia 地图上的位置。从这个图片我们能看出来 Serindia(蓝色)和 Innermost Asia(绿色)的遗址地点与 GE 上的位置都不一致。图四是以 Mazār-Tāgh 为例表示 GE、Serindia、Innermost Asia 地图上遗址周围的情况。因为地形情况都很一致,所以我们能够认定这三幅图表示的是同一个遗址。可是与图三类似,将地图重叠起来的话,现在 GE 表示的遗址地点跟古地图的遗址地点在位置上都不一致。因此,我们通过计算这种偏差,可以评价斯坦因地图的精密度。

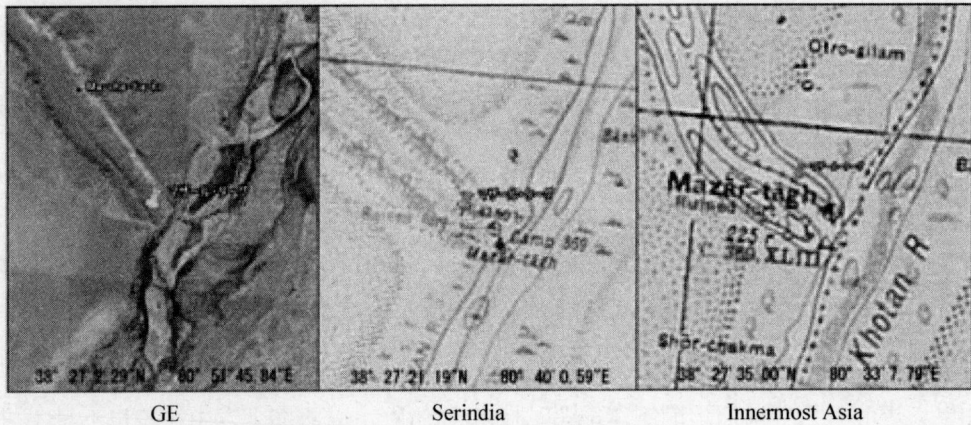

| GE | Serindia | Innermost Asia |

图四　Mazār-Tāgh 遗址

　　在同样的条件下,我们搜集了能成为标准点的遗址地点,条件是绘在一幅以上的斯坦因地图中并可以在现在的 GE 卫星照片上确定位置,符合条件的共 105 个地点。为了确定这些地点,我们主要利用了两种实地考察的报告[冈内 2004][西村、铃木 2005]。①

　　另一方面,在斯坦因地图中,用拉丁字母标注了斯坦因所记录的当地语言(维吾尔语)的绿洲的地名。因为这些绿洲的地名到现在还可以用汉字追溯,所以绿洲地点也成为我们参照的对象。为了确定绿洲地点,除了斯坦因地图和 GE 以外,我们还利用了中国出版的现代地图。结果,绘在一幅以上的斯坦因地图中,并且能在现代的 GE 以及其他地图上确定的地点增加到约 200 个。

　　但是因为有以下的几个理由,我们应当注意绿洲地点的可靠性不如遗址地点:

　　1. 因为河道的变动,绿洲也存在变动的可能性。

　　2. 因为绿洲的范围一般比遗址大,而且在现代多数绿洲的范围扩展很大,如果我们选择绿洲中任意一点的话,那么可能并不具有可比性。

　　因此,我们首先调查了在斯坦因地图上绿洲地点的误差倾向,得到绿洲地点与遗址地点具有同样误差倾向的结果。据此,本文假定绿洲地点基本上没有变动,并且比较时尽量选择绿洲的中心地点。

5.2　误差分布图的特征

　　使用这样选择的标准点,我们测定了现在位置(在 GE 卫星照片上的位置)与斯坦因地图上的位置偏差。图五用地图表示了这些偏差的结果(误差分布图)。在这幅图中,以现在位置为标准(箭型符号的起点),图示斯坦因地图上的位置(箭型符号的终点)。由于如果按照实际尺寸,很难看清误差特征,所以在确定偏差方向的基础上,将偏差的距离放大了十倍。因为斯坦因地图有两种图,而选择标准点的方法也

---

　　① 除了这些报告以外,还利用了 2005 年西村、铃木的陕西、甘肃考察记录以及 2003 年森美智代在库车的考察记录等。

有两种,所以一共有四种误差分布图。

从这个结果,我们能看出来所有地图具有同样的误差倾向。我们以现在位置与斯坦因地图上位置之间的距离来定义斯坦因地图的误差大小,从整体来说遗址地点的误差只限于几公里左右,但各个地点的误差大小不稳定,最少 250 米,最大达到 32 公里之巨。从图五来看,整体性误差倾向有以下六点特征。

(1) Serindia 地图与 Innermost Asia 地图的误差具有同样的特征。

(2) 东西方向的误差很大,南北方向相对于东西方向,误差极小。

(3) 随着斯坦因考察路线的延伸,误差逐渐的增大。

(4) 在天山南路西部的绿洲城市——阿克苏向西的误差很大。

(5) 在河西走廊的城市——甘州,向东的误差很大。

(6) 各地的误差分布不一样。

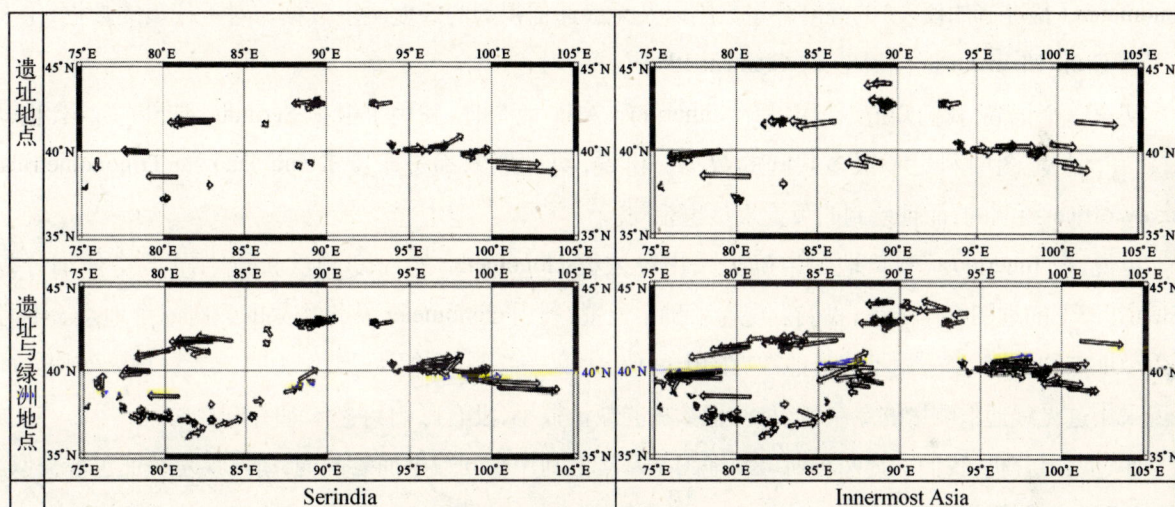

图五　斯坦因地图的误差分布图

六、误差分布图的分析

那么,我们在第五章提示的误差分布图的特征是由于什么原因而造成的呢? 如果只研究地图的话,我们难以解释这一问题,但斯坦因地图所幸还保存着与之相关的线索,即斯坦因本人所写的相关论文——[Stein1911]与著作[Stein1923]。

论文[Stein1911]是关于 Serindia 地图(1906～1908)的论文。因为正文部分只是短短的六页,所以没有包含关于地图具体的绘制信息,而只是概括了地图的制作方法与测量的概略。

著作[Stein1923]是关于 Innermost Asia vol.4 中地图制作的记录。在这幅地图中包含斯坦因三次探险(1900～1901,1906～1908,1913～1915)中获得的所有地理信息,还包含有对分幅图的详细注解。

于是我们通过参考斯坦因本人留下的这些著作,对照误差分布图的特征与斯坦因本人地图制作或测量过程,说明地图误差的发生原因。

6.1　Serindia 与 Innermost Asia 地图的共同性

图五的第一个特征是 Serindia 地图与 Innermost Asia 地图的误差表示出同样的倾向。我们依据斯坦

因本人的著作进行如下分析：

首先，在文献[Stein1911]中，对 Serindia 的地图制作方法有以下记述：

（1）以斯坦因等的实地考察为基础，在印度的 Dehra Dūn 的 Trigonometrical Survey office 来实际绘制地图。

（2）在考察时，以平板测量为主体，利用天体观测得到的纬度数据并以三角测量（只限于昆仑山脉部分）为补充。[1]

在文献[Stein1923]中，对 Innermost Asia 的地图制作方法，有以下记载：

（1）作为地图制作的标准，利用了第二次、第三次探险中的三角测量数据与所有三次探险中所获得的依据天体观测得到的纬度数据。

（2）在 Serindia 地图中，基本上没有做到经度测量，但在 Innermost Asia 地图中，利用过依据 clonometer（很准确的仪表）的经度测量数据以及无线通信得到的经度测量数据。对于仪表的数据，主要利用了 Cecil Clementi 的测量结果[Clementi1911]。[2]

从第一个记载，我们知道斯坦因制作 Innermost Asia 地图时，利用了很多 Serindia 地图的数据，也就是说，在两种地图中利用了很多共同的数据。再说，两种地图都是印度 Dehra Dūn 的 Trigonometrical Survey office 绘制的，而且绘制的负责人员也相同。

再说，在 Innermost Asia 地图中确实采用过依据 clonometer 的经度测量新技术，[3]但是仔细分析[Stein1923]的地图制作记录，我们发现为了确定位置，利用 clonometer 测量结果的只有六个地点。而且这六个地点的位置，都采用了与其他数据的中间值，因此在绘制中并不一定作为基本数据加以使用。此外还采用过无线通信测量的结果，这种测量数据的数量很小，没有影响到整体地图的形成。

通过以上分析，我们认为两种斯坦因地图是基本上利用相同数据而绘制的，所以误差特征也很类似。

6.2　东西方向的误差

东西方向的误差比南北方向大的原因就在于当时的测量方法。在[Stein1911]中斯坦因认为：

（1）在塔里木盆地的平地沙漠中，很难以交点或三角形确定地点，所以为了准确测量行车距离，使用以车轮回转来测定距离的行车距离计（cyclometer），由此能够有效地测量距离。

（2）因为气象条件恶劣、移动速度高（一天40公里）、包含范围广大，经度的测量实际上是不可能的。[4]

（3）纬度根据天体观测来测量。

关于纬度测量，当时的技术可以保证相当的精密度，而经度，对于当时的技术而言，测量有很大的困难。尤其是像斯坦因本人所写的那样，遇到了塔里木盆地的种种不利条件，有些部分实际上就不能测量经度。东西方向（经度）误差很大的原因，主要来源于经度测量的困难。

6.3　随着斯坦因考察路线延伸，误差逐渐增大的原因

图六是利用 Serindia 地图中所画的露营地信息绘制的斯坦因第二次考察的路线图。把这幅图与图五 Serindia 的误差分布图对照的话，我们能看出随着斯坦因考察路线的延伸，地图误差有逐渐增大的倾向。

---

① Stein1911，第276页。
② Stein1923，第55～57页。
③ 参看ソベル1997。
④ Stein1911，第276页。关于经度的测量，参看ソベル1997。

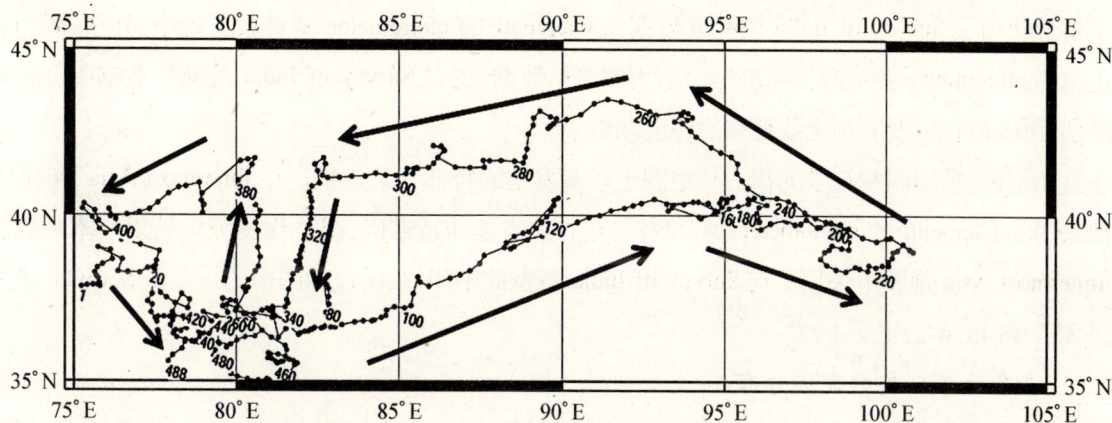

图六　第二次探险时(1906~1908)的考察路径图

这个原因,我们首先猜想可能是使用行车距离计的结果。如我们在 6.2 讨论的那样,作为经度的测量方法,在部分地区斯坦因利用了行车距离计。如果用这个测量方法的话,只能采用先把车轮的回转数量转换为距离,然后把距离转换为经度等较复杂的方法。这样一来,很可能随着车轮回转数量的增多,误差也被积蓄而增大起来。因此,我们认为如果使用了这个方法,随着考察路线的延伸,误差必定也会逐渐增大。

6.4　在阿克苏的误差

关于阿克苏的误差,在[Stein1911][Stein1923]的两种文献中都有记载。首先在[Stein1911]中,提到如下情况:

(1)关于阿克苏,为了确定位置而利用的数据(Captain Deasy · Stein 1900－1901、Stein 1906－1908)之间互相都有差异,所以采用了三个数据的中间值。斯坦因认为阿克苏的实际位置,与以前地图绘制的位置相比,可能更为偏东。

(2)另一方面,在[Stein1923]中更明确地记载了测量的错误。

(3)包括库尔勒(Korla)、轮台(Bugur)、库车(Kucha)、阿克苏(ak-su)的天山南路的经度测量有误,斯坦因的测量结果对比赫定的数据偏西 29 分(约 45 公里)。因为采用了 1908 年地图(Serindia 地图)同样的绘制方法,即使用了几个数据的中间值,因此误差只限于 8 分以内。但很可能所有位置都有向西的误差。[①]

图五的误差倾向与上述斯坦因的担心非常一致。两种地图都有误差,但 Innermost Asia 地图存在更大的误差。我们可以认为,这些误差反映了测量上的问题。

6.5　在甘州的误差

地图中发生的最大误差是在甘州附近。关于这一点,斯坦因在[Stein1911]中陈述过以下内容:

(1)在甘州(张掖)附近,由于对从西方到东方的移动距离的估计过大,必须要修正经度,以使之与 Survey of India 所认定的甘州的经度相适应。[②]

(2)随着甘州经度的调整,依据天体观测的数据调整了位于楼兰和甘州之间的其他地点的经度。然后,在[Stein1923]中说明如下:

在肃州、甘州等河西走廊的地区,使用了绘制 Serindia 地图时的第二次探险中所获得的数据,为了最

---

① 　Stein1923,第 81~82 页。

② 　Stein1911,第 279 页。

后确定位置使用了 Survey of India 的经度数据与 Clementi 的 clonometer 测量数据的中间值。因为有关河西走廊的 clonometer 测量数据与斯坦因本人的测量数据,还有 Survey of India 的测量数据中存在着很大的差别,所以应该需要利用无线通信的经度测量。[①]

在甘州附近,斯坦因所记录的担心与地图上误差发生的特征非常一致。在 Innermost Asia 地图中,第一次被采用的 Clementi 的 clonometer 测量数据,在甘州附近非常准确,跟现代的测定结果基本一致。因为在 Innermost Asia 地图中采用了与 Survey of India 数据的中间值,所以地图中的误差从 Serindia 地图的 32 公里减半到 15.6 公里。

6.6 在各地不一样的误差分布

从图五,我们能看出误差大小在各个地方存在差异。在进行三角测量的地方,误差相对小一些,同时,以车轮测量距离的地方,误差相对较大。这样,各地误差大小很可能受到测量方法较大的影响。此外,如上所述,还有测量的错误和技术的限制等种种原因,地图整体的误差分布表现出很复杂的模式。

斯坦因地图的误差在各地具有不一样的模式。所以为了地图的利用,我们不能施行同样的修正,在各个地区应当施行不同的修正,然后才能加以利用。因此,我们在第 7 章详细地分析了各个地区的误差模式,总结地图利用中应注意的问题。

七、斯坦因地图在各地的精密度

为了总结斯坦因地图的精密度,产生应该选择什么地点等问题。作为标准点,应当选择斯坦因地图绘制过程中使用过的那些重要地点,而且最好平均的分布在丝绸之路的全部地区。

因此,我们决定利用 Innermost Asia 地图的制作报告书[Stein1923]中所提到的斯坦因地图的调整位置点。调整位置点是绘制地图时候为了决定地图上的位置而利用过的地点,包括塔什库尔干、喀什、阿克苏、库车、库尔勒、轮台、吐鲁番、哈密、巴里坤、和田、尼雅、若羌、米兰、安西、甘州、肃州等绿洲城市,还有城市附近的三角测量地点。

图七表示了为调整位置而使用的绿洲的位置。

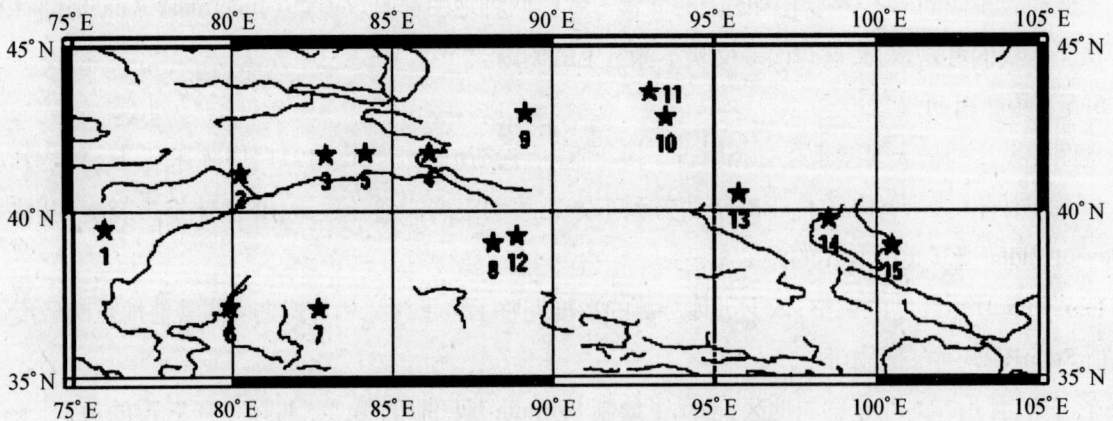

图七 调整位置地点(地图中的号码与表一对应)

① Stein1923,第 104 页。

【表一　斯坦因地图的各地的误差】

城市地点 （绿洲）	附近的遗址	Serindia		InnermostAsia	
		方　向	距离（km）	方　向	距离（km）
1　喀什 Kāshgar		南西	4.5	西北	1.2
	三仙洞	南西	8.53	南	6.19
	罕诺依古城			东南东	9.05
	莫尔佛塔			东南东	4.5
2　阿克苏 Ak-su		西	17	西	26.7
3　库车 Kuchā		西	19	西	3.2
	克孜尔尕哈石窟	西	16.99	西	2.86
	库木吐拉石窟	西	20.06	东	1.7
	森木塞姆石窟	西	21.41	西	4.7
4　库尔勒 Korla		东南	4.3	西南	20.3
5　轮台 Bugur		西	17.93	西	6.5
	轮台故城			西北西	8.5
6　和田 Khotan		北东	5.1	北	1.2
	约特干遗址	北东	5.29	北东	2.57
7　尼雅 Niya		东	2.6	东	3.1
	尼雅佛塔	东	2.7	东	3.8
8　若羌 Charkhlik		东北东	4.4	西北西	10
	Charklik Stupa mound	东北东	3.6	西北西	12.39
9　吐鲁番 Turfān		西南	4.9	西南西	8.2
	高昌故城	西北西	3.23	西南	5.87
	交河故城	西南	7.7	西	6.41
10　哈密 hāmi		西南	6.2	西南	6.2
	庙儿沟（Ata-ram temple ruins）	西南	9.1	西南	8.6
11　巴里坤 Burkul				西	12.9

续　表

	城市地点 （绿洲）	附近的遗址	Serindia		InnermostAsia	
			方　向	距离（km）	方　向	距离（km）
12	米兰 Miran		东北	2.67	西北	12.34
		米兰要塞	东北	2.9	西北	11.79
13	安西 An-xi		东	13.3	东	15.2
		榆林窟	东	4.3	东	6.3
		锁阳城	东	8.5	东	9.71
14	肃州 Lan-chou		东	4.7	东	3.5
15	甘州 Kan-chou		东	32	东	15.6

表一以上述的调整位置点为对象,表示了这些地点误差的方位与距离。但是,这些地点基本上是绿洲地点,所以存在着我们在5.1讨论的问题。因此,我们用包括遗址和绿洲郊区在内的地点表现了同一个地区内的误差,以此减少了绿洲地点存在的可靠性问题。其次,详细地分析各个地区的误差模式。因为在某些地区存在多个可以对照的地点,所以在同一个地区内的误差发生倾向中,可能有以下四种模式:

(1) 全部的方向与距离一致。

(2) 方向一致,距离不一致。

(3) 方向不一致,但距离很短。

(4) 完全不一致。

在表一中表现了各个地区的误差在方向与距离基本一致的模式。这表明在同一个地区内,地图带有基本上一样的误差,所以我们认为,为使用者提示各个地图的误差信息是有意义的。

作为例子,在图八中提示了天山南路的绿洲库车与位于其郊区的遗址地点的误差。中央的★符号表

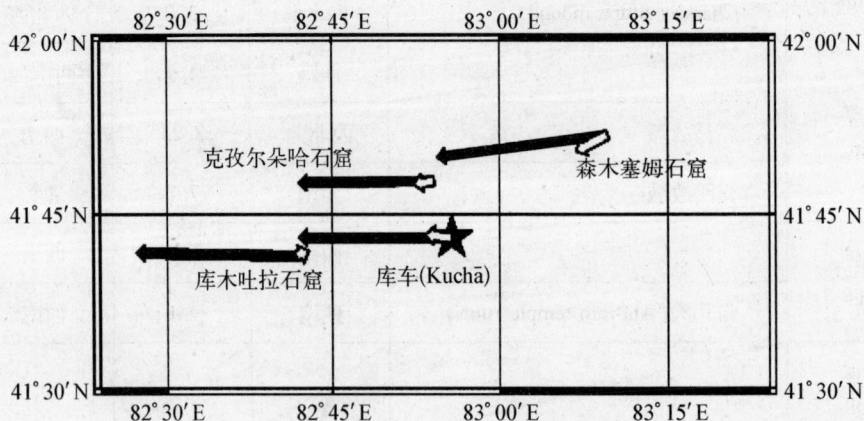

图八　库车附近的遗址的误差

示现在库车的位置,黑色的箭型符号表示与现在位置比较的 Serindia 的误差,白色的箭型符号表示与现在位置比较的 Innermost Asia 的误差。在库车郊区两种地图的遗址地点的误差都表现出同样的倾向。所以利用这个信息,我们可以分别提示 Serindia 的库车地区的校正信息与 Innermost Asia 的库车地区的校正信息。

另一方面,在图九的喀什以及郊区的遗址地点,我们发现不一样的倾向,即各个地点误差的方向与距离都不一致。我们现在还不能解释这个原因,但如果在一个地区内的误差不一致的话,我们就不能总结各个地区的误差特征。关于喀什地区我们还需要更详细的调查。

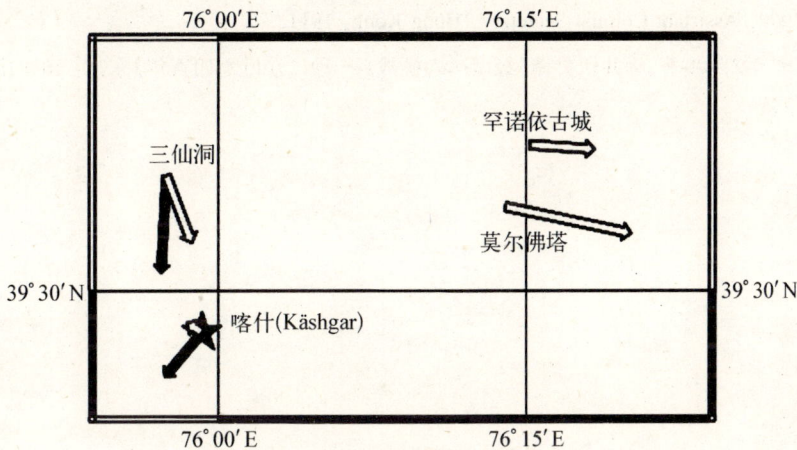

图九 喀什附近的遗址的误差

八、结 束 语

本文以丝绸之路古地图为分析对象,具体阐述了从古地图阅读条件的改善到精密度评价的一系列方法,并介绍了把古地图作为信息平台应用的一个例子。在每个研究阶段中,GE 都发挥了很大作用,所以可以认为 GE 是应用古地图时非常有用的工具。然后,通过参考制作地图的记录,阐明地图误差发生的原因,因而提出了可靠的总体校正信息。配合上述一系列的分析与在第七章所提示的各个地区的精密度信息,我们认为可以做到为学术研究而使用的地理信息平台。

今后的研究课题,包括通过从地图中搜集更多标准点,更详细地评价各个地区的精密度,以及由于这次我们搜集的遗址的位置信息还可以利用于其他的研究,所以这些信息应制作成能利用的数据库等等。

还有,比如 Ancient Khotan 或赫定的报告等书中的地图,可以用同样的方法来进行类似的研究,这也是今后的一个课题。但是,类似于斯坦因地图,留下地图制作记录的例子是很罕见的。利用这次研究的成果,我们希望以后能做成包括丝绸之路地区的合乎实用的学术信息平台。通过上述研究,我们期待结合新技术的古地图作为新的学术工具,可以应用到考古调查、历史地理研究等领域。

参考文献略号表

冈内 2004:冈内三真《汉代西域都护府の综合的调查》(平成 12 ~ 14 年度日本学术振兴会科学研究费补助金基盘研究 B

（2）研究成果报告书,2000～2002 年,2004 年）。

西村、铃木 2005：西村阳子、铃木桂《吐鲁番地区遗址调查报告（2004 年 10 月 14 日～11 月 1 日）——以麹氏高昌国、唐西州时期の古城、墓葬、石窟、宗教遗址の空间的把握を目指して—》《アジア史研究》29 号,2005 年,第 1～41 页。

Stein1911：M. Aurel Stein, Note on Maps illustrating Dr. Stein's Explorations in Chinese Turkestan and Kansu. *The Geographical Journal*, vol. 37, No. 3, Mar. , 1911, pp. 275－280.

Stein1923：M. Aurel Stein, *Memoir on Maps of Chinese Turkestan and Kansu: From the Survey made during Sir Aurel Stein's Explorations. 1900－1901, 1906－1908, 1913－1915*. DehraDūn, Trigonometrical Survey office, 1923.

Clementi1911：Cecil Clementi, M. A. , *Summary of Geographical Observations taken during a journey from Kashgar to Kowlun, 1907－1909*, Assistant Colinial Secretary, Hong Kong, 1911.

ソベル1997 ：デーヴァ・ソベル著,藤井留美译《经度への挑战：一秒にかけた四百年》东京：翔泳社,1997 年。

新疆洋海古人类牙齿人类学研究报告

韩康信

中国社会科学院

一、牙齿人类学（Dental Anthropology）

牙齿人类学主要关注人类牙齿冠和齿根特征的变异性，包括牙齿大小尺寸及形态结构方面。有的学者在观察内容中还包括了牙齿病理、人工畸形及拔牙等，是体质人类学专注于牙齿研究的一个分支领域。许多学者认为，牙齿形态结构的相对稳定受遗传因素的控制，因此牙齿人类学的研究可以为绝灭和现存人群之间提供直接的证据。

从上世纪七八十年代以来，虽然有许多学者从事了这方面的研究并有大量论文或调查报告发表，其中美国 C. L. Brace、G. R. Scott 以及 C. G. Turner II 等人的研究比较受到重视。前者的研究着重牙齿大小的测量学方面，[①]后两者侧重牙齿结构形态学方面。[②] Scott Turner II The Anthropology of Modern Human Teeth-Dental Morphology and Its Variation in Recent Human Populations（Cambridge University Press，1977）一书将牙齿人类学的研究扩展和综合到世界不同的地理人群。

二、人骨出土的地理位置

人骨出土的洋海古代墓地位于新疆吐鲁番地区鄯善县火焰山南麓的戈壁滩上。地理坐标为北纬 42°28′ ~ 42°49′，东经 89°39′ ~ 89°40′。墓地曾多次被盗掘。2003 年吐鲁番地区文物局与新疆考古所联合挖掘 509 座墓葬（另有千余座墓葬尚未发掘），是一处长期形成的大型墓地，据称其营造年代在公元前 10 世纪——公元初。[③]

---

① 新疆文物考古研究所、吐鲁番地区文物局：《吐鲁番考古新收获——鄯善洋海墓地发掘简报》，《吐鲁番学研究院》2004 年第 1 期，第 1 ~ 66 页；韩康信：《丝绸之路古代居民种族人类学研究》，新疆人民出版社，1993 年。

② 张帆：《中国古代人群的 mtDNA 多肽性研究》（博士论文，待发表）；Brace C L, 1967. Enviroment, tooth form, and size in the Pleistocene, Journal of Dental Research, 46: pp. 809 - 816.

③ Turner C G II, Nichol C R, Scott G R, 1991. Scoring procedures for key morphology traits of the permanent dentition: the Arizona State University dental anthropology system. In: Kelley M A, Larsen C S eds. Advarces in Dental Anthropology. Nek York: Wiley-Liss, 1991, pp. 13 - 31.

三、研 究 材 料

本文调查的人牙材料源自吐鲁番地区文物局在发掘中采集的头骨标本。经清理，共计489具完整和部分保存的头骨及82具游离的下颌骨。

观察齿种包括上、下门齿(Incisors，I)，犬齿(Canine，C)，前臼齿(Premolars，P)和臼齿(Molars，M)。

每个齿种可供观察的样本数最少61例，最多340例。合计约5 066例次。是一组具有相当充分统计价值的样本。

四、研 究 方 法

本文一共观察了27项齿冠和齿根形态特征。各项形态特征的定义和登记标准根据美国亚利桑那州大学人类学系C. G. Turner II等人建立的"亚利桑那州大学牙齿人类学系统(Arizona State University Dental Anthropology System)"简称"ASVDAS系统"的规定。[1] 出现率的计数采用"个体纪录方法"(Individual Count)。[2]

27项齿冠或齿根特征列于下：

1. 上第一门齿翼状排列(UI1 Winging)
2. 上第一门齿铲形(UI1 Shoveling)
3. 上第一门齿双铲形(UI1 Double shoveling)
4. 上第二门齿斜切痕(UI2 Interrup groove)
5. 上第二门齿齿结节(UI2 Tuberculum dentale)
6. 上犬齿舌面近中边缘脊(UC Mesial ridge)
7. 上犬齿舌面远中副脊(UC Distal accessory ridge)
8. 上第二臼齿第四次尖(UM2 Hypocone)
9. 上第一臼齿第五尖(UM1 5 - cusp)
10. 上第一臼齿卡氏尖(UM1 Carabelli's cusp)
11. 上第三臼齿旁结节(UM3 Parastyle)
12. 上第一臼齿釉质延伸(UM1 Enamel extention)
13. 上第一前臼齿单根性(UP1 1 - root)
14. 上第二臼齿三根性(UM2 3 - roots)
15. 上第三臼齿退化或先天缺失(UM3 Peg-shaped and congenital absence)
16. 下第二前臼齿多尖性(LP2 Lingual cusp variation)
17. 下第二臼齿Y型沟(LM2 Y-groove pattern)

---

[1] 张帆：《中国古代人群的mtDNA多肽性研究》(博士论文，待发表)。

[2] Brace C L, 1967. *Enviroment, tooth form, and size in the Pleistocene, Journal of Dental Research*, 46：pp. 809 - 816.

18. 下第一臼齿第六尖(LM1 6 - cusp)

19. 下第二臼齿四尖型(LM2 4 - cusps)

20. 下第一臼齿屈曲隆脊(LM1 Deflect wrinkle)

21. 下第一臼齿下次小尖(LM1 Protostylid)

22. 下第一臼齿第七尖(LM1 7 - cusp)

23. 下第一前臼齿托马斯根(LP1 Tome's root)

24. 下犬齿双根化(LC 2 - roots)

25. 下第一臼齿三根化(LM1 3 - roots)

26. 下第二臼齿单根化(LM2 1 - root)

27. 下前臼齿中心结节(LP1 - 2 Odontome)

(注：上述特征的括号中"U"和"L"表示上和下，"I"、"C"、"P"、"M"分别代表门齿、犬齿、前臼齿和臼齿的缩写字母，齿号后边的阿拉伯数字代表该齿种的顺序好，如 I1 代表第一门齿，M2 代表第二臼齿等，依此类推。)

统计特征的出现率不分性别年龄因素。特征出现的取舍等级按 C. G. Turner II 的规定(参见"结果和比较"一节中的列表"有效级"栏)。左右侧取级别大的一侧计数。出现率用百分比(%)。

比对资料引用 G. R. Scott 和 C. G. Turner II 对世界五个地区人群的调查数据。[1] 这五个地区的人群是(参见图一)：

1. 欧亚大陆西部人群(Western Euasia)(包括西欧、北欧、北非)。

2. 撒哈拉以南非洲人群(Sub-Sabarn Africa)(包括西非、南非、桑人)。

3. 中国—美洲人群(Sino-Americas)(包括中国-蒙古，现代日本人，日本绳文人，东北西伯利亚，南西伯利亚，北极美洲，北美西北，北美和南美印第安人)。

4. 巽他—太平洋人群(Sunda-Pacific)(包括东南亚史前、东南亚现代、波利尼西亚、密克罗尼西亚)。

5. 萨呼尔—太平洋人群(Sahul-Pacific)(包括澳大利亚、新几内亚、美拉尼西亚)。

牙齿形态出现率的组间距离的计算公式为 $d = \sum |x_1 - x_2| / m$。

五、结果和比较

1. 洋海人牙齿的 27 项特征的出现率(%)如下表：

观 察 特 征	有效级	有效数/观察数	出现率
UI1 翼状排列(Winging)		4/61	6.7
UI1 铲型(Shove)(0~6)	>3	5/98	5.1
UI1 双铲型(Double shovel)(0~6)	>3	2/64	3.1
UI2 斜切痕(Interrup)(1~4)	D. Med.	27/28	31.0

① Brace C L, 1967. *Enviroment, tooth form, and size in the Pleistocene*, *Journal of Dental Research*, 46: pp.809 - 816.

观　察　特　征	有效级	有效数/观察数	出现率
UI2 齿结节(Tuberculum)(0～4)	>2	2/90	2.2
UC 近中脊(Mesial)(0～3)	>1	3/98	3.1
UC 远中副脊(Distal accessory ridge)(0～5)	>2	0/100	0.0
UM2 第四次尖(Hypocone)(0～5)	>2	187/262	71.4
UM1 第五尖(5 - cusp)(0～5)	>1	9/226	4.0
UM1 卡氏尖(Carabelli's cusp)(0～7)	>2	44/149	29.5
UM3 臼齿旁结节(Parastyle)(0～5)	>1	6/102	6.0
UM1 釉质延伸(Enamel extention)(0～3)	>2	19/329	5.8
UO1 单根性(1 - root)	1	176/261	67.4
UM2 三根性(3 - roots)	3	193/308	62.7
UM3 退化-先天缺失(P./C./CA)	P. C. C. A	186/244	76.2
LP2 舌侧多尖性(>1Lingual cusp)(0～9)	>1	70/180	38.9
LM2 Y 型沟(Y-groove)(Y. t. x)	Y	0/246	0.0
LM1 第六尖(6 - cusp)(0～5)	>1	3/246	1.2
LM2 四尖型(4 - cusp)	4	217/226	81.6
LM1 屈曲隆脊(Deflect wrinkle)(0～3)	>3	4/72	5.6
LM1 下次小尖(Protostylid)(0～7)	>1	3/207	1.4
LM1 第七尖(7 - cusp)(0～4)	>1	14/295	4.7
LP1 托马斯根(Tome's root)(0～5)	>1	24/228	10.5
LC 双根化(2 - roots)	>1/3	8/244	3.3
LM1 三根化(3 - roots)	3	6/340	1.8
LM2 单根化 LP1 - 2(1 - root)	1	56/304	18.4
LP1 - 2 中心结节(Odentome)(0～1)	>1	0/187	0.0

2. 洋海组与世界五个地区人群的 1 项特征在同一频率等级(分高、中、低频率段)中共同出现的频率最多的是与西部亚欧人群。与其他地区人群共出的频数相对少得多。具体数据如下(参考图二)。

与西部欧亚人群共出频数　　　　19 项　　　　占 90.5%

与撒哈拉以南非洲人共出频数　　6 项　　　　占 28.6%

与中国-美洲人群共出频数　　　　11 项　　　占 52.4%

与巽他-太平洋人群共出频数　　　8 项　　　　占 38.1%

与萨呼尔-太平洋人群共出频数　　12 项　　　占 57.1%

3. 洋海组与其他世界各组人群在 21 项特征的综合形态距离的比较也证明与西部欧亚人群的最小，尤其是与这个人群中的西部欧洲人群最小(0.052)，与北部欧洲人群的距离也很小(0.064)，与北部非洲的人群也不大(0.079)。与其他地区人群的距离都明显增大(0.096～0.267)(参见图三)。

4. 洋海人的齿系结构特点：

低频率的 12 项，包括 UI1 翼状排列，UI1 铲型，UI1 双铲型，UC 近中脊，UM1 第五尖，UM1 釉质延伸，LM2 Y 型沟，LM1 第六尖，LM1 屈曲隆脊，LM1 第七尖，LM1 三根性，LP1 - 2 中心结节等，这些特征的低出现使牙齿结构向简化的方向发展。

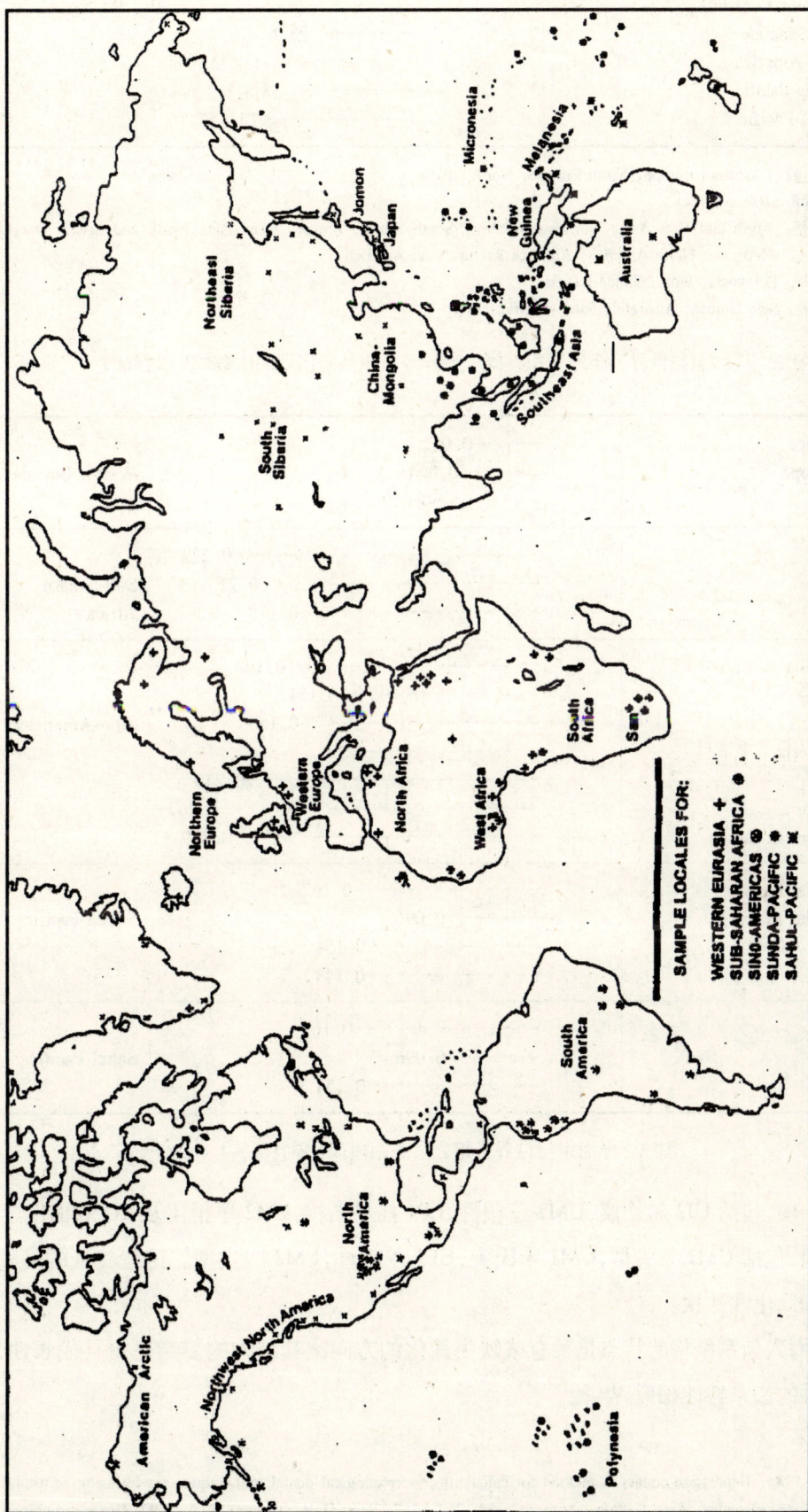

图一 世界五个地区牙齿样本分布图（引自 G．R．Scott 和 C．G．Terner Ⅱ，1997）

Western Eurasia 欧亚大陆西部人群 Sub-Sahsran Africa 撒哈拉以南非洲人群 Sahul-Pacific 萨哈尔-太平洋人群
Sino-Americas 中国-美洲人群 Sunda-Pacific 巽他-太平洋人群 异他-太平洋人群

Western Eurasia	--------------------19 90.5%
Sub-Saharan	------6 28.6%
Sion-America	-----------11 52.4%
Sunda-Pacific	--------8 38.1%
Sahul-Pacific	-----------12 57.1%

"Western Eurasia" 包括：Western Europe, North Europe, North Africa.

"Sub-Saharan" 即 Sub-Saharan Africa.

"Sion-America" 包括：North and East Asia, Northeast Siberia, South Sibria, Joman, East Asia, North and South American Indian, Northwest North America, America Arctic, Sino-America.

"Sunda-Pacific" 包括：Polynesia, India, Sunda-Pacific.

"Sahul-Pacific" 包括：New Guinea, Australia, Sahul-Pacific.

图二　洋海组与世界五个地区组在同一变异等级中共同出现的次数(21 项特征)

Western Europe	-----0.052	
Northern Europe	------0.064	Wester Eurasia
North Africa	-------0.079	
West Africa	----------------------0.222	
South Africa	---------------------0.21	Sub-Saharn
Khoisan	------------------0.178	Africa
China-Mongolia	--------------------0.193	
Jomon(Japan)	---------------0.151	
Recent Japan	-------------------0.186	
Northeast Siberia	--------------0.14	Sino-Americas
South Siberia	--------------------------0.243	
America Arctic	----------------------------0.267	
N. & S. American Indian	--------------------------0.259	
Southeast Asia(Early)	---------------0.167	
Southeast Asia(Recent)	-------0.096	Sunda-Pacific
Polynesia	-------------0.154	
Micronesia	-------------0.148	
Australia	---------------0.167	
New Guinea	-------0.096	Sahul-Pacific
Melanesia	-------------0.154	

图三　洋海组与世界各组之形态距离(21 项特征)

中等频率的 5 项,包括 UI2 斜切痕,UM2 三根性,LP1 托马斯根,LM2 单根化及 LC 双根化。

高频率的 4 项,包括 UM2 三尖型,UM1 卡氏尖,UP1 单根性,LM2 四尖型。这些特征的高频率化也属于牙齿的退化和简化性性状。

总的来看,洋海人齿系结构的特点是稀有或缺失简化的方向比其结构的复杂化更具代表性,而这样的特征与欧洲人种的齿系特性相似。[1]

---

① Turner C GⅡ, 1985. Expression count: A method for calculating morphological dental trait frequencies by using adjustable weighting coefficients with standard ranked scales. Am. J. Phys. Anthrop. , 68: 263–267. Scott G. R, Turner C GⅡ ,1997. The anthropology of modern human teeth: Dental morphology and its variation in recent human populations. Cambridge University Press.

六、结　论

　　洋海人的齿系的简化特性,各种特征出现率更多与西部欧亚人群的相似以及多项特征的形态距离也与西部欧亚人群的最小,这些都证明:中国新疆境内至少在距今 3 000 多年前已经出现了与西部欧亚人群相似的齿牙人类学系统。这一研究结果和以往对新疆古人骨的种族形态学研究[1]以及已经有的新疆古人骨的 mtDNA 多肽性分析似相符合。[2]

　　[1]　Mayhall J T, Saunders S R, Belier P L, 1982. The dental morphology of North American whites: a reappraisal. In Teeth: Form, Function, and Evolution, ed. B. Kurten, pp. 245 - 58, New York: Columbia University Press.
　　[2]　Zubov. A. A, Khaldeeva N I, 1979. Ethnic Odontology of the USSR. Moscow: Nayka(In Russian).

鄯善吐峪沟 81SATM2 陶棺人颅

王 博

新疆维吾尔自治区博物馆考古部

1981 年吐鲁番地区文物保护管理所在鄯善县火焰山南,吐峪沟河谷出山口西面的一条小沟里发现了一片墓地。这里被雨水冲刷形成了一条条大体是东西走向的沟壑,墓葬即分布沟壑的崖壁上,从外表看有 15 座之多。吐鲁番地区文物保护管理所清理了两座墓葬,出土了 2 具陶棺(81SATM1 陶棺、81SATM2 陶棺),都是泥质灰陶,在形制上略有些变化。[①] 1988 年文物普查时,我们也专门调查了吐峪沟墓地,墓葬是土洞墓室,墓门面向沟壑,生土坯封门。墓室不大,平面呈长方形,室顶略显弧形。葬俗是两种:一种是无葬具的仰身直肢葬,一种是陶棺葬。[②]

本文研究的是 81SATM2 陶棺人颅骨。81SATM2 陶棺呈横圆桶形,在腹壁纵向等分装饰着四条

图一 鄯善县吐峪沟墓地 81SATM2 陶棺

附加堆纹,同时在盖上面又多加了一条的附加堆纹,由此纵向的附加堆纹共是五条。陶棺长 66 cm、直径 30 cm。棺口开在上面的中部,很明显棺盖是制作过程中直接从棺体上切下来的,长 33.5 cm、宽 20 cm。盖上面还塑了横向的两条附加堆纹纽。陶棺内骨架呈叠压形式,基本完整,头骨在最上面(图一)。骨架上除残留少量的筋皮、肉外,大多都非常干净,似经过清洗。由此推测,在埋葬过程中首先对尸体经过了特殊的脱骨处理,或是自然腐烂之后叠压装入棺内的。

一、性别和年龄

81SATM2 人颅骨牙齿为一级磨损,颅顶缝比较清晰,为成年(或青年,年龄 23～26 岁)个体。眉弓稍显,乳突中等,下颏方形,为男性个体。

---

① 吐鲁番地区文管所:《新疆鄯善县吐峪沟发现陶棺葬》,《考古》1986 年第 1 期。岑云飞主编:《吐鲁番博物馆》,新疆美术摄影出版社,1992 年,第 71 页图 136。“陶棺”,俄文作“Оссуарии”,英文拼写作“Occuaril”。汉语意译形式非常多,除写作“尸骨瓮”、“纳尸罐”、“盛骨瓮”、“骨灰罐”外,还有“尸棺”、“陶瓮”、“陶尸坛”、“赤陶尸坛”、“遗骨棺”、“骨罐”、“沉默塔”、“无声塔”、“安息塔”、骨灰盒等;音译作“奥苏阿里”。王博:《丝绸之路上的祆教陶棺》,载于赵丰主编:《丝绸之路艺术与生活》,香港艺纱常服饰,2007 年,第 31～40 页。
② 自治区文物普查办公室吐鲁番地区文物普查队:《吐鲁番地区文物普查资料汇编》,《新疆文物》1988 年第 3 期,第 70 页。

二、形态观察和测量分析

81SATM2 人颅骨保存完整,带有下颌骨。下面进行形态观察和测量特征的分析。

(一)非测量性形态特征的观察

81SATM2 人颅骨额、顶结节平缓,最大宽的位置在后 1/3,枕部弯度平缓,颅形呈楔形。无额中缝,颅顶缝微波型或深波型,非常简单。颅顶形状呈圆穹式,颅侧壁形状呈弧形外凸。翼区呈 I 型(颞-额式)。眉弓凸度稍显,眉间突度不显,鼻根点凹陷浅,梨状孔形状呈梨形。眶形呈斜椭圆形,四边呈弧形,眶宽明显大于眶高。眶腔呈敞开形,眶口前倾。犬齿窝浅,鼻前棘中等,梨状孔下缘钝型,鼻骨形状中部缩狭,鼻额缝和额颌缝弧形上凸。乳突中等。下颌颏形呈方形,枕外隆凸稍显。颅顶前囟点至人字点之间,没有明显的正中矢状隆起。鼻梁冠状隆起为 2 级,鼻骨略隆起(图二)。

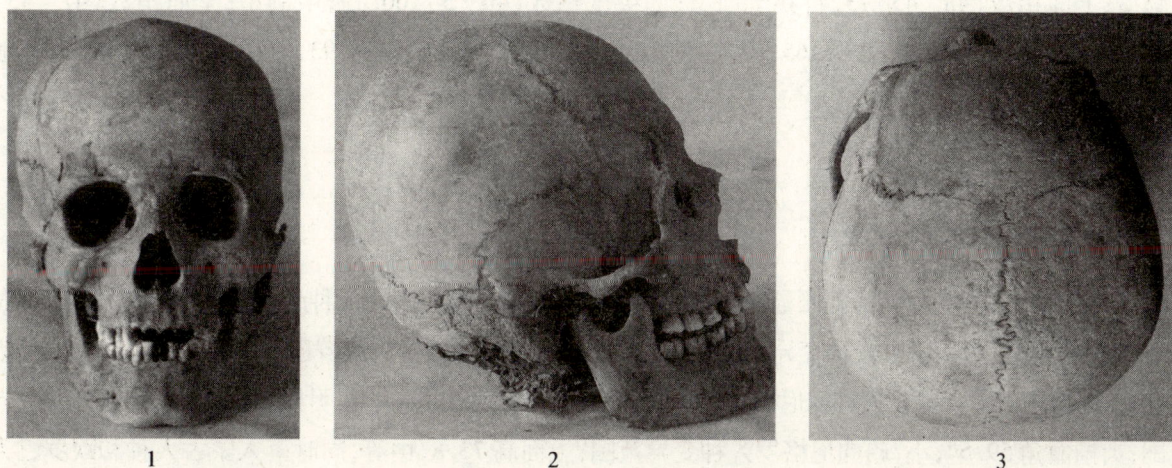

图二　81SATM2 人颅骨

1. 正面观　　2. 侧面观　　3. 顶面观

(二)颅面测量特征

81SATM2 人颅骨的测量见附表一,指数见表一。

表一　吐峪沟 2 号陶棺人颅测量表(男性)

项　　目	数　据	项　　目	数　据
1. 颅指数(8:1)	89.49	7. 眶指数 I(52:51)	78.95
2. 颅长高指数(17:1)	83.48	8. 垂直颅面指数(48:17)	53.09
3. 颅长耳高指数(21:1)	71.47	9. 上面指数(48:45)	52.64
4. 颅宽高指数(17:8)	93.29	10. 全面指数(47:45)	87.73
5. 鼻指数(54:55)	50.48	11. 中面指数(48:46)	75
6. 鼻根指数(SS:SC)	33.33	12. 额宽指数(9:8)	65.10

项 目	数据	项 目	数据
13. 面突度指数(40:5)	100.19	17. 鼻尖指数(SR:O_3)	40.84
14. 颧额宽指数($43_①$:60)	101.22	18. 齿槽弓指数(61:60)	118.93
15. 颅面宽指数(45:8)	94.09	19. 中面扁平指数	26.83
16. 上面扁平指数(n 至 fmo-fmo:43)	14.56	20. 眶间宽高指数(DS:DC)	34.39

81SATM2 人颅骨头最大长较短,颅宽较宽,颅指数(8:1)89.49,特圆颅型;颅长高指数(17:1)83.48,高颅型;颅宽高指数(17:8)93.29,正颅型;颅长耳高指数(21:1)71.47,高颅型。81SATM2 人颅骨鼻高中等,鼻宽中等,鼻指数(54:55)50.48,中鼻型;眶高较低,眶宽中等,眶指数Ⅰ(52:51)左78.95,中眶型;上面指数(48:45)75,特狭上面型;面突度指数(40:5)100.19,中颌型;全面指数(47:45)87.73,中上面型;额宽指数(9:8)65.10,狭额型;齿槽弓指数(61:60)118.93,短颌型;总面角83.5,中颌型;齿槽面角59.5,超突颌型。

三、比较分析

1. 通过表二的 14 项人面部测量项目将吐峪沟 2 号陶棺人颅与三大人种颅面测量特征进行比较:鼻指数 50.48,中等,落入蒙古人种变异范围;鼻尖指数 40.84,较大,落入欧罗巴人种变异范围;鼻根指数 33.33,中等,同时落入蒙古人种和尼格罗人种变异范围;鼻颧角 147°,上面明显扁平,落入蒙古人种变异范围;齿槽面角 59.5°,小,趋向尼格罗人种变异范围;上面高 73.8,中等,同时落入蒙古人种和欧罗巴人种变异范围;颧宽 140.2,大,落入蒙古人种变异范围;眶高(左)33,中等,同时落入欧罗巴人种和尼格罗人种变异范围;齿槽弓指数 118.93,大,落入蒙古人种变异范围;垂直颅面指数 53.09,中等,同时落入蒙古人种和欧罗巴人种变异范围;颧上颌角 123°,中面明显突出,趋向欧罗巴人种变异范围;上面扁平指数 14.56,落入蒙古人种变异范围;前颌指数 26.83,趋向欧罗巴人种变异范围;最小额宽 97,宽,落入欧罗巴人种变异范围。

表二 吐峪沟 81SATM2 人颅与三大人种颅面测量特征比较(男性)　　单位:毫米、度、%

序 号	比较项目	SATM2	蒙古人种	欧洲人种	尼格罗人种
1	鼻指数	50.48	43~53	43~49	51~60
2	鼻尖指数	40.84	30~39	40~48	20~35
3	鼻根指数	33.33	31~49	46~53	20~45
4	鼻颧角	147°	145°~149°	135°~137°	140°~142°
5	齿槽面角	59.5°	73°~81°	82°~86°	61°~72°
6	上面高	73.8	70~80	66~74	62~71

序　号	比较项目	SATM2	蒙古人种	欧洲人种	尼格罗人种
7	颧宽	140.2	131～145	124～139	121～138
8	眶高(左)	33	34～37	33～34	30～34
9	齿槽弓指数	118.93	115～120	116～118	109～116
10	垂直颅面指数	53.09	52～60	50～54	47～53
11	颧上颌角	123°	141°～142°	124°～127°	—
12	上面扁平指数	14.56	13.7～16.2	18.5～20.3	16.7～20.6
13	前颌指数	26.83	不超过20	30左右	—
14	最小额宽	97	89～96.9	96.2～103.7	

这里有5项(鼻指数、鼻颧角、颧宽、齿槽弓指数、上面扁平指数),落入蒙古人种的变异范围;有1项(鼻根指数),同时落入蒙古人种和尼格罗人种的变异范围;有2项(上面高、垂直颅面指数),同时落入蒙古人种和欧罗巴人种的变异范围。落入或趋向欧罗巴人种变异范围的有4项(鼻尖指数、颧上颌角、前颌指数、最小额宽);有1项(眶高)同时落入欧罗巴人种和尼格罗人种的变异范围。另外,还有1项(齿槽面角)趋向尼格罗人种的变异范围。

在观察项目上,81SATM2人颅骨眉弓凸度稍显,眉间突度不显,鼻根点凹陷浅,眶腔呈敞开形,眶口前倾,犬齿窝浅,鼻前棘中等,鼻梁冠状隆起为2级。这里除眶口前倾趋向欧罗巴人种特征外,其余的都倾向蒙古人种特征。

这样一来,81SATM2人颅骨在观察和测量项目上显现出相对的一致,可以将他归入蒙古人种类型。另外,鼻尖指数和最小额宽两项数据也接近蒙古人种的上限。不过,也可以看出来有的项目明显是趋向欧罗巴人种特征的,如颧上颌角、前颌指数等。

2. 81SATM2人颅与亚洲蒙古人种地区类型颅、面测量特征组间差之比较

以上观察和测量特征的分析,初步推定81SATM2人颅属蒙古人种类型。下面将他放入苏联学者制作的有关亚洲东部蒙古人种各地区类型的主要颅、面测量特征组间18个项目的变异范围,进行比较。

1) 库车古墓组与全部亚洲蒙古人种组间变异的比较,颅长、颅指数、额倾角、颅长高指数、鼻骨角等5项都脱离出亚洲蒙古人种组间差异界值,这是一个值得注意的现象。

2) 81SATM2人颅与北蒙古人种组间差异的比较,有9项落入其变异范围;81SATM2人颅与东北蒙古人种组间差异的比较,有7项落入其变异范围;81SATM2人颅与东蒙古人种组间差异的比较,有7项落入其变异范围;81SATM2人颅与南蒙古人种组间差异的比较,有7项落入其变异范围。由此看来,81SATM2人颅在颅、面体质特征上更趋向于北蒙古人种类型,同时81SATM2人颅的额倾角、鼻骨角数据也接近北蒙古人种类型。

表三　81SATM2 与亚洲蒙古人种地区类型颅、面测量特征组间差之比较

测量项目	SATM2	北蒙古人种	东北蒙古人种	东蒙古人种	南蒙古人种
颅长(1)	166.5	176.7～192.7	181.8～192.4	175.0～180.8	168.4～181.3
颅宽(8)	149	142.3～154.6	134.3～142.6	137.6～142.6	135.7～143.6
颅指数(8:1)	89.49	75.4～85.9	69.8～79.0	77.1～81.5	76.6～83.4
颅高(17)	139	125.0～135.8	133.8～141.1	136.4～140.2	134.0～140.9
颅长高指数(17:1)	83.48	67.4～74.8	73.2～75.6	75.3～80.2	75.8～80.2
颅宽高指数(17:8)	93.29	83.5～94.5	92.1～100.0	96.8～100.3	94.4～101.3
最小额宽(9)	97	89.0～97.0	94.6～98.2	89.0～93.7	89.7～95.4
额倾角(32)	77	77.5～84.2	77.9～80.2	83.3～86.4	82.5～91.7
颧宽(45)	140.2	139.0～143.7	137.5～142.4	130.6～136.7	131.4～136.2
上面高(48)	73.8	73.3～79.6	74.5～79.2	71.0～76.6	59.8～71.9
垂直颅面指数(48:17)	53.09	56.1～61.2	54.1～58.5	51.7～54.9	43.8～52.5
上面指数(48:45)	52.64	51.2～55.4	51.3～56.2	51.7～56.8	45.1～53.7
鼻颧角(77)	147	144.3～151.4	146.2～152.0	144.0～147.3	141.0～147.8
总面角(72)	83.5	84.8～89.0	83.1～86.3	80.6～86.5	80.6～86.7
眶指数(52:51)	78.95	79.6～86.0	81.3～84.5	80.7～85.0	78.2～86.8
鼻指数(54:55)	50.48	47.2～50.7	42.7～47.3	45.2～50.3	47.7～55.5
鼻根指数(SS:SC)	33.33	26.7～49.2	34.8～45.8	31.7～37.2	26.1～43.2
鼻骨角(75<1>)	25	16.9～24.9	14.8～23.9	13.7～19.8	12.0～18.3

结　语

　　1981 年吐鲁番地区文物保护管所发掘出土的 81SATM2 陶棺,关于它的年代许多学者都认为属于麴氏高昌国时期(公元 460 年至 640 年),[1]同时认为其属于祆教徒的墓葬。祆教传入新疆的时间,多根据吐鲁番市安乐古城出土的《金光明经》卷 2 题记上写有"城南太后祠下胡天",推断至迟在 5 世纪祆教传到了新疆。[2] 唐代祆教在新疆传播的已比较普遍,《旧唐书》卷一百九十八记载,于阗国"好事祆神",《魏书·西域传》记载焉者"俗事天神"。可以说在这一时期,从今天的吐鲁番、焉者,一直到于阗,都有信仰

　　① 李肖主编:《吐鲁番文物精粹》,上海辞书出版社,2006 年,第 114 页。陶棺,麴氏高昌国时期(公元 460 年至 640 年),内葬成年人骨骼一具,为拜火教徒(祆教)的葬俗。
　　② 王素:《高昌火祆教论稿》,《历史研究》1986 年第 3 期。

袄教的信徒居住。

对 81SATM2 陶棺所葬人骨族属的研究,多有学者涉及。吐鲁番阿斯塔那出土的 6 世纪文书中有"萨薄"一词,有学者认为"萨薄"是古代波斯语 Sartavaho 的汉字音译,是袄教寺庙的主持者的职称,我国古代又译作萨宝、萨保。应该说,在古代新疆萨保是管理粟特人信奉袄教宗教事务主持者的职称,陶棺葬也应当是粟特袄教徒的埋葬形式。由出土陶棺的分布来看,从粟特本土、今天的泽拉夫善河一带沿着丝绸之路向东、向西都有发展的趋势。同时,从出土文物和古代文献的研究情况来看,在古代的新疆几乎每一个大的城镇或者是处于重要的交通干道上的一些小城镇,都有粟特人的身影。①

粟特人,在中国史籍中又被称为昭武九姓、九姓胡、杂种胡、粟特胡等等。从人种上来说,他们是属于伊朗系统的中亚古族;从语言上来说,他们操印欧语系伊朗语族中的东伊朗语的一支,即粟特语(Sogdian),文字则使用阿拉美文的一种变体,现通称粟特文。②

81SATM2 陶棺葬的人骨是一具成年男性,他所表现出的基本特征:在观察项目上,弓凸度稍显,眉间突度不显,鼻根点凹陷浅,眶腔呈敞开形,眶口前倾,犬齿窝浅,鼻前棘中等,鼻梁冠状隆起为 2 级。在测量项目上,属特圆颅型,高颅型,正颅型,中鼻型,中眶型,狭额型,短颌型及眶高低等特征。虽然他有较多的北蒙古人种类型特征,但其中的颅、面部所显示出的如鼻尖指数、颧上颌角、前颌指数、最小额宽和眶高低等,欧罗巴人种特征还是很明显。81SATM2 陶棺葬人骨只是从个例说明这一时期吐鲁番袄教信徒居民在人种特征上的特殊性,也是今后研究吐鲁番古代居民体质特征研究上要注意的问题。

附表一　吐峪沟 2 号陶棺人颅测量表(男性)　　　单位:毫米、度、%

马丁号　项目	数据	马丁号　项目	数据
1 颅长(g—op)	166.5	43 面宽(fmt—fmt)	106
2 颅长(g—i)	164.5	43(1)两眶内宽(fmo—fmo)	99.6
5 颅底长(enba—n)	102.8	鼻根点至两眶内宽矢高	15
8 颅宽(eu—en)	149	46 中部面宽(zm—zm)	98.4
9 额最小宽(ft—ft)	97	颧上颌角	33.5
10 额最大宽(co—co)	123	40 面底长(pr—enba)	103
11 间宽(au—au)	134	72 总面角(n—pr—FH)	83.5
12 星点间宽(ast—ast)	115.9	73 鼻面角(n—ns—FH)	89
17 颅高(ba—b)	139	74 齿槽面角(ns—pr—FH)	59.5
18 颅高(ba—v)	140.8	额倾角(m—g—FH)	77

① 荣新江:《西域粟特移民聚落补考》,《西域研究》2005 年 2 期,第 1~11 页。影山悦子:《东トルキスタン出土のオシサリ(ゾロアスター——教徒の纳骨器)について》,第 78~80 页。林梅村:《高昌火袄教遗迹考》,《文物》2006 年第 7 期,第 59~59 页。钱伯泉:《从祀部文书看高昌曲氏王朝期的袄教及粟特九姓胡人》,《新疆文物》1990 年第 3 期,第 93~101 页。
② 荣新江:《从撒马尔干到长安——中古时期粟特人的迁徙与入居》,载荣新江、张志清主编:《从撒马尔干到长安——粟特人在中国的文化遗迹》,北京图书馆出版社,2004 年,第 3~8 页。

续　表

马丁号　项目		数　据	马丁号　项目		数　据
21 耳上颅高		121	额倾角(m—n—FH)		84
47 耳上颅高(b)		119	32 前囟角(b—g—FH)		50
47 全面高(n—gn)		123	前囟角(b—n—FH)		55
48 上面高 (n—sd)		73.8	32 额角(m—g—op)		70
上面高(n—pr)		70	75 鼻梁侧面角(n—rhi—FH)		59
45 颧宽(zy—zy)		140.2	鼻额角(fmo—n—fmo)		147
鼻高(n—ns)		52.5	颧上颌角(zm—ss—zm)		123
鼻宽		26.5	鼻骨角(pr—n—rhi)		25
眶高	左	33	57(1)鼻孔高(rhi—ns)		33.8
	右	33.5	57(2)鼻骨上宽		13.9
眶宽 (mf—ec)	左	41.8	57(3)鼻骨下宽		17.3
	右	41.5	鼻骨最大高		9.1
上齿槽弓长		56	眶中宽(O₃)		47.5
上齿槽弓宽(ecm—ecm)		66.6	鼻尖高(SR)		19.4
眶间宽(mf—mf)		19.1	鼻骨长(n—rhi)	左	22.35
鼻梁至眶间宽的矢高		6.5		右	24.75
57 鼻骨最小宽		9	鼻骨最小高		3

交河故城保护加固

李最雄

敦煌研究院

一、交河故城概况

交河故城遗址是国务院 1961 年公布的第一批全国重点文物保护单位,位于新疆维吾尔自治区吐鲁番市西 10 km 的雅尔乃孜沟村。交河故城地处吐鲁番盆地西部,自古以来就是连接内地与西域的门户,也是沟通塔里木、准噶尔两大盆地的通道,故城坐落在高达 30 m 的台地上,台地正当火焰山与盐山交接处,控扼着两山之间的天然豁口。交河故城是丝绸之路上具有近两千年悠久历史的名城,它自公元前 2 世纪直到公元 14 世纪一直是西域重镇,是古代西域政治、经济、文化中心之一,在东西方文化交流中起过十分重要的作用。交河故城对研究西域历史、宗教历史、古代西域交通史、丝绸之路史、中西方文化经济和政治交流的历史有重要价值,其城市布局、遗存的雄伟建筑及出土的文物对于研究古代建筑史具有重大意义。

交河故城总面积 35 万余平方米,建筑面积 22 万平方米,现今保存在地面的建筑遗迹大多是公元 3 ~ 6 世纪所建。经初步调查认定,故城内现存佛教遗迹 52 处,古井 316 眼,窑洞 106 孔,房舍 1 389 间(其中较完整的 356 间),制陶窑址 7 处,城门 4 处,街道长度 1 908 m,巷道 34 条,共计 2 241 m,防护墙遗址 1 041 m,墓葬区 15 万 m²。交河故城在一柳叶形台地上,它与建在宽阔的平原地带的城市的最大区别是受地形条件的制约,只能因地制宜规划营建市区。交河城区位于台地的中南部,以中心大街为中轴线,将整个市区大致可分为 6 个区(图一)。中心大街北端为中心佛塔,南端为瞭望台。中心佛塔以北至东北佛寺为寺庙区;中心大街西侧为西城区,东侧以东西大街为界,以北为东城区,以南为官署区;瞭望台以南为南城区;东北小佛寺以北为墓葬区。

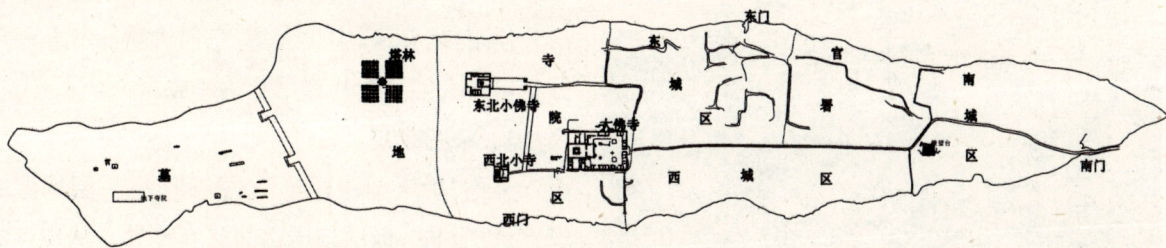

图一 交河故城城市布局图

二、交河故城的建造工艺及结构

交河故城遗址的建筑形式从建造工艺上主要分为两大类,一类为是从地表向下从生土中挖成的,这类建筑多为窑洞式建筑、地穴、半地穴、井等,少量为庭院式建筑;另一类是挖、夯、堆砌三种工艺方法结合或者挖和堆砌两种工艺方法结台构筑的建筑物,这类建筑多为庭院式建筑及佛塔、佛坛等。

1. 夯土建筑

现存较为完整的夯土建筑有:衙署台地北沿护墙、一些佛殿的中心柱、塔林、护墙、交河最北端夯土台基等。从以上遗迹中可以看出,夯土技术可分为两种情况存在于交河故城中。一类是位于原生地面上,不掺杂其他建筑技法的纯夯土建筑(图二);另一类则作为诸如"减地法"建筑的辅助技术而存在(图三)。这两类夯土建筑有着本质上的差别,其时代可能相差甚远。夯筑技法差异很大,其夯层厚度、所用材料均不一样(素土及加掺和料两种),如东门北侧门墩为素土夯成,内加芦苇作筋,而南侧的门墩则加掺和料夯成,内加树枝作筋。

图二　纯夯土建筑(东门)

图三　夯土找平层(大佛寺)

2. "减地法"建筑

在地面上事先规划好建筑物的布局、确定了墙壁的位置之后,把墙内外的土挖去,这样竖起墙来,由此挖出房间、院落及街道等建筑(图四)。城中除了寺院外的大部分建筑,如大型院落区、衙署区的部分建筑、街巷区、中央大道、东西大道、东门、一部分护墙及大部分街巷都用此法建成。

图四　减地法(官署自东向西望)

3. 垛泥建筑

又称"板筑泥法建筑"(图五),每一层垛泥的厚度是均匀的,但层与层之间略有差异。从现存的情况看,每层的厚度在 50～90 cm 左右,以 70 cm 左右的层高为多见。垛泥墙每层均有若干条同一斜向的干缩裂缝,相邻两条干缩裂缝之间称为垛,垛

交河故城保护加固

宽约45~60 cm,同层相邻两垛之间看不出刻意衔接的痕迹。相邻两层垛的方向相反,上下相邻两层相对的垛之间也无有意识压缝的迹象,立面裂痕呈"人"字形。

4. 土坯、生土块建筑

在交河城中使用土坯砌墙是极个别的现象(图六),土坯材料虽然一直未占据主导地位,但作为辅助材料却被广泛使用,而且贯穿整个交河城的建筑史。除了土坯之外,城里的建筑物还可见到使用生土块进行砌墙(图七)、补洞等工程,生土块一般都切削成大小适中的正方体,边长约在15~25 cm(图八)。

图五　垛泥(东北小佛寺南墙外)

图六　土坯砌墙(官署地面残墙)

图七　土块砌墙(大佛寺东30 m)

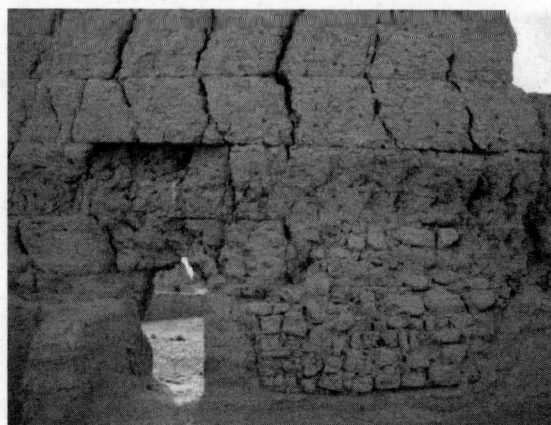
图八　土块补洞(大佛寺东墙北端)

三、遗址的主要病害

1. 文物本体病害

（1）片状剥离

① 雨蚀剥离

在交河故城可见两种类型的雨蚀剥离病害。一种是在暴雨作用下土体崩解成泥流附着在墙体上,在强烈的干湿交替作用下形成泥皮(图九),由于风等外力的作用,泥皮脱落。发育不同程度的墙面片状剥蚀,主要发育在墙体的西北面,生土墙体、垛泥墙体和夯土均有发育。另一种是龟裂纹,主要分布在垛泥

· 315 ·

墙表面,在大佛寺、东北小寺和西北小寺发育最为普遍。

② 风蚀剥离

风蚀剥离病害在交河故城发育较为广泛,主要发育在土遗址的西北面,垛泥墙面主要表现形式是墙面被风吹蚀成凹凸不平的蜂窝状(图十),在生土墙面主要表现为墙体表面残留有大量的结石小突起。

图九　雨蚀形成的泥皮(塔林小佛塔东面)　　　　图十　垛泥墙面风蚀剥离病害

(2)掏蚀

① 酥碱

由于土体中含有较多的易溶盐,在水的作用下,土遗址土体中的可溶盐尤其是 Na_2SO_4 发生反复的溶解收缩后结晶膨胀,土体结构不断疏松(图十一)。这种类型主要分布在台地的中部和南部,在地势较低处的墙基较为发育,在生土墙基多见。

② 风力掏蚀

交河故城的风力掏蚀主要有两种形式。由于地层岩性的差异,胶结差的地层容易被风吹蚀,形成典型的风蚀病害。层状风蚀病害主要发生在生土地层(图十二)。棒槌墙是墙基根部由于酥碱作用下结构变得疏松,在风的作用下墙基被掏蚀凹进(图十一),主要分布在生土墙基。

图十一　酥碱掏蚀凹进(瞭望台东200 m)　　　　图十二　风蚀地貌(大佛寺外东40 m)

（3）裂隙

① 卸荷裂隙

在土遗址本体上，卸荷裂缝主要分布在一些宽大、高耸的土台上，土台一般近直立，裂缝宽，破坏性大。

② 构造缝

交河故城的构造缝主要有两种表现形式。一种是新构造活动的结果，延伸长，分布广（图十三）。还有一种是生土墙基的节理构造以及受其影响发育在上部墙体的构造缝。

③ 变形裂隙

交河故城的变形裂隙主要有两种形式。一种是由于窑洞的开挖，引起应力重分布导致的洞顶纵向裂缝和洞口变形裂缝（图十四）。另一种是由于基础的不均匀沉降引起的变形裂隙，如塔林大金刚塔，基础是对自然地面略加整理，然后用夯土层进行找平。

图十三　构造裂缝（官署区街道旁）

图十四　洞顶变形裂缝（东城区）

④ 建筑结构裂缝

交河故城建筑工艺裂缝主要有墙体之间的接槎缝和垛块之间的施工缝。主要分布在垛泥墙体上。垛泥墙由于施工时的垛缝以及墙间互不接槎，墙体干燥收缩在风和雨的作用下，裂缝不断加宽（图十五、图十六）。

图十五　垛泥墙接槎缝（东北佛寺南墙）

图十六　垛泥缝（东北佛寺东墙外面）

（4）冲沟

交河故城的冲沟主要是径流型冲沟。径流型冲沟主要发育在一些宽大厚实的生土台顶部和台地中央，台地的中央大道就是沿自然冲沟地形布置。

（5）人为破坏

由于历史的原因，交河故城遗址曾受到严重的人为破坏，给遗址带来无法弥补的破坏。

2. 文物载体病害

交河故城台地崖体的病害是一个岩土工程问题，主要病害有崩塌和地表水的冲刷。

（1）崖体的崩塌

① 裂隙的特征

交河故城崖体主要有两类破坏裂隙：构造裂隙—节理、次生卸荷裂隙。整个崖体区，发育三组节理：NE 向组，走向 15°～35°，均值 25°，倾角近直立；NNW 向组，走向 310°～330°，均值 325°，倾角近直立；NWW 向组，走向 275°～295°，均值 285°，倾角近直立。其中以走向 25°和走向 325°两组发育严重，走向 285°组次之。发育一组卸荷裂隙，其优势破坏产状：走向 NW，均值 328°，倾角近直立，平行崖体走向。崖体裂缝在平面上主要形态有：锯齿状、弧形、平直三类，以平直类为主，占裂缝总数的一半以上。

② 崩塌的类型

交河故城台地东南边裂隙切割崖体多为连续大段崩塌破坏，局部出现裂隙切割孤立体崩塌破坏，西北边多为裂隙切割孤立体崩塌破坏。历史上崖体的崩塌主要是错断式崩塌。根据崖体的工程地质条件分析，崖体主要是崩塌破坏，崩塌模式有错断式崩塌、拉裂式崩塌和倾倒式崩塌（图十七～图二十）。

（2）崖体的崩塌

交河故城遗址所在的台地位于雅尔乃孜沟中央，直接受洪水危害。尤其是洪水主要流经台地东南侧河沟，洪水量大而河道急剧变宽，河水直接冲刷的崖壁面积骤增。在凶猛的洪水冲击下，故城周缘崖体不断坍塌。

图十七　错断式崩塌（大佛寺西西崖体）　　　　图十八　倾倒式崩塌（台地南端东崖）

图十九　崖边卸荷裂缝（台地北部东崖）

图二十　拉裂式崩塌（塔林东东崖体）

四、遗址加固的主要工程技术措施

1. 文物本体加固

（1）土坯砌补

土坯砌补技术主要是针对遗址局部悬空失稳、掏蚀凹进严重且下部具有支撑空间的土遗址，均采用与遗址本体相同材料的土坯支顶、填充，尽量最少干预的结构补强措施，达到防止进一步风化掏蚀和遗址坍塌的目的。

（2）锚固

锚杆锚固是指遗址本体在失去一定的黏聚力而局部失稳后，通过锚杆给失稳本体新的连接力的技术措施，遗址本体可依赖锚杆连接提高本体的整体稳定性。这种工艺技术方便、简洁、隐蔽性好、强度提高较明显，是遗址本体保护工程的重要技术措施之一。

（3）裂隙灌浆

锚固后的裂缝必须进行灌浆填充，否则一旦裂缝中入渗雨水会导致土体软化，使锚杆失去锚固作用；另外，裂隙中不断填充沙土，或裂隙两壁长期风化，也会影响锚固效果。因此，锚固后裂隙灌浆填充的密实与否，是保证锚固作用的关键。

（4）表面防风化渗透加固

根据遗址土体表层风化的状况、严重程度及风化的深度等病害情况，设计要求及相关的规范等，以不同模数、不同浓度、不同配比，选适宜的气温条件，对遗址表层的风化土进行 PS 渗透加固。做旧是土遗址本体加固的最后一个环节，通过一定的技术措施使遗址本体整体协调一致。

（5）其他特殊工艺

针对遗址体的破坏特征，在官署西洞口还采用了钢梁吊顶加固措施。此外对于个别遗址体采取了多种结构形式结合加固的措施。

2. 文物载体加固

交河故城崖体的加固具有地质工程高边坡加固的属性，同时又属于文物加固的范畴，因此，崖体加固所采取的措施及施工工艺具有复杂性、专业性和特殊性。根据崖体加固的施工设计文件和施工过程中的调整优化,形成了科学合理的加固工程措施与加固施工工艺。崖体加固的总体施工方法如图二十一。

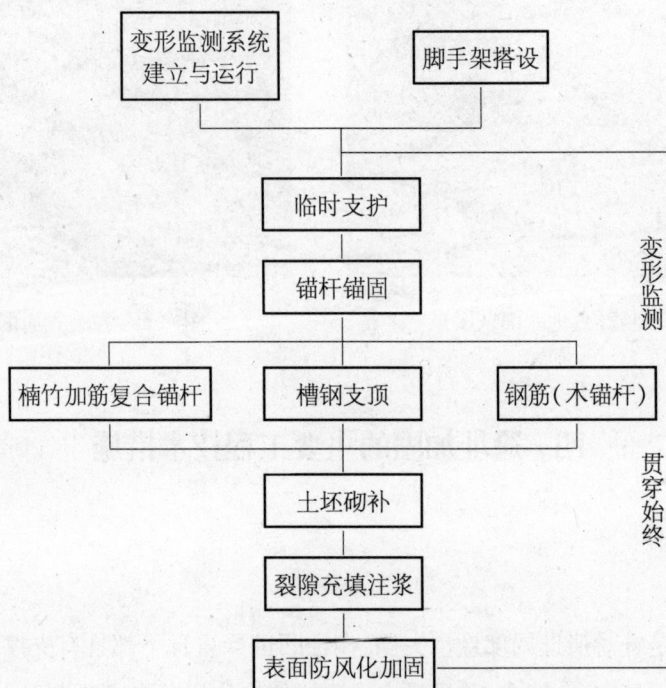

图二十一　交河故城崖体加固施工措施结构图

崖体加固根本目的在于大幅度提高崖体稳定性问题,同时,增强崖体的抗风化能力,以延长遗址的寿命。提高崖体稳定性所采取的工程措施包括锚杆锚固(楠竹复合加筋锚杆、槽钢支顶、钢筋和木锚杆等)、裂隙充填灌浆和土坯砌补。同时,运用表面防风化加固措施和少量的土坯砌补来增强崖体表面的抗风化能力。脚手架工程是后续施工的平台,临时支护是锚固灌浆施工的安全储备和保障。此外,崖体作为一类特殊的边坡工程,严格遵循信息化施工的原则,根据崖体的破坏特点和现场条件,建立了变形监测系统,且变形监测贯穿崖体加固全过程。

此外局部还采取了框架(三角支架)锚固、静压注浆等工程措施。

五、遗址保护加固工程实例

1. 东北佛寺保护加固

(1) 主要工程措施

东北佛寺地处交河故城台地东北角,常年受到季风的影响,东北佛寺主要突出性病害为:严重风化、裂隙发育。针对其突出性病害,东北佛寺主要采取的工程措施为:3~5%的 PS 溶液喷洒渗透,采用当地粉土和3%的 PS 溶液,按水灰比为0.2~0.3进行裂隙砌补,采用5~8 mm 的塑胶管根据裂隙深度布设注浆管,用5%的 PS 溶液和和当地粉土按照水灰比为0.6拌制并灌浆。有效地防治了东北佛寺遗址本体裂隙的发育,提高了本体强度,即抗风化能力。

（2）主要的施工工艺组织

根据东北佛寺的实际地形，及东北佛寺 S5 墙和 W6 墙裂隙发育，有随时坍塌的危险，结合现场的实际情况，东北佛寺自西侧 S5 墙和 W6 墙顺时针旋转组织施工按照不同的遗址本体情况进行加固。施工工艺的组织形式基本按照先结构后西部的加固组织方法。以东北佛寺 S5 墙为例说明东北佛寺保护加固工艺(图二十二)。

（3）加固效果

加固前后的对比见图二十三～图二十六。

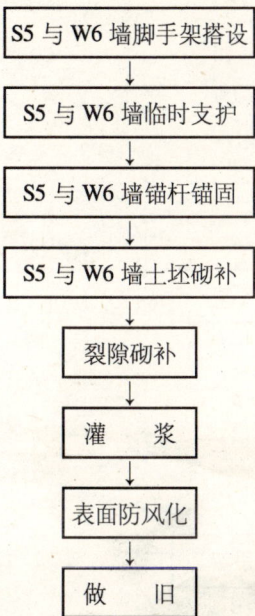

图二十二　S5 墙施工工艺流程图

S5 与 W6 墙脚手架搭设
↓
S5 与 W6 墙临时支护
↓
S5 与 W6 墙锚杆锚固
↓
S5 与 W6 墙土坯砌补
↓
裂隙砌补
↓
灌　浆
↓
表面防风化
↓
做　旧

图二十三　东北佛寺 S5 南立面(加固前)

图二十四　东北佛寺 S5 南立面(加固后)

图二十五　东北佛寺 S5 北立面(加固前)

图二十六　东北佛寺 S5 北立面(加固后)

2. 57 区加固工程实例

（1）加固施工方案

崖体 57 区主要病害是裂隙深度大,崩塌体体量大,大多处于极限平衡状态,表面风化严重,崩塌体根部不断掏蚀,崖体高度大,近直立,缺乏支护空间。针对它的病害,采用楠竹加筋复合锚杆锚固、裂隙注浆、土坯砌补等措施加固稳定崖体,通过表面防风化加固来解决崖体表面尤其是胶结能力差的土体的抗风化能力,防止进一步风化。施工设计严格按照动态设计的要求进行。

（2）加固施工工艺

根据施工设计图纸和施工组织设计文件,57 区的加固施工顺序和工艺如图二十七。

图二十七　57 区施工流程图

（3）加固效果

57区的崖体加固施工，严格按照信息化施工的思路开展。变形监测信息的采集、分析与反馈对57区-2的安全施工起到决定性的作用。同时施工勘察与设计的一致结合也是57区顺利施工的重要原因。根据施工勘察的成果，在原设计基础上，增加了#字框架梁的锚固，有效地解决了57-2崖体中下部崖体破碎难以加固施工的困难。同时，根据实际崖体的形态与破坏特征，进行了科学合理的施工放样，从而确保了锚固的效果。因地制宜的脚手架搭设方案也为后续的类似场地的脚手架施工提供了重要价值的参考。通过这些措施，有效地达到保护的目的，体现了保护设计的理念(图二十八、二十九)。

图二十八　57区加固前整体图

图二十九　57区加固后整体图

吐鲁番台藏塔遗址保护研究

梁 涛

新疆文物古迹保护中心

台藏塔遗址位于吐鲁番盆地北缘与火焰山南麓戈壁滩接壤的冲积平原地带,周围地势平展。行政区划属于新疆维吾尔自治区吐鲁番市三堡乡尤喀买里村。西距吐鲁番市约40公里,东南距高昌故城遗址1.2公里。2001年6月25日,国务院批准公布台藏塔为第五批全国重点文物保护单位。

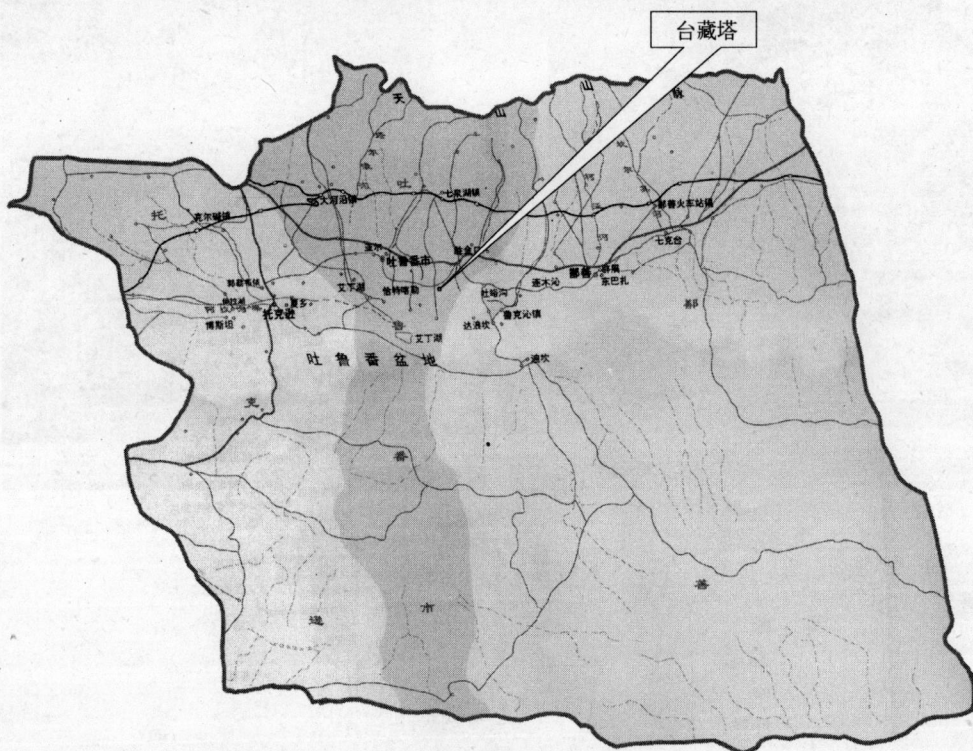

作为吐鲁番地区著名的佛教建筑,千百年来,受自然和人为因素影响,台藏塔遗址不断遭受破坏。目前,遗址的保护与安全问题日益突出。在日常保护管理工作中,明显反映出仅靠一些人防保护措施已经很难保证台藏塔遗址的安全。我们赴现场进行了必要的勘查,结合这座建筑存在的病害问题进行了分析。在参考国内外类似生土建筑遗址的保护方法后,我们认为,对台藏塔采取必要的保护和加固措施,将会减少遗址遭到破坏的几率,进而延长其存续的时间。

一、台藏塔遗址的保存现状

台藏塔遗址周围为村民住宅区的民房和菜园,地势平坦。遗址东侧为居民宅院,内有窖穴及晾棚等;

北侧紧贴居民宅院的土坯围墙;西侧围有土坯墙,内为羊圈,墙外有南北向道路;南侧紧邻居民宅院后部的菜地。

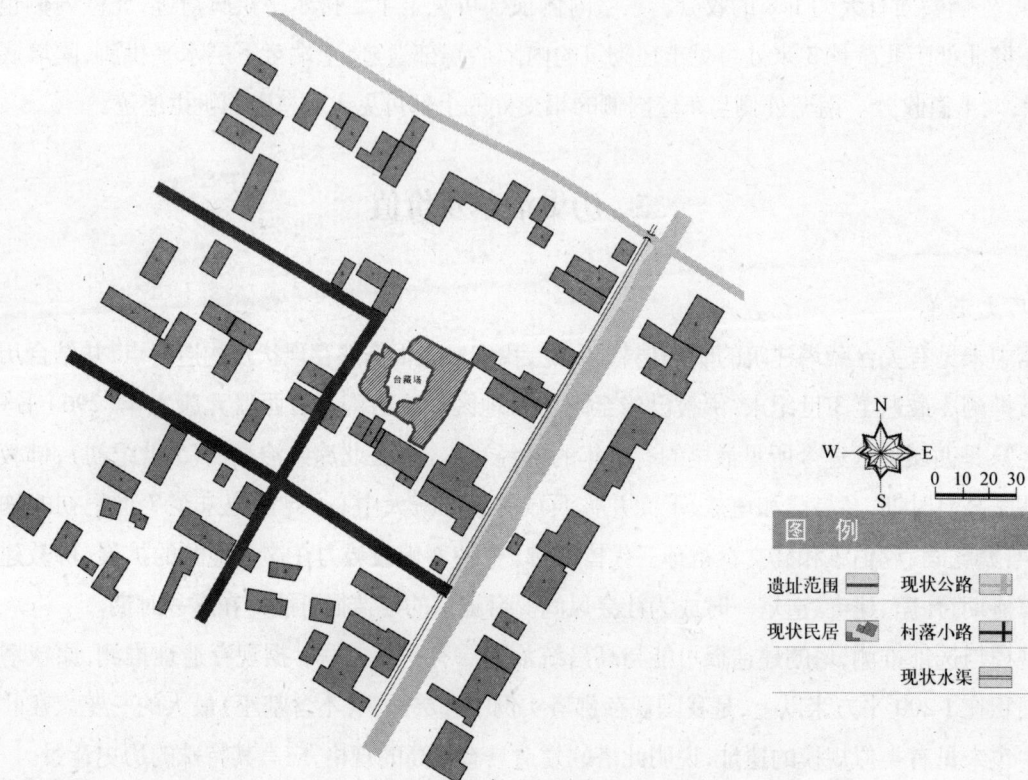

遗址塔基占地面积为 939 平方米。残高约 20 米。遗址塔身平面略呈口字形,朝向南偏西。塔基底部外边南北长约 36 米,东西残长 34 米,塔壁基部厚 8~12 米。塔内中空,内边方约 15 米。南向正中有宽约 3 米的缺口。

东壁长约 36 米,南端伸出南壁外约 5 米,北端与北壁平直相交;北壁残长 23 米,西北转角墙体残缺,缺口内角宽 3 米;西壁残长 20 米;南壁残长 25 米。东壁、北壁残高约 20 米,西壁残高约 15~17 米,南壁不详。东壁可辨上下三层列龛:底层存 7 座方口浅龛,高约 3 米,之间以扶壁垛状的墙体相隔,似于收分极大的塔身下部掏挖而成;二层亦存 7 座券龛,立面位置与下层龛相错,高约 3 米,深约 1 米,龛口以土坯砌筑,外部存留浅色泥皮,像皆不存;三层存 5 座内外两重的券龛,立面位置与下层龛相对。外龛高约 3 米,深约 1 米;于外龛后壁更开内龛,龛口高约 1.5 米,上饰火焰券龛楣,龛内深度及设像情况不详。北端一龛保存相对完整,外龛顶部彩绘尚存。东壁二层的南、北端可见宽约一间、深约半米、高为一层的角墩遗迹。北壁外侧下部无龛,上部存有二排残龛:下层存 5 龛,上层存 4 龛,水平位置、高度、形式与东壁的二、三层龛基本相同,但上下层龛的立面位置相错。下层龛内尚残留少量浅色泥皮,上层外龛顶部隐约有彩绘痕迹;西壁北端不存,中部残缺,南半段墙体在与东、南壁底层高度相当的位置上有一条水平状的边台,但上下壁面上均未见与东壁类似的佛龛遗迹。塔身西南转角墙体上部残损;南壁表面亦未见佛龛遗迹。

遗址塔身内外地面高差在 1.7 米左右(塔内地面标高 -36 米,塔外地面标高 -37.7 米),南面缺口处现状有坡道连通内外。塔内西壁正中 1 米高处凿有长方形纵券顶式壁洞,穿墙而出(墙厚达 13 米),在壁

洞内两侧又有两个深入的壁洞。疑该券洞为后人破坏所致。

遗址塔身用夯土筑成,内外壁表面皆留有上下交错排列的觚木孔洞,内衬土坯,呈方孔状。内侧壁面基本直立,外侧壁面有大约1/8的收分。东壁内侧顶部可见上下二排水平拱脚遗迹,北壁内侧也有类似遗迹。东壁北部距北壁约3米处可见土坯砌筑的内隔墙端部遗迹,上端至下层水平拱脚,隔墙底部宽度约1米余,向上有收分。南壁外侧与东壁内侧的相交处的上部可见土坯垒砌的帆拱遗迹。

二、历史沿革及价值

1. 历史沿革

史籍中未见有关台藏塔建筑的明确记载,因此,我们只能根据遗存现状及构造特点,并结合历史文化背景来做推测。最迟至3世纪末,佛教已传至吐鲁番地区。吐峪沟出有西晋元康六年(296)书写的《诸佛要集经》,是西域地区迄今所见最早的有纪年的佛经写本。[①] 至北凉统治高昌(5世纪初),佛教已成为国教。麹氏高昌时期,高昌已和龟兹、于阗并称西域佛教的三大中心。6世纪末至7世纪初的麹氏高昌统治者中,麹乾固、麹伯雅和麹文泰祖孙三代皆崇佛。[②] 随着佛教势力在这一地区的扩展,佛教建筑活动也进入繁盛期,开窟、建寺、造塔一时成为社会风尚。台藏塔的建造很可能即在这一时期。

从规模与选址推测,塔的建造很可能与高昌统治阶层有一定关联。据现存遗址推测,原状塔身底层的占地面积在1 200平方米以上,是我国现存佛塔实例中底层面积(不含基座)最大的一座。在吐鲁番现存遗址中也未见有类似规模的遗址,说明此塔的建造具有极高的规格,应有其特殊的历史背景。

据学术界探讨,高昌王陵的位置有可能位于阿斯塔那古墓群的南缘一带,则台藏塔的位置正在高昌王陵的南面(北距疑为麹文泰墓的TAM336号墓约1 000米),亦即自高昌城前往高昌王陵的途中,[③]故推测此塔及所在的寺院在麹氏高昌时期可能与王室有关。根据塔内四壁围合、南壁正中缺口的现状,推测塔的中部原来很可能是一座面积达200余平方米的佛殿,据塔身内侧壁上部发券遗迹推测,殿顶有可能采用纵券结构。而南壁外侧与东壁内侧的交角处上部出现帆拱,表明塔门上方可能为半穹顶结构的门廊(门头)。这种隔角帆拱的穹顶结构是中亚伊朗、阿富汗一带历史上曾广为流行的建筑结构形式。从遗址现状,可以见到塔身各面的外观形式有所不同:南面(正面)带有前廊及入口,东、西面(侧面)应对称地有上下三层龛,北面(背面)下部实墙、上部有二层龛。这种情况不见于高昌、交河等处佛塔遗址,亦为国内已知佛塔遗存中仅见。另外,塔身东壁的角墩遗迹与塔身底层连为一体,上部券龛与底层浅龛的形式不同,推测塔的下部(高度在10米左右)可能为塔身整体的基座部分。因此,台藏塔的整体外观形式很可能与国内已知的佛塔实例有较大不同。塔身东、北壁上层的龛形为内外双重券龛,内口上饰火焰券龛楣,这种做法为此塔所仅见。已知当地大型佛塔实例(如高昌、交河大寺佛塔和已毁的色尔克普大塔)中,均为直接在塔身表面开并列浅龛、龛内设像外露的做法。虽然台藏塔上层龛内设像的情况不明,但相比之下,这种内外双重龛口的做法无疑更为讲究,应属更高的规格。

① [日]香川默识编:《西域考古图谱》,学苑出版社影印,1999年,第112页。
② 田卫疆主编:《吐鲁番史》,新疆人民出版社,2004年,第139~140页。
③ 柳洪亮:《高昌王陵初探》,《西域考察与研究续编》,新疆人民出版社,1998年;吴震:《TAM336墓主人试探》,《新疆文物》1992年4期。

麹氏高昌之后的唐西州与回鹘高昌时期,佛教一直是高昌地区流行的主要宗教。回鹘时期,从出使高昌的宋人王延德所记当地仍保留大量唐代佛寺的情况分析,[①]台藏塔及其所在的寺院这时亦应完好存在。

14世纪末,察合台汗国统治者黑的儿火者强迫高昌居民信奉伊斯兰教。吐鲁番地区的佛教消亡,佛寺大都被毁,台藏塔也未能幸免。

2. 价值

台藏塔遗址虽不见于史籍记载,但无疑是一处具有重要文化(历史、文物、艺术、学术)价值的遗存,在中西文化交流史以及建筑史、宗教史的研究中应具有重要的地位。

台藏塔遗址是新疆境内目前发现的规模最大、保存较好的一座唐宋时期的佛塔建筑。它是高昌国时期的重要佛教遗迹,同时是佛教沿丝绸之路传播及发展的重要见证。塔的规模与现状反映出高昌历史上佛教活动之兴衰。

塔身造型独特,三面各异的立面、殿堂式的内部空间、带有异域风格的外观等,在新疆地区乃至我国现存古代佛塔中是一个孤例。塔身周壁用夯土筑成,内侧上部留有土坯发券痕迹,暗示佛塔内部结构做法,显示出很高的工程技术水平,是十分罕见、极为珍贵的大型夯土建筑实例,具有重要的文物价值。

塔的形式则反映高昌地区宗教文化融汇东西的一个侧面及其与龟兹佛教建筑艺术的联系,具有重要的历史价值。台藏塔对于研究高昌国佛教文化以及中西佛教文化的交流,对于研究西域佛教建筑艺术风格以及吐鲁番地区早期生土建筑的发展和演变,具有特殊的学术参考价值。

三、台藏塔遗址存在的病害及成因

1. 病害

台藏塔遗址被包围在居民宅院之中,周围环境杂乱,不利于遗址的保护、管理,同时对遗址景观造成不良影响。遗址东侧的住宅院内掘有多处地下窖穴,其上覆土坯券顶或木构覆土平顶;院落之间的土坯隔墙直抵塔身;遗址北侧、西侧紧靠塔壁堆积杂物,圈养羊群,局部有搭建痕迹;遗址南侧塔基外虽设有简易围栏,但仍有羊群进入塔内、遗留粪便的现象;紧贴遗址塔身东壁的南端建有居民住房;遗址塔身西壁的顶端立有木杆,其上架设扩音器;遗址塔身东、西侧均有距离较近的架空电线。

从外观看,遗址塔身仅东、北壁相对完整,西、南壁残缺、颓圮严重,塔基周围均为居民宅院用地。主要的破坏状态有:

(1)颓圮,即上部倒塌、外形浑然。遗址塔身西壁、南壁的残存夯土墙体,表面颓圮严重。与东壁相对照,推测原西壁亦应有上下三层龛像,可能因顶部和外侧墙体的颓塌,现皆不存。

(2)裂隙,即因物理作用而导致的表面开裂。遗址塔身东壁内外可见多道较细微的横向裂隙,与南壁相交的内转角处有一道自上而下的较深弧形凹槽;北壁西部可见自上而下的较大横向裂隙,东侧自二层龛下至底部有表面裂隙,深度不详;西壁现状北端墙体表面可见纵横双向裂隙。

(3)塌落,即局部离析、失稳或倒塌。遗址塔身表面以土坯垒砌的部分严重塌落,佛龛券口大都破损,仅个别相对完整。

---

① 《宋史》卷490《高昌传》。

（4）销蚀，即表层磨蚀。台藏塔遗址的表面都存在严重的销蚀现象。

（5）剥落，即表层（泥皮）与主体脱离。主要指墙面表皮的剥落，包括粉刷层与壁画。在遗址东壁三层外龛顶部、北壁下层龛内和上层外龛顶部等处，零零星星地保留了台藏塔遗址仅见的壁画遗存。

（6）冲刷，台藏塔遗址东壁上下层龛之间可见明显的因水流冲刷造成龛形破损的痕迹。

2. 病害成因分析

根据实际踏勘和深入研究当地的环境、气象和水文资料，主要的破坏因素有：

（1）自然因素

① 风蚀，是造成建筑遗址毁坏的主要破坏因素。风蚀不仅剥蚀地表，使地面建筑遗迹的外表逐渐颓平，同时也可能造成建筑物的坍毁。

吐鲁番地区是著名的风口，据有关资料记载，1961 年 5 月该地区曾发生特大风灾，其中 12 级风力竟持续了数日，风速达 40 米/秒。1998 年 4 月，又曾遭遇特强沙尘暴的浩劫。这两场风灾与沙尘暴均可能对台藏塔遗址造成过严重损害，但未见有关具体损害情况的资料。

② 雨侵，是造成建筑遗址坍毁的主要因素之一。吐鲁番地区虽然干旱少雨，但对于夯土或土坯砌筑的建筑物来说，偶遇暴雨或连续降雨就可以造成房屋倒塌。对于已经失去屋顶罩覆的建筑遗存来说，则使墙体坍塌或冲出明显的裂隙。台藏塔遗址表面的横向与纵向开裂，也应与之相关。近年来，吐鲁番地区降水量有逐年递增的趋势。

③ 水融，在湿度较大的情况下，土质遗存的表层在水分作用下融化，干燥后结成薄片，形成一层脆弱的外壳。在践踏、触碰或热胀冷缩时，便出现大面积剥落。这种情况多发生于建筑遗址表面、接近地面的部位以及风口等特殊部位。

④ 温差，吐鲁番地区的地面昼夜温差最大可达 40 度以上。长年处于急剧变化的气温之中，必然导致遗址的频繁涨缩，在风蚀、雨侵的共同作用下，造成遗址开裂、出现裂隙、泥皮脱落等现象。

⑤ 鼠穴，台藏塔遗址地面存在鼠穴洞口，与塔址周围的居民生活有关。其对建筑遗存的具体危害程度尚有待进一步详查。

（2）人为因素

① 台藏塔遗址北侧底部壁面有拆除搭建后存留的构件卯孔及掏挖痕迹。

② 关于台藏塔遗址塔身西壁下部的券洞，应再经考察确认是原有形貌还是人为破坏遗迹。

③ 当地居民在台藏塔遗址塔身西侧及塔内空地上圈养羊群，对塔基夯土造成损害与威胁。

④ 台藏塔遗址塔顶上方架设的扩音器以及周围架空电线等对遗址总体景观造成损害。

⑤ 台藏塔遗址塔顶经常有鸟类停落，造成一定程度的污损与腐蚀。

⑥ 周围居民生活炊烟、污水和垃圾对台藏塔遗址造成污染。

⑦ 周围居民宅院对台藏塔遗址总体造成不良景观。

四、台藏塔遗址的保护和加固

1. 保护和加固的目标

（1）采取有效手段，改善台藏塔遗址的内外环境条件，防范并减轻人为因素和自然力对遗址的损害。

（2）针对损毁现象,分析破坏因素,经过科学实验,采取适当措施,遏制或减缓台藏塔遗址颓毁态势的进一步发展。

（3）在管理与保护加固中,采取一系列严格要求和措施,消除或减少人为破坏因素。

（4）通过环境治理,强调生态保护的概念,力求文物资源的永续利用,并使与文物相关的产业,特别是旅游业,能够可持续发展。

（5）通过旅游配套设施和其他配套基础设施的建设,充分发挥文物保护工作对构建当代中国先进文化的突出价值和作用,显著发挥文物资源的社会效益和经济效益。

2. 保护和加固的内容

（1）保护范围的确定

台藏塔遗址被包围在居民宅院之中,周围环境杂乱,不利于遗址的保护、管理,同时对遗址景观造成不良影响,因此制定合适的保护范围是台藏塔保护的关键。

根据台藏塔遗址目前的破坏状况,主要是与人为的破坏因素密切相关,在开发旅游中所面临的主要问题,也是游人活动可能对遗址带来的损害;另外,环境气候条件的恶化,也是造成遗址毁败的重要因素之一;再者,旅游发展所要求的配套设施建设和文物资源的展示要求,都是以确定台藏塔遗址的保护范围为先决条件的。

台藏塔遗址保护范围的南、北、东三面以现状道路内侧为界：南北 144 米,东西 120 米,占地面积 1.65 公顷。与遗址之间距离：北侧约 70 米、西侧约 50 米、南侧约 40 米、东侧约 30 米。台藏塔遗址保护范围的实际勘察总面积为：23 149.011 平方米（34.72 亩）,约为 2.32 公顷。

（2）保护范围的生态绿化

为增大台藏塔遗址周围地带的地表粗糙度,以减低风速、减少气流携沙量,最大限度地减少风蚀的破坏作用,同时考虑到高昌故城遗址周围应具有良好的景观与开敞的视野,以及当地的气象资料,确定在遗址保护范围西北两面做生态绿化,植被的裸土面积不得超过 10%,秋冬季节仍须保留植物的枯干枝茎;植物配置应以低矮、耐旱的灌木为主,并配以适当比例的乔木与草本植物;植物种类的选用,首选历史上高昌国时期的当地植物种类,如羊刺;考虑到绿化带的观赏效果,可按照植物花期,合理选用吐鲁番地区现已引种的植物品种;植物株距暂按平均为 3×3 米考虑。

（3）保护范围的边界防护围栏

考虑到台藏塔遗址外围经常出现游散畜群,为防止其对遗址基部及林木幼苗（绿化带）等造成损害,沿遗址保护范围的边界设置防护围栏。围栏外观应尽量淡化、无需基础或浅小基础,可采用金属网一类简易有效的形式。

（4）旅游配套设施

在展示区的东面设置游人出入口。参观台藏塔遗址的游客从公路沿遗址东侧的道路到达展示区,进入展示区之后,按逆时针方向环绕遗址一周,然后返回出入口处,结束参观。一般游客的参观时间约在 15～30 分钟。

为提高台藏塔遗址的保护与管理水平,必须彻底改变台藏塔遗址保护范围内的交通现状,规范道路的走向、宽度与做法。在遗址周围距离遗迹 25 米处,设环行参观步道,步道宽 5.0 米,在现状地面上铺设立砖路面,路牙采用立砖干摆,高出现状地面 5 cm 左右,路面做旧与遗址周围地表颜色一致。台藏塔遗址每一侧人流较集散的地点,设置 20×10 米的小型广场,地面做法为相邻路面的延伸。

（5）护坡护坎防水保护

台藏塔遗址塔身的外侧均为民居,受生活用水的侵蚀,多处出现基础塌陷与塔体滑坡的损毁现象,因此有必要沿塔身外侧采用夯土方式铺设散水带。沿塔身外侧采用夯土方式铺设散水带,宽度 2 米,表面斜度 3% ,边缘以土坯砌筑防水护坎,高出周围地面 5 cm。护坡与护坎的做法可采用泥坯夯筑,泥坯中可掺入具有防水性能的材料成分。并根据加固部位夯土的化学组成、矿物质成分和干密度,并经过试样加固后的强度变化和风洞试验结果,确定保护剂的填充料成分与配比。

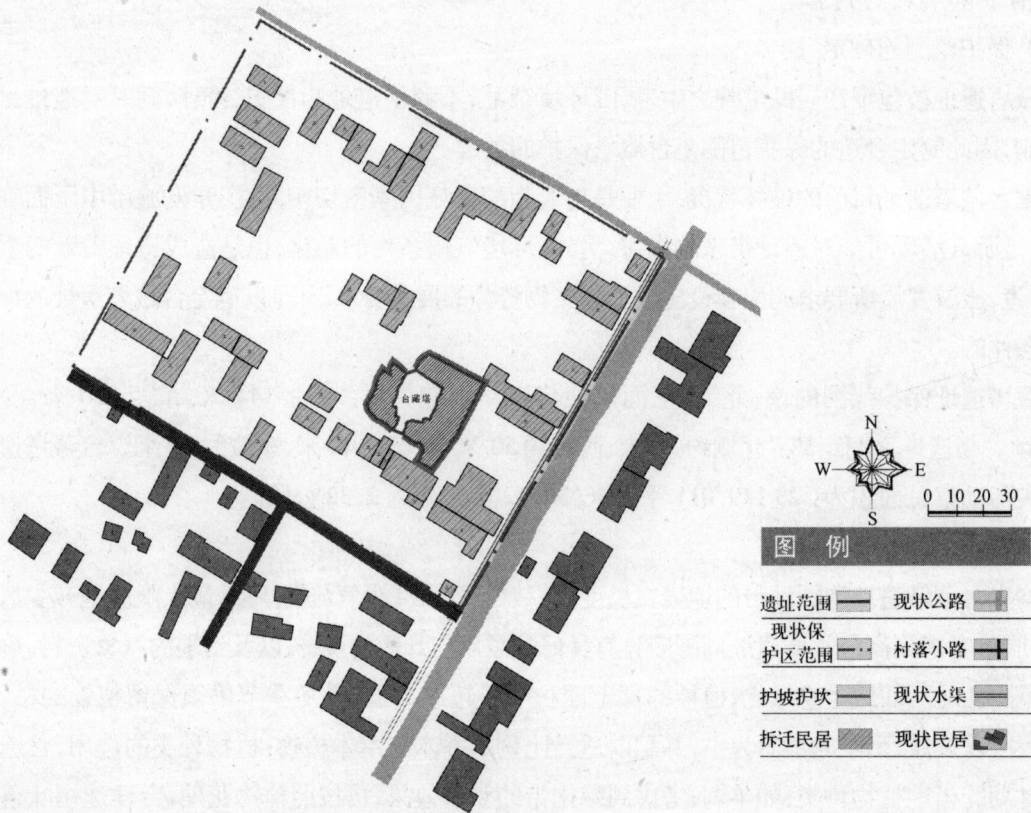

（6）塔顶防水

在塔顶覆盖一层土工布后,再抹一层草泥。草泥层要形成一定的坡度,以利于塔顶积水有组织的排放。

（7）风蚀防治

风蚀破坏主要发生在生土建筑的遗存上,它是台藏塔遗址所面临的最普遍、最严重的自然破坏因素之一。因此,风蚀防治是台藏塔遗址保护的根本措施。为此,主要从两个方面考虑:一是削减大风的侵蚀能力,二是增强文物本体的抗侵蚀强度。前者需与生态环境治理密切结合,并辅以局部的工程手段;后者目前主要依赖化学技术。目标是建立一个由工程、生物、化学措施组成的多层次、多功能的综合防治风蚀的体系。

风蚀的环境治理,根据目前的研究结论,主要是增加地表粗糙度,即:减少裸土面积、增加植被覆盖率。

风蚀防治的化学措施主要是对文物本体采取 PS 喷涂。PS 喷涂不但能够防治风沙的风蚀破坏作用,而且能够提高文物本体防止雨水冲刷的能力。[1] PS 稀释比例不大于 10%，工艺为喷涂三遍以上。应用时一定要避免不可逆的强度过高问题。

　　考虑到该措施实施费用较高，将其实施程度分为两级：一是对位于风蚀严重地区的重要遗存采用迎风面、顶面喷涂，二是对风蚀程度不突出或文物价值不突出的遗存采用酌情局部喷涂。塔体的表面加固应针对遗址的保存状况和展示过程中可能受损的情况，确定施用 PS 保护剂的部位与面积，并根据遗址的材质，选择适当的材料配比。墙体的顶部可考虑采用较高配比的 PS 保护剂，以提高耐水性（抗水崩解性）；墙体侧面建议采用低浓度、多次喷涂的加固方式。在确定了遗址的 PS 保护剂配比方案之后，应先选择一般性遗址的次要部位进行 PS 保护剂配比的试验，试验期限应在 1 年以上。

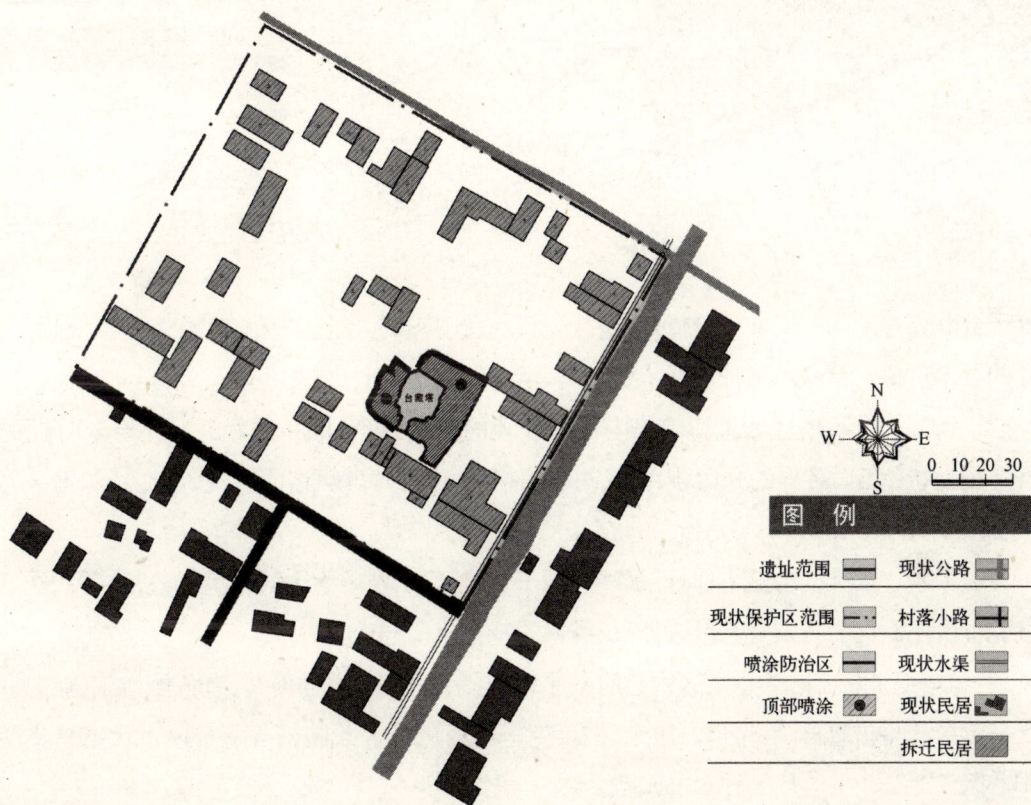

　　（8）考古调查和勘探

　　台藏塔的考古工作还不详细，考虑到台藏塔遗址周围有可能存在早期寺院遗址，建议在遗址周围方圆 200 米范围内进行考古勘探，探明地下是否存在有关遗迹及其分布状况、范围。台藏塔遗址的考古勘探和清理要充分利用高科技保护手段进行物探、航测、遥感，以全面掌握地面遗迹和地下遗存情况。

五、保护和加固的效益评估

1. 保护后旅游发展价值评估

　　现存遗址周围环境条件较差，遗址本身缺乏保护、管理与展示设施，是影响遗址展示的两个主要方

---

① 李最雄：《PS 加固土质石质文物的稳定性和强度问题》，《敦煌研究》1996 年第 3 期。

面。但鉴于台藏塔遗址的重要文化价值，及遗址现状所反映出的大量历史信息，该遗址虽残损严重，但仍具有很高的展示价值。台藏塔遗址的展示资源可以包括两个方面：

（1）建筑遗址。台藏塔遗址是新疆境内目前发现的规模最大、保存较好的一座唐宋时期的佛塔建筑。塔身造型独特：三面各异的立面、殿堂式的内部空间、带有异域风格的外观等，在新疆地区乃至我国现存古代佛塔中是一个孤例。

（2）废墟景观。宏大的台藏塔遗址，那些跨越千年，伫立于空旷之中的残垣断壁，随着四季、朝夕、光影、角度的变换，不断向游人展现着令人惊叹、震撼的特殊氛围与奇异景观。

另外，台藏塔遗址位于吐鲁番地区中心的平原地带，东临公路，交通便利，有条件与东侧的高昌故城、阿斯塔那—哈拉和卓古墓群、胜金口石窟寺、柏孜克里克石窟寺等共同构成一个以古代高昌文明为主题的展示中心区。

综上所述，台藏塔遗址具有便利的交通条件和优越的地理位置，遗址本身虽然没有良好的展示环境，但却拥有充足的展示资源。如果对台藏塔遗址进行保护和加固，完全可以具备旅游发展的条件，但目前尚缺乏必要的管理、展示及旅游服务等设施，文物古迹资源亟待保护和加固。

2. 保护和加固后预期的效果评估

台藏塔遗址中所包含的历史信息对于社会史（政治史、经济史、军事史、民族史等）、科技史（城市史、建筑史、技术史等）、文化史（宗教史、艺术史等）等领域以及考古学、地理学、人类学等学科研究均具有重要的学术价值。因此，台藏塔遗址不仅对于新疆历史的发展演变具有重要的历史和学术价值，而且，由于众所周知的原因，其现实的政治意义尤为突出。

台藏塔遗址的保护和加固，是针对此遗址的保存现状和旅游发展的要求而采取的系统的保护和加固，将有效地改善国家级重点文物保护单位台藏塔遗址的保存现状，完全具备旅游发展的条件。同时，进一步避免了遗址的破坏，从而使台藏塔遗址得以有效的保护，能更好地进行科学研究和社会教育，促进与文物相关产业的发展,对于改善投资环境,发展旅游业,扩大对外经济贸易和科技、文化交流,促进产业结构调整,缓解就业压力,带动当地致富奔小康,具有十分重要的积极作用。因此,保护和加固不仅具有极大的经济效益,而且具有极大的社会效益,不但有效地保护了文物,同时也积极促进了两个文明建设,是非常可行和必要的。

六、结 论

经过现场勘察,认真分析,我们找出了台藏塔现存的主要病害,并从自然因素和人为因素两个方面探讨了其成因。针对病害情况,我们制定的保护加固的目标以及拟采取的具体措施,既有科学性,又有可行性,完全符合《中国文物古迹保护准则》所规定的维修保护"不改变文物原貌"的原则,同时,在切实保护好文物的前提下,充分考虑了旅游开发的实际需要,此举也与我国文物工作"保护为主,合理利用"方针的精神实质相一致。

Консервация и реставрация деревянной подвески из Берельского кургана № 11 (по материалам курганов Казахского Алтая)

Крым Алтынбеков

Научно-реставрационная лаборатория

ТОО «Остров Крым»   Алматы, Казахстан

В ходе археологических исследований кургана № 11 некрополя Берел в Восточно-Казахстанской области, датируемого III–IV вв. до н. э., обнаружено 13 коней в парадном убранстве (археолог З. С. Самашев). Конское убранство, представляющее большую художественную ценность, выполнено из дерева, украшенного резным орнаментом, плакированного металлической фольгой. Конструкция кургана должна была обеспечить стабильный микроклимат захоронения и хорошую сохранность предметов материальной культуры. Повреждение ее при грабительских раскопках кургана вызвало появление разрушающих факторов (проникновение талых вод, колебания температуры и влажности), способствующих деградации древесины.

Деревянные изделия, извлеченные из раскопа, имеют высокую степень водонасыщенности, различные дефекты и деформации, нередко утрачены первоначальная форма и цвет. Для их сохранения и дальнейшей музейной экспозиции необходимо проведение комплекса консервационных работ, которые выполняет научно-реставрационная лаборатория «Остров Крым» — специализированная организация по консервации и реставрации археологических находок из различных материалов.

Процесс консервации деревянных предметов показан на примере одного из изделий, имеющем типичные повреждения, характерные для берельских находок из дерева (всего в кургане №11 их обнаружено более 900). Деталь конского убранства представляет собой подвеску в виде головы горного барана, помещенной на прямоугольной планке. Сохранился фрагмент плакировки желтого цвета и следы фольги серого цвета. Изделие фрагментировано. Древесина характеризуется высокой степенью деградации и водонасыщенности. Металлическая фольга скручена, покрыта окисными пленками.

Консервация изделия проводилась с использованием состава и технологии пропитки, на которые получен патент Республики Казахстан. Состав содержит полиэтиленгликоль (ПЭГ), полиэтилметакрилат, этилированный алкилфенол, этанол. Разработанный консолидант обладает большой проникающей способностью в древесину, что создает хорошие условия для полного заполнения ее внутренних пор.

Особенность метода консервации состоит в отсутствии предварительной сушки деревянного предмета, пропитка начинается в водонасыщенном состоянии с постепенным вытеснением водного почвенного раствора консервантом.

Выбор технологии консервации зависит от степени деградации материала, которая оценивается на основе химических анализов древесины. Был проведен физико-химический анализ древесины, оперативный качественный микроанализ металлов плакировки, спектральный анализ клея для крепления фольги. Исследования показали, что степень деградации древесины составляет более 30%. Основным компонентом фольги желтого цвета, использованной для покрытия дерева, является золото. Фольга серого цвета, имитирующая серебро, состоит из олова, этим и объясняется ее плохая сохранность, так как олово деградирует при температуре $-13℃$. Для крепления фольги был применен белковый клей, возможно, осетровый. По результатам анализов определены технология и режим консервации, состав для пропитки дерева.

Вначале изделие было промыто дистиллированной водой для удаления остатков почвы и других поверхностных загрязнений, после чего обработано дезинфицирующим составом.

Пропитка дерева с целью его укрепления проводилась по определенной схеме в термостате при температурах $40-60℃$. В процессе пропитки регулярно определялись масса и плотность изделия, степень пропитки ПЭГ и глубина его проникновения. Мягкие и сильно деградированные места пропитывались дополнительно ПЭГ с метакрилатом. Для исправления изгибов и придания изделию начальной формы использованы каркасы из твердого пластика.

Древесина после пропитки имеет прочную структуру, гладкую поверхность с четко выраженной текстурой. Цвет дерева — натуральный, но несколько темный. Поверхность древесины не крошится. Влага и газы из атмосферы не поглощаются. Степень пропитки консолидантом составила около 70%.

Пропитанное изделие прошло длительную стабилизацию вначале в специальном боксе, затем в помещении лаборатории при обычных условиях. Стабилизация — постепенный процесс адаптации артефактов к новым условиям хранения. В течение периода стабилизации производится регулярный осмотр состояния предметов. При недостаточной прочности дерева выполняется допропитка, излишки консерванта удаляются.

Укрепление древесины позволило соединить разрозненные фрагменты подвески. Сохранившийся фрагмент фольги очищен от окисных пленок, выправлен и установлен на первоначальное место.

Процесс консервации подвески продолжался более года. В результате деревянное изделие защищено от дальнейшей деградации, подготовлено к длительному сохранению внешнего вида и внутренней структуры материала. Разработанная технология обеспечила экономичные условия хранения экспоната, не требующие создания искусственного климата: находки, прошедшие консервацию, хранятся в обычных музейных условиях.

Консервация оригинала и проведенные исследования дали возможность выполнить реконструкцию подвески — создать ее точную копию в другом материале. Реконструированные детали конского убранства используются для воссоздания полного парадного убранства коней из берельских курганов.

Аналогичным образом проведена консервация еще 300 деревянных изделий из берельского кургана №11.

1. Общий вид берельского кургана.

2. Раскоп захоронения.

3. Деревянные изделия в раскопе

4. Подвеска до консервации.

5. Подвеска после консервации.

6. Реконструкция подвески.

7. Реконструкция парадного убранства берельского коня.

土蜂对高昌故城造成的病害分析

杨 华

新疆吐鲁番学研究院

一、高昌故城简介

高昌故城遗址坐落在吐鲁番市东面约四十公里的哈拉和卓乡所在地附近,北距火焰山南麓的木头沟沟口约6.5公里。

高昌故城距今有两千多年的历史,是西汉王朝在车师前国境内的屯田部队所建。全城平面略呈不规则的正方形,布局可以分为外城、内城和宫城三部分。高昌故城自始建到13世纪废弃,使用了1 300多年,留下了期间各个历史时期的城市建设遗址。故城周长5公里多,总面积约220公顷,现存建筑遗址面积约40公顷。

高昌故城所在地气候属于典型的大陆性暖温带荒漠气候,日照充足,热量丰富,降水稀少,极端干燥。年降水16.6毫米,蒸发量2 800毫米以上,空气湿度30%左右。正是由于极端干燥的气候条件才使得高昌故城得以保存到今天。

在高昌故城里的生物种类稀少单一,主要有:

1. 主要的野生植被以刺山柑、骆驼刺等抗旱植物为主,还有少量苦豆、菟丝子等野生植物。

2. 野生动物中常见的有猫头鹰、刺猬、蛇、野兔、猫头鹰、土蜂、蚁蛉、蜥蜴、甲虫等。

二、高昌故城建筑工艺

高昌故城是一座早期土建筑城市遗址,以夯筑和土坯垒砌为主要建造方法,再辅以少量木结构而建造的。但是现存的高昌故城遗址,木结构已损毁、佚失,只见大量的残墙、颓土,依稀可辨故城当年的繁华。

1. 夯筑

高昌故城主要以夯土筑成,其外城墙墙基厚12米、高11.5米,周长约5公里余;夯层厚8～12 cm,间杂少量的土坯,可见清楚的纴木孔;故城外围夯筑的马面如今大多还保存完好。

2. 土坯垒砌

故城内大量的佛寺遗址、居民建筑等用土坯垒砌而成,表面再抹泥层。外围城墙在历史的各个时期均有修缮,部分修缮亦采用土坯垒砌。

三、土蜂介绍

土蜂属膜翅纲膜翅目,世界性分布,热带尤多。体小至大形,体长一般 10～20 毫米,大者可达 50 毫米左右。多被密毛,体黑色,并有白、黄、橙、红色斑纹。头部略成球形,通常较胸部狭。复眼完全或凹入。通常两性均有翅,后翅有臀叶。触角短,雌虫 12 节、弯曲,雄虫 13 节、直。前胸背板两侧角伸达肩板。中胸小盾片大而明显。中、后胸腹板形成一连续的板,盖住中、后足基节。足短而粗,胫节扁平,有长鬃毛。腹部长,有带纹,第 1～2 腹节间深缢,各腹节后缘有毛,翅脉多伸达不到翅的外缘。雄蜂腹部末节有 3 个刺。土蜂常见于植物的花上,取食花蜜。

土蜂在土下数十厘米或更深处筑巢,巢室内部涂以蜡和唾液的混合物,以保持巢室内的湿度。土中筑巢的结构、巢室的数量、入口处的形状因不同的种而异。土蜂筑巢后,于巢室内产卵,将猎物放于巢室内,封闭巢室,幼虫孵出后取食猎物,直至老熟化蛹。①

四、土蜂对高昌故城土遗址的破坏分析

土蜂对高昌故城的主要破坏作用是筑巢,土蜂筑巢选择夯土建筑的中下层,一般是某一层或局部土质结构松软的部分。在高昌故城多见的是呈层状分布的蜂穴,而在其他一些整体土质强度较差的区域产生大量虫穴的现象则相对较少,这与故城的建造技艺有很大关系。遗址采用夯筑技术,在建造的过程中,不可能保证每一夯层的夯实系数一致,总会出现某一夯层或连续几个夯层的夯实系数较小,这些相对松软的土质则成为土蜂筑巢的首选对象,因此我们可以在故城中看到许多呈层状分布,且延续很长的穴孔遗迹(见图)。局部区域所产生的虫穴则往往是因为该建筑块体使用了较差的土质,一般表现为含沙量较高,这样就无法达到较高的夯实度,这些也成为土蜂筑巢的理想场所。

土蜂蛀蚀的大量巢穴可使遗址内部变得疏松多孔,土体成为蜂窝状,使其失去支撑作用,进而引起一系列的病变。破坏类型总体可分为两大类:一种是土蜂筑巢等活动对遗址本体造成的直接破坏作用,筑巢改变了遗址的内部结构及受力分布,从而使遗址本体产生剥蚀、裂隙发育、坍塌等重要病害。另一种是土蜂对遗址产生的危害可与其他自然力破坏作用产生协同作用,从而加速其他病害的发育速度,加剧其破坏作用,最终导致遗址的大面积坍塌损毁。

1. 直接破坏作用

首先,土蜂在遗址本体上的筑巢过程是一个由表及里的过程,当表层 10 多厘米的土体遭到蛀蚀时,表层土与内部土体的结合力遭到破坏。内外密实度的不同又将产生收缩率的较大差异,进而产生开裂,在重力等的作用下,表土难以支附则导致大面积的剥落(见图)。

其次,土蜂的进一步筑穴,可深及遗址内部,局部深达到 30 cm 以上。这使得遗址本体变得疏松多孔,大大降低了遗址的承载强度,改变了遗址本体的受力分布。遗址在建成后,经过长时间的平衡调整,基本处于稳定状态,但是遗址在被蛀蚀后,土体内部的应力重新分布,当应力集中在某一区域时则产生卸荷裂隙。

---

① 吴燕如:《中国动物志》《膜翅目 准蜂科 蜜蜂科》第二十卷。

最后,在一些整体土质较差的区域所产生的大量虫穴,完全破坏了遗址基部的承载强度,往往内部又有较多裂隙在不断发育,当裂隙发展到一定程度或遇到外力的诱发时,遗址将出现大体量的坍塌(见图)。

2. 与其他病害的协同作用

任何病害都不会孤立的存在和作用于遗址本体,它们之间必然有着种种联系,并且协同发展,这是一种严重的破坏方式。就土蜂的破坏作用而言,它在与其他破坏方式的互相作用中起到加速风化、促进裂隙发育、导致坍塌等重要作用。并且这种作用是一个连续的过程,其可分为四个阶段:

第一,土蜂筑巢引起的遗址结构、强度的变化为风化、风蚀提供了更加有利的条件。筑穴部分的土体强度远远小于周围土体的强度,筑巢造成的遗址表面使得风化的破坏作用大大提高,原本已难以附着的表土,在风力的作用下成片剥落,这在蜂穴区随处可见。

另外造成的遗址强度的不均匀,必然导致差异风化的形成,并加速、加剧这一过程。使遗址出现凹蚀。凹蚀可分为坑状凹蚀和连续槽状凹蚀(见图)。

第二,高昌故城中可见许多因土蜂筑巢,又在风蚀的作用下形成的凹蚀体。土蜂在筑巢的过程中为了保持巢穴内的湿度,分泌一种粘液用以加固穴壁,这使得穴壁有着比其他夯土较高的抗风蚀能力,在风蚀的作用下,最终只残留下那些纵横交错的孔道(见图),但这并不能阻止凹蚀的进一步发展,相反在风的作用下,凹蚀不断地向遗址内部延伸。凹蚀最终打破了遗址原本的稳定状态,应力的集中使遗址本体产生卸荷裂隙(见图)。

第三，裂隙发育。高昌故城所处的吐鲁番盆地属于干旱少雨的典型内陆气候，但是这里气候的又一特点是时而会发生暴雨，暴雨沿着正在发育的裂隙对遗址本体产生强烈的冲刷，不断雨蚀使裂隙进一步发育，分割土体，使多处遗址成为危崖。

第四，遗址在基地蜂蛀凹蚀，支撑力不断降低和裂隙不断发育等多重破坏作用下，难免面临坍塌的命运。

五、结　论

土蜂对高昌故城土遗址有着极强的破坏作用，它所引起的凹蚀、坍塌等破坏作用足以与自然风蚀、雨蚀等所造成的破坏作用相媲美，而且在一定程度已经超过自然力的破坏作用。

高昌故城屹立千年，至今仍保存了大量的夯土建筑遗址。其中一些风蚀体头大脚小却依然屹立不倒（见图），为何我们看似坚固的其他城墙等遗址却频频倒地，只留下一堆颓土让我们追忆故城昔日的辉煌，这不得不值得我们去深思……

吐鲁番博物馆馆藏文物的保存情况

古丽努尔·汗木都

吐鲁番博物馆

吐鲁番地区的文物保护工作始于 1954 年,当时由马义提先生一个人进行文物管理。1956 年吐鲁番成立了文物保护小组,承担吐鲁番地区的文物遗址管理工作。1959 年成立了吐鲁番文管所。1965 年改为吐、鄯、托三县文管所,1978 年正式成立吐鲁番地区文物保护管理所。1990 年吐鲁番博物馆成立。1993～1994 年成为文物中心。1995 年正式成立地区文物局。[①] 2005 年成立了吐鲁番学研究院。在这个过程中我局从一个只有一个人工作的文物小组发展到现在拥有一支一百多人的保护队伍,及保护和研究为一体的单位。馆藏文物数量也从 1966 年前的几百件增加到现在的数千件。

吐鲁番的文物 20 世纪初就开始被发掘了,但是发掘出土文物并没有保存在吐鲁番,而是被世界十几个国家的博物馆分别收藏。

解放后,新疆文物工作者培训班的学员 1956 年曾先后在交河故城、阿斯塔那古墓等地进行文物发掘。随后,自治区博物馆对阿斯塔那和哈拉和卓墓地进行了先后 13 次的发掘,出土了大量的文书和其他文物。

随后,在自治区考古所的带领下于 1988 年、1992 年实施了多次发掘。2003 年又进行了更大规模的抢救性清理发掘。

随着发掘工作的频繁进行,库房内的文物数量也越来越多,而文物保管也成了一个主要问题。吐鲁番干旱少雨的气候条件使得地下各种文物保存下来。出土后进入库房后,由于保存条件发生变化,库房的文物达不到文物保存所需要的标准,而夏季的湿度往往高出文物保存所需条件的一倍。造成了陶器表面的脱落、表面裂缝和变形。丝毛织品的硬化和纤维的断裂。针对这些现象,我们采取了最简单的保存措施——用加湿器加湿,我们用空调降温的方式应对夏季的高温环境。

不同质地的文物所需要的湿度、温度条件也不一样,比如说陶器所需要的温度在 18～24℃、湿度 50%～60%,木器温度为 16～20℃、湿度 55%～65%,纺织品温度 16～18℃、湿度 50%～55%,金属器温度 18～24℃、湿度 45%～50%,纸质品温度 16～18℃、湿度 50%～55%。[②]

室内温度在上述标准范围内逐渐正常波动,一般不会造成藏品损坏。但温度剧变对藏品是危险的。如:在相对湿度为 50%,温度为 25℃的环境中,纸张仅能保存 100 年;若在相对湿度不变,温度降至 15℃的环境中,则纸质文物可保存 581 年。[③]

漆、木、竹器、纸张和丝织品对干燥最敏感。它们一般都含有水分,在干燥到与周围环境处于平衡状

---

① 王天文主编:《吐鲁番文史》(第一期),阿里木编写:《吐鲁番地区文物管理机构概况》,第 111 页。
② 王宏钧主编:《中国博物馆学基础》(修订本),第二节《藏品的保存环境》,第 204 页。
③ 王宏钧主编:《中国博物馆学基础》(修订本),第二节《藏品的保存环境》,第 204～205 页。

态时,仍含有一定比例的水分。如,木材含水量为本身重量的 12% ~ 15%,若含水量低于其应有的比例,纸张会酥脆断裂,木材则翘曲变形。木材随空气相对湿度的变化而伸缩,相对湿度在 55% ~ 65% 之间变动,对一般木质文物不会有显著影响。但空气相对湿度降至 45%,文物面临干裂危险,30% 以下,造成木质文物的损坏。所以把此类文物所需相对湿度的安全下限定为 50%。①

而我馆文物库房温度在夏天一般在 40℃ 左右,相对湿度在 20% 以下,而且不同质地的文物混放在一起,这给文物的加湿、调温工作带来了不便。我认为文物应该首先按质地、出土地点进行分类,然后按照出土时间进行分类保存。以保证同一质地的文物保存在同一库房内,根据文物保存的需要进行加湿、调温。

我们文物库房的丝毛织品保存工作还存在问题,前几年在自治区考古所的带领下,对洋海墓地实施了大规模的抢救性考古清理发掘,出土了大量的毛织品。在自治区博物馆专家和我单位技术保护室工作人员的细心清理下,重现了这些毛织品精美的图案。经清洗后的丝、毛织品入库以后,我们把毛织品撂在一起,库房内现有的存储柜无法容纳这些毛织品,因为这些毛织品尺寸较大。所以我们只能采取定期翻动这些丝毛织品及放置樟脑球等驱虫药剂的方式来加以保存,尽管我们很小心以避免造成纤维断裂,但随着翻转次数增多,丝、毛织品纤维断裂的现象也随之增多,这对丝、毛织品造成了很大的损坏。我们需要专制的保存柜来存放这些文物。在藏品保存设备选材问题上,国际博物馆界有两种不同的观点和倾向,以日本和美国、加拿大为代表。日本对使用木材作藏品库房设备有很大的兴趣,强调木材具有吸收释放空气中水分的特征,可调解库内湿度。使用金属材料制作库房设备,在美国、加拿大等西方国家备受赞赏,普遍使用。② 现在国内较大的博物馆已使用防止生虫的木材制造的存储柜来保存这些丝、毛织品,真正实现了每件丝、毛织品隔离保存。

如果我们无法定做这种保存柜,也可以尝试定做其他材质的保存柜子加以保存,但必须要保证每一件丝、毛织品放置在独立的柜子进行保存,同时存储环境需要放置驱虫药剂,以防止生虫。

总之,文物都有相当久远的历史,能够保存至今而且被发现更实属不易。这些文物出土后进入库房或展厅陈列,我们就有责任和义务把他们保管好。文物越珍贵,我们的责任也越重大,更需要学习国内外先进的保存经验,购置必要的保存设施,制定切实可行的保存方案,使库存文物得到妥善的保管。

---

① 王宏钧主编:《中国博物馆学基础》(修订本),第二节《藏品的保存环境》,第 205 页。
② 同上书,第 212 页。

The Origin of Nomadic Powers in the Eurasian Steppes

Hayashi Toshio

Soka University, Japan

1. Introduction

When did the first mounted nomadic power appear in the Eurasian steppes? Some scholars think that the Proto-Indo-European (PIE) horse riders emerged with strong military powers in the western part of the Eurasian steppes in the late fifth-fourth millennia BCE (Gimbutas 1997: 355 – 356; [1] Anthony 2007: 236 – 237[2]). Others consider that mounted horsemen to battle came out just at the beginning of the first millennium BCE (Khazanov 1994: 90 – 95; Drews 2004: 68 – 69ff).

In the ancient world the kings of first unified kingdoms often built monumental structures like gigantic tumuli. Those grandiose structures must have played a role as a symbol which let people to know the birth of first kingship. The earliest kings of the Egyptian Old Kingdom built the biggest pyramids. In Japan the biggest *kofun* 古墳-tumuli were built at the first stage of Yamato Kingdom in the second half of the 3rd— the 5th centuries. Various sizes of *kofun*-tumuli reflect clearly the difference of the ranks of the buried persons. Can we observe the same situation in the Eurasian steppes?

In Mongolia there are many stone mounds of various sizes with round or square stone enclosures, called *khereksur*[3] in the Mongolian archaeological literature. The dating[4] and the function[5] of *khereksur*s are not so clear. In any ways these *khereksur*s, especially big ones, might have been the signs of the first nomadic powers. Our Japan-Mongol joint archaeological expedition[6] set our goal to elucidate the dating and the function of khereksurs for the study of the origin of nomadic powers.

---

[1] The work cited is a previously unpublished article of Marija Gimbutas (1921 – 1994).

[2] But David Anthony considers Eneolithic mounted raiders as tribal fighters (not as organized later cavalrymen).

[3] Mongolians call it *khirgiskhüür*, "Kirgis (people) corpse (or tomb)". In the 19th century, Russian archaeologist heard it from local people and transcribed *khereksur*. After that the term of *khereksur* has been used by Russian archaeologists. The Mongolians of Yulduz Highland in Central Tianshan, China, call this type of site as khirgisyas, "Kirgis bone".

[4] There are two reasons of difficulties of the dating. One is that excavated khereksurs are very few and the second is that almost nothing has been found from them.

[5] Some archaeologists believe that *khereksur*s are not tombs but ritual sites for the sun (Grach 1980: 62).

[6] The head of the Japan side is Professor Takahama Shu of the University of Kanazawa and the head of Mongol side is Dr. Diimaajav Erdenebaatar of the University of Ulanbator. Our researches were performed in 1999, 2003 – 2006 (Takahama et al. 2006).

2. Ulaan Uushig I

We chose a site at the foot of Mt. Ulaan Uushig ("Red Lung") near from the city of Mörön, the center of Khövösgöl aymak, 550 km northwest of Ulaanbaatar. Our survey revealed 10 groups (I - X) of various archaeological remains around the mountain. Most of them are concentrated on the eastern and southern sides of the mountain and there is no group on the northern side. This distribution is analogous to that of stone heaps around a *khereksur* (see later).

In each group there are various sizes of *khereksur*s: big, medium and small. Generally speaking, bigger khereksurs are located on the lower flat foot of the mountain and smaller ones are located on the upper slopes. The difference of sizes probably indicate the hierarchical systems of social organization.

We have researched mainly in Ulaan Uushig I, which includes 15 *kherekur*s, 15 stag (deer) stones 鹿石 and many small stone circles and stone heaps. One of stag stones is very famous for having a relief of human face. [1] This site was surveyed in 1970 by Russian archaeologists, V. V. Volkov and E. A. Novgorodova (Volkov, Novgorodova 1975; Volkov 1981: 61 - 66, 195 - 202; Volkov 2002: 78 - 83, 187 - 194; Novgorodova 1989: 203 - 212). They drew a plan and a reconstructed picture of this site with small excavations around stag (deer) stones. But their plan and picture are not accurate. They named it Ushkiin-Uver ("South of Uushig"). But now we know several groups of sites on the southern side of the mountain. So we have changed the site name to Ulaan Uushig I.

3. Ulaan-Uushig Kh - 1

We have excavated Kh - 1 (medium-small size of khereksur) with stone heaps, Kh - 12 (small size) without stone heap, Stag Stone 4 and 7 with stone circles.

The central mound has the diameter of 13 m and the height of 1.5 m. The mound has "horn" — like two protrusions on the east. This type of mounds with protrusions may have a relation with a kurgan "with whiskers" (kurgan "s usami") in Kazakhstan (Hayashi 1999). During the excavation of Kh - 1 we found two important relics for dating Kh - 1. The first is pottery fragments which were distributed among the stones of mound. They belong to one or two vessels and are quite similar to the pottery of "Slab grave culture. [2]" (TSybiktarov 2001: ris. 29) Our pottery is of the same age or later than Kh - 1.

The second is a stag stone (length 82 cm, width 36 cm, thickness 13 cm) on which two (large and small) circles are engraved. It was unearthed at the edge of the stone mound. V. V. Volkov divided stag stones into three types. A stag stone without animal representations belongs to his first type (Volkov

---

[1] Stag stones with human face are very rare: only 4 or 5 examples of over 600.

[2] Slab grave culture is dated to the Late Bronze and Early Iron ages: the end of the 2nd millennium — the middle of the 1st millennium BCE.

2002：19）.

At the center of the mound we found a square stone cist (141 × 72 cm) on ground level. Inner space of the cist is small but sufficient for Hocker position. Unfortunately we could not find any remains in the cist. We continued digging under the cist and found only soft fresh grass, modern bootlaces and cotton gloves which we used the year before. This is a *tarbagan*[①]'s nest. The bones of corpse might have been bit off by a *tarbagan*. Dr. Erdenebaatar told us that it is very rare to unearth human bones from stone cists because of *tarbagan*'s biting.

On the eastern side of Kh－1 there are distributed 21 stone heaps. In 17 stone heaps except Nos. 1, 6, 19 and 21 we found a set of horse bones: skull, mandible, row of cervical vertebrae (neck bones), and sometimes the third phalanges (hooves) and caudal vertebrae (tail bones) in one case.[②] The muzzles are always oriented toward the east. Horse skulls were put on the ground or dug in a small pit. Stone Heaps Nos. 1, 6, 19 and 21 were heavily disturbed. Therefore horse bones must have been placed in all of the stone heaps. This situation means that 17－21 horses were slaughtered for sacrifice around Kh－1.

4. Ulaan-Uushig Kh－12

Next our target was Kh－12. The central mound is 9 m in diameter, surrounded by a circular enclosure of 16 m in diameter. During the excavation we found an iron knife among the stones of mound. Its length is 16.7 cm. The general shape resembles to that of the bronze knives of Spring and Autumn — Warring States period. A similar iron knife was found at Maoqinggou 毛庆沟 in Inner Mongolia (Tian, Guo 1986: 295). But it is uncertain that this knife has a direct relation with Kh－12.

At the center of the mound there appeared a stone cist shaped in oval (ca. 120 × 60 cm) on the ground level. Inside the cist we discovered bones. Most of the bones were judged to be those of human child of 5 or 6 years old.[③] This judgment is very important, because it supports that *khereksur*s must have been basically burial sites. According to Dr. Erdenebaatar, this is the fourth case of human remains to be found inside a cist of *khereksur* in Mongolia.

5. Ulaan-Uushig Stag Stone Nos. 4 and 7

Stag stones often stand near *khereksur*s, but the relationship between them is uncertain. So we have excavated the areas around two stag stones (Stag Stone Nos. 4 and 7), and searched whether there are any relations or not.

Stag Stone No. 4 has representations of earrings, shield, belt, axe, knife and Karasuk type dagger except

---

① *Marmota bobak*: a kind of marmot.
② We could not find any remains from the stone heaps on four corners of enclosure.
③ The bones were judged by anthropologist Dr. D. TÜMEN, Professor of the National University of Mongolia.

stag representations. Karasuk Culture is dated to the end of the 2nd millennium — the beginning of the first millennium BCE. The animal depiction is similar to the early Scythian animal style: 8th– 6th centuries BDE.

We excavated 8 stone circles around Stag Stone No. 4. From 6 of 8 stone circles we discovered horse skulls with neck bones and in one case accompanied with hooves. The muzzles are always oriented toward the east just like those of Kh – 1.

Near Stag Stone No. 7 we found 5 sets of horse bones (skull, neck bones, and hooves) in stone circles and stone heaps. The muzzles are of cause oriented toward the east.

We confirms that the same ritual of horse sacrifice was conducted in the stone heaps of *khereksur*s on one hand, and stone circles and heaps around stag stones on the other hand. And both of *khereksur* and stag stone are dated to the same age: approximately the 1st half of the 1st millennium BCE.

6. Conclusion

There are many bigger khereksurs than our Kh – 1 in Mongolia. One of them is located in Urt Bulagyn am, Öndör-Ulaan *sum*, Arkhangay *aymak*. This huge khereksur has a large square enclosure (longer side is 200 m) and is surrounded by more than 1700 stone heaps and stone circles (Allard and Erdenebaatar 2005: 549; Fitzhugh 2006: 3). Central mound is 4.9 m tall at its highest point and about 30 m in diameter at ground level (Allard et al. 2006: 209). Mongol-American (Pittsburgh University) Expedition excavated 7 stone heaps and they found a set of horse bones, skulland cervical vertebrae, oriented to east-south-east, just like our site in each heap (Allard et al. 2006: 214). [1]

This suggests that about 1700 horses were sacrificed for the specific person. He must have been a first king of the steppes. In conclusion we notice that a strong power and hierarchical system of social organization were born in Mongolia about at the beginning of the first millennium BCE.

Bibliography

Allard, F. and D. Erdenebaatar 2005. "Khirigsuurs, Ritual, and Mobility in the Bronze Age of Mongolia." *Antiquity* 79: 547 – 563.

——, —— & J.-L. Houle. 2006. "Recent Archaeological Research in the Khunuy River Valley, Central Mongolia." D. L. Peterson et al. ed., *Beyond the Steppe and the Sown: Proceedings of the 2002 University of Chicago Conference on Eurasian Archaeology* (*Colloquia Pontica 13*), pp. 202 – 224. Leiden-Boston: Brill.

Anthony, D. W. 2007. *The Horse, the Wheel, and Language: How Bronze-Age Riders from the Eurasian Steppes Shaped the Modern World*. Princeton: Princeton University Press.

Drews, R. 2004. *Early Riders: The Beginnings of Mounted Warfare in Asia and Europe*. New York: Routledge.

---

[1] Radiocarbon dates from horse remains excavated from two stone heaps at Urt Bulagyn am have been dated at ca. 1040 – 850 BC and 975 – 680 BC (Allard and Erdenebaatar 2005: 551).

Fitzhugh W. W. 2006. "Deer Stones and Khirigsuurs: A Bronze Age Ceremonial complex in Hovsgol, Mongolia." Draft for the *Eurasian Steppe Archaeology Symposium*, Feb 10 – 11, 2006, organized by Bryan Hanks, University of Pittsburgh.

Gimbutas, M. 1997. "The Fall and Transformation of Old Europe: Recapitulation 1993," in *The Kurgan Culture and the Indo-Europeanization of Europe: Selected Articles from 1952 to 1993*, pp. 351 –372. Washington, D. C.: Institute for the Study of man.

Grach, A. D. 1980. *Drevnie kochevniki v tsentre Azii*. Moskva: Izdatel' stvo "Nauka".

Hayashi Toshio 1999. "Distribution of Kurgans "with Whiskers": A Culture beyond borders." (in Japanese) *Bulletin of the National Museum of Ethnology*, Special Issue 20: 409 –461.

Khazanov 1994. *Nomads and the Outside World*, 2nd edition. Madison: University of Wisconsin Press.

Novgorpdova, E. A. 1989. *Drevnyaya Mongoliya*. Moskva: "Nauka".

Takahama Shu 高濱秀, Hayashi Toshio, Kawamata Masanori 川又正智, Matsubara Ryuji 鬆原隆治, Erdenebaatar, D. 2006. "Preliminary Report of the Archaeological Investigations in Ulaan Uushig I (Uushigiin Övör) in Mongolia," *Bulletin of Archaeology*, The University of Kanazawa 28: 61 –102.

Tian Guangjin 田廣金, Guo Suxin 郭素新 1986.『鄂爾多斯式青銅器 *Ordos Bronzes*』, Beijing: Wenwu Publishers.

Tsybiktarov, A. D. 2001. *Buryatiya v drevnosti istorii*. Ulan-Ude.

Volkov, V. V. 1981. *Olennye kamni Mongolii*. Ulan-Bator.

—— 2002. *Olennye kamni Mongolii*. Moskva: Nauchnyi Mir.

Volkov, V. V., Novgorodova, E. A. 1970. "Olennye kamni Ushkiin-Uvera." *Pervobytnaya arkheologiya Sibiri*, ss. 78 –84. Leningrad: "Nauka".

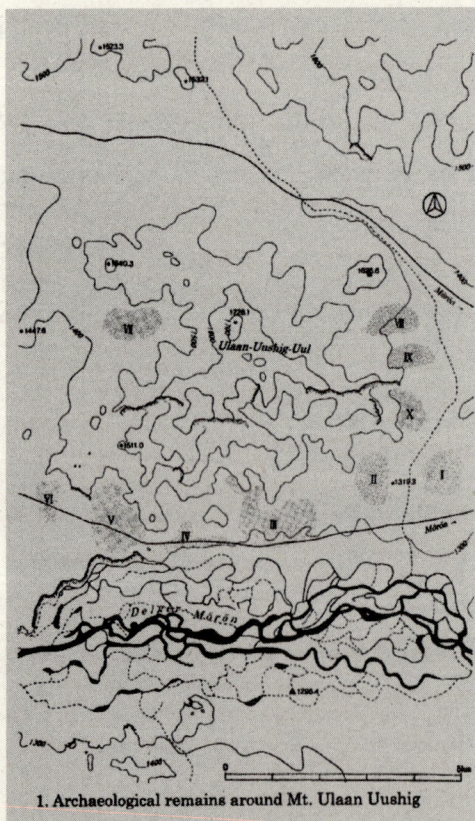

1. Archaeological remains around Mt. Ulaan Uushig

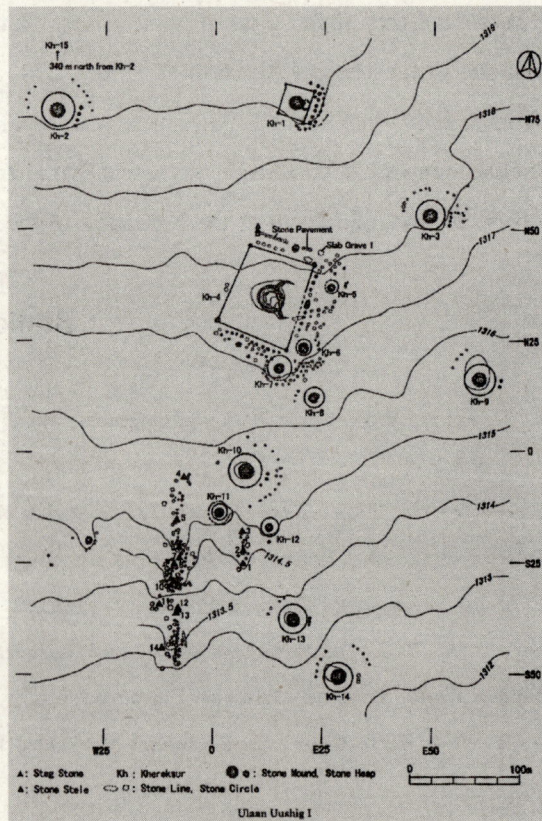

Ulaan Uushig I

Mt. Ulaan Uushig　　　　　　　Ulaan Uushig I

2. Khereksur1

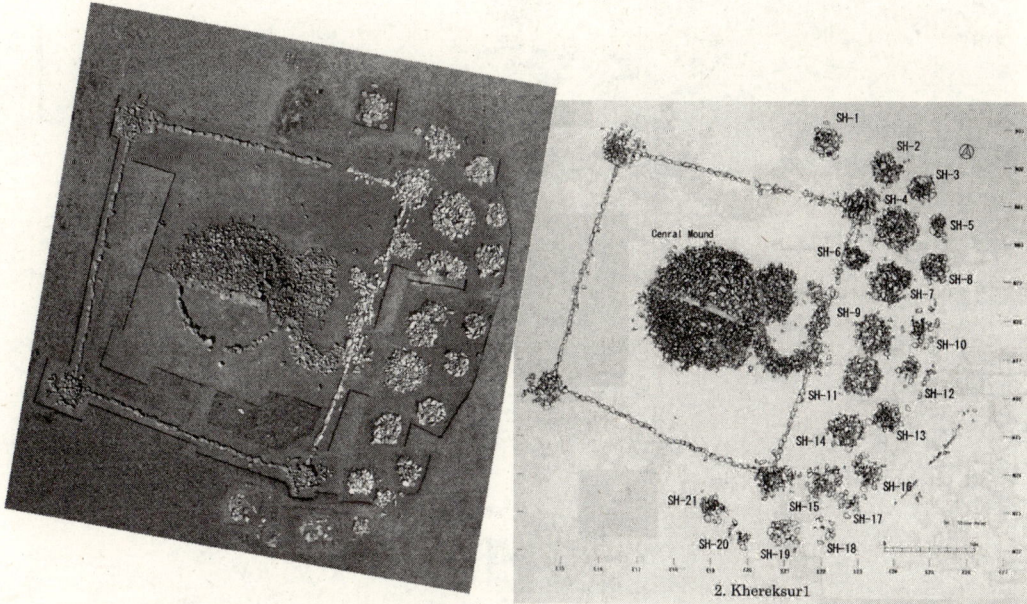

Kh－1 (Central Mound, Square Enclosure, 21 Stone heaps) 2003

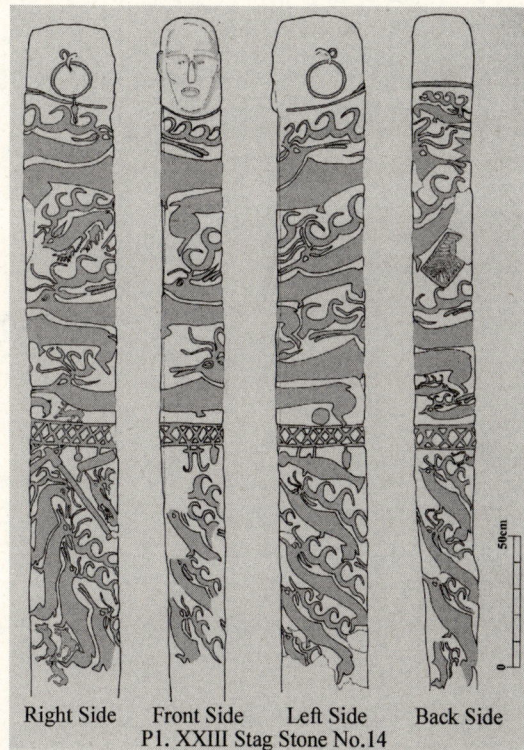

Right Side   Front Side   Left Side   Back Side

Pl. XXIII Stag Stone No.14

No. 14 Stag Stone with a human face

South(Google earth)　　　　　　　　　North(ALLARD et al. 2006)

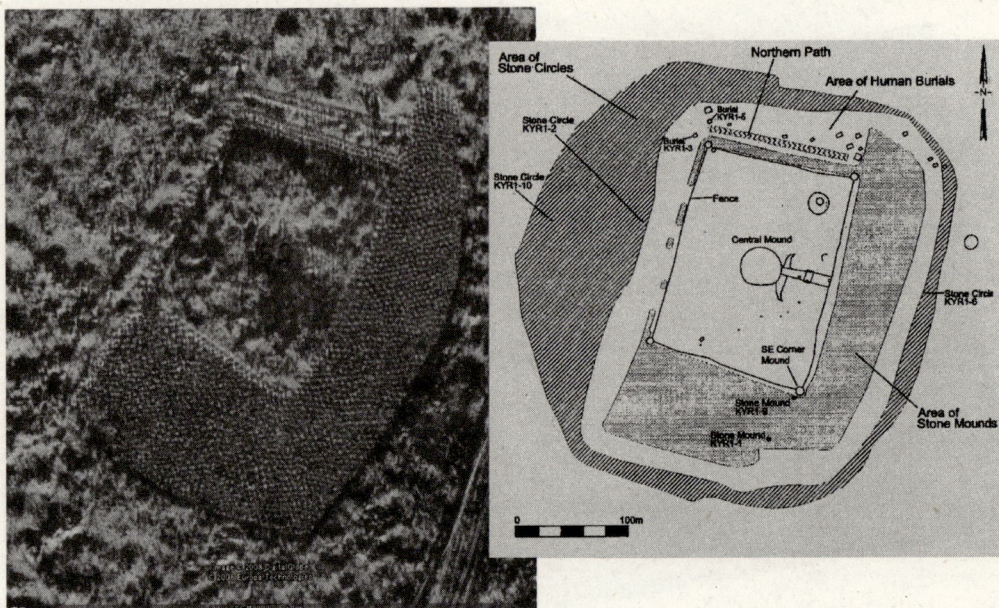

Biggest *Khereksurs*, Urt Bulagyn am

The Eastern Factors in the Development
of Eurasian Nomadic Culture

Ludmila Koryakova

The Institute of History and Archaeology, Ural Division of Russian

Academy of Sciences, Ekaterinburg, Russia

In my paper I intend to discuss some eastern aspects of Eurasian nomadic world. I will particularly dwell on the area of Central-Northern Eurasia, including Urals and Kazakhstan steppe and western Siberia forest-steppe I will discuss some elements of the following issues: 1) the origin of Eurasian nomadism, 2) the social consequences of this phenomenon, and 3) the role and influence of trade system "east-west" meaning above mentioned area.

In Eurasia, in the first millennium BC several cultural worlds were formed up (Fig. 1). Among them the Nomadic World was the biggest; it constituted the close periphery of Ancient States and transformed the cultural and historical situation in the steppe and forest steppes (Fig. 2). This world, stretching from

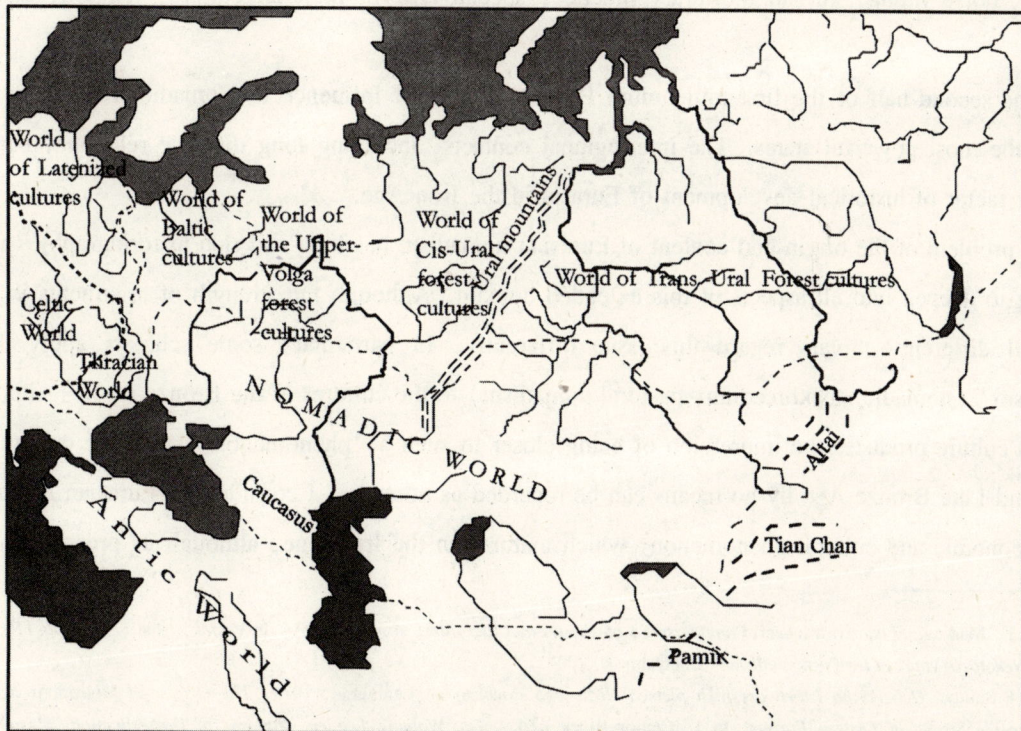

Fig. 1　Cultural Worlds of Eurasia in the first millennium BC.

700 BC 600 500 400 300 200 100 0 100 200 300 AD

European stepppe — **Scythians**

Sauromatians — Sarmatians — Alanians

Asiatic steppe

Central Asia — Sacae (Saka) — Dahi — Kangh-Ku State — Kushan State — Chorasmia

Cis-Urals (Kama area) — Ananyino cultural groups — Pyanobor cultural groups

Western Siberia — Sargat Cultural Groups

China — Spring-Automn (710-481 BC) — Eastern Zhou (771-221 BC) — Warring States (480-221 BC) — Western Han (206 BC-AD 9) — Eastern Han (AD 25 -220)

Anatolia, Iran — Assiria (883-612) — Neo-Babilonian Kingdom — Achaemenid Empire (559-330 BC)

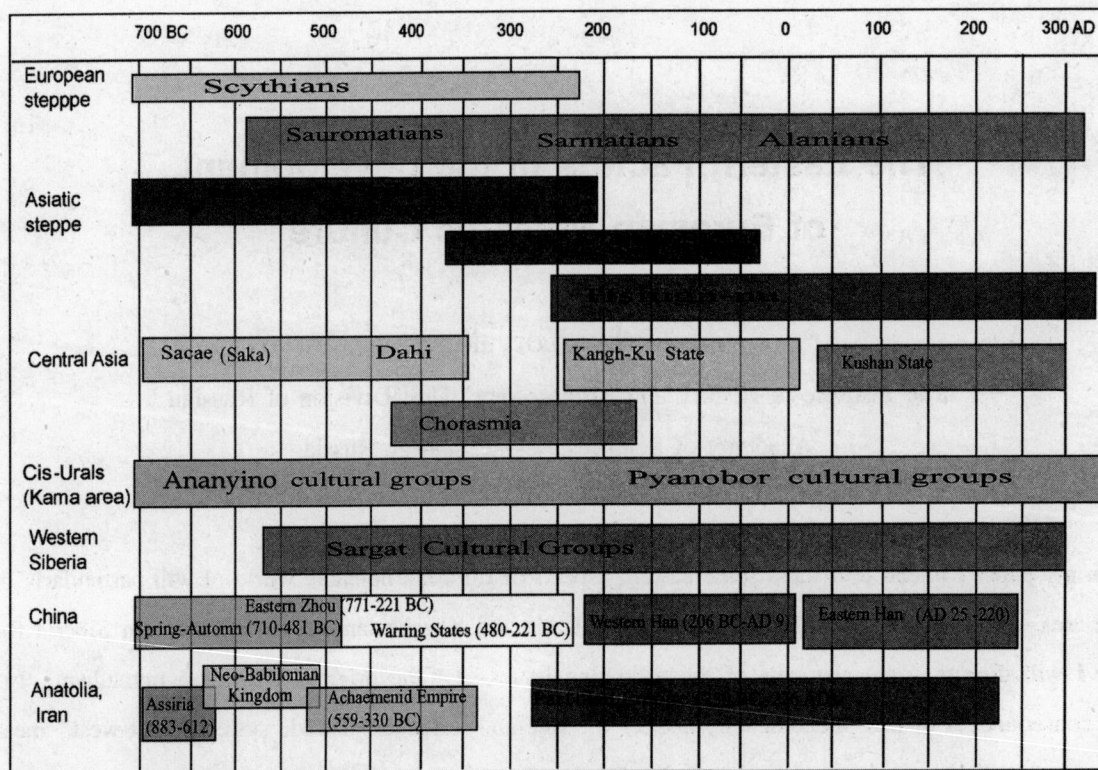

Fig. 2　Chronology of cultural and social formations of Eurasia in the first millennium BC.

Mongolia to Hungarian Pushta, was composed by various cultures, which changed their spacial and temporal configurations, but were united by definite number of cultural attributes: mobile mode of life, animal herding economy, horse riding, kurgan morturary practice, special type of material culture, religion, and a sign system.

In the second half of the first millennium BC the spheres of influence to Nomadic world were divided between the most powerful states. The interregional contacts, including long distance relations, became an important factor of historical development of Eurasia in the Iron Age.

The problem of the origin and content of Eurasian nomadism has long and rich historiography[1] and I am not going to deepen into all aspects of this extended domain. Although the strength of arguments is basicaly over, still different scholars regard this issue differently. In particular, some scholars apply the term "nomadism" (nomadic stockbreeding, pastoral nomadism) to the cultures of the Bronze Age.[2] Although the Yamnaya culture produces the impression of being closer to such a "phenomenon", then the cultures of the Middle and Late Bronze Age by no means can be regarded as nomadic. I consider the Eurasian nomadism as social, economic and cultural phenomenon, which matured in the Iron Age, although its preconditions were

① G. E. Markov. *Iz istoriyi izucheniya nomadisma v otechestvennoi literature: voprosy teoriyi.* In *Vostok,* 1998 (n 6), pp. 110-123; V. I. Zaitov. *Nekotorye voprosy teoriyi nomadisma.* Chelyabinsk, 2004.

② V. P Shilov. *Ocherki po istorii drevnikh plemen Nizhenego Povolzhy'a.* Leningrad, 1975; *The Origin od Migrations asnd Animal Husbandry in the Steppe of Eastern Europe.* In J. Clutton-Block (ed.) *The Wolking Leader. Patterns of Domestication, Pastoralism and Predation.* London, 1989; N. I. Shishlina. *Eurasian Steppe Nomads.* In P. N. Peregrine & M. Ember(eds) *Encyclopedia of Prehistory.* London, 2000; E. N. Chernykh. *Kargaly: Phenomen i paradoksy razvitiya (Tom V).* Moscow, 2007, p. 30.

originated in the Bronze Age. An integral part of Eurasian nomadism is the definite form of social organization. [1] Very important factor of establishment of pastoral nomadism in its classical form in the Eurasian steppe was the interregional division of labour or the corresponding level of global economic and political structuring. [2]

The comparative environmental studies showed that in the eastern steppes (Mongolia and eastern Turkista and northern and western China) the conditions for transition to mobile pastoralism under the influence of ecological factor might have been started earlier than in the west. In about eights century BC, Mongolian steppe was in transition from dry (3000 – 2700 BP) to humid (2700 – 2300 BP) climatic phases. A. D. Tairov, who summarized all available paleoclimatic data, has noted that in the turn of the second and first millennia BC the eastern regions, including Mongolia, northern and north-west China experienced rather sever aridity whereas in Central Kazakhstan and southern Urals ecological conditions were better (Fig. 3). [3]

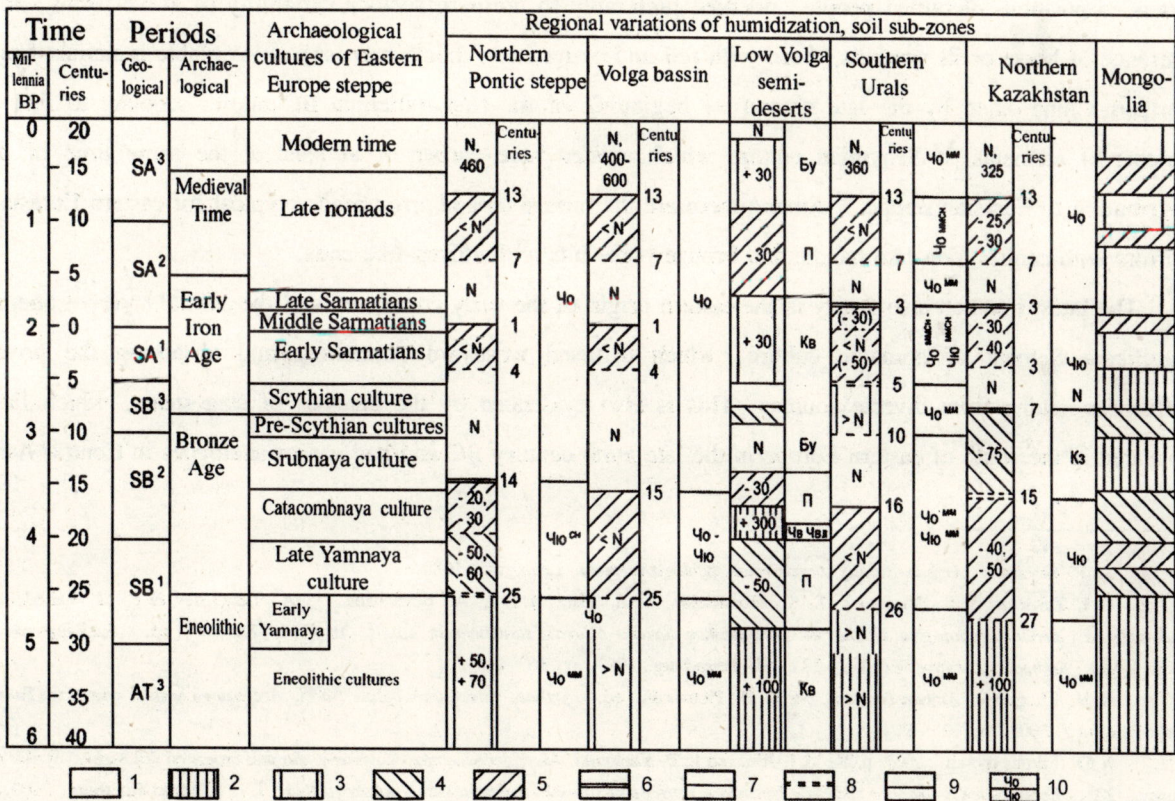

Time		Periods		Archaeological cultures of Eastern Europe steppe	Regional variations of humidization, soil sub-zones						
Millennia BP	Centuries	Geological	Archaeological		Northern Pontic steppe	Volga bassin	Low Volga semi-deserts	Southern Urals	Northern Kazakhstan	Mongolia	

Figure content: The chart shows columns for Northern Pontic steppe (N, 460), Volga bassin (N, 400-600), Low Volga semi-deserts, Southern Urals (N, 360), Northern Kazakhstan (N, 325), and Mongolia, plotted against Time (Millennia BP 0–6, Centuries 20–40), Geological periods (SA³, SA², SA¹, SB³, SB², SB¹, AT³), Archaeological periods (Medieval Time, Early Iron Age, Bronze Age, Eneolithic), and Archaeological cultures of Eastern Europe steppe (Modern time, Late nomads, Late Sarmatians, Middle Sarmatians, Early Sarmatians, Scythian culture, Pre-Scythian cultures, Srubnaya culture, Catacombnaya culture, Late Yamnaya culture, Early Yamnaya, Eneolithic cultures).

Legend: 1, 2, 3, 4, 5, 6, 7, 8, 9, 10

Ecological epochs: 1-normal, 2-optimal, 3-strong crisis, 4-dramatic crisis, 5-gradual crisis. Climatic changes: 6-dramatic improvement, 7-gradual improvement, 8-dramatic degradation, 9-gradual degradation. Annual precipitation: N, 460-modern. mm/year. Soils: u_0-chernozen normal. u_0^{mm}-chernozem thin, K-brown, Π-sandy desert.

Fig. 3 The chart of climatic variations in Eurasia (after A. D. Tairov, 2007).

[1] G. E. Markov. *Kochevniki Aziyi. Struktura khozyaistva I obshchestvennoi organizatsiyi.* Moskva, 1976; S. I. Vainshtein. *Istoricheskaya etnographiya tuvintsev. Problemy kochevogo khozyaistva.* Moskva, 1972; N. E. Masanov. *Kochevaya tsivilizatsiya kazakhov: osnovy zhiznedeyatelnosti nomadnogo obshchestva.* Almaty-Moskva, 1995; A. M. Khazanov. *Kochevniki i vneshni mir.* Almaty, 2000.

[2] L. N. Koryakova and A. V. Epimakhov. *The Urals and Western Siberia in the Bronze and Iron Ages.* Cambridge, 2007.

[3] A. D. Tairov. *Izmemeniya klimata stepei i lesostepei Tsentralnoi Evraziyi vo II – I tys. do n. e.: meterialy k istoricheskim rekonstruktsiyam.* Chelyabinsk, 2003; *Kochevniki Uralo-Kazakhstanskikh stepei v VII-VI v. do n. e.* Chelyabinsk, 2007, p.55.

Repeated overpopulation above the carrying capacity of the Mongolian steppe caused the effect which is called the "Mongolian generator of peoples". It stimulated some groups of population to move westward. Therefore the early elements of Scythian culture are traced in the east and, in particular, expressed in such an early site as Arzhan – 1[①] (Gryaznov 1980), which is dated by the end of the 900 cal BC. [②] Recently excavated complex of Arzhan – 2 is dated by the seventh century BC and has demostrated rather developed attributes of the Schythian-type culture. [③]

Comparative analysis of cultures of Altai, Central Asia, and north-west China of eights-seven centuries BC demonstrats, first — their relative similarity, second — their discrete distribution in westward direction. Some scholars believe that this occurrence was due to pulsating movement of people from north and north-west China and Mongolia, that participated in the formation of Saka cultures. [④]

This was reflected in such traits of funeral rituality as use of stone in funeral constructions, back-lying extended positions of buried people, oriented preferably to northern sector, variability of grave forms, and presence of horse or its symbols (head with fell and extremities, horse harness). [⑤] Available materials from northern China dated by the late second — beginning of the first millennia BC allows scholars to find a number of elements of Scythian culture which existed here earlier or at least at the same time of its distribution to Eurasian steppe. [⑥] Among them are the bronze tanged arrowheads, typical for eastern Eurasia, mirrors with central loop-like handle and bronze horse bits with stirrup-like ends.

The latest research also testify to the eastern origin of the early components of the animal style — one of significant element of nomadic culture, which diffused westward, enriching and absorbing the novel influences issuing from diverse sources. This is also evidenced by the analysis of stag steles, which first appeared in the south of eastern Europe in the late ninth century BC and had earlier analogues in Central Asia

① M. P. Gryaznov. *Arzhan-tsarskij kurgan ranneskifskogo vremeni.* Leningrad, 1980.

② G. I. Zaitseva, S. S. Vasily'ev, L. S. Marsadolov, v. d. Pliht, I., A. A. Sementsov, V. A. Dergachev & L. M. Lebedeva. *Radiouglerod i dendrokhronologiya kluchevykh pamyatnikov Sayano-Altaya: statisticheski analiz.* In G. I. Zatseva (ed.) *Radiouglerod i arkheologiya* (*Arkheologicheskiye vesti*,. V. 37). St.-Petresburg, 1997, pp. 36 – 44.

③ K. V. Chugunov. *Arzhan-istochnik.* In M. B. Piotrovski (ed.) *Arzhan. Istochnik v doline tsarei. Arckeologicheskiye otkrytia v Tuve.* Sankt-Peterburg, 2004, pp. 10 – 39.

④ A. D. Tairov, op. cit., 2003, p. 24; M. I. Itina and L. T. Yablonski. *Mavzolei Severnogo Tagiskena. Pozdnii bronzovyi vek Nizhnei Syrdar'i.* Moskva, 2001; *Epokha bronzy-rannego zheleza v Priaraly'e i problema proiskhozhdeniya kultur sakskogo tipa* (T. 2). Sankt-Peterburg, 2003.

⑤ N. A. Bokovenko. Asian Influence on European Scythia. In Ancient Civilizations from Scythia to Siberia (V. Ⅲ), Rome, 1996, pp. 97 – 122; Nekotorye osobennosti formirovaniya pogrebalnogo obryada rannikh kochevnikov Sayano-Altaya i Kazakhstana. Papar presented to the conference Skifskaya epokha Altaya. Barnaul, 1986, pp. 46 – 48; A. D. Tairov, op. cit., 2007, pp. 26 – 32.

⑥ D. Erdenebaatar. *Burial materials related to the history of the Bronze Age in the territory of Mongolia.* In K. M. Linduff (ed.) *Metallurgy in Antient Eastern Eurasia from the Urals to the Yellow River.* Chinese Studies. Lewiston. 2004; S. Khudyakov,. & S. Komissarov. *Kochevaya tsivilizatsiya Vostochnogo Turkestana.* Novosibirsk, 2002; Yu. F. Kirushin,. & A. A. Tishkin. *Skifskaya epokha Gornogo Altaya. Kultura nacleniya v ranneskifskoye vremya.* Barnaul, 1997; A. A. Kovalev. *Proiskhozhdeniye skifov soglasno dannym arkheologiyi.* Paper presented to the conference *Mezhdu Aziyei i Evropoi. Kavkaz v Ⅵ – I tys. do n. e.*, St.-Petersburg, 1996. Uberlegungen zur Herkunft der Skythen aufgrund archaologischer Daten. *Eurasia Antiqua*, 4, 1998. pp. 247 – 272; G. N. Kurochkin & A. V. Subbotin. *Boyevye chekany (klevtsy) s golovkoi khishchnoi ptitsy mezhdu boikom i vtulkoi v aziatskoi i evropeiskoi chastyakh skifskogo mira.* In B. A. Rayev (ed.) *Antichnaya tsivilizatsiya i varvarski mir.* Novocherkassk, 1993; V. E. Larichev & S. A. Komissarov. *Drakonicheskij mir, drakonicheskoye vremya (r probleme semantiki svernutogo kol'tsom khishchnika).* Paper presented to the conference *Istoriya i kultura Vostoka Aziyi*, Novosibirsk, 2002; A. D. Tairov, op. cit., 2007.

and southern Siberia (Mongolia, Tuva, Altai, Xingjian) where there are numerous representations.[1] It is worthwhile to remind that these regions were in close contacts in the Late Bronze Age due to influence of Karasuk culture.[2] Some scholars believe that mass nomadic migrations in the Northern Zone were caused by political events in Western Zhou.[3] I think that A. D. Tairov saying that this process embraced much wider area, was right.[4] These migrations influenced Kazakstan and Uralian steppes and stimulated the involvment of local population into nomadic pastoralism.

In the 1983, M. P. Gryaznov put forward the theory that this period, which he called the Arzhan-Chernogorovo stage, corresponded to the process of the formation of the Saka and Scythian cultures in Eurasian steppe.[5] Despite local variations, some common attributes of material culture (Fig. 4) characterize the spread of some similar ideological, social and economic patterns in the ninth-eighth centuries BC and marked, first of all, by the birth of a new semantic and artistic system — the animal style.[6] It means the initial forming of the cultural complex of the early nomads occurred in Central Asia in late tenth — early ninth century BC, and it passed, in Bokovenko's expression, in a hidden form.[7] What is especially significant is that a new form of funeral ritual reflecting a new concept of the after-life took shape in the burials of mounted warriors stressing their distinctive social status.

For later time scholars reconstruct at least two waves of migration from the east. The first one (preferably the late ninths century BC) covered the Tuva and Minussinsk areas. The more massive was the second wave (the eights — seventh cent. BC), when the area from Altai to northern Pontic steppe became linked by similar material complex.[8] As Dirksen & van Geel fairley noticed: " Since the 9th century BC the human population density increased sharply and the Scythian nomads expansion to the Asian steppe zone occurred. We suggest that the reason for this cultural phenomenon was the strong late Holocene humid pulse, which changed initially arid expressions into attractive living area for the stockbreeding nomads. This 3 — 2 ka period of more-humid-than-today climate can be regarded as optimal for steppe vegetation growth that provided the much higher biomass production and consequently, triggered the increase in human population

[1] N. A. Bokovenko, op. cit., 1996; Migrations of early nomads of the Eurasian steppe in the context of climatic changes. In E. Marian Scott, A. Y. Alekseyev & G. Zaitseva (eds) Impact of the Environment on Human Migration in Eurasia. London, 2004, pp. 21 – 34; A. A. Kovalev. O proiskhozhedeniyi olennykh kamnei zapadnogo regiona. In V. S. Olkhovsky (ed.). Arkheologiya, paleoekologiya i paleodemografiya Evraziyi. Moscow, 2000, pp. 138 – 179.

[2] S. Legrand. Karasuk metallurgy: technological development and regional influence. In K. M. Linduff (ed.) Metallurgy in Ancient Eastern Eurasia from the Urals to the Yellow River. Chinese Studies. Lewiston, 2004; 139 –156. J. Mei. Copper and Bronze Metallurgy in Late Prehistoric Xinjiang: its Cultural Context and Relationship with Neighboring Regions (BAR Inetrantional Series, 865). Oxford, 2000.

[3] D. G. Savinov. Vozmozhnosti sinkhronixatsiyi pismennykh I arkheologicheskikh dat v izucheniyi kultury Yuzhnoi Sibiri skifo-sarmatskogo vremeni. In Yu. Kirushin (ed.) Problemy khronologiyi i periodizatsiyi arkheologicheskikh pamyatnikov Yuzhnoi Sibiri. Barnaul, 1991, pp. 93 – 96; A. A. Tishkin. Altai v epokhu pozdnei drevnosti, rannego I razvitogo srednevekovy'a. Avtoreferat dissertatsiyi ... doct. istoricheskilh nauk. Barnaul, 2006.

[4] A. D. Tairov, op. cit., 2007, p. 24.

[5] M. P. Gryaznov. Nachalnaya faza razvitiya skifo-sibirskikh kultur. In A. I. Martynov (ed.). Arkheologiya Yuznoi Sibiri. Kemerovo, 1983, pp. 3 –20.

[6] D. S. Rayevsky. Model mira skifskoi kultury. Moscow, 1985.

[7] N. A. Bokovenko, op. cit., 1996, pp. 97 – 122.

[8] A. D. Tairov, op. cit., 2007, pp. 34 – 35.

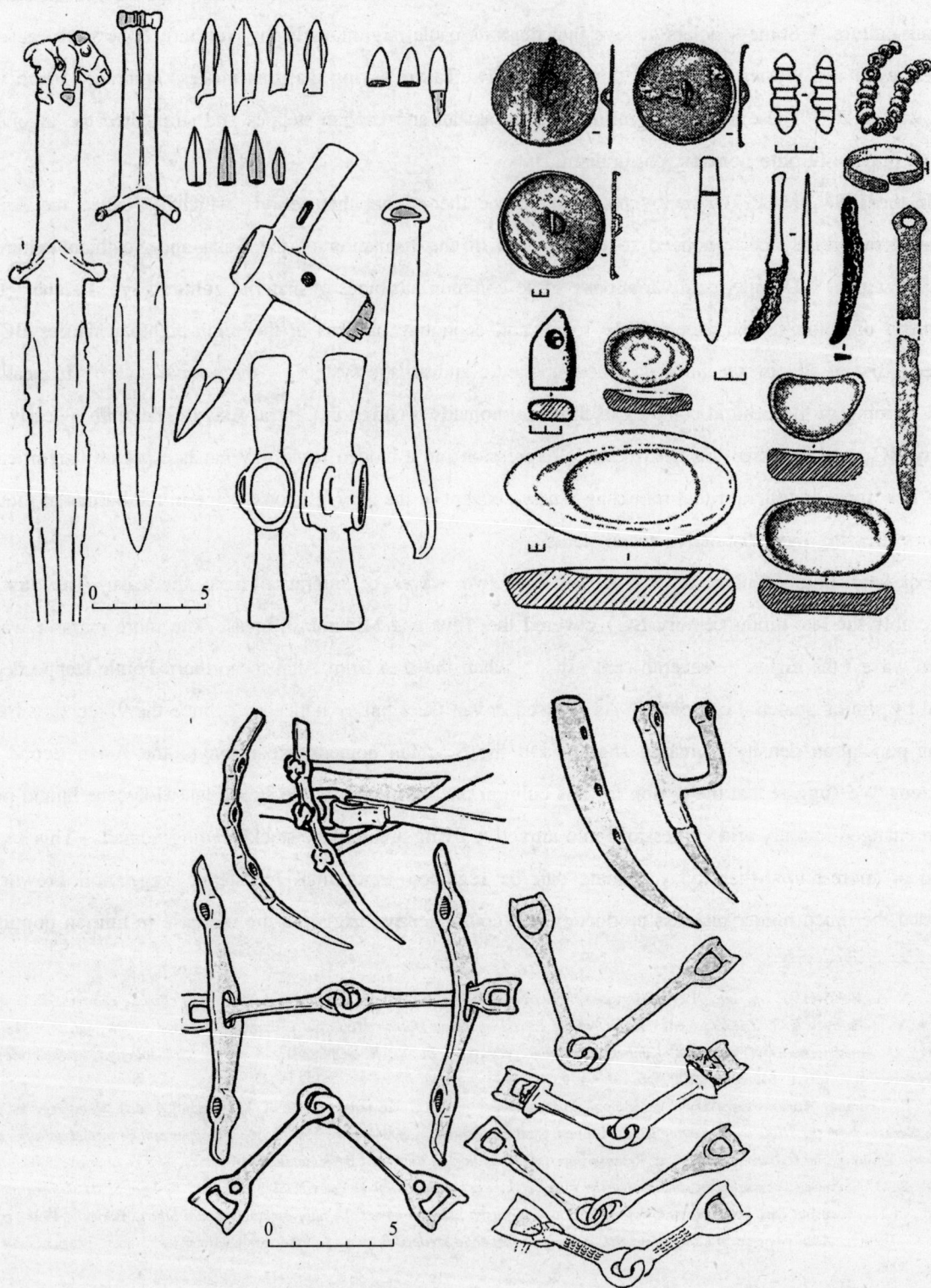

Fig. 4   Materials from different areas of Eurasia: 1 — from Tuva area (after M. P. Gryaznov, 1983, Fig. 1), 2 — from northern Kazakhstan (after A. D. Tairov, 2007, Fig. 3), 3 — horse bits from central Kazakhstan (after M. P. Gryaznov, 1983, Fig. 7).

density and the blooming of impressive Scythian culture". [1]

This process left its mark in the southern Urals as well. In particular, the Big Gumarovo kurgan contained a burial with a stag stone, which preserved the engraved depictions of weapons (a sword with a straight guard and mushroom shaped top and Scythian type bow) and a rather specific set of early type of bronze arrowheads (Fig. 5). [2] Close set of arrowheads is discovered in the Prygovo kurhans in Trans-Urals that can be regarded as the most northern evidence of nomadic penetration to western Sibera forest-steppe. [3] Similar finds, as well as specific forms of horse harnesses, swords, daggers, disk shaped mirrors with loops, and archaic arrowheads indicate the westward movement of the so-called "proto-Scythians"[4] or "Early Scythians of Aristeas and Diodorus". [5]

Archaeologically, the early nomads, who occupied the southern Urals in the seventh to sixth centuries BC, are represented by standard kurgans and some occasional finds. All these remains relate to the Bobrovka stage of the early nomadic culture belonging to the Tasmola cultural tradition characteristic for central and northern Kazakhstan. The mounds were constructed from earth or stone or a combination of the two. The burials were placed into rectangular or oval pit-graves, some of which were furnished with special niches (podboi) constructed on the longitudinal wall. The deceased were supine, in extended position with their heads oriented to the north-west. Signs of organic bedding or a sprinkling of ash were found under the deceased, who were accompanied by traces of meat or a sheep's hind leg and grave goods, including daggers, socketed and tanged, bilobate or trilobate arrowheads, composite belts, mirrors, stone altars, knives of a Central Kazakhstan type, and amulets. [6]

Spread of nomadic population over Ural-Kazakhstan and western Siberia inevitably entailed their interest to neighboring regions and their communications with various aboriginal populations. They were also active in western Siberia because the forest-steppe was attractive in periods of environmental instability in the steppe.

Mapping the nomadic sites around the southern Urals demonstrates that, during the early period (the seventh to fifth centuries BC), their territory was limited to only the steppe landscapes. However, in the west, by the fourth century BC, the forest-steppe area of the Don and Dnepr basins was included culturally and politically into the Scythian kingdom. To the east of the Volga River, the sites of the "Sauromatians" (Cis-Uralian nomads) are mostly situated in the steppe area rather than in the forest-steppe. There was no direct contact between them and the Volga Finno-Volgaic population of the Diyakovo and Gorodetskaya cultures. The Ananyino culture occupied the forest area and was open to association with the Cimmerians and

① V. G. Dirksen & B. van Geel. *Mid to late Holocen climate change and its influence on cultural development in central Siberia*. In E. Marian Scott, A. Y. Alekseev & G. Zaitseva (eds) *Impact of the Environment on Human Migration in Eurasia*. Dordrecht: 2004, p. 304.

② R. Ismagilov. *Pogrebeniye Bolshogo Gumarovskogo kurgana v Yuzhnom Priuraly'e i problema proiskhozhdeniya skofskoi kultury*. In *Archeologicheski Sbornik Gosudarstvennogo Ermitazha* (29), 1988, pp. 28 – 46.

③ M.-Y. Daire & L. N. Koryakova (eds). *Habitats et necropoles de l'Age du Fer au carrefour de l'Eurasie*. Paris, 2002, pp. 18 – 20.

④ Murzin, V. Y. *Proiskhodgdeniye Skifov: osnovnyje etapy formirovanija skofskogo etnosa*. Kiev, 1990.

⑤ A. Y. Alekseev. *Chronologiya Evropeiskoi Skifiyi (7 – 4 vv. do n. e)*. Sankt-Peterburg, 2003.

⑥ A. D. Tairov. *Rannij zheleznyi vek*. In N. O. Ivanova (ed.) *Drevnyaya istoriya Yuzhnogo Zaural'ya*. Chelyabinsk, 2000, pp. 4 – 205.

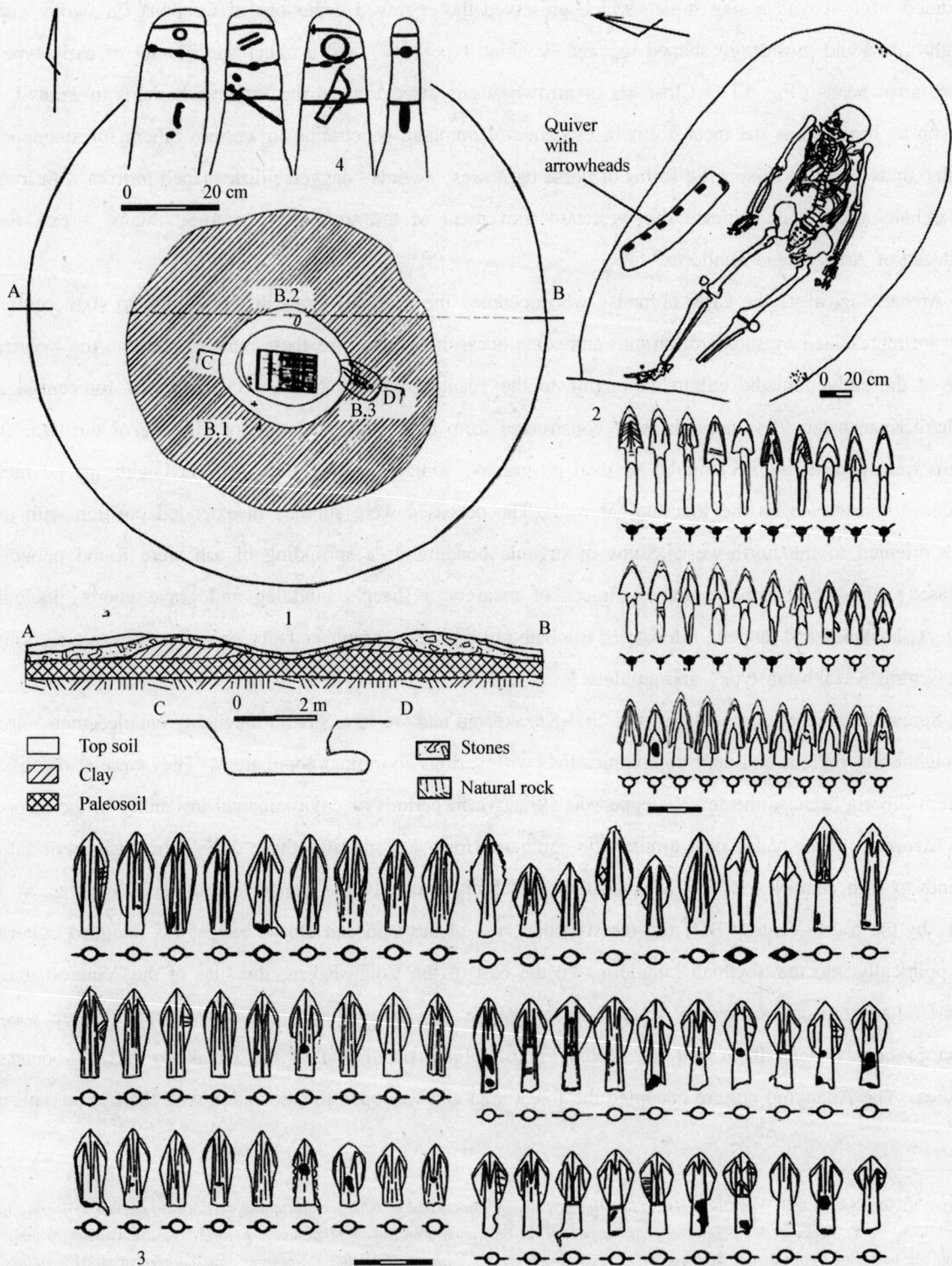

Fig. 5　Big Gumarovo kurgan (redrown from R. Ismagilov, 1988).

Scythians but was almost closed for the south Uralian nomads.

We can also see that at least a part of the forest-steppe was not populated during some time between the eighth and seventh centuries BC. The south Uralian nomads who were more involved in relations with the Saka tribal groups, used metalwork made in Trans-Uralian (Itkul culture) workshops. Of particular interest is that these two participants of interaction remained culturally different, as is seen in their absolutely different archaeological material culture, sign system, and funeral rituals.

By the fifth century BC, a turning point for north-central Eurasia, the western Siberian forest steppe experienced the direct impact of the nomadic population. The synthesis of new cultures is represented by numerous sites displaying a settlement hierarchy and burial grounds which show an almost completely nomadic model of mortuary practice. It gives us a clear example of relationships between different economic systems and social structures. This culture has been formed through interaction between nomads and the aboriginal population. [1]

Social consequences of transition to pastoral nomadism were very significant. The appearance of back riding has entailed the whole range of technological innovation and change of social organization. New social order, based on strong leadership, combined with clan system, which became strongly hierarchical when the nomads were drawn into complex political units or when they had to have long and active contacts with urban societies, was established for many centuries. The "Great Steppe Empires" which were formed by nomads produced an impression of highly despotic states. [2] Another important factor which started to work with help of pastoral nomadism is an activization of interregional connections. War, trade and diplomacy became an integral part of the new social and economic order which was created with participation of Eurasian nomads.

From the final centuries BC, a number of objects of an eastern origin appeared in the Eurasian steppe and forest-steppe: turquoise and gold zoomorphic objects, Chinese mirrors, raw opium, nephrite fastenings for sword scabbards, lacquer objects, silk, gold works, bronze things, small purple beads. Their remains were registered in robbed graves and concentrated in some intact rich tombs. Such a rich material is recorded in several regions, in particular, in Bactria (Tilla-Tepe), western Siberia (Sidorovka and Isakovaka), and the Lower Don area (Khokhlach, Sadovyi, Kobyakovo, Zhutovo, Vysokhino, Dachi and others), which seems to be the centre of the powerful nomadic union, supposedly headed by the Alans, connected archaeologically with middle Sarmatian culture. As A. S. Skripkin noted, characteristic feature of Sarmatian sites is evident eastern influence, manifested in material culture and funeral rites. [3] The same observation has been made by S. A. Yatsenko. [4] Foreign objects may reflect trade along the northern branch of the Silk Route, which began

---

[1] L. N. Koryakova & A. V. Epimakhov, op. cit. , pp. 312 – 314.

[2] N. N. Kradin. *Nomadic Empires in Evolutionary Perspectives*. In N. N. Kradin, A. V. Korotayev, D. M. Bondarenko, V. De Munk & P. Wason (eds). *Alterantives of Social Evolution*. Vladivostok, 2000.

[3] A. S. Skripkin. *K voprosu ob etnicheskoi istoriyi sarmatov pervykh vekov nashei ery*. In *Vestnik Drevnei Istoriyi* (1). 1996, pp. 160 – 168.

[4] S. A. Yatsenko. *Alanskaya problema I tsentralnoaziatskiye elementy v kulture kochevnikov Sarmatiyi rubezha* I – II *vv. n. e*. In M. Shchukin (ed.) *Peterburgski arkheologicheski vestnik*. Sankt-Petreburg, 1993, pp. 60 – 70.

in 36 BC. Some of these objects could have come this way, but it is unlikely that the massive gold sacred decorations of the rich barrows in the Lower Don basin and in the Dnepr region would have been mercantile trade items. Some of the objects have parallels in Siberian collections and among the Hunnic objects. The origin of this art goes back to Central Asia, as yet Ristovtsev supposed.[1] The international (not necessarily ethnic) military aristocracy was the most likely group to disperse the turquoise and gold style artifacts.

Such a material was yielded by unrobed elite graves which were excavated in the Tobol and Irtysh areas, in particular, in the Tutrino,[2] Isakovka,[3] and Sidorovka[4] cemeteries. These graves relate to the Sargat culture occupying the forest-steppe of western Siberia. It embraces the period from the fifth century BC to the second-third centuries AD.

Interesting discovery was at Sidorovka kurgan 1, which had, apart from the destroyed central burial, a well-preserved peripheral burial. There were two interments in the large pit; the upper grave was completely robbed, but it protected a lower well-preserved one. It is difficult to say whether this burial was deliberately or accidentally preserved, but its contents were intact and rich. On the other hand, one can note that such a custom corresponds to the type of secrete elite burials known in Central Asia (Tilla-Tepe, Kargalinka).[5]

This grave contained a number of "eastern" objects, including golden belt plaques similar to which were found in Xiongnu sites and made with bronze[6] and Hotung collection (Fig. 6 – 9).[7]

Another elite burial was excavated by Pogodin in 1989 in the Isakovka cemetery, Omsk oblast'.[8] Especially rich was grave 6 in kurgan 3. It was at the periphery of the kurgan and overlapped its circular outer ditch. The grave was covered with a massive wooden roof. The bottom covering rested on a wooden frame forming a fairly large funeral chamber. A wooden bed (2.2 × 1 m) held the remains of a man wrapped in golden textiles; his head was oriented to the northwest. Outside the chamber, between its wall and the northern wall of the pit, were two large bronze cauldrons holding a wooden spoon and the remains of horse meat and bones.

A closed clay pot with five tubes and white powder inside, used for smoking, hung by an iron chain on the north wall. A large vessel of Central Asian origin and a leather vessel stood in the southwest corner, and a small handmade Sargat-type pot (symbol of the Sargat culture identity) was placed near the head of the deceased. Near the skull, a large silver phial, identical to one found in the Kazanluk district in Bulgaria,[9]

① M. I. Rostovtseff. *The Animal Style in South Russia and China* (Princeton Monographs in Art and Archaeology 29). Princeton, 1929.

② N. P. Matveyeva. *Sargatskaya kul'tura na Srednem Tobole*. Novosibirsk, 1993.

③ L. I. Pogodin. *Otchet ob arkheologicheskikh issledovaniyakh v Nizhneomskom a Gorkovskom raionakh Omskoi oblasti v 1989*. Manuscript. Archive of the Institute of Archaeology RAN. Omsk. 1989. P – 1, 13932; L. I. Pogodin & A. Y. Trufanov. *Mogilnik sargatskoi kultury Isakovka – 3*. In V. M. Kulemzin (ed.) *Drevniye pogrebeniya Ob'-Irtyshy'a*. Omsk, 1991, pp. 98 – 126.

④ V. I. Matushchenko & L. V. Tataurova. *Mogilnik Sidorovka v Omskom Priirtyshye*. Novosibirsk, 1997.

⑤ S. A. Yatsenko, *op. cit.*, p. 63.

⑥ A. V. Davydova. *K voprosu o khunnskikh khudozhestvetnnykh bronzakh*. In *Sovetaskaya arkheologiya* 1, 1971, pp. 93 – 105.

⑦ E. C. Bunker, T. S. Kawami, K. M. Linduff & W. En. *Ancient bronzes of the eastern Eurasian steppes*. New York, 1997, p. 274.

⑧ L. I. Pogodin, *op. cit.*, 1989; L. N. Koryakova. *On the Northern Periphery of Nomadic World: Research in the Trans-Urals*. In A. Farcas (ed.) *Golden Deer of Eurasia*. N. Y., 2006, pp. 102 – 114.

⑨ I. Marazov. *Ancient Gold: The Wealth of the Tracians. Tresures from the Republic of Bulgaria*. New York, 1998.

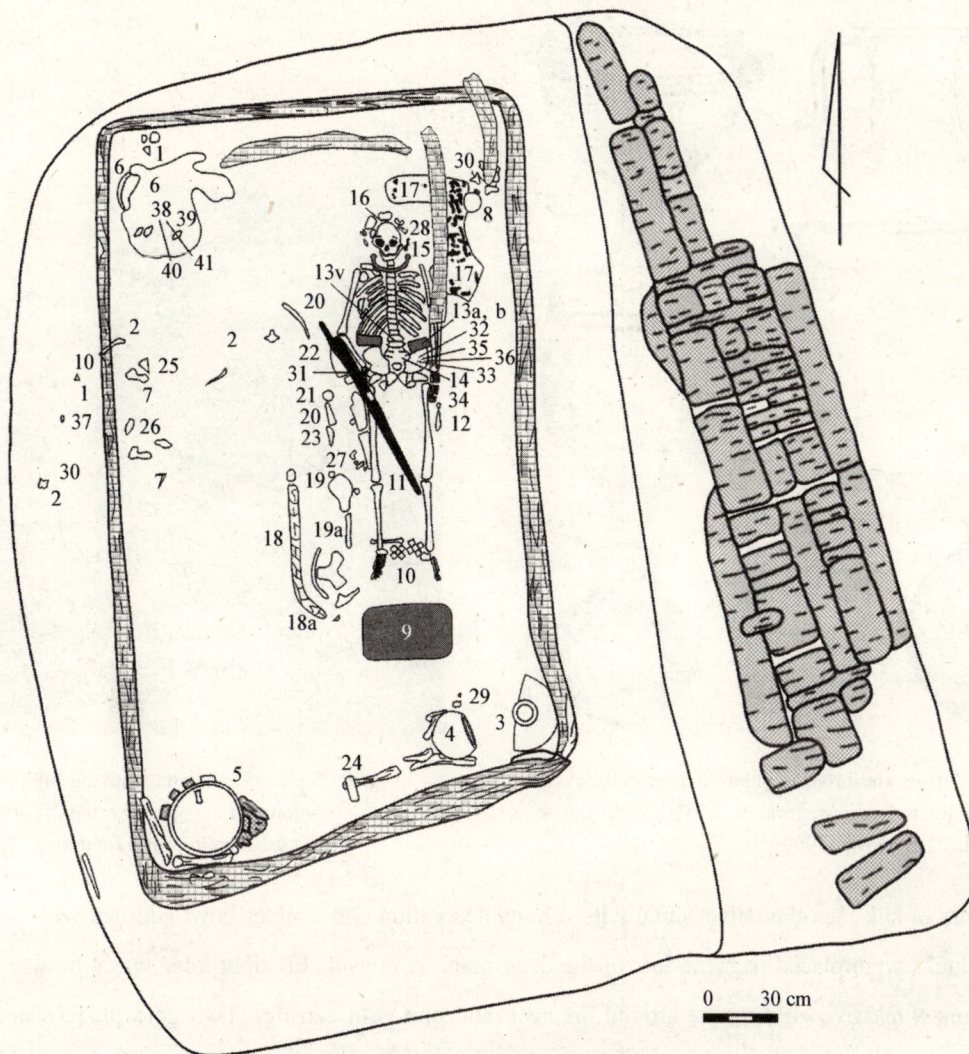

Fig. 6　Sidorovka kurgan 1, grave 2 (the Sargat culture) (after L. N. Koryakova & A. V. Epimakhov, 2007, Fig. 8. 16).

Fig. 7　Sidorovka kurgan 1, grave 2. The gold belt plaque with semiprecious stones.

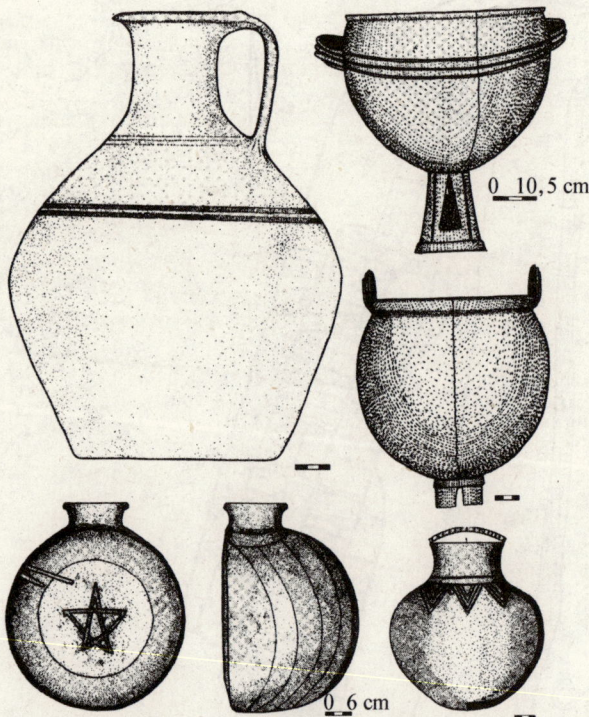

Fig. 8　Vessels and bronze couldrons from Sidorovka kurgan (redrown from V. I. Matushchenko & L. Tataurova, 1999).

Fig. 9　Silver vessels and smoking pipe from the Sidorovka kurgan 1, grave 2 (after V. I. Matushchenko & L. Tataurova, 1999).

held remnants of silk, another silver phial with a lotus decoration and a silver bowl adorned with dolphins and swimming ducks were placed near the feet of the dead man. Alongside his right knee was a bronze kettle. The deceased wore a massive gold torque around his neck and one gold earring. Two gold plaques decorated his red belt, to which was attached by a stone staple a lacquer-covered scabbard holding a long iron sword. An iron dagger adorned with stone-inlaid gold plaques hung from the belt as well. Beside the western wall were iron armour and a large iron belt. [1]

These graves and other graves in the Isakovka cemetery produced rich material, including heavy weapons, gold objects decorated with turquoise, silver phaleras, bowls or phials,[2] and beautiful bronze cattle and vessels of the Han dynasty period (type Hu). [3]

On Matveyeva's estimation, 10% of goods, coming from Sargat sites, have the analogies in the west, among the Sarmatian material, 25% point to southern direction and 15% are imported from the east (Altai, eastern Siberia and China). [4] Special research undertaken by Pogodin, extends the list and amount of Chinese

[1]　L. I. Pogodin, op. cit., 1989; *Vooruzheniye naseleniya Zapadnoi Sibiri rannego zheleznjgj veka*. Omsk, 1998; *Zolotoye shity'e Zapadnoi Sibiri*. In A. V. Yakub (ed.) *Istoricheski ezhegodnik*. Omsk, 1996, pp. 123 – 134; *Lakovye izdeliya iz pamyatnikov Zapadnoi Sibiri rannego zheleznogo veka*. In L. I. Pogodin (ed.) *Vzaimodeistviye sargatskikh plemen s vneshnim mirom*. Omsk, 1998, pp. 26 – 38.

[2]　Livshits, V. A. *Three silver bowles from he first burial ground of Isakovka*. In *Vestnik Drevnei Historiyi* n 2, 2002, pp. 43 – 56; L. N. Koryakova, *op. cit.*, 2006; L. N. Koryakova & A. V. Epimakhov, *op. cit.*, 2007.

[3]　L. I. Pogodin, *op. cit.* 1989.

[4]　N. P. Matveyeva. *O torgovykh svyzyakh Zapadnoi Sibiri i Tsentralnoi Azii v rannem zheleznom veke*. In *Rossiiskaya arkheologiya*, n 2, 1997, pp. 63 – 77.

goods in Sargat graves. [1] In particular, he distinguished about 14 sites where the remains of silk with gold stitching were found. Thus, the Sargat culture constitutes the most northern region of the area where such a material was diffused, including Afganistan (Tilla Tepe) and northern Pontic. The silk from Isakovka1 burial ground is close to silk from Tilla-Tepe. [2]

One can note that if the prestige goods system of the fifth-fourth centuries BC was predominantly oriented to the local nomadic culture, the main feature of which was the Animal Style, then by the end of the first millennoum BC it was transformed. Foreign valubale objects became exclusive symbols of high social statuse. This fact can be regarded as a result of an influence, coming from close relationships, first with classical civilizations, then also with Parthia and China.

This tendency became rather noticeable in the last centuries BC and at the beginning of the first millennium AD, when the interregional trade system was fully established. Interestingly, the elite burials of this time were located not only in the centre as was traditionally accepted, but often on the periphery of the funerary space. Sometimes they were arranged at the bottom of a deep hole, under a second burial, which was destined to distract the robbers' attention.

The graves which contained the "visit card" of that epoch — objects of Sarmatian Animal Style, are recorded in several Eurasian regions: 1) Mongolia and Ordos, 2) the Sayan and Altai mountains, 3) the forest-steppe and steppe between the Urals and Irtysh rivers, 4) the Seven Rivers basin, 5) Iran, 6) Bactria, 7) the Lower Syrdarya basin; and 8) Sarmatia. [3] The finds of such style coming from Uralian and western Siberian unrobed graves are close to the Chinese and Hunnic traditions. [4] These graves also contained direct Chinese imports (mirrors, bronze vessels, long iron swords, lacquer scabbards, nephrite braces, and peaces of silk fabric with golden stitching).

By force of various factors (environmental, political, economic and some others which we cannot determine so far) some Eurasian societies became organized within the regional economic system. An example of such relations is found in the territory of Central Asia — Kazakhstan and western Siberia. Recent research has shown that around the Silk Road there existed a system of trade routes which partly coincided with paths of traditional nomadic transmigrations. [5] Luxury objects, found in Trans-Uralian graves, came from advanced southern centres, including China and Iran. Late written documents report which goods were exported from western Siberia to Central Asia. Except fur, these included: treated horse leather, honey, nuts, birch bark, fish glue, and fish teeth. [6] Trade connections between the southern Chinese state of Chu, Central Asia and Siberia existed in the fourth-third centuries BC. Besides that, a great number of long

---

[1] L. I. Pogodin, *op. cit.*, 1996; 1998.

[2] L. I. Pogodin, *op. cit.*, 1996, pp. 127 – 130.

[3] M. Y. Treister & S. A. Yatsenko. About the Centers of Manufacture of Certain Series of Horse-Harness Roundels in 'Gold-Turquoise Animal Style' of the 1st – 2nd Centuries AD. In Silk Road Art and Archaeology, Vol. V, 1997/1998, pp. 51 – 106.

[4] L. N. Koryakova. *op. cit.*, 2006.

[5] A. D. Tairov. *Torgovyje kommunikatsiyi v Zapadnoi chasti Uralo-Irtyshskogo mezhdurechy'a*. Chelyabinsk, 1995.

[6] A. D. Tairov, *op. cit.*, p. 34.

Chinese iron swords was found in the Eurasian steppe and Trans-Uralian forest-steppe in the last centuries BC when, as we know, there was a state monopoly on the production of iron and weaponry trade in Han Dynasty China. The finds from the Pasyryk culture and other Eurasian cultures reveal that the Chinese silk, bronze mirrors, jewellery and these were not rare. [1]

Chinese objects penetrated into Europe by the southern route via Persia and further via the Mediterranean. This way is best known. There is no doubt that Chinese goods were in commerce before the Silk Road officially began to function. Without this early commercial foundation, the system of long-distance trade could not have been formed so quickly. Unfortunately, the northern direction of this trade is not well studied, except for the "steppe" route, which led from China and probably Mongolia to the west around the Caspian Sea. [2] One part of this route led from eastern Turkistan across the Pamir and then along the middle Syr-Darya to the north-west (Fig. 10). It is thought that the Great Silk Road in the early phases may have run in an broken line. Trade may have been conducted by stages. [3]

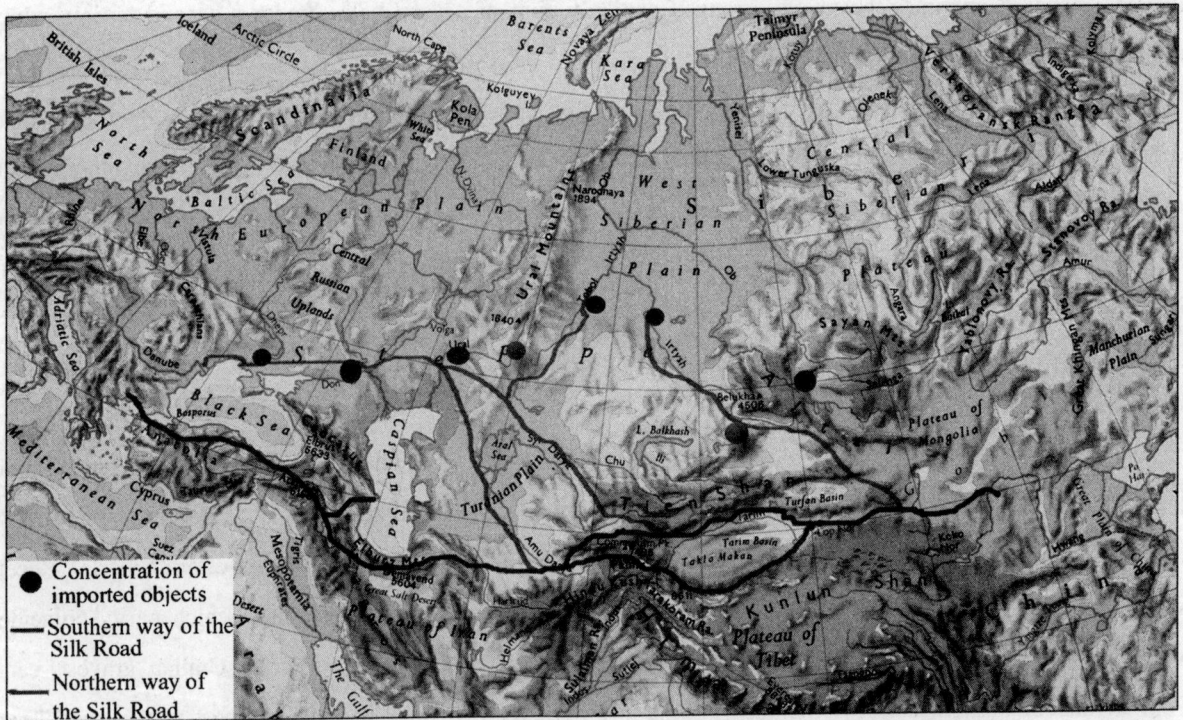

Fig. 10   Trade routes in Eurasia in the Iron Age (after after L. N. Koryakova & A. V. Epimakhov, 2007, Fig. 9.2).

Tairov supposes that the most effective trade routes were established in the late first millennium BC and

① E. I. Lubo-Lesnichenko. *Veliki shelkovyi put'*. In *Voprosy istoriyi*, n 9, 1985, pp. 13－20; *Pazyryk i Zapadnyi Meredianalnyi put'*. In *Strany i narody Vostoka*, Vol. XXV, 1987, pp. 237－44; *Kitai na Shelkovom Puti*. Moscow, 1994; N. V. Polos'mak. *Steregushchiye zoloto griphy*. Novosibirsk, 1994.

② B. Y. Stavisky. *Velikij shelkovyi put*. In P. G. Muradov (ed.) *Cultural Values*. Biblioteka Turkmenica. Sankt-Peterburg, 1997, p. 22.

③ N. Gorbunova. Traditional Movements of Nomadic Pastoralists and the Role of Seasonal Migrations in the Formation of Antient Trade Routes in Central Asia. In Silk Road Art and Archaeology, Vol. III, 1993/1994, pp. 5－10.

existed without any major changes up until the 19th century AD. [1] The main trade centres of central Eurasia were situated in the states of Central Asia through which the main branches of the Silk Road passed. In the sixth-third centuries BC their northern trade was oriented to south-eastern Europe, but after the second century BC, caravans went to western Siberia, where the Sargat culture represented the most powerful political union and trade agent. It is quite probable that this is a reflection of the competition for control over the northern branch of the Silk Road, which led to the Volga River. Later, in 700 – 800 AD again the more significant stretches connected Central Asia and eastern Europe (Volgan Bulgaria), in 1400 – 1500 AD when new states appeared in western Siberia (the Siberian Tatar Kingdom) the trade routes led there again. That is to say, organized trade was established when the main partners attained the level of statehood or at least complex chiefdom.

In conclusion I should stress that the role of so-called "eastern" factor in the development of Eurasian cultures of the first millennium BC was very significant. It started to act at the end of the Bronze Age, but entered into an active phase in the Iron Age, in the first millennium BC. It acted on different levels and was of different expression. The strength of its influence depended on environmental, social and political situation, but it has never disapeared from Eurasian development.

---

[1] A. D. Tairov, *op. cit.*, 1995, p. 32.

On a Traditional Reutilization among Old Turkic Monuments and the Cult and Cultural Background among Nomad Peoples in the South Siberian Steppe-Through the International Joint Expeditions-

Takashi Osawa

OSAKA University of Foreign Studies, Department
of the Foreign Studies, Turkic Studies, Japan.

Preface

As well-known, from the Bronze Age human beings created many kinds of their own drawing and painting in the Rock mountains or caves to express their own thought and feeling or show the spiritual respects toward the sacred existence. This scene can be observed also in the South Siberian Area including Mongolia, Tuva, Hakasiya, Altai, Kazakhstan, and China etc. Especially we can point out that Old Turkic nomadic peoples created several unique funeral complex and stone statue including the Old Turkic Runic epitaphs in the Eurasian Steppe. One of the most interesting to researchers is the nomadic cultural element, which had been spread widely in the several areas of these regions under the almost same nomadic political and military strength. Of course, it seems normal that they have several differences in their shape and expressions, however, it seems obvious that they have essentially common elements in their shamanistic cult and culture, because they have generally sent their own way of lives on the basis of the dry and cool climate and many kinds of variety composed of the sky, rivers, trees, mountains, hills, earth etc. which are peculiar to the northern Asian Steppe. In this circumstance, how the Old Turkic nomadic peoples have feel and think to the older monuments?

To answer to this question, I would like to introduce the condition of several historical monuments of the Old Turkic nomadic peoples in the South Siberia, and analysis how to conserve these historical cultural heritages.

1. What a relationship the nomadic peoples have with the monuments of the different times?

As long as we can know, in the southern Siberia there are many cultural heritages of the Old Turkic

periods including the tombs, sites, shrines, architectures, cities, stone statues, petrography, coins, Old Turkic Runic epitaphs and inscriptions. At a glance, it seems normal that several historical sites are remained in the original places with not so much damages as if they were established at that time, however, it is astonishing thing. Why these monuments have been conserved until now? What a relationship the nomadic peoples generally treated toward these monuments? They are destroyers of cultural heritages as some peoples think so? To answer this question, we have to observe monuments from the archaeological and historical points of views with no bias of the settled peoples of the neighboring countries. During the last 10 years, I have continued on the international expeditions with the specialists of the South Siberian including the members of Mongolia, Tuva, Hakasiya, Gorno-Altai regions of Altai Republic, Altai county or Yili district of Xinjiang Autonomous Regions of Chinese Republics etc. As a result of my researches, I can mention the reasons of the monuments conservation and classify into four groups naming the name of sites as follows:

(1) Their location of some monuments has good condition such as that they are constructed in too dangerous districts so that everyone cannot reach there easily. As to this, I can say that they are rock carvings or Runic Epitaphs of the Tepsey Rock along the Yenisei River of Hakasiya, Runic epitaphs of the Bigel Rock in the Southwest Mongolia, Old runic epitaphs of the Kosh Agach County of the Gorno-Altaisk region and the rock carving of the Qinhe regions of the Chinese Altai region etc.

(2) Some monuments reconstructed by the Old Turkic peoples reusing of the older monuments. For example I can say Tonyukuk inscription, Ikhu khoshtou inscription, many of the Yenisci inscription in the Yenisei Steppe, Bunghbur epitaphs of the Bayan-Khongor Aymak in the Southwest Mongolia, Bain Tsagan site in the Ar-khangay Aymak in the Middle Mongolia, and Chamurchak sites in the Chinese Altai region.

(3) Some monuments conserved or maintained by the nomadic believing in dwelling of the spirits in the tomb or shrine, so they were coming into contact with them although a part or many parts of the monument had been already destructed by war or plunder before. To this relation, I can say Orkhon monuments of Mongolia, Kalbak Tash rock carving of Unguday County in the Gorno-Altaisk regions etc.

(4) Some monuments conserved by the reason that they originally were built as the capital, cities or towns of the settled peoples under the powerful nomadic governments such as the Old Turkic Kaghanate, the Uyghur nomadic empire and other Turkic Kaghanate or the Mongol Empire. Capital of the city or the settlement of the peoples. Most of them have been forgotten in the earth for a long time as the result of the natural phenomenon. To this, I can mention Karabalgasun site, Bay Balik site and Tsagaan Sumiin Balgas belonged to the Uyghur Empire in Mongolia, Alga site and Karakorum of Mongolia, the Gongyue city of the Xinjiang Uyghur Autonomous regions of China etc.

These monuments mentioned above, of course, has very important historical significances, however, we should consider why there could be remained there with several damage as if when they had been built in the first time. Through the analysis, we may have a key to solve the problem such as how to conserve the world cultural heritages in the Eurasian Steppe. In next chapter, I would like to show the condition of monuments of every group mentioned above, and analysis the cause why they could been conseraved from the historical viepoints until mow.

2. Observation and background of monuments conservation

In the following, I would like to inform the result of general survey of monuments mentioned above in ever group from the first group to the fourth group:

(1) Monuments of the first conservation group

(1-1)　Runic Epitaphs of the Tepsey Rock along the Yenisei River of Hakasiya

This epitaphs are discovered in the surface of rock wall in the Mountain namde Tepsei along the middle Yenisei River. I tried to investigate this epitaphs in 2005, however my Russian archeaolog V. Blenchev (The researcher of the Minusinsk regional Museum) advised me no better go to this site alone, because to arrive at this Rock, it is necessary to get on the boat and climb up the deep slope of rock, this is too dangerous. According to D. D. Basiliev's phtographs [Basiliev 1983: 122], it seems quite true. Why the Kirghiz peoples of this region had climed up this deep slope and carved several epitaphs? To this question, we can explane some phrase such as names of God, epithet, title or place name as the sacred one. For example, I can translated the Old Turkic epitaphs of the Tepsey Rock Mountain as follows:

(1) bedizlig Kaya (Rock having ornament) [Tepsei Ⅰ-E-111]①

(2) çigsi (a title or name of inscription's writer) [Tepsei 113, E-113]②

(3) Tebsei keçig kutlug keçig (The crossing place of the Tebsei Mountain, and the crossing place having the charisma) [Tepsei Ⅳ-E-114] ③

(4) ... Tängride kutlug tebsei tängri (The God Tebsei that has acqired the the charisma from the Tängri) [Tepsei 115-E-V]④

(5) ... Täbsëy Käçigsän, käçäring ä! Tängrim ä! Öçük ä! Yärim ä! (You are the crossing place of the Tebsey, Please cross, a! My God Tängri,a! Roof a! My earth a!)[E-116]⑤

(6) kut (Charisma) [Tepsei Ⅶ-E-117]⑥

(7) öz apa! Uyusï asïng! urï enis ïlma! isig küçügün bering! [Apa of ravine! Walk on a curve and cross! Not descend to ravine and valley! Do give your work and your strength (i. e. Give your services)]⑦

From Old Turkic epitaphs mentined above, the Tepsei Rock Mountain where Old Turkic epitaphs were

---

① Basiliev 1983: 43.
② Basiliev 1983: 44.
③ Basiliev 1983: 44.
④ Basiliev 1983: 44.
⑤ Basiliev 1983: 44. In translation, I doubted Basiliev's reading, so I tried to investigate them and I orrected his reading of the runic letters according to the phtographs of Basiliev [Basiliev 1984: 123].
⑥ Basiliev 1983: 44.
⑦ Basilev 1983: 44. As for this interpretation, I reconsidered and corrected Bsiliev's transliteration on the basis of his phtographs of estampaj [Basiliev 1983: 123].

carved can be regarded as the sacred < crossing place > that the peoples can go into the new road. This can be explained as the special gate into the Sacred Mountain as we know the expression of [sacred crossing place Tebsei], [God Tängri], [My earth], [My roof]. And to this rock mountain, describers addressed in the second personal pronpun or the second personal possessive suffix. And from the term of < bedizlig kaya > [Rock having the monument (or adorment or pictures)], we can understand that the Kirghiz peoples considered this Rock Mountain as the rock having [ornament or pictures], that is, petrogryphs including the hunting scene by the worriers and several tribal tamgas. Therefore, we can suppose that at that time the Kirghiz peoples had been respect and worshipped the spirit of the crossing place named [Tepsei Tengri] where the petrogriphs had been drawn in the bronze age. So, this monument can be continued until now.

(1-2)　Runic epitaphs of the Bigel Rock in the Southwest Mongolia

This historical site is located in the Shgar sum, Gobi-Altai Aymak of the Southwest Mongolia. According to the data of GPS that the Japanese and Mongolian international joint expedition researchers had estimated then, it is situated in lat. 45°, 33′, 24,5″ N. ; Long. 97°, 09′, 12,6″ E. There they found and investigated the rock epitaphs including the Old Turkic Runic letters, some tamgas and petrography in two places from 100 - 200 m high from the foot of the mountain in the 8th September, 2004. [1] From this landscape, this epitaph is situated in the high place of the deep slope of the Bigel Mountain that is not easy to find for foreigners. And according to the transliteration of one epitaph, it can be translated such as < Köl ... Yurtu > (This place is camp place of the nomadic people named Kül ...). [2] So we can assume that this place can be camping place of a nomadic person named < Kül ... > of the Old Turkic tribes. And the Mongolian peoples have worshiped this mountain, so we can suppose that this mountain can be one of the sacred mountains also among the Old Turkic tribes. So the epitaphs and the many petrography's' including the hunting animals such as sheep, mountain goats, deer etc. can be maintained until now.

(1-3)　Old runic epitaphs of the Kosh Agach County of the Gorno-Altaisk region

As one of the monument, I introduce the rock inscriptions of the Onguday and Kosh-Agach counties of Gorno-Altai regions of Altai Republic, where I went to expedition with Russian archaeologists V. D. Kubarev and D. G. Kuvarev of Nobosibirsk Archaeological and Ethnical Institute of Nobosibirsk in September, 2005. Then I could investigate many Old Turkic petrogryphs and funeral monuments with stone statues. At the same time, aside the petrogryphs of the Bronze Ages, there were also Old Turkic epitaphs and several tamgas belonged to the Old Turkic periods carved. For example, in Kosh-Agach county, we could investigated two lines of Old Turkic epitaphs in a rock board near the peak of the Rock Mountain named Zharguz Tebe. This site is situated in Lat. 49°, 52′, 33,3″ N. , Long. 88°, 41′, 13,5″, and 1 922 m Height. As far as we know, as to this epitaphs, there are not understandable reading in the philological and historical ponts of view, because there is unresolved runic letter that can be regrded as one of the western

---

① Preliminary Report on the Medieval Studies in East Asia, MURAOKA, S. (ed.), Ryokoku University, Kyoto, Japan, 2006, p. 18.
② MURAOKA 2006;18, phto.

Runic letters. In my view, however, it is important to mention that these two lines of letters had been carved from bottom to upside in the rock cave which has a surface of 2 m width, 1,8 m height to escape the place of petrogryphs of the Bronze Ages where had been graved in the hunting scene and mountain goat or deer. When V. Kubarev talked me as an episode, 20 years ago when he investigated this site with Dr. Nadelayev, he was too hard to access to this peak of the Montnain through the way behind the north slope of this mountain. In my view, this location presearved this site from the invaders from outside. And from this sample, we can also understand that the Old Turkic inscribers had been respectful toward the petrogryphs, then escaped the place of this pictures carved his Turkic letters.

(1 – 4)   and the rock carving of the Qinhe regions of the Chinese Altai region etc.

In September of 2006, I visited Altai region of Xinjiang Autonomous Regions of Republic of China and investigated Old Turkic Sites and some petrography in Altai county with two Chinese senior researchers named Huan of Altai Cultural Museum, and then I researched sites and petrography of the Bronze Ages and Old Turkic periods with a Chinese senior researcher named Jiaokemin of Altai Culture an Relics Institute of Qinghe county.

Especially as to sites of Qinghe County, there are many interesting petrography of the Bronze Ages and Old Turkic periods and a large kurgan and monuments with deer stones of the Bronze Ages of hill of the mountain. There are the winter camping places of the Kazakh nomadic peoples near the narrow steppe along a road and the Shao Qing he river. In rock walls of rock hills there are petrography composed of animal figures of deer, ox, sheep, Mountain goats and Bactrian camels named Qiaoxia, which belongs to the periods from the 9th to the 1st Century BC. in Lat. 46°, 44′, 34,2″ N, Long. 90°, 29′, 04.1″, and 1 289 m Height. And aside this rock scene, there are also petrography of Old Turkic periods where wolves figure of attacking the mountain goat or sheep. According to Jiaokemin's information, in recent years this site becomes worse in the conservation by the development of the regions around this site. However, on the way to the downtown of Qingnhe city, we could observed some petrography of mountain goats or deer, a incantation phrase of Old Tibetan Buddhism in high rock wall of the mountain near the Shaoqing he River. This is a deep rock wall, then we cannot easily access to this place, so it can be conserved until now.

The other hand, as to the site and a large kurgan with the Deer Stones, there are in the large swamp steppe named Sanhaidaozi. One of the Deer Stones of the Bronze Ages is situated in Lat. 46°, 47′, 06,5″ N, Long. 90°, 54′, 31,8″, and 2 644 m Height. This is named Huahaizi. Around here, there are similar sites with the Deer Stones, that have rock carving the typical deers ornaments of the Early Scytians Periods. And as to a large kurgan, it is situated in Lat. 46°, 48′, 11,8″ N, Long. 50°, 52′, 23,5″, and 2 656 m Height. The center of this kurgan has 15 – 16 m Height and ca. 150 m diameter. This kurgan has in four direction, there are every square sites having some Deera stones. According to Jiaokemin's information, this place is summer camp for the Kazakh nomadic peoples, so we could come across many Kazakh peoples that are moving back to the autumn camp or winter camp from here. Frankli speaking, it was too hard to arrive at these sites, because there are not a level road, but rogh road that Kazakhs caravan only can walk on, as a result, these sites could be maintained under the natural condition.

(2) Monuments of the second conservation group

This sites can be conserved under the reusing, that is, the first site of the Bronze Ages were reused as the materials of being described Old Turkic runic letters or the ornaments in the Old Turkic periods. One hand, it can be destruction, however, the other hand, in my view; it could be conserved by the way of replacing like that.

(2-1) Tonyukuk inscription, and Ikhu khoshtou inscription

I investigated this site and inscription in the summer season of 1996, 1997 and 2006 as a member of the Mongol-Japanese International joint Expedition. As well known, there are two Old Turkic Runic inscriptions in the east side of the Mound arranged from north to south. The front side can be the western side. In the western side of the mound are two sarcophagus of the square that can be considered as the funeral tombs for Tonyukuk and his wife. And it is possible that stone figure of Tonyukuk and his wife were established in the front place of every sarcophagus. And from the gate of eastern side, it can be supposed that there is one road to go to the sarcophagus area. And along the road five or six stone figures, which face each other, were set.

Now, we should pay attention to the inscription's surface and the shape. As to the sites of the Old Turkic Kaghanate periods, in my view, they had been influenced from the Chinese dynasties such as Beiqi, Beishu, Sui and Tang. And to the site and inscription of the Turkic Kaghans of the royal family of the Ashinas, it is generally that the site was built in the mound that has a ditch and a bank around it. And in the western side of the mound was established a shrine-house building to be placed the cremated body or his spirit, that has a Chinese typical roof tiles and bricks, and the flower ornaments as demonstrated by the Orkhon sites and inscriptions of Köl Tigin and Bilgä Kaghan, Ongi site and Inscription of Eltmis Yabgu, Mukhar site and inscription of Kapgan Kaghan, Idel site and inscription of Mukhan Kaghan or Ishvara Kaghan (?) as well as the Bugut site and inscription of the 1st Old Turkic Kaghanate of Tatpar Kaghan. And as to the inscription, it had a stone head that had two or some dragon's sculptures and the base of a stone tortoise for inserting by the pivot. However, to the peoples of high ranking titles except the Old Turkic Ashinas family under Kaghans' classes, their tomb or shrines has no dragons stone head nor a stone tortoise base that can shown by the Ikhu-Khoshutu site of Küli Çor and Unget site of Sientaou tribes of non Ashinas tribes etc. As to the shape of the Tonyukuk inscription, it reminds us the shape of the Deer Stones of the Bronze Ages. From the researching the surface condition, we can point out that a part of the surface of this stone pillar was came off, however, Runic inscriber wrote the letter avoiding the damaged part. This shows that the stone pillar before the Old Turkic periods originally has a damaged part like that. From this condition of this stone pillar, it can be the Deer Stone of the Bronze Ages. If my idea is accepted, it seems obvious that Old Turkic peoples would like to use again the Old stone pillars while there are some rock hills fro the inscriptions materials that are not so far from here. From there, we should assume that the Old Turkic peoples intend to reuse the stone materials of the Bronze Ages possessing the purpose of respecting the nomadic ancestors spirit without concerning tribal attribution. Furthermore, we should investigate and excavate this site from the archaeological point of view as well as inscription.

(2-2)   Yenisei inscription in the Yenisei Steppe

Turkic epitaphs of this category can be generally recognized that Old Turkic Runic epitaphs was carved in the Deer Stone (Olen Kamenniya) or the Stone pillars that had been built in the front side or the stone circle monuments of the Bronz Age. Therfore among almost archaeological researchers of the Bronze Age, it seems natural that Old Turkic runic letters should be different from the monuments including the Deer Stoen and the Stone Sarcophagus, so most of them hasa tendency not to attention to the Old Turkic runic letters, while all philologists and historians of the Old Turkic Nomadic Peoples have only interpreted and analysed the Old Turkic letters although they neglected the Deer Stone and the Stone Sarcophagus. This may be explained that there are not so much stone materials that the writers of the Old Turkic periods can carve the runic letters for their dead, so this can be reused case. This is fact, however, is it no hesitating to dare inscribe the letters on the deer stone, or stone saracophagu or stone pillars of the Bronze Age? In my view, it seems obvoius that Old Turkic peoples have a tendency to respect the natural spirit and the soul of the dead from the traditional shmanistic cul and culture. So we can assume that Old Turkic peoples such as the Kirghiz peoples along the Yenisei Basin have also respected the spirit of this monument that had been built in the Bronze Age. For example, some Old Turkic Runic letters can be engraved in the surface of the Deer Stone or in the border of the Stone sarcophagus as if the letters escaped from the ornaments or the lines of the scenes of hunting the beast animals like deer, marals, oks, mountain goat, sheep, wild boars and etc (E-1; E-2; E-3; E-5; E-108; E-109; E-64; E-6; E-7; E-8;E-9; E-10; E-53; E-70; E-52; E-53;E-11; E-14; E-16; E-17; E-18; E-19; E-20; E-21; E-22; E-23; E-25; E-104;E-26; E-30; E-31; E-32; E-34; E-98; E-41; E-42; E-49; E-43; E-49; E-45; E-44; E-45; E-46; E-48; E-51; E-50; E-55; E-57; E-58; E-59; E-60; E-61; E-62; E-65; E-66; E-68; E-69; E-122;E-89; E-90; E-92; E-93; E-94; E-95; E-97; E-99; E-96; E-100; E-105; E-106; E-107; E-105; E120; E-119; E145; E-135;E-141; E-34). [①] In my view, carving way like this cannot be accident, necessarry to pay their attenstion to the symbol of the spirit of the Bronze Age, though they didnot know which periods the Deer stone had been built or to which ethnical groups they had been belonged. Analysed as philologyical and historical sources of the Kirghiz Peoples of the Yenisei Basin, aparting from the monuments including the Deer Stone and the Stone sarcophag etc.

(2-3)   Bunghbur epitaphs of the Bayan-Khongor Aymak in the Southwest Mongolia

On the date of 20, August, under the Japanese and Mongolian International joint Expedition, I tried to find this site with a Japanese collegue SUZUKI Kosetus and a Mongolian archaeologist Mönkhtulga, however, the data of the location (GPS) recorded was wrongly recorded, so we needed many time to find this site on 19, August, 2006. Next day, at last we could find it, then we investigated this site and stele archaeologically and philologically. This is situated in Lat. 46°, 07′, 08,4″ N, Long. 99°, 31′, 51,1″, and

---

① This number of Old Turkic epitaphs along the Yenisei Basin is based on [D. D. Yasiliev 1983].

1 940 m Height. As to this site, there was a question whether this is tomb or not. Firstly the runic letter was carved in a lower part of a stone pillar that had cut in the half line. This inscription can be interpreted as follows:

Üzä tängrikä, asra yerkä yükünükün bar erti, yangïltukum yok, basmïlïg bodunug

utup artattïng. el besh äli kunçuyung utu altunï alu karluk kuvrap utu altun aldï.

[I had done obeisance to the sky (Heaven)above and the earth below. (In addition) I have not committed a fault. Defeating the peoples of Basmïl, you (=leaders of Karluk) broke them up. (As a result,) The real, m (of Karluk) acquiring your forty five (future) princesses and getting their (= the Basmïls') gold, (then) the Karluks assembling and getting (them), they acquired the gold] (SUZUKI 2006: 84 - 85, 92).

Behind this inscriptionlillar, there was another half stone pillar, so we can conclude that this stone pillar was the same ston epillar that had been established in the front side, that is the eastern side of this mound of the Bronze Ages. So we can assume that this is reused inscription of the Deer stone of the Bronze Ages. This assumption can be supprted by the situateion that in the western part behinnd the center there was a stone hill that the body of the dead had been originally buried, now it was found that robbers had dug this part illegually before. And around this mound, there are several Deer Stones circle of the Bronze Agestone, from which we can conclude that this site had been constructed in the Bronze Ages. Then it seems undoubted that this site used again for the memorial stele in Old Turkic periods.

From this contents such that Karluk tribal leader called to his peoples (turk. bodun) that they got the victory against the Bashmil tribe and perished them in the war, then they could plunder the 45 daughters and gold. This situation reminded us there was a war between the Basmil tribe and the Karluk tribe, and this historical situation can be placed after the destruction of the Eastern Turkic Kaghanate and alliance among Uighur, Bashmil and Karluk. And we know that the Uighur tribe and the Karluk peoples drove the Basmil tribe out of their country, and then the Uighur tribe constructed the Uighur Steppe Empire with the Karluk in 744 in Mongolia. Later the Uighur tribe attacked the Karluk tribe in 746, and could get hegemony in Mongolia. As long as we consider this, it is probable that Bunghbur inscription was built the periods from 744 when Basmil Kaghanate's destruction to 746 when Uighurs' triumph upon Karluk and Karluk's running away from Mongolia A. D. [SUZUKI Kousetsu 2005]. In anyway, from the first sentence, we can know that Karluk tribes respected and worshipped not only the sky < **Tängri** > , but also the earth < **Yer** > as Old Turks, Uighurs and Yenisei Kirghizs etc. From this phrases, the Karluk peoples respect the spirit of the Tangri and the Earth, and it seems nature that they respected the ancinet nomadic ancestors spirit that could go and come back to this site. So I can suppose that the Karluk peoples had respected this site and reused the Deer Stone of the Bronze Ages to write down their memorial issues on this surface. We can say that this may be destruction, however, on the other hand, this site can be conserved by the fact of that the Karluk peoples reused this Deer stones as the own inscriptions materilas.

(2－4)　Bain Tsagan site in the Ar-khangay Aymak in the Middle Mongolia

This site was researched by a Russian Archaeologist V. Voitov with Mongolian colleagues and was classified as one of the Old Turkic peoples belonged to the 2st Eastern Turkic Kaghanate in the 8th century. This cause of this chronological view is based on the site that has an Old Turkic typical mound with two stone sarcophagi, southern one of which has a rough stone statue and from outside of the eastern mound there were balbal stones that were built in a straight line in eastern direction. And he points out that this stone statue was roughly remade of a Deer Stone.[①] In August of 2006, I have also investigated this site as one member of the Japanese Mongolian international Expeditions. This sarcophagus is situated in Lat. 47°, 45′, 19,6″ N, Long. 101°, 20′, 38,7″, and 1 551 m Height. Then I also could confirm Voitov's view on the stone statue remade of the Deer Stone. In details, this stone statue is made of the picture carved of human being on the southern surface. Especially what we should say is that reusing the old monument is not only on the stone statue, bit also on the sarcophagus. In other words, we can find Old Turkic typical sarcophagus reused of the stone circle kurgan of the Bronze Ages. This is a sample that the Old Turkic peoples conserved the historical monument of the Bronze Ages although at a glance this condition can be regarded the destruction.

(2－5)　Chamurchak sites in the Chinese Altai region.

I researched several site with stone statues in the village of Hainar, in Qiemurqiek township (Chamurchak) in Altai County in September in 2006 with a Kazakh archaeologist named Huan of Altai Culture and Relics Institute and a Chinese senior researcher Sun of Altai Cultural Museum of Altai County in the Xinjiang Autonomous Region of China. A site and stone statues of the Hainar village is situated in Lat. 47°, 49′, 20,2″ N, Long. 87°, 51′, 0,4″, and 770 m Height. When we visited here, there are five stone statues stood along the eastern outside of this mound, and has a stone circles in the center and the western place in the mound. This site is surrounded with stone square that has a scale of 35,5 m[②] from east to west side and of 20,4 m from north to south side, square stone is made of granit stone and has a 50 cm height from the ground. As to the stone circle of the center, it is a elliptical shape that has a diameter of 6－7,2 m. And in a place of the western mound there are some broken pieces of a black meteorite that can remind us the historical accidents that meteorite stones had fall down near the steppe of Camurchak township in the 19th century. Stone statues are made of granit and quartz materilas. And it has characteristic features in carving method. From these materials, we can point out that part of the face is shaped with the method of simple relief. And parts of eyes, bears, lip, neckless and breast are also carved with a relief, and in front of the abdomen both hands are carved in relief. Especially it seems chracteristic that this nose relief is tied with eyebrows in the same line. A stone statue of the left side is a woman, and has a scale of ca. 1,7 m height, 86 cm width, 40 cm thin, the second one is damaged in head over an half part, so it is hard to distingushed the sev, however, it has a same beast, so we can assume this is shown as woman, thatt has a scale of 1.8 m

---

① Voitov 1996: 50, tab. 2, 51.

② This scale was estimated by the counting my foot step, According to the researching report of Chinese, it has 25 m from east to west [Wan & Bo 1995: 116].

height, 90 cm width and 40 cm thin. The third one is also much damaged in the half part of the right side, so we cannot say this is man or woman. This has a scale of 1,6 m height, 53 cm width and 40 cm thin as a remained part. The fourth one is completely remained, however it is difficult to distingush this sex, maybe it is man because it show the bear under the lip. It has a scale of 1m height, 50 cm width and 40 cm thin. The fifth one is also remained well and has a scale of 132 cm height, 52 width and 29 cm thin, it is also difficult to distingush this sex, however according the expression of bear, it can be a man. Until now, it has been discussed on the problem whether it belongs to the Bronze Ages or not. Chinese researchers insist on this stone statues are to be belonged to the period of the 10th Century BC, i. e. the Bronze Ages[①] based on the materials excavated from the elliptical stone circles in the center of the mound and the characteristic shape of this stone statues. However, it is possible to be belonged to the Old Turkic periods on the location of this stone statues where were placed in the eastern side of this mound, turning the face to the east as well as many stone statues of the Old Turkic periods. Then it cannot be accepted the chronological view of monument of the Bronze Age that has been supposed by the Chinese researchers until now. Beside this site, I could investigated Karatas site near the Chamurchak River along the road of Altai-Borochin where is far from ca. 8 km in the southwest from the administrative office of Chamurchak township. This is situated in Lat. 47°, 46′, 42,7″ N, Long. 87°, 51′, 14,7″, and 814 m Height There are two black stone statues of syenite stones lined from north to south along the eastern side of a square mound. By the expression of the bear, left stone statue can be a man and the other one can be a woman. This mound has a scale of 11 m × 11 m. And there is a stone hill that has a diameter of 6 m in the center of the mound. Until now, this site has been supposed that it can be belonged to the 5 − 2 BC of the Bronze Ages by Chinese archaeologists.[②] In my view, however, these two stone can be a reused Deer Stone of the Bronze Ages by the reason of that these stone statues were broken in two stone parts in the half line of a Deer Stone which had been originally built at the present place. Later every broken part was reused as stone statues of a man and a woman. And the position of stone statues where were established in the eastern outside of the mound turning the front side to the eastern direction can be regarded as the typical aspect of the Old Turkic sites. Therefore I suppose that these stone statues were made of original Deer Stone that were established in the east side of the mound of the Bronze Ages. From this, we can assume that these Bronze Ages' monument was reused as the Stone statues and mound of the Old Turkic periods. And the first monument of Hainar village can be also the reused monuments of the Bronze Ages in Old Turkic periods. In my view, the stone statues having the typical way of relief on the face expression like that of the Haynar region of Altai county should be belonged not to the Bronze Ages, but to the Old Turkic Periods as Japanese Prof. Hayashi suggested before.[③] Thus elder monuments can be maintained as new monument under the conservation by the Old Turkic peoples. Additionally we can say that the stone statue like the Hainar type under the discussion can be also belonged to the Old Turkic periods.

---

① XWGD 1999: 338; 404 − 405; Wan & Qie 1995: 116 − 118.
② XWGD 1999: 344, Fig. No. 0964; Wan & Qie 1995: 116.
③ HAYASHI 2005: 159 − 164.

（3）Monuments of the third conservation group

（3－1） Orkhon monuments of Mongolia

The Orkhon monuments of Köl Tigin and Bilgä Kaghan along the steppe of the Kosho Tsaidam Basin are very famous among the Old Turkic researchers since the July of 1889 that had been discovered by a Russian ethnographical and archaeological researcher N. M. Yadrintsev, that was also one of the Orkhon Expedition under the Russian imperial Geographical Association under W. Radloff.[1] Then it has partly been excavated by the Orkhon Expedition of the Fin-Ougour Society under the Finish Archaeologist O. A. Heikel,[2] then W. Kotvich,[3] D. D. Bulinich, Ser-Odzhav, and L. Jisl[4] etc. But it is historically important that the Turkish and Mongolian International Expedition excavated archaeologically the mound of Bilge Kaghan during the 2000－2005 years under the help of Turkish International Cooperation Association (TIKA). And this process and the excavated results have been published in every year.[5] On this subject of the conservation, especially attention should be paid to the fact that there were excavated a horse bone in some pieces from the front area of the shrine of the Bilge Kaghan's mound. According to the report of excavation, this horse bone is found on the destructed pieces of the shrines, that is, this bone was sacrificed to the destructed shrine of the Bilge Kaghan in the later periods. And Mongolian Archaeologist D. Bayar tells that this is similar to the method of the scarifying toward the sacred monuments such as oboo. This also suggested us that maybe Turkic or Mongolian peoples had a habit of sacrificing toward the Bilge Kaghan's spirit that had been came back to his stone statue or the sarcophagus although it is unknown that they know to whom this monument has belonged in Old times. And it is known that Mongolian nomadic peoples of the local regions have worshipped stone statues of Old Turkic periods as if they pray and worship the statue of Buddha even in recent years as reported by the archaeologists of the last periods of the 19th century and the early periods of the 20th century such as N. M. Yadrintsev, O. A. Heikel, V. D. Kotvich etc. that had been visited this sacred regions. From this, we should consider that the Orkhon sites including the inscription and stone statues have been conserved on the basis of the local Turkic or Mongolian nomadic people respecting the sacred monuments.[6]

（3－2） Kalbak Tash rock carving of Unguday County in the Gorno-Altaisk regions.

Moreover as another examples, I would like to mention the rock inscriptions named ＜Kalbak Tash＞ of Gorno-Altai regions of Altai Republic, where I went to expedition with Russian archaeologists V. D. Kubarev and D. G. Kuvarev of Nobosibirsk Archaeological and ethnical Institute of Nobosibirsk in two weeks of September, 2005.

＜Kalbak Tash＞'Stone (mountain) like spoon' in modern Altai dialect that has the another name of ＜Yalbak Tash＞ meaning 'flat stone (mountain)' is situated in Ungudai district of Gorno Altaisk regions,

① RadAtlas 1892.
② FinAtlas 1982.
③ Kotvich 1914.
④ Jısl 1963.
⑤ Yadrintsev 1892; TIKA 2001; TIKA 2003; Bahar 2002; Bayar 2004; Sertkaya et al, 2001; Alyilmaz 2006; OSAWA 2007.
⑥ OSAWA (Forthcoming 3).

in Lat. 50°, 23′, 52,7″ North, Long. 86°, 48′, 53,2″ East, and 830 m Height in our measurement of GPS. This rock carving are curved in four stone rock place stood vertically, in our estimation, we can attest about 29 inscriptions including little inscription there. This rock inscription which visited and investigated by Russian archaeologists and philologists like V. Potanin, N. M. Nadelyaev, D. D. Vasiliev, I. L. Kyzlasov, B. D. Kubarev, E. Jacobson etc. is famous among specialists, however, it is not so good interpretation in my view. This reason can be caused by the fact that these runic letters show bad condition and curved not so deeply, therefore they cannot be so easy to be distinguished, moreover, the little writing of the forth rock is located too dangerous area, where is registered on the high rock.

However, I tried to climb the mountain and took these inscriptions by photos and videos. And as for the part, I took a rubbing it. At this present I can present some part of this inscription as follows:

(1) Yer bänggü ermis, Atam bädük a! isigin bertig, a! Ürem, a! Ataçïmda, yer-yïs a! [It is said that the place is eternal. My father was great, ah! You served your strength, ah! My highland (i. e. This rock), ah! From my dear father, ah! Place and wooded Mountain, ah!]　　　　　[Kalbak Tas I-1]

(2) Yägän, [etdim], Apa er, a! [Yägän, I organized (this country?), Apa-Er, ah!]

[Kalbak Tas I-2]

(3) Sü ilin yägän bän etdim a! [Army and country, I, organized, ah!]　　[Kalbak Tas II-10]

(4) Apa er bang(ü)si ayagda [This is Apa-Er's inscription, by order]　　[Kalbak Tas II-10]

(5) Yagïz yer! İduk yerim a! atanïgma! [Brown place, ah! My sacred place, ah!　Who be sacrificed!]　　　　　　　　　　　　　　　　　　　　　　　　　　[Kalbak Tas II-4]

(6) Er Apa bän, yägän a!, atam a!, äning a! [I am Er-Apa, Yägän, ah! My father, ah! You, come down, ah!]　　　　　　　　　　　　　　　　　　　　　　　　　　　[Kalbak Tas II-6]

(7) Ürüng a! bitidim a! anaçïm a! adrïldïmïz a! [Ürüng, I wrote, ah! My mother, ah! We departed (from you), ah!]　　　　　　　　　　　　　　　　　　　　　　[Kalbak Tas IV-7]

(8) Er atï yägän a! yägän isigin bertig. yägän a! [His adult name is Yägän. Ah! Yägän, you served your strength, Yägän, ah!]　　　　　　　　　　　　　　　　　[Kalbak Tas IV-10]

From these sentences, we can consider that this inscription was constructed for the person named < Yägän > that had organized a tribal country, and this can be written by a person named < Apa-er/ er-Apa >. And what is important is calling the dead Yägän and maybe he was the father of Apa-er and the rock itself as < Yer >. This certificates my consideration mentioned in the 2nd chapter of this paper that < Yer > of Orkhon inscription includes the Mountains. And in this Kalbak Tash, we can 31 tribes' tamgas in the first rock places according to the D. G. Kubarev's research. This indicates us that the tribal leaders gathered under the rock inscription, and by the description of [Kalbak Tash II-4] we can guess that peoples of this country sacrificed the animals to this rock Mountains.

(4) Monuments o the fourth conservation group

This group of sites is chiefly historical cities for the settled peoples such as Chinese and Iranian and Sogdian traders, artists or farmers that moved or were brought here through the networks in all directions under the Old Turkic or Mongolian nomadic Kaghanates But as a result of the excavation or field researches in recent years, it seems that historical functions of these monuments have been gradually begun to be clarified.

(4-1)　Karabalgasun site

As well know, this site was named ＜Huihu-shanyucheng＞ i. e. the castle of the Uigur Kaghan or ＜Bu-gu-Han-cheng＞ i. e. the castle of Bögü Khan, or ＜Wo-Lu-Duo＞, i. e. Orda in the Tang Chronicle named Shin-Tang-Shu or Jiu-Tang-Shu, or ORDU-Balik from the Islamic Geographies. In archaeological researches, it is knowledge among the researchers since the Orkhon Expedition under V. Radloff of 1892. Then N. M. Yadrintsev investigates this in July 1901, then by Kotwich in 1914, and then by Kiselev 1957. This is situated in 30 km north from Karakorum site, of Kharakholin city of Arkhangai Aymak of Mongolia. It is situated in Lat. 47°, 24 - 26′ North, Long. 102°, 38 - 39′ East. I also investigated the Karabalgasun Inscription and site as one of the Japanese and Mongolian international joint researchers under the Japanese Scientific researching Association and Mongolian Historical Institute of the Mongol Scientific Academy in 1996 and 1997 years. Then we could take rubbings and read the fragments of inscription Chinese, Runic Turkic and Sogdian parts. As to the details of this site, we wrote down in our preliminary report, so I do not feel need to be reported here. However, it is cautious that first W. Radloff considered that this site can be reused by the Mongolian peoples, and then had been added to the castle of the bank as the regions of the prayer places of the Buddhist. To this view, we cannot assume his view, and should consider that this part can be defense of the Eastern Uigur Empire in the first periods of the 9th century. However, it seems possible that this site could be used as the settled Chinese farmers or Iranian, i. e. Sogdian merchants or crafts arts, industrial arts even in the later periods because there is the fact of that a Chinese envoy Buddhist monk named Wanyante of the Sung Dynasty reported there was an old Uigur city near the Arkhangai region near the Orkhon under the Liao Empire, that we can consider that castle was reused by the Kitan peoples or the Uigur peoples. And we discovered this site named Tsgaan-Sumiin-Balgas, i. e. the White temple city, however it is different from Karabalgasun city itself. This site is situated in in Lat. 47°, 04′, 14,8″ North, Long. 102°, 15,0′, 53,2″ East, and 1 713 m Height in the center place, in Tsgaan som of the Arkhangai Aymak when I researched this site as one of the Japanese and Mongolian International Joint researchers in August, 2006. Beside it, there are another castle of the Uigur Empire where is situate in Lat. 47°, 03′, 35,7″ North, Long. 102°, 06′, 10,0″ East, and 1 707 m Height in the center place of the inner place. From this, it seems possible that this site had been reused in the Liao Empire, and maybe even in Mongolian Empire as the basic camp for the settled peoples of Chinese and Muslims.

(4-2)　Bay Balik site and Tsagaan Sumiin Balgas in Mongolia

This name is well known as the city that had been built in the second kaghan named Moyuncur of the Eastern Uygur nomadic Empire in Mongolia on the based of the information of Sine Us inscription that had been established in 757 - 758 yeras AD. And in the geographical information of the Nothwestern region from Tang Dynasty, this castle city is placed in the northern steppes along the Selenge River.

As to this site, I investigated and estimated it in summer of 1997 as one of the Japanese and Mongolian

International Joint researchers under the Japanese Scientific reseaching Association and Mongolian Historical Institute of Mongolian Scientfic Academy. This site is placed where is 11 km westerward far from Hotag-Öndür-som in Bolgan Aimak, today this is also call Bii-Bulag and this complex is composed of three sites. One site is situated in Lat. 49°, 23′ North, Long. 102°, 48′, 33′ East, the second and third one are situated in Lat. 49°, 22 – 24′ North, Long. 102°, 31 – 34′ East. The castle bank has 235 m length in four direction, 7 m height width 3^4 m. And this site has a gate in the eastern part of the south side and outside this gate there are tracks of the another gate named Yancheng in the typical gate of Tang Dynasty for defending invaders. And the banks are strengthened the foundation by the typical method named < Hanchiku > of the Tang Dynasty's architecture. Inner mound there are five stone statues of lions, coins of the Qing Dynasty, fragments of the ware vessel adorned with the combed ornament Kitan Empire periods. According to information of the local Mongolian nomadic peoples, there were 9 Buddhist temples in the Qing Dynasty, later in the revolution peiods in th eearly 20th century, they were definitly destructed.

And the second one is mesured of 140 m sides in every side. This site is call Bor-Tolgoi, i. e. gray hill. And from the innerside mound of this, a gray vessels, many roof bricks and tiles of the Uygur Empire periods have been found.

The third site was measured of 305 – 318 m in every sides. It is call Arslan-Üüd, i. e. Gate of Lions. From inner side of this site, brown vessel with stamped ornament of the Uighur Empire periods, the ware vessel adorned with the combed ornament Kitan Empire periods, porclains of the Sung Dynasty, grazed brown-green pod, white porclain, roof bricks were excavated. From these condition we can understand that these sites belongs to the Eastern Uygur Empire, then was reused in the Kitan Dynasty, until the Qing Dynasty.

And by the Chinese information of < Yuan-Wen Lei > vol. 42 and < Yuan-shi > vol. 6, under the Khubilai Khan, Baybalik site is registrated as the city of the Mongolian setppe where industrilas and crafts arts had resident in the name of < Bai-Ba-Li >, i. e. in the simplised placename from Baybalik in Chinese characters. Khubilei Khan ordered an imperial command to bring and gather the crafs arts of in Daidou (then the odl capital of the Jin Dynasty named Zhong dou) as well as Karakorum. From these documents and archaeological evidences, we can conclude that Baybalik city has been build in 570 years of the Eastern Ugur Empire, then reused in Kitan peoples of the Liao Empire, then Mongol Empire, then Qing Dynasty. It seems evident that this site were partly damaged by the cause of the flood from the Selenge River, and in the early periods of the 20th century of the social revolutional movements Buddhist temples were entirely destructed, however, through the almost of the past periods from the Eastern Uygur Empire to the Qing Dynasty, the nomadic peoples has a custom reusing the historical site as his own settled places. This can be also a kind of the conservation of the historical monument.

(4 – 3) Aulga site and Karakorum in Mongolia

Thishostorical monument is known by the partly excavation of Mongolian archaeologist Perlee in 1961, 1966, 1967, 1968 and 1976, however there are not special name of this site. Then, under the sponsorship of the Japanese YOMIURI Foundation, the Gorban Gol project was begun under the superviser of Japanese Prof. Dr. KATO Shinpei, then this site was mesured by the joint researchers partly.

Later this site was entirely excavated by the Mongolian and Japanese International joint researchres under the leadership of Prof. Dr. KATO Shinpei and Prof. Dr. SHIRAISHI Noriyuki and Mongolian Archaeological Institute Prof. Dr. Tsevendorji of the Mongolian Scientific Academy in Summer of 2001. This is placed in the southern flat slope area of a hill between the Rashaan-Ukha hill and the Avragin River in the Deliger-khan som of the Khentey aymak, where is 250 km eastward from Ullanbaatar of the Mongolian capital city. This site is situated in Lat. 47°, 05′, 49″ North, Long. 109°, 09′, 42″ East, and 1 205 m Height, and is composed of the square having the 1 200 m length in the side from East to West and 500 m length in the side from South to North. And inside it there is the ceremonial moundof square having the size of 30 m in every side. ①

This site can be attested with the Ordu of Chingiz Khan on the basis of the registration on the Chinghiz Khan's built his Ordu along the Khelren River in 1211 year of the Yuanshi vol. 1 and his coming back to his Ordu near the lu-qu-he River in 1218 year of Yuanshi, vol. 1, and his successor of Chingiz Khan, the second Mongol Emperor Ögädäi Khan went to the Ordu of his father, Chingiz Khan in the December of 1232 year and etc. Since summer season of 2001, the archaeologist of Mongolian and Japanese Joint Expedition under Prof. Dr. SHIRAISHI and Mongolian colleagues excavated this mound for six years. According to SHIRAISHI's excaveted reports, it is clarified that this site is composed of four layeres as follows: (1) The first layer from the surface of the ground has the sacred shrine that can be belonged to the periods from the fourth-fourth period of the 13th century to the third-fourth periods of the 15th century; (2) The second upper layer has the sacrifycing place in the fourth-fourth quarter of the 13th century; (3) The third layer has a building of Ordu of Ögädäi-Khan first, then the sacred shrine in the second-fourth quarter of the 13th century to the fourth-fourth quarter of the 13th century; (4) The fourth layer has the Ordu of Chinghiz Khan in the fourth-fourth quarter of the 12th century to the second-fourth quarter of the 13th century. ②

As to the old layer, that has relationship with the fourth layer mentioned above, this site can be attested with Ordu and around mound, horse bone of 300 pieces were excavated, is to be sacrificed to worshipp the Chingiz Ordu, it seems probable that this site has turred to his shrine after the priod of Ögedei. According to the Yuanshi, vol. 153, in the 1229, when Ögedai Khan sat a enthronement, he orduerd the architecturers made resotre his fathers Ordu, then he also ordered make the Karakorum. Thus we can assume that this site turned to the sacred shrine to be worshipped for the aristoctatic peoples of Chingiz families after the Karakorum city was built in 1235 year. Acccording to the Yuanshi vol. 3, in July of 1257, Üogedei Khan visited Chingiz's Ordu and he prayed the banners and drums (of his father).

Then according to excavated materilas from the first and second layer from the surface of the ground,

① SHIRAISHI 2002: 179; SHRAISHI 2005: 3 - 5.
② SHIRAISHI 2002: 179 - 194; SHIRAISHI 2005: 1 - 8. Cf. KATO & SHIRAISHI 2005.

there are many bones of oxes and horses marked by cutting the sharpe blade. From this, his grandsons of the Yuan Dynasty has been worshipped this shrine sacrfycing the special oxes and many horses. This supposition can be supported by the Rashid — Uddin's registration of Tamür Khan named QAMARA as follows: He, Khan of Shin region of Chinese subjected the prohibition of hunting named Burkhan-Khaldun. There are four large Ordu of Chingiz Khan remained. These ones are conserved under the command of QAMARA. There are four large Ordu and another five ones (Ordus) remained. This area is prohibbited from acsessing to here because this is near the prohibition of hunting. There his former Khans' portraits are decoreted, and there inscence was always burned. And from the Yuanshi vol. 115, we can read that in 1292, again he, (Great Khan) commanded the Khan of Shin region and moved and controled the northern area and subjected four Great Ordus of Chinghiz Khan and the terittory of Tata(r), then the Khan died in the forty years old in the first day of the January in 1302. [1]

Thus we can conclude that ordu of Chingiz Khan has been conserved as the sacrficing place and the shrine of the Mongol Empire, then the Yuan Dynasty under the shanamistic cultural background respecting the spirits of their ancestors. [2]

(4-4) Gongyue city in the Xinjiang Uyghur Autonomous regions of China etc.

This site was investigated by the Northwest regions of Chinese Expedition under the leadership of a Chinese archaeologist Huanwenbei in 1950 years. And in 1960 years this was measured and investigated by the archaeologist Prof. Dr. Menfaren of Xinjiang Uygur Autonomous region. As a result of comparative researching with the sites of city, Prof. Dr. Menfaren attested this old city named Uch-Turfan by the local peoples with a city named Gonyuecheng, i. e. a city named the Gonyue tribe in the Tang Chronicles such as XinTangshu or JiuTangshu and other records. Especially it is well known that this site has been recorded in the Old Chinese documents of the 7th century excavated from the Astana tomb of the Turfan Basin. According to the historical documents, many Sogdian and Chinese merchants visited and traded in this market town, and then they went to the cities of Turfan, Kucha and Suiab through some trading cities along the steppe roads of the northern regions of the Tienshan Mountains. In September of 2005, I visited and investigated this site with a Chinese archaeologist named Anyinshin of the Yili historical and Cultural Museum. This eastern part inside is situated in Lat. 43°, 59′, 47,8″ North, Long. 81°, 30′, 40,4″ East, and 825 m Height. There are many apple trees inner mound. And now it seems that the local Uygur farmers utilizes it. Until now, there are not entirely excavated researches, so we cannot say that this is real or not the old city of the Gongyue. However, near here, there is a remained town of Almalik city of the Chagatai Kaghanate, then also the historical tracks of the Qing periods. So we can only say that this place is one of the most important places among the Old Turkic and Mongolian peoples from the political and economical points of views.

---

① SHIRAISHI 2005: 8-15.
② Cf. OSAWA 2005.

Conclusions

As mentioned above, as long as I could research, there are interesting historical monuments that has been conserved among the Steppe people. If we enlarge the region, it can be counted much more sites than we suppose. As a cause that site has been conserved, it seems undoubted that the Old and Middle nomadic peoples has a custom of respecting the natural spirit of the mountain, trees and the soul of the ancestors[1] although they had no relationship with his own genealogy. For example, when we investigated sites, the local nomadic peoples came to us and watched our activities cautiously, and when we ask him if they know on the condition and episode of this, they were willing to narrate us the history on this monuments. In my view, as long as they send their nomadic peoples, old historical monuments can be maintained under the influences of their traditional shamanistic cult and culture, however, if the way of their lives were damaged from the cause of the political and economical issues such as capitalism that was spread under the name of globalization. To this problematic issue, it is most effective to establish the conservative networks among the all over the world under the UNESCO as well as the help to the nomadic peoples economically.

Abbreviations

Finatlas 1892 = *Inscriptions de L'Orkhon, Recueilles Par L'Expédition Finnoise 1890*, (Ed.) Société Finno-Ougrienne, Helsingfors.

JMJAE 2001 – 2003 = Preliminary Report on Japan-Mongol Joint Archaeolojical Expedition < New Century Project 2003 >, Department of Archaeology, Faculty of HUMANITIES, Niigata Univesrsity, March 2004.

RadAtlas 1892 = *Atlas der Alterthümer der Mongolei*, (Ed.) W. Radloff, St. Petersburg.

TIKA 2001. Treasury of Bilge Khagan was revealed by TICA, *Eurasian File* 145, pp. 1 – 3.

TIKA 2003. Mogolistan'daki Türk Anıtları Projesi 2001 Yılı Çalısmaları, yayın No. 67, TIKA. Ankara.

XWGD 1999 = Chonguo Xinjiang Wenwu Guoji daguan (A G rand View of Xinjiang's Cultral Relocs and Historic China), Xinjian meishusheyingsyubanhse, Urumqi, 1999.

TCG = Alaaddin Ata Melik Cüveynî, Tarihi Çihan Güsa 1 (Trns. Öztürk, M) KTB, Ankara, 1988.

Bibliography

Bahar, H. et al. 2002. 2001 Bilge Kagan Külliyesi Kazıları, *Türkler* 2, Yeni Türkiye Yayınları, pp. 182 – 190.

Bayar, D. 2004. Novye Arkheologicheskie Raskopki na Pamyatnike Bil'ge-Kagana, *Arkheologiya, Étnografiya i Antropologiya Evrazii* 4, pp. 73 – 84.

---

① On the belief and worshipping sacred mountain among the Old nomadic peoples, cf. OSAWA 2003; OSAWA 2006 a; OSAWA 2007; Roux 1999; YAMADA 1950; Cenzhonmian 1939; Inan 1987. And the belief toward the Deer or another wild animals cf. Jacobson 1993; Kubarev & Jacobson 1996; Pelliot 1929.

HAYASHI T. 2004. *Yuurashia no Sekijin* (*Stone statues of Eurassian Steppe*) , Tokyo.

Inan, A. 1987. "OBA" , "OBO" sözleri hakkında, *Makaleler ve Incelemeler*, TTK, Ankara, s. 614 – 616.

Jisl, L. 1963. Kül-Tegin Anıtında 1958'de yapılan Arkeoloji Arastırmalarının Sonuçları, *Belleten* 27, pp. 387 – 410.

Jacobson, E. 1993. *The Deer Goddess of Ancient Siberia in the Ecology of Belief*, Brill.

Kotvich, V. D. 1914. V Khusho Tsaidame. *Tr. Troitsko-Kyakhtinsckogo otd. Rys. Geogr. Rus. ob-va.* -T. 15, vyp. 1. -pp. 50 – 54.

Kubarev, V. D & Jacobson, E. 1996. *Répertoire des Peetroglyphes D'Asie Centrale*, *Fascicule No.: SIBERIE Du Sud 3: Kalbak-Tash I* (*République de L'Altai*) , Paris.

Kyzlasov, I. L. 2002. *Pamyatniki Runicheskoi Pisımennosti Gorno Altaya*, Gorno-Altaisk.

Lingan. 1987. Gu Tujue bei ming zha ji(Aspect of the Old Turkic inscriptions) (In Chinese) , Selected historical articles on the old Turkic and Uighurs, shang, Zhong hua shu ju, Beijing, pp. 582 – 594.

Meng Fanren, 1985. *Beitingshide Yanjiu* (The historical geographical study of Beiting) (In Chinese) , Urumqi, Xinjiangrenming.

MORIYASU, T. & Ochir, A. (ed.) 1999. Provisional Report of Researches on Historical sites and Inscriptions in Mongolia From 1996 to 1998 (in Japanese), The Society of Central Eurasian Studies, OSAKA University.

MURAOKA, S. 2006. *Medieval Studies in East Asia The report on the Archaeological and historical researches of the sites of the Middle Age in Mongolia, 2004 – 2005*, (in Japanese) Ryuukoku University, Kyoto.

Nadelyaev, V. M. 1981. Drevnetyurkskie Nadpisi Gornogo Altaya, Izvestiya *Sibirskogo Otdeleniya Akademii nauka CCCR*, No. 11/3, pp. 65 – 81.

OSAWA, T. 2003. Aspects of the cult and culture of Tengri upon the ancient Turkic inscriptions of the Yenisei Basin, Tengri Ordo Foundation, *The 1st International Scientific Conference < Tangrianity is the worldview of the Altaic people >*, 10 – 13th November 2003 (Collection of papers in Russian and English languages) , Abstract. pp. 45 – 50, Beshkek, Kyrgyz Republic.

OSAWA, T. 2006. *Minami Siberia Chiikino Kodaihibunn to Ibutsu karmita Enisei Kirgiz zokuno Rekishiteki Saikentoo* (The Historical reconsideration on the Yenisei Kirghiz peoples on the basis of the Old Turkic insciptions and archaeological data in the Southern Siberia-Preliminary report of the Scientific Reserahes on the Japanese Scientific Foundation) (In Japanese) , OSAKA University of Foreign Studies.

OSAWA, T. 2006 a. On the belief and worship toward the sacred Mountains in Old Turkic Peoples, *Proceedings of the 49th PIAC – 49, July – 4 August 2006*, Freiburg University, Berlin.

OSAWA, T. 2006 b. Mogolistan'daki Orhon Anıtlarını— durumu ve bununla ilgili inançlar-Eski Cin kaynaklar ve arkeolojik detaya göre – 1st International Symposium on the Chenghiz Khan and his descendents-, Istanbul University, Turk Edebiyat Fakultesi, Türkiyat Arastırmalar Enstitüsü, 7 – 8 Aralık, 2006, Istanbul.

OSAWA, T. 2007. On the Archaeological investment of the Bilge Kaghan Site in the recent years and the relationship toward the Tang dynasty on the basis of the direction of the stone tortoise and inscription, Shihoo 39, pp. 14 – 38, Hokkaido University, Department of the Oriental Historical studies.

OSAWA, T. (Forthcoming) , A philological and historical investigation and researches on the worship toward the sacred Mountain in the Old Turkic Periods in the Gorno-Altaisk region (In Japanese) , Osaka.

Pelliot, P. 1929. Le Mont Yu-Tou-Kin (ütükän) des anciens Turcs (Neuf Notes sur des Questions d'Asie Centrale III) , *T'oung Pao* 26, pp. 212 – 219.

Roux, J. P. 1999. *Altay Türklerinde Ölüm*, Kabalcı yayınevi, Istanbul.

Radloff, V. V. 1894. *Die Alttürkischen Inschriften der Mongoleri*, I. Lieferung, St. Petersburg.

Sertkaya, O. F. et al., ed. 2001. *Moaolistan'daki Türk Anıtları Projesi Albümü*, Ankara.

SHIRAISHI N. 2002 *Mongoru teikokushi no Kookogakuteki Kenkyuu* (*Archaeological Studies on the Mongol Empire*) (In Japan), Tokyo, Dooseisha.

SHIRAISHI N. 2005. Chinghisu Haan Byoo no gneryuu (The sources of the Chinghiz Khaan's sacred shrine) (In Japanese), *Tokyooshi Kenkyuu* 63 – 64, pp. 1 – 20.

KATO, S., SHIRAISHI, N. 2005 Aulaga Site 1, Tokyo, Dooseisha.

SUZUKI, K. 2006. Mongorukoku Bayanhongoru/aimaku hatugenno bunguburu hibun (Bunghbur Inscription discovered in Bayankhongor Aymak, Mongolia) (In Japanese), MURAOKA 2006, pp. 82 – 93.

Teveendorzh, D., Mönkhtulga, R. 2004. Chuin khotogorin Shneer Oldson Runi Bichees, *Arkheologiin Sudlal*, 2/22, Ulaanbaatar, pp. 151 – 154.

Tsogtbaatar, B. 2005 "Abargin balgas" — in Arkheologiin Sudalgaani Tovch Toim, *Arkheologiin Sudlal* 2/22, Ulanbaatar, pp. 204 – 207.

Vasilev, D. D. 1995. Da^a lık Altaylardaki Kalbak-Tas Mabedinin Göktürk Yazïtları (A. – 47, 48, 49, 50), *Türk Dili Arastırmaları Yıllıg Belleten*, Ankara, pp. 91 – 97.

Wanbo, Qi Xiaoshan, 1995. *A Reseach on the Glassland Stone Figures along the Silk Road* (In Chinese), Xinjiang Uygur Autonomous region, Xinjian renmin shupashe, Urumqi.

Yadrintsev, N. M. 1892. Otchet ekspeditsii na Orkhon, sovershennoi v 1889 godu. *Sb. tr. Orkhonckoi Ékspeditsii*, Vyp. 1, pp. 51 – 111.

YAMADA, N. 1950. Tyuruku no Seizan Utyukenzan [The sacred Ötükän Mountain] (in Japanese), The Belleten of The Liberal Arts Faculty, Shizuoka University [Series A: Human Science] No. 1, Japan, pp. 65 – 74.

Cen Zhongmian. 1939. Wai meng yu dou djin kao, *Li shi yu yan yan jiu ji* 8/3, pp. 357 – 369.

The Tomb of the Sogdian Master Shi:
Insights into the Life of a *Sabao*

丁爱博(Albert E. Dien)

美国斯坦福大学

The most interesting evidence of the Sogdians in China thus far is the tomb of Master Shi which was found in 2003 in Xi'an, in an area where other such tombs have been excavated, in what may have been a cemetery for high-ranking Sogdians who lived in Chang'an during the Northern Zhou dynasty. Besides being so important as a source of information concerning the Sogdians in China, the tomb also provides new information concerning the office of *sabao* or merchant chief, the head of the Sogdian communities in China. In this paper I wish to offer an interpretation of scenes of the life of the deceased, Master Shi, and point out why the interpretation of the French scholar, Frantz Grenet, is not correct.

The tomb had been robbed in the past, only a few items remained of whatever grave goods had been deposited in it. The robbers had disturbed the contents such that some bones were found scattered about, that of a male and a female. There is also mention in the report of animal bones but nothing more was said on that topic.

The total length of the tomb was 47. 26 m, and it was made up of a long ramped passageway, with five air shafts along its length, an entry way that had been blocked up with bricks and a stone door, that then led into the tomb chamber itself, 3. 7 × 3. 5 m. The walls of the passageway, entry and chamber had been covered with a thin layer of white plaster on which murals of some sort had been painted but nothing of this survived.

What was so exciting was this stone vault, the *shitang* 石堂 or "stone hall" as it was called, 2.5 × 1.55 m, that was covered with reliefs to which paint and gold foil had been added.

Usually in China the epitaph, if there is one, is on a stone slab that stands alone, but in this case it was incised on the lintel above the door of this stone vault. Additionally, it was a bilingual one, in Chinese and in Sogdian, the only one in Sogdian thus far known.

The Chinese text, less well-preserved than the Sogdian, says that the deceased was surnamed Shi 史, that he held the title of *sabao* of Liangzhou of the Zhou dynasty, that is, of the Northern Zhou, that he was a man of the state of Shi (that is, Kesh, the modern Shahr-I Sabz in Uzbekistan), that he had lived in the Western Regions but had moved to Chang'an. His grandfather, Ashipantuo 阿史盤陀, had been a *sabao* in his native land, his father's name was A'nujia 阿奴伽, but no office is listed for him. Master Jun (whose Chinese name is not legible and so in Chinese publications he goes by his surname with the honorific *jun* or "master". by which he is termed in the epitaph) early in the Datong reign (535 – 551) was appointed as chief of the judicial department of the *sabao* bureau (*panshicao zhu* 判事曹主), then in the 5th year of some reign (not legible) he was made *sabao* of Liangzhou. He died in 579 at the age of 85. His wife, née Kang (= Samarkand origin) died a month later. The tomb was built by their three sons, and the interment took place the next year.

The Sogdian contains basically the same information.

There is much to be said about the religious aspects of the scenes on the vault, but I want to turn to life on earth, at least as depicted here, the topics include receptions and banquets at home often with music, scenes of hunting, processions, and caravans.

There is much variety in the reliefs found in these Sogdian tombs, such that one may argue that these have an autobiographical element. That may explain why Turks, with whom the Sogdians had close relations in their commercial dealings, appear in some of these tombs. The tomb of An Jia, a *sabao* who also died in 579, was near to that of Wirkuk. A central panel at the back of the coffin couch from An Jia's tomb features a meeting between whom we can assume is An Jia and a Turkish leader, both on horseback, accompanied by aides, and we see them below in discussion.

As a sabao, or head of a Sogdian community composed primarily of merchants, these contacts may have been in line with An Jia's official duties, or it may relate to his personal dealings. If we knew more about his life, we might be able to construct a vita as depicted in these panels.

The French scholar Frantz Grenet has attempted to do exactly that with the panels from the sarcophagus of Master Shi. In what he calls a continuous narrative he traces the life of Master Shi. (W2) Here he believes Master Shi as a youth and his father came by horse to call on a regal couple, denoted by the crowns that they wear. Note the child that is being held on the lap.

The ruler hunts as a caravan moves at the bottom of the panel. Note the man using a telescope to look out for bandits that may be lurking about.

The caravan now rests by a river as the Sogdians, presumably still Master Shi and his father, visit yet another ruler sitting in his yurt.

The regal couple (the ruler's crown is the same as in the first scene, though the queen's is different) have a grand reception, with music and dancer. Here we see no evidence of Master Shi, but there are three ladies in the wings who seem to be bringing presents.

Here we no longer see the foliage typical of the previous scenes, as Master Shi, now grown, rides with his wife, both shielded by umbrellas. Master Shi exchanges a gesture of blessing with one of the riders. Is this the marriage of that is mentioned in the epitaph?

A party, with five men at the top, sitting on a carpet, and exchanging toasts. Musicians and servants with large dishes of food surround them. Below, five women also sit on a rug and drink. Grenet's interpretation is that Master Shi followed the family tradition and travelled in several countries, trading in both the cities and the steppe, and came to marry and was appointed sabao in Guzang, or Liangzhou as in the

Chinese epitaph. The party scene, Grenet believes, is perhaps a celebration at Nowruz, the Iranian New Year, for he is now a high dignitary and needs not travel any more, he can just sit back and enjoy the good life.

This is rather ingenious and may well be accurate, though there is no way to say for certain and other narratives may be possible. For example, why is the central panel, N2, without evidence of Master Shi?

In an article by Grenet and a student of his published jthis year, much is made of the crowns shown in these scenes, where they are identified as being worn by the rulers of the Hephtalite state whom Master Shi would have visited in his journeys. The Hephtalites had established a state in the Oxus watershed in the late 5.th century, and had expanded their rule over Sogdia, Afghanistan on into northern India. They were driven from power by a joint attack of the Turks and Byzantium in 556—560.

One problem with this dependence on the crown for the interpretation is that there are no depictions of Hephthalite crowned figures; it does resemble that of Peroz, the Sasanian king who ruled 457 to 484 and came to be a tributary of the Hephthalites until he turned on them but lost his life as a result. The crown in Master Shi's tomb closely resembles that on a massive issue of coins by Peroz in 476 – 477 when he was paying tribute to the Hephthalites, as well as on some other coins of the post-Hephthalite period. Grenet's hypothesis is that the style was set by the Hephthalites themselves, though there is no direct evidence. Frankly I think this is a reach but it is necessary if the scenes with crowned figures are to be seen as Master Shi's visits to the Hephthalite court. But we should remember that Peroz's coins which could have served as a model in Master Shi's tomb were available in large numbers in China; in an article published in 1974, 122 of his coins were reported found in China.

At this point it would be useful to pay particular attention to the information contained in the Chinese epitaph.

The name of the reign title during which Master Shi received his appointment as *sabao* is missing in the epitaph but there are a number of reasons why I believe the date of his appointment is 565. Because the appointment took place in the fifth year of a Northern Zhou dynasty reign title, the possible dates are 539, 565, 570 and 576. One needs to note that Chinese texts do not repeat a reign title, and since Datong (535—557) was mentioned earlier in the epitaph, the date 539 is unlikely, and the two missing characters should be of one of the later reign titles. Master Shi was born in 494 (he was 86 *sui* in 579), so he would have been 71, 76 and 82 in those years. Of the three, the first then may be the more probable simply because it is the least advanced in age.

If Grenet is correct that there is a biographical narrative here, and I think he is, then the observation by Yoshida Yutaka, the Japanese scholar, is significant. He has noted that there are several panels in which Master Shi is accompanied by three people who could be his three sons. In my reading of this as a biographical narrative, following the panels in a clockwise manner starting with the west side, after the Manichaean pane, in W2 one finds a couple seated in a dwelling, attendants to the side and a groom and horse below. The couple are shown wearing crowns but I see the crown as a sign of elevated status, not of royalty.

When Master Shi and his wife are depicted on their way to Paradise, they are shown wearing those crowns. Grenet did not mention this.

The style of the crown would have been known at the time from the coins, such as that of Peroz which we saw earlier. The man holds an infant on his lap. I see the crowned couple as a reference to Master Shi's grandfather who had also served as a *sabao*, and the child then is the grandson Master Shi. The epitaphs of the Sogdians in China are certain to record whether the deceased or any progenitor held the office of *sabao*, and the depiction of the *sabao* as wearing the crown would confirm the importance of the office and the high esteem in which the office was held by the Sogdian community.

The next panel (W3) depicts a caravan with Master Shi and his three sons. Above is a scene of hunting both with archery and with hawks. Master Shi, born in 494, was in his 40's before his first official appointment, and this scene may represent those decades of his life.

Rounding the corner, N1, the caravan has stopped at a river bank. Master Shi holds up a finger as he instructs one of his sons. Above, a crowned man sits in a tent, accompanied by three men while a fourth, bearded, kneels as he and the crowned person in the tent exchange toasts. I take this to represent Master Shi's appointment in 535 as Chief of the Supervising Affairs Section of the Sabao Bureau. The person facing him is bearded, and so is not to be confused with Master Shi who is not shown with a beard elsewhere in these reliefs. The relatively lowly office would explain the modest size of his dwelling.

In N2 we see a crowned couple surrounded by attendants and musicians. The elegant dwelling and host of entertainers may then represent the Master Shi's promotion to be *sabao* at Liangzhou. The three sons are nowhere to be seen — there are three young women, perhaps he had three daughters who are not listed in the texts.

Then we see the couple in transit, again with his three sons. The person in the rear is bidding farewell to Master Shi. Finally in Chang'an, when Master Shi can spend his retiring years, again the three sons, and an elderly guest. Below is his wife presiding over a meal with the three who may be daughters. Both Wirkuk and his wife each are hosting a guest.

To review, I see here a depiction of Master Shi's career with an emphasis on his appointment as sabao. For the first time we have specific dates of appointment, how they were chosen, the age at appointment, and a vivid depiction of the honor in which that position was held. What we need here are some labels to settle the matter, but up to now such are not forthcoming.

粟特人史君墓：萨宝生活管窥

丁爱博
美国斯坦福大学亚洲语言学系

墓葬形制 迄今为止，粟特人在中国最有趣的证据当推史君墓。2003 年，该墓在西安发掘，其所在的地区还发掘出了其他类似的墓。这里可能是北周时期居住在长安的粟特名门墓地。该墓除了是粟特人在中国的主要信息来源外，还提供了关于萨宝也就是商人首领，即在华粟特人聚落首领这个官职新的信息。大约在一个月前左右法国学者葛乐耐（Frantz Grenet）发表了一篇关于史君墓的文章。在对故去的史君的生活景象作一种解释。本文打算指出 Grenet 的解释错误原因之所在，并提出我自己的解释。

该墓过去被盗过，墓中的物品所剩无几。盗墓者弄乱了墓内的东西，男尸和女尸的骨头四散。发掘报告还提到里面有动物的骨头，不过没有更多的信息。该墓总长 47.26 米。

墓道 由一个长的斜顶墓道组成，有五个天井。

砖砌封门 是用砖和一扇石门封住的甬道，门通往 3.7×3.5 米的墓室。墓道、甬道、墓室的墙上涂有一层薄白灰泥浆，上面绘有壁画，但没有保存下来。

石堂 最令人振奋的是这个石质 2.5×3.5 米的石堂，石堂上是彩绘金饰装饰的浮雕。

题铭 一般说来，如果有题铭的话，是刻在一块独立的石板上的，但该墓的题铭却是刻在石堂门上面的门楣上。此外，题铭是双语的，用汉文和粟特文写成，这是迄今唯一一个用粟特文写的题铭。

铭文 汉文铭文保存的不如粟特文的完整。汉文铭文说，死者姓史，是周朝也就是北周凉州的萨宝，系史国人（今乌兹别克斯坦的萨尔伊萨布），本居西域，但迁居长安。其祖父阿史盘陀曾做过本地萨宝，其父阿奴伽没有官号。史君（汉文铭文里看不清他的名字，因此汉语出版物里就用题铭里面的尊称"君"作为他的名字）在大统（535～551）初年授萨宝判事曹主，接着在某年间（铭文里似乎有两个字看不清）的第五年，授凉州萨宝。他去世于 579 年，享年 85 岁。他的妻子康氏（Samarkand 人）在一个月后去世。他们的三个儿子建造了该墓，并在第二年举行了葬礼。粟特文铭文内容与汉文的基本相同。

石堂上描绘的场景里的宗教内容很值得研究，但我想把目光转向尘世生活，至少是这里描绘的生活。绘画的主题包括家内的招待客人和宴饮，还常常伴有音乐、狩猎和出行及商队等场景。

安伽 这些粟特人墓中的浮雕主题多样，以至于我们可以说这些浮雕带有自传的成分。这可以解释为什么其中的一些墓中有突厥人。粟特人与突厥人有着密切的商贸关系。安伽墓距史君墓不远，他也是一位萨宝，同样在 579 年去世。安伽墓中石棺床后面的石屏中央有一幅浮雕，是安伽和一位突厥人首领会晤的场景，他们都骑在马上，旁边有扈从。

安伽 w/突厥人 我们在下面看到他们在交谈。作为一位萨宝，也就是主要由商人组成的粟特人聚落的首领，这些有可能是安伽的公务，或者可能是他私人的事务。如果我们对他的生活了解得多些，或许能够为他建构出一个像这些石板上描绘的那样的传记。

W2 法国学者 Grenet 正试图用史君石棺上的浮雕画建构出一个史君的传记。在他所谓的连续性的叙述中,他追溯了史君生活的轨迹。他在这里相信史君年幼时与他父亲一起骑马拜访一对国王夫妇,其标志是他们戴的宝冠。注意怀中抱着的孩子。

W3 Grenet 以为在石板底部当商队行进时,首领正在狩猎。注意那个正在用千里眼观察有可能藏在附近的强盗的人。

N1 Grenet 认为商队现在在一条河边休息了,此时粟特人可能仍是史君和他的父亲,他们又拜访了另一位坐在自己的圆顶帐篷中的首领。

N2 Grenet 以为这是一对国王夫妇(首领的宝冠与第一个场景中的相同,尽管王后的不一样)在举行一个盛大的宴会,有伎乐和伎舞。可是看不到史君的踪影。Grenet 没有说为什么。在两翼有三位女子,似乎正在呈上礼物。

N3 已经成年的史君与妻子一块骑着马,都遮着伞盖。史君在与其中的一位骑马者互赠临别祝福。在这儿 Grenet 问了会不会这就是题铭里面所说的婚礼。

N4 这是一个宴饮聚会,顶部的五个人正坐在毯子上饮酒。周围是伎乐和盛满食物的大盘。下面是五位妇女,也坐在圆形毯子上饮酒。

Grenet 的解释是,史君遵循家庭传统到一些国家旅行,在城市和大草原做贸易,然后结婚,并被任命为姑臧的也就是汉文题铭里的凉州的萨宝。Grenet 认为,宴饮聚会的场面可能是在庆祝伊朗新年诺鲁兹节(Norwuz),因为现在他是高官了,不用再旅行了,可以坐下来享受生活了。

这种解释确实非常有独创性,也有可能是非常正确的,尽管无法确定,尽管也存在着其他叙述的可能性。

宝冠 Grenet 在他的文中对这些场景里出现的宝冠非常关注,这些宝冠被视为史君在旅途中拜见过的嚈哒国王的王冠。公元 5 世纪末,嚈哒人在乌浒河流域建立了一个国家,其统治的范围从粟特、阿富汗直到北印度。公元 556~560 年,他们被突厥人和拜占庭联合击败。

金币 这种依赖宝冠的解释有一个问题,那就是没有关于戴王冠的嚈哒人物形象的叙述。它确实像萨珊王卑路斯(Peroz)的王冠,他在位的时间是 457~484 年,曾向嚈哒人纳贡称臣,后来又背叛了他们,并最终丧命。史君墓里的宝冠与卑路斯在 476~477 年间大量发行的钱币上的王冠非常像,那时卑路斯还在向嚈哒进贡,也像以后嚈哒的一些其他钱币上的王冠。葛乐耐的假设是,王冠的样式是由嚈哒人自己确定的,但没有直接的证据。如果把戴宝冠人物的场景视为史君拜访的嚈哒人王廷的话,那这就是必要的。但是,我们必须记住,卑路斯的钱币在中国非常多,在 1974 年发表的一篇文章中,据说在中国发现了 122 枚他的钱币。所以这些钱币很容易作为史君墓里面宝冠模型的。

汉文题铭 在这儿我要提上一些汉文墓志铭里面包含的信息。

史君接受萨宝官位时的皇帝的年号在碑文中遗失了,但我认为是在 565 年,理由如下。因为任命是在北周一位皇帝年号的第 5 年,可能的年份有 539 年、565 年、570 年和 576 年。据我所知,所有的汉文献内,年号都不会重复提,因为前面的题铭里已经提到了大统(535~57),所以,不可能是在 539 年,看不清的两个汉字应该是后来的一个年号。史君生于 494 年(579 年他 86 岁),因此,在这些年里他应该是 71 岁、76 岁和 82 岁。在这三个年份中,第一个 71 岁最有可能,原因很简单,这是年纪最小的。

W2 Grenet 认为这里有自传的成分,这点我同意他的意见,可是我有另外一个解释:日本学者吉田丰注意到，这些浮雕里有几块是史君与三个人在一起的场面，他以为这三个人可能是史君的儿子。那我们从西侧的那块开始，沿着顺时针方向则会看到，有一对夫妇坐在一个居室中，旁边是仆人，下面是马夫和马。这对夫妇戴着宝冠，我认为这宝冠是身份高贵的象征，而不是王室的象征。

E3　在史君和他的妻子到天堂去的路上的场景里，他们也戴着那些宝冠。

E3/细节　Grenet 并没有提到这个。

W2　当时宝冠的样式本应该从钱币上知道的，比如我们前面看到的卑路斯的钱币。那位男的怀里抱着一个孩子。我认为戴宝冠的夫妇指的是史君的祖父，他也是一位萨宝，而那个孩子则是他的孙子史君。在中国的粟特人的墓志铭里一定会记载死者或任何一位祖先是否做过萨宝，把萨宝描绘成戴宝冠的形象则会确立该官位的重要性，以及粟特人聚落对该官位的尊敬。

W3　下一个石板上描绘的是史君和他的三个儿子与一个商队。上面是用弓箭和猎鹰狩猎的一个场景。生于 494 年的史君在他接受第一个官职前有 40 多岁，这个场景可能表现的就是那些岁月里的生活。

N1　下一个石板上一个商队环绕在拐角 N1 上，停在一条河的岸边。史君竖起了一根手指。上面有一位戴宝冠的男人坐在一个帐篷里，由三个男人陪伴着，第四个留胡子的男人跪着，与帐篷里戴宝冠的人干杯。我认为这表现的是史君在 535 年被任命为萨宝判事曹主。他对面的人被画上了胡子，免得与史君混淆了，这些浮雕里面的其他场景中史君都没有胡子。相对较小的官职则说明了他的住处并不宽敞。

N2　下一个石板上我们看到一对戴宝冠的夫妇，周围是仆人和伎乐。宽敞优雅的住处和款待艺人们则可能表现了史君在凉州升为萨宝。三个儿子并没有出现在这里——有三个年轻的女子，也许他有三个女儿，但文献里面并没有记载。

N3　接下来，我们看到这对夫妇的出行，又是与他的三个儿子一起。后面的一个人正在向史君告别。最后在长安，史君能安度致仕后的岁月，又是与他的三个儿子，还有一个年长的客人在一起。下面是他的妻子和三个可能是女儿的人一起在主持饭局。史君和他的妻子分别在招待一位客人。

65A　回顾上文，我认为这里描绘的是史君的职业生涯，突出的是他被任命为萨宝的事。我们首次知道了任命的特殊日期，它们是如何被选定的，任命时的年龄，以及一个活灵活现的对于拥有该职位的荣誉的描绘。这里我们需要的是一些来解决问题的标签，但迄今这些东西还没有出现。

（刘林海译）

试析5世纪塔里木盆地诸绿洲国存在状况对
各游牧势力在西域角逐的影响

李艳玲

中国社会科学院历史研究所

张骞"凿空"开启东西文化交流的新篇章,塔里木盆地的绿洲则成为这种交流的中转站。其特殊的自然环境及重要的地理位置,使之往往成为周边诸势力的争夺对象。在公元5世纪,除来自东方的中原势力触及该地,力图经营西域外,柔然、吐谷浑、高车及嚈哒等游牧势力在西域积极扩张,展开激烈角逐而相交于塔里木盆地。目前学界对柔然、高车、吐谷浑、嚈哒等在西域的势力扩张多有论述,并强调其对塔里木盆地绿洲国的影响。[①]但未将与游牧势力生产方式不同的塔里木盆地诸绿洲作为主体,所以不曾论述该时期塔里木盆地诸绿洲国的存在状况对诸游牧势力在西域角逐所产生的影响。本文试图在已有的研究成果基础上,主要从塔里木盆地诸绿洲国的政治、经济、生态环境方面对此加以简单考察。

一

自东汉末年中原势衰,塔里木盆地再度陷入相互征伐、诸国争霸的境况,如鄯善、焉耆、龟兹、疏勒、于阗等之间展开了激烈的斗争。魏晋短暂经营后,塔里木盆地先后受前凉、前秦、后凉的管辖。进入5世纪,西凉、北凉相继经营于此,后又有北魏势力介入塔里木盆地,但其对该地的有效经营甚为短暂。所以,在5世纪,塔里木盆地内部仍延续着诸国争霸的现象,[②]诸绿洲的政治形势变动不居。这为游牧势力在西域大肆扩张提供了良机。

5世纪初,西凉政权建立后,因有北凉的迫压,只有高昌受其实际控制。北凉于420年灭西凉后,高昌即处于北凉的直接控制之下,[③]盆地内的其他绿洲意识到北凉的影响力,永初三年(422)"鄯善王比龙入朝,西域三十六国皆称臣贡献"。[④] 但此时北凉因东有西秦及其后来的北魏政权的威胁,无力对高昌以

---

① 冯承钧:《高车之西徙与车师鄯善国人之分散》,载《西域南海史地考证论著汇辑》,中华书局香港分局,1976年,第36~47页。段连勤:《丁零、高车与铁勒》,上海人民出版社,1988年;余太山:《柔然与西域关系述考》,载《嚈哒史研究》,齐鲁书社,1986年,第193~216页;松田寿男著、陈俊谋译:《古代天山历史地理学研究》,中央民族学院出版社,1987年,第167~191,241~259页;钱伯泉:《从〈高昌主簿张绾等传供状〉看柔然汗国在高昌地区的统治》,载《吐鲁番学研究专辑》,敦煌吐鲁番学新疆研究资料中心1990年;王素:《高昌史稿——交通编》,文物出版社,2000年,第364~386页。薛宗正:《丁零——铁勒的西迁及其所建立政权》,《喀什师院学报》1992年第3期;《柔然汗国的兴亡——兼论丁零、铁勒系族群的西迁与崛起》,《西域研究》1995年第3期;《高车与西域》,《喀什师范学院学报》2000年第3期;《吐谷浑与西域》,《西域研究》1998年第3期。马曼丽:《论吐谷浑与周邻的关系》,《甘肃社会科学》1987年第4期。王欣:《麴氏高昌王国与北方游牧民族的关系》,《西北民族研究》1991年第2期。荣新江:《阚氏高昌王国与柔然、西域的关系》,《历史研究》2007年第2期。

② 余太山:《两汉魏晋南北朝正史西域传研究》,中华书局,2003年,第502~505页。

③ 参见王素:《高昌史稿——统治编》,第202~203页。

④ 《宋书·大且渠蒙逊传》。

外的塔里木盆地诸绿洲施加实际的影响力。塔里木盆地总体上成为一片政治真空地带,使柔然在西域的扩张极为顺利。《魏书·蠕蠕传》中记有柔然早在社仑天兴年间(398～404)即不断兼并周边诸游牧部落,由此"号为强盛。随水草畜牧,其西则焉耆之地,东则朝鲜之地,北则渡沙漠,穷瀚海,南则临大碛。其常所会庭则敦煌、张掖之北。小国皆苦其寇抄,羁縻附之"。① 则柔然的势力已于 5 世纪初越过天山,占据焉耆之北,并以敦煌、张掖之北为其势力中心。因元强大势力支持塔里木盆地诸绿洲对抗柔然,除高昌外,诸绿洲逐渐沦为柔然的附庸,所以到大檀可汗时期,塔里木盆地的"焉耆、鄯善、龟兹、姑墨东道诸国,并役属之。"②而高昌被柔然势力从东、北、西三面包围,不可避免地受到柔然的影响。北凉在"缘禾"四年(435)3 月 29 日,依北魏"太延"年号改为"太缘"时,高昌阚爽未随之改奉,仍奉"缘禾"年号,表明高昌逐渐对北凉产生了离心倾向。③ 柔然在西域的影响力显著增强,以致出现太延元年(435)五月,北魏遣使王恩生等出使西域被柔然阻隔之事。④

但因塔里木盆地诸绿洲国积极交通北魏(其力图借助北魏势力摆脱柔然的侵扰为重要原因之一),北魏改变以往的政策,锐意进取,使塔里木盆地的政治形势出现新的变动,柔然在西域尤其是在塔里木盆地的扩张因此受阻,南部的吐谷浑也无法在该时期向塔里木盆地扩张势力。

在北魏派董琬、高明成功西使后,塔里木盆地诸绿洲除高昌外,都密切了同北魏的交往。太延三年(437)三月即有"龟兹、悦般、焉耆、车师、粟特、疏勒、乌孙、渴槃陀、鄯善诸国各遣使朝献"。⑤ 柔然在西域的势力由此受到一定程度的影响,因此其极力阻止北魏的势力进入西域。太延四年(438)乐平王丕随世祖征伐柔然后,柔然遣使至西域诸国宣称"魏已削弱,今天下唯我为强,若更有魏使,勿复恭奉",⑥促使各绿洲国离心于北魏。其后,在北魏的打击下,北凉残余势力于太平真君二年(441)十一月、次年四月分两批流亡到鄯善,⑦鄯善王比龙则自率一半国人逃亡且末,使且末役属鄯善。此时面对从伊吾逃亡而来的唐契、唐和等西凉残余势力,自立为高昌太守的阚爽震恐不已,向盘踞鄯善的沮渠无讳求援,意图使其两败俱伤。结局是高昌被北凉沮渠无讳占有,阚爽逃亡柔然。⑧ 至此,塔里木盆地的鄯善、且末、高昌由北凉残余势力

① 《魏书》卷 103《蠕蠕传》,第 2290～2291 页。

② 《宋书》卷 95《索虏传》,第 2735 页。

③ 有关缘禾、太缘年号的探讨及其反映出的北凉对高昌郡的统治问题,具体参见王素:《高昌史稿——统治编》,第 190～198;202～208 页。另外王素先生认为因北魏干涉,沮渠氏北凉被迫放弃高昌。如果是因北魏干涉所致,则高昌应有归诚北魏的表示,但此后高昌既没有改奉北魏的"太延"年号,也没有护送经由此地的北魏使者,而且北魏再次遣使时改经鄯善。北魏的势力尚不及于高昌。所以,不妨认为此时高昌已倾向于割据自保。

④ 《魏书》卷 102《西域传》,第 2260 页。定为太延元年五月,参见余太山:《两汉魏晋南北朝与西域关系史研究》,中国社会科学出版社,1995 年,第 151～152 页。

⑤ 《魏书》卷 4《世祖纪》,第 88 页。

⑥ 《魏书》卷 102《西域传》,第 2260 页。

⑦ 北凉残势逃亡没有首选生产条件相对较好的高昌,可能是考虑到柔然及其扶植下的唐契等势力,惧其趁机攻击自身。另外,大海道不适合于大规模行军,无讳似乎也知明了高昌阚爽并不是真心归顺奉其年号,而北凉在鄯善地区一直有影响力,且该地没有强大的对抗势力。按余先生之说是阚爽担心将无立足之地的北凉势力会首先将矛头指向高昌,所以自太平真君二年(441)三至七月间开始奉行北凉的"建平"年号。见余太山:《关系史研究》,第 280～283 页。王素先生认为是阚爽既不敢公然独立,又不愿受到其他政权直接控制的心态使然。见王素:《高昌史稿——统治编》,第 235 页。

⑧ 其中关于柔然援助阚爽击败唐契及北凉残余势力进据高昌与唐和作战的记载存在着诸多矛盾。王素先生注意到,《资治通鉴》将上述史料中唐和与沮渠安周交战系于宋文帝元嘉十九年(442)四月,据此则在同年八月,无讳应阚爽之邀经焉耆赴高昌前,安周已先抵高昌,但如此与记载及事理不合,所以应从白须净真之说,即事应发生在无讳统治高昌时期。但王先生也认识到如此理解,则唐和如何从交河出发绕过无讳统治的高昌城,攻击其东的横截、高宁、白力三城的情况不明。(见王素:《高昌史稿——统治编》,第 249 页及该页注①。)冯承钧先生则指出唐和先攻高宁,闻契战殁,乃收余众奔前部王国。中途攻拔横截。与车师取得联系,复率众东攻,连下高宁、白力二城。由是高昌国北境与东境皆为和据。(见《高昌事辑》,载《西域南海史地考证论著汇辑》,第 62 页。)按唐和所率人口并不多,(转下页)

控制,但高昌西部的车师前部与逃至该地的唐和势力联合交好北魏。这种情况下,柔然只能继续在焉耆、龟兹等绿洲、准噶尔及其以西地区施加影响。太平真君六年(445),鄯善又为北魏控制。此间,南部的吐谷浑势力因北魏的追袭,其首领穆利延西逃,经且末到达于阗,大肆杀戮。但其北有柔然势力的威胁,东部又有北魏军队的屯守,此孤军终难以稳固在于阗的统治。所以在北魏的招抚下,吐谷浑慕利延于太平真君七年(446),"遂还旧土"。[①] 北魏于太平真君九年(448)"夏五月甲戌,以交趾公韩拔为假节、征西将军、领护西戎校尉、鄯善王,镇鄯善,赋役其民,比之郡县"。[②] 鄯善成为北魏经营西域的基地。塔里木盆地西北的悦般国又曾遣使请求北魏共同讨伐柔然。随之,焉耆、龟兹两大绿洲先后被北魏讨平,且北魏在焉耆设镇。与此同时,北凉"(沮渠)安周乘虚引蠕蠕三道"围攻其西部的车师,车师陷落成为北凉残余势力的辖区。[③] 柔然在西域的扩张势头因此受到北凉及北魏两方势力的遏制,其势力被排挤出塔里木盆地。

柔然在西域的重新雄张是在北魏势力退出塔里木盆地之后。北魏在焉耆、鄯善所设立的军镇撤销,[④]盘踞高昌的北凉残余势力于460年灭亡于柔然,高昌被纳入柔然的统治之下,柔然在西域的扩张更为强劲。于阗使素目伽素目伽于468年左右朝献北魏时,上表称"西方诸国,今皆已属蠕蠕,奴世奉大国,至今无异。今蠕蠕军马到城下,奴聚兵自固,故遣使奉献,延望救援"。[⑤] 表明柔然独霸西域,影响地域甚广,中亚、南亚的一些政权与之积极往来。[⑥]

5世纪后期,因高车副伏罗部叛柔然西迁,[⑦]塔里木盆地诸绿洲转而附属之,使柔然在西域的统治遭受沉重打击。塔里木盆地的政治形势再次动荡,为6世纪初嚈哒、吐谷浑等游牧势力在西域的扩张打开了方便之门。

"(太和)五年,高车王可至罗杀首归兄弟,以敦煌人张孟明为王。"[⑧]此处的"五年"应为"十二年"(488)之误。[⑨] 高昌转受高车的控制,而焉耆则可能在此前已臣属高车。因为高车反柔然西走时即到达

(接上页)似乎并没有力量镇守高昌的北境与东境。另外,《宋书》中记载:"八月,无讳留从子丰周守鄯善,自将家户赴之。未至,而芮芮遣军救高昌,杀唐契,部曲奔无讳。九月,无讳遣将卫寮夜袭高昌,爽奔芮芮,无讳复据高昌。"[①]将柔然杀唐契之事系于该年八月,与《魏书》不同。在此,若唐契等于四月进攻高昌,阚爽向无讳求救,无讳与安周八月才出军,让人难以理解。如果《宋书》记载不误的话,参照《魏书·唐和传》则可理解为:在阚爽向无讳发出求援信号后,无讳派遣安周带领部队前去救援,所以才有唐契被柔然杀死后,唐和西逃车师前部过程中遭遇沮渠安周之事,唐和在击败沮渠安周势力后,西至车师前部。此时,高昌阚爽认为在唐和与北凉残余势力相残杀的情况下,高昌之围已解,从而对留于此地的北凉残余势力的态度必会发生变化。由此才有八月份,无讳率军去往高昌之事。这可与无讳策问于僧人法进之事相联系,无讳曾"今欲转略高昌为可克不?"在得到法进答曰"必捷。但忧灾饿耳"之后,无讳"回军即定"。(《高僧传》卷十二《法进》。王素先生将"今"字系于阚爽求援之时,认为其最可能在太平真君三年(442)离鄯善趋高昌之前。见《高昌史稿——统治编》,第242~243页。)其中的"回军"也表明此前北凉残余势力已出兵高昌,此次八月份出兵已是第二次,而且这次是带家口的大规模行动,增援安周,意在占据高昌地区。鄯善地区相对恶劣的自然环境也是无讳决定转略高昌的重要原因。经长途跋涉,无讳于九月占领高昌,阚爽只得逃奔柔然。

① 《魏书》卷101《吐谷浑传》。松田寿男则认为穆利延占有于阗前约两年。见《古代天山历史地理学研究》,第177页。薛宗正先生指出吐谷浑此次逃亡未导致西域拓宇,见《吐谷浑与西域》,《西域研究》1998年第3期。

② 《魏书》卷4《世祖纪下》。

③ 《魏书》卷30《车伊洛传》。

④ 余太山先生指出焉耆镇撤正平元年(451)或二年,而不妨认为鄯善镇撤于延兴二年(472)前,最早可能与焉耆镇同时废撤。见余太山:《两汉魏晋南北朝与西域关系史研究》,第171页。王素先生认为北魏撤离鄯善在459年以前。见王素:《高昌史稿——交通编》,第232页及其注①。

⑤ 《魏书》卷102《西域传》,第2263页。余太山先生认为于阗朝献在466~468年间,见《两汉魏晋南北朝与西域关系史研究》,第173页。

⑥ 参见荣新江:《阚氏高昌王国与柔然、西域的关系》,《历史研究》2007年第2期。

⑦ 《魏书》卷103《高车传》。关于高车副伏罗部起义西迁的时间考释,见冯承钧:《西域南海史地考证论著汇辑》,中华书局香港分局,1976年,第39页;段连勤:《丁零、高车与铁勒》,上海人民出版社,1988年,第219~223页。

⑧ 《魏书》卷102《西域传》,第2243页。

⑨ 王素:《高昌史稿——统治编》,文物出版社,1998年,第271~274页。冯承钧先生以为是"十五年"之误,见《西域南海史地考证论著汇辑》,第40页。相较而言,王素先生的论证更为充分。

了前部西北,且在扶立高昌王时,将车师前部"胡人"徙"入于焉耆"。① 另据萧齐"益州刺史刘悛遣使江景玄使丁零,宣国威德。道经鄯善、于阗,鄯善为丁零所破,人民散尽"②可知,鄯善已为高车所掠,于阗也不免受高车的影响。而太和十二年(488)十二月,原柔然控制下的伊吾地区内属北魏,这与高昌臣属高车不无关系。太和十四年(490),高车派胡商越者出使北魏,以对抗柔然,使北魏的势力间接介入塔里木盆地。柔然在西域的势力也因此被高车及北魏阻断。但柔然并未就此放弃对西域的争夺,加之高昌等地政局的动荡,使高车在西域的统治极不稳固。高昌国人不满高车所立王,于太和二十年(496)杀之,立马儒为王。因惧怕高车势力的报复,马儒遣使北魏要求内徙,又为国人弑杀,麴嘉随之被立为王。③ 即是这一状况的反映。正是在塔里木盆地诸绿洲如此复杂的政治形势下,西来的嚈哒与南上的吐谷浑两大游牧势力在西域扩张极为迅速,使诸游牧势力在西域的角逐也更为激烈。

二

除塔里木盆地诸绿洲的政治形势对诸游牧势力在西域的角逐产生影响外,我们还必须考虑当时诸绿洲国的经济状况与生态环境。《汉书·西域传上》记有"西域诸国大率土著,有城郭田畜,与匈奴、乌孙异俗,故皆役属匈奴。匈奴西边日逐王置僮仆都尉,使领西域,常居焉耆、危须、尉黎间,赋税诸国,取富给焉"。则塔里木盆地诸绿洲与游牧民族经济生产方式不同,以农业为主的绿洲国能够为经济类型较为单一的游牧势力提供经济上的补充,特别是在游牧势力同中原对峙时期,据有塔里木盆地绿洲对西域的游牧势力更为重要。5 世纪时,高昌、焉耆、龟兹、于阗等绿洲的农业、手工业、商业都较为发展,对游牧势力有较强的产品输出与交换能力。所以这些经济状况较好的绿洲成为诸游牧势力争夺的焦点,由此使诸游牧势力在西域角逐的激烈程度大为增加。

魏晋动荡之时,高昌地区与河西走廊及与内地的联系并没有中断,其偏处一隅,未卷入中原各势力间的混战,境内相对安定,关陇一带及凉州的居民大批涌入高昌。而在 5 世纪初,北凉残余势力又进入高昌,高昌地区人口大幅增加,先进的生产技术也被引进于此,为高昌地区的发展注入新的活力,该地的农业生产水平会有所提高。《魏书·西域传》记载高昌"厥土良沃,谷麦一岁再熟,宜蚕,多五果,又饶漆。有草名羊刺,其上生蜜而味甚佳。引水溉田。……多葡萄酒"。表明高昌具有相对优越的耕作条件,水利灌溉已较为发达,④当时肥沃土地之作物可一年两熟。⑤焉耆"土田良沃,谷有稻粟菽

① 《魏书》卷 102《西域传》。对于高车迁徙前部胡人入焉耆的时间,有不同争论。在此依冯承钧之说,见《西域南海史地考证论著汇辑》,第 43 页;另外,段连勤则认为是在 498～500 年之间,见《丁零、高车与铁勒》,上海人民出版社,1988 年,第 239 页,但其论述有不合理之处。王欣亦从其说,见《麴氏高昌王国与北方游牧民族的关系》,《西北民族研究》1991 年第 2 期。

② 《南齐书》卷 59《芮芮传》,第 1025 页。冯承钧先生指出高车破鄯善地区疑在 493 年前。(冯承钧:《西域南海史地考证论著汇辑》,中华书局香港分局,1976 年,第 45～46 页)段连勤先生认为可能就在 492 年,即与魏军破柔然的时间同时或稍后。(段连勤:《丁零、高车与铁勒》,上海人民出版社,1988 年,第 232～233 页)总之,高车袭破鄯善距离通好北魏不远。

③ 关于马儒请求内徙是因害怕高车报复的论述,见王素:《高昌史稿——统治编》,第 303～305 页。王素先生对麴嘉为王的时间做了较为详细的考订分析,以为在 501 年,见《高昌史稿——统治编》,第 307～329 页。

④ 柳洪亮:《十六国时期高昌郡水利考》,《新疆社会科学》1985 年第 2 期;《略谈十六国时期高昌郡的水利制度——吐鲁番出土文书研究》,《新疆大学学报》1986 年第 2 期。

⑤ 参见王素:《高昌史稿——交通编》,第 88～90 页;关于该时期高昌的农业耕作参见宋晓梅:《高昌国——公元五至七世纪丝绸之路上的一个移民小社会》,中国社会科学出版社,2003 年,第 33～41 页。

麦，……俗尚蒲萄酒，……有鱼盐蒲苇之饶"。龟兹"物产与焉耆略同"，于阗"土宜五谷并桑麻"，①疏勒"土多稻、粟、麻、麦"，②这些绿洲国拥有较为发达的农业种植。

正史中没有关于两汉时期塔里木盆地蚕桑丝织业的明确记载。《魏书·西域传》中则有高昌"宜蚕"，焉耆"养蚕不以为丝，唯充绵纩"，于阗"土宜五谷并桑麻"。其中未记龟兹、疏勒的蚕桑丝织业的情况，但龟兹"物产与焉耆略同"。另外，吐鲁番出土的北凉时期的文书中有"丘慈锦"、"疏勒锦"的记载，③龟兹与疏勒拥有较为发达的纺织技术，能生产出具有自身特色的纺织品。④ 该技术在塔里木盆地绿洲间得以传播，并在高昌地区逐步发展。《西凉建初十四年严福愿赁蚕桑券》⑤反映出高昌地区蚕桑业的发达。所以，5世纪时，高昌、焉耆、龟兹、疏勒、于阗等绿洲地区的蚕丝业及相应的纺织业已经普遍发展起来，成为当时重要的丝织品产地，其所生产的丝织品也成为重要的贸易商品。⑥

这些绿洲还拥有其他资源且较为丰富。高昌有赤盐和白盐，高昌与焉耆间的银山"皆是银矿，西国银钱所从出也"。⑦《魏书·西域传》记龟兹"出细毡，饶铜、铁、铅、麞皮、氍毹、饶沙、盐绿、雌黄、胡粉、安息香、良马、犎牛等"。《水经注》中也提到龟兹"北二百里有山，夜则火光，昼日但烟。人取此山石炭冶此山铁，恒充三十六国用"。⑧ 可知龟兹冶铸业之发达。于阗"国人善铸铜器"，疏勒亦有铜、铁等。

绿洲国所拥有的丰富资源及其所生产的物品，其中一部分需供奉于控制自身的游牧势力。《北史·西域传》记载疏勒"土多稻、粟、麻、麦、铜、铁、锡、雌黄、锦、绵，每岁常供送于突厥"。就是此种状况的反映。《高昌主簿张绾等传供帐》记有：

4]出行㲲五疋，付左首兴，与若愍提懃。

5]出赤違（韦）一枚，付爱宗，与乌胡慎。

7]疋，付得钱，与吴儿折胡真。

8]赤違一枚，付得钱，与作都施摩何勃。

9]㲲一疋，赤違一枚，与秃地提懃无根。

14]行㲲三疋，赤違三枚，付隗已隆，与阿祝至火下。

15]张绾传令，出疏勒锦一张，与处论无根。

16]摩何□□。

17]㲲一疋，毯五张，赤違□枚，各付已隆，供鍮头[　　　。⑨

经钱伯泉先生研究，该文中的行㲲、毯、绢、疏勒锦、赤違等物品是高昌向柔然使者提供的。⑩ 联系疏勒贡

① 《魏书》卷102《西域传》。

② 《北史》卷97《西域传》。

③ 见《吐鲁番出土文书》第一册《北凉承平五年道人法安弟阿奴举锦券》、《北凉承平八年翟绍远买婢券》第181、187页；第二册《高昌主簿张绾等传供帐》，第17页。

④ 参见唐长孺：《吐鲁番文书中所见丝织业手工业技术在西域各地的传播》，《出土文献研究》，文物出版社，1985年。

⑤ 《吐鲁番出土文书》第一册，第17页。

⑥ 参见唐长孺：《吐鲁番文书中所见丝织业手工业技术在西域各地的传播》；武敏：《从出土文书看高昌地区的蚕丝与纺织》，《新疆社会科学》1987年第5期。

⑦ 《大慈恩寺三藏法师传》卷二。

⑧ 《水经注·河水篇》引《释氏西域记》。

⑨ 《吐鲁番出土文书》第二册，第17~18页。

⑩ 钱伯泉：《从〈高昌主簿张绾等传供状〉看柔然汗国在高昌地区的统治》，载《吐鲁番学研究专辑》（内部资料），1990年，第96~111页。

奉突厥,将此归为高昌对属主柔然的贡奉应不为过。

《隋书·高昌传》记有"铁勒恒遣重臣在高昌国,有商胡往来者,则税之送于铁勒"。则高昌的过境贸易的商业收入相当可观,这当在柔然牢牢控制高昌时期已然。因为随政治形势的变化,高昌在5世纪已成为天山南北、中亚、西亚各政权同中原往来的交通枢纽,商业贸易必将随之繁盛,其税收也必将在整个经济收入中占有很大比重。高昌西部的焉耆、龟兹、疏勒、于阗的商业贸易亦有不同程度的发展。龟兹曾自铸多种货币,流通于这一时期的龟兹无文小铜钱,目前在库车、巴楚、拜城、新和、轮台、温宿、柯坪、于阗、策勒、民丰以及楼兰遗址都有发现,①可见其流通范围甚广,于阗"有屋室市井",②反映出这些地区商品经济的发达及市场交换的活跃频繁。在此扩张势力的诸游牧民族能从中得到巨额利润,自身实力增强。另,鄯善地区"地多沙卤,少水草",③北凉残余势力流亡鄯善时使鄯善"大乱",后又为高车所破,"人民散尽",生产环境遭到破坏,"其地崎岖薄瘠"。④ 但其为丝绸之路南道的必经之地,也是"河南道"的一部分,⑤所以商业利润的刺激是吐谷浑将势力积极扩张到这一地区并西至且末的重要原因。

高昌、焉耆、龟兹、疏勒、于阗等较为发达的绿洲将当地物产源源不断输入游牧民族,游牧势力的经济需求得到一定程度上的满足,促使其在西域的统治得以稳固,巨额的商业税入对增强游牧民族在西域的竞争实力具有重要意义。这正是柔然等游牧势力在西域展开争夺,以图垄断丝绸之路贸易的关键原因,也是该时期诸游牧势力尤其在高昌、焉耆绿洲展开激烈角逐的重要原因所在。

诸游牧势力在西域进行角逐而形成的对峙格局,除同各游牧势力的实力相关外,与塔里木盆地绿洲的生态环境有密切联系。

原塔里木盆地的一些绿洲不再见于有关5世纪的文献记载,如塔里木盆地南部的精绝、东部的楼兰、山国等,这几个绿洲国都处于河流的末端或下游的沿岸地带,结合与此相关的考古资料,我们不难发现:经过汉末魏晋的长期动乱,塔里木盆地绿洲的生态环境在5世纪已发生剧烈变化。

《后汉书·西域传》记载"出玉门,经鄯善、且末、精绝三千余里至拘弥"。精绝是塔里木盆地南部交通的重镇。在精绝并入鄯善、扜弥并入于阗后,精绝成为鄯善与于阗两大绿洲东西往来的必经之地,这在佉卢文书中有明确反映。⑥《汉书·西域传下》记载龟兹"南与精绝、东南与且末、西南与扜弥、北与乌孙、西与姑墨接","贰师将军李广利击大宛,还过扜弥,扜弥遣太子赖丹为质于龟兹"。⑦ 又精绝居民有逃亡龟兹者。⑧ 因此不排除当时精绝绿洲的居民通过尼雅河直接达到龟兹。而考古资料表明,两汉魏晋时期的于阗、扜弥之北,从麻扎塔格——丹丹乌里克——喀拉墩——精绝以至且末一线,都有同时代的人类活

① 张平:《再论龟兹的地方铸币》,《西域研究》1999年第1期。

② 《梁书》卷54《西北诸戎传》。

③ 《魏书》卷102《西域传》,第2261页。

④ 《高僧传·法显传》。

⑤ 参见唐长孺:《南北朝期间西域与南朝的陆路交通》,载《魏晋南北朝史论拾遗》,中华书局,1983年,第168~195页;周伟洲:《古青海路考》,《西北大学学报》1982年第1期;王叔凯:《古代青海中西交通考》,《青海社会科学》1983年第3期;王育民:《丝路"青海道"考》,《历史地理》(第4辑),出版社,1986年;薄小莹:《吐谷浑之路》,《北京大学学报》1988年第4期;吴焯:《青海道述考》,《西北民族研究》1992年第2期;罗新:《吐谷浑与昆仑玉》,《中国史研究》2001年第1期;王超云:《试析吐谷浑在中西交通史上的作用》,《陇东学院学报》2004年第4期。

⑥ 见佉卢文书第14、22、223、253、367、135、214、306号,林梅村:《沙海古卷——中国所出佉卢文书(初集)》,文物出版社,1988年,第14、44、73、78、103、65~66、71、90页;佉卢文书第637号,T. Burrow, *A Translation of the Kharoṣṭhi Documents from Chinese Turkestan*, The Royal Asiatic Society, London 1940, p.132,参见王广智译:《新疆佉卢文残卷译文集(初稿)》,第170页等。

⑦ 《汉书》卷96《西域传下》。

⑧ 见佉卢文书第621号,林梅村:《沙海古卷——中国所出佉卢文书(初集)》,文物出版社,1988年,第141页。

动遗存,可推断这些地点相连甚或有路可通。① 所以两汉魏晋时期,精绝及其西部的扜弥成为沟通鄯善、于阗乃至龟兹三大绿洲区的中间地带。魏晋前凉时期,分别作为于阗、鄯善边境的扜弥和精绝处在了两大绿洲国的冲突之下,战乱不断。佉卢文 713 号中记有:

> 彼等现已结束了一场前所未见的空前的战争。这次空前的战斗结束,终于使一切都得到解决。诸战士现俘获所有的东西。一些人在战斗中被杀,另一些人被彼等生俘,故一切事情均获解决。汝听到此事,一定不胜欣喜。②

正是当地战争中杀戮抢掠的写照,这不可避免地使当地的生产遭到破坏。尼雅逐渐在此状况下废弃、荒芜。③ 其西部的扜弥之地也经历着同样的灾难。根据目前的考古发掘,尼雅遗址发现的文物均为汉晋时期,而无唐代的,王炳华先生将其定为晋代。④ 与尼雅遗址同时代的喀拉墩遗址,属于当时于阗境内的扜弥绿洲范围内,其年代同样为晋——南北朝时期。⑤ 则塔里木盆地南部沟通鄯善、于阗、龟兹的尼雅绿洲、部分扜弥绿洲已经被废弃。从而玄奘东归时,自"媲摩川东入沙碛,行二百余里,至尼壤城,"而不再经由精绝。但尼壤已成为于阗的东部边境,其"泽地热湿,难以履涉。芦草荒茂,无复途径。唯趣城路,仅得通行,故往来者莫不由此城焉"。⑥

精绝以东的绿洲的生态环境也同样恶化。《大唐西域记》卷 12 中记载从尼壤城东行四百余里,"至覩货逻故国。国久空旷,城皆荒芜。"斯坦因指出安迪尔遗址即为该"覩货逻故国",与尼雅遗址属于同一个时代,废弃于公元 3~4 世纪。⑦ 该遗址可能为汉小宛国王治所所在。⑧ 由尼壤至该地的途中,流沙漫漫,"聚散随风,人行无迹,遂多迷路。四远茫茫,莫知所指,是以往来者聚遗骸以记之。乏水草,多热风。风起则人畜惛迷,因以成病。时闻歌啸,或闻号哭,视听之间,怳然不知所至,由此屡有丧亡,盖鬼魅之所致也"。⑨ 路途艰险可见一斑。自该地东至且末之地的路途状况也是如此。《魏书·西域传》记有"且末西北方流沙数百里,夏日有热风为行旅之患。风之所至,唯老驼豫知之,即鸣而聚立,埋其口鼻于沙中,人每以为候,亦即将毡拥蔽鼻口。其风迅驶,斯须过尽,若不防者,必至危毙"。

综上,塔里木盆地南部绿洲沟通东西的扜弥故地(喀拉墩遗址)、精绝、小宛等绿洲被废弃,环境恶化,使且末与于阗间为流沙横亘,成为两地区间交通往来的巨大障碍,这自然影响到诸游牧势力在盆地内部的扩张,使吐谷浑与嚈哒相互间难以突破且末、于阗的势力范围。

塔里木盆地东部的绿洲生态环境的变化主要体现为楼兰绿洲的废弃。楼兰绿洲,位于罗布泊西北的孔雀河尾间三角洲上,其作为魏晋时期西域长史府的驻地,是中原经营西域的基地,当时在政治、交通、军

---

① 见殷晴:《湮没在沙漠中的扜弥古国》,《和田绿洲研究》,第 220~221 页。
② 林梅村:《沙海古卷——中国所出佉卢文书(初集)》,第 316 页。
③ 参见于志勇:《关于尼雅聚落遗址考古学研究的若干问题》,《新疆文物》2000 年第 1、2 期。
④ 王炳华:《尼雅考古新收获》,载《新疆文物考古新收获(续)1990~1996 年》,第 486 页。于志勇:《关于尼雅聚落遗址考古学研究的若干问题》,《新疆文物》2000 年第 1、2 期,第 49 页。
⑤ 李吟屏:《克里雅河末端古遗址踏察简记及有关问题》,《新疆文物》1991 年第 1 期。
⑥ 《大唐西域记校注》卷第 12,第 1030 页。
⑦ A. Stein,Serindia: Detailed Report of Explorations in Central Asia and Westernmost China, vol. 1, Oxford at the Clarendon Press 1921, p. 277,286;塔克拉玛干综考队考古组:《安迪尔遗址考察》,载《新疆文物考古新收获(续)1990~1996 年》,第 529 页。
⑧ 见余太山:《楼兰、鄯善、精绝等的名义——兼说玄奘自于阗东归的路线》,《两汉魏晋南北朝正史西域传研究》,第 483 页。
⑨ 《大唐西域记校注》卷第 12,第 1030~1031 页。

台下令在所有各地区设立驿站,称之为"塔阳站",①命倡举此事的阿剌浅、脱忽察儿主负其责。

这条道路从拔都境内(不里阿耳、罗斯诸公国、克里木、伏尔加河下游)到原花拉子模的河中地区,再经察合台汗国(不花剌、撒马尔罕、阿力麻里)、窝阔台领地(叶密立、霍博)到哈喇和林,即可从黑海西岸渡顿河经萨莱抵咸海、里海北,再沿锡尔河东岸至中亚阿拉木图、江布尔,过伊犁河经霍博、乌苏、轮台,穿准噶尔盆地边缘之占木萨尔或科布多谷地北上阿尔泰山北麓、杭爱山南麓到达蒙古高原的中心哈喇和林,将当时蒙古人所控制的地区全部连接起来了。

对于驿站管理也作了详细规定。如规定驿站马夫数(20 人)、车马用度,②每一驿程(一程约 25 ~ 30公里)置一千户(后又设通往汉地的帖里干、木邻、纳邻三条驿道,从哈喇和林到当时的中都城之间设立37 个纳邻站,每五程一站)。③ 驿站每年都要经过检查,有损缺时要及时补齐。④ 驿路的设置为商人的长途旅行提供了便利,他们不仅可以安全通行(在察合台治下的突厥斯坦和河中,商旅甚至无需保镖和卫士就可畅通无阻,志费尼还记录了当时一个夸张的说法:一个头顶黄金器皿的妇女可以不用害怕地单独行走)。⑤ 商旅还可以乘骑驿马来往于高原各地。⑥ 对于他们带来的货物,窝阔台下令不管好坏全部收下,并如数付酬。⑦ 即使商人开出十倍甚至更高的价码。同时,他给商人本钱(斡脱)和驿符,让他们专门采购各种商品,有时甚至是埃塞俄比亚的奴隶。⑧ 窝阔台的慷慨好施和对商人的优待,吸引了各地的商人纷纷前往欧亚草原的中心城市哈喇和林,使窝阔台的府库中堆满了报达和不花剌等地的织物、珠宝,印度的象牙,中原的丝绸粮食等,并且每天有五百辆车载着食物和饮料从汉地供应哈喇和林。

此外,窝阔台继续让花拉子模大商人马合木·牙拉瓦赤⑨掌管河中,畏兀儿人阔儿吉思掌管呼罗珊。牙拉瓦赤废除了扯里克、签军等强制兵役以及许多临时赋税和摊派,不仅减轻了居民的负担,也刺激了市场的复苏,大大有利于商贸的开展。

继窝阔台之后的贵由由于在位时间较短,在管理国家上少有作为,不过他继承了其父的慷慨大度,无节制地采购,以致国库货物堆积如山而没有足够的现金来支付,而不得不向各地开出支付票。⑩ 在其影响下,贵由的后妃子女及各宗王皆仿效之,向商人乱发牌子,向各地乱开支票。可以说,这一时期的大蒙古国的财政管理相当无序,经常随意而为,在入库和发放方面常常不经司账和稽查。⑪ 迨蒙哥即位后,针对国家经济的无序状况进行了以下几个方面的革新:

(1)下令禁行成吉思汗之后的诏令和牌子。这项规定的用意正如巴托尔德所观察的那样,即否认窝阔台系的合法性,⑫以巩固他与拔都的联盟。

---

① 《史集》第 2 卷,第 60 ~ 61 页。
② 《蒙古秘史》第 280 节,第 447 页。
③ 《史集》第 2 卷,第 69 页。
④ 志费尼:《世界征服者史》(上),内蒙古人民出版社,1980 年,第 34 页。
⑤ 《世界征服者史》(上),第 321 页。
⑥ 《史集》第 2 卷,第 259 页。
⑦ 《世界征服者史》(上),第 249 ~ 250 页;《史集》第 2 卷,第 94 页。
⑧ 《世界征服者史》(上),第 258 页;《史集》第 2 卷,第 100 页。
⑨ 关于牙拉瓦赤事迹考述,可看看何高济、陆峻岭《元代回教人物牙老瓦赤和赛典赤》一文,《元史论丛》第 2 辑,中华书局,1983 年,第 225 ~ 231 页。
⑩ 《世界征服者史》(上),第 302 页;《史集》第 2 卷,第 220 ~ 221 页。
⑪ 《世界征服者史》(上),第 238 ~ 239 页。
⑫ 参见巴托尔德著,张锡彤、张广达译:《蒙古入侵时期的突厥斯坦》(下),第 555 页,上海古籍出版社,2007 年。

（2）规范驿站和驿路的管理。禁止各宗王利用驿站的便利来从事商贸活动，并废除商人乘骑驿马的特权。其实早在窝阔台时期就已经注意到这个问题，1229年，他曾对商人乘驿马作出限制，"商贾做客之人，勿骑驿马，违者断按答奚罪"，但同时又说，"如有送丝线颜色物料，并外国使臣将礼物缎匹及有急速勾当来者，应付铺马"，①因此，这种限制实际上如同虚设。

（3）整顿税收、规定税率。窝阔台、贵由时期，汉地世侯府库中的钱粮储备比哈喇和林都要多，②而河中地区的税收也受到察合台系的干涉和包税商的侵吞，所以在诛杀察合台、窝阔台两系的成年男性后，蒙哥把有征税经验的马合木·牙拉瓦赤调到汉地，而让其子马思忽惕伯接管突厥斯坦（Turkestan）、河中诸城（Transoxiana）、畏兀儿诸城、费尔干纳、花拉子模等地。蒙哥所关心的是减轻百姓的赋税，而不是增加库藏中的财富。③ 为了不让税务总管随意更改赋税，他又下令制定年计划，根据各地的情况以及贫富来制定税率，如汉地、河中、呼罗珊等农耕定居区实行大致相同的税率，按贫富最高征11个的那，最低征1个的那。牧区则征忽卜绰儿，为百税一，不满百不征。④ 同时废除商人免征课赋和赐给札儿里黑（圣旨）的优待，并不许拖欠和少缴交易税。⑤ 王恽《乌台笔补》中记录了蒙哥当时的圣旨节概："斡脱做买卖、畏吾儿、木速蛮回回，交本住处千户百户里去者。若称有田产物业不去呵，依前圣旨体例里，见住处不拣大小差发、铺马、抵应、与民户一体当差。钦此。"⑥

（4）设立专门的商人管理机关。蒙哥委派专职近臣管理商人和商贩（尤其是对斡脱商人的管理⑦），让他们负责分派商人牌子，并充当商业纠纷的诉讼中介。此外，设专人负责为货物估价和鉴定金钱（其中验货师分得很细，有专门验珠宝的、外衣的、皮货的等等），专人掌皮货、金银现钱。⑧

经过蒙哥的整顿，窝阔台、贵由时期混乱的财物状况得到了扭转。尤其难能可贵的是，为了安抚商人，使政治上的动乱不致影响到商贸活动的正常开展，蒙哥下令从新的赋税收入中偿还贵由时所开出的未能兑现的支票，金额达五十万银巴里失（《史集》为五十多万金银巴里失）。⑨ 这一做法赢得了商人们信任和尊重，世界各地的商旅络绎不绝于草原之路，我们从普兰·迦儿宾和鲁布鲁克等西方使节的回忆报告中亦可得知，当时他们的长途旅行并不是寂寞的，而是行走在一条繁忙的商道上。与他们结伴而行或相遇的有来自拜占庭君士坦丁堡、波兰、奥地利、热那亚、威尼斯等地的商人，他们或是穿过蒙古人治下的畅通的草原之路去黑海沿岸的乞瓦（基辅）、地中海，或是前往蒙古汗廷做交易，享受着驿站所带来的种种便利。

大蒙古国时期对商贸的重视，还体现在都城选址和被征服地区商业城市的重建方面，这与商道、驿站以及具体的商贸管理政策一样，都经过了一个转变过程。

（1）都城选址。对于建立城郭，成吉思汗的态度一直是审慎的，他不赞成其后代进入土墙围成的城市，认为这将会让他们耽于享乐，忘掉传统。⑩ 所以他一直将在怯绿涟河（今克鲁伦河）曲雕阿阑的斡耳

---

① 参见《经世大典》，《永乐大典》卷19416，中华书局，1986年影印本，第7192页上。
② 参看韩儒林《耶律楚材在大蒙古国的地位和所起的作用》一文，《穹庐集》，河北教育出版社，2000年，第188～205页。
③ 《世界征服者史》（下），第701页。
④ 《世界征服者史》（下），第701页。
⑤ 《世界征服者史》（下），第701、722页。《史集》第2卷，第260页。
⑥ 《秋涧大全集》88，《为在都回回户不纳差税事状》。
⑦ 关于斡脱，可参看爱宕松男《斡脱钱及其背景——十三世纪蒙古元朝白银的动向》一文，《东洋史研究》第32卷第1号1973年六月。
⑧ 《世界征服者史》（下），第722页。《史集》第2卷，第263页。
⑨ 《世界征服者史》（下），第703、719～720页。《史集》第2卷，第262～263页。
⑩ 参见《史集》第一卷第二册，商务印书馆，1986年，第357页。

朵作为自己的老营,也即大蒙古国的政治中心。但因蒙古地区没有任何城镇,无法使商旅聚集起来,形成固定的商贸中心。① 窝阔台的看法与其父不同,他在设置驿站的同时,便考虑将政治中心西迁至回鹘都城故地——哈喇和林。哈喇和林一直是游牧民族活动的中心区域,先后为匈奴、突厥、回纥(回鹘)、黠戛斯、克烈部等占据。1234 年,他将斡耳朵西移,在原克烈部王汗的夏营地答兰答八思建筑行宫;1235 年,又确立哈喇和林为都城,并任命燕京工匠大总管刘敏率领汉地工匠在此建立新城。② 1238 年,又在和林城南一程远的地方建图苏湖城,为进入和林使节、商旅休憩与准备觐见的前站。哈喇和林因此成为草原之路的起点,成为南控长城,西通地中海、黑海、里海、咸海的交通网络中心,到蒙哥汗时,又扩展至波斯湾和辽东半岛。从哈喇和林西行的路线有多条③(海屯一世朝见贵由汗时有着清晰的记载④),"哈喇和林城成为世界真正的政治和经济中心。在通往该城的大道上,挤满了去向蒙古皇帝表示敬意的人们和到蒙古都城经商的人"。⑤

术赤、察合台、窝阔台以及后来旭烈兀的汗国在都城选址上也都有如此考虑。拔都把金帐设在伏尔加河下游的主要原因就是因为萨莱处于东西方贸易干线上,⑥察合台将政治中心放在阿力麻里、窝阔台系放在叶密立,进入伊朗的旭烈兀家族也把统治中心放在帖必力思,⑦其用意也都是要依存商道。

(2)重建被毁的商业城市。蒙古人在西征中尽堕城邑的做法并不是不重视商业的表现,而是出于军事的考虑,是为了避免分散军队,削弱战斗力。而在征服过后,为了尽快恢复和平,在疏通商路的同时便着手重建城市。如金帐汗国境内的不里阿耳、伏尔加河河口的亦的勒城、克里木及其港口、花拉子模的都城玉龙杰赤等都很快地得到重建,仍然是当时东西方商贸交汇的中心。察合台领地的河中地区诸城如不花刺、撒马尔罕,突厥斯坦诸城阿力麻里等,在察合台及其后王的努力下也很快恢复了商业繁荣。当然这也与前四汗派到上述地区的总督、八思哈等的治理分不开。到了海都控制中亚地区时,他在费尔干纳地区建立了新城安集延,巴托尔德认为,这是中亚史上少有的统治者不为一己之私利而专为商业建造的城市。⑧

从以上梳理和分析不难看出,前四汗时期为了巩固新生的游牧帝国而在贯通草原商路、发展商贸上付出了极大努力,而商路也确实在蒙古社会文明进程的轨道上起到了重要的推动作用。

三、草原之路对蒙古文明进程的影响

草原之路并不仅仅是物质交换的通道,同时也是知识、技术、理念等传播的媒介,兹从以下几个方面进行论述:

---

① 《世界征服者史》(上),第 90 页。

② 可参看陈得芝《元岭北行省建置考》(上)一文,原载《元史及北方民族史研究集刊》(九),《蒙元史研究丛稿》,人民出版社,2005 年,第 113~136 页。

③ 周清澍先生对这三条路线考论甚详,参见其《蒙元时期的中西陆路交通》一文,《元蒙札记》,内蒙古大学出版社,2001 年,第 237~270 页。

④ 《海屯行纪》,中华书局,2002 年,第 1~27 页。

⑤ 鲁克、克文敦:《游牧帝国》,《中亚史丛刊》第 2 期,第 35 页。

⑥ 《金帐汗国兴衰史》,第 55 页。

⑦ 伊利汗国的北部(伊朗)和南部的阿塞拜疆都有大量的草原,如木干草原(Mūghān,今阿塞拜疆阿拉斯河下游南)等,这就让建立汗国的蒙古人依然能够过着游牧的生活,并以大不里士和苏坦尼亚为中心建立了游牧中心区。

⑧ 《中亚简史》,第 53 页。

（一）货币、汇票和支票的引进，对大蒙古国时期经济的影响。

蒙古在统一之前是没有货币的，主要是物物交换。《蒙古秘史》中记载了成吉思汗在与王汗的战争中战败后在额尔古纳河畔遇到回回商人阿三赶着一千头羯羊和一匹白骆驼去蒙古地区换皮货的故事，[①]由此可看出当时从事中间贸易的伊斯兰和畏兀儿商人在蒙古地区的支付手段。待成吉思汗建立国家后，货币自然提到日程上来了。当时在大蒙古国境内中亚、西亚、汉地的钱币都可以使用，并有专门从事兑换的商人，鲁布鲁克就曾亲眼在和林的市场上看到南宋的纸钞。而蒙古国自己的计量货币是巴里失（金、银），也即金银锭，志费尼认为，"巴里失值五十个金的或银的密思合勒（misqal），约等于其十五个鲁克尼（rukni）的那（dinar，波斯哈里发鲁克那丁的铸币），其金位为三分之二"。[②]此外，蒙古仿中亚钱币铸造了带有各汗徽记的硬币（金、银、铜）。[③]至忽必烈与阿里不哥争夺汗位时，各汗国已实际上脱离了大蒙古国而独立，铸币开始盛行。由于大蒙古国时期钱币的研究较多，故不作重点论述。

在此需要特别指出的是，对蒙古经济影响较大的是汇票、支票这一商业信用系统的引进。8世纪以后，阿拔斯王朝以巴格达（Baghdad）为中心构筑了一个笼盖伊斯兰世界并贯通东西方的商业网。中国的丝绸和大黄、东南亚的香料、印度的木材，西方自斯堪地纳维亚输入的毛皮、蜜糖，非洲的黄金、象牙、奴隶等，都由这个庞大的商业网在中间操作，为了便利大宗贸易，支票和汇票便出现了，并早于西欧建立了类似于近现代的银行系统的商业网络，巴格达的支票可以在其他地区兑现。到了12～13世纪初，虽然阿拔斯王朝早已名存实亡，但是这种商业信用体系却被继承下来。而蒙古对伊斯兰世界的征服，又使这种信用体系得以移植到蒙古本土。如前面提到的贵由汗及各地宗王都十分娴熟地使用汇票，在各地都有专门从事兑换业务的商人。可以说，汇票的使用是蒙古本土融入当时世界贸易体系的一个明证，在一定程度上推动了刚刚完成国家化的蒙古经济的进程。

（二）对蒙古文字创立过程的影响。

畏兀儿文成为蒙古文的基础，并不是偶然的。除了原蒙古语向古蒙古语过渡的过程中经历了几百年深刻突厥化的因素外，[④]与畏兀儿文（回鹘文）自10世纪起便作为商业文书用语通行于许多蒙古语和突厥语部落密切有关。南宋孟珙《蒙鞑备录》载："其（指蒙古）俗既朴，则有畏兀儿为邻，每于两河博易，贩卖于其国。迄今文书中自用于他国者，皆用回鹘字，如中国笛谱字也。"[⑤]另外，早在成吉思汗征服王汗之前，他的身边就聚集了不少畏兀儿伴当，负责翻译和文书，出身于高昌商人世家的克烈人田镇海便是其中一位。所以在征服乃蛮后，成吉思汗选择乃蛮国的掌印官畏兀儿人塔塔统阿负责创制蒙古字，并不仅仅是因为他掌管文书和印章的身份，更主要的是他对于畏兀儿文已经十分熟悉了，"掌握这种文化既不破坏这个阶层的统一，又不破坏他们对草原传统的热忱"。[⑥]因此在一定程度上可以说，蒙古文字的创立是商贸活动的结果。"经济流通的需要本身会决定这个国家的语言，为了商业交往的利益，懂得这种语言对大

---

① 参见《蒙古秘史》第182节，第240页。

② 《世界征服者史》（上），第24页。另可参见《多桑蒙古史》（上）"巴里失之价值"，中华书局，2004年，第417页。

③ 以大英博物馆的收藏为著，该馆并编有《大英博物馆东方钱币目录》（*Catalogue of Oriental Coins in the British Museum*）之《蒙古钱币》，1881年。

④ 《畏吾体蒙古文和古蒙古语语音》，《亦邻真蒙古学文集》，第511～543页。

⑤ 王国维：《蒙鞑备录黑鞑事略笺证》，文殿阁书社，936年，第68～69页。

⑥ 参见瓦·符·巴托尔德《成吉思汗帝国的建立》，见余大钧译《北方民族史与蒙古史译文集》，云南人民出版社，2003年。第436～450页。

多数人来说都是有利的。"①我们知道，畏兀儿文是由粟特文字母演变过来的粟特体突厥文，②它正是在粟特人进行频繁商业活动的影响下形成的。其后在伊斯兰化突厥语的基础上形成的察合台语，以及在元代通行的波斯语，都可以说是商贸活动选择的结果。叶列梅耶夫在论述《游牧民族在民族史上的作用》时对游牧民族这种有意识地选择"在大民族中间能够听懂和推广的语言"的做法给予积极评价，认为这可以克服氏族和部落语言的多样性，是游牧民族文化进步道路上重要的一步。③

当然，造字并非塔塔统阿一人之功，而是当时蒙古与其他民族的智者集体合作的结果，这一点15世纪的阿拉伯史学家伊宾·阿剌卜沙早已言明，④在此不赘述。

（三）对蒙古行政规范和制度的影响。

畏兀儿不仅给蒙古人带来了文字，而且将整套文书、印章牌符制度也引进到蒙古的行政管理中去，这大大便利了蒙古的政令、军报的通达。⑤大批的畏兀儿人在大汗的身边充当必阇赤的角色，如前面提到的镇海便是大必阇赤，负责回回地面文书，耶律楚材负责汉地文书，二人在大蒙古国时期文书制度和文官体系的确立上起到了重要的作用。

而大批穆斯林则充当了蒙古人的斡脱商、军事向导、被征服地区的税务官和政务官。蒙古人是以实利性的财富观念来统治国家的，他们懂得从城市居民和土地所有者那里所能得到的税收要远多于从游牧民那里所得到的，因此为了避免农耕区税收减少，他们尽量避免自己直接介入管理中去，⑥而是采取培植中间人的方式进行治理。伊斯兰商人由于经常往来于草原之路，熟悉地理环境和伊斯兰国家的内部情况，很自然便被引为中介。蒙古人一方面把他们当作最信任的顾问和行军向导，甚至委以使臣的重任，通过他们的说服，来减少蒙古军的损失。如《史集》中提到的很早就为成吉思汗效力的商人忽辛·哈只（巴托尔德认为此人就是阿三），在成吉思汗西征时，被术赤派往锡尔河畔的速黑纳黑城游说；另一方面又把战争掠夺的财物委托其行商，以坐取巨额收益，同时又以包税的形式将各省区的税收承包给他们。当时穆斯林世界有最有效率和最先进的行政管理制度——底万制度，西征后，为了高效有致地管理广大的国土，成吉思汗及后继者大批起用伊斯兰商人作为地方政务官和税务官，如前面已提到的牙拉瓦赤父子，以及阿里火者、答失蛮哈只卜、奥都剌合蛮、畏兀儿人佛教徒阔儿吉思等都被委以重任。这些诸文明地区人士的加入，不仅使蒙古人从繁琐的具体管理制度中解脱出来，同时也扬长避短，使被征服地区在较短的时间内恢复秩序。由此可以看出，游牧民族天生具有的联合与吸收属性，以及善于利用其他文明的长处来保证自身利益的开放心态，使其在政治技术和手段的运用上呈现出务实和圆通的特点，从而也提升了国家的行政效率。

（四）宗教传播及其对帝国政治的影响。

传教实际上是伴随着商业活动进行的。⑦以基督教为例。基督教对东方的影响要早在蒙古人西进

---

① 《列宁全集》中文版第20卷，第2页。

② 亦邻真认为这种粟特体的畏兀儿文在回鹘汗国之前就已使用，而畏兀儿体蒙古文亦指这种文字借用于畏兀儿文，而非畏兀儿独创。参见其《畏吾体蒙古文和古蒙古语语音》文中注，《亦邻真蒙古学文集》，第514页，内蒙古人民出版社，2001年。

③ Д·Е·叶列梅耶夫著，冯丽译：《游牧民族在民族史上的作用》（下），《世界民族》1987年第5期，第33～39页。

④ 参见瓦·符·巴托尔德《关于畏吾儿文献及其对蒙古人的影响问题》，《北方民族史与蒙古史译文集》，第457～461页。

⑤ 关于畏兀儿文对蒙古文化的影响，罗贤佑先生作过梳理，可参看其《畏兀儿文化与蒙古汗国》一文，《中央民族学院学报》2005年第5期，第30～36页。

⑥ 参上引书，第47页。

⑦ 巴托尔德：《中亚简史》，第128～129页。

苏贝希文化木器和木材加工工艺

祖力皮亚·买买提

吐鲁番地区文物局

前　言

吐鲁番,古称车师(姑师),系我国汉代司马迁笔下的所谓西域"三十六国"之一。若将汉代的《史记》、《汉书》对西域的记载作为信史时代的肇始,那么公元前 2 世纪以前即为吐鲁番地区的史前时代。

苏贝希是吐鲁番盆地中火焰山北麓吐峪沟口一个行政村名,在维吾尔语中为"水流的上游"之意。由于天山冰雪融化而形成的水源,经由"坎儿井"引到苏贝希村流出地面形成吐峪沟河,横断火焰山后注入南部绿洲,苏贝希因为该河的源头而得名。1980 年至 1992 年间,在苏贝希村境内共发现墓地 3 处,居住址 1 处。此后,在吐鲁番地区又有许多新的发现,其中有洋海、三个桥、喀格恰克、艾丁湖、阿拉沟、交河沟北、沟西墓地等。墓葬型制、埋葬习俗、随墓器物和服饰都趋同。在英亚依拉克、恰什塔格、乔拉克坎儿、克尔间、东巴扎、伙什江扎、墩买来、三坎克日、吐格曼博依、奇格曼、胜金口、阿斯塔那等地点的调查中都采集到较多的陶片,从陶器的器型和彩陶纹样看与上述经过发掘的遗址和墓地属同一文化系统。这些地点地域相连,文化面貌一致,其中的苏贝希是由遗址和多个墓群组成的完整聚落体系。遗址在Ⅲ号墓地发现之后即被全部发掘,取得了一个完整墓地的资料,而Ⅰ号墓地又是发掘最早的一处。根据考古学文化命名原则,学界将其命名为"苏贝希文化"。

吐鲁番是一个神奇而又极具魅力的地区。由于其独特的地理环境、气候和自然资源,造就了它极具个性的人文历史。干燥、少雨、多风的气候环境,使其地上、地下保存了大量文物资源,木器就是其中的一个重要项目,这种条件是其他地区所不具备的。上述各墓地在考古发掘中出土了较多的木器,而且基本都见有报导,材料丰富,值得认真研究。

一、人类木材加工史

古猿用拣来的木棍击落树上的果实,这种木棍不能称其为木器,因为木棍不是按人的意愿有意识的加工成的器物。但人类使用木器的时间和石器一样久远,可以追溯到石器时代。木材和石块一样,在大自然中到处都有分布。但要说到加工,就必须用加工工具,人类所能使用的最早的加工工具,也只能是石器。但到了青铜时代和早期铁器时代,由于金属工具广泛使用,用作木材加工的金属工具应运而生,出现了各式各样的木材加工工具,技艺也不断进步,形成了渐进式的木材加工史。

二、苏贝希文化墓葬建筑和葬具

埋葬代表的是一种宗教信仰。最早的墓葬起源于旧石器时代晚期,已有在山顶洞人阶段埋葬的人骨化石被发现,并撒有红色赤铁矿粉。但一直到龙山文化晚期,至今还没有发现木结构的墓葬建筑遗存。在我国,或者具体到新疆,墓葬的木构建筑是从青铜时代才开始的。最著名也是最早的当数孔雀河太阳墓和小河墓地。在吐鲁番盆地的苏贝希文化墓葬中,用圆木做建筑材料和制作葬具自始至终都非常普遍。

1. 墓口盖木的木材种类和加工

从我区墓葬发掘资料中得知,无论是沿天山一带伊犁河流域的土墩墓、和静察吾呼文化的石围石室墓、哈密五堡的二层台墓,还是昆仑山北麓的且末扎滚鲁克墓地、洛浦山普拉墓地,无不大量使用加工过的木材作墓葬建筑材料。苏贝希文化中的墓葬也是一样,几乎哪一座墓都使用木材。

苏贝希文化墓葬有三种基本形式:二层台墓、竖穴墓和偏室墓,而且有一个递进的发展演变过程,可以设想这个过程是这样:最初,人们在修建墓葬时,为了使其更像一个住所,必须中空有顶,为了使篷盖顶部深埋地下,在墓室壁的中部必须有一个二层台。洋海墓地所在台地地层黄土细腻坚硬,很方便地可以挖出二层台。察吾呼文化墓葬所在地层为砂质的戈壁砾石,在这样的地方不可能挖出规整的竖穴二层台,即便可以,也承载不了墓顶篷盖物的重量。所幸附近有各种大小的砾石,就采用砾石砌出二层台,上面是篷盖石板或圆木。而焉不拉克墓地是二者的结合,土质硬的地方用生土二层台,土质松散的砂砾层必须加固修筑,附近又不方便取石,但是有黏土,那么就采用土坯。我在洋海一号墓地 M168 号墓的发掘中,就发现该墓四壁中一部分用了土坯,这在洋海墓地是很特殊的现象。研究认为,人们在挖竖穴坑时东、北壁偶遇沙层而塌边,因而用土坯修筑,另两面因为土层坚硬而用自然的生土壁。

目前发现的墓口盖木的木材种类主要是胡杨木。可见当时人们的居留地及周围一定大量生长着这种树木。从前面列举的史前墓葬分布情形来看,几乎遍布吐鲁番盆地的各个绿洲。也就是说,史前的吐鲁番盆地中,到处都生长着胡杨。这也正符合吐鲁番盆地的地理气候特征,因为胡杨喜欢沙漠干燥的地理气候环境。

在封盖墓口的圆木中,还有一些松木、冷杉木、柽柳木,柽柳木容易理解,因为生长胡杨之地往往都长着柽柳。而生长松木和冷杉木的地方,最近也要到北面 80 千米的博格达山北坡去找。可见,当时居住在洋海的居民的活动范围已经到达了山北。他们到那里决不会只是为了砍树,而是为了放牧和狩猎,只是归来时捎带一些而已。在制作器具所用木料中,还有绣线菊木,这是一种生长在山上的灌木,俗称"兔儿条",是现代工具柄用木,强而有韧性,弓体均用此木。还有杖、鞭杆、马镳等。

2. 木床、床罩的结构和制作

木床是为安葬人的尸骨而设计的,根据墓葬的大小而有伸缩,分单人和双人两种,当然,双人用的木床会宽一些。样式可分为平板式和靠背式,但以平板式为主。所谓平板式,是四条短粗的木腿(直径 15 cm、长 30 cm 左右)用榫头卯眼接合一个长方形木框,木框内也同样用榫头卯眼方式等距离安装 2 根横撑,上面竖向铺排木棍或树枝条,并用牛皮条缠绕固定在横撑和床框上。靠背式数量较少,均为单人设计。也就是以给平板式木床同一长边的 2 根腿加长至 65 cm 左右,比床面高出部分的木腿上安装 2 根横木棍为基本形式。

床罩为长方拱弧形,用带毛的牛皮条和柳树枝捆扎而成。底座木棍较粗,用榫头卯眼接合成长方形木框,在木框长边上各凿出 5 个卯眼,插入 5 根拱弧形的细木棍,用 4 根竖向的长木条与拱弧形的柳树枝等距交叉固定,形成正方格。床罩上覆盖着毛毡。由于制作时牛皮条和柳树枝都是湿的,干后一般都整体变形扭曲。

木床和床罩的制作都运用了榫头卯眼法,榫头可用铜斧或铜刀砍、削而成,而卯眼用铜凿更容易打成,观察卯眼内壁,即可看出窄而锋利的工具痕。发掘出土有带直銎或横銎的铜斧,被盗墓葬中还见有平板式铜斧(铜锛),但从未出土过铜凿。

三、随葬器物中的木器分类

苏贝希文化随葬器物中木器数量大,种类也很多,涵盖了人们生产、生活的方方面面,分类复杂甚至难以分类。这里从器形和用途两方面入手。

1. 木容器

即盛物品的器具。有盘、盆、豆、臼、杯、桶、勺等。这些器物都是用胡杨树的圆木加工成,盘较浅,盆较深,豆深腹有柄。都经过了挖、刻、切、削的工序和过程。有些木盘底部阴刻着怪兽或北山羊的图像。臼的个体都较大而壁厚,外沿都有成对分布的四个大方鋬,用于系牛皮带加固臼体和口部。由于经长期使用的缘故,所见木臼底部都已磨得很薄。木杯和木桶都是深腹器物,所以全部掏成筒状后再安装圆平底,并且不惜功夫在器表雕刻精美的纹样。尤其是洋海墓地出土的木桶,往往雕刻有成群结队的山区、草原和沙漠动物图形,有北山羊、马、狼、虎、狗、鹿、骆驼、野猪等,洋海木器上的雕刻画是发现中的又一亮点。在木桶的外壁,阴刻、线刻出成组的动物形象,它们均成组的分布,用以组成一个完整的画面。比如有的是狼和北山羊的组合,另一个则是骆驼、野猪、麋鹿、岩羊的组合。在一些木钵、盆、器柄上也雕刻有山羊、狼、怪兽的形象。当多种动物组合在一件器物上时,尽管动物种属不同,但雕刻技法是一样的。当然,同种动物组合在一件器物上,不但雕刻技法相同,而且神似。个别木桶外口沿还粘贴小花紫草草籽组成连续的三角纹。在一个口径只有 2 cm 的小木臼外表,圆雕出三个盘羊的形象,形态各异,有站立者,也有卧姿后肢向上翻转。还有木盘底部的动物形态也很生动。木勺都有一个粗柄,有直也有曲,阿拉沟出土的 1 件更是将柄部雕刻成马蹄形。

2. 简朴的器形和小件器物

按出土数量的多少依次列举如下:钉、橛、纺转、梳、钻木取火器、杖、鞭杆、镳、扣、器柄、直角器、俑等。木钉长度不足 20 cm,出土数量最多,多胡杨木,少柽柳木,除少数出土时还钉在墓壁上之外,大多落在墓底,可知入墓时是用来挂随葬品的。木橛长 60 cm 左右,多用直而光洁的柽柳木棍削出尖头,顶上有重物敲击痕。少部分在墓室,大多数在墓葬盖木上面,用途不明。最大可能或是用作墓葬的选址桩。纺转,由纺轮和线轴组成二件套,线轴用绣线菊木,打磨光滑。纺轮用胡杨木削制,有些上面阴刻纹样。木梳为流线形和长方形的扁平体,真可谓各种各样,有些还在柄部线刻或彩绘纹样。史前时期的吐鲁番居民似乎还不会制作篦子。钻木取火器也是二件套,由取火板和取火棍组成,木制的钻木取火器的标准名称叫"燧"。是由两个单件器物组成(火绒不易保存下来),取火板和取火棒。取火板一般为木制的小长方体,表面打磨光,沿两个长边等距刻出凹槽,有时在槽的两面先钻出直径 1 cm 左右的小圆圈,在小圆圈的位置实施取火操作;取火棒锥形,一般长不足 10 cm,直径同样为 1 cm 左右,表面磨光。在出土样品中,取火棒的粗头顶端和取火板两边的钻孔凹槽中都有碳化痕。用木头把火钻出来,实施起来也不是一件太容易的事情,取火板两侧的凹槽必不可少,这是用来夹持艾、绒等易燃物的。当用拇指和其他手指捏住取火棒的细端高速旋转摩擦时,产生的高温就会点燃火绒。但是,如若认为用任何木头都能钻出火来,那就错了。我有幸观察过大量的取火板和取火棒,它们都是用一种木头作成的,这种木头的木质松紧不一,非常粗糙。均用同一种木料削制,木质松软粗糙。木杖是助行工具,一般顶端都有短的弯柄,绣线菊木制成,打磨光滑。鞭杆也多为绣线菊木制,长 40 cm 余,一头刻槽,便于系鞭梢。镳、扣、器柄都较少,均用绣线菊木制成,打磨光滑。直角器以前都称作"直角形木器"、"鞣皮工具"等,不妥。这种器物呈 90 度折角,折角两边体长短略有差别,短头稍钝,长 15 cm 左右;较长的一头较尖,长 20 cm 左右,通体磨光。除苏贝希遗址、墓地和洋海墓地出土以外,民丰尼雅遗址出土最多,有人叫它"木钥匙",因为它的确有点像当地农民当时还在使用着的开木锁的木钥匙。尼雅遗址 95 墓地 4 号墓有一件,出土时和短把木锹放在该墓箱式木棺之上,好像是随手放上去的,并且上面都粘满了干泥巴。而木棺盖和侧板的条条缝隙中都抹进了同样的泥土,可见其作用相当于泥抹子。苏贝希遗址一号房址出土一件,土坯墙壁上抹有草泥。俑用圆木雕刻成,长不足 10 cm,多用色彩画出面部,作用不详。

3. 弓、箭和弓箭袋撑板

人类在旧石器时代晚期就开始使用弓箭了,但考古学证据只有石镞,包括整个新石器时代也都仅仅发现石质的箭头以及木箭头,弓也都是木制的单体弓。发展到青铜时代,才有了复合弓,也就是多种材料制成的弓。弓箭兼有狩猎工具、作战武器、健身器械多种功能,古人特别注重其性能。据成书于春秋战国之际的《考工记》载:弓者制弓,一定要按照时令选取六种材料,也只有六种材料都具备齐全的基础上才能开始制造。这六种材料是杆、角、胶、筋、漆、丝,但吐鲁番盆地缺少后两种材料,用鹿皮胶和羊肠衣替代。杆使箭射得远,角使箭射得快,筋使箭射得深,胶使各材聚合为弓身,肠衣使弓身坚固。选用牛角制弓片,秋季的牛角厚,春季的牛角薄,青色坚韧有力,根部发白、中部发青、末端丰满,这是最为理想的材质。鹿胶青白色、牛胶火红色、鱼胶微黄色,时间越久颜色变深且有光泽,黏性越大。小筋要成长条,大筋要连在一起并且有光泽,取做筋的动物要跑得快。在制弓的流程中,冬季制作弓杆,使其细密;春季浸泡牛角,使其润泽;夏季制作弓筋,使其不续结杂乱;秋天合角、丝、漆三材,则坚固致密。初冬微寒时再进一步加固弓体,弓便不会变形。材料备齐后,开始制弓。弓的加工步骤是先制作弓胎(杆),在制弓材料中弓杆最强,所以用韧性最强的绣线菊(俗称兔儿条)木,火烤弯曲成型,调制好后张弓才会像流水一般。牛角是用来支撑弓体的,其要弯曲而不要弯斜,先将牛角撕开,火烤压平,弯曲成型后两面都划出条纹,以利用胶粘合,粘贴在弓杆的内侧。筋是增加强度的,将筋放在水中浸泡变软,用温水洗净后平放在温热的胶锅中浸沾,梳理平整使筋条展开,铺在弓杆的外侧。铺完一道筋等阴干后再铺第二道,最少要铺三道。要制作力量更大的弓,那就多铺几道。弓梢制成三角形,呈倒钩状,弦反向挂在弓上,烘烤弓体给弓定型。通体再反复缠牛筋、肠衣,刷胶。弓弦用牛筋合成,两端作成固定的环,环上再缠羊皮条,弦的中段也同样要缠皮条,以防过早将弦磨断。弦的长短要反复调试松紧度才能合适。

要作成一支箭一般要分三截加工成型后接合,有很长的一段粘牛皮胶后互为插入,接口处缠以很细的牛筋或羊肠衣。箭尾有挂弦的槽,并有尾羽三四枚,等距分粘在接近尾槽处四周。箭杆必须磨光,是用刻有半圆形槽的两块长方形木板夹持,槽里粘有细砂粒,反复拉动箭杆可达目的。

因为弓箭袋是用柔软的皮革制成,所以必须安装支撑板,这样才便于携带和出入弓箭。撑板用胡杨木板作成,在一个边上打孔穿绳固定在皮袋上。撑板一般长 55 cm,底宽上窄,宽 5~8 cm。往往在一个面上浅浮雕连续的羽状涡纹,大量重复地使用这同一种纹样,总觉得当事人在祈求着什么,愿射出的箭像长了翅膀一样远飞。

在史前的最后阶段,人们以畜牧经济为主,畜群是他们赖以生存的基础和生命线。在外出放牧时为保护畜群的安全必须要进行狩猎,弓箭是不可或缺的利器。因此,他们在制造弓箭上投入大工夫是可以理解的。

4. 竖琴(箜篌)

吐鲁番盆地史前墓葬中,只有洋海墓地发现了 4 件竖琴,其中有一件基本完整,是用整块胡杨木雕刻挖成,并经过打磨抛光。由音箱、颈、弦杆和弦组成,音箱和琴颈连为一体,通长 61 cm。音箱上口平面长圆形,底部正中有三角形发音孔,口部蒙羊皮。蒙皮正中竖向穿一根加工好的柽柳棍,再用 5 根小枝等距分别穿在竖棍下,枝、棍交叉呈"十"字形露出蒙皮,再分别引一根用羊肠衣做的琴弦到弦轴上。琴弦仅存半根,弦轴杆首正好也有 5 道弦痕。从器物类型学角度作比较,其他 3 件也基本类似,都由整块木料挖削而成,音箱上口呈平面长圆形,底部正中有三角形发音孔。从承弦杆上存有明显的 5 道系弦痕迹看来,这应是经长期使用的结果。我们也注意到,洋海出土竖琴的墓葬主人的身份都很一般,竖琴的制作工艺水平也较低,材质为当地胡杨,应是民间使用的普及型乐器。

古代文明中的美索不达米亚人、埃及人和印度人主要演奏竖琴。在公元前 15 世纪的埃及墓室壁画中,乐队的竖琴手总是处于最前面。公元前 7 世纪,亚述王赛纳克里布把首都迁到尼尼微,宫墙石雕中有乐师在花园中演奏竖琴。音乐是所有印度宗教仪式中的组成部分,发现于印度河河谷文明中的雕像显示,这里的人们演奏的也是竖琴,时间在公元前 20 世纪左右。可见,竖琴为多弦拨弦乐器,其早期形式出现于公元前 3 世纪末。当然,结构最简单的早期竖琴发现较少,洋海一号墓地 90 号墓较完整的那件尤其显得珍贵。

5. (飞)旋镖

曲棍形器物,也可叫做投掷棒,只有洋海墓地出土 10 余件。大小形状近似,这种器物呈 85~120 度折角,折角两边棒体长短有较大差别,短头较宽扁,长 25 cm 余;较长的一头厚圆,长 50 cm 左右,顶端有扁圆形手柄,通体磨光。为较重而结实的榆木和柽柳木制作,因出土时多有断裂,又有手柄,因此可认为是投掷器,叫旋镖。器型稍大些,与"飞去来器"最大的区别是两边棒体不等长,也不够扁平,投掷出去也不可能返回来。但用来打兔子是很好的工具。在青铜时代岩画中就往往见到一人手扬持该器,前方不远处一只兔子倒地的图形。

而飞去来器是澳大利亚土著居民最有名的狩猎工具之一。用木头加工成微弯的、扁扁的形状,通体磨光,为两头圆润的木制投掷棒。由于棒的一侧扁平另一侧圆,使投掷出的飞旋镖所走路线是曲回的。当这种武器飞出去后,如果碰不上障碍物就会自行飞旋回到投掷的起始点。当欧洲人到达澳洲以后,他们有机会看到当地土著居民的狩猎活动,并留下了大量文字和摄影资料,其中就有猎人在有稀疏灌木丛的草地上一手持飞去来器,另一只手握旋镖形器物全神贯注观察前方动静的照片。可见二者之区别。

6. 冠饰

吐鲁番盆地内的三个桥、苏贝希、洋海、胜金店墓地都有遗存。男女有别，男性冠饰通体用薄木板加工粘合而成，呈四方长筒状，中空，高 60 cm 左右。底口近方形，因为四个面中只有一个面是平直的，其他三个面都略弧，向外先鼓出后又逐渐细收成尖状体，中间略粗，与直面相对的那个斜面上方安装一个三角形"尾鳍"或"翼"——像船之尾舵状的薄木片。冠饰通体染成黑色。冠体下端有前后对应的小孔，可插入木销钉，用来固定一枚安装在筒中的木条。木条为细长方体，上面有条形孔，并缠绕头发，以便将木冠饰固定在头顶上。女性冠饰有一个像帽子一样的圆形筒，用宽而薄的木板弯曲粘接成筒状。近圆形顶盖与圆筒组装在一起，顶盖中部有 2 个半圆形或长方形孔，便于发辫从双孔内穿出后打结，好将木桶一样的冠帽稳定在头顶之上。口微敞，口沿上有两段突起，薄沿，像一个倒扣的木桶。桶顶两侧分别安装一根微曲的圆木棍或直木板（冠翅），并向两侧叉开一定角度。木冠冕成型后，通体外包羊皮，并染成黑色，类似于长着动物双角的木冠饰才算作成。类似的冠饰还有皮革和毛毡制作的，它们的基本形态、用途、用法也相同。

四、木材加工工艺

木材加工工艺是指把圆木加工成器具的方法、技术和过程，但整体受加工工具的制约，由工具决定产品。反向思维，只要达到一定的技术水平，可以创造出新的工具。

1. 加工工具

要把圆木加工成器具，必须有相适应的工具。古人云：工欲善其事，必先利其器。就是这个道理。没有工具时可以发明工具。木床和床罩的制作都运用了榫头卯眼法，榫头可用铜斧或铜刀砍、削出，而卯眼用铜凿更容易打成，观察卯眼内壁，即可看出窄而锋利的工具痕。发掘出土有带直銎或横銎的铜斧，被盗墓葬还见有平板式铜斧（铜锛），但从未出土过铜凿。同样道理，观察木床的四只粗短腿，面上非常的平整，似乎是锯出来的茬口。再说，苏贝希文化就是以大量锯齿纹为显著特征的考古学文化，他们在陶器上、木器上乃至服饰毡毯上装饰锯齿纹，难道说就缺乏那么一点将纹样变成实物的灵感，何况这时鲁班都已经过世了。刻削有铜刀和铁刀，锥刺有铜锥铁锥，微雕用什么工具来完成？大概用小刻刀吧，哈密黑沟梁早期铁器时代墓葬中就发现这种小型青铜工具。但吐鲁番盆地考古中一直未见。还有钻孔工具，主要是给木纺轮钻孔，用铜刀可以做到。墓地还出土不少玛瑙珠、滑石珠都有更加难钻的孔。以前有人认为是用管状物加金钢砂而为之，这完全可能，在洋海墓地就发现了木打磨器和木锉刀，使用面上都粘有细砂粒。

2. 砍削

这是大动作的作业，同样适用于制作较大件的器物。如竖琴的制作，都是用整块的木料削、挖而成。音箱上口在一个平面，这是该器最高的部分，音箱底最低。从上口到器底的厚度就是最初选料的厚度，长度和宽度确定之后，首先加工好一个长方体形的厚木板，再经过砍、削、挖的工序。盖木和木床的制作，都离不开大刀阔斧的砍削。当然还包括许多的木容器和旋镖。

3. 雕刻

这种技法适应于细致的图形和小件器物，特别是动物图形和图案。有圆雕、浅浮雕、透雕和阴刻、线刻、挖刻等。有一件小木盅,口径和高都不足 3 cm,通体圆雕三只蜷曲的盘羊和格里芬,而且这些动物都栩栩如生。还有一件肖形印,高仅 3 cm,上半部印钮透雕成一头大象,大耳、长鼻、柱腿,造型绝妙之极。浅浮雕技法主要用在木撑板上,雕刻出连续的羽状涡纹,流畅而有动感。线刻和阴刻主要作用在木桶和盘底的动物图像上,有一个木桶上线刻 6 只动物,其中 2 只狼匍匐在上,下面有 4 只半立的北山羊。另一件上面雕刻了 2 只动物,1 只半卧的麋鹿和 1 只半立的北山羊。木桶上阴刻动物也很多,其中有个上面阴刻 4 只动物,2 只龇牙咧嘴的狼和 2 只温顺的北山羊,狼牙、羊角和羊的鬃毛都用锯齿纹表示。还有 1 个木桶上雕刻了 10 只动物,5 只北山羊,3 峰骆驼,1 头野猪和 1 只麋鹿。另 1 个上雕刻了 2 只老虎,虎尾、双腿和身体轮廓采用线刻,阴刻连续三角纹代表鬃毛,并用红、粉、白三色施彩。

4. 钻孔

钻孔的技术非常成熟,能打出各种大小的圆孔,主要作用在纹轮上。从大量遗存的纺轮上观察,中间穿孔好像不是挖出来的,而是钻成的。在木容器柄顶和口沿上,往往也有穿孔,用于系绳,这些孔都比较小,似乎更不容易钻出。有些带裂缝的木容器,在裂缝两侧钻 2 排小孔,穿入细绳进行捆绑,类似于陶器上的铜补方式。在竖琴和木梳柄上,有较大的孔洞,因已磨得十分光滑,很难判定到底是钻出来的还是刻挖形成。

5. 粘合

能体现粘合技法的木器标本,最好的就是复合弓了。从文献记载和实物观察,所用均为动物皮胶。一直到复合弓出土时,弓杆两面的牛角片和筋条还牢牢地敷着在木质弓杆上。一支箭是先分三截作成的,箭头连 10 cm 长的箭杆,箭尾也差不多同样长度,中间是 60 cm 长的箭杆。粘接时一端削成长楔状,另一端削成等长的鱼嘴,用皮胶牢固地粘合在一起,至今都有不会脱节。弓箭的表面也都刷了一层胶,显得光洁明亮,但不能着水,必须加强保护,这也是当初人们下大工夫制作弓袋箭囊的动力所在。据说鹿胶青白色、牛胶火红色,而且时间越久越有光泽,黏性也越大。在哈密青铜时代的艾斯克霞尔墓地,就出土过装了半杯的皮胶。

6. 抛光

在苏贝希文化各墓地中,出土了大量磨光木器,如木箭、木线杆、木鞭杆,也包括木容器的口沿、外表、器柄等。在洋海墓地,我们发现了加工上述器物的工具:木锉刀和打磨器。木锉刀的造型类似于现在的钢锉,为长条形较扁的木板,长 30 cm 余,宽 2.5 cm,带一个较窄而椭圆的手柄,使用部分有一个平面,上面还用胶粘了一层沙粒。木打磨器是两件一套的长方体,两面各有多个长条形凹槽,扣合后形成多个笔直的圆筒,内壁同样用胶粘一层沙粒。这样,可将木箭杆、木线杆、木鞭杆等类似的器物半成品放入拉伸,很容易就能磨光了。以前其他地区也发现过相同用处的器物,但不得要领。

结　论

当我最初涉猎考古学文献的时候,就发现新疆的史前墓葬中保存下来大量的木质器物。如苏贝希墓地、五堡墓地、孔雀河墓地、山浦拉墓地、扎滚鲁克墓地等。近些年来,特别是洋海墓地和小河墓地的发掘,出土了更多的木器,甚至不见陶器。上述地点都气候干燥少雨,那么像伊犁河流域墓地、和静察吾呼墓地、哈密焉不拉克墓地的情况又是怎么样呢?只要哪一座墓保存好一点,同样也一定会有木器出土。

可见木器在史前人们的生活中起何等作用,它的重要性是不言而喻的。尤其是 2003 年对洋海墓地的发掘,发现出土了数以千计的木器。我自始至终参加了田野发掘和最初的室内整理及简报编写工作,并在很大程度上受益于这项工作。由于苏贝希文化所处的吐鲁番盆地特殊的地理环境因素,使大量不易保存的木质器物都完好无损地保存下来,这是我们得以进行研究的基础。

木器与史前人类的生活息息相关,那么他们就会在木器加工和工艺上下大工夫,所以我们才能见到体现在木器加工上的诸多技艺。

在中国古代社会中所体现的是男耕女织,而洋海墓地中夫妇合葬墓占墓葬的绝对多数,体现的是男牧男木作女织。所以一直到唐朝,阿斯塔那出土的"飞天衣"人物绢画,仍然是夫握直角尺、妇持剪刀而双双升天的图像,历史就是如斯延续。

可萨族源考*

桂宝丽

新疆师范大学人文学院历史系

可萨人（Khazars），[①]也称为哈扎尔人，是6~11世纪活跃在欧亚大草原西部的一个游牧民族。6世纪后期可萨人作为西突厥汗国的属部出现在南俄罗斯草原。西突厥汗国覆亡以后，可萨人成为一股独立的政治力量，在西突厥汗国的废墟上建立了强大的汗国。大约在7世纪中叶，可萨汗国已是北高加索和伏尔加河下游地区一个重要的国家。9世纪前期可萨汗国势力最为强大，先后使得东斯拉夫人、马扎尔人、佩切涅格人、布尔塔斯人、北高加索匈人臣服。在可萨最盛时，领有西至基辅，东到花剌子模草原，北到伏尔加保加尔，南到北高加索的广大土地。965年，罗斯大公斯维亚托斯拉夫对可萨发起毁灭性的攻击，大败可萨军队，摧毁了可萨的要塞萨尔克尔以及阿得尔、萨曼达尔等城。同年，古斯人也越过伏尔加河乘机攻打可萨人。在罗斯人与古斯人的双重打击下，可萨汗国最终覆亡。部分可萨人向南退至他曼半岛地区。1016年，拜占庭联合罗斯进攻"可萨地区"，消灭了可萨人的残余势力。从此，可萨人逐渐融入其他民族间，消失在人们的视野中。

对于可萨人的族源，学者们进行了许多的研究，也提出了不少观点。目前学术界对于可萨的族源主要有突厥说、回纥说、阿卡齐尔（Akatzir）说、乌古尔（Ogur）说和萨比尔（Sabir）说等说法。由于有关可萨的史料很少涉及可萨人的起源问题，所以直到今天为止，对可萨族源的研究仍然没有定论。

可萨汗国是由许多部落组成的一个军事联盟，但是其核心部落是起源于萨比尔人的可萨人。10世纪的阿拉伯地理学家马苏第就认识到了萨比尔人和可萨人之间的联系，据他记载，"可萨人在突厥语里称为萨比尔人，而在波斯语中称为可萨人"。[②] 在马苏第看来，萨比尔人和可萨人是同一个民族，只是不同的民族对他们的称呼不一样。

可萨人与萨比尔人同种可以从可萨国王约瑟夫给西班牙御医沙普鲁的信件中看出。[③] 约瑟夫在回

---

* 本文为2008年度新疆维吾尔自治区高校科研计划青年教师培育基金项目"可萨汗国史研究"（项目编号：XJEDU2008S43）的阶段性成果。

① 可萨是我国史料中对Khazar的称呼。《旧唐书》卷198《西戎传》之"波斯"条云："波斯国，在京师西一万五千三百里，东与吐火罗、康国接，北邻突厥之可萨部。"《新唐书》卷221《西域传》中亦有对可萨的记载，其中的《波斯传》称"波斯，居达遏水西，距京师万五千里而赢，东与吐火罗、康接，北邻突厥可萨部"；《拂菻传》云："拂菻，古大秦也，居西海上，一曰海西国。去京师四万里，在苫西，北直突厥可萨部"；《大食传》云："大食之西有苫国者，亦自国。北距突厥可萨部，地数千里。"从地望和对音上看，可萨应该就是西方史料中的Khazar。西方学者中最早把中国史料中可萨一名考订为Khazar的是法国汉学家德金（De Guignes），之后吉本（Gibbon）著《罗马衰亡史》（*Decline and Fall of the Roman Empire*）时又引用了德金的说法，从此学术界都赞同此说，无人提出异议。参见邓禄普：《犹太可萨人历史》（D. M. Dunlop, *The History of the Jewish Khazars*, Princeton, NJ：Princeton University Press, 1954），第34~36页。

② Al-Mas'ūdī, *Kitāb at-Tanbīh*, ed. De Goeje, p.83, 转引自Peter Golden, *Khazar Studies: An Historico-Philological Inquiry into the Origins of the Khazars*, Akademiai Kiado, Budapest, 1980, p.57.

③ 犹太人哈斯代·伊本·沙普鲁（Hasdai ibn Shaprut）是西班牙科尔多瓦的伍麦叶王朝著名的御医，生于915年，卒于970年。他听说东方的可萨国是个犹太王国，于是去信和可萨人联系，询问可萨的历史、地理和宗教信仰。可萨可汗约瑟夫大约在960年左右回信给沙普鲁，信中介绍了可萨汗国统治的民族以及可萨人信仰犹太教的情况。有关信件的详细情况可参见Paul E. Kahle, *The Cairo Geniza*, Basil Blackwell, 1959, pp.30－32.

答沙普鲁有关可萨人属于什么民族的问题时说："我们是 Japhet 的儿子 Togarma 的后代。我们从祖先留下的系谱书上得知，Togarma 有十个儿子，他们的名字是——Agijoe，Tirus，Ouvar，Ugin，Bisal，Zarna，Cusar，Sanar，Balgad 和 Savir。我们是 Cusar 这一支，在我们祖先生活的时代我们这一支人数非常少"。① Savir 人显然指的是萨比尔人，这进一步表明可萨人与萨比尔人同族。

约瑟夫的回信接下来记载了可萨人与翁乌古尔人（Onogur）的战争，但是却没有提到可萨人与萨比尔人的战争。根据拜占庭史料的记载，萨比尔人主要活动地域与可萨人的活动区域一致，都在北部高加索地区。萨比尔人利用自己的地理位置，经常周旋于波斯人和拜占庭人之间，而这与可萨人所处的战略地位完全一致。如果可萨人和萨比尔人是敌人的话，可萨人崛起的时候首先要对付的就是萨比尔人，但是无论约瑟夫的信件还是拜占庭史料都只提到可萨人与翁乌古尔人（保加尔人的主体）的战争，却丝毫没有提及对萨比尔人的进攻，这又从侧面说明了可萨人与萨比尔人同族。

萨比尔人和可萨人两个名称在不同民族的史料中记载不一样。萨比尔一名主要见于拜占庭史料，从 5 世纪中期第一次出现在拜占庭史料中，到 6 世纪晚期逐渐消失在拜占庭史料的记载中。但是在同一时期的亚美尼亚史料中却看不到关于萨比尔人的记载，其中只保存了对可萨的记载：由于阿尔巴尼亚人的土地在 6 世纪前期多次遭到可萨人的攻击，教堂和福音毁于战火。于是在万王之王库萨和一世统治的第二年（532），阿尔巴尼亚人的首都从 Cholay 城迁移到了 Partaw。② 穆斯林史料中也保存了同一时期可萨人的活动。巴拉祖里在叙述库萨和一世的父亲古巴兹修建的城市时说："可萨人过去常常攻击远至 ad-Dinawar 的地方。鉴于此，古巴兹·伊本·卑路斯（Kubadh ibn-Fairuz）国王派遣了他的一个杰出的将军率领 12 000 人蹂躏了 Arran 的土地，征服了位于 ar-Rass 河和舍尔宛之间的地区。然后古巴兹紧随其后，在 Arran 建立了拜义赖甘城（al-Bailakan）、白尔泽阿城（Bardha'ah）——这是整个前线地区的首府——以及垓白拉城（Kabalah），即可萨城。之后他在舍尔宛和 al-Lan 之门之间立起了赖班水坝（Sudd al-Libn）。沿着水坝建立了 360 个城市，这些城市在建立巴布·艾布瓦布城（al-Bab wa-l-Abwab）之前都成为废墟了。"③ 古达玛的《税册》中也记载了古巴兹之子阿尔努舍尔旺（即库萨和一世，531 年至 578 年在位）在打耳班地区修建军事要塞，抵抗可萨人的事情。④ 亚美尼亚史料和阿拉伯史料对可萨的记载很早，但是拜占庭史家在萨比尔人活动的 5～6 世纪期间却从没有提到过可萨人，可萨人第一次出现在拜占庭史料中，是在 7 世纪 20 年代希拉克略与可萨人联合攻打波斯时。

萨比尔和可萨的名称在同样的历史时期各自见于不同系统的史料，说明马苏第关于二者乃同名异译的记载是可信的。因此，可萨人的起源问题实际上就是萨比尔人的起源问题，只要考证出萨比尔人的来源，可萨的来源问题也就迎刃而解了。

关于萨比尔人的来源，目前学术界还没有定论，也有很多问题需要进一步研究。学者们往往笼统地说萨比尔人是从中亚迁徙到南俄罗斯草原的，但具体是什么民族则没有进一步说明。已故学者普利查克（Omeljan Pritsak）在萨比尔人的来源问题上曾提出了一个假说，他认为萨比尔人来源于我国史书中记载

① Elkan Nathan Adler, ed. *Jewish Travellers*. London：George Routledge & Sons, 1930, p. 34.
② Movsēs Dasxuranc'i, *The History of the Caucasian Albanians*, trans. C. Dowsett, London：Oxford University Press, 1961, p. 70.
③ Philip Khūri Hitti, *The Origins of the Islamic State*, a partial translation of the *Kitāb Futūh al Budān of al-Balādhuri*. vol. 1, New York：AMS Press, 1968, p. 305.
④ ［阿拉伯］伊本·胡尔达兹比赫著，宋岘译注：《道里邦国志》所附《税册》，中华书局，1991 年，第 275～277 页。

的鲜卑人。① 由于对中文史料的认识有限,他没能充分挖掘中文史料来进一步证明自己的观点,论据仅限于对音的一致性,因此这一假说并没有引起太多的关注。其实,普利查克的观点是比较合理的,萨比尔人很有可能就是我国历史上西迁的鲜卑人的后裔。

第一,萨比尔和鲜卑从对音上来看,是完全符合的。萨比尔在拜占庭史料中主要有如下写法:在普里斯库斯(Priscus)和塞奥非拉克特·西蒙卡特(Theophylactus Simocatta)的记载中作 Σαβιροι(Sabiroi),在普罗柯比(Procopius)、阿卡塞亚斯(Agathias)和米南德尔(Menander)的记载中作 Σαβειροι(Sabeiroi),在约尔丹尼斯(Jordanes)的记载中作 Saviris。② 由于在中世纪希腊语中的字母"阿尔法"(α)经常被用作希腊语中没有的外来音 ä 的替代字母,因此,去掉希腊语后缀-οι,Σαβιροι 这一名称应被译解为 Säbir。在 Säbi-r 一词中,最后的 r 是阿尔泰语的集合后缀,若去掉这个 r,则可以拟订为 Säbi。③

鲜卑在我国史料中有师比、犀毗、胥纰、私铌、斯比等称呼。王国维《胡服考》云:"黄金师比者具带之钩,亦本胡名。《楚辞·大招》作鲜卑,王逸注:鲜卑,绲带头也。《史记·匈奴传》作胥纰,《汉书》作犀毗,高诱《淮南》注作私铌头,皆鲜卑一语之转。"④鲜卑一名,伯希和认为与后来的室韦对音相同,应该拟订为 Särbi,Sirbi,Sirvi。⑤ 因此,我国史书中的鲜卑与拜占庭史料中的萨比尔从语音上是可以勘同的。

第二,萨比尔人名与鲜卑人名具有对应关系。在拜占庭文献中主要记载了五个萨比尔人名,其中有四个可以和鲜卑的人名或部落名对应起来。

1. Balaq

这是 527 年与拜占庭皇帝查士丁尼结盟的萨比尔女首领波丽克丝(Boarex)已故丈夫的名字,在塞奥发尼斯的编年史中作 Βαλαχ,在马拉拉斯的编年史中作 Βλαχ。此名应该就是拓跋鲜卑勋臣八姓中的步六孤氏。步六孤,步鹿孤,伏鹿孤,可以拟为 baliukkua,孤的韵母可以省去,即为 baliuk,这与 balaq 是可以对上的。《魏书·官氏志》云:"步六孤氏,后改为陆氏。"《魏书·陆俟传》中记载东平王陆俟乃代郡人,"曾祖干,祖引,世领部落。父突,太祖时率部民从征伐,数有战功。"传后所附俟孙陆叡,据姚薇元先生考证,就是《南齐书·魏虏传》记载的"伏鹿孤贺鹿浑"。⑥ 北周大司空陆滕以及隋太子洗马陆爽均是陆俟的玄孙,而陆爽正是《切韵》的作者陆法言的父亲。东平王陆氏一门出自步鹿孤部落,后以部落名为姓氏,遂称步鹿孤氏,到元魏统治时期才改为陆氏。拜占庭史料中记载的这位首领的名字也应该就是其部落名。

2. Boarex

这是与查士丁尼结盟的萨比尔女首领的名字。在马拉拉斯的编年史中作 Βωαρηζ,在塞奥发尼斯的编年史中作 Βωαρηξ。这个名字应即随拓跋鲜卑内入诸姓中的拨略。拨略,也作拔略,拨和拔为同音字,皆与跋同音,⑦拟音为 buatliak,与上文的 boarex 完全可以对应。

3. Iliger

这是阿卡塞亚斯(Agathias)的编年史中提到的在 555 年率领萨比尔人作战的将军的名字,在书中记

---

① Omeljan Pritsak, "From the Säbirs to the Hungarians", *Studies in Medieval Eurasian History*, Variorum Reprints, 1981, Ⅴ, p. 22.
② Peter. B. Golden, *Khazar Studies*, p. 256.
③ [美] 普雷特萨克著,陈一鸣译:《"失必儿"一词之来源》,《蒙古学信息》1996 年第 1 期,第 4 页。
④ 王国维:《胡服考》,《观堂集林》卷 22,中华书局,1959 年,第 1073 页。
⑤ 伯希和:《吐火罗语与库车语》,见冯承钧译《吐火罗语考》,中华书局,2004 年,第 143 页注释 12。
⑥ 姚薇元:《北朝胡姓考》,科学出版社,1958 年,第 28～30 页。
⑦ 姚薇元:《北朝胡姓考》,第 62 页。

作 Ιλιγερ。此名与拓跋鲜卑宗族十姓中的伊娄具有对应关系。伊娄是拓跋鲜卑先祖献帝的二弟所统领的部落的名称。《魏书·官氏志》云："伊娄氏后改为伊氏。"《周书》中的"伊娄穆"、"伊娄训"，后魏将军伊谓，宰官令伊娄愿等都是伊娄部的族人。娄，音缕，因此伊娄，可拟为 iliu，正好和 Iliger 名字的前半部分 Ili 相同，这位将军很有可能出自伊娄部。

4. Kutilzis

这是阿卡塞亚斯（Agathias）的编年史中提到的在 555 年率领萨比尔人作战的将军的名字，希腊文作 Κουτιλζις。此名可以对应《后汉书·乌桓鲜卑列传》中所记载的檀石槐军事联盟中东部大人阙机的名字。阙机，也作阙居，可以拟为 kiuatki，从音值上可以和 Kutilzis 对上。

从上面的分析可以看出，拜占庭史料中记载的萨比尔人名大都与我国史书中记载的鲜卑人的人名和部落名具有对应关系。

第三，从语言上看，萨比尔人和鲜卑人都使用突厥语。巴托尔德曾提出"突厥语本身的最早的发展阶段很可能就是匈奴人的东邻——鲜卑"的假说。[1] 克劳森在研究了《南齐书》收录的拓跋鲜卑的十几个词语后认为，这些词语属于突厥语中的 l/r 方言，并得出"拓跋讲突厥语"的结论。[2] 鲜卑人说突厥语也可以在《魏书·官氏志》中找到证据。《官氏志》记载，"屋引氏后改为房氏"，《新唐书》卷 71 下又记"河南房氏，晋初有房乾，本出清河，使北虏，留而不遣，虏俗谓房为屋引"。这里的"北虏"指的是鲜卑，可见鲜卑语中房子称为"屋引"，而这个读音可以对应突厥语族对"房屋"的称呼 Yu。由此也可看出拓跋鲜卑使用的是突厥语。

萨比尔人的语言在史料中没有留下太多信息，有关可萨人语言的书面材料也没有保存下来，美国学者 Peter Golden 从历史语言学的角度研究了散见于各种文字史料中的可萨词汇，写成了《可萨研究——对可萨人起源的历史语言学研究》一书。书中最后作者得出如下结论："大部分可萨的称号总的说来都和当时突厥语世界的称号一样，尤其与西突厥的称号几乎完全一致。多数人名是突厥语，只有两个名字可能来自伊朗语。许多名称和头衔还无法解释，这主要是因为我们的材料中有很多混淆的地方，而且我们缺乏相比较的材料。从北高加索一直到伏尔加河下游的草原的可萨水文名称和地名，都来自突厥语。"[3]目前，研究可萨历史的学者们大都同意戈登的看法。

可萨人使用的可汗、可敦、特勒这些称呼也很早就见于鲜卑人中。可汗的称号过去认为始自柔然的社仑可汗，但是实际上应该来自鲜卑。《宋书》卷 96《鲜卑吐谷浑传》记慕容鲜卑乙那楼对吐谷浑言"处可寒"，并解释说"宋言尔官家也"。这里的"可寒"即可汗。《晋书》卷 125《乞伏国仁载记》，记魏晋之际陇西鲜卑的纥干被部众推为"统主，号之曰乞伏可汗托铎莫何"。《旧唐书》卷 29《音乐志二》记："后魏乐府始有北歌，即《魏史》所谓《真人代歌》是也。今存者五十三章，其名目可解者六章……其不可解者，咸多可汗之辞。按今大角，此即后魏世所谓《簸逻回》者是也，其曲亦多可汗之辞。北虏之俗，皆呼主为可汗。吐谷浑又慕容别种，知此歌是燕魏之际鲜卑歌。"可见可汗一词在鲜卑语中早已存在。1980 年在鄂伦春自治旗阿里河镇的嘎仙洞石壁上发现太平真君四年（443）魏武帝拓跋焘派遣李敞等人前往祭祀时

① ［苏］威廉·巴托尔德著，罗致平译：《中亚突厥史十二讲》，中国社会科学出版社，1984 年，第 27 页。
② ［英］G·克劳森著，牛汝极、黄建华译：《突厥、蒙古、通古斯》，《西北民族研究》1991 年第 2 期。
③ Peter Golden, *Khazar Studies*, p. 262.

镌刻的《石刻祝文》,其中有"皇祖先可寒"及"皇妣先可敦"之语,[1]这更从实物上证实了拓跋鲜卑在5世纪中期仍然使用可汗的称号。鲜卑人的可汗称号后来经柔然、嚈哒、突厥等民族的传布,成为欧亚草原民族广泛使用的一个称谓。可敦与可汗的称呼同见于李敞的《石刻祝文》,可见鲜卑语中很早也就存在这一称谓。而突厥的特勤则来源于鲜卑的"直勤"。[2]

第四,从人种上看,萨比尔人和鲜卑人都同属蒙古利亚种。萨比尔人在拜占庭史料中通常被称为是匈人。塞奥发尼斯的编年史中记载,515年"以萨比尔一名著称的匈人穿越过里海之门,蹂躏了亚美尼亚";在527年,那位与拜占庭人结盟的女首领Boarex,也被称为"萨比尔匈人"。[3] 普罗柯比的《战史》中也记载了在530年波斯入侵拜占庭控制的亚美尼亚领土时,波斯军队中有一支三千人的匈人队伍,他们被称为萨比尔人,是最好战的民族之一。[4] 约翰·马拉拉斯(John Malalas)的编年史中也把萨比尔人称为匈人。[5] 在西方历史上影响巨大的匈人属于蒙古利亚种已经成为公论,萨比尔被视为匈人,其种族特征一定与匈人相似,因此,可以推断萨比尔人也属于蒙古利亚种。亚美尼亚史料载提到可萨人时,也经常称呼他们为匈人,而且还留下了可萨人形象的简单描述。据《高加索阿尔巴尼亚史》记载,梯夫利斯的居民在可萨人和拜占庭人联合围攻他们之时,为了羞辱可萨人,于是"他们取来一个巨大的南瓜,在上面画出了一腕尺宽和一腕尺长的匈人国王的像,在画睫毛的地方,因为没人看得见他的睫毛,所以他们画了一条细细的线;该画胡须的地方,他们带侮辱性地让那里光秃秃的,他们把他的鼻孔画得有一指距那么宽,鼻孔下面有很多毛发作为髭须"。[6] 阿尔巴尼亚史家还把入侵自己国家的可萨人称为"丑陋的、粗野的、宽脸庞的、没有睫毛的拖着像女人一样的长发的暴徒"。[7] 宽脸庞、少须和短睫毛显然都属于蒙古利亚人种的特点。

鲜卑人也属蒙古利亚种,这为国内的考古发现所证实。目前国内出土的有关鲜卑人的古人种学资料,已经发表的共计11批,分别出自内蒙古呼伦贝尔盟的完工墓地、扎赉诺尔墓地、赤峰市巴林左旗的南杨家营子遗址、乌兰察布盟的三道湾、七郎山、东大井、叭沟墓地,辽宁省朝阳市的十二台营子、喇嘛洞墓地,吉林省大安县的渔场墓地和山西省大同市南郊的北魏墓地。这些墓葬的年代大致为东汉至北魏时期。其中除了朝阳墓葬属于慕容鲜卑外,其他墓葬研究者一般认为属于拓拔鲜卑。吉林大学边疆考古研究中心的朱泓教授经过多年的研究,得出以下结论:"除完工、喇嘛洞、大同3组存在争议的资料之外,其他汉、晋时期鲜卑族居民的人种类型,均应属于低颅高面类型的西伯利亚蒙古人种"。[8]

综上所述,与萨比尔人同种的可萨人来源于西迁的鲜卑人。

从我国史料中的记载还可以追寻到鲜卑人迁徙的路径。我国的史料主要记载的是大漠以南的游牧民族与中原王朝发生的联系,对于北迁的游牧民族的记载微乎其微。因此,通常我们关注的鲜卑人主要

---

① 米文平:《鲜卑史研究》,中州古籍出版社,1994年,第30页。

② 关于拓跋鲜卑的直勤与突厥的特勤之间的关系,可参看罗新:《北魏直勤考》,《历史研究》2004年第5期。

③ Cyril Mango and Roger Scott, *The Chronicle of Theophanes Confessor: Byzantine and Near Eastern History A. D. 284 - 813*, Oxford: Clarendon Press, 1997, pp. 245, 266.

④ H. B. Dewing, *Procopius*, vol. 1: *History of the Wars*, London: William Heinemann, 1914, p. 129.

⑤ K. Czegledy, "Pseudo-Zacharias Rhetor on the Nomads", *Studia Turcica*, ed. Lajos Ligeti, Budapest: Akadémiai Kiadó, 1971, p. 147.

⑥ Movsēs Dasxuranc'i, *The History of the Caucasian Albanians*, p. 85.

⑦ *Ibid*, p. 83.

⑧ 朱泓:《东胡人种考》,《文物》2006年第8期,第76页。

是活跃在北部边塞地区的鲜卑,而那些由于种种原因向更北的方向迁徙的鲜卑人则鲜能进入我国史官的视野。其实,认真检查一下正史中关于鲜卑人的记载,我们不难推测出鲜卑人的迁徙。

应该说从鲜卑人进入蒙古草原后,鲜卑人在欧亚大草原上的迁徙就开始了。《后汉书·鲜卑传》:"和帝永元(89~105)中,大将军窦宪遣右校尉耿夔击破匈奴,北单于逃走,鲜卑因此转徙据其地。匈奴余种留者十余万落,皆自号鲜卑,鲜卑由此渐盛。"匈奴的西遁,使鲜卑成为了蒙古草原上的主体民族。十余万落的匈奴人"自号鲜卑",进一步壮大了鲜卑人的力量。逐水草而居的游牧生活方式使鲜卑人向广袤的西伯利亚平原迁徙并非是不可能的事情。

2世纪中叶鲜卑首领檀石槐成立了一个草原部落军事大联盟,他"南抄缘边,北拒丁零,东却夫余,西击乌孙,尽据匈奴故地,东西万四千余里,南北七千余里,网罗山川水泽盐池"。① 檀石槐领导下的部落军事大联盟的范围很广,包括了整个蒙古草原的东部、中部和西部。从右北平以东至辽东,与夫余、獩貊接壤,为东部,共二十多个邑。大人有四:弥加、阙机、素利、槐头。从右北平以西至上谷,为中部,共十多个邑。大人有三:柯最、阙居、慕容等。从上谷以西至敦煌,西接乌孙,为西部,共二十多个邑。大人有五:置鞬、落罗、日律、推演、宴荔游。上述十二个大人皆为大帅,都制属于檀石槐。灵帝光和年间(178~184),檀石槐死,其子和连代立。《后汉书·鲜卑传》云:"和连才力不及父,亦数为寇抄,性贪淫,断法不平,众畔者半。"从此,鲜卑军事联盟开始分裂。和连后被人射杀,因其子骞曼年幼,遂立和连兄长之子魁头。骞曼长大后,与魁头争国,众益离散。魁头死后,弟步度根立。此时,西部鲜卑各部相率叛去,迁徙到漠北或是西迁到乌孙地界。漠南自云中郡以东分裂为三部分:一为步度根集团,拥众数万落,占有云中、雁门、北地、代郡以及太原等郡的全部或一部分;一为轲比能集团,拥众十多万落,据有自高柳以东的代郡、上谷郡边塞内外各地;另外,在辽西、右北平、渔阳塞外,还有素利、弥加等原来所谓"东部大人"的若干小集团,他们也从部落大联盟分化出来,"割地统御,各有分界"。在漠北草原上形成了许多鲜卑军事小集团,直到3世纪初,史称"小种鲜卑"的轲比能逐渐强大,重新统一漠北,"尽收匈奴故地"。② 但是,这种统一的局面终因轲比能被刺杀而宣告结束。2世纪后期至3世纪前期先后出现的檀石槐军事联盟和轲比能军事联盟虽然只是暂时的统一了鲜卑,但是却在蒙古高原上产生了巨大的影响,促进了鲜卑人与蒙古高原上其他部族的融合。随着这两大鲜卑军事联盟的解体,从此,鲜卑"种落离散,互相侵伐,强者远遁,弱者请服。由是边陲差安,漠南少事,虽时颇钞盗,不能复相扇动矣"。③ "强者远遁"恰恰说明了许多势力强大的鲜卑人向着远离漠南草原的方向迁徙,因此才会出现"漠南少事"的局面。我们的史料记载的多是那些归降的"弱者",而对于远遁的"强者"则所知甚少。鲜卑人的"远遁"势必沿着欧亚草原之路向北、向西迁徙。

虽然没有直接的史料记载了鲜卑人向北方和西方的迁徙,但是从《魏书》中我们可以找到一些蛛丝马迹。《魏书·高车传》中提到了高车的两个部落——护骨和乙旃。《魏书·高车传》云:"其种有狄氏、表(袁)纥氏、斛律氏、解批氏、护骨氏、异奇斤氏。……高车之族,又有十二姓:一曰泣伏利氏,二曰吐卢氏,三曰乙旃氏,四曰大连氏,五曰窟贺氏,六曰达薄干氏,七曰阿仑氏,八曰莫允氏,九曰俟分氏,十曰副伏罗氏,十一曰乞袁氏,十二曰右叔沛氏。"护骨,在《隋书·铁勒传》中作"纥骨",正好是拓拔鲜卑宗族十

---

① 《后汉书》卷90《乌桓鲜卑列传》。
② 《三国志·魏志》卷30《乌桓鲜卑东夷传·序》。
③ 同上。

姓之一。乙旃也是拓拔鲜卑宗族十姓之一。目前许多学者都认为拓拔鲜卑宗族十姓中的这两姓来自高车的两个部落,是高车融合到拓拔鲜卑中的明证。① 其实从《魏书》相关的记载中不难看出,应该是拓拔鲜卑中的两个部落融合到高车中。要想弄清楚这个问题,首先应认真分析一下《魏书·官氏志》中的记载。《魏书》卷113《官氏志》云:

> 初,安帝统国,诸部有九十九姓。至献帝时,七分国人,使诸兄弟各摄领之,乃分其氏。自后兼并他国,各有本部,部中别族,为内姓焉。年世稍久,互以改易,兴衰存灭,间有之矣,今举其可知者。献帝以兄为纥骨氏,后改为胡氏。次兄为普氏,后改为周氏。次兄为拓拔氏,后改为长孙氏。弟为达奚氏,后改为奚氏。次弟为伊娄氏,后改为伊氏。次弟为丘敦氏,后改为丘氏。次弟为侯氏,后改为亥氏。七族之兴,自此始也。又命叔父之胤曰乙旃氏,后改为叔孙氏。又命疏属曰车焜氏,后改为车氏。凡与帝室为十姓,百世不通婚。太和以前,国之丧葬祠礼,非十族不得与也。高祖革之,各以职司从事。②

拓拔鲜卑原来有九十九姓,但是到献帝时候,"七分国人"。这里的"国人"指的是拓拔鲜卑的主体,后分为宗族十姓,而文中的"他国"则是相对"国人"而言,指的是先后进入拓拔鲜卑的其他部落(包括拓拔鲜卑之外的其他鲜卑部落和鲜卑以外的其他部族),这些部落后来称为"内姓"。显然宗族十姓和内姓是有很大区别的。宗族十姓在拓拔鲜卑中的地位是很特殊的,他们"百世不通婚,太和以前,国之丧葬祠礼,非十族不得与也"。十姓当中除了车焜氏被称为"疏属"之外,其余八姓均为献帝的至亲统领。高车诸部怎么又可能是拓拔鲜卑的宗族呢? 高车应属于"他国",高车诸部进入拓拔鲜卑后应成为"内姓",而不可能进入宗族十姓。一般认为,献帝就是2世纪中期檀石槐鲜卑军事同盟中的西部大人推演。可见,宗族十姓的确立是很早的。然而高车的"护骨氏"和"乙旃氏"最早见于《魏书》的记载,在此之前没有任何史料提到过高车中存在这样两个部落。从时间的先后顺序上也不难看出,《高车传》中提到的"护骨"和"乙旃"并非高车原有的部落,而应是拓拔鲜卑融入高车后形成的。

《魏书·序纪》记载力微在神元元年(220)遭到西部大人的内侵,力微无力抵抗,只好投靠没鹿回部大人窦宾,以至于"国民离散",这时部分的拓拔鲜卑部众亡入高车或其他部落联盟是完全有可能的。应该就是在这个时候,拓拔鲜卑宗族十姓中的纥骨与乙旃两姓中的部分人进入高车,与高车人融合后形成了高车的两个部落。融入高车的拓跋鲜卑人,应该是鲜卑军事联盟解体后向北迁徙的鲜卑人中的一部分。只是由于后来拓跋鲜卑建立了北魏政权,所以才在《魏书·官氏志》中记载了纥骨和乙旃两部的名称,而更多北迁的鲜卑其他部落的名称则湮没在历史的汪洋之中了。部分的鲜卑人与高车相融合,另一些鲜卑人则先后到达西伯利亚平原,把自己的名字留在了这里。③ 鲜卑人在西伯利亚平原上一直生活到5世纪中期,因受到阿瓦尔人的进攻才被迫向里海草原一带迁徙。据拜占庭史家普利斯科斯(Priscus)记载,公元463年前后,"Saraguri,Urogi 和 Onoguri 派遣使者到东罗马。萨比尔人的进攻使他们离开了原来居住的土地。而后者又是被阿瓦尔人驱赶,阿瓦尔人则是被居住在海边的部落所取代"。萨拉古尔人

① 姚薇元:《北朝胡姓考》,第23~24页。段连勤:《丁零、高车与铁勒》,上海人民出版社,1988年,第136~138页。
② 《魏书》卷113《官氏志》。
③ 包尔汗、冯家昇:《"西伯利亚"名称的由来》,《历史研究》1956年第10期,第57~62页。

(Saragur),乌古尔人(Ogur)和翁乌古尔人(Onogur)派遣使者到东罗马。萨比尔人的进攻使他们离开了原来居住的土地,而萨比尔人又是被阿瓦尔人驱赶,阿瓦尔人则是被居住在海边的部落所取代。乌古尔诸部原来居住的地方一般认为就是今天的西西伯利亚和哈萨克斯坦草原一带,萨比尔人受到阿瓦尔人的进攻,迫使乌古尔人越过伏尔加河,进入南俄草原,[1]终于在6世纪初定居到北高加索地区,成为影响拜占庭和波斯在高加索地区征战的一股重要的力量。而当西突厥汗国衰落后,这些西迁的鲜卑人于7世纪中期联合其他部族共同组建了可萨汗国,通过一系列的对外扩张战争,在8到10世纪称雄于南俄草原。

　　鲜卑人沿着欧亚草原的大迁徙以及由此所引起的其他游牧民族的迁徙是欧亚史上一种非常普遍的现象。普利查克把这称为"类民族迁徙的反应链",正如他所说的:"该迁徙链的决定性的启动因素是追求草原霸主权的部落组织对蒙古地区的征服,或是类似的政治组织对中国北部的占领。直到蒙古时代(13~15世纪),草原各民族仍将沿鄂尔浑河或克鲁伦河一带地区,公认为欧亚草原的统治中心。……欧亚新霸权——或相对而言,逃避蒙古旧霸权——的下一站,首先是西西伯利亚低地,而后是伏尔加盆地和北高加索(如果这个新的草原帝国打算讹诈罗马帝国的话),或先经今塞米列策(Semirece)至咸海地区的图兰(Turan)低地,此乃通向控制伊朗的第一步。"[2]

---

① *The Cambridge History of Early Inner Asia*, edited by Denis Sinor, Cambridge: Cambridge University Press, 1990, p.257.
② [美]普雷特萨克著,陈一鸣译:《"失必儿"一词之来源》,第2页。

The Interests of the Rulers, Agents and Merchants behind the Southward Expansion of the *Yuan* Dynasty

Mukai Masaki

School of Letters Osaka University, Japan

Introduction

Among the migrations of the peoples in the pre-modern Eurasian history, what common or special features can we see in the Mongolian expansion during the 13th – 14th centuries? The Mongolian expansion is one of the most complex movements in the Inner Eurasian history that brought about large-scale migrations and left a deep impression to the societies around the Eurasian landmass. On the other hand, their later expansion cannot be described only in the context of the Inner Eurasian history. Especially, the Mongol empire after Qubilai Khan's accession, i. e. the *Yuan* 元 dynasty, tried to expand their influence beyond the sea and carried out expeditions (both military campaigns and dispatches of embassy) to the regions in the maritime world such as Dai Viet, Champa, Burma, Java, Ma'abar (Colomandel coast) and Kūlam (Quilon). [1] But we can still find a lot of Inner Eurasian features in these activities.

This paper deals with the Mongolian maritime expansion during the late 13th — to the early 14th century as an example of Eurasian nomadic empires paying attention to the interests and roles of various groups such as members of the court, agents of the ruler and the followers including merchants. As many other Eurasian nomadic empires, expeditions seem to be planned and directed solely by the eminent figures at the center. But the ruling class was not monolithic and furthermore, the agents of the ruler and the followers at the peripheral regions also actively took part in the expeditions for their own interests and sometimes made a significant contribution. Nevertheless, the previous studies haven't focused enough attention to the unique features of the periphery.

As for the groups at the center, this paper will focus on the larger context of the southward expansion of the *Yuan* China and the process of the reconciliation among the interests of various groups in the background of transition of the foreign policy. As for the groups at the periphery, it will focus on the figures in the Fu-jian 福建 region where Quan-zhou 泉州 was a major international entrepôt at that time. I will study officials of the mobile secretariat who had strong connection with Qubilai and behind them was competition among

---

[1] For detailed account of the Qubilai's overseas expeditions, refer Rossabi (1988: 219 – 220).

traders of the *Nan-hai* or the Southern Sea[1] including the descendants of Arab-Persian shippers and Muslims from Central Asia each having strong interests for the commercial chance.

At the Center of the Mongol Empire in the Southward Expansion

(i) The traditional pattern of the Monglian Expansion

The topics related to the groups at the center have been well studied. According to the preceding studies, the Mongol empire's expeditions were projects that all members of the Mongolian nobility had a concern in. As Peter Jackson wrote (1999: 12).

> The Mongol conquests were regarded not as the possessions of the emperor or Great Khan (*qaghan*, *qa'an*) but as the joint property of the imperial family (*altan orugh*) as a whole, including female members.

So it was taken for granted that the spoils from a conquered territory were distributed to each branch of the Chinggisid family, whether they had taken part in the original campaign of a conquest or not. In relation to this, each representative of the armies was sent to garrison newly conquered territories or to reduce new territories.[2]

The prince in command of an expedition would be accompanied by contingents representing, or perhaps led by, princes from each of the other Chinggisid lines. The system was found to be in operation as early as Chinggis Khan's great expedition against Khwārazmshāh. This system of representation was applied when Güyüg Khan had sent general Eljigidei to Persia in 1247 and when Möngke Khan had sent Hülegü to Persia in 1254 – 1260 and sent Qubilai to Yun-nan 云南 in 1252 (Jackson1999: 22).

But the situation seems to have changed after Qubilai's conquest of the *Southern Song* 南宋. There is still left possibility that the system was operated in a more confined fashion though we have few examples of the existence of representation in the overseas expeditions. Then the previous studies have seen that the Mongolian southward expansion had more concern at the personal interests of the Khan and his advisors and many observations have been made in this direction.

(ii) Why did the Mongols proceed southward?

Regarding the aim of the overseas expeditions, several points have been proposed by Japanese scholars. For example, Prof. Sugiyama Masaaki said that the fleets sent by Qubilai to Southeast Asia were only demonstrations stimulating international trade and persuading each country to subordinate or to send a tributary

---

[1] A Chinese name of the broad ocean to the South of China roughly containing the South China Sea, Maritime Southeast Asia, sometimes extending to the Bay of Bengal, Indian ocean, Persian gulf and Swahili coast. This paper will use the term in a broad sense roughly including the seas from South China to South India. Some scholars define the term in a narrow sense or prefer the term "Southern Ocean" in a broad sense. For a detailed account on the Chinese concept of the Southern Sea or Southern Ocean, refer Wang (1958: 5 – 6), Wolters (1971: 19 – 38).

[2] The grant of appanages or domains to the members of each Chinggisid lines after the conquests of the Chin and the *Southern Song* was studied by Matsuda (1978), Li (1992), Muraoka(1997) etc.

to the *Yuan* while roughly after 1287 peaceful relations were established because of the shift of foreign policy (Sugiyama 1995: 194 – 195).

On the other hand, a specialist of Southeast Asian history Prof. Momoki Shiro said that the Central Eurasian fashion to demand substantial tributary relation and military assistance was hard to accept for the Southeast Asian countries that had been familiar with the trade leading relation under the formal subjection from the *Song* period (Momoki 1990: 245).

Despite the differences of the standpoints between two scholars, both views shared the point that the control of the trade routes was more important than the occupation of the lands. Then the next question is what meaning the grasp of the sea routes had not only for the Khan and his advisers but also for the other groups in the ruling class and around the coastal region who were concerned with the southward expeditions?

(iii) A geopolitical analysis: the shifts of the gravity in the *nanhai trade* network

In this respect, Abu-Lughod offered an interesting hypothesis. She pointed out that the "natural" role of the ports along the Straits (of Malacca; e. g. , Palembang, Jambi and so on) was that of *comprador*, a role that is both politically contingent and economically unstable. And especially in relation with Chinese maritime development, we can observe a sea-saw like transitions in the importance of the ports in the Straits.

Whenever the Chinese moved aggressively outward, the intermediary ports paradoxically became more prosperous but less important. Whenever the Chinese pulled back from the western circuit or, even worce, interdicted direct passage of foreign ships into their harbors, the ports in the straits flourished, but only because Chinese vessels took up the easternmost circuit slack by meeting their trading partners at Palembang, Kedah, or, later, Malacca (Abu-Lughod 1989: 311).

The Chinese overseas expansion and the destiny of the Straits were interrelated. Moreover, the role of *comprador* was not only for the ports of the Straits but also for those of the South China coastal region that had been the main base for the Chinese overseas endeavor. So what is crucial for the prosperity and the decline of the ports of the Straits and the South China coastal region was a shift of gravity of the whole trade network in the Maritime Asia. And it was also the case for the situation around the southward expansion of the *Yuan* dynasty.

It is said that Quan-zhou suffered the decline of the maritime trade from the early 13th century and traders there were moved to Guang-zhou. Soon after that, since Guang-zhou became the place of growing military tension and a final battle between the *Song* and the *Yuan*, the *nanhai* (the Southern Sea) trade of the two main ports in the South China coastal region should be seriously damaged in the middle of 1270s.[①] Not only did this cause the diminished trade activity of the Chinese merchants, but also invited the decreased number of

---

① As for the damage of Guang-zhou, *Da-de nan-hai-zhi* 大德南海志 6 says, "During the war of *Song* to *Yuan* transtion, countless people were injured by arrowheads and spears, abducted, captured, killed by bandits or transferred to other areas."

the trade ships visiting Chinese ports or the escape of foreign immigrants to seek a safer base for their commercial activity. And considering above-mentioned characteristics of the shifts in the maritime world, some ports on the Straits could have become their new home. [1]

In 1276, Qubilai first ordered Suo-du (Mo. Sögedü? Sogatu of *Marco Polo*: 162) 唆都 and Pu Shou-geng 蒲寿庚 to sent envoys to the kingdoms of South India and Maritime Southeast Asia. The purpose of this is obviously to revive maritime trade. His imperial edict ordered them to dispatch traders to bring Qubilai's message abroad. The edict said,

> Since every barbarian countries ranged along the Southeastern Islands are attached to loyalty, dispatch foreign traders to convey my message as follows. If you can truly come to greet me, I will show you a favor and politeness. And the traffics and trades are permitted freely in accordance with your desire. [2]

From the view point of Abu-Lughod's hypothesis, it can be understood as an attempt of the *Yuan* dynasty to take back control of trade routes for the benefit of Chinese ports. The vigor of the Chinese ports, however, would reduce (if not perfectly destroy) the importance of the Straits. So it is inevitable to bring about contradiction between the interests of the peoples of the Southern Sea and that of China including the population around the coastal region and the Mongols who wanted to extract profits from the ports.

(ⅳ) The grand overseas expedition and the "block" of Champa

In course of Qubilai's attempt, Champa appeared to be the first obstacle in a substantial way. Champa was one of the most influencial states around the Southern Seas because it controlled the main route from Quan-zhou to the Strait of Malacca though the state itself is considered to be nothing but a confederation of the small polities. In the tenth month of 1281, Qubilai assigned Suo-du, Liu Shen and Yu-hei-mi-shi (*Turk.* Yïγmïš?) as the oficials of the mobile secretariat (*xing-sheng* 行省) at Champa to undertake a preparation for the coming grand overseas expedition to the Southern Sea decided to start in the first month of 1282. Planning to mobilize 100 ships and 10 000 soldiers and sailors, Qubilai ordered the king of Champa to supply the fleets joining the expedition. But the son of Champa king rejected and arrested the embassies sent by Qubilai to further countries, which caused war against Champa then against Dai Viet who had rejected the offer of assistance to attack Champa. [3]

(ⅴ) The Bengal route and the "block" of Burma?

The southeast coastal region was not the only gateway for the *Yuan* to the outer world. Yun-nan in the

---

[1] A Similar phenomenon was seen at the rebellion of Huang Chao 黄巢 in 878 C. E. Foreigners resident at Guang-zhou were massacred and escaped abroad, then Kalaf (Keda) of Malay Peninsula flourished as a major entrepot.

[2] *Yuan shi* 10, p. 204 (the eith month of the 15th year of *Zhi-yuan* 至元 [1278] period, *Shi-zu ben-ji* 世祖纪 [Basic annals of emperor Shi-zu], Zhong-hua shu-ju 中华书局 edition).

[3] For detailed process, see Yamamoto (1950,1975).

southwestern border of the dynasty was another dynamic frontier having similar position as Fu-jian. For the *Yuan* dynasty already subjugated Tibet and Yun-nan, the *Mian* 缅国 (Burma) appeared as the only obstacle to reach the Bay of Bengal. According to the geographical source, *Dao-yi-zhi-lüe* 岛夷志略 (section of Tian-Tang 天堂: Mecca), there existed the route for Yun-nan muslim's pilgrimage to Mecca, which probably was passing through the Bay of Bengal (Wang 1981: 352; Chen 2005: 423).

The *Yuan* court undertook successive campaigns against "the kingdom of *Mian*," which were opened in 1277 by Nasr al-Dīn, a muslim official of the mobile secretariat at Yun-nan[1] and battles were recorded in 1280, 1283, 1286, 1300. [2] But the situation was not simple as seen in Chinese historical sources. It is said that the first attack was against the Pagan dynasty and the others were against *Shan* leaders who had expanded their territories and built polities in Burma. But the effect of the Mongolian incursion seems not so crucial for the decline of the Pagan dynasty as had been considered before (Lieberman 2003: 119). In any way, judging from intensive expeditions to strategically important trade areas, the *Yuan* court was trying to approach the trade routes of the Southern Sea simultaneously by both (southeast and southwest) sides of the dynasty.

(vi) When was the "Pax Mongolica" in the Southern Sea established?

When the *Yuan* was actually engaging Champa on the battle field, there was a diplomatic "war" at the same time. Qubilai sent embassies to the further areas including Cambodia 干不昔, Nakonsithammarat 探马礼, Java 爪哇, Ma'abar (?) 马八, Kūlam 俱蓝, Samudra 苏木都剌, Siam (Ayuthya?) 暹, Perlak 法里郎 (Ferlec of *Marco Polo*: 166), Aru 阿鲁, Kampei 乾伯 around 1282. They were dispatched to seek association for the grand expedition to the Southern Sea planed to start by the first month of 1282, while Champa which rejected the *Yuan*'s order of assistance also dispatched embassies to seek alliance with the surrounding kingdoms like Dai Viet (Tran Dynasty 陈朝 1225–1400), Cambodia 真腊, Java 爪哇, that had been rivals and had fought each other in the past. The *Yuan*'s "failed" overseas campaigns and the dense communications in the Southern Sea made traffics without matching the *Yuan*'s demands an accomplished fact. As a result, *de facto* trade-leading relations were reappearing in the Southern Sea.

What was important for an establishment of peaceful relation is the end of military tension between the *Yuan* and powerful kingdoms around the sea routes. Champa had been a major obstacle for the *Yuan*'s access to the Southern Sea. After the campaigns failed, the *Yuan* court could not help accepting the foreign relation in rather compromising way, which made easier for other independent polities in the Southern Sea to have trade relation with China.

From a viewpoint of the gravity in the trade network, it still meant a triumph of the *Yuan* China because if they had failed to grasp sea route substantially, now obtained safer path to the Straits while the maritime kingdoms could only content themselves in a position of *comprador* instead of the "king of the sea" or an

[1] He is a son of Sayyid Ajall Shams al-Dīn and his ancestor was said to be the prophet Muhammad's son-in-low, Alī.
[2] See *Yuan shi* 210, pp. 4655–4660 (*Wai-yi zhuan* 外夷传 [Biographies of foreign country] 3, the section of *Mian* 缅).

independent ruler of the sea routes.

Prof. Sugiyama considers that the peaceful situation was brought about around 1287 because of the shift of the foreign policy of the *Yuan* court from an aggressive to a peaceful one (1995: 195). In relation to this, it was a symbolic event that the embassies from 10 countries ranged from the east and west coast of South India to Malay Peninsula arrived in the tenth month of 1286. This was the result of Yang Ting-pi 楊庭壁's overseas mission from 1283 to travel around these countries and ask for subjection. But it is impossible to consider that the foreign policy had perfectly changed by that time only from the circumstantial evidence.

There remained another "king of the sea" in the Straits, the kingdom of Majapahit, whose king Kertanagara had been rejecting subjection and became the next target of the *Yuan*'s overseas campaign. Its strong influence on the Straits of Malacca appeared to be an obstacle of the traffic for the *Yuan* to South India or to Iran. After the *Yuan* troops were defeated at Java in 1292, peaceful relation was reestablished and there remained no substantial "block" challenging the Chinese access to the Straits. Though, it is still doubtful to consider that the stable condition of the Southern Sea was accompanied by the shift of diplomatic policy.

(vii) Demands of subjection and transition of foreign policy

The Mongols offered the subordinates a set of demands, which appeared as "six demands" in the Chinese sources on Korea and Dai Viet though a comparison of the related accounts shows that the demands were seven in all. [1] It is obvious that if the Mongols were to establish relations in any way, they must give up these demands and that Qubilai could not help to follow Chinggis in forcing the overseas polities to agree to the same demands Chinggis had set nearly half a century ago. Then, why did Qubilai had tried to keep this outdated protocols nevertheless it seems nearly impossible to apply to kingdoms of the Southern Sea?

One possibility is that Qubilai was "pretending" as if he was pursuing to get a new territory for the members of the Chinggisid family in order to win the support of the Mongolian nobility. Because Qubilai had obtained throne through a *coup d'état*, he had failed to have a broad support from members of each Chinggisid line. Though in fact, Qubilai had planed overseas expeditions not to discover a new territory but to rule the trade routes, we cannot perfectly deny the existence of the representation system. We have one weak but telling evidence. Li Heng 李恒, a military chief from the loyal family of the Tanghut kingdom, had been a representative of the family of Jöchi Qasar, a younger brother of Chinggis khan, during the early period of Qubilai's reign. Later, he joined the war against *Southern Song* and the campaigns to Japan and Dai Viet but there is no indication to tell us his role as a representative. [2]

Although a substantial campaign was never carried out after Qubilai's reign, the "hard line" was never given up until later period. Another plan of overseas campaign was discussed at the *Yuan* court soon after the death of Qubilai. The successor Temür (Cheng-zong 成宗) took up an active foreign policy. In the ninth

---

① Matsui Dai showed that the polities under the Mongol rule were required to (1) give hostage, (2) assist military operations, (3) tribute grains as land tax or military provisions, (4) build stations for the relay postal system, (5) take a census of the population, (6) accept to put *daruya*(*či*), (7) make a visit to khan and express subjection by the king (2002: 87).

② I'd like to thank Yamazaki Shinichi of Osaka University for introducing this example.

month of 1294, the very year of succession, the *Yuan* court sent embassies to Ge-lan 阁蓝 (Kūlam?). And in the tenth month, the court let the embassies of Lamuri 南巫里, Samudra 速木答剌, Malayu 继没剌矛 and Tamiang 毯阳 back to their countries. They had been invited by Yïɣmïš 也黑迷失 during the campaign against Java (Majapahit) and remained at capital because of the maritime ban. ① In the ninth month of 1295, the embassy of Java came and in the eleventh month, Tamiang, Perlak and Aru sent the King's relatives. ② In 1296, when the *Yuan* court discussed to attack the countries that had not subordinated, Karunadas 伽鲁纳答思, an Uigur Buddhist official at the court, opposed. His biography in *Yuan shi* says,

(In the 2nd year of *Yuan-zhen* 元贞 period [1296]) When the *Yuan* court discussed to mobilize the army and to attack kingdoms of Siam 暹 (Ayuthya or other polity of Thais), Luo-hu 羅斛 (Lopburi; Lochac of *Marco Polo*: 164), Ma'abar 馬八児, Kūlam 俱藍 and Samudra 蘇木都剌, Karunadas advised, "all these are tiny countries. What merit does it have if we indulgingly seize them? Mobilizing the army only means murdering the people in vain. It would be better to send messengers first to persuade them to submit reasonably. It wouldn't be too late to attack them after they rejected to submit." The emperor accepted his advise and ordered Yüe-la-ye-nu 岳剌也奴, Tie-hui 帖灰 and others to go as a messenger. As a result, they subjugated more than twenty countries. ③

In fact, on New Year's Day of 1299, Siam, Malayu (southern part of Sumatra Island), Lochac and other countries sent a tributary to the *Yuan* court. ④ Karunadas' "soft line" was followed during the reign of Hai-shan 海山 (Wu-zong 武宗)⑤ and finally came to be the formula of the dynasty as seen in *Jing-shi da-dian* 经世大典 (Compendium for governing the world)⑥ compiled in 1331,

In former times, our state was facing all directions. If there were [countries] who had not paid a courtesy visit, our state sent messenger and persuade them to subject. If there were countries that did not subject, our state attacked them.

The "soft line" was formulated and no military attack to the countries in the Southern Sea was planned

---

① *Yuan shi* 18, pp. 387 – 388 (the 31th year of *Zhi-yuan* period [1294], *Cheng-zong ben-ji*).

② *Yuan shi* 18, pp. 396 – 397 (the 1st year of *Yuan-zhen* period [1295], *Cheng-zong ben-ji*). The last three countries are on the eastern shore of Sumatra Island.

③ As for Karunadas, see Matsui (2008: 39). *Yuan shi* (134, p. 3260) says he was an Uigur and worship Tibetan Budhism. And *Jāmi ' al-tavārīkh* of Rasīd al-Dīn says that he (QRNT'S in Arabic) is from Kashmir (Boyle 1971: 302; Blochet 1911: 546). Yüe-le-ye-nu 岳乐也奴 (another variation of the same name as Yüe-la-ye-nu) was sent to Ma'abar in the seventh month of 1298 (*Yuan shi* 19, p. 405, the 2nd year of *Yuan-zhen* period, *Cheng-zong ben-ji*).

④ *Yuan shi* 20, p. 425 (the first month, the 3rd year of *Da-de* period [1299], *Cheng-zong ben-ji*).

⑤ *Yuan shi* 23, p. 517. Ga-lu-na-da-si and others required Emperor to send embassy to overseas countries Palembang, Pasai, Champa etc.

⑥ *Jing-shi da-dian* 41, p. 429 (section of "Qian-shi" 遣使 [dispatching embassies] in *Li-dian* 礼典 [Book of ritual], Si-bu cong-gan 四部丛刊 edition).

anymore even though none of them had met the original demands of subjection set by Chinggis and the *Yuan* court seemed to content with the simple expression of subjection.

To sum up above investigation on the roles and the motives of the center, it seems reasonable to conclude that the Mongolian overseas expeditions were aimed to get access to the trade route but the foreign policy was by no means monolithic even in the *Yuan* court and the measure of using military power was never perfectly given up after Qubilai's reign. The major transition to the "soft line" in the foreign policy was observed during Cheng-zong and Wu-zong's reign. On the other hand, we cannot neglect the silent pressure of the tradition of the "collectiveness" of the Mongols. In this sense, it can be said that the Mongolian southward expansion was not only a matter of Qubilai's (and the leading figures') planning and not confined to his reign. The characteristic of "collectiveness" of the Mongolian expansion is also important in a different meaning at the periphery. The Mongolian southward expansion was not only an affair of the center. The roles and interests of the followers, agents and immigrants at the periphery will be studied in the following part.

At the Periphery of the Mongol Empire in the Southward Expansion

We can see at least two sorts of groups at the periphery. The first of them are traders who became supporters or followers in the Mongolian expeditions from their own interests, the second are the agents of Khan also having their own interests. We will observe the situation of Fu-jian region introducing some figures and groups.

(i) Pu shou-geng's contribution and his local network

From a viewpoint of the role of commercialism and competition in the Mongolian expansion, the involvement of Uigur merchants in the campaign to the West of Chinggis was recently pointed out. [1] As for the Mongolian southward expansion, it has been said that the role of Muslim traders in the Southern Sea was important, among which Pu Shou-geng was said to be an exponent (e. g. Sugiyama 1995: 184 − 186).

Generally speaking, Pu Shou-geng, an influential foreign merchant of Quan-zhou, surrendered to the *Yuan* dynasty in the twelfth month of 1276 and went on to make a significant contribution in the transition from the *Song* to the *Yuan* regime. However, recent studies threw a new light on the roles and characteristic of Pu Shou-geng.

Some of the titles and authority he is considered to have held under the late *Southern Song* dynasty have now been called into question (So 2000: 108, 301 − 305). Cases of appointments of local military leaders to the post of *zhao-fu-shi* 招抚使 (pacification commissioner) of the Fu-jian region during the late *Southern Song* period suggests that Pu, a *zhao-fu-shi* of that region contemporaneously, also commanded a private

---

[1] For more detailed account of Uigur involvement and their trade network, see Moriyasu (1997) and Muraoka (2006).

militia (Mukai 2007: 69 – 71). [1] And Several branches of Pu family of Quan-zhou seemed to be granted the privilege of participating in official trade under the initiative of prime minister, Jia Si-dao 贾似道, which should form the basis of Pu's *shi-bo-shi* 市舶使 (superintendent of maritime affairs) title and 30 years of involvement in maritime trade. A late *Southern Song* official Fang Hui 方回's blame for Jia Si-dao says, [2]

> The third (of ten reasons to require Jia Si-dao's execution) is greediness . . . various Pu families 诸蒲 in Quan-zhou which had been running traders (贩舶) for 30 years accommodated with 10 million *guan* 贯 (by Jia Si-dao) and paid back a half (5 million guan) from the profit every year. It makes no matter for him to pay 800 *hu* 斛 peppers every times.

The relation between Pu families and Pu Shou-geng is obvious because the latter is also said to run trader business for 30 years. According to *Song shi* 宋史, [3] "Pu Shou-geng had been handling a profit of *fan-bo* 蕃舶 (ships engaging in foreign trade) for 30 years." Furthermore, the Pu Shou-geng formed a tie with a rich foreign merchant from the Southern Sea, Fo-lian 仏莲 through the marriage of Fo-lian and Pu's daughter.

It was crucial for Qubilai to ally with Pu Shou-geng in order to expand Mongol dominance to the maritime sphere. Pu family's trade network worked in the missions to Southeastern countries during the early years of the Qubilai's reign. As I already mentioned, Qubilai's imperial edict in 1274 ordered Pu Shou-geng and Suo-du to dispatch *fan-bo zhu-ren* 蕃舶诸人 (peoples of *fan-bo* trade) while Pu Shou-geng was said to have been handling *fan-bo* 蕃舶 trade for 30 years.

Whereas Pu shou-geng took an active role in the overseas missions for the Mongols, he was utilizing his connections with the Mongols to expand his own personal trade network. For example, in the twelfth month of 1279, returned Zhao Yu 赵玉 whom Suo-du (and Pu Shou-geng) had sent to She-po 闍婆 in the previous year. She-po was Chinese transcription for Java commonly used in the *Song* textual sources but in the sources of the *Yuan* period, Zhua-wa 爪哇 was common (Fukami 2004: 105 – 106). It seems that this Zhao Yu's mission to She-po was conducted depending on Pu Shou-geng's trade network continuing from the Song period and Pu Shou-geng seems to have had a trade relation with Java. According to Fang Hui, Pu families were engaged in pepper trade and Java was known as a major entrepot for pepper produced there and imported from India during the *Song* period (Mukai 2008: 5).

Pu Shou-geng and Suo-du sometimes tried to dispatch embassies to foreign countries by themselves. In 1280, Suo-du requested a permission to their mission to eight countries including San-fo-qi 三佛齐. [4] "San-fo-qi" is considered to be a generic name of the countries around the Straits of Malacca and, as "She-po" for

---

[1] A contemporary source shows that Pu not only owned a private fleet, but also possessed a sizable entourage consisting of "zi-nan 子男" (children) and "jia-tong 家僮" or "jia-ren 家人" (domestics, or servants with specialized skills).

[2] *Tong-jiang-ji* 桐江集 (Fang Hui's anthology) ch. 3.

[3] *Song shi* 47, p. 942 (29 of eleventh month, the first year of *Jing-yan* 景炎 period [1276], *Ying-guo-gong ben-ji* 瀛国公本纪, Zhong-hua shu-ju edition).

[4] *Yuan shi* 11, p. 225 (the eighth month of the 17th year of *Zhi-yuan* period [1280], *Shi-zu ben-ji*).

Java, commonly used by *Song* textual sources but rarely used in the sources of the *Yuan* period (Fukami 2004: 103 – 104). Utilizing the trade network from *Southern Song* period, the mission to San-fo-qi should have been conducted by merchants (probably by Pu Shou-geng). In the same year, one of Suo-du's subordinate, Gu Zong-guan 顾总管 was punished for piracy. [1] Kuwata Rokurō pointed out that this might be an explosion of his complaints against the policy of the *Yuan* court to conduct overseas missions by initiative of the center (Kuwata 1993: 143). But considering the commercial nature of the overseas missions, Gu Zong-guang's piracy could be seen as a compensation for diminished chances for their private trade under the disguise of official diplomatic missions.

Even though Qubilai rejected the propose of Suo-du and Pu Shou-geng and ordered to put missions under the initiative of central government, many of the embassies sent to these countries continued to be subordinate of Pu Shou-geng and former *Southern Song* local elites that Pu had recommended and got the *Yuan*'s official post (Mukai 2008: 9). According to *Wan-li chong-xiu quan-zhou-fu-zhi* 万历重修泉州府志 (Prefecture gazetteer of Quan-zhou), [2] "Pu Shou-geng became Zhong-shu zuo-cheng 中书左丞 after his surrender to the *Yuan* and appointed the former *Song* officials to their original post."

(ii) Mongolian officials and their connections

It is clear that under facial centralized organization, functioned Pu Shou-geng's various connections and these connections made overseas missions possible to carry on.

The alliance with a Jalayir (tribe of the Mongols) commander, Suo-du 唆都 is one of these important connection. Suo-du once engaged in suppression of disorder at south Fu-jian 福建 under the title of *xing-sheng* (mobile secretariat) and became an ally of Pu Shou-geng and conducted Qubilai's overseas missions at Quan-zhou together with Pu. As for Suo-du's connection, except for above mentioned Gu Zong-guan, There was a standing figure Yang Ting-bi 杨庭壁, who was Suo-du's former subordinate and later took long voyages to South India which led to simultaneous tributary from ten Southeast Asian — and South Indian kingdoms in 1284.

On the contrary, there had also been a gap between different connections or alliances. As well as the Suo-du / Pu Shou-geng alliance, another strong alliance in Fu-jian region was that of Mangγudai 忙兀 台, but he seems to have been a competitor rather than a collaborator. In the seventh month of the 19th year of *Zhi-yuan* 至元 period (1282), *xuan-wei* (*shi*) 宣抚 (使) (pacification commissioner) Meng Qing-yuan 孟庆元 and *wan-hu* 万户 (myriarch) Sun Sheng-hu 孙胜夫 was arrested by Mangγudai when they returned from Java. Sun was a Pu Shou-geng's subordinate and seems to have been dispatched to Java by Pu Shou-geng. [3]

Mangγudai was a Tatar (tribe of the Mongols) in origin and was assigned to *ping-zhang* 平章, the chief official of the mobile secretariat at Fu-zhou 福州, the capital of Fu-jian region. He once was the

---

[1] *Yuan shi* 11, p. 224 (the sixth month of the 17th year of *Zhi-yuan* period, *Shi-zu ben-ji*).

[2] ch. 18, *Ren-wu zhi* 人物志 (Biographies), part of the *Song* period, Zhuang Mi-shao 庄弥邵.

[3] *Yuan shi* 12, p. 244 (*Shi-zu ben-ji*).

superintendent of maritime affairs at Quan-zhou at the beginning of the Mongol rule. He later moved to Jiang-huai 江淮 region (around lower Yangze River), the economic center of whole China and the important node of financial artery connecting the South East China coastal region including Fu-jian to the empire's political center, Da-du 大都 (Beijing).

Mangγudai once advanced a suggestion about the maritime trade in 1283 though he was not in charge of maritime affairs at that time[①] and after his movement to Jiang-huai in 1284, his concern with the maritime trade could be continued in relation to his brother Jalayildai's commission of Fu-jian's salt monopoly and maritime trade from 1284 as a chief of *Fu-jian-deng-chu yan-ke shi-po du-zhuan-yun-si* 福建等处盐课市舶都转运司 (bureau of salt distribution and matirime affairs at Fu-jian) (Tsutsumi 2000: 26 - 27). It is important to discover this kind of informal connections working under the facial Chinese-style bureaucratic organization.

Mangγudai also had a connection with Shihāb al-Dīn, who was a muslim from Central Asia and a member of the group of Sangha 桑哥, one of the capable and influencial financial ministers in the early *Yuan* period. A document from the section of *shi-bo* 市舶 (maritime affairs) in *Da-yuan sheng-zheng guo-zhao dian-zhang* 大元圣政国朝典章 (*Yuan-dian-zhang* 元典章) mentioned interference in maritime trade by the combination of Mangγudai with Shihāb al-Dīn (Yokkaichi 2006: 143 - 144).

We cannot deny the possibility of a significant commercial concern behind them that try to get rid of precedent maritime commercial force from the Southern Sea. And the gap between Suo-du (with Pu Shou-geng) and Mangγudai could be just a refrain of the larger structure of commercial confliction. It is also possible to see that Mangγudai himself had an interest in maritime trade. At least, the maritime low of the early *Yuan* period did not ban the personal involvement of local officials in maritime trade only if they paid regular tax and not bother normal merchants' activities. [②]

In any way, competing among different groups made Qubilai and his brain's attempts not able to carry out without collision and adjustment. But neither of Suo-du, Pu Shou-geng nor Mangγudai had constituted perfectly independent maritime force out of central control. This is mainly because they have a strong personal tie with the Khan. For example, according to his biography, Suo-du was in *su-wei* 宿卫 (*kešig* "imperial guard") of Qubilai and at the time of appointment and assignment of several missions, he went to meet Qubilai and directly received his order. [③] It shows that his activity had the characteristic of that of agent of the Khan.

Although we cannot find a firm evidence to testify his relation with *kesig*, Mangγudai also had the characteristic of Khan's agent. His biography shows his occasional meeting with Khan and his presenting of

---

① See biography of Mang-wu-tai 忙兀台 (Mangγudai) in *Yuan shi* 131, p.3188. According to the bipgraphy of Suo-du in *Yuan shi* 129 and other sources, it seems that Bai-jia-nu 百家奴, Suo-du's son, and Pu Shi-wen 蒲师文, Pu Shou-geng's son, were in charge of maritime affairs with the title of *shi-po Ti-ju* 市舶提举 (superintendent of maritime affairs) since 1278.

② See a document dated 13th of the fourth month of the 30th year of Zhi-yuan period from the 23 articles of maritime low (shi-bo ze-fa 市舶则法) in the section of *shi-bo*, *hu-bu* 户部 8, *Yuan-dian-zhang* 22.

③ *Yuan shi* 129, pp.3150 - 3152.

pearls to his master as a courtesy of obedience. [1] These pearls were probably obtained through his commitment or involvement to the maritime trade. This kind of present and courtesy is commonly observed among Qubilai's immediate liege like Yïɣmïš, Gao Xing 高兴 and others. [2] The personal ties like *khan-kešigden* (pl. of *kešigdei*, "member of *kešig*") relation worked as a strong bond between center and periphery and make a whole system possible to work efficiently.

(iii) The Periphery and the role of commercialism

As for the commercial force behind the southward expansion, as we have seen already, Pu Shou-geng's trade network had an important role to rebuild the trade relation between the Chinese ports and that in the maritime world. Pu Shou-geng seems to have lost his strong connection with the Mongols after Suo-du's death and corruption of Suo-du's army at coastal region through the battle at Champa. [3] Pu Shou-geng's activity disappeared in the sources and the campaign to Java was conducted by the new members of the Fu-jian mobile secretariat like Yïɣmïš, Gao Xing and Shi Bi 史弼.

Even so, it is possible to consider that Pu Shou-geng quitted from the facial political circle to "camouflage" his participation in the military mission in order to carry on his business at Java and around the Straits. According to Java, Marco Polo says,

It is subject to a great king of the country, and the people of it they are all idolaters and do tribute to no man in the world. This island is full of very great wealth. They have pepper in this island and nutmegs and spikenard and galingale and cubebs and cloves and in short of all other kinds of good and dear spicery which one could find in the world. And unto this island come very great numbers of ships and of merchants who come there to trade and buy many goods there and make very great profit there and very great gain. There is so great treasure in this island that there is not a man in the world who could believe or tell or say it. Moreover I tell you that the great Kaan can never have it subjected to his rule because of the long way and for the danger that it was to sail there. And from this island the merchants of Çaiton [Quanzhou] and of Mangi [South China] have formerly drawn very vast treasure and still draw every day. And the greater part of the spices which are carried through the world are brought from this island (*Marco Polo*: 163).

The account tells us that there were many Chinese ships (probably including *fan-bo* or Pu families' trade ships) engaged in trade with Java as early as Qubilai's reign when the *Yuan*-Java formal relation was not in stable condition. We must pay attention to the force of commercialism and competition behind the Mongolian

---

[1] This kind of greeting and presenting to the lord called *a'uljamïšï* the word appears in the persian historical sources which is, according to Doerfer, derived from a Mongol word *a'ulja- ~ aɣulja-* "to greet the lord and send a present" (Honda 1991: 411 – 414).

[2] *Yuan shi* 131, p. 3199 (biography of Yi-hei-mi-shi 亦黑迷失, the 29th year of *Zhi-yuan* period [1292]), 162, p. 3804 (biography of Gao Xing, the Fall of 16th year of *Zhi-yuan* period).

[3] See *Yuan shi* 129, p. 3153 (biography of Suo-du) and Yamamoto (1975: 118).

expedition. There was Central Asian merchants' embarkation to maritime trade, especially after the conquest of the South China. According to *Yuan shi*,

'Alī 阿里 wanted to prepare ships and to participate in the troop attacking Java 爪哇 with Zhang Cun 张存 in order to visit Champa and Cambodia to persuade subjection. Give 'Alī the paiza of tiger with three pearls and Zhang Cun the one with one pearl and exempt him from debts of 3000 ding *ortoq chao* (*chao* = paper money) 斡脱钞 that his father Bu-bo 布伯 had made. ①

Here can be seen an example of *ortoq* merchant who was seeking a business chance in the campaign against Java. ②

Table 1.   Number of regular officials with Islamic name in the administrations of Fu-jian during the *Yuan* period (not including clerical officials)

	Xing-sheng；Xuan-wei-si (Mobile secretariat; Pacification office)	Su-zheng-Lian-fang-si (The surveillance office)	Du-zhuan-yun-yan-shi-si (Bureaus of salt distribution)	Shi-bo-ti-ju-si (Office of maritime affairs)
1274 – 1307	13/103	2/37	14/34	2/12
1308 – 1334	7/32	6/66	8/24	14/38
1335 – 1367	1/25	5/96		1/17
Total	21/160 13%	13/199 7%		17/67 25%

Table 2.   Number of regular officials with Islamic name in the circuits and counties of Fu-jian during the *Yuan* period (not including clerical officials)

	Lu (Circuit)			Xian (County)	
	Quan-zhou	Fu-zhou	Shao-wu	Jin-jiang	De-hua
1274 – 1307	9/35	9/35	14/34	11/53	4 /13
1308 – 1334	12/56	12/56	8/24	5/32	3 /19
1335 – 1367	2/28			1/15	2/23
Total	23 /119 19%			17/100 17%	9/55 16%

Source：*Ba-min tong-zhi* 八闽通志30, Zhi-guan 秩官, Yuan 元

---

① *Yuan shi* 17, p. 365 (6th of the seventh month in the 29th year of *Zhi-yuan* period [1292]).

② *Ortoq* is originally a Tukish word meaning "partner" (Moriyasu 1997). The merchants having a partnership with the Mongolian nobilities and carrying on commercial activities by their investment was called *ortoq*. This 'Alī could be the same person appears in *Yuan shi* 13, p. 277(sixth month in the 22th year of Zhi-yuan period[1285]) as a court merchant dispatched to Ma'abar to buy curiosities with 1000 *ding*. He was accompanied by Mas'ūd who should be a muslim merchant engaging in a long-distance trade.

Another important movement of commercial force behind the Mongolian southward expansion is the migration of Central Asian muslims. Through a statistical analysis on the number of Islamic names in the list of officials of administrations in Fu-jian region during the *Yuan* period, there are several findings as seen below. First, the number of officials bearing Islamic name is relatively high in the administrations in Fu-jian. For example, according to the table 2, the percentage of the officials with Islamic name in the circuits of Fu-jian region is 17% ~ 19%, that of counties is 16% ~ 17% while the percentage of the *hui-hui* 回回(many of them are considered to be Muslims from Khwārazm) plus *mu-su-lu-man* 木速鲁蛮 (Muslims) of the circuit of Zhen-jiang 镇江 is 13% and average of three counties in Zhen-jiang circuit is 10%. Second, although the number of high rank officials with Islamic name decreased from the middle *Yuan* period, the numbers in the administrations like *shi-po-ti-ju-si* 市舶提举司 (office of maritime affairs) and *du-zhuan-yun-yan-shi-si* 都转运盐使司 (bureaus of salt distribution) continued to be high (see Table 1). These are the administrations dealing with maritime trade and salt monopoly. It suggests that descendants of muslim officials in Fu-jian region who had originally been merchants were in charge of both tax collection and transportation of these taxes, and constituted local ruling class.

The movement of muslim migration focusing on the Fu-jian's 福建 coastal region shows that the frontier region of the *Yuan* dynasty were the places of intensive migration. Both the textual sources like Ibn Battuta's itinerary (Defrémery et Sanguinetti, t. 4: 269,274,285) and the archaeological remains discovered in various cities of either in or near the south China coastal region such as Quan-zhou 泉州, Guang-zhou 广州, Hang-zhou 杭州, Yang-zhou 扬州, San-ya 三亚 in Hai-nan Island 海南岛 testify the existence of the muslim towns in China during medieval times. Among them, the tombstones having Arabic-Persian inscriptions excavated in those South China coastal regions mainly belong to 13th – 14th centuries, so-called the Mongol period (Chen 1999). It suggests that there was intensive migration to the Southeastern frontier region at that time.

The Mongol period was the age of flourished international communication and a variety of foreign people migrated into China, and were known as *se-mu-ren* 色目人. Especially the migration of muslim officials of the Iran-Turkistan origins was crucial and they were active in financial administrative duties. They were often both merchants and officials simultaneously. One example of them is in *Gao-shi-zhuan* 高士传 (Biography of a magnificent person) in *Jiu-ling-shan-fang-ji* 19 (Si-bu cong gan edition).

(Ding) He-nian 丁鹤年 was a Westerner. Both the great-grandfather 'Alā al-Dīn and his younger brother 'Umar were the giant merchants of the early *Yuan* period. When the Shi-zu emperor tried to subjugate the Western land and suffered from discontinuity of food supply, they ran to the military camp by horse to help the army. They surrendered by their wealth. They joined the [Mongolian] army and conquered the Western and Northern countries as easy as snapping an unsound twig. The court once discussed to give 'Alā al-Dīn an official position but he would not serve because of the old age. The court gave him fields and residence and let him stay in the capital. 'Umar answered the imperial request to appoint to be an official of *xuan-wei-si* (pacification office) at somewhere ... The grand father Shams al-Dīn was appointed from a servant official of prince Bei-jin-wang 北晋王, to be a *daruyači* at the circuit of Lin-jiang 临江, ...

This illustrative story of a muslim family from the Western region (*xi-yu* 西域) is the early example of the alliance of the Mongols and commercial power and the evidence of that they had two faces as a merchant and as an official. We can find other examples of muslims who supply the Mongolian army.[1] It is easy to understand if they were originally merchants.

The muslims of Java around 15 – 16th centry were said to have migrated from Fu-jian or Yun-nan in Chinese records on Zheng-he's expedition and the Malay annals of Sěmarang and Cěrbon (Ptak 2004; Kumar 1987: 610; de Graaf and Pigeaud 1984: 2, 13 – 16). It seems possible to say that the *Chinese muslims* as a mixed or hybrid group active in Southeast Asia seen in those later sources were appeared as a result of intensive migration of the muslims into the empire's frontier regions, especially Yun-nan and Fu-jian and of the various types of exchanges between them and indigenous *Han Chinese*.

Conclusion

It is clear that the Mongols' southward expansion was not merely an attempt of Qubilai himself or of some leading figures in the central government but there are working several interests of several groups or people in the center and the periphery of the empire. The expansions in the pre-modern Eurasian history should be studied as a total of the movements and interests of the followers, the agents, the commercial forces and the immigrants both at the center and the periphery of the empire's realm.

There is an important topic left untouched in this paper, the effect of global climatic shifts on the Eurasian southward movement. It is also an important topic of comparative study because there were preceding examples of southward migration caused by the change of temperature.[2] It can be said that the Mongolian southward expansion is one such trend caused by environmental change. 13 – 14th century was a period of cold temperature and under that condition there were many places dried up and which became grassless and we can see some examples about the movement of nomadic leaders from Mongolia to North China in the *Yuan* sources.[3] In this sense, the Mongols' southward expansion was a part of larger trend of the world history that covers both central Eurasia and Maritime Asia.

---

① See an anecdote of the surrender of Bayan, the son of Sayyid Ajall, to Qubilai Khan (Boyle 1971: 287).

② E. g. the southward movement of Wuhu 五胡 tribes and the climatic change.

③ According to Prof. Li Zhi-an, there were two types of such nomadic princes. Some were settling permanently in North China. The others stayed North China temporarily (1992: 112).

Works Cited

[Japanese]

Fukami Sumio 深見純生. (2004). "Gendai no marakka kaikyō: Tsūro ka kyoten ka 元代のマラッカ海峡—通路か據点か— (Passage or Emporium?: The Malacca Straits during the *Yuan* Period)." *Tōnan ajia: rekishi to bunka* 東南アジア—歴史と文化—(Southeast Asia: History and Culture) 33: 100-118.

Honda Minobu 本田實信. (1991). *Mongoru jidai-shi kenkyū* モンゴル時代史研究 (Studies on the Mongol Domination). Tokyo: Tōkyō daigaku shuppankai 東京大学出版会.

Kuwabara Jituzō 桑原隲藏. (1989). *Hojukō no jiseki* 蒲壽庚の事蹟. Tokyo: Heibonsha 平凡社 (Rpt. of *Sō-matsu no teikyo-shihaku saiiki-jin hojukō no jiseki* 宋末の提擧市舶西域人蒲壽庚の事蹟. shanhai tōa-kōkyūkai 上海東亜裕攻究會. 1941).

Kuwata Rokurō 桑田六郎. (1993). "Gensho no nankai keiryaku nitsuite 元初の南海経略について (Maritime Military Expeditions of the Early Yuan Dynasty)." *Nankai tōzai kōtsūshi ronkō* 南海東西交通史論考 (*Studies on the History of East-West Maritime Trade*). Tōkyō: Kyūko shoin 汲古書院: 139-150.

Matsui Dai 松井太. (2002). "Mongoru-jidai uigurisutan no zeieki-seido to chōzei-shisutemu モンゴル時代ウイグリスタンの税役制度と徴税システム(Taxation and Tax-collecting Systems in Uiguristan under Mongol Rule)." *Hikokutō-shiryō no sōgōteki-bunseki ni-yoru mongoru-teikoku — Genchō no seiji/ keizai-shisutemu no kisoteki-kenkyū* 碑刻等史料の総合的分析によるモンゴル帝国・元朝の政治・経済システムの基礎的研究 (Research on Political and Economic Systems under Mongol Rule)(Report of the Scientific Research Project, Grant-in-Aid JSPS, Basic Research (B)(1), 2000-2001), 87-128.

——. (2008). "Tōzai-chagatai-kei sho-ōke to uiguru-jin chibetto-bukkyōto: Shin-hatsugen mongoru-go monjo no saikentō kara 東西チャガタイ系諸王家とウイグル人チベット仏教徒—新発現モンゴル語文書の再検討から—(The Chaghataids and Uigur-Tibetan Buddhists: Re-examination on a Mongolian Decree Newly Discovered at Dunhuang)." *Nairikuajia-shi kenkyū* 内陸アジア史研究(*Inner Asian Studies*) 23: 25-48.

Matsuda Kōichi 松田孝一. (1978). "Mongoru no kanchi tōchi seido: bunchi bunmin seido wo chusin toshite モンゴルの漢地統治制度—分地分民制度を中心として—." *Machikaneyama Ronsō* 待兼山論叢 11: 33-54.

Momoki Shirō 桃木至朗. (1990). "10-15 seiki-no nankai-kōeki to vetonamu: chū-etsu kankei heno ichi-shikaku 一〇—一五世紀の南海交易とヴェトナム—中越関係への一視角—." *Series sekaishi heno toi 3: Idō to kōryū* シリーズ世界史への問い3 移動と交流. Tōkyō: Iwanami-shoten 岩波書店, 225-256.

Moriyasu Takao 森安孝夫. (1997). "Orutoku to uiguru shōnin オルトク(斡脱)とウイグル商人." *Kinsei kindai chūgoku oyobi shūhen-chiiki niokeru shominzoku no idō to chiiki-kaihatsu* 近世・近代中国および周辺地域における諸民族の移動と地域開発 (Report of the Basic Research (B) (2), 1995-1996, Grant-in-Aid for Scientific Research). Nara: Tenrijihōsha 天理時報社, 1-48.

Mukai Masaki 向正樹. (2007). "Hojukō gunji-shūdan to mongoru kaijō seiryoku no taitou 蒲壽庚軍事集団とモンゴル海上勢力の臺頭(The Role of Pu Shougeng's Private Militia in the Emergence of Mongol Sea Power)." *Tōyōgakuhō* 東洋学報 89.3: 67-96.

——. (2008). "Kubirai-cho shoki nankai-shōyu no jitsuzō: Senshū ni-okeru gunji-kōekishūdan to konekushon クビライ朝初

期南海招諭の實像―泉州における軍事・交易集團とコネクション―(Another Aspect of the Legation to the Southern Seas during the Early Part of Khubilai's Reign: Military and Trade Groups and Their Connections)." *Tōhōgaku* 東方学 106: 127 - 145.

Muraoka Hitoshi 村岡倫. (1997). "Gendai kōnan tōkaryō to mongoria no yūboku shūdan 元代江南投下領とモンゴリアの遊牧集団." *Ryūkoku kiyō* 龍谷紀要 18.2: 13 - 30.

――. (2006). "Chinkai-tonden to chōshun-shinjin arutai-goe no michi: Haruzan-shiregu iseki-chōsa no sōkatsu チンカイ屯田と張春真人アルタイ越えの道―ハルザン・シレグ遺蹟調査の総括―." *Chūsei hokutō-ajia kōko-iseki no dēta-bēsu no sakusei wo kiban to suru kōko-gaku rekishi-gaku no yūgō* 中世北東アジア考古遺蹟のデータベースの作成を基盤とする考古学・歴史学の融合 (Report of the Project 2004 - 2005, Chūsei kōkogaku no sōgō-teki kenkyū: Gaku-yūgō wo mezashita sin-ryōiki sōsei, 中世考古学の総合的研究―学融合を目指した新領域創生―, Grant-in-Aid for Scientific Research, JSPS). Kyōto, 35 - 45.

Sugiyama Masaaki 杉山正明. (1995). *Kubirai no Chōsen* クビライの挑戦. Tokyō: Asahi Shinbunsha 朝日新聞社.

Tsutsumi Kazuaki 堤一昭. 2000. "Daigen-urusu chika kōnan shoki seiji-shi 大元ウルス治下江南初期政治史." *Tōyōshi Kenkyū* 58 (4): 1 - 32.

Yamamoto Tatsurō 山本達郎. (1950). *Annanshi kinkyū* 安南史研究 Vol. I, Tokyo: Yamakawa Shuppansha 山川出版社.

Yamamoto Tatsurō (ed.). (1975). *Betonamu chugoku kankeishi* ベトナム―中国関係史. Tokyo: Yamakawa shuppansha.

Yokkaichi Yasuhiro. (2006). "Genchō nankai kōeki keiei kou: Monjo gyōsei to senka no nagare kara. 元朝南海交易經営考―文書行政と錢貨の流れから―(The YUAN Government's Control and Management of the Nanhai Trade: from the aspect of transmission of formal documents and flow of trading capital)." *Kyūshū daigaku tōyōshi ronshū* 九州大学東洋史論集 (Oriental Studies) 34: 133 - 156.

[Chinese]

Chen De-zhi 陈得芝. (2005). "Yuan-dai hai-wai jiao-tong de fa-zhang yu ming-chu Zheng-he xia-xi-yang 元代海外交通的发展与明初郑和下西洋." *Meng-yuan-shi yan-jiu cong-gao* 蒙元史研究丛稿. by Chen De-zhi. Beijing: Ren-min chu-ban-she 人民出版社. 411 - 423 (orig. in Zheng-he xia-xi-yang lun-wen-ji 郑和下西洋论文集. Vol. 2. Nan-jing da-xue chu-ban-she 南京大学出版社. 1985).

Li Zhi-an 李治安. (1992). *Yuan-dai fen-feng zhi-du yan-jiu* 元代分封制度研究. Tianjin: Tianjin gu-ji chu-ban she 天津古籍出版社. (rpt. *Nan-hai da-xue Shi-xue jia lun-cong* 南开大学史学家论丛. Vol. 3. Ed. Liu Ze-hua 刘泽华. Beijing: Zhong-hua shu-ju 中华书局. 2007).

Wang Da-yuan 汪大渊. (1981). *Daoyi Zhilüe Xiaoshi* 岛夷志略校释. Ed. Su Ji-qing 苏继庼. Beijing: Zhonghua Shuju.

[Others]

Abu-Lughod, Janet. L. (1989). *Before European Hegemony: The World System A. D. 1250 - 1350*. New York: Oxford University Press.

Blochet, E. (ed.). (1911). *Djami el-Tévarikh: Histoire générale du monde, par Fadl Allah Rashid Eddin; Tarikhi moubarek-i Ghazani, Histoire des Mongols*, Leiden-London: Brill.

Boyle, John Andrew. (1971). *The Successors of Genghis Khan: Translated from the Persian of Rashīd al-Dīn*. New York: Columbia University Press.

Chen Da-sheng et Kalus, Ludvik. (1991). *Corpus d'Inscriptions Arabes et Persanes en Chine 1: Province de Fu-Jian (Quan-*

zhou, *Fu-zhou*, *Xia-men*), Paris.

Defrémery, C. et Sanguinetti (trans. et eds.). (1853 – 58). *Voyages d'Ibn Battûta*, tome1 – 4, Paris.

de Graaf, H. J. ; Pigeaud, Th. G. Th. (1984). *Chinese Muslims in Java in the 15th and 16th Centuries: The Malay Annals of Sĕmarang and Cĕrbon*, Monash Papers on Southeast Asia No. 12.

Jackson, Peter. (1999). "From *Ulus* to Khanate: The Making of the Mongol States c. 1220 – c. 1290." *The Mongol Empire and its Legacy*. Ed. Reuven Amitai-Preiss and David O. Morgan. Brill.

Kumar, Ann L. (1987). "Islam, the Chinese, and Indonesian Historiography: A Review Article." *Journal of Asian Studies* 46: 603 – 616.

Lieberman, Victor. (2003). *Strange Parallels: Southeast Asia in Global Context, c. 800 – 1830 Vol. 1: Integration on the mainland*, New York: Cambridge University Press.

Liu Xin-ru and Lynda Norene Schaffer. (2007). *Connections Across Eurasia: Transportation, Communication, and Cultural Exchange on the Silk Roads*. New York: McGraw-Hill.

Ptak, Roderich. (2004). *China, the Portuguese, and the Nanyang: Oceans and Routes, Regions and Trade (C. 1000 – 1600)*. Variorum.

Polo, Marco. (1938). *Marco Polo; The Description of the World*. 2Vols. trans. and annot. by Moule, A. C. Moule and Paul Pelliot. London: Routledge.

Rossabi, Morris. (1988). *Khubilai Khan: His Life and Times*. University of California Press.

Shaffer, Lynda. (1994). "Southernization." *Journal of World History* 5: 1 – 21.

So, Billy K. L. (2000). *Prosperity, Region, and Institutions in Maritime China: The South Fukien Pattern, 946 – 1368*, Cambridge (Massachusetts) and London: Harvard University Press.

Wang Gung-wu. (1958). "The Nanhai Trade: A Study of the Early History of Chinese Trade in the South China Sea." *Journal of the Malayan Branch of the Royal Asiatic Society* 31(2): 1 – 135.

Wolters, O. W. (1970). *The Fall of Srivijaya in Malay History*. Kuala Lumpur: Oxford University Press.

Sarmatians-People from Central Eurasian Steppes-On their Westernmost Territory

Halina Dobrzańska

Institute of Archaeology and Ethnology, Polish Academy

of Sciences, Cracow Branch, Poland

The Sarmatians were nomads of Iranian origin who had formerly inhabited the steppes beyond Volga river and the Aral-Ural steppes. At the beginning of the 2nd century BC Sarmatians occupied the territory between Volga and Don rivers and they started to move westwards to the north coast of the Black See. Their culture flourished on the steppes of the northwestern part of the Pontic See in the 1st century AD.

Several Sarmatian waves from the North Pontic steppes formed the Sarmatian culture on the Great Hungarian Plain (Alföld) between the 1st century AD and the beginning of the 5th century AD. It is generally accepted that Sarmatians who moved to Alföld had lost individual character of their culture.

Main issues of the paper are related to activity of Sarmatians on the margin of their main areas in Central and Eastern Europe as contacts and interactions between Sarmatians and Germanic peoples, Dakians and other tribes. In the Polish area (Przeworsk culture) we can distinguish two main periods basing on archaeological evidences. The first one spans the second half of the 1st century AD, the second period encompasses the second half of the 2nd century to the beginning of the 4th century AD.

The first one spans the second half of the 1st c. A. D. , especially the last quarter. Among the artefacts belonging to that period the following must be mentioned: a gold necklace and an assemblage of wheel-made vessels found in the high-status elite grave in Giebułtów; a silver plate and wheel-made vessels from the richly furnished burial of a warrior, who was also provided with a bow, found in Sandomierz-Krakówka and comparable to the high-status elite grave in Giebułtów; and the coins from the incompletely preserved hoard in Gorlice-Glinik Mariampolski. All of them belong to the so-called "valuable objects", or "valuables". These are the finds that point to some contacts between the social elites of the nomadic Sarmatians (as they resemble the rich burials of the Porogi type) and the local people of the Przeworsk Culture. The artefacts under discussion undoubtedly show that there existed some links with the North Pontic region. The accumulating archaeological evidence of close chronology might reflect the events that occurred only a little earlier. It is at the beginning of the last quarter of the 1st c. that we witness the decline of a tribal political body (a proto-state) founded by King Pharzoios around 49 A. D. , and since 70 ruled by his successor, Inismeos. The royal seat was in Olbia. We know from the writings of Dio Chrysostomos, a Greek philosopher who arrived in Olbia in 83 A. D. , that the city was already "free" from "Scythian" rulers (SHCHUKIN 1989B, 333 – 324). Thus the contacts between the population of the Przeworsk Culture and the Sarmatians, who must have been among the tribes unified by King Pharzoios, occurred during the period of the decline of the Sarmatian rulers in Olbia, or in other words during the decline of the proto-state political structure founded by King Pharzoios. It is therefore conceivable that it was precisely in the territories of Southern Poland that the Sarmatian rulers sought allies at the beginning of the last quarter of the 1st c. , while they were striving to preserve the unity of their proto-state. It is equally possible that there were also peaceful contacts, the aim of which was to broaden spheres of influence and to develop trade relations.

The second period encompasses the second half of the 2nd c. and particularly the first three decades of the 3rd c.

In comparison to the first period, the contacts between the local community of the Przeworsk Culture and the Sarmatians were broader. Among the Przeworsk finds we observe a bronze fibula (A VII type) identified as "Sarmatian" and worn by women as a part of their clothing. Some of those fibulas were locally made of iron, a metal often used by the population of the Przeworsk Culture. The heads of weapons with wooden shafts are often carved with Sarmatian tamga-signs which must have been adopted from the North Pontic cultural milieu. However, in accordance with the local custom, they were carved on weapons. To complement the image, we could point to some characteristics of steppe cultures, such as a burial with a horse found in the cemetery in Grzybów and the arrowheads that were found on the same site. All these occurrences might have been a consequence of the turmoil caused by the Marcomanic Wars and the resulting migrations of various peoples.

The majority of the above-mentioned facts must have been synchronous with the appearance of the Goths in the North Pontic region, which probably occurred at the beginning of the 3rd c. (SULIMIRSKI 1979, 146; MĄCZYŃSKA 1996, 61, 289). In the face of the "Gothic" invasions into the Sarmatian territories in Ukraine and Moldavia, the people of the Przeworsk Culture living in South and Central Poland and the Sarmatians living in the basins of the Prut and Dniester rivers might have drawn closer together. Neither can we reject the possibility that at that time there were small groups of Sarmatians inhabiting the territories of the Przeworsk Culture and undergoing assimilation in the local cultural environment.

We must emphasize that in the existing archaeological sources there is better evidence for contacts between the community of the Przeworsk culture and the Sarmatians occupying the northwestern part of the Black Sea basin than with those living on the Great Hungarian Plain. In this context, we ought to draw particular attention to a shield-shaped brooch, covered with white enamel and decorated with the image of a stag, found in grave 345 at Grabice, the cemetery of the Luboszyce Culture (DOMAŃSKI 1992, 78, rys. 1: 10, 79), which can be dated to the times of the Marcomanic Wars or shortly thereafter. Similar brooches with the image of a deer are known in the culture of the Sarmatian Jazyges who occupied the Great Hungarian Plain (VADAY 1989, 82 – 83, 306, Abb. 14: 11). As far as contacts between the Sarmatians and the Masłomęcz group in southeastern Poland, Kokowski (KOKOWSKI 1998, 18) has placed them in the 2nd to

4th c. and related them to the Jazyges.

A lack of interest among Polish researchers in the problems concerning Sarmatians within the context of the culture studies of communities inhabiting our territories during the Roman Period has resulted in an unsatisfactory state of knowledge concerning contacts between the tribes living in the widely-understood northwestern region of the Black Sea and the Great Hungarian Plain. Improved knowledge of those contacts depends on further fieldwork and studies on hitherto unpublished or wrongly interpreted archaeological sources from the territory of Poland. It is also contingent on progress in the study of Sarmatian peoples inhabiting the northern and northwestern territories of the Black Sea basin and the Great Hungarian Plain. In the context of our discussion, it is of particular interest how the Sarmatians related to a cultural milieu that was alien to them, a process that was accompanied by the tendency to adopt some of the alien elements.

九、十世纪西域北道的粟特人

荣新江

北京大学中国古代史研究中心

从公元 3 世纪到公元 10 世纪,中亚河中地区的粟特人大量东迁,在丝绸之路沿线建立殖民聚落和贸易网络,控制了陆上丝绸之路的贸易。同时,随着大量粟特人及其后裔在移民当地入仕于各级军政部门,对西域、北亚、中原王朝的政治进程都有程度不等的影响,也给这些地区的社会生活和宗教文化吹拂了一阵阵强劲的"胡风"。

最近十多年来,笔者在前辈学者研究的基础上,利用近年来大量公布的胡语文书、敦煌吐鲁番汉文文献,中原发现的墓志、石椁或石榻围屏的图像材料等,努力追索粟特人的踪迹,力图把零散的信息集中在一起,构筑粟特人的迁徙路线、聚落分布和贸易网络。笔者就此问题先后发表《古代塔里木盆地周边的粟特移民》[①](后改订为《西域粟特移民考》[②])、《北朝隋唐粟特人之迁徙及其聚落》[③]、《西域粟特移民聚落补考》[④]、《北朝隋唐粟特人之迁徙及其聚落补考》[⑤]、《魏晋南北朝隋唐时期流寓南方的粟特人》[⑥]等专论,还有一些相关的文章[⑦]。但由于资料分散,新材料不断涌现,所以这项工作仍在进行中,还有一些区域没有得到充分的考察。

本文所探讨的九、十世纪西域北道粟特人的活动情形,就是这项努力的一部分。

一、安史之乱后粟特人没有退出西北的历史舞台

安史之乱不仅是中国历史的一个分水岭,也对入华粟特人产生了巨大的影响。其中有关他们在中原王朝的情形,我在《安史之乱后粟特胡人的动向》一文中有详细的分析,主要是想说明,由于发动叛乱的安禄山、史思明都是出身粟特的胡人,所以在唐朝平定安史之乱后,中原地区弥漫着一种批评"胡化"的风潮,胡人也受到不同程度的冲击,于是利用改姓改宗、移民他乡、隐瞒祖籍等方式,来磨灭自身的胡人特征,有的则前往河北三镇,在安史部将的藩镇中求得生存的空间[⑧]。

---

① 《西域研究》1993 年第 2 期,第 8～15 页。

② 马大正等编《西域考察与研究》,新疆人民出版社,1994 年,第 157～172 页。收入《中古中国与外来文明》,北京:三联书店,2001 年,第 19～36 页。

③ 初刊于北京大学中国传统文化研究中心编《国学研究》第 6 卷,北京大学出版社,1999 年,第 27～85 页;收入《中古中国与外来文明》,第 37～110 页。

④ 《西域研究》2005 年第 2 期,第 1～11 页。

⑤ 《欧亚学刊》第 6 辑,中华书局,2007 年 6 月,第 165～178 页。

⑥ 韩昇编《古代中国:社会转型与多元文化》,上海人民出版社,2007 年 12 月,第 138～152 页。

⑦ 荣新江:《隋及唐初并州的萨保府与粟特聚落》,《文物》2001 年第 4 期,第 84～89 页;又《新出吐鲁番文书所见的粟特人》,《吐鲁番学研究》2007 年第 1 期,第 28～35 页。

⑧ 纪宗安、汤开建主编《暨南史学》2,暨南大学出版社,2003 年 12 月(2004 年 4 月),第 102～123 页。

至于唐朝的西北地区,由于安史之乱后吐蕃陆续占领了陇右和河西东部,阻断了唐朝与河西西部、西域地区的往来,中原地区那种排斥胡人、胡化的风潮,对于西北地区并没有特别明显的影响,胡人仍然在这个他们原本拥有相当势力的地域内,发挥着自己的作用。

敦煌留下的材料较多,因此我们知道即使在786年吐蕃占领敦煌以后,当地的粟特人仍然保持着相当的势力,显然是粟特后裔的康再荣曾任沙州大蕃纥骨萨部落使,可见粟特上层人士在吐蕃时代的敦煌,仍然占据着很高的行政地位①。

在西域地区,情形应当也和敦煌相似,只是我们目前看到的材料不如敦煌文书那么多而已。

在吐蕃阻断西域经河陇到中原的通道以后,西域的唐朝军队仍然在坚守。十多年中,唐朝并不知道西域的唐朝守军的情形,也不知道安西、北庭两镇节度使都换了哪些人。

《资治通鉴》卷二二七德宗建中二年(781)六月条记载:

> 北庭、安西自吐蕃陷河、陇,隔绝不通,伊西、北庭节度使李元忠,四镇留后郭昕帅将士闭境拒守,数遣使奉表,皆不达,声问绝者十馀年。至是,遣使间道历诸胡自回纥中来,上嘉之。秋,七月,戊午朔,加元忠北庭大都护,赐爵宁塞郡王;以昕为安西大都护、四镇节度使,赐爵武威郡王;将士皆迁七资。元忠姓名,朝廷所赐也,本姓曹,名令忠;昕,子仪弟之子也。

笔者颇疑这里的北庭节度使曹令忠原本是粟特曹国人的后裔,原因是如果他是一个汉族出身的将领,唐朝没有必要让他改从皇家的李姓,只有这个曹姓是出身胡族的曹姓,才有可能像武威的安氏那样,改作李姓。据日本有邻馆藏《唐开元十六年(728)庭州金满县牒》,开元中庭州郭下的金满县三分之一的人口是兴胡②,即粟特商胡,这为曹令忠可能为粟特人的后裔提供了某些背景。不过他作为北庭节度使这样的高官,完全可能来自西北其他地区。

786年,吐蕃占领敦煌以后,开始向西域进军。唐朝的西域守军在漠北回鹘汗国的帮助下,奋力抵抗。791年,吐蕃与回鹘在北庭发生激烈的争夺战。虽然北庭之战中回鹘失败,但其后不久,回鹘即打败吐蕃,控制了天山东部地区,从北庭、高昌,一直到焉耆、龟兹,均纳入漠北回鹘汗国势力范围③。到回鹘保义可汗在位时期(808~821),回鹘的势力范围一直沿塔里木盆地北缘扩张到疏勒(今喀什)甚至葱岭以西。于是,回鹘汗国也把自己信奉的摩尼教的势力,推广到这些新占领的地域。

德国吐鲁番探险队所获编号为 M 1 的中古波斯语《摩尼教赞美诗集》(*Mahrnāmag*)跋文中,罗列了保义可汗时期漠北回鹘大量的王族成员(可汗和王子们)、与王族密切相关的宰相权臣,以及北庭、高昌、龟兹(包括伕沙和拨换)、焉耆、于术等地一些官员、贵族或地方首领的名称,其中个别人物是摩尼教的所谓"听者首领"(niyōšāgčān),而大多数是一般的听者,即普通的摩尼教信众。从人名的拼写可以看出塔里木盆地北沿各城镇中的上层人士有回鹘人、汉人、粟特人、波斯人等。过去,笔者曾经利用这条史料来

---

① 郑炳林:《吐蕃统治下的敦煌粟特人》,《中国藏学》1996年第4期;此据《敦煌归义军史专题研究》,兰州大学出版社,1996年,第374~390页;又《〈康秀华写经施入疏〉与〈炫和尚贷卖胡粉历〉研究》,《敦煌吐鲁番研究》第3卷,1998年,第191~208页。
② 《北朝隋唐粟特人之迁徙及其聚落》,《中古中国与外来文明》,第49~50页。
③ 森安孝夫:《增补:ウィグルと吐蕃の北庭争夺战及びその后の西域情势について》,流沙海西奖学会编:《亚洲文化史论丛》第3卷,东京,1979年,第201~226页。

论证上述地区粟特人的存在,但没有具体列举名表中哪些是粟特人。① 王媛媛在她的博士论文《从波斯到中国:摩尼教在中亚和中国的传播(公元 3—11 世纪)》中,在缪勒(F. W. K. Müller)、博伊斯(Mary Boyce)、克林凯特(H.-J. Klimkeit)和 D. Durkin-Meisterernst 转写、翻译的基础上,把这个重要的跋文做了全部的汉译,为我们提供了一份极其重要的原始材料的完整汉译。② 我这里把她整理的各个城镇中摩尼教信徒名表中属于粟特人名的部分摘出,以见当时粟特人的情况:

(1)在北庭部分(除回鹘王室成员外)所列 9 人中,有如下 2 名粟特人:

mašiyān 蜜始延(粟特人名)

zāryūd 座利佑(粟特人名)

(2)在高昌部分列举的 24 人中,有 9 位拥有纯粟特式的人名,另有 1 位是伊朗语的人名,估计也是粟特人:

wiγašemāx 于贺施莫(粟特人名)

wanōmāx 越奴莫(粟特人名)

wanōšēr 越怒失(伊朗人名)

pūtyān 伏帝延(粟特人名)

γāw pāq 豪白(粟特人名)

dšāpat 地舍拨(非摩尼教范畴的粟特式人名)

yišōwarz 夷数越寺(粟特人名)

māxyān 莫贺延(粟特人名)

bändäk 槃陀(粟特人名)

aspast 安萨波悉(粟特人名)

(3)龟兹包括伕沙和拨换,共 25 人,其中 16 位是粟特人:

xumār čör 呼末啜(粟特人名)

yišōwarz 夷数越寺(粟特人名)

βagerēz 薄列(粟特人名)

kāyfarn 继芬(粟特人名)

dšāpat 地舍拨(粟特人名)

freštwarz čapiš 拂夷瑟越寺车鼻施(粟特人名)

tsu silang 曹侍郎(粟特人名)

gōtam 胡(或俱)耽(印度式人名,但可能为粟特人所借用,实为一粟特人名)

nawemāq 怒莫(粟特人名)

qazān 诃瓒(粟特人名)

zuānak 如缓诺(粟特人名)

① 《西域粟特移民聚落考》,《中古中国与外来文明》,第 29~34 页。
② 王媛媛:《从波斯到中国:摩尼教在中亚和中国的传播(公元 3—11 世纪)》,北京大学历史系博士论文,2006 年 6 月。在人名的汉字构拟上,日本京都大学的粟特文专家吉田丰教授和笔者本人都提供了帮助。王媛媛近刊《中古波斯文〈摩尼教赞美诗集〉跋文译注》,即 M 1 跋文的转写、翻译和注释,文载朱玉麒主编:《西域文史》第 2 辑,北京:科学出版社,2007 年 12 月,第 129~153 页。

βagežwān 薄如缓(粟特人名)

dēn frād šādak 电拂剌沙陀(粟特人名)

wiɣašefarn 于贺施芬(粟特人名)

βagefarn 薄芬(粟特人名)

βagebīrt 薄毗(粟特人名)

（4）焉耆部分共32人，可以看作是粟特人的有13位：

yišōyān 夷数延(粟特人名)

satōyān 萨吐延(粟特人名)

rōxšyān 阿了黑山延(粟特人名)

byāmanwarz čör ïnanču 浮夜门越寺啜伊难珠(粟特人名)

rēžyān il-tutgu wančīk 列而延颉咄吐胡缓职(粟特人名)

māqfarn 莫芬(粟特人名)

tsu pangwan 曹判官(粟特人名)

bōg 仆(粟特人名)

lāfarn 罗芬(粟特人名)

zernwāk 绝怒(或射怒迦)(粟特人名)

yāxē 也希(粟特人名)

tograk 笃勒(突厥人名)

fattaq 发铎(伊朗人名)

（5）于术部分共22人，粟特人有15位，占大多数：

anžirki 安日鸡(汉化粟特人名)

naweyān 怒延(粟特人名)

ālāu 安老(汉化粟特人名)

wiɣaše 于贺施(粟特人名)

xūnzāk 昆昨(粟特人名)

nawefarn 怒芬(粟特人名)

wisāx 于索(粟特人名)

wiɣašefarn 于贺施芬(粟特人名)

βag-anut 薄贺讷(粟特人名)

tūnak wahman-čör 顿诺于呼嘎啜(伊朗人名)

tišfarn 呬尸潘(粟特人名，其身份是医生、抄写人)

yišōzēn 夷数前(粟特人名)

wāsēndan 咮辛檀(族属不明)

βāmyān 凡延(粟特人名)

salīgām qüilčör 萨利甘(?)阙啜(突厥人名)

这个名表要分析的方面很多，这里先指出两点：第一，表中大量粟特式人名的存在，说明了塔里木盆地北沿各绿洲城镇中居住着大量的粟特人。第二,有些粟特人的名字前面有汉姓,拥有汉姓显示了他们一定程度的汉化。

二、活跃在西州回鹘王国的粟特人

840 年,漠北回鹘汗国破灭,其中相当一部分部众随庞特勤西迁天山东部地区。大中二年(848),沙州张议潮率众起义,赶走吐蕃守将,收复瓜、沙二州,遣使前往唐朝都城长安报捷,沙州使者于大中五年(851)方才到达长安。同年冬,唐朝下《沙州专使押衙吴安正等二十九人授官制》,文字出自杜牧。在杜牧的《樊川文集》卷二十中,上述《授官制》的前面,还收录了一首《西州回鹘授骁卫大将军制》,现抄录如下:

> 敕:古者天子守在四夷,盖以恩信不亏,羁縻有礼。《春秋》列潞子之爵,西汉有隰阴之封,考于经史,其来尚矣。西州牧守颉干(于)伽思、俱宇合、逾越密施、莫贺都督、宰相安宁等,忠勇奇志,魁健雄姿,怀西戎之腹心,作中夏之保障。相其君长,颇有智谋。今者交臂来朝,稽颡请命。丈组寸印,高位重爵,举以授尔,用震殊邻。无忘敬恭,宜念终始。可云麾将军、守左骁卫大将军、〔员〕外置同正员,馀如故。[①]

拥有着颉于伽思(il ügäsi)、俱宇合(külüg alp)、逾越密施(ügämïs)、莫贺都督(baγa tutuq)、宰相等一系列回鹘文高级官员头衔的安宁,是当时的西州牧守,即西州(吐鲁番)地区的最高首领,从他的姓来看,无疑是出身安国(布哈拉)的粟特后裔。

对于安宁的归属,主要观点有二:一种观点认为安宁系由住在焉耆的庞特勤派遣治理西州的,[②]另一种认为安宁受沙州张议潮控制。[③] 笔者曾在《归义军史研究》中做过分析:"如果安宁果真是庞特勤的属部,此次西州使者入朝,应当已经把庞特勤的消息报告给唐朝,但据《唐大诏令集》卷一二八所载《大中十年二月议立回鹘可汗诏》,唐朝在大中十年方才得到安西庞特勤的消息。因此,安宁不应是庞特勤的部属。从西州此前的历史背景来看,安宁等很可能是原漠北回鹘汗国的守土封臣。"[④]

虽然漠北的回鹘汗国已经在 840 年被黠戛斯击破,但这个冲击可能没有马上波及到西域的天山东部地区。安宁作为回鹘汗国的西州牧守,也就是吐鲁番地区的最高行政长官,拥有宰相这样的高级称号,说明他在回鹘汗国当中并非等闲之辈。大概在知道漠北的汗国破灭以后,他追寻沙州张议潮入朝唐朝,希望得到唐朝的支持。

大中五年后的西州情形没有史料记载,到咸通七年(866)二月,北庭回鹘仆固俊尽取西州、北庭、轮台、清镇等城,"胡汉皆归伏",[⑤]于是"使达干米怀玉朝",[⑥]入唐朝报捷。一般认为,仆固俊才是西州回鹘

① 《樊川文集》,上海古籍出版社,1987 年,第 304~305 页。
② 森安孝夫:《ウイグルの西迁についつ》,《东洋学报》第 59 卷 1.2 号,1977 年,第 120 页。
③ 刘美崧:《论归义军与回鹘关系中的几个问题》,《中南民族学院学报》1986 年第 3 期,第 131 页。
④ 荣新江:《归义军史研究——唐宋敦煌历史考索》,上海古籍出版社,1996 年,第 354 页。
⑤ 《资治通鉴》卷二五〇咸通七年春二月《通鉴考异》引《实录》。
⑥ 《新唐书》卷二一七下《回鹘传》。

王国的真正创立者。在仆固俊取得全面性的胜利后,他派往唐朝献捷的使者叫"米怀玉",这显然是一个米国(Māymurgh,弭秣贺)出身的粟特人,表明粟特人在仆固俊创建西州回鹘王国的过程中,也是主要的一支力量,史籍所谓归伏的"胡汉"民众中,一定有原在这一地域内生存的大量粟特胡人。

让米怀玉出使唐朝,可能还有另外一层考虑,那就是粟特人擅长作为使者在不同国家、民族之间充当沟通的角色,因为他们通晓不同民族的语言,像米怀玉应当就是能够在回鹘和唐朝之间的沟通上没有语言障碍的粟特人。

粟特人作为使者的例子在史籍中屡见不鲜,在材料不多的西州回鹘对外交往的有关记录中,我们也可以找到不止米怀玉一个例子。敦煌发现的回鹘语文书 P. 2988 + P. 2909 号,是西州回鹘使臣在出使沙州归义军时在敦煌写的发愿文,其中依次为 tangri taβγac xan "圣天桃花石汗"(中国皇帝)、tangri uyγur xan "圣天回鹘汗"、沙州之 tangri taypü bäg "圣天太傅匐"等祝福。沙州太傅匐指 10 世纪曹氏归义军节度使中某人无疑。在这批西州回鹘使臣中,有籍属吐鲁番的安姓粟特人(turpan-liγ An enčü),有名为 Māxu-čor 者,还有其他一些高级官吏,如都督(totoq)、地略(tiräk)、将军(sangun)、啜(čor)、刺史(čigši)、特勤(tegin)等,[1]可见这位安姓粟特人也是这个使团的高级官员之一。

相反,沙州归义军出使西州回鹘的使者,也有的以粟特后裔充使。如 P. 3501 背(9)《戊午年(958)六月十六日康员进贷绢契》:"戊午年六月十六日立契,兵马使康员进往于西州充使。"[2]

一般来讲,当时的使者都是兼带着从事贸易活动的,因此,在西州回鹘对外的贸易交往中,粟特人也扮演着重要的角色。敦煌发现过一些年代属于 9 ~ 10 世纪的回鹘语或回鹘-粟特语(Turkish-Sogdian)所写的商业文书,其中有些应当就是西州回鹘王国的粟特商人留在敦煌的。[3]

三、西州回鹘王国中的粟特摩尼教徒和基督教徒

10 世纪波斯佚名作者的《世界境域志》记载:

> 在今吐鲁番附近有五个属于粟特人的村落,其中住着基督徒、祆教徒和萨毗。[4]

这个记载为 20 世纪初叶以来吐鲁番的考古发现所证明,而根据考古材料,应当补充的是这里还有大量的摩尼教徒。

在吐鲁番出土的摩尼教伊朗语残片中,大约 70% 是以摩尼教的教会用语——中古波斯语(Middle Persian)和帕提亚语(Parthian)书写而成,但也有大约 30% 的粟特语摩尼教文献。[5] 研究这些伊朗语摩尼

---

① J. R. Hamilton, *Manuscrits ouigours du IXe - Xe siècle de Touen-houang*, I, Paris 1986, pp. 83 - 92.

② Yamamoto Tatsurō and Ikeda On, *Tun-huang and Turfan Documents Concerning Social and Economical History*, III, Contract, A, Tokyo, 1987, p. 358. 年代据陈国灿:《敦煌所出诸借契年代考》,《敦煌学辑刊》1984 年第 1 期,第 8 页。

③ Hamilton, *op. cit.*; N. Sims-Williams, & J. Hamilton, *Documents turco-sogdiens du IXe - Xe siècle de Touen-houang*. London 1990. 参看森安孝夫:《シルクロードのウイグル商人—ソグド商人とオルトク商人のあいだ》,《岩波讲座世界历史》第 11 卷《中央ユーラシアの统合:9—16 世纪》,东京,岩波书店,1997 年 11 月,第 365 ~ 389 页。

④ V. Minorsky, *Hudud al-'Alam. The Regions of the World*, Oxford University Press, 1937, p. 95.

⑤ 王媛媛:《从波斯到中国:摩尼教在中亚和中国的传播(公元 3—11 世纪)》,第 136 页。

教文献的学者认为,书写中古波斯语和帕提亚语文献的摩尼教教徒未必是波斯人,就像唐朝的景教徒可以书写他们的教会用语叙利亚文,但他们实际上是波斯人或粟特人;或者像今天中国的天主教徒可以书写他们的教会语言拉丁文,但他们是汉人。高昌出土的大量粟特文摩尼教文献表明,使用这些文献的人的母语应当是粟特语。① 而且,有一些中古波斯文和帕提亚文的摩尼教文献中,也有一些用粟特文加以提示哪里要吟唱,哪里要重复的文句,还有一些这两种教会语言所写文献的后面有粟特文的题跋。② 这些都表明即使是这些中古波斯文和帕提亚文摩尼教文献,他们的所有者恐怕也是粟特人(和部分回鹘人)摩尼教徒。③ 另外,在吐鲁番出土摩尼教文献当中,还有一些中古波斯语-粟特语双语、帕提亚语-粟特语双语、粟特语-突厥语双语术语表,④其中尤以中古波斯语-粟特语居多。据伊朗语专家的看法,这些术语表是摩尼教徒在翻译经典语言时的工具。从历史的角度来看这些术语表,粟特人显然在中古波斯文和帕提亚文摩尼教文献向粟特文,或从粟特文向突厥-回鹘文的转译时,起着中间的桥梁作用。

这里只举一个例子,即柏林藏吐鲁番出土摩尼教文书 M 5779(T II D 123),内容是有关摩尼教最高的宗教节日——庇麻节(Bema)的仪式程序,主要用帕提亚文、中古波斯文书写,而仪式主持者所使用的指示性说明文字则是粟特文。现将其译文摘引如下:⑤

正面:

……[帕提亚文]:我主摩尼将从天堂降临。哦,主啊,当您降临,请让我们免受轮回之苦。哦,摩尼,弥勒佛,您降临了,请拯救我。

[中古波斯文/粟特文]:念诵两遍。

[粟特文]:稍后。[帕提亚语]:我们呼唤您,拥有美妙名号的神和庄严的王者,大德摩尼!(哦)您,光明的赐予者,我们大声赞美您!

[粟特文]:当念到灵魂的名字,赞美诗结束时,稍作停顿。然后从《福音》中取·⤳·…并向神使(摩尼)和正义者(选民)致敬。再开始忏悔。

背面:

唱颂这三首赞美诗:[帕提亚文]:"大德摩尼,庄严的君王,美妙的仪相(dīdan)";"明父,我向您忏悔,请饶恕我的罪过";"至善的大德摩尼,哦上帝,请回应我!"

[中古波斯文/粟特文]:念诵两遍。

---

① W. Sundermann, "The Manichaean Texts in Languages and Scripts of Central Asia", S. Akiner & N. Sims-Williams (eds.), *Languages and Scripts of Central Asia*, School of Oriental and African Studies University of London, 1997, pp.41-45.

② 如 M 481 可能就是某一帕提亚文经书的粟特语跋文部分,见 W. B. Henning, *Ein manichäisches Bet-und Beichtbuch*, APAW X, 1937, p.12; M. Boyce, *A Catalogue of the Iranian Manuscripts in Manichaean Script in the German Turfan Collection*, Berlin, 1960, p.32.

③ W. Sundermann, "Iranian Manichaean Turfan Texts concerning the Turfan Region", *Turfan and Tun-huang, the texts*, Firenze, 1992, p.74.

④ W. B. Henning, *Sogdica* (James G. Forong Fund, XXI), London, 1940; M. Boyce, *A Catalogue of the Iranian Manuscripts in Manichaean Script in the German Turfan Collection*, p.148; W. Sundermann, "'The Book of the Head' and 'The Book of the Limbs'. a Sogdian List", *Iran Questions et Connaissances. Actes du IVᵉ Congrès Européen des Études Iraniennes Organisé par la Societas Iranologica Europaea Paris*, 6-10 Sept 1999, Vol. I: La période ancienne, Association Pour L'avancement des Études Iraniennes, pp.135-161.

⑤ 译文是王媛媛以亨宁的德译本为基础,并参考了克林凯特的英译本翻译出来的。"[ ]"中提示了紧跟其后的内容所用的语言。原文见 W. B. Henning, *Ein manichäisches Bet-und Beichtbuch*, pp.45-46; H. -J. Klimkeit, *Gnosis*, p.150. 汉译文见王媛媛:《从波斯到中国:摩尼教在中亚和中国的传播(公元 3—11 世纪)》,第147~148 页。

[中古波斯文]：哦，摩尼，拥有美妙名号的救世主，请拯救我，哦，请拯救并宽恕我的罪过。

[粟特文]：当念完"封印之信（Letter of the Seal）"后，在神使面前吟诵这首赞美诗。[帕提亚文]：我的明父，大德摩尼，升入天堂吧。

[粟特文]：圣餐之后唱颂这三首赞美诗：

[帕提亚文]"拥有美妙名号的王者，大德摩尼神！""哦，主，您离开了，请带我升入天堂。""神使降临……

这是一个庇麻节仪式上的指导性文书，文中以中古波斯文、特别是粟特文写出了详细的提示，如诗歌的念诵次数，何时该暂停、礼拜、忏悔或进行圣餐等等，以提示仪式主持者在什么时点上做什么事情。从大多数提示性的文字都用粟特文书写这一点来看，这位主持者或许就是一位粟特人。

还可以举一组高昌回鹘王国时期的摩尼教文书，就是 1980 年柏孜克里克石窟出土的三封粟特文书信，其中两封都是高昌回鹘境内某地的拂多诞寄给教团更高一级的领袖慕阇的。两封信写于摩尼教的斋月当中，除了拂多诞向慕阇问候的语句外，其中充满了虔诚的套语。我们从中可以得知，在年终、年初的斋月里摩尼教徒的宗教生活情景，他们有的"咏唱了四首赞美诗，反复朗读和歌唱了二十条教规和三百首歌，拜读了优秀的教典《夏普夫尔冈》"；有的则是"用粟特语两次咏唱了名为《没有过失》的赞美诗，反复朗读和歌唱了四十条教规和三百首歌"。[①] 由此可见，这些高昌回鹘地方上的摩尼教团，已经用粟特文来吟诵摩尼教的赞美诗，而不是用中古波斯文或帕提亚文，说明其教会的成员可能主要是粟特人。至少我们从该教会的首领拂多诞的信件用粟特文书写这一点上，可以知道该教团的领袖是粟特人。而收信的这位名为马尔·阿鲁亚曼·普夫耳的慕阇，也即高昌回鹘王国内最高的摩尼教僧团领袖，恐怕也是一个粟特人。

西州回鹘也为景教徒提供了良好的生存环境，德国探险队在高昌城东和今吐鲁番市北葡萄沟（布拉依克）北部水旁遗址，发现两所景教寺院，其中后者发现了大量景教经典，包括成册的粟特文景教文献，另外，还有少数写本来自木头沟（Mutoq）、库鲁塔格（Kurutaq）以及吐峪沟（Tuyuq）。

关于高昌回鹘景教教团遗存下来的各种语言书写的文献，陈怀宇《高昌回鹘景教研究》一文根据欧美学者的研究成果做了整理，现将其中粟特语文献留存的情况转述如下：[②]

（1）圣经文献：《马太福音》（Mathew）：第 1 章，10～13 节（叙利亚-粟特语双语）；第 5 章，30～33 节，38～41 节；第 10 章，14～19 节，21～33 节；第 13 章，17～19 节，24～25 节；第 16 章 24 节～第 17 章 2 节；第 20 章，17～19 节；第 21 章，28～43 节；第 24 章，24～26 节，32～33 节；第 24 章，31～45 节。《约翰福音》（John）：第 1 章，19～35 节；第 3 章，18～21 节，26～27 节；第 5 章，25～31 节，33～40 节；第 9 章，9～16 节，30～38 节；第 10 章（只有一句）；第 15 章，18～20 节；第 16 章，20～33 节；第 17 章，24～26 节；

---

① 吉田丰：《粟特文考释》，柳洪亮主编《吐鲁番新出土摩尼教文献研究》，北京：文物出版社，2000 年，第 98 页。

② J. P. Asmussen, "The Sogdian and Uighur-Turkish Christian Literature in Central Asia before the Real Rise of Islam: A Survey", L. A. Hercus, J. F. B. Kuiper & T. Rajapatirana & E. R. Skrzypczak (eds.), *Indological and Buddhist Studies. Volume in Honour of Professor J. W. de Jong on his Sixtieth Birthday*, Canberra 1982, pp. 11–29. Reprint: Sri Satguru, Delhi 1984. 陈怀宇汉译《前伊斯兰时代中亚粟特语和回鹘突厥语基督教文献概述》，《国际汉学》第 4 辑，郑州：大象出版社，1999 年，第 345～366 页；N. Sims-Williams, "Die christlich-sogdischen Handschriften von Bulayïq", H. Klengel & W. Sundermann (eds.), *Ägypten, Vorderasien, Turfan. Probleme der Edition und Bearbeitung altorientalischer Handschriften. Tagung in Berlin, Mai 1987*, Akademie-Verlag, Berlin 1991, 119–125；陈怀宇：《高昌回鹘景教研究》，《敦煌吐鲁番研究》第 4 卷，北京大学出版社，1999 年，第 179 页。

第 20 章,19～25 节。《路加福音》(Luke):第 1 章,1～4 节(叙粟双语),63～80 节;第 6 章,12～17 节;第 9 章,13 节以下;第 10 章,34～42 节;第 12 章,24 节,31 节见于摩尼教文献,35～39 节,42～44 节;第 13 章,3～4 节;第 16 章,15～27 节;第 21 章,1 节,5～7 节。《哥林多前书》(I Corinthians):第 5 章;第 7 章 (这两章为叙粟双语);第 11 章,23～25 节。《加拉太书》(Galatians):第 3 章 25 节～第 4 章 6 节(叙粟双语)。《诗篇》(Psalms):第 5 篇 4 节～第 6 篇 4 节;第 19 篇 1 节～第 20 篇 1 节;第 23 篇 4 节～第 24 篇 10 节;第 29 篇 1 节～第 30 篇 1 节;第 50 篇 15 节～第 51 篇 5 节。

(2) 非《圣经》文献:"基督教写本第二组"(即 C 2,经辛姆斯-威廉姆斯的研究,这组写本实际是来自一本书①):《佩提昂轶事》(The Story of Pethion)、《达德依苏·卡特拉亚"论阿巴以赛亚第十五布道书"》(Dadiso Qatraya's Commentary on the Fifteenth Homily of Abba Issiah)、《马尔巴拜"论最后不祥时刻"韵文布道书》(A Metrical Homily "On the Final Evil Hour" by Mar Babay)、《使徒教规》(The Apostolic Canons)、《洗礼和圣体礼拜书注释》(A Commentary on the Baptismal and Euchristic Liturgies)、不明来源的《论上帝之慈布道书》(A Homily "On the Maercy of God")、来自《尊者言论》(Verba Seniorum)的部分、《沙普尔二世治下的波斯殉道者》(The Persian Martyrs under Sapur II)、《以弗所之眠者》(The Sleepers of Ephesus)、《欧斯塔提乌斯轶事》(The Story of Eustathius)、《论谦卑》(On Humility)、庞提科斯的《镇魔真言》(The Antiiheticus of Evagrius Ponticus)、《佩提昂轶事引言》(Incipit of the Story of Pethion)。

(3) 杂撰:《赫拉那女王之十字架传奇》(The Cross Legend of Helana Queen)、《巴尔沙巴》(Bar-Shaba)残卷、《薛尔吉思》(Sergios)残卷、《西蒙》(Simon)残卷、《但以理》(Daniel)残卷、《论基督教忍耐之劝告》、《阿佩伦》(Apellen)残卷、《反邪心之布道书札记》、《圣乔治受难记》(St. George Passion)、一页《生命书》(The Book of Life)、《三威蒙度赞》(Glora in Exesis Deo)、《拉班·谢敏言论集》(Rabban Schemin)、《塞拉皮昂轶事》(The Story of Serapion)、《论护教与预言》、《宗主教言论集》(Apophothegmata Patrum)、约翰-戴拉马亚(Johanan Dailamaya)的一件作品、《赞美诗之源》(C19)、《圣徒名单》、《主对门徒论诺亚(Noah)与抹大拉的玛丽亚(Maria Magdalena)》、可能提到焉耆('rgn)的《教会史》残卷。

据前人研究,集中出土景教文献的水旁景教寺院遗址发现的文献所用的语言计有六种:叙利亚语 (Syriac)、粟特语、中古波斯语、钵罗婆语(Pahlavi)、新波斯语(New Persian)、回鹘突厥语(Uighur-Turkish)。其中,叙利亚语作为景教的教会用语而使用最为广泛,一些粟特语、中古波斯语、钵罗婆语和新波斯语、回鹘突厥语写本的题目是用叙利亚语来写,而且还有许多先用叙利亚语书写,接着用粟特语书写的所谓"叙粟双语"文献,表明了已经慢慢不太懂得叙利亚语真正含义的高昌回鹘景教徒,把叙利亚语景教经典翻译成他们能够读懂的粟特语,这部分景教徒很可能就是粟特人。

这里出土的粟特语景教文献也相当之多,而且题材广泛,它们当然是操粟特语的景教徒所使用的文献。从现存的高昌回鹘景教文献来看,高昌回鹘王国的景教教团主要应由粟特人和回鹘人组成。敦煌保存的一封回鹘-粟特语的书信,是高昌回鹘王国某人寄给敦煌的一位景教徒的,②表明两地的粟特教徒也

---

① N. Sims-Williams, *The Christian Sogdian Manuscript C2* (Berliner Turfantexte XII), Berlin, 1985.

② N. Sims-Williams & J. Hamilton, *Documents turco-sogdiens du IXe－Xe. siècle de Touen-houang*, London, 1990, pp. 63－76; N. Sims-Williams, "Sogdian and Turkish Christians in the Turfan and Tun-huang Manuscripts", Alfredo Cadonna (ed.), *Turfan and Tun-hunag: the texts*, Firenze 1992, p.55; 中文本见陈怀宇译《从敦煌吐鲁番出土写本看操粟特语和突厥语的基督教徒》,《敦煌学辑刊》1997 年第 2 期,第 142 页。

有联络。

　　以上主要根据吐鲁番出土的属于高昌回鹘时期的文书,来看九、十世纪西域北道、特别是吐鲁番盆地的粟特人情况。这里原本就是东来粟特人比较集中的地方,加上回鹘汗国的影响和西迁回鹘中的粟特民众的注入,粟特人拥有相当强大的势力,在北庭、高昌、焉耆、龟兹,一直到疏勒的丝路北道上,一些粟特人成为各个地方政权中的骨干,有的甚至是当地的首脑人物,如西州牧首安宁。在西州回鹘王国成立以后,吐鲁番盆地成为粟特人继续生存的肥沃土壤,他们继续在政府中担任外交使臣的角色,也是当地流传的摩尼教、景教的主要信徒,沟通着西方教会和当地民众之间的联系。随着历史车轮的前进,丝路北道的粟特人也逐渐走上回鹘化的过程,不过这个问题已经跃出本文的范围,在此不做讨论。

(2008 年 6 月初稿,2009 年 1 月 17 日修订)

Chinese Classical Works in Uighur Tradition

Peter Zieme

Berlin-Brandenburg Academy of Science and Humanities

The title of my paper may raise some astonishment as it is well-known that the Old Uighur literature was religiously dominated by the three world religions of Christianity, Manichaeism and Buddhism. But there are some traces of classical Chinese works, and it seems to be worth to bring them together. I use here "classical" in the broad sense that includes any Chinese literary work of the pre-Republican period. I would like to show where and to which extent Chinese classical works were known or used by Old Uighurs. In so doing I begin with indirect data proceeding to translations or re-workings of classical scriptures. This survey remains preliminary in many aspects. First of all, because the existing collections of Uighur texts are by far fully studied, discoveries among the unpublished texts are still possible, and in the course of time more finds will come to light either by excavations in Xinjiang and Gansu or even in other regions of China. The reconstruction of the Old Uighur culture and literature is an ongoing process.

The first section

In the course of the fast acculturation of Buddhism into the Chinese culture the incorporation of Chinese literature played a certain role. By this way many quotations from Chinese literary works found its way into the Chinese Buddhist corpus. Were such Buddhist works translated into Old Uighur, it was unavoidable to translate these citations, too. Thus we can get if only indirect evidence of translations of Chinese classics. The 大慈恩寺三藏法师传 Da ci'ensi sanzang fashi zhuan (Biography of Xuanzang) is a work of the latter half of the seventh century which is an example of a high literary standard. A. Mayer who examined the Biography of Xuanzang in great detail, concluded that the work is the result of a mixture of annalistic, canonical and Buddhist styles. [1]

In the first book of the Biography of Xuanzang we find a quotation from 孝经 the Xiaojing (Book of filial piety): "From his childhood the Master showed magnanimity of nature and outstanding brilliance. Once when he was a child of eight, his father, who was sitting at a small table, was teaching him orally from the Book of Filial Piety. When he came to the passage relating how Zengzi stood up respectfully from the mat on which he was sitting, the Master got up and straightened his dress. Being asked why, he replied, ' Since

---

[1] Mayer 1992, p. 11.

Zengzi stood to listen to the lectures of his teacher, why should I sit comfortably while receiving instructions from my father?' His father was greatly pleased with the reply and had no doubt that his son would make great achievements in his life. When he invited his clansmen and told them about this incident, they complimented him, saying, 'He is a filial son indeed!' This was an instance of the Master's precocity."[1]

In the seventh century, at a time when the *Biography of Xuanzang* was written, the incorporation of the concept of filial piety into Buddhism, had already been well-established as Kenneth Ch'en has shown in his book "The Chinese Transformation of Buddhism".[2] He argued that Chinese Buddhists reacted on the criticism, mainly from the side of Confucianists, against them for not obeying the principle of filial piety by pursuing three methods: 1) by pointing out that numerous Buddhist sutras were indeed talking on filial piety by presenting exemplary people, 2) by creating a large body of apocryphal sutras that emphasise Chinese conceptions like that of filial piety, 3) by contending that the Buddhist concept of filial piety was superior than that of the Confucianists in that it aimed at universal salvation contrasting the Confucianists' aim to one family.[3]

As shown in my recent article on some fragments of the *Xuanzang Biography*,[4] the fragment B 49: 4 - 1 of the Northern Mogao Caves[5] refers to the quotation given above.[6] In other parts of the Biography we find quotations from the *Book of Changes*, the *Book of Songs* etc. And there are some allusions to classical passages without reference to their origin.

Other Buddhist texts like some *śāstra*s written by Chinese authors sometimes refer to classical Chinese works, as it is the case in the text published as "Ten ten reasons of belief"[7] which was identified by K. Kudara as a part of the famous commentary to the Lotus sutra 妙法莲华经玄赞 *Miaofa lianhua jing xuanzan* written by 窥基 Kuiji (632 - 682) a pupil of 玄奘 Xuanzang.[8]

In this commentary two times sayings of 孔夫子 Kong Fuzi (Confucius)[9] are cited.

1) *el tutdačı bäg ärkä süüli ašlı kertgünčli üčägü täŋ kärgäk. temin ök elin tutgalı uyur. antag ugrı bolup bo üčägüdä birisin birisin titgülük ıdalaguluk käzigi kälsär. ašnukı ikinti titsär ıdalasar bolur kertgünčüg ar(ı)tı titsär ıdalasar bolmaz. ašnukı ikigükä tayaklıg tirig bolmak ögdisiz ol. kertü köŋülin b(ä)k tutup ölmäk ögdilig tetir.*

_____

① Li 1995, pp. 11 - 12.
② Ch'en 1973.
③ Ch'en 1973, p. 18.
④ Zieme 2008, pp. 480 - 482.
⑤ Peng/Wang I, pl. XLIII, p. 354.
⑥ Not mentioned by Yakup 2006, p. 265.
⑦ TT V B: Mainz 732.
⑧ Kudara 1980.
⑨ TT V B, 103 - 104: *tsuan ni atl(ı)g bögü kuŋ vutsi*. In his fn. to l. 103 K. Kudara writes: "*tsuan ni* is not a transliteration of 仲尼 [*Zhong Ni*, his courtesy name] but of 宣尼 [*Xuan Ni*]." (Kudara 1980, p. 65) 宣尼 is a part of his posthumous name given in the first year of the *yuanshi* period of Han: 宝成宣尼公 [*Baochengxuan ni gong*] "Laudable declarable Lord Ni". B. Csongor retained the derivation of tsw'n ny from 仲尼 *Zhong Ni* as proposed in a note in TT V B (Csongor 1953, p. 119, numbers190 and 191), but observed its irregularity (p. 105 n. 14). In the light of swyn for 宣 in 宣使 (BT XIII, p. 169; Shōgaito 1987, pp. 34, 137) Csongor's emendation of tsw'n to tswyn (p. 81) can be accepted as indeed in the ms. there is rarely a difference between the letters' and y.

"A lord ruling the realm needs army, food and faith, these three equally. Then he can immediately rule his realm. If it happens that the turn comes to give up one of these three, it is possible, if one gives up the first and the second one. It is not possible if one gives up the faith! To live supported by the first and the second one is praiseless. To die while keeping tight the faith is praiseworthy."

One has to compare this passage first with 论语 *Lunyu* XII/7:

子贡问:"政。"子曰:"足食,足兵,民信之矣。"子贡曰:"必不得已而去,于斯三者何先?"曰:"去兵。"子贡曰:"必不得已而去,于斯二者何先?"曰:"去食;自古皆有死;民无信不立。" *Zigong wen zheng, zi yue zushi, zubing, minxin zhi yi. Zigong yue, bibudeyi er qu, yu si sanzhe he xian? yue qu bing. Zigong yue, bibudeyi er qu, yu si erzhe he xian? yue, qu shi, zigu jie you si, min wu xin bu li.*

Zigong asked about ruling. Confucius said, "Sufficient food, sufficient arms, and the trust of the people."

Zigong said, "If one had to be dispensed with, which of the three should be first?" Confucius said, "Dispense with arms."

Zigong said, "If one had to be dispensed with, which of the remaining two should be first?" Confucius aid, "Dispense with food. Death has always been since the beginning of time. but without trust, the people could not establish their stand."

Now, the text of the 妙法莲华经玄赞 *Miaofa lianhua jing xuanzan* alludes to this text but shortens it rather sharply as follows:[1]九:建名道之良资。宣尼云:兵食信三。信不可弃,自古皆有死,人无信不立。 *jiu jian mingdao zhi liangzi. xuan ni yun bing shi xin san. xin buke qi. zigu jie you siren wuxin bu li.* "Ninth. Establishing excellent means for the famous way. Xuanni said: weapons, food, and faith, three. One cannot abandon faith. Already in old times it was that dead people cannot stand up without faith." Somehow, after enumerating the three items, the text immediately concludes that one cannot abandon faith.

In the *Lunyu* the essential words are: 食 *shi* "food", 兵 *bing* "weapons", 民信 *minxin* "trust of the people". The order in the *Miaofa lianhua jing xuanzan* changing the order of the first two items is 兵 *bing*, 食 *shi*, 信 *xin*. The substitution of the original 民信 *minxin* by 信 *xin* "belief" shows a clear shift into the religious sphere.[2]

As the Uyghur text is a translation of the *Xuanzan*, it also has only "faith". A slight difference for the first term is apparent in the Old Uighur version insofar as it has "army" instead of "weapons".[3] But as a whole the Uighur translation gives more room to a kind of further explanation which resembles the exposition in the *Lunyu* itself. It is difficult to say that the translator had direct access to a written work, but probably he knew the story by heart.[4]

---

[1] T. 1723, p. 662b28 - c1.

[2] Mr. Wang Ding who read a first draft and gave me much encouragement adds two points: 1) the omission of the character *min* is due to a taboo since 627; 2) the character *xin* if used solely has not necessarily a religious connotation.

[3] Mr. Wang Ding pointed out to me that Classical Chinese *bing* has both meanings, "weapon" and "army", he refers to the famous *Sunzi Bingfa* "The Art of War".

[4] Mr. Wang Ding noted that in Astana and Turfan several mss. of the *Lunyu* in the commentary of Zheng Xuan 郑玄 were found, cf. Wang Su 王素, *Tang Xieben Lunyu Zhengshi zhu jiqi yanjiu* 唐写本论语郑氏注及其研究, Beijing 1991.

2）*kaltı ulug kaŋlınıŋ boyundurukı yok ärsär kičig kaŋlınıŋ kızgačı boguz bagı yok ärsär ol kaŋlı yorıyu umaz*

"It is as if the yoke of a large cart is missing, or as if a small cart has no shafts or throat band, the cart cannot move."

The 论语 *Lunyu* passage：大车无輗,小车无軏,其何以行之哉 *dache wu ni, xiaoche wu yue, qi heyi xing zhi zai*[①] "I know not what a man without trustworthiness may accomplish. Be it large or small, how could a carriage move without its yoke-bar?"[②]

In the English translation the difference of 輗 *ni* and 軏 *yue* was disregarded. Indeed, the two words are very near in their meanings. The first word *ni* is translated as "rings on the yokes",[③] while *yue* means "the cross-bar at the end of the pole of a carriage".[④] But the Uighur translator tried to make a strict difference between *ni* and *yue*: for *ni* he used *boyunturuk* "yoke", while *yue* is translated by two expressions：*kızgač* "pongs" and *boguz bagı* "throat band".[⑤] This bipolar expression which may be regarded as a kind of alternative translation shows the translator's accurateness.

In line 120 of the same text another work, the 春秋 *Chunqiu* is quoted：*k(a)ltı čuan tsiu atl(ı)g bitigdä sözläyür* "like it is said in the book called Chunqiu". The text quotation is the following：*kimnäŋ birök bar ärsär yaruk yašuk kertgünči ol kertgünči üzä özlärdäki özäklärdäki yava čigidäm suvlardakı ögänlärdäki sargan otı yašı yaš bolarnı alıp kut vahšik t(ä)ŋrilärkä agır ulug ulug eliglärkä hanlarka ančolasar tapınsar bo tapıgı yarayur tep.*[⑥] "Who has a clear and bright belief and takes in this belief *yava čigidäm* plants of brooks and rivers and *sargan* plants of rivers and channels freshly and offers them to ghosts and gods as well as to high kings and lords, this his offering is apt."

This Uighur text agrees to the following passage in the Chinese *Xuanzan*：[⑦]春秋言苟有明信,涧嵠沼沚之毛,蘋蘩蕴藻之菜,可荐于鬼神,可羞于王公。*chunqiu yan, gou you mingxin, jian xi zhao zhi zhi mao, pin fan yun zao zhi cai, ke jian yu guishen, ke xiuyu wanggong.*

The editors Bang and v. Gabain saw already that the quotation is not taken from the *Chunqiu* itself, but from the 左传 *Zuozhuan* mostly regarded as one of the three commentaries to the *Chunqiu*, but other scholars believe that it is an independent work. This is a shortened passage from the *Zuozhuan*：[⑧]苟有明信,涧谿沼沚之毛,蘋蘩蕴藻之菜,筐筥锜釜之器,潢汙行潦之水,可荐于鬼神,可羞于王公。*gou you ming xin, jian xi zhao zhi zhi mao pin fan yun zao zhi cai kuang ju qi fu zhi qi, huang wuxing lao zhi shui, ke jian yu guishen,*

---

① Lunyu II/22.
② From a Confucius website.
③ Mathews 4674. Cf. Ricci 8177："Pièce servant à fixer le joug à l'extrémité du timon d'une grosse voiture."
④ Mathews 7705. Cf. Ricci 13332："Cheville servant à fixer le joug à l'extrémité du timon d'une voiture; taquet." Cf. Ricci 8177［b］compound *ni yue* "1. (anc.) Pièce servant à fixer le joug à l'extrémité du timon d'une grosse voiture (à boeufs), *et* servant aussi à fixer le joug à l'extrémité du timon d'une voiture de voyage (à chevaux)."
⑤ ED 322a："if a small cart has no shafts or throat band."
⑥ TT V B 121–126.
⑦ T. 1723, 662c2–4.
⑧ TT V B, p.356.

ke xiuyu wanggong.

"The *Chuanqiu* says: If there is clear belief, (it is possible to take) vegetation of mountain streams, brooks, ponds, sand-banks, vegetables like duckweed, pond-weed, aquatic plants in vessels like bamboo baskets or round baskets, pots with legs, metal cooking-pots, water of lakes, stagnant pools, flooded tracts and offer it to the ghosts or to the kings and dukes."[①]

The second section

As already mentioned before, one purpose of creating new sutras that are nowadays usually named "apocryphal sutras", was the sinification of Buddhism or in other words the incorporation of traditional Chinese concepts into Buddhism. For my topic I would like to stress that such apocryphal sutras composed by Chinese monks may contain quotations from classical works or may expound Chinese traditional concepts without special reference.

1. The 八阳经 *Bayangjing* and the concept of 阴 *yin* and 阳 *yang*

For the latter fact that Chinese apocryphal sutras easily could incorporate Chinese classics a good example is found in the exposition of 阴 *yin* and 阳 *yang* in the *Bayangjing*. Its Uighur translation as *Säkiz yükmäk yaruk sudur* was widespread and very often copied.[②] Here the theory of *yin* and *yang* is incorporated into sayings of the Buddha:

täŋri burhan inčä tep yarlıkadı tözün oglanım, inčä ukuŋlar koduru tıŋlaŋlar bo yertinčüdä

üstün täŋri yaruk tetir, altın yagız yer kararıg tetir

kün täŋri yaruk tetir, ay täŋri kararıg tetir

ot yaruk tetir, suv kararıg tetir,

är yaruk tetir, tiši kararıg tetir,

bo yerli täŋrili tišili irkäkli birgärü kavıšıp

kamag tınlıglı tınsızlı iki türlüg äd tugar bälgürär

tınlıg käntü beš ažun tınlıg tetir

tınsız ärsär kamag ı ıgač yaš ot tetir

künli aylı karıšu kavıšu yorıyur

---

① Legge 1872, p. 13 (Book I Year III): "When there are intelligence and sincerity, what is grown by streams in the valleys, by ponds, and in pools, the gatherings of duck-weed, white southernwood, and pond-weed, in baskets round and square, and cooked in pans and pots with the water from standing pools and road hollows, may be presented to the Spirits, and set before kings and dukes". Here I would like to cite also the German translation (TT V, p. 356): "Wenn es strahlenden Glauben gibt, so kann man Gewächse, die an Bergbächen und Teichen (wachsen), Pflanzen (wie) marsilia quadrifolia, weiße Artemisia, Hanf und ruppia rostellata, in eckigen und runden Körben, in Dreifüßen oder flachen Schüsseln, (mit) Wasser aus stehenden Gewässern oder aus Pfützen den Geistern darbringen und Königen und Herzögen darbieten." The Manchu version has: *unenggi genggiyen akdun bici. holo uhaliyan. omo. niyamašan-i orho. pianggari. empi jici zoo-i sogi. šoro. nionioro* [Hauer 2007, p. 371a: *nionioru*]. *mucen. hacuhan-i tetun. tehe. eyehe. bisaka muke seme. hutu enduri de doboci ombi. wang gung de tukiyeci ombikai.* (Bauer 1959, p. 14).

② Oda 2009.

ötrü yaylı kıšlı tört üd bolur

tört üd ičintä yana ikirär üd adrılur säkiz yaŋı kün bolur

otlı suvlı bir ikintikä küč basut bolup

ötrü kop türlüg ı tarıg yemiš ulatı bıšarlar etilür

tišili irkäkli kavıšıp kiši oglı yalaŋuklar ulatı tugar bälgürär

bo alku yertinčü yer suvdakı ädgüli ayıglı käntünüŋ iki türlüg kılınč ugrınta törütmiš törü tetir. ①

"The Devabuddha deigned to say：My dear sons！Thus understand, carefully listen！In this world it is that above the heaven is light, beneath the brown earth is dark. The Sun is light, the Moon is dark. The fire is light, the water is dark. The man is light, the woman is dark. When earth and heaven, female and male join, all will appear as two types of matter, animate and inanimate. The animate are the living beings of the five *gati*s. The inanimate are all plants and the fresh grasses. When sun and moon join each other and wander, then summer and winter, the four seasons appear. In the four seasons again each two are separated, thus eight first days appear. When fire and water give strength each other, then all kinds of cereals and fruits will ripen and be made. When female and male join, human beings, sons of men, will be born and come up. This is the state come into existence through bad and good in this world, the two kinds of deed. Ó

2. 父母恩重 Fumu enzhong

Direct evidence can be achieved through reference to Buddhist works based on Chinese treatises. One brilliant example is the *Fumu enzhong*. This text is widely known from Chinese Dunhuang versions. The author of the first version is unknown, later it was widespread and became popular in different ways. The length of the text differs, as Ch'en writes, from 39 lines to 122 lines. As a real sutra the text begins as a saying of the Buddha, who declares that parents are the closest to children. The parents nourish and caress the children. Ānanda asks the Buddha how one can repay for the parents' care. Buddha answers that a filial son should prepare sutras and distribute them or he should prepare a 盂兰盆 *yulanpen* offering to the Buddha. After expounding other examples of parents' love and repay of children Buddha answers that the sutra is to be called 父母恩重经 *Fumu enzhong jing*. Love of parents and filial piety are two sides of the same medal, both principles were declared as sayings of the Buddha. Renowned monks and scholars from Zongmi to Shandao used them in their writings. ② Its Uighur translation is well documented among the Turfan texts, in 1985 I collected a large number of manuscripts and prints preserved in Japanese and German collections. One rather long manuscript broken or cut into dozens of pieces, was studied by one of my students but is still not published. The Uighur versions are all written in alliteration verses. This shows that the text had a high reputation.

There is no time to give examples, but as a whole the reworking of the Chinese text in Uighur gives the impression that the Uighur poet revelled in poetical pictures demonstrating how far mother's care can go.

---

① TT VI, 316－330.

② Ch'en 1973, pp. 40－41.

I should at least also mention the exemplary life of Maudgalyāyana who turned into the well-known Chinese of Mulian rescuing his mother from hell. As a study of such an Uighur text is in print, here I refer only to it. [1]

The third section

After having shortly mentioned some examples of the usage of Chinese classical texts in Buddhist literature I turn now to the direct testimonies, namely texts that can be shown as translations or re-workings of classical Chinese texts.

1. The Book of Changes (易经 *Yijing*)

A little book from Yarxoto approximately half of which is preserved, is if not a translation a reworking of the well-known Chinese 易经 *Yijing*. It contains the hexagrams known from the Chinese as well as prophecies, but rarely one finds similar text passages not to mention exact matches. The whole text makes the impression that it either represents a totally unknown Chinese version which seems to be improbable, or what is more reasonable, the Uighurs have used the composition to rework the book in their own style. The Uighur text was the first edited in the series Türkische Turfantexte, and later it was often re-edited. A new edition by Semih Tezcan is in preparation. [2] Here I would like to show the correspondence between the two versions. As many lacunae exist, it is difficult to find a complete set. One is the following. It starts with the hexagram 45 on leaf 32 (*iki kırk*): *utru kälmäk* = Chin. 萃 *cui* / Gathering Together. The Uighur text:

Birök utru kälmäk atl(ı)g ırk kälsär savın inčä ter

utruŋda asıg tusu yedärü kälti

ätözüŋdä ayag čiltäg ünäšü[3] berdi

köŋülüŋtäki küsüšüŋ barča kantı

atıŋ atayu kut süü[4] özin kälti

äski atıŋ tägšilip yaŋı boltuŋ

bogdam atıŋ tägšilip tatıglıg boltuŋ

täprätük sayu iš kütküŋ tapıŋča

olurtuk sayu orun yurt özüŋčä[5]

ulug ärk kälti

tört yıŋak tüzülti köŋülüŋčä

kidirti täprämiš küčlüg yagı kitdi

---

① Zieme (forthcoming).

② Tezcan (forthcoming).

③ TT I 114 *ornaŋyu*, ETŞ 82 (p. 294) *ornanu*.

④ TT I qïw, ETŞ 82 (p. 294) *kıv*. My reading *süü* is based on the assumption that *kıv* is never written with a final-w, but on the other hand one has not to forget that the first letter is rather a q-, not s-.

⑤ TT I *ögüngčä*, ETŞ 86 *ögüngçe*.

öŋdürti täprämiš oot yalını öčti

olurup körünčlägil inčgä yügürük atlarıg

tapıŋča alıp išlätgil yenik ädgü lalarıg

tümän sav tügüni sinidä boltı

yıl ay etilü älgiŋdä kirdi

üstünki altınkı tapladı

örüki kudıkı sävinti

bäg tamgası älgiŋdä

ornaglıg orun anıŋta

yerkä t(ä)ŋrikä sävinč tut

*burhanlarka tapıg kıl*①

"If the omen called 'Coming towards' appears, it says in word thus:

towards you profit and favour follow you immediately,

about yourself fame and renown resound quickly,

your wishes in your heart are all fulfilled,

calling your name bliss and fortune came by itself, your old name changed, you became new,

your bad name changed, you became lovely,

each time you move your deeds are according your wish,②

each time you sit ho me and country are like yours,

great might came,

the four directions were arranged according your heart,

when moving westward the strong enemy flew,

when moving eastward the flame of fire expired,

sit down and observe fine racing horses,③

take according to your wish light and good mules and let them work,

the knot of ten thousand things was in you,

years and months were arranged by your hands and entered,

above and beneath agreed,

high and low enjoyed,

the seal (*tamga*) of the lord was in your hands,

a settled place (was assured) by this,

---

① TT I, 112 – 132.

② For line 119 Bang/v. Gabain refer to Gua 42 Legge 149: there will be advantage in every movement which shall be undertaken. Vgl. auch Gua 24, Legge 108.

③ Cf. the proverb (?) (Ch/U 6500) *bilgä kiši* […] *yügrük atka bir kamčı bergä* […] "[For] wise man […], for a racing horse a whip […].

keep thankfulness to earth ad heaven,

do service to the Buddhas. "

A translation of the Chinese text of the 45th hexagram (萃 *cui* / Gathering Together) :[1]"GATHERING TOGETHER. Success.

The king approaches his temple.

It furthers one to see the great man.

This brings success. Perseverance furthers.

To bring great offerings creates good fortune.

It furthers one to undertake something. "[2]

If we compare these two texts we can observe at the utmost a similar general outline of the content. There is nearly no exact match between these two passages. What strikes most is that the Uighur text is much more lengthy than its Chinese counterpart.

Here follows another example.

allıg čävišlig kišilär altayu turur üsküŋdä

kün ay yarukın tıda katıglanur[3]

"Tricky people are always betraying you

(like clouds that) strive to hinder the light of sun and moon. "

In their notes W. Bang and A. v. Gabain[4] assure an allusion to the 5th chapter of the 新语 Xinyu a work of 陆贾 Lu Jia: 邪臣之蔽贤,犹浮云之鄣日月也。*xie chen zhi bixian*, *you fuyun zhi zhang riyue ye* "Ein schlechter Minister stellt einen Weisen in den Schatten, wie ziehende Wolken Sonne und Mond verdecken".

The first editors[5] hoped that scholars familiar with Chinese classical literature will find the original texts of some passages or of the whole booklet. [6] But as far as I can see no progress is in sight, and thus one may even assume that it never will be possible to find a real "original" text, probably one has to regard this omen book as genuine.

2. 千字文 *Qianziwen*

Very different is the *Qianziwen*, the *Thousand-Character Essay*. This is a text ascribed to the historiographer 周兴嗣 Zhou Xingsi (fl. 550). It served for learning Chinese and i. a. as shelf numbers in libraries. The use of the book was widespread in neighbouring countries, too. Only since the turn of the last centuries Uighur fragments of translations of the *Qianziwen* including parts of a four character group came to light. They were introduced by M. Shōgaito and Abdurishid Yakup. [7] Here the translations are very strict and

---

① In the *Mawangdui Yijing* it is hexagram 43, cf. Hertzer 1996, 231 – 236.

② The I Ching or BOOK OF CHANGES The Richard Wilhelm Translation rendered into English by Cary F. Baynes (internet).

③ TT I, 24.

④ TT I, p.256.

⑤ TT I, p.242.

⑥ TT I, p.4.

⑦ Shōgaito/Yakup 2001.

follow the original text. That makes the Qianziwen an excellent tool for word equations. As these texts have been published recently I can dispense with examples.

3. 管子 *Guanzi* (?)

My third example is still very dubious, and I have to put a question mark. But I want to draw the attention to a small fragment of the Turfan Collection in Berlin that belongs to the finds of the first expedition in 1902/1903. As far as I know, it was totally neglected up to now. But if my preliminary observations are correct, this small piece is of great importance insofar as it might show that Uighurs also translated or used real Chinese literary texts. But one has to be cautious because it is also possible that the fragment is part of quite a different book and contains a passage only as a quotation.

My observations on this fragment can be summarised in the following items.

1) The fragment seems to be unique. I could not find another fragment belonging to the same handwriting.

2) The fragment is written in a carefully executed type of calligraphic Uighur script.

3) The layout of the manuscript makes the impression of a Manichaean text, as it has the typical syntagma marker: a double stroke in black surrounded by a circle in red. The fragment was not included into the catalogue of Manichaean Turkic texts by J. Wilkens. [1] Although the majority of text fragments of this type indeed belong to the Manichaean corpus, it is not always the case. There are some examples of clear Buddhist content. Therefore a Buddhist affiliation is also possible.

4) Line 3 of the supposed verso side contains a transcription of a Chinese name.

5) Guided by the interpretation of this name, I looked into the *Guanzi* and found there some similar sentences. This is not a final proof that the fragment represents a translation of the *Guanzi*, but may be regarded as a first hint.

If we now take a closer look at the text, there are more problems. The text of the side which I regard as recto, speaks of relations between man and woman, a topic which is not expressively treated in the *Guanzi*. On the other hands, there we find several strings of nine kinds, inter alia the *jiu bai* 九败 "Nine Ways of Failure". [2] But in connection with "nine kinds of ..." I could not find any allusion to the topic of the Turkic text.

Although it is clear that on the supposed verso side the transcription in line 4 is one of a Chinese name, there are problems. The author of the 管子 *Guanzi* is 管仲 Guan Zhong. Phonetically the first syllable *čo* can stand for *zhong*, but then one has to assume the transcription of the first part, i. e. *guan*, in a lacuna before *čo*. This Guan Zhong is usually called Guanzi (Chin. 管子；*? – † 645 BC). [3] The following two syllables may indeed represent this name, i. e. Guanzi. One could explain both name forms side by side only

[1] Wilkens 2000.
[2] Rickett 1985, pp. 109 – 113.
[3] He was a famous politician and philosopher of the 春秋 *Chuan qiu* period. His *ming* was Yiwu (Chin. 夷吾). Guan originated from Yingshang (颖上). He was chancellor of the state Qi for 14 years. Many texts have sayings and records of him.

as an explanatory addition which is not rare in Uighur translation texts. ①

I include here a full edition of the text fragment U 2391 (T I x 514).

recto (?)

01 [ ] är [   ]   [ ] man [   ]

02 [uzun]tonlug [   ]   [wo]man [   ]

03 ävtin alp är [   ]   from the house the brave man [ ]

04 tokuz türlüg [   ]   nine kinds [   ]

05 kertü yolın [   ]   on the true way [   ]

06 [bä]g är yut[uz]l[   ]   [hu]sband and wife [   ]

07 ayur: čıgay är' [   ]   speaks: Poor man [   ]

08 [ko]lulamaz:② bilgä [ ]   does not consider. Wise [ ]

09 [ ] asagl(a)g [   ]   [ ] useful [   ]

10 [ ] özüŋ [   ]   [ ] yourself [   ]

11 [   ]   [   ]

verso (?)

01 [čax]ša[pt]larıg   [the co]mmands (acc.)

02 [arıg] tutsar asag-ı   keeping [purely], its profit

03 [... bolur iki]n ara ögdilig   [is sure(?).] Between the praiseworthy

04 [ ] čo kua[n]tsi (?)   [ ] Zhong Guanzi,

05 [ö]tläyü täginürm(ä)n   I dare to give my advice.

06 [bilgä ä]r kor kötürm[äz]   A wise man does not bring damage.

07 [ ] kiši tod äšidmäz   A [?] person does not hear shame.

08 [ädgü] savl(ı)g kiši ayag   A person of [good] words gains reputation.

09 [-lıg bo]lur: kat(ı)glan[gučı]   [A] striving

10 [ ]gäy③ bolu[r]   [man] will be [ ]

For comparison I quote here from Rickett's edition of the *Guanzi*:④

中情信诚 *zhong qingxin cheng*

If within [a person's heart] there is a feeling for trustworthiness and honesty,

则名誉美矣 *ze mingyu mei yi*

his fame will be great.

修行谨敬 *xiuxing jin jing*

If he has cultivated diligent and respectful conduct,

---

① Cf. the unusual treatment of Confucius' courtesy name above: 宣尼 as the middle part of 宝成宣尼公, fn. 10.

② Or: [t]alulamaz "does not choose".

③ Or: *täŋri* "god"?

④ Rickett 1985, p. 78.

则尊显附矣 *ze zunxian fu yi*

honor will be associated [with his name].

中无情实 *zhong wuqing shi*

But if within [his heart] there is no feeling for truth,

则名声恶矣 *ze mingsheng'e yi*

his reputation will be notorious.

行慢易 *xiuxing man yi*

If he has cultivated an indolent and easygoing conduct,

则汙辱生矣 *ze wuru sheng yi*

shame will result.

References

W. Bang / A. v. Gabain, Türkische Turfantexte I, SPAW 1928, Berlin 1928.

W. Bauer, Tsch'un-ts'iu mit den drei Kommentaren Tso-tschuan, Kung-yang-tschuan und Ku-liang-tschuan in Mandschuischer Übersetzung, Wiesbaden 1959 (Abhandlungen für die Kunde des Morgenlandes XXXIII,1).

G. Clauson, An Etymological Dictionary of Pre-Thirteenth-Century Turkish, Oxford 1972.

B. Csongor, Chinese in the Uighur Script of the T'ang-Period, in: Acta Orientalia Academiae Scientiarum Hungaricae II (1953), pp. 73–121.

Grand dictionnaire Ricci de la langue chinoise, I–VII, Paris-Taipei 2001.

Kenneth K. S. Ch'en, The Chinese Transformation of Buddhism, Princeton/N. Jersey 1973.

J. R. Hamilton, Manuscrits ouïgours de Touen-Houang. Le conte bouddhique du bon et du mauvais prince en version ouïgoure, Paris 1971.

E. Hauer (ed. by O. Corff), Handwörterbuch der Mandschusprache, 2., durchgesehene und erweiterte Auflage), Wiesbaden 2007.

D. Hertzer, Das Mawangdui-Yijing. Text und Deutung, München 1996.

K. Kudara, ウイグル訳『妙法蓮華経玄賛』(1) Uiguru-yaku "Myōhōrengekyō genzan" (1). [Uigur translation of the Miao-fa-lian-hua-jing Xuan-zan (1)], in: 仏教学研究 Bukkyōgaku kenkyū [Studies in Buddhism] 36 (1980), 49–65.

J. Legge, The Chinese Classics with a Translation. Critical and Exegetical Notes, Prolegomena, and Copious Indexes, Vol. V, Part I, Hongkong/London 1872.

Li Rongxi, A Biography of the Tripitaka Master of the Great Ci'en Monastery of the Great Tang Dynasty, Berkeley 1995.

R. H. Mathews, Chinese-English Dictionary, Cambridge/Mass. 1972.

A. Mayer, Xuanzangs Leben und Werk. Teil 1: Xuanzang, Übersetzer und Heiliger, Wiesbaden 1992.

J. Oda, A Study on the Buddhistic Sūtra named *Säkiz yükmäk yaruq* or *Säkiz törlügin yarumïš yaltrïmïš* in Old Turkic, Kyoto (forthcoming).

Peng, Jinzhang/Wang, Jianjun, 敦煌莫高窟北区石窟 [*Dunhuang Mogaoku beiqu shiku* Northern Grottoes of Mogaoku, Dunbuang] I–III, Beijing 2000–2004.

W. Allyn Rickett, Guanzi 管子. Political, Economic, and Philosophical Essays from Early China. A Study and Translation,

Princeton, N. Jersey 1985.

M. Shōgaito, ウイグル文献に導入された漢語に関する研究 [uiguru bunken ni dōnyū sareta kango ni kansuru kenkyū], in: 外国学研究 [Gaikokugaku kenkyū] XVII (shōwa 62), pp. 17–156.

M. Shōgaito/Abdurishid Yakup, Four Uyghur Fragments of *Qianziwen* 'Thousand Character Essay'., in: Turkic Languages 5 (2001), pp. 3–29 + 4 pl.

Ş. Tekin, Eski Türk Şiiri, Ankara 1965.

S. Tezcan, Das uigurische Insadi-Sūtra, Berlin 1974 (Berliner Turfantexte III).

S. Tezcan, Neue Interpretationen des alttürkischen Wahrsagebuches, in: R. Emmerick et alii (ed.), *Turfan*, *Khotan und Dunhuang*. Vorträge der Tagung "Annemarie v. Gabain und die Turfanforschung", veranstaltet von der BBAW in Berlin (9.–12. 12. 1994), Berlin 1996, 335–341.

S. Tezcan, Re-edition of the Omen book (TT I) (forthcoming).

TT I = W. Bang/A. v. Gabain, *Türkische Turfan-Texte. I.* Bruchstücke eines Wahrsagebuches. SPAW. Phil. -hist. Kl. 1929: 15, 241–268.

TT V = W. Bang/A. v. Gabain, *Türkische Turfan-Texte. V.* Aus buddhistischen Schriften, SPAW Phil. -hist. Kl. 1931: 14, 323–356.

TT VI = W. Bang/A. v. Gabain/G. R. Rachmati, *Türkische Turfan-Texte. VI.* Das buddhistische Sūtra *Säkiz yükmäk*, SPAW Phil. -hist. Kl. 1934: 10, 93–192.

J. Wilkens, Alttürkische Handschriften Teil 8: Manichäisch-türkische Texte der Berliner Turfansammlung, Stuttgart 2000.

Abdurishid Yakup, Uighurica from the Northern Grottoes of Dunhuang, A Festschrift in Honour of Professor Masahiro Shōgaito's Retirement: Studies on Eurasian Languages, Kyoto 2006, 1–41.

P. Zieme, Buddhistische Stabreimdichtungen der Uiguren, Berlin 1985 (Berliner Turfantexte XIII).

P. Zieme, Some bilingual manuscripts of the *Xuanzang Biography*, in: Aspects of Research into Central Asian Buddhism. In memoriam Kōgi Kudara, Turnhout 2008, 475–483.

P. Zieme, Buddhistische Unterweltsberichte-alttürkische Varianten aus der Turfan-Oase (forthcoming).

吐 蕃 与 突 厥

周伟洲

陕西师范大学西北民族研究中心

公元 6 世纪中叶后,在中国北方蒙古草原和西南青藏高原,先后兴起了两个强大的民族及其所建的政权,即突厥人所建的突厥汗国和吐蕃人所建之吐蕃王朝。在这两大政权之间,是先后崛起的隋、唐王朝。因而,在 7~9 世纪,唐朝、突厥和吐蕃三个政权之间对中亚地区(西域)的激烈争夺,就成为中亚和东亚的历史上最重要的一页,也成为相距甚远的青藏高原的吐蕃与漠北的突厥发生关系的契机。关于这段历史,过去中外学者的研究论著中,从不同的角度和主题,多有涉及。本文则以吐蕃与突厥相互关系为主题,依据唐代汉、藏等文献,试作一番梳理和探索。

一、吐蕃联合西突厥与唐朝争夺西域

突厥,是公元 6 世纪中叶兴起于北方蒙古草原的游牧民族。中国史籍记载了一些关于它起源的传说,尽管中外学者对其族源的看法,意见分歧,但是大多数学者认为,突厥是以狼为图腾的部落,其原居地在匈奴之西北,其语言系属阿尔泰语系突厥语族。突厥(turk、turuk)一词原意有"气力"或"权力"之意。以后,突厥又迁于金山(今阿尔泰山)之阳,故中国史籍又记:"金山形似兜鍪,其俗谓兜鍪为'突厥',遂以为号。"此时,突厥为蒙古草原强大的柔然(又作"蠕蠕"、"茹茹"等)所役属,为其冶铁之"锻奴"。

到 6 世纪中叶,突厥首领土门自称伊利可汗,始正式建立汗国。其子科罗(乙息记可汗)、燕都(木杆可汗)先后继立,于西魏恭帝二年(555)灭柔然汗国;"又西破嚈哒,东走契丹,北并契骨,威服塞外诸国"。其疆域,"东自辽海以西,至西海(今里海),万里;南自沙漠以北,至北海(今贝加尔湖),五六千里;皆属焉"。而突厥控制西域,将势力伸入中亚,是由木杆可汗弟室点密可汗(又译作"瑟帝米")带领十部落完成的,故中外学者以此可汗为西突厥始祖。大约到隋开皇三年(583),东西突厥始正式分立。最早与吐蕃发生关系的即是统治西域的西突厥。

吐蕃于 6 世纪末兴起于青藏高原后,与远在蒙古草原的突厥汗国几乎没有什么交往。但是,在敦煌发现的古藏文历史文书赞普传记(P. T1287)中,却记载了 6 世纪末松赞干布父论赞赞普(后称"郎日论赞")攻杀于那城(今西藏拉萨北彭域)的古陕森波结,"芒布杰松木布(王子)逃往突厥(Dru-gu)"。在古藏文文献中,"Dru-gu"一词确系这一时期吐蕃对突厥的称谓,系由突厥(turk)一词转写而来,故中外学者大都认为,这是吐蕃与突厥发生关系之始。也有的学者认为,此事"在多大程度上符合史实现在还很难判断,在这件事上,很可能突厥之境并不意味着真正的突厥领域,而只是不为人知的遥远的北方地区而已"。1954 年法尊大师在翻译近代藏族著名学者根敦琼培撰《白史》时,却直接将此句译作:"芒波结松布逃往吐谷浑。"或许法尊大师的理解更符合当时的历史,因上引敦煌藏文献是 8 世纪后的作品,故用"突厥"一词代替早已亡于吐蕃之吐谷浑。

7世纪初,吐蕃名王松赞干布大约在唐贞观十八年(644)最终兼并了西边的象雄(Zhang-zhung,唐代文献称为"羊同",地在今西藏阿里地区),杀其王李聂秀,将象雄各部收于治下。这样,吐蕃象雄北部就与西突厥统治下的西域地区相接。当时吐蕃象雄通西域有三道:一即由象雄北穿过喀喇昆仑山,可至于阗(今新疆和田地区);二由象雄西部、今阿克赛钦地区或拉达克,向北翻越喀喇昆仑山山口,至朱俱波(今新疆叶城一带);三由象雄西经勃律(今克什米尔西北巴尔提斯坦、吉尔吉特),再北至中亚或由葱岭(今帕米尔高原)入今新疆地区。因此,事实上吐蕃在兼并象雄之后,即与西域的西突厥各部有了交往,只是汉、藏文献没有记载而已。更为重要的是,唐朝在贞观四年(630)灭亡了东突厥汗国之后,即向西突厥统治下的西域扩展,暂时抑制了吐蕃向西域地区的渗透。

贞观二十二年(648),唐朝派军击降西域龟兹(今新疆库车),徙安西都护府于此,统领新设置的龟兹、于阗、焉耆、疏勒四镇(安西四镇)。到唐高宗显庆二年(657),唐朝一举灭亡西突厥汗国,统一西域地区,"西尽波斯,并隶安西都护府"。在原西突厥十姓部落及其属部之地,唐朝先后设置了一批羁縻府州,以原西突厥首领为都督、刺史,统属于安西都护府管辖。如在碎叶水(今中亚楚河)之东的西突厥五咄陆部,设有六个都督府,归新置之昆陵都护府直辖,任命原西突厥首领阿史那弥射为昆陵都护、兴昔亡可汗;在碎叶水之西的西突厥五弩失毕部,设都督府若干,归新置之濛池都护府直辖,任命阿史那步真为濛池都护、继往绝可汗。是时,西域的西突厥各部与吐蕃还未发生直接的关系。

可是,到7世纪60年代吐蕃芒松芒赞在位时,噶尔·禄东赞父子掌政,即向唐青海、西域及剑南等地扩张,遂与西域的西突厥各部发生了直接的关系。事实上,自唐朝灭亡了西突厥汗国后,西突厥各部上层贵族大多不甘心接受唐朝的统治,他们不仅内争一直没有停息,而且企图"反叛"唐朝,重新自立,并与向西域扩张之吐蕃联合。据唐代史籍载,龙朔二年(662)前后,吐蕃先策动龟兹叛唐,唐高宗诏飓海道总管苏海政率昆陵都护阿史那弥射、濛池都护阿史那步真击龟兹。因弥射与步真原有矛盾,步真诬告弥射反,苏海政不查,竟诱杀弥射及诸酋长。五咄陆之鼠尼施部、五弩失毕之拔塞干部叛走。海政与步真率军追击,讨平之,还至疏勒南,西突厥别种弓月部就引吐蕃之众阻击唐军,海政以师老不敢战,"以军资赂吐蕃,约和而还"。这一事件表明,吐蕃势力早已深入西域,且在西突厥诸部中进行策动反唐的活动。而唐朝西域的官吏、将帅,如苏海政之流,处理西突厥内部事务不当,枉杀兴昔亡可汗弥射,引起西突厥部众的不满,由是"各有离心"。不久,继往绝可汗步真死,"十姓无主,有阿史那都支及李遮匐收其余众,附于吐蕃"。

从此,西突厥诸部多倒向吐蕃,危及唐在西域的统治。龙朔三年至麟德二年(663~665)吐蕃与弓月、疏勒等多次攻唐四镇之一的于阗,安西都护高贤领兵击弓月以救于阗,后又命西州都督崔知辩等率兵救之,但收效不大。此时,吐蕃已灭青海吐谷浑,可由青海路入西域,并占据原属吐谷浑的鄯善(今新疆若羌)、且末,在西域的势力大增。到咸亨元年(670)吐蕃遂"入残羁縻十八州(属安西都护府),率于阗取龟兹拨换城(今新疆阿克苏),于是安西四镇并废"。这是唐安西四镇设置以来第二次废置,安西都护府还治于西州。敦煌藏文吐蕃历史文书纪年部分,记此年吐蕃"于且末国击唐军多人",似与吐蕃取安西四镇有关。唐朝罢四镇后,积极争取西突厥十姓及西域诸国,以与吐蕃抗衡,规复四镇。咸亨二年(671),唐朝以西突厥阿史那都支为左骁卫大将军兼匐延都督,以瓦解其与吐蕃之联盟,委其统五咄陆之众。咸亨四年(673),原已附吐蕃之疏勒、弓月入唐请降;上元元年(674),于阗王伏阇雄入唐朝见,次年(675),唐在于阗置毗沙都督府,以伏阇雄为都督;又先后在焉耆、疏勒设立督府。一时,唐在西域的势力有所恢复。敦煌藏文历史文书纪年部分,记上元二年(675),"突厥(指西突厥)地方有内乱";次年(仪凤元年,676),"论赞悉若(禄东赞子)领兵赴突厥"。可能即指上述西突厥部及于阗等降唐之事("内乱"),故吐蕃重臣论赞悉若领兵至西突厥(西域)。

仪凤元年(676),吐蕃赞普芒松芒赞卒,其子墀都松赞普立。唐朝于仪凤四年(679年,此年六月改元调露)初,方知吐蕃赞普去世消息,高宗欲命裴行俭乘间图吐蕃,行俭认为,"钦陵(禄东赞子)为政,大臣辑睦,未可图也"。然而,是年六月,情况发生了变化:西突厥阿史那都支及李遮匐复叛,煽动十姓部落,联合吐蕃,侵逼安西。裴行俭向朝廷献策,以送波斯王子泥涅斯返国为由,出其不意平息西域动乱。唐朝遂遣裴行俭依策而行,行俭率军出其不意擒都支、遮匐,立碑碎叶(今吉尔吉斯斯坦托克马克阿克别希姆遗址)而还。唐朝遂于此年第二次复四镇,移安西都护府还治龟兹。此时,四镇中碎叶代焉耆。

到永淳元年(682),又有西突厥阿史那车薄等率十姓叛,后为安西都护王方翼击败。垂拱二年(686),西突厥再次掀起反唐浪潮,吐蕃在西域势力再度增长,则天武后不得不再次放弃安西四镇,移安西都护府还治于西州。敦煌藏文历史文书纪年部分记:垂拱二年,"大论钦陵声言领兵赴突厥,实延缓未行";次年,"大论钦陵领兵赴突厥龟兹之境"。这均有吐蕃支持西突厥迫使唐第三次放弃四镇有关。吐鲁番出土的《延载元年氾德达告身》中,也有:"准垂拱二年敕金牙军拔于阗、(安西、疏)勒、碎叶四镇"的记载。

安西四镇关系着唐朝西部边疆的安全,唐朝自然势必与吐蕃展开激烈争夺。垂拱二年前后,武后以继往绝可汗步真子斛瑟罗为右玉钤卫将军,袭继往绝可汗号,押五弩失毕部;以兴昔亡可汗弥射子元庆为左玉钤卫将军,袭兴昔亡可汗号,押五咄陆部。永昌元年(689),武后又以韦待价为安息道大总管,率军与吐蕃激战于寅识迦河(在今新疆霍城西南),但为吐蕃所败,安西副都护唐休璟收余众,武后即以休璟为西州都督。由于吐蕃这次战争的胜利,故敦煌藏文历史文书纪年部分,记此年"大论钦陵自突厥引兵还"。天授二年(691),武后再以岑长倩为武威道行军大总管击吐蕃,后中道召还,军未出。这一系列的军事行动都是针对吐蕃的,目的是夺回四镇。终于在长寿元年(692),王孝杰、阿史那忠节等率军大破吐蕃,一举夺回安西四镇,移安西都护府还治龟兹,用汉兵三万以镇之。此乃唐朝第三次复置四镇。

到延载元年(694),因阿史那元庆被诬处死,西突厥十姓遂拥立元庆子阿史那俀子为可汗,与吐蕃联合攻安西。阿史那俀子遂被吐蕃封为"东叶护可汗(ton-ya-bgo-khagan)"。同年,武威道总管王孝杰破吐蕃与俀子于冷泉(在今新疆焉耆东南)和大岭,各三万余人;碎叶镇守使韩思忠又破吐蕃及西突厥泥熟俟斤等万余人。万岁通天元年(696),吐蕃遣使请和,并请唐罢四镇兵,分十姓突厥之地。武后遣郭元振与吐蕃伦钦陵商议,唐朝廷议而未决。元振遂上疏建议:以吐蕃归还吐谷浑青海之地,则可将西突厥五俟斤(即五弩失毕部)归吐蕃为条件,塞钦陵之口。武后从之。

此时,吐蕃因连年争战,引起国人的不满;加之噶尔家族长期专政,逐渐年长的赞普对此也甚为不平。因而,终于酿成了圣历元年(698)赞普迫钦陵自杀,赞婆(禄东赞子)等降唐的事件。敦煌藏文吐蕃历史文书纪年部分还记载:圣历二年(699),"东突厥可汗将来致礼";次年(700),"遣送东突厥可汗往突厥"。如上述,此"东突厥可汗"即阿史那俀子,在延载元年为唐王孝杰击破后,至是到吐蕃朝见,次年又为吐蕃遣还突厥(西域)。大约在8世纪初,阿史那俀子还出现于西域,因唐税甲税马于拔汗那(今中亚撒马尔罕),拔汗那不胜侵扰,而南招引俀子与吐蕃,"重扰四镇"。但是,对唐安西四镇并未构成大的威胁。也正因为西突厥一些上层贵族投附吐蕃,故敦煌藏文吐蕃历史文书赞普传记中,记墀都松赞普灭噶尔家族之后,说"赞普掌执政事权位高于往昔诸王,突厥等天下别部均一一降归治下,征其贡赋"。长安四年(704),墀都松赞征南诏时卒,至此,吐蕃联合西突厥与唐争夺西域的斗争暂告一段落。

二、吐蕃与后突厥汗国的关系

自贞观四年唐灭东突厥汗国后,经五十余年,原东突厥颉利可汗族人骨咄禄于永淳元年(682)率部反唐,自称颉跌利施可汗,重建突厥政权,后世史家称为后突厥汗国或第二突厥汗国。不久,骨咄禄在老臣暾欲谷的帮助下,用其计谋,东征契丹,北服九姓铁勒,建牙乌德犍山(今蒙古杭爱山东麓),以其弟默啜为"杀"(官号)。武周天授二年(691)骨咄禄卒,弟默啜立,称默啜可汗,不时与吐蕃联合,寇扰唐边境。长安元年(701)年"突厥(指默啜)、吐蕃联兵寇凉州",武后以主客郎中郭元振为凉州都督、陇右诸军大使。长安三年(703),默啜向西征服拔悉密,后又威服黠戛斯,又南下杀西突厥突骑施部娑葛。此时,后突厥汗国势力已达西域天山以北地区。据汉文文献记载,唐开元三年(715)二月,时任北庭都护的郭虔瓘"累破吐蕃及突厥默啜,斩获不可胜计,以其俘来献"。因而得到玄宗的嘉奖。由此可知,吐蕃曾与后突厥默啜联合,不断寇扰西域及河西等地。

又据敦煌藏文吐蕃历史文书纪年部分载:"及至猴年(开元八年,720)……默啜(bug-cor,或作 vbug-cor)之使者前来致礼"。中外学者大多将"bug-cor"译为后突厥可汗默啜,但默啜可汗早于开元四年(716)征拔曳固时被杀,故认为此指后突厥汗国(即东突厥)。也有的学者据敦煌发现的一份文书《北方若干国君之王统叙记》(P. T. 1283)中,记突厥的 bug-cor 包括十二个部落。

到开元十五年(727),后突厥毗伽可汗遣其大臣梅录啜入贡于唐,揭发此年九月吐蕃寇瓜州(治今甘肃安西东南)时,曾遗毗伽可汗书信一封,约其共发兵入寇。毗伽献此书于唐朝廷。玄宗嘉之,允其于西受降城互市。此后,汉、藏史籍再未见吐蕃与后突厥汗国交往之事。古突厥文《阙特勤碑》,即后突厥汗国第三任毗伽可汗(默啜侄)为其弟阙特勤记功而立,内记述其功时说:"……我向南征伐,直至九曲(今青海黄河河曲),我几乎达到吐蕃(tuput)。"又记:开元十九年(731)阙特勤卒后,"从吐蕃可汗那里来了一位论"。由此,亦反映出后突厥与吐蕃是有交往的。

三、吐蕃与西突厥突骑施的关系

8世纪初,在西域的原西突厥中的突骑施部逐渐强大。突骑施包括三个核心部落,即突骑施、车鼻施和处木昆,原居于今伊犁河流域。武周久视元年(700),武后以继往绝可汗步真子斛瑟罗为平西大总管,进驻碎叶,以统西突厥各部。斛瑟罗为政残暴,十姓不服。这就为突骑施的兴起创造了条件。

首先兴起的是突骑施首领乌质勒及其子娑葛,其尽统十姓之地,唐朝曾封娑葛为十姓可汗。到开元二年(714)因娑葛内部发生内讧,娑葛为后突厥默啜所攻杀,西突厥十姓大乱,纷纷降唐。然而不久,十姓之地很快又被突骑施中车鼻施部首领苏禄所据有。开元三年(715),苏禄遣使向唐朝贡,玄宗即封其为左羽林大将军、金方道经略大使。同时,苏禄又南与吐蕃,东与后突厥汗国联盟。开元五年(717),苏禄遂"勾引大食(阿拉伯帝国)、吐蕃,拟取四镇,见围拔换城及大石城(今新疆乌什)"。唐安西副大都护

汤嘉惠发三姓葛逻禄兵与阿史那献(唐封之西突厥十姓可汗)击之。开元六年(718),吐蕃遣使奉表至唐盟誓,其表文云:

> ……又以北突厥骨吐(咄)禄共吐蕃交通者,旧时使命实亦交通。中间舅甥(指唐与吐蕃)和睦已来,准旧平章,其骨吐禄,阿舅亦莫与交通,外甥亦不与交。今闻阿舅使人频与骨禄交通,在此亦知为不和。中间有突厥使到外甥处,既为国王,不可久留外国使人,遂却送归,即日两国和好,依旧断当。吐蕃不共突厥交通,如舅不和,自外诸使命,何入蕃,任伊去来?阿舅所附信物并悉领。外甥今奉金胡瓶一,玛瑙杯一,伏维受纳。

显然,此表文系唐朝由藏文译为汉文之作。内“北突厥骨吐禄”是指突骑施苏禄,因唐册封突骑施可汗多用“骨咄禄毗伽”可汗号,这早为学者所指出。从表文可知,苏禄不仅与唐朝多有“交通”(交往),而且已派使人到吐蕃(表文自称“外甥”)处,吐蕃已即将使人遣还。因此,吐蕃在表文中,要求唐朝与吐蕃和好,双方都不要与突骑施苏禄交往。然而,双方此后均未遵行。唐朝仍对苏禄倍加笼络,于开元七年(719)封其为“忠顺可汗”,并从其居碎叶之请,以焉者代碎叶为四镇之一。开元十年(722),唐又以阿史那怀道女为金河公主妻苏禄。而吐蕃仍阴与苏禄相结,与唐争夺西域。

开元十五年(727)闰月,苏禄遂与吐蕃赞普发兵围安西城(今新疆库车),为唐安西副大都护赵颐贞击走。次年初,安西大都护赵颐贞即击败吐蕃于曲子城。据敦煌藏文吐蕃历史文书纪年部分记,吐蕃大论穷桑于蛇年(开元十七年)“征集、增加预备军旅之数字,引兵赴突厥地,还”。这很可能是当时吐蕃进攻河西瓜州及西域,急需增加兵力;而大论穷桑之赴突厥(指西突厥),可能与前一年兵败于西域曲子城有关。此后,吐蕃加强了与突骑施苏禄的联盟,敦煌藏文吐蕃历史文书纪年部分先后记载:

> 及至猴年(开元二十年,732年)……大食与突骑施(Dur-gyis,指苏禄)之使者均前来赞普王廷致礼。
> 及至狗年(开元二十二年,734年)……王姐卓玛遣嫁突骑可汗(苏禄)为妻。

苏禄不仅娶唐金河公主,而且又娶后突厥汗国可汗女及吐蕃赞普姐卓玛为妻,正如《新唐书》卷二一五下《突厥传》所说:苏禄“又交通吐蕃、突厥,二国皆以女妻之,遂立三国女并为可敦,以数子为叶护”。就在开元二十二年,突骑施阙俟斤以羊马入朝贸易,行至北庭,为北庭都护张焕所杀。唐朝为平息苏禄之怨,借口杀张焕。苏禄并不满足,遂于开元二十三年(735)进攻北庭及四镇。次年(开元二十四年,736),据敦煌藏文吐蕃历史文书纪年部分记,有吐蕃“属庐莽布支绮穷领兵赴突厥”。此年春正是北庭都护盖嘉运大破突骑施之时,吐蕃遣军赴突厥(指西突厥之地),或与此有关。

苏禄年老多病,敛聚为己,部内百姓又分为黄姓(即自谓娑葛部者)和黑姓(即自谓为苏禄部者),更相猜疑;部内大首领莫贺达干、都摩支争权不已,故势力大衰。开元二十六年(738),苏禄为属下莫贺达干所杀,其子骨缀立为吐火仙可汗,与都摩支据碎叶,与黑姓可汗连兵拒唐。次年,唐朝遣安西都护盖嘉运,联合莫贺达干,擒吐火仙可汗,收金河公主。唐朝遂以阿史那怀道子昕为十姓可汗,派兵护送至十姓地。这引起莫贺达干的不满,发兵拒之。开元二十八年(740),唐朝遂立莫贺达干为可汗,以统突骑施部众。至天宝元年(742),莫贺达干击杀唐遣至十姓地的阿史那昕,旋其又为唐安西节度使所击杀。突骑施部遂立黑姓伊里底密施骨咄禄为可汗。在突骑施内乱及纷争的过程中,似仍与吐蕃有所交往。据敦煌藏文吐蕃历史文书纪年部分记:天宝三年(744),有"突骑施使者前来致礼"。此使者可能是上述突骑施黑姓可汗所派遣。天宝十载(751),时任安西四镇节度的高仙芝在与吐蕃争夺大、小勃律的战争胜利后,又攻占中亚的石国(今乌兹别克斯坦塔什干),入朝所献俘获中,有"生擒突骑施可汗、吐蕃大首领及石国王并可敦及羯师王"等。此"吐蕃大首领"与突骑施可汗等并列,从一个侧面也反映出两者的关系。天宝十二载(753),突骑施黑姓更立登里伊罗密施为可汗,势力更加衰落。

至天宝十四载(755),安史之乱爆发后,吐蕃先后占据唐陇右、河西诸州;至8世纪末,又占据西域天山以南大部分地区。以上这些地区的突厥部落也均为吐蕃所统治。因史籍记载不多,故所知甚少。仅在新疆米兰、玛扎塔格等地发现的8世纪及以后的藏文简牍中,有关于吐蕃统治天山以南一些突厥人活动的记载。如王尧、陈践编号70号木简记"突厥(Drug)人芒顿之妻领取谷子六升"。编号118号木简记"……在凉包抚服突然入境之汉人与突厥人",编号134号木简记"给巴本以下突厥啜尔(Drugu-vjor)以上斥候之木牍……"。编号223号木简记"那雪部落二十名汉属突厥人及零旧生小部之埭乌玛桑和门结穷二人派往布拉林去替换"。编号262号木简记"贪通向甲珑以上及实厥君门(郡)以下之驿吏悉诺等禀报"。此外,编号269号记有"突厥啜尔",289号记有"汉属突厥人向于阗……",334号有"……查看突厥人住处"等。这些藏文简牍所记,反映出吐蕃统治今新疆南部地区仍有不少的突厥部落,以及他们为吐蕃服役及生活的片断。

最后,还必须提及的是,上述敦煌发现的一份藏文文书,即《北方若干国君之王统叙记》(P. T. 1283),中外学者对此文书研究成果颇多。学者们大多认为,这份文书大致书于回纥汗国兴起时期,即8世纪中叶。文书开首记,"往昔,回鹘(Hor)王颁诏:北方究竟有多少国君? 命五名回鹘(Hor)人前往侦察。此即其回报文书,系取自玉府也。"即是说,吐蕃所获得的关于北方诸族的情况是来自回鹘人。文书中提到,在汉人称之为"室韦(ji-ur)"的方向,有"突厥(Dru-gu)默啜(Bug-chor)十二部落:王者阿史那部(Rgyal-po-zha-ma-mo-ngan)、颉利部(ha-li)、阿史德部(A-sha-sbe)、舍利突利部(shar-du-livi)、奴剌部(lo-lad)、卑失部(Par-sil)、移吉部(Rngi-kevi)、苏农部(So-ni)、足罗多部(Jol-to)、阿跌部(Yan-ti)、悒怛部(He-bdal)、颉跌部(He-bdal)、葛罗歌布逻部(Gar-rga-pur)"。如前所述,默啜,即藏文Bug-chor,是指后突厥汗国(主要是原东突厥汗国)的突厥部落。

文书还记:"自默啜(Bug-chor)而西,番人(吐蕃)称之为突厥(Drg-gu)九姓。九姓部落联盟之首长,名之为'回鹘都督'(Vu-yi-kor-du-tog),汉人册封为'Kha-gan'。其族姓为'药罗葛'(yag-le-ker),门上均竖有九面幡标。"此"突厥九姓",如学者指出,即是"九姓铁勒",包括回鹘(回纥)、同罗、思结、拔野古、浑、契苾、仆骨、拔悉密、葛逻禄等(不一定只指此九部)。以外,文书还记述了一些其他的突厥部落,不再一一列出。从这份藏文文书,可知当时吐蕃对北方突厥了解的情况,此乃系吐蕃与突厥及铁勒诸部建立关系的基础。

高昌回鹘国始末

钱伯泉

新疆社会科学院

高昌回鹘是中世纪吐鲁番盆地的主体居民,曾经建立自己的国家,在此生产、生活前后长达七百余年之久,为发展吐鲁番的政治经济,创造吐鲁番的文化艺术,作出过卓越的贡献。本文根据文献记载和考古资料,拟对高昌回鹘国的历史进行比较系统的研究。

一、回鹘与吐蕃争夺北庭获胜,始迁高昌

早在秦汉之际,吐鲁番盆地是车师前王国的领土,车师人是这里的主体民族,他们多为欧罗巴白色人种,也含有少量蒙古黄色人种的成分,似操突厥语,[1]半农半牧。

汉朝统一西域后不久,即在高昌前王国设立戊己校尉府,幕府即在高昌壁(今吐鲁番市高昌故城东部),派遣河西和陇右的汉族将士携带眷属,在此屯田戍边。有些将士屯戍期满后,贪恋这里肥美的土地,即与家属留居在戊己校尉府周围。于是,吐鲁番盆地始有汉族居民,而且随着时间的变迁而日益增多。

魏晋和南北朝前期,中原板荡,内地战乱频仍,河西和陇右的大批民众扶老携幼,西逃至戊己校尉府的治所——高昌城四周避难,汉人的数量不断增多,于是车师前王国的东部领土皆成汉人的聚居地,村落相连,禾黍遍地。车师人则在西域的民族纷争中日渐衰落,不得不退居以交河城为政治中心的吐鲁番盆地西部。于是,两者在吐鲁番盆地"平分秋色",友好相处。

东晋咸和二年(327),前凉王张骏派兵平定戊己校尉赵贞的叛乱,即以其地设置高昌郡,下辖田地县(柳中城,故址在今新疆鄯善县鲁克沁)。北魏太延五年(439),河西的北凉王朝为北魏所灭,其贵族沮渠无讳和沮渠安周西迁高昌,建立流亡的北凉小王朝。沮渠安周与柔然汗国联兵,逐走车师前王车夷落及其民众,兼并其地。北魏和平元年(460),柔然汗国击灭北凉小王朝。吐鲁番盆地先后出现阚氏、张氏、马氏统治的短暂王朝。北魏景明元年(500)左右,麹嘉成为高昌王,建立麹氏王朝,子孙相继十代。

贞观十四年(640),唐太宗派兵击灭麹氏王朝高昌国,即以其地设西州。唐朝鼎盛时,先后在西域分设安西和北庭两大都护府。西州虽然划归安西大都护府管,但因紧靠北庭,与北庭都护府的关系也颇为密切。

回纥原来游牧于婆陵水(今蒙古高原北部的色楞格河),始为高车族的一个大部族,后来南迁至鄂尔浑河游牧,役属于柔然汗国。隋唐之际,突厥强大,回纥成为九姓铁勒之首,归附于东突厥汗国。7世纪前期,回纥崛起,先后助唐朝击灭东突厥汗国、薛延陀汗国和西突厥汗国,为唐朝统一蒙古高原和西域立下汗马功劳。天宝三年(744),回纥首领骨力裴罗率众打败拔悉蜜汗国,征服葛逻禄部,自立为骨咄禄毗

---

① 参看钱伯泉:《车师语言和车师种族初探》一文,见《新疆大学学报》1997年第3期。

伽阙可汗,建牙帐于郁督军山(今蒙古杭爱山脉中段),创立了回纥汗国。由于其属部拔悉蜜游牧于阿尔泰山东西两麓,属部葛逻禄游牧于东部天山内外,不少回纥部落也西迁至阿尔泰山和天山内外,监督拔悉蜜和葛逻禄二部。所以,即使回纥汗国建立之初,回纥的实力即已扩展到唐朝北庭都护府所管辖的准噶尔盆地东部,西迁回纥与吐鲁番盆地仅有一山之隔。

天宝十四年(755),唐朝发生"安史之乱",叛军攻占了东京洛阳和西京长安,回纥葛勒可汗磨延啜主动派兵助唐收复两京,肃清叛军,恢复了唐朝的统治。葛勒可汗遣使求婚,唐肃宗将其女儿宁国公主嫁给他为妻,并册封他为"英武威远毗伽可汗",回纥与唐朝的关系空前亲密。

由于抽兵平叛,唐朝的西部边防空虚,吐蕃与唐为敌,乘机攻占了河西和陇右,使得北庭和安西两都护府孤悬天边,与唐朝多年失去联系。后靠回纥帮助,绕道蒙古高原,至京都长安报告边情,北庭、安西与朝廷的联系才得以恢复。吐蕃不断发兵进扰西域,而北庭和安西兵力单薄,又是多靠回纥相助,才得以艰难苦守。

贞元五年(789),吐蕃大举侵犯北庭,回纥大相颉干迦斯与唐朝北庭都护杨袭古联兵抵抗。由于原属回纥的葛逻禄人和沙陀人不堪回纥统治者的剥削和压迫,反戈一击,投归吐蕃,回纥和唐军大败,颉干迦斯逃归本土,杨袭古南奔西州,北庭为吐蕃所占。次年,颉干迦斯再次统兵西征,与吐蕃争夺北庭,又遭败北。又次年,颉干迦斯集全国精兵,又至北庭,终于大败吐蕃,克复北庭。从此北庭和西州正式成为回纥汗国的疆土,回纥部落不断迁居西州,人数越来越多,逐渐超过残留的汉人。

据龟兹石窟汉文题记的纪年可知,吐蕃大约于贞元十二年(796)攻占了安西大都护府。但是,原为安西大都护府属地的西州,却因紧靠北庭,始终牢牢地掌握在回纥人的手中。因为有一份外国探险家在吐鲁番发现的有关摩尼教的古突厥文写本这样记载,说高昌地区是摩尼教东方教区的一个中心,回纥的怀信可汗曾于"羊年"(803)亲自到高昌来,邀请三位 Maxistak 级别的摩尼教经师前往蒙古高原的汗国中心地区传教。[①] 此"羊年"相当于贞元十九年,距吐蕃占领安西大都护府已经七年,回纥的怀信可汗仍然可以十分从容地进出高昌。

根据《九姓回鹘爱登里罗汩没蜜施合毗伽可汗圣文神武碑》记载,保义可汗在位时,回纥大败吐蕃和葛逻禄的联军,"奔逐至珍珠河"。"珍珠河"即中亚锡尔河的上游纳伦河。保义可汗在位之初(公元808~812年左右),回纥"攻伐葛(罗)禄、吐蕃,搴旗斩馘,追奔逐北,西至拔贺那国"。拔贺那国即唐朝的泼汗国,汉朝的大宛国,故址在今乌兹别克共和国东部的费尔干纳盆地。[②] 保义可汗又征服西突厥"十姓"、"三姓突骑施"。至此回纥统一西域,西境远达咸海东南的锡尔河、阿姆河流域全境。高昌及其北方的北庭,成了回纥汗国联系西域和统管西域的重地。武功煊赫的保义可汗遣使唐朝,请求将"回纥"回的译名改作"回鹘","义取迴旋轻捷如鹘也"。[③]

二、高昌回鹘国的建立和发展

保义可汗死后,回鹘汗国天灾频繁,内乱不断,国势遽衰。唐开成五年(840),黠戛斯出兵十万,攻克

---

① 德国探险家勒柯克在吐鲁番所得的摩尼教文书,编号为 T. Ⅱ,D173 号。
② 转引自林干、高自厚:《回纥史》附录该碑的汉文部分,内蒙古人民出版社,1994年,第405页。
③ 《旧唐书》卷一九五《回纥传》。

回鹘的牙帐,回鹘汗国破灭,部落四散奔逃。接着,黠戛斯又与吐蕃联兵,攻取回鹘汗国的北庭和安西。黠戛斯收兵回国,北庭和安西为吐蕃所占,高昌地区因此落入吐蕃之手。北庭和高昌的回鹘避入天山自保。

大中二年(848),敦煌、晋昌(即瓜州,今甘肃安西县)爆发张议潮的起义,逐走吐蕃的"节儿"(相当于唐朝的"节度使")。次年,起义军收复了酒泉、张掖。在张议潮起义的影响和支援下,回鹘也出兵收复了西州,并遣使随张议潮的使团到长安向朝廷报捷。唐宣宗大喜,即命杜牧起草了《西州回鹘授骁卫大将军制》,给予表彰和奖励,其原文是:

> 敕:古者天子守在四夷,盖以恩信不亏,羁縻有礼。《春秋》列潞子之爵,西汉有隰阴之封,考于经史,其来尚矣。西州牧首颉干迦思、俱宇合、逾越密施、莫贺都督、宰相安宁等,忠勇奇志,魁健雄姿,怀西戎之腹心,作中夏之保障,相其君长,颇有智谋。今者交臂来朝,稽颡请命,丈组寸印,高位重爵,举以授尔,用震殊邻。无忘敬恭,宜念终始。可云麾将军、守左骁卫大将军,外置同正员,余如故。①

从这篇制文看,收复西州的回鹘首领名叫"安宁",他原是回鹘汗国九宰相之一,又是可汗任命的"西州牧首"(西州长官)、莫贺都督(大都督)。

在此同时,有一支从蒙古高原西逃的回鹘人,在庞特勤的率领下,从东部天山南下,攻占了焉耆九城,建立了安西回鹘。因为当时蒙古高原本土有了遏捻可汗,庞特勤不能自立为可汗,只是自称比可汗要低一级的"叶护"。《旧唐书》卷一九五《回纥传》记载:

> 开成初,其相有安允合者,与特勤柴革欲篡萨特勤可汗,萨特勤可汗觉,杀柴革及安允合。又有回鹘相掘罗勿者,拥兵在外,怨诛柴革、安允合,又杀萨特勤可汗,以厖馺特勤为可汗。有将军句录末贺恨掘罗勿,走引黠戛斯,领十万骑破回鹘城,杀厖馺,斩掘罗勿,烧荡殆尽,回鹘散奔诸蕃。有回鹘相馺职者,拥外甥庞特勤及男鹿并遏粉等兄弟五人、十五部,西奔葛逻禄,一支投吐蕃,一支投安西。

"特勤"是回鹘汗国官爵名称,凡是可汗的兄弟子侄,统称为"特勤"。因此,"庞特勤"必是可汗的子侄,其舅父宰相馺职拥护他及亲人五位,统帅十五个部落西逃葛逻禄人的故地——东部天山,一支南奔河西的吐蕃地区,一支西奔安西都护府境内。《新唐书》卷二一五《突厥传》记载:"斛瑟罗余部附回鹘,及其破灭,有庞特勤居焉耆城,称叶护;余部保金莎岭,有众二十万。"斛瑟罗是唐朝任命的西突厥十姓可汗,因施政残暴,为新兴的属部突骑施所驱逐,东归唐朝时,将其统率的西突厥残部寄放在东部天山。回鹘汗国强盛时,西突厥十姓残部归附于回鹘汗国。"金莎岭"指北庭城南的东部天山高峰,今乌鲁木齐市东的博格达山。据上述引文可知,当庞特勤西迁,在焉耆建立安西回鹘国时,金莎岭一带尚有回鹘和附属的十姓西突厥残众二十万人,听命于庞特勤。

不久,蒙古高原回鹘汗国本土的遏捻可汗因故逃亡,下落不明。回鹘失去了共主,于是庞特勤乃自立

---

① 杜牧:《樊川文集》卷二十。

为可汗,并不断遣使唐朝,请求册命,但是,或因路途不清,或因唐皇多难,一直未能取得联系。直到大中十年(856),庞特勤的使者才辗转到达长安,唐宣宗详加询问,得知:"庞特勤今为可汗,尚寓安西,众所悦附,飏宰相以忠事上,誓复龙庭。杂虏等以义向风,颇闻靡至。"①唐宣宗很高兴,当即遣使安西回鹘国,慰问庞特勤可汗。唐朝的使者刚到灵武(今宁夏灵武县),又碰见庞特勤派来进贡和请求册命的三批使者。唐朝使者带领这三批使者回朝复命。于是,唐宣宗立即发布册命:"今遣使臣朝议郎、检校秘书监兼卫尉少卿、御史中丞、上柱国、赐紫金鱼袋王端章,副使臣朝议郎、检校尚书工部郎中兼国子礼学博士、赐绯鱼袋李浔持节备礼,册命为九姓回鹘温禄登里罗汩没密施合俱录怀建可汗。尔其服我恩荣,膺兹爵位,勉修前好,恢复故疆,宜克己于蹛林,长归心于魏阙,无怠尔志,永孚于休。"②

此后吐蕃发动反扑,一度重新占领西州等地。但是为时不久,即被回鹘收复。《资治通鉴》卷二五〇记载:"(咸通七年)二月,归义节度使张议潮奏:北庭回鹘固俊克西州、北庭、轮台、清镇等城。"③咸通七年即为公元866年。北庭城在今新疆吉木萨尔县,轮台城在今乌鲁木齐市,清镇城在今新疆玛纳斯县。关于同一事件,《新唐书·回鹘传》也说:"懿宗时,大酋仆固俊自北庭击吐蕃,斩论尚热尽取西州、轮台等城,使达干米怀玉朝且献俘,因请命。诏可。"④前一引文的"固俊",当为此引文中的"仆固俊"之误。《新唐书》明确地说"仆固俊"是"北庭大酋",意为北庭一带的回鹘大酋长,可见他是回鹘贵族,地位不低。由前引《议立回鹘可汗诏》中"庞特勤今为可汗,众所悦附",而且敢于"誓复龙庭",可见其国力甚强,作为北庭大酋的仆固俊,原来必然"悦附"于庞特勤可汗,诸如西州、轮台、北庭、清镇等地,原来也一定归属于庞特勤可汗的安西回鹘国。那么,仆固俊的"北庭大酋",也许就是庞特勤可汗所任命的。仆固俊克服西州、北庭、轮台、清镇,胜利是巨大的,战功是显赫的,理应向可汗庞特勤邀功请奖,但是他却采取了不正当的做法,居然无视庞特勤可汗,擅自派遣米怀玉至唐朝"献俘"和"请命"。这个"请命"有两种理解,一种是"请求任命唐朝的官职";另一种是"请求册命为回鹘可汗",这是不可容忍的。前者仅仅表示仆固俊怀有独立和分裂的倾向,后者则显示仆固俊有着篡夺庞特勤的汗位,准备取而代之的野心。

此后唐朝内乱不断,逐渐失去了与西域的联系,有关庞特勤可汗和北庭大酋仆固俊的事情,再不见于唐朝的历史记载,但在11世纪波斯学者加尔底吉(Gardizi)所编写的《记述的装饰》(Zayn al-AKhbar)一书中,有这样的一段记载:

　　说起九姓乌古斯,该王自称九姓乌古斯可汗。在他的一族中,有个叫库尔特勤(Kül tegin)的著名人物,他母亲是阿尔钦(Archin),是个自由人。库尔特勤的异母兄长是可汗,哥哥要杀害库尔特勤,把他的喉咙砍了后弃置于山上。库尔特勤的乳母把他送到摩尼教的经师那里,经过医治,逐渐好转,终于痊愈。后来,库尔特勤到九姓乌古斯可汗的都城焉耆(Azal)隐居起来,派人尽力去讨好可汗,让可汗心里高兴。可汗终于回心转意,答应不再杀他,但不准他进王宫去,派他当了五城(Panjikath,突厥和回鹘人称Bexbalik,即北庭城)的总督。他在那里积聚力量,与当地人交朋友,经常对他们施以恩惠,暗地里等待时机。这时听到可汗要去狩猎的消息,于是便集合了大批队伍,去袭击可汗。库尔特

① 《唐大诏令集》卷一二八《议立回鹘可汗诏》。
② 《唐大诏令集》卷一二九《大中十一年册回鹘可汗文》。
③ 《资治通鉴》卷二五〇"咸通七年二月"条。
④ 《新唐书》卷二一七下《回鹘下》。

勤打败了可汗,可汗逃回城里固守。库尔特勤命令放水淹城,城墙坍毁。库尔特勤宣布,凡投降者一律赦免。城内居民因饥饿而疲惫不堪,均出城投降,所有人都被恩赦。由于九姓乌古斯可汗待在城内,库尔特勤便命部下将他绞死,于是他便接了可汗的位置。

故事下面接着说:"从波斯到库尔特勤处,必须经过温宿、库车,到焉耆;由焉耆再经一地,便到秦人城(高昌),秦人城周围有二十多个小城镇。"

加尔底吉虽然是11世纪中叶的人,但他在编写《记述的装饰》时,凡是讲到突厥诸族、中国和吐蕃的历史时,都是选取著名历史学家穆卡法父子、忽儿达兹比赫、贾伊哈尼等人的著作。贾伊哈尼记述的,主要是公元870年左右的突厥和九姓乌古斯的历史。西方称回鹘为九姓乌古斯,九姓乌古斯可汗建都于焉耆的,只有安西回鹘国可汗庞特勤,而仆固俊又是"北庭大酋",与库尔特勤的身份和地位相同。因此,《记述和装饰》讲述的这个故事,无疑记录了庞特勤可汗和库尔特勤的斗争历史。最后仆固俊取得了胜利,成为可汗,并把都城搬迁到高昌,正式改称其政权为"高昌回鹘国";因为高昌地区是唐朝的"西州",所以五代和宋朝的汉文史料又称之为"西州回鹘国"。

三、高昌回鹘国的发展和繁盛

回鹘原是"随畜牧,逐水草"的游牧民族,受自然条件的约束,生产方式落后,自身实力起伏很大。回鹘汗国的衰败,就是连年天灾,羊马多死而引发的。回鹘西迁,建立高昌国,政治稳定之后,由于地理环境和自然条件大变,他们的生产方式和生活习惯也因之大变。高昌回鹘国的疆土包括吐鲁番盆地、焉耆盆地和准噶尔盆地东南部。这些地方水土肥美,适宜于农耕。早在回鹘迁入之前,人数众多的汉族平民和军垦屯户即在这些地方从事耕作,农业生产的历史,长久者约达千年,短暂者也已数百年。到处呈现村落相望,阡陌相连,禾黍遍野,桑麻茂盛的景象。高昌回鹘拥有这样优越的地理条件和自然环境后,在汉族农民的影响和帮助下,大多数人很快改营农业,开始定居。先进的农业生产方式,大大促进了高昌回鹘的经济繁荣和国力强盛。

高昌回鹘建国后的前二百年(约848~1048),四周国家和民族的形势对其保持政治稳定和经济发展十分有利。高昌回鹘国的东方隔一伊州,始与瓜、沙归义军地方政权相邻,该政权地小民贫,自顾不暇,只能和平相处;后与甘州回鹘国接界,二者种族相同,关系亲密。11世纪中期,大国西夏攻灭甘州回鹘国,征服伊州,一度虎视高昌。高昌回鹘审时度势,俯首称臣。西夏又忙于东与宋、辽争斗,于是,高昌回鹘躲过战乱的浩劫,得以平安无事。这时,辽朝占据蒙古高原,隔阿尔泰山,与高昌回鹘相望。高昌回鹘采取柔顺的态度,按时遣使进贡称臣,取得了长期的和平。高昌回鹘国的东南原为吐蕃的属部龟兹回鹘。吐蕃衰微,退回青藏高原南部后,龟兹回鹘得以独立建国,后来改称撒里畏兀儿。他们与高昌回鹘种族相同,始终和睦相处。高昌回鹘国的西南与佛国于阗隔着大漠相望,交往很少。高昌回鹘国的西面原是龟兹佛国,后为葛逻禄所建的"割禄国"所代替,其族也信佛教,与多信佛教的高昌回鹘友善相处。11世纪初期,喀喇汗王朝西回鹘先后击灭于阗,征服割禄国,与高昌回鹘国在布古尔(今新疆轮台县)对峙。由于宗教信仰的不同,伊斯兰化的喀喇汗王朝西回鹘将信仰摩尼教和佛教的高昌回鹘视为仇敌,多次对其进行"圣战",但未得到多少便宜。后来,喀喇汗王朝忙于西方的战事,无暇东顾,高昌回鹘的西方边境始得长时期的平静和安宁。11 世纪后期至 13 世纪中期,高昌回鹘采取一贯的和平外交政策,遣使向宋、辽、西夏、金纳贡称臣;又先后长期归附于西辽和成吉思汗及其子孙创建的大蒙古国和元朝,从而政治稳定,经济发达,使国家一直处于比较繁荣的境地。

宋朝初建,高昌回鹘国即遣使朝贡。宋太祖建隆三年(962),高昌回鹘国派出以阿都督为首的 42 人组成的庞大使团,向宋朝进献方物。宋太宗太平兴国六年(981),其王始称"西州外生(甥)王阿厮兰汉(汗)",遣都督麦索温至宋朝进贡。① 宋太宗鉴于高昌回鹘可汗的真诚态度,即以供奉官王延德为正使,殿前承旨白勋为副使,出使高昌。王延德在其国内停留十月,走遍全境,对其国情了解得一清二楚。东归之后,他撰文记录其出使过程,今摘录有关其国家情况的部分内容如下:

> 高昌即西州也,其地南距于阗,西南距大石、波斯,西距西天、布露沙、雪山、葱岭皆数千里,地无雨雪而极热每盛暑,人皆穿池(地)为穴以处。飞鸟群萃河滨,或起飞即为日气所烁,坠而伤翼。屋室覆以白垩,开宝二年,雨及五寸,即庐舍多坏。有水出金岭,导之周绕国城,以溉田园,作水碓。地产五谷,惟无荞麦。贵人食马,余食牛及凫雁。乐多箜篌。出貂鼠、白氎、绣纹花蕊布。俗多骑射。妇人戴油帽,谓之苏幕遮。用开元七年历,以三月九日为寒食,余二社、冬至亦然。以银或鍮为筒,贮水激以相射,或以水交泼为戏,谓之阳阴气去病。好遊(游)赏,行者必抱乐器。佛寺五十余区,皆唐朝所赐额,寺中有《大藏经》、《唐韵》、《玉篇》、《经音》等。居民春月多遊(游),聚众遨乐于其间,遊(游)者马上持弓射诸物,谓之禳灾。有敕书楼,藏唐太宗、明皇御札诏敕,缄锁甚谨。后有摩尼寺、波斯僧,各持其法,佛经所谓外道者也。统有南突厥、北突厥、大众慰、小众慰、样磨、割禄、黠戛斯、末蛮、格多族、预龙族之多甚众。国中无贫民,绝食者共振(赈)之。人多寿考,率百余岁,绝无夭死……狮子王邀延德至其北廷,历交河州,凡六日,至金岭口,宝货所出;又两日,至汉家寨。又五日,上金岭、温岭,即多雨雪,上有《龙王刻石记》云:"小雪山也。"岭上有积雪,行人皆服毛罽。度岭一日,至北廷,憩高台寺,其主烹羊马以具膳,尤丰洁。地多马,王及王后、太子各养马,放牧于平川中,弥亘数百里,以毛色分别为群,莫知其数。北廷川长广数千里,鹰鹞雕鹘之所生,多美草,下生花砂鼠,大如兔,鸷禽扑食之。……北廷山中出硇砂,山中常有烟气涌起,而无云雾,且又光焰若炬,照见禽鼠皆赤。采硇砂者,着木底靴,若皮为底即焦。下有穴,生青泥,出穴外即变为砂石,土人取以治皮。城中多楼台草木。人白皙端正,惟工巧,善冶金银铜铁为器及攻玉。善马值绢一匹,其驽马充食者,才值一丈。贫者皆食肉。……②

从高昌"地产五谷",北廷"地多马",人"好游赏,行者必抱乐器","居民春月多游,聚众遨乐于其间","国中无贫民,绝食者共振(赈)之;人多寿考,率百余岁,绝无夭死","贫者皆食肉"等记载来看,高昌回鹘国真是和平安宁,富裕欢乐。比起烽火不断、恶战连年、民不聊生的内地宋、辽、金、西夏等国,真可谓是人间无上的世外桃源,实实在在的理想之国。

高昌和北庭都是处于丝绸之路的要地。高昌是"伊吾路"的终点和"安西路"的起点,北庭是"回鹘

---

① 《宋史》卷四九〇《外国六·高昌》。
② [宋]王明清:《挥麈录·前录》卷四,中华书局 1961 年 10 月版,第 36～38 页。

路"的终点和"碎叶路"的起点。高昌回鹘十分繁荣的丝路贸易,显示了这个国家的经济非常发达。以五代末年高昌回鹘国与后周进行的一次官方贸易为例:广顺元年(951),春二月"辛丑,西州回鹘遣使贡方物……丁巳……回鹘遣使贡方物"。[1] 这两条记载过分简略,仅记遣使事实,未记进贡物品。但是宋朝所编的《册府元龟》却记载得十分具体和详细:

> 广顺元年二月辛丑,西州回鹘遣都督来朝,贡玉大小六团,一团碧、琥珀九斤、白氎布一千三百二十九段、白褐二百八十段、珊瑚六树、白貂鼠皮二千六百三十二、黑貂鼠皮二百五十、青貂鼠皮五百三、旧貂鼠袄子四,白玉环子、碧玉环子各一,铁镜二、玉带铰具六十九、玉带一、诸香药称是。回鹘遣使摩尼贡玉团七十九、白氎段三百五十、青及黑貂鼠皮共二十八,玉带、玉鞍辔、铰具各一副,氂牛尾四百二十四、大琥珀二十四、红盐三百斤、胡桐泪三百九十斤,余药物在数外。[2]

西州回鹘国与后周、宋朝和辽朝之间,名义上是"朝贡关系",实则上为"官方贸易"。使者携带货物东行,进入后周和宋朝、辽的边境后,不但一路受到官方的招待,住驿馆,供饮食,而且到达京都后,既能受到皇帝的宴见和重赏,又能得到朝廷的"优给货价",获利无数。因此,高昌回鹘国的统治者乐此不疲,往往超出中央王朝"两年一次"的规定,总是年年遣使,甚至如"广顺元年"一样,一年即达两次。从上引记载看,高昌国使者所带的货物,也是五代和宋、辽时期诸藩属国朝贡使者所带货物最多的一次。这些货物,有的产自本土,诸如白氎布(棉布)、褐布、貂皮、红盐、胡桐泪等;有的来自国外,诸如于阗的玉,波斯湾和地中海的珊瑚,伊朗高原、阿拉伯半岛的琥珀和香药(乳香、鸡舌香、龙涎香等)。当年内地的玉价奇贵,轻软保暖的白氎布也是高档衣料,至于貂皮,只有皇亲贵戚才能享有。高昌回鹘使者带着这么多的贵重物品,其价值是相当巨大的,完全反映了高昌回鹘国繁荣的经济与强大的物力、财力。

四、高昌回鹘国的分离及其消亡

公元1206年,铁木真统一蒙古高原,被尊为"成吉思汗",创建了大蒙古国。接着,成吉思汗着手经营西域,于公元1209年派大将军忽必来西征巴尔喀什湖南海押立地区的葛逻禄部,其部首领阿儿思兰罕不战而降。高昌回鹘国亦都护(王)巴而术阿而忒的斤听说成吉思汗的威名,主动遣使大蒙古国,表示归附。《蒙古秘史》对此记载说:

> 畏兀儿部的亦都兀惕罕遣使臣阿惕乞敕黑、答儿伯二人来谒见成吉思合罕,奏说:"如云开见日,如冰消河清。成吉思合罕恩赐:我给你扯拉你的金带扣子,我给你扶持你的圣洁袍子,做你的第五个儿子,给你效力!"听了这话,成吉思合罕赐答,使人去告说:"把我的女儿嫁给你,你做我的第五个儿子,请献来金银、珠宝、金缎子、亮刺绣、绸缎等物!"亦都兀惕获得恩赐,很高兴,就预备了金银、珠宝、绸缎等物,拿来拜见成吉思合罕。成吉思合罕赏赐亦都兀惕,把女儿阿勒阿勒屯别乞嫁给了他。[3]

---

① 《旧五代史》卷一一一《周书二·太祖本纪》。
② 《册府元龟》卷九七二。
③ 《蒙古秘史》第238小节,见策·达木丁苏隆编译,谢再善译,中华书局,1956年5月,第283页。

此后,蒙古统治者改称高昌回鹘国为"畏兀儿国"。成吉思汗分封诸子时,作为"第五子",畏兀儿国的亦都护巴而术阿而忒的斤得以保有其原来的疆域。从此巴而术阿而忒的斤及其子孙始终效忠于大蒙古国和元朝,为征伐西域,击灭西夏、金朝和南宋建立了丰功伟绩,深受大蒙古国和元朝统治者的器重和优待。畏兀儿国因此长期处于政治稳定、经济发展的状态,人民群众也都过着平安而富裕的生活。

成吉思汗死后,始由幼子托雷监国,继则由三子窝阔台即位为大汗,蒙古最高统治集团因而形成两大派系,权力之争愈演愈烈。公元1259年,托雷之子、蒙哥之弟忽必烈继位为大汗;不久建立元朝,又成为皇帝。窝阔台汗海都拉拢察合台汗都哇,发动叛乱,反对忽必烈。于是,忠于大汗和皇帝的畏兀儿国成了叛军重点打击的对象,经历四百多年和平和安宁的城乡一再遭受战火的洗劫,损失惨重。亦都护火赤哈尔的斤入朝报告情况,元世祖忽必烈奖励他的忠诚,拨巨款赈济他的难民。公元1280年,火赤哈尔的斤西归,刚刚到达哈密力(今新疆哈密市),叛军侵占高昌,继续东进。双方一场鏖战,火赤哈尔的斤阵亡。其子纽林的斤收集残众,东退河西走廊,奉忽必烈之命,长住永昌。早在唐高宗龙朔年间(661~663),即有众多回鹘人从蒙古高原内迁于此,这里又是甘州回鹘国的发祥之地。因此,可说是回鹘人的第二故乡,历来颇多回鹘遗民生活于此。从此,畏兀儿国的主体即在甘肃永昌重新立国,与高昌和北庭的故国分离为二。这段历史事实详见于《元史》卷一百二十二的《巴而术阿而忒的斤传》中。

不久,元朝出兵驱逐叛军,收复天山南北,畏兀儿国的故土得以重归。元朝下令各地搜集畏兀儿流民,将他们遣返高昌和北庭,西部畏兀儿国的政治和经济得以逐渐恢复。但因当时青海东部的脱思麻地区局势不稳,吐蕃人连年作乱,元朝特任纽林的斤为吐番(蕃)宣慰使,率领本部探马赤军长驻脱思麻地区,以资弹压。纽林的斤军务倥偬,无暇西顾,故土的治理只得委托他的亲信子弟负责。

公元1308年,海都和都哇的叛乱彻底平息,纽林的斤因为功劳卓著,接连受到元朝皇帝的奖赏,并曾一度奉命率军西归,重整故土的城池。《亦都护高昌王世勋碑》记载:"武宗皇帝召还,赐为亦都护,赐之金印;复署其部押西护司之官。仁宗皇帝始稽故实,封为高昌王,别以金印赐之,设王傅之官,王印行之内郡,亦都护之印则行诸畏吾而之境。八卜义公主薨,尚公主兀敕真,阿难答安西王之女也。领兵火州。复立畏吾而城池。"[①]按,"畏吾而"为"畏兀儿"的异译。元武宗册封纽林的斤为亦都护,赐亦都护金印,并以北庭城设押西护司,是他刚即位的至大元年(1308)的事。元仁宗册封纽林的斤为高昌王,并赐高昌王金印,是他即位的次年,即皇庆元年(1312)的事。纽林的斤领兵返回火州,重建畏兀儿城池,则在皇庆二年。但是重建故土各城之后,纽林的斤仍然率军返回甘肃永昌,五年之后,即死于该地,并埋葬于该地的石碑沟中。可见在亦都护家族的眼中,甘肃永昌已是高昌王的封国重地,是畏兀儿国的主体,而高昌和北庭的故土,则已退居次要的地位,仅由亦都护高昌王指派亲族或官员代理而已。

纽林的斤去世后,其长子帖睦尔补化继位为亦都护、高昌王。帖睦尔补化曾领本部军马镇守襄阳,后又长期驻守湖广行省,至今湖南常熟市和桃源县一带仍有一批畏兀儿人后裔生活着。后来,帖睦尔补化又受元文宗之召,带兵北上勤王,入汴时与河南行省的军民一起,抗御上都集团诸王南扰的叛军,部分畏兀儿户驻屯于河南西部,因此,今河南渑池县境内也生息着一批畏兀儿人的后裔。接着,帖睦尔补化又率所部趋至京师,削平大难,彻底镇压了上都集团诸王的叛变,留居大都,畏兀儿军户驻守于京西。因此,元明之际,京西一带都是畏兀儿人的聚居地,不过随着历史的发展,其后裔逐渐融合于汉族中。东部畏兀儿

---

① 黄文弼:《亦都护高昌王世勋碑复原并校记》,见《文物》1964年第2期。

国的精壮部分,就这样逐渐分散于各地,留居甘肃永昌的畏兀儿人,多为老弱或家累沉重的少数人。

元朝末年,年少的和赏继位为亦都护、高昌王,坐镇甘肃永昌。公元 1368 年,朱元璋创立明朝,元顺帝逃归蒙古高原,元朝灭亡。洪武三年(1370),明将冯胜率大军攻克兰州,和赏审时度势,乃手捧亦都护和高昌王金印,率王府官属至兰州的明军辕门请降。冯胜派兵护送和赏入朝南京,明太祖即以高昌王封地设置"高昌卫",任命和赏为怀远将军、高昌卫同知指挥使司事,立足于甘肃永昌的东部畏兀儿高昌王国即告结束。

元朝末年,中原板荡,无力顾及西域,察合台汗国的势力东渐,将原属元朝的东部天山南北之地,包括北庭、高昌一带的西部畏兀儿国,置于其势力范围之内。察合台汗国分裂为东、西两部分后,秃黑鲁帖木儿汗虽然建都于阿力麻里(今新疆伊犁地区的霍城县),但他属下的主要部众则东迁游牧于北庭地区的天山内外,北庭成了东察合台汗国第二个重城。突厥语称北庭为"别失八里",因此,明朝就直称东察合台汗国为"别失八里国"。于是北庭地区的畏兀儿遗民被迫南迁高昌地区。至秃黑鲁帖木儿汗之子黑的儿火者执政时,大力推广伊斯兰教,对笃信佛教的高昌畏兀儿进行多次"圣战",攻占高昌及其周围的村镇,强迫残留的畏兀儿遗民改信伊斯兰教。[①] 为了加强对高昌地区的统治,黑的儿火者将都城迁至交河城东的安乐城,改称之为"土鲁番",同时分派亲信为柳城(今鄯善县鲁克沁)、高昌(明朝称之为"火州")、土鲁番的城主。当永乐四年(1406),明成祖派遣刘帖木儿出使别失八里国,分赐其属下时,柳城的城主名"瓦赤敕",火州的城主为"王子哈散"(黑的儿火者之子,"哈散"为伊斯兰教的教名),土鲁番的城主名"赛因帖木儿",都是蒙古族人名,不是畏兀儿人名。由此可知,西部畏兀儿国灭亡于黑的儿火者的"圣战"中。这里的畏兀儿人或者被杀,或者被迫改信伊斯兰教,融合于维吾尔族,或者辗转东逃,加入撒里畏兀儿人中,后来成了裕固族人的祖先。

五、高昌回鹘国的政治经济、宗教信仰和文化艺术

高昌回鹘国的前期,其最高统治者为"可汗"(khan),又以狮子(arslam)为美称,合谓"arslam khan",音译为"阿斯兰汗",意译为"狮子王"。高昌回鹘国的后期,其最高统治者改称为亦都护(iduq),其早年的原音为"Idikut",意为"国之福王"。"亦都护"为突厥汗国的官号,约略与低可汗一级的"叶护"相当。由"可汗"改称"亦都护",一定有其变故在,留待日后再作考证。回鹘汗国时期,由于国境广大、事务庞杂,特设内外宰相九人,分管国族大事。西迁高昌之后,国小事少,故只设宰相一人,号称"伂俚杰忽底"(bilge kuti),意为"智福大相"。宫廷各类官员总名为"达干"(dargan),其中主管议论的"达干"号称"乌鲁阿吾只"(ulug awuz),直译为"大咀巴"。此外,领兵的官员号称"都督"(tutuq),领部落的官员号称"梅录"(bulug),地方官员总称"别吉"(begi),突厥汗国和回鹘汗国时称"匐"(beg),清朝时称"伯克"(beg)。因此综观高昌回鹘国的制度,官制是健全的,职掌是分明的,政治效率是较高的,国家是治理得井

---

① 米尔咱·马黑麻·海答尔著,新疆社会科学院民族研究所译,王治来校注《中亚蒙兀儿史·拉史德史》第一编《第二十六章秃黑鲁帖木儿汗之子黑的儿火者汗统治的开始》说:"黑的儿火者汗在位时,曾经举行过圣战(ghazat),进攻契丹。他亲自攻占了契丹的两个边陲重镇哈拉和卓和吐鲁番,强迫当地居民皈依伊斯兰教。因此,这两个地方现在被称为'达尔·阿勒·伊斯兰'(Dar al Islam)。作为蒙兀儿汗的驻地来说,这个地区的重要性仅次于哈什哈尔。"新疆人民出版社,1983 年 6 月版,第 225 页。"契丹"指明朝。由这条记载可知,亦都护高昌王和赏投归明朝后,其属下的今吐鲁番地区的畏兀儿国也曾一度归属明朝,直至被黑的儿火者攻占为止。

井有条的。

汗国时期的回鹘是一个游牧民族,自古以来即在他们发祥的游牧天国——蒙古高原世代游牧,"随畜牧,逐水草",住毡房,饮乳食肉,马、羊、牛是他们牧放的主畜,冬闲时也以狩猎为副业。当汗国强盛时,一些回鹘部落即已西迁至北庭城外的浮图川(今新疆吉木萨尔县的草原)中游牧。回鹘与吐蕃争夺北庭,北庭被吐蕃攻占,浮图川的草原被吐蕃的盟友葛逻禄占据,这里的回鹘牧民只得东逾阿尔泰山,迁回到蒙古高原西南部避难。① 公元 792 年,回鹘战胜吐蕃,夺回北庭,同时取得天山以南的高昌地区(即唐朝的"西州")。于是大批回鹘部落不但迁回浮图川,而且进占高昌。但是,这时的回鹘移民仍旧从事游牧。由于北庭和高昌水源充足,土地肥沃,气候适宜,汉族军民自汉至唐的八百多年中开展屯田戍边或农耕,积累了丰富的生产经验,开发出星罗棋布的农耕区。由于农耕生产的收获比畜牧业生产要多得多,而且比较稳定。于是,北庭和高昌的回鹘牧民大多迅速改变生产方式,改营农业,定居村镇;只有少数人坚持游牧,为王家、贵族和富人牧放马羊。《宋史·高昌传》记载:"有水,源出金岭,导之周围国城,以灌田园,做水硙。地产五谷,唯无荞麦。"②高昌回鹘国的主要农作物是小麦、水稻、黍、稷、菽,足供国民食用。其经济作物主要是"白氎",白氎是草本棉花,早在南北朝时,这里即以盛产"白氎"、纺线织布而著名。唐、宋时期,内地尚无棉花,富穿锦绣,穷穿麻衣,轻柔细软的白氎布是高昌输入内地的珍贵衣料,价值很高,所以种植颇多,并因此促进了高昌回鹘国的棉纺织手工业。五代后周广顺元年,高昌回鹘国通过两次官方贸易,输入中原的白氎布居然达到一千五百七十九段匹,可见其种植、纺织、印染、出口白氎之多。高昌的园艺业也十分发达,葡萄、瓜类的质量好,产量多。元朝宫廷和贵族喜饮葡萄酒,均由畏兀儿国生产和进贡。③中国上古没有西瓜,西瓜原产于西亚,辽宋时期始传入高昌回鹘国,因吃瓜瓤,故称"瓤瓜"。后传入辽朝,再经辽朝传入中国北方,但因水土气候不同,质量大减,日益小而不甜。至于甜瓜,古称"甘瓜",更是高昌回鹘国的特产。公元 1221 年,长春真人丘处机赴中亚进见成吉思汗,于阴历秋九月到达畏兀儿国的昌八敕城(今新疆昌吉市),"其王畏午儿与镇海有旧,率众部族及回纥僧皆远迎。既入,斋于台上。泊其夫人劝葡萄酒,且献西瓜,其重及秤。甘瓜如枕许,其香味盖中国未有也"。④ "及秤"指重达一百市斤,一个西瓜一百斤,只有吐鲁番盆地才可能种出。甜瓜兼有浓香,也只产于高昌地区,明朝时期才东传哈密,并俗称"哈密瓜"。

高昌回鹘国的手工工场生产和家庭手工业,只要有白氎纺织业,马皮、貂皮等皮革鞣制和加工业,雕琢玉器的手工业等等。由于高昌多有中亚的粟特移民,其中来自康国(撒马尔罕城)的粟特手工工匠,善于用金、银、鍮石、铜等制作装饰品、实用盘罐及刀剑、锁子甲等武器,回鹘工匠也学得了他们的技艺。

早在麴氏王朝高昌国和唐初,高昌地区的汉族居民皆信佛教,粟特族九姓移民则信祆教。唐朝初期,随着粟特九姓新移民的东来,摩尼教也进入了高昌地区,但因受佛教和祆教的抑制,并不兴盛。回纥未建国前,流行和信仰萨满教,巫师在族中颇有地位。回纥建国后不久,助唐平定"安史之乱",在收复东京洛

---

① 《新唐书》卷二一七下《回鹘下》:"吐蕃因沙陀共寇北庭,颉干迦斯与战不胜,北庭陷……葛禄又取深图川,回鹘大恐,稍南其部落以避之。""深"为"浮"字之误,"深图川"应作"浮图川"。北庭西汉时为车师后国之地,车师后王主牙帐在"务塗谷",指北庭以南的天山山谷。"浮图"为"务塗"的异译,"川"指平川。因此,"浮图川"即北庭周围的草原。由以上记载可知,早在回纥汗国创立后不久,就有许多回纥部落西迁至北庭周围游牧。

② 《宋史》卷四九〇《外国六·高昌》。

③ 《元史》卷四十一《顺帝四》:"(至正七年十月)戊戌,西蕃盗起,凡二百余所,陷哈剌火州,劫供御葡萄酒,杀使臣。"

④ 转引自张星烺编注,朱杰勤校订《中西交通史料汇编》第五册,中华书局,1977 年,第 98 页。

阳时,首先接触到摩尼教,牟羽可汗极感兴趣,当即邀请睿息等四名摩尼教经师前往蒙古高原传教,回纥立时掀起信仰摩尼教的高潮。不久之后,摩尼教竟然成了回纥汗国的国教。① 回纥战胜吐蕃,占领北庭和高昌后,仍然笃信摩尼教,对众多的佛寺和僧人视而不见,听而不闻。西方的摩尼教廷听说回纥笃信其教,新占丝路重镇高昌和焉耆,即派大批传教士东来。于是,经过短短数年,焉耆和高昌即成了摩尼教廷东方教区的两个中心城市。根据吐鲁番出土的摩尼教文书记载,怀信可汗曾在"羊年"(803)亲至高昌,邀请三名摩尼教经师到蒙古高原的可汗龙庭去宣教。回鹘汗国崩溃,高昌回鹘西迁建国后,仍然笃信摩尼教,其教仍占有国教的地位。因此,吐鲁番出土过大量用回鹘文写成的摩尼教经典和文书,其中最著名的有《牟羽可汗入教记》、《摩尼教赞美诗集》、《摩尼教寺院经济文书》,以及附有手绘工笔彩图的摩尼教经典残书。但到高昌回鹘国后期,大约是公元1036年甘州回鹘国灭亡,大批甘州回鹘贵族和部众迁入高昌回鹘国后,宗教状况大变。甘州回鹘原来也信摩尼教,但与瓜、沙曹氏归义军割据政权建立姻亲关系后,受敦煌及曹氏统治者的影响,很快改信佛教。甘州回鹘灭国和西迁之时,汗国上下都已笃信佛教,摩尼教已处于无足轻重的地位。由于西迁的甘州回鹘首领出身于药罗葛氏可汗家族,是回纥祖先卜古可汗的嫡系子孙,高昌回鹘可汗即让位于他,退居国相之位。于是,甘州回鹘首领成了高昌回鹘国主,改称号为"亦都护",他和贵族、部众们利用高昌地区旧有的佛寺,继续开展佛教活动。原来的高昌回鹘居民在他们的影响下,很快都改信佛教,摩尼教失去了国教的地位。高昌城北的柏孜克里克石窟寺、北庭古城西侧的高台寺,都成了回鹘王家的寺院,至今存留有大量供养人像和回鹘文题记。吐鲁番还出土过大量的回鹘文佛经。高昌回鹘国后期,尤其是归属于大蒙古国和元朝后,随着部分留居于畏兀儿国的蒙古贵族和官吏改信景教,回鹘人或畏兀儿人中也出现了少量的景教徒,吐鲁番还曾出土过一些回鹘文写的景教典籍和文书。用回鹘文译成的《伊索寓言》,也一定是回鹘景教徒所为。

回鹘的语言属阿尔泰语系突厥语族,创立汗国之前,没有自己的文字。创立汗国之后,借用粟特文和突厥文来记事。回鹘汗国鼎盛时期,疆域扩张,事务繁杂,感到借用粟特文和突厥文多有不便,于是利用粟特字母拼写本族语言,创造了回鹘文,并在回鹘人中迅速普及起来。从此,回鹘人写史、记事、撰写文学作品,无一不使用回鹘文。回鹘汗国崩溃,高昌回鹘建国后,其大量的历史记载、文学作品、公私文书和契约,都是用回鹘文写成的。

高昌回鹘国用回鹘文写成的历史作品有《乌古斯可汗的传说》、《牟羽可汗入教记》、《亦都护高昌王世勋碑》等。其中《乌古斯可汗的传说》、《亦都护高昌王世勋碑》皆为史诗,记史多神奇,写诗有韵律。以《亦都护高昌王世勋碑》为例,卜古可汗的降生和西迁的经过皆为神话和传说,记载投归成吉思汗之后的几代亦都护的近现代史则十分写实。全文由61首"四行诗"组成,都按回鹘古诗的风格,押头韵而排列;少数段落受汉文古诗的影响,使用押脚韵的技巧。全诗词藻华丽,感情丰富,是史诗中的上乘之作。服务于元朝的畏兀儿历史家偰哲笃曾参与编写《辽史》,而纂修官则是廉惠山海牙;沙敕班则曾参与编写《金史》;岳柱、全普俺撒里则担任《宋史》的提调官。他们为我国二十四史的编写做出了贡献。

高昌回鹘国的文学创作十分繁荣。吐鲁番发现的大量回鹘文遗书中,除佛经、公文、契约外,还有不少故事和民歌,其中尤以民歌最为优秀,不但情趣隽永,文字优美,语言流畅,而且哲理深邃。例如:《箴言》:②

---

① 《九姓回鹘爱登里罗汨没蜜施合毗伽可汗圣文神武碑》汉文部分第5~8行:"可汗乃顿军东都,因观风俗,敕民弗师,将睿息等四僧入国,阐扬二祀,洞彻三际。况法师妙达名门,精通七部,才高海岳,辩若悬河,故能开正教于回鹘。"
② 选译自葛玛丽、拉希德拉赫曼托1933年的论文《高昌民歌》。

对于尚未做过的事情，
应该三思而后行。
如果不经考虑而做错了，
莫要抵赖脱身。

脏衣服上的油污，
用清水才能洗净。
语言的污秽难洗，
有什么办法可寻？

真理就是真理，
为它值得献出生命。
事实就是事实，
不必为其多做说明。

交友要交好人，
他会把正道向你指明。
莫因树弯而举刀乱砍，
果实正好结在树荫。

可惜这些高昌回鹘的古代文学作品，都被外国探险家偷运到国外去了，我们无法加以全面地整理、欣赏和研究。在元朝的宫廷内外，不少畏兀儿人对汉文诗词有深刻研究和很高造诣，他们用汉文创作了许多诗词和散曲，其中偰玉立有《玉立诗集》、偰哲笃有《世玉集》，散曲大家贯云石有《酸斋乐府》等流传古今。而我国最古老的回鹘文剧本《弥勒会见记》，则是高昌盛行佛教戏剧的明证，它对研究我国戏剧发展史具有重大意义。

翻译是一种重要的文化种类，它也含有丰富的文学加工，可以称之为"二手创作"。高昌回鹘的翻译事业特别发达，成果十分丰富，许多回鹘高僧都精通六国语文（梵文、藏文、回鹘文、契丹文、西夏文、汉文），他们都是高明的翻译家，由他们翻译的佛经真是不计其数。高昌国唆里迷城的智护法师翻译《弥勒会见记》，别失八里城（即北庭）的僧古萨里都统翻译《菩萨大唐三藏法师传》，即是其中的典型。元朝的畏兀儿大翻译家安藏，将汉文的《尚书》、《贞观政要》、《资治通鉴》等政治史籍，《难经》、《本草》等医学著作译成回鹘文，其意义和作用更无法估量。

根据历史记载，高昌回鹘十分爱好音乐。他们"好游赏，行者必抱乐器"，"乐多琵琶、箜篌"。奏乐的形式多为独奏或二三人的小型合奏，其乐谱则已湮灭，至今未曾发现。有人认为其音乐与维吾尔族古典音乐"十二木卡姆"相近，这是错误的。"十二木卡姆"形成和发展于喀喇汗王朝后期和察合台汗国的喀什噶尔一带，其采用的乐器和演奏形式与高昌回鹘完全不同。高昌回鹘的奏乐着重"自娱"的独奏，受内地汉风的影响颇深。又，宋朝使者王延德在北庭，回鹘可汗盛情招待他，"泛舟于池中，池四面作鼓乐"。

大型奏乐场合以鼓为主奏乐器,更是唐宋时期河西、陇右民间乐舞的形式,这与高昌回鹘国后期大量甘州回鹘西迁其地有关。

　　高昌回鹘的绘画艺术水平颇高,他们的作品大多遗留于佛寺和石窟的遗址中。高昌回鹘的壁画,无论技法和布局,深受敦煌壁画的影响,它们都是细腻繁复的线条画作轮廓,内填对比强烈的鲜红艳绿色彩,例如伯孜克里克第 20 窟的《佛本行经变图》,中为高大的立佛,约占画面的一半。两侧侍立七尊菩萨,菩萨的下方跪着捧盘献金银的粟特胡商二人,献马的唐朝官员一人。菩萨和供养人约占画面的一半。全画主次分明,人像大小适宜,色彩鲜艳富丽,令人观感强烈。北庭回鹘王大寺中的壁画《出征图》,上下皆为起伏的山峦,中间夹着一片翠绿的草原,将军们披挂整齐,或持武器,或秉牙旗,身跨雄健的战马,簇拥骑着白象的亦都护前行,画面充满威武的气象。高昌回鹘的洞窟和佛寺壁画,也像敦煌壁画一样,多画有供养人像。例如伯孜克里克第 16 窟,在一宽大的画面中,上画一列头戴桃形金冠的亦都护及其特勤兄弟的八位供养人像,下列前面画着戴有三叉戟银冠的国相兄弟四位供养人像;后面画着带扇形银冠的四位达官供养人像。在伯孜克里克第 27 窟中,更画有头戴"姑姑冠"的蒙古公主、亦都护夫人的供养人像。这些供养人像右侧,都有长方形的榜题,题着他们的官爵和姓名,这种形式完全来自敦煌壁画。①

---

　　① 上列画面皆见于霍旭初、祁小山著《丝绸之路·新疆佛教艺术》,第 126~129 页。

西汉征讨西域楼兰、姑师军事力量考

李 方

中国社会科学院中国边疆史地研究中心

西汉武帝时期,汉军与西域楼兰、姑师爆发了一场战争。《史记·大宛列传》将这场战争的起因、过程、结局叙述得很清楚:"楼兰、姑师,小国耳,当空道,攻劫汉使王恢等尤甚。而匈奴奇兵时时遮击使西国者。使者争遍言外国灾害,皆有城邑,兵弱易击。于是天子以故遣从骠侯(赵)破奴将属国骑及郡兵数万,至匈河水,欲以击胡,胡皆去。其明年,击姑师,破奴与轻骑七百余先至,虏楼兰王,遂破姑师。因举兵威以困乌孙、大宛之属。还,封破奴为浞野侯。王恢数使,为楼兰所苦,言天子,天子发兵令恢佐破奴击破之,封恢为浩侯。于是酒泉列亭鄣至玉门矣。"①知这场战争的原因是,姑师、楼兰常常攻劫汉使,阻碍了西汉王朝与西域大宛等国的交往,汉武帝听说这些小国兵弱易击,于是兴兵讨伐之。姑师、楼兰之所以常常攻劫汉使,是因为它们处于汉通西域的南北交通孔道,汉使频繁来往于道,增添了他们的供给负担,又听从了匈奴的挑唆和指使。战争的过程是,汉将赵破奴等率大军先至匈河水击匈奴,不遇,然后到西域,破楼兰,再破姑师。战争的结局是,楼兰王、姑师王皆被擒,汉军不仅取得了军事上的胜利,而且取得了政治上的巨大胜利,汉朝在西域树立了声威,西域诸国为之震动。《史记·大宛列传》未载这场战争的时间,但"封破奴为浞野侯"下有《集解》引徐广注:"元封三年";"封恢为浩侯"下有《集解》引徐广注:"捕得车师王,元封四年封浩侯。"此二注乃据《史记》卷二〇《建元以来侯者年表》,②知这场战争发生在武帝元封三年(前108)。

赵破奴等率属国骑及郡兵击楼兰、姑师,对于西域来说是一件具有划时代意义的大事。因为,这不仅是西汉与西域之间的第一场战争,而且是姑师历史的终结。姑师从此分裂为八国,③姑师之名不再见于史书,而以后,"车师"前后国等国则频显于史。关于这件事件的重大意义,学术界有充分认识和精辟阐述,如王素先生说:"此役影响极为重大。对汉王朝而言,亭鄣从酒泉列至玉门,势力愈益逼近西域。对姑师而言,破败之余,难逃进一步被分裂的命运。"④田余庆先生说:"汉朝势力向西发展经历了两个阶段,即元封和太初;两个步骤,即楼兰之役和大宛之役。这是战略形势使然。"⑤余太山先生说:"楼兰、姑师之役

---

① 《汉书》卷九十六《西域传上》、《汉书》卷六一《张骞传》略同。

② 该年表从"骠侯"(赵破奴)条云:"以匈河将军元封三年击楼兰功,复侯。"该年表"浩侯"条云:"以故中郎将将兵捕得车师王功,侯。"同条下"元封"栏又云:"四年正月甲申,侯王恢元年。"《汉书·景武昭宣成功臣表》所载略同。可见赵破奴、王恢破楼兰、姑师在元封三年,封侯在三、四年。王素先生根据赵破奴、王恢的封侯指出:"可知赵破奴是以击楼兰功复侯,王恢是以捕得车师王功封侯。也就是说,此西征之役,赵破奴只是击楼兰的主将,王恢才是破姑师的主将。"此说当是,见其著《高昌史稿·统治篇》,文物出版社,1998年,第10页。

③ 关于姑师分裂时间,学术界大致有三说:一为宣帝时(前73~前49)说,一为宣帝神爵(前61~前58)中说,一为宣帝神爵二年(前60)秋说。王素先生说:"这些说法均不可取。实际上,姑师分裂的时间,就在前述姑师被击破的元封三年(前108)或稍后。"其分析论证有理有据,可以信从。见其著《高昌史稿·统治篇》,第11页。

④ 《高昌史稿·统治篇》,第10页。

⑤ 《论轮台诏》,原载《历史研究》1985年第1期,后收入其著《秦汉魏晋史探微》,中华书局1993年版,第45页。

获胜之后,'汉列亭鄣至玉门',为下一步向西域的发展作了准备。"①但是,对于赵破奴、王恢击姑师所率领的属国骑及郡兵等问题,则未见学者措意。这是因为,前人更多关注的是西汉在西域的进展,西汉与楼兰、姑师之间的战事,姑师、车师名称所蕴含的政治变迁、地理范围等问题。然而,这个问题对于我们研究西域东、南部与西汉的关系却是十分重要的,因为它是武帝决心开通西域以后,第一次大规模派兵在此地进行的活动,而此前自张骞出使西域以后,西汉虽然频繁遣使西域,"使者相望于道,一岁中多至十余辈",②但规模都很小,至多几百人,这一次西汉派数万人来到西域,无疑是西汉与西域东、南部民族大规模接触的机会,借此我们可以了解,在武帝前期,内地有哪些人马来到过西域东、南部,并与当地民众打过交道,留下印记。

关于赵破奴、王恢击姑师所率之兵的问题,史书记载十分简略,仅有"武帝遣从骠侯(赵)破奴将属国骑及郡兵数万击姑师"③一句记载。然而,这个所谓"属国骑",正是我们研究问题的突破口。按《史记·大宛列传》此句下无注,《汉书·西域传上》此句下有颜师古注:"属国谓诸外国属汉也。"未言所率"属国骑"的具体所指,我们只能从其他记载中求证之。

武帝元封三年(前108)之前西汉所设属国,史书有明确记载的,仅有元狩二年(前121)所置五属国。《汉书·武帝纪》载:元狩二年"秋,匈奴昆邪王杀休屠王,并将其众合四万余人来降,置五属国以处之。以其地为武威、酒泉郡"。可见,元狩二年,武帝因匈奴昆邪王率四万余众来降,设"五属国"以安置之,并在昆邪王、休屠王的原驻地设置武威郡、酒泉郡。不过,《汉书·武帝纪》未记载这五属国的具体名称和方位。颜师古作注在"置五属国以处之"下云:"凡言属国者,存其国号而属汉朝,故曰属国",仅说明了"属国"的含义和性质,亦未说明这五属国的名称、方位,或设置在哪个郡县。关于武帝所设五属国,《汉书》其他传亦有记载,但皆语焉不详。如同书《卫青霍去病传》载:"乃分处降者于边五郡故塞外,而皆在河南,因其故俗为属国。"这里记载武帝将五属国分置于"边五郡故塞外",并说明此五郡皆在河南,比《武帝纪》详细,但仍未说明这五属国的名称或方位。同书卷七三《韦贤传》记载,太仆王舜、中垒校尉刘歆议论武帝南、北、东、西的武功:"孝武皇帝愍中国疲劳无安宁之时,乃遣大将军、骠骑、伏波、楼船之属,南灭百粤,起七郡;北攘匈奴,降昆邪十万之众,置五属国,起朔方,以夺其肥饶之地"云云,将置五属国作为武帝在北方攘匈奴的结果,知五属国置于北方,但亦未说明具体方位。其他史书,如《两汉纪》未载此事,《西汉会要》下"典属国"仅据《汉书·武帝纪》所载记设五属国事,而《史记·卫将军骠骑列传》、《资治通鉴》卷一九武帝元狩二年正文亦未明载,唯两书之注详记之。《史记·卫将军骠骑列传》正文与《汉书·卫青霍去病传》正文所载相差无几,谓:"分徙降者边五郡故塞外,而皆在河南,因其故俗为属国。"其下正义注:"五郡,谓陇西、北地、上郡、朔方、云中,并是故塞外,又在北海西南。"《资治通鉴》正文与《史记》相同,注亦引之,然在"五郡,谓陇西、北地、上郡、朔方、云中"后接云:"故塞,秦之先与匈奴所关之塞。自秦使蒙恬夺匈奴地而边关益斥,秦、项之乱,冒顿南侵,与中国关于故塞。及卫青收河南,而边关复蒙恬之旧。所谓故塞外,其地在北河之南也。"是二书之注皆谓五属国在陇西、北地、上郡、朔方、云中五郡之中。然则赵破奴、王恢所率之"属国骑"也应是这五郡的属国骑。

---

① 《西域通史》,中州古籍出版社,2003年,第53页。
② 《汉书》卷九十六上《西域传上》。
③ 《汉书》卷九十六上《西域传上》。此与前引《史记·大宛列传》意同,文字稍有差别,在"遣从骠侯(赵)破奴将属国骑及郡兵数万"后直接缀上"击姑师"三字,更精练,故引之。

西汉时期还有五原属国、西河属国、金城属国、天水属国、张掖属国、安定属国的记载,但这些属国之设,大约都在元封三年之后。如《汉书》卷一七《景武昭宣元成功臣表第五》载:辉渠忠侯仆朋"元鼎四年(前113),侯雷电嗣。……延和三年,以五原属国都尉与贰师将军俱击匈奴,没"。[①] 这里记载了五原属国,时间在延和三年,即武帝征和三年(前90)。[②] 延和三年虽然并非五原属国设置时间,但距元狩二年(前121)已三十余年,距元封三年(前108)亦近二十年,此时五原属国乃见于史乘,估计所设时间应该较晚。同书《地理志》载,五原郡"蒲泽,属国都尉治",是五原属国又可称为蒲择属国。又如《汉书·宣帝纪》载,五凤四年(前54),"置西河、北地属国以处匈奴降者"。是西河属国设在宣帝五凤四年(前54),而"西汉王朝先后设置过两个北地属国",[③]此为第二次设置。同书同卷载:神爵二年(前60),"夏五月,羌虏降服,斩其首恶大豪杨玉、酋非首。置金城属国以处降羌"。是金城属国置于神爵二年(前60),且为处降羌而置。同书《张放传》:"出放为天水属国都尉。永始、元延间,比年日蚀,故久不还放。"永始(前16~前13)、元延(前12~前9)为成帝年号,天水属国所设亦应较晚。同书《匈奴传上》载:"明年,单于使犁污王窥边,言酒泉、张掖兵益弱,出兵试击,冀可复得其地。时汉先得降者,闻其计,天子诏边警备。后无几,右贤王、犁污王四千骑分三队,入日勒、屋兰、番和。张掖太守、属国都尉发兵击,大破之,得脱者数百人。属国千长义渠王骑士射杀犁污王,赐黄金二百斤,马二百匹,因封为犁污王。属国都尉郭忠封成安侯。自是后,匈奴不敢入张掖。"这里的"明年",据上文推算,应是昭帝始元七年(前80年,一说元凤元年即公元前79年),是张掖属国所设时间亦应较晚,且属国中有义渠王千长,当以义渠人为主,至少有一部分是义渠人。按同书《地理志》与《武帝纪》载张掖郡之设时间不同(前者在武帝太初元年即公元前104年,后者在元鼎六年即公元前111年),学术界对河西四郡的设置时间亦有不同意见,[④]但无论如何,张掖郡属国之设,应在设郡之后,说其设在元封三年之后大约无误。同书《楚元王传》载:刘歆"以病免官,起家复为安定属国都尉。会哀帝崩,王莽持政",是刘歆任安定属国都尉在哀帝末年(前2~前1)。同书《地理志》载,安定郡有三水县,"属国都尉治",是安定属国又称三水属国。[⑤]《后汉书·卢方传》载,"王莽末,乃与三水属国羌胡起兵"。所见时间更晚。此中"羌胡"并提,属国中当有羌、胡两种。总之,这些属国设置时间大约都在武帝元封三年(前108)之后。

武帝设五属国之后,大约很长时间内未设新属国,所以,史书叙述这段史实时,一般径称"属国"而不名详称。《史记·卫将军骠骑列传》载骠骑将军霍去病"元狩六年卒,天子悼之,发属国玄甲军,陈自长安至茂陵,为冢象祁连山"。这里亦径称"属国",而不详指,其下《正义》亦注曰:"属国,即上分置边五郡者也。玄甲,铁甲也。"将"属国"亦解释为边郡五属国,正所谓无独有偶吧。关于这个问题,《汉书·景武昭宣元成功臣表》表现得最为明显。其在记武帝元封三年(前108)前所封侯,凡涉及受封者的属国时皆径

---

① 《史记·建元以来侯者年表》仆朋作仆多。索隐谓:"汉表作仆朋,此云仆多,与《卫青传》同。"

② 陈直先生曾对征和当为延和年号问题作过专门考证,其著《汉书新证》"武纪第六"征和元年条谓:"征和当为延和,形近而误,西安汉城遗址中,曾出延和元年瓦片,笔画很分明。又居延汉简释文卷二,第七十页,有简文:'……延和三年十月丁酉朔',……见于其他木简者,无不作延和。"并举《汉书》《高惠功臣表》《景武昭宣功臣表》等例证,说"皆作延和而不作征和。又按《隶释》卷六,《袁良碑》叙征和三年叙反者公孙勇事,可见在东汉中晚期,已普遍作征和"。(天津人民出版社,1959年,第38~39页)

③ 李大龙:《汉唐藩属体制研究》,中国社会科学出版社,2006年,第87页。此说甚确。

④ 请参阅张维华:《汉河西四郡建置年代考疑》,原载《中国文化研究汇刊》第2卷,现收入《汉史论集》,齐鲁书社,1980年,第309~328页。周振鹤:《西汉河西四郡设置年代考》,《西北史地》1985年第1期,第19~25页。王宗维:《汉代河西四郡始设年代问题》,《西北史地》1986年第3期,第88~98页。

⑤ 李大龙先生认为,安定郡由北地郡分置,其属县有三水,应该是武帝时期所设置北地属国所在(见其著《汉唐藩属体制研究》,第87页),可备一说。

称之,而不冠以具体郡属,而以后子孙嗣侯涉及属国时,则冠以详称。如载元鼎五年(前112)封侯:"昆侯渠复累(?),以属国大首渠击匈奴侯","骐侯驹几,以属国骑击匈奴捕单于兄侯","梁期侯任破胡,以属国都尉间出击匈奴将军累(?)缔缦"。而其后嗣侯者,如前举辉渠忠侯仆朋之子雷电,则详载其为延和三年(前90)的"五原属国都尉"。既然史书所载武帝前期属国皆指五属国(陇西、北地、上郡、朔方、云中五郡属国),那么,赵破奴、王恢击楼兰、姑师所率之"属国骑"也就应该是这五郡的五属国骑。① 唯不知赵破奴、王恢是尽发五属国之兵,还是仅发其中一部分属国兵?从他们所率兵有"数万"来看,发五属国兵的可能性比较大。另外,赵破奴、王恢所率还有郡兵。这郡兵是何郡之兵,史书亦未详载。但根据史料上下文文意来判断,这郡兵应该与属国骑同郡,即皆为陇西、北地、上郡、朔方、云中五郡之兵。不能想象,赵破奴、王恢发这五郡属国骑,同时还发其他郡兵而史书不载。然则,元封三年(前108)从赵破奴、王恢到西域东、南部来开战的汉军是陇西、北地、上郡、朔方、云中五郡之兵及五属国骑。

这五郡之兵及属国骑名义上是汉军,其中当然有不少汉人,但是,也有不少少数民族。首先,五属国为匈奴降者所设,这些随赵破奴、王恢进入西域东部的属国骑就应该是匈奴人。我们颇疑"破奴与轻骑七百人先至,虏楼兰王"的"轻骑七百人",就是属国骑匈奴人,至少,其中有一部分是匈奴人。如然,则在西域东、南部这片土地上,在西汉前期与西域东、南部民族打交道的人群中,既有来自匈奴势力的匈奴人,又有来自汉朝势力的匈奴人,这两种势力虽然在政治上、军事上是对立的,但在种族成分上却有相同部分。其次,这支队伍中可能还有狄、氐、羌、义渠等族人。我们知道,这五郡中有不少"道",而"道"正是少数民族居住的地方。如陇西郡有11县(道与县同级),其中就有狄道、氐道和羌道,等等。《汉书·地理志下》卷二八下略载:"陇西郡,秦置。莽曰厌戎。……县十一:狄道,白石山在东。莽曰操虏。……氐道,禹贡养水所出,至武都为汉。莽曰亭道。……予道,莽曰德道。大夏,莽曰顺夏。羌道,羌水出塞外"云云。师古注"狄道"曰:"其地有狄种,故云狄道。"注"氐道"曰:"氐,夷种名也。氐之所居,故曰氐道。"而北地郡有"义渠道"。同书同卷略载:"北地郡,秦置。莽曰威成。……县十九:……除道,莽曰通道。……略畔道,莽曰延年道。……义渠道,莽曰义沟。"可见这五郡有狄人、氐人、羌人、义渠人,等等。这些少数民族作为五郡之民,是否一定会当作郡兵而被派到西域来,我们不清楚,但是这种可能性是不能排除的。

随赵破奴、王恢进入西域东、南部的汉族也非常广泛。仅就其征发的郡兵可能涉及五郡来说,范围就已经很广泛了,然而,其中除了原住民之外,可能还有不少来自关东(或山东)等地的汉民。《汉书·武帝纪》载:元狩"四年冬,有司言关东贫民徙陇西、北地、西河、上郡、会稽凡七十二万五千口,县官衣食振业,用度不足"云云,可见在元封三年(前108)之前,陇西、北地、上郡等地已迁来了大量关东人口。《汉书》卷二四下《食货志下》亦载此事,且可以与《武帝纪》此载互为补充。其载:"其明年,山东被水灾,民多饥乏,于是天子遣使虚郡国仓廪以振贫。犹不足,又募豪富人相假贷。尚不能相救,乃徙贫民于关以西,及充朔方以南新秦中②七十余万口,衣食皆仰给于县官。"此处"明年",据前文推算,应为元狩二年(前121)(《武帝纪》所谓"四年冬",是有司上奏的时间),是武帝徙民在元狩二年(前121)。徙民的原因,则是因为山东水灾,民多饥乏,国家以郡国仓廪振贫而不足;募豪富人相假贷,亦不能相救,不得已而迁徙民众。所不

----

① 《汉书·李广利传》载:"太初元年,以广利为贰师将军,发属国六千骑及郡国恶少数万以往。"此举乃伐西域大宛。太初元年为公元前104年,距元封三年仅4年,此"属国骑"估计也是五属国骑。

② 应劭注曰:"秦始皇遣蒙恬攘却匈奴,得其河南造阳之北千里地甚好,于是为筑城郭,徙民充之,名曰新秦。四方杂错,奢俭不同,今俗名新富贵者为'新秦',由是名也。"

同的是,《食货志下》载所徙之民为山东之民。山东、关东大约可以相通吧。另外,《食货志下》迁徙地点似乎还包括了朔方郡。朔方郡为武帝元朔二年(前127)新开。《汉书·武帝纪》载:其年"夏,募民徙朔方十万口"。明年秋,"城朔方"。这十万民来自何方不详,估计也来自内地。《汉书·食货志下》载:"又兴十余万筑卫朔方,转漕甚远,自山东咸被其劳",说明朔方设郡、筑城,劳役之甚,已远达山东。综合这些材料看,说朔方郡也有来自山东等地的汉民应不为过。

率兵前来的将军赵破奴,史书载是"故九原人",①即西汉五原郡人。② 辅佐赵破奴的王恢,籍贯不详。武帝时期有两个王恢,一个为大行令,一个为浩侯。大行令王恢因首倡马邑之谋,遇匈奴兵多而不敢进,于元光二年(前133)自杀。浩侯王恢知名度不及前者,在《汉书》中凡五见,其事迹主要有二,一是本件,一是太初元年(前104)随贰师将军李广利伐大宛事。其籍贯虽然不详,但与赵破奴共同率军出征楼兰、姑师,丰富了汉军的郡属来源当无疑问。

元封时期,西汉派五属国骑及五郡兵到西域东、南部来是有原因的。我们知道,五属国为安置匈奴昆邪王所率四万余降众而设(昆邪王所率降众包括了休屠王部下),而昆邪王、休屠王原驻地就在河西走廊(汉在此设武威郡、酒泉郡,后分置敦煌郡、张掖郡),此地与西域东部紧密相连,这些人对西域东部并不陌生,起码不是很隔膜,因此,派这些人来西域东、南部讨伐楼兰、车师,是比较有利于行军作战的。而且,匈奴人作为游牧民族骁勇善战,也是一个有利条件。除此而外,派他们来西域还应有两个原因,一是这些匈奴人投降汉朝以后,汉朝政府对他们给予了优厚待遇,史载:"胡降者数万人皆得厚赏,衣食仰给县官,县官不给,天子乃损膳,解乘舆驷,出御府禁臧以澹之。"③西汉政府不仅给予这些降胡数万人每个人以优厚赏赐,而且还承担了他们每个人的衣食供给,地方政府财力不足,武帝甚至不惜减少膳食,解乘舆驷,出御府禁臧的物资以付担之。汉朝政府当然是需要回报的;二是经过持续的周边作战,汉朝政府可以征发的力量已经有限,史载:"法既益严,吏多废免。兵革数动,民多买复及五大夫、千夫,征发之士益鲜。"④西汉政府需要新的力量加入作战队伍。这些降胡正好是一支可以利用的新力量。于是,攻打楼兰、车师等国,就自然而然落在了这些五属国骑兵的身上。

陇西、北地、上郡、朔方、云中这五郡由于迫近游牧民族,其民风本身也是崇尚武力、好射猎的。《汉书·地理志》载:"天水、陇西,山多林木,民以板为室屋。及安定、北地、上郡、西河,皆迫近戎狄,修习战备,高上气力,以射猎为先。故秦诗曰:'在其板屋';又曰'王于兴师,修我甲兵,与子偕行'。及车辚、四载、小戎之篇,皆言车马田狩之事。汉兴,六郡良家子选给羽林、期门,以材力为官,名将多出焉。孔子曰:'君子有勇而亡谊则为乱,小人有勇而亡谊则为盗。'故此数郡,民俗质木,不耻寇盗。"又载:"定襄、云中、五原,本戎狄地,颇有赵、齐、卫、楚之徙。⑤ 其民鄙朴,少礼文,好射猎。"五郡这种民风,自然也促使他们加入到征讨西域姑师等国的行列中。也正因为这五郡兵和五属国骑骁勇善战,所以,在赵破奴、王恢的率领下,他们一到西域就旗开得胜,不仅"虏楼兰王,破姑师",而且"暴兵威以动乌孙、大宛之属",为西汉下一步进军西域奠定了基础。而与此同时,也为西域东、南部民族与西汉内地民族的接触交往,揭开了新的一页。

---

① 《史记》卷一一一《卫将军骠骑列传》。
② 《汉书·地理志》:"五原郡,秦九原郡,武帝元朔二年更名。"
③ 《汉书》卷二四《食货志下》。
④ 《汉书》卷二四《食货志下》。
⑤ 颜师古注曰:"言四国之人被迁徙来居之。"

尼雅考古资料中所见汉王朝"安辑"精绝故实

王炳华

中国人民大学国学院西域历史语言研究所

自公元前 2 世纪,西汉王朝逐步进入并统治西域,面对种族、民族殊异,经济生活类型不同,语言、文化心态有别,政治倾向各异的大小城邦,如何实现稳定统治,是一个全新问题。历经几个世纪的统治实践,经过不少成功、失败的经验、教训后,《后汉书·西域传》对此进行总结,结论是"可安辑,安辑之;可击,击之"。另一种表达方式,是分别对象,根据形势"或兵威肃服",或"财赂怀诱"。这软硬两手,"安辑"是核心。"兵威"之后,往往还是要用"安辑"、"怀诱"手段收拾残局。手段不同,但目标不变,这就是使"西域服从",使汉之号令可以颁行于西域。

两汉王朝,在统治西域时实施的"安辑"政策,曾取得很大成功。相关"安辑"的具体措施,文献中略见涉及,但都语焉不详,少有完整叙述。至于如弹丸之地的"精绝"这类小城邦,曾如何在汉王朝"安辑"政策下一步步发展,在汉文化传统中寻找到新的精神寄托,文献中则根本不见一字一句的涉及。

20 世纪的西域考古,精绝故地尼雅遗址,是考古工作做得比较多、收获也比较丰富的一个地点。爬梳相关考古资料,就两汉王朝在精绝曾经有过的"安辑"实践,进行分析,颇可捕捉这一政策的要领、主要内容。自然,汉代西域精绝,只能算在最小城邦之列。但是麻雀虽小,五脏俱全。以之进行汉王朝"安辑"政策实践的剖析,反有其更易于深入的优点。

一

本文论及的"西域",基本局限在今天的新疆境内。即使如此,这也是一片境域十分广大的地区。

从考古资料看,这片土地上,古代居民种族多源,既有欧罗巴人种,也有蒙古人种。民族成分更其复杂。已经掌握的体质人类学资料,就白种人讲,既有欧洲北部古典欧洲人种,也见地中海周围、印度、伊朗高原地带的白种人。蒙古人种成分,同样并不单纯。后期语言学资料,可与此呼应:既有印欧语系,也有阿尔泰语系、汉藏语系,不同语种的存在。其复杂程度,可以说是远过于任何一个相对独立的自然地理单元。从社会发展角度分析,自公元前一千年后期,这片地区已逐渐步入文明:金属器,尤其是青铜、铁器冶炼、铸造已比较成熟;在一些地点,已见早期城市,城址作圆形。这些分踞天山南北的居国、行国,与周邻的南西伯利亚、西亚、南亚,东边的黄河流域也都存在程度不等的经济、文化联系。在天山以南,沙漠广布,分居于内陆河尾闾地段、屈指可数的大小绿洲,彼此为戈壁、沙漠隔阻,交往、联系困难,自然形成大小不等、相对独立的城邦;天山以北,则为游牧王国所统治。这样一片民族殊异,政治、经济状况不同的土地,自公元前 2 世纪初,匈奴及匈奴统属下的乌孙已逐渐进入准噶尔盆地,乌揭、车师均受匈奴制约。塔里木盆地,自公元前 176 年起,也入于匈奴王国的统治之下。匈奴将统治西域的军政中心——"僮仆都尉"府,置于中部天山南麓之焉者盆地内,这里位居西域之中。东向车师前部,入楼兰,南下昆仑山北缘,西向天山南麓,北与乌孙及匈奴右部联系,均得其便。至此,西域大地,虽与匈奴"不相亲附",政治上终是已入于匈奴的控制之下。

面对这一形势,汉王朝要进入西域,并在西域立足,没有军事力量开拓,政治上自然是不可能保持影响的。

自公元前2世纪末,西汉王朝取河西走廊,设敦煌四郡;取楼兰,发大军远征大宛,灭轮台,攻焉者,与匈奴五争车师以取得对吐鲁番盆地的控制权,发大军与乌孙联兵击匈奴右部……半个多世纪中,自河西走廊西部至西域大地,可以说是征战不绝、战火连绵。经过相当长时间的军事打击后,匈奴势力后退,西域大地上林立的大小城邦,对汉王朝的军威感到"震惧"。公元前60年,汉置"西域都护",汉之号令可以颁行于西域大地。

在汉设西域都护之前,取楼兰,并迁楼兰于扜泥,设鄯善。西汉王朝力求避开匈奴重点经营的天山中部,着力经营沿阿尔金山、昆仑山西走的丝绸之路南道。楼兰、鄯善、于阗,南道上的这几个国家,曾是两汉王朝重点关注、"安辑"、"赂遗怀诱"的重点。其中精绝,虽只是南道上的小"国"之一,它虽深处沙漠,但地理位置冲要,是丝路南道上无法逾越的关键站点,所以也颇得中原王朝之重视,得"安辑"、"怀诱"之惠。西汉时,它曾经保有独立地位。东汉时,先后在于阗、莎车、鄯善争夺南道统治地位的角逐中沉浮。但不论处于何种状况,均曾是笼罩在两汉王朝"安辑"政策之下的一个绿洲城邦。从这一角度观察,对汉王朝当年安辑政策的实际运作,解剖精绝,就具有更加典型的意义。

二

关于"精绝",见于史籍的相关记录,几乎只是《汉书·西域传》中有关的短短81个字。[①] 说了精绝所在地理环境、人口、王国主要职官等。《后汉书》中,已不见精绝专条,它已没入于"鄯善传"的文字之中了。对这么一处真正只能算是弹丸之地的小小绿洲,当年的实际历史状况,几乎全部得之于相关考古资料。两汉王朝对精绝的"安辑"、"怀诱",从并不完整的考古资料中,约略可见以下数端。持续相当长的"安辑",所产生的社会效果,也可在实际生活中见到痕迹。

(一)实施屯田。1959年,在尼雅故址中,曾获炭精质"司禾府印"一枚。[②] "司禾府",文献失录。但顾名思义,当是与屯田相关的机构,表明在精绝,中原王朝也曾经有过屯田之举。而揆诸历史实际,在"丝路南道"为交通主体的汉代,从后勤供应角度分析,择地屯田,实际也是势在必行之举。

精绝故国所在的尼雅废墟,深处沙漠之中。距今天的民丰县,直线距离在120公里以上。故址依尼雅河谷南北铺展,最长约25公里,东西宽约3~7公里。整个面积不过100多平方公里。因处在汉代尼雅河尾闾地段,水流还是比较丰沛的。农业及附属于农业的家庭饲养、园艺,是精绝王国的基础产业。这样一个小绿洲,汉代时居民仅有480户、3360人。实际也就是一个不大的村寨。但因为地居于吐火罗故国安迪尔与扜弥(今于田)之间,不论缘丝路南道东走,还是西行,沙漠途程均有100多公里,以骆驼来去,

① 《汉书·西域传·精绝》。
② 史树青:《说新疆民丰尼雅遗址》,《文物》1962年第7~8期。

得行一周左右。因此,不论自故吐火罗绿洲西走,还是从扜弥东行,至精绝,人、畜都必须补充水、草秣、粮食给养,稍事休息,恢复精力。在丝路"南道"作为主要交通路线,"驰命走驿"、"商胡贩客"不绝于途,驿导、粮秣供应,对精绝城邦是一个不堪其重的负担。这一客观形势,加之尼雅河尾闾地带,也不乏可供新屯之地。在这里设"司禾府",堪谓既有可能、也有需要。而设"司禾府",组织屯田,可以免除对精绝王国新增税赋。精绝可得"丝路"开通,自然带来的利益,而不必负责难以承受的负担。汉之"安辑"精神,此乃首要一端。

(二)"财赂怀诱"。据 1959 年新疆博物馆发现的贵族夫妇合葬墓,[①]1995 年中日尼雅联合考古队中方成员发现、发掘的东汉精绝王陵,[②]汉王朝对精绝的"财赂怀诱",是倾其全力、不稍吝惜的。日用漆器、藤器、铜镜、丝绸锦绣等,均是当年官府手工作坊中的上品。以 1995 年精绝王陵三号墓男女主人为例,可以说从头到脚、由内及外,无不是丝绸锦缎:身盖锦被,头戴锦帽、锦质组带,面覆锦质面衣,全身内外锦衣、锦袍、锦裤,贴身则为绮、绢内衣,脚着钩花锦鞋、锦𦆲毡靴。全部丝质衣物达 31 件,其中匹值万钱,贵可与黄金等价的锦质衣服,即达 17 件,占一半以上。许多锦料,从花式至吉祥文字,均为既往所不见。男主人使用的龙虎纹铜镜,出土时不锈,光彩熠熠,仍可照人影像,显为当年造镜之上品。这只是一个典型例证,说明汉王朝在"怀诱"这些小城邦的统治上层时,确实是倾府库之所有,不遗余力。这些当年居于世界物质文明前列的制品,对深处沙漠,实际只是一个小聚落的头人来讲,不啻是人间天堂的奇珍,它们所产生的相当强大的吸引力,是不可轻估的。

(三)和亲。"和亲",是怀诱的重要手段。与精绝和亲,不见任何文字记录。向这样一个深处沙漠之中的荒僻小村下嫁"公主",大概实际也没有可能。但在已发掘的 1995 年尼雅三号墓中,男女主人合盖的全新锦被,穿插在锦纹间的"王侯合昏千秋万岁宜子孙"吉祥用语,它明显是为"和亲"这类政治婚姻而由汉王朝工房准备的专用织物,清楚宣示了在这沙漠小村中,确也曾经有过"和亲"的一幕。下嫁给这位精绝王的自然不会是真正的公主或宗族贵胄,更大可能只不过是宫廷中活动能力较强的一位普通宫女。但她却确曾承担了联络、增进汉王朝与精绝王室感情的使命。这一和亲事实,给我们的重要信息是:在当年的西域大地任何一处接受了汉王朝统治的绿洲上,"和亲"十分可能就是一种普遍性存在。当然,在"和亲"的旗帜下,任何一位所谓"公主"的到来,不仅会带来相当财富,而且会带来浸透在生活细节中的种种汉文化精神。

三

与物质怀诱同步,是精神文化层面的推行、灌输。这是有深远影响的举措,对精绝王国精神文明的影响,不可轻估。这方面已见于考古文物的,如汉文字学习、汉文化教育、相关礼制(如服饰制度、葬制、食具等)的变化等。

(一)汉文字学习、汉文化教育。与"屯田"、"财赂怀诱"这类稳定社会经济、改善物质生活措施相比较,进行汉文字学习、汉文化教育,对精绝社会的影响,是更为重要的环节。

---

① 新疆博物馆:《新疆民丰县北大沙漠中古遗址墓葬清理报告》,《文物》1960 年第 6 期。
② 王炳华:《95 尼雅一号墓地三号墓发掘报告》,《新疆文物》1999 年第 2 期。

在公元前 2 世纪,精绝并没有自己的文字。西汉王朝进入,同时带来了汉语文字。为适应统治的需要,精绝极力推行汉文字的学习、教育。很快,汉语文就成为了精绝上层掌握、使用的文字工具。这一结论的证明是多方面的。既有这里出土的"苍颉篇"木简,[①]隶书精妙,具有早期特点。A.斯坦因在 N14(精绝王宫所在)的垃圾堆上,发现了 8 件精绝王室成员间互相赠礼的木简,王国维判定,时代最晚到东汉晚期。[②] 汉文、佉卢文简牍的封缄形式,也都明显来自中原大地。这些资料十分有说服力地表明:精绝王室在学习汉文字,并利用汉文字为思想交流工具。在东汉以后,佉卢文传入,在精绝王室的政治生活中,汉文、佉卢文并行,汉文在社会生活中仍然具有重要地位。

(二)接受中原王朝的礼仪规制。随汉文字传入,汉王朝尊奉的礼制,也同样受到精绝王室贵胄的崇奉,这是文化领域的一种变化,值得重视。

袍服右衽,适应沙漠地区的特点。尼雅遗址出土的服饰极具土著特点:如包覆头部、耳翼深长的单帽,束颈、小袖、套头的上衣,颈部高领、有三对或三对以上的衣带互相交系,可防沙土浸入的对襟、束腰长袍,既左衽,也右衽内衣等。但在 1995 年发掘的精绝王陵,[③]保存完好的精绝王夫妇的服饰,却明显为右衽深衣、右衽上衣、右衽长袍。从严重磨损痕迹观察,多为平日长期服用的衣物。这右衽的锦袍、深衣等,明显是接受了中原汉王朝服制的影响,是对传统服饰的一种变革。

男女不同楎椸。男女衣物,不能同置于一架,这是中原汉王朝尊奉的礼制,体现着男女有别、男尊女卑的精神。这在《礼记·内则》中有明确的规定:"男女不同椸枷,不敢悬于夫之楎椸,不敢藏于夫之箧笥……。"[④]精绝故址内已经出土的贵族墓,均夫妇合葬,男女主人之衣物等,均分别挂附在男女主人身旁不同的木杈上。这"丫"形木杈根部尖锐,可随处楔插在地。平日插在土室中,可作为衣物之架。入葬后,这种简易衣架,随殉入棺。男女身侧,最重要的就是这一木杈,男女主人不同随葬衣物,几乎都悬挂在这杈形木架上。木杈,是尼雅本地的造型;功能,则是衣物架,是与中原楎椸同一类型器物。而男女衣物,是置于不同木杈之上,则明显是汉代礼制中男女有别精神的生动体现。[⑤]

葬制。尼雅遗址,曾发现过一批早期墓葬,土葬、殉陶器等物,但保存不好。保存稍好的精绝土著居民墓葬,多用胡杨木掏空而成的"船"形棺,和衣入殓。或有一件日用器皿入殉。这与精绝王国上层贵族使用长方形木棺,棺外有象征木椁的矩形木"栏"(大小规模,视木棺而定,总是较木棺稍大一点)有关。入葬的男女主人,均复面衣,头枕鸡形枕,盛妆盖被,多层衣服,务求豪奢。面盖覆锦质面衣这一习俗,明显是袭用《仪礼·土丧礼》中规定的"布巾"[⑥]制度的表现。[⑦] 这是尼雅绿洲土著居民从来不见的,是精绝上层集团接受汉王朝礼制的有力证明。

饮食制度。大量考古资料表明,两汉以前,包括两汉时期,西域大地的游牧行国、绿洲城邦居国,很普遍的现象之一是以木盆、陶钵盛羊肉,羊肉旁边或插在羊排上的是一柄小铜刀、小铁刀。粮食制品则是烤

① 王樾:《略说尼雅发现"苍颉篇"汉简》,《西域研究》,1998 年第 4 期。
② 罗振玉、王国维编著《流沙坠简》,中华书局,1993 年影印本,图版见第 69 页,考释见第 223～225 页。
③ 王炳华:《95 尼雅一号墓地三号墓发掘报告》,《新疆文物》1999 年第 2 期。
④ 《礼记》"内则第十二"。
⑤ 王炳华:《楎椸考——兼论汉代礼制在西域》,《西域研究》1997 年第 2 期。
⑥ 《仪礼》"土丧礼第十二"。
⑦ 武伯纶:《关于复面》,《文物》1961 年第 1 期;王炳华:《复面、眼罩及其他》,《文物》1962 年第 7～8 期。

饼、蒸饭,饭食置于陶、木盆、碗中。而到汉代,在楼兰、精绝,斯坦因、李遇春均发现了木筷。[①] 斯坦因所见木筷,出土于他所编号的 NX 遗址,李遇春所见则是在另一房址之中,这表现当年尼雅遗址中,筷子并不少见。用木筷进食,明显受到了中原文化的影响。

(三)度量衡制度的变化。两汉时期,沿昆仑山西走的"丝绸之路"南道,是自黄河流域进入西、南亚洲的主要交通干线,是汉王朝重点经营的地区。呼应着丝路商贸活动的开展,在度量衡制度方面有怎样的发展,是我们关注的问题。文献中未有记录。20 世纪初,大家都注意到在于阗、鄯善王国境内通行的汉佉二体钱,是一种打制的铜币。除标示佉卢文外,钱体上还用汉文标明重"六铢"、"二十四铢"。这样,汉佉二体钱可以与中原通行的五铢钱方便地折算、交换。这是表现在货币上的衡制变革,以"铢"为重量单位,实际呼应了贸易、商品交换的要求。作为丝路南道上的精绝,在这一背景下,会有怎样的改变。在尼雅考古期间,我们曾有意识进行探求,方法是具体测量一些重要遗迹,如 N2、佛塔、N13、精绝王陵中的棺木等,分析其遵循的度制。佛塔东侧的 N2,在尼雅遗址中部,是一组环绕一处广场呈环形分布的居址,现存房址 19 处。在这组遗存东、南,可以观察到 5 段以圆弧形展开的土墙。土墙用块状、不规则淤泥垒成,东边最长一段,长不足百米、基宽 4 米多、顶宽 2 米多、残高可达 8 米,似为土城残留;北、西边为沙土覆盖。虑及它不同寻常的地位,又傍近尼雅标志性建筑物——佛塔,故曾经对这区遗址中的一号、八号、十三号、十九号房址,进行了详细测量。其旁侧佛塔,可能与精绝后期王宫存在密切关联的第十三号建筑,精绝王陵中的棺木等,同样进行了精细测量。结果发现一个有趣的现象:在精绝,两种长度单位并行。如 N2 遗址中的多处房址、佛塔台基的高度,都可以与精绝传统的度制 Hasta(约当一肘长,相当于 43 cm)相对应,成为一个整数;而第十三号房址及精绝王墓(95MNM3)的棺木,以 Hasta 度量,完全无序。而以东汉尺(以每尺为 23.5 cm 计)为单位换算,则是规整的数据。如十三号房址,建筑范围是 200 尺 × 300 尺;精绝王墓棺木,则是 10 尺 × 4 尺 × 4 尺。[②] 这说明,第十三号建筑及王墓棺木都是依据汉制,是以东汉的尺度为单位进行设计、加工的。这清楚表明,至东汉后期,汉尺也是精绝王国内使用的度制之一。

精绝,是丝路南道上居于沙漠深处的弹丸小村,人口虽只区区数千,但除土著成分外,这里还有"于阗人"、"山地人"、偶尔前来的"汉人";分析一些居民名字的佉卢语语音,有吐火罗语的特征;[③]文字,又使用着汉文、佉卢文,呈现着相当复杂的面貌。这在西域具有典型性。两汉王朝实践证明,"安辑"政策在这里取得了成功。终两汉之世,晚至魏晋,不论作为尼雅绿洲上的精绝王国,或沦为鄯善王国境内的一个州,它都与中原大地保持相当密切的关系。甘肃悬泉置出土的汉简,不少表现了汉代西域进入中原的情况,其中,精绝所占比重非小。足以显示当年精绝与中原王朝关系相当紧密。

两汉王朝持续努力进行安辑,终于收获了西域各城邦"思汉威德,咸乐内附"。在政治上,取得了可以稳定统治的思想基础,这是任何兵威所不能比拟的成功。在这一相当长的历史时段中,有过因为汉王朝政治、军事力量不济,有效统治中断的时期,但总体形势却没有因为这种失落而逆转,"安辑"政策的影响,不可轻估。

还应看到,"安辑"政策实施的过程,也是两汉王朝占统治地位的文化,在相关地域拓展其影响的过

① 斯坦因:《古代和田》,NX 出土物,《尼雅考古资料》,第 62 页;李遇春:《尼雅遗址和东汉合葬墓》,载《尼雅考古资料》,第 28 页。
② 《中日共同尼雅遗迹学术报告书》第二卷,第 215~222 页。
③ 韩森:《尼雅学研究的启示》,载《汉唐之间文化艺术的互助与交流》,文物出版社,2001 年,第 278 页。

程。"安辑"政策实施之处,可以同时看到中原文明在同一地域的点点浸润、渗透,以至逐渐生根、发芽,生长出华夏文明的新枝。精绝,茫茫沙漠中的小绿洲,算得一个典型。公元前2世纪初,因种族、民族殊异,语言不通,文化不同,不可避免会出现种种排异心理,经过几个世纪的努力,变成心向汉王朝,这实在是精神文化领域巨大的成功。

剖析精绝各方面变化,在边疆史、少数民族史研究中,也可以得到方法上的启迪:一定要十分努力地深化、细化对考古资料的分析,不能放掉任何一个可以剖析的细节。一百年尼雅考古,涉足尼雅的中、外考古学者实在不能算少,都曾在房址、佛塔中徘徊、凭吊。但真正不计风沙寒冷,一点点测量、分析它们的长度、高度,探求背后的度制,还真少见。要在看似平常处寻觅求新的精神,这不仅要求知识、理论储备,也要求严谨、认真的态度,如是面对西域大地上丰富的历史遗存,分析任何一处不同的细节,在西域史研究、少数民族史研究中,肯定有望呈现新的光明。

兴复哈密与明正德朝宫廷朋党之争

施新荣

新疆师范大学历史系暨西域文史研究中心

如所周知,明代党争盛行,而明孝宗弘治二年(1489)两京御史案,正式揭开了有明一代宫廷内部的朋党斗争。① 但弘治朝之党争,尚未在兴复哈密的问题上产生激烈交锋,因而明成化、弘治时期,面对土鲁番地区的不断东侵,明王朝上下尚能齐心协力共同应对,三度兴复哈密。但是,到了"嗜酒而荒其志,好勇而轻其身"②的明武宗当政的正德朝(1505—1521),宫廷内部的派系之争愈演愈烈,在围绕兴复哈密及肃州失事等问题上展开了激烈交锋。有关正德朝时期哈密与明朝宫廷内部斗争之间的关系,似仅见于田澍先生的《明代哈密危机述论》、《彭泽与甘肃之变》③二文。本文拟进一步讨论之。

一、忠顺王拜牙即叛入土鲁番

弘治十二年(1499),虽然哈密忠顺王陕巴顺利返回哈密,但哈密卫积贫积弱,以及忠顺王孱弱的状况依然如故。因而,哈密卫内部政局不稳的情况依旧。据《明史·哈密传》载:

> 陕巴嗜酒掊克,失众心,部下阿孛剌等咸怨。(弘治)十七年(1504)春,阴构阿黑麻迎其幼子真帖木儿主哈密。陕巴惧,挈家走苦峪。奄克孛剌与写亦虎仙在肃州,边臣以二人为番众所服,令还辅陕巴,与百户董杰偕行。杰有胆略。既抵哈密,阿孛剌与其党五人约夜以兵来劫。杰知之,与奄克孛剌等谋,召阿孛剌等计事,立斩之,其下遂不敢叛。乃令陕巴还哈密。④

据此,知陕巴重归哈密后,有失众心,不能服众,因而导致其部下阿孛剌等勾结土鲁番速坛阿黑麻,并迎立阿黑麻之子真帖木儿入主哈密。后经明朝使臣对阿孛剌等人的惩治,哈密卫政局才有所安定。事后,甘肃"守臣令都指挥朱瑄率兵送陕巴入哈密,抚送真帖木儿还土鲁蕃。时阿黑麻已死,其子速坛满速儿新立,诸兄弟相仇杀,真帖木儿惧不敢归,乃曰:'奄克孛剌,我外祖也,愿依之,暂住哈密。'朱瑄恐陕巴怀疑生变,携真帖木儿羁居甘州"。⑤

① 商传:《从朋党到党社——明代党争之浅见》,《学习与探索》2007 年第 1 期,第 222 ~ 227 页。
② [明] 王思:《谏猎虎疏》,[明] 黄训编《名臣经济录》卷一〇,《景印文渊阁四库全书》第 443 册,台北:商务印书馆,1986 年,第 168 页上栏。
③ 田澍:《明代哈密危机述论》,《中国边疆史地研究》2002 年第 4 期,第 14 ~ 23 页;又见氏著:《嘉靖革新研究》,北京:中国社会科学出版社,2002 年,第 213 ~ 229 页;田澍:《彭泽与甘肃之变》,《西域研究》2004 年第 1 期,第 11 ~ 16 页。
④ 《明史》卷三二九《西域一·哈密传》,第 28 册,北京:中华书局点校本,1974 年,第 8520 页。
⑤ [明] 严从简:《殊域周咨录》卷一三《土鲁番》,余思黎点校,北京:中华书局,1993 年,第 436 页。

弘治十八年(1505),哈密忠顺王陕巴去世,明朝"立其子速坛拜牙即为忠顺王,给冠服、彩段、盔甲、弓箭等物,命都督奄克孛剌仍掌哈密卫印信,偕都督写亦虎仙协力佐之"。① 这样,土鲁番进入"桀黠变诈踰于父,复有吞哈密之志"的速坛满速儿时期,而哈密则进入"昏愚失道"②的拜牙即阶段。

拜牙即之昏愚无道,在《四夷广记·哈密》所载《正德八年哈密卫大小头目卜儿罕虎力参政、右头目也写克、左头目虎都六马黑麻等番文》中有非常贴切地描述,不妨迻录如下:

> 速坛拜牙即害人,每家夺麦三石,肥壮牛羊都夺了杀喫。又要去肃州下札丹,把屎谷霜打了。到了晚间,土剌上不睡下来人家好妇女强奸。众人与都督奄克孛剌说了,他脑著,穿上盔甲,要杀。奄克孛剌慌了,走出城外土剌上坐了三日,往肃州来了。有甘州差卜儿罕虎力驮十个段子、四十个梭布与他,嫌少,每家要梭布一匹,又要马十匹,不顺中国,投土鲁番去,要领人马来抢甘肃。③

如此"昏愚失道","又被奸回诱引与番酋结好"④的拜牙即,在明武宗正德八年(1513)秋"弃城叛入土鲁番"。⑤ 随后,土鲁番速坛"满速儿令头目火者他只丁",以及正德八年春护送真帖木儿回土鲁番,而滞留在此的写亦虎仙、满剌哈三"入哈密取金印"。火者他只丁"又令哈密都指挥火者马黑木等至甘州索赏。哈密诸酋译书言拜牙即弃国从番,乞即差人守哈密"。对此,"巡抚赵鉴谬谓满速儿忠义,令火者他只丁、写亦虎仙、满剌哈三守城勤劳,差抚夷官送土鲁番诸酋金币二百"。⑥ 据此可见,拜牙即之昏愚,而明朝甘肃巡抚赵鉴之糊涂。

二、彭泽与肃州失事

正德九年(1514)正月,当"抚夷官才至哈密,番酋(满速儿)已率众亦至,分据剌木等城,日夜聚谋侵甘肃,又索段子万万匹赎城、印。且言:'如不与,即领兵把旗插在甘州门上。'总制邓璋乃请官经略"。⑦ 是年五月,朝廷遂"敕都御史彭泽总督军务,量调延绥、宁夏、固原官军驻甘肃御之"。⑧ 而《吾学编·四夷考》云:"时总制都御史邓璋请专敕大臣一人经略哈密,大将督兵战守。"⑨似乎《皇明资治通纪》的记载更清楚,曰:"总制三边都御史邓璋、巡抚甘肃都御史赵鉴以土鲁番书阅,乞照先年差张海故事,差官往经略。时彭泽在四川征盗适平,兵部遂奏差泽往总督经略。"⑩

---

① 《明实录·武宗实录》卷六,弘治十八年十月丙辰条,黄彰键校勘,台北:"中央研究院"历史语言研究所校印本,1975年,第192页。

② 《明史》卷三二九《西域一·土鲁番传》,第28册,第8533页。

③ [明]慎懋赏辑《四夷广记·哈密》,《玄览堂丛书续集》第九十八册,南京:"国立中央"图书馆,1949年影印,第721页。

④ [明]严从简:《殊域周咨录》卷一三《土鲁蕃》,第437页。

⑤ 《明史》卷三二九《西域一·哈密传》,第28册,第8521页。

⑥ [明]郑晓:《吾学编·四夷考》卷下《哈密》,载《北京图书馆古籍珍本丛刊》12,北京:书目文献出版社,1990年据明隆庆元年履淳刻本影印,第720页下栏。

⑦ [明]严从简:《殊域周咨录》卷一三《土鲁蕃》,第437页。案:"索段子万万匹赎城、印"一句,似衍一"万"字。

⑧ 《明实录·武宗实录》卷一一二,正德九年五月己丑条,第2291页。

⑨ [明]郑晓:《吾学编·四夷考》卷下《哈密》,第721页上栏。

⑩ [明]陈建撰,卜世昌、卜六典校正《皇明资治通纪》卷一三,载《皇明资治通纪三种》,北京:中华全国图书馆文献缩微复制中心,2000年据湖北图书馆藏明万历刻本影印,第444页下栏。

由上可见，就邓璋、赵鉴二人向朝廷所奏初衷而言，并无要求派遣总督之请，而是奏请朝廷照弘治时差张海故事，委派一名专臣经略哈密事宜。但兵部任命彭泽以总督之职前往甘肃，使得甘肃一地在总制、巡抚之外，又有总督。如明人陈建所论："今甘肃有巡抚，又有总制矣！经略哈密岂非巡抚、总制者之责乎，乃复另差大臣总督经略之，岂以当时居巡抚、总制者为不足任此乎！夫不足任则当易置，而责成不宜复另差经略，重为烦扰也。"①

其实，彭泽对出任此职，是心存疑虑的。《武宗实录》卷一一五，正德九年八月戊申（十八日）条载："右都御史彭泽既平蜀寇，且还，会陕西土鲁番之变，复命泽总制经略。泽自谓：'久典军务，又陕为乡土，且已用都御史邓璋总制及咸宁侯仇钺皆可任。'遂引疾上疏辞，诏不允，且曰：朕亦念卿久劳于外，宜勉为朕一行，以安边境，其毋固辞。"②又，《彭泽墓志》曰："甫离汉中至褒城，又奉敕令总督陕西、甘肃等处军务，盖以西域土鲁番酋速坛满速儿侵夺哈密忠顺王城、印，欲占取甘肃；北虏亦卜剌等二枝大扰甘肃地方，占据西海，且地方饥馑尤甚，镇巡诸公莫保朝夕。"③可见，彭泽清楚地知道担任此职责任重大，因而任前一再推辞。彭泽以这种心态担任经略哈密之重任，多少为其后来草率行事埋下了隐患。

正德十年（1515）春正月，彭泽肩负收复哈密城、印之重任至甘州，时值土鲁番速坛满速儿部将火者他只丁等深入肃州边外的赤斤等地抢掠。他只丁得知彭泽已至甘肃调集兵马，"不敢深入，假写番文称被赤斤抢了贡物，与他报仇，不敢侵犯甘肃，只讨些赏赐回去"。然而，"彭泽不察其诈"，④却"以为番夷可以利哈"，⑤随"即措段绢、褐布共三百，遣马骥与通事火信、抚夷百户马昇并马驯捧前敕二道，同马黑木、（写亦）虎仙等到哈密，邀他只丁同往土鲁番。他只丁嫌赏薄，先将金印与（写亦）虎仙、（满剌）哈三等，及将所掠去赤斤铜印一颗付马驯等，议遣骥并火信持回添取赏赐"。⑥

事后，彭泽向朝廷奏称："甘肃兵粮颇集，道路开通，土鲁番虽欲侵扰甘肃，决不可能。今又差官往谕归还城印，地方安静，乞要放归田里。"但武宗未允。火信等回到甘州，"纳抚还赤斤铜印，并报添取赏赐"。彭泽"又备罗段、褐布共一千九百，银壶、银碗、银台盏各一副，令火信等复持往谕"。⑦

待火信等人二次出使土鲁番后，彭泽"遂奏远夷悔过，献还城印"。⑧"未得报，辄奏事平，乞骸骨。召还理院事。"⑨此时（正德十年四月），原户部尚书王琼出任兵部尚书，⑩对彭泽事未毕即回朝，提出异议未果，"（彭）泽之憾（王）琼始此"。⑪彭泽于正德十年闰四月回京，并向朝廷奏称："通事马骥等往谕土鲁番，要以重赏。其酋速坛满速儿悔过效顺，乃付哈密金印及城池于都督满剌哈三、写亦虎仙掌守之，召监守头目火者他只丁还，仍献所夺赤斤卫印。哈密王速坛拜牙即尚匿于其弟把巴叉营，因其兄弟不睦，故未释也。必量给赏，令颁之族众，以相和辑，事乃就绪。"⑫

---

① [明]陈建撰，卜世昌、卜六典校正《皇明资治通纪》卷一三，载《皇明资治通纪三种》。
② 《明实录·武宗实录》卷一一五，正德九年八月戊申条，第2332页。与《明史·彭泽传》（第5236页）略同。
③ 《彭泽墓志》，载薛仰敬主编《兰州古今碑刻》，兰州大学出版社，2002年，第30页。
④ [明]严从简：《殊域周咨录》卷一三《土鲁番》，第437～438页。
⑤ [明]陈建撰，卜世昌、卜六典校正《皇明资治通纪》卷一三，载《皇明资治通纪三种》，第444页下栏。
⑥ [明]严从简：《殊域周咨录》卷一三《土鲁番》，第438页。
⑦ 同上。
⑧ 同上。
⑨ 《明史》卷一九八《彭泽传》，第17册，第5236页。
⑩ [明]陈建撰，卜世昌、卜六典校正《皇明资治通纪》卷一三，载《皇明资治通纪三种》，第446页下栏。
⑪ [明]陈洪谟：《继世纪闻》卷六，盛冬铃点校，北京：中华书局，1985年，第112～113页。
⑫ 《明实录·武宗实录》卷一二六，正德十年六月庚午条，第2523页。

由上可见,彭泽在处置收复哈密城、印事宜时,如明人陈建所论:"轻信幸功,欲以厚币啗之,赎取城印,误矣!"①彭泽如此草率行事,实乃急欲尽快了结,以期还朝心态的必然结果。彭泽之举,不仅使"哈密城池不可复赎",②而且给明朝的西北边防造成了更大的危机。

当火信等人持物抵达土鲁番后,满速儿复"嫌其赏薄"。而且同行的写亦虎仙因与满速儿有隙,"满速儿欲杀之,大惧,求他只丁为解,许赂币千五百匹,期至肃州界之,且啗之入寇,曰肃州可得也。满速儿喜,令与其婿马黑木俱入贡,以觇虚实,且徵其赂"。③《明史·彭泽传》称:"写亦虎仙者,素桀黠。虽居肃州,阴通土鲁番酋速檀满速儿,为之耳目,据城夺印皆其谋。泽初不知而遣之。"④然而,当写亦虎仙及其婿马黑木,以及土鲁番索贿贡使入关后,遂引发了土鲁番围攻肃州的事变。据《武宗实录》卷一四五,正德十二年(1517)正月壬寅(二十六日)条载:

> (甘肃)守臣以随贡头目火者撒者儿为火者他只丁弟,惧其有变,乃并其党虎都写亦羁之甘州,而督写亦虎仙出关。虎仙惧,弗去。火者他只丁遂复诱夺哈密城,请速坛满速儿移居之,分兵协据沙州,纠众入寇。至兔儿坝,(芮)宁与参将蒋存礼,都指挥黄荣、王琮各率所部往御之。宁先进至沙子坝,遇贼,贼以大兵围宁,而分兵缀存礼等,令不得合。宁势孤援绝,遂为所败,死焉。一军皆没,凡七百人。贼既败我军,又遣斩巴思等十余人以驼马至肃州,诡言乞和,而阴赍阿剌思罕儿、写亦虎仙等书,约举火内应。兵备副使陈九畴廉得其情,执阿剌思罕儿等并斩巴思付狱,令通事毛鉴等防守。鉴等故缓之,令与其党通,欲伺隙而逸。时初闻宁败,城中恟惧,及贼薄城,军士皆出战,众夷果欲为变。九畴备严,不得发。乃戮鉴等数人于市以徇,并系其通谋者二百余人。贼久驻无援,恐谋泄为我所乘,遂遁去。⑤

当土鲁番围攻肃州城之时,甘肃巡抚"李昆等亦恐甘州藏有奸夷内应,将(写亦)虎仙、(火者)撒者儿、(虎都)写亦及各家属并各起夷人四十四名俱捕下狱。……失拜烟答病死,贼起营西去"。⑥

《彭泽墓志》将肃州失事系于丁丑(1517)春,⑦《皇明资治通纪》卷一三系于正德十一年(1516)冬,⑧而《明朝纪事本末·兴复哈密》、《明史·武宗本纪》均系于正德十一年九月。⑨ 清人夏燮已注意到土鲁番据哈密、围攻肃州的时间问题,他在《明通鉴》卷四六,正德十一年九月条"考异"中指出:"《明朝纪事本末》系土鲁番复据哈密于是月,无日。《实录》书于明年之正月,盖据奏报之月日。而所叙据哈密、攻肃州事,皆在此前一年,故诸书皆系之是年九月,《明史·哈密传》言'十二年正月,羽书至闻',则奏报之至在明年正月。"但夏燮也将土鲁番复据哈密与肃州失事,一同系于正德十一年九月。⑩

---

① [明]陈建撰,卜世昌、卜六典校正《皇明资治通纪》卷一三,载《皇明资治通纪三种》,第447页上栏。

② 同上。

③ 《明史》卷三二九《西域一·哈密传》,第28册,第8522页。另参见[明]谢贲:《后鉴录》,《明史资料丛刊》第1辑,南京:江苏人民出版社,1981年,第88~89页。

④ 《明史》卷一九八《彭泽传》,第17册,第5237页。

⑤ 《明实录·武宗实录》卷一四五,正德十二年正月壬寅条,第2842~2843页。

⑥ [明]严从简:《殊域周咨录》卷一三《土鲁番》,第441页。

⑦ 《彭泽墓志》,载薛仰敬主编《兰州古今碑刻》,第31页。

⑧ [明]陈建撰,卜世昌、卜六典校正《皇明资治通纪》卷一三,载《皇明资治通纪三种》,第449页上栏。

⑨ [清]谷应泰:《明朝纪事本末》卷四〇《兴复哈密》,北京:中华书局点校本,1977年,第593页;《明史》卷一六《武宗本纪》,第2册,第208页。

⑩ [清]夏燮:《明通鉴》卷四六,正德十一年九月条,北京:中华书局点校本,1958年,第1740~1741页。

据王琼在正德十二年四月初二日所上《为斩获犯边回贼首级追逐远遁事》云:"……甘肃地方去年十一月内土鲁番贼役,死游击进军芮宁,损折官军数多。"①

王琼《为抚谕夷悔过献还哈密城印遣使进贡事》称:"本年(正德十一年)十一月十六日,土鲁番犯肃州,杀死芮宁等官军一千余员名,攻陷城堡,杀虏人畜以数万计。"②

王琼《为斩获犯边回贼首级追逐远遁事》曰:"至十一月十六日,土鲁番贼至肃州城西十里,杀死芮宁官军。至十九日,贼势渐退,陈九畴方将斩巴斯等打死。"③

《边政考》称:正德十一年"十一月,满速儿、牙木兰领兵会合罕东左卫土巴部落,凡万余骑入嘉峪关,十六日游击芮宁领军出南门御之,败绩。官军死者八百四十二人……"。④

上引王琼《晋溪本兵敷奏》"皆其官兵部尚书时所上",⑤当是据第一手材料而成,最接近事实,可信度极高。因而,土鲁番围攻肃州及肃州失事应发生于正德十一年十一月中旬,《明朝纪事本末》、《明通鉴》、《明史·武宗本纪》系于是年九月,不确,而《彭泽墓志》系于正德十七年春,误。不过,将土鲁番复据哈密之事系于正德十一年九月,是可以接受的。

如所周知,公元1514年(明武宗正德九年),满速儿的弟弟赛德在东察合台汗国的西部建立起了一个割据政权,即所谓的叶尔羌汗国。这样,东察合台汗国就一分为二,满速儿汗在东;赛德汗在西。这种局面的出现对满速儿来说非常不利,穆斯林史料称:满速儿汗"已退到土鲁番和察力失,这时他既无力反抗,也没有地方可以避难"。⑥然而,两年(即正德十一年)后,东察合台汗国发生了一件有利于满速儿的大事。据穆斯林史料《拉失德史》说:满速儿汗非常害怕速檀赛德汗,因为速檀赛德汗的亲兄弟速檀哈里勒之死,就是他促成的,而且头目之间也曾发生过多次激烈的冲突。满速儿汗深信这一点将会使他们之间永世不能和好,但是,和他的预料相反,速檀赛德汗派人护送一个使者到他这里来请求会晤。他们于伊斯兰历922年(1516)在阿克苏和苦先之间举行会见。会见时速檀赛德汗宣布臣服于满速儿汗,同意在虎土白中郎诵其兄的名字,并以满速儿之名铸造钱币。于是,他们两兄弟之间完全言归于好,结果使两个地面在二十年之间完全安享太平。⑦这就使得土鲁番速檀满速儿无西顾之忧,可以全力东向扩张。因此,正德十一年后,土鲁番长驱深入河西围攻肃州城等城池,就是在这样的背景下进行的。

三、朋党之争与彭泽等人去职

鉴于土鲁番公然围攻肃州城,明军初战失利,"甘肃告急",明朝政府于正德十二年二月,命"彭

① [明]王琼:《为斩获犯边回贼首级追逐远遁事》,《晋溪本兵敷奏》卷六,载《四库全书存目丛书》史部第59册,济南:齐鲁书社,1996年据明嘉靖二十三年廖希颜刻本影印,第163页上下栏。

② [明]王琼:《为抚谕远夷悔过献还哈密城印遣使进贡事》,《晋溪本兵敷奏》卷六,载《四库全书存目丛书》史部第59册,第176页上栏。

③ [明]王琼:《为斩获犯边回贼首级追逐远遁事》,《晋溪本兵敷奏》卷七,载《四库全书存目丛书》史部第59册,第189页下栏至第190页上栏。

④ [明]张雨:《边政考》卷一一《西域经略》,载《续修四库全书》第738册,上海古籍出版社,2002年据国立北平图书馆善本丛书第一集明嘉靖刻本影印,第179页下栏。

⑤ 《钦定四库全书总目》卷五六,四库全书研究所整理,北京:中华书局,1997年,第781页。

⑥ 米儿咱·马黑麻·海答儿:《拉失德史》第2编,新疆社会科学院民族研究所译,王治来校注,乌鲁木齐:新疆人民出版社,1986年,第262页。

⑦ 米儿咱·马黑麻·海答儿:《拉失德史》第1编,新疆社会科学院民族研究所译,王治来校注,第345、356页。

泽提督陕西等处三边军务,镇守宁夏右都督郤永充总兵官。……以太监张永总制提督,孔学监管神枪"。① 但,是年四月,兵部接到甘肃巡抚李昆奏报称土鲁番人马已遁去,甘肃"地方稍宁"。于是,明武宗命"张永、彭泽、孔学并纪功等官且不必去"。但令郤永继续"统领原带官军前去甘肃邻近地方暂且住扎,以便赴援"。② 同时,武宗"命给事中黄臣会同巡按赵春行委陕西参议施训、副使高显、金事董琦勘问,将(写亦)虎仙问拟谋叛具奏。(写亦)虎仙诉,行肃州兵备再审。奄克(孛剌)恐其脱放,乃告(写亦)虎仙及其丈人哈即构引土鲁蕃坏事,今不曾正法,恐贻后患。……诏提解(写亦)虎仙等到京会审"。③ 至此,因肃州失事而造成的危机暂告结束,但土鲁番入关围攻肃州城事件,却给明王朝朝野上下以极大的震动,围绕此事,朝廷内部的派系斗争亦凸现了出来。

兵部尚书王琼于正德十二年二月初六上书奏事曰:"看得土鲁番为因先许贮丝一千五百疋取出给金印,贮丝未曾送去,以此启衅,酿成今日之祸,大坏地方。造谋之人,合当查究。"④王琼在同日的另一份奏书中又说:"及查先前许与段疋之人,因何轻许失信,致启边衅,就彼拿问明白,解京发落。"⑤

身为兵部尚书的王琼,在奏书中提出追究处置哈密事宜不当,而酿成肃州失事之祸官员的责任,本无可厚非,属其职责范围内之事。况且从奏文用语来看,亦在情理之中,未有不妥之处,纯粹是为朝廷着想。但史称"(王)琼为人有心计",⑥而且王琼与彭泽有隙。

关于王、彭二臣矛盾之由来,文献有不同的记载。王世贞《弇州史料前集·王琼传》称:王琼与彭泽因"议哈密事相矛盾",⑦此说似据明人陈洪谟专记正德一朝见闻的《继世纪闻》(见前)。但清人所修《明史·彭泽传》则云:"初,兵部缺尚书,廷臣共推泽,而王琼得之,且阴阻泽。言官多劾琼者,由是有隙。"⑧对于这两种不同说法,笔者更倾向于前说。

不论怎样,彭泽"经略哈密事颇不当"⑨是事实,因此身为兵部尚书的王琼,就是在奏文中明确提出惩治彭泽处置哈密失宜也不过分,但就王琼"为人有心计"的个性来说,奏文用没有倾向性的词语,不排除含有打击、报复彭泽之嫌疑。彭泽面对来自王琼的压力,以及难以推卸的责任,遂于正德十二年五月乙未(二十一日)"以率病乞休"。对此,彭泽自言道:"及岁,夫月米优典,更奉旨允弟冲侍疾于家。科道交章留之,未之允。"⑩显然,彭泽的言语中已流露出被迫离职之意。《武宗实录》评述道:"盖(彭)泽之去,实为兵部尚书王琼所挤,举朝虽惜之,而不能留也。"⑪可见,彭泽以"病乞休",实乃王琼逼迫所致。

但事情到此并未结束,据《武宗实录》卷一六○,正德十三年(1518)三月壬子(十三日)条载:

勒致仕太子太保左都御史彭泽为民,逮甘肃巡抚都御史李昆、兵备副使陈九畴至京治之。初,兵

① 《明实录·武宗实录》卷一四六,正德十二年二月庚戌条,第2850页。
② [明]王琼:《为斩获犯边回贼首级追逐远遁事》,《晋溪本兵敷奏》卷六,载《四库全书存目丛书》史部第59册,第163页下栏。
③ [明]严从简:《殊域周咨录》卷一三《土鲁蕃》,第441~442页。
④ [明]王琼:《为夷情事》,《晋溪本兵敷奏》卷六,载《四库全书存目丛书》史部第59册,第158页下栏。
⑤ [明]王琼:《为夷情事》,《晋溪本兵敷奏》卷六,载《四库全书存目丛书》史部第59册,第158页上栏。
⑥ 《明史》卷一九八《王琼传》,第17册,第5232页。
⑦ [明]王世贞:《王琼传》,《弇州史料前集》卷三○,载《四库禁毁书丛刊》史部第48~50册,北京出版社,2000年据明万历四十二年刻本影印,第199页上栏。
⑧ 《明史》卷一九八《彭泽传》,第17册,第5236页。
⑨ 同上。
⑩ 《彭泽墓志》,载薛仰敬主编《兰州古今碑刻》,第31页。
⑪ 《明实录·武宗实录》卷一四九,正德十二年五月乙未条,第2907页。

部尚书王琼既奏遣科道官详勘哈密事,欲中泽以危法,及勘至于泽,一无所劾。琼又遣其属储询、路直嘱会同馆主事张灿簇夷人之拘馆中者,令暴泽短。不可。琼计阻,乃自直言:"泽擅遣使,妄增金币,以敕谕及钦赏自遣书议和,失信起衅,辱国丧师,并(李)昆、(陈)九畴,俱宜逮治。"诏以事体重大,下廷臣集议之。及议,众多不平,然畏琼不敢言。①

又,同月戊午(十九日)条载:

> 传旨,调工科都给事中石天柱、刑科都给事中王爌于外任。初,廷议彭泽事,两人忤兵部尚书王琼意。未数日,遂假内批谪之。科道复疏言:两人无可指之,罪去之何名? 恐传之天下,后世不能无议,亦不纳。竟调为推官。天柱云南临安府,爌广东惠州府。②

由此可见,王琼继续深究彭泽等与肃州失事有关官员,并三番五次地设法治以重罪。而且不惜唆使番夷,借其口达到打击政治异己的目的,甚至对对其做法提出异议的官员进行恶意的报复。至此,王琼的所作所为已远远超出其兵部尚书的正常职责范围了,演化为利用处置肃州失事官员之机,行打击政治异己之实。这样到明武宗正德朝时,边疆的哈密危机已演化成了明朝宫廷内部政治派系斗争的工具。

更令人难以置信的是,正德十四年(1519),肃州失事的祸首"写亦虎仙亦减死,遂夤缘钱宁,与其婿得侍帝左右。帝悦之,赐国姓,授锦衣指挥,扈驾南征"。③ 由此可见武宗朝时期明朝政治的黑暗。

---

① 《明实录·武宗实录》卷一六〇,正德十三年三月壬子条,第3093~3094页。
② 《明实录·武宗实录》卷一六〇,正德十三年三月戊午条,第3096页。
③ 《明史》卷三二九《西域一·哈密传》,第28册,第8523页。

吐鲁番对传统中医药学的贡献

宋 岘

中国社会科学院

本文所言的是今吐鲁番市所辖地面的古代吐鲁番。在中国,吐鲁番位于中原内地与西域边疆之间;从国际角度上讲,吐鲁番位于中外文化交流的通道——丝绸之路上。由此,吐鲁番成为各种文化交流的枢纽,在这里的医药交流也独具特色。

一、唐代高昌曾是抗击国际流行病——"天行发斑疮"的前哨阵地

唐玄宗天宝十一载(752)成书的方剂书——《外台秘要》①卷三言:

> 文仲陶氏云:"天行发斑疮,须臾遍身,皆戴白浆。此恶毒气方。云永徽四年,此疮从西域东流入海内。但煮葵菜叶、蒜韭,啖之则止。鲜羊血入口亦止。初患急食之。少饭下菜亦得。"出二十五卷中。

此"恶毒气方"所言的西域,当指如今中国的新疆及其以西的中亚、西亚地区。当时的吐鲁番(西州)、喀什(疏勒),皆在唐代中国的版图之内,故皆属海内。因此,此"天行发斑疮"应是发生在中国安西都护府辖区以外的西域——波斯、阿拉伯一带。

众所周知,巨大的自然灾害,如地震、海啸、洪灾、雪灾、蝗灾;或巨大的人祸,如战乱、种族仇杀,等等,均会严重破坏原本的生态环境。人们因逃难而流离失所,甚至长途迁徙。这一切变故,均会产生和传播时疫,比如天花,就在唐代以前的世界上多次流行。那么,"永徽四年"前后的波斯、阿拉伯地面上也发生了此类变故。

由于 626 年波斯君主撕毁了穆罕默德的国书,羞辱了阿拉伯人,因此,新生的阿拉伯伊斯兰政权决计消灭波斯国。634 年阿拉伯人攻入波斯。637 年 6 月阿拉伯人攻波斯国的首都——泰西封。卫戍部队跟着波斯末代君主——伊嗣俟(叶兹德吉尔德,Yezdjerd,见《册府元龟》)弃城而逃。唐高宗永徽元年前后(649~650)阿拉伯人攻占了波斯腹地柏塞波利斯(今舍拉子一带)。永徽二年(651)伊嗣俟携带皇冠、财宝和少数侍从,逃到木鹿(今土库曼斯坦的马里)。一个磨房主见财起异,将伊嗣俟杀害在磨房里。与他走散的皇子——卑路斯(Peyrooz,"得胜者"之意)、孙子——泥涅师师(Narses)等波斯皇室遗族,则继续东逃。据《旧唐书·西域传》可晓,皇子卑路斯先投奔吐火罗叶护。龙朔元年(661),唐高宗置疾陵城(今

---

① 王焘:《外台秘要》卷三,人民卫生出版社,2002 年版,第 119 页。

伊朗境内的扎黑丹),为波斯都督府,授卑路斯为都督。咸亨(670~674)中,卑路斯自来入朝,高宗甚加恩赐,拜右武卫将军。……景龙(707~710)初,泥涅师师来朝,授左威卫将军。卑路斯、泥涅师师父子均客死中国。波斯萨珊王朝的末代君主及其子孙均客死他乡的情景十分悲凉,造成如此情形的原因还在于阿拉伯人对波斯国的战争,并不满足于攻城略地,而是要对伊嗣俟当年羞辱阿拉伯政权一事必欲进行彻底的报复。因此651年伊嗣俟死后,阿拉伯人又向木鹿以东地区进行征战。《新唐书·西域传》卷二三八言:"米,或曰弥末,曰弥秣贺。北百里距康。其君治钵息德城。永徽(650~655)时,为大食所破。"此米国(Maimargh)所治钵息德,即今乌兹别克斯坦境内的朱马巴扎尔(Guma-a-Bazar)。其中的康,即隋唐时期的昭武九姓胡国之一的康国,即以撒马尔罕为都城的粟特人的城邦国家,其地今属乌兹别克斯坦。《唐会要》卷九九"康国"条:"永徽中,其国频遣使告为大食所攻,兼征赋税。"由此可知,永徽四年(653)及其之前这几年的波斯、中亚,正进行着一场残酷的战争。《外台秘要》所言的"从西域东流入海内"的"天行发斑疮"正是这场令波斯人亡国灭种的战争引起的,也正是由那些躲避这场战争而逃入中国的中亚波斯人将此病传入中国内地的。

言及此,我们再看看当年的吐鲁番——唐代的高昌、西州是否有与此相关的事情发生?

据新疆社会科学院考古研究所编《新疆考古三十年》介绍,1959年10~11月新疆博物馆东文物工作组在吐鲁番的阿斯塔那(Āstānā,波斯语词,意为:皇陵、圣墓)对六座古墓葬进行了发掘,其中编号为TAM302的墓内,有永徽四年墓志。此墓有尸首三具,1男2女。男在外,头向东;1女在内,头向西,另1女在西壁下,头向南。在服饰上,男女都于头顶束髻。1女尸裹麻布,外以素绢连头包裹。上身穿直领对襟齐膝外套,下系裙,均用茄紫色绢缝制,胸上露出的部分缝"对马织锦"一方。在阿斯塔那的这六座古墓中,唯在此302号墓内才有"对马纹锦"(二件)。一为1女尸覆面及胸饰。橙黄地显蓝、浅绿、粉红色花纹。在长径9 cm、短径8.5 cm的近圆形边圈内昂颈相对的带翼双马,一只前蹄腾空,栩栩如生。编者言:这类花纹"显然不是汉族风格,大约是波斯文化影响的产物。"在这六座古墓的诸多陪葬物中,也唯独在这座302号墓中发掘有波斯银币两枚,即那两具女尸嘴里各含的一枚。[①]

在此TAM302号墓内,有用汉文题写的墓志铭。朱书八行:

> 唯永徽四年,岁次癸丑十一月;己酉朔十三月辛酉,新除都官主簿赵松柏,行都官参军事,属大唐启运,泽被西州,蒙授武骑卫,方将竭诚奉国,荫蔽家门,何图一旦奄然殡逝,遂使亲族悲号,乡间嗷泣。春秋五十九
>
> ……呜呼哀哉!

此墓志铭讲,其中的男尸乃墓主人,59岁,新近才被朝廷委任为都官主簿、行都官参军事、武骑卫,正当他在吐鲁番地面的西州履新,却不幸突遭变故,而"奄然殡逝"于一旦。据墓志铭可知,他与同穴的那两位女子,暴卒于永徽四年。前文所言,《外台秘要》记录的天行发斑疮从西域流行入海内的时间,也恰恰是永徽四年。再有,同穴的那两位女子颇多波斯文化特征。这一切表明,这位时值壮年的赵松柏是死于这次国际流行病——天行发斑疮的可能性极大。当然,此事于今,已过去了1 300多年了。若确审此

---

① 新疆社会科学院考古研究所编《新疆考古三十年》,新疆人民出版社,1983年,第74~78页。

事,则须对那 1 男 2 女三具古尸做一番科学检测才行。阿斯塔那 TAM302 号墓很可能是当年吐鲁番地区流行过天行发斑疮的一个例证。而当年,西州地区亦确实为传统中医药从根本上防治这种国际流行病提供过宝贵的病情信息。

二、唐代西州的医方

王焘《外台秘要》记录了一些汉唐年间的非中原内地的少数民族的方剂。比如,"古今录验匈奴露宿丸"、[①]"崔氏疗三五十年眼赤并胎赤方。西域法。太常丞吕才道效"。[②]

王焘《外台秘要》又言:

古今录验"西州续命汤"。疗中风入藏。及四肢拘急不随。缓急风方:

麻黄三两去节　石膏二两　芎藭一两　生姜三两　黄芩一两　甘草一两　灸　芍药一两　桂心一两

郁李仁三两去皮　防风一两　杏人(仁)四十枚　当归一两　右十二味切,以水九升煮麻黄,去上末,内诸药煮取三升,分四服,初服取汗,米粉于衣里粉之,忌海藻菘菜生葱,出第四卷中。[③]

其中的"西州"即唐太宗贞观十三年平高昌而设的西州都督府。此"西州续命汤"乃是唐代吐鲁番对中医的贡献。

王焘《外台秘要》曰:必效疗阴生疮脓出做臼方:

高昌白矾一两

右一味捣。细研之。炼猪脂一合。于滋(磁)器中和搅作膏。取槐白皮切。作汤洗疮上。及以楸叶贴上。不过三两度。永差。[④]

这个仅有一味药——高昌白矾的方剂,当与吐鲁番的高昌有关系。

《本草纲目》卷二十五"酒"一节言:"米酒[气味]苦、甘、辛,大热,有毒。(士良曰)凡服丹砂、北庭石亭脂、钟乳诸石、生姜,并不可长用酒下,能引石药气入四肢,滞血化为痈疽。"这表明,北庭所产的石亭脂已被列为石药。古人已掌握了服丹砂、石亭脂、钟乳石时忌讳伴着生姜服用,更忌讳以米酒为药引子的经验。

(清)赵学敏《本草纲目拾遗》卷二上部"开元钱"一节言:《槐西杂志》:"交河黄俊生言,折伤接骨者以'开通元宝'钱烧而醋淬,研为末,以酒服下,则铜末自接而为圈,周束折处,曾以折足鸡试之,果接续如故。及烹此鸡验其骨,铜束宛然。此钱,唐初所铸。欧阳询所书其旁微有一偃月形,乃进样时,文德皇后误掐一痕,因而未改也。其字当回环读之。俗以为开元钱,则误矣。"显然,此接骨方法,得之于唐代的吐鲁番。

---

① 王焘:《外台秘要》,第 333 页。
② 同上,第 567 页。
③ 同上,第 527 页。
④ 同上,第 716 页。

三、土产于吐鲁番的古代中药

本节讲述的,是一些原产于吐鲁番的,或原产于与高昌、吐鲁番相关联的地面上的古代中药。

前述的高昌白矾,应是吐鲁番地面上的土产。或者,它是吐鲁番人民就地取材,加工制造出的矿物药,抑或是通过吐鲁番而采购到的非吐鲁番本地产的矿物药。

《外台秘要》卷三十一曰:"西州蒲暴。"意思是西州(吐鲁番)地面出产药物——"蒲暴"。[①] 此"蒲暴"为何物? 是否指葡萄? 待查。

李时珍《本草纲目》卷十一石部的"光明盐"一节言:"《梁四公子记》云:高昌国烧羊山出盐,大者如斗状,白如玉。月望收者,其纹理粗,明澈如水。非月望收者,其纹理密。"高昌的"烧羊山"今在吐鲁番何处? 待察。

《本草纲目》卷十一石部的"戎盐"一节言:"《梁杰公传》言:交河之间,掘碛下数尺有紫盐,如红如紫,色鲜而甘。其下丈许,有璺珀。"文中的"交河"即吐鲁番地面上的交河。

《本草纲目》卷十一石部的"硇砂(北庭砂)"一节言:[集解](时珍曰)张匡邺《行程记》云"高昌北庭山中,常有烟气涌起而无云雾,至夕光焰若炬火,照见禽鼠皆赤色,谓之火焰山,采硇砂者,乘木屐取之,若皮底即焦矣。北庭即今西域火州也"。

该节又言:[发明]张杲《玉洞要诀》云:"北庭砂秉阴石之气,含阳毒之精,能化五金八石,去秽益阳,其功甚著,力并硫磺。"

该节附有一疗"噎膈反胃"的方子:"邓才兴用北庭砂二钱,水和荞麦面包之,煅焦,待冷,取中间湿者焙干一钱,入槟榔二钱,丁香二个,研匀,每服七厘,烧酒送下,日服,愈即止。后吃白粥半月,仍服助胃丸药。"

《本草纲目》卷十一石部"石硫磺(黄硇砂)"一节言:张华《博物志》云:"西域硫磺出且弥山,去高昌八百里有山,高数十丈,昼则孔中状如烟,夜则如灯光。"

《本草纲目》卷二十六菜部"胡萝卜"一节言:金幼孜《北征录》云:"交河北有沙萝卜,根长二尺许,大者径寸,下支生小者如箸,其色黄白,气味辛而微苦,亦似萝卜气,此皆胡萝卜之类也。"

《本草纲目》卷三十三记"给勃罗",并言唐代本草学家陈藏器(8世纪人)记之为刺蜜,又名草蜜。陈藏器《本草拾遗》言:"交河中有草,头上有毛,毛中生蜜,胡人名为给勃罗。"此给勃罗即甘露蜜。其学名: Alhagi desortorum。此本草亦出现于《回回药方》,被呼作"他阑古宾"。

《本草纲目》卷三十三"葡萄"一节言:"西边有琐琐葡萄,大如五味子而无核。"此琐琐葡萄,即吐鲁番产的可制为葡萄干而品名为"无核白"的小粒葡萄。李时珍言,葡萄主治"筋骨湿痹",有"益气、倍力、强志、令人肥健、耐饥、忍风寒。久食,轻身、不老、延年、可作酒"等功能。然而李时珍未明确指出此葡萄及葡萄酒的产地。

《饮膳正要》卷三言:"葡萄酒益气、调中、耐饥、强志。酒有数等,有西番者,有哈剌火者,有平阳太原者,其味都不及哈剌火者田地酒最佳。"《饮膳正要》乃元代人忽思慧于1330年的作品,其所记的哈喇火

者正是元代对高昌的称谓。忽思慧于元代延祐至天历（1314～1329）年间担任饮膳太医。《本草纲目》卷二十五"葡萄酒"一节言：葡萄烧酒，乃"唐时破高昌始得其法"。可见，吐鲁番的葡萄酒早已被列入中国医药。

《本草纲目》卷三十四"阿魏"言："按《（大明）一统志》所载，有此二种，云出火州及沙鹿海牙国者，草高尺许，根株独立，枝叶如盖，臭气逼人，生取其汁熬作膏，名阿魏。"

《本草纲目》卷三十六"木棉"言："李延寿《南史》所谓高昌国有草实，如茧中丝，为细纑，名曰白叠，取以为帛，甚软白。"

《本草纲目》卷三十七"醫"言："[集解]（恭曰）今西州南三百里碛中得者，大则方尺，黑润而轻，烧之腥臭，高昌人名为木醫，谓玄玉，为石醫。共州土石间得者，烧作松气，功同琥珀。……（慎微曰）《梁公子传》柰公云：'交河之间平碛中掘深一丈下有醫珀，黑逾纯漆，或大如车轮，末服攻夫人小肠症瘕诸疾'。"

《本草纲目》卷五十"羊"之[附录]"大尾羊"有言："（时珍曰）羊尾皆短，而哈密及大食诸番有大尾羊，细毛、薄皮，尾上旁广，重一二十斤，行则以车载之。《唐书》谓之灵羊，云可疗毒。"

《本草纲目》卷五十一"跳鼠"言："鼹鼠（李时珍曰）今契丹及交河北境有跳兔，头目毛色皆似兔，而爪足似鼠，前足仅寸许，后足近尺，尾亦长，其端有毛，一跳数尺，止即蹙仆。此即鼹鼠也。"

《本草纲目拾遗》卷五草部下"一支蒿"言："绍郡府佐李秉文久客西陲，言巴里坤出一种药，名'一枝蒿'，生深山中，无枝，叶一枝，苗土气，味如蒿。四月间，牧马卒驱马入山，收草携归，煎膏以售远客。有贩至兰州货卖者。活血、解毒、去一切积滞沉疴、阴寒等疾。驱风理祛。"

《本草纲目拾遗》卷七花部言：雪荷花（雪莲花）"亦产巴里坤等处"。

《本草纲目拾遗》卷十虫部言："雪虾蟆《忆旧游诗话》：巴里坤雪山中有之。医家取作性命之药，军中人争买之，一枚价至数十金且不易得也。朱退谷曾于吴门见之，云遍身有金线纹，其身绝似虾蟆。"

以上诸种矿物药与植物药被收录于唐代到清代的中医文献中。

四、中外医药交流在吐鲁番

据麹氏高昌时期的《高昌内藏奏得称价钱账》的记述可知，吐鲁番是中外药品的交易市场。其中有硇砂、鍮石、郁金根、石蜜。又据池田温研究的《天宝二年交河郡估案》可知，在吐鲁番交易的外来药还有（波斯）青黛、阿魏煎、没石子、胡榛子、一日子、庵摩勒、郁金花、丁香、沉香、白檀香、白石蜜、硇砂、质汗、诃梨勒、犀角、高良姜、胡姜、青木香、甘松香。[①]

永乐三年（1405）正月壬戌……火州回回满剌（Maola，义为"首领"）、乞牙木丁（Qiyam al-Deen，意为"宗教的支柱"）等来朝贡马及方物。[②] 所谓方物，即土特产。火州的方物，应是前面提及矿物药、植物药。这是吐鲁番地面的穆斯林同中原内地的中央政府进行的一次物质文化交流。

永乐八年（1410）十一月乙丑，撒马儿罕并火州等处回族者马儿等献玉璞、硇砂。[③] 其中的硇砂即氯化铵，即前已述及的北庭砂，为高昌（火州）地面上的土产，是当时中土极为难得的药材。

① 参见陈明撰《殊方异药》，北京大学出版社 2005 年版。
② 见田卫疆编《〈明实录〉新疆资料辑录》，第 13 页。
③ 同上，第 29 页。

永乐十三年(1415)十一月丁酉,赐哈烈、撒马尔罕、火州、吐鲁番、失剌思、俺都准等处使臣不花等及郎古卫指挥速苦等宴。① 由此可见,吐鲁番在丝绸之路上与很多国家保持着联系。

成化十六年(1480)十一月戊戌,吐鲁番、兀隆各并撒马尔罕遣使臣满剌马黑麻母的来朝贡马。② 又有弘治三年(1490)三月丙辰,撒马尔罕马黑麻王,天方国速坛阿黑麻王,吐鲁番速坛阿黑麻,哈密卫左都督罕慎及把丹沙等地面失保丁等,各遣使贡马驼、玉石等物。③ 嘉靖二年(1523)九月癸巳,撒马尔罕并吐鲁番、天方等国番王头目宰纳等各备马驼方物差使臣土鲁孙等来贡。④ 显然,吐鲁番在中外物流方面起到了招引和陪行陪送的作用。

仅从以上几个事例即可看到,古代吐鲁番对丰富和发展传统中医药,发挥了独到的积极作用,作出了重大的历史贡献。

---

① 见田卫疆编《〈明实录〉新疆资料辑录》,第40页。
② 同上,第174页。
③ 同上,第190页。
④ 同上,第244页。

西汉伊循的两套职官

贾丛江
新疆社科院历史研究所

伊循位于西汉鄯善国境内。有关西汉伊循职官的情况,目前模糊不清之处有二:

一、西汉曾在伊循设置都尉。学界对此伊循都尉性质的认识,随着新材料的出土,有一个逐步深入的过程。往昔,学界一般认为伊循的职官隶属于西域都护。上世纪40年代,论者据新出土的罗布淖尔汉简,提出伊循都尉为属国都尉,负有镇抚鄯善国职责的观点。[1] 这种新认识,对学界重新审视楼兰地区的行政隶属问题,产生了积极影响。上世纪90年代悬泉遗址出土大批汉简,论者据此新材料,先后提出伊循都尉受敦煌太守节制,[2]以及该都尉具有属国都尉和敦煌郡部都尉之双重性质的两种新观点。[3] 学界对伊循都尉的认识已日渐深入。

二、笔者发现,伊循地区除了伊循都尉及其属吏之外,还存在另外一套职官。

伊循职官的性质和系统,关乎人们对西域都护府体制和敦煌边郡职官系统的认识。本文欲在前贤和时俊已有研究成果的基础上,略作增补,以就教于同仁。

一

伊循屯田,始自元凤四年(前77)或其后不久。《汉书·西域传》记其事曰:

> 元凤四年,大将军霍光白遣平乐监傅介子往刺其(楼兰)王。……介子遂斩王尝归首。……乃立(王弟)尉屠耆为王,更名其国为鄯善。……王(尉屠耆)自请天子曰:"身在汉久,今归,单弱,而前王有子在,恐为所杀。国中有伊循城,其地肥美,愿汉遣将屯田积谷,令臣得依其威重。"于是汉遣司马一人、吏士四十人,田伊循以填抚之。其后更置都尉。伊循官置始此矣。

所谓"伊循官置始此矣"之原意,学者均认为是起自"更置都尉"而非始于司马屯田。[4] 笔者亦持此论。始于元凤四年(前77)或其后不久的司马屯田,只是40名吏士自给自足的临时性措施,和后来的伊循屯田不能同日而语。此"司马",不是针对伊循城所设立的专门职官。所谓"伊循官",非指此"司马",而是"其后更置"之"都尉",即见诸汉简的"伊循都尉"和"伊循城都尉"——两种称谓为同一职官。"伊循官

---

① 黄文弼:《罗布淖尔考古记》,北京,1948年,第188页。
② 张德芳:《从悬泉汉简看两汉西域屯田及其意义》,《敦煌研究》2001年第3期。
③ 李炳泉:《西汉西域伊循屯田考论》,《西域研究》2003年第2期。
④ 张德芳和李炳泉均持此论,见前揭文。

置始此矣"的文意表达方式,和"都护之起,自吉置矣"(同传)相类似,说明了"伊循官"的重要地位和特别之处。

对伊循都尉设立的时间,有论者考订为地节二年(前68)或其后不久。① 依据是《汉书·冯奉世传》所记:"前将军增举奉世以卫侯持节送大宛诸国客。至伊循城,都尉宋将言莎车与旁国共攻杀汉所置莎车王万年。……都护郑吉、校尉司马熹皆在北道诸国间。"而冯奉世送大宛客,《汉书·西域传》系于元康元年(前65),说明伊循都尉设置于此年之前。论者将伊循更设都尉,放在地节二年汉廷遣郑吉屯田渠犁、加强经略西域的政治背景之中,进而推定其时间在地节二年或其后不久。② 笔者赞同这种推定逻辑和结论。伊循都尉的设置,也标志着伊循城及周边地区,已从行政隶属上由原鄯善国领地改为敦煌郡之辖区。

二

伊循职官的性质,决定于伊循都尉的性质。伊循都尉属于西汉职官中的何种"都尉",是问题关键之所在。

汉代的都尉有多种,各种都尉的职权、隶属,学界早有论述。多见于史籍和简牍的常设之都尉,有郡都尉、部都尉、属国都尉、农都尉;另外,也有少数见诸文献的关都尉(皆专指函谷关)、骑都尉、三辅都尉。有论者指出,单称都尉者,是指郡都尉(郡尉),③验之于文献,确然如此。《汉书·百官公卿表》记其职事:"郡尉,秦官,掌佐(太)守典武职甲卒,秩比二千石;有丞,秩比六百石;景帝中二年更名都尉。"郡都尉,是各郡辅佐太守掌管军事的最高武职。西汉时期,内郡一般设一个都尉。而边郡除设郡都尉外,又分为若干部,每部设一部都尉,如东部都尉、西部都尉、南部都尉、北部都尉、中部都尉等。部都尉,汉简中亦称"守部都尉",它与郡都尉均隶属于郡太守。《汉书·百官公卿表》记:"农都尉、属国都尉,皆武帝初置。"属国都尉是属国的最高长官,掌管各属国内的少数民族事务,隶属于中央的典属国。④ 属国,是汉代在郡县制区域内为归附或内迁的少数民族设立的行政区划的名称,其政治地位不同于作为西汉边疆地区的内臣。农都尉属田官系统,隶属于中央大司农。但是,各郡的农都尉和属国都尉的职权,又受郡太守节制。⑤ 另外,按汉代属部制度,朝廷对边疆地区的"内臣"诸国,如西域城廓诸国,也仿照汉制改造其原有职官系统——其中也设都尉,由朝廷授予印绶。但是,内臣与属国之间,内臣之都尉与属国都尉之间,性质完全不同。

关于"伊循(城)都尉"的性质,我们依次来做分析。

其一,该都尉不属于鄯善国的职官,即不同于作为内臣的城廓诸国职官系统中"都尉"。这一结论,我们可以从《汉书》和汉简中所见伊循都尉均为汉人就可以确知,如《汉书·冯奉世传》中的"宋将"、悬泉简中的"大仓"⑥等。另外,《汉书·西域传》专记鄯善国之都尉为"鄯善都尉",而其他城廓诸国均记为"都尉"、"左右都尉"——内臣职官系统中的常设职官,而对于那些随汉朝征战有功的城廓诸国,朝廷还

---

① 孟凡人:《楼兰新史》,中国光明日报出版社、新西兰霍兰德出版有限公司,1990年,第84~85页。
② 孟凡人:《楼兰新史》,第84~85页。
③ 陈梦家:《西汉都尉考》,《汉简缀述》,中华书局,1980年,第131页。
④ 王宗维:《汉代的属国》,《文史》第20辑,中华书局,1983年。
⑤ 陈梦家:《汉简所见居延边塞与防御组织》,《汉简缀述》,第41页。
⑥ "大仓"为人名,汉简中省去了姓氏,这是汉代习惯格式,即"职官+名字",史籍和汉简中多为此格式。

有特封的有专门名称的都尉,如"击车师都尉"、"却胡都尉"。① 除"鄯善都尉"外,诸国均无以国名作都尉名称的。这种特例,有可能是班固为了将伊循都尉与鄯善国的都尉相区别而有意为之。

其二,该都尉不是属国都尉。参证史册和简牍,凡属国都尉,文献均明确标明"属国都尉"字样。《汉书·地理志》全部写明"某地,属国都尉治"。而大量见诸居延简的属国都尉,也是如此:"属国都尉千秋、丞充"(68·48)、②"敢告居延属国、部、[农都尉]"(216·1)。③ 这是汉代的固定格式。而汉简所记伊循都尉者,却从未见过标有"属国"字样,罗布淖尔简、居延简、悬泉简、疏勒河流域所出汉简中,凡涉及伊循都尉者,均是如此(详见下文)。

其三,该都尉归敦煌太守领属,是敦煌郡的部都尉。

《汉书·地理志》"敦煌郡"只记录该郡有四个部都尉:中部都尉、宜禾都尉、阳关都尉、玉门关都尉,未记伊循都尉。但是,正如论者所说的,出土汉简已经清楚地表明,伊循都尉受敦煌太守领属,并且属于敦煌郡的部都尉。因论者已有详论,本文只简略举例以示之。

简1:口敦煌伊循都尉臣大仓上书一封……。甘露四年六月庚子上……。(II0216③:111)④

简1明确在伊循都尉前面标明"敦煌"郡名,其隶属关系不言自明。

然而,虽然我们认定伊循都尉受敦煌太守领属,但是,这和认定它就是敦煌郡的部都尉之间,还是有区别的。悬泉简中就提供了质疑的线索。

简2:敦煌太守千秋、长史奉憙、守部候修仁行丞事,下当用者小府、伊循城都尉、守部都尉、尉官候移县泉、广至、敦煌郡库,承书从事,下当用者如诏书。(V1312③:44)⑤

简2是敦煌太守府的下行公文,虽然公文表明伊循城都尉是受太守府节制,但录文将"伊循城都尉"和"守部都尉"并列,而"守部都尉"即部都尉,这似乎向人们彰显着两者之间的某种差别。有论者认定伊循都尉归敦煌太守领属,却不明言它是该郡之部都尉,这显然是谨慎之论。⑥

然而,笔者检索河西出土的汉简资料,找到一条可以明确研判伊循都尉身份的资料:

简3:敦煌太守常乐、长史布口、丞口口口循城部都尉临口官,承书从事,下当用者,如诏书口言。(T.Ⅵ.b.i.250,217,正面)⑦

此简是斯坦因在疏勒河下游地区吐火洛泉西南第10烽隧(斯氏自编号)遗址中发现的汉简,简文中"口循城

① 此"胡"指匈奴。
② 谢桂华、李均明、朱国炤:《居延汉简释文合校》,文物出版社,1987年,第118页。
③ 谢桂华、李均明、朱国炤:《居延汉简释文合校》,第346页。
④ 胡平生、张德芳编撰《敦煌悬泉汉简释粹》,上海古籍出版社,2001年版,第125页。
⑤ 胡平生、张德芳编撰《敦煌悬泉汉简释粹》,第126页。
⑥ 张德芳:《从悬泉汉简看两汉西域屯田及其意义》,《敦煌研究》2001年第3期。
⑦ 林梅村、李均明编《疏勒河流域出土汉简》,文物出版社,1984年,第45页。简号前为斯坦因原编号,后为本书所编序号。

部都尉"显然是指伊循城都尉。在敦煌西部地区,除伊循城外,再无其他地区符合"□循城部都尉"之条件。所以,此简虽为残简、孤证,却是坚实的证据。由此,我们可以断定,伊循(城)都尉是敦煌郡的部都尉。

三

既然我们已经明确伊循都尉属于敦煌郡部都尉,那么,按常理论,西汉伊循地区的职官性质,就不应再有疑问。但是,汉简材料反映,这一地区还存在不属于敦煌郡的职官。

　　简4:伊循农……(II 90DXT0215C:38)①
　　简5:入上书一封,车师己校、伊循田臣强。(V1310③:67)②

简4所录"伊循农……",是属于西汉田官系统的职官,应指"伊循农令"。这不属于作为边郡候望系统的部都尉的属官,都尉属吏中没有以"农"为名的职官。简5反映,车师己校和伊循田官,由一个名"强"的人兼任。"田臣"已表明他是田官。如果我们认为此"伊循田臣"是伊循都尉的属官,则等于认定戊己校尉是伊循都尉的属官。而多枚悬泉简明确记载了戊己校尉府的军吏,在更代之后返回北军的情况,这已为人所周知。笔者曾有专文讨论西汉戊己校尉实为直属中央的职官,在制度上隶属于北军,在屯田事务上受大司农领导,在镇守职责上受都护节制。③ 中央军北军的校尉,不可能做敦煌郡部都尉的属官,这不符合汉代的官秩品阶。这个名"强"的人能够兼任己校和伊循田官的原因,正在于戊己校尉和伊循田官,在组织制度上都由中央直辖、在屯田事务上均由中央大司农掌管。我们知道,西汉在各边郡设有农都尉及其所属田官系统,以管理屯田事务。它们不隶属郡县系统,而是直属中央大司农。《汉书·叙传》载:"(班况)举孝廉为郎,积功劳,至上河农都尉,大司农奏课连最,入为左曹越骑校尉。"按汉代上计考课制度,每年由郡国考课县道,由中央考课郡国,而田官系统不属于此考课系统,是由所属上级单位大司农直接考课。戊己校尉和伊循田官,均是如此。当然,笔者认为,这种一人兼两职的情况,不是常态,而是特殊时期的产物。

　　"伊循农"和"伊循田臣"都是隶属于大司农的田官系统的职官。"伊循田臣"虽然是"强"的自称,但是,它已经透露出伊循地区存在着一个官秩和戊己校尉平级的田官,其官职名称可能就是"伊循田官"。"田官"作为职官名称,常见诸河西出土的汉简,前面冠以地名,是表达职权范围的常见格式。这个伊循田官领导着伊循地区的屯田事务,受大司农主导的田官系统的领导。悬泉汉简反映了这一方面的信息:

　　简6:五凤四年九月己巳朔戊子,渊泉丞贺敢言之:大司农卒史张卿所乘传车一乘。……张卿
　　　　乘,西付冥安,皆完,今张卿还至。(II 0114③:461)④
　　简7:西合檄四,其一封凤博印,诣破羌将军莫(幕)府,一封□□侯印,诣太守府……一封欒延

---

①　转见吴礽骧《敦煌悬泉遗址简牍整理简介》,《敦煌研究》1999 年第 4 期。
②　胡平生、张德芳编撰《敦煌悬泉汉简释粹》,第 124~125 页。
③　贾丛江:《西汉戊己校尉的名和实》,《中国边疆史地研究》2006 年第 4 期。
④　胡平生、张德芳编撰《敦煌悬泉汉简释粹》,第 87 页。

寿印,诣大司农卒史张卿治所。□□□封阳关都尉□□。(Ⅱ0113⑤:152)①

两简均提到一个人——"大司农卒史张卿"。简6记载张卿在五凤四年(前54)九月因公事在敦煌郡西部地区奔波,而大司农卒史的职责就是管理屯田事务,其因之奔波各地的公事,自然与屯田有关。简7是一份悬泉置吏员对四份传递公函途经悬泉置时所做的例行登记。而此简提供了两条有价值的线索:其一为时间线索。一份"封凤博印"的公函,送达的目的地是"破羌将军莫(幕)府"。而西汉只有辛武贤两度出任过破羌将军。据《汉书·辛武贤传》,他出任该职的时间,分别是神爵元年(前61)至二年、甘露元年(前53)至二年。不论此简出现在哪一个任期,它都与"五凤四年九月"相隔了一段时期。换言之,出现于另一份公函中的张卿,曾经在敦煌郡停居过一段时间。再参证以简中所记"张卿治所"一句,可知张卿在敦煌郡是有固定公署的。其二是方位线索。此简登记的最后一份公函是"□□□封阳关都尉□□",联系前面公函的登记格式,此处可以复原为"□□一封阳关都尉印□"。阳关都尉的治所位于悬泉置的西面,这说明这四份公函均是从西面向东传送并途经悬泉置的,正如简文开头所说"西合檄四"。换言之,"封欒延寿印"的公函,是从悬泉置(今敦煌市与安西县的中间)的西面传送到张卿治所的。而寄呈张卿的公函,自然是有关屯田事务的。由此,我们可以得出以下结论:大司农的卒史张卿,在敦煌郡拥有固定公署;其职责就是负责敦煌郡——至少是包括悬泉置以西地区的屯田事务;伊循的屯田,也在卒史张卿的管辖之内。

我们知道,西汉在边郡的屯田,一般是由设立在各郡的农都尉及其所属田官系统负责。西汉在诸边郡广设农都尉的情况,在一枚居延简中有反映:"武□以东至西河郡十一农都尉官二调物钱谷漕转粲为民困乏愿调有余给不……"(214·33正面)。②简中"武□",学界一般认为是"武威",武威以东至西河,设有十一个农都尉,其中并未包括敦煌郡。这和现存各种文献和出土资料所反映的敦煌郡的情况相互吻合,即西汉政府没有在敦煌郡设立农都尉。所以,前文提到的负责伊循屯田的"强",才自称"车师己校、伊循田臣"而非"农都尉"。

然而,这并不能掩盖敦煌境内存在大规模屯田的事实——这已被众多出土的汉简所证实。我们认为,敦煌郡和其他边郡一样,境内的屯田分为两类,一类是隶属于大司农的田官系统(田官和屯田士)的屯田,一类是隶属于边郡候望系统(部都尉和戍卒)的戍卒屯田。而屯田的主体是田官系统的屯田。伊循地区是西汉时期重要的屯田区,这从多枚为人熟知的记载向伊循输送施刑士的汉简就可以确知。

我们将张卿的活动,与"强"兼任己校、伊循田官所反映的伊循和车师在屯田事务上的紧密关系的状况,综合起来考量,不由使人感到,伊循屯田的主旨,不是为了解决敦煌郡的军需,而是为了支撑西汉在西域的驻屯。而罗布淖尔土垠遗址出土的"伊循卒史黄广宗 二□"(11)③等西汉简牍,也许正反映了伊循屯田区支持居卢訾仓(土垠遗址)的某些讯息。人们有理由认为,在行政区划上隶属于敦煌郡的伊循城,作为一块向西突入塔里木盆地的战略要地,是支撑西域驻防的重要后勤基地。

综上所述,本文认为,西汉所设伊循都尉是敦煌郡的部都尉;伊循地区在行政上隶属于敦煌郡辖区;伊循地区除了存在隶属于敦煌郡候望系统(都尉)的职官外,还存在隶属于中央大司农的屯田系统的职官。

---

① 胡平生、张德芳编撰《敦煌悬泉汉简释粹》,第133页。
② 谢桂华、李均明、朱国炤:《居延汉简释文合校》,第337页。
③ 黄文弼:《罗布淖尔考古记》,第188页。

晋唐时期吐鲁番地区饮食文化交流初探

贺菊莲

中国人民大学国学院

吐鲁番地区先民依凭独特的自然地理环境、特定的政治历史文化、无法替代的交通位置等创造了绚烂多彩的饮食文化。晋唐吐鲁番地区饮食文化是中华饮食文化的重要组成部分;是吐鲁番地区文化不可或缺、不能轻忽的重要组成部分;是生活在该地区的各族人民共同创造的,一种处于东西方文化交汇的多源发生、多维发展的地域文化,不仅是该地区各民族饮食文化交融的成果,而且是与祖国内地、周边游牧民族及西方饮食文化相互交流的结晶,是在中西文化交融的过程中吸纳了游牧文化因素而形成并繁荣起来的饮食文化。深入研究晋唐时期吐鲁番地区饮食文化,可深入认识吐鲁番地区的文化,进而弘扬中华饮食文化,也能为深入探讨东西方文明交流及草原文明与绿洲文明之间的关系提供另一视角。

一、晋唐吐鲁番地区饮食文化交流的可能性和必然性

1. 吐鲁番地区在地理位置方面具有特殊优势。吐鲁番盆地周围山脉山口谷道多,故自古以来这里就是东西和南北交通的十字路口,是古代丝绸之路上四通八达的重要交通枢纽,此为包括饮食文化在内的文化交流提供了便利条件。在一定程度上说,丝绸之路也是饮食文化交流之路。作为丝绸之路重要驿站的高昌就是典型例子。"高昌实际上处于东西、南北交通的十字交叉点上。这种重要的战略位置为东方、西方和北方游牧文化的汇聚创造了条件。如果说西域文化是一种十字路口文化的话,那么这一特点在高昌地区表现得最为突出。"①

2. 吐鲁番地区特定的自然地理环境也决定了其必然存在饮食文化交流。吐鲁番地区古称高昌,其中心区在吐鲁番盆地,是西域绿洲农业文明的典型代表。绿洲特定的地理环境决定"绿洲居民并不单纯是农耕民,而兼有商业民的性质","绿洲是浮现在沙漠中的岛屿,是个可以耕作的土地。但是这里的农耕受到自然条件的强烈制约:第一,享受不到雨水的恩惠;第二,由于依赖于地下水和河水,所以水量有限;第三,由于水量有限,所以耕地不能无限度地扩大。诚然,绿洲由于地理条件所决定的孤立性和封闭性,在最初的时期,起到了保护、组织、统治绿洲生活的'蛋壳'作用。但是无奈因土地狭小,水量、耕地有限,迟早会发生人口和耕地失去平衡的状态,并且资源丰富也谈不上能满足生活提高的需要。也就是说随着历史的发展,绿洲地理上的封闭性便成为障碍。在这里,当地居民依靠与其他绿洲或其他生产地区的交往突破了这个难关。因此,我们应该说克服了沙漠的艰难险阻的队商的发

---

① 余太山:《西域文化史》,北京:中国友谊出版社,1995年,第111页。

展是极其自然的"。① 吐鲁番地区亦是如此。

3. 吐鲁番地区特定的政治历史文化决定了吐鲁番地区的饮食文化史就是一部饮食文化交融史。民族迁徙与融合通常是饮食文化交流的重要途径。吐鲁番地区是以东来移民——汉人为主体民族的移民地区。吐鲁番大地曾为古车师人的天堂。公元前104年,西汉贰师将军李广利西征大宛,进入吐鲁番盆地后,为安顿军中伤病者建立了"高昌壁"。后来,以此为中心,人口逐渐增多,成为汉政府设置在西域的戊己校尉屯驻之地。魏晋时期,高昌仍是戊己校尉驻地,长期隶属于敦煌郡管辖,以后逐渐成为中央政府在西域的政治中心。东汉末年、三国时期、西晋之初,内地许多汉族为避中原战乱移居高昌地区。他们与车师族和其他族共同构成了高昌的社会基础。公元640年,唐军平定高昌,将其改为西州。除了汉族,在漫漫历史长河中,吐鲁番大地还迎来了吐鲁番周边其他西域移民及游牧民族移民,乃至西来移民,如粟特人。吐鲁番地区在晋唐时期可以说是一个移民区。移民社会的形成,涉及政治、经济、文化方方面面,但从深层次探析,其更主要是一种文化、社会和生活方式的变迁和适应过程。

二、晋唐时期吐鲁番地区饮食文化交流的具体体现

1. 吐鲁番本地区各族人民饮食文化间的交融

"关于古代新疆——西域的文化特色,各国学者有多种观点。认真分析、剖析各种论述,其中比较引人注意的倾向之一,是明显强调周邻地区发育较高的先进文化(如黄河流域古代文明、古印度文明、古伊朗文明、古希腊、罗马文明等)对新疆大地的影响,而对本地土著文化的发育、发展、特点等,注意不够,认识不清。""古代新疆孕育、成长了有自身鲜明特色的地域文化,显示了古代新疆人民的聪明才智。这一文化,有自身优点、特点,但又不是一种封闭的存在,而是与周邻地区存在多方面的交流,吸收它们的积极因素,为己所用;自身有特色的创造,也在这一交流中介绍给周邻地区,为人类文明发展做出了积极贡献。"②从吐鲁番阿斯塔那随葬品中大量出土的纺织品中可以看到:"作为一种文化现象,尽管受到地理环境,文化氛围的限制。在丝绸之路的沟通中,高昌在晋唐时期对世界文明所做的贡献是巨大的。"③此贡献也包括绚烂多彩的饮食文化。

吐鲁番地区是一个多民族地区,这决定了在民族交融的过程中必然存在饮食物资和饮食文化的交流。"隋唐时期高昌(西州)居住着大批汉族,通行汉语、汉文,汉族是高昌的主体民族,但也有许多汉化程度不同的各族居民。其中主要有来自西域本土各国的居民,如帛氏或白氏(龟兹人)、龙氏(焉耆人)、裴氏(疏勒人)、鄯氏(鄯善人)等;有来自北方草原或西北地区的古代民族的成员,如沮渠氏(匈奴人)、支氏(月氏人)、秃发氏(鲜卑人)等;还有大量来自葱岭以西河中地区的昭武九姓人曹、何、史、康、安、石、米等。突厥人是特别值得指出的唐代高昌居民中的重要成分。""翻开吐鲁番出土的隋唐时期的汉文文书,就如同走进了一个门类齐全的民族博物馆。"④

---

① [日]松田寿男著,陈俊谋译《古代天山历史地理学研究》,北京:中央民族学院出版社,1987年,第4~5页。
② 王炳华主编《新疆古尸:古代新疆居民及其文化》,乌鲁木齐:新疆人民出版社,1999年,第14页。
③ 新疆博物馆考古队:《阿斯塔那古墓群第十次发掘简报》,《新疆文物》2000年第3、4期,第128页。
④ 余太山主编《西域文化史》,第193页。

另,值得一提的是,柳洪亮先生对迁居吐鲁番盆地的吐谷浑人的研究。阿斯塔那153号墓所出《高昌入作人、画师、主胶人等名籍》①曾数次提及"浑善相"其人。《高昌计人配马文书》②中有人名"浑神救"。又阿斯塔那206号墓所出《高昌义和五年(618)延隆等役作名籍》③第二行记:"……康相谦、浑德……。"柳洪亮先生认为:"高昌国时期的'浑'姓人在当地充任作人、承担赋役,已成为盆地的居民,而且从其姓名看,已有相当程度的汉化,如浑善相、浑神救即是如此,这说明他们来到吐鲁番盆地已有一段时日。因此,高昌王国时期的'浑'姓人,应该就是吐谷浑人。"④吐鲁番出土文书中也有有关唐西州时期吐鲁番盆地的吐谷浑人的记载,如《唐神龙二年(706)主帅浑小弟上西州都督府状为处分马口料事》⑤中之"主帅浑小弟"及《唐西州蒲昌县牒为申送健儿浑小弟马赴州事》⑥中之"健儿浑小弟"等。"唐代西州时期,吐鲁番盆地有吐谷浑人定居并活动,这应是不争之事实。至于他们的人数及规模,出土文书及文献都没有明确记载。不过,浑小弟由健儿升至主帅,说明他还是颇有能力的。……这些都从侧面暗示出唐代西州的吐谷浑人拥有一定的实力。他们与当地汉人杂处,共同租佃官府屯田,并熟悉汉文化,实际上在很大程度上已经汉化了,与唐末以后迁入盆地的吐谷浑人恐怕并不完全相同。"⑦

"吐鲁番出土的古尸,多有墓志、纪年文书等共出,不仅墓主人生活时代,甚至生卒年月都很明确,他们多为汉族,但又是吐鲁番地区的居民。古代吐鲁番是一个多民族杂居的地方,各民族都曾为吐鲁番的开发建设奉献过智慧与汗水,通过有关的文物,可得清楚的说明。⑧ 在出土文书第四册中,文书《唐西州高沙弥等户家口籍》,反映出王国内平民的婚姻状况,说明吐鲁番地区已出现各民族相互婚嫁的现象,这必然会导致文化,包括饮食文化间的交融。

同时,高昌本地区各族人民间的文化交融,也包括原土著居民与后来移民于此的新居民间的文化的交融,当然其在一定程度上体现为该地区饮食文化的传承性与变异性间的辨证关系。"移民群体的文化移植与文化传统之延续是移民在一个新的文化环境中普遍面临的问题,在一种新的文化和社会环境中,移民能够直接认同新环境的主体文化吗? 是保持传统,拒绝同化,还是放弃传统与环境融合,这是移民群体不得不面临的选择。"⑨这些都影响到吐鲁番大地上呈现出怎样的饮食文化面貌。关于移民与移民区饮食文化状况的关系、移民对原居住地饮食文化的影响及移民的饮食心理等问题值得深入探讨。

"罗阁"是传承吐鲁番地区土著文化的一个典型例子。"据二酉堂藏版《凉州风物志》记:'高昌僻土有异于华,寒服冷水,暑啜罗阁,《太平御览》原注,阁,受车切,此鄙人取糜粥啜之,俗号罗阁者也。'按高

---

① 国家文物局古文献研究室、新疆维吾尔自治区博物馆、武汉大学历史系编《吐鲁番出土文书》,第二册,北京:文物出版社,1981年,第334页。

② 国家文物局古文献研究室、新疆维吾尔自治区博物馆、武汉大学历史系编《吐鲁番出土文书》,第二册,第331页。

③ 国家文物局古文献研究室、新疆维吾尔自治区博物馆、武汉大学历史系编《吐鲁番出土文书》,第五册,北京:文物出版社,1983年,第259页。

④ 柳洪亮:《迁居吐鲁番盆地的吐谷浑人》,《吐鲁番学研究》2004年第2期,第118页。

⑤ 国家文物局古文献研究室、新疆维吾尔自治区博物馆、武汉大学历史系编《吐鲁番出土文书》,第八册,北京:文物出版社,1987年,第56页。

⑥ 国家文物局古文献研究室、新疆维吾尔自治区博物馆、武汉大学历史系编《吐鲁番出土文书》,第八册,第59页。

⑦ 柳洪亮:《迁居吐鲁番盆地的吐谷浑人》,《吐鲁番学研究》2004年第2期,第123~124页。

⑧ 王炳华主编《新疆古尸:古代新疆居民及其文化》,第174页。

⑨ 金云峰:《对文化生长与文化生态关系的几点思考——以海外华人社区和中国穆斯林社区为例》,载于王继光主编《中国西部民族文化研究2003年卷》,北京:民族出版社,2002年,第658页。

昌乃汉人聚居区,罗阁非汉语,必是从古车师人继承下来的一种食俗,唐之西州必因袭不变,据判断,罗阁大约是一种发酵的酸粥,有解暑的功能。"①苏贝希墓地典型地体现了古代车师居民日常饮食。在该墓地中曾出土"一种相当重要的食品是粟糊。墓穴出土陶器中,罐碗底部,多见这类糊状物在水分挥发后的余淀,干结成糊块。在天气十分干燥的吐鲁番地区,养分的补给,水分的吸收,这种糊状物,实在也是不错的形式。新疆农家早餐常有'乌玛希',糊状可稠可稀,用它伴饼而餐,至今仍是新疆农民早餐的形式"。②

2. 吐鲁番地区饮食文化与中原饮食文化的互动

早在魏晋南北朝时期,鉴于这里的居民及其生产方式和生活习惯与内地相同,前凉王张骏平定叛乱后,将其改设为高昌郡,这是西域首次推行郡县乡里制。隋唐时期,儒家文化成为高昌汉文化的主体。在高昌麴伯雅受封于中央担任高昌王时,下令"改行内地风俗",在当时的高昌王宫中"画鲁哀公问政于孔子之像",推行儒家礼治。在高昌古城出土的隋唐时期文物中,还有《毛诗》、《论语》、《孝经》、《三国志》等一些手写本。如《古写本〈论语集解〉残卷》及《古写本〈孝经〉残卷》③及《唐景龙四年(710)卜天寿抄孔氏本郑氏注〈论语〉》。④考古发现证明晋唐时期吐鲁番地区文化与中原文化的一脉相承。如新疆博物馆考古队在阿斯塔那古墓群第二次发掘,发掘了30座墓葬,出土纪年最早者为章和十八年(548),最晚者为唐咸亨五年(674)。"墓葬形制均为斜坡墓道洞室墓。西州时期出现了天井、甬道,并开凿耳室置放俑像。其埋葬方式与中原保持一致。……葬式上,保存好的尸体均呈仰身直肢葬,尸体脸部普遍盖覆面及手持握木。关于覆面习俗,根据《仪礼·士丧礼》记载,秦汉以前就已有了,到了唐代,死人覆面盛行,此次发掘证明了死人覆面的葬俗在吐鲁番同样盛行。握木,史籍中也有载,称'握手',《仪礼义疏·士丧礼上》:'握木用玄缠裹长尺二寸,广五寸,牢中旁寸,著组系。[正义]郑氏康成曰:谓削约握之中史以安手也。刘氏熙曰:'握,以物著尸手中,使握之也。'从出土握木看其制作方法均是截一段细圆木,经削制而成,表面还往往缠一层锦片,与史籍吻合。……据考古资料和文献记载,我国在殷周时代就已有死者口中含贝的风俗,以后逐渐被铜钱所取代。唐代时,这种风俗仍旧流行,吐鲁番阿斯塔那这种死者口中含钱的习俗应源于中原。凡此种种,都说明高昌在唐代前后与中原文化一脉相承。"⑤另,阿斯塔那古墓群第三次发掘的是"一座典型的聚族而葬的茔院,其形制上基本一致,均是斜坡墓道洞室墓。反映了在麴氏高昌至唐西州时期,其埋葬方式与中原有着千丝万缕的联系,是中原文化的延伸"。⑥这些都决定了中原汉地饮食文化对吐鲁番地区饮食文化浸染的必然性。

中原饮食文化西传吐鲁番地区,主要体现在以下几个方面:

(1)具体食物品种的西传。如桃、杏类果品,均来自内地。曾有人认为"吐鲁番地区古遗址中却没有发现桃。从考古发掘和史籍记载,古代吐鲁番地区可能种有核桃和棉桃,但未种桃。从《吐鲁番

① 《中国西北文献丛书》,《西北稀见古籍》,第二卷,转引自薛宗正主编《中国新疆古代社会生活史》,乌鲁木齐:新疆人民出版社,1997年,第246页。
② 王炳华:《吐鲁番古代饮食文化初探》,《吐鲁番学研究》2001年第2期,第77页。
③ 国家文物局古文献研究室、新疆维吾尔自治区博物馆、武汉大学历史系编《吐鲁番出土文书》,第七册,北京:文物出版社,1986年,第304~308页。
④ 国家文物局古文献研究室、新疆维吾尔自治区博物馆、武汉大学历史系编《吐鲁番出土文书》,第七册,第533~548页。
⑤ 新疆博物馆考古队:《阿斯塔那古墓群第二次发掘简报》(1960年11月),《新疆文物》2000年第3、4期,第35~36页。
⑥ 新疆博物馆考古队:《阿斯塔那古墓群第二次发掘简报》(1960年11月),《新疆文物》2000年第3、4期,第77页。

出土文书》看,古代吐鲁番地区葡萄的名称有写作蒲陶、蒲桃、浮桃、蒱桃、陶、桃的,而桃则是这一地区葡萄的特称。"①但桃在汉晋时期的楼兰城遗址内,吐鲁番晋、唐古墓中均见。汉代尼雅遗址中亦见。出土物均是桃核。②可见,桃应是吐鲁番人们的口中美味之一。吐鲁番古墓地内也曾见到杏核。从吐鲁番阿斯塔那随葬品中发现属于唐西州时期杏干(22件,72TAM223:31,残)。③出土文书《古写本医方一》④中也有"杏人"(应是杏仁)入药的记载。

在新疆吐鲁番阿斯塔那唐墓中发现了唐代饺子和馄饨实物,形状与现代的同类食品几乎没有多少区别。⑤1959年发掘的吐鲁番县阿斯塔那墓葬中发现了食物,如"301墓发现面制饺子三个,分盛于三个陶碗内。饺子长约5 cm、中宽1.5 cm。301墓和302墓都出有面制龙形(?)残段,是用面皮捏合成的,外面压划文饰。另有面条、面饼之类,并有面制插座。至于粮食,除上述粟、黑豆之外,还发现有紫穗麦"。⑥阿斯塔那古墓群第十次发掘"饺子5件。72TAM151:88。薄皮、内有馅。长4.5 cm、宽2.2 cm、厚1.1 cm。另还发现面俑2件"。⑦《〈新疆维吾尔自治区博物馆〉画册》中也有"饺子"的图文介绍。"饺子,唐(618~907),长6 cm、宽2.3 cm,1960年自吐鲁番阿斯塔那339号墓出土。为小麦面质,形如月牙,皮薄,内有馅,与现在水饺无异。饺子在当时称'水角'、'角子'或'牢丸'等。作为中华民族的传统美食之一,早在唐代就已成为吐鲁番地区居民普遍食用的一种面食。"⑧

(2)食生产技术、日常饮食用具等的西传。如吐鲁番晋墓中发现的陶器中常见釜和甑,这是内地常见的一套炊器。"在挖造阿斯塔那墓葬的时代,人们似乎使用过漆成黑色的木盘。木盘呈四边形,边角都做成了圆形,备有两个鱼尾形的把柄。在已被断代为541年的一座墓葬中也曾发现过一件这样的器皿(出土自阿斯塔那36号墓葬,见《文物》1960年第6期)。在阿斯塔那古墓葬中发现的日用品形状的古老性使所有的考古学家们都感到震惊,因为这些物品与中国汉代所使用的器皿常常具有惊人的相似性。""在吐鲁番地区,经常使用的似乎就是汉地的器皿,至少在高昌城完全是这样的,人们曾经在那里发掘到了一些筷子。某些女供养人就餐时所使用的就是典型的汉地碗和汤匙(见《和卓传》书中图版64i)。"⑨

(3)汉饮食礼仪、观念的西传。晋至南北朝阿斯塔那墓葬随葬器物普遍为灰陶、有灯、釜、甑、罐、壶、盆、瓮、盘、碗等,器型较大。瓮上有墨书"黄米一"、"白米一",反映了汉魏原地区风尚在这里的影响。⑩

汉饮食礼仪、观念的西传的另一具体体现为中原内地节日饮食礼俗在吐鲁番大地的再现。端午节是中华民族的传统节日,其最主要的节令食品是粽子。"在南北朝时,粽子的名称已逐渐代替了角黍,其制

---

① 陈习刚:《吐鲁番文书中葡萄名称问题辨析——兼论唐代葡萄的名称》,《农业考古》2004年第1期,第154~162页。

② 王炳华:《新疆农业考古概述》,《农业考古》1983年第1期,第106页。

③ 新疆博物馆考古队:《阿斯塔那古墓群第十次发掘简报》,《新疆文物》2000年第3、4期,续表附1《出土器物登记表》第147页。

④ 国家文物局古文献研究室、新疆维吾尔自治区博物馆、武汉大学历史系编:《吐鲁番出土文书》,第四册,北京:文物出版社,1983年,第273~277页。

⑤ 新疆社会科学院考古研究所:《新疆考古三十年》,乌鲁木齐:新疆人民出版社,1983年,图版第277。转引自吴玉贵:《中国风俗通史·隋唐五代卷》,上海文艺出版社,2001年,第28页。

⑥ 新疆维吾尔自治区博物馆:《新疆吐鲁番阿斯塔那北区墓葬发掘简报》,载于新疆社会科学院考古研究所:《新疆考古三十年》,第78页。

⑦ 新疆博物馆考古队:《阿斯塔那古墓群第十次发掘简报》,《新疆文物》2000年第3、4期,第111页。

⑧ 新疆维吾尔自治区博物馆、新疆百石缘工美有限公司主编《〈新疆维吾尔自治区博物馆〉画册》,香港金版文化出版社,2006年,第112页。

⑨ [法]莫尼克·玛雅尔著,耿昇译《古代高昌王国物质文明史》,北京:中华书局,1995年,第181页。

⑩ 新疆维吾尔自治区博物馆:《吐鲁番县阿斯塔那-哈拉和卓古墓群发掘简报》,载于新疆社会科学院考古研究所:《新疆考古三十年》,第80~81页。

作原料也由黍米改为主要用大米了,而且粽子也成为夏至和端午两个节日的节令食品。""汉代至魏晋是端午节初步形成的阶段,而南北朝至隋唐则是端午节定型化、成熟化的阶段。"①几千年来,这一民间习俗广泛地流传。每逢端午,凡炎黄子孙,几乎都在沿袭之。旅顺博物馆工作人员在整理拣选新疆(吐鲁番)出土的唐代文书碎片时,曾发现了混入于文书纸屑中的一件草编粽子(是目前已知仅有的一件)。粽子是采用草篾编制而成,大小共有五枚,均呈等腰三角形,与今日北方部分地区民间所食用的粽子的形状如出一辙。经测量大者底长1.37 cm、高1.35 cm;小者底长1.1 cm、高1.01 cm。五枚粽子由一根手捻棉线穿挂于一起,线的一端打有一结。经肉眼仔细观察,我们发现该粽子系类似于麦秸秆这样一种植物。从中剖开后,用赶角叠压的方式编制而成的,因此在其表面仍保留有草秸秆的光泽。粽子虽小,但其编制工艺可谓精细,且非常逼真。从这件草编粽子的形式上,我们认为是悬挂于儿童身上的饰物。其实时至如今,在端午节这一天还是有很多人要将用五彩线编成的小粽子挂在孩子们的胸前以讨个欢喜和吉利,而旅顺博物馆所收藏的吐鲁番出土的古尸中也恰恰有一具儿童干尸,这或许可以从中得到印证。② 端午节吃粽子这一民俗事项是何时传入新疆地区的已无据可查,但至迟在高昌时期就已经得以流传想来已是无疑。

另如寒食节。寒食的形成源于周代仲春之末的禁火及春秋时晋国故地山西一带祭奠介子推的习俗,在寒食节的形成及传承过程中,后一源头的影响越来越大。寒食节在清明之前一二日。从先秦以迄隋唐,寒食节均为一个大节日。隋唐五代时期,"无论贵贱贫富,对过寒食节都是非常重视的"。③ 吐鲁番出土文书《唐课钱帐历》共41件,其中第34件记有"张三便二百文,许过寒食五日内分付了"。④ 说明唐代吐鲁番人们也过寒食节。

吐鲁番地区与中原饮食文化的交流是双向的,形成了互动。吐鲁番地区在接受中原饮食文化影响的同时,其饮食文化也东渐中原。如太宗破高昌,获取葡萄酒酿造法就是典型例子。《册府元龟》记载:及破高昌,收马乳蒲桃实,于苑中种之,并得其酒法。帝自损益,造酒成,凡有八色,芳辛酷烈,味兼缇盎,既颁赐群臣,京师始识其味。

另,高昌向中原王朝的朝贡其实是饮食文化交流的重要手段和形式之一。朝贡是古代中国边疆诸族以及地方政权向中原中央政权表示臣属的一种特殊形式,也是当时特定条件下一种有报偿的物质交换方式。来自边疆各地的贡物,多为当地土特产、宝物。而中原王朝也会回赠一些物品,其中有些也是中原特产。朝贡贸易中的物品有很多与饮食有关,如高昌的葡萄及葡萄酒、刺蜜等就曾作为贡品。如《旧唐书·西域传》记载唐玄宗时,"西州交河郡……天宝元年为郡,土贡:丝、叠布、毡、刺蜜、'蒲萄五物酒浆煎皱干'"。朝贡贸易丰富了两地人民,有时主要是上层阶级的物质文化生活,同时也促进了中国各地区之间经济文化的交流,包括饮食文化的交流。

3. 吐鲁番地区饮食文化与周边游牧饮食文化的互动

吐鲁番盆地处于天山北部游牧的行国通往塔里木盆地城郭诸国交通要道之一,两汉时期,曾是中原王朝与匈奴民族政权争夺的焦点地区。晋唐时期,环绕吐鲁番地区四周的是以柔然、高车、铁勒、突厥等

---

① 姚伟钧:《汉唐节日饮食礼俗的形成与特征》,《华中师范大学学报》1999年第38卷第1期,第73页。
② 王珍仁、孙慧珍:《吐鲁番出土的草编粽子》,《西域研究》1995年第1期,第116~117页。
③ 吴玉贵:《中国风俗通史·隋唐五代卷》,第650~651页。
④ 国家文物局古文献研究室、新疆维吾尔自治区博物馆、武汉大学历史系编《吐鲁番出土文书》,第五册,第307页。

为代表的草原民族游牧文化。魏晋以来,高昌曾被迫依附于外部的一些游牧民族政权。游牧民族也想方设法从各方面影响高昌。婚俗上,高昌王室上层必须遵从突厥的收继婚制就是具体体现之一。《隋书》卷八三《突厥传》记载,隋开皇十年(590)"(麹)伯雅立,其大母本突厥可汗女,其父死,突厥令依其俗,伯雅不从者久之。突厥逼之,不得已而从"。另,曾有专家考证"高昌吉利"钱币中的"吉利"两字,应为突厥语 ilik 或 ilig 的汉语音译,意思为"王",文献上一般译作"颉利发"或"颉利","高昌吉利"对应的汉语意思为"高昌王"。"高昌吉利"钱币是农耕的汉文化与游牧的突厥等文化相互之间交汇、融合的结果。正是在这两种完全不同类型文化的相互影响下,形成了以"汉胡交融"为特色的高昌文化,"高昌吉利"钱币便是这种文化交融的具体表现。[1] 高昌王麹伯雅两次出使隋朝,回国后曾颁布"解辫削衽"令,但最终失败。这说明游牧文明在吐鲁番地区人们生活中的影响之深。总之,汉胡交融是吐鲁番地区文化的重要特色之一,这与当时政治、经济紧密关联,对饮食文化自然会产生不可轻估的影响。

可以说,吐鲁番地区畜牧业在经济生活中的比重、其居民食肉方式及食酪等在一定程度上是受游牧民族的影响。如乳酪,系用牛、马、羊等乳浆炼制成的食品,有干、湿两种。晋唐时期,酪也已成为吐鲁番地区市场的商品之一,《高昌乙酉丙戌岁某寺条列月用斛斗帐历》中记载"麦二斛七斗,得钱三文,麦一斛五斗作面,麦口斗买落(酪)。栗五斗,作饭……尽供七月七日食"。[2] "酪"应是游牧民族的传统食品。元代著名的维吾尔族农学家鲁明善在所著的《农桑衣食撮要》中提到造酪的方法。如谓"五月,晒干酪。将奶酪于锅内,慢火煞,令稠,去其清水,摊于板上,晒成小块,候极干收贮"。

另,《梁书·高昌传》:"人多噉麨。"《高昌众保等传供粮食账》中有"麨五斗"、"麨七斛五斗"、"面五斗、麨二斛"等记载。[3] "延昌末年正值隋朝初年,西域地区主要处在室点密系突厥的控制之下","这一时期往来于高昌的客使以突厥和粟特人居多,突厥和粟特客使都是高昌国人的座上客,客使离开高昌,由高昌负责为其提供到达下一个目的地途中所需要的粮食,其品种以携带方便为要"。上述传供粮食账"账目显示面、麨各半,还有少量的粟米"。"麨是一种炒熟后即食的食品。按《本草拾遗》:'河东人以麦为之,北人以粟为之,东人以粳米为之,炒干饭磨成也。'麨的食法最早流行于游牧民族,为了适应常年随水草逐牧的生活,饮食主要考虑加工简便和携带方便。麨即可干食,或可以乳冲食,故随身携带很方便。"[4] 吴震先生在分析高昌某寺月用斛斗帐历曾注意到"以麦为麨",最初认为此"即干粮、炒面",并"似主要用于作、使餐外的补充食物",[5]后来认为该帐历"凡单称'麦'者皆为大麦的省称",而此麨麦指"经蒸或炒熟之后磨粉,犹今之'炒面'"。[6] 王素先生认为"高昌的麨是一种仅用麦炒熟后磨成粉的干粮",并引用延寿二年(625)十月末至延寿三年(626)九月初某寺条列月用斛斗帐历屡次提到"麦伍斗,作麨麦";"麦壹斛,作麨麦";"麦贰斛伍斗,作麨";"麦叁斛,作麨"作证。其指出"麨应为当时主食之一,而非补充食物。又,青稞本为大麦之一种,高昌文书未见其名,或亦包含在'麦'的称谓中"。[7]

① 王永生:《"高昌吉利"钱币考——兼论隋唐之际高昌地区的文化融合》,《西域研究》2007 年第 1 期,第 57~64 页。
② 国家文物局古文献研究室、新疆维吾尔自治区博物馆、武汉大学历史系编《吐鲁番出土文书》,第三册,第 231 页。
③ 国家文物局古文献研究室、新疆维吾尔自治区博物馆、武汉大学历史系编《吐鲁番出土文书》,第二册,第 283~286 页。
④ 宋晓梅:《高昌国——公元五至七世纪丝绸之路上的一个移民小社会》,北京:中国社会科学出版社,2003 年,第 42 页。
⑤ 吴震:《吐鲁番出土高昌某寺月用斛斗帐历浅说》,《文物》1989 年第 11 期,第 64 页。
⑥ 吴震:《7 世纪前后吐鲁番地区农业生产的特色——高昌寺院经济管窥》,《新疆经济开发史研究》上册,乌鲁木齐:新疆人民出版社,1992 年,第 56 页。
⑦ 王素:《高昌史稿》(交通编),北京:文物出版社,2000 年,第 90~91 页。王素先生还在注释中举例指出唐西州文书中,青稞也每与大麦合称。

吐鲁番地区与周边游牧饮食文化的交流应也是双向的。在吐鲁番地区饮食生产活动中,绿洲农业占据主导地位;园艺业占有特殊地位;畜牧业及家庭饲养业占有重要地位。而游牧民族一般以畜牧业为主要饮食生产方式。史书记载突厥"其俗畜牧为事,随逐水草,不恆厥处"。"突厥兴亡,唯以羊马为准。"南疆、东疆与北疆不同的自然地理环境、生计方式决定了其饮食文化具有差异性、互补性。而在此基础上的饮食文化交流成必然趋势。史书就曾明确记载疏勒"土多稻、粟、麻、麦、铜、铁、锦、雌黄,每岁常供送于突厥"。

4. 吐鲁番地区饮食文化与西方饮食文化的交流

德国学者克林凯特指出:"几乎没有其他哪个绿洲,在文化面貌上像吐鲁番这样丰富多彩,它位于一条东西大道和一条南北大道的交汇点上。因此它就很特殊地成为东西方许多不同文化的相会地点。从文化上说吐鲁番好像一块海绵,它从各个方面吸收精神内容与文字形式,而并不一定要把它们统一化、规范化。引人注目的是,这个绿洲的文化传统极富国际性。"[①]如1959年发掘的吐鲁番县阿斯塔那墓葬中发现丝、麻织品标本。各种花纹织锦可分为七种,其中鸟兽树木纹锦、双兽对鸟纹锦、树纹锦及对马纹锦四种花纹显然不是汉族风格,大约是受波斯文化影响的产物。[②]新疆博物馆考古队在阿斯塔那古墓群第二次发掘中,发现墓葬中出土有萨珊银币及铜钱,均出自死者口中。吐鲁番是当时丝绸之路上的交通要道,中西贸易往来,文化交流必经于此。这些萨珊银币,便是实物证据。[③]

众所周知,葡萄是外来的物质文明,其原生地在黑海和东地中海沿岸一带及中亚细亚地区。高昌栽种葡萄的历史悠久。"考古人员在洋海古墓中发现了一根保存完好的葡萄藤。这根古葡萄藤呈深褐色,略有弯曲,有五个芽节。专家认为,这根葡萄藤的具体年代应在公元前500年前,这相当于中原的春秋战国时期。'这是迄今为止发现的吐鲁番地区种植葡萄最早的实物见证。'有关专家说:'当时的人们已经知道,葡萄的传播不是用葡萄种子,而是靠葡萄藤来无性繁殖的。所以墓主人要带一根葡萄藤到另外一个世界去种葡萄,然后继续安享葡萄美味。'吐鲁番位于天山东部的山间盆地,以其独特的气候和特有的沙质土壤造就了悠久的种植历史,这一点在考古中也得到了印证。历年来,吐鲁番出土的葡萄实物标本是新疆发现有关葡萄文物最多的地区,证明从东汉至唐高昌王国时期,吐鲁番地区种植葡萄就已十分普遍。在洋海古墓群其他古墓的发掘中,再没有出土葡萄藤。考古专家推断,出土葡萄藤的古墓墓主有可能是最早掌握葡萄栽培技术的'园艺师'。"[④]在吐鲁番地区晋唐时期古墓葬中,往往以葡萄入殉,可以看到历史上它一直就是人们珍视的果品。其栽植之盛,从墓葬壁画中有葡萄园,出土文书中有"卖"、"租"葡萄园的契纸、有关葡萄酒的记录等,均可透见这一果品在当时人们日常生活中具有重要地位。

值得一提的是,葡萄酒酿造工序在吐鲁番地区考古中的再现。吐鲁番出土一壁画"庄园生活图"的"右下角的方形框内绘有密集的藤类植物,旁边写有'蒲陶',应象征着葡萄园",同时在一"磨面人的后面似乎是一幅压榨葡萄汁的画面;在一个曲足案上放置有大桶,旁边有一人用弯曲的棒状物伸向桶内。桶内下部三分之二是许多圆球,可能代表葡萄;上面三分之一处画一横线,可能代表压榨出的葡萄汁。曲足

---

① [德]克林凯特著,赵崇民译《丝绸之路古道上的文化》,乌鲁木齐:新疆美术摄影出版社,1994年,第176~177页。

② 新疆维吾尔自治区博物馆:《新疆吐鲁番阿斯塔那北区墓葬发掘简报》,载于新疆社会科学院考古研究所:《新疆考古三十年》,第73~74页。

③ 新疆博物馆考古队:《阿斯塔那古墓群第二次发掘简报》(1960年11月),《新疆文物》2000年第3、4期,第35~36页。

④ 马玉矞:《洋海葡萄古藤:吐鲁番人早已享受葡萄美味》,《丝绸之路》2007年第5期,第25页。

案的下方安置有一个陶罐,用于承受桶内流出的葡萄汁。为了形象地反映出葡萄汁的过滤过程,曲足案地侧面被特意画成网格状,象征着大桶的滤网。在'榨汁图'的右侧上下排列着两个图案,只有放置的器物,没有人物形象,或也与'榨汁图'有关:下面的图案是一个三足釜上放置着容器,可能象征着酿酒之前煮葡萄汁的工序;上面的图案是一个三层塔状的曲足案,下承一罐,与发酵酿造以致装罐的工序有关"。①

"据新疆博物馆历史文物陈列,唐代吐鲁番地区还出土了芝麻、巴旦杏。芝麻原产非洲,巴旦杏原产伊朗。看来,新疆地区引进、栽培的历史也是很久的。"②在吐鲁番的晋唐古墓里还出土过巴旦杏。③

关于"叵罗",蔡鸿生先生作过详细考证:"叵罗"又写作"破罗"、"颇罗",同音异译。叵罗是粟特语,碗状酒杯。④ 73TAM193:15(b)唐天宝某载(749~756)行馆器物帐⑤记有"破大屈椀贰拾[枚]"屈椀,即有屈柄的碗。⑥ "按照《中国古代器物大辞典》的解释,此'屈碗'当是著名的叵罗的另一种叫法。"⑦岑参也有诗云:交河美酒金叵罗。由此可知唐代西域交河风行叵罗酒具。

三、结　语

1. 饮食文化交流是饮食文化发展的重要动力。饮食文化发展的原因是综合的。如一个国家、地区或民族生产力的发展是其饮食文化发展的物质基础;良好的民族素质、民族饮食心理及社会风尚是饮食文化健康发展的重要条件。而饮食文化交流是推动西域饮食文化,乃至中华饮食文化、世界饮食文化发展的重要动力之一。

吐鲁番出土的点心系列,体现了吐鲁番先民生活精细一面,至少已反映他们中的一部分人的饮食生活已不单单是为了填饱肚子,而有了更高的精神追求。而这很大程度上得益于饮食文化的发展。晋唐时期吐鲁番地区饮食文化发达的具体表现之一即饮食市场的出现和发展。

随着农业生产有了相当的发展之后,有较多的农产品进入市场,特别是为市场提供社会所需的商品粮食。《高昌乙酉、丙戌岁某寺条列月用斛斗帐历》⑧中可见该寺用于购买生产、生活用品以及缴纳官府的各种"剂"钱,都是出售粮食所得。货币交易体现商品经济进一步发展。如《唐家用帐》中记载"买菜用九文。……五日,六十余面,卅买酱,十八买酢"。⑨ 在吐鲁番阿斯塔那第4号墓中,总共出土了二十三件社会经济文书,其中的两件《唐支用钱练帐》,其中一件体现了唐代吐鲁番用货币购买麦、米、麨、肉等现象,同时也存在用实物,如白练购买米的现象。如:"用钱拾文,憧籴麦。""用练一匹,籴麨来迥河头。""用练半匹,籴米,买婢,缺练一匹。""买肉。""更用同钱六文,籴麨。""钱一十八文,籴麨。""用银钱二文,买一脚肉。更用钱廿一文,买麨。"⑩如另一件中:"用练一匹,曹愿住处买羊,用钱还买肉""拨换城用练

① 李肖:《吐鲁番新出壁画"庄园生活图"简介》,《吐鲁番学研究》2004年第1期,第126~127页。
② 王炳华:《新疆农业考古概述》,《农业考古》1983年第1期,第106~107页。
③ 张玉忠:《新疆出土的古代农作物简介》,《农业考古》1983年第1期,第125页。
④ 蔡鸿生:《隋书康国传探微》,《文史》第二十六辑,第106~107页。蔡鸿生:《唐代九姓胡与突厥文化》,北京:中华书局,2001年,第31页。
⑤ 唐长孺主编图录本《吐鲁番出土文书》,第四册,北京:文物出版社,1992~1996年,第240页。
⑥ 王启涛:《吐鲁番出土文书词语新考(二)》,《新疆师范大学学报》2007年第28卷第4期,第24页。
⑦ 高启安:《唐五代敦煌饮食文化研究》,北京:民族出版社,2004年,第101页。
⑧ 国家文物局古文献研究室、新疆维吾尔自治区博物馆、武汉大学历史系《吐鲁番出土文书》,第三册,第225~233页。
⑨ 国家文物局古文献研究室、新疆维吾尔自治区博物馆、武汉大学历史系编《吐鲁番出土文书》,第八册,第294页。
⑩ 国家文物局古文献研究室、新疆维吾尔自治区博物馆、武汉大学历史系编《吐鲁番出土文书》,第六册,第434~435页。

半匹,籴米,买婢"、"愿住处买肉"。"用钱三文,作斋。""用同(铜)钱廿二文,买麨。"①钱伯泉先生曾把《唐支用钱练帐》两件文书中有关帐目体现的物价与阿斯塔那214号墓出土两件《唐和籴青稞帐》所体现的物价对照,得出货币与一些实物的比价,推算出:一斗麦约值银钱1文或0.8文。"用练一匹,籴麨",练一匹相当于银钱十文,麨为炒麦粉,若麦去麸三成算,则一斗麨值银钱1.3至1.5文,一石麨值银钱13至15文。"用练一匹,曹愿住处买羊",可知一只大羊值银钱10文。"用练半匹,籴米",米价略高于麺粉价,可以推知一斗米约值银钱1.5文至1.8文。②

有关饮食的手工业专门作坊的出现,如"制盐业、酿酒业(附制醋、制酱业)"③等的出现也体现了社会分工的进一步扩大,饮食市场经济的发展。作坊除寺院、官府所有的之外,还有私人作坊。《延寿九年(632)范阿僚举钱作酱券》中,"从道人元某举银钱20文的范阿僚,便是酿造酱、酢(醋,或称"苦酒")的作坊主。甜酱与醋都是调味品,范阿僚一次借银钱20文,可能用于扩大生产,定期以生产实物偿付,说明所造酱醋并非为自家食用,而是为市场上提供食品"。④

商品经济的发展促使很多有关饮食的行业专业化。如文书《唐枣贩残书牍》⑤体现唐代已经出现专门卖枣的商人。另,《唐何好忍等匠人名籍》第二件中记有"油匠"、"杀猪匠"。⑥

买卖饮食的市和行的出现。市的出现是商品经济发展到一定程度的结果。唐朝在西域的州县设有市。《唐开元廿一年(733)正月西州百姓石染典买马契》说:"马一匹骝敦六岁。开元廿一年正月五日,西州百姓石染典交用大练十八匹,今于西州市,买康思礼边上件马。"(后略)⑦出土文书不仅说明西州有市,而且还记载了西州市的许多行名。行是商业活动中的一种组织形式,也是各行业专门化的社会分工。西州出现了如此多的行,这是前所未有的事,反映了商业经济的发达。据日本学者统计,西州市有不少的行,如菓子行、彩帛行、铛釜行、米面行、菜子行、帛练行等。市上各行出售的商品有布帛类、酢类、畜类、皮制品、食物、干果、粮食、菜种、药物、香料、化妆品、器具、炭草及大粪等。⑧ 总的来说,"交河郡的农牧业已经突破了小农生产自给自足的樊篱,成为商品经济的一个组成部分。此地市场经济发展的水平,显然在全国也可列为先进。从中我们还可以看出,随着社会的进步,产业分工的发展和交通条件的改善,进入流通领域的商品,已在一定程度上突破了奢侈品的范围,逐渐扩大到有关国计民生的广大群众生产、生活中的必需品"。⑨

2. 吐鲁番地区饮食文化是曾经生活在这里的以汉族为主的各个民族在适应和改造独特的自然环境的过程中,充分发挥主观能动性共同创造的丰硕果实,交融性是其重要特点之一。"高昌地处中西文化交流的要道,许多民族在此杂居,高昌文化在全面承袭汉文化同时,不可避免受到其他文化的影响。""在民间的生活习俗上,高昌人受他族影响不少,如《周书·高昌传》记载高昌人'服饰,丈夫从胡

① 国家文物局古文献研究室、新疆维吾尔自治区博物馆、武汉大学历史系编《吐鲁番出土文书》,第六册,第436~437页。
② 钱伯泉:《从〈唐支用钱练帐〉考察唐初西域的政治经济状况》,《新疆社会科学》2005年第5期,第106页。
③ 王素:《高昌史稿》(交通编),第110~114页。
④ 武敏:《5世纪前后吐鲁番地区的货币经济》,载于殷晴主编《新疆经济开发史研究》上册,乌鲁木齐:新疆人民出版社,1992年,第235页。
⑤ 国家文物局古文献研究室、新疆维吾尔自治区博物馆、武汉大学历史系编《吐鲁番出土文书》,第九册,第186页。
⑥ 国家文物局古文献研究室、新疆维吾尔自治区博物馆、武汉大学历史系编《吐鲁番出土文书》,第四册,第16页。
⑦ 池田温:《中国古代籍帐研究》,北京:中华书局,2007年5月,第220页。
⑧ 《西域文化研究》第三《敦煌吐鲁番社会经济资料》,转引自雷学华:《略述唐朝对西域的商业贸易管理》,《敦煌学辑刊》1983年,第100期,第117页。
⑨ 殷晴:《唐代西域的丝路贸易与西州商品经济的繁盛》,《新疆社会科学》2007年第3期,第99~105页。

法,妇人略同华夏'等。但同样不可否认的是,在接受他族文化影响和承袭汉文化传统二者之间,毕竟是后者占据主流。"①该地区饮食文化亦如此。当然,由于特定的地理环境、历史文化及交通位置,其与中原汉人饮食文化存在千丝万缕联系的同时,又凸显其独特性,为中华饮食文化增添了瑰丽的一页。

3. 饮食文化交流的意义何在呢? 饮食文化交流通常包含物质文化及精神文化两方面。物质方面的饮食文化交流能提高世界人民的生活水平。而精神方面的饮食文化交流,它能提高世界人民的精神境界,能促进世界饮食文化创造的繁荣,更重要的是能促进世界上不同民族的相互了解,增强他们之间的友谊和感情。季羡林先生曾认为:"我为什么对文化交流情有独钟呢? 我有一个别人会认为是颇为渺茫的信念。不管当前世界,甚至人类过去的历史显得多么混乱,战火纷飞得多么厉害,古今圣贤们怎样高呼'黄钟毁弃,瓦釜雷鸣',我对人类的前途仍然是充满了信心。我一直相信,人类总会是越来越变得聪明,不会越来越蠢。人类历史发展总会是向前的,决不会倒退。人类在将来的某一天,不管要走过多么长的道路,不管要用多么长的时间,也不管用什么方式,通过什么途径,总会共同进入大同之域的。我们这些舞笔弄墨的所谓'文人',决不应煽动人民与人民,国家与国家,民族与民族之间的仇恨,而应宣扬友谊与理解,让全世界的人们都认识到,人类是相互依存,相辅相成的。大事如此,小事也不例外。像蔗糖这样一种天天同我们见面的微不足道的东西的后面,实际上隐藏着一部错综复杂的长达千百年的文化交流的历史。"②文化交流是历史研究中的一个重要课题,但饮食文化交流的专题研究还有待大大加强。

---

① 孟宪实:《汉唐文化与高昌历史》,济南:齐鲁书社,2004 年,第 15 页。
② 季羡林:《〈糖史〉自序》,《社会科学战线》1995 年第 4 期,第 255~256 页。

司马懿之崛起试探

杨晓东

武汉大学历史系

"高平陵之变"是曹氏与司马氏之争中的关键事件。历来的研究者多着意于正始年间双方的斗争及高平陵之变后司马氏对曹氏的镇压,以及正始改制、双方斗争的原因等问题,[①]而对魏文帝、明帝时期的司马懿留意较少。其实这一阶段正是司马懿地位奠定和巩固的重要时期,而对此问题的阐释也正是本文的主旨所在。

一

关于司马懿在魏武帝时期的活动,《晋书》卷一《宣帝纪》只记寥寥数语,并说:

> 汉建安六年,郡举上计掾。魏武帝为司空,闻而辟之。帝知汉运方微,不欲屈节曹氏,辞以风痹,不能起居。魏武使人夜往密刺之,帝坚卧不动。及魏武为丞相,又辟为文学掾,敕行者曰:"若复盘桓,便收之。"

周一良先生《曹氏司马氏之斗争》一文中引叶适《习学记言》卷二十九曰:"懿是时齿少名微,岂为异日雄豪之地,而操遽惮之至此?且言不屈节曹氏,尤非其实。史臣及当时佞谀者意在夸其素美,而无词以述,亦可笑也。"[②]建安十三年(208)魏武帝为丞相再辟司马懿时,其不过二十九岁,叶适谓之"齿少名微"并不虚错,至于曹操两次辟举司马懿,也并非因为司马懿在当时享有诸葛亮"卧龙"般的高名,据《三国志》卷一《魏书·武帝纪》注引《曹瞒传》,司马懿之父司马防为曹操孝廉之举主,故曹操辟举司马懿在很大程度上带有报恩之意。这种现象在汉末不足为奇,后汉樊儵曾"上言郡国举孝廉,率取年少能报恩者,耆宿大贤多见废弃,宜敕郡国简用良俊",[③]甚至有孝廉不为举主服丧而受贬议,同年孝廉互举子弟者。[④] 而司马懿之兄司马朗,也正为曹操所辟,[⑤]况且也没有不应征辟就派刺客谋害的道理。至于司马懿拒绝征辟的原因,真相不得而论,[⑥]但在清议鼎盛的汉末,拒辟以养名,几乎是每一个被征辟者所默认的"潜规则"。

---

① 如周一良先生的《曹氏司马氏之斗争》一文,文见《魏晋南北朝史札记》,中华书局,1985年,第26~37页;王晓毅:《正始改制与高平陵政变》,文载《中国史研究》1990年第4期;王晓毅:《司马懿与曹魏政治》,文载《文史哲》1998年第6期;王永平:《曹爽、司马懿之争真相考论》,文载《扬州大学学报》1999年第3期。

② 文见《魏晋南北朝史札记》,第26页。

③ 见《后汉书》卷三十二《樊儵传》。

④ 可参应劭:《风俗通义校注》,卷四《过誉》"南阳五世公为广汉太守"条,第192页;及卷五《十反》"豫章太守汝南封祈武兴"条,第231页,王利器校注,中华书局,1981年版。

⑤ 参《三国志》卷十五《魏书·司马朗传》:"年二十二岁,太祖辟为司空掾属,除成皋令"。

⑥ 王晓毅认为司马懿"似乎是受儒家正统观念影响,准备为汉王朝效忠",而拒绝曹操的辟举,见《司马懿与曹魏政治》,文载《文史哲》1998年第6期,可备一说。但我认为这中间不排除有被征辟者对举(辟)主的观望,但更多的是期望达到"少年名士"的效果。

这也可以解释司马懿在魏武时期并未受到特别重视的原因,建安十三年辟为文学掾之后,据《晋书》卷一《宣帝纪》:

使与太子游处,迁黄门侍郎,转议郎、丞相东曹属,寻转主簿。

曹丕立为魏太子是在建安二十二年(217),那么司马懿似乎在近十年时间中位处闲职,这一点也不难解释,建安十三年(208)赤壁战后三国鼎立的格局基本形成,曹操的功业也接近巅峰,除了建安十六年(211)平定关中和建安二十年(215)征张鲁外,中间基本没有大的军事举措,此时期作为文学掾的司马懿既无军功也无资历,况且曹操一直着重"唯才是举"、"任贤惟能",自然对其没有大的升任。《晋书》记载司马懿从讨张鲁,言于魏武顺势取蜀,魏武曰:"人苦无足,既得陇右,复欲得蜀!"①而不从其言,也是当时司马懿人微言轻的反映。至于后来司马懿任丞相东曹属、主簿的具体时间,史无明文,那么他很可能在建安末年出任此二职,又迁"军司马",也就是说,在魏武末年,司马懿开始进入曹操的丞相幕府。对此,《晋书》又有一段记载:

魏武察帝有雄豪志,闻有狼顾相。欲验之。乃召使前行,令反顾,面正向后而身不动。又尝梦三马同食一槽,甚恶焉。因谓太子丕曰:"司马懿非人臣也,必预汝家事。"太子素与帝善,每相全佑,故免。帝于是勤于吏职,夜以忘寝,至于刍牧之间,悉皆临履,由是魏武意遂安。

这段中所谓的"三马同食一槽"的描述,颇有干宝《搜神记》的色彩,显然是后来的人附会宣、景、文三父子,《晋书》于曹操与司马懿之间的关系,以疑忌始,以猜忌终,但随着曹操的去世,司马懿的命运也随之改变。

二

黄初元年(220),曹丕代汉自立。众所周知,曹丕是与曹植经过激烈角逐之后被立为太子,故曹丕即位之初,在中央及地方多拔置其党与,如以贾诩为太尉(黄初元年),以桓阶为尚书令(黄初元年),以陈群为尚书左仆射(黄初元年,二年桓阶卒后迁尚书令),以钟繇为廷尉(及文帝践祚,又于黄初四年贾诩薨后代为太尉),以司马懿为督军、御史中丞(黄初元年,二年迁尚书右仆射),以朱铄为中领军(黄初二年,直至曹丕去世);②在地方上则以吴质为振威将军、假节都督河北诸军事(黄初元年),曹真为镇西将军,都督雍、凉州诸军事(黄初元年,三年还京师后迁上军大将军、都督中外诸军事、假节钺),夏侯尚为征南将军、领荆州刺史、都督南方诸军事(黄初元年,二年迁征南大将军),曹休为镇南将军、都督扬州诸军事(黄初元年)。③ 翻检以上诸人本传,他们或是"太子之争"过程中曹丕的支持者,或是与曹丕私情无间者,如贾

---

① 《晋书》卷一《宣帝纪》。

② 以上参万斯同:《魏将相大臣年表》,收《后汉书三国志补表三十种》中册,中华书局,1984年版,第949～982页。

③ 以上参万斯同:《魏方镇年表》,收《后汉书三国志补表三十种》中册,第985～1006页。而唐长孺:《西晋分封与宗王出镇》一文(文见《魏晋南北朝史论拾遗》,中华书局,1983年版,第123～140页。)中所引《隶释》卷十九《魏公卿上尊号奏》中记曹真、曹休、夏侯尚的职衔分别为:使持节、行都督、督军、镇西将军、东乡侯;使持节、行都督、督军、领扬州刺史、征东将军、安阳乡侯;使持节、行都督、督军、征南将军、平陵亭侯。

诩,《三国志》卷十《魏书·贾诩传》:

> 是时,文帝为五官将,而临菑侯植才名方盛,各有党与,有夺宗之议。文帝使人问诩自固之术,诩曰:"愿将军恢崇德度,躬素士之业,朝夕孜孜,不违子道。如此而已。"文帝从之,深自砥顾。太祖又尝屏除左右问诩,诩嘿然不对。太祖曰:"与卿言而不答,何也?"诩曰:"属适有所思,故不即对耳。"太祖曰:"何思?"诩曰:"思袁本初、刘景升父子也。"太祖大笑,于是太子遂定。

又同书同传注引《魏略》曰:"文帝得诩之对太祖,故即位首登上司。"其次如桓阶,《三国志》卷二十二《魏书·桓阶传》:

> 时太子未定,而临菑侯植有宠。阶数陈文帝德优齿长,宜为储副,公规密谏,前后恳至。

而司马懿、陈群、吴质、朱铄则号曰"太子四友";[1]至于钟繇,文帝在东宫时候就赐之五熟釜,又曾向其索要玉玦;[2]曹真、曹休两人就是在曹丕为魏王后与吴质书中所称的"南皮之游,存者三人,烈祖龙飞,或将或侯"者;[3]夏侯尚,《三国志》卷二十三《魏书·杜袭传》提到他"暱于太子,情好至密"。在这样一种大背景下考察当时的司马懿,也能看出他并不是出类拔萃者,在曹魏初年都督制开始形成时期,司马懿也没有掌握军权。

文帝在位的近六年时间里,可谓军国务繁,不断来往于许昌、洛阳之间。黄初三年孙权复叛之后,战事增频,在这种情况下,自然需要可靠且有谋略之人来稳定后方,时任尚书令的陈群和尚书右仆射的司马懿,当是最合适的人选,《三国志》卷二十二《魏书·陈群传》说:

> (陈群)在朝无适无莫,雅仗名义,不以非道假人。文帝在东宫,深敬器焉,待以交友之礼,常叹曰:"自吾有回,门人日以亲。"及即王位,封群昌武亭侯,徙为尚书。制九品官人之法,群所建也。及践阼,迁尚书仆射,加侍中,徙尚书令,进爵颍乡侯。

陈群世为颍川名族,也是魏武帝时期的重要谋臣,曾向曹操举荐多人,有知人之誉。而司马懿更是"每与大谋,辄有奇策,为太子所信重",[4]因此在黄初六年(225)时候,两人对录尚书事,《三国志》卷二《魏书·文帝纪》注引《魏略》载诏曰:

> 今内有公卿以镇京师,外设牧伯以监四方,至于元戎出征,则军中宜有柱石之贤帅,辎重所在,又宜有镇守之重臣,然后车驾可以周行天下,无内外之虑。吾今当征贼,欲守之积年。其以尚书令颍乡

---

① 见《晋书》卷一《宣帝纪》。
② 见《三国志》卷十三《魏书·钟繇传》注引《魏略》:"后太祖征汉中,太子在孟津,闻繇有玉玦,欲得之而难公言。密使临菑侯转因人说之,繇即送之。"
③ 见《三国志》卷二十一《魏书·吴质传》注引《魏略》。
④ 见《晋书》卷一《宣帝纪》。

侯陈群为镇军大将军,尚书仆射西乡侯司马懿为抚军大将军。若吾临江授诸将方略,则抚军当留许昌,督后诸军,录后台文书事。镇军随车驾,当董督众军,录行尚书事;皆假节鼓吹,给中军兵骑六百人。

这也是司马懿正式进入权力中心的开始。继而,黄初七年,文帝疾笃,《三国志》卷二《魏书·文帝纪》载:

> 夏五月丙辰,帝疾笃,召中军大将军曹真、镇军大将军陈群、征东大将军曹休、抚军大将军司马宣王,并受遗诏辅嗣主。[1]

文帝崩时,武帝朝之旧将诸曹、夏侯氏已相继零落。曹纯薨于建安十五年,夏侯渊战死于建安二十四年,夏侯惇薨于文帝初,曹仁薨于黄初四年,夏侯尚薨于黄初六年。当时宗室尚存曹洪、曹休与曹真,而曹洪因得罪文帝而险遭丧命,后免官削爵土,[2]自然不以之辅政;宗室之中曹爽、曹肇、夏侯玄等资历尚浅,故皆不在顾命之列。[3]而文帝敢以陈群、司马懿为顾命,自然也是由于曹真、曹休手握兵权之故。又王夫之在《读通鉴论》卷十《三国》中评论说:

> 魏之亡,自曹丕遗诏命司马懿抚政始。懿之初为文学掾,岂夙有夺魏之心哉?魏无人,延懿而授之耳。……丕之诏曹真、陈群与懿同辅政者,甚无谓也。子叡已长,群下想望其风采,大臣各守其职司,而何用辅政者为?其命群与懿也,以防曹真而相禁制也。然则虽非曹爽之狂愚,真亦不能为魏藩卫久矣。以群、懿防真,合真与懿、群而防者,曹植兄弟也。[4]

船山先生因其时代之故,多作愤激之辞。考察当时情势,曹丕设立辅政十分必要,明帝即位之时虽已二十二岁,但因其为太子日浅,《三国志》卷三《魏书·明帝纪》载:“(黄初)七年夏五月,帝病笃,乃立为皇太子。丁巳,即皇帝位,大赦。”又注引《世语》曰:

> 帝与朝士素不接,即位之后,群下想闻风采。居数日,独见侍中刘晔,语尽日。众人侧听,晔既出,问“何如”?晔曰:“秦始皇、汉孝武之俦,才具微不及耳。”

试想,明帝从立为太子到即位为帝不足一月,况“与朝士素不接”,曹丕以四人辅政自在情理之中。至于王夫之认为要合真与懿、群以防范曹植兄弟,又大可不必,时曹植兄弟实是朝不保夕。兹引《三国志》卷

---

① 此处文帝召四人辅政,但《晋书》卷一《宣帝纪》记为:“及天子疾笃,帝与曹真、陈群等见于崇华殿之南堂,并受顾命辅政。诏太子曰:‘有间此三公者,慎勿疑之。’”辅政者无曹休,又说“间此三公”,无曹休明矣。《通鉴》卷七十《魏纪二》似采用《晋书》,记为:“夏,五月,帝疾笃,乃立叡为太子。丙辰,召中军大将军曹真、镇军大将军陈群、抚军大将军司马懿,并受遗诏辅政。丁巳,帝殂。”本文采用《三国志》的记载。

② 参《三国志》卷九《魏书·曹洪传》:“始,洪家富而性吝啬,文帝少时假求不称,常恨之,遂以舍客犯法,下狱当死。群臣并救莫能得。卞太后谓郭后曰:‘令曹洪今日死,吾明日敕帝废后矣。’于是泣涕屡请,乃得免官削爵土。”

③ 参《三国志》卷九《魏书·诸夏侯曹传》。

④ 王夫之:《读通鉴论》卷十,中华书局,2002年版,第268页。

二十《魏书·武文世王公传》可见魏时王公情形：

> 魏氏王公，既徒有国土之名，而无社稷之实，又禁防壅隔，同于囹圄；位号靡定，大小岁易；骨肉之恩乖，常棣之义废。为法之弊，一至于此乎！

又注引《袁子》曰：

> 魏兴，承大乱之后，民人损减，不可则以古始。于是封建侯王，皆使寄地，空名而无其实。王国使有老兵百余人，以卫其国。虽有王侯之号，而乃侪为匹夫。县隔千里之外，无朝聘之仪，邻国无会同之制。诸侯游猎不得过三十里，又为设防辅监国之官以伺察之。王侯皆思为布衣而不能得。既违宗国藩屏之义，又亏亲戚骨肉之恩。

曹魏朝对宗室的政策，陈登原在《国史旧闻》卷十七"曹魏苛待宗室"条有说明，此不多论。①

三

考察魏明帝其人，并非庸碌无为者，前面刘晔所说秦皇汉武之俦，才具微不及的话也不为夸毗，其治国方略，儒法并用，而非文帝的"通达"作风，②《三国志》卷三《魏书·明帝纪》注引《魏书》："帝生数岁而有岐嶷之姿……好学多识，特留心于法理。"又同纪："（太和三年）冬十月，改平望观曰听讼观。帝常言'狱者，天下之性命也'，每断大狱，常幸观临听之。"又《三国志》卷二十二《魏书·陈矫传》载：

> 明帝即位……车驾尝卒至尚书门，矫跪问帝曰："陛下欲何之？"帝曰："欲案行文书耳。"矫曰："此自臣职分，非陛下所宜临也。若臣不称其职，则请就黜退。陛下宜还。"帝惭，回车而反。

明帝留心法理及欲案行文书，都说明他谙熟于治国之道。在这种情况下，明帝与辅政大臣之间的关系也颇值得注意，《三国志》卷三《魏书·明帝纪》注引孙盛曰：

> 闻之长老，魏明帝天姿秀出，立发垂地，口吃少言，而沉毅好断。初，诸公受遗辅导，帝皆以方任处之，政自己出。

明帝既以方任处辅政的情况，"政自己出"，则势必与辅政之间有所龃龉，对此时之政局，当时人孙权在与

---

① 参陈登原：《国史旧闻》，中华书局，2005年，第476～477页；又可参王永平：《曹魏苛禁宗室政策之考论》，文载《许昌师专学报》2001年第3期；而曹植之结局也证明这种政策的有效性，《三国志》卷十九《魏书·曹植传》载："植每欲求别见独谈，论及时政，幸冀试用，终不能得。既还，怅然绝望。时法制，待藩国既自峻迫，寮属皆贾竖下才，兵人给其残老，大数不过二百人。又植以前过，事事复减半，十一年中而三徙都，常汲汲无欢，遂发疾薨，时年四十一。"

② 有关"魏武好法术，而天下贵刑名；魏文慕通达，而天下贱守节"，前人论述较多，此处不论。

诸葛瑾书中曾有评论,《三国志》卷五十二《吴书·诸葛瑾传》:

> 近得伯言表,以为曹丕已死,毒乱之民,当望旌瓦解,而更静然。……闻任陈长文、曹子丹辈,或文人诸生,或宗室戚臣,宁能御雄才虎将以制天下乎?……又长文之徒,昔所以能守善者,以操笮其头,畏操威严,故竭心尽意,不敢为非耳。逮丕继业,年已长大,承操之后,以恩情加之,用能感义。今睿幼弱,随人东西,此曹等辈,必当因此弄巧行态,阿党比周,各助所附。如此之日,奸谗并起,更相陷怼,转成嫌贰。一尔已往,群下争利,主幼不御,其为败也焉得久乎?所以知其然者,自古至今,安有四五人把持刑柄,而不离刺转相蹄啮者也。强当陵弱,弱当求援,此乱亡之道也。

这段话中,曹魏政权在明帝时期虽不至"乱亡",但孙权所论的主弱臣强的局势大致不差,我们可以从太和四年曹真伐蜀一事以见一斑。

曹真在明帝即位之初"迁大将军";太和四年,曹休已死,曹真又"迁大司马,赐剑履上殿,入朝不趋",此于曹真则人臣之贵已极,但同年曹真伐蜀,则执意而行。《三国志》卷二十二《魏书·陈群传》中载:

> 太和中,曹真表欲数道伐蜀,从斜谷入。群以为"太祖昔到阳平攻张鲁,多收豆麦以益军粮,鲁未下而食犹乏。今既无所因,且斜谷阻险,难以进退,转运必见钞截,多留兵守要,则损战士,不可不熟虑也"。帝从群议。真复表从子午道,群又陈其不便,并言军事用度之计。诏以群议下真,真据之遂行。

"诏以群议下真,真据之遂行",《通鉴》胡三省此处评注曰:

> 诏以议下真,将与之商度可否也。真锐于出师,遂以诏为据而行。①

曹真之"锐于出师",是否存心朝廷,不得而知,但很有伐蜀立威的嫌疑,且曹真出师之后,又有太尉华歆、少府杨阜、散骑常侍王肃等多人疏陈出师之弊,②最终曹真虽听诏班师,但实是因为当时"大霖雨三十余日,或栈道断绝"。③曹真太和四年八月出师,而太和五年三月卒。其负气而出,未捷而返,跋扈之行迹已露,明帝对之实属无奈,这正应孙权所说的"主幼不御"之语。

再来看曹休,因太和二年曹休已死,明帝时期并没有太多事情可述,但若细心考察,还是有可疑之点,《三国志》卷十四《魏书·刘放传》注引《资别传》:

> 资曰:"陛下思深虑远。……文皇帝始召曹真还时,亲诏臣以重虑,及至晏驾,陛下即阼,犹有曹休外内之望,赖遭日月,御勒不倾,使各守分职,纤介不间。"

---

① 见《通鉴》卷七十一《魏纪三》。
② 三人上疏见《通鉴》卷七十一《魏纪三》。
③ 见《三国志》卷九《魏书·曹真传》。

关于"曹休外内之望",清人何焯认为:

> 《孙资别传》有文皇帝晏驾,陛下即阼,犹有曹休外内之望云云。(何焯)按:明帝与曹休无间,知《资别传》为妄。①

何焯之言,似未深考。曹休之死,史载其为吴诈败:

> 休上书谢罪,帝遣屯骑校尉杨暨慰谕,礼赐益隆。休因此痈发背薨,谥曰壮侯,子肇嗣。②

败军而不治,反礼赐益隆,但又何至于"痈发背薨"?因此我们虽不确知曹休当时之隐情,但明帝与曹休不为"无间"可知!

四

同为辅政的陈群在当时的处境,我们也可以从下面材料中看出大概,《三国志》卷二十一《魏书·吴质传》注引《资别传》曰:

> (质)太和四年,入为侍中。时司空陈群录尚书事,帝初亲万机,质以辅弼大臣,安危之本,对帝盛称"骠骑将军司马懿,忠智至公,社稷之臣也。陈群从容之士,非国相之才,处重任而不亲事"。帝甚纳之。明日,有切诏以督责群,而天下以司空不如长文,即群,言无实也。……

"帝甚纳之"说明对陈群的积怨已非一日,故有明日督责陈群的"切诏"。而司马懿的命运似乎不同,《晋书》卷一《宣帝纪》:

> 太和元年六月,天子诏帝屯于宛,加督荆、豫二州诸军事。

司马懿之掌握军权,实始于此时,前虽以抚军大将军辅政,但并不掌兵,也正是在都督荆、豫之时,司马懿初步显示了其军事才能,西擒孟达、兼讨申仪,并于太和二年协助曹休伐吴。吴质为文帝宠臣,"侍中"又为近密之职,或许也是这番话的作用,明帝以时任骠骑将军的司马懿为"大将军,加大都督,假黄钺,与曹真伐蜀",③用来牵制曹真。太和五年曹真死后,又直接以司马懿西屯长安,都督雍、梁二州诸军事,担负起曹魏最强劲的对手诸葛亮的进攻。此时的司马懿威望卓著,已有震主之威,《三国志》卷十七《魏书·

---

① 何焯:《义门读书记》中册,卷二十六,中华书局,1987年,第438页;祝总斌《都督中外诸军事及其性质、作用》(《见材不材斋文集》下编,三秦出版社,第289页。)一文中认为此处之"外内"与都督中外诸军之"中外"涵义相同。似可商讨。此处"外内之望"似应指权臣之威望。
② 《三国志》卷九《魏书·曹休传》。
③ 《晋书》卷一《宣帝纪》。

张郃传》注引《魏略》曰：

> 亮军退，司马宣王使郃追之，郃曰："军法，围城必开出路，归军勿追。"宣王不听。郃不得已，遂进。蜀军乘高布伏，弓弩乱发，矢中郃髀。

张郃是武帝旧将，立赫赫战功，"识变数，善处营陈，料战势地形，无不如计，自诸葛亮皆惮之"，[1]官拜车骑将军，然正是司马懿亲促其死，赵翼也在其《廿二史札记》"《三国志》多回护"条中据此为证：

> 五年亮出军祁山，司马懿遣张郃来救，郃被杀，亦皆不书。……由此可见其书法，专为讳败夸胜为得体也。[2]

但明帝也只有叹息而已。[3] 司马懿于青龙三年（235）"迁太尉，累增封邑"，[4]屯长安将近八年，数与诸葛亮对垒，以智谋和持重屡建奇功，直至景初元年（237）公孙渊反叛，才被再次召回京师。作为异姓功臣，司马懿自然有危机之感，在此之前，《三国志》卷二十二《魏书·陈矫传》注引《世语》：

> 帝忧社稷，问矫："司马公忠正，可谓社稷之臣乎？"矫曰："朝廷之望；社稷，未知也。"

可见明帝对司马懿是有猜疑之心的，在景初二年（238）司马懿前往辽东路过温县宴请父老时，据《晋书》卷一《宣帝纪》：

> 帝叹息，怅然有感，为歌曰："天地开辟，日月重光。遭遇际会，毕力遐方。将扫群秽，还过故乡。肃清万里，总齐八荒。告成归老，待罪舞阳。"

司马懿时封舞阳侯，故有"待罪舞阳"之言，这首诗也可见其忧虑之深。

正是此年十二月，明帝寝疾不豫。景初三年正月，司马懿还至河内，"帝驿马召到，引入卧内，执其手谓曰：'吾疾甚，以后事属君，君其与爽辅少子。吾得见君，无所恨！'宣王顿首流涕"。[5] 这就是历史上聚讼纷纭的"登堂把臂"之托，《三国志》卷十四《魏书·刘放传》载之较详：

> 其年，帝寝疾，欲以燕王宇为大将军，及领军将军夏侯献、武卫将军曹爽、屯骑校尉曹肇、骁骑将军秦朗共辅政。宇性恭良，陈诚固辞。帝引见放、资，入卧内，问曰："燕王正尔为？"放、资对曰："燕王实自知不堪大任故耳。"帝曰："曹爽可代宇不？"放、资因赞成之。又深陈宜速召太尉司马宣王，以

① 《三国志》卷十七《魏书·张郃传》。
② 赵翼：《廿二史札记校证》卷六，王树民校注，中华书局，2005年版，第124页。
③ 《三国志》卷二十五《魏书·辛毗传》注引《魏略》曰："帝惜郃，临朝而叹曰：'蜀未平而郃死，将若之何？'"
④ 《晋书》卷一《宣帝纪》。
⑤ 《三国志》卷三《魏书·明帝纪》。

纲维皇室。帝纳其言，即以黄纸授放作诏。放、资既出，帝意复变，诏止宣王勿使来。寻更见放、资曰："我自召太尉，而曹肇等反使吾止之，几败吾事！"命更为诏，帝独召爽与放、资俱受诏命，遂免宇、献、肇、朗官。太尉亦至，登床受诏，然后帝崩。

而《三国志》卷三《魏书·明帝纪》注引《汉晋春秋》与此略有不同。因史料的不足，本文不拟揣测当时之真相，但《三国志》卷十四《魏书·刘放传》注引《资别传》中有一则材料值得注意：

帝诏资曰："吾年稍长，又历观书传中，皆叹息无所不念。图万年后计，莫过使亲人广据职势，兵任又重。今射声校尉缺，久欲得亲人，谁可用者？"

也就是说，明帝曾有过以宗室据兵任的想法，而最后似乎也得以实现，本欲以之辅政的领军将军夏侯献、屯骑校尉曹肇、骁骑将军秦朗以及后来辅政的武卫将军曹爽，都掌握重要的禁卫军权。[①] 但在最后时刻，由于掌机密达三十年的孙资、刘放拉拢司马宣王再次加入辅政之列，从而改变了曹魏王朝的命运。不过可以肯定的就是，当时宗室并没有杰出人物来做支撑，也是实情。王夫之评曰：

司马懿之于魏，掾佐而已，拒诸葛于秦川，仅以不败，未尝有尺寸之功于天下也；受魏主睿登床之托，横翦曹爽，遂制孱君、胁群臣，猎相国九锡之命，终使其子孙继世而登天位，成一统之业。其兴也不可遏，而抑必有道焉，非天下之可妄求而得也。曹氏之驱兆民、延人而授之也久矣。[②]

船山先生认为司马懿"未尝有尺寸之功于天下也"显然是过言，但又承认"其兴也不可遏，而抑必有道焉"，则是确论。至于正始年间曹、马之争，研究已多，则不多论。

① 领军将军、屯骑校尉、骁骑将军、武卫将军在当时都是重要的禁卫武官，可参张金龙：《魏晋南北朝禁卫武官制度研究》第四章《曹魏禁卫武官制度》，中华书局，2004年版，第99～149页。
② 参王夫之：《读通鉴论》卷十，中华书局，2002年版，第289页。贺昌群：《魏晋清谈初论》中也有类似的话："司马懿之于魏，起于掾佐之间，及拒诸葛亮于秦川，仅以不败，未尝有煊赫之功，继征辽左，仓皇遁返，而受明帝'登床把臂'之托，横翦曹爽，遂制弱君，猎相国九锡之命，终使其子孙继世而登大位，成一统之业，亦必有故焉。盖司马氏执政之初，即一反曹氏刻薄寡恩之政，用贤恤民，务从宽大，以结天下之心，而士大夫乃稍知有生人之乐，其谋险而小惠，盖已周矣。"（商务印书馆，2000年版，第38页）可能就引自船山此论。这里即是说司马懿以宽大得人心，而曹氏以苛恩失天下，当时情势是否如此，则另论。

试论清初治理新疆的政策

张付新
新疆塔里木大学经济与管理学院

清朝是中国少数民族建立的第二个统一的中原王朝,也是中国最后一个封建王朝。清朝建立后,随着实力的逐渐增强,与新疆的各民族联系逐渐增多,经过康熙、雍正、乾隆三朝终于平定了准噶尔贵族及大小和卓的叛乱,逐渐统一了天山南北,制定并实施了一系列行之有效的统治政策。学术界关于清王朝的边疆政策和民族政策的研究一直都比较广泛,尤其是新疆的治理政策更是学术界关注的重点,也取得了丰硕的研究成果。但新疆地处边疆,又是多民族聚居的地区;边疆政策与民族政策通常是二位一体的。

一、清初治理新疆政策的背景

(一)清初边疆政策形成的社会环境

在整个中国政治舞台上,后金政权到清初的势力依然相对弱小。后金要改变这种不利地位,在政治角逐中争取更多主动,必须坚持巩固和发展自己的实力,采取行之有效的方法来聚集政治和社会资源,以增强实力、扩大政权基础。在文化上。满族处于文化相对落后状态,需要通过学习先进文化来发展自己。清朝时期,多民族的社会生存环境促使满族作为统治民族,必须团结一切可以团结的力量,切实做到人尽其才,以处理各种民族矛盾与问题的挑战。清朝皇帝必须突破"华夷之防",社会进步方能进步。上述背景都对清代民族政策的形成和发展产生了不同程度的影响。

(二)清初新疆的局势及演变

明末清初,是中国历史上的大动荡、大分化时期。居住在中国西北的蒙古族分为漠南蒙古、漠北喀尔喀蒙古和漠西卫拉特蒙古三部分。天山北路主要以卫拉特蒙古(元代称"斡亦剌惕",或"斡亦剌"、"外剌"、"外剌歹",明代称为瓦剌,清代称"卫拉特"、"厄鲁特"、"额鲁特")为主,天山南部的居民主要以维吾尔族为主。

统治天山南路是察合台后裔建立的叶尔羌汗国,其首领阿不都拉哈汗早在顺治帝时期就与清朝建立了朝贡关系。但随着中亚伊斯兰教苏非派的不断渗入,宗教势力开始逐渐影响新疆政局。伊斯兰教传入新疆后,在天山南路形成了两个不同的派系:白山派和黑山派。两派之间互相斗争。在争战中处于劣势的白山派首领阿帕克和卓经过中亚逃往西藏寻求帮助,五世达赖喇嘛写信准噶尔部首领噶尔丹出兵帮助阿帕克和卓。于是,噶尔丹在白山派教徒的支持和响应下,率部攻克叶尔羌城,并将其迁往伊犁,噶尔丹逐渐控制了天山南路。噶尔丹扶持代理人为其收取赋税,实行间接控制。新疆地区的民族分布格局至此有了细微的变化,即在天山北路除了有蒙古族之外,也有了被准噶尔部强行迁到此地的一小部分维吾尔族。原来"南回北准"的民族分布格局事实上已经被打破。

康熙年间,卫拉特四部之一的准噶尔部日益强大,噶尔丹逐渐合并了其他三部,并不断东进攻击漠北喀尔喀蒙古。清政府当时忙于平定"三藩之乱"(云南的平西王吴三桂、福建的靖南王耿精忠、广东的平南王尚可喜),无奈采取安抚的妥协政策。1681年,清政府平定"三藩之乱"后,立即投入了歼灭噶尔丹的斗争,1690年,清军在乌兰布通大败噶尔丹,1697年,噶尔丹势穷自杀。十年中双方发生过数次大规模战争,各有胜负,时战时和。准噶尔等人夺取中央政权的企图虽没得逞,但清朝也未能完全统一我国西北广大地区。

从外部来看,15世纪中叶,楚河流域兴起了哈萨克汗国,到16世纪20年代,哈斯木汗统一哈萨克各部,汗国处于鼎盛时期。17世纪卫拉特四部之一的准噶尔部兴起后,哈萨克汗国在准噶尔部的侵扰下逐渐衰落,形成以血缘为纽带的三个玉兹。其中,大玉兹(乌勒玉兹)在伊犁河至巴尔喀什湖周围;中玉兹(奥尔塔玉兹)在锡尔河以北;小玉兹(克什玉兹)在咸海西北至伏尔加河以东地区。雍正元年(1723),准噶尔军队侵袭,大玉兹全部及中玉兹部分被击溃,臣服于准噶尔汗国。乾隆五年(1740),准噶尔军队西进至乌拉尔河,中玉兹大部亦臣属于准噶尔汗国,小玉兹则被迫向更西迁徙。至此,哈萨克各部落已大多归属准噶尔汗国。

16世纪中叶,沙皇俄国征服喀山汗国和阿斯拉罕汗国,不断南进。至17世纪,沙皇的权力大大加强,走上了急剧殖民扩张的道路。1648年,沙俄的势力已经到达亚洲的东北角。与此同时沙俄的探险家来到黑龙江流域,开始侵占中国领土,但遭到中国军队的抗击,被迫同意和平谈判,1689年签定了中俄《尼布楚条约》,双方明确划定疆界。1694年,彼得一世亲政,实行了著名的具有现代化性质的改革,国力大增。沙俄此时成为威胁中国北部安全的一个劲敌。

清朝在统一新疆前,因为沙俄势力的膨胀,清政府施政的重点在天山北路卫拉特蒙古聚居区,所实行的是以怀柔、羁縻为主的民族政策。但是,随着准噶尔部势力逐渐增强以及噶尔丹个人野心膨胀,清朝在北方和西北边疆的统治受到了严重威胁,遂被迫调整其对天山南北的民族政策。

清朝"平准"战争的彻底胜利及战略方针的转变,使天山南北广大地区开始处于清朝政府的直接统治之下。随后,清廷在这里设官置守,驻军屯田,征收赋税,最终结束了我国西北地区长期动荡割据的局面,使中国的统一在新的条件下又向前迈进了一步。

二、清初治理新疆的基本政策

清代前期是学术界公认的历史上治边最有成效的朝代,对西北边疆民族地区的管辖也是如此。清朝统一新疆后,结合新疆实际和其他边疆地区治理的经验,实行了一系列稳定和开发新疆的政策和措施。笔者将从政治体制与管理、军事政策、经济政策和宗教政策四方面进行总结。

(一) 政治体制与管理

1. 札萨克制

札萨克制是清朝在新疆地区最早实行的行政管理体制。康熙三十五年(1696)哈密地区的维吾尔人首领额贝都拉就率部归附清廷,并协助清军击败准噶尔。此后,札萨克制不断在东疆地区推广和完善。雍正年间,吐鲁番地区的维吾尔首领额敏和卓不断遭受准噶尔部的侵扰,臣服于清政府,清廷以为"额敏和卓,著封为札萨克辅国公"。[①] 这样,清朝在吐鲁番地区的札萨克制正式建立了。清朝对当地的维吾尔族贵族封贝

---

① 《清世宗实录》雍正十年十一月乙未,卷一二五《清实录》,中华书局影印本,1986年,第8册,第644页。

子、贝勒等爵位,且均为世袭。这两地的维吾尔族首领在清朝后来平定新疆期间,协助清朝平叛,功不可没。

清朝统一新疆以后,远徙伏尔加河流域的土尔扈特部于公元1771年迁回天山北路故地,随后部分和硕特蒙古也陆续回到了新疆。清朝将回到新疆境内的土尔扈特部分为新、旧土尔扈特,由渥巴锡率领的被称为旧土尔扈特,由舍棱领导的被称为新土尔扈特。在行政管理上,旧土尔扈特部隶书于伊犁将军,新土尔扈特部则受制于定边左副将军。清朝一律对该地区实行的是札萨克制。清朝对各部首领进行了汗、王、台吉等爵位的册封,并赋予其管理本部事务,并且准许各部首领到北京朝觐。清朝对归附的卫拉特蒙古实行札萨克制的目的在于强化管理、分而治之。而对哈密、吐鲁番地区实行札萨克制则带有一定的嘉奖、拉拢其部众的因素。

2. 伯克制

清朝在除哈密、吐鲁番以外的广大维吾尔族聚居区则实行伯克制度,并派兵驻防。苗普生先生曾指出:"伯克制度"是我国维吾尔族和中亚地区一些操突厥语族语言的民族历史上的一种官制,它在我国维吾尔族地区发展的最为完备、严密。[1] 据侯丕勋研究:"'伯克'作为官名,在清初康熙时业已存在。"[2]苗普生认为:"伯克制度经过14至16世纪的发展,至赛依德王朝就基本形成了,17世纪初臻于完善。伯克制度的形成,主要是蒙古贵族及其后裔的统治,和伊斯兰教在新疆传播的结果。"[3]刘志霄认为,伯克制度是"构成清朝在天山南北的主要行政建制","它是介于札萨克制和郡县制之间的一种行政建制","伯克制度既避免了札萨克过分的封建色彩,同时,也顺应了当地维吾尔居民的习惯"。[4] 清朝统一新疆之初,大小和卓的叛乱,使清政府借助宗教上层人物统摄南疆的政策无法实现。清朝平定了回部叛乱之后,首先派兵驻防,以保证边疆安全和社会稳定。叛乱平息后,清朝继承南疆地区旧有的伯克制,使其成为清朝在新疆地方官制的一个重要组成部分。但出于强化中央集权考虑,清政府对伯克制采取了一系列改革措施,如"废除伯克世袭,由朝廷任免升调"、以"对清政府的效忠态度"为选任标准、"实行回避制度"、"制定品级,颁发印记"、"各城伯克均统于当地驻扎大臣"。这些措施的实行,使"伯克在身份上发生了重大变化,从原来的贵族官僚逐渐转化为清政府的地方官"。[5] 由此可见,清朝前期在经略西北边疆过程中,"伯克"制的实行,对新疆地区的稳定一度起了十分重要的作用。

3. 府县制

府县制是清朝在新疆东部汉族、回族聚居区实行与内地基本相同的管理制度。"于乌鲁木齐设立同知一员,通判一员,仓大使一员,巡检两员,令其分任管理,统听哈密兵备道管辖。"[6]乾隆帝还规定,乌鲁木齐地区同知一职定为满缺。随着清初所实行的一系列移民实边政策,使得很多内地农民、商人等流入新疆,且大多居住在乌鲁木齐、哈密、吐鲁番等地。因内地人口的不断增加,使府县制这种行政体制得以实行并越加完善。

4. 法律制度

清朝统一前的新疆天山南北两路各民族的文化传统、风俗习惯与法律制度各不相同。清初依据"因

① 苗普生:《伯克制度》,新疆人民出版社,1995年,第1页。
② 侯丕勋:《历代经略西北边疆研究》,甘肃文化出版社,1997年,第20页。
③ 苗普生:《关于伯克制度的形成和发展》,载《西北历史研究》,1987年。
④ 刘志霄:《维吾尔族历史》,民族出版社,1985年。
⑤ 马汝珩、马大正:《清代的边疆政策》,中国社会科学出版社,1994年,第338~339页。
⑥ 《乾隆朝上谕档》,乾隆二十五年五月初三日,档案出版社,1998年。

俗而治"的传统原则,制订了一系列符合天山南北各民族不同特点的法规和制度,主要涉及政治、经济、宗教、文化各方面。这样,保证了清朝在新疆地区各项政策的顺利实施,使各项政策在执行过程中都可以做到有法可依。

清朝对蒙古地区的立法,起源于皇太极时期。清初虽然在天山南路并未制订相关的法律制度,但是"乾隆朝进行了一系列以皇帝谕旨或经皇帝批准的臣工条奏为形式的单项立法"。① 乌什之变之后,清朝对南疆地区的政治、经济进行了较大改革,从而形成了一系列的规章条例。这些皇帝谕旨和规章条例后来被直接收录到了《回疆则例》中,反映了清政府对南疆地区统治的不断深入。在尊重少数民族习惯法的同时,也将《大清律例》渗入其中。因此,新疆地区的法律制度呈现出了多元性的特点。但《回疆则例》的编纂又进一步强化了所谓的"汉回隔离"、"边政与民政分离"政策,这种不平等的民族政策在客观上不利于回疆与内地的政治、经济与文化联系。加之军府制下"北重南轻"的格局,使清代的回疆地区动乱频生。1864 年,新疆各族农民大起义爆发,清朝在新疆地区的统治体系全面瓦解,《回疆则例》亦随之寿终正寝。② 纵观清朝在新疆实行的各项民族政策,利弊参半。就清朝在新疆初期的统治来说,这些政策起到了一些积极作用;随着社会发展,其弊端渐渐显露了出来,对后来也产生了一定的负面影响。

清朝所实行的以上政策使新疆原有的民族分布格局发生了较大的变化。天山北路是遭受战乱破坏最为严重的地区,原来卫拉特部众或亡或迁,人口损失大半。因伊犁地区以前为准噶尔部的活动中心,所以清朝在此地驻扎了比任何地方都多的官兵。清朝从内地调集满蒙八旗官兵组建"惠远城满营"、"惠宁城满营"、锡伯营、索伦营、厄鲁特营。清朝还在天山北路的重镇如乌鲁木齐、巴里坤等地方,调集满、汉、蒙等各族官并共同驻守,并在当地屯田,发展生产。在天山北路驻防的官兵多为"携眷永驻",不断成为天山北路众多民族中的一员。

其他一些邻近少数民族也在这一时期迁入天山南北。哈萨克族在清朝统一新疆前是准噶尔部的属民,统一新疆以后,部分哈萨克族人迁入天山北路,成为清朝的臣民。此外,还有一些内地的回族商人、农业人口自行流动到新疆,部分也逐渐成为当地的永久居民。柯尔克孜族曾经也是卫拉特的臣民,在统一新疆以后成为清朝的臣民。清朝在乾隆年间曾两次将柯尔克孜族东迁至黑龙江地区。

清朝统一新疆之后,由政府组织及各族人民自发的各种类型的民族迁徙活动,基本上形成了近代新疆各民族大杂居、小聚居,各民族交错杂居的分布格局。此种民族分布格局所产生的影响在其后发生的1864 年新疆农民起义中表现得最为明显。

(二) 军事政策

清王朝是由一个马背上的民族建立起来的,但已经继承了中原王朝的传统的军事防御政策。阿睦尔撒纳和大小和卓的叛乱平定后,清朝根据天山南北政治形势以及民族分布格局发生重大变化的实际情况,本着"因俗而治"的方针,在新疆地区实行了"军政合一、以军统政"③的军府制,还实施了派重兵、筑城堡、建台站、设卡伦等措施。

清朝统一新疆后,建立了以伊犁将军为统帅的最高军事机构。军府制下的札萨克制、伯克制、府县制等行政管理体制。清朝在平定准噶尔和回部叛乱后,认为天山北路系准噶尔部的活动区域,也是新疆动

---

① 白京兰:《清代回疆立法——〈钦定回疆则例〉探析》,《中南民族大学学报》(人文社会科学版),2004 年第 4 期。
② 王欣:《〈回疆则例〉研究》,《中国边疆史地研究》2005 年第 3 期。
③ 管守新:《清代新疆军府制度研究》,新疆大学出版社,2002 年,第 2 页。

乱的源头,只有将统摄天山南北的最高行政机构设在此处,才能稳定北疆,北疆稳则全疆安。因此将最高管理机构设在了天山北路的伊犁地区,并设重兵驻防。但伊犁距内地路途遥远且崎岖难行,为解决送粮问题,清朝就令在伊犁驻守的官兵"在镇边驻守的同时,还要屯垦生产,以解决自身粮秣供应问题。这样,驻军就肩负起了巩固边防与建设地方的双重任务"。① 由此可以看出,军府制是新疆地区集军事、民政于一身的管理体制。伊犁将军为新疆地区的最高长官,总揽军事与民政事务。下设伊犁参赞大臣、塔城参赞大臣一,喀什噶尔参赞大臣、乌鲁木齐都统共同管理新疆各项事务。军府制下各级官员的主要职责是管理全疆的军事事务,同时权限范围也涉及北疆和东疆地区政治、经济、文化、法律等各方面,但对南疆维吾尔族地区的民政事务则很少触及。

清朝在南疆实行换防制的主要目的,在于不令维吾尔族人民与其他各族官兵久处,避免因风俗习惯不同而产生矛盾。但是这种驻军形式也在后来带来了不利影响。另外,清朝还在南北各地分建回城、满城,其目的就在于不令各族人民尤其是维吾尔族人民与其他各民族杂居,同时对前往内地办事的各族官员的活动也作了一定的限制。由此可以看出,清朝同样不准新疆人民在内地久留。

(三)经济政策

清朝在统一新疆之后为了巩固统治、发展地方经济,制定了相应的经济政策。

1. 屯田政策

新疆的屯田可分为兵屯、民屯、犯屯、回屯、旗屯等五种形式,其中最早的应该是兵屯。清初在天山南北的主要地区都派有驻兵。当时清朝在新疆的驻军体制有换防制和驻防制两种,为了屯田的需要,清朝还将某些地区的驻军由换防制改为了驻防制。这种屯田方式在一定程度上虽然解决了一些实际问题,发展了经济,但是却削弱了军队的战斗力,在需要作战时很难将屯田的军队调动、整合在一起,最后兵屯不得不走向民屯。

民屯是清朝在新疆的第二种屯田形式。清朝统一新疆之后,乾隆帝认为在新疆"办理屯种亦抵因地制宜之举"。② 为了改变战后天山北部人烟稀少、土地荒芜、经济凋敝的状况,清朝于乾隆二十七年(1762)在乌鲁木齐开始屯田。清朝对这些屯田人士均登记造册,严格管理户口,最后他们就都成了新疆的永久居民。此后民屯的范围逐渐从天山北路向天山南路发展。

犯屯,顾名思义就是由流犯所从事的屯田活动。清初将人犯大都发配到东北等地。后来,清朝将犯人遣送新疆,使其充实边疆人口、开发边疆。清朝一般都是将犯人发往有重兵把守、易于防范的地方。当遣犯刑满之后,清朝允许其为民,留在新疆继续垦种土地。这些犯人的身份随之转为平民,成为民屯的一部分。

回屯指新疆维吾尔族人民的屯田活动。清初回屯的范围主要集中在哈密、吐鲁番、伊犁等地。如前所述,伊犁地区的回屯自准噶尔统治时期就已经存在。清朝统一新疆以后又从南疆地区调遣一批维吾尔族人前往伊犁,与绿营兵共同屯田。吐鲁番、哈密地区的回屯则早在清朝与准噶尔作战时就开始了。

旗屯指的是八旗官兵的屯田活动,主要包括驻防在伊犁地区的锡伯、索伦、察哈尔、厄鲁特四营官兵。

清朝的上述屯田活动,不仅发展了当地经济,解决了官兵和百姓的生活问题,更重要的是减轻了各族人民的负担,客观上也有利于边疆地区的稳定和发展。

---

① 管守新:《清代新疆军府制度研究》,第19页。
② 《乾隆朝上谕档》,乾隆二十五年五月初九日。

2. 货币政策

清朝统一新疆后,在新疆实现了不同的货币政策。在天山北路及东路采用了与内地相同的制钱,但在天山南路继续沿用维吾尔族人民所使用的普尔钱,这也是其"因俗而治"民族政策的具体体现。

在准噶尔统治时期,"回旧亦用钱名曰普尔,以红铜为之。以腾格计数,每五十文为一腾格。普尔之式小于制钱,而厚中无孔,一面用帕尔西字铸叶尔羌字,一面用托武字铸策妄阿拉布坦及噶尔丹策凌字样,重一钱四五分至二钱不等"。[①] 统一新疆以后,清朝下令销毁以往准部统治时所用的旧普尔钱,改铸新钱。随后清朝首先在南疆叶尔羌地区开局造钱,其钱币"每百文为一腾格,每文重两钱,一面铸乾隆通宝,一面铸清字及回子字,叶尔羌字"。[②] 随着经济的发展,清朝先后又在阿克苏、乌什、库车、喀什噶尔等地开局铸钱。舒赫德在乾隆二十五年(1760)奏"阿克苏现需鼓铸钱文所有器皿,业经行文。该督办解应用至匠役一项,若从叶尔羌分拨,恐两处人数不敷,亦请于内地再行拨往等语"。[③] 通过对普尔钱形制、重量的改革,清朝一方面尊重了当地的传统,另一方面也维护了中央政府的主权。但这种不同的钱币也造成了经济流通中的困难,难以形成稳定的经济联系。

3. 赋税与贸易政策

清朝统一新疆后,对天山南路的赋税政策也重新调整,南疆的各项赋税都有所减轻。随着新疆社会经济的发展,各族人民之间的贸易活动也日益频繁,清朝前期对此基本持积极态度。乾隆三十年(1765)南疆乌什地区爆发了维吾尔族人民的暴动后,清朝的态度开始发生转变。只准许内地商民在有驻军的地方贸易,且明确规定他们不能与维吾尔族人民杂处,否则视为犯法。这就限制了商民在新疆贸易的自由,同时限制了南疆地区与其他地区的经济交流。

(四)宗教政策

清朝在宗教政策上采取利用与限制并举、拉拢与管理并重的措施。清朝首先拉拢藏传佛教的上层首领,依此控制了天山北路的蒙古部众。在政治上对学识渊博且忠于朝廷的藏传佛教上层首领封以国师等名号,或赐以班第达、诺门罕、呼图克图等职衔,而且允许藏传佛教上层首领统辖一方。经济上免除喇嘛的一切赋税、赋予大喇嘛向人民收取赋税的特权、厚赏藏传佛教上层人士、补贴藏传佛教寺院经济,这也是黄教寺院能长期存在的原因。清朝还在藏传佛教盛行的地方广修寺庙,以满足信教群众的需要。由于清朝对喇嘛实行的各项优惠政策,致使新疆卫拉特蒙古族当中喇嘛的人数不断增加。除了优待与扶植外,清朝同时也加强了对藏传佛教管理,创立了金瓶掣签的转世制度,进一步完善了藏传佛教的活佛转世制度。这种改革既尊重了信教人民的习俗,也将喇嘛的任免权牢牢地掌握在了清朝手中,同时也遏制了蒙藏地区由于选取转世灵童而随之膨胀的地方势力。此外,清政府又对喇嘛进行了如下规定:喇嘛格隆等穿黄色、金黄红色衣服,班第等穿红衣,违者进行处罚;每年喇嘛念经由院领赏银赏给喇嘛,禁止喇嘛班第等私行;喇嘛给人看病需先禀明大喇嘛,不许留宿在病人家里,违者进行处罚;禁止喇嘛留宿妇人家内,同时寺院内同样不能容留妇女,否则进行处罚;对犯罪的喇嘛进行革退处理;喇嘛若留贼盗于寺内与贼盗者一同治罪。[④]

---

① 永贵等:《新疆回部志》卷四钱法,《中国西北文献丛书》,第118册,第67页。
② 永贵等:《新疆回部志》卷四钱法,《中国西北文献丛书》,第118册,第67页。
③ 《乾隆朝上谕档》,乾隆二十五年十一月初三日。
④ 《蒙古律例》,《中国边疆史地资料丛刊综合卷》,全国图书馆文献缩微复制中心,1988年。

清初对待伊斯兰教的政策也是如此。清朝利用伊斯兰教在回疆地区的影响力,采取保护伊斯兰教圣地、尊重其教法教规等措施,赢得广大维吾尔信众的支持。在平定大小和卓的叛乱后,清朝对在喀什噶尔的和卓陵园却加以保护。对伊斯兰教法、教规,清朝也给予了足够的尊重。清朝在统一新疆之后,对于伊斯兰教法中规定的穆斯林所要遵守的规定,不加任何干涉,尊重民族习俗。因此,清朝在天山南路办理一切事务基本上都参照"回例"办理,很少使用《大清律例》。这样,就尊重了维吾尔族人民的宗教感情,为清朝在南疆统治打下了较好的基础。清朝还加强了管理与限制:规定实行严格政教分离政策。清朝统一新疆前,南疆当地的宗教首领执掌当地事务,各地阿訇甚至掌握着伯克的生杀大权。通过政治体制的改革,各城伯克的地位明显提高;清朝加强了对伊斯兰教职业宗教人事的管理,制定了明确的阿訇选取制度,并对之进行监督管理;此外,清朝还将伊斯兰教的上层人物安置在京师,赏官授爵,既表达对其尊重,也限制他们在南疆地区的影响力。

三、清初治理新疆政策的反思

清前期形成的边疆政策,其核心是促进边疆地区与内地的一体化。清政府能妥善解决蒙古问题,安定了北疆;推行改土归流,巩固了西南边疆;更能迎来土尔扈特部的回归。

1. 入关的清朝统治者改变了传统的华夷观,对其他边疆少数民族在思想感情上更容易接近。这正好成为清初制定边疆政策制定的重要思想基础之一。理藩院的设置、年班制度的实施方能较好执行。乾隆十九年(1754),在改建承德避暑山庄丽正门时,以满、蒙、汉、维、藏五种民族文字并行题写门额,有力地证明清政府转变传统华夷观。

历代统治者多用"以夷治夷"来解决边疆问题,也成为历代治边思想的一个重要内容。其核心是通过少数民族来治理少数民族,从而解决边疆问题。其表现形式及采取的相应措施,则随着时代的进步有所变化。其实,这是以乱夷来安华,是放弃了对边疆的治理。这就使"因俗而治"得以实现,"修其教不易其俗,齐其政不易其宜"。对于中央政权来说,只是对边疆地区实现了间接的统治,而远未像内地那样实行直接的统治。但因条件所限制,封建统治者采取"因俗而治"的方针来实现"以夷治夷"的目的,已是历史的一大进步了。

2. 必须尊重边疆和少数民族的历史文化传统。在"以汉化夷"的治边思想逐渐成为主导思想后,清政府的边疆政策中仍保留了"因俗而治"这一方针。雍正皇帝曾经明确指出:"从俗从宜","各安其俗"。[①] 此时清政府采取"因俗而治"的方针是强调在"因俗"基础上的"治"。如在新疆地区实施并改革伯克制。这种政策上创新,在某种程度上具有改土归流的特征。

3. 必须妥善处理民族、宗教问题,务必掌握宗教话语权。其政策可以概括为:"区别对待,因俗而治",特别是在统治政策、行政管理政策、民族宗教政策等方面。这是我国少数民族地区在行政制度、风俗习惯、社会组织和宗教信仰等方面存在明显差异的产物,强调了不应改变少数民族地区的这些方面而进行统治。

4. 必须使固边向富边、强边过渡,实现经济、政治、文化、社会全面进步。从处理当前新疆面临的各

---

① 《清世宗实录》卷六二,雍正五年十一月癸卯条,第956页。

种民族问题分析,清代前期治理政策提供了宝贵的历史借鉴。我国是历史悠久和文化灿烂的国家,长期以来,新疆各族人民创造了非常丰富的政治智慧,为我们留下了弥足珍贵的文化遗产,这是其他国家所不能企及的。而清代前期的治理政策就是珍贵文化遗产的组成部分。如今,我们要全面建设小康社会,实现各民族共同繁荣和中华民族的伟大复兴,必须正确认识和妥善处理我们所面临的各种国内外民族问题,协调好民族关系,不断增强中华民族的凝聚力,团结一切可以团结的力量,调动一切可以调动的积极因素,充分集中各民族的智慧和力量进行现代化建设。在我国,只有实现了民族团结和各民族共同繁荣,才能真正确保社会的稳定,才能粉碎国内外反华势力"西化"和"分化"中国的图谋,才能使我们聚精会神搞建设,一心一意谋发展。因此,必须充分借鉴和吸收人类文明进步的成果,这其中也包括我们祖先留下的文化遗产。这正是"以铜为鉴可以正衣冠,以人为鉴可以知得失,以史为鉴可以知兴替"的意义所在,我们研究探讨清代民族政策的主要目的也正在于此。

吐鲁番的学童读本与"侧书"

——重读吐鲁番所出"卜天寿抄本"札记

柴剑虹

中华书局

吐鲁番阿斯塔那 363 号唐代墓葬所出文书,经整理编入《吐鲁番出土文书》第七册者有如下 7 件:

1. 唐麟德二年(665)西州高昌县宁昌乡卜老师举钱契(67 TAM363:9)

2. 唐仪凤二年(677)西州高昌县宁昌乡卜老师辞为诉男及男妻不养赡事(67 TAM363:7/1)

3. 唐仪凤二年(677)西州高昌县宁昌乡某人举银钱契(67 TAM363:7/2)

4. 唐仪凤年间(676~679)西州蒲昌县竹住海佃田契(67 TAM363:7/4)

5. 唐残书牍(67 TAM363:7/3)

6. 唐景龙四年(710)卜天寿抄郑氏注《论语》(67 TAM363:8-1a)

7. 唐景龙四年(710)卜天寿抄《十二月新三台词》及诸五言诗(67 TAM363:8-2a)

从上述 7 件文书编号看,该墓葬似乎还应该有其他文书,但目前资料不全,难下判断。① 从内容看,该墓葬应与某卜姓人有关,"卜老师"应系卜天寿前辈,但究竟是什么关系,亦难下结论。

从编号看,该墓葬文书应出土于 1967 年,后来许多研究者都误写为 1969 年,大概是将初步整理出来的时间当作出土年代了。到 1972 年初,郭沫若先生先后在《新疆日报》(3 月 15 日)、《考古》杂志(当年第 1 期)和《文物》(当年第 3 期)发表了《卜天寿〈论语〉抄本后的诗词杂录》一文,后又由人民出版社出版《出土文物二三事》单行本,吐鲁番出土文书遂始为世人所知,在那个文化学术资讯极端贫乏的年代,引起的轰动是可想而知的。当时我正在乌鲁木齐工作,因为同在一所中学教书的陈戈兄调到离学校不远的新疆博物馆考古队,我和他们常来往,得以预先看到郭老论述"坎曼尔诗签"和"卜天寿抄本"的征求意见稿,在感兴趣的同时,也产生一些疑问,记得当时还很冒昧地给郭老写了一封信求教,当然并未得到回复。我后来得知,在 1972 年、1973 年,对卜天寿抄本进行释读的国内专家还有夏鼐、龙晦、潘吉星、韩国磐等先生;80 年代后,又有刘铭恕、张广达、穆舜英、周菁葆、薛宗正、张涌泉、王素、徐俊等学者发表了相关的研究成果。应该说,对该写卷文本本身的整理、释读还是比较充分的。但是,随着敦煌藏经洞文献的全面刊布、整理,一些敦煌写本和吐鲁番文书之间的关联被更多地揭示出来,其中就有敦煌学士郎某些诗抄和卜天寿诗抄近似而引发的思考,促使我去重新研读这个抄本。下面就将我的一些粗浅的体会写出来以求教于学界同仁。

---

① 67 TAM363:7 原是 7 个碎片,后来经整理可缀合成四部分,所以现在的编号是 67 TAM363:7/1-4,但 67 TAM363:1-6 是文书还是别的物品,我目前尚无法得知。

一

卜天寿所抄郑氏注《论语》177 行后有一行题记:"景龙四年三月一日私学生卜天寿[抄]",其后所抄《十二月三台词》及六首五言诗和《千字文》(一行)间又题署云"西州高昌县宁昌乡淳风里义学生卜天寿年十二"(其卷背则有"景龙四年崇贤管(馆)义学生"字样)。敦煌莫高窟藏经洞所出 P. 2643 号《古文尚书》写本卷末有乾元二年(759)"义学生王老子"的题记。可见初、盛唐之际已经以"义学"来通称馆塾一类"私学",即便是远在敦煌、西州亦如此。据《唐会要》卷三十五载:玄宗"开元二十一年五月敕……许百姓任立私学"。开元二十六年(738)朝廷再次下诏书,规定"每乡之内,各里置一学"。而在玄宗颁布此敕令前三十年,卜天寿所在的吐鲁番宁昌乡淳风里就已经开办私学了,是一点也不落后于敦煌及中原地区的。①

关于卜天寿所抄六首诗词的作者问题,徐俊曾在《敦煌学郎诗作者问题考略》(《文献》1994 年第 2 期)一文中做了考辨,指出《写书今日了》、《他道侧书易》两首在敦煌学士郎诗抄里有近似之作,因此,"这些五言通俗诗极有可能是唐五代间流行于西域地区学士郎中的一种儿童语体诗,相当于今天的儿童歌谣"。这就比郭沫若的考订又进了一步。我在若干次讲座和文章中对这些学郎诗抄均略有分析,兹不赘述。这里只想补充说明,这类诗歌常常是抄写在学童自己抄录并使用的启蒙教材上的,和今日流行的童谣不尽相同,或可称作学童诗抄。

我现在推测,吐鲁番出土文书中的儒家经籍、韵书、字书、书仪、史籍、诗文等,大多是做学童的教材之用。这一情况与敦煌写本基本相同,说明了两地的儒学传承均与公、私学校的教学读本密切相关,只是唐五代时期的敦煌除了公学(郡、州、县学)、私学外,还有为数不少的寺学,因其师资力量强、教学水准高而更具特色,容当另文分析,兹不旁述。下面先就国内所藏和德、英、俄、美等国所藏吐鲁番出土文书中的这些读本作一个不十分完整的统计。

(一) 国内所藏,上世纪 70~90 年代整理的,主要根据 10 册《吐鲁番出土文书》(文物出版社,1985~1992 年)统计,数量不多,因为这些材料大家比较熟悉,所以只列读本名称,略去了收藏编号。近年来新出土及征集的,已有刚刚出版的图录本《新获吐鲁番出土文献》(荣新江、李肖、孟宪实主编,中华书局,2008 年 5 月)可以查看,我在相关写本后括注了收藏编号。

诗经(毛诗) 孝经(孝经解) 礼记 尚书 论语(郑注)

急就章 千字文 开蒙要训 书仪 典言 晋阳秋 诗文赋(残篇)

(以下新出)

千字文(2004 TBM 115:10)

急就篇(2004 TBM 203:30-4)

论语 (97 TSYM1:12、2006 TSYIM4:5)

孝经义(97 TSYM1:12)

---

① 卜天寿抄《学问》诗前有"口觉寺学"四字,根据前面的诗抄,前三字应是"玄觉寺",第四字"学"下接下一行之"问"字,并非说明当地有寺学;下行"问"字上错开被认为是俗字的"孝"字实为"冬"字讹写,因为整个写卷里的"学"字都无一例外均写成正楷的繁体"学"字,故《学问》诗全诗应为:"学问非今日,维须迹(积)年多。冬看仟荫水,万合始成河。"

易·杂占(97 TSYM1:13)

诗经(2006 TSYIM4:2-1-4)

古诗习字(2006TZJI:006v、007v、073v、074v)

另据陈国灿教授介绍,在由旅顺博物馆和日本龙谷大学合作编选的《旅顺博物馆藏新疆出土汉文佛经选粹》(京都法藏馆,2006年3月)中也包含了少数吐鲁番地区所出的儒家经籍残卷,如《毛诗》(LM20-1504-472)、杜预注《春秋左传》(LM20-1455-14-12,LM20-1514-410)、郑玄注《论语》(LM20-1505-705)、荀悦《前汉纪》(LM20-1455-07-01)等。[①]

(二)欧美四国所藏这类读本,系据荣新江主编的《吐鲁番文书总目(欧美收藏卷)》(武汉大学出版社,2007年)统计,数量较多,为便于查考,书名后也列注了部分收藏地编号。[②]

诗经(毛诗·小雅)Ch121、Ch2254r

春秋经传集解 Ch1044r、Ch1298v

礼记 Ch2068、Дх16721+16839+16884

周易注 Ch1331r

御注孝经疏 Ch2547r

尚书 Ch3698、Or.8212/630r、Or.8212/631、Or.8212/1044-1045

春秋左传正义 Or.8212/1355

论语(何晏集解)Or.8212/632v

经义策问(礼记、孝经、论语、春秋等)7b-s、Frame1a-b

经典释文(论语)Ch3473r

庄子(成玄英疏)Ch773v

史记(仲尼弟子列传)Ch938v(李斯列传)Дх2670

汉书(张良传)Ch938r

新唐书(石雄传)Ch3623v、2132v

春秋后语注本 Ch734

文选李善注(七命)Ch3164v、Дx1551r

文选白文本(卷四、五)MIK Ⅲ520r

(柟)子赋 Ch2378

幽通赋注 Ch2400r+3693r+3699r+3865r

魏晋杂诗 Ch3693v+3699v+2400v+3865v

唐诗文残片 Or.8212/599

散花乐 Ch3002r

曲子词(?)Ch3010、3629

---

① 见陈氏未刊论文《古高昌大乘信仰盛况的再现——对旅博藏吐鲁番出土佛经整理评介》,《中国敦煌吐鲁番学会2008年度理事会议暨"敦煌汉藏佛教艺术与文化学术研讨会"论文集》。

② 这里涉及德国国家图书馆藏的下列5种编号:Ch、Ch/U、U、Mainz、Tlb、MIKⅢ;英国藏的Or.8212编号;俄国藏的Дx和SI编号;美国藏的7b-s和Frame编号。

大唐西域记卷十 Ch/U7224a

书仪(？)Ch1221r

切韵 Ch323r、343r、1072v、1106v、1150v、1246r、1538r、1577r、2437、2917r、3533、3715

韵书 Or. 8212/620v

尔雅音义 323v、343v、1246v、1577v、2917v、3716；Ch/U6783

尔雅(郭璞注)Ch/U 560、564、6779、7111；U560r

玉篇(部首) Ch1744、2241

龙龛手鉴(刻本)Ch1874

千字文 Ch640r、1234r、1805、2922、3004r、3457r、3716；Ch/U6789、6925、7296；SI 4b Kr181、182、185、194 等

九九歌诀 Ch/U 6448

习字 Ch1986r、2061r、3002v、3800、3801

又另据陈国灿、刘安志主编之《吐鲁番文书总目(日本收藏卷)》(武汉大学出版社,2005 年),日本所藏其中的这类读本大同小异,除《千字文》习写数量较多外,品种及数量均较少;但也有别的收藏地尚未见到的《太公家教》、《孙子》、《初学记》、《驾幸温泉赋》、《后汉书·杨震传》等数种,只是《驾幸温泉赋》(大谷大宫 3170、3227、3506、5789 等号)与《太公家教》(大谷大宫 3167、3507、4371 等号)出土地点不明,我颇怀疑是敦煌藏经洞写本掺入者。

从这些读本可知,在吐鲁番地区的童蒙教育中,儒家传统的识字教学(形、音、义)与诗歌教学(读、写、作)是占了很大比重而且二者密切结合的。这种教学内容与方法,既有孔子时代的"诗教"渊源可寻,又是长期实践经验积累的结果,符合中国汉文字本身蕴涵丰富文化内涵的规律,因此是科学的、成功的。例如《切韵》的普遍使用,说明韵书类工具书是诗歌教学最基本的教材,而这恰恰是我们今天中文教学中几乎已经丢失了的传统。吐鲁番出土的卜天寿抄本绝非一个孤立、偶然的现象,如果我们将它放在儒家文化教育的大背景中来观察,应该具有更普遍的意义。同样,我们将它作为例证来观察唐诗传播的途径,进而探究唐诗繁荣的原因,也可以得出更令人信服的结论。另一方面,如果我们以此来比照今天中小学校的语文教学、高校的文史教学,乃至全民的文化素养培育,就能明显地感觉到因优秀传统的断裂而造成水准的下降,值得引以为鉴。

二

现在再回到卜天寿诗抄中的《侧书》诗。诗云:"他道侧书易,我道侧书[难]。侧书还侧读,还须侧眼[看]。"郭沫若将"侧书"误校作"札书",后来的研究者均从龙晦的解释,认为是写字"姿势不正,甚至有侧起写字的习惯"。[1] 我以前也觉得这个解释大致不差,不久前在阅读敦煌 P. 3189 号三界寺学郎张彦宗所抄《开蒙要训》卷末的题诗《侧书》时,有了新的想法。该诗曰:"闻道侧书难,侧书实是难。侧书须侧立,还须侧眼看。"与卜抄应为同一诗而略有异文。所谓"侧读"、"侧眼"、"侧立",显然并非单纯的写字、

---

① 见龙晦:《卜天寿〈论语〉抄本后的诗词杂录研究和校释》,《考古》1972 年第 3 期。

阅读姿势,而涉及某种书写方式。我于是联想到敦煌、吐鲁番写卷中不仅有许多的"胡语"写本,也有不少的胡汉双语(乃至多语)写本。因为古代书写汉字的习惯是从右到左竖写,而作为拼音文字的古藏文、梵文等则是从左到右横写,如果在同一张纸上既写汉文又写藏文、梵文,就必须在转换时将身体或纸张横过来书写,即是"侧写";阅读时也得"侧立"、"侧眼"、"侧读"。这对于张彦宗、卜天寿这样的汉人学童来讲,当然不是件容易的事,故有"实是难"之叹。日本高田时雄教授在《敦煌发现的多种语言文献》、《汉语在吐鲁番》、《藏文音译〈寒食诗〉残片》、《〈杂抄〉与九九乘法表》等论文中,关于敦煌所出粟特、于阗、梵、回鹘语文献及汉藏文书写有不少精辟的论述,①具有启示意义。我们知道吐蕃占领敦煌时期推行汉语同时使用藏语言文字,后来的归义军时期仍双语并行,所以在当时的学校教学中开展双语教学是很普遍的事,这可以从许多汉藏对照读本、汉藏习字残卷中得到证明。国家图书馆善本部敦煌学资料中心的萨仁高娃女士为我提供了一张《汉藏对译千字文》的照片,其收藏编号为:Ch. 86. ii. back(IOC. C. 132),虽然还不能最后确证它的抄写年代,却肯定是敦煌藏经洞所出的写本,也最能说明这种正写汉字、侧写藏文的情形。我认为,作为丝路门户的古代吐鲁番系"西域三十六国"各种语言的交汇之地,双语乃至多语同时抄写读本的情况不仅更加普遍、突出,②而且似已在公、私学校形成制度。

《北史·西域传》关于隋代时麹氏高昌有如下记载就颇值得注意:"隋时,城有十八。其都城周回一千八百四十步,于坐室画鲁哀公问政于孔子之像。……其风俗政令,与华夏略同。……文字亦同华夏,兼用胡书。有《毛诗》、《论语》、《孝经》,置学官弟子,以相教授。虽习读之,而皆为胡语。"(中华书局,1974年版,第3214~3215页)这段话并非编者凭空穴来风之杜撰,不但说明了高昌地区的儒学源流,而且非常明确地反映了文字"兼用胡书",学校用胡语"习读"《毛诗》等儒家经典的事实。

据前引《吐鲁番文书总目(欧美收藏卷)》列目,欧美所藏吐鲁番文书中有这样一些原系汉人童蒙读物译成胡语或胡汉双语、多语的写本:

回鹘文音注汉文难字 Ch696v、1221v、2757、3582、6781

汉、回鹘文杂写 Ch1954v

回鹘语千字文 Ch6701r

回鹘语汉语千字文 SI 3Kr. 14v

藏语回鹘语双语文献 Tib 102

千字文及、回鹘文粟特语—回鹘语词汇对照表 Ch3716、Ch/U8152v

回鹘文粟特语—回鹘语词汇对照表 Ch/U6051v、6561v、7202v、7113v

回鹘语佛教诗歌 Ch/U6089v、6335v、6337v

汉、梵、回鹘语《长阿含经》词汇对照 Ch/U6092a-b

回鹘语《五更转》译本 Ch/U6223v;U472v、2302、5664、6200、6152;SI Kr. 1/15

回鹘语《大慈恩寺三藏法师传》(卷十)U1504b、1873;Ch/U6052v、6061v、6265、6268v

回鹘语荀居士抄《金刚经灵验记》 U3107

---

① 见高田时雄:《敦煌·民族·语言》一书,中华书局"世界汉学论丛",2005年版。例如他着重分析了吐鲁番出土的各种版本的《切韵》,不仅强调了《切韵》在汉字文化传统上的地位,而且指出了对回鹘的语言和社会都产生了广泛的影响;他特别提及:"像敦煌这样的佛教社会,初等教育往往在寺院中开展,因此可以考虑藏文字也会常常拿来供童蒙之用。"这些意见无疑是极具启发性的。

② 本文暂不涉及佛经的各种"胡语译本",但下面要列举的一些词语对译写本显然和翻译、诵读佛经有着最直接的关系。

回鹘语《五台山赞》U5684a‒c

所涉及的语言有汉、藏、回鹘、梵、粟特,仅此数斑,虽然还不足以使我们清晰窥见晋唐时期吐鲁番地区开展多民族语言教学的全豹,却已经可以大致了解其概貌。这不禁让我想起二十多年前在读了俄、英、法藏敦煌《长安词》(礼五台山偈)写卷后的推测:汉僧离五台山西行求法,胡僧西来至五台山礼拜,都用了相近的诗句来表达自己的心情,说明了中原汉民族与西域各民族在思想文化上的交流。① 张彦宗、卜天寿等年轻学郎们在敦煌、吐鲁番广泛传抄《侧书》诗,又是一个生动的例证。

---

① 请参见撰写于 1983 年初的拙文《列宁格勒藏敦煌〈长安词〉写卷分析》(《敦煌吐鲁番学论稿》,浙江教育出版社,2000 年 5 月,第 73 ~ 79 页)。高田时雄教授在《敦煌发现的多种语言文献》一文中也专门提及了伯希和收集的《梵—藏文对照表》和《梵—于阗语会话练习簿》,认为均和到五台山朝圣的印度和尚有关。

对一件西州回鹘时期汉文造佛塔记的研究

陈国灿   伊斯拉菲尔·玉苏甫

武汉大学   新疆维吾尔自治区博物馆

上世纪 80 年代,吐鲁番鄯善县吐峪沟的农民在一座寺庙遗址里,发现并上交了一件残纸片,不久转入新疆维吾尔自治区博物馆收藏。残纸片上残存有 7 行墨笔楷书的汉文文字。

现将其内容转录于下:

1 □教末代迴鶻愛登曷哩阿郍骨牟里彌施俱錄闋蜜伽　聖　可汗時

2 □子四月　日清信士佛弟子鄢耆鎮牟虞蜜伽長史龍公及娘子溫氏

　　　　　　　　　　　　　　男都典效達干

3 □□□山門勝地敬造佛塔其時□牧主多害伊難主 骨 都祿都 越

4 　_] 真訶達干　宰相　攝西州四府五縣事清信弟子伊 難 [主]

5 　　_] 釋門法獎念三歲乃業該經史學洞古今　[_

6 　　　_] 蘊 海納　 因 其 願 日　羯磨律師廣嚴弟子[_

7　　　　　　_]憑此舍利造□□　　為求佛道勝福善　　普施[_①

此纸前后均为齐边,文字为预先在纸上打好乌丝条栏七条后,书写于栏条上的楷书。从第3行"山门胜地,敬造佛塔"和第7行"凭此舍利造……为求佛道胜福善"等语判断,这应是一件造舍利佛塔记。

此造佛塔记缺纪年,从文中一连串的回鹘官员姓名及职务看,属于西州回鹘王国时期的文书无疑。然而究竟具体书写于何时? 则是须要首先弄清楚的。其次,通过本件内容中提到的一些回鹘官员姓名、职务及机构建制等,能说明什么? 再次,透过本件内容对认识西州回鹘社会及其对佛教的信仰又能提供些什么? 这都是本文希望探讨解决的问题。

一、关于佛教"末代"问题

本件第1行开头写有"□教末代",教字前所缺,推测为"释"字。将佛教称为"释教",是因为回鹘社会有多种宗教流行,对某一教均以其创始人名相称,如"摩尼教"、"释教"等。释教乃是指释迦牟尼所创之教。

"末代",乃是佛教系统的一种专有的概念,即指末法时代。本件造佛塔记写于释教末代——僧界认定的末法时代。这为本件的断代提供了一个重要的线索。然而在中世纪的中国,特别是在我国北方或西北地区对于佛教的"末代",是如何认定的? 这是解决本问题的关键之所在。

据《杂阿含经》、《贤劫经》等佛典所云:在释迦牟尼佛涅槃后,由"教法住世",教法会经历着正、像、末三个时期的变迁,依教法修行,即能证果,称之为正法;虽有修行,多不能证果,称之为像法,即相似之意;虽有禀教,而不能修行证果,称之为末法。对三个时期的划分,诸经论说法不一,大体可分为四类:1. 按《贤劫经》卷三、《大乘三聚忏悔经》的说法是正法五百年,而后是像法五百年。2. 按《中观论疏》及释净土的《群疑论》卷三的说法是正法一千年,像法一千年。3. 按《大方等大集经》卷五六、《摩诃摩耶经》卷下的说法是正法五百年,而后是像法一千年。4. 按《悲华经》卷七、《大乘悲分陀利经》卷五的说法是正法一千年,像法只有五百年。以上四种说法对于佛法进入末代的时间,实可分为三种,即释迦涅槃之后一千年说;一千五百年说;两千年说。大体都认为,像法转入末法后的末法期有一万年。

在古代中国的北方,大体流行后两说,即在中原地区早期流行的一千五百年说,和在民族地区流行的两千年说。

在北京房山雷音洞洞门左壁上,有唐贞观二年(628)静琬的一道题刻,转录如下:

> 释迦如来正法、像法凡千五百余岁,至今贞观二年,已浸末法七十五载。佛日既没,冥夜方深,瞽目群生,从兹失导。静琬为护正法,率己门徒知识及好施檀越,就此山顶刊华严经等一十二部,冀於旷劫,济渡苍生,一切道俗,同登正觉。②

这是按正法、像法经一千五百年后转入末法的准则,依据释迦牟尼于中国周朝昭王、穆王间在世说推

---

① 本件文书(以下简称《造佛塔记》),现藏于新疆维吾尔自治区博物馆。
② 北京图书馆金石组、中国佛教图书文物馆石经组编《房山石经题记汇编》,北京,书目文献出版社,1987年,第1页。

算出来的。

　　从现存的一些敦煌写经题记中,也能证实民间流行的末代观与静琬石刻说的一致性。如西魏"大统十七年(551)岁次辛丑五月六日抄"的司马丰祖写《十方佛名》题记中即云:

　　　　是以白衣弟子祀马部司马丰祖,自维宿墨弥深,生遭末运,若不归依三尊,凭援圣典,则长迷二谛,沉沦四流。故割减所资,敬写《十方佛名》一卷。①

所谓"生遭末运",是说生逢佛法的末代。司马丰祖写经的大统十七年(551),正是静琬所云进入末法的这一年。在此前几年,已有许多写经也提到"末代"问题,如西魏大统十一年(545),比丘惠袭写《法华经文外义》一卷的题记是:

　　　　大统十一年岁次乙丑九月廿一日,比丘惠袭於法海寺写讫,流通末代不绝也。②

比丘惠袭写《法华经文外义》,目的是为了使此经在进入末代以后流通不绝。此外,北魏永熙二年(533)比丘惠恺写《宝梁经》题记中所云"自惟福薄,生罹运末";③北魏建明二年(531)前后东阳王元荣多部写经题记中的"既居末劫"、"生在末劫"④等,都是说的面临末法时代。由此看,古代中国北方,包括西北地区,一度流行的是公元551年转入末法时代说。

　　然而,如按正法一千年、像法一千年再转入末法的标准来考虑,则进入"末代"的时间,就应该是公元1051年。我们发现,在11世纪的北中国,确有如此认识并付诸行为的实践者。1988年在辽宁朝阳北塔修缮中,考古工作者清理了这座辽代佛塔中的天宫和地宫,在天宫中发现的金、银四层套装的经塔上,第三层金套上除刻有一佛八菩萨外,还刻有题记3行:

　　　　重熙十二年四月八日午时葬,像法只八年。提点上京僧录宣演大师赐紫沙门蕴跬记。⑤

在天宫石函门板外侧,立有"石匣物帐与题名志石",在物帐末尾又刻有:

　　　　大契丹重熙十二年四月八日午时再葬,像法更有八年入末法,故置斯记。⑥

在地宫清理中,发现有石雕经幢,在第四节幢身的幢文最后刻记有:

　　　　司司轩辕亨勘梵书,东班小底张日新书。大契丹国重熙十三年岁次甲申四月壬辰朔八日己亥午

　　① 池田温:《中国古代写本识语集录》,东京,大藏出版株式会社,1990年,第125页。
　　② 同上,第123页。
　　③ 同上,第118页。
　　④ 同上,第115页。
　　⑤ 朝阳北塔考古勘察队:《辽宁朝阳北塔天宫地宫清理简报》,《文物》1992年第7期,第6页。
　　⑥ 同上,第17页。

时再葬讫,像法更有七年入末法。石匠作头刘继克镌、孟承裔镌。①

辽代重熙十二年,为公元 1043 年。按当时建塔者的观念,再过八年即进入末法,即是说到公元 1051 年,就进入末法时代了。

对 11 世纪中进入末法时代的认定,在当时恐怕已经遍及整个北中国的僧俗各界,在敦煌文书S.5520 号《敦煌社条(文样)》中记有:

> 今乃时登末代,值遇危难,准章程须更改易,佛法议诚,誓无有亏,世上人情,随心机变。②

又 P.4651 号《张愿兴王祐通投社状》中也称:"右愿兴祐通等,生居末代,长值贫门。"③敦煌文书中所云的末代,虽均无纪年,然从须改易社条章程看,应属归义军晚期敦煌地区的观念。因为从公元 10 世纪以来的一些敦煌文书里,已见有"末代"之说。S.0529 号是后唐同光二年(924)"定州开元寺参学比丘归文"往西天取经途中致沙州的一组牒启状文,在五月廿九日的状上文中即言:"归文自恨生末代,谬厕玄风。"④可见 10 世纪接近末代的新说,由河北定州到敦煌的佛教界都是相通的,且具有一致性。

10 至 11 世纪的契丹辽政权,与回鹘的关系十分特殊,因为帝后多出自回鹘述律氏,在后族的推崇影响下,契丹贵族才更深地敬奉佛教。辽太祖时与皇后述律氏于弘福寺共施观音画像,辽太宗又在此寺为皇后回鹘萧氏饭僧。⑤ 这些都说明回鹘对辽国宗教信仰的影响。在这种特殊历史背景下,西州回鹘与辽国的关系自然也就密切起来,成为辽国"外十部"之一,"附庸於辽,时叛时服,各有职贡,犹唐之有羁縻州也"。⑥ 有时以和州回鹘名义,或阿尔斯兰回鹘、或高昌国、或师子国名义,贡使于辽国。不仅在政治上为辽之附属国,而且在经济上、佛教信仰上,交往也很密切。宋人洪皓在《松漠纪闻》中记载说:

> 回鹘……多为商贾於燕。……奉释氏最盛,共为一堂,塑佛像其中,每斋必刲羊,或酒酣以指染血涂佛口,或捧其足而吮之,谓为亲敬。诵经则衣袈裟,作西竺语,燕人或俾之,祈祷多验。……其在燕者皆久居业成,能以金相瑟瑟为首饰。⑦

宋人所称的"燕",即是辽国的南京。从所记看,在辽国的南京,居住着不少回鹘商人,他们信仰释教,而且影响到当地居民。辽圣宗统和十九年(1001),"春正月甲申,回鹘进梵僧名医"。⑧ 咸雍三年(1067),"十一月壬辰,夏国遣使进回鹘僧、金佛、梵觉经",⑨表明到了 11 世纪,回鹘的佛教对西夏、对辽政权都在

---

① 朝阳北塔考古勘察队:《辽宁朝阳北塔天宫地宫清理简报》,《文物》1992 年第 7 期,第 22 页。
② 宁可、郝春文辑校《敦煌社邑文书校注》,南京:江苏古籍出版社,1997 年,第 47 页。
③ 同上,第 703 页。
④ 唐耕耦、陆宏基:《敦煌社会经济文献真迹释录》,全国图书馆文献缩微复制中心,1990 年,第五辑第 9 页。
⑤ 《辽史》卷三《太宗纪》,中华书局,1974 年,第 37 页。参见杨富学:《回鹘之佛教》第一章第六节"回鹘佛教对北方诸族的影响",新疆人民出版社,1998 年,第 67 页。
⑥ 《辽史》卷三三《部族下》,第 393 页。
⑦ [宋]洪皓:《松漠纪闻》卷一,文渊阁《四库全书》本,第 5 页。
⑧ 《辽史》卷一四《圣宗纪》,第 156 页。
⑨ 《辽史》卷二二《道宗纪》,第 267 页。

进行着交流并相互影响着。在旅顺博物馆藏的大批来自吐鲁番出土的佛经残片中,有不少木刻经文残片,其中"不乏辽代刻本",属辽代雕版刻印的《契丹藏》。①《契丹藏》在吐鲁番的寺庙遗址中的出土,不仅印证了西州回鹘与辽国佛事交往的密切,而且表明教义信仰的一体性。由此不难看出,西州回鹘造佛塔记中所云的"释教末代",应是与辽国末代说具有一脉相承的关联。在教义义理的见解上也应是一致的。

辽国的佛教僧团既然认定重熙二十年(1051)进入了末法时代,那么西州回鹘造佛塔记中所云的"释教末代",也应是指的公元1051年起始的末代。而回鹘爱登葛哩阿郁骨牟里弥施俱录阙密伽圣可汗在位的时间,亦应在1051年的前后。遗憾的是第2行"子四月日"之前一字全缺,否则,依据具体干支是可确定本件书写的年月的。

二、造塔记中的回鹘职事官及机构建制

造塔记第1行提到的"回鹘爱登葛哩阿郁骨牟里弥施俱录阙密伽圣可汗"②是史籍及出土文献中从未见过的汗王名,但却出现过相近似的名字。据学者们研究,被认为是漠北回纥汗国(744～840)的第11位可汗"爱登里啰汩没密施合句录毗伽可汗(ay tängrid ā qut bulmïš alp külüg qaɣan),即为公元832～839年出现在漠北高原上的彰信可汗胡特勤"。③ 显然,此合句录毗伽可汗不是西州回鹘的阙密伽圣可汗。

从《造佛塔记》中确定的"释教末代"看,阙密伽圣可汗应属于公元11世纪中期前后的西州回鹘国的一位国王。在《辽史·道宗纪》中,记载了道宗在平定一场政变后,发布嘉奖加封者的名单中,有"回鹘海兰纽斡哩……并加上将军",④时间为清宁九年(1063)。"海",相当于"爱";"兰纽斡哩"亦与"登葛哩"音近;"海兰纽斡哩",有可能是回鹘语 ay tängri 之契丹语读音的音译。不知《辽史》所记被加上将军号者,是否就是这里的阙密伽圣可汗? 如果是的话,则可确定此可汗在公元1063年仍在汗位上。

程溯洛先生曾作《高昌回鹘亦都护谱系考》,将其王室谱系分为两个阶段,即唐末至西辽为第一阶段;元代为第二阶段。他仅依靠汉文史料列举了属第一阶段的五位汗王。其中,这一阶段真正属于西州回鹘王者,仅有庞特勤、仆固俊、毕勒哥三人。⑤ 此处的密伽圣可汗,应该属于仆固以后、毕勒哥以前的一代汗王,至于究竟属于西州回鹘王室的第几代? 则恐怕是难以查考了。不过,我们还是想对此提出自己

① 李际宁:《关于旅顺博物馆藏吐鲁番出土木刻本佛经残片的考察》,旅顺博物馆、龙谷大学共编:《旅顺博物馆藏新疆汉文佛经研究论文集》,京都,2006年,第236页。

② 这位回鹘可汗的称号中,除"圣"字表示意译外,其余均为回鹘语音译,还原成回鹘语应是:回鹘—uyɣur,爱—ay,登葛哩阿郁—tängridä,骨—qut,牟里弥施—bulmïš,俱录—külüg,阙—köl,密伽—bilgä,圣—ïduq,可汗—qaɣan;即 uyɣur ay tängridä qut bulmïš külüg köl bilgä ïduq qaɣan(可意译为:从月天得到福位的著名智库圣可汗)。须指出,此可汗称号中的"登葛哩阿郁"(回鹘语 tängridä 之音译)在蒙古人民共和国哈喇巴勒哈逊出土的《九姓回鹘爱登里啰汩没密施合毗伽可汗圣文神武碑并序》(见罗振玉:《和林金石录》罗振玉校补,辽居杂著本)中出现的几位可汗称号里和《新唐书·回鹘传》所提及的回纥可汗称号中,均以"登里啰"形式出现。在回鹘可汗称号中,一般在"爱登里啰"与"汩没密施"之间不会出现 alp(音译为合,意为英武)一词,在"爱登里"与"汩没密施"间更不会有之;一般音译为"爱登里啰汩没密施"之回鹘语,在《造塔记》中音译成"爱登葛哩阿郁骨牟里弥施",可见"登里啰"和"登葛哩阿郁"均为回鹘语 tängridä 之音译。"登葛哩阿郁"等五个字分别为 tän(登)+ g(葛)+ r(哩)+ i(阿)+ dä(郁)[或 täng(登葛)+ ri(哩阿)+ dä(郁)]等的音译。这里,"阿郁"(ē nuó)不该是 alp 的音译。

③ 森安孝夫:《ウイグル゠マニ教史の研究》,日本大阪大学学刊,1991年,第182～183页。

④ 《辽史》卷二二《道宗纪》,第263页。

⑤ 程溯洛:《高昌回鹘亦都护谱系考》,《西北史地》1983年第4期,第13～17页。

的初步认识。

众所周知,目前就高昌回鹘王室谱系而言,其第二阶段较清楚,因为学者们业已从已研究整理好的汉文、回鹘文《亦都护高昌王世勋碑》、史籍以及波斯史料等为依据解决了不少问题。[①] 但是第一阶段尚不太清楚。学者们为了弄清这一问题,亦付出了努力。特别需要指出的是,日本学者森安孝夫根据回鹘文文献的汗王称号,已整理出 10 世纪 50 年代左右至 11 世纪 60 年代左右间的高昌回鹘汗王顺序(以下简称"汗王顺序")。[②] 显然,这对高昌回鹘王室属第一阶段汗王谱系的建立,具有较高的参考价值。对于《造佛塔记》中的汗王在"汗王顺序"中的排位,我们的考虑是:

1. 在本文的第一部分中,我们已论述了《造佛塔记》所云的"释教末代"应指的是公元 1051 年开始的年代。而回鹘爱登曷哩阿郁骨牟里弥施俱录阙密伽圣可汗在位的时间,亦应该在 1051 年前后这个时段来作出考察。

2.《造佛塔记》中的回鹘可汗称号与《汗王顺序》中排列在?—1017?—1019—1020—1031?—? 年间在位的可汗称号,即"kün ay tängridä qut bulmïš uluɣ qut ornanmïš alpïn ärdamin il tutmïš alp arslan qutluɣ köl bilgä tängri xan"(意译为:从日、月、天得到福位,置身于福位上,以勇敢与品德治国的勇猛狮子——有福的智海天〈可〉汗)有相似之处。譬如:前者为"从月天得到福位……智海圣可汗",后者则是"从日、月、天得到福位的……智海天可汗"。可见两者中有一定的联系。

3. 回鹘文哈密本《弥勒会见记》的抄成时间是"qoyn yï zün ücünc ay iki otuzqa(羊年闰三月二十二日)",即"tängri bögü il bilgä arslan tängri uyɣur tärkän"(回鹘天圣国智狮子天王)在位期间。[③] 有学者曾论述过这里的羊年应指丁未年(1067)的理由,并认为"tängri bögü il bilgä arslan tängri uyɣur tärkän"的在位时间在?—1067—? 年间。[④]

新疆维吾尔自治区博物馆与德国法兰克福大学、日本京都大学共同合作,对馆藏的《吐火罗文 A〈弥勒会见记〉》和《回鹘文哈密本〈弥勒会见记〉》无文字之碎片进行了碳素年代测定。结果《回鹘文哈密本〈弥勒会见记〉》之碳素年代在公元 980 ~ 1035 年间(可能性为 95.4%)。[⑤] 我们依据《二十史朔闰表》[⑥]的查找结果看,在公元 980 ~ 1035 年间只有己亥(999)闰三月,而癸未(983)、乙未(995)、丁未(1007)、辛未(1031)中均无闰三月。自"20 世纪 90 年代以来,尽管常规碳十四测年技术有了改进,又发明了加速器质谱记数法(AMS),采用了系列样品高精度曲线拟合法,但其测定数据有误差的弊端,并未从根本上改变"。[⑦] 故以上的碳素测年数据只可作为参考。

至于丁未年(1067),此年就有闰三月。因此,"回鹘天圣国智狮子天王"在位于?—1067—? 年间的理由可以成立。我们根据以上三点,认为《造佛塔记》所提及的"阙密伽圣可汗",应该是在"从日、月、天得到福位的……智海天可汗"之后,而在"回鹘天圣国智狮子天王"之前的西州回鹘可汗。

---

① 程溯洛:《高昌回鹘亦都护谱系考》,《西北史地》1983 年第 4 期,第 13 ~ 17 页。

② 森安孝夫:《ウイグル=マニ教史の研究》,第 182 ~ 183 页。

③ 伊斯拉菲尔·玉苏甫等:《回鹘文〈弥勒会见记〉》1,乌鲁木齐:新疆人民出版社,1987 年,第 114 页。

④ 森安孝夫:《トルコ佛教の源流と古トルコ語佛典の出現》,《史学杂志》98-4,1989 年,第 1 ~ 35 页。

⑤ 《On the radiocarbon — dating of the samples related to Tohaea characters(3)》,TITUSproject.(Representative:Tatsushi TAMAI, Frankfurt University)报告者:河野益近(京都大学),2005 年 9 月。

⑥ 陈垣:《二十史朔闰表(附西历回历)》,中华书局,1962 年,第 121 页。

⑦ 张国硕:《考古学年代与碳十四年代的碰撞》,《中国文物报》2005 年 4 月 8 日,第 7 版。

《造佛塔记》第2～3行有"清信士、佛弟子鄢者镇牟虞蜜伽、长史龙公及娘子温氏……山门胜地,敬造佛塔"。表明造塔主是鄢者镇长史龙公及娘子温氏,牟虞蜜伽(为回鹘语美称 bögü bilgä 之音译,是贤明之意)是给龙公的回鹘语官封号。鄢者,即焉者,始置镇于唐贞观末年。《旧唐书·西戎龟兹传》载:"先是,太宗既破龟兹,移置安西都护府于其国城,以郭孝恪为都护,兼统于阗、疏勒、碎叶,谓之四镇。"此条未列焉者而列碎叶,岑仲勉先生考订说:"碎叶列四镇,是高宗时事;此处当作焉者,唐是时势力未达碎叶也。"①焉者镇自建立后,一直存在到公元九世纪回鹘人的到来。《新唐书·突骑施传》载:"有特庞勒居焉者城,称叶护,余部保金娑岭,众至二十万。"特庞勒,即庞特勤,这是指的"公元840年,庞特勤率领十五部西奔阿尔泰山、西至中亚楚河流域葛逻禄人的住地十多年,在856年至857年之间,他本人大概想在西域开辟疆土,于是又东返天山南麓安西四镇中的焉者定居下来,自己当上回鹘的可汗,人数有二十万"。② 由此可见,焉者镇在回鹘人到来后,一度成为王国经营发展的基地,当然也是西州回鹘王国统治下的一个部分。"长史龙公",是指焉者镇的长史。据《旧唐书·职官志》,唐镇设有镇将、镇副,而无长史。然而,此焉者镇属唐安西四镇之一的镇,具有都督府一级的规格,则有都督一员,长史一员。从长史一称看,西州回鹘王国实际上仍保持着唐焉者都督府的建置。《旧唐书·焉者传》称:"焉者国……其王姓龙氏。"由此知长史龙公,应是原焉者国的王族龙姓人。透过这一点不难看出,西州回鹘王国继承了唐的民族自治政策,很注意用本族人统治本族地区。北宋太平兴国六年(981)以后,王延德出使西州回鹘,亲见"所统有南突厥、北突厥、大众熨、小众熨、样磨、割录、黠戛司、末蛮、格哆族、预龙族之名甚众"。③ 对于这众多的民族,想必也采用了同样的统治方式,唯其如此,才能保持西州回鹘王国东起伊州、西抵安西广大地域内的稳定统治。

随同焉者长史龙公造塔的有"牧主多害,伊难主骨都录都越,男都典效达干"。牧,应是指的州牧,唐制:"京兆、河南、太原等府,三府牧各一员。"④此乃沿于古制,如《旧唐书·职官志》所载:"牧,古官,舜置十二牧是也。秦以京城守为内史,汉武改为尹。后魏、北齐、周、隋又以京守为牧。武德初,因隋置牧,以亲王为之。"⑤据此得知,唐京都的最高长官称为牧,且以宗室亲王为之。西州乃西州回鹘王国国都之所在,故西州的最高州官,也仿效唐制,称牧为"牧主"、"牧首"。唐大中五年(851)西州回鹘首领安宁等至长安朝贡,为此唐宣宗下《西州回鹘授骁卫大将军制》,制文云:

> 西州牧首颉干迦思俱宇合逾越密施莫贺都督宰相安宁等,忠勇奇志魁健雄姿,怀西戎之腹心,作中夏之保障,相其君长,颇有智谋。今者交臂来朝,稽颡请命。丈组寸印,高位重爵,举以授尔,用震殊邻。无忘敬恭,宜念终始,可云麾将军守左骁卫大将军,外置同正员,余如故。⑥

这道制文将回鹘在西州的最高长官称为"西州牧首",这应是"牧主"称号的一个具体来源。本记中的西

① 岑仲勉:《西突厥史料补阙考证》,中华书局,1958年,第29页。
② 程溯洛:《高昌回鹘亦都胡谱系考》,《西北史地》1983年第4期,第15页。
③ 王延德:《西州使程记》,杨建新主编《古西行记选注》,宁夏人民出版社,1987年,第160页。
④ 《旧唐书》卷四四《职官志·州县官员》,中华书局,1975年,第1915页。
⑤ 同上,第1915～1916页。
⑥ 杜牧:《樊川文集》卷二〇,《全唐文》卷七五〇,中华书局,1983年,第7770页。

州牧主名多害，①其下的"伊难主骨都录都越"，②应该是多害的副手。在骨都录都越名的右侧，有一行小字："男都典效达干。"从都典一词观察，其职务类似于唐之州录事参军；其古音"效"不像回鹘语人名的音译；都典效达干，当是骨都录都越之子，故在其名前冠一"男"字。达干系回鹘的一种官号，张广达先生说："从实际例证来看，它是专统兵马的武职官称，回鹘文的原文作 Tarqan。"③从效达干的职事为都典看，西州回鹘时期的达干，亦存在当人名使用的现象，但不排除成为一种勋号的可能性。再说，统兵马的武职官员称号之 Tarqan，如果在这里表示人名或勋号的话，那么都典或许与"都监"（宋代兵马都监的简称）有所关联。

《造佛塔记》第4行有"宰相摄西州四府五县事、清信弟子伊难[主]……"，伊难[主]是西州回鹘王国的宰相，同时又兼管着西州四府五县的事务。西州回鹘王国统治的地域，如前所论，远比唐西州的境域要大得多。然而，西州四府五县却是王国的核心地区，故其事务也须王国的宰相兼摄过问，前揭唐宣宗时西州牧首宰相安宁即是先例。"西州四府五县"是指唐初建西州以后，在吐鲁番盆地建立的高昌、交河、柳中、蒲昌、天山等五个县，和相继建立的前庭、岸头、蒲昌、天山等四个府兵折冲都尉府。唐代的这一建制，基本上维持到公元8世纪末唐政权退出西州。此后的情况，由于史籍缺载而不清楚。通过本记才得知，回鹘人来到西州建立王国时，对西州的地方建制，仍保持着唐制而未改，直到11世纪中叶，还存在着"西州四府五县"的名称和事务。

我们也注意到，成书于11世纪70年代的《突厥语大辞典》里，没有西州"四府五县"的记载，只提及高昌回鹘的唆里迷（即焉者）、高昌、彰八里、别失八里、仰吉八里等五座城市，④至于四府五县中每个县的具体建制是否还存在？由于资料的缺乏，目前尚无法作出判断。不过，从今天的现实生活中，仍能找到唐县名的影子，如高昌，经回鹘语发音逐渐转写为"火州"；柳中，经回鹘语发音逐渐转写为"鲁克沁"；蒲昌，经回鹘语发音转写而为"辟展"等。⑤ 这些仍能反映出回鹘人对唐代建制名称的继承。

三、西州回鹘对唐文化的承袭

从《造佛塔记》中看到，一批西州回鹘的官员和焉者地方的官员，于11世纪中，来到本记的出土地——吐峪沟，敬造舍利佛塔的情景。造舍利佛塔的目的在本记的第7行已有表述："为求佛道胜福善，普施……"表明了这批回鹘官员们对佛教的虔诚信仰。回鹘原本信仰摩尼教，来到西州后，遇到了此地十分兴旺的佛教信仰和较发达的唐文化，对此，回鹘统治者们不但没有排斥，反而由尊重、敬仰，进而步入接受、信奉。敦煌文书 S.6551 号讲经文，经张广达、荣新江先生共同研究，确定为公元930年前后、来自西

---

① 多害，"多"之古音为 ta，"害"之古音则是 ɣai 或 ɣät（见郭锡良：《汉字古音手册》，北京大学出版社，1985年，第33、123页）。多害的古音 taɣai 相合于回鹘语 taɣay。Taɣai 本义为"舅、伯叔，有时亦当人名使用"，如："ikinti oɣlum taɣay ygän"（"我次子塔奈依·依甘"；参见伊斯拉菲尔·玉苏甫：《回鹘文〈弥勒会见记〉》1，新疆人民出版社，1987年，第114页）。

② "伊难主骨都录都越"："伊难主"（亦作伊难珠。参阅耿世民《古代突厥文碑铭研究》，中央民族大学出版社，2005年，第135~136页）为回鹘语 ïnancu 或 ïnanc 的音译，指大臣或宰相官号；"骨都录"（史籍中作骨咄禄）为回鹘语 qutluɣ 之音译，是人名；"都越"，由于与之相连贯的第4行开头的几字缺失，故不好解释，是否为近似于唐宋时期的勋官"都尉"的一种勋号？

③ 张广达、荣新江：《有关西州回鹘的一篇敦煌汉文文献——S6551讲经文的历史学研究》，张广达：《西域史地丛稿初编》，上海古籍出版社《中华学术丛书》，1995年，第229页。

④ 参见麻赫默德·喀什噶里：《突厥语大词典》（汉文译本，校仲彝　刘静嘉译）第1卷，北京：民族出版社，2002年，第121~122页。

⑤ 参见于维诚：《新疆建置沿革与地名研究》，乌鲁木齐：新疆人民出版社，1986年，第28、32~33页。

州回鹘的一篇汉文文献。他们指出:"这篇讲经文说明,930 年前后,佛教在西州回鹘已经具有相当大的势力,以致这位外来的僧人敢于否定包括回鹘曾立为国教的摩尼教而极力颂扬佛教。"①在《讲经文》中有一段话,颇值得注意:"天王乃名传四海,德布乾坤,卅余年国泰民安,早受诸佛之记。"②这是将国泰民安归之于受诸佛授记的结果。由此看,在公元 10 世纪初,以西州回鹘天王为首的统治者及贵族,已经接受了佛教信仰。

上世纪初在高昌故城 X 遗址寺院废墟中出土的回鹘文木杵铭文,经研究判定为公元 948 年回鹘"公主殿下"和"沙州将军"二人的造寺祈福文。③文有 20 行,其中说道:

> 我们心中怀着一种决不离开,也不放弃"三宝"的纯洁意念。……当我们听说了如此高尚的壮举之后,我们二人就恭恭敬敬地为修建一座寺庙而夯入了一根 sat 木杵以为基础。但愿这一功德善业所产生的力量能使我们以后与崇高的弥勒佛相会;但愿我们能从弥勒佛那里得到崇高的成佛的祝福;但愿我们借助这一祝福所产生的力量,在永劫间和三无量限中将六条解脱之路走完。但愿以后(重新)诞生在一个佛国世界中!

从这段祈福文中,可以看到回鹘贵族们对弥勒佛信仰的无限虔诚。同时参与祈福者,列有公主和可敦者 15 人,都督、将军、达干等官员者约 25 人,"他们当为该寺院的施主,可见政府官员对佛庙兴建活动的支持"。④

也是在 20 世纪初,在吐鲁番胜金口寺庙遗址中,出土了一根类似的汉文木杵文书,写于"岁次癸未之载五月廿五日辛巳",经研究判断为公元 983 年,相当于北宋太平兴国八年。回鹘"天特银、天公主"在"新兴谷内高胜岩嵧福德之处"施建伽蓝所写的功德记,目的也是"引将弥勒下生之时",能与弥勒相会,能"安至天上远权菩提,一时成佛"。⑤ 这一方面反映出到 10 世纪末,佛教信仰在西州回鹘地区的方兴未艾;另一方面也表明汉语言文字和唐文化,伴随着佛教的流行,仍在这里使用着、流传着。

就在上述汉文木杵文书书写的同时,适逢宋朝的使臣王延德来到了西州,他所见到的情形是:"用开元七年历,以三月九日为寒食,余二社、冬至亦然。……佛寺五十余区,皆唐朝所赐额,寺中有《大藏经》、《唐韵》、《玉篇》、《经音》等。……有敕书楼,藏唐太宗、明皇御札诏敕,缄锁甚谨。"⑥五十多座佛寺"皆唐朝所赐额",寺中藏的佛典及其他汉籍自然也是唐朝留下的,反映出西州回鹘王国不仅完好无损地保存了唐代留下的佛教文化遗产,而且还让其在继续发挥着作用。

以上属于西州回鹘对唐佛教文化方面的继承,而在政治方面,回鹘与唐至宋的中央王朝关系一

---

① 张广达、荣新江:《有关西州回鹘的一篇敦煌汉文文献——S6551 讲经文的历史学研究》,载张广达:《西域史地丛稿初编》,第235、218 页。另有李正宇:《S6551 讲经文作于西州回鹘国辨正》一文(《新疆社会科学》1989 年第 4 期,第 88 ~ 97 页),认为此文写于唐末天复、天祐间(901 ~ 907)。此处从张、荣说。

② 张广达、荣新江:《有关西州回鹘的一篇敦煌汉文文献——S6551 讲经文的历史学研究》,载张广达:《西域史地丛稿初编》,第218 页。

③ 杨富学:《吐鲁番出土回鹘文木杵铭文初释》,《西域敦煌宗教论稿》,兰州:甘肃文化出版社,1998 年,第 257 ~ 276 页。

④ 同上,第 257 ~ 276 页。

⑤ 关于此汉文木杵文书,勒柯克(A. von Le Coq)、缪勒(F. W. K. Müller)、伯希和(P. Pelliot)、葛玛丽(A. von Gabain)、哈密顿(J. R. Hamilton)、安部健夫、森安孝夫和岑仲勉等均有过考释与研究,此处所录据岑仲勉:《吐鲁番木柱刻文略释》,载《金石论丛》,上海古籍出版社,1981 年,第 453 ~ 456 页。

⑥ 王延德:《西州使程记》,杨建新主编《古西行记选注》,银川:宁夏人民出版社,1987 年,第 158 ~ 161 页。按王延德于北宋太平兴国六年(981)五月出使,于七年四月至高昌,八年春始别高昌东返,可见 983 年初,他还在西州回鹘王国活动。

直很好,长期保持着贡使关系,自唐乾元、至德以降,经几代公主和亲后,"谊为舅甥,岁有通和,情无诡计",①五代以后,回鹘"世以中国为舅,朝廷每赐书诏,亦常以'甥'呼之"。②西州回鹘国的可汗们,正是以唐王朝统治的继承者、代唐执政的唐外甥心态来统治西州的,所以对唐太宗、唐明皇以来的历代诏敕、御札等,都当作法权上的圣物,而加以特别珍惜宝藏之。由此才好理解回鹘来到西州后、全盘承袭唐朝政治制度的背景。不仅如此,而且对于西州流行已久的佛教,也是当作唐文化而全盘加以接受的。从王延德的记载中,还可看到,回鹘人来到西州后,用的是唐开元七年的历法,也开始过起了寒食节。所谓"余二社、冬至亦然",是说春、秋祭社的聚会和冬至节,也和寒食过节一样。这些本是汉、唐以来汉民族的民间节令风俗,到10世纪也都被西州回鹘的广大群众所接受,这恐怕与受到西州原住汉民生活习俗的感染有关。

在了解到10世纪以来的西州回鹘社会状况后,再来看本《造佛塔记》中对法奖和尚的赞扬,就更好理解了。《造佛塔记》第5行云:"释门法奖念三岁,乃业该经史,学洞古今。"法奖,属于释门的法名,此人二十三岁,即对经、史的学问兼备,且对古今世事都能洞悉了解,由此看,他是出自汉族的一位学问僧。联系到第7行"凭此舍利造……",推测此舍利有可能是法奖圆寂后的火化之物,凭此舍利而造佛塔。在11世纪的西州回鹘王国,仍有这样"业该经史,学洞古今"人物的存在,并且受到地方官员们的崇敬,说明唐文化在这里不但没有泯灭,而且伴同着佛教一起在继续传扬着。

《造佛塔记》第6行列有"羯磨律师广严,弟子……",律师,乃是释门中指通晓律藏之人,亦可称之为持律师,在中国佛教史上,著名的律师不少,见于诸《高僧传》中的"明律篇",如唐代的道宣、怀素等。③羯磨一词,原出梵语 karman,意译称之为"业",乃指办事、作法、行为之意;亦可指受戒、忏悔等有关戒律行事之场合。④羯磨律师,是指负责戒坛指导受戒者明律、作礼、乞戒的僧人。造舍利佛塔时,羯磨律师及其弟子均到场,表示了此事的隆重庄严,这也是对唐佛事传统的因袭。

释门僧界有一套僧官系统,它始于魏晋,发展完善于唐朝。西州回鹘也建立了一套僧官系统,敦煌文书 P.3672 号是一件西州回鹘《赏紫金印检校廿二城胡汉僧尼事内供奉骨都录沓密施呜瓦伊支都统大德致沙州宋僧政等状》,状文云:"昨近十月五日,圣 天恩判:补充都统大德,兼赐金印,统压千僧。为缘发书慰问。"⑤作为僧官的"大德",起于何时?据《续高僧传·释吉藏传》载:"武德之初,僧过繁结,置十大德,纲维法务,宛从物议,居其一焉。"⑥由此知,设置大德这一僧官来统领僧尼,始于唐武德初年。然而,自唐中宗以后,大德一称"已是对德劭位尊者的荣宠之称"了。⑦关键在于"都统"一称上,都统,可以看作是都僧统的简称,僧统始置于北魏,唐代沿袭此称,沙州归义军时期置"河西都僧统"以统全境僧尼。西州回鹘的都统大德实际上是对境域内廿二城胡汉僧尼事进行管理的僧官,由回鹘圣天可汗所任命,看来这套系统也是从敦煌引进过来的。本件状文无纪年,从所涉人名推测,或许属10世纪后半纪至11世纪初的文献,⑧它反映出在西州的廿二城有着大量的胡汉僧尼。汉籍僧尼的存在,也反映了汉族百姓的存

① 杜牧:《西州回鹘授骁卫大将军制》,《全唐文》卷七五〇,北京:中华书局,1983年,第7770页。
② 《旧五代史》卷一三八《回鹘传》,北京:中华书局,1975年,第1841页。
③ 释赞宁:《宋高僧传》卷一四,中华书局,1987年,第327~330页、第334~335页。
④ 慈怡主编《佛光大辞典》,台北:佛光出版社,第7册,第6137~6138页。
⑤ 唐耕耦、陆宏基:《敦煌社会经济文献真迹释录》第5辑,第35~36页。
⑥ 释道宣:《续高僧传》卷一一《释吉藏传》,《高僧传合集》,上海古籍出版社,1991年,第194页。
⑦ 张弓:《汉唐佛寺文化史》卷上,中国社会科学出版社,1997年,第359页。
⑧ 森安孝夫在《敦煌与西回鹘王国——寄自吐鲁番的书信及礼物》(陈俊谋译本,载《西北史地》1987年第3期)一文中认为"可以断定此书简乃是10世纪后半期前后数十年间的东西"。

在。这正是西州回鹘时期仍有汉文文献产生的基础。

另外需要说明的一点是，由于有些回纥或回鹘语词在《九姓回鹘爱登里啰汩没密施合毗伽可汗圣文神武碑并序》、各类史籍（简称《神武碑》）与《造佛塔记》中的音译用词不同。如：tängridä、qut、bulmiš、bilgä、bögü、qutluɣ 等，在《神武碑》及各类史籍中作登里啰、汩、没密施、毗伽、牟羽、骨咄禄，而在《造佛塔记》里作登曷哩阿郁、骨、牟里弥施、密伽、牟虞、骨都禄。因此我们不能排除《造佛塔记》出自懂汉文的回鹘人之手的可能性。因为 11 世纪的著名维吾尔学者麻赫默德·喀什噶里曾明确指出："回鹘人的语言是纯粹的突厥语，但他们彼此交谈时还使用一种方言。回鹘人使用本书开头部分谈到的二十四个字母的突厥文（指回鹘人还有和秦人文字相似的另一种除了非穆斯林的回鹘人和秦人外，其他人是不认识这种文字的。"[1]

四、结　语

西州回鹘时期的这件汉文造佛塔记，是一件十分珍贵的地下出土历史文献。通过对它的考察和研究，我们可以获得以下几个方面的认识：

首先，关于造佛塔记的写作年代，记中所写释教"末代"，提供了一个大的时限。佛教末世，即末代说，在古代中国的北方有两种，一种是稍为早期流行于中原地区的佛灭后一千五百年，即公元 551 年转入末世说；一种是稍晚多流行于北方民族地区的佛灭后两千年、即公元 1051 年转入末世说。有充分证据证明契丹建立的辽国及归义军政权下的敦煌都是信奉的佛灭后两千年转入末世说，而与辽国和敦煌有着密切佛事往来的西州回鹘，也受其影响，奉行佛灭后两千年即公元 1051 年转入末世说，由此可以判定，本《造佛塔记》写于公元 11 世纪中期之前后。而本《造佛塔记》中写的"回鹘爱登曷哩阿郁骨牟里弥施俱录阙密伽圣可汗"在位的时间，亦应在 11 世纪中期之前后。

其次，《造塔记》所提及的"阙密伽圣可汗"，应该是在 1031 年还在位的"从日、月、天得到福位的……智海天可汗"之后，而在 1067 年在位的"回鹘天圣国智狮子天王"之前的西州回鹘可汗。从《造佛塔记》中所列官人职称看到，西州回鹘汗国不仅继承了唐统治机构，还延续着唐的一套政策。"长史龙公"，是指焉耆镇的长史，从长史一称看，西州回鹘王国仍保持着唐焉耆都督府的建置。长史龙公，应是原焉耆国的王族龙姓人。由此看，西州回鹘王国继承了唐的民族自治政策，很注意用本族人统治本族地区。西州乃西州回鹘王国国都之所在，故西州的最高州官，也仿效唐制，称为牧或"牧主"、"牧首"。本记中的西州牧主名多害就是一例。记中所列"宰相摄西州四府五县事、清信弟子伊难[主]……"，反映出回鹘人来到西州建立王国后，对西州的地方建制，仍然保持唐制而未改，直到 11 世纪中叶，仍然存在着"西州四府五县"的名称。由于四府五县属王国核心地区，故由宰相兼管。

第三，《造塔记》中记载的一批西州回鹘的官员和焉耆地方的官员，参与造佛塔活动的虔诚，表明到 11 世纪中，西州回鹘的汗王以及贵族、官员，已将宗教信仰完全转向了佛教。从吐鲁番出土的几件汉文佛事文献看，早在 10 世纪中期，就有一些回鹘贵族，成了虔诚的佛教徒。西州回鹘对佛教文化的迅速接受，与西州原有住民对佛教传统信仰的影响不无关系，宋朝的使臣王延德来到西州，见到五十多座"唐朝

---

① 麻赫魔德·喀什噶里：《突厥语大词典》第一卷，第 32 页。

所赐额"的佛寺及所藏佛典、汉籍保存完好,反映出西州回鹘王国不仅完好无损地保存了唐代留下来的佛教文化遗产,而且还让其在继续发挥着作用。西州回鹘国的可汗们,常以唐外甥自称,他们到西州是以唐王朝统治的继承者、代唐执政的唐外甥心态来统治西州的,所以对唐太宗、唐明皇以来的历代诏敕、御札等,都当作法权上的圣物,而加以特别珍惜宝藏之。由此才好理解回鹘来到西州后、全盘承袭唐朝政治制度的背景。进而才能认识到西州回鹘接受佛教文化,是作为接受唐文化来进行的。随着对佛教的崇拜,而附着在佛教上的礼仪制度、僧官制度及汉文化传统的东西,也一起被西州回鹘统治者们所全盘继承,这从对一位有学问的汉族僧人修舍利佛塔的礼仪中,已得到了充分的体现。

吐鲁番所出夫役文书与唐代杂徭研究

程喜霖

湖北大学历史系

关于唐代杂徭问题,由于史载零散或阙漏,导致它成为唐史研究中的疑难问题之一。我因多年整理研究吐鲁番文书,注意到唐代赋役文书中的夫役文书,发现夫役文书乃研究唐代杂徭史所罕见的新鲜资料,补充了史载的阙漏,在杂徭的实施方面填补了空白。我利用这些新鲜的文书资料,兹著《唐代西州杂徭研究》之一、之二、之三。① 虽然如此,若从宏观全方位观察夫役文书的价值还有未尽之言,故特作是文对这组夫役文书在研究杂徭的重要意义及解决何种问题,作一综合考察。

一、唐代杂徭研究述略

要梳理吐鲁番所出夫役文书与唐代杂徭一些问题,知其学术价值,必先明乎唐代杂徭的研究状况。唐长孺先生有云:"关于杂徭的研究,国内唐耕耦、张泽咸、程喜霖诸同志均有专文。日本堀敏一氏列举日本学者的研究成果。""杂徭的问题相当复杂,诸家之说有颇大分歧……。我以为广义的杂徭包括正役以外的各种劳役,一般恐怕只指带有地方性的劳役。"②

堀敏一《均田制研究》专设杂徭一节,③将日本学者研究杂徭的成果归纳为丁中皆要服杂徭,"历来争论最激烈的是关于杂徭的日数问题":

"曾我部静雄氏的四十天说(《均田法及其税役制度》第二一六页以下)。"

"宫崎市定氏的不满四十天,仅三十九天的说法(《唐代赋役制度新考》)。"

"浜口重国氏的五十天说(《论唐代杂徭的义务天数》)。……正役一天 = 杂徭二天。"

"吉田孝氏观点(《日唐律令中的杂徭的比较》)……认为在三十九日以内是地方官可以无偿使役的劳动。"堀氏"认为吉田氏的说法是合理的"。

概而言之,日本大多数学者认为杂徭的重要史料是《白氏六帖事类集》卷二二《征役第七》所收《充夫式》注引《户部式》佚文,附议宫崎氏将"四十日免"后补"役"字,推测杂徭以三十九日为限,是地方临时性徭役。

---

① 程喜霖:《对吐鲁番所出四角萄役夫文书的考察——唐代西州杂徭研究之一》,《中国史研究》1986 年第 1 期,第 50~63 页;《吐鲁番文书所见唐代杂徭(上篇)——唐代西州杂徭研究之二》,《宁可先生祝寿论集》,北京:中国社会科学出版社,2008 年 10 月;《吐鲁番文书所见唐代杂徭(下篇)——唐代西州杂徭研究之三》,《吐鲁番学研究》2008 年第 1 期(创刊号)。因本文是综合考察吐鲁番所出夫役文书对研究杂徭的学术价值,故在阐述重要问题时难免节引上列三文的有关资料和论述,在此特作说明,下不另注。

② 唐长孺:《唐代色役管见》,《山居存稿》,北京:中华书局,1989 年 7 月,第 166~194 页。

③ [日]堀敏一著,韩国磐等译《均田制研究》,福州:福建人民出版社,1984 年 3 月,第 224~283 页。

中国学者关于杂徭的专题论文有唐耕耦《唐代前期的杂徭》:①"杂徭一项,属地方掌管。"支持宫崎市定的"三十九日说"。

张泽咸《关于唐代杂徭的几个问题》:②采纳宫崎市定"三十九天说",认为唐中央掌管杂徭征发。

程喜霖《唐代西州杂徭研究之一》,③征引《充夫式》,参考宫崎、唐、张三氏的解释,重新补正录文;考证西州官萄役夫,役期五日。

二十世纪九十年代,有两部涉唐朝杂徭的经济史方面著作,郑学檬主编《中国赋役制度史》设"杂徭、色役、资课"一节:④"丁男正役之外,不另服杂徭";"中男服杂徭(夫役)的法定役期为十天"。

李锦绣《唐代财政史稿》(上卷):⑤据吐鲁番所出"夫役"文书说明杂徭日数,西州以"十日"为限。

综上所述,中日学者关于唐代杂徭的研究主要集中在征役日数、是地方或是中央执掌的徭役等问题,诸家有颇大分歧,由于文献对杂徭的具体实施语焉不详,导致众说纷纭,莫衷一是。所幸的是吐鲁番出土的唐代西州夫役文书,给我们提供了研究唐代杂徭史所罕见的资料。

二、吐鲁番所出夫役文书对唐代杂徭研究的重要意义

关于唐代杂徭的记载主要集中在《唐六典》、《唐会要》、《唐律疏议》、《白氏六帖事类集》等四部书,⑥记载零散,且《充夫式》又有脱讹。不仅如此,对杂徭如何实施更是史无明文。因此,诸家解释不一,推论各异。杂徭研究迹近停顿。余通检吐鲁番出土的大量唐朝赋役文书,仔细梳理拣出三十八件夫役文书,兹制作《唐代夫役文书一览表》。⑦ 这组夫役文书,乃研究杂徭弥足珍贵的资料,它将杂徭研究推进一个新的阶段,其学术价值不可估量。

第一,夫役文书揭示了唐代西州杂徭实施的全貌,填补了史载的空白。

细检《唐代夫役文书一览表》所列文书三十八件,明确记载"夫"或"夫役"者二十件,余者由文书内容推知为夫役文书。文书时限自太宗经高宗、武则天、中宗、睿宗、玄宗、代宗,即唐代前期诸朝,在西州普遍征发夫役。实际上在诏令中通常将杂徭称为夫役,盖唐朝前期夫役是杂徭的通称或代称。在唐朝将近三百年的历史中杂徭的内涵与外延,前期与后期是不同的,特别反映在杂徭与色役上。这不是几句话说得清楚的,本文不拟讨论。在此仅征引唐长孺先生所言:"在最广泛的意义上,所有色役不管哪一类都属杂徭。"因为"除了正役以外,律令上便只有杂徭"。"但在唐代前期,二者是有区别的。(案:当指狭义的杂徭与色役的区别)……但自两税法施行后,色役这个专词的内容发生了变化。那时色役与差役,差科往往互称,实际上成为杂徭的代用语,或者包括了杂徭和差科。"⑧因为夫役文书皆属唐代前期,故本文只研究

① 唐耕耦:《唐代前期的杂徭》,《文史哲》1981 年第 4 期,第 34~38 页。
② 张泽咸:《关于唐代杂徭的几个问题》,《中国社会经济史研究》1985 年第 4 期,第 11~21 页。
③ 程喜霖:《对吐鲁番所出四角萄役夫文书的考察——唐代西州杂徭研究之一》,《中国史研究》1986 年第 1 期,第 50~63 页。
④ 郑学檬主编《中国赋役制度史》,厦门大学出版社,1994 年 8 月,第 219~225 页。
⑤ 李锦绣:《唐代财政史稿》(上卷)第二分册,北京大学出版社,1995 年 3 月,第 420、421、607、608、711、766、767、768、787、788、789、793 页。第三分册第 882、989、1039、1075、1076、1086、1087、1088、1089 页。
⑥ 《唐六典》卷三户部郎中员外郎。《唐会要》卷八三《租税上》。《唐律疏议》卷二八"诸丁夫杂匠在役"条《疏议》。《白氏六帖事类集》卷二二《征役第七》,又《白孔六帖》卷七八《征役七》。
⑦ 参见程喜霖:《吐鲁番文书所见唐代杂徭(上篇)——唐代西州杂徭研究之二》,《宁可先生祝寿论集》。为了节省篇幅,本文不另附表,径直引表内容,凡本文称"表"者,皆出自此表,下不另注。
⑧ 唐长孺:《唐代色役管见》,《山居存稿》,北京:中华书局,1989 年 7 月版,第 171~172、180 页。

唐代前期杂徭。

我们检索《唐代夫役文书一览表》获知,唐西州都督府所征发的杂徭名色繁夥,粗略统计有门夫(子)、烽夫(子)、仓夫(子)、库夫(子)、官菊(田)夫、堤夫、堰夫、渠夫、水夫(子)、桥夫、修墙夫、筑城夫、炭夫、柴夫、苇夫、茭夫、藏冰夫、取土夫、造箭夫、车牛夫、墓夫等等二十一种,当只是一部分征夫名目,真可谓诸色百役,称为杂徭名符其实也! 我们发现自门夫、烽夫至桥夫十种役是相对固定的名色,即常年定期征发;墙夫、城夫之后十余种为临时性夫役,比如蒲昌县驿墙临时坍塌,随机征发,带有临时性征发的特点,这类地方临时所须杂徭很多,不胜枚举。

这组夫役文书给我们展示,上至西州都督府(表·一)、高昌县(表·四)、蒲昌县(表·七)、天山县(表·一二)、柳中县(表·一三),下至武城乡(表·五)、顺义乡(表·一五)、宁大乡(表·二九)、宁戎、丁谷寺等(表·三一),到百姓马寺尼法慈为父张无价身死请给墓夫赗赠事牒(表·二八),或如西州都督府直接征夫给所属诸司厅配役,或县、乡、百姓向西州都督府申请征发夫役。

由是观之,吐鲁番所出夫役文书将唐代西州都督府征发杂徭展现在我们面前,揭示了杂徭实施的全貌,填补了史载的阙漏。

第二,夫役文书揭示了唐代杂徭若干重大问题。

细审前揭表列三十八件夫役文书,勾勒出唐代杂徭的清晰轮廓,将杂徭具体实施的方方面面展现在我们面前。

其一,关于杂徭的性质与称谓:唐代徭役分为正役和杂徭,与正役相对应而言,杂徭是诸种杂役的总称,又称为轻徭与小徭。或如吐鲁番文书记载的"夫",通称"夫役",即《唐律疏议》所载:"夫谓杂徭"之谓欤!

其二,夫役文书说明,唐代杂徭征发丁中,而在西北边陲西州杂徭征发的对象为当州所有编户,即包括农民、牧户、庄坞(部曲、奴及佃户),商人及夷胡户中的丁男、中男、残疾,或许唐朝诸州亦如兹,至少边州如此。

其三,关于杂徭征役日数:据表列夫役文书所记,唐朝西州征发夫役少者役一、三、五、六日,多者役十、十五日。

其四,夫役文书说明,唐代西州杂徭有固定性(如表·二所记"烽夫"、表·九所记官菊役夫)和临时性(如表·七记临时征夫修缮驿墙)两种。

其五,关于杂徭是地方性还是中央执掌的徭役,史无明文,但夫役文书给我们提供的信息是西州都督府和所属诸县、乡依据官府日常所需杂徭:或修缮水利工程,或依"往例"征发夫役,征夫内容十分丰富。

其六,从夫役文书所见,唐代西州杂徭主要征发丁中,然在表列三十八件夫役文书中有四件按户征夫文书,这只能说有按户征夫的案例,但不能称为户役。

其七,表列三十八件夫役文书记有车牛役者,如表·二、五、六、九、一六、一七、二三、三〇、三一等九件文书明确记载,西州征发车牛并夫役,承担维修水利工程,官田耕作及官府所需柴草、炭、冰等运输夫役,乃唐代杂徭一大特色。

其八,表列夫役文书反映唐代西州都督府所征发的杂徭可纳资代役(钱或物),如表·五《运海等赁车牛契》、表·六《唐史玄政等纳钱代车役帐》、表·一九记"刘定师、令派建行等纳资(率皮)代夫役",就是实例。

由此可见,吐鲁番所出夫役文书揭示了唐代杂徭研究中的八个重大问题,填补了空白。诚如史学大师陈寅恪所言:"一时代之学术,必有其新材料与新问题。取用此材料,以研求问题,则为此时代学术之新潮流。……敦煌学者,今日世界学术之新潮流也。"①研究吐鲁番学亦如斯,我们运用吐鲁番所出新鲜资料推进史学研究,对吐鲁番学发展有不可估量的意义。

三、吐鲁番所出夫役文书在拓展唐代杂徭研究上的进展

我们细审夫役文书涉及唐代杂徭的称谓、性质、征役对象(丁中)、征役日数,是临时还是固定之役、是中央还是地方徭役,是否是户役、纳资代役、车牛役、杂徭的名色等等若干问题,也就是说杂徭各个方面的问题都全方位展现在我们面前。

可是研究杂徭最重要的核心问题:一是杂徭日数,二是中央或地方性徭役? 这也是诸家争论不休,歧异最大的问题。夫役文书揭示了杂徭研究中这两个最疑难的问题:

第一,关于唐代杂徭的服役日数。文献缺载,是杂徭研究中最疑难的问题。上举记载杂徭的四部书,仅《白氏六帖事类集》卷二《征役第七·充夫式》注引《户部式》佚文,有涉及徭役满四十日,折免有差的记载,兹参考前揭宫崎市定、张泽咸、唐耕耦文重新补正录文为:

> 诸正丁充夫四十日免[役]。七十日并免租,百日以上课役俱免。中男充夫满四十日已上免户内地租,无他税(地租之误),折户内一丁,无丁,听旁折近亲户内丁。②

研究者依《充夫式》所载,对杂徭日数进行形形色色的推论。前文已述:日本曾我部静雄"四十天说",滨口重国"五十天说",宫崎市定"三十九天说";中国学者唐耕耦、张泽咸采纳宫崎市定"三十九日说",郑学檬、李锦绣则提出"十日说"。诸家的观点歧异很大,可谓众说纷纭,莫衷一是。实际上《充夫式》注引《户部式》佚文,多有脱讹,虽经补正亦难读懂。前揭张文有言:"现存《户部式》的文字存在不少讹误。唐耕耦同志撰文备引日本学者对它所作不同的解释,并据宫崎市定意见,在'免'字下补一'役'字,使式文稍可通读。即使如此,仍存在不少疑难点。"唐文称:"现存《充夫式》在传写过程中有错漏,又无其他记载可以帮助订正,而且《白氏六帖事类集》本身,系为应付考试需要而辑,辑集时往往掐头去尾。因而文义多有断漏。要想把握《充夫式》的原意,已极困难。这个问题的最终角决,有待于新材料的发现。"由是解通《充夫式》成为杂徭研究的难题。如果按宫崎市定"三十九天"说,那么杂徭征役日数为三十九天,服役满四十日免役,也就是说超期服役一日,就免二十天役,令人难以置信;如若依曾我部静雄"四十天"说,即杂徭义务日数为四十天,这与《充夫式》规定的"诸正丁充夫四十日免[役]"相抵牾;我们再看滨口重国氏的"五十天"说,即杂徭义务日数五十日,若按滨口重国所论杂徭二日折正役一日,显然与《充夫式》四十日役相矛盾。前揭郑、李二君提出的杂徭"十日"说,虽各有所据,但未据《充夫式》,姑不论。

---

① 陈寅恪:《陈垣敦煌劫余录序》,《金明馆丛稿二编》,上海古籍出版社,1980年10月版,第236页。
② 又参见《白孔六帖》卷七八《征役七·充夫式》。

余基于三条理由提出《充夫式》新的解释：

其一，检唐朝典籍虽然没有发现杂徭的役期，但却有记载正丁所承赋役，《唐六典》卷三"户部郎中员外郎"条：

> 凡赋役之制有四：一曰租、二曰调、三曰役、四曰杂徭。
>
> 课户每丁租粟二石，其调随乡土所产，绫、绢、絁各二丈，布加五分之一……
>
> 凡丁岁役二旬，有闰之年加二日。
>
> 无事则收其庸，每日三尺，布加五分之一。
>
> 有事而加役者，旬有五日，免其调；三旬则租调俱免。通正役，并不得过五十日。[①]

我不厌其烦地征引是条，是要说明唐代凡编户中各类人户丁所承之役皆如律令，给人启示。细审唐朝徭役有正役与杂徭二项，"凡丁岁役二旬"。即丁负担的力役，每年二十日，与之并列的杂徭日数不明。或许是立法者将正役与杂徭并列，役期亦相同，故在规定前者岁役二十日，而省略了后者日数。若余揣测无误，唐代杂徭日数当似二十日为最高限额。唐制，十八岁以上中男与残疾一样受田，不服正役，而承杂徭是合理的。但十六、七岁的中男不受田，也要承杂徭则是不合理的。虽然杂徭就劳动强度而言，称轻徭、小徭，以二日抵一日正役，但是像筑城、修水利工程则是重劳动，故杂徭日数二十日为最高限额，适合残疾及十八岁以上中男，特别是十六、七岁中男承役。这对减轻丁男承役的负担也有利，符合唐初李世明吸取隋亡的教训，所制定的"轻徭薄赋"的国策。又凡丁服正役二十日，超期十五日免调，三十日租调俱免。换言之，正役二十日，加上超期服役的三十日，总共五十日，这是正役的最高极限。综上所论，我们比对《唐六典》记载与《充夫式》文式，可以帮助我们理解《充夫式》的含义。

细审《充夫式》，正丁服夫役满四十日免役，七十日免租，百日以上课役俱免，超期服役折免的役差是三十日，其最高时限是百日。这与正丁所承正役超期服役折免十分相似，只不过后者折免役差是十五日，其最高时限为五十日而已。杂徭日数恰好是正役的一半。或许前揭滨口重国文所论正役一日等于杂徭二日，来源于此吧！

其二，我们再仔细阅读前揭宫崎市定的论文注（二）《追记》有云："杂徭日数是三十九日。……政府在继续命令征收杂徭时，就将其缩短为二十九日了。由此可知唐代的法制不单是法理这一条原则，同时它还适应实情，顾及到一些人民的利益。并且在将它变成法律文字时，立法者不经意地使用了一种独特表现手法。……附言一句，我还认为在以六十日杂徭代纳了三十日租调之后，原来的杂徭恐怕就更缩短为不满二十日了。"又郑学檬、李锦绣氏提出杂徭征役十日，各有所据，则与宫崎博士的真知灼见都给人启迪。

其三，吐鲁番所出三十八件夫役文书记载征夫，日数皆没有超过十五日、二十日者，更没有一件文书记载征夫达到三十九日的征役日数。

由是我推断："诸正丁充夫满四十日免（役）"，包含杂徭义务日数和超期服役折免役的日数两项。似

[①] 《唐会要》卷八三《租税上》所载略同。《通典》卷六《食货门赋税下》"大唐"条："诸丁匠岁役工二十日，有闰之年加二日。须留役者，满十五日免调，三十，租调俱免（从日少者，见役日折免）。通正役，并不过五十日（正役谓二十日庸也）。"依此凡编户各种人户丁所承正役，一如律令。

乎唐朝正丁服杂徭义务日数为十日或二十日,若为十日则超期三十日共满四十日免役;若为二十日,则超期二十日共满四十日免役。比照《唐六典》所载"正丁所承赋役"条,我倾向唐代前期杂徭的法定日数为二十日。我们解通了《充夫式》前半段,正丁充夫及折免事项。那么后半段,"中男充夫满四十日已上免户内地租",自然包含杂徭义务日数和超期服役折免租的日数两项,即中男服杂徭法定日数二十日,超期服二十日折免"户内租"。唐制,中男不承租调与正役,只承杂徭,故云超期服杂徭二十日折免"户内租"。若无"户内租"或折户内一丁,或听折"近亲户内丁"之役。

以上重新诠释了《充夫式》,那是否可以获得这样的认识:唐代杂徭法定征役日数似为二十日,那么吐鲁番所出夫役文书又给我们提供何种实证呢?通检《唐代夫役文书一览表》,兹将记载征役一至十日的文书条列如次:

表·一《配役名籍》记:"门夫",据《通典》载:门夫"每番一旬"。①

表·七《某驿修造驿墙牒》记:"修驿墙制砖","用单功六十人,一日役";垒墙"用单功六十人,一日役"。

表·九《四角菊役夫牒》记:"四角官菊",役夫"七十八人","各合伍日";"九乘"车牛,"各一日役"。

表·二〇 a《差人夫修堤堰牒》记:高昌县维修兴新谷、草泽堤堰及箭干渠,征夫一千四百五十人,似用单功,一日役。

表·二一《给城夫斋料符》记:供"筑城夫斋料"四十六石,可供一千三百八十人或一百三十八人食用一日或十日,也就是说,一千三百八十名城夫,役一日,或一百三十八名城夫,役十日。

表·二八《请给墓夫牒》记:"墓夫",依制,五品以上官吏给营墓夫,"皆役十日"。

表·二六 a《夫役名籍》记:"已役上第八户,各夫一人,六日。"意即名籍所列的八等户,各征夫一人,人别役六日。

表·一六《运苇书牍》记:苅苇、车牛运苇夫役三日。

表·一九 a《率皮名籍》记:唐刘定师等率皮代夫役十日。

表·一九 b《率皮名籍》记:唐令狐建等按户率皮代夫役一日。

表·二二《开元水部式》规定:置浮桥征夫,"准户均差,役各不得过十日"。

由以上征引的十一件文书揭示:维修堤堰等水利工程、坍塌驿墙夫役,"一日役";苅苇、车牛运苇夫役,"三日役";官菊役夫,"五日役";征八等户人夫,"六日役";筑城夫,一日或十日役;门夫、墓夫,"十日役";桥夫"十日役"。可见征发夫役的名色不同,役种不同,劳动强度不一,因此所需的"单功"亦不同。导致征役日数有一日、三日、五日、六日、十日之别。

我们细审夫役文书发现烽夫(子)上番十五日,为西州杂徭的最高征役日数,兹节录相关文书如次:

1　表·三《唐安西判集》(前略)(节录)

比闻烽夫差遣,是残疾中男。

(后略)

伯(P)·2754

---

① 《通典》卷三五《职官·碌秩二》"门夫"条。

2 《唐西州高昌县武城乡张玉埬雇人上烽契》①

（节录）

1 ☐☐☐☐☐正月廿八日，武城乡 ☐☐☐☐☐

2 ☐☐☐☐银錢八文，雇同乡人解知德當柳中☐ ☐☐☐☐

3 ☐☐☐☐壹次拾伍日。其錢即日交付☐

4 若烽上有遗留，官罪，壹仰解知德

5 當。张玉埬悉不知。☐有先悔者，一罰

6 贰，入不悔人。☐☐☐☐☐ 指为記。

（后略）

60TAM326: 01/1, 01/2

本件出自阿斯塔那 326 号墓，纪年已残，同墓出有高宗总章元年（668）文书，又本契文中见有柳中（县），乃唐改高昌之田地县为柳中，还有武城乡名，立契时间当在唐初。

3 兹迻录吐鲁番阿斯塔那 389 号墓所出（表·四 b）《唐西州番上烽铺文书》②

（前缺）

1 ☐☐☐☐合上烽　分五幡　余有六人

☐☐☐☐　　人别三幡，计当四十五日上烽。

2 　　三幡

　　☐☐三百十九日不役。

（后缺）

86TAM389: 22/4

余著文《吐鲁番新出唐代烽铺文书考释——新出烽铺文书研究之一》，③对新出烽铺文书之时代、释文、定名、内容的考释，在此不赘述。据考，本件当是唐高宗时期文书，文云"幡"，据《说文解字注》七篇下巾部"幡"："从巾，番声"，"幡信"，"旌旗类也"。也就是说，幡、番同音，可指旗帜。唐西州有使用绯幡作为烽号预警，吐鲁番所出《唐西州都督府牒为诸府县警备寇贼事》："见贼骑即点幡绯……从北来，向北点；壹人点壹下……若拾人已上，百人已下，急多点。"④或许在西州幡为烽号之一，又幡、番同音，故将上番烽铺之番写成幡，在吐鲁番文书中借用同音字是常见的，又同出《番上烽铺名簿》将上烽之"番"书写本字。因此，本件"幡"当指番期，与番同义。

上举三件文书，关于文书的时代、烽夫（子）上番日数、是否为杂徭征发，我的论著考证已详，⑤本文不赘述。在此仅作扼要说明：第 1 件判集有"奉判裴都护"语，裴即裴行俭，任安西大都护应是麟德二年

---

① 《吐鲁番出土文书》简本第五册，第 164～165 页、真本第二册，第 254 页录文图版。
② 柳洪亮：《新出吐鲁番文书及其研究》，乌鲁木齐：新疆人民出版社，1997 年 4 月版，第 86、452 页，图版 71。
③ 《第二届吐鲁番学国际学术研讨会论文集》，上海辞书出版社，2006 年 10 月版，第 60～68 页。
④ 程喜霖：《汉唐烽堠制度研究》，台北：联经出版事业公司，1991 年 10 月版，真本第 239～249 页《雇人上烽》，第 461 页：宁 7(2)。
⑤ 程喜霖：《从吐鲁番出土文书中所见的唐代烽堠制度之一》，《敦煌吐鲁番文书初探》，武汉大学出版社，1983 年 10 月，第 275～315 页。《汉唐烽堠制度研究》真本，第 239～253 页。P·2754 号文书皆转引东洋文库《敦煌吐鲁番文献关于社会和经济的历史》I 法律文书 1978 年版，断本件"吐鲁番所出"，乃误。实则本件为敦煌所出 P·2754 号，特此纠正，这是余作此注的初衷！
程喜霖：《唐代烽铺上番番期新证——新出烽铺文书研究之三》，《新疆师范大学学报》2006 年第 2 期。

(665)至乾封二年(667)间,判集当是此时之物。判集称"烽夫",征发残疾中男。按称"夫"即烽子,当征发杂徭,据判集烽夫之称可以证明烽子一般不是兵役而是杂徭,我们知道唐代杂徭是征发中男残疾的。第2件《张玉堈雇人上烽契》,乃高宗总章元年(668)左右文书,与第1件年代相近。吐鲁番出土十七件雇人上烽契,其中太宗贞观年间三件,占15%,高宗、武则天时期十一件,占65%,另三件纪年不能确指,但知为唐前期的契券。由此看到早在贞观年间就出现了烽子雇人替上,到高宗、武则天之世至少有相当一部分应上番的烽子已雇人代上。我们从雇人上烽契所见,凡应上番烽子代上"壹次拾五日",此"壹次"系指一个番期而言,即烽子每烽番为十五日。第3件番上烽铺文书与上二件同属唐高宗朝文书,其第2行:"三幡(番):人别三幡(番),计当四十五日上烽。"此条意为:凡上烽烽子三番,注明:人别三番,计当四十五日,即烽子番期十五日。本件是唐官府档案,与上引《雇人上烽契》所记,替人代上"壹次十五日",相印证。又与日本《养老军防令》所云:

　　　　凡烽,各配烽子四人,若无丁处,通取次丁,以近及远,均分配番^{谓以二人为一番也},以次上下。①

这虽是日本情况,古代日本法令可能所据即是唐令。此条说明烽子征自民间,每月四人上番,二人为一番,即每番十五日。互为印证,说明唐边州烽子上烽必依据定制征发,可证唐令原有烽子上番十五日的令文,我认为日本《军防令》烽子上番条文原本唐令也。烽夫(子)上番文书补充了史籍的缺漏。

我们知道唐朝烽子涉边陲军防,放烽须一定技能并涉军事通讯秘密,烽子相对固定。因此,役期两年,番期十五日。所云"人别三番",似指烽子(夫)每年上三番,计四十五日。也就是说,当征为烽夫者,在役期二年内上六番,年别三番。如果按《充夫式》规定,满四十日者折免有差。上三番的烽夫则超时限五日以上,若依上文对《充夫式》的重新诠释,那么超时限二十五日,无论如何对超时限的日数,官府应给予折免或经济补偿。当然,烽夫是涉军防的役,乃属特例。虽然如此,但是烽夫(子)是一种役,乃属杂徭役。应当说明,前揭唐长孺先生文认为唐初门夫、烽子原"本是杂徭",后"转化为色徭",是值得研究者注意的。至于何时转化成色役,本文姑且不论,将拟专文讨论。有唐一代三百年,若以百年为一段可划分为初、中、晚(前、中、后)唐,那么上举三件文书属于初唐之物,故所载夫役盖属杂徭无疑。

综上所论,我们通检《唐代夫役文书一览表》所列三十八件夫役文书所见,在西州都督府所属诸县广征胡汉编户中的丁中、残疾、商贾、工匠及庄园中的佃客、部曲、奴等为夫役,满足官府所需要的夫役劳动者。因此,在西州出现各色不同的夫役所征发日数亦有一、三、五、六、十、十五日之差别,一般以十日或十五日为限。概而言之,在唐西州杂徭日数当十五日为最高限额,抑或这就是唐代杂徭实际征发日数为十五日,至少边州如此,西州杂徭征发日数就是实证。

第二,唐代杂徭是地方性、临时性徭役,还是中央执掌的徭役。

关于唐代杂徭是地方性的临时征发,还是中央直接执掌,史无明文。由是研究者各自提出自己的看法,前揭堀敏一氏文记录,越智重明氏推测为"地方性徭役"、"临时性的徭役"。其他日本学者附议者有之,如宫崎市定推测杂徭是地方临时性徭役。中国学者唐耕耦认为:"杂徭一项,属地方掌管。"张泽咸先生则认为:"唐中央掌管杂徭征发。"究竟熟是,我们通览唐朝文献,如上举记载杂徭的四部书对此语焉不

---

① 《令义解》卷五《军防令》。

详,关于如何征发杂徭更是缺载。若无新鲜资料,研究陷于停顿。那么吐鲁番所出夫役文书透露了什么信息呢?

我们仔细分析吐鲁番赋役文书,包括夫役文书,没有见到唐中央政府发布征发杂徭的诏令,也没有西州都督府接到中央或安西、北庭都护府征发西州夫役的令符,或西州都督府征发杂徭的请示奏章或备案表文,凡此皆没有发现。

细审夫役文书,发现《唐代夫役文书一览表》所列三十八件文书,有不少记载西州临时征发夫役和固定名目征发夫役两种,即如门夫、烽夫、田夫、水夫为固定性杂徭,又临时修缮驿墙及墓夫、城夫、柴夫等却是官府所需的临时性杂徭。对此《唐代西州杂徭研究之三》有详细考述,在此不赘述。本文仅集中对夫役文书揭示西州都督府及所属诸县征发夫役作一考察:

其一,夫役文书揭示西州都督府直接征发夫役:

表·一《唐西州都督府诸司厅、仓、库等配役名籍》:[①]

本件共(八)段,节录相关条文如下:

    (二)

1 □塞子铜匠 以上并配本司

    (三)

1 牛怀愿

2 魏海伯 以上仓子

    (四)

1 右件人等并门夫

    (五)

1 □□□ 以上都督 厅

2 □□志 长史厅

3 □□欢 司马厅

    (六)

3 □□住 功曹库

4 □□欢 仓曹库

5 □□仁 桃(萄)库

6 □□□ 油库

    73TAM210:136/12-1

本件出自阿斯塔那210号墓,纪年已残,据同墓所出有纪年者为贞观二十三年(649),可知本件当是贞观十四年(640)至贞观二十三年之间的文书。乃唐初之物,故所云"门夫",当是杂徭。(清)赵翼《陔余丛考》卷三六"门子"条:"唐时则守门之人谓之门子",即门夫也。在吐鲁番文书中某夫、子互称不止一见,烽夫称为烽子就是一例。由是本件所记的"仓子及诸厅、功曹库、仓曹库、桃(萄)库、油库"的服役者,

---

① 《吐鲁番出土文书》图录本,第三册,第45~48页,前揭《唐代西州杂徭研究之二》对本件及下文所引表·七、表·二〇a、表·二八文书有详考,下不另注。

"守当"诸门者称门夫,劳作者可称厅夫(子)、仓夫(子)、库夫(子)。我们从文书内容分析,此"名籍"中的人员服的是夫役。也就是说,这件"名籍"是西州都督府征发西州百姓(含工匠)夫役,配所属诸司、仓、库驱使。

又表·八《武周证圣元年(695)前官阴名子牒为官萄内作夫役频追不到事》、表·九《武周圣历元年(698)前官史玄政牒为四角萄已役未役人夫及车牛事》、表·一〇《武周圣历元年(698)四角萄所役夫役名籍》载:西州为四角官萄征夫役作。表·二一《唐开元二十三年(735)高昌县申西州都督府为给城夫斋料事》记,西州征发夫役一千三百八十人或一百三十八人维修州县城墙,可谓征发城夫规模之大矣;表·三一《唐西州下宁戎、丁谷等寺帖为供车牛事》记,西州为宁戎、丁谷等寺征发车牛并夫劳作。

上举诸件夫役文书,皆是西州都督府直接征发杂徭的实例。

其二,夫役文书见有高昌、蒲昌等县向西州都督府申请征发夫役:

1　表·七《唐开耀二年(682)西州蒲昌县上西州都督府户曹牒为某驿修造驿墙用单功事》:[①]

1　　　　　　　丞

2　例,具检高下步数如前者,准状,追□料功,得泥匠冯

3　明隆状称:一步料须塈五百颗,计用塈一万五千,用

4　单功六十人,一日役,造塈人别二百五十颗。垒墙并口

5　用单功六十人,一日役。

6　　　　　　　一丈二尺,阔五尺。

7　　　　　　　检前件驿墙见倒,具检高下步数

　　　　　　　(中略)

11　内上件驿　　　　　　县营造,今以状申

12　以前料用功壹佰陆　　　　　壹日役。

13　　　　　　　　　丞惠

14　都督府户曹件状如前,谨依録申,请裁,谨上。

15　开耀二年三月十七日主簿判尉　庞礼

16　十八日入　　　　　　事翟欢武

　　　　　　73TAM517:05/1(a)、1(b)

本件盖有"蒲昌县之印"七处,骑缝背处有"礼"字签署,并钤"蒲昌县之印"一方,又牒尾书"开耀二年三月",今据"历史年表":高宗开耀二年二月癸未十九日,改称永淳元年。似当敕书未达西州,故仍用旧号。

我们考察文书内容得知,这是高宗开耀二年(682)蒲昌县"驿墙见倒",即驿墙临时坍塌,牒上西州都督府户曹申请征役"营造",由泥匠冯明隆编制用工预算,所修驿墙"计用塈(未烧制的土砖)一万五千,用单功六十人,一日役,造塈,人别二百十五颗"。垒墙"用单功六十人,一日役"。由是本件第12行可补阙为:总共"用功壹佰陆(拾人,人别)壹日役"。显然蒲昌县某驿墙坍塌是偶发事件,申请所需人工,是临时性征役,与番上二十日的正役有区别。似当为夫役。

---

① 《吐鲁番出土文书》图録本,第一册,第268页。

2 (表·二〇 a)《唐开元二十二年(734)西州高昌县申西州都督府牒为差人夫修堤堰事》:①

1 高昌县 　　　　　　为申修堤堰人 □□□□□

2 新兴谷内堤堰一十六所,修塞料单功六百人。

3 城南草泽堤堰及箭幹渠,料用单功八百五十人。

4 　　　右得知水官杨嘉恽、鞏虔纯等状称:前件堤堰

5 　　　每年差人夫修塞。今既时至,请准往例处分

6 　　　者。准状,各责得状,料用人功如前者。依检案

7 　　　□□□□□ 例取当县群牧、莊坞、底(邸)店及夷、胡户

8 　　　□□□□□ 日功 修 塞,件检如前者。修堤夫

　　　　　　(中略)

11 宣 德郎行令上柱国处讷　　　朝议 □□□□

12 □督府户曹件状如,谨依録申,请裁,谨上。

13 　　　　　　开元廿二年九月十三日登仕郎行尉白庆菊上

14 　　　　　　録 □□□

15 　　□□□ 賓 □□□□

16 　　　　　　録事 □□□

17 下高昌县为修新兴谷内及 □□□□□

73TM509:23/1-1(a)、1-3(a)
　　　　　　1-2(a)、1-2(b)

　　本件出自阿斯塔那 509 号墓,上盖有“高昌县之印”五处,第 12、13 行间骑缝背钤“高昌县之印”一方,并押署“虔”字。细审文书知是高昌县水官杨嘉恽、鞏虔纯呈县状文称:“新兴谷内堤堰十六所”和“城南草泽堤堰及箭幹渠”。预计须用“人夫”一千四百五十人整治、维修,“请准往例处分”,“差人夫修塞”。高昌县令处讷等审核“料用人功”属实,具牒向西州都督府户曹参军事申报,请批准按“往例”征发。牒尾第 17 行:“下高昌县为修新兴谷内及 □□□□□ ”,缺文当为(城南草泽堤堰及箭幹渠)准往例征发人夫。这是西州都督府的批文,所以用大字书写。

　　这件文书说明:① 高昌县内堤、堰、泽、渠等水利工程,由县设水官统一管理。每年三至九月农忙季节行水,农闲季节即九月之后维修,常年如此。② 高昌县征发维修水利工程的夫役,必须申报州府批准施行。也就是说征夫权掌握在州府。仅高昌一县常年维修水利工程的人夫达一千四百五十人,所征发的夫役,乃当县编户丁中,包括农耕的百姓,牧户,庄坞(庄园)中的佃户、雇工、部曲、奴等,还有邸店的商人及“夷、胡户”。即征发当县所有编户丁中,特殊人户亦不例外。

　　概而言之,本件所记西州高昌县维修水利的夫役,是由县向州户曹参军呈牒申请并获批准按“往例”征发的一种杂徭。

　　其三,百姓依制向西州都督府申请“赙赠墓夫”:

　　表·二八《唐大历七年(772)马寺尼法慈为父张无价身死请给墓夫赙赠事牒》:②

---

① 《吐鲁番出土文书》图录本,第四册,第 317~318 页。

② 《吐鲁番出土文书》图录本,第四册,第 396 页。

```
1 _____袋上柱国张无价
                              为家贫子然[一]

2 _____廿七日不幸身亡。其父先
                  比日收将在寺安养[二]   伏乞[三]

3 _____准式,身死合有墓夫赗赠。请处
   _____多少,田第人夫

4       分〇人夫葬送。贫尼女人即得济辦。

5       大历七年六月  日百姓马寺尼法慈牒
```

73TAM506：07

本件注[一]"为家贫子然",此五字似补在二行"其父"上。[二]"比日收将在寺安养",此八字当补在三行"准式"以上,但因上残,具体位置不详。[三]"伏乞",此二字当补在三行"请处"上。这样似可连读,获知本件记载,马寺尼法慈为父上柱国张无价身死,"准式,身死合有墓夫赗赠"。请西州征墓夫营造坟茔安葬。据考张无价曾任散官五品游击将军、武职事官夏集府折冲都尉,据所任官职,依唐制至少可以享受营墓夫十至二十人的待遇。

从本件内容推断,张无价只有出家为尼的法慈一个孤女,死后无人问津,故法慈将其灵柩停灵于马寺,并"准式"即依唐制,呈牒西州都督府申请"赗赠墓夫"。由文书三处夹行字和第4行圈改字,疑此件为牒稿,想必法慈必具正式文牒上承州府,西州当依制征拨墓夫,安葬了张无价。今天在吐鲁番阿斯塔那古墓群中存有506号张无价坟墓,当是西州征发的墓夫营造的。

另外,表·二四《唐西州抄目》记:"户曹符,为给张玄应墓夫十人。"可能张玄应是五品散官,减现任职事之半,获赠墓夫十人。凡此说明,唐朝五品以上高级官吏给墓夫制度是实行了的,吐鲁番文书提供了实证。值得注意的是营墓夫,乃西州都府户曹参军下符征发的。

由是观之,吐鲁番所出夫役文书揭示,西州都督府杂徭由户曹参军事掌管,其具体征发分两类:一是州府直属的官厅、官田等,当由户曹直接征发人夫驱使;二是县管的水利工程和馆驿及其他事项须用人工者,由县向西州户曹申请征发权。

细审唐朝存世的文献,如上举《唐六典》、《唐会要》、《唐律疏议》、《白氏六帖》四部书规定了唐之徭役分设正役与杂徭,"夫谓杂徭";又《充夫式》注引《户部式》佚文:丁中役满四十日,折免各有差,即杂徭实施的原则,盖为杂徭的立法。但是究竟杂徭是否由中央或地方执掌实施没有明文,也找不到唐中央政府向全国诸州县征发杂徭的律令。然而却见有某皇帝出巡过州县征发夫役的诏文,仅举唐玄宗曾去河东为证,诏云:

> 郑、卫、雒、相、宜、沁、慈、隰等州佐助夫役,虽日不多,终是往还辛苦,各免户内今年差科。①

显然是征发所过州县的夫役,并非跨州府道征发。表·二二《唐开元水部式》载:"龙首、泾堰、五门、升原等堰,令随近县官专知检校,仍堰别各于州县差中男廿人,匠十二人,分番看守。"若有破损,随即修

---

① 《全唐文》卷二九《幸河东推恩诏》。唐代前期武则天、玄宗朝这类诏书不止一件。参见前揭《唐代西州杂徭研究之三》、张泽咸《关于唐代杂徭的几个问题》。

理,"任县申州,差夫相助"。又诸置浮桥处,"所须人夫采运榆条造石笼及绲索等杂使者",先役当津水手、镇兵不足者,征发"侧州县人夫充"。即桥在两州两县间者,亦于两州两县准户均差","役各不得过十日"。这与夫役文书所载西州县征夫相似。唐朝立法有律、令、格、式,"式以轨物程事",[①]乃工部水部郎中和都水监管理全国江湖河渠的法规。《水部式》明确规定凡修治桥梁、堤堰,须人夫者,在当州县征发,与律令相一致,《唐律疏议》载:

> 依《营缮令》;"近河及大水有堤防之处,刺史、县令以时检校。若须修理,每秋收讫,量功多少,差人夫修理"。[②]

由此可见《律令式》所载,唐中央政府制定关于杂徭的立法及施行法规,而地方州县则依法具体征发杂徭。既有立法,就有中央政府对地方州县征发杂徭是否违时过限,进行督察、处罚的权力。《唐律疏议》卷一六"诸非法兴造及杂徭役"条《疏议》曰:

> "非法兴造",谓法令无文;虽则有文,非时兴造亦是,若作池、亭、宾馆之属。"及杂徭役",谓非时科唤丁夫。驱使十庸以上,坐赃论。

中央政府督察地方州县非法兴造池、亭、宾馆者,或违农时或过限征发杂徭,要依法处治。

然而,我从唐朝典籍确实未发现唐中央尚书省所属部门不仅户部郎中员外郎职掌设有征发杂徭事项,其他的部门职掌亦未见杂徭一项。而仅见地方州府执掌杂徭的一条记载。《新唐书》卷四九下《百官志》"府州户曹司户参军事"条:

> 掌户籍、计帐、道路、过所、蠲符、杂徭、逋负、良贱、刍藁、逆旅、婚姻、田讼、旌别孝悌。

依此户曹参军主办十三项事务,杂徭为其一,役夫文书为其执掌杂徭提供了证据。

若以上考察无误,唐朝典籍所载,地方府州户曹司户参军执掌有杂徭一项,与吐鲁番夫役文书所记西州都督府户曹参军执掌杂徭征发,互为印证。我们可以得出如下认识:唐朝中央政府制定杂徭的立法、施行原则以及监察纠违法规,其具体实行征发之权则下给府州户曹司户参军执掌,吐鲁番所出夫役文书提供西州都督府户曹参军征发杂徭的实证! 我们从夫役文书看到,唐代西州杂徭有固定和临时征发两种,特别是供西州及所属诸县官府所需要的临时差役占相当大的比重,凡此又带有临时性的地方徭役的特点,这也是不争的事实。

四 余 论

众所周知,唐代杂徭,由于典籍记载零散或阙漏,导致杂徭研究为唐史研究中的疑难问题之一,研究

---

① 《唐六典》卷六"刑部郎中员外郎"条。
② 《唐律疏议》卷二七《杂律》"诸不修堤防及修而失时者"条《疏议》。

者从文献考察难以取得进展,几近停顿。所幸的是吐鲁番所出夫役文书对唐代杂徭研究有不可估量的意义。综上所论,夫役文书,给我们廓清了迷雾,揭开了杂徭的神秘面纱,将唐代西州杂徭的具体实施全方位展现在我们面前。特别是揭示杂徭日数、实际征发最高限额十五日,抑或是唐代杂徭的实际征发日数;又揭示唐中央政府执掌杂徭的立法和监察,而具体实施则由地方府州户曹司户参军执掌征发之权。由此将唐代杂徭研究向前推进到新阶段,可以说取得突破性进展。

诚然如此,关于杂徭仍有一些问题还须进一步探讨,比如有的学者提出"烽子"、"门夫"在唐初原本为杂徭,后来转化为色役。究竟何时转化为色役呢? 又唐代前期与后期杂徭的内涵与外延究竟有否变化? 杂徭与色役究竟有何区别? 凡此种种,都有待深入研究,因囿于篇幅,本文姑不作深论!

吐鲁番出土高昌郡文书所见的"胡"与"虏"

王 素

故宫博物院

众所周知,岳飞《满江红》所说"壮志饥餐胡虏肉,笑谈渴饮匈奴血",其中"胡虏"甚至"匈奴",实际上都是泛指。但东晋十六国时期,也就是吐鲁番历史上的高昌郡时期,在当时的中国,特别是在河西、高昌地区,"胡"与"虏"却是有特定含义的。了解当时"胡"与"虏"的特定含义,对于了解当时河西、高昌地区的民族关系,一定会大有裨助。

一、从"胡贼"说起

1979 年 4 月下旬,吐鲁番地区文管所在阿斯塔那清理了一座编号为 382 的十六国墓葬,出土了不少颇有价值的文书,其中,阚爽政权《缘禾五年(436)二月四日民杜犊辞》尤为重要。该辞后缺,存文 6 行,迻录如下:

1　缘禾五年二月四日,民杜犊辞:犊
2　有赀七十八斛,自为马头。宋相明
3　有赀十六斛,在犊,马著身即
4　自乘。去前十月内胡贼去后,
5　明共犊私和义(议),著有赀,义身
6　自□取马之[际],困义□[往]□□□①

其中提到"胡贼",颇受学者关注。柳洪亮先生认为:此处"胡贼"只能是指"北凉沮渠氏"。② 这一见解得到大多数学者的赞同,并将"胡贼去后"的缘禾四年(435)十月作为沮渠氏北凉统治高昌的终结和阚爽政权统治高昌的开始。③

关于北凉沮渠氏称"胡",传世文献颇多记载。如:

---

① 新疆吐鲁番地区文管所(柳洪亮):《吐鲁番出土十六国时期的文书——吐鲁番阿斯塔那 382 号墓清理简报》,《文物》1983 年第 1 期,图第 9、21 页;柳洪亮:《新出吐鲁番文书及其研究》,新疆人民出版社,1997 年,第 8 页(文)、第 391 页(图);岑云飞主编《吐鲁番博物馆》,新疆美术出版社,1992 年,第 59 页、彩图 99。按:原释文稿有漏误及问题,此处进行了增订。

② 柳洪亮:《吐鲁番出土文书中缘禾纪年及有关史实》,原载《敦煌学辑刊》1984 年第 1 期,第 52~53 页,收入前揭柳洪亮:《新出吐鲁番文书及其研究》,第 248~249 页。

③ 王素:《高昌史稿·统治编》,文物出版社,1998 年,第 213~221 页。

沮渠蒙逊,临松卢水胡人也。其先世为匈奴左沮渠,遂以官为氏焉。(《晋书》卷一二九《沮渠蒙
逊载记》)

胡沮渠蒙逊,本出临松卢水,其先为匈奴左沮渠,遂以官为氏。(《魏书》卷九九《卢水胡沮渠蒙逊传》)

大且渠蒙逊,张掖临松卢水胡人也。匈奴有左且渠、右且渠之官,蒙逊之先为此职,羌之酋豪曰
大,故且渠以位为氏,而以大冠之。世居卢水为酋豪。(《宋书》卷九八《胡大且渠蒙逊传》)

沮渠氏出身卢水胡,《晋书》、《魏书》、《宋书》记载均同,《魏书》、《宋书》更在北凉开国主沮渠蒙逊传名中
加"胡"字,沮渠氏称"胡"自是毫无疑问。关于卢水胡的血缘,学者见解不同,主要存在四说:一为匈奴
说,[①]二为月氏说,[②]三为杂胡(含匈奴、月氏及西域胡)说,[③]四为匈奴、月氏、羌和大胡(即西域胡)融合形
成说。[④] 此外还有鲜卑说。如《晋书》卷九五《艺术·郭瑞传》云:"瑞尝曰:'凉州谦光殿后当有索头鲜卑
居之。'终于秃发傉檀、沮渠蒙逊迭据姑臧。"但这是后人附会,秃发傉檀确为鲜卑,沮渠蒙逊却并非鲜卑,
因而此处不取。至于前揭四说,我曾明确表示后二说更有道理。[⑤]

从理论上说,卢水胡既为"杂胡",则其各种成分都应有"胡"名。匈奴历来称"胡",已为人所熟知。
如《史记·秦始皇本纪》太史公曰:"蒙恬北筑长城而守藩篱,却匈奴七百余里,胡人不敢南下而牧马。"月
氏亦历来称"胡"。如《汉书》卷六一《张骞传》"匈奴降者言匈奴破月氏王"条师古注曰:"月氏,西域胡国
也。"又《后汉书》卷二三《窦融传》"融率五郡太守及羌虏小月氏等"条李贤注云:"小月氏,西域胡国名。"
西域亦历来称"胡"。如前引《张骞》、《窦融》二传的师古、李贤二注已指出凡西域之国均称"胡国"。又
《汉书·武帝纪》天汉二年秋"渠黎六国使使来献"条注引臣瓒曰:"渠黎,西域胡国名。"前引同书《张骞
传》"发使抵安息、奄蔡、犛轩、条支、身毒国"条师古注曰:"自安息以下五国皆西域胡也。"还有同书《元帝
纪》建昭三年秋条云:"使护西域骑都尉甘延寿、副校尉陈汤挢发戊己校尉屯田吏士及西域胡兵攻郅支单
于。"《后汉书》卷二四《马援传》云:"伏波类西域贾胡,到一处辄止。"李贤注云:"言似商胡,所至之处辄
停留。"尤其《三国志·魏书·仓慈传》记慈为敦煌太守云:

常日西域杂胡欲来贡献,而诸豪族多逆断绝。既与贸迁,欺诈侮易,多不得分明。胡常怨望,慈
皆劳之。欲诣洛者,为封过所,欲从郡还者,官为平取,辄以府见物与共交市,使吏民护送道路,由是
民夷翕然称其德惠。数年卒官,吏民悲感如丧亲戚,图画其形,思其遗像。及西域诸胡闻慈死,悉共
会聚于戊己校尉及长吏治下发哀,或有以刀画面,以明血诚,又为立祠,遥共祠之。

后来粟特昭武九姓均称"胡",也与该族来自西域有关。据《魏书》卷九九《私署凉州牧张寔附子骏传》、
《晋书》卷八七《凉武昭王李玄盛传》、前引《宋书·大且渠蒙逊传》,前凉杨宣、西凉李暠,都曾官"西胡校
尉"。此"西胡校尉"顾名思义也是管理西域胡国的。唯羌不称"胡"(羌称"虏",见下文)。值得注意的

① 马长寿:《北狄与匈奴》,生活·读书·新知三联书店,1962年,第126页;黄烈:《中国古代民族史研究》,人民出版社,1987年,第312页。
② 姚薇元:《北朝胡姓考》,中华书局重印本,2007年,第394页;周一良:《北朝的民族问题与民族政策》,《魏晋南北朝史论集》,中华书局,1963年,第156页。
③ 唐长孺:《魏晋杂胡考》,《魏晋南北朝史论丛》,生活·读书·新知三联书店,1955年,第413页。
④ 周伟洲:《试论吐鲁番阿斯塔那且渠封戴墓出土文物》,《考古与文物》1980年第1期,第101页。
⑤ 王素:《北凉沮渠蒙逊夫人彭氏族属初探》,《文物》1994年第10期,第45页。

是,羌虽不称"胡",却与"胡"关系密切。如《史记》卷一一〇《匈奴列传》云:"是时汉东拔秽貉、朝鲜以为郡,而西置酒泉郡以隔绝胡与羌通之路。"说明羌原本与"胡"交通频繁,关系密切。至于《汉书·宣帝纪》神爵二年五月"羌虏降服,斩其首恶大豪杨玉、酋非首"条注引文颖曰:"羌胡名大帅为酋,如中国言魁。"前引《晋书·沮渠蒙逊载记》云:"羌胡多起兵响应。"此处的"羌胡",实际是"羌"与"胡"两个概念,所以并称,也是因为二者关系密切。据此,可以认为:东晋十六国时期,在当时的中国,特别是在河西及高昌地区,传世文献和出土文献称"胡"都是有其特定含义的,大致包括匈奴嫡系和西域各少数民族及其政权,与高昌关系最为密切的则主要应是曾经统治过高昌的沮渠氏北凉和邻近的车师、焉耆等少数民族及其政权。[①]

高昌建国之后,情况才似乎稍有变化。姜伯勤先生曾指出:"在吐鲁番所出十六国时期文书中,可以依稀看到一些胡人姓名,如车都末当系车师人。翟阿富、翟定,可能属于高车。竺国奴、竺黄媚,属于天竺或月氏。可是我们没有明确看到昭武九姓的人名。"[②]吐鲁番新出阚氏王国《永康十二年(477)闰月十四日张祖买奴券》始载"张祖从康阿丑买胡奴益富一人"。[③] 柳方氏最早对该买奴券进行探讨,但对该"胡奴"出身何族没有进行解说。[④] 荣新江先生接着对该买奴券进行探讨,由于认为"康阿丑应当是一个出身中亚康国的粟特人",而"粟特人一直是丝绸之路上的人口贩子,特别是把中亚粟特地区、西域塔里木盆地周边绿洲王国、北方草原游牧民族地区的男女奴隶,倒卖到高昌、敦煌甚至长安",所以断定:"这里称被买的奴隶为'胡奴',显然也是中亚粟特地区来的奴隶。"[⑤]也就是说,高昌建国之后,吐鲁番出土文献所见的"胡",才主要是指粟特的昭武九姓胡。传世文献如《周书·高昌传》所云:"文字亦同华夏,兼用胡书。有《毛诗》、《论语》、《孝经》,置学官弟子,以相教授。虽习读之,而皆为胡语。"(《北史·高昌传》、《通典·车师高昌附》同)其中"胡书"、"胡语"之"胡",也主要是指粟特的昭武九姓胡。

二、"虏使"与"虏奴"、"虏婢"

前述 1979 年 4 月下旬吐鲁番阿斯塔那 382 号墓还出土了一件阚爽政权《缘禾六年(437)二月廿日阚连兴辞》,也很重要。该辞完整,存文 4 行,迻录如下:

1 缘禾六年二月廿日,阚连兴辞:所具赍

2 马,前取给虏使。使至赤尖,马于彼不还。

3 辞达,随所给贾(价)。谨辞。

4   诶[⑥]

---

① 按:《魏书》卷三〇《车伊洛传》云:"车伊洛,焉耆胡也。"车伊洛原为车师前国王,后流亡至焉耆,故史书称为"焉耆胡"。据此,则车师国人亦可称为"车师胡"。

② 姜伯勤:《敦煌吐鲁番文书与丝绸之路》,文物出版社,1994 年,第 154 页。

③ 荣新江、李肖、孟宪实主编《新获吐鲁番出土文献》,中华书局,2008 年,第 125 页。

④ 柳方:《吐鲁番新出的一件奴隶买卖文书》,《吐鲁番学研究》2005 年 1 期(总第 11 期),第 122~126 页。

⑤ 荣新江:《新获吐鲁番文书所见的粟特》,《吐鲁番学研究》2007 年第 1 期(总第 15 辑),第 30 页。

⑥ 前揭新疆吐鲁番地区文管所(柳洪亮):《吐鲁番出土十六国时期的文书——吐鲁番阿斯塔那 382 号墓清理简报》,图第 7、21 页;前揭柳洪亮:《新出吐鲁番文书及其研究》,9(文)、第 392 页(图);前揭岑云飞主编《吐鲁番博物馆》,第 59 页、彩图 98;李肖主编:《吐鲁番文物精粹》,上海辞书出版社,2006 年,第 90 页(彩图)。按:"随所"之"所",柳洪亮原作"□",朱雷改作"请(?)",见《吐鲁番出土文书所见的北凉"按赍配生马"制度》,《文物》1983 年第 1 期,第 35 页;又,《敦煌吐鲁番文书论丛》,甘肃人民出版社,2000 年,第 25 页。但均有问题。此字极为清楚,实为"所"之草书,因改。

其中提到"虏使",也颇受学者关注。柳洪亮先生认为:此处"虏使"应指"其他少数民族的使者",①朱雷先生认为应指"柔然使臣"。② 我曾明确表示朱雷先生的见解更有道理。③

关于柔然称"虏",传世文献也颇多记载。如:

> 侍臣受斤亡入蠕蠕,诏眷追之,遂至虏庭。(《魏书》卷二六《尉古真附诺子眷传》)
>
> 自索虏破慕容,据有中国,而芮芮虏有其故地,盖汉世匈奴之北庭也。芮芮一号大檀,又号檀檀,亦匈奴别种。(《宋书》卷九五《索虏附芮芮传》)
>
> 芮芮虏,塞外杂胡也。编发左衽。晋世什翼圭入塞内后,芮芮逐水草,尽有匈奴故庭,威服西域。(《南齐书》卷五九《芮芮虏传》)

按:柔然又称蠕蠕、芮芮。《魏书》称柔然为"虏",还有很多例证。如同书卷九九《卢水胡沮渠蒙逊附子牧犍传》记北魏指责牧犍,谓牧犍"北托叛虏",此"叛虏"就是指柔然。《宋书》直称"芮芮虏"。《南齐书》更在芮芮传名中加"虏"字,柔然称"虏"也是毫无疑问。关于柔然的民族,《宋书》谓为"匈奴别种",《南齐书》谓为"塞外杂胡",似乎都是得自传闻。唯《魏书》卷一〇三《蠕蠕传》称柔然为"东胡之苗裔",应较可信。因为拓跋氏亦属"东胡"一派,也被称为"虏"。④

关于拓跋氏称"虏",传世文献也颇多记载。如:

> 索头虏姓托跋氏,其先汉将李陵后也。陵降匈奴,有数百千种,各立名号,索头亦其一也。(《宋书》卷九五《索虏传》)
>
> 魏虏,匈奴种也,姓托跋氏。晋永嘉六年,并州刺史刘琨为屠各胡刘聪所攻,索头猗卢遣子曰利孙将兵救琨于太原,猗卢入居代郡,亦谓鲜卑。被发左衽,故呼为索头。(《南齐书》卷五七《魏虏传》)

《宋书》、《南齐书》均在拓跋氏传名中加"虏"字,拓跋氏称"虏"也是毫无疑问。关于拓跋氏的民族,《宋书》谓为"汉将李陵后",《南齐书》谓为"匈奴种",也都是得自传闻。唯《南齐书》后称"亦谓鲜卑",始得其正。当时鲜卑支派众多。既然拓跋鲜卑称"虏",则其他鲜卑也都应称"虏"。

东晋十六国时期,鲜卑国家和鲜卑部落众多,除北魏拓跋氏外,还有西秦乞伏氏、南凉秃发氏、前燕慕容氏、后燕慕容氏、南燕慕容氏以及吐谷浑、乙弗勿敌等等。关于西秦乞伏氏称"虏",未见明确记录。关于南凉秃发氏称"虏",传世文献则颇多记载。如《宋书》卷九八《胡大且渠蒙逊传》云:"蒙逊与西平虏秃发傉檀共攻凉州。"由于秃发为拓跋之异译,故秃发亦称"索虏"。如《晋书》卷一二五《乞伏乾归载记》云:"索虏秃发如苟率户二万降之。"关于前、后、南三燕慕容氏称"虏",传世文献也颇多记载。如《晋书》卷一一五《苻坚载记下》云:"秦人呼鲜卑为白虏。"据《魏书》卷九五《徒何慕容廆附从孙永传》云:"西人

① 前揭新疆吐鲁番地区文管所(柳洪亮):《吐鲁番出土十六国时期的文书——吐鲁番阿斯塔那382号墓清理简报》,第21页;前揭柳洪亮:《新出吐鲁番文书及其研究》,第139页。
② 前揭朱雷:《吐鲁番出土文书所见的北凉"按赀配生马"制度》,第37页;前揭朱雷:《敦煌吐鲁番文书论丛》,第30页。
③ 前揭王素:《高昌史稿·统治编》,第221页。
④ 按:拓跋氏出身鲜卑(参见下文),与柔然族属原甚近密,以致《晋书》卷一三〇《赫连勃勃载记》称柔然开国之祖"杜(社)崘"亦为"河西鲜卑"。可见二者族属自古就很难区分。

呼徒何为白虏。"知所谓"白虏",均特指三燕慕容氏。关于吐谷浑称"虏",传世文献也颇多记载。如《晋书》卷九七《四夷·吐谷浑传》云:"西北杂种谓之为阿柴虏,或号为野虏焉。"《宋书》卷九六《鲜卑吐谷浑传》云:"阿柴虏吐谷浑,辽东鲜卑也。"关于乙弗氏称"虏",传世文献也有记载。如《魏书》卷九九《鲜卑秃发乌孤附弟傉檀传》云:"神瑞初,傉檀率骑击乙弗虏,大有擒获。"

此外,羌也一直称"虏"。前引《汉书·宣帝纪》神爵二年五月条云:"羌虏降服,斩其首恶大豪杨玉、酋非首。"同书卷六九《赵充国传》"羌虏瓦解,前后降者万七百余人"条师古注曰:"羌虏即羌贼耳,无豫于胡也。"说明当时对"虏"与"胡"是有较严格的区别的。又《晋书》卷一一四《苻坚载记下》记王猛临终对苻坚说:"鲜卑、羌虏,我之仇也,终为人患,宜渐除之,以便社稷。"又记苻融谏苻坚曰:"陛下听信鲜卑、羌虏谄谀之言,采纳良家少年利口之说,臣恐非但无成,亦大事去矣。"说明直至东晋十六国时期,羌也是称"虏"的。

据此,可以认为:东晋十六国时期,在当时的中国,特别是在河西及高昌地区,传世文献和出土文献称"虏"也都是有其特定含义的,大致包括柔然、鲜卑、羌等少数民族及其政权,与高昌关系最为密切的则主要应是鲜卑和柔然。

吐鲁番新出《前秦建元二十年(384)三月高昌郡高宁县都乡安邑里籍》见有"虏奴"、"虏婢"。[①] 荣新江先生认为:"'虏'字本来是战争或掠夺而得的战俘,被降服的人也称作'虏',这种战俘在古代社会往往变成奴隶,受主人役使。'虏'另指敌人或叛逆者,还有就是对北方少数民族的蔑称。《建元二十年籍》中的这些'虏奴'、'虏婢',不可能是主人劫掠来的,这是违法的行为,那么这个'虏'字更可能是一种对北方少数民族的蔑称。……因此,可以把这里的'虏奴'、'虏婢'看作是当地百姓购买的外族奴婢,从高昌的地理位置来说,这些虏奴、虏婢主要来自西北地方。"[②]这种推测是有道理的。我认为:此处"虏奴"、"虏婢"的"虏",应指北边的鲜卑。

我们知道:《魏书》卷一〇三《蠕蠕传》云:"社仑……号为强盛。随水草畜牧,其西则焉耆之地,东则朝鲜之地,北则渡沙漠,穷瀚海,南则临大碛。其常所会庭则敦煌、张掖之北。小国皆苦其寇抄,羁縻附之,于是自号丘豆伐可汗。"社仑称可汗,在公元402年。[③] 据此,则前秦时期,柔然尚未与高昌为邻。此时在高昌北边活动的,仍为魏晋以来传统的鲜卑。如《三国志·魏书·鲜卑传》注引王沈《魏书》云:"鲜卑西部,西接乌孙。"《晋书·武帝纪》咸宁元年(275)六月记载:"西域戊己校尉马循讨叛鲜卑,破之,斩其渠帅。"又咸宁二年(276)七月记载:"鲜卑阿罗多等寇边,西域戊己校尉马循讨之,斩首四千余级,获生九千余人,于是来降。"而根据《太康元年(280)十月二日凉州都尉鲁铨墓表》、咸宁四年(278)六月,凉州刺史杨欣还与鲜卑树机能进行过一次武威之战,损失惨重并不幸阵亡。[④] 关于凉州鲜卑的由来及其为患,学者已有专门研究,[⑤]《晋书》卷八六《张轨传》、卷八七《凉武昭王李玄盛传》以及相关"载记"也还有一些记载,这里不拟赘述。

① 前揭荣新江、李肖、孟宪实:《新获吐鲁番出土文献》,第177、179页。
② 荣新江:《吐鲁番新出〈前秦建元二十年籍〉研究》,《中华文史论丛》2007年第4辑(总第88辑),第20~21页。
③ 中国科学院历史研究所史料编纂组:《柔然资料辑录》,中华书局,1962年,第81页。
④ 参阅王素:《西晋鲁铨墓表跋》,《出土文献研究》第6辑,上海古籍出版社,2004年,第271~278页。
⑤ 参阅王国维:《尼雅城北古城所出晋简跋》,《观堂集林》卷一七,中华书局重印本,1984年,第865~869页;周伟洲:《魏晋十六国时期鲜卑族向西北地区的迁徙及其分布》,《西北历史资料》1983年第1期(总第8期),第35~45页。

三、高昌"外接胡虏"解读

《晋书·吕光载记》云:"群议以高昌虽在西垂,地居形胜,外接胡虏,易生翻覆,宜遣子弟镇之。光以子覆为使持节、镇西将军、都督玉门已西诸军事、西域大都护,镇高昌,命大臣子弟随之。"此事《通鉴》卷一○八系于东晋孝武帝太元十九年(394)七月。这里提到的高昌"外接胡虏",与前述吐鲁番出土高昌郡文书所年见的"胡"与"虏"正相印证,值得我们重视。

按所谓高昌"外接胡虏",意思是说高昌与"胡虏"为邻,或者说与高昌为邻的均为"胡虏"之国。我们知道:关于高昌的邻国,魏晋南北朝时期的史籍,仅《梁书》卷五四《高昌传》曾进行概括,原文为:"南接河南,东连敦煌,西次龟兹,北邻敕勒。"《南史》卷七九《高昌传》同。但这是麹氏王国时期的情况,高昌郡时期情况与此不同。根据记载,高昌郡时期,高昌北边的邻国先后为鲜卑、柔然,如前所说这都是"虏"国;西边的邻国为车师,西南的邻国为焉耆,如前所说这都是"胡"国。此外,高昌接受过八个割据政权的统治,其中前凉、西凉、段氏北凉及阚爽政权为汉族,前秦、后凉为氐族,沮渠氏北凉和沮渠氏北凉流亡政权为卢水胡。汉族不属"胡虏",可以不用讨论。氐族偶尔称"虏",多称为"贼",均属蔑称,也可以不用讨论。唯卢水胡称"胡",如前所说属于"胡"国。这样就清楚了。所谓高昌"外接胡虏",联系前述吐鲁番出土高昌郡文书所见的"胡"与"虏",可见前文所说,"胡"指东边的沮渠氏卢水胡、西边的车师、西南的焉耆,"虏"指北边的鲜卑、柔然,是正确的。

罗布泊海头遗址出土的著名的《前凉李柏致焉耆王书稿》,共有二封:一封记载:"王使回复罗从北虏中,与严参事往,想是到也。"(538A)一封记载:"王使招直俱共发,从北虏中,与严参事往,不知到未?"(538B)其中提到的"北虏",究竟指何民族,学者见解不一,存在匈奴遗种、戊己校尉赵贞等多说。[1] 但根据上述考证和分析,可以认为,自然也应指北边的鲜卑。解决了这一长达百年的疑问,可以说是本文对吐鲁番出土高昌郡文书所见"胡"与"虏"的特定含义进行探讨取得的新收获。

此外,还需要指出两点:(一)东晋十六国时期,称"胡"、称"虏"者,当然不止前文所说的那些少数民族及其政权。譬如后赵石氏出身羯族,前赵刘氏、大夏赫连氏出身匈奴,自然也都称"胡"。东晋十六国各政权多置征虏、平虏、讨虏、破虏、扫虏等将军,包含更加广泛。但这些与河西特别是高昌没有关系,所以本文不多涉及。(二)史籍常有"胡"、"虏"混淆情况,需要认真分析,不能轻易认为当时称"胡"、称"虏"没有区别。譬如《宋书》卷九六《鲜卑吐谷浑传》云:"晋末,金城东允街县胡人乞伏乾归拥部众据洮河、罕开,自号陇西公。"我们知道:乞伏氏出身鲜卑,只能称"虏",不可能称"胡"。这段记载属于后来追述,实有混淆"胡"、"虏"之嫌。又譬如《高僧传》卷一二《释法进传》称:"(沮渠蒙)逊卒,子景环(无讳)为胡寇所破。"沮渠氏自身就称"胡",怎么可能为"胡寇所破"?这里的所谓"胡寇",实际是指鲜卑拓跋氏,即所谓"索虏"。前引《宋书·大且渠蒙逊传》载刘宋太祖诏曰:"往年狡虏纵逸,侵害凉土,西河王茂虔(牧犍)遂至不守。"称为"狡虏",才是正确的。

---

① 前揭王素:《高昌史稿·统治编》,第123~133页。

吐火罗语文献释读百年纪念

徐文堪
汉语大词典编纂处

提　要

　　19 世纪末至 20 世纪初,德、法、英、俄、日等国考古队在我国新疆发现了一种用北印度婆罗谜字母书写的前所未知语言的大量写本,俄国学者奥登堡(S. F. Oldenburg)于 1892 年首次发表该语言写本的残页。怎样称呼和解读这种语言,成为学者们关注的焦点。对这种语言的定名和释读,开始是与对回鹘语《弥勒会见记》(*Maitrisimit nom bitig*)的研究联系在一起的。根据回鹘文本《弥勒会见记》的一则题记,这种以前未知的语言在 1907 年被定名为“吐火罗语”(英语 Tocharian,来自德语 *Tocharisch*,希腊语 *Tokharoi*,拉丁语 *Tochari*,回鹘语 *twqry*)。1908 年梵语学家西格(Emil Sieg)和西格林(Wilhelm Siegling)发表著名论文《吐火罗语考》(*Tocharisch. Die Sprache der Indoskythen*),确定了该语言属印欧语西支(kentum 语组),分为两种。刊布了吐火罗语 A 种方言的《弥勒会见记剧本》(*Maitreyasamiti*)的几个片断。这标志着“吐火罗学”(Tocharology)的诞生。本文对百年来吐火罗语研究史作了回顾,概述了吐火罗语文献收藏、译释、断代和数字化的现状,也涉及与此有关的古文书学和历史学、考古学、人类学、语言学问题,并对未来的探索和研究略作展望。

　　有关塔里木盆地存在后来被称为“吐火罗语”的印欧语的信息首次传到西方世界是在 1892 年。这一年俄国学者奥登堡(S. F. Oldenburg)在《俄国考古学会东方部会刊》(*Zapishi Vostochnago Otdyleniya Imperatorkago Russkago Archeologicheskago Obshchestva7.*)上刊布了一张用北印度婆罗谜字写成、来自俄国驻喀什领事彼得罗夫斯基(Petrovsky)收集品的未知语言写本的照片。次年即 1893 年,英国学者霍恩勒(A. F. R. Hoernle)在一篇谈“韦伯写本”(Weber Manuscripts)的论文[1]末尾,对这同一页写本作了拉丁转写,并对其进行了分析,认出了其中的几个梵文词语。

　　在这前后,由于英、德、法、俄、日、瑞典等各国探险队在新疆、甘肃等地进行的考古探测,发现了大量多种语言文字的古代写本,其中最引人注目的是用以前未知的印欧语书写的残卷,[2]从而开始了欧洲学者对这些文献的研究热潮。德国学者劳于曼(Ernst Leumann)1900 年在《圣彼得堡帝国科学院纪录历史——语文学类》第 4 卷第 8 期上发表《中亚一种不知名的书面语》(Über eine von den unbekannten Literatursprachen

---

① A. F. R. Hoernle, "The Weber Manuscripts, Another Collection of Ancient Manuscripts from Central Asia", *JASB* 62/1, 1893, 1–40.

② 贺昌群:《近年西北考古的成绩》,原载《燕京学报》第 12 期(1932 年),收入《贺昌群文集》第 1 卷,北京:商务印书馆,2003 年,第 54~97 页。

Mittelasiens），刊布了上述第一张写本的照片，并从俄国收集品中找到了另一张写本照片，进行了讨论。劳氏的转写比较正确，比定了一些梵文词语，后来的研究表明该写本是一种佛赞（Buddhaṣtōtra）的译文残卷。

霍恩勒和劳于曼研究的印欧语以前不为人所知，所以劳氏称其为第一种不知名语言（Unbekannte Sprache Ⅰ），后又改称为喀什语（Kaschgarische），但这些名称又都被放弃了。

继续研究这种语言的当时主要是柏林突厥学家缪勒（F. W. K. Müller）和梵学家西格（Emil Sieg）。缪勒在 1907 年发表了一篇不长的论文《对进一步确定中亚不知名语言的贡献》（Beitrag zur genaueren Bestimmung der unbekannten Sprachen Mittelasiens，载于 *SBAW*，958 - 960.），提出依据回鹘文《弥勒会见记》（*Maitrsimit*）的题记，把这种语言定名为"吐火罗语"。其他学者如爱沙尼亚的钢和泰（Baron Alexander von Staël Holstein）和挪威的柯诺（S. Konow）则认为吐火罗这一名称应该用来称属东伊朗语的和阗塞语。

次年即 1908 年，西格和另一位学者西格林（Wilhelm Siegling）发表著名论文《吐火罗语考》，[①]赞同缪勒的命名。特别重要的是，两位学者清楚地证明了这种语言是印欧语系中独立的一支，分为两种方言即吐火罗语 A 和吐火罗语 B，并且发现此种地处东方的印欧语有西方印欧语特别是意大利语和凯尔特语的一些特点，例如，该语言保留了假设的印欧语硬软颚音如 $^*\hat{K}$，$^*\hat{g}$，$^*\hat{g}^h$ 的软颚音特征（吐火罗 A 的 känt、吐火罗 B 的 kante 近于希腊语的 hekaton，拉丁语的 centum）。这标志着"吐火罗学"（Tocharology）的诞生，今年正好是一百周年。

吐火罗语的发现和译释是 20 世纪印欧语历史比较语言学的一件大事，其意义完全足以与赫梯语和安纳托里亚诸语的发现与释读相提并论。吐火罗语和赫梯语也有共同之处，如以"r"为标志的中被动态，这在若干年之后才被认识到。但从总体来说，赫梯学和安纳托里亚诸语的研究在近一个世纪的时间里较吐火罗学发展得更加成熟，而且由于有历史悠久的亚述学的成果作为铺垫，赫梯学研究更加受到印欧语学者的关注，吐火罗学的研究要迎头赶上，还必须作出更大的努力。

在吐火罗语文献的刊布和研究成果的出版方面，自 1908 年后也有相当进展。1921 年西格和西格林发表了《吐火罗语残卷》（*Tocharische Sprachreste*），公布了柏林所藏吐火罗语 A 的写卷并附有许多图版。1931 年他们与语言学家舒尔慈（W. Schulz）合作，出版了 500 多页的《吐火罗语语法》（*Tocharische Grammatik*）。至于吐火罗语 B 文书的出版工作则延迟了，直到 1949 年（*Tocharische Sprachreste*）和 1953 年（*SpracheB*）才先后出版了两卷，其时西格林和西格已先后去世。他们的学生托玛士（Werner Thomas）在这方面也做出了重要的贡献。[②] 直到他去世前不久，还发表了有关吐火罗语 A《弥勒会见记》的论文。[③]

在法国，印度学家烈维（Sylvain Lévi）在著名语言学家梅耶（Antoine Meillet）的帮助下，早在 1911 年就刊布伯希和（Paul Pelliot）所获吐火罗语文书，至 1933 年出版了关于吐火罗语 B 即龟兹语的专集（*Frgments de textes koutchéens*）。1948 年印度学家费辽扎（Jean Filliozat）刊布了一些医学和巫术文书。但总的说

---

① Emil Sieg & Wilhelm Siegling, Tocharisch, die Sprache der indoskythen, vorläufige Bemerkungen über eine bisher unbekannte indogermanische Literatursprache, *SPAW*, Berlin, 1908, pp. 915 - 932.

② Werner Thomas, *Tocharische Sprachreste*. Sprache B. Teil I: Die Texte. Band 1. Fragmente Nr. 1 - 116 der Berliner Sammlung, by v. Emil Sieg und Wilhelm Siegling, neubearbeitet und mit einem Kommentar nebst Register versehen v. Werner Thomas, Göttingen, 1983.

③ Werner Thomas, "Bemerkungen zu den Fragments of the Tocharian A Maitreyasamiti-Nāṭaka", *Indogermanische Forschungen* 108, 2003, pp. 305 - 329.

来,自1953年以来,虽然在吐火罗语语文学和语言学的研究上都有相当进展,一直至20世纪90年代,没有大量刊行吐火罗语原典。吐火罗学前50年的情况,美国学者蓝恩(G. S. Lane)曾在1958年发表的文章里作了很好的概述。① 这一时期的主要研究者,除上面已经提到的外,还有丹麦的裴德生(H. Pedersen)、英国的贝利(H. W. Bailey)、德国的克劳泽(W. Krause)、比利时的顾物勒(W. Couvreur)、温德肯(A. J. van Windekens)、捷克的普哈(P. Poucha)、苏联的伊凡诺夫(Vjaceslav V. Ivanov)等,日本学者如井之口泰淳等也陆续发表了一些日本收藏的吐火罗语文书。我国的季羡林先生在20世纪40年代留德期间,曾在哥廷根大学跟随西格教授认真研治吐火罗语,取得显著成绩。

1975年在我国新疆焉耆出土了44张88页吐火罗语A《弥勒会见记剧本》残卷。季先生从20世纪80年代初开始,经过十多年的艰苦努力,对全部残卷进行释读,分别用中文和英文发表论文多篇,并在德国学者温特(Werner Winter)和法国学者皮诺(Georges-Jean Pinault)的帮助下,于1998年用英文出版了《吐火罗文〈弥勒会见记〉译释》。② 同年出版的《季羡林文集》(南昌:江西教育出版社)第11卷收入此书,并加上了中文长篇导论。这是吐火罗学研究史上的空前之举,受到国际学术界的高度赞誉。

众所周知,依据回鹘文题记,回鹘文本的《弥勒会见记》是自吐火罗文译为回鹘文的,而吐火罗文则是据印度文原本"编译"的。印度文原本没有发现。因此,利用汉译平行异本和回鹘语本的《弥勒会见记》来解释吐火罗语本,是一种行之有效的方法。季先生在工作中就参考了中外学者关于回鹘文《弥勒会见记》的著作。还应该提及的是,我国著名突厥学家耿世民教授自20世纪60年代初开始研究新疆哈密发现的回鹘文《弥勒会见记》写本,1978年后先后用汉文、维吾尔文、德文(与德国同行H. -J. Klimkeit、J. P. Laut,法国学者皮诺合作)发表、出版了研究专著两部(三卷)和论文十余篇,最近又加修订、补充,出版了完整的中文版本,③与季羡林先生的《吐火罗文〈弥勒会见记〉译释》堪称双璧。季先生曾一再指出,通过仔细分析,可以看出关于弥勒的著作有两大类:一类是《弥勒会见记》,另一类是《弥勒授记经》(Maitreyavyākraṇa);属于《弥勒授记经》一类的汉译佛经为数不少,有存有佚,而《会见记》的标本,则是元魏慧觉等译《贤愚经》卷十二《波婆离(梨)品》第五十,这在汉译佛经中几乎是仅有的。这两类著作在吐火罗文写卷中都有,所以西方学者至今往往不加区别。但是,这两类文献毕竟关系密切,研究时可以相互参证。值得一提的是,近年留学慕尼黑大学的刘震博士在哈特曼(Jens-Uwe Hartmann)教授指导下,以四个梵文本与义净译《佛说弥勒下生成佛经》及波斯文译本对校,写成论文《梵本〈弥勒下生成佛经〉及其译本对勘》,这是很有意义的。

现存吐火罗语文书据统计总数在7 600件以上,其中包括为数不少的小残片。为数约1 500件的吐火罗语A写本的主要部分已经发表,但至少还有640件残卷未经编辑,其中有的非常小。许多值得关注的吐火罗语B文书尚待译释发表。收藏地主要是柏林、伦敦、④巴黎、圣彼得堡,还有日本大谷探险队所

① George Sherman Lane, "The present state of Tocharian research", *Proceedings of the 8th International Congress of Linguists* (*Oslo August 1957*), Oslo, 1958, pp. 252－261.

② Ji Xianlin, *Fragments of the Tocharina A Maitreyasamiti-Nāṭaka of the Xinjiang Museum, China.* Transliterated, translated and annotated by Ji Xianlin in collaboration with Werner Winter and Georges-Jean Pinault, Berlin/New York: Mouton de Gruyter (Trends in Linguistics, Studies and Monographs 113), 1998.

③ 耿世民:《回鹘文哈密本〈弥勒会见记〉研究》,北京:中央民族大学出版社,2008年。

④ 英国所藏吐火罗语写卷,有不同编号系统,其中霍恩勒部分,列维、西格和西格林、蓝恩、顾物勒等都作过研究,但系统处理这批材料的是J. W. Broomhead,其著作作为剑桥大学三一学院1962年学位论文(共2卷),至今尚未正式出版。

得,现藏于京都龙谷大学和东京国立博物馆等处。[①] 中国北京、乌鲁木齐和新疆各地文物机构也有一定数量的收藏品,除前述《弥勒会见记剧本》外,有的已见于公开出版物和图录中。此外还有壁上的粗刻(graffites)、铭文和木简(现藏龟兹石窟研究所)、钱币等。我国所藏各类吐火罗语文献已经引起国外学者如德国的瓦尔德施米特(S. Waldschmidt)、施米特(Klaus T. Schmidt)和法国的皮诺等的关注,先后撰文予以讨论和译释。最近奥地利学者 Melanie Malzahn 编辑出版了一部论文集,[②]收入美、奥、法、荷兰等国学者撰写有关吐火罗语语文学的论文 10 篇,对我们全面了解吐火罗语文献的收藏、研究现状很有帮助,可以参看。

吐火罗语文献的数字化工作近年已获得长足进展,特别是通过伦敦的"国际敦煌研究项目"和法兰克福的"TITUS 项目"及柏林德国科学院的"吐鲁番研究项目",大部分收藏于英、德等国的吐火罗语文书已经可以通过因特网获得,这将大大推动吐火罗学的进展。德国学者吉伯特(J. Gippert)和在德工作的日本学者玉井达士(Tatsushi Tamai)和乌普沙拉大学(Uppsala Universitet)的 Christiane Schaefer 博士等为此作出了极大的努力。在吐火罗语文献的断代方面,通过对婆罗谜字母的字象学和古文书学考察及 C[14] 测定,现存吐火罗语 B 文书年代最早的在公元 400 年以前,年代最晚的在 1178 年和 1255 年之间;吐火罗语 A 文书的年代约为公元 700 年至 1000 年。[③] 概括地说,约开始于公元 400 年,终止于公元 1200 年。在婆罗谜字母的古文书学研究方面,L. Sander 和近年的 Dieter Maua 等学者有突出贡献。

当今的吐火罗学研究,较之赫梯学研究虽有逊色,但并无"曲高和寡"之感。资深学者除上文已提及者外,如美国的 Eric P. Hamp、Douglas Q. Adams(亚当斯,吐火罗语专家,所编《吐火罗语 B 词典》于 1999 年出版)、J. H. Jasanoff,德国的 S. Zimmer、O. Hackstein,荷兰的孔甫烈(Frederik Kortlandt)、A. M. Lubotsky,比利时的 Lambert Isebaert,捷克的 V. Blažek,波兰的 K. T. Witczak 等都在近 20 年中有相关论著发表。美国的 Donald Ringe 等用计算语言学方法对吐火罗语在印欧语系中的地位进行探索。英年早逝的冰岛学者 J. Himarsson(1946~1992)1987 年在雷克雅未克创办了世界上唯一的吐火罗语专业刊物《吐火罗语和印欧语研究》(Tocharian and Indo-European Studies),现仍继续在哥本哈根出版。俄国的 Svetlana Burlak、Ilya Itkin,法国的 X. Tremblay,美籍韩国裔学者 Ronald Kim 等都在吐火罗语及相关研究中取得引人注目的成绩。[④] 进入 21 世纪,又有较年轻学者崭露头角,如自 2000 年起,瑞典的 Gerd Carling、日本的斋藤治之、俄国的 S. A. Burlak、荷兰的 M. Peyrot 都有专著问世。[⑤] G. Carling 正与皮诺和温特两位教授合作编纂吐火罗语 A 词典,现已进行 5 年,其第一卷即将出版。2008 年 8 月 25 日至 28 日在莫斯科—圣彼得堡召开了纪念吐火罗语文献译释百年的国际学术会议,我国台湾留法学人庆昭蓉出席会议并宣读了论文。

对吐火罗语的定名问题的讨论始于 20 世纪初,它牵涉到我国新疆等西北地区古代历史、地理、民族

① 荣新江,"Japanese Collections of Dunhuang and Silk Road Manuscripts", IDP Newsletter 10, at: http://idp.bl.uk, 1998.

② M. Malzahn, Instrumenta Tocharica, Heidelberg: Winter, 2007.

③ D. Adams, "Some implications of the Carbon-14 Dating of Tocharian Manuscripts", Journal of Indo-European Studies 34, 2006, 381–389.

④ Ronald Kim, "The Duke of York Comes to Xinjiang: Ablaut, Analogy, and Epenthesis in Tocharian Nasal Presents", Historische Sprachforschung 120, 2007, pp. 66–104.

⑤ G. Carling, Die Funktionen der lokalen Kasus im Tocharischen, Berlin/New York: Mouton de Gruyter, 2000; H. Saito, Das Partizipium Präteriti im Tocharischen, Wiesbaden: Harrassowitz, 2006; M. Peyrot, Variation and change in Tocharian B, Amsterdam/New York: Rodopi, 2008.

分布与迁徙、东西文化交流等一系列复杂问题,①所以至今仍为学者所关注。"吐火罗"在汉语中亦作"兜佉勒"、"吐呼罗"、"覩货逻",原是民族名,后转为地名,指乌浒水(今阿姆河)上游即缚刍河流域,以今昆都士为中心的阿富汗北部地区。缪勒、西格为了证明回鹘文题识中的 twqry 就是吐火罗而连续撰文申述己见。② 后经伯希和、羽田亨、贝利、亨宁(W. B. Henning)等卓越学者和我国王静如教授的考证,③说明缪勒当初的读法有失误,并使许多相关问题得到了澄清。现在多数学者都不反对把吐火罗语 A 称为焉耆—高昌语,把吐火罗语 B 称为龟兹/库车语。但是问题并没有彻底解决。

近半个世纪的争论围绕着藏于圣彼得堡的一件残损的梵语/龟兹语双语文书展开。④ 这件文书里有一个梵语词 tokharika "一个吐火罗妇女"与龟兹语词 kucaññe işcake 对应。对第二个龟兹语词有各种不同解释,但把第一个词读成"龟兹"的对应词似乎是有把握的。这样,就龟兹语本身来说,可以在 tokharika 也就是"真正的"巴克特里亚的吐火罗人和龟兹人之间画上等号。我们既然已经在回鹘语《弥勒会见记》中找到了可以与焉耆等同的 twqry,又在此文书中发现把吐火罗人解释为龟兹人,这就提供了证据,表明焉耆和龟兹两方面都把自己看成吐火罗人。

上述看法遭到一些学者的反对。有人认为双语文书中龟兹的 kucaññe 指龟兹的读法可疑。更重要的是,梵语词清楚地指"吐火罗妇女",而对应的龟兹语词则是阳性或中性名词,这就使任何把这个词翻译作"妇女"的企图无法成立。⑤ 因此,在回鹘文题记 twqry 与古典文献记载的 Tokharoi、Tochari 之间没有明确肯定的联系,这些名称相互之间的类同可能是偶然的。也有学者认为回鹘文题记所指 twqry 是某种伊朗语,也就是说《弥勒会见记》首先从印度文译成伊朗语,然后才译成吐火罗语 A 和突厥语。

与此有关的所谓"四 twgr"(见于古突厥语碑铭、回鹘语、中古波斯语和粟特语文献等),是指塔里木盆地一个带有"吐火罗化"名称的政治实体,有的学者认为这些地区说的语言可以论证是吐火罗语,但也有学者将此与唐代的"四镇"联系起来,其中包括疏勒和于阗,这二者说的都是伊朗语。

关于龟兹人和焉耆人的自称也引起了一些讨论。龟兹王室的汉姓是"白",有的语言学家认为 Kuci 与梵语、阿维斯塔语中表示"白"、"光辉的"等意义的词同源,但至今没有在龟兹语文献里得到充分证明,而且常见的龟兹王的名字里都有 Suvarṇa 这样一个成分(即龟兹语的 Ysāṣṣe),意为"金"(《大唐西域记·屈支国》:"近代有王,号曰金花。"金花即 suvarṇapuṣpa,《旧唐书·龟兹传》作"苏伐勃駃"),所以并不与"白"相联系。⑥ 至于焉耆语的 Ārśi,有的学者认为与《阙特勤碑》、《毗伽可汗碑》的 toquz ärsin 即"九 ärsin"有关。也有学者认为这个词来自佛教混合梵语的 ārya-,转为一种语言时指梵语而非焉耆语。按美国学者亚当斯的意见,焉耆人的自称更像是许多资料所称的类似 *ākñi(阿耆尼)的形式,来自印欧语的 āke,意为"边缘"、"边界",也就是说,焉耆地区的人是"边地居民"、"终点之人",这一类名称在欧洲其他地区也可以找到,例如"乌克兰"、"莫西亚"(Mercia,原英格兰中部和南部的一个盎格鲁—撒克逊王国)

---

① 张广达、耿世民:《唆里迷考》,原载《历史研究》1980 年第 2 期,第 147~159 页;收入《张广达文集·文书典籍与西域史地》,桂林:广西师范大学出版社,2008 年,第 25~41 页。

② F. W. K. Müller mit E. Sieg, "Maitrisimit und Tocharisch", SPAW, 1916, pp. 395-417; F. W. K. Müller, Toxrï und Kuišan (Küšän), SPAW, 1918, pp. 566-586.

③ V. S. Vorob'ev-Desjatovskij, "Pamjatniki central'no-aziatskoj pis'mennosti", UZLGU 16, 1958, pp. 280-308.

④ 王静如 "Arsi and Yen-ch'i, Tokhri and Yüeh-shih", Monumenta Serica 9, 1944, pp. 81-91; W. B. Henning, "The Name of the 'Tokharian' Language", Asia Major, 1949/1950, pp. 158-162.

⑤ 吐火罗语专家皮诺对此另有解释,请参看,见 Indo-Iranian Journal, 45, 2002, pp. 311-345.

⑥ 季羡林:《龟兹国王金花考》,《文史知识》2001 年第 3 期,第 14~18 页。

的语源就是如此。

最后略谈一下吐火罗人的起源问题,这一问题是与印欧人的起源和迁徙问题紧密相关的。

对印欧语和印欧人的起源问题,各国学者已关注多年,但现在还远未解决。著名考古学家伦福儒(Colin Renfrew)认为印欧人起源于中东,安纳托里亚是其故乡,早期农耕者在不断扩张中把古印欧语带到了欧洲。格鲁吉亚语言学家 Thomas V. Gamkrelidze 和俄国语言学家伊凡诺夫有类似看法。与此相对的是金布塔斯(M. Gimbutas)主张的"Kurgan 假说",认为印欧人起源于南俄黑海草原。① 如果印欧语的共同祖先不在欧洲,则欧洲语言的洪流中应该有反映基因变化的波浪。但是近年的 DNA 研究却表明此种"农业先导"对欧洲的基因库影响很小,似乎只限于临近中东的地区。另据一项新的基因研究成果,今天的欧洲人几乎没有遗留多少来自古代中东"肥沃新月地带"居民的基因,所以很可能当年的农耕迁徙者已被早先的狩猎采集居民所代替,狩猎人群学会了农耕者的农业技能,但没有把他们的基因流传下去。此前的研究也证明,从捷克到阿尔泰地区,一直向南贯穿中亚,M17 这个标记出现的频率都很高,"微卫星定位"多样性显示,它最早起源于俄罗斯南部和乌克兰。所有这些基因数据和种种考古发现,都证实印欧语最早起源于南俄的假说是可能成立的。现在也有学者把以上两种假说加以折中,认为欧洲的印欧语源于约 9 000 年前的安纳托里亚农民,但由于环境与生态的变化,约始于 6 000 年前的 Yamnaya 文化已由农耕转为游牧,并引起了早期游牧民族从乌拉尔以西地区向东方的迁徙和印欧语的向东扩张。

著名伊朗学家亨宁曾在其遗作《历史上最初的印欧人》②中将吐火罗人与楔形文字中经常出现的古提人(Guti)等同起来,假定 Tukri 和 Guti 是两个关系紧密的兄弟部族,他们在公元前三千纪之末离开波斯西部,经过长途跋涉到了中国,其中一部分定居下来,其他的仍过着游牧生活,是即后来中国史书记载的"月氏"。Gamkrelidze 和伊凡诺夫发展了亨宁这一观点,波兰学者 K. Witczak 和美国学者 J. K. Choksy 表示赞同并予以讨论。我们认为此说虽富于启发性,但现在还难以证明。

新疆各处的墓葬遗址曾挖掘出许多保存完好的古代人类遗体,其中年代最早的可追溯至约公元前 2000 年,多数具有明显的高加索人种特征。③ 虽然还存在争议,但国内外不少学者都认为这些古尸与吐火罗人的祖先可能存在某种联系。可以设想,原始印欧人约在公元前 5 千纪发生分裂,说安纳托里亚语的部族首先脱离出去,约八、九百年后,说原始吐火罗语的部族约从多瑙河与第聂伯河之间地区逐渐东迁,与阿凡纳羡沃(Afanasevo)文化的居民融合,到达萨彦—阿尔泰地区,然后沿额尔齐斯河、阿勒泰进入准噶尔盆地。这条路线沿途河湖纵横,山川秀丽,克尔木齐古墓群表明这是吐火罗人进入新疆的主要通道。④

---

① M. Gimbutas, Primary and secondary homeland of the Indo-Europeans, *Journal of Indo-European Studies* 13, 1985, pp. 185 – 202. 美国学者 David W. Anthony 在其新著 *The Horse, the Wheel, and Language: How Bronze-Age Riders from the Eurasian Steppes Shaped the Modern World* (Princeton and Oxford: Princeton University Press, 2007) 从语言学、考古学、人类学等诸方面对相关问题进行了全面分析,请参看。

② W. B. Henning, "The First Indo-Europeans in History", in G. L. Ulmen, ed., *Society and History, Essays in Honor of Karl August Wittfogel*, The Hague-Paris-New York, 1978, pp. 215 – 230. 印度学者 A. K. Narain 则认为吐火罗—月氏人起源于中国,见其所著 *The Tokharians: A History without Nation-State Boundaries*, Shillong: North-Eastern Hill University Publications, 2000.

③ E. W. Barber, *The Mummies of Ürümchi*, New York-London: Norton, 1999; J. P. Mallory and V. H. Mair, *The Tarim Mummies*, London: Thames and Hudson, 2000. 对新疆古尸的 DNA 研究,参看:崔银秋:《新疆古代居民线粒体 DNA 研究》,长春:吉林大学出版社,2003 年。对现代维吾尔族的基因研究,见 Shuhan Xu, Wei Huang, Ji Qian, and Li Jin, Anaysis of Genomic Admixture in Uyghur and Its Implication in Mapping Strategy, *The American Journal of Human Genetics* 82, 2008, pp. 883 – 894.

④ 林梅村:《吐火罗人的起源与迁徙》,载《丝绸之路考古十五讲》,北京:北京大学出版社,2006 年,第 12 ~ 34 页;陈致勇:《再论丝绸之路古代种族的起源与迁徙》,《现代人类学通讯》第 1 卷,2007 年,第 92 ~ 105 页。

语言学研究表明,原始吐火罗语与芬—乌戈尔语有长期接触,①这种接触应多半发生在中亚北部地区。

我国史籍所载的(大)月氏人与吐火罗人有渊源关系,目前多数学者都持肯定态度。最近澳大利亚学者本杰明(C. G. R. Benjamin)出版了关于早期月氏史的专著,②可以参看。

总的说来,百年以来的吐火罗学研究取得了重大进展,我国学者也为此作出了艰巨努力,取得不少成绩。但遗留下来的许多问题有待解决。例如,吐火罗语中有不少来自中世伊朗语特别是大夏语(Bactrian)的借词,③其历史背景究竟是什么,我们感到疑惑,应深入研究。又如英国学者布洛(T. Burrow)早已指出楼兰、尼雅所出佉卢文文书的语言中有吐火罗语成分,④亚当斯等一些吐火罗语学者称之为吐火罗语C。这种说法能否成立,现在还没有把握,希望继续探讨。至于吐火罗语在印欧语系中的地位及与各种非印欧语(包括汉藏语)的语言接触,也是需要在前人基础上着力研究的。近年来一些学者采用和借鉴数理统计、计算机科学和与基因测定有关的生物计量学和分支分类学(cladistics)领域的新进展,从事印欧语系语言年代学和谱系学(phylogenesis)的研究,⑤也应该引起我们的关注。目前吐火罗语文书数字化的工作有较大进展,由于其主体部分数量有限(吐火罗语A约500件;吐火罗语B约3 200件,包括洞壁题刻和木简等),如果能通过国际合作的方式,把各国所藏汇聚在一起,编辑和影印出版一部《吐火罗语文献集成》,那对未来的研究将是非常有益的。

附记:

吐火罗学研究应该包括与吐火罗语文献和吐火罗人相关的石窟艺术的研究,但由于笔者本人知识的局限,未能涉及,特此说明。

---

① V. V. Napol'skikh, Tocharisch-uralisch Berührungen: Sprache und Archäeologie. In: *MSFOU*, 242, 2001, pp. 367 – 383.

② Craig G. R. Benjamin, *The Yuezhi: Origins, Migration and the Conquest of Northern Bactria*, Turnhout: Brepols, 2007. 书评见 V. H. Mair, *The Journal of Asian Studies*, 2008, pp. 1081 – 1084.

③ Xavier Tremblay, Irano-Tocharica et Tocharo-Iranica, *BSOAS*, 68/3, 2005, pp. 421 – 449.

④ Thomas Burrow, Tokharian Elements in the Kharosthī Documents from Chinese Turkestan, *JRAS*, 1935, pp. 667 – 675.

⑤ R. D. Gray, Q. D. Atkinson, Language-tree divergence times support the Anatolian theory of Indo-European origin, *Nature*, 426, 2003, pp. 435 – 439; L. Nakhleh, Don Ringe and T. Warnow, Perfect Phylogenetic Networks: A New Methodology for Reconstructing the Evolutionary History of Natural Languages, *Language*, 81(2), 2005, pp. 382 – 420; D. Ringe and T. Warnow, "Linguistic History and Computational Cladistics", In: *Origin and Evolution of Languages: Approaches, Models, Paradigms*, Edited by Bernard Laks, Equinox Publishing, 2008, pp. 257 – 271.

回鹘文《金刚般若波罗蜜经》的版本、原典及其重构

阿不都热西提·亚库甫

柏林勃兰登堡科学院吐鲁番学研究中心

引　言

　　般若文献在回鹘文佛教文献当中构成单独一类,在翻译方法和佛教术语的使用方面具有一些独特的特点。其范围覆盖经、注、感应录等不同类型文献并以抄本和印本的形式在回鹘得以较广的流传。据目前的研究结果,这一文献群至少包括以下九个回鹘文佛典:

　　(一)《金刚般若波罗蜜经》

　　(二)《梁朝傅大士颂金刚经》

　　(三)《般若波罗蜜心经》

　　(四)诗歌体《大般若波罗蜜经》

　　(五)《八千般若波罗蜜经》

　　(六)《说心经》

　　(七)《观心经》

　　(八)《金刚般若波罗蜜经注解》以及

　　(九)《金刚般若波罗蜜经感应传》等。

　　此外,还有一些头韵诗。其中一首似是根据龙树(梵文名 Nāgārjuna)的《金刚般若波罗蜜多颂》(*Nirvikalpa-stotra)创作的头韵诗由土耳其学者阿拉特(R. R. Arat)在其名著《古代突厥诗歌》(简称ETŞ)加以刊布。[1]

　　至今发现的回鹘文《金刚般若波罗蜜经》(以下简称《金刚经》)大多译自该经的汉文简译本。对这一点,我准备在下一节做较详细的探讨。实际上,当提到回鹘文《金刚经》时,学者们首先想到的一般来说是《梁朝傅大士颂金刚经》(《大正藏》,第八十五册,Nr. 2732)的回鹘文译文。其实,这是一种以颂的形式对鸠摩罗什译《金刚经》进行解释的经注,它至少有两种回鹘文译文:经文夹颂的全译本和选译本。其中,全译本由序、净口业真言、虚空藏菩萨普供养真言及奉请八金刚、发愿文、经颂(经、颂夹杂)、五歌等七个部分组成,而选译本则只包括序、颂和歌,其中也没有经文夹杂。后者在结构上酷似伯二二七七、斯四一零五等

---

　　① 参见 ETŞ,第 15 号。

敦煌汉文文献。跟这两个敦煌汉文文献所不同的是,除五十颂外,回鹘文选译本还包括一些不见于相关汉文文献的颂和歌。例如,在汉文本里,《法界通化分第十九》只有经,并不包括偈,而回鹘文选译本却在此处还加有一偈。此外,在汉文本的开头部分"万代古今传"后的经文在回鹘文选译本里以诗体形式出现。目前还不清楚这些不见于汉文的颂和歌是回鹘文译者的创作或源于某种不明汉文文献,有待进一步探讨。①

最近,笔者在柏林所藏回鹘文文献当中确认一些《金刚经》的回鹘文经注残片。其中保存较好的是编号为 Mainz 726(T II D 85)的长卷,其注解的主要是第十六分的后半部和第十七分的前一部分。据笔者初步研究,《金刚经》曾存在过至少四种不同的回鹘文注解。可惜,没有一本能够完整地流传至今。尽管如此,《金刚经》回鹘文注解的发现在学术界尚属首次,其意义较大。

柏林所藏编号为 U 5336(T III 289)的一本回鹘文小书展现的是《般若波罗蜜心经》(以下简称《心经》)简本的完整译本。回鹘文本的底本既不是梵文本也不是五世纪由鸠摩罗什翻译的早期汉文译文,而是玄奘的译本(《大正藏》,第八卷,Nr. 251)。但回鹘文译本在经文后还带有一个较长的陀罗尼。这一陀罗尼的前半部分与梵文原本相同,而其后半部分尚需确定。除以上提到的小书外,柏林还藏有一些属于《心经》的其他回鹘文残片。

至今,诗体本回鹘文《大般若波罗蜜多经》(以下简称《大般若经》)通常被看作是回鹘人自己的创作,②也有些学者暗示,它可能译自梵文。③ 可是,就像庄垣内正弘教授所指出的那样,诗体本回鹘文《大般若经》里夹杂的大量汉字是从玄奘汉译《大般若经》(《大正藏》,第七册,Nr. 220)当中抽出来的。这说明,回鹘文本实际上是以玄奘的汉文译本为蓝本,以韵文形式改写的佛教文学作品。④

《八千般若经》或《小品般若经》也被译成回鹘文。其现存残片都出自同一印本,分别藏在柏林勃兰登堡科学院吐鲁番学研究中心和伊斯坦布尔大学文学院图书馆。该文献残片破损十分严重,只保存一些单词或字母。⑤

此外,还有两件只以回鹘文经名得知的回鹘文文献也可看作是回鹘文"般若"类文献群的特殊成员。一件为所谓的 *Xin tözin ukıtdačı nom*,国内学者一般译作《说心经》。它是用草体回鹘文写成的小书,其正文由长达四百多行的头韵诗组成。该文献于上世纪初被发现在敦煌藏经洞,现藏于大英图书馆(编号为 Or. 8212(108))。另一件为 *ätözüg köngülüg körmäk atlg nom bitig*,可译作《身心见经》或《观身心经》,其残片出自一个回鹘文印本,均保存在柏林。后者的主要部分相当于智顗(538~597)作《关心论》(《大正藏》,第八十五册,Nr. 2833)和《达摩大师破相论》(《新纂续藏经》,第六十三册,Nr. 1220)的部分内容。⑥

本文重点探讨回鹘文般若文献中的核心佛典之一回鹘文《金刚经》的一些问题。首先,对其主要译本进行分类和介绍,并就其原典或底本提出笔者的看法。然后简要讨论梵文原文对回鹘文《金刚经》的作用,同时涉及回鹘文《金刚经》的引用、断代等问题。最后,根据可能的材料试就回鹘文《金刚经》的全貌进行重构。

---

① 见井口 1995,第 375 页。
② 见 Tekin 1980,第 156 页;Zieme 1992,第 43~44 页。
③ 参见 Zieme 1991,第 191~193 页;Elverskog 1997,第 8 页。
④ 详见庄垣内 1995。
⑤ 至于该文献的详细描写见 Sertkaya 1983 和 Yakup 2009。
⑥ 笔者在 Yakup 2008 里,把该文献当作《心经》残卷,不妥,应订正。

一、《金刚经》回鹘语译本的种类及其原典

就像以上所提到的那样,很长一段时间学者们把带有《金刚经》经文的回鹘文残片一律归并到《梁朝傅大士颂金刚经》。[①]直到 1992 年,德国学者皮特·茨墨教授(Peter Zieme)提到,在柏林收藏品中存在一些《金刚经》简本的回鹘文译文。[②] 两年前,日本学者庄垣内正弘教授首次刊布两件属于《金刚经》简本的回鹘文残片。其中,编号为 U 4820 的木刻本残片藏于柏林,另一篇(SI Kr. II 37/1)保存在圣彼得堡。其中后者出自一个两面书写的手抄本。[③]

据笔者初步统计,至少有 10 件回鹘文残片属于《金刚经》简本的回鹘文译文。其中包括四件手抄本残片和六件印本残片。除一件手抄本残片和一件印本残片分别藏在圣彼得堡和巴黎,其余残片均保存在柏林。通过对这些残片的内容和语言进行分析并把它们跟其他语言同类文献做初步比较,笔者确认《金刚经》简本的回鹘文译文至少存在三种。

(一) 以笈多译《金刚能断般若波罗蜜经》为底本的直译本

《金刚经》的所有六件回鹘文木刻本残片,分别编号为 U 4815、U 4820、U 4813、U 4434、U 4789 及 Pelliot 215,都出自同一印本,其底本为笈多(Dharmagupta)译《金刚能断般若波罗蜜经》(《大正藏》,第八册,Nr. 238)是一种直译本。该本比较忠实地再现笈多本所用的佛教术语和各类语素。在这一点上,回鹘文本的译法跟笈多本所采用翻译方法基本相同。[④] 为说明这一观点,下面笔者对两个重要语言现象进行简要分析。

该回鹘文译本用 *nom sakınč* 和 *nom ärmäz sakınč* 来再现由梵文 *dharma-saṃjñā* 和 *na-dharma-saṃjñā* 来体现的佛教概念(见 U 4815 第三行、第六行和 U 4820 第一行、第三行)。在梵文里,这两个术语的第二部分,即 *saṃjñā* 具有"涵义、概念、思想、外部世界的一切"等意义。[⑤] 鸠摩罗什一贯用"相"来翻译这两个术语中的 *saṃjñā*,即在鸠摩罗什本里 *dharma-saṃjñā* 和 *na-dharma-saṃjñā* 的对等术语分别为"法相"和"无法相"。笈多在翻译这两个术语后一成分时所采用的汉字跟鸠摩罗什不同,他分别用"法想"和"无法想"来再现这两个术语。假若该回鹘文本的底本是鸠摩罗什本,那么译者用的不是 *nom sakınč* 和 *nom ärmäz sakın*,而应该是 ** nom b(ä)lgü* 和 ** nom ärmäz b(ä)lgü* 或 ** nom lakšan* 和 ** nom ärmäz lakšan*。因为,在回鹘文佛教文献里,"相"有固定的对等词 *b(ä)lgü* 和借自梵文的 *lakšan*,而用来翻译"想"的通用术语为 *sakınč*。值得提到的是,我们在回鹘文文献里找不到 *sakınč* 和 *b(ä)lgü* 或 *lakšan* 被混用的任何例子。当然,鸠摩罗什有时候也用"想"来翻译 *saṃjñā*,例如"相想"(= Skr. *nimitta saṃjñā*),但在翻译 *dharma-saṃjñā* 和 *na-dharma-saṃjñā* 时,他却未用过"想"。[⑥]

在该回鹘文本里,必须是附加成分 *-GUlUk* 用来翻译汉文的"应",[⑦]例如:*lakšanlıg čog yalın üzä mü*

---

① 见 Hazai/Zieme 1971,第 9 页;Zieme 1985,第 166 页;Zieme 1990,第 38 ~ 39 页。

② 见 Zieme 1992,第 29 ~ 30 页。

③ 见庄垣内 2005。

④ 关于笈多本的翻译方法见 Mayer 1989,Zacchetti 1996 和 Lehnert 1999 的第 294 ~ 305 页。

⑤ 参见 Edgerton 1953,551b。

⑥ 至于鸠摩罗什翻译方法的分析参见 Lehnert 1999,第 296 ~ 297 页。

⑦ 实际上,应在笈多本里用来翻译梵文的副动词附加成分 *-tavya*;关于有关分析参见 Mayer 1989,第 86 ~ 87 页。

ančulayu kälmiš körgülük ärür 一句中的 *körgülük* 再现的是汉文的"见应",而且整个句子的语序也跟其汉文原文"相具足如来见应"大体相同。有所不同的是,回鹘文的译者在"相具足"的对等词 *lakšanlıg čog yalın* 之后加了表示工具的后置词 *üzä* 和疑问助词 *mü*。在此句里,汉文好像是用语序来体现工具意义,而疑问似乎是通过语调来表示的。从这个意义上讲,回鹘文译文的两个追加成分所表达的语法意义实际上是汉文原文所含有的。这里,最有趣的是 *lakšanlıg čog yalın* 这一术语的结构。它是笈多本用来翻译梵文 *lakṣaṇa-sampadā* 的术语"相具足"的直译,构成回鹘语术语的三个词的排列顺序跟汉文的"相具足"完全相同。假若回鹘文本的底本是鸠摩罗什本的话,译者采用的不是 *lakšanlıg čog yalın*,而似乎是 **čog yalınlıg lakšan*,因为,鸠摩罗什用"具足相"来翻译梵文的 *lakṣaṇa-sampadā*。[①]

该回鹘文译文的另一特点是,它在一些方面比起汉文更接近梵文。比如说,在该版本残片 U 4820 里,我们有次碰到 *nomlug käzig* 这一术语(见 U 4820 第十一行)。很明显它在此处是用来翻译梵文的 *dharmaparyāya*。换言之,它是梵文术语 *dharmaparyāya* 的选择性复制。其中,*nomlug* 相当于 *dharma*(等于汉文的"法"),而具有"转、轮"等意义的 *käzig* 再现梵文里具有"回转、旋转、反复"等意义的 *paryāya*。[②]《金刚经》的不同汉译本用不同术语来翻译梵文的 *dharmaparyāya*:笈多本用"法本"(《大正藏》,第八册,Nr. 238,767b)作为对等词,义净本有"法门"(《大正藏》,第八册,Nr. 239,772b20),而鸠摩罗什简单用一个"法"字来翻译这一术语。很显然,回鹘文的 *nomlug käzig* 很难直接来源于这些汉文术语,而其结构和意义跟梵文术语一致。这说明,该回鹘文本的译者虽以笈多本为底本,但同时也参考过梵文原文。作为蓝本,我们以下只提供柏林所藏印本残片 U 4820(现存两页)的转写、译文及与其对应的梵文和汉文原典。

U 4820 的转写(原文见图版一)

01. sakınčı ävrilsär: ol [tınl(ı)]gl(a)rnıng m(ä)n körümi

02. bolgay: tınl(ı)g körümi ÿašaglı körümi putgali

03. körümi bolgay: birökči nom ärmäz sakınčı ävrilsär: ol ok

04. olarnıng m(ä)n körümi bolgay: tınl(ı)g körümi yašag-

05. lı körümi putgali körümi [bolga]γ: munčulayu nä

06. tıltagın tep tesär: anın i[nči]p yana subudi ya:

07. bodis(a)t(a)v üzä m(a)has(a)t(a)v üzä näng nomug tätrü

08. tutguluk ärmäz: näng nom ärmäz ymä ärmäz: anın bo

09. savıg ugrap ančulayu kälmiš üzä sav sözlätilmiš

10. ärür: kola upam[③] tegmä tar kemi yöläštürüglüg[④]

---

① 至今刊布的回鹘文文献里只有 *lakšanlıg čog yalın*,似乎是个固定术语。但这并不等于说,* *čog yalınlıg lakšan* 不能成理。请参见庄垣内 2008,第 543 页的 *čoglug yalınlıg ridi* 和 *čoglug yalınlıg küči*。

② 关于 *paryāya* 的意义参见 Monier-Williams 1899,第 605b 页;狄原 1986,第 764 页。

③ *kola upam* < Skt. *kola upama*"如筏",见 Edgerton Ⅱ,194b;Hirakawa 920b。该术语在梵文原文的形式为 *kolopama*,回鹘文残片以 *tar kemi* 来意译其第一成分 *kola*"筏",其第二成分 *upama*"象"却没有翻译。

④ *yöläštürüglüg* 由 *yöläštür-*"比喻、比较"(Erdal 1991:818)+ 名词性合成词尾-(X)glXg 构成,这里相当于汉语的"喻"。至今刊布的回鹘文文献未见该词。

11. nomlug k(ä)zikig biltäčilär ü[čü]n: nomlar ok

12. tarkarguluk ärürlär: takı nä ayıtmıš k(ä)rgäk nom ärmäz

汉文译文:

······假若(那些众生的法)想转,那些众生可有我见、众生见、寿见和人见。假若他们的非法想转,他们也有我见、众生见、寿见和人见。若问:"为何如此?"须菩提!这是因为,又是菩萨和摩诃萨不应把任何法取反,任何非法也是如此。所以,因此言故,如来说:"知我说法,如筏喻者,法尚应舍,何况非法。"

该段相当于梵文原文的以下部分:

[na hi Subhūte teṣāṃ bodhisattvānāṃ mahāsattvānāṃ] ātma-saṃjñā pravartate na sattva-saṃjñā na jīva-saṃjñā na pudgala-saṃjñā pravartate. na-api teṣāṃ Subhūte bodhisattvānāṃ mahāsattvānāṃ dharma-saṃjñā pravartate, evaṃ na-adharma-saṃjñā. na-api teṣāṃ Subhūte saṃjñā na-asaṃjñā pravartate. tat kasya hetoḥ? sacet Subhūte teṣāṃ bodhisattvānāṃ mahāsattvānāṃ dharma-saṃjñā pravarteta, sa eva teṣāṃ ātma-grāho bhavet, sattva-grāhō jīva-grāhaḥ pudgala-grāho bhavet. saced a-dharma-saṃjñā pravarteta, sa eva teṣāṃ ātma-grāho bhavet, sattva-grāho jīva-grāhaḥ pudgala-grāha iti. tat kasya hetoḥ? na khalu punaḥ Subhūte bodhisattvena mahāsattvena dharma udgrahītavyo na-adharmaḥ. tasmād iyaṃ Tathāgatena sandhāya vāg bhāṣitā: kolopamaṃ dharma-paryāyam ājānadbhir dharmā eva prahātavyāḥ prāg eva-adharmā iti. (Conze 1974: 第 31~32 页)

以下为与其相应的汉文佛典段落:

善實!菩薩摩訶薩,法想轉,無法想轉;不亦彼等,想、無想轉不。彼何所因? 若,善實! 彼等菩薩摩訶薩法想轉,彼如是,善實。彼等菩薩摩訶薩法想轉。彼如是彼等我取有。眾生取壽取人取有。若無法想轉。彼如是彼等我取有。眾生取。壽取。人取有。彼何所因。不復次時。善實。菩薩摩訶薩。法取應不非法取應。彼故此義意如來說筏喻法本。解法如是捨應。何況非法。(《大正藏》,第八册,Nr. 238,767b25 - 767c3)

(二)以鸠摩罗什译文的标题本为底本的回鹘文译文

就像《金刚经》的梵文原文一样,鸠摩罗什、菩提流

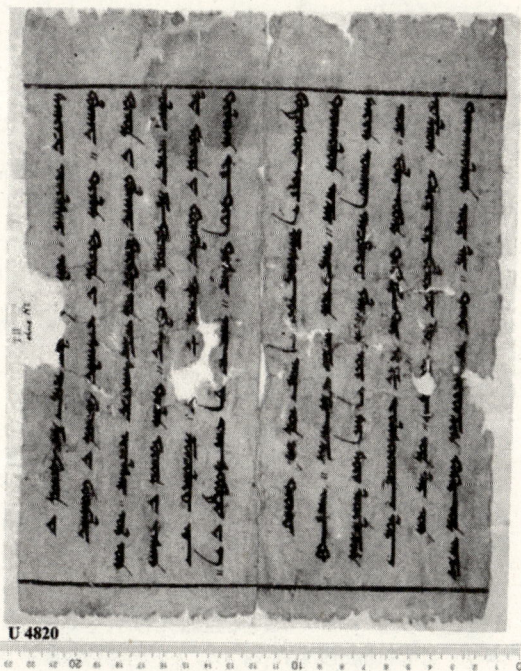

U 4820

图版一:柏林所藏回鹘文木刻本《金刚经》残片 U 4820

支等人的汉文译文根本没有分章分品,当然也没加章分标题。带有章分标题的《金刚经》译文据说出现于五六世纪之间。据说,梁朝的昭明太子萧统(501~531)把鸠摩罗什的《金刚经》译文分为三十二章分并加章分标题。后来,这一带有章分标题的版本(以下简称标题本)比较流行。①柏林所藏回鹘文《金刚经》残片当中至少有五件出自一种标题本译文的手抄本。其中编号为 U 5107 的残片属于一种忠实地再现标题本的译文。其保存的是第十六分的前一部分。有趣的是,恰恰是这一段被回鹘文《慈悲道场忏法》的译者所引用。我将在下一节进一步涉及这一点。

虽然是个小残片,U 5894 代表标题本的另一种回鹘文译文。它原先应属于一个长卷,因为其正面的第八分和背面的第九分之间差很长一段经文。该残片用草体书写,并用 *ülüš* 来翻译汉文标题中的"分"。在这一点上,它跟用 *bölük* 来翻译"分"的注解文残片 U 3347 以及属于《梁朝傅大士颂金刚经》的许多残片有明显的不同。

大体上,U 5894 忠实地再现汉文原文。有趣的是,它包括不存在于鸠摩罗什本的 *hurhanlar nomı tetir*,即"它们是佛法"这一句。实际上,这是第八分的最后一句,除了孔泽(Edward Conze)出版的梵文本外,至少笈多的译本和包培(Nicholas Poppe)出版的《金刚经》的蒙古语译文也包括此句。②另外,在翻译 *nirjāta* 一词时该本使用具有"生"这一意义的[*tug*]*ul*-一词。这说明,译者在翻译过程中也曾参考笈多本。因为,只有笈多用"生"来翻译 *nirjāta*,而鸠摩罗什在翻译该词时却用"出"。需要指出的是,在回鹘文文献语言里,"出"的对等词不是 *tugul*-,而是 *ün*-。③下面是 U 5894 的拉丁字母转写和汉文译文。

U 5894(T III M 353.50(?))的转写(原文见图版二):

01. l'r [nom-]

02. ın t[ayan]m[a]k(?) ü[n]miš ülüši s[äkizinč]

03. ymä subudi nä ukarsız④ k[a]yu [kiši üč ming]

04. ulug ming yertinčü yer suvug [yeti]

05. ä[r]dinin a[g]ısın barımın toš[gurup bušı]

06. bersär ädgü k[ıl]ınč utlısı üküš [ärür mü]

07. [   ]/ [bo nomtı]n [tug]ul[mıš ärür: subu]di

08. [nä üčün tep tesär burhanl]ar nomı tetir. ol *bu*rhanlar

09. [nomı ärmäz] tep. burhanlar nomı tetir.

10. [alku barča] b(ä)lgüsüz ülüši tokuzunč.

11. [   ] subuti nä ukars[ız] sortapan⑤

12. [inčä] s[a]kınč turguru uyur mu

---

① 见 Conze 1978,第 63 页;Lehnert 1999,第 48~49 页。
② 参见 Conze 1974,Poppe 1971 及《大正藏》第八册,Nr. 238。
③ 参见庄垣内 2008,第 711~712 页。
④ 需要注意的是,这里的人称词尾不像跟其他残片那样为-*sän*,而是 -*sız*。
⑤ *sortapan* < Skt. *srotāpanna*"入流"。

汉文译文:

[……依法]出生分第[八]

"复次,须菩提! 你如何理解,若有[人以七]宝和其财富满[三千]大千世界,并(用它)给布施,其善业之得果多不?"

[一切诸佛及诸佛阿耨多罗三藐三菩提法,](皆)出于[此法]。[须菩]提! 若问["为何?"]它们是[佛]法。所谓[非]佛[法]即谓佛法。

[一切]五相分第九

……须菩提! 你怎么理解? 须陀洹能这样想吗:

该段文字相当于鸠摩罗什本的以下部分:

依法出生分第八①

「须菩提! 於意云何? 若人满三千大千世界七寶以用布施,是人所得福德,寧為多不?」(《大正藏》, 第八册, Nr. 235, p. 749b18–19)

一切五相分第九

一切諸佛,及諸佛阿耨多羅三藐三菩提法,皆從此經出。須菩提! 所謂佛法者,即非佛法。須菩提! 於意云何? 須陀洹能作是念:(《大正藏》, 第八册, Nr. 235, p. 749b23–26)

图版二:柏林所藏《金刚经》残片 U 5894(T III M 353.50(?))

---

① 《大正藏》, 第八册, Nr. 235 无此标题, 下同。

圣彼得堡收藏的残片 SI Kr. II 37/1 很有可能也属于这一类。至于圣彼得堡残片的情况庄垣内正弘教授已做过较详细的分析,不再赘述。需要提到的是圣彼得堡所藏残片带有章分标题的部分没有保存下来。另外,圣彼得堡残片出自另一种手抄本。

（三）不以单一底本为基础的回鹘文译文

笔者最近确认,柏林所藏回鹘文残片 Mainz 323 也是《金刚经》回鹘语译文的一种,但它的底本却不易确定。它在不同程度上跟鸠摩罗什和笈多译文的相关部分比较接近,但跟这两个译本又不完全一致。例如,在该残片里,用来翻译梵文 *abhisaṃbuddha* 的回鹘语术语为 *tanuklamakta* [*tuy-*],应该是模仿笈多本中的"证觉"造出来的。它是汉文"证觉"这一术语的直译,也就是说,其中的第一个动词 *tanukla-*"证明" 是汉文术语的第一个字"证"的对等词,而 [*tuy-*]"感觉"再现汉文术语的第二个字"觉"。很显然,回鹘语的 *tanuklamakta* [*tuy-*] 依据的不可能是鸠摩罗什本的音译词"阿耨多罗三藐三菩提"。可是,在同一残片里我们发现 *otgurak nom* 这一术语。我们可以把它看作是鸠摩罗什本用来翻译梵文 *kaścid dha*(*r*)*ma* 的术语"定法"的仿造词。因为,该回鹘语术语所依据的模型不可能是笈多译文中的"一法",因为"一法"在回鹘语佛教文献语言里的可能对等词为 *bir nom,而不是 *otgurak nom*。在回鹘佛教文献语言有很多用 *otgurak* 来翻译"定"的例子,①却没有用 *otgurak* 来翻译"一"的任何例证。总之,*tanuklamakta* [*tuy-*]这一术语仿造的是笈多本的"证觉",而另一术语 *otgurak nom* 依据的却是鸠摩罗什本的"定法"。这显示,在该残片所代表的回鹘文译文所依据的并不是某种单一底本。下面是 Mainz 323 的拉丁字母转写和汉文译文。

Mainz 323（T II S. 2 - 502）的转写（原文见图版三）

01. {[   ]k tarıglg② yer orun yetinčsiz bulgus[u]z}

02. [   ]: ötrü t(ä)ngri t(ä)ngrisi burhan subudika

03. [inčä tep y(a)rlıka]dı: subudi ya säning köngülüngdä nätäg ol

04. [kertüdin käl]miš čın kertü tözüg tanuklamakta

05. [tuyup tüz]gärinčsiz yeg tüzü köni tuymakıg bulyuk-

06. [miš mu ol azu kertüd]in kälmišning čın kertü töztä

07. [öngi nomlaguluk otgurak] nomı ymä bultukar:

08. [ärti   subudi inč]ä tep ötünti:

09. [t(ä)ngrim sizin]g y(a)rlıkamıš y(a)rlıgıngıznıng yörügin mäning ukm[ıš-]

10. [ım inčä ärür: yok ärür] otgurak nom: čın kertü tözüg tanuklamak*ta*

11. [tuyup tüzgär]inčsiz yeg tüzü kertü köni tuymıš atlg ymä ök

12. [yok ärür] otgurak nom čın kertü tözdä öngi kertüdin

13. [kälmiš no]mlaguluk sözlägülük nä üčün tep tesär

---

① 参见庄垣内 2003,第 152 页,注 34～36。

② 该词暂读作 *tarıgl*(ı)*g*,意为"种的",通常跟 yer"地,处"一起使用表示"种地"之义。遗憾的是,《金刚经》的梵文原文和汉文译本都没有跟它相应的词。故此处的确切意义无法确定。

14．［kertüdin kälmišning no］mlaguluk nomı alku barča tutgalı bolmaguluk

15．［sözlägäli bolmaguluk ol nom］ ärmäz nom ärmädin① ymä ärmäz tetir

汉文译文：

［……］{种地［……］无法得到的［……］}然后天中天佛(＝世尊)对须菩提这样说道：须菩提！你怎么想？如来已得无上正遍知证觉吗？或者除真理之外如来还别有定法讲解？［……］须菩提说：据我理解，世尊所说法之义是如此：既没有定法，也没有无上正遍知证觉这么一法，如来可说。若问："何故？"如来所说法，皆不可取、不可说，是非法，又是非非法。

下面似乎是作为该译文底本的鸠摩罗什和笈多译文的相关部分：

　　復次，世尊，命者善實邊如是言："彼何意念？善實！有如來、應、正遍知，無上正遍知證覺？無上正遍知證覺？有復法如來說？"善實言："如我，世尊！世尊說義解，我，無有一法若如來無上正遍知證覺；無有一法若如來說。彼何所因？若彼，如來法說，不可取，彼不可說，不彼法，非不法。"(《大正藏》，第八冊，Nr. 238，p.767c3－9)

　　"須菩提！於意云何？如來得阿耨多羅三藐三菩提耶？如來有所說法耶？"須菩提言："如我解佛所說義，無有定法名阿耨多羅三藐三菩提，亦無有定法，如來可說。何以故？如來所說法，皆不可取、不可說、非法、非非法。"(《大正藏》，第八冊，Nr. 235，p.749b12－16)

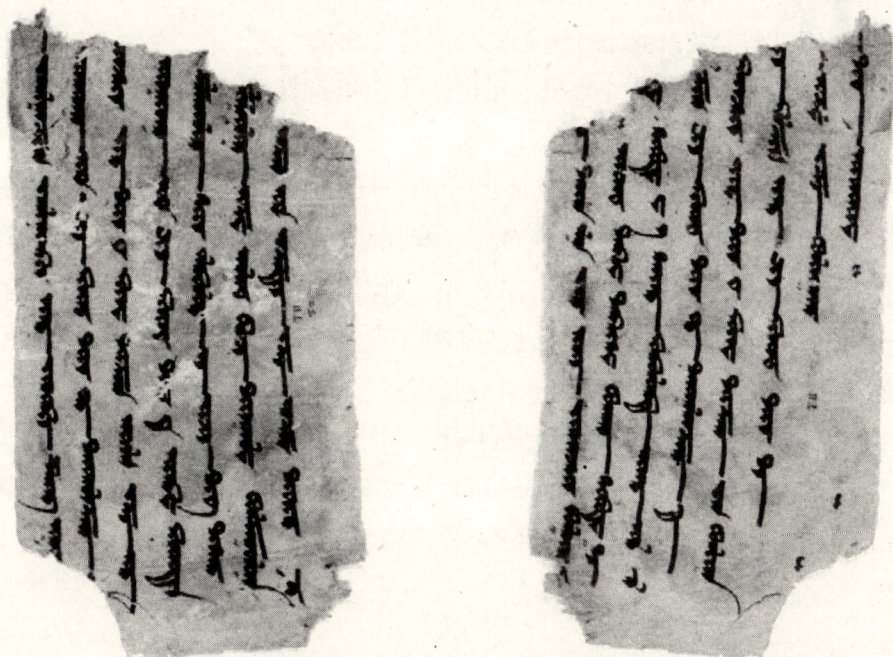

图版三：柏林所藏《金刚经》残片 Mainz 323（T II S. 2－502）

---

① 一般来说，此处出现的是 ärmäz，而不是动词 är-的否定副动词形式 ärmädin。这里的 ärmädin ＋ ... ärmäz 结构并不典型。

除此之外,还应存在过用回鹘文书写的汉语《金刚经》。柏林所藏残片 U 8004(MIK 031775)就出自这一类文献。看来,回鹘人除了直接利用汉文《金刚经》及其回鹘语译文外,还曾用反映中古汉语语音特点的回鹘汉字音来朗读《金刚经》。虽然是个小残片,U 8004 在研究中古汉语语音研究方面具有较高的价值,需专门研究。①

二、《金刚经》梵文原文的作用和回鹘文译文的年代

上面在讨论 *nomlug käzig* 这一术语时笔者已经提到,回鹘语《金刚经》的译者曾参照过《金刚经》的梵文原文。这里还有其他一些实例可支撑这一观点,但不再一一列举。需要指出的是,《金刚经》的各类译本参照梵文的程度有所不同。有些回鹘语译文是否曾参照过梵文,我们没有证据说明。比如说,标题本的各类译文依据的肯定是鸠摩罗什的汉译本,但在翻译过程中,回鹘文的译者是否参照过梵文原文,我们却无法确定。但我们可以断言,比起《金刚经》的其他回鹘文译文,以笈多的译文为底本的直译本更多地参照过梵文原文。关于梵文在《金刚经》的回鹘语翻译过程中所起的作用问题,皮特·茨墨教授曾发表过一些有益的意见,②但其中一些看法,值得商榷。由于这一问题的讨论将不可避免地涉及一些细微的语言现象,笔者不准备这里一一讨论。

这里,我想简单地提到一点。虽然笔者非常赞同茨墨先生"回鹘文《金刚经》的译者曾参照梵文原文"这一观点,但以笔者来看,由他作为该观点旁证来讨论的 *kola upam* 这一词(见残片 U 4820)不是像他所谈到的那样来源于梵文的 *kolopam*,而是来自具有"像筏一样"这一意义的梵文短语 *kola upama*。即便是该词确实源于《金刚经》的梵文本所出现的连声(sandhi)形式 *kolopam*,回鹘文本的译者正确地把它还原为其原形。另外,就像以上所说,作为茨墨先生分析对象的《金刚经》的回鹘文木刻本,即直译本的底本并不是像他所指出的那样是鸠摩罗什的汉文译文,而是笈多本。

为《金刚经》的回鹘语译文确定一个准确的年代是很难的。很显然,《金刚经》的回鹘文印本产生的时间应不早于十三世纪后期或十四世纪初期,大约跟大批回鹘文印本的印刷时间相一致。但至少有一个手抄本产生于早期回鹘语佛教文献时期,也就是九至十一世纪之间。首先,这一抄本使用的是一种相当古老的写经体。其次,在该抄本里,表示"菩萨"的词为早期回鹘语文献语言特有的 *bodis(a)v(a)t*,其在后期回鹘语文献里一般以 *bodis(a)t(a)v* 的形式出现。遗憾的是,从这一抄本只剩下一些残片。此外,还有一些带有古老语言特征的《金刚经》残片,但它们都属于《梁朝傅大士颂金刚经》。除此之外,另一残片,即 U 5894 的产生年代也不应晚于十二世纪。它是用相当古老的回鹘文字体来书写的。

虽然跟本节的内容无关,这里笔者想顺便提到一点。布里特(Judith Ogden Bulitt)在其介绍普林斯顿大学盖斯特图书馆(The Gest Library, Princeton)所藏敦煌文献时提到的所谓回鹘文《金刚经》残片(见 Bulitt 1989,第 18 页,图片 7)实际上跟《金刚经》无关,属于著名的回鹘文佛教故事集成《十业道譬喻故事花环》。

---

① 庄垣内正弘教授已完成该残片的初步研究,其最终成果会近期发表。
② 见 Zieme 1990,第 38~40 页。

三、回鹘文《金刚经》的引用及相关问题

本节简要论及《金刚经》回鹘文译文的引用及其他一些相关问题。众所周知,著名的回鹘文忏悔文献《慈悲道场忏法》(*Kšanti kılguluk nom bitig*)①包含一段引自《金刚经》的经文。最近,庄垣内正弘教授把该段当作《金刚经》的一部分加以刊布。② 该段引文实际上出自《金刚经》第十六分的开头。该段文字是否直接引自汉文或不明回鹘文译文,历来学术界没有确切的看法。最近,笔者在柏林收藏品中发现一个回鹘文残片,正好相当于《慈悲道场忏法》中的引文。经比较,笔者倾向于认为,回鹘文《慈悲道场忏法》的引文并不是直接译自汉文,而是引自《金刚经》的回鹘语译本,即回鹘文残片 U 5107(T M 258)。首先让我们把这段引文(请重点看黑体字部分)跟柏林残片 U 5107 简单做一比较。

回鹘文《慈悲道场忏法》中的《金刚经》引文(= U 2724 v + U 2696 r)

: : subudi kayu tözünlär [o]glı tözünlär kızı birök bo nom ärdinig tutar bošgurur okıyur sözläyür ärkän yana adınagutın tutka učuzka tägsär: bo kiši öngrä ažuntakı ayıg kılınč tıltagınta: bo ažunta ätöz kodup üč y(a)vlak yolta tugguluk ötäki bar ärsär: bo ažundakı ol tutka učuzka tägmäki üzä ök ol öngrä ažundakı tsuy ayıg kılınčları [tar]ıkar ketär öčär amrılur: keningä yana kamagta yeg [tü]zgärinčsiz tüzü köni tuymak burhan kutın bulur

U 5107(T M 258)的拉丁字母转写:

takı ymä subudi tözünlär oglı tözünlär kızı birök bo nom ärdinig tutar bošgunur okıyur sözläyür ärkän inčip yana adınagutın tutka učuzka tägsär: bo kiši öngrä ažuntakı ayıg kılınčı tıltagınta bo ažunta ätöz kodup üč y(a)vlak yolta tugguluk ötäki bar ärsär: bo ažuntakı ol tutka učuzka tägmäki [...]

汉文译文:

"须菩提! 若善男子、善女人,受持读诵此经,就说是他们被人轻视或贬低,就说是他们因其先世的罪行,死后应重生于恶道,由于他们已在今世受到别人轻视和贬低,[他们在先世所反下的罪行将会消灭,最终得到阿耨多罗三藐三菩提。]"③

该段文字相当于鸠摩罗什本的以下部分:

復次,須菩提! 善男子、善女人,受持讀誦此經,若為人輕賤,是人先世罪業,應墮惡道,以今世人輕

---

① 至于其较完整的、最新的刊布本见 Wilkens 2007。
② 参见庄垣内 2005,第(7)1148~(9)1146 页。此外,Zieme 1990,第 23 页和 Wilkens 2007,第 86~87 页等也包括该段的研究。
③ 方括号内的部分是根据 U 2696r 补译的。

贱故,先世罪业则为消灭,当得阿耨多羅三藐三菩提。(《大正藏》,第八册,Nr. 235,750c24-27)

很显然,回鹘文《慈悲道场忏法》中的《金刚经》引文跟回鹘文《金刚经》残片 U 5107 基本上是相等的,其间的差异极小。比如,《金刚经》残片 U 5107 在 yana"又、再者"一词之前还有 inčip"这样"这一词,但《慈悲道场忏法》中的引文却不没有这个词;U 2724 当中的 kılınč"所做、行为"一词也不带第三人称领属附加成分。但这类出入是在抄写过程中很容易发生的。

笔者最近发现,另一柏林所藏回鹘文残片 Mainz 580(T III B TV 51/8)也包括引自《金刚经》的一句。引人注目的是,在这件破损严重的残片里《金刚经》的经名不像在《慈悲道场忏法》中的引文那样为 kimkoke atlg vačrakčedak sudur[汉文]叫做"金刚经"的金刚经,而是 v(a)žir bilgä nom,可译作《金刚般若经》。这译名有可能译自梵文的 Vajracchedikā-prajñāpāramita-sūtra,也有可能是根据汉文经名《金刚般若波罗蜜经》翻译出来的。因为,其中来自梵文的 v(a)žir 在回鹘语里属于常用佛教术语,为回鹘佛教徒并不陌生。以下为柏林残片 Mainz 580 的拉丁字母转写和汉文译文。

拉丁字母转写:

1. [　　　kı]lgalı asıg tusu kılgalı todmaz kanmaz ol bodis(a)t(a)v yorıkı [　　　　　]
2. [　　　]q bä(1)güsüz tep ter：v(a)žir bilgä nom ičintä tört t[örlüg sakınč ärür]
3. [ašnukı] m(ä)n sak[ınč ikinti kiši sakınč üčünč tınlg sakınč[t]örtü[nč öz yaš sakınč]
4. [　　　]/// b[o] tört törlüg sakınč ičin[tä　　　　　　　　　　　　　]

汉文译文:

> ……不满足于做有益之事。菩萨行……说是无相。在《金刚般若经》里[有]四[想。第一为]我想、第二为人想、第三为众生想、第四[为寿想]。在这四想中……

我们无法判断这段引文也是否引自《金刚经》的回鹘文译文,因为,目前为止能够确定的《金刚经》的各类回鹘文译文都缺相应段落。但有一点是可以断定的:该引文跟鸠摩罗什本无关。因为,引文中的回鹘语术语 m(ä)n sakınč"我想"、kiši sakınč"人想"、tınlg sakınč"众生想"、[öz yaš sakınč]"寿想"等只能跟笈多本特有的汉文术语我想、人想、众生想、寿想等联系起来。对等术语在鸠摩罗什本却有不同的形式,即我相、人相、众生相及寿相。关于这一点,上面已作过一些分析,这里不再赘述。但有一点需要提到,在赖尼特(Martin Lehnert)看来,笈多本的"想"并不像有些人所主张的那样是"相"的假名,而像其构造本身,即心+相=想所显示的那样,反映一种心(citta)取相(nimitta)等于"想"这么一个教理。[①] 回到我们的论题,假若 Mainz 580 的引文也引自《金刚经》的回鹘文译文的话,那么这个译文很可能是上面所提到的直译本。当然,我们不能完全排除笈多本另一种回鹘文译文存在的可能性。

最后,笔者还想顺便提到另一个相关事实。《梁朝傅大士颂金刚经》的回鹘文译文也为其他回鹘语

---

① 关于赖尼特的讨论见 Lehnert 1999,第 294~305 页。

文献所引用。柏林所藏编号为 Mainz 844 的残片包含一个跟《柏林吐鲁番文献研究丛书》第一卷(以下简称 BT I,等于 Hazai/Zieme 1971)所刊布的《梁朝傅大士颂金刚经》回鹘文译文相同的偈。Mainz 844 的引用文和 BT I 本之间的唯一差别是引文用 *sözlä-* 来翻译汉文的动词"言",而 BT I 本在翻译"言"时却使用与其同义的另一回鹘语动词 *savla-*。请比较。

Mainz 844(T III TV 59 − b)(原文见图版四)

1. čın savıg sözläsär äzüg bolmaz :
2. kertü sözüg sözläsär igid b[olmaz]:
3. bašlagı [üzüki tägšilmäki] adısıgsız ä[rür:]
4. tözi [(ä)]l[güsi södinbärü čın kertü tetir]:

U 2986(T II S 90.6)

1. čın savıg savlasar äzüg bolmaz :
2. kertü sözüg sözläsär igid bolmaz :
3. bašlagı üzüki tägšilmäki adısıgsız ärür :
4. tözi b(ä)lgüsi södinbärü čın kertü tetir :

这一偈相当于《梁朝傅大士颂金刚经》第三十六颂的以下部分:

真言言不妄　　實語語非空

始終無變異　　性相本來如(《大正藏》,

第八十五册,Nr. 2732,5b23 − 24)

当然,我们不能完全否定 Mainz 844 也可能出自《金刚经》的一种回鹘语注解。因为,《梁朝傅大士颂金刚经》实际也是一种带有注疏性质的佛典。难怪《金刚经》的有些汉文注疏,如《金刚经注解》(注见《新纂续藏经》,第二十四册, Nr. 468)等把《梁朝傅大士颂金刚经》当作注疏加以引用。

图版四：柏林所藏引有《梁朝傅大士颂金刚经》
第 36 偈的回鹘文残片 Mainz 844 正面

四、回鹘文《金刚经》的构拟

皮特·茨墨教授在其《古代厥语"金刚经"的一些问题》(*Probleme alttürkischer Vajracchedikā-Übersetzungen*)一文里提及回鹘文《金刚经》的构拟问题。他认为,依据《金刚经》残片、《梁朝傅大士颂金刚经》的经文部分和一些引文可把《金刚经》三分之二的内容构拟出来。[1]笔者并不清楚,他想用来构拟回鹘文《金刚经》的经文残片和引文到底包括哪些。不管怎样,一般来讲,重构《金刚经》是可能的。但其基础应是回鹘文《金刚经》本身。此外,除了茨墨教授所提到的诸文献外,《金刚经》的回鹘文注疏残片也应列于参照范围,因为,这些注疏在进行注解之前往往引经文段落。当然通过这种方法重构的《金刚经》是虚构的、很不自然的,但它有助于理解回鹘文《金刚经》的全貌。笔者参照《金刚经》的各类回鹘语译文、

---

① 见 Zieme 1990,第 38 页。

《梁朝傅大士颂金刚经》全译本的经文部分、《金刚经》的回鹘文注疏残片以及一些《金刚经》引文,尝试性地对回鹘文《金刚经》进行了构拟。构拟文的基本面貌如下(为节省篇幅,这里不提供各残片的拉丁字母转写和译文):

第一分	U 2981 正面	001 – 008
第二分	U 2786 + 2787	009 – 024
	U 1757	025 – 028
第五分	U 1768	029 – 030
第六分	U 4815	031 – 036
	U 4820	037 – 048
第七分	Mainz 323	049 – 062
	U 2785	063 – 064
	U 5894	065
第八分	U 5894 + U 2249 + ˙U9242	066 – 088
第九分	U 3344v + U 5894	089 – 095
	Mainz 124 Hr + U 2036r	096 – 103
	U 736 + SI Kr. II 37/1 + Mainz 124Hv + U 2036v	104 – 123
第十分	U 3214 + U 3352	124 – 128
第十二分	U 2464	129 – 138
第十三分	U 2499	139 – 145
	U 3066	146 – 155
第十四分	U 3342	156 – 163
第十五分	U 4813	164 – 169
	U 4434	170 – 175
	U 2201	176 – 193
第十六分	U 5107 + U 2724v + U 2696r	194 – 203
	U 759	204 – 205
第十七分	U 759	206 – 235
	Mainz 726 (ll. 1 – 39)	236 – 238
	Mainz 726 (ll. 21 – 30)	239 – 248
	U 3068 + U 2490	249 – 262
第十八分	Pelliot 155	263 – 268
第十九分	U 3126	269 – 273
第二十分	U 4789 (ll. 1 – 8)	274 – 281
第二十一分	U 4789 (ll. 9 – 12)	282 – 285
	U 3392	286 – 299
第二十三分	U 3127	300 – 301

第二十四分	U 3127	302 – 304
第三十分	U 3357 ＋ U 3106 ＋ U 3400	305 – 324
第三十一分	U 2300	325 – 329
第三十二分	3347	330 – 343
	U 2675 ＋ U 2248	344 – 358
跋文	U 3204	359 – 376

构拟文大约相当于《金刚经》的五分之四。从第三分、第四分、第十一分和第二十二分没有留下任何残片。从第二十五分到第二十九分的各分经文没有保存下来。从有些部分，尤其是从第八分和第十八分只是很小一部分内容得以生存。需要重申的是，笔者这里重构的只是从未以这种形式存在过的虚构版本。它是由具有不同风格、不同语言特征和不同书写特点的残片拼凑而成的。

当然，我们也可以用同样的方法来构拟回鹘文《梁朝傅大士颂金刚经》的基本面貌。但构拟文不可避免地重复回鹘文《金刚经》构拟本的大部分内容。但回鹘文《梁朝傅大士颂金刚经》的构拟问题不属于本文的讨论范围。

五、小　结

回鹘文《金刚经》作为"般若"类文献群的核心文献之一，曾在不同时期多次译成回鹘语。其中有以笈多的汉文简译本文为底本的直译本，也有以鸠摩罗什本为基础的各类译本。六世纪左右产生的《金刚经》标题本也被译成回鹘文。有些回鹘语译文的底本不易确定。例如，柏林残片 Mainz 323 既表现笈多本的术语特点又带有参照鸠摩罗什本的迹象。

《金刚经》的有些回鹘文译本所使用的部分佛教术语明显地区别于汉文本所使用的术语：其中，有些直接借自梵文，有些则是根据梵文术语仿造的。这说明，尽管回鹘语《金刚经》都译自同经的不同汉文简译本，但有些回鹘语译本，尤其是直译本的译者曾在翻译过程中不同程度地参考过该经的梵文原文。

虽然回鹘语《金刚经》木刻本的年代相对较晚，但该经的有些回鹘文残片却带有早期回鹘语的一些典型特点，用于书写这些残片的也是早期回鹘文佛典常见的写经体和古式草体。从此可以推测，《金刚经》早期回鹘语译本的产生年代不晚于十一世纪。

回鹘文《慈悲道场忏法》的《金刚经》引文跟柏林残片 U 5104 基本一致。《慈悲道场忏法》中的《金刚经》引文很可能不是译自汉文，而是引自《金刚经》的回鹘文译本。假若 Mainz 580 中的《金刚经》引文也引自回鹘语译本，那么这暗示，除已知的木刻本外，笈多本曾在另一回鹘语译本。

参照《金刚经》的各类回鹘语译文、《梁朝傅大士颂金刚经》经文部分和《金刚经》的回鹘文注疏残片以及一些《金刚经》引文，我们可以把《金刚经》回鹘语译本大约五分之四的内容构拟出来。但构拟本体现的只是一种从未以这一形式存在过的虚构版本。虽然构拟本有助于认识回鹘语《金刚经》的全貌，但它忽视各类文献特有的风格、语言特征和书写特点。

参 考 文 献

Arat, Reşit Rahmatı 1965. *Eski Türk Şiiri*. (Türk Tarih Kurumu yayınları. 7, 45.) Ankara: Türk Tarih Kurumu Basımevi.

Bulitt, Judith Ogden 1989. Princeton's manuscript fragments from Tun-Huang. *The Gest Library Journal* volume III, numbers 1 – 2: 7 – 29.

Conze, Edward 1974. *Vcjracchedikā Prajñapāramitā*. Edited and translated with introduction and glossary. 2nd edition with corrections and additions. (Serie Orientale roma XIII.) Roma: Is. M. E. O.

Conze, Edward 1978. *The Prajñapāramitā literature*. Second edition, revised and enlarged. Tokyo: The Reiyukai. (The Reiyukai Liabrary Bibliographia Philologica Buddhica Series Maior I.)

Edgerton, Franklin 1953. *Buddhist Hybrid Sanskrit grammar and dictionary*. II. Dictionary. New Haven: Yale University Press.

Elverskog, Johan 1997. *Uygur Buddhist Literature*. Turnhout: Brepols. (Silk Road Studies I.)

v. Gabain, Annemarie 1967. *Die Drucke der Turfan-Sammlung*. Berlin 1967. (SDAW. Klasse für Sprachen, Literatur und Kunst. 1967, 1.)

Harrison, Paul 2006. Vajracchedikā Prajñāpāramitā: A new English translation of the Sanskrit text based on two manuscripts from Greater Gandhāra. In: Jens Braarvig et al. (eds.), *Manuscripts in the Scheyen Collection: Buddhist manuscripts*. Vol. III. Oslo: Hermes Publishing, pp. 89 – 132.

Harrison, Paul and Shogo Watanabe 2006. Vajracchedikā Prajñāpāramitā. In: Jens Braarvig et al. (eds.), *Manuscripts in the Scheyen Collection: Buddhist manuscripts*. Vol. III, Oslo: Hermes Publishing, pp. 133 – 159.

Hazai, Georg/Peter Zieme 1971. *Fragmente der uigurischen Version des, Jin'gangjing mit den Gāthās des Meister Fu* "nebst einem Anhang von Taijun Inokuchi. (Berliner Turfantexte I.) Berlin: Akademie Verlag.

Inokuchi, Taijun 井口泰淳 1995. 金剛般若経伝承の人形式. 载: 井口泰淳著《中央アジアの言語と仏教》, 京都:法藏館, 第 364 ~ 377 页.

Lehnert, Martin 1999. *Die Strategie eines Kommentars zum Diamant-Sūtra* (*Jingang-boruo-boluomi-jing Zhujie, T. 1703*). (Freiburger Fernöstliche Forschungen 4.) Wiesbaden: Harrassowitz Verlag.

Mayer, Alexander L. 1989. Dharmagupta (ca. 545 – 619) und das Vajraccedikāsūtra-unreifes Frühwerk oder perfektionistische Wiedergabe der Vorlage? In: E. Wagner / K. Röhrborn (Hrsg.) *Kaškūl*. Festschrift zum 25. Jahrestag der Wiederbegründung des Instituts für Orientalistik an der Justus-Liebig-Universität Giessen. Wiesbaden: Otto Harrassowitz.

Monier-Williams, Monier 1899. A Sanskrit-English dictionary. Oxford: Oxford University Press.

Ogihara, Onrai 荻原云来 1986.《汉译对照梵和大辞典》, 东京:讲谈社。

Poppe, Nicholas 1971. *The diamond sutra. Three Mongolian versions of the Vajracchedikā Prajñāpāramitā texts*, *translations*, *notes*, *and glossaries*. (Asiatische Forschungen.) Wiesbaden: Otto Harrassowitz.

Sertkaya, Osman F. 1983. Turfanda bulunan Uygur metinleri Türkiye kütüphanelerine nasıl geldi? 载: *Türk Kültürü Dergisi* 247, 第 740 ~ 746 页.

Shōgaito, Masahiro 庄垣内正弘 1995. ウイグル文サダ−プラルデイタ菩薩とダルモ−ドガタ菩薩の物語の内容構成について[1-2]。《神戸外大論叢》, 第 46 巻第 3 号, 第 1 ~ 18 頁; 第 46 巻, 第 5 号, 第 1 ~ 12 頁。

Shōgaito, Masahiro 庄垣内正弘 2003. ロシア所蔵ウイグル語文献の研究 [英文附标题:Studies on the Uyghur texts preserved in Russia — Chinese texts written in Uyghur script and Uyghur Buddhist texts.] 京都:京都大学研究生院文学

分院。

Shōgaito, Masahiro 庄垣内正弘 2005. ロシア所蔵ウイグル文'金剛般若経'断片一葉について. 载:石塚晴通教授退職記念会編《日本学敦煌学漢文訓読の新展開》,东京:汲古書院,第(1) 1154 ~ (27) 1128 页。

Shōgaito, Masahiro 庄垣内正弘 2008. ウイグル文アビダルマ論書の文献学的研究[英文附标题: *Uighur Abhidharma texts: A philological study*]. 京都: 松香堂.

Soothill, William Edward and Lewis Hodous 1939. *A Dictionary of Chinese Buddhist Terms.* With Sanskrit and English Equivalents and a Sanskrit-Pali Index. London: Routledge & Kegan Paul Ltd.

Tekin, Şinasi 1980. *Buddhistische Uigurica aus der Yüan-Zeit.* (Bibliothera Orientalis Hungarica XXVII.) Budapest: Akddémiai Kiadó.

Wilkens, Jens 2007. *Das Buch von der Sündentilgung.* Teil 1 - 2. (Berliner Turfantexte XXV 1 - 2). Turnhout: Brepols.

Yakup, Abdurishid 2008. *Alttürkische Handschriften Teil 12: Die uigurischen Blockdrucke der Berliner Turfansammlung. Teil 2: Apokryphen, Mahāyāna-Sūtren, Erzählungen, Magische Texte, Kommentare und Kolophone.* (Verzeichnis der Orientalischen Handschriften in Deutschland, Bd. XIII 20.) Stuttgart: Franz Steiner Verlag.

Yakup, Abdurishid 2009. *Alttürkische Handschriften Teil 15: Die Uigurischen Blockdrucke der Berliner Turfansammlung. Teil 3: Stabreimdichtungen, Kalenderstücke, Bilder, Unbestimmte Fragmente und Nachträge.* (Verzeichnis der Orientalischen Handschriften in Deutschland, Bd. XIII 20.) Stuttgart: Franz Steiner Verlag. [即出]

Yang, Fuxue 杨富学 2004. 回鹘文《荀居士抄〈金刚经灵验记〉》研究.《吐鲁番学研究》第二期, 第 56 ~ 61 页。

Zaccchetti, Stefano 1996. Dharmagupta's unfinished translation of the Diamond-Clearer (*Vajracchedikā Prajñapāramitā-sūtra*). *T'oung Pao* LXXXII, pp. 137 - 152.

Zhang, Yong 张勇 2000. 傅大上研究. 成都: 巴蜀出版社.

Zieme, Peter 1985. *Buddhistische Stabreimdichtungen der Uiguren.* (Berliner Turfantexte XIII.) Berlin: Akademie Verlag.

Zieme, Peter 1990. Probleme alttürkischer Vajrachchedikā-Übersetzungen. In: ALFREDO CADONNA 编 *Turfan and Tun-Huang. The texts. Encounter of civilizations on the Silk Route.* Firenze 1992. S. 21 - 42. (Orientalia Venetiana. 4.)

Zieme, Peter 1992. *Religion und Gesellschaft im Uigurischen Königreich von Qočo. Kolophone und Stifter des alttürkischen buddhistischen Schrifttums aus Zentralasien.* Opladen. (Abhandlungen der Rheinisch-Westfälischen Akademie der Wissenschaften. 88).

Zieme, Peter 1999. The scolar Mr. Xun of the district Xinfan. A Chinese tale in an Old Turkish translation. 载《耿世民先生七十寿辰纪念文集》. 北京:民族出版社, 第 276 ~ 288 页.

Zieme, Peter 1999b. The "Sūtra of Complete Enlightenment" in Old Turkish Buddhism. In: FOGUANGSHAN FOUNDATION FOR BUDDHIST & CULTURAL EDUCATION (ed.): *Collection of Essays 1993. Buddhism Across Boundaries. Chinese Buddhism and the Western Regions.* Sanchung (Taiwan). S. 449 - 483.

Manichaean Terminology in Sogdian

Desmond Durkin-Meisterernst

Turfanforschung, Berlin Brandenburg Academy, Berlin

First of all, I would like to thank Li Xiao and all the organizers of this very interesting conference for the opportunity to talk to you here in Turfan. The Manichaean text material in the Turfan Collection in Berlin contains a significant number of Sogdian texts and Sogdian passages or remarks in texts in the other Iranian languages, Middle Persian and Parthian used by the Manichaeans in Central Asia. The Sogdian Bezeklik letters published in 2000 also belong to this community. Other texts (either as texts, captions, names etc. or in what they depict, e. g. the dignaitaries of the court listed in M1 and MIK III 36) show clearly that, in Turfan, even the use of Sogdian was secondary: Many of the Manichaeans were Uigurs who used texts in their own language but also those in Sogdian, Middle Persian and Parthian. We therefore have the possibility of gaining insights from the Turfan material into Manichaean Sogdian as such, but also into the specific constellations in which the Manichaean literature in Sogdian arose and was used.

The spread of speakers of Sogdian along the Silk Road certainly began earlier than the spread of Manichaeism. While we could naturally assume that Manichaeism spread from the Parthian-speaking areas of the northern Sasanian empire to the neighbouring area of the Sogdiana (from time to time under Sasanian control) to the north, we have no direct evidence for this and cannot determine the time when this may have happened. The Parthian mission started during Mani's lifetime, but none of the missionary texts (preserved only in fragments) mentions a Sogdian mission, rather all the fragments indicate that the missions stayed within the frontiers of the Sasanian empire, something that can also be observed for a long time on the western frontiers of the Sasanian empire and which may confirm a specifically Sasanian policy adopted by Mani at least up to a certain period. In any case, there is no missionary history for the time after Mani's death. The lack of sources and the complex military and political developments in Central Asia in the 4th – 6th centuries make it extremely difficult to make any tenable assumptions about the date of the arrival of Manichaeism in the Sogdiana. [①] The only direct historical evidence we have is late: An-Nadim (late 10th c.) says that there was an unspecified number of Manichaeans in cities of the Sogdiana; however, he gives no history of the development of the Manichaean communities in these cities. Al-Beruni mentions Manichaeans in Turkestan, China, Tibet and India, but says nothing about Manichaeans in the Sogdiana.

---

① If the date of the name *s"nk* on a seal from Čāč is correct, 5th or 6th c. , it is the earliest documentation of Manichaean activity to the north of the Sogdiana.

But we do have, in the texts, a direct source of linguistic information.

Looking at the Sogdian fragments listed in Boyce's *Catalogue of the Iranian Manuscripts in Manichean script in the German Turfan Collection*, 1960 and those in Sogdian script in Reck's catalogue *Berliner Turfanfragmente manichäischen Inhalts in soghdischer Schrift*, 2006 we find roughly 1000 fragments of various sizes and in a wide variety of conditions. Digital images of all these fragments are online in the Digitales Turfanarchiv at turfan. bbaw. de The texts on these fragments include a few fragments of works by Mani and parts of a church history but in the main they comprise various homilies and treatises (Kephalaia type expositions), sermons and tales, as well as hymns and prayers, some letters and documents (s. the list of texts according to content in Reck 2006, 332 – 338 and Morano 2007, 240 – 266). Most of this Manichaean literature was translated from Middle Persian and Parthian, even if the originals do not always survive.

When we look closer, some details are very indicative. The double page M172 contains on page I part of the Middle Persian text of Mani's Gospel, a text also attested in part in Greek in the Cologne Mani Codex from Egypt, which confirms that the text goes back to Mani and will have existed in Aramaic but also in Middle Persian, which therefore attained a particular status. In consequence, the Middle Persian text was retained in M172 I together with a Sogdian interlinear version which clearly shows that the user of the book needed an interpretation of the Middle Persian text but probably also needed to be able to recite the Middle Persian in the original. The second page M172 II contains an Old Turkish Manichaean text, documenting the language of the Uigur patrons of Manichaeism in Central Asia, for whom Sogdian was at least in part a *lingua franca*. The Sogdian captions on many of the pages containing the small number of Middle Persian and the much larger number of Parthian hymns shows again the use of Sogdian by the Manichaean community. Sogdian transcriptions of Parthian hymns and the Sogdianised cantillations (indicating the chanting or singing of the hymns) of Parthian hymns show the need for versions of the hymns in a script that specific people could read, allowing them to follow and reproduce the sound of the hymns without necessarily knowing what the words meant. There do not seem to be any original Sogdian hymns, i. e. the community sang mostly Parthian hymns and hymn cycles and had, for example, a Sogdian translation of the first part of the Parthian *Huyadagmān* but not of the whole text[1]; the great mass of Parthian hymns was not translated. Perhaps some of the names of the melodies given in the captions indicate Sogdian melodies; for lack of further details we cannot judge this. Sogdian versions of some Parthian prose texts survive: These are the sermon texts. It seems unlikely that 'independent' Sogdian prose texts existed, though if there was a Manichaean mission in the Sogdiana it should have resulted in some developments in the Manichaean literature. The Turkish confessional text *wxāstwānift* has a Parthian title and some Parthian elements but was surely translated by someone with a knowledge of Sogdian or using a Sogdian version, of which a part has survived. Some of the Sogdian tales

---

[1] In M815 the Parthian and Sogdian texts of AR Ia 7 – 8 and 12 – 13 are presented on the same page. There, the Sogdian *šm'rynd* (AR Ia 7b) seems to contain a Parthian spelling for the ending of the 3rd plural!

may have had a Parthian or Middle Persian background, the use of the conjunction *kt* to introduce speech in the 'Tale of the Pearl borer' may be due to a Middle Persian or Parthian original, because this feature does not regularly occur in Sogdian texts otherwise. [1]

There are significant Sogdian texts without a Parthian original. These are Sogdian versions of texts in Middle Persian such as the above-mentioned beginning of Mani's Gospel in M172/I/, Sogdian parts of the Book of Giants, the cosmogonical text M178/. The lack of a Parthian version of these texts can be explained by a high regard for Middle Persian as a language probably spoken by Mani and used by him, e. g. in the *Šābuhragān* and also by the closeness of Parthian and Middle Persian, which probably meant that educated Parthian-speakers were able to make sense of Middle Persian. This could not apply to Turkish-speakers who needed a proper interpretation of the Middle Persian texts.

When were the Sogdian versions of these texts made? If in the Sogdiana, then to continue the work of translating Manichaean texts into the local language. If not in the Sogdiana but in Eastern Central Asia, the translations chose a *lingua franca* possibly even instead of a local language, Turkish, to emphasize the non-local importance of the texts. The result in Turfan is the same: To a certain extent, Sogdian is paired with Middle Persian, and Parthian with Turkish, to continue a situation that arose in the Manichaean Parthian mission during which only certain texts were translated (mostly from Aramaic) into Parthian whereas texts by Mani in Middle Persian were retained in the original. It seems that Sogdian may have taken over something of the role of Middle Persian.

What is the status of M178? This is a beautiful double page written on white leather and containing part of a Sogdian cosmogonical text. No such text has survived in Parthian, the known texts of this kind are all in MP, though none preserves the original of the Sogdian text. [2] The luxurious presentation of the double page indicates that it was produced for a special purpose, perhaps for presentation at the Uigur court. The use of leather is also unusual, since the Manichaen fragments in Turfan are all on paper with a few exceptions on silk or ramie. The Manichaen Bactrian page is also written on leather. Is that incidental or is the use of leather intended to refer to Western book materials?

Let us now move on to the terminology. Most of the following is a presentation of the work of others and may already be familiar to you.

Manichaean terminology: Terms common to Sogdian and Parthian (in some cases also Middle Persian)

As related Middle Iranian languages, Sogdian and Parthian have common features and a common inherited vocabulary. Some of the religious vocabulary in both languages is identical.

---

[1] Christian Sogdian texts are excepted from this statement because the use of the conjunction there is due to the Syriac particle *d* in the originals of those texts. Some other Sogdian tales also exhibit this feature, which may mean that all came from the same Middle Persian or Parthian source.

[2] Henning 1948 accordingly assumes a translation from MP. Concerning the term. *'βtkyšpy xwt'w* he points to MP *haft kišwar* and notes that the term is used for the usual *w'd jywndg*. This shows an independent tradition but the Sogd. *'βtkyšp* actually is closer to Parth. *qyšpr* than MP *kyšwr* and the spelling *wyyndyy* in line 51 with its unjustified *γ* may suggest a late Parthian form with a fricativised *γ* for g from *k. *'rd'w'n m't* is also a Parthian term in the text. Does all this affect the source and dating of the text?

Identical terms in Sogdian and Parthian

Sogd.	Parth.
"βryn-	*'fryn-* 'to bless' [cf. *sfryn* 'to create' and *sfrywn* 'creation'].
"prywn, *'frywn*	*"frywn* 'blessing' [this may be a Parth. loanword, because the native term seems to have the form *'fryw*, i. e. without the final *n*, in Ancient Letter 1].
δynh	*dyn* 'religion' with a difference in the initial consonant. Similarly *δ'm* and *d'm* 'creature, creation'; *δyw* and *dyw* 'demon'; *γryw* and *gryw* 'soul'.
frn	'glory', general Iranian.
rw'n	*rw'n* 'soul'.
tm-	*tm* 'darkness'.
tnp'r	*tnb'r* 'body'.
w'xš 'word'	*w'xš* 'spirit' (referring to the occurrence in *w'xš ywjdhr* 'holy spirit' MacKenzie 1994, 189 says: 'seems to take the meaning of MP *w'xš* 'spirit', instead of its normal Sogd. one 'word'. The same applies to *w'xš ' y βxtgyy* 'the spirit of division/schism', s. below under language switching).
wyγr's	*wygr's-* 'to wake', a central term in Manichaeism, indicating the wakening of the soul to divine revelation. Here also with the difference *γ ~ g*.

Manichaean terminology: Names of mythological figures

Sundermann 1979 gathered the names of mythological figures in the Iranian Manichaean texts. He groups the names according to their type. Only the Sogdian terms in his list are reproduced here. Also included here are the names Sundermann published in a further article 'Eine Liste manichäischer Götter in soghdischer Sprache' (Sundermann 1994) with the names of the deities from a Sogdian list. For the attestations and commentaries please consult Sundermann 1979 and Sundermann 1994.

1. retention of a Syriac name[1]

'δ'm	Adam
'hw'y	Eve
β'm βγ-	the Great Builder, Aramaic *bān*.
mšyh'	the Messias[2]
s't'nh	Satan (fem. ! s. Wendtland 2005 following Henning 1944)
š'qlwn	Saklas
yyšw	Jesus[3]

2. translation of a Syriac name or term. These are descriptive names some of which are very general words with a specific Manichaean use.

---

[1] *m'ny*, *m'nyxyws* the name of the prophet Mani is also Semitic; the second form has retained a Greek ending.

[2] This and the next term are not in Sundermann's list.

[3] Misplaced in Sundermann under group 3.

''p*	'water' and ''pβγ-*, the deified name of an element.
''ṯr*	'fire', also the name of an element.
''z*	'greed' < MP/Parth. ''z*.
'rδ'yp'y βγ-	'god radiance', probably Jesus the Light, Syriac *yyšw'zyw'*.
'štykw pr'yšt'k	'third messenger' < Parth. *hrdyg fryštg* (translation of the first part, retention of the second).
β'mystwn	'column of glory' < Parth. *b'mystwn*.
βr'nk'n βγ-	'god aether', the god of the first light element.
fryy rwšn βγ-	'god beloved of the light(s) < Parth. *fryhrwšn*.
gryw jywndg	and *jwndy γryw* 'living soul' from Parth. *gryw jwyndg*.
qnygrwšn	'maiden of light' < Parth. *knyqrwšn*.
m'x	and *m'xβγ-* 'god moon' < Parth. *m'ḥ*.
mnwhmyd rwšn	'light-nous' > Parth. *mnwhmyd rwšn* (note the retention also of Parth. *rwšn*).
pδw'xtq	'answer' (lit. the answered) and *pδw'xt'kk βγ-* a transcription of Parthian *pdw'xtg bg* 'god Answer'.
rštyy 'xtw	'just judge' < Parth. *d'dbr r'štygr*.
rwxšn'βγpwryc	'light princesses', containing Parth. *pwhr* 'son, child'.
w'ṯ	'wind', and *w'ṯ βγ-* following Parthian *w'd* 'wind'.
w'd jwyndg	and *w'δ jywndyy* 'living spirit' < Parth. *w'd jywndg*.
w'xš ywz-txr	'holy spirit' < MP *w'xš ywjdhr* (a rare case of retention of a MP term).
wjyd w'd	'chosen spirit' < Parth. *wjyd w'd*; also *wjyδw'δ* (s. also M172 and the note by MacKenzie 1994, 189).
xrwštg	'call' (lit. called) and *xr'wšt'kk βγ-* a transcription of Parthian *xrwštg bg* 'god Call'. Together with *pδw'xtg*, this refers to the central gnostic element in Manichaeism, the call of the deity to the slumbering soul and its answer.
xwr	and *xwr βγ-* 'god sun' < MP *xwr*.
zprṯ w'xš	and *zprtw'ṯ* 'holy (pure) spirit', s. *w'xš* above.
XII βγpwryšt	'the twelve princesses', s. *rwxšn' βγpwryc* above.

3. identification with Mazdaean mythical figures, i. e. usually the retention of a Parthian or Middle Persian term where this identification had already taken place.

'rt'w frwrtyy	'air' Parth. *'rd'w frwrdyn*.
'rtxwšṯ	'light' Zor(oastrian) MP *Ardawahišt*.
δšny w't βγ-	'god of the right (south?) wind', a Zoroastrian deity who greets the dead soul or one of the Manichaean five light elements (Sundermann 1994).
mrδ'spnd	'the light element(s)' and *mrδ'spnt βγ-*, MP *'mhr'spnd'n, mhr'spnd'n*.
mrtynh	'Eve' MP *mwrdy'n* [Zor. MP *mašyānag*].

myšyy βγ-	ˈgod sunˈ MP/Parth. *myhr*.
nr'y-sβyzδ	and *nryšnx βγ-* Parth. *nrysfyzd* and Zor. MP *Nēryōsang*.
pt'ycy βγ-	ˈfacing godˈ, the goddess (*daēnā-*) who receives the soul after death, the Manichaean Maiden of the Good Deeds (ˈJungfrau der Guten Tatenˈ) (Sundermann 1994).
pysws	ˈPēsūsˈ
srwšrt̲ βγ-	ˈgod just Obedienceˈ MP *srwšhr'y*.
šmnw	ˈAhrimanˈ MP/Parth. *hrmyn*.
whmn rwšn	ˈlight-nousˈ MP *whmn*.
wšγnyy βγ-	ˈAdamasˈ, Zor. MP *Wahrām*.
wyšprkr	ˈliving Spiritˈ Av. *vaiiuš uparō. kairiiō.* (Humbach)
xwrmrt'βγ	ˈFirst Manˈ, MP *'whrmyzd by*, Parth. *'whrmyzdbg*.
z'y spnd'rmt̲	ˈthe splendid earthˈ Zor. MP *spendārmad*.
(')zrw' βγ-	ˈZurwān, Father of Greatnessˈ, MP *by zrw'n*, Parth. *zrw'βγ-*.

4. ˈdefinitionˈ and unclear cases. some of these are descriptive names.

"δβγ-	s. below under Indian loan-words.
"wqršnyy	ˈof the same formˈ, the Column of Glory.
'βtkyšpy xwt̲'w	ˈlord of the seven world regionsˈ = *w'd jywndg*.
'δδm't	ˈmother of the Livingˈ, apparently modelled on *"δβγ-*.
'rδ'w'n m't̲	ˈmother of the justˈ < Parth. *'rd'w'n m'd*.
δynmzt̲'yzn βγ-	ˈgod of the Mazdaean religionˈ.
δynyfrn	ˈglory of the religionˈ Parth. *dyn frh̲*.
pδf'ry βγ-	possibly for MP *pd pryyg yzd ˈgod carried on the shoulderˈ, translation of a Syriac term equivalent to Greek 'Ωμοφόρος (Sundermann 1994).
r'mr' t̲wxβγ-	ˈpeace-giving godˈ MacKenzie 1994, 187: ˈneither element is otherwise found in Sogdianˈ.
sm'n xšyδ	ˈlord of heavenˈ.
rwxšn'γrδmncyk 'xšywnyy βγ-	ˈgod ruler of the paradise of lightˈ MP *whyštwšhry'r*, Parth. *whyšt šhrd'r*, but the term is closer to Avestan *γarō. δəmāna-*.
(')xš'yšpt βγ-	< *xšaθra-pati- baga-* ˈgod lord of the landˈ, apparently the equivalent of MP *dhybyd* (Skjærvœ apud Sundermann 1994).

Concerning the names in the list published by him in Sundermann 1994, 461 −465 Sundermann notes the remarkable independence of some of the Sogdian names from the Middle Persian and Parthian names of the same entities and their closeness to Zoroastrian terms. He concludes (p. 462): ˈThe Sogdian divine terminology that certainly was made in the first half of the first millennium AD in the Sogdiana, creates the impression that it arose in a country definitely shaped by Zoroastrianism, in which Buddhism played no prominent role. [1] Is this a specific Sogdian contribution to Manichaean terminology and therefore evidence for the Manichaean mission in the Sogdiana, as Sundermann suggests? Unfortunately, the names are preserved only in a list. The lack of specific sources — in particular of Sogdian texts using these names and the Middle Persian or Parthian originals of these texts makes it impossible to judge if these names are Sogdian developments or rather continuations of Middle Persian and Parthian names that may well have existed beside the attested ones. This also raises the further question of how relevant the Manichaean mission in the Sogdiana may have been for the development of Manichaean literature in Sogdian. As is well known, in the sphere of Buddhist literature, some of the earlier translators from Indian to Chinese were Sogdians who were active outside of the Sogdiana and were not writing down Sogdian versions of these texts; later, Sogdian translations of Chinese texts were made in Eastern Central Asia rather than in the Sogdiana. It seems therefore to be a possibility that at least some of the Sogdian Manichaean texts were also products of the Sogdian diaspora or perhaps even of Sogdian as a lingua franca.

Manichaean personal names

P. Lurje (Vienna) is currently preparing a volume on Sogdian personal names. These include the names of Sogdian Manichaeans. Naturally, the Sogdian Manichaeans display a wide variety of names, most of which are assumed Middle Persian and Parthian or even mixed names, as well as native Sogdian ones.

Manichaean concepts apart from names

The following groups of words are titles and designation of the Manichaean hierarchy and its community; a clearly identifiable group of Indian loanwords; and an area of vocabulary difficult to define between borrowing, reinterpretation of native words (calques) and language switching.

Titles and designations

The titles used in the Manichaean hierarchy: *δyns'rδ'r* 'leader of the religious community', *mhystk* 'presbyter', *mwj'k ~ mwz"k* 'teacher', *xrwhxw'n* 'preacher', *xwyštr* 'presbyter' are, with the exception of the last, borrowed from Parthian and Middle Persian. The same applies to the designations *nγwš'k* 'hearer, auditor', *wyct'y* 'chosen, elect' and the terms *δyn'βr* and *δynδ'r* 'bringer/holder of the (true) religion'. The

---

[1] 'Die soghdische Götterterminologie, die gewiß in der ersten Hälfte des ersten Jahrtausends n. Chr. in der Sogdiana geschaffen wurde, erweckt den Eindruck, daß sie in einem eindeutig zoroastrisch geprägten Land entstand, in dem der Buddhismus keine auffallende Rolle spielte.' His remark contains not only 1, the presence of Zoroastrianism, which applies to the Sogdiana but also to the Sasanian Empire but also 2, the absence of Buddhism which should exclude Turfan and might be taken to exlude eastern Iran, where Parthian may have picked up some of its Indian loanwords. But of course, there are some Indian loanwords in the Sogdian terminology. Some of these are dependent on Parthian, some probably arose in Turfan.

words *m'nyst'n* 'monatery' and *'wnglywn* 'Evangelium, gospel' are also loanwords, the first from MP/Parth. the second from Greek via Syriac.

Indian loanwords

The Indian loanwords (mostly from a Buddhist context) occurring in Manichaean Sogdian texts were listed by Sims-Williams 1983, 140 – 141, to which I refer. The list is restricted here to religious terms. These include:

'βc'npδ	'world' < *jambudvīpa*-.
'δδβγ	'supreme deity' < *adhideva*- or *atideva*- (Sims-Williams 1983, 139).
βwsndyy	'fast' < *upavasatha*-.
bwt̤	'Buddha' < *buddha*-.
cxš'pδ	'moral precept', <*śikṣāpada*- with a Parthian sound-change (Sims-Williams 1979).
δrmh	'dharma' < *dharma*- and *δrmyq* 'legal'
ykšyšt	pl. 'yakšas' <*yakṣas*-.
krm, qrm	'karma, bad deed' and *krmšwhn* 'forgiveness' lit. 'the washing off of karma' < *karman*-.
mx'pwtty	'element' < *mahābūta*- (Sundermann 1997, 142 (§ 119,3)).
mytr'gr	and *mytrcytr* and *mytrg* < Maitreya.
p'šyk	'hymn' < *bhāṣā*-.
rtn	'juwel' < *ratna*-.
smyr γr-	'Mount Sumeru' < *sumeru*-.

Reinterpretation of native words and language switching

An important part of Manichaean terminology in Sogdian is the use of native words in a technical Manichaean sense. The term for the sacred meal *xw'n* entered Sogdian as part of a borrowed MP phrase *xw'nyzd'n* < *xwān ī yazdān* 'meal of the gods' but may also have met with a native Sogdian word of the same basic meaning, now narrowed into the Manichean sacred meal. This and other cases are difficult to decide. Is, for example, *'n'wš* 'immortal' a loanword contrasting with the native form *nwš'k*? Is *'nž'wny* 'saviour' (lit. 'who causes to live') modelled on MP *zyndkr*? The words *wyδβ'γ* 'exposition, sermon' and *xwyck'w'k* 'clarification (esp. of a parable)' have specific Manichaean usages but can be expected to have existed outside of Manichaean contexts. The same applies to other words whose meanings do not change, but by being placed within a fixed Manichaean scheme they acquire new references, as for example in the various lists in the Sogdian version of the Sermon on the Light-Nous (s. Sundermann 1992, 137 – 141). Simple terms for 'body' and 'soul', 'light' and 'darkness' are given new, specifically Manichaean nuances and contexts. There is some variance here: M 14 shows that the lists could also be kept in the original language, and simply glossed by Sogdian words. For a Sogdian-speaking Manichaean the Sogdian words just refer back to the corresponding Parthian terms that are the primary technical terms, removed, as it were, from daily use in the spoken language. Some of the Parthian terms are never translated (or the translations have not survived); others are translated more than once, e. g. in the Sermon on the Light-Nous Parthian *mnwhmyd* 'mind, understanding' is translated by *'šy'h* and *jn'* (Sundermann 1992, 137); the unattested Parthian term for 'patience' is translated by *wyt'wp'zn'kyh* and *βwrt'rmyky'* (Sundermann 1992, 139).

Language switching is particularly clear in BBB ('Bet- und Beichtbuch', M801a Henning 1937) where various MP quotations are given, introduced by remarks such as: BBB 476 *c'nw npykyy frm'yt* 'as he (= Mani) says/commands in a book' or BBB 547 *c'nw frm'yt* 'as he says/commands'. MP is clearly the language of canonical texts and is revered as such. It may have been accessible to most of the Sogdian-speaking Manichaeans, who may have used MP with their trading partners. But this may no longer have applied to the Uighur-speaking Manichaeans in Turfan, who may have needed a translation. No Parthian quotations are introduced in this way in the text — i. e. Parthian texts going back to Mani do not exist and Parthian does not have the same standing — but Parthian hymns and the phrase *hyrzwm 'st'r* 'forgive my sins' are part of the liturgy. As mentioned above, there are Parthian passages in Sogdian texts, such as M 14 where a list of Parthian terms is included in the text. This language switch shows the importance of Parthian in an exposition of dogmas. On the other hand, the two Sogdian letters complaining about the behaviour of Syrian Manichaeans in Turfan (Sundermann 2007) contain some MP terms, the most important of which is *w'xš' y βxtgyy* 'the spirit of division/schism' of which the Syrians are accused in the second letter. This specific term may reflect a predominance of Persian speaking Manichaeans in Turfan in the tenth century[①]; it could be once only quotation or a standard term. The MP title *s'r'r* 'leader' and the Parth. *dyncyhryft* 'religiosity, proper religious behaviour' also occur in the first letter.

Adaptation of Zoroastrian terminology

There are clear instances of an adaptation of Manichaean terminology to Zoroastrian terminology. This starts from the Sasanian background of Manichaeism, where Mani and his disciples clearly attached Middle Persian Manichaean texts to Zoroastrianism in terms of concepts, literary forms and vocabulary adapted to suit Manichaeism. This adaptation was also carried into the Parthian texts as an ongoing development, as the Sermon on the Soul shows by quoting the names of Avestan texts. The fact that a Zoroastrian vocabulary was certainly also available in Sogdian would have allowed the continuation of this development. The names published by Sundermann 1994 quoted above may show that this did occur. There has been a lot of debate

---

① Some of the names in the text are Persian.

about the Zoroastrian fragment from Dunhuang, now in the British Library under the signature Or. 8212/84. This is not restricted to the Sogdian form of the Avestan prayer *ašəm vohū*; the accompanying text depicts *zrwšc* 'Zarathushtra' in a context that is generally Indian or Buddhist but is full of Avestan terms (Sims-Williams 1976, 46 – 48 and I. Gershevitch there, Appendix, 75 – 82.). Even if this specific fragment were not to be Manichaean, the form of the name and many of the terms occur in clearly Manichaean texts.

How extensive the specific Sogdian development was is hard to judge from the damaged texts. If it was not very extensive this can be for two reasons: The terminology was already established and was not free to be developed further or Manichaeism did not have the vitality or the intellectual impetus to adapt itself to Sogdian Zoroastrianism. This might mean that the numbers of Manichaeans involved were too small or that their background was not Zoroastrian.

Sundermann published 'Bruchstücke einer manichäischen Zarathustralegende' (Sundermann 1986) which shows an interest in tales about Zarathustra; again there is also a Turkish fragment (Le Coq 1908) with a similar content; the form of the name *zrwšc* occurring there is clearly Sogdian and attested in Sogdian texts, as we have already seen (Sundermann 1986, 476 n. 18[1]). In this connection, Sundermann (1986, 466) makes the interesting suggestion that the form of the name *zrwr* for Zarēr as he is known in MP may indicate an independent, Sogdian, tradition of the Avestan name *zairi-vari-*.

Parthian loan-words in Sogdian

Parthian words in Sogdian versions of 'canonical' Middle Persian texts show the importance of Parthian. The opening words of Mani's Gospel, preserved in Middle Persian with a Sogdian translation in M172 I, has on line V/14/ *wjyδw'δδ* 'living spirit' in the Sogdian text as a translation of the Middle Persian *w'xš ywjdhr* 'living spirit'. In line V/15/ in the Sogdian part, the words *zprt w'xš* 'holy spirit' follow. As MacKenzie 1994, 189 remarks, *w'xš* will be a borrowing from Middle Persian in the Sogdian text and *zprt w'xš* therefore the translation of Middle Persian *w'xš ywjdhr*. The addition of the Parthian *wjyδw'δδ*, placed before *zprt w'xš*, by either the translator or a later copier of the text, suggests that the Parthian term was felt to be clearer. No written Parthian translation of this text seems to have survived. It seems quite likely that Middle Persian texts attributed directly to Mani were not translated into Parthian. The use of a Parthian term in the Sogdian translation suggests that the Parthian term had entered the Sogdian Manichaean vocabulary. It may also point to an informal Parthian translation of the Middle Persian text as the medium through which the Sogdian version was made. Similarly, the Middle Persian version of the Book of Giants seems to have been held in high regard and to have remained without a Parthian translation. Nevertheless, in the Sogdian version in M7800 (Text 'G' in Henning 1943, 52 – 74) in line 24 *w'δjyw[nd](yh)* again occurs. Henning 1943, 69 n. 6 points out that the text here is certainly a translation and that the corresponding Middle Persian is *myhryzd*,

[1] But is a Parth. intermediary necessary, as he suggests?

and Parthian *w'd jywndg*. He refrains, however, from drawing the conclusion that the Sogdian version was translated from a Parthian one, because no Parthian version of the Book of Giants is attested and therefore the same things will apply as in the case of M172, i. e. that this is evidence for Parthian loanwords in Sogdian Manichaean terminology beyond the translation of specific texts.

Indirect evidence from Turkish and Chinese texts.

Parthian and Sogdian loan-words in the Turkish *xwāstwānift*

The Turkish text, *xwāstwānift*, is a confessional text which gives detail of sins not to be committed by Manichaeans — these sins mostly concern the denial of Manichaen doctrines and the failure to fulfill the obligation to celebrate the Manichaean rites. The text is well preserved in a number of copies and was clearly important to the Turkish speaking Manichaean community. In his edition of the text, Asmussen 1965, 134 points to the Parthian title *wx'stw'nyft* and the recurrent Parthian formula *mnst'r xyrz'* = Parth. *man astār hirzā* 'forgive my sins' (the equivalent Middle Persian verb is hil-)[①] On p. 204 commenting on the first occurrence of this phrase, he rightly remarks: 'The presence of the Parthian words in the text does not indicate. that the original was Parthian, but is due to the fact that the ecclesiastical language of Eastern Manichaeism was Parthian until, probably in the latter half of the sixth century, it was replaced by Sogdian farther East (W. B. Henning, BSOAS XII, 1947, p. 49). But this means that the established cultic apparatus (especially phrases and designations of institutions), which originally first of all was Parthian, was preserved also after the change of language. ' Two fragments of a Sogdian *wxāstwānīft* were found and published by Henning 1940, 63 – 67 but no Parthian text has been found. This may never have existed or it was simply never written down. Asmussen rightly points to the occurrence of the Sogdian form *zrw'* of the name Zurwān in the text as an indication of a Sogdian original.

Mikkelsen 2006, 102 – 109 lists the words from other languages transcribed in the Chinese Manichacan texts. Apart from names and some Aramaic terms, the Iranian words occurring here are from Middle Persian and Parthian. Only in the case of two calendrical terms does Mikkelsen refer to Sogdian (Chin. transcribed *mi-ri* 'Sunday' from Sogdian *mīr* and Chin. transcribed *mo-ri* 'Monday' from Sogdian *māx*). Many of the MP and Parthian terms occurring here are also attested as loanwords in Sogdian. Clearly, the Chinese texts show the particular position of these words and confirm the appreciation of them in the Sogdian/Uigur context in which the Chinese texts were created.

Conclusions

We find in Sogdian Manichaean terminology an indicator of the internal history of Manichaeism in Central Asia — a history for which we have nearly no direct sources. Although the religious texts cannot

---

① There he also points out the dependance of Sogdian terminology on Parthian using the examples of Parth. *w'd jywndg* and *myšyy βyyy* and Sogdian *njyδ w'δδ* from Parthian *njyd w'd*.

replace the lack of historical sources they do show us stages in the adaptation of Manichaeism from Aramaic, Middle Persian and Parthian originals to Sogdian, apparently with only a restricted Sogdian contribution as far as actual texts are concerned. Where this adaptation took place is also unclear. At least some of it must have taken place in the Sogdiana, some of it definitely took place in Turfan to contribute to the extraordinary linguistic mixture that we find in Manichaean texts, the survival and discovery of which here in Turfan is of such great importance.

Bibliography

J. P. Asmussen: X*ᵘāstvānīft. Studies in Manichaeism*, Copenhagen 1965 (Acta Theologica Danica 7).

M. Boyce: *Catalogue of the Iranian Manuscripts in Manichean script in the German Turfan Collection*, 1960.

W. B. Henning: Ein manichäisches Bet- und Beichtbuch, *Abhandlungen der Preußischen Akademie der Wissenschaften* 1936, 10, Berlin 1937 [= W. B. Henning: *Selected Papers I*, 417 - 558].

W. B. Henning: *Sogdica*, London 1940 (James G. G. Forlong Fund, XXI) [= W. B. Henning: *Selected Papers II*, 1 - 68].

W. B. Henning: The Book of the Giants, *Bulletin of the School of Oriental and African Studies* 1943, 52 - 74 [= Selected Papers II, 115 - 137].

W. B. Henning: The Murder of the Magi, *Journal of the Royal Asiatic Society* 1944, 133 - 144 [= *Selected Papers II*, 139 - 150].

W. B. Henning: Two Manichaean Magical Texts, with an Excursus on The Parthian ending -ēndēh, *Bulletin of the School of Oriental and African Studies* 12, 1947, 39 - 66 [= *Selected Papers II*, 273 - 300].

A. Le Coq: Ein manichäisch-uigurisches Fragment aus Idiqut-Schahri, *Sitzungberichte der Preußischen Akademie der Wissenschaften* 1908, 398 - 414.

D. N. MacKenzie: 《I, Mani .. 》, in: H. Preißler, H. Seiwert (eds.), *Gnosisforschung und Religionsgeschichte. Festschrift K. Rudolph*. Marburg, 1994, 183 - 198.

G. Mikkelsen: Dictionary of Manichaean Texts in Chinese, Turnhout: Brepols 2006 (Corpus Fontium Manichaeorum. Dictionary of Manichaean texts. Vol III. Texts from Central Asia and China. Part 4).

E. Morano: 2007, A working catalogue of the Berliner Sogdian fragments in Manichaean script, in: M. Macuch, M. Maggi, W. Sundermann (eds.) *Iranian Languages and Texts from Iran and Turan. R. E. Emmerick Memorial Volume*, Wiesbaden 2007, 239 - 270 (Iranica 13).

C. Reck: *Berliner Turfanfragmente manichäischen Inhalts in soghdischer Schrift*, 2006.

N. Sims-Williams: The Sogdian fragments of the British Library, *Indo-Iranian Journal* 18, 1976, 43 - 82.

N. Sims-Williams: A Parthian sound-change, *Bulletin of the School of Oriental and African Studies* 42/1, 1979, 133 - 136.

N. Sims-Williams: Indian Elements in Parthian and Sogdian, in: K. Röhrborn, W. Veenker (eds.), *Sprachen des Buddhismus in Zentralasien*. Vorträge des Hamburger Symposions vom 2. Juli bis 5. Juli 1981, Wiesbaden 1983 (Veröffentlichungen der Societas Uralo-Altaica 16), 132 - 141.

W. Sundermann: Namen von Göttern, Dämonen und Menschen in iranischen Versionen des manichäischen Mythos, *Altorientalische Forschungen* 6 (1979), 95 - 133 [= W. Sundermann: *Manichaica Iranica 1*, pp. 121 - 159 and pp.

160 - 163].

W. Sundermann: Eine Liste manichäischer Götter in soghdischer Sprache, in: C. Elsas (ed.), *Tradition und Translation* (Festschrift C. Colpe), 1994, 452 - 462 [= W. Sundermann: *Manichaica Iranica 2*, 833 - 845].

W. Sundermann: Bruchstücke einer manichäischen Zarathustralegende, in: R. Schmitt, P. O. Skjærvœ (ed.), *Studia Grammatica Iranica*. München 1986, 461 - 482 [= W. Sundermann: *Manichaica Iranica 2*, 853 - 874 and 875 - 876].

W. Sundermann: *Der Sermon vom Licht-Nous*. Eine Lehrschrift des östlichen Manichäismus. Edition der parthischen und sogdischen Version, Berlin 1992 (Berliner Turfantexte XVII).

W. Sundermann: *Der Sermon von der Seele*. Eine Lehrschrift des östlichen Manichäismus, Turnhout 1997 (Berliner Turfantexte XIX).

W. Sundermann: Eine Re-Edition zweier manichäisch-soghdischer Briefe, in: M. Macuch, M. Maggi, W. Sundermann (eds.) *Iranian Languages and Texts from Iran and Turan. R. E. Emmerick Memorial Volume*. Wiesbaden 2007, 403 - 321 (Iranica 13).

A. Wendtland: Ist der Satan weiblich? Zur Interpretation von soghdisch xH, in: G. Schweiger (ed.), *Indogermanica. Festschrift G. Klingenschmitt*, Taimering 2005, 689 - 698.

从吐鲁番、撒马尔罕文书看丝绸之路上的贸易

——本文献给年初逝世的吐鲁番考古学家吴震先生

韩森 著 王锦萍 译

耶鲁大学历史系

吐鲁番的历史重要性是什么？这取决于历史学家个人对吐鲁番的看法。有学者将吐鲁番看作唐朝历史的延伸,他们所问的问题是:吐鲁番在什么方面与唐朝其他 300 多个州郡具有相似点？在什么方面又有不同？一个明显的区别在于资料的性质:吐鲁番发掘的汉文文书使吐鲁番成为 755 年以前唐朝所有州中资料记载最好的一个, 而其他地区类似资料的缺乏使我们很难评估吐鲁番的典型性。在缺乏直接证据的情况下,我们中的许多人只能跟着感觉走:要么认为 640 年之后吐鲁番和其他唐朝的区域一样,要么不是。如果我们相信吐鲁番具有典型性,我们可能会得出这样的结论:唐朝政府能够在全国范围内贯彻均田制。而如果我们相信吐鲁番不具典型性,我们可能会认为,因为政府对边疆地区的控制力度比内地更强,唐朝内地的官员们并没有像在吐鲁番那样严肃对待均田制的种种规定。此类争论大概读者已经很熟悉了吧。

本文将从一个不同的,我希望也是新的角度来对待吐鲁番的典型性问题。与将吐鲁番只看成唐朝境内的一个州相比,本文更倾向于将吐鲁番看成丝绸之路上的一个重要据点。塔克拉玛干沙漠南路和北路上的著名停驻点包括:北路上的敦煌、吐鲁番、焉耆、龟兹、喀什,以及南路上的敦煌、楼兰、米兰、尼雅、于阗、喀什。旅人到达喀什之后,他们可以西行至撒马尔罕或南行至印度。在这些地点,特别是在龟兹和穆格山(Mount Mugh)(在跨越今天乌兹别克斯坦边境的撒马尔罕城外,今塔吉克斯坦境内),发现了与吐鲁番文书同期的文书,这并非因为如同吐鲁番和敦煌的居民那样,将回收的旧纸用于制作为死者准备的纸衣物,而是出于不同的原因,且每个地点起因各异。

很少有学者将中亚地区发掘的文书作为一个整体来研究,很大程度上是因为这些文书是用不同语言写就的,其中一些非常难懂,只有极少数学者有信心解读它们。幸运的是,每种语言的文书都吸引了一小群专家的注意,他们翻译并发表了最重要的出土文书。在简单介绍关于这个问题的最重要的吐鲁番文书之后,本文将注意力转向龟兹和撒马尔罕地区发现的公元 500 年至 800 年间的一批文书,并提出以下的问题:这些文书反映了丝绸之路上贸易的哪些方面？是谁在购买和出售什么商品？为什么？是谁频繁地行走在这些路线上？

吐鲁番出土文书

考虑到本文的读者对吐鲁番文书已经非常熟悉,我将只简单罗列几份对丝绸之路贸易有最重要反映的文书:

记录主要由粟特商人带到吐鲁番的商品的 37 件称价钱文书①

记载曹禄山代表其亡兄和其亡兄的汉人合伙人李绍谨之间的诉讼文书②

过所文书③

市场上出售商品的价格列表④

三百份汉文契约文书,特别是那些属于左崇义的契约文书⑤

一份来自阿斯塔那的粟特文契约文书⑥

请允许我在这里总结我以前发表过的观点。⑦ 传统的看法是,在公元一千年中,许多富裕的商人在丝绸之路上交易他们的货物。但如果将吐鲁番文书作为一个整体来看,这种习见将会被颠覆,因为它们清楚地记载了农民进行简单商品的实物交易这种经济形式的大量存在。吐鲁番文书几乎没有提及任何传说中丝绸之路上的丝绸、金银和珠宝的长途贸易。

当吐鲁番农民向丝路上的商人借钱或购物(通常为动物或奴隶)时,他们经常立契。六至七世纪的契约,甚至是那些记载最小量交易的契约,反映了丝绸之路上商业意识的影响:许多价格是以萨珊王朝(统治时间为公元 224 年至 651 年,统治领土位于今伊朗境内)所铸的银币结算的,这些契约收每个月百分之十的罚金。

唐朝统治时期的丝绸之路贸易对吐鲁番经济有一定的影响,即高度的货币经济,以及所有交易都要支付高额利率。即便是实物交易的契约文书也反映出,六至八世纪的吐鲁番经济更为商业化。童丕(Eric Trombert)认为唐朝中央政府在丝绸之路贸易的兴起中扮演了重大角色。⑧ 他指出,我们应该注意的不是在塔里木盆地活动的许多私商,而是政府财政。当唐王朝决定将大量丝绸运往中亚地区作为支付给其驻军和官员的军费,丝路贸易顿时繁荣起来。而当唐王朝在 755 年突然从中亚撤军的时候,它停止了向该地区支出的大量军费(通常以调布的形式)。当中国政府继续向西北地区以高价买马时,⑨丝路贸易的规模就大大缩小了。

而即便是 640 年至 755 年这段唐朝控制丝绸之路的鼎盛时期内,许多人也并非靠丝路贸易,而是靠

---

① 参见朱雷:《魏氏高昌王国的"称价钱"》,《魏晋南北朝隋唐史资料》4,第 17~24 页;Jonathan K. Skaff 斯加夫,"Sasanian and Ara-Sasanian Silver Coins from Turfan: Their Relationship to International Trade and the Local Economy 吐鲁番发现的萨珊银币和阿拉伯—萨珊银币:它们和国际贸易及地方经济的关系", *Asian Major*, 3rd series, XI. 2 [1998],第 67~115 页。

② 参见黄惠贤:《"唐西州高昌县上安西都护府牒稿为录上讯问曹禄山诉李绍谨两造辩辞事"释》,唐长孺主编:《敦煌吐鲁番文书初探》,武汉大学出版社,1983 年,第 344~363 页。

③ 参见程喜霖:《唐代过所研究》,北京:中华书局,2000 年。

④ 参见池田温:《中国古代籍帐研究》,东京大学东洋文化研究所,1979 年,第 447~463 页。

⑤ 山本达郎、池田温, *Tun-huang and Turfan Documents Concerning Social and Economic History III Contracts A Introduction and Texts* 敦煌吐鲁番社会经济史文书 3:契约 A:导言与文书,东京:东洋文库,1987 年。

⑥ 吉田丰、森安孝夫、新疆维吾尔自治区博物馆:《麴氏高昌国时代ソグド文女奴隶买卖文书》,《内陆アジア言语の研究》,IV,1998 年,第 1~50 页;英译文见 Y. Yoshida, "Appendix: Translation of the Contract for the Purchase of a Slave Girl Found at Tufan and Dated 639," *T'oung Pao*, 89/1-3, 2003, pp. 159-161.

⑦ 韩森:《丝绸之路贸易对吐鲁番地方社会的影响:公元 500~800 年》,王锦萍译《粟特人在中国——历史、考古、语言的新探索》,北京:中华书局,2005 年,第 113~140 页。

⑧ Éric Trombert 童丕, Le crédit à Dunhuang: vie materielle et societé en Chine médievale, Paris: Collège de France, 1995. 中译本:余欣、陈健伟译《敦煌的借贷:中国中古时代的物质生活与社会》,北京:中华书局,2003 年。

⑨ Éric Trombert 童丕, "Textiles et tissus sur la Route de la soie: Eléments pour une géographie de la production et des échanges 丝绸之路上的丝织品和布:生产和交易的地理因素," in *La Serinde, terre d'échanges: Art, religion commerce du Ier au Xe siècle XIVes Rencontres de l'Ecole du Louvre* 贸易之地中亚:1 至 10 世纪的艺术、宗教和商业. Paris: La Documentation française, 2000, pp. 107-120.

耕地来谋生。这些农民除了向放债者借银币或长途贸易者购买动物和奴隶之外,基本上与丝路贸易关系甚微。我的假设是:丝路贸易在中亚地区的整个经济中只扮演了一个很小的角色。让我们现在来考察一些来自库车(即龟兹)和粟特的证据来分析该假设。

库车出土文书

库车位于吐鲁番西面,但并没有出土和吐鲁番一样多的文书,可能是因为还没有发现墓地。然而法国学者伯希和在 1907 年 10 月考察库车地区时发现了几处由两种方言(一为焉耆语,或称吐火罗语 A,一为龟兹语,或称吐火罗语 B)及汉语写的文书的窖藏。与斯坦因不同的是,伯希和在生前并没有发表这些文书,也没有详细记录这些文书的发现点。① 大约在六世纪前后,大多数住在龟兹的人说龟兹语,但贸易时也使用印度西北俗语(Prakrit)。焉耆语作为重要佛教介语言之一的梵语,在龟兹境内的某些宗教场合中也曾经使用,不过,出土文献同时证实了,也有一些仪式以龟兹语进行。

库车文书包括两种类型:一种是关于寺院支出的(发现于苏八什[Subashi]附近和玉其吐尔[Duldur Aqur]),另一种则是与过所文书类似的。伯希和在玉其吐尔附近的寺院发现汉文文书,这些文书后来由童丕和张广达在《库车汉文文书》中发表了。②

一组文书列出了佛教寺院的支出、收入和收支差额,所以能反映龟兹经济是如何运作的。在苏八什,伯希和在一个 10×54 cm 的木片上发现了一组此类文书。③ 木片记录了日期(龟兹国王 Dharmacandra 统治的第三年),草拟该文书的作者(最可能是官员),以及文书的目的——列出支出和收入。由于我们对该国王一无所知,故无法对这些文书精确定年,但很可能在 650 年左右。

伯希和在玉其吐尔发现了烬余和残破的文书,包括寺院的纸收据。④ 这些帐目中的条目表明寺院使用称为 cāne 的铜币。龟兹人也从汉人那里借用了十进制。玉其吐尔的帐目列出了购买糖、酒以及雇用在仪式上表演的乐人所费现金的清单。该寺院还采购用于仪式的油,还雇磨坊主来舂米。另外,寺院也列出了几组为寺院提供食物的供养人,这些食物既供应僧侣,也供应依靠寺户。这些文书表明,购买这些物品的人至少可以在当时龟兹的寺院中使用钱币或谷物。

另外三件从寺院发现的龟兹语文书残片(现存圣彼得堡),纪年大概在公元七世纪后半期,肯定了我们此前对寺院中存在实物经济的推断。这些文书记载了村民向寺院赠送绵羊和山羊,其中一些用于还债。在一个例子中,一个人向一位长者为浇地的事情支付了一头"梳了两遍羊毛的"母羊。⑤ 另一个例子

---

① 这些文书在伯希和死后在 "Mission Paul Pelliot 伯希和考古丛刊"中发表了。关于库车的一卷名为"Sites divers de la region de Koutcha 分布于龟兹地区的各个遗址,"Paris:College de France,1987.

② 本书为法文,但包括了图片和汉文文书的完整转录。童丕、池田温、张广达 *Manuscrits chinois de Koutcha: Fonds Pelliot de la Bibliothèque nationale de France* 库车汉文文书:法国国立博物馆的伯希和收藏, Paris:Institut des hautes études chinoises du Collège de France, 2000.

③ 文书号:Pelliot Kouchéen Bois, série C, 1. Georges-Jean Pinault, "Aspects de bouddhisme pratiqué au nord de désert du Taklamakan, d'après les documents tokhariens 从吐火罗语文书看塔克拉玛干沙漠北端的佛教活动的方面," in Fukui Fumimasa and Gérard Fussman (ed), Actes du colloque "Bouddhisme et cultures locales 会议论文:佛教和地方文化. " Paris:École français d'Extrême-Orient, 1994.

④ 文书号:PK DA M. 507。Georges-Jean Pinault 1994 年一文在第 91 页上将此文书翻译成法语,在第 94 页上讨论了文书的日期。第 93 页上使用了汉语中的量词,第 95 页则是关于寺院买卖的。

⑤ Georges-Jean Pinault, "Economic and Administrative Documents in Tocharian B from the Berezovsky and Petrovsky Collections 别列佐夫斯基和彼得罗夫斯基收藏中龟兹语的经济和行政文书," *Manuscripta Orientalia* 4.4 (1998):1-19, 第 8 页。

中一些长者用 250 磅大麦买了两头山羊,200 磅谷物买了一头绵羊。在这里大麦和谷物充当了货币,而文书没有提及任何钱币。显然,这些长者在国王和当地百姓之间处于中间的管理层的位置。也许有人会好奇在这样的经济形式中人们使用什么样的词汇,事实上龟兹语中有描述绵羊和山羊的丰富词汇,包括:雌的、雄的、幼崽期的、壮年期的和老弱期的(按字面翻译的话为"有大牙的",因为成年动物有永久性的中间的门牙)。[①] 这些寺院文书只提到了本地商品,给我们留下了一个印象,即寺院并不参与长途贸易。

另一类同样由伯希和发现,Pinault 发表的文书,说明了进出龟兹的商队交通。1907 年 1 月,一个当地人给了伯希和六个有婆罗谜语手稿的木片,这些桦树皮发现于距查尔德朗(Shaldïrang)关口不远的佛教废墟。[②] 伯希和又去了查尔德朗附近一个还在被使用的名为托拉(Tourâ)的税所。托拉是库车北边山里的一个小地方,是通过山区去往拜城的必经之地。在位于一个悬崖的废弃烽火台中,伯希和在雪地下 20 cm 的地方发现了 130 份"过所"文书。

早在 1913 年,法国学者 Sylvain Lévi 就解读了伯希和发现的文书:由龟兹国官员发给商队的"过所"。这些官员记录了每个商队中的每个人和每头动物,但不记录商队所携带的货物。显然,政府官员只检查商队成员,但并不检查货物。在每个关卡,商队需上交他们现有的"过所",然后得到新的"过所"。Lévi 意识到,正因为此才能在查尔德朗发现一百多个被丢弃的"过所"。库车的"过所"可能是模仿中国的"过所"而造。

尽管纸在龟兹很常见,并用于记录寺院账单和书写信件,官员们所作的"过所"是由白杨木片制成的。这些木片要比纸便宜,大小平均为 10×5 cm,但也几份大小稍有不同。如同在尼雅发现的佉卢文文书木片一样,这些龟兹语文书由合在一起的两部分组成。外面的木制封套装着里面的一份木片(有时为几片)。这样,文书的内容从外面看不出来,而封套上只可见驿站官员的名字。[③]

尽管"过所"的大小各异,其内容则遵循着一个固定的格式:记录寄件人的姓名、收件人的姓名和地址、介绍性的问候语,以及携带此"过所"的旅行者的姓名。同行成员则按如下顺序条列:男子、女子、驴、马和牛。[④] 使用大写的数字表明,这些是正式的行政文书。[⑤] 这些文书通常以劝诫性的话语结尾:"让他们过关。如果他们的成员超过了所列总数,则不允许他们过关。"最后,文书会给出在位国王的统治年份、月份和日期,以及一个证人的证词。所发现这些文书的纪年都在 Suvarn. adeva (reigned 624 - 646)国王统治的最后几年中,即 641 ~ 644 年。[⑥]

Pinault 作了关于这些"过所"的有用的表格,列出了每个商队中的人和动物。

① Georges-Jean Pinault, "Economic and Administrative Documents in Tocharian B from the Berezovsky and Petrovsky Collections," *Manuscripta Orientalia* 4.4 (1998):pp.1 - 19.

② Georges-Jean Pinault, "Épigraphie koutchéenne:I. Laisser-passer de caravans passes;II. Graffites et inscriptions 龟兹题铭:第一章:过所;第二章:涂鸦与题记" In *Mission Paul Pelliot VIII. Sites divers de la région de Koutcha* 伯希和考古丛刊 8:分布于龟兹地区的各个遗址。Paris:Collège de France, pp. 59 - 196. 第 67 页注 4 引用了伯希和 1907 年一月写给 Émile Senart 的信。

③ Pinault,《龟兹题铭:过所》,第 69 ~ 71 页。显然,并没有完整的文书存世。见该书图版 XL - LII 的现存文书照片。

④ Pinault (1987) 第 72 ~ 74 页为一张表格,显示 130 份过所文书的每一份包括哪些要素,结果没有一份是完整包括所有的要素。第一份文书是最为完整的,只缺了最后证人的证词。

⑤ Pinault,《龟兹题铭:过所》,第 79 页。

⑥ Pinault,《龟兹题铭:过所》,第 84 ~ 85 页。

表（Pinault 1987:78）

文书号	男 子	女 子	驴	马	牛
1	20		3	1	
2					4
3	2				
5	10			5	1
12				3	
15				3	
16	4				2
21	3		15		
25	5	1			
30	6	10	4		
31					5
33	32			7	
35	3		12		
37	2		2		
44	3			4	
50	8			17	
64		X	X		3
79					2
80	40				
95				10	

在十三份给出男子人数的文书中，我们看到，其中十人以下的有九份，其他四份则各为十人、二十人、三十二人和四十人。动物数目最多的是十七头驴，有八个男子随行。驴对商队来说非常重要，一些商队只由男子和驴组成。两份"过所"列了随行的孩子，另外两份列了被称为 kapyâre 的劳动力。很可能，这个词与汉语中的"净人"很接近，指"为（僧）作净者"。[1] 有一个商队完全由妇女组成，由一个男子的商队头目带领，可想而知，这些妇女正被卖往龟兹的人口市场，这个市场在正史中被称作"女市"。[2] "过所"没有显示商队所携带的货物，但它们确实反映了龟兹国王对进出龟兹的商队进行严格的监控，以确保他们在固定的路线上行进。

简而言之，库车发现的文书有两类：一类是寺院记账文书，一类是一百多份"过所"文书。648年，当唐朝军队进入龟兹的时候，设立了龟兹都督府，但在位六个多世纪的白氏家继续统治库车。在玉其吐尔，一组汉文文书被保存了下来，在这组文书中，最早的为692年，最晚则至784年。

这段时间是相当不稳定的。唐王朝在七世纪时努力维持其对龟兹的控制，679年重新占领，然后又再次失去了。在七世纪末，吐蕃成为挑战唐朝在中亚统治的强有力扩张帝国，唐王朝直到692年才能收复龟兹。尽管唐朝在755年安史之乱后大大衰弱了，但唐朝从中亚撤军的时候，安西都护府管理下的唐

---

① 庆昭蓉，1/10/09，电子邮件。
② 魏收：《魏书》卷一〇二，北京：中华书局，1974年，第2267页。

朝军队继续驻扎在龟兹。在766年与781年之间,一个名为郭昕的汉官为安西都护时,安西都护府就设在龟兹,但郭昕与长安的唐朝廷之间已经失去了联系。781年郭昕派使者前往长安,重建了与唐朝廷的联系,但继续独立统治着龟兹。至792年时,唐朝完全失去了对龟兹的统治。

伯希和在玉其吐尔发现的资料中,214件文书上有汉字。如龟兹语文书一样,这些文书因被焚毁,大多只是很小的残片。童丕在池田温和张广达的帮助下已从这些残片上解读出了相当可观的信息。① 龟兹语文书有佛经和寺院记账文书两种,而汉文文书则不同,几乎完全是有关世俗社会的。童丕解释到:"从证据来看,在玉其吐尔曾有一个管理性的军营,很可能是一支中国来的驻军,在那里汉人负责管理驻军和他们的村庄,而这些驻军和村庄中人都是从中国移民而来,并留在龟兹生活的人。"②

这些资料,如龟兹语的"过所"文书一样,记载了商队的活动。而这些商队,则是很多人的信使(见121号和131号文书)。其中一个写信者显然他自己也在旅途中,为了及时将信拿给一群回龟兹的汉人,他写得飞快,甚至一再重复某些习语(131号文书)。

这些文书中提到的主要商品为马,如114号文书记载中国人用约600公斤的铁粉买马,129号文书则记载用约310米的布买马。108号文书记载了寄给政府官员饲马粮草的数量和种类(如碾碎的谷物,及大豆、糠麸或大麦)。41号文书指出,当地民兵、各种远征军队,以及驿站和中转站都要用到马。121号文书是一个马商报告一匹马生病、随后又康复的信。这些不同的材料都表明了贸易的存在,但这些人所需要的商品,特别是马,都是中国官员购买的。玉其吐尔的文书尽管多为残片且难读,但仍反映了官方资助贸易的存在。

这些残片资料略微暗示了粟特人在龟兹的存在。玉其吐尔出土的220号文书留有粟特文手稿的痕迹,而77号文书则不是粟特文就是回鹘文(由于回鹘文采用了粟特语的字母,所以并不总能区分这两种语言)。112号文书是一份汉文契约,提到了"便立胡书契"。这是另一份没有留存下来的契约,是用非汉文的语言写的,很可能是龟兹语或粟特语。112号文书规定了偿付一笔贷款需付两匹练。显然,某人的妻子支付了其中的一匹练,但没有支付另一匹。原始交易可能涉及粟特人,但很难确定。

尽管玉其吐尔出土的材料残缺不全,它们仍然记录了一种人们花费大量铜钱进行私人交易的货币经济。一个没有官位的人付了1000文税钱以免除某种差役,另一个人则付了1500文钱。24号文书列出了一组欠债人,并记录了他们向某人(他们的名字出现在该文书中)借款的数目:4800文钱、4000文(可能更多)钱、2500文钱。136号文书记载某人欠了4000文钱。这些描述与正史中对龟兹居民始终在市场上使用钱币的描述相吻合。

库车除玉其吐尔之外的地区还发现了另外11件契约。如同本文讨论的其他文书一样,这些契约也是残片。三件保存最好的文书都是借贷1000文钱的契约,贷款者都同意付给借款人200文钱的利息。很可能这里说的钱,是低劣仿制唐朝钱币的货币,并在755年之后在龟兹地区流通。在同中国的联系被断绝之后,龟兹的统治者自己铸造钱币,并仍在钱币上铸唐朝皇帝的大历(766～769)和建中(780～783)年号。与长安失去联系后,安西都护无法再从唐朝廷获得钱的供给。于是他们用一枚"开元通宝"做了一个模子,来铸造自己的中国式钱币。他们磨掉"开元"来作"大历"或"建中"通宝,然后以此模铸

---

① 童丕:《丝绸之路上的丝织品和布:生产和交易的地理因素》列出了所有有纪年的文书,第141页。张广达关于水利的论文见张广达:《文书、典籍与西域史地》,桂林:广西师范大学出版社,2008年,第71～79页。

② 童丕、池田温、张广达:《库车汉文文书:法国国立博物馆的伯希和收藏》,第35页。

造新的钱币。币上的新字比模上的字更为粗劣,而且有一些错误。这些龟兹钱另有一些标记说明它们不是唐朝中央政府铸造的,如这些钱币中央的孔经常是八角形而非四角形。与中原地区流通的钱币相比,这些龟兹钱中赤铜的成分更多,这也是说明这些钱由本地铸造的另一个标志。在目前发现的一千多枚龟兹钱中,整整 1 000 枚是在新疆地区发现的,其中 800 枚来自库车地区,只有两枚来自内地。①这些考古发现说明了 760 年至 780 年之间铸币的增长,而库车地区发现的 11 份汉文契约文书也说明了这一点。②

钱币学家们经常争论政府和商业在钱币发展史上的作用。一些罗马史学家强调政府是钱币的主要生产者(除了国家还有谁需要支付古罗马军团士兵的军费呢?),而另一些学者则将钱币的出现看作是地方经济商业化和市场成熟的自然结果。我们对龟兹八世纪晚期历史的部分认识,很难解释为何当时钱币的使用呈明显增长趋势,但 755 年后龟兹地区军事化程度的增加,可能导致钱币使用的增加。

毫无疑问,玉其吐尔地区发现的汉文资料是非常有限的。这些文书总共有 208 件,且许多只有几个汉字。即便如此,它们涉及的活动范围之广,仍然令人惊讶。28 号至 30 号文书为驻龟兹的汉人士兵所写,它们包括了写给家乡的信,以及三封称赞战死士卒的讣告。5 号文书中,一位佛教徒列举了各种违反佛教戒律的行为,包括饮酒、吃肉、破坏素食斋戒、损坏寺院财物及士兵杀生。21 号文书谈到了寺院僧侣的诵经,43 号文书讲到一个妇女写信的事,19 号文书提到了屯田的规模,55 号、119 号及 132 号文书提及了折冲府的事务,125 号文书记载了道教仪式中所用幅的数量,117 号文书则提到了对一位官员治绩的考评。

然而所有这些活动都没有提及传统印象中的丝路贸易——即没有私人商旅携带大量货物长途跋涉。童丕总结到:"伯希和及大谷探险队收集的玉其吐尔汉文文书的一个特点,是缺乏明显的商业文书。文书没有提交任何可买卖的商品名单。没有如在查尔德朗附近的驿站发现的许多'过所'那样的'过所'文书。即便有少量的契约文书,也多数是农民之间的交易。"③童丕认为,龟兹是一个商业中心,但来往龟兹的商人都呆在龟兹城内或者绿洲以外。由于这些商人并不在玉其吐尔停留,所以这个地方没有商业文书被保存下来。但我们必须考虑到另外一个可能:即因为没有贸易存在,所以没有记录留下。

所有在库车地区发现的汉文和龟兹语文书总共不到五千件。也许只有几百份文书保存较好,可供解读。它们提供的是一些假设性的结论:龟兹地区确实存在着贸易,但是"过所"文书表明,这是由政府官员监控的贸易。而汉人驻军地发现的资料也证明,贸易经常是由这些官员直接经营的。如果确实存在能证明由私人商旅经营长途贸易的资料,那么它们还有待被发现。

---

① François Thierry, 1997 "On the Tang coins collected by Pelliot in Chinese Turkestan (1906 – 09) 伯希和 1906 年至 1909 年在新疆发现的唐代钱币," In Joe Cribb, Katsumi Tanabe, Helen Wang (ed.), *Studies in Silk Road Coins and Culture: Papers in honour of Professor Ikuo Hirayama on his 65th birthday* 丝绸之路钱币和文化研究:平山郁夫教授六十五华诞祝寿文集. Kamakura:The Institute of Silk Road Studies, pp. 149 – 179;关于库车钱币的讨论见第 151 页。

② Helen Wang 汪海岚, *Money on the Silk Road: the evidence from Eastern Central Asia to c. AD 800*, including a catalogue of the coins collected by Sir Aurel Stein (London:The British Museum Press, 2004) 第 85 ~ 87 页分析了库车钱币,第 87 页上的表格非常有用,列出了每件翻译中钱币的纪年和数量。山本达郎、池田温在《敦煌吐鲁番社会经济史文书 3:契约 A:导言与文书》第 74 ~ 76 页转录了库车发现的契约。参见笔者在 "The Place of Coins -and their Alternatives—in the Silk Road Trade(中译文《钱币和其他形式的钱在丝绸之路贸易中的位置》,王锦萍译)"一文中学者们对该问题研究的讨论。本文即将由上海博物馆出版。

③ 参见童丕:《丝绸之路上的丝织品和布:生产和交易的地理因素》第 35 页关于敦煌的讨论。

粟特地区发现的文书

在丝绸之路北路上行走的人，大多都经过吐鲁番和龟兹去往撒马尔罕。不同语言的文书证实了粟特人的重要性，对这些文书研究最深入的要数魏义天(Etienne de la Vaissière)和荣新江。[①] 目前出土的粟特语文书数量特别少。撒马尔罕及其周边地区的气候不如塔克拉玛干沙漠那样干燥，土壤酸性更大，许多资料在八世纪早期伊斯兰的征服中被毁掉了。目前出土的粟特语文书，有两组最重要：一是斯坦因(Aurel Stein)在敦煌城外发现的八封四世纪初的粟特古信札，一是二十世纪三十年代在撒马尔罕外一个曾被围攻的堡垒中发现的八世纪初的近百件文书。其他的粟特语材料也仅见于银碗或纺织品上的文字、绘画题记以及吐鲁番发现的宗教文献。[②]

到最近为止，学者们一直都主张，斯坦因在敦煌附近的发现的废弃邮包是现存最早的粟特语文书。但是从1996年至2006年之间在哈萨克斯坦南部的库尔托别(Kultobe)进行发掘的考古学家们发现了10件带粟特语文字的烧硬的砖瓦。粟特语专家辛姆斯·威廉姆斯(Nicholas Sims-Williams)认为这些文本比上述粟特文古信札更早，但他不确定究竟有多早。在修这面墙的时候，至少存在四个粟特城邦国家，而这些文本太过零碎，很难说明更多的问题。[③]

斯坦因是在一个丢弃的邮包中发现粟特语文书的。发现地点位于敦煌北部90公里，楼兰东部550公里。因为其中有一封信是寄往撒马尔罕的，表明在信件丢失时信使正在去往撒马尔罕的路上(英文版魏义天书法文本67页，地图中显示了信札中提到的城镇名称)。斯坦因是在1907年调查一系列长城烽燧时发现这组信札的。烽燧之间间隔3公里左右，为中原王朝为防守边疆而建。烽燧最低6米，一般都会附带建一个小规模的守卫士兵的住地。有一个斯坦因编号为TXII.A(T表示敦煌/Tun-huang)的烽燧高2.4米，由晒干的土坯和芦苇建成。在结实的烽燧基址和坍塌的围墙之间有不到0.5米宽、3.35米长的通道，其中布满了垃圾。由于没有发现任何特别的东西，斯坦因派他的中国助手蒋师爷和印度测量员清理通道，他则开始发掘另外一座烽燧。当他傍晚返回时，工作人员向他展示了他们的发掘成果：一些彩色的丝绸、一个木制的容器、公元一世纪早期的汉文文书、一匹写有公元400年以前使用的带有佉卢文文字的丝绸，以及一团"整齐折叠在一起、用某种西方文字书写的纸卷"。[④] 上面的文字看起来像是阿拉米语，斯坦因想起他在楼兰曾经找到过类似的东西。只是到后来，这种语言才被断定为粟特语。

解读这些文字并非易事。由于残缺严重，信札上的字母很难辨认。世界上仅有很少的人能读懂粟特语，直到今天，他们仍在不停地争论每句话的意思，解释着过去一个世纪里始终困扰着他们的某个短语。

---

① 参见荣新江：《中古中国与外来文明》，北京：三联出版社，2001年；Étienne de la Vaissière 魏义天, *Histoire des marchands Sogdiens* 粟特商人的历史. Paris：Collège de France, Institut des Hautes Études Chinoises, 2002；英文版见 *Sogdian Traders: A History* 粟特商人的历史, Leiden：Brill, 2005. 可惜的是，该书还没有中译本。

② Klimkeit 1993；Sims-Williams 1992.

③ Nicholas Sims-Williams and Frantz Grenet 葛乐耐，"The Sogdian inscriptions of Kultobe 库尔托别的粟特题铭," *Shygys* 2006. 1 [2007], pp. 95 – 111.

④ Aurel Stein 斯坦因, *Ruins of Desert Cathay: Personal Narrative of Explorations in Central Asia and Westernmost China* 沙漠契丹废址记：中亚和中国西部考古的个人叙述, London, Macmillan and co., limited, 1912：II, p. 113.

五封信札中的四封最近已经被翻译成了英文。[①]

斯坦因的发掘方法在他生活的时代已算是先进的了,但并非没有缺点。他的工人并没有记录他们在哪一地层发现了哪些材料,因此带来了无法确定信札纪年的问题。2 号信札为我们给这些文书纪年提供了唯一的线索:"最后一位天子,据他们说,因为饥馑逃离了洛阳。有人在宫殿和城市里放了火,宫殿被付之一炬,城市也遭到毁灭。洛阳已不复存在,邺(河南彰德府)也不复存在!"[②]洛阳被攻破的时间有公元190 年、311 年和 535 年,大部分研究粟特语的学者都认为信中所指的应该是公元 311 年。[③] 信的作者称呼入侵者为"匈奴(Huns)",事实上他们的领袖石勒(274~333),就属于匈奴部落联盟中的一支。

八封信并没有被装在信封中,而是如斯坦因所描述的"折叠成整齐的小卷",长 9~13 cm,直径为2.5~3 cm。其中五封基本完整,尽管来自中国不同的城市,但是信纸的尺寸相同,大约长为 39~42 cm,宽 24~25 cm,这说明纸的生产规格可能已经定型了。考虑到直至公元 3 世纪纸才在中国被广泛使用,这已是相当快的发展速度了。有三封信被放在单独的丝袋里;第四封信,即 2 号古信札,则是放在一个亚麻包裹的丝袋里,上面写着"寄往撒马尔罕",但是却没有发信人地址。另外一封没有收信人地址,这说明投递者可能清楚地知道收件人。有两封信(1、3 号)是一位住在敦煌的妇女给她可能住在楼兰的母亲和丈夫写的,5 号信札是从武威寄出的。这些信札表明,早在四世纪初,粟特人的"聚落"就已经存在于洛阳、长安、兰州、武威、酒泉和敦煌等地。第二封信提到在一个地方有一个由 40 个粟特人组成的居住区,另外一个地方(这些地名都已经不能辨认)有 100 个来自撒马尔罕的"自由人",洛阳的居住区里包括粟特人和印度人。当粟特人的数量达到一定的规模,即大概 40 人时,他们的首领便会组织修建一座火祆教的寺庙。在中文文献中,这个首领被称为萨宝,萨宝调解纠纷,具有火祆教祭司的职能,即管理火坛以及主持与火祆教有关的节日庆典。

从名叫 Mīwnāy 的妇女所写的 1 号和 3 号信札我们得知,Mīwnāy 被她的丈夫抛弃,还背负他的债务。她在信中强烈地发泄着对她丈夫的失望:"我遵从你的命令,来到敦煌,却没有接受我母亲或者我兄弟的劝导。在我跟着你的那天,神灵们一定对我生气了。我宁愿是一只狗或一头猪的妻子,也不愿意是你的妻子!"[④]Mīwnāy 困在敦煌有三年之久,其间她有五次机会可以离开,可能是和启程的商队一起走,但是她没有足够的钱,即 20 个斯忒特(stater,一种货币)来支付她的旅费。我们从她给丈夫的信里她女儿的附言中可以得知,这对母女为贫穷所困,靠为人养羊为生。

Mīwnāy 先是向一位官员(显然是一位收税的官员)求救,然后是她丈夫的一位亲戚,而第三个男人,则显然是一个商人。她所接触到的男人的名单提供了背井离乡的粟特人的简单概况。每一个人都以帮助她是她丈夫的责任,而不是他们的责任为由拒绝了她。最后,Mīwnāy 找到"庙里的祭司",他许诺给她

① 关于发现的背景,参见 Stein 1921: 669 - 677, map 74;对信札的总体介绍,参见 de la Vaissière 2002: 48 - 76; Sims-Williams 1987; Grenet and Sims-Williams 1987. Nicholas Sims-Williams (2004) 已经将 1~3 信札和 5 号信札的译文发布在网上,网址如下:http://depts. washington. edu/uwch/silkroad/texts/sogdlet. html. 关于这些古信札最新的翻译见:

1 号信札:Letter 1, Sims-Williams 2005;

2 号信札:Sims-Williams 2001:267 - 280; 2001a:47 - 49;

3 号信札:Whitfield 2004:249;

5 号信札:Grenet, Sims-Williams, de la Vaissière 1998:91 - 104.

② Sims-Williams 2001:261.

③ 3~5 号信札可能写于公元 313 年 5 月 11 日和 314 年 4 月 21 日之间,也可能从公元 313 年 6 月到 12 月(Grenet at al (1998):102),也参见 de la Vaissière 2002:51, 51n5.

④ Sims-Williams 2004:249.

一匹骆驼和一名男子陪他。

2 号古信札——即谈到洛阳被毁的那封信——的作者是一个过着背井离乡生活的粟特代理商,他在信中向撒马尔罕的主人汇报他在甘肃酒泉和武威所雇不同手下的情况。它证明了贸易体系中三种等级的存在:老板(在撒马尔罕的一对父子),为老板监管生产者的代理人(信件作者),以及为代理人制作商品的生产者。在信中,代理人授权撒马尔罕的商人从他在撒马尔罕的财产中"取出 1 000 或者 2 000 斯忒特,帮助一个他照顾着的孤儿"。该代理人看来是很富裕的。

学者们对斯忒特的价值并不确定。不知道这种钱币是不是像当时流通的某些斯忒特一样,有 12 克重或者是更轻一点,就像撒马尔罕曾流通过的银币一样只有 0.6 克。无论如何,我们可以看出,代理人比困在敦煌、只需要 20 斯忒特来支付旅费的妇女 Mīwnāy 要富裕得多。①

2 号信札提及了当时交易的一些商品,包括羊毛织物和亚麻制品。写信的人提到,他已经送了 32 包(vesicles,一种不太确定的价值单位)麝香到敦煌,麝香大概重 0.8 公斤,确实是数量不小。② 麝香由麝香鹿的腺体加工而成,用来作为香水和定色剂,大概从西藏和甘肃的交界处得来。2 号信札还提到了羊毛织物和麻制品,但是没有提及数量。

5 号信札反映了姑臧和敦煌之间当地的商业情况,这封信是寄给一位商队首领的(中文中写作萨宝/保,粟特语 s'rtp'w)。信中提到少量的钱:写信人提到他只收到了本属于他的 20 斯忒特中的 4.5 斯忒特。他还提到商队从姑臧运到其他地区的几种货物,很可能是 1 400 公里以外的楼兰。这些货物包括:一种称为"白"的东西,很可能是铅粉,为一种白色粉末的化妆品,此外还有胡椒粉、银子和词意不明的"rysk"。这些物品的数量都不确切,大多数学者认为数量很小,很可能只在 1.5 公斤到 40 公斤之间。③

某些商品来自很远的地方:胡椒(5 号信札)和樟脑(6 号信札)只能在东南亚或者印度才能够买到,而麝香(2 号信札)则来自西藏和甘肃的交界处。6 号信札只保存了部分内容。在信中,写信人要求收信人买一些东西,大致是"来源于蚕",意思即丝织品或者丝线。如果丝(?)买不到,那收信人可以买些樟脑来代替。如果 Sims-Williams 的解释正确,那么这就是粟特义古信札中唯一提到"丝"的地方。④

粟特文古信札的发现意义重大,因为它们是丝绸之路文书中仅见地由商人写成,而非由管理或征收贸易税的官员所写。这些信札描述了粟特人作为商人、农夫,甚至农仆的安居生活,尽管当时的中国处于动荡分裂的时期,朝代更替频繁,这些散居的粟特人仍然从事着商业和长途贸易。

在随后的几个世纪里,粟特人继续使用着他们自己的语言,但通过改变服饰和发型来顺应新的环境——即新的游牧民族征服者。六世纪时匈奴、寄多罗(Kidarites)、嚈哒(Hephthalites)和突厥相继控制了撒马尔罕。在西面,萨珊王朝(224~651)统治着以今天巴格达附近的泰西封(Ctesiphon)为首都的大帝国。萨珊王朝为了打败另一个民族,经常在不同时期和统治撒马尔罕的政权结盟。公元 509 年,萨珊王朝在败给了嚈哒人(有时被称为白匈奴,是蒙古草原上伊朗和突厥民族的部落联盟),被迫放弃了撒马尔罕。公元 565 年,萨珊又和新兴起的突厥联兵打败了嚈哒。565 年之后,撒马尔罕处于西突厥控制之下。尽管已经有了自己的书写语言,突厥人仍然经常选择使用粟特语。因此突厥和粟特之间的文化联系

① 参见 de la Vaissière 2002:60-61 中的讨论;关于重量单位的研究,参见 Marshak and Raspapova 2005.
② 此处假设 1 vesicule 有 25 克,de la Vaissière 2002:58.
③ Grenet, Sims-Williams, de la Vaissière 1998:100; de la Vaissière 2002:59.
④ Sims-Williams 2005:182.

是非常紧密的。

在这几个世纪多次的政治变化中,粟特人逐渐从他们的老家撒马尔罕和布哈拉往外扩张。自五世纪开始,粟特人在泽拉善夫河(Zerafshan River)北岸和东岸计划新的定居点时,建造了粟特风格的建筑和水利灌溉工程。五世纪中期粟特地区经济飞快增长,到六、七世纪时,粟特已经成为中亚最富裕的地区。

但是撒马尔罕以及整个中亚的政治走向即将面临翻天覆地的变化。632 年穆罕默德死后,在四大哈里发和此后的倭玛雅(Ummayad caliphate,661~750)统治时期,阿拉伯人征服了北非、西班牙南部以及伊朗地区。阿拉伯人在 651 年击败了萨珊王朝,随后继续东进中亚,目标就是撒马尔罕。671 年阿拉伯人首次占领撒马尔罕,681 年阿拉伯统治者第一次可以在该地区过冬。[①] 在 705 年和 715 年之间,阿拉伯将领屈底波(Qutayba b. Muslim)攻打粟特地区,并最终在 712 年攻占了撒马尔罕。

在粟特本土发现的唯一用粟特文写成的文书正属于这一时期。1933 年苏联考古学家在撒马尔罕东 120 公里的穆格山发现了一处特别的窖藏。[②] 穆格山文书从被征服者而非征服者的角度,提供了对伊斯兰征服的独特描述。文书描述了一位统治者为了阻挡阿拉伯军队,在已无退路的情况下,如何急切地与突厥、中国和其他当地统治者进行磋商。这提醒我们,伊斯兰对中亚的征服过程既漫长而又不稳定,而唐朝在该地区八世纪早期的政治中扮演了一定的角色,但具体怎样的角色则不明。

穆格山是一座偏僻的小山,海拔 1 500 米。穆格山文书的发现只在苏联统治时期。在沙俄统治时期,6 公里以外的库姆(Kum)某村庄的村民得知,穆格山的山顶上藏着某种宝藏。1932 年春,当地几个牧羊娃来到了这个地方。他们围着一个洞坑挖掘,并发现了几件写在皮革上的文书。他们将最完整的几张带回了村庄,而将剩下的放回了洞里。[③]

当地的官员 Abdulhamid Puloti 曾经在塔什干学习历史。当他风闻此发现之后,许诺一个村民如果能帮他找到这些文书,就给他一份警察的工作。Puloti 最后被带到一个村民家里,主人从一面墙和门柱的缝隙间取出了一份文书。Puloti 把这个情况报告给了他的上级,后者旋即通知了文化部门。于是这份后来被编号为 1.1 的文书被送到了塔吉克斯坦首都杜尚别(Dushanbe)。[④]

和许多亚洲民族一样,粟特人用在位统治者的年号来记录文书的时间。多数的穆格山文书的年代在统治者 Dēwāštīč 在位元年至十四年之间。但是,由于 Dēwāštīč 的统治时间不为人所知,所以学者们无法给文书精确纪年。在穆格山发现的 97 件文书中,有 92 件用粟特文书写,3 件用汉文书写,1 件用阿拉伯文书写,1 件用一种不明具体何种语言的鲁尼文(北欧文字)书写。[⑤] 一件汉文文书纪年为 706 年,表明这批

---

① Grenet & de la Vaissière 2002:155.

② 穆格山发现的文书已出版三卷:The Freiman 1962, Livshits 1962, Bogoliubov and Smirnova 1963.

③ Ilya Yakubovich(2002)报告说,村民们将粟特文手稿当成了阿拉伯文本,他们相信这些文书会指引他们发现一个古代宝藏。

④ 上述内容来自我和艾米塔什博物馆中亚和高加索部部长马尔沙克于 2000 年 3 月 25 日在宾夕法尼亚州大学的谈话。马尔沙克教授认识 Puloti 本人,Puloti 亲口告诉他这些细节。Vladimir A. Livshits, *Iuridicheskie dokumenty i pis'ma. Sogdiiskie dokumenty s gory Mug 2*(Legal documents and letters). Sogdian Documents from Mount Mugh 2(Moscow: Izdatel'ctvo Vostochnoi Literatury, 1962)在第 108~109 页上对此有一个简单的介绍,第 112 页上有文书 1.1 的照片 Yakubovich(2002)后来 1.1 文书 1933 年消失。

⑤ 这是 O. I. Smirnova(1970:14)给出的全部文书数目。穆格山文书根据他们所发现的时间编号:文书 1.1 发现于 1932 年春天;文书 B 是 Puloti 于 1933 年 3 月发掘的;文书 A 是 A Vasil'ev 于 1933 年夏天发现的;标注俄文 ß 的文书是 Freiman 考察队 1933 年 11 月发现的;编号为"新"的文书是 Puloti 于 1934 年赠送的。当发掘结束以后,Freiman 考察队返回列宁格勒,Puloti 被迫交出了他在 Freiman 探险队到达之前得到的一批文书,即:一个乱七八糟的篮子里装着的六份皮革文书,包括在穆格山找到的最长的文书,为一份婚约以及"新娘"所持有的副本。

文书的时间可能为八世纪早期,但学者们并不知确切的年份。[1]

前苏联著名的阿拉伯学者 I. Y. Kratchkovsky (1883~1951) 在他的论文集里指出,唯一一份阿拉伯语文书是确定这批文书日期的关键。[2] 当 Kratchkovsky 读到这份文书时,他意识到,穆格山文书中的 Devastich,就是来自撒马尔罕的土地贵族 Diivashnii,塔巴里(al-T. abarī)在其详尽的伊斯兰编年史中提到过这个名字。[3] 这个关键的证据使穆格山文书的时间可以定在 709~722 年。

在获知发现文书的消息后,列宁格勒的社会科学研究院就派出了由 A. A. Freiman (1879~1968) 领导的考察队前往塔吉克斯坦,A. A. Freiman 是前苏联当时众所周知的研究粟特的学科带头人。从 1933 年 11 月 10 日至 23 日,他带领来自科学院的考察小组发掘了这个堡垒遗址。这座堡垒位于今塔吉克斯坦片治肯特城东 120 公里外的山里。[4] 这是一个非常合适作堡垒的地方:库姆(Kum)河和泽拉夫善河环绕着堡垒的三面,居民修筑内墙和外墙做进一步的防御。

在考察完遗址上发现的器物之后,考古学家们就能够判定这个只有五间屋子的小堡垒内不同房间的用处了。四间四方形的房间有 17.3 米长,1.8~2.2 米宽,天花板距地面 1.7 米高。整个建筑并不奢华。房间只能从南边采光,现已不存的墙上原本应该开有窗户。

堡垒的防备能力极其脆弱,只有一些大的土罐用于储水,清楚地表明,住在堡垒中的人依靠附近村子的村民为他们从 500 米外的小溪中取水。这个堡垒的空间太小,不可能容纳一支军队,应该是统治者为自己及家人和仆人居住而设计的。但是如果挤在一起的话,该堡垒的大屋和庭院还是可以暂时容纳一百户人家。

让发掘者奇怪的是,遗址内基本没有留下有价值的东西。内院是个垃圾坑,表面覆盖有一层 0.5 米厚的骨头、陶土和织物等废弃物。1 号房间内有 1 米厚的堆积物,是九层明显不同的用黄土隔开的动物粪便,表明堡垒被使用了大概 9 年到 10 年。由于房间内还存有木料残余,因此发掘者推断 1 号房间曾经是一个木料加工作坊,而在冬天兼作牲口棚使用。2 号房间是厨房,存有大量家用器具:陶土罐、盘碟的碎片、芦苇编制的篮子、小陶土杯、大豆、大麦种子,旁边还有火的痕迹。奇怪的是,3 号房间除了一些小的玻璃瓶子和一把梳子之外,基本上空无他物。这间屋子是谷仓,墙上装饰着白色的石膏图案。4 号房间有大部分的古器物,包括三个陶土罐、很多家用器具、三枚硬币(一枚为银币)、箭头、金属箭头、几匹布料以及一个腰带搭扣。所有这些都是在上面一层发现的,都倒塌在下面一层的顶上。[5]

4 号房间的北边有一个巨大的陶土罐倒在那里,旁边散落着 23 根刻着文字的柳条棍,看起来像是从陶罐口掉到地上的。这些棍子上刻有管家为主人记录的家庭支出情况。[6] 他使用柳条棍而非纸张或皮革,是因为柳条棍很便宜且很容易得到。

管家记录了每次招待不同的客人时所花费的酒和小麦的不同数量,我们可以通过他的帐目推算出当地经济的概况。附近的居民多次给堡垒的主人运来成车的谷物,这可能是以谷物来交税。而管家的帐历同样记载了他们从堡垒主人那里得到谷物。

---

[1] Polyakov 1934:103;文书图片在第 99 页上。

[2] I. Y. Kratchkovsky, 1953:142-150.

[3] Powers 1989:171, 177-178, 183.

[4] Freiman 1962:7.

[5] Krachkovskii and Freiman 1934:29.

[6] Bogoliubov and Smirnova 1963.

放牧在当地经济中扮演着很重要的角色：人们吃绵羊和山羊，他们用动物的皮毛制成衣服，有时候需要 50 只动物的皮毛，但通常数量要少一些。文书 A17 列出了各种消费明细帐：一匹马 200 迪拉姆，给房屋加顶 100 迪拉姆，给琐罗亚斯德教祭司 50 迪拉姆，给医生和倒酒的人 15 迪拉姆，为新年宴会准备的牛花费 11 迪拉姆，给起草文件的人 8 迪拉姆，纸张、丝绸、黄油花费 8 迪拉姆，给刽子手 5 迪拉姆。尽管学者们不确定当时在撒马尔罕流通何种钱币，但迪拉姆在当时取代了萨珊银币，是流通于整个阿拉伯语世界的主要银币。除了纸张和丝绸来自中国之外，基本上所有在柳条棍帐历上出现的商品，都是产自本地。这留给我们的印象是，如同临近的龟兹人那样，粟特本土的人也用钱币购买本地物品。

除柳条棍之外，这个遗址还发现了六十件写在纸上或者皮革上的文书，它们都散落在 2 号房间和 3 号房间内一楼和二楼倒塌的天花板的废墟里，表明它们原本是被存放在 2 号房间上面二楼的某个地方。①第三个发现皮革文书的地方就是牧羊男孩们最初发现的篮子。

穆格山 97 份文书中，有三件是写在呈梯形的皮革片上的法律契约。它们反映了这个时期复杂精密的法律机制。尽管在我们看来皮革是一种使用不便的书写材料，但是我们必须记住，皮革在整个阿拉伯语世界中一直都被使用（欧洲人在同时期使用羊皮纸），经验丰富的抄写员能在皮革上记载详细的协议。到目前为止，在穆格山文书中篇幅最长、内容最丰富的，是一份婚约以及附带的文件，即"新娘"持有的副本，内容是丈夫陈述他对新娘家庭的责任。这两份文件都是在 Puloti 于 1934 年上交给官方的篮子里发现的。②

婚约和新娘所持副本可定为国王突昏统治的第十年，即 710 年。两份文书合起来有满满的 90 行，分别用了 21 cm 和 15.5 cm 长的两张皮革。这两份文书明确地列出了粟特妇女查托（Chat）从她的监护人笈赤建（Navikat），七河流域地区的一个粟特城邦城主的统治者 Chēr 移交到她的新丈夫乌特特勤（Ottegin）之手时所需注意的事项，她丈夫的名字很清楚地表明他是一个突厥人。

这份伊斯兰征服以前的文书揭示了当时社会中关于义务的严格的互惠原则，故非常引人注目。丈夫可以在某种情况下提出离婚，而妻子也可以在同样情况下要求离婚。③ 如同现代的婚前协议，这份婚约也写明了如果婚姻出现问题后该如何应对。如果丈夫娶了"另外一个妻子或者小妾，或者另外一个查托不喜欢的女人"，就要许诺付给他的妻子相当多一笔钱，即"30 个上好的、纯的、Dēn 形制的迪拉姆"，并且送她离开。

如果他决定结束婚姻，当然他可以这么做，他必须给他的妻子提供食物，归还她的嫁妆以及所有他给她的礼物。不管是丈夫还是妻子都不应欠对方任何赔偿。然后丈夫就可以自由地再婚了。尤其值得注意的是，妻子也有结束婚姻的权利，但是只有在她归还了她丈夫的一切礼物之后；她可以保留她自己的财

---

① *Sogdiiskii sbornik* 1934：29.

② 3 号文书（婚约）和 4 号文书（新郎的义务）最初是由里夫谢茨（V. A. Livshits）转写和翻译（Livshits, *Dokumentys gory Mug* 2：21 - 26.）。最新的翻译参见 Ilya Yakubovich, "Marriage Sogdian Style 粟特人的婚姻模式," *Iranistik in Europa — Gestern, Heute, Morgen* 欧洲的伊朗学：昨天、今天和明天（ed. H. Eichner at al.）, Vienna：Verlag der Österreichischen Akademie der Wissenschaften, 2006, pp. 307 - 344. 简介另见 Ilya Gershevitch, "The Sogdian Word for 'Advice', and some Mugh Documents," *Central Asiatic Journal 7* (1962)：77 - 95, 讨论见第 90 ~ 94 页；W. B. Henning, "A Sogdian god," *Bulletin of the School of Oriental and African Studies* 1965：242 - 254, 讨论见第 248 ~ 254 页。

③ 3 号文书（婚约）和 4 号文书（新郎的义务）非常独特。Yakubovich 在 "Marriage Sogdian Style 粟特人的婚姻模式"中考察了大量婚约，但只发现了另外一组婚约契约，即在埃及大象岛（Elephantine）犹太人定居点发现的亚兰文协议，该协议允许妻子提出离婚。他提出了两种可能性。一种可能性为：与其他相邻的社会相比，粟特人社会提供给妇女更多的权利。另一种可能性为：Chēr 可以为其被监护人赢得异常优惠的条件。

产以及从她丈夫那里得到的补偿。一旦婚姻结束,没有一方需为另一方的罪行负责,而只有犯罪一方有义务接受任何处罚。

乌特特勤许诺如果他们离婚,而他又未能毫发无伤地将查托送回 Chēr 家,他需要赔偿一百个上等迪拉姆。如果他没有及时交纳违约金,他需在未付余额的基础上再付 20% 的罚金。这份文书的大部分内容清楚明白地说明了监护人能获得付款的程序:如,文书指定了一个监护人选出的保证人,并命令全社会的都来共同监督这个在公所里,在众多证人面前签署的协议。该婚约表明,在 7 世纪早期,也可能更早,粟特人的协议已经发展成复杂细密的法律文件,其中充斥着复杂的处罚条款。

穆格山发现的另外两件契约,一份为有关磨坊的租金(B-4),另外一份为买卖墓地的协议。这两份契约和婚约相比短一些,但是在总体结构上是一样的,都给出了日期(国王统治的年月日)、契约双方的名字、具体条款、见证人和起草人的名字。

Devashtich 把自己的三个磨坊出租给一个男人,这份契约载明租金是每年 460 单位的面粉。[①] 如同柳条棍上的文件一样,这份契约也要求以实物付款,此处为面粉。但是这份契约超出了简单的租借的陈述。契约有 42 行,是很严谨的法律文件。契约指出,如果租借者在指定日期内没有向管理者交纳全额租金,就要承担法律后果。

第三份契约中讲到一处墓地的租金是 25 迪拉姆。[②] 根据 Ilya Gershevitc 的译文,[③]这份契约记录了一家的两个儿子向另一家的两兄弟以 25 迪拉姆的价格租借墓地的条款。

穆格山契约让我们知道,这个堡垒中保存的,不仅仅是统治者 Devashtich 的私人文件。有些文件,如指出租用磨坊者必须付给磨坊主人的租金总额的协议,明显属于他自己。但是他为什么要保留一份一个突厥人及其粟特新娘之间的条款繁杂的婚约呢?

很可能,穆格山的居民,包括新娘查托,或许是在堡垒被围攻的最后日子,随身带着他们所有的重要的合法文件,以便安全保管。他们或者希望在阿拉伯人的威胁被消除以后,他们还可以重新履行他们的协议。但是这些契约在穆格山的堡垒里面,一直尘封未动,直到 1932 年牧羊的男孩们发现它们。如果这个假定属实,就可以解释为什么穆格山不仅有 Devashtich 本人的信札,还有在堡垒里面避难的其他几位较低等级的领主的信札。

把塔巴里(al-Tabari)详细的编年史提供的信息和来自穆格山的文件结合起来看,我们可以推想导致穆格山堡垒陷落的事件。[④] 编年史记载了一名新的统治者在 720 年秋及 722 年春和粟特人发生过战争。粟特人和突骑施人(Türgesh)结成联盟。突骑施原来属于西突厥,但在 715 年到 740 年之间控制了原属西突厥的部分领地。[⑤] 公元 721 年,Devastich 在做了片治肯特差不多 14 年的统治者以后,被正式加冕为"粟特之王,撒马尔罕之主"。[⑥]

Devastich 声称自己是突昏的继承者,突昏是撒马尔罕的上任统治者。709 年,他向白衣大食呼罗珊总督屈底波投降,但是紧接着当地发生了一次起义,710 年他不是自杀就是被处决了。屈底波打着为突

---

① Livshits 已将 B-4 文件转写并翻译成俄文(Livshits 1962:56-58);同时参见 Gershevitch (1962, p. 84)的简要讨论。
② Livshit (1962:47-48)已将 B-8 号文件转写并翻译成俄文;Ilya Gershevitch (1975:195-211) 校订了里夫什茨的译文。
③ Gershevitch 1975:205-206.
④ Grenet and de la Vaissière 2002 在弄清这些令人迷惑的事件方面取得了真正的突破。
⑤ de la Vaissière 2002:197.
⑥ de la Vaissière 2002:157.

昏报仇的旗号，不断攻打撒马尔罕城，并且在 712 年取得了控制权。当粟特首领乌勒伽(Ghuurak)投降的时候，他签定了一份条约，约定一次性支付 2 000 000 迪拉姆，以后每年支付 200 000 迪拉姆。[①] 屈底波和几位地方贵族接受了乌勒伽希望接任突昏位置的请求，但撒马尔罕西南部的人则支持 Devastich。两位竞争者共存了十年，但这段时期发生的事很多不为人所知。根据穆格山出土的阿拉伯语文书，719 年 Devastich 给呼罗珊的阿拉伯总督写信，谦恭地承认他自己是其属下。但到了 721 年夏，Devastich 乐观地以为他有机会打败阿拉伯人。据 V - 17 文书，当时 Devastich 给撒马尔罕西南 12 公里至 16 公里的 Khākhsar 的统治者 Afshūn 写信，信中提到"突厥和中国大军都来了"。显然突骑施人、部分中国以及东边的拔汗那(Ferghāna)的国王，组成了一支对抗伊斯兰军队的联盟。穆格山出土的书信提供了中国人卷入这场事件的唯一证据，另外一封信(V - 18)里提及"中国"侍人("侍人"一词模糊不清)。"中国"一词可能指来自当时唐朝西域地区的中国人，而不一定是由长安中央政府派出的军队。[②]

一年以后，很可能是 722 年，文件揭示出，情况已经完全发生了变化。据一位使者报告，突厥人消失得无影无踪。而另一个人，可能是一位驿差，描述了拔汗那为在伊斯兰军队击溃，14 000 多人投降。[③] 塔巴里编年史记载，粟特人分成了两拨。人多的一拨至少有 5 000 人，他们去了拔汗那，但是被拒绝入境，结果就惨遭伊斯兰军队的屠杀。[④] 人少的一拨，可能只有几百户人，和 Devastich 一起，逃到了穆格山的堡垒里面。[⑤]

在遭到阿拉伯军队最后屠杀之前，人多的一拨中，只有商人有能力向侵略军交付赎金来换得他们的生命安全。对于新被征服的中亚地区的人们来说，课税是一个重要的问题。他们为了躲避沉重的税金而皈依伊斯兰教，接受给予穆斯林教徒的优惠税率。然而在 8 世纪，阿拉伯统治者急切地需要征税以供应战争，个别地区的统治者并不总是给那些新皈依的穆斯林教徒以优惠税率。结果，许多粟特人逃到突厥所管辖的地区及中国境内。

Devashtich 和其随从，大概只有一百个男人以及他们的家庭，搬到了穆格山的堡垒里(塔巴里书中称为 Abghar)。[⑥] 他们派出了很小规模的兵力到堡垒外抗击伊斯兰军队，伊斯兰军队将他们赶回堡垒，围困在内并最终打败了他们。在被打败以后，Devashtich 请求 Saᶜid al-Haraši 保证他们的安全，Saᶜid al-Haraᵛsi 最初答应了他的请求。留在堡垒里面的一百个家庭交出了堡垒里的物品以换取自由。塔巴里记载说，阿拉伯军队的指挥官拍卖了堡垒里的东西，并且如伊斯兰法律所规定的，留下堡垒财富的五分之一上交国库。这就是 1933 年前苏联考古学家发掘这个堡垒时，里面几乎空无一物的原因。所有值钱的东西都已被移走，而纸张和皮革文件则没有引起注意。

尽管阿拉伯指挥官曾许诺 Devashtich 的安全，但却食言了。他将 Devashtich 钉在十字架上处死了，并且砍下他的头送给伊朗的指挥官，而将他的左手送给阿富汗的指挥官。[⑦] 处死 Devashtich 的方法表明

① Yakubovich 2002.

② Grenet 1989:17.

③ A - 14, A - 9, Grenet/de la Vaissière 2002:168 - 169, 172.

④ Powers 1989: 172 - 174; Gernet and de la Vaissière 2002:156.

⑤ Zeimal 1983: 259 - 260.

⑥ Richard Frye, "Tarxun-Turxun and Central Asian History 塔尔逊-吐尔逊和中亚历史," 112 - 113; E. V. Zeimal, "The Political History of Transoxiana 河中地区的政治史," in Ehsan Yarshater, ed. *The Cambridge History of Iran*, volume 3 (Ⅰ) *The Seleucid, Parthian, and Sasanian Periods* 剑桥伊朗史，卷3：赛琉古王朝、帕提亚和萨珊时期 (New York: Cambridge University Press, 1983) 259 - 260; Powers, *The History of al-Tabari* 塔巴里的历史 171, 177 - 178, 183.

⑦ 参见 *The History of al-Tabari*, 178。该书英译者 Powers 把 Devashtich 在阿拉伯语中的名字翻译成 al-Diwashini，而 Kratchkovsky 在解读穆格山出土的阿拉伯语文书时，则将其名读作 Divashni。

他不是一个小角色。因为 Devashtich 代表了粟特人的反抗,阿拉伯指挥官选择了一种极端的方法处置他的尸体。[①] 但他随后因为使用如此残忍的处罚而被解职了。

Devashtich 的死只是伊斯兰征服撒马尔罕中的一个小片段。在接下来的几十年中,伊斯兰军队控制了这个地区,阿拉伯人取代了粟特人,伊斯兰教取代了琐罗亚斯德教。公元751年,在怛逻斯(Talas),即今天哈萨克斯坦的江布尔(Dzambul),伊斯兰军队打败了一支唐朝军队。四年以后,唐朝节度使安禄山叛乱,唐廷被迫将军队从中亚撤回以镇压这场叛乱。这两件紧接着发生的事件意味着,在8世纪中叶以后,撒马尔罕以及粟特周边地区不再指望东边的中国。同时,粟特地区的伊斯兰化,使得很多居住在中国的粟特人难以重返他们的家乡。

纸 之 路

穆格山文书的年代先于中亚的伊斯兰化及造纸技术在这个地区的传播。穆格山文书使用不同材料书写表明,当地的统治者因为中国纸耐用并且方便,很愿意出钱使用中国纸,但是就像 Krachkovsky 翻译的唯一的用阿拉伯语写成的信札那样,当地居民继续使用皮革来记录重要文件,用柳条棍记载如家庭账簿之类不太重要的文件。

穆格山存在长途贸易的珍贵证据,就是在那里发现的中国纸张。8片残片被拼成了三件汉文文书,都为写在来自中国的回收再用的纸上。在穆格山其实并没有人能写汉语。有一件文件(A-21)最早是写于凉州的官文书,这是中国境内丝绸之路上的一个重要城市。在它废弃不用之后,就被当成纸卖掉(另一面是空白的,还可以使用),丝路商人把它从3600公里外的东方带到了穆格山。[②]

另外一个发现纸的遗址在前苏联境内,即 Moschevaia Balka,字面意思为"木乃伊或者尸体的峡谷",可见八九世纪时中国的纸张深入中亚地区程度之深。黑海东北岸是目前发现中国纸张到达最远的地方了。遗址由坟墓构成,这些坟墓不是在石灰石的阶地上,就是在山坡上被发现的。20世纪早期的发掘者找到了一些写有汉字的纸片。最完整的一份文件,15×8 cm,有几行手书的汉字,记录了各种花费的时间和数量(2 000文钱,及400文钱)。尽管非常残缺不全,这份文书看上去很像某种官文书。[③] 这个遗址还发现了别的物品,所有的物品都很明显来自中国。这些物品包括:一幅绢画,上面画着一个佛教的神以及一个骑马的男子(可能是离宫之前的悉达多王子),还有一片佛经残片,以及混凝纸浆制的信封残片。这些物品清楚地表明,至少中国的纸张和丝绸,或者甚至是中国的商人,在8世纪至10世纪之间的某个时候到过高加索地区。[④]

8世纪的某个时期,中亚人学会了制造纸张。一篇阿拉伯文文献记载,在751年的怛逻斯之战中,阿巴斯王朝的哈里发彻底打败了中国的一支军队,并把战俘带回他们的首都巴格达。有些战俘将造纸技术传授给了他们。[⑤]

---

① Yakubovich 2002.
② Polyakov 1934.
③ Ierusalimskaja and Borkopp 1996：Catalog item #120.
④ Knauer 2001.
⑤ Tha < aaliibii 1968；140.

和其他有关技术传播的传说一样,这个故事也并不一定可信。① 通过将植物和破布等原料挫捣后制成纸浆,然后在某种平面上晒干的造纸技术并不难学。造纸技术从中国向外慢慢地传播,直到 8 世纪才达到中亚。到 8 世纪晚期,伊斯兰世界中纸张逐渐取代皮革成为书写的主要材料。纸张比皮革有更多的优势:花费低、生产快、远比皮革方便,并且比只生长在埃及的莎草纸容易获得。在 11 世纪晚期和 12 世纪早期,通过在西班牙和西西里的伊斯兰世界,纸张进入了欧洲基督教世界。

毫无疑问,是中国发明的纸张——而非丝绸——改变了它所接触的社会。丝绸在现代社会之前,不管具有多么大的吸引力,主要还是用于穿着或者装饰的目的。如果不可得,其他的纺织品也可以很轻易地代替它,如在中亚,棉花就经常是丝绸的代用品。相比之下,纸张标志着书写材料的一个真正的大突破。随着便宜的纸张的引进,书本就从奢侈品变成了很多人都用得起的物品,教育水平因此相应提高。与羊皮纸或者皮革不同,纸张易吸墨,因此可以用来印刷。如果没有引进造纸技术,印刷术的革命——无论是中国的木版技术还是欧洲的活字印刷都不可能发生。

结　论

研究龟兹及粟特地区出土文书的众多学者都同意,这些文书很少提及贸易。驻扎在龟兹的中国军队买马的行为,促成了绝大部分现存的有关龟兹贸易的文书记载。粟特文古信札尽管由商人写成,但也只证明了小规模贸易的存在。② 同样地,穆格山文书记录了各种实物交易,这些交易让 Devastich 可以在712 年撒马尔罕沦陷之后的困难时期经营自己的财产。

每个学者都在为丝绸之路大规模贸易缺乏文字资料作出尽可能合理的解释。他们主张这种贸易的存在。但到如今,我们应该对这一迹象有别样的解释。与其竭力解释为何材料没有提及贸易,我们何不考虑一种真实的可能性,即我们的材料实际上是在描述当时存在的贸易。

我下面要提出三个结论,尽管一个比一个大胆。

首先,即使最坚信丝绸之路贸易数量巨大、交易频繁的学者都必须承认,很少有证据能证明那种程度贸易的存在。学者也可以对这些片断的证据做出与本研究不同的解释,即丝路贸易还是有相当规模的。但是不可否认,所争论的证据只是一些残缺不全的碎片,而非大量的。多数持怀疑态度的人,会说这项研究的材料覆盖面窄,而更多反映大规模贸易内容的证据还没有发掘出来,还保存在地底下。这或许如此吧。

但是,与此同时,我们有必要以批判的眼光对已拥有的证据进行仔细审察。本文所用的考古发掘资料是真实的、第一手的材料:与商人所付的实际税单或批准商人通关的"过所"相比,一般的概括性论说显得苍白无力。尽管这些考古证据数量不多,并常常缺乏关键部分,但却来自不同的遗址,比起只从一个遗址选取材料来看,其可靠性毕竟更大一些。库车出土的文书发现自不同的地方,记录了寺院和中国驻军的经济活动。粟特文古信札不可能是伪造的:2 号和 5 号信札中确实有来自粟特的商人在讨论商业活动。穆格山文书被发现在堡垒中,但是位于三个不同的地点:来自 4 号房间的罐子旁边的柳条棍,2 号房

---

① Bloom 2001.
② Grenet, Sims-Williams, de la Vaissière 1998:101.

间和 3 号房间倒塌的天花板中散落的纸张和皮革文件,以及装在一个单独篮子里面的 6 件皮革上的文书。

这些证据引出第二个结论:不管丝绸之路的贸易规模如何,它对丝路沿线居民的影响极小。农民继续在土地上耕作,实物交易也从来没有停止过。尽管如此,商队始终行进在丝绸之路上。在 3 号粟特文古信札中,从 4 世纪初开始,Miwnay 说她有 5 次单独的机会离开敦煌。在接下来的世纪里,玄奘及其他朝圣者不管去往何处,都可以和商队结伴而行。

商队的常规活动,以及因逃避家乡的战争或政治冲突而导致的频繁的人口流动,同时也意味着技术在东西方之间的传播,如造纸和生产丝绸的技术从中国由东往西传播,而玻璃制造技术则从西往东传入中国。与其只盯着某类商品的大规模贸易,我们更应该将注意力放在一波又一波的难民身上,他们带着某种技术离开家乡,并在其新的居住地方使用这种技术。

是不是有可能,我们被丝绸、珠宝等奢侈品的浪漫所蒙蔽,而误解了丝绸之路贸易的根本性质? 除了看到来去自由的私商在能带来利润的地方随便做生意,我们更应该关注使者之间的常规交往,以及库车和吐鲁番发现的过所文书所反映的对贸易的严格控制。这是一种受到严格管制的贸易,由政府官员谨慎地监控着。在这种贸易中,政府作为各种商品和服务的购买者扮演了主要的角色。

新获吐鲁番出土文献词语考释

王启涛

四川师范大学文学院

由荣新江、李肖、孟宪实主编的《新获吐鲁番出土文献》于2008年4月由中华书局出版。这些文献是我们研究中古史、汉语史的重要语料。其中一些词语不被前代和当今字典辞书收录，或即使收录但释义有漏、有误，今特依词首音序，拈出"剥兰"、"打投"、"绀清"、"候次、候人、更次"、"鸡弊"、"挍断"、"康念"、"尅贼"、"略良"、"论台"、"迁延"、"取受"、"上条、事条"、"司正"、"鍮瑄叉"、"望请"、"奄葛留亭"、"掩"、"夈"、"燕明"、"爰"、"轵当"以做诠释。

【剥兰 bō lán】

裂开（皮裂），梗塞。97TSYM1：13－5背面古写本《甲子推杂吉日法》（拟）（156）：①"病咽喉剥兰，金釜妄鸣。"请比较97TSYM1：13－5背面古写本《甲子推杂吉日法》（拟）（156）："家有病咽喉閇塞，汤火所兰。"考"剥"本来有"撕裂"义，《墨子·非攻下》："夫取天之人，以攻天之人，此刺杀天民，剥振神之位。"《诗·小雅·楚茨》："或剥或亨，或肆或将。"朱熹注："剥，解剥其皮也。"又有"伤害"义，《书·泰誓中》："剥伤元良，贼虐谏辅。"孔传："剥，伤害也。""兰"即阻隔、梗塞，《战国策·魏策三》："河山以兰之，有周、韩以间之。"《史记·扁鹊仓公列传》："夫以阳入阴支兰藏者生，以阴入阳支兰藏者死。"

【打投 dǎ tōu】

投奔。"打"已经成为动词的前缀，用在表示人的行为动作动词前。2006TZJ1：124＋2006TZJ1：103唐龙朔二、三年（662、663）西州都督府案卷为安稽哥逻禄部落事（四）（322）："但前件［部］　　［后］打投此部落居住。"请比较《祖堂集》卷七："今日共师兄到此，又只管打睡。"

【绀清 gàn qīng】

绀綪，青红色。2006TSYIM4：8北凉缺名随葬衣物疏（174）："绀清结发一枚，桐杈一枚。"请比较59TAM305：8缺名随葬衣物疏一（1－3）："绀綪尖一枚，紫縺枕一枚。"②75TKM96：15龙兴某年宋泮妻翟氏随葬衣物疏（1－29）："故绯碧绀綪结发六枚，故鸡鸣枕一枚，故银钗二枚，故耳中珠四枚。故帛縺尖一枚，故绀綪尖一枚。""绀"是微呈红色的深青色。《说文·糸部》："绀，帛深青扬赤色。"段玉裁注："绀，含也，青而含赤色也。"《正字通·糸部》："绀，深青赤色。"綪，本指赤色的缯，也指"青赤色"。《说文·糸部》："綪，赤缯也。"《广韵·霰韵》："綪，青赤色。"在吐鲁番出土文献中，"糸"旁和"氵"旁常常混用不别，如"漏併"又写成"编併"，参考拙著《吐鲁番出土文献词典》"漏併"、"编併"条。

---

① "（156）"表明该件文书原卷图版见于荣新江、李肖、孟宪实主编《新获吐鲁番出土文献》，第156页，下同。

② "（1－3）"表明此件文书图版见于唐长孺主编图录本《吐鲁番出土文书》第一册，第3页，下同。

【候次 hòu cì】【候人 hòu rén】【更次 gēng cì】

"候次"即担任"候"这种差役的班次,"候"即在军种负责侦察敌情,在府中值宿担任警卫和服务的人员,甚至包括整治道路、稽查奸盗和迎送宾客的人员;"候人"即从事"候"这一差役的人;"更次"即承担巡更(巡夜)的班次。2006TSYIM4:3-3北凉高昌郡高宁县差役文书(一)(197):"　口口张相富、翟紛。右二家户候次,[逮][三]口口　　火,与高昌、田地承　　七日,候廿日[竟]口　　曹阚禄白。"2006TSYIM4:3-4北凉高昌郡高宁县差役文书(二)(198):"右二家户候次,逮三日为更。　口高昌、田地相承保,无失＆脱＆军　　[到]乃下。　[谨]条次取候人名[如]　行。"2004TAM398:6-2唐某年二月西州高昌县更簿(一)(9):"更次交付怀[欢]　。""候"有"侦查"、"巡逻守夜"、"守望报警"义,《墨子·号令》:"候出越陈表,遮坐郭门之外内。"请比较唐张九龄《敕北庭经略使盖嘉运书》:"近敕彼军与天山计会,常审观事势,远著候人。"也指稽查小吏。《墨子·号令》:"诸吏卒民非其部界而擅入他部界,辄收以属都司空若候,候以闻守。"孙诒让间诂:"此候为小吏。""次"有"顺序"、"依次"义,《国语·周语中》:"抑晋国之举也,不失其次,吾惧政之未及子也。"也有"行列"义,《国语·晋语三》:"失次犯令,死。"韦昭注:"次,行列也。"

【鸡弊 jī bì】

契弊、契苾,属于北方游牧民族特勒部。2004TMM102:47c唐残牒(121):"辛舍[门]　鸡弊埴奴依[捡]上件　谨牒。"检吐鲁番出土文献中还有"鸡弊零"。60TAM307:5/3(a)高昌竺佛图等传供食帐(一)(1-413):"次昌僧忠传,面六斗,广禾米一斗二升,供鸡弊零。"60TAM307:4/4(a)高昌口善等传供食帐(二)(1-416):"供鸡弊零出军　斗。"考《隋书·铁勒传》:"铁勒……种类最多。自西海之东,依据山谷,往往不绝。独洛河北,有仆骨、同罗、韦纥、拔也固、覆罗,并号俟斤;蒙陈、吐如纥、斯结、浑、斛薛等诸姓,胜兵可二万。伊吾以西,焉者之北,傍白山,则有契弊、薄落、职乙咥、苏婆、郁曷、乌讙、纥骨、也咥、于尼讙等,胜兵可二万。"(引文参考马长寿《突厥人与突厥汗国》第3页)《新唐书·回鹘传》:"武后时,突厥默啜方强,取铁勒故地,故回纥与契苾、思结、浑三部度碛,徙甘、凉间。"又:公元605年后,高昌八代王麹伯雅臣于铁勒,当时统治高昌的铁勒人,主要是紧邻高昌的天山地区的契弊(契苾)可汗和阿尔泰地区的薛延陀可汗。但是王素指出:"'鸡弊零'似乎只能作为契苾羽的异译,而不能作为契弊、契苾的异译。'鸡弊'才是契弊、契苾的异译。《通典·边防十五》契苾羽条云:'契苾羽在多滥葛南,两姓合居。'《唐会要》卷七二诸蕃马印条有'苾羽马'和'契苾马',岑仲勉先生据此认为:'似契苾、苾羽各一姓。'"(王素《高昌史稿·交通编》第496页。所引岑文见岑仲勉《突厥集史》下册,中华书局1958年,第857页)我们检索了吐鲁番出土文献,发现"鸡弊"主要用作姓(可能表明此姓人来自同一名称的部落)。除了我们在以上文中所举"雞弊埴奴"外,在吐鲁番出土文献中还有"张埴奴",见于64TAM134:17、18高昌麹阿留科钱帐(2-215);还有"康埴奴",见于64TAM5:84唐诸户主丁口配田簿(甲件)(一)(3-186),正好可以和"鸡弊埴奴"相对照。而"鸡弊零"没有做姓的现象,依然作为一个独立的部落名称使用。

【挍断 jiào duàn】

考量、裁断。2006TSYIM4:3-5背面北凉义和三年(433)文书为保辜事(七)(196):"　口保辜三　口主者召蒲挍断。　"《广雅·释诂一》:"挍,度也。"

【康愈 kāng yù】

平安舒适。2005TST33唐书信(265):"严寒,不审使[君]口履康愈。襄帷务广,愿口口口口口口口口口[旅]　　　。"请比较《说文·心部》："念,喜也。"《玉篇·心部》："念,悦也。"又《玉篇·心部》："念,豫也。"《广雅·释诂一》："休,喜也。"晋王羲之《夫人帖》："夫人涉道康和,足下大小皆佳。"《晋书·艺术·鸠摩罗什》："罗什未终少日,觉四大不念。"吐鲁番出土文献还有与之意义相近的词语,请参考拙著《吐鲁番出土文献词典》"康和"、"康休"、"清休"条。

【尅贼 kè zéi】

尅贼。伤害。同义连用。97TSYM1:13-5背面古写本《甲子推杂吉日法》(拟)(156)："少不秋矣。所以然者,祟是太父母先人来尅贼子孙,亦言不祀祭。""尅"即"砍伐",考《淮南子·说山训》："至伐大木,非斧不尅。"《玉篇·戈部》："贼,伤害人也。"罗竹风主编《汉语大词典》(第1030页)收有"尅贼",但漏释"伤害"义,今补。

【略良 luè liáng】

强抢平民。2004TBM207:1-4唐仪凤三年(678)九月西州功曹牒为检报乖僻批正文案事(78)："大素自考[后]以来,诸司所有乖僻处分随案,并捉得略良胡数人及财物等,官口之日,并皆不通,请捡附状者。"考《方言》卷二："略,强取也。"《小尔雅·广诂》："寒、探、钩、掠、采、略,取也。"《唐律疏议·名例》："诸略、和诱人,若合同相卖。疏议曰:不和为'略'。前已解讫。和诱者,谓彼此和同,共相诱引,或使为良,或使为贱。"《资治通鉴·后晋齐王天福八年》"禁压良为贱"胡三省注："买良人子女为奴婢,谓之压良为贱,律之所禁也。"吐鲁番出土文献还有与之类似的词语,参考《吐鲁番出土文献词典》"压良"、"压良詃诱"、"寒良詃诱"、"寒詃"条。

【论台 lún tái】

轮台。唐庭州属县之一,永徽五年(654)唐将程知节伐西突厥阿史那贺鲁置,后为北道征收西域商胡的关卡与西陲边防重镇,下领四乡。关于其具体地址,一说在今昌吉以东唐代破城子,一说今米泉县古牧地一带,一说今乌鲁木齐以南乌拉泊故城遗址。2006TAM607:2-2背面唐景龙三年(709)后西州勾所勾粮帐(46)："二石六斗小麦,论台运欠,徵杜口。二石六斗米,中舘妄破,苏仁折纳。"2006TAM607:2-4唐神龙元年(705)六月后西州前庭府牒上州勾所为当府官马破除、见在事(32)："三疋,长安四年六月给论台声援兵随北庭讨击军不迴。"请比较"轮台"。73TAM509:8/4-2(a)之二唐开元二十一年(733)唐益谦、薛光泚、康大之请给过所案卷(4-272)："唐益谦牒,请将人拾马　　[福][州],[薛]光泚人叁,[驴]　　来文,并责保识有口准给所由过所,唐口从西自有　别给。由康大[之]　　　往轮台徵[债]

同,牒知任去,谘[元]。十四日。"检《集韵》平声第十八"谆"韵中,既有"论",又有"轮"。所以二字同音。关于"轮台",参见纪大椿主编《新疆历史词典》第388页。但该著和冯志文等编著的《西域地名词典》都未收"论台"。

【迁延 qiān yán】

拖延时间。2004TAM396:14(1)唐开元七年(719)四月某日镇人盖嘉顺辞为郝伏憙负钱事(15)："开元七年四月日镇人盖嘉顺辞:同镇下等人郝伏憙负钱壹阡文,府司:前件人去三月内,于嘉顺便上件钱,将前蒙司马判命就索,其人迁延与,既被将藏避,请乞处分,谨辞(后缺)。"请比较与之相关的"延引"。69TAM134:9唐麟德二年(665)牛定相辞为请勘不还地子事(2-216)："从嗦地子,延引不还。请付宁昌乡本里追身,勘当不还地子所由。""引"本有"拉长"、"延长"义,北魏郦道元《水经注·江水》："时有高猿长啸,属引凄异。""迁"有移动、变易、避开义,《广雅·释言》："迁,移也。"《玉篇·辵部》："迁,易也。"

【取受 qǔ shòu】

（痛苦）遭遇。97TSYM1:13-5背面古写本《甲子推杂吉日法》（拟）（156）："若任身者，台伤；若无台者，更取受起，病瘦连延。""取"、"受"都有"遭受"义，《杂阿含经》卷一七："譬如空中狂风卒起，从四方来：有尘土风，无尘土风，毗湿波风，脾岚波风，薄风，厚风，乃至风轮起风。身中受风，亦复如是。种种受起：乐受，苦受，不苦不乐受。"又请比较"受病"。《周礼·考工记·弓人》："斲目不荼，则及其大修也，筋代之受病。"又有"取病"。《晏子春秋·内杂下十》："王笑曰：'圣人非所与熙也，寡人反取病焉。"罗竹风主编《汉语大词典》第1108页收有该词，但释义为"拿取和收受"，今补一新义项。

【上条 shàng tiáo】【事条 shì tiáo】

"上条"即逐一罗列陈述，呈报；"事条"即事项，但从字面上讲，依然含有"逐一罗列之事"的意义。2004TMM102:6唐显庆元年（656）西州宋武欢移文（104）："悉平生上条所用之物　　上所求好去。"2004TMM102:6背面唐永徽四年（653）八月安西都护府史孟贞等牒为勘印事（三）（107）："　　口[前]件事条如前，谨牒。永徽四年八月廿日史孟贞牒。功曹参军事令狐京伯勘印，隆悦白。"请比较2004TMM102:41c+2004TMM102:42b唐永徽四年（653）八月安西都护府史孟贞等牒为勘印事（四）（109）："　　[壹]条为关[仓][士][户]三曹给使口　　牒肆条，一为沙州勘合马事，二为　　一为牒纳[职]给使　　[叁]条，一为牒柳中给使口事，一为下高　　驰事。　　一为关口　　。"《资治通鉴·唐德宗兴元元年》："朕欲遣使宣慰，卿宜审细条流以闻。"胡三省注："条，分也。"按，罗竹风主编《汉语大词典》第233页收录"事条"，但释为"条例，法规"，引用语例是唐吴兢《贞观政要·纳谏》："陛下初即位，诏书曰：'逋租宿债，欠负官物，并悉原免。'即令所司，列为事条。"释为"条例"近是，"法规"则误。准确地讲，此处之"事条"还是"事项"。又参考拙著《吐鲁番出土文献词典》"条"、"条列"条。

【司正 sī zhèng】

宴会中的监礼官。2004TBM207:1-5a唐上元三年（676）六月后西州残文书（74）："酒匠　　造V浆酒，好口　　司正监其隐截。"考《仪礼·乡饮酒礼》："主人降席自南方，侧降；作相为司正，司正礼辞许诺，主人拜，司正答拜。"又参见《礼记·乡饮酒义》。考《国语·晋语一》："公饮大夫酒，令司正实爵与史苏。"韦昭注："司正，正宾主之礼者也。"

【鍮瑄叉 tōu xuān chāi】

有鍮石和瑄的钗子。2004TAM408:17令狐阿婢随葬衣物疏（20）："故落緤结发一枚，故鍮瑄叉一枚。""鍮"是金属名，从域外引进，主要用来作为妇女首饰、铸造佛像，唐代又用鍮石制造官章饰，如九品官员的袍带。《新唐书·车服志》："八品九品服用青，饰以鍮石。"《格古要论》："鍮石乃自然铜之精者。炉甘石所炷炼者为假鍮。崔昉云：铜一斤炉甘石一斤，炼之以成鍮石。真鍮出波斯。鍮石如金，火炼成红色，不变黑。""鍮"可能是锌铜合成的黄铜。"瑄"即六寸璧。《说文新附·玉部》："瑄，璧六寸也。""钗"是妇女的首饰。用金、玉、铜等制作。《新唐书·车服志》："庶人女嫁有花钗，以金银琉璃涂饰之。"关于"鍮石"的传入及其在高昌和中国内地的使用，参考林梅村《古道西风——考古新发现所见中西文化交流》第210~230页。又参考拙著《吐鲁番出土文献词典》"鍮石"条。

【望请 wàng qǐng】

希望、请求。2004TMM102:35c、2004TMM102:36d、2004TMM102:35b唐永徽五年（654）九月西州诸府主帅牒为请替番上事（三）（116）："秋[收][时]忙，望请　　口替[处]，谨以牒[陈]。"2004TMM102:33

唐永徽六年(655)某月西州诸府主帅牒为请替番上事(二)(118):“配在口[平]仓皺掌,种麦时忙,望请雇左[右]辛武俊替上。”请比较 OR. 8212/545Ast. III. 4. 078b 武周长寿二年(693)为麹寿年充头官事牒残片(沙 1-85):[①]“右口麹寿年(武周)望请充头官事　　口口谨以牒陈,请裁处分,谨牒。”OR. 8212/1866M. Tagh. 80(1)(2)唐牒于阗军贮纳熟粮残牒(沙 2-264):“　　烂望请给　　出来请取当　　。”73TAM518:2/4-1 唐阿麹辞稿为除出租佃名事(3-469):“望请附感佃名,除。”又请比较“望乞”。75TAM239:9/13 唐景龙三年(709)十二月至景龙四年(710)正月西州高昌县处分田亩案卷(3-562):“其户内更两人,户见未绝,地未出,望乞处分。”

【奄葛留亭 yān gé liú tíng】

强迫停止,停留,阻止。2004TMM102:4+2004TMM102:6 唐显庆元年(656)西州宋武欢移文(荣104):“不得奄葛留亭,急急汝律令。”“奄”乃“占领、关闭、久留、停止”义,《广韵·琰韵》:“奄,取也。”又:“奄,藏也。”《汉书·礼乐志·郊祀歌》:“盛牲实俎进闻膏,神奄留,临须摇。”颜师古注:“奄,读曰淹。”南朝宋谢灵运《登永嘉绿嶂山》:“践夕奄昏曙,蔽翳皆周悉。”黄节《谢康乐诗注》:“奄,久留也。”《汉书·司马相如传》:“与波摇荡,奄薄水渚。”而“葛”亦为“阻止”、“掩盖”义,《逸周书·酆保》:“葛其戎谋,族乃不罚。”孔晁注:“葛,古通蓋,掩覆也。”(请比较《三国志·魏志·曹衮传》:“其微过细故,当掩覆之。”)“亭”即“停”。清朱骏声《说文通训定声·鼎部》:“亭,字亦作停。”《汉书·西域传上》:“其水亭居,冬夏不增减。”吐鲁番出土文献还有不少与“奄葛留亭”在意义上相关的词语,参考拙著《吐鲁番出土文献词典》“呵留”、“诃留”、“奄遏停留”、“留难”、“奄歇留停”、“诃禁”、“谒留”、“奄歇留亭”、“遏留停”、“案留亭”、“奄遏留停”、“奄遏留亭”、“奄渴留亭”、“留亭”条。

【掩 yǎn】

突然。2004TMM102:12 唐显庆元年(656)二月十六日宋武欢墓志(103):“计当与金石同固,保守长年,掩然迁化,春秋六十一。”2004TBM217:12 唐垂拱二年(686)十一月二十七日口如节墓志(384):“怀秀不实,掩及茔穴。”考《方言》卷二:“奄,遽也。”《文选·潘岳〈西征赋〉》:“啚万载而不倾,奄摧落于十纪。”李善注:“奄,忽也。”而“奄”、“掩”古通用,《方言》卷三:“掩,同也,江淮、南楚之间曰掩。”戴震疏证:“案:掩、奄古通用。”检吐鲁番出土文献,还有相关词语,参考拙著《吐鲁番出土文献词典》“奄及”、“奄至”、“奄然”、“奄尔”、“奄便”、“淹然”、“掩然”、“勿尔”、“忽”条。

【夵 yǎn】

帽子或固定头发的巾类用具。2006TSYIM4:8 北凉缺名随葬衣物疏(174):“枣疏一枚,绀大+小一枚。帛縺夵一枚,绯覆面一枚,紫繻一领。”这里关键是“夵”的训释,此字虽然在《广韵》和《集韵》等韵书中有释,但是没有列举任何语言实例。荣新江、李肖、孟宪实认为吐鲁番出土文献“夵”与“尖”同(见《新获吐鲁番出土文献》第174页)。是。但还需要沟通他们之间的关系,我们寻得以下证据,首先是文献证据(将吐鲁番出土文献互证),请比较 75TKM96:15 龙兴某年宋泮妻翟氏随葬衣物疏(1-29):“故绯碧紺綪结发六枚,故鸡鸣枕一枚,故银钗二枚,故耳中珠四枚。故帛縺尖一枚,故紺綪尖一枚,故帛縺衫一[领]。”此处之“帛縺尖”正好与我们讨论的“帛縺夵”相比较。其次是训诂证据。考《广韵·琰韵》:“夵,上大下小。”《集韵·琰韵》:“本广末狭谓之夵。”但又考《玉篇·大部》:“尖,小细也。”《正字通·小部》:

① “(沙 1-85)”表明此件文书图版见于沙知、吴芳思《斯坦因第三次考古所获汉文文献(非佛经部分)》第一册,第85页。

"尖。末锐也。"所以两字意义颇为接近,我们认为吐鲁番出土文献中的"夵"与"尖"可能是异体字(上下两个组成部分交换位置),都表示头帽或头巾类。关于"尖"帽和"尖"巾,廖名春指出:"唐刘言史《夜观胡腾舞》诗云:'织成番帽虚顶尖。'可见,胡帽是一种尖顶帽。Kutoba 银瓶上斯基泰武士、沂南画像石中的匈奴武士、莫高窟 43 窟盛唐壁画中的胡商、唐嗣圣十年杨氏墓出土的胡俑、礼泉唐李贞墓出土的女骑俑、开元六年韦顼墓石椁线雕中的女像,特别是吐鲁番阿斯塔那 230 号唐张礼臣墓出土屏风绢画上的乐人,以及吐鲁番出土唐三彩骑泥俑,吐鲁番出土唐彩马伏木俑,戴的都是这种很显目的尖顶帽。由于吐鲁番人中盛行这种尖顶帽,自然,他们就有可能借帽子的特征来代替帽子本身,称帽为尖。"(《吐鲁番出土文书新兴量词考》,《中国学术史新证》第 336～337 页)其实,早在公元前 10 世纪,吐鲁番地区以及新疆地区就有高尖帽,为用褐色毛毡支制成的筒状,帽端缝成鸟头状,高尖帽在中亚和西亚地区也比较流行,见田卫疆《吐鲁番史》第 37 页。《三国志·魏志·管宁传》:"宁常着皂帽,布襦袴,布裙,随时单複。"又请比较《太平广记》卷二五五张鷟(出《朝野佥载》):"高巾子,长布衫。"颇疑"尖"与上文所言"高巾子"以及"帻"也有关。又参考拙著《吐鲁番出土文献词典》"尖"、"清尖"、"精尖"、"绀精尖"、"帛缝尖"、"帛尖"、"造尖"、"紫罗尖"条。

【偃明 yàn míng】

偃明,一种枕头,形状像仰卧的一轮弯月。2004TMM102:4＋2004TMM102:6 唐显庆元年(656)西州宋武欢移文(荣 104):"金眼笼具,燕明一枚,孝经一卷,笔研具,石灰三斛五谷具,[鸡][鸣]一[枚],玉坠一双,耳[抱]具。"考《墨子·备穴》:"令陶者为月明,长二尺五寸,六围,中判之,合而施之穴中,偃一覆一。"孙诒让间诂引毕沅:"偃,仰。"《说文·人部》:"偃,僵也。"段玉裁注:"凡仰仆曰偃。引申为凡仰之称。"《龙龛手鉴·人部》:"偃,仰也,仆也,倒也,息也。"所以,"月明"可能都是一种形似弯月的枕头,吐鲁番出土文献还有"偃明"、"偃鸣"形式(参考拙著《吐鲁番出土文献词典》"偃明"、"偃鸣"条),也是一种枕头。而"燕"与"偃"音近。因为"燕"又作"宴"。《集韵·铣韵》:"宴,《尔雅》:'宴,宴居,息也。'或作'燕'。"而"宴"与"偃"乃同声旁之字。而"燕"在《广韵》中有一音是于甸切,影母霰韵开口四等去声山摄,"偃"音于幰切,影母阮韵开口三等上声山摄(详见郭锡良《汉字古音手册》第 200～201 页)。声母相同,韵则相近(均属开口,只是一为三等,一为四等),声调有上去之别,但根据廖名春的研究,早在公元 6 世纪的吐鲁番出土文献中,就发生"浊上变去"的现象(见氏著《中国学术史新证》之《考信篇》"从吐鲁番出土文书的别字异文看'浊上变去'",引用文字见该著第 361 页),所以,"燕"与"偃"音近相通。

【爰 yuán】

更换。2006TSYIM4:1 北凉缘禾二年(433)高昌郡高宁县赵货母子冥讼文书(荣 171):"缘禾二年十月廿七日,高昌郡高宁县都乡安邑里[民][赵]货辞:行年卅,以立身不越王法,今横为叔琳见状枉死,即就后世。衔[恨]入土,皇天后土,当明照察,盐罗大王,平等之主,愿加威神,召琳夫妻及男女子孙捡挍。冀蒙列理,辞具。货命母子白大公、已父,明为了理,莫爰岁月。"请比较《汉书·食货志》:"休二岁者,再易下田,三岁更耕之,自爰其处。"

【戠当 zhí dāng】

负责,承当任务(官差)和职责。2004TMM102:34g、2004TMM102:35a、2004TMM102:38d、2004TMM102:34e、2004TMM102:35d 唐永徽六年(655)某月西州诸府主帅牒为请替番上事(一)(118):"牒:叠举身当今月十六日番　　虞候戠当,即时种麦,　　　憧护替处,谨以牒陈,　　　　。永徽六

年　　　。依替□　　。”请比较“臧掌”。72TAM187：197 武周追当番职掌人文书（一）（4-204）：“右被［符］　　到职掌追来［者］，　　元未赴臧掌者。”请宁乐八（2）号唐开元二年七月二十二日蒲昌府贺方为诸事上州听裁判（72）：“其来月诸臧掌阙　　听裁。诸烽戍交替兵勘过。”考《晋书·纪瞻传》：“臣之职掌，户口租税，国之所重。”《汉语大词典》“职当”条释义：“犹正当，正处于。”引用语料是唐杜甫《醉为马坠诸公携酒相看》诗：“职当忧戚伏衾枕，况乃迟暮加烦促。”今据吐鲁番出土文献补充另一义。

参 考 文 献

冯志文、吐尔迪·纳斯尔、李春华、贺灵、石晓奇等编著《西域地名词典》，新疆人民出版社，2003 年。

郭锡良：《汉字古音手册》，北京大学出版社，1986 年。

纪大椿主编《新疆历史词典》，新疆人民出版社，1996 年。

廖名春：《中国学术史新证》，四川大学出版社，2005 年。

林梅村：《古道西风——考古新发现所见中西文化交流》，生活·读书·新知三联书店，2000 年。

罗竹风主编《汉语大词典》，汉语大词典出版社，2002 年。

马长寿：《突厥人与突厥汗国》，广西师范大学出版社，2006 年。

荣新江、李肖、孟宪实：《新获吐鲁番出土文书》，中华书局，2008 年。

沙知、吴芳思：《斯坦因第三次考古所获汉文文献（非佛经部分）》，上海辞书出版社，2005 年。

唐长孺主编图录本：《吐鲁番出土文书》，第一册，文物出版社，1992 年；第二册，文物出版社，1994 年；第三册，文物出版社，1996 年；第四册，文物出版社，1996 年。

田卫疆主编《吐鲁番史》，新疆人民出版社，2004 年。

王启涛：《吐鲁番出土文献词典》（即出）。

王素：《高昌史稿·交通编》，文物出版社，2000 年。

《编 年 史》评 介

苗普生

新疆社会科学院

  《编年史》,是沙·麻赫穆德·朱拉斯撰写的一部关于叶尔羌汗国历史的重要著作,成书于清康熙十一年至十五年(1672~1676)。因该书前半部分主要辑录《拉失德史》的内容,故又称《拉失德史续编》。后半部分则是作者自己的著述,记述从阿不都·拉失德汗(1510~1559)至伊斯马因汗(?~1680)等9位汗王时期的叶尔羌汗国的政治、经济、社会等方面的情况,特别是涉及苏非派首领在这一时期的活动,以及白山派与黑山派争夺教权的斗争。所以,它对研究叶尔羌汗国时期新疆伊斯兰教,特别是苏非派活动情况具有重要的学术价值。该书一经发现便引起了学术界的高度重视。

一、关于《编年史》的作者、版本

  《编年史》的作者沙·麻赫穆德·朱拉斯的生平资料很少。只是在该书的《前言》中,他自称沙·麻赫穆德·本·米尔咱·法则里·朱拉斯,他的父亲是麻赫穆德·米尔咱·法则里·朱拉斯。我们从沙·麻赫穆德·朱拉斯的姓氏可以知道,他出身于察合台汗国时期的蒙古贵族。朱拉斯家族的代表人物曾经反对秃黑鲁·帖木儿汗(1347/1348~1362年在位)皈依伊斯兰教。[①] 在此后相当长的时间里,有关朱拉斯家族的消息并不多。只是根据朱拉斯家族一些成员在叶尔羌汗国时期的任职情况,有的学者认为,朱拉斯家族的艾米尔大概参加了赛义德汗进攻朵豁剌惕部异密阿巴·乩乞儿的活动,是开国功勋,[②]所以在论功行赏时,他们被分封到了阿克苏-乌什一带的某个地方。朱拉斯家族的成员曾经长期担任阿克苏、乌什的阿奇木伯克。在穆罕默德汗(生于1536/1537年,于回历999年登位,相当于公元1590/1591~1608/1609年在位)和阿黑麻汗(1608/1609~1618/1619年在位)统治时期,朱拉斯家族的地位上升。穆罕默德汗先任命米儿咱·海答儿·朱拉斯为远征军统帅,远征和田,后又让他做了喀什噶尔的统治者。在这一时期,朱拉斯家族的著名成员还有米儿咱·哈西木·朱拉斯及其兄弟们。他们在反击月即别人、吉尔吉斯人袭击的战斗中,起了重要作用。在阿不都拉汗时期(1638~1667),则有米儿咱·沙西得·朱拉斯、米儿咱·穆罕默德·阿敏·朱拉斯、米儿咱·法西尔·朱拉斯,分别担任阿克苏、乌什、巴楚的阿奇木。所以,沙·麻赫穆德·朱拉斯说,他们的家族是个大家族。

---

  ① 参见米尔咱·马黑麻·海答儿著,新疆社会科学院民族研究所译,王治来校注《中亚蒙兀儿史——拉失德史》(新疆人民出版社,1983年)第一编第164~165页载:"黑的马特大毛拉主持汗的入教仪式,汗诵读了信仰真主的祷词,成了穆斯林。接着,他们决定:为了传播伊斯兰教,他们决定一个一个地会见众王公贵人。……就这样,他们一个一个地考验了众王公。他们全都接受了伊斯兰教,轮到札剌思的时候,他不答应。"此处"札剌思"即"朱拉斯",是一位蒙古王公贵族的名字。

  ② 参见魏良弢:《叶尔羌汗国史纲》,黑龙江教育出版社,1994年5月,第7页。

朱拉斯家族不仅在政治上与世俗政权关系密切,而且与宗教上层有着千丝万缕的联系。沙·麻赫穆德·朱拉斯在书中谈到伊斯哈克·外力在阿克苏传教时记述道:忽都鲁克·穆罕默德·米儿咱·朱拉斯对阿克苏人说:"朋友们,海则莱提们能来到这里,是当今世界的荣誉,来世的希望,朝拜这些艾孜赞们是今世和来世的幸福。"可是,一个人却说:"从维拉耶特(指河中地区——注者)到这儿来的每个人都称自己是和卓或艾孜赞。"刚说到这里,乌什吐尔·哈里发和艾孜赞们一起开始在阿克苏人之中走来走去,过了一会,他拿手杖把那个否认和卓者打倒在地。阿克苏人从乌什吐尔·哈里发的身上看到这个神奇的同时,重新认真崇拜海则莱提·艾孜赞,并在忽都鲁克·穆罕默德·米儿咱·朱拉斯的带领下成为他们的信徒。(见本书正文"海则莱提·艾孜赞的到来和他们后裔的叙述"一节相关内容)这段文字所讲述的故事,虽然有些离奇,但却告诉人们,为了让伊斯哈克·外力在阿克苏顺利传教,忽都鲁克·穆罕默德·米儿咱·朱拉斯做了不少工作,并带领大家成为他的忠实信徒。忽都鲁克·穆罕默德·米儿咱·朱拉斯就是沙·麻赫穆德·朱拉斯的曾祖父。据说,为报答忽都鲁克·穆罕默德·米儿咱·朱拉斯的支持,和卓伊斯哈克在巩固地盘以后,任命他为大哈里发,赋予他领导所有穆里德(信徒)的权利。

实际上,在此之前,即在赛义德汗时,朱拉斯家族就出现了一个著名人物,名叫马黑麻·朱拉斯。"这些学者中有大毛拉马黑麻·失剌思,他是一位伟大的宗教律士,不但博览群书,而且精于医道。""他为蒙兀儿诸汗立过杰出的功勋,并被任命为'大断事官'",[1]终生侍奉赛义德汗。[2] 所以我认为,朱拉斯家族开始被分封到了阿克苏-乌什一带的某个地方,与其说是因为立有军功,倒不如说是因为马黑麻·朱拉斯渊博的学识和医道。只是由于资料所限,还不能比较详细地说明这一点。

沙·麻赫穆德·朱拉斯虽然出身名门望族,但关于沙·麻赫穆德·朱拉斯本人情况的资料却不多。苏联学者阿基穆什金根据有限的资料,对其生平曾经作过一个简单的介绍。他认为,沙·麻赫穆德·朱拉斯大约生于17世纪20年代,死于1696年之后不久。他的父亲初被阿不都拉汗任命为右翼乌赤别吉(军队右翼先锋),后升任为大将军。他的哥哥也跻身军界,是当时有名的将领之一。根据其父兄的情况,沙·麻赫穆德·朱拉斯也应该立功疆场,但是却走上学术之路,阿基穆什金因而怀疑他生有残疾。根据著述情况,可以推测,沙·麻赫穆德·朱拉斯年青时学习过阿拉伯语和波斯语,学习过《古兰经》及其他一些宗教著述。

沙·麻赫穆德·朱拉斯著述颇多,但传至现在的只有两部:一是《编年史》,一是《寻求真理者之友》。后者是关于黑山派和卓的圣者传记,大概完成于1696年。

1913年,在塔什干一位名叫巴基·江·巴依的私人藏书中,发现了沙·麻赫穆德·朱拉斯的《编年史》抄本。《俄国考古学会东方部集刊》对此进行了报道,引起了学术界的高度重视。1916年,著名学者B·B·巴托尔德利用出差的机会,从巴基·江·巴依的手中借到该书抄本,带回圣彼得堡"拍照"。本来计划正式出版该书,但一直没有实现,后来连唯一的传世抄本也不知去向。1945年,列宁国家图书馆手稿部得到了这部书的抄本,可是学者们并不知情。1961年以后,学者们再次发现了该书,并开始利用它提供的资料,研究15~17世纪的中亚史。阿基穆什金将该书翻译成俄文,并进行了校订、注释。1976年,苏联科学出版社出版了《编年史》俄译本,后附有校勘过的波斯文原文,还有阿基穆什金写的长篇研究

① 见《中亚蒙兀儿史—拉失德史》第二编第270页,此处"马黑麻·失剌思"即马黑麻·朱拉斯,他的事迹参见该书第五十五、五十六和五十七章。
② 见《中亚蒙兀儿史—拉失德史》第二编第272页。

导论。

《编年史》俄文版的出版,为各国学者研究 15～17 世纪的中亚史提供了极大方便,人们进一步认识到了该书的史料价值,特别是对研究新疆历史的学者来讲,情况更是如此。所以,1987 年,新疆学者将《编年史》俄文版后附的波斯文译成维吾尔文,并以《叶尔羌汗国史料》为名,由喀什维吾尔文出版社出版。我们这次将《编年史》译为汉文时,依据的底本是这个维吾尔文本,参照了该书的俄文本,利用和吸收了这两个版本中的研究成果。

二、《编年史》的主要内容

《编年史》的叙事年代,上起 1428 年歪思汗之死,下至 17 世纪 70 年代中期,即伊斯马因汗统治时期,包括了东察合台汗国后期和几乎整个叶尔羌汗国的历史。全书由导论和上下两部分组成。导论包括颂词和黑山派和卓世袭。上半部分有七十七章,主要是对米尔咱·马黑麻·海答儿《拉失德史》中七十七章(第一编中的第一章至第三十四章、第二编中的前四十三章)内容的简要复述。因为已经有《拉失德史》全书的汉文译本,所以我们没有重新翻译这一部分。下半部分有七十一章,是沙·麻赫穆德·朱拉斯自己的著述。我们翻译并进行注释的主要是这一部分。

《编年史》下半部分,主要包括以下几个方面的内容:

1. 关于叶尔羌汗国的政治演变。《编年史》首先从叶尔羌汗国的创立者速檀·赛义德汗(1514～1530 年在位)开始,按其在位年代,讲述了以后十位汗王的承袭情况和他们统治的历史,以及当时发生的一系列重大事件,赞扬了他们的业绩和高尚美德。这些内容占了全书的大部分章节,每一位汗都有三四章的篇幅。在记述每一位汗的事迹时,其撰述形式几乎是相同的,先记述汗即位前发生的种种事件,接着讲述汗即位及其以后的统治情况,最后介绍汗的生平及其在位的时间,有时还专用一章的篇幅赞扬汗的高尚美德和行为。如作者称赞穆罕默德汗(也作马黑麻汗)"是位公道、虔诚和公正的国君"(见正文"穆罕默德汗的品德和高尚的行为"一节相关内容),称述疏扎丁·阿黑麻汗十分关心臣民,"在他执政时,狼和羊、老鹰和鸽子可以一起生活,相安无事"(见正文"疏扎丁·阿黑麻汗,他登上了汗位,治理国家的方式和那个时期所发生的事件"一节相关内容),等等。当然,书中也有对汗及各位速檀行为不满的记述。如作者说阿黑麻汗之子帖木儿速檀"生性专横暴力、嗜酒",称"速檀·阿黑麻汗是个软弱的男人,不怎么明智,军队和平民都厌恶他"(见正文"阿不都拉汗在阿克苏领地的统治,速檀穆罕默德汗的逝世和速檀阿黑麻汗的事业结局"一节相关内容);尧勒瓦斯汗(尤勒巴尔斯汗)"对臣民大搞暴政,贪婪是他的本性,残暴是他的天性,以致在暴政嗜杀方面,哈孜逊色于他,哈贾吉·本·尤素甫和左哈克都甘拜下风"(见正文"尧勒瓦斯汗事业之结局,阿不都剌帖夫速檀的执政和阿里·沙赫伯克比克奇克的遇害"一节相关内容)。显然,沙·麻赫穆德·朱拉斯对尧勒瓦斯汗残酷镇压黑山派极为愤慨。

2. 关于当时的宗教领袖人物海则莱提·艾孜赞们活动的记述。叶尔羌汗国时期,是和卓势力在新疆迅速发展的时期。拉失德汗时期(1533～1559),中亚纳合西班底耶教团首领玛合图木·阿杂木为了调解月即别(乌兹别克)人与喀什噶尔人的冲突,以"圣者"的身份来到喀什噶尔主持谈判,并进行传教活动,受到推崇。拉失德汗聘其为宫廷顾问,并馈赠给他大片土地。然而,由于当时以穆罕默德·谢里甫为首的苏非派势力正盛,玛合图木·阿杂木难有作为,仅发展了一些门徒并娶了一位据说是萨图克·布格拉汗后裔的女子为妻之后,便返回了中亚。1542 年,玛合图木·阿杂木去世,其长子伊禅卡朗名正言顺地成为纳合西班底耶教团首领,玛合图木·阿杂木与萨图克·布格拉汗后裔妻子所生之爱子伊斯哈克·外力则应阿不都·哈林汗(1559 ~ 1591)邀请,来到喀什噶尔。但他并未受到重用,只好离开汗廷,先后在喀什噶尔、叶尔羌、和田、阿克苏等地传教,并向各地派遣了六十四位哈里发(代理人),发展信徒。十二年后,伊斯哈克·外力返回撒马尔罕。

1591 年,阿不都·哈林汗去世,其五弟马黑麻(即穆罕默德汗)即位为汗。[①] 马黑麻汗曾经是阿克苏的统治者,在伊斯哈克·外力初来喀什噶尔时,即已成为其忠实门徒,又在阿克苏隆重接待过他。马黑麻即位为汗以后,伊斯哈克·外力即将自己七岁的儿子和卓夏迪(原名为穆罕默德·叶海亚)派往叶尔羌。马黑麻汗遂以其为精神导师,建造府第,赐给村庄土地。和卓势力随之兴起。

和卓夏迪历马黑麻汗(1591 ~ 1610)、阿黑麻汗(1610 ~ 1619)、阿不都剌帖夫汗(1619 ~ 1631)、速檀阿黑麻汗(1631 ~ 1639)诸汗,被奉为他们的导师,上入汗廷,下浸民间,势力无所不在,玩汗权于股掌之间。然而,他的权威却受到了和卓玛木特·玉素甫的挑战。

和卓玛木特·玉素甫,与和卓夏迪都是玛合图木·阿杂木的孙子。和卓玛木特·玉素甫在父亲伊禅卡朗去世后,便遵父嘱来到叶尔羌汗国境内传教,从而把伊禅卡朗与伊斯哈克·外力之间的矛盾争斗扩大到了新疆,[②]逐渐形成了两个针锋相对的派别。后人称以伊斯哈克·外力为代表的一派为黑山派,称伊禅卡朗为代表的一派为白山派。黑山派又称黑帽派,白山派亦称白帽派。其实,两派在对宗教教义的理解方面并没有本质的区别,但为了控制世俗政权而相互残杀。

《编年史》记述了黑山派和卓是怎样从一个外来的传教者发展成为一重要宗教派别首领进而控制世俗政权的过程。这一方面的内容不仅占有大量的篇幅,而且摆在了突出的位置。《编年史》把和卓世系置于颂词之后、当今汗王的世系之前,且在书中列有数章,专门论述和卓的活动,赞颂他们的品质,宣扬他们的神奇。这种情况在其他类似著作中是少见的。

3. 关于政权与教权即汗与和卓关系的记述。叶尔羌汗国时期,和卓势力迅速发展,是与历任汗的推崇分不开的。历任汗之所以推崇和卓,同样是因为其取得政权和巩固政权的需要。沙·麻赫穆德·朱拉斯在叙述阿不都·哈林汗创业之初发生的种种事件时说:他是苏非派和卓穆罕默德·谢里甫朋友的信徒,因而在与其父拉失德汗之间发生信任危机时,宗教人士让他知道,"宗教上层人物是会把您推举上汗位的"。后来的事实表明,阿不都·哈林汗不仅依靠和卓穆罕默德·谢里甫等宗教上层的支持,抢先登上汗位,而且又从中亚请来和卓伊斯哈克·外力,以便寻求更多的支持和帮助。马黑麻汗更是想借用宗教上层的力量巩固自己的统治。在他执政阿克苏的时候,就曾专程到喀什噶尔与和卓伊斯哈克·外力"这位德高望重的辟尔(导师)会谈并结拜"(见正文"海则莱提·艾孜赞的到来和他们后裔的叙述"一节相关内容)。马黑麻即位为汗以后,又邀请伊斯哈克·外力七岁的儿子和卓夏迪到喀什噶尔。当和卓夏迪在舒图尔哈里发陪伴下到达时,马黑麻汗远出城外欢迎他们,并"把穆罕默德·叶海亚和卓的马缰套在自己的脖颈上,引领到宫中,举行了三日大庆"(见正文"阿布·赛义德速檀之死和当时发生的种种事件"一节相关内容),并拜和卓夏迪为精神导师。

---

① 马黑麻汗:《中国新疆地区伊斯兰教史》等著作译为穆罕默德汗。
② 伊斯哈克·外力因没能继承父位成为纳合西班底耶教团首领,便怀恨其兄伊禅卡朗。根据《大和卓传》记载,伊斯哈克·外力返回撒马尔罕后,曾企图毒死伊禅卡朗。故伊禅卡朗嘱咐其子和卓玛木特·玉素甫避走叶尔羌。

但是,随着和卓势力的发展,和卓对朝政的干预日益加强。开始,和卓只是以能够对汗施加影响而心满意足,到后来他们就想"既控制思想又控制国家事务"。①1610年,马黑麻汗去世。这时,和卓夏迪24岁,已是一个血气方刚的青年。在激烈的争夺汗位的斗争中,他一手把阿不都·拉失德第六子阿布·赛义德之子、喀什噶尔统治者疏扎丁·阿黑麻扶上汗位,由此也确立了自己在统治集团中的地位和权威。阿黑麻汗执政十年,活到50岁,1619年被叛乱的艾米尔杀害。和卓夏迪亲自前往喀什噶尔,与当地艾米尔一起,拥立阿黑麻汗最小的儿子、喀什噶尔统治者阿不都剌帖夫(俗称阿帕克汗,也作阿不都·拉提夫汗)为汗(参见正文"阿不都剌帖夫汗的事业之初"一节相关内容),并出兵叶尔羌,平息了叛乱。从此,和卓开始操纵朝政。阿不都剌帖夫汗死后,和卓拥立疏扎丁·阿黑麻汗兄弟之子速檀·阿黑麻为汗,但仅过了两年就被其弟速檀·穆罕默德汗(也作速檀·马合木汗)赶下了台。兄弟二人不和,据沙·麻赫穆德·朱拉斯的说法,是因为速檀·穆罕默德汗在准备与和卓拉提夫的女儿举行婚礼时,速檀·阿黑麻汗抢走了和卓拉提夫的女儿,"速檀·穆罕默德汗把对其兄的怨恨记在心里"。这样的政变,并不危及宗教上层的利益。所以,和卓夏迪并没有对速檀·穆罕默德汗采取什么措施,只是在速檀·阿黑麻汗受到阿不都拉汗追击时,请求速檀·穆罕默德汗网开一面,放速檀·阿黑麻汗一条生路。但是,后来速檀·穆罕默德汗却采取了对和卓家族不利的政策。于是,和卓夏迪亲自主持策划暗杀了速檀·穆罕默德汗,恢复了速檀·阿黑麻的汗位。然而,速檀·阿黑麻汗"软弱"、"不明智",大概是也开始对和卓夏迪不敬了。所以,他们转而又同情、支持阿不都拉汗。受和卓的影响,"有名气的巴哈都尔(勇士)们也逃离喀什噶尔和叶尔羌,投奔阿不都拉汗了"(见正文"阿不都拉汗在阿克苏领地的统治,速檀穆罕默德汗的逝世和速檀阿黑麻汗的事业结局"一节)。于是,阿不都拉汗势力强大了,并夺取喀什噶尔,最终迫使速檀·阿黑麻汗"放弃了国家,去了巴里黑",阿不都拉汗被和卓夏迪等人拥立为汗。和卓夏迪通过操纵汗位的更迭,削弱了汗的权力,加强了自己在统治集团中的权威,实现了对权力的控制。

和卓操纵汗位,而世俗的汗为了维护自己的地位和权力,也在不断寻求新的精神领袖的支持。这样,两派政治势力、两个宗教派别的争斗,使叶尔羌汗国陷于四分五裂的境地,并最终导致了它的灭亡。沙·麻赫穆德·朱拉斯对后来各位汗的褒奖,正好反映出了汗与白山派和卓关系的变化。

4. 关于周邻民族的记述。叶尔羌汗国与吉尔吉斯、哈萨克、乌兹别克和卫拉特诸族为邻,《编年史》中有不少关于这些民族及其相互关系的内容。

《编年史》用了不少篇幅记述吉尔吉斯人及其与叶尔羌汗国的关系。"吉尔吉斯人被称为蒙兀儿斯坦戈壁滩上的野狮子"(见正文"阿不都拉汗下令消灭吉尔吉斯人"一节)。按照沙·麻赫穆德·朱拉斯的说法,在阿不都·拉失德汗时期,其子阿不都·拉提夫进攻吉尔吉斯和哈萨克首领阿克·那孜儿汗(又作哈克·奈斋儿汗),先胜后败,被俘后死亡。阿不都·拉失德汗为了给儿子报仇,征伐阿克·那孜儿汗。阿不都·拉失德汗大获全胜,俘获阿克·那孜儿汗及其他首领,并将他们处死。"在历史上,昔班人、②哈萨克人和蒙古人之间发生过很多战争,通常哈萨克人和昔班人战胜过对方,蒙古人从未战胜过,但阿不都·拉失德汗把他们全部打败了,这荣誉至今还保持着。"(见正文"阿不都·拉提夫速檀的结局,阿不都·拉失德汗为儿子报仇而出征"一节)看来,通过这次征战,吉尔吉斯人臣服了阿不都·拉失德汗,成

① 参见伊莱亚斯:《和卓传·导言》。
② 即月即别。

为了叶尔羌汗国的属民。阿不都拉汗时期(1638～1667),叶尔羌汗国与吉尔吉斯人又发生激烈冲突,其原因可能和速檀·阿黑麻汗在安集延的复辟活动有关。1639 年,阿不都拉汗进攻并攻克奥什,"让他的人马大肆抢掠洗劫了该城"。但是,他们遭到了吉尔吉斯人的顽强反击。双方厮杀了五天五夜,"最后,汗的军队失败了,而吉尔吉斯人成了胜利者"(见正文"阿不都拉汗征讨并攻克奥什;汗从另一条路返回来;诸艾米尔跟随汗征战,他们被吉尔吉斯人击败"一节)。一年以后,阿不都拉汗再次率军征讨吉尔吉斯人。由于和卓的神奇,在"阿克赛之战"中,吉尔吉斯人被打败,臣属了阿不都拉汗。但是,阿不都拉汗怀疑吉尔吉斯的艾米尔"仍有异心",于是又对吉尔吉斯人"开始了不分青红皂白的大屠杀"。吉尔吉斯人被迫接受叶尔羌汗国的统治。

《编年史》也用了不少篇幅记述乌兹别克人及其与叶尔羌汗国的关系。乌兹别克人与叶尔羌汗国的关系在汗国初期就存在了,速檀·赛义德汗就是为了躲避乌兹别克人的攻击而进入喀什噶尔建立政权的。阿不都·哈林汗去世三年后(约在 1594 年前后),乌兹别克人大举进攻喀什噶尔、叶尔羌,但无功而返。乌兹别克人与叶尔羌汗国再次发生激烈冲突,也是在阿不都拉汗时期。在征服吉尔吉斯人以后,乌兹别克人自然成为他的下一个目标。1643 年,阿不都拉汗调集了 4 万军队,率领当地所有的著名宗教上层人士和各城阿奇木,远征安集延。他们攻破安集延城,大肆抢掠和洗劫穆斯林后返回奥什。这一次征伐,可以说是凯旋而归。但是,"阿不都拉汗从安集延返回来后,那里的居民就又背叛了阿不都拉汗,因此汗又再度遣军"。当他们再次攻打安集延城时,塔吉克人和乌兹别克人则联合起来,进行顽强抵抗,坚守不出。"汗不得已退了回去,返回了叶尔羌。"(见正文"阿不都拉汗是怎样第二次领军征讨安集延的,他又是如何未达到目的而返回的"一节)

从《编年史》的记述,我们知道,在阿不都拉汗即位不久,汗国尚不稳定的时候,准噶尔即乘乱侵入叶尔羌汗国,甚至深入到了和田地区。以后,其势力便逐渐深入到了汗国内部,干预汗国政治。尧勒瓦斯汗就是在准噶尔的支持下登上汗位的,后来准噶尔又支持人们除掉了这个暴君。最终,准噶尔灭亡了叶尔羌汗国。

总之,《编年史》的内容是比较丰富的。沙·麻赫穆德·朱拉斯不仅是所载许多重大政治事件和军事冲突的见证人,而且可能还是其中某些事件的参与者。又由于他出身名门望族,能够读到同时代人难以读到的书籍,得到同时代人难以得到的信息资料。所以,《编年史》的抄本一经发现,便受到学者们的重视,应该说是非常自然的。

三、《编年史》的史料价值

早在 19 世纪末,中亚史专家伊莱亚斯在为《和卓传》写导言时就非常感慨地指出:他们当时仅有的一部关于中亚蒙兀儿人的史籍——《拉失德史》,叙事的截止年代是在拉失德汗执政时期。由于资料所限,从 1546 年起直到拉失德汗去世以后相当长的时间里,人们不知道蒙兀儿斯坦发生了什么事情。后来,一些学者们,如哈特曼、博斯沃思等利用《和卓传》、《喀什噶尔史》等提供的资料,研究这段历史,取得了一些进展,但仍留下了许多未能解答的问题。直到上个世纪 60 年代,在翻译、校订、注释《编年史》以后,阿基穆什金告诉人们,如果我们现在觉得从 16 世纪起至 17 世纪 70 年代这一时期的新疆历史还比较有头绪,不那么模糊不清,应该归功于沙·麻赫穆德·朱拉斯的著作。《编年史》的史料价值主要在于:

1. 关于诸汗在位的时间及汗位的承袭。《编年史》比较详细地记述了诸汗的承袭情况及各汗在位的时间。如"阿不都·拉失德汗是速檀·赛义德汗之子","当了27年独立的君主,终年52岁";"阿不都·哈林汗是阿不都·拉失德汗的次子","在位30年……他也在63岁时离开了这个世界";"穆罕默德汗是阿不都·拉失德的第五子","阿不都·哈林汗去世3个月后,穆罕默德汗远征回来继承了汗位","他独立执政18年……终年72岁";"疏扎丁·阿黑麻汗执政10年,活了50岁";"阿不都刺帖夫汗是疏扎丁·阿黑麻汗最小的儿子,是穆罕默德汗之孙","独立执政12年,他活了26岁",等等。关于此后各汗的记载,情况基本都是如此。特别是在讲到穆罕默德汗时,沙·麻赫穆德·朱拉斯明确指出,"回历整999年,汗登上了王位"。在讲到速檀·穆罕默德汗时,他又指出,"回历1045年(1635~1636)的一个月,在汗城叶尔羌,速檀·穆罕默德汗出了这样可怖的事件(指因饮酒过度而死)。他活了22岁,执政近3年"。参照米儿咱·马黑麻·海答儿关于速檀·赛义德汗的生卒的记载,[①]我们就掌握了三个基本的数据,从而推算出了叶尔羌汗国诸汗即位时间和生卒年代。

另外,从《编年史》的记述中,我们可以得知,自阿不都拉汗开始,汗位的继承转到了阿不都·拉失德汗的三儿子阿不都刺因速檀的后代手中。阿不都拉汗是阿不都刺因速檀的长子。1667年,阿不都拉汗被迫退出汗位以后,其子尧勒瓦斯汗夺得汗位。尧勒瓦斯汗被处死以后,"阿里·沙赫伯克被推举主政叶尔羌,让阿瓦孜伯克当了伊沙噶伯克,宣布尧勒瓦斯汗的儿子阿不都刺帖夫速檀为汗"。(见正文"尧勒瓦斯汗事业之结局,阿不都刺帖夫速檀的执政和阿里·沙赫伯克比克奇克的遇害"一节)

2. 关于东察合台汗国。1504年,东察合台汗国阿黑麻汗病死,长子满速儿当权。为巩固汗位,满速儿汗将其弟速檀·赛义德驱逐至中亚。速檀赛义德先后投奔其伯父马合木汗和姑表兄巴布尔帕的沙,[②]后因巴布尔在与月即别人的战争中失败,遂率军进入喀什噶尔,击败朵豁刺惕部首领阿巴·乣乞儿,占领南疆西部,自立为汗,建立叶尔羌汗国。1516年,赛义德汗在阿克苏会晤其兄满速儿汗,同意在虎图拜(伊斯兰教祈祷仪式)时朗诵满速儿的名字,并以他的名字铸钱,以表示臣服。满速儿汗则表示不再追究赛义德汗以往的活动,承认现实,与赛义德汗分别统治东察合台汗国的东部和西部。但是,满速儿汗死后,东察合台汗国的东部形势是如何发展的,人们知之甚少。从汉文史籍中仅仅知道,满速儿汗死后,长子沙为速檀。1565年(明嘉靖四十四年),沙速檀在与瓦刺作战时,"中流矢死",其堂弟马速"拥众嗣立"。[③] 然而,由于马速与沙速檀是"远房伯叔,不该做王子",结果被"绑在牙儿坎(叶尔羌)地方去了",沙速檀弟马黑麻遂即位为王。[④] 其后,便世系不明。《编年史》不仅补充了这方面的资料,而且可以和汉文资料相互印证。沙·麻赫穆德·朱拉斯告诉我们,沙速檀因"在战场上勇敢牺牲而成了殉教者"。沙速檀死后,马速拥众嗣立,显然不符合蒙古人的传统,所以受到了阿不都·哈林汗的讨伐。结果,马速父子被俘,马黑麻被扶立为吐鲁番地区的统治者。至此,吐鲁番地区,即原东察合台汗国的东部实际上已经被叶尔羌汗国所兼并。所以,到穆罕默德汗时,"叶尔羌、喀什噶尔、阿克苏、乌什、库车、察力失和吐鲁番、哈密,还有和田、萨里库尔[⑤]及拉拉矿等地的虎图拜和图章,都刻着穆罕默德汗的尊名"(见正文"有关穆罕

---

① 《中亚蒙兀儿史—拉失德史》第二编第431~432页载:"速檀·赛义德汗生于892年/1487年,卒于939年/1533年,在位20年。"
② 巴布尔,即印度莫卧尔王朝的创立者巴布尔大帝。他的母亲是东察合台汗国羽奴思汗的女儿忽都鲁·尼格尔·哈尼木,故与速檀·赛义德是姑表兄弟。
③ 《明世宗实录》卷五五六。
④ 殷士儋:《远夷谢恩求贡疏》,转引自陈高华:《明代哈密、吐鲁番资料汇编》,第4页。
⑤ 今塔什库尔干。

默德汗执政时代和他年龄的最后记述"一节)。穆罕默德汗派阿不都·拉失德汗最小的儿子、他的弟弟阿不都刺因汗"统治了察力失和吐鲁番,并享有满速儿汗所拥有的那些特权"。自此以后,原东察合台汗国的东西部之间的矛盾,便逐渐演变为阿不都·拉失德汗子孙之间为争夺叶尔羌汗国的领导权而进行的斗争了。

3. 为研究叶尔羌汗国时期伊斯兰教的传播及黑山派与白山派的斗争提供了非常有价值的资料。如前所述,《编年史》用大量的篇幅记述了宗教领袖人物海则莱提·艾孜赞们的活动,以及他们和世俗政权的关系。

首先,我们从中了解到了和卓家族的世系。沙·麻赫穆德·朱拉斯说:"海则莱提和卓·穆罕默德·阿卜都拉是海则莱提和卓·穆罕默德·叶海亚之子,穆罕默德·叶海亚是海则莱提和卓·穆罕默德·伊斯哈克之子,穆罕默德·伊斯哈克是毛吾拉那·哈加克·卡萨尼之子。他以玛合图木·阿杂木(愿真主保佑他们的灵魂)这个名字而闻名。"(见正文"关于海则莱提·艾孜赞的神圣血统与道统的叙述"一节)这是黑山派和卓的世系,是完全正确的。但是,他又接着说:"海则莱提·玛合图木·阿杂木的系谱经过了十个阶段。"在可追溯到他们的祖父海则莱提·沙赫·布喇尼丁以后,又向上追溯了九代。人们对这个系谱可能会有很多疑问,但他毕竟给人们提供了可以比较的资料,仍然是有价值的。

其次,我们从《编年史》的记述中,了解到了黑山派和白山派的形成过程,以及他们之间的矛盾和斗争。沙·麻赫穆德·朱拉斯告诉我们,和卓伊斯哈克·外力是在阿不都·哈林汗时期从撒马尔罕到喀什噶尔的,由于伊禅卡朗信徒的挑拨,伊斯哈克·外力与阿不都·哈林汗之间产生了隔阂,被迫到和田传教,"在一个叫策勒的地方呆了三年"。后又因与和田统治者忽来失速檀产生矛盾,遂奔向阿克苏,最后从库车返回故乡撒马尔罕,派舒图尔·哈里发去了吐鲁番。伊斯哈克·外力在叶尔羌汗国境内传教十二年,除发展了大批信徒外,最重要的是与穆罕默德汗建立了联系,并取得了他的尊重和信任,为以后和卓夏迪的活动奠定了基础。和卓夏迪时期无疑是黑山派势力迅速发展的时期,也是宗教上层开始操纵政权的时期。和卓夏迪企图通过操纵汗位的更迭,加强自己在统治集团中的权威,实现对权力的控制。而世俗的汗为了维护自己的地位和权力,同样在寻求新的精神领袖的支持,这就为白山派和卓玛木特·玉素甫在叶尔羌汗国境内的活动提供了条件。和卓玛木特·玉素甫是在阿不都剌帖夫汗时期来到喀什噶尔,并利用"正统"和卓的身份传教,发展信徒的。也就在这个时候,和卓夏迪去了撒马尔罕,"朝拜了他祖父的麻扎尔"。显然,他是在宣示自己的身份,巩固自己的权威。回到喀什噶尔以后,他不但除掉了自己的政治对手舒图尔·哈里发,还迫使阿不都剌帖夫汗将和卓玛木特·玉素甫驱逐出喀什噶尔。阿不都拉汗时期,和卓玛木特·玉素甫又来到喀什噶尔。虽然,"阿不都拉汗没有臣服和卓玛木特·玉素甫,叶尔羌人都没有臣服他",但当时喀什噶尔的统治者阿不都拉汗的长子尧勒瓦斯汗,因与父亲不和而以和卓玛木特·玉素甫为导师。和卓玛木特·玉素甫死后,其子阿帕克和卓继承道统。"尧勒瓦斯汗属于并崇拜阿帕克和卓",他在阿帕克和卓和准噶尔首领僧格支持下,逼迫阿不都拉汗放弃汗位,夺得政权。"他下令杀绝留在叶尔羌的居民,连妇女和儿童也不能幸免,还有那些曾随同海则莱提·艾孜赞一起去了阿克苏的人众。"(见正文"尧勒瓦斯汗登上了国家的汗位"一节)和卓夏迪的儿子玛木特·阿布都拉则跑到阿克苏,支持阿不都拉汗的四弟伊斯马因汗。尧勒瓦斯汗在被黑山派策划的政变杀死以后,"(伊斯马因)汗在海则莱提(玛木特·阿布都拉)和卓的帮助下,登上了祖父的汗位"。伊斯马因汗上台后,不仅处死了尧勒瓦斯汗诸子,且对白山派和卓进行镇压。阿帕克和卓被迫流亡他乡。在《编年史》作者的笔下,不管白山派多么"正统",但在与黑山派的争斗中,整体上是处于下风的。

第三,从《编年史》的记述中,我们可以找到有关政权与教权,即汗与和卓关系的资料。和卓势力迅速发展,无疑是与历任汗的推崇分不开的。历任汗之所以推崇和卓,同样是因为其取得政权和巩固政权的需要。但是,汗与和卓之间也存在着矛盾和斗争。如上述和卓夏迪去撒马尔罕朝拜其祖父麻扎尔一事,一方面说明由于和卓玛木特·玉素甫的到来,他的权威受到挑战,另一方面可能也表明阿不都剌帖夫汗和舒图尔·哈里发对他操纵朝政不满。沙·麻赫穆德·朱拉斯写道:和卓夏迪想去撒马尔罕,请求阿不都剌帖夫汗准予远行。"汗一直不予允诺,但却未能阻止住他,海则莱提·艾孜赞还是动身去了撒马尔罕,为的是祭祈祖父们发光的麻扎尔。"(见正文"海则莱提·艾孜赞们的出走及当时发生的事件"一节)在朝拜了他的祖父的麻扎尔以后,"有人向他告发哈里发舒图尔和米儿咱·穆罕默德·尤素甫"。和卓夏迪返回喀什噶尔,"当他们过了沙尔特大坂时,舒图尔哈里发和米儿咱·穆罕默德·尤素甫的死讯传来了"。研究者大都认为,由于和卓夏迪对米儿咱·穆罕默德·尤素甫伯克独揽朝政不满,同时对大哈里发舒图尔在教内操纵一切的愤恨,于是用暗杀手段除掉了他们。[①] 这时,黑山派和卓与汗的矛盾已经初露端倪。以后,便逐渐演绎为两种政治势力、两个宗教派别之间错综复杂的斗争。

4. 为研究16～18世纪新疆及中亚地区的民族关系提供了许多有价值的资料。叶尔羌汗国时期,塔里木盆地缘边地区居民经过长期的同化、融合,已经形成了一个新的民族共同体——维吾尔族。所以,叶尔羌汗国与吉尔吉斯、哈萨克、乌兹别克和卫拉特诸族的关系,实际上可以说是维吾尔族与上述各民族的关系。如前所述,《编年史》中有不少关于这些民族之间互相征伐的记述。但是,这只是问题的一个方面。《编年史》中还有不少记述表明,上述民族,特别是在这些民族的上层之间,存在着某种血缘关系。沙·麻赫穆德·朱拉斯告诉我们,"阿不都·拉失德的妻子曲曲克·哈尼木是哈萨克部加尼别克之子阿的黑速檀的女儿。曲曲克·哈尼木的母亲是速檀·羽奴思汗第四女——速檀·尼格尔·哈尼木"(见正文"关于速檀·赛义德汗之子阿不都·拉失德汗登上汗位"一节)。在阿不都拉汗时期,哈萨克加罕格尔汗又将自己的女儿嫁给了尧勒瓦斯汗。阿不都拉汗曾经多次进攻乌兹别克人,看来主要是因为阿黑麻汗的问题。阿黑麻汗被迫放弃汗位以后,去了巴里黑,但并不甘心失败,他到达河中以后,伊玛目·库里汗"派纳扎尔·布鲁特和近七万人的军队一起同速檀阿黑麻汗去攻打喀什噶尔",自然会引起阿不都拉汗的不满。所以,"当速檀阿黑麻汗自撒马尔罕来到安集延时,有关他的消息就传到了阿不都拉汗那里。汗怀疑大臣和高官们,在喀什噶尔杀了和卓米尔、和卓穆罕默德·拉乌弗、米儿咱·卡马尔·巴鲁剌思、米儿咱·阿不都赛买提·朱拉斯、米儿咱·阿里夫比克奇克,总共杀了近200个有名望的人。在叶尔羌他也杀了阿訇·和卓纳斯尔,愿真主垂怜他,还有米儿咱里扎·伊·西拉里、伊斯基塔基部的米儿咱沙赫·穆罕默德、巴邻部的塔西尔和卓,他总计除掉了近百人"(见正文"阿不都拉汗即位称汗"一节)。直到速檀阿黑麻汗在进攻安集延时被杀的消息传到叶尔羌以后,"纷争才逐渐缓和了下来"。所以说,阿不都拉汗远征安集延事出有因。从这一事件当中,我们可以看出他们之间的政治联系中互相干预对方的内部事务是常有的事。至于吉尔吉斯人,在大部分时间里,他们是叶尔羌汗国的臣民,但往往游移于维吾尔和乌兹别克政权之间。《编年史》向人们提供了准噶尔早期在南疆活动的资料:早在僧格时准噶尔的势力就已经渗入叶尔羌汗国,与白山派和卓一起支持尧勒瓦斯汗,取得政权。从这个时候起,他们之间就已经建

---

① 参见魏良弢:《叶尔羌汗国史纲》,第132页。

立了联系,白山派和卓已对准噶尔不陌生。看来,以后阿帕克和卓跑到西藏,请求达赖写信给噶尔丹,噶尔丹引领准噶尔军队进入南疆,俘伊斯马因汗,灭叶尔羌汗国,就不是偶然的了。

四、《编年史》的缺陷与问题

《编年史》内容比较丰富,给我们研究叶尔羌汗国史提供了非常有价值的资料,首先是应该肯定的。但是,作为一部史学著作,它存在的缺陷和问题也是明显的。

首先,作为一部史学著作,内容应该比较全面,有政治、经济、社会文化等方面的记述,而《编年史》仅涉及政治。就政治而言,也缺乏制度方面的系统内容。所以,想通过《编年史》了解当时的社会全貌是困难的。

其次,《编年史》记述了叶尔羌汗国时期发生的许多重大事件,但只有几件重大事件标明了具体的日期。像其他较早的穆斯林著作一样,人们在使用它提供的资料时,必须首先参照其他史籍,考证出事件发生的年月日期。否则,是无法利用的。

第三,从《编年史》的记述不难判断,沙·麻赫穆德·朱拉斯是一位忠实的黑山派教徒,宗教偏见令人吃惊。首先,他对白山派的记述很少。很难从他的记述中,全面了解白山派的活动。众所周知,白山派是新疆伊斯兰教的一个重要派别,是叶尔羌汗国时期一支与黑山派相抗衡的社会政治势力。缺少对他们的记述,即便是作为一部政治史,也是不全面的。这不能不说是一个缺憾。

第四,像多数穆斯林著作一样,作者在前言中总是谦虚一番。沙·麻赫穆德·朱拉斯也是如此,说如果他不是受到阿尔格伯克的鼓励和支持,"无本无能的鄙人,穆罕默德·米儿咱·法则里·朱拉斯之子怎能有本领在这奇迹般的篇章上写出文字呢"(第24页)。但实事求是地讲,他的史学修养与文学修养都显得不足,许多事情记述得并不全面、清楚。有的学者指出,这种情况大概与当时这一地区文化的普遍下降有关。① 应该说,有一定的道理。

但是,《编年史》的主要问题还不在上述几个方面,而是在于他对黑山派和卓"神奇"故事的宣扬及盲目崇拜。一是宣扬和卓可以预知未来,某某人及其后代可以成为君王,某某人的后代当不了君王。沙·麻赫穆德·朱拉斯还讲到,因为和卓额拜都拉的挑拨,黑山派和卓伊斯哈克·外力没有能够与阿不都·哈林汗晤面。所以,和卓伊斯哈克指示说:"哎,和卓额拜都拉!(愿真主保佑他)你们没有敬仰我们。有一天,我们的一个乞丐会将你用金子建造起来的宫殿用作驴圈的。"结果,到了穆罕默德汗时,舒图尔·哈里发带着海则莱提和穆罕默德汗的指示来了。那时额拜都拉汗已经去世,汗把他的家属和亲戚都驱赶到了和田。舒图尔·哈里发(愿真主保佑他)有一匹很大的驴,他以一种陶醉的感觉把这头驴拴在大臣家里的一个地方,自己就在他家的凉棚里睡觉了。二是宣扬和卓可以为人祈求多子多福。沙·麻赫穆德·朱拉斯讲到,一些米儿咱向海则莱提·艾孜赞们祈祷,请求生育男孩。于是,艾孜赞们满足了他们的请求。"经过祈祷之后,忽特鲁克·穆罕默德·米儿咱有了八个儿子、四个女儿;莫莫克·米儿咱有了五个儿子、七个女儿。"(第43页)三是宣扬和卓的"神智",可以异地作法。沙·麻赫穆德·朱拉斯在讲到舒图尔·哈里发在吐鲁番传教时说,舒图尔·哈里发到达了吐鲁番,并会见了吐鲁番人,但他们未臣服。他们崇拜海则莱提·阿里甫·阿塔,闪光灿烂的舒图尔·哈里发到阿里甫·阿塔·哈孜坟墓并骑在上面,坟墓开始震动,并把舒图尔·哈里发抛掷在地上。舒图尔·哈里发站起来又骑在坟墓上,又被抛掷下来。坟墓裂开后出现了一只狮子,海则莱提·艾孜赞的神智保护并营救了舒图尔·哈里发。四是宣扬和卓可以让死人复活。《和卓传》载:和卓伊斯哈克在巴里黑时,巴里黑之王有一个儿子,名叫夏·穆罕默德·苏力唐。和卓伊斯哈克·外力去看望他,回来一个小时后,和卓伊斯哈克·外力向国王告诉他儿子将要"病逝"的消息。国王赶紧跑到儿子跟前,看到他无力地躺着,心里很难过。国王将儿子抱起放在和卓伊斯哈克·外力的面前,对他说:"大人啊!您在真主的面前是尊贵的,也有一些挚友。所以,只要您做祈祷,因您祈祷之尊,我儿子定会起死回生的。"和卓伊斯哈克·外力为了真主天庭的荣耀,从心底里发出这样的话:"主啊!请您不要以无比的力量和高贵的品质使我这可怜的人出丑。请您发发慈悲,为了诸圣人的尊严,接受我的祈祷。"祈祷之后,天使也发出叹息声,真主也接受了他的祈祷。王子站立起来,父子俩向和卓伊斯哈克·外力表示了感谢之意。其后,在巴里黑城流传着"依禅大人使死人复活"的话。但是,在和田和卓伊斯哈克·外力的法术却失灵了。沙·麻赫穆德·朱拉斯在讲到和卓伊斯哈克·外力在和田传教时说,和田的统治者忽来失速檀热情地迎接了他们,并把自己的一个儿子交给了和卓伊斯哈克·外力,"以便为他们效劳,成为忠诚信徒"。忽来失速檀的妻子死后,他"向海则莱提·艾孜赞提出了'复活妻子的请求'"。但是,和卓伊斯哈克·外力却以为时已晚为由予以拒绝。因此,双方关系破裂,和卓伊斯哈克·外力只好奔阿克苏。五是宣扬和卓手杖的"神力"。传说穆罕默德的女儿法蒂玛得了痼疾顽症,人间无法医治,于是真主派了七个人为她治病。治好病以后,先知给了他们一把手杖,说手杖发芽处就是你们落脚的地方。这七个人到过许多地方,手杖都没有发芽。最后,他们到了叶尔羌,把手杖往地上一插,就发出了绿芽。于是,他们便留了下来,手杖则变成了和卓传教的工具。按照和卓伊斯哈克·外力的指示,如果有人反对他们,舒图尔·哈里发"就用手杖打他。被打的那个人倒下以后,叫着他的名字站起来,并变成了他虔诚的信徒"。有关黑山派和卓"神奇"的故事还有很多,在这里就不再一一列举了。但必须指出,在许许多多离奇、荒诞故事的背后,是和卓在向人们展示威严和权威,并以此攫取地位和特权。

尽管《编年史》存在着这样那样的问题,但仍然应该肯定它是记述叶尔羌汗国历史最有价值的文献之一。基于此,我们就不能过于苛求古人了。

突厥语《摩尼大颂》考释

——兼谈东方摩尼教的传播特色

芮传明

上海社会科学院历史研究所

　　《摩尼大颂》①见于吐鲁番出土的摩尼教文书中,可能撰成于公元 10 世纪初期。它显然是用突厥语直接书写,而并非译自伊朗语。全诗共计一百二十颂,当是迄今所见的最长的摩尼教突厥语赞美诗。从该诗采用的措辞来看,佛教色彩十分浓重,许多术语都是直接借自佛经梵语,故是东传摩尼教深受佛教文化影响的明显佐证。然而,在大量使用佛教术语的表象之下,它仍隐含了清楚的摩尼教教义,这是摩尼教传播方式的一大特色,故本文在考释和研究《摩尼大颂》之内容的同时,也将对这一特色进行探讨。

一、《摩尼大颂》之汉译文②

　　1. 啊,夷数③之原始教义的导师! ／我们将以虔诚的心灵崇拜你。／啊,我尊敬而名声卓著的父尊,／我的摩尼佛!④

　　2. 我们已经准备好 ／以谦卑之心崇拜你。／我们的希望和信赖者,⑤请接受 ／我们每个人的一切崇拜吧。

　　3. 我们向你鞠躬,／发自内心深处的信仰。／但愿我们每次崇拜时都洁净异常。／……

　　4～13. (残缺厉害,只剩零星辞句)你解释了恶业的后果……你阻挡了通往地狱之路……传播妙法⑥……

---

　　① 其内容分见于 T Ⅲ D 258、T Ⅲ D 259 和 T Ⅲ D 260 等文书中,突厥语的拉丁转写和德译文,见 W. Bang & A. von Gabain, *Türkische Turfan-Texte III*, APAW, April 1930, pp. 184－205;英译文则见 Klimkeit, *Gnosis*, pp. 280－284。该赞美诗标题的德译名作 *Der große Hymnus auf Mani*,英译名则作 *Great Hymn to Mani*。

　　② 本译文主要根据克林凯特的英译文(*Gnosis*, pp. 280－284)转译,并亦参看邦格与葛玛丽之德译文(*Türkische Turfan-Texte III*, pp. 184－205)以及克拉克的英译文(*Pothi-Book*, pp. 180－189)。

　　③ 在此之所以将 Jesus 译作"夷数"而非"耶稣",是因为摩尼教借用此神,并在汉语典籍《下部赞》中译作"夷数",故从之,以区别于纯粹的基督教神灵。

　　④ 此名的拉丁转写为 mani burxan,邦格与葛玛丽的德译文取音译名 Mani Burchan(p. 185),克林凯特的英译文则意译作"佛"——Buddha Mani(p. 280),克拉克虽亦作意译,但取"先知"之义——Prophet Mani(p. 180)。盖按公元 7～8 世纪的古突厥语,习惯于将汉语"佛"字读作 bur 音,再与具有"王者"之义的 xan(汗)构成组合词 burxan,以翻译佛经中相当于"佛"一类的高级神灵;后来便被摩尼教借用,用以指称如摩尼之类的"先知"(见 *Etymological Dictionary*, p. 360)。既然 burxan 一名源出突厥语佛经,那么,在此取"摩尼佛"之汉译名,则更利于彰显摩尼教文献的佛教影响。

　　⑤ 古突厥语 umuɣ ïnaɣ,义为众生寄托希望和信赖的对象,频见于突厥语佛经中,即是指佛陀。这一专名被摩尼教借用,在此显然成为摩尼的尊称。

　　⑥ 突厥词 edgü 为善、好、仁慈等义;nom 则是外来词,借自希腊 nomos,义为"法",作为摩尼教的专用术语,则有法、教义等更广泛的含义,而在突厥语佛经中,则几乎专译梵语 dharma。所以,突厥语 edgü nom 所对译的,当是佛经中常用梵语 sad-dharma,亦即汉语妙法、净法、正法等,也就是佛陀所说之教法。

你拯救……遭受八难①的众生……疯狂、野蛮和有毒的兽类。

14. 处于野蛮状态的兽类，/ 不断地沉没在 / 重复转生的失忆尘埃中，/ 他们永久地疯狂。

15. 当他们被贪欲②毒害，/ 正在死亡和毁灭时，/ 你为他们制备了/禅定③的药方。

16. 瞋怒④而咆哮，/ 他们毫无知觉或思想，/ 你聚合起他们的思想，/ 使得他们理解了自己的出身。

17. 对于五趣⑤众生，/ 你使之脱离愚痴。⑥ / 你赐予他们智慧，/ 引导他们趋向般涅槃。⑦

18. 形形色色的情感，/ 诸如仇恨与怨望/ 全都见于这些有情身上，/ 导致他们产生邪见。

19. 但是当你，我们的神圣父尊，/ 从天而降，/ 一切有情之族 / 全获安宁涅槃。⑧

20～25.（严重残缺）

26. ……/ 没有希望的我辈受苦众生，/ 只能继续遭受轮回⑨的折磨，/ 找不到你的大道终端。

27. 你设置了智慧之梯，/ 你允许我们超然于五趣之上，/ 拯救了我们。/……

28. 我们……/ 遭囚禁而受难的众生 / 被救而脱离轮回。/ 为了见到如佛般的日神，⑩/……类似于你。

29. 对于沉湎于无常之乐的众生，/ 你传播了无上正法；⑪/ 你引导他们渡过苦海，⑫/ 带领他们达到完美涅槃。

30. 对于受制于贪爱之源的众生，/ 你指示了通往诸佛之界的道路。/ 你建造了功德的须弥山，⑬/ 你允许他们找到这……永恒欢乐。

31. 对于陷入慢见⑭之水的众生，/ 你指示了正法之桥。/ 你使其内心理解了妙法；/ 你把他们托付给……神圣集会。

---

① 从字面解释，突厥语 sekiz tülüg emkek 的意思为八种苦难、痛苦，为佛经梵语 aṣṭāv akṣaṇāḥ 的对应译语，汉译佛经简称"八难"，指不得遇法、不闻正法的八种障碍。本文书显然借用了佛经术语，但具体所指，却不得而知。

② 突厥词 az 直接借自中古波斯语"z，义为贪婪。这在突厥语古文书中用得相当普遍，往往对译佛经中的梵语 lobha（贪求名声、财物等而无厌足之意，汉译作"贪"）或 tṛṣṇā（贪恋执著于一切事物之意，汉译作"爱"）。是为佛教的"三毒"之一。

③ 突厥词 amwrdšn 直接借自帕提亚语 'mwrdyšn，通常义为"聚合"、"聚集"（释见 Boyce, Word-List, p. 11）。但是葛玛丽则持异说，认为 amwrdšn 与 cxšapt、boštgut 一起，分别对应于佛经中的梵语词 dhyāna、šīla 和 prajñā，即禅、戒、慧（见 Clark, Pothi-Book, p. 193）。

④ 突厥语 ot 原义为"火"，有时则引申为"恼怒"、"愤怒"，在此显然是对译佛教术语 dveṣa，即"三毒"之二的"瞋"。

⑤ 突厥语 biš 义为五；ažun 源自帕提亚语"jwn，原义为诞生、再生。故词组 biš ažun 便义为五种生存形态，也就是对应于佛教术语"五趣"（梵语 pañca gatayaḥ）——轮回的五种去处：地狱、饿鬼、畜生、人、天。

⑥ 突厥词 biligsiz 义为无知、缺少智慧，在此显然是对译佛教术语 moha，即"三毒"之三的"痴"。

⑦ 突厥词 frnibran 借自帕提亚语 prnybr'n，源出梵语 parinirvāṇa，即佛教术语"般涅槃"（圆满诸德，寂灭诸恶）之意。

⑧ 突厥词 nirvan 是梵语 nirvāṇa 的直接借词，为佛教术语，与"般涅槃"之意相若，指燃烧烦恼之火灭尽，完成悟智的境地。

⑨ 突厥词 sansarta 直接借用了梵语 saṃsāra，即佛教的常用术语"轮回"——在六道迷界（天、人、阿修罗、饿鬼、畜生、地狱）中生死相续，与"涅槃"恰成对照。

⑩ 突厥语 burxanıɣ kün tngrig，克拉克译作"日神先知（the Sun-God of Prophets）"（Pothi-Book, p. 182），不似"如佛般的日神"贴切。克林凯特认为，此"日神"是指摩尼教主神之一的"光辉夷数（Jesus the Splendor）"（Gnosis, p. 287, note 14）。

⑪ 突厥语 eššiz 有"无比的"之义（Pothi-Book, p. 194）；kšni:义为正直的、真正的（Etymological Dictionary, pp. 726 - 727）；nom 则义为法、教义。故 eššiz könii nomuγ 一语，当即佛教术语"无上正法"（也就是最高智慧"佛智"）的对译。

⑫ 突厥词 emkek 义为苦难，taluy 义为海，二者构成的词组经常用来对译佛教术语"苦海"，故此语显然借鉴自佛经。

⑬ 突厥词 Sumir 系借自伊朗诸语的外来词：帕提亚语、粟特语均作 smyr；梵语则作 sumeru。汉译佛经通常作须弥山、苏迷卢山等，或者意译为妙高山，为印度神话及佛教中的神山。

⑭ 突厥词 küfenč 义为傲慢，常用以对译佛教术语 māna，为轻蔑他人，自负之义，汉译佛经作"慢"，有诸多讲究。

32. 对于六根①感知惑乱的众生，／你展示了上下诸种生存状态。／你告知他们阿鼻地狱②的受苦情况；／你允诺他们再生于幸福的五重天。③

33. 为了寻找拯救众生的种种途径，／你走遍四面八方的地域。／当你见到需要获救的众生，／你就毫无例外地拯救他们每一个。

34. 对于我辈这样曾经虚度光阴的众生，／你详细地宣讲《福音书》④之宝。／我们懂得了自由与获救的种种途径，／我们从那书中了解了一切。

35. 如果你未曾以如此彻底的方式／传播这种净法，⑤／世界及诸有情岂非／就会走到尽头？

36. 你在四佛⑥之后降世，／获得无上正等觉。⑦／你拯救了亿万生灵，／将他们救离暗狱。

37. 你净化他们，使之不再狡诈、欺骗，／并使他们从事利他之业。／你成为迷途者的向导。／你救助他们脱离事恶之魔⑧的利爪。

38. 你营救了那些曾是邪恶的人，／你治愈了那些双目失明的人。／你使他们从事光荣之业，／你为他们指明了通往神界的正确道路。

39. 你作为世界的希望和信赖者而诞生，／你教导众生理解七种宝藏⑨的涵义。／此外，你还阻止了／那些本来会与邪魔结盟的人。

40～49.（严重残缺）

50. 人们边走边呼唤着你的名字，／他们赞扬你，称颂你，／他们全都敬爱你，／犹如孩子们敬爱其母亲和父亲。

51. 你以大慈悲之心，／拥抱他们所有的人，／你赐予他们大利益。／……

52. 无分亲疏，／你对待他们全都如同亲生。／你将自己的忠告给予／无数的生灵。

53. 你以……之心／于一切众生为善。／你所施之善的结果是，／所有受折磨者都消除了忧伤。

---

① 突厥词 altı 义为六，qačıγ 义为感官，故词组 altı qačıγ 意为"六种感官"，而它作为专用术语，则是对译佛教术语 ṣaḍ indriyāṇi 或 ṣaḍ āyatana。前者的汉译作六根、六情，指六种感觉器官（眼、耳、鼻、舌、身、意）或认识能力（视、听、嗅、味、触、思）；后者的汉译作六处、六入，指心所依止处，或者识之所入。

② 突厥语 awiš 是源自梵语 avici 的借词，指佛教所谓的无间地狱（也音译作"阿鼻"），也就是"八热地狱"中的第八个地狱，刑罚、痛苦、生、死无间断。

③ 突厥语词组 biš qat tngrii yirinteh 意为"五重天"，其所指有些模糊不清，因为按摩尼教的宇宙学说，只有"十天"，故或许这五重天只是指"十天"的上半部分。（说见 Pothi-Book, p.195）

④ 突厥词 awngliwn 系源自伊朗诸语的借词：帕提亚语、粟特语均为 'wnglywn，义为福音、福音书（Evangel, Gospel）。此名在这里是特指摩尼所撰的七本书中的第一本《生命福音》（Living Gospel，汉语典籍《仪略》作《彻尽万法根源智经》）。

⑤ 突厥语 arıγ 义为清洁的、纯净的，引申为精神方面的形容词，则含有宗教性"洁净"的意思，如摩尼教称其专职修道者"选民"为 arıγ。这里的"净法"是佛教"妙法"的对译。

⑥ 突厥词 tört 义为四，burxan 义为佛，故词组 tört burxan 意为"四佛"。尽管形式上借用佛教术语"佛"，但所指者则是摩尼教神学中位于摩尼教之前的四个"先知"或光明使者，可能是：塞思（Seth）、琐罗亚斯德（Zarathustra）、佛陀（Buddha）、耶稣（Jesus）。（说见 Pothi-Book, pp.196－197）

⑦ 突厥语词组 tözkerinčsiz burxan qutın 的意思是"无与伦比的完善之觉悟"，在突厥语文书中，几乎专门用以对译佛经的梵语词组 anuttara-samyak-sambodhi，亦即汉译"阿耨多罗三藐三菩提"，意为无上正等觉、无上正真道、无上正遍知等，是佛陀所觉悟的智慧，最为圆满、至高。

⑧ 突厥词 šmnu 源自伊朗语（粟特语作 šmnw），并与中古波斯语、帕提亚语 'hrymn（ahrēman）为同源词，都义为敌对和邪恶的精灵。在摩尼教文书中，šmnu 几乎总是指称伊朗语的 Ahriman（即 'hrymn 等）；在佛教文书中，则对应于印度梵语中的 Māra（"魔"）。所以，突厥语词组 ayıγ qılınčlıγ šmnu 便意为"从事恶业之魔"。

⑨ 突厥词 yitih 义为七；aγılıq 义为宝藏，在佛经翻译中，是为专译梵语 garbha（汉译"藏"）的术语。故词组 yitih aγılıq（七种宝藏）实际上是指教主摩尼亲撰的经典——七本书。

54. 你持续不断，永久地以这种方式，/ 赐予我们巨大的利益和幸运。/ 由于你的功德，/ 你获得了正遍知。

55. （残缺严重）

56. 你以其无上圣言，/ 慷慨地赐予 / 我辈可怜的众生 / 以"善"之法宝。

57~58.（严重残缺）

59. 众生诸族 / 曾经因其黑暗情感，/ 而完全丧失心智，/ 但是他们此后再生……

60~77.（缺失或严重残缺）

78. 你以大慈悲之心，/ 拥抱一切众生；/ 你营救他们脱离转生循环，/ 拯救他们跳出轮回。

79. 具有清净心的有福者 / 不断地逐步获得洞察力，/ 克服了邪恶之念，/ 取得阿罗汉①果。

80. 六尘②之妄想，③ / 导致狡诈和欺骗；/ 对于那些…… / 你带给他们利益与幸运。

81. …… / 对于忘却出身来源的那些人，/ 你露现自己的本相，/ 改变你的状貌……

82. 当一切众生 / 见到你的示现时，/ 他们都被激发了 / 逃离轮回之苦的愿望。

83. 对于人类的孩子们，/ 你显示慈祥之相，/ 使他们不再从事恶业，/ 使他们脱离受其奴役的俗世的欲爱。

84. …… / …… / 在全界④的蓝天的视野下，/ 你作为诸师之佛而诞生。

85. 一见到你，众生就高兴成分，/ 就不再有任何疑虑。/ 他们怀着勤勉之心，/ 遵奉你所制定的戒律。

86. 随着他们的持戒…… / 他们心灵中的善念 / 与日俱增，/ 犹如日神那样光辉照耀。

87. 他们的光亮知识发射照耀，/ 怜悯之心愈益增长；/ 他们遵奉无罪的戒律，⑤ / 从而逃离了烧炙地狱。⑥

88. …… / 他们努力持奉正法，/ 他们遵守真实戒律，/ 不犯不净之罪。⑦

89. 领悟了躯体的无常，/ 他们于是出家。⑧ / 他们奉行善法，/ 他们遵守使躯体净化的戒条。⑨

90. 他们努力使自己实施净法，/ 以免陷入危险之地。/ 为了再生于无生界，⑩ / 他们遵奉使口清净

---

① 突厥词 arxant 系借自粟特词 rhnd，但其真正的来源却是梵语 arhat，亦即汉译的佛教术语"罗汉"或"阿罗汉"。意指断尽三界见、思之惑，证得尽智，而堪受世间大供养的圣者。

② 突厥词 fišay 直接借自梵语 visaya，后者为佛教术语，汉译作"尘"、"境"，为引起六根之感觉思维作用的对象，即色、声、香、味、触、法。

③ 突厥词 atqaɣ 被用来对译梵语 vikalpa，也是佛教术语，汉译作"妄想"，意指由于心之执著，而无法如实知见事物，从而产生谬误的认识。

④ 突厥词原作 ililig，但显然是 illig（＝éllig）的错误拼写，义为王国、界域（见 *Etymological Dictionary*，pp. 141，145），在此则当指明界，故汉译作"界"。

⑤ 突厥词 čxšapt 是佛教梵语词 śikṣāpada 的借词，后者意为"所学之处"，通常即是指比丘、比丘尼学习戒律时所遵循的戒条。摩尼教或佛教的突厥语文书，多以此词指戒律；在此列数对于选民的"五戒"，第一即是"不犯罪过之戒"。

⑥ 突厥词 tamu 乃是粟特词 tmw 的借词，并可探源至其他伊朗语。但是，在突厥语佛经中，此名则相当普遍地对译梵语 naraka（地狱），故将本文书"永燃之狱"（ever-burning Hell 或 the hell which is ever aflame）译成佛教术语"烧炙地狱"，即"八热地狱"之六，铁城中大火永燃，烧炙罪人，皮肉焦烂，痛苦不堪。

⑦ 不犯不洁净之罪，是摩尼教选民"五戒"中的第二条。

⑧ 突厥词组 evtin barqtın untiler 为典型的佛教术语，即"出家"（ev 义为家、住所；barq 义为家庭财物）。其对应的佛教梵语是 pravrajyā，专指出离家庭生活，潜心修沙门净行。本文书使用这一术语，显然是摩尼教对佛教因素的借鉴。

⑨ 净化身体，是摩尼教选民"五戒"中的第三条。

⑩ 突厥词 anwšagan 当是借自中古波斯语 'nwšg，义为不朽的，永恒的；ortu 则义为营帐、宫殿。故词组 anwšagan ortu 意为永生之宫，显然是指称摩尼教神学中的明界。由于文书在此不是直接称"明界"，而是借用佛教"永断生死"的描述方式，故汉译作"无生界"，以佛教之永离生灭的极乐净土喻指摩尼教同一含义的明界。

的戒律。①

91. 他们全都祈求福祉，／行走在幸福之路上……／为了逃避可怕的轮回，／他们遵奉清贫之福②的戒条。

92. 他们认识到伪法的无常，／并且惧怕堕入三恶趣，③／他们遵奉三印④之戒，／以再生于最高之所。⑤

93～113. （缺失或者严重残缺）

114. 你亲自命令他们，／要念赞语，唱颂歌，／要为其恶业忏悔，／要聚合起来，从事禅定。

115. 一直迷惑不清的众生，／一旦闻听你的命令，／便会导致功德如海，⑥从而再生于佛土。

116. 其他天真质朴之人，／行走于清净道上，／从事禅定，／并再生于无生界。

117. 向着你，我们的最高神灵，／我们鞠躬，我们崇拜，／但愿世上的众生／自今以后再生涅槃！

118. 我们以虔诚之心崇拜；／但愿世上的一切众生／全都脱离灾难；／但愿他们获得安静涅槃。

119. 我们赞美与崇拜之功德／但愿上下诸神／和各类精灵／的神圣力量得以增强。⑦

120～121. （残缺）

二、《摩尼大颂》"佛教化"的表现形式

就《摩尼大颂》全文的表现形式而言，佛教术语的使用之多，是毫无疑问的。即使概要地观察一下，也可发现众多明显的佛教词汇。

首先，频繁地将摩尼教神灵称为"佛"。例如，"摩尼佛"（第 1 颂）、"如佛般的日神"（第 28 颂）、"通往诸佛之界"（第 30 颂）、"四佛"（第 36 颂）、"诸师之佛"（第 84 颂）、"佛土"（第 115 颂）等。其中，"摩尼佛"当然是指摩尼教的创建者摩尼。"日神"是指摩尼教的主神之一夷数，亦即从基督教移植而来的耶稣（Jesus），但在摩尼教神学中，他有时被指为司管太阳，故称日神。由于"诸佛之界"指的是摩尼教的光明乐土"明界"，故所谓"诸佛"，也就是泛指明界的一切神灵。至于"四佛"，如前文注释所言，当是指摩尼降世之前，由大明尊派遣的四位使者或先知，即塞思、琐罗亚斯德、佛陀、基督。⑧塞思（Seth）原是见于基督教《圣经》的神话人物，为亚当与夏娃的儿子，生于该隐杀死亚伯之后；琐罗亚斯德原为琐罗亚斯德教的

---

① 使口洁净，是摩尼教选民"五戒"的第四条。

② 摩尼教选民"五戒"的第五条，是生活清贫，但是快乐而有幸福感。

③ 突厥词组 üč yavlaq yolqa 意为三种邪恶的生存形态，即是佛教术语梵文 trīni durgati 的对译，汉译作三恶趣（或作三途、三恶道），通常指地狱、饿鬼、畜生三种生存形态，是众生造作恶业所感得的世界。

④ 突厥词组 üč tmqalar 是摩尼教的专用术语，意为三种印记。所谓"印记"（seal），是喻指摩尼教信条的象征符号，总数共有七种。在此所言的"三印"属于日常生活的道德范畴，即口、手、胸三者；另有"四印"则属于精神或教义范畴，即爱、信、惧（神）、智。关于"七印"的详说，可参看 Jackson, *Researches*, pp. 331 – 337。

⑤ "最高处"即是指摩尼教的永生乐土"明界"。

⑥ 突厥词组 buyanlïγ taluy ögüzüg 为佛教术语梵文 guṇasāgarar 的对译，即"功德海"，譬喻功德之深广似海。

⑦ 这是见于丝绸之路上突厥语佛教文书中的典型结语。（说见 *Gnosis*, p. 287, note 38）

⑧ 这一说法只见于中古波斯语的《巨人书》中："但是，神（楚尔凡？）在每个时代都派遣使者：塞思、琐罗亚斯德、佛陀、基督……"（But God［Zrwān?］, in each epoch, sends apostles: Šītīl, Zarathushtra, Buddha, Christ, ...），见 Henning, *Giants*, p. 63。但是在较早时期的文献中，却声称在摩尼之前只有三位使者或先知，例如，摩尼在其著述《沙卜拉干》（*Shābuhragān*）中称，明尊不时派遣使者降世，某一时期是佛陀降世印度，某一时期是琐罗亚斯德降世波斯，某一时期是耶稣降世西方，"而这一时代的先知便是我摩尼，真诚之神的使者，降临于巴比伦之地。"（见 Ort, *Mani: Personality*, pp. 117 – 118）故摩尼教的"四佛"之说或许起源较晚。

创建者;佛陀原为佛教之缔造者;基督即耶稣,原为基督教的创建者;显然,这些异教神灵都被摩尼教所借鉴,并在此成了"佛"。"诸师之佛"也是指称摩尼。由于"佛土"指的是明界,故此语中的"佛"也就泛指摩尼教诸神了。不难看出,几乎所有神灵都被冠以"佛"号,是为本摩尼教文书"佛教化"的一个明显标志。

其次,不妨归纳一下本文书中清楚借用佛教术语的词汇和词组。

"妙法"见于第4~13颂、31颂;"净法"见于第35颂、90颂;"正法"见于第29颂、31颂、88颂。前文已经谈及,突厥词 könii 义为正直的、合乎正道的、真正的等,故词组 könii nom 便用以对译佛教的梵文术语 sad-dharma。在佛经中,佛陀所说之教法被认为是真正之法,故称正法;此外,凡是契当于佛法正理之法,均称正法。鉴于佛法妙不可言,且决非所有其他之法可以比拟,故又称妙法,突厥语便以 edgü nom 对译之(edgü 为善、好之义);盖因梵语 sad 为不可思议、不能比较等意思,遂称无法比较而不可思议之法为妙法。至于"净法"(突厥词组 arïγ nom)则也是对应了佛教术语:指称佛陀所说之正法,因其法能令众生超三界,得解脱,身心清净,故名。由此可知,本文书中,无论是 könii nom,还是 edgü nom,抑或 arïγ nom,实际上都是确切地各自对译了佛教术语"正法"、"妙法"和"净法",也就是佛教对于佛陀所说之教法的诸异称,而这是十分典型和普及的佛教术语。不过,必须指出的是,本文书只是借用了这一佛教术语,而并非真的指佛陀的教法。

"般涅槃"见于第17颂;"涅槃"见于第19颂、29颂、117颂、118颂。突厥词 frnibran 为外来借词,清楚地对译梵语 parinirvāṇa,亦即佛教术语"般涅槃"。而此词则意为灭尽诸恶、圆满诸德,本来专指佛陀之死,即灭尽烦恼而进入大彻大悟的境地,也就是脱离生死之苦,全静妙之乐,穷至极的果德。因此,汉译佛经除译此词为"般涅槃"外,还常译作圆寂、灭度、入灭、入寂等。至于突厥词 nirvan 则是梵语 nirvāṇa 的直接借词,其意与 parnirvāṇa(般涅槃)相仿,也就是指超越生死迷界,到达悟智境界(菩提),为佛教的终极实践目标。汉名涅槃也是音译,与般涅槃的区别,是后者多一前缀 pari,为完全、圆满之意。当然,本文书多次出现的"涅槃",同样只是借用佛教术语,其所指的实际含义,毕竟不同于佛教。

"轮回"见于第26颂、28颂、78颂、82颂、91颂。突厥词 sansarta 是佛教梵语 saṃsāra 的直接转写,故是完全的外来词,汉译佛经作"轮回"。佛教认为,一切众生由于"业因"的缘故,往往始终在天、人、阿修罗、饿鬼、畜生、地狱这样六种生存形态中循环转生,永无穷尽,饱受生死之苦,所以称轮回。

本文书中,与"轮回"关系密切的佛教术语是"五趣"(见第17颂、27颂)和"三恶趣"(第92颂)。突厥词组 biš ažun 义为五种生存形态,用以对译佛教术语 pañca gatayaḥ,汉译佛经作五趣、五道,或五恶趣等;"趣"为所住之义。大乘经多持"六趣"说,小乘则持"五趣"说,即不列阿修罗一道。但无论是六趣说还是五趣说,都将地狱、饿鬼、畜生列为"三恶道"(三恶趣),本文书中的突厥词组 üč yavlaq yolqa(意为三种邪恶的生存形态)便是用以对译佛教术语 trīni durgati(三恶趣)。

与"轮回"关系密切的另一术语便是"地狱",如第4~13颂、32颂、87颂等均见此名。实际上,本文书不仅仅用泛指的突厥词 tamu 对译佛教术语 naraka(汉译作"地狱"),并且更具体地借用了佛教的地狱专名"阿鼻"(突厥词 awiš 借自梵语 avici)。阿鼻地狱为"八热地狱"中的第八个地狱,也称无间地狱,意谓堕此地狱者,所受之苦无有间断,一劫之中,始终受苦而不间断,身形遍满地狱而无间隙,如此等等的"无间"。总而言之,苦不堪言。第87颂所言之地狱显然也是某个特定地狱:其"永远燃烧"的特征与八热地狱中的第六地狱"烧炙"、第七地狱"大烧炙",或者第八地狱"无间"吻合,[①]虽然其确切所指尚不得而知,但是借用了佛教的地狱说,却没有疑问。

本文书中还有一些专用词组,尽管只出现过一次或两次,但从形式上看,都是十分明显的佛教术语。其中主要者有:

见于第4～13颂的"八难"。突厥词组 sekiz tülüg emkek(八种苦难)对应于佛教术语 aṣṭāv akṣaṇāh,但后者指的是众生无缘见佛闻法的八种障难:堕于地狱、陷于饿鬼道、沦于畜生道、在心想不行的长寿天、在不受教化的边地、盲聋瘖哑、耽习外道经书、生在佛降世之前或其后。所以,本文书虽然也用"八难"术语,但其内涵显然不会同于佛教。

见于第15颂和第114颂的"禅定"、第17颂的"智慧"及第87颂的"戒律"。突厥词 ạmwrdšn 对译佛教术语 dhyāna,汉译佛经作"禅那",亦即"禅定"或"定",意为专注于某一对象,心不散乱的精神境界。突厥词 bilig 对译梵语 prajñā,汉译佛经作"慧"或"般若",即最高智慧。突厥词 čxšapt 则对译梵语 śikṣāpada,汉译佛经作"戒"或"戒律"。戒、定、慧三者合称佛教的"三学"或"三胜学",是佛教的实践纲领(由戒生定,由定发慧)。显然,本文书很巧妙地借鉴了这些重要的佛教术语,以表述摩尼教本身的教义。

分别见于第14颂、16颂、17颂的"贪欲"、"瞋怒"和"愚痴"。本文书使用了突厥词 az、ot 和 biligsiz 分别对译佛教梵语 lobha、dvesa 和 moha,也就是汉译佛经所称的贪、瞋、痴,是为毒害众生出世善心中的最甚者,故合称"三毒"、"三垢"或"三不善根"等。贪、瞋、痴在连续三颂中分别叙说,显然是有意识地借用佛教文化。

见于第30颂的"须弥山"。突厥词 Sumir 虽然并非直接借自梵语 Sumeru,但是源自佛教的这一重要宇宙观,却毫无疑问。此名在汉译佛经中作须弥、须弥卢、苏迷卢等,意译则作妙高山、好光山、善高山、善积山、妙光山等,最初是印度神话中的山名,后则被佛教沿用,以其为世界中央的高山,周围绕有八山、八海,从而形成一个"须弥世界",亦即"三千大千世界"(一佛之化境)之一。须弥山高出水面八万四千由旬(梵语 yojana,其长度诸说,为十余里至数十里不等),山顶有三十三天宫,乃帝释天所居之处。本文书以须弥山譬喻功德,则是借用了佛教须弥山极高的特色。

见于第79颂的"阿罗汉"。突厥词 arxant 是间接借自梵语 arhat 的外来词,汉译佛经作阿罗汉、阿罗诃、阿卢汉等,简称罗汉,意译则作应供、杀贼、无生、无学、真人等,是指断尽三界见、思之惑,证得尽智,堪受世间大供养之圣者。狭义而言,阿罗汉只指小乘佛教中所获之最高果位;广义而言,则泛指大、小乘中的最高果位。同时,由于或称阿罗汉通摄三乘的无学果位,因此这也是佛陀的异名,亦即如来的十号之一。本文书以取得佛教的阿罗汉果来譬喻摩尼教修道者的成功,足见佛教色彩之浓烈。

见于第32颂的"六根"。突厥词组 altı qačıγ 对译的佛教术语是梵语 ṣaḍ indriyāṇi,汉译佛经作六根或六情,是指六种感觉器官或六种认识能力:眼(视觉器官)、耳(听觉器官)、鼻(嗅觉器官)、舌(味觉器官)、身(触觉器官)、意(思维器官)这样六根,具有视、听、嗅、味、触、思这样六种认识能力。佛教要求修

---

① 八热地狱之第六地狱"何故名为烧炙大地狱? 尔时,狱卒将诸罪人置铁城中,其城火然,内外俱赤,烧炙罪人,皮肉燋烂。苦痛辛酸,万毒并至,余罪未毕,故使不死。是故名为烧炙地狱";第七地狱"云何名大烧炙地狱? 其诸狱卒将诸罪人置铁城中,其城火然,内外俱赤,烧炙罪人,重大烧炙,皮肉燋烂。苦痛辛酸,万毒并至,余罪未毕,故使不死。是故名为大烧炙地狱";位列第八的无间地狱则"有大铁城,其城四面有大火起,东焰至西,西焰至东,南焰至北,北焰至南,上焰至下,下焰至上,焰炽回邅,无间空处。罪人在中,东西驰走,烧炙其身,皮肉燋烂,苦痛辛酸,万毒并至"。诸语并见[后秦]佛陀耶舍共竺佛念译《佛说长阿含经》卷十九《第四分世记经·地狱品第四》,《大正藏》第1册,第1号,第124页中、124页下、125页上,大正十三年六月版。

道者达到身心充满种种功德而清净,故有"六根清净"之说。

与"六根"关系密切的另一佛教术语是"六尘",本文书第 80 颂则以突厥词 fišay 对译梵语 viṣaya,这显然是直接移用了佛教梵语。汉译佛经将 viṣaya 译作尘、境或境界,此指分别引起"六根"之感觉思维作用的六种对象、境界,即色、声、香、味、触、法。由于这六种境界具有染污情识的作用,因此或以带有贬义的"尘"译称之。与"六尘"同时使用的还有另一个源自佛教的术语:突厥词 atqaγ,它对译梵语 vikalpa,汉译作妄想、妄想颠倒、虚妄分别,其义与妄念、妄执同,意谓以虚妄之心念去认识和理解诸法之相,于是产生错误的思想,遂远离一切法的真实义,远离觉悟境界。

以上所列,只是见于本文书的佛教术语的主要者,其他尚有不少常用佛教术语也见于此,如无常、有情、恶业、苦海、魔、功德海、慈悲、出家、无上正等觉、正遍知等等,以及佛教突厥语文书的习惯用语,由于大多在注释中加以简释,故在此不再重复。总的说来,本文书的佛教色彩的浓厚,是显而易见的。

三、《摩尼大颂》的摩尼教教义内涵辨析

尽管上文列举了本文书中使用的诸多佛教术语,显得相当"佛教化",但是,细加辨析,便不难发现,文书的撰编者基本上只是借用了佛教术语这一"躯壳",而在其中则换成了摩尼教自身的"灵魂"。今略举数例如下。

首先,尽管通篇有诸多的"佛"称,但读者很容易知道,"摩尼佛"清楚地是指其教主摩尼;"四佛"所指,乃是摩尼教神学中提及的琐罗亚斯德、耶稣等摩尼教神灵,并在其他文献中被称为先知,而非"佛";至于"佛土",则显然指的是摩尼教神学中的光明天堂"明界",这不会真被理解为佛教的"西方佛国"。

本文书中的"轮回"(突厥语 sansarta)虽然是梵语 saṃsāra 的直接移植,但是其细微含义实际上与佛教的"轮回"颇有区别;与之关系密切的"地狱"、"苦海"亦然。

在佛教看来,凡是在人世间犯错、犯罪的(包括不孝敬父母、不信教、杀生等等),都会因过错和罪行的大小而堕入各种地狱。所以,它的"地狱",主要是用来恐吓和惩罚现实世界中不好自为之的"恶人"的。此外,堕入三恶道之其他二道"鬼道"(= 饿鬼道)和"畜道"(= 畜生道)的人,也是因其人世间的罪、过而致;而在"三善道"(天、阿修罗、人)轮回的,则颇多生生世世积了"福德"的人。因此,佛教的轮回说实际上主要对俗世居民进行"劝善罚恶",旨在改善现实的社会环境。相应地,其"冥府"和"地狱"也主要是惩罚"坏人";易言之,并不反对在俗世为人,相反,却颇为鼓励。

然而,摩尼教最为厌恶和力图避免的"轮回",却是在现实世界中转世为人或其他生物;它所谓的"地狱"、"苦海"等等,指的也就是这个物质世界,并主要包括人类本身的躯体。例如,摩尼的教谕声称:

> 当恶人临终时,他被贪欲所主宰,魔鬼伴随着他,抓着他,斥骂他,向他展示恐怖之象。由于善神穿着同样的衣服出现在他面前,恶人便误以为他们是来拯救他的。然而,善神们却申斥他,使他想起自己的邪恶行为;善神并证实他从未帮助过选民。然后,恶人继续徘徊在这个世界上,遭受折磨,直到最后审判时,被投入地下黑狱。[①]

---

① *Fihrist*, Chapter Nine, p.796.

显然,对已死恶人的惩罚便是让他"继续徘徊在这个世界上,遭受折磨"。则摩尼教把灵魂的再世为人——即"轮回"——视作最大的痛苦;而"轮回"之所即是人间！这是与佛教的轮回观、地狱观截然不同之处。所以,不能因摩尼教文书借用了佛教的"轮回"术语,就混淆了二者的实际内涵。①

又,文书虽然声称日神"如佛一般",但他决不是指古印度的日神(即"日天"或"日天子",梵语 Āditya)或太阳神(梵语 Sūrya),以及佛教密宗的大日如来,而是特指摩尼教的某位主神,该神灵或为"夷数"(Jesus),或为三明使(the Third Messenger,亦作"第三使");当然,有时亦以其他次要神祇当之。不过,一般说来,是以三明使当日神,而以夷数当月神,亦即是说,主司日、月两"光明宫"的神或两"船"的"船主",分别是三明使和夷数。如《克弗来亚》所言:"他们将三明使称作'父尊'。他的伟大是他所生活的活灵火之光明舟,他在其中被创建。又,光辉夷数本人也被称为'父尊'。他的伟大是他所生活的活灵水之舟,他在其中被创建。"②在此,"活灵火之舟"与"活灵水之舟"分别是太阳与月亮的别称。

本文书中的"戒律"虽然借用了佛教的术语(突厥词 čxšapt 是梵语 śikṣāpada 的音译),但是其戒条的内容则完全属于摩尼教本身。如本文书逐一描述的那样,对于选民(摩尼教的专职修道者)的五条戒律分别是:不犯罪过、不犯不洁、身体净化、口净化,以及生活清贫,但快乐而幸福。此外,尚有针对听众(摩尼教的世俗修道者)的十项戒条:禁止崇拜偶像、不准撒谎、戒绝贪婪、不得杀生、禁绝淫欲、不得偷盗、不行邪道和巫术、不能对宗教信仰有异见、办事不得怠惰,以及每天祈祷四次或七次。③其中,三条针对口,三条针对心,三条针对手,一条针对身。

本文书多次使用佛教术语涅槃(nirvan)或般涅槃(frnibran),但是它们的含义毕竟有其摩尼教的特殊性。例如,见于吐鲁番的一份摩尼教帕提亚文书说道:"醒悟吧,弟兄们,尊神的选民,在精神获救之日,即密尔(Mihr)月的第十四天,是为尊神之子夷数进入涅槃之时。"④显然,夷数在此的"涅槃",是借用了基督教主神耶稣的"复活",而这一"涅槃"的意义也就是摩尼教徒所理解的"精神获救",亦即光明分子回归明界。又如,见于中亚的摩尼教帕提亚语文书中,还有一整套礼仪文书,称为《般涅槃颂诗》(*parnißbrānig bāšāhān*),专为纪念摩尼的去世,亦即前赴明界,在每年一度的庇麻节(Bema Festival)上唱颂,其中有"光明使者进入般涅槃,是痛苦之日和悲伤之时。他留下了领袖们,以庇护本教。他告别了大众。这位高贵神灵始终在履行着他亲口答应我们的诺言。"⑤所以,摩尼教文书中的"涅槃"通常是指俗世之神或信徒最终"回归明界"或"得救",其内涵自有本教的特色。

以上所述,是本文书使用的佛教术语之形式后面隐藏的摩尼教教义;另一方面,文书中还有不少名称和术语,本身的形式就是摩尼教或非佛的,如五重天(可能是摩尼教"十天"中的上面五层天)、福音书(摩尼所撰七书中的《生命福音》)、三印(摩尼教信条的象征符号)等,则它们都展示了典型的摩尼教含义。

至于有的句式,初看之下并无什么特异之处,但实际上是摩尼教神学内涵的体现,例如,本文书第 81 颂有"你露现自己的本相,改变你的状貌"之说,其实是指摩尼教高级神灵的一种奇特能力。盖按摩尼教

①　有关佛教与摩尼教之轮回观、地狱观之区别的详细论述,可参看拙文《摩尼教"平等王"与"轮回"考》,《史林》2003 年第 6 期。

②　*Kephalaia*, Ch. XX, 63^{35}~64^{4}, p.66.

③　*Fihrist*, Chapter IX, p.789. 但是,此文献只列了九条戒律;第十条戒律则据 *Manichees*, p.61 补入。

④　文书号 M 104,原文转写见 *Reader*, text, bx, p.127. 英译文见 Hans-J. Klimkeit, *Jesus Entry into Parinirvāna: Manichaean Identity in Buddhist Central Asia*, p.225, *Numen*, Vol. 33, 1986.

⑤　文书号 M 5,英译文见 *Mani: Personality*, p.240。

创世神话,大明尊第二次"召唤"出净风(Living Spirit)在创造天地时,曾"对暗魔诸子露现出本相,并将它们吞自五明子的光明分子净化,制成了太阳、月亮,以及千万颗明星"。又,大明尊第三次"召唤"出的三明使(the Third Messenger)也曾在半空中"露现出本相,男身和女身,为一切雌、雄暗魔所见。暗魔见到三明使的美丽相貌后,全都性欲大盛,雄魔垂涎于女身,雌魔贪恋于男身,于是全都喷泄出它们此前吞自五明子的光明分子"。①

在此的"露现本相"一词,叙利亚语原文作 ṣūrāthēh,有揭露、暴露、显露等义。从三明使之"露现本相"看,当即裸体,因为这样才能引发诸魔的性欲;至于净风,虽未见诱惑诸魔的描述,但从此后"净化光明分子"的做法来看,似乎也与三明使一样,是诱其因性欲过盛而"泄出"的,或许只是原文曾经有意无意地略作删节而已。所以,这是摩尼教诸神的"露现本相"能力。此外,三明使既能现男身,也能现女身,便是"改变状貌"的能力了。

四、小　结

通过以上的考释和辨析,可以得到如下几点结论:

第一,摩尼教自创立之始,就融入了不少佛教因素,但在传播至中亚以及更东地区之后,其佛教色彩更为浓重。这与佛教在当地流行的时间更早、更普及有着密切的关系。

第二,摩尼教突厥语文书《摩尼大颂》约成于公元 10 世纪初期,亦即契丹政权太祖(907～926)执政的那段时期内,②而当时距离佛教初传中国内地也已经八九百年了,佛教在中亚地区之传播则时间更为久远。所以,成于吐鲁番盆地的《摩尼大颂》受到佛教的巨大影响是势在必行的;该文书的许多佛教术语都移植自突厥语佛经,便是极好的证明。

第三,尽管突厥语《摩尼大颂》在形式上有意无意地借用了大量佛教术语乃至佛教概念,但是其内藏的含义仍然可以辨别出摩尼教神学;另一方面,也确实还保持了不少摩尼教本身的术语和句式。所以,总的说来,这类文书的"佛教化"并未从根本上改变其文化要素。

第四,无可否认的是,东方的摩尼教为了传教的方便,十分积极主动地利用当地的语言和文化来传布本教教义,这是摩尼教得以迅速普及的重要原因之一。然而,一个很大的负面影响是,毕竟形式上浓厚的佛教色彩会误导信众,特别是普通的新皈依的徒众,更不易辨别和领会"佛经"形式后面所隐藏的摩尼教教义,因此,摩尼教的"原始教义"逐步走样、歪曲乃至消失,也就不足为怪了。这或许正是摩尼教比较特殊的传播方式的悲剧所在。

略　语　表

APAW

Abhandlungen der preussischen Akademie der Wissenschaften

---

① 见成于约公元 8 世纪的叙利亚语 *Mani's Teachings*, pp. 236－237, 244。

② 此说源出葛玛丽,见 *Pothi-Book*, p. 160;但是克林凯特则归之于 13 或 14 世纪的蒙古人时期(见 *Gnosis*, p. 280)。似以前说为是。

BSOAS

Bulletin of the School of Oriental and African Studies

Etymological Dictionary

Sir Gerard Clauson, *An Etymological Dictionary of Pre-Thirteenth-Century Turkish*, Oxford, 1972.

Fihrist

Bayard Dodge, *The Fihrist of al-Nadīm — A Tenth-Century Survey of Muslim Culture*, Volume 1, Chapter IX, Section I, "Manichaeans", Columbia University Press, 1970.

Giants

W. B. Henning, *The Book of the Giants*, in BSOAS, XI, 1943, pp. 52 – 74; also *W. B. Henning Selected Papers II* (Acta Iranica 15), Leiden, 1977, pp. 115 – 137.

Gnosis

Hans-Joachim Klimkeit, *Gnosis on the Silk Road: Gnostic texts from Central Asia*, New York, 1993.

Kephalaia

Iain Gardner, *The Kephalaia of the Teacher — The Edited Coptic Manichaean Texts in Translation with Commentary*, E. J. Brill, Leiden, 1995.

Manichees

F. C. Burkitt, *The Religion of the Manichees*, London, Cambridge University Press, 1925.

Mani: Personality

Lodewijk Josephus Rudolf Ort, *Mani: A Religio-Hostorical Description of His Personality*, E. J. Brill, Leiden, 1967.

Mani's Teachings

Theodore Bar Khoni (c. 800 A. D.), *On Mānī's Teachings Concerning the Beginning of the World* (tr. From the Syriac by Dr. Abraham Yohannan, in Jackson, *Researches*, pp. 221 – 254).

Pothi-Book

Larry V. Clark, *The Manichean Turkic Pothi-Book*, Altorientalische Forschungen, IX, 1982, Berlin.

Reader

Mary Boyce, *A Reader in Manichaean Middle Persian and Parthian*, E. J. Brill, Leiden, 1975.

Researches

A. V. Williams Jackson, *Researches in Manichaeism — with Special Reference to the Turfan Fragments*, New York Columbia University Press, 1932.

Word-List

Mary Boyce, *A Word-List of Manichaean Middle Persian and Parthian* (Acta Iranica, 9a), E. J. Brill, Leiden, 1977.

高昌摩尼教圣像艺术之宗教功能辨析

王媛媛

中山大学历史学系博士后

引　言

本文题目所用"圣像"一词,盖类于西文之 icon(源自希腊语 eikōn)。按 icon 一词的意义很宽泛,指东欧和中东的基督教徒所崇拜的所有神像。它与神像的制作材料无关,可以是石质或金属雕塑、壁画或纸画等,即从形态上,包括立体的偶像和平面的画像。西文的 idolatry,一般被汉译为"偶像崇拜"。而在宗教学上,idolatry 的概念最初来源于一个特殊的历史宗教环境:以色列的一神论。它指的是人对神的替代品的崇拜,即对由人制造出来的神的形象的崇拜,而这个"神的替代品"自然包括了偶像或画像,其代替了对无形的造物主的崇拜。[①] 由于在汉语中,"偶像"和"画像"毕竟是两个不同的词汇,有不能互替的明显区别,因此,通常用"偶像崇拜"来对译 idolatry,便不免略欠谨严。职是之故,本文拟用"圣像崇拜"来对译 idolatry,庶几能更准确地反映该词的本来含义,也可避免与当今世俗意义的偶像崇拜混淆。按"崇拜"一词,其宗教意义和世俗意义也是有区别的,前者指的是礼仪,即用某种宗教仪式,诸如祈祷、祭祀、顶礼膜拜等方式来表达对神的敬畏或自己的愿望;后者不过是表示对人对物的高度敬重或依赖。本文讨论所采用"崇拜"一词的内涵,自指前者。

不少宗教,都有自己的圣像系列,其中或为本教所崇拜的神,或为本教的创立者、本教历史上的领袖或杰出人物等等,不一而足。本文所要探讨的高昌摩尼教,根据考古发现的该教艺术残存,可窥见其确实也有圣像系列的存在。不过,该等圣像多已残缺不全,或模糊不清,而且数量很有限;加之笔者学力不逮,要对其进行全面考察,实无可能,故本文仅拟从宗教功能的角度,在既往学者研究的基础上进行讨论。讨论的重点是:该等圣像究竟是如某些学者所认为那样,作宗教仪式崇拜之用,抑或只限于宗教宣传。

一、摩尼教绘制神灵画像的传统

吐鲁番出土的摩尼教赞美诗《胡威达曼》(*Huyadagmān*)曾警示其他的圣像崇拜者:"没有任何期望和幸福的抚慰会来帮助处于炼狱般境地中的他们……没有任何一个(他们的)偶像、圣坛或神像,会把他

[①] *The Encyclopedia of Religion* Vol. 7, New York: Macmillan Publishing Company, 1987, pp. 67, 73. 又,《宗教大辞典》中将"偶像崇拜"释为:对所奉之神灵塑造其形象而加以崇拜。详见任继愈主编《宗教大辞典》,上海辞书出版社,1998 年,第 582 页。

们从地狱中解救出来。"①一篇针对圣像崇拜者的辩论文痛斥"这世间被误导（他们）的偶像、被墙上由木石（制成）的形象所惑乱。他们畏惧欺妄，他们膜拜它、礼敬它。他们已抛弃天堂的明父，向欺妄祈祷"。② 在摩尼教中，"欺妄"（wiftagīh，或"诳语"）被视为圣像崇拜的共性，是十二黑暗领土（或十二种邪恶本性）之一。③ 因此，这实际是在告诫人们，偶像是一种误导和欺骗，而崇拜它的那些异教徒"会进地狱，因为他们自身就是罪孽的根源和作恶者的祸因（?）……到最后，世界末日那天，他们会蒙受耻辱，所有崇拜偶像的人，他们终将走向灭亡"。④ 这些严厉抨击圣像崇拜的言论，均出自高昌摩尼教会，这不仅说明该教在入华之后的高昌仍抄录、保留着原始教义，同时，也从宗教经典的层面体现了高昌教徒应该依旧遵守着不拜圣像的戒律。

克里木凯特曾以泉州草庵雕像的存在为唯一凭据，上溯至高昌时期，认为当时也已存在用于膜拜的摩尼塑像。⑤ 可事实上，在吐鲁番出土的该教细画、壁画等艺术品中，至今尚未发现一例塑像。我们推测，教中诸神的形象在当时的高昌教会中，可能还没有被塑成圣像供人膜拜。当然，排除了塑像的可能性之后，还应考虑到摩尼教的光明诸神仍有可能在绘画作品中被保留下来，并流传于高昌教会之中。

擅长绘画的渊源可追溯至摩尼本人，他曾亲著"大门荷翼图一，译云《大二宗图》"。⑥尽管叙利亚基督教神父 Ephraem 恶意攻击："摩尼也用颜料在纸卷上作画——据他的一些门徒所说——他所画的是自己思想中邪恶的东西。"他的画催生了这种备受谴责的信仰。⑦ 但历史学家 Mīrxond 仍客观地评价摩尼是独一无二的画家，并给我们讲述了一则传说：摩尼在东方旅行时发现了一个山洞，仅有一个出口，洞外林壑幽美。他悄悄地将一年所需的食物放入洞中，然后告诉随行弟子："我将去天堂一年，十二个月后再回来，并将神的启示带给你们。来年初就在此处等我。"于是，他进入山洞用一年的时间作画，并称之为摩尼教的阿达罕（Ardahang）。当他再次现身于人前，手中便拿着一本画册，色彩绚丽，幅帙繁多，震惊了所有的人。摩尼宣称："这是我从天堂带来的预言。"从此，人们皈依了他。⑧ 既是神启福音，那它自然是一本摩尼教宇宙神学的完整图解，亦即摩尼将原本复杂的神学体系用直观的艺术手法予以简化。

《克弗来亚》记载，摩尼在画册中描绘了犯有罪孽的人堕入地狱，正直的选民上升光明王国的命运，却不画一般听者的形象。⑨ 然而，我们在吐鲁番的摩尼教艺术品中发现了很多回鹘听者、供养人，且穿着多似贵族官员，而非寻常百姓。这一有悖于教主原意的变化，体现了高昌教会在回鹘羽翼之下，对于统治

① M. Boyce, *The Manichaean Hymn-Cycles in Parthian*, Oxford University Press, 1954, pp. 62 -65; D. N. MacKenzie, "Two Sogdian Hwydgm'n Fragments", *Acta Iranica* 25, 1985, pp. 421 -428; H.-J. Klimkeit, *Gnosis on the Silk Road: Gnostic Parables, Hymns & Prayers from Central Asia*, New York, 1993, p.104.

② 文书编号 M 28, M. Boyce, *A Reader in Manichaean Middle Persian and Parthian*, Téhéran-Liège: Bilbliothèque Pahlavi; Leiden: E. J. Brill, 1975, p.174; H.-J. Klimkeit, *Gnosis on the Silk Road: Gnostic Parables, Hymns & Prayers from Central Asia*, p.126.

③ 在帕提亚语文书 M 34 中提到了"十二黑暗领土（或十二种邪恶本性）"的伊朗语名称。参 F. C. Andreas & W. B. Henning, "Mitteliranische Manichaica aus chinesisch-Turkestan II", *Sitzungsberichte der (Königlich-) Preussischen Akademie der Wissenschaften Philosophisch-Historische Klasse*, Berlin, 1933, pp. 311f; H.-J. Klimkeit & Schmidt-Glintzer, "Die türkischen Parallelen zum chinesisch-manichäischen Traktat", *Zentralasiatische Studien* 17, Wiesbaden, 1984, p.114.

④ M. Boyce, *A Reader in Manichaean Middle Persian and Parthian*, pp.174 -175; H.-J. Klimkeit, *Gnosis on the Silk Road: Gnostic Parables, Hymns & Prayers from Central Asia*, p.127.

⑤ H.-J. Klimkeit, "the Fair Form, the Hideous Form and the Transformed Form: on the Form Principle in Manichaeism", M. Heuser & H.-J. Klimkeit, *Studies in Manichaean Literature and Art*, Brill, 1998, p.149.

⑥ 《摩尼光佛教法仪略》"经图仪第三"，林悟殊：《摩尼教及其东渐》，台北：淑馨出版社，1997年，第285页。

⑦ Lodewijk Josephus Rudolf Ort, *Mani. A Religio-Historical Description of His Personality*, Brill, 1967, p.32.

⑧ Geo Widengren, *Mani and Manichaeism*, p.109; 克里木凯特著，林悟殊译《古代摩尼教艺术》，第39页。

⑨ Iain Gardner, *The Kephalaia of the Teacher*, pp. 241 -242.

者的政治庇护,必须回馈以宗教利益,更为重视听者。目前,尚无确凿证据可证明此画册中是否有摩尼的自画形象,但既然他宣称自己是继琐罗亚斯德、释迦牟尼、耶稣之后的第四位先知,[①]作为上天派入世间传布"灵知"(gnosis)的神使,按常理而言,应当会在这本画册中有所体现。因此,创教伊始,摩尼教会中便已存在光明诸神的平面形象,他们均有客观模样可寻,并非虚无缥缈。同时,摩尼既已宣扬不拜圣像,那么,他图画神像的本心就定然不是要使之成为信众崇拜的对象,或后世教会塑制圣像的粉本,而是为了让人们更易于理解其深奥教义。尽管摩尼教没有塑制圣像的传统,但教会中流传有神灵的画像确是事实,由是,我们便不能排除后世教徒绘制神灵(包括摩尼)画像进行崇拜的可能性,毕竟,如前所述,对着画像进行礼拜也可算作圣像崇拜的一种形式。

二、庇麻节仪式中的"宝座"

唯一可能与摩尼画像有关的宗教仪式是为纪念摩尼殉道,于每年十二月底或斋月的最后[②]举行的庇麻节。奥古斯丁曾记录下西方摩尼教中庇麻节仪式的相关场景:"……你们向庇麻(祭日)致以崇高的敬意,那天即摩尼的殉道日,你们立了一个有五层阶梯的台子,用贵重的幕布覆盖住,它的位置醒目,面向礼拜者……"[③]这个五层台就是"庇麻"(Bema,希腊语"宝座"之义),审判者的圣座。它象征着已去世的摩尼仍活在选民之中,他将代替夷数,直到后者以审判者的身份重新降临人间。[④] 一种观点认为,在空着的圣座上可能摆放着摩尼的画像,[⑤]另一种观点则认为上面放的应该是那本摩尼画册。[⑥] 这两者的依据应该都是摩尼教科普特语布道文,因为文中将庇麻与摩尼的图画(drawings)[⑦]联系在一起:

① Hans Jonas, *The Gnostic Religion: The Message of the Alien God and the Beginnings of Christianity*, Boston, 1963, p. 207. 详参粟特语摩尼教譬喻文书 T III T 601(Ch/U 6914)、T III 2015[So. 15000(5)]及 T II D 2(Ch 5554)上的阐述,见 W. Sundermann, *Ein manichäisch-soghdisches Parabelbuch, mit einem Anhang von Friedmar Geissler über Erzählmotive in der Geschichte von den zwei Schlangen.* (*Berliner Turfantexte XV*), Berlin, 1985, pp. 19 – 36.

② Geo Widengren, *Mani and Manichaeism*, London:Weidenfeld and Nicolson Ltd., 1965, p. 103; Christiane Reck, *Gesegnet sei dieser Tag. Manichäische Festtagshymnen. Edition der mittelpersischen und parthischen Sonntags-, Montags- und Bemahymnen.* (*Berliner Turfantexte XXII*), Brepole, 2004, p. 28. 但这一日期根据的是科普特语赞美诗,而非东方摩尼教文献,因此还可作进一步探讨,而各地教会也可能有不同的时间安排。见 W. Sundermann, "Manichaean Festivals", E. Yarshater (ed.), *Enıran IX*, Costa Mesa, 1999, p. 548. 确实,从10世纪后半期开始,高昌的摩尼教徒将庇麻节往后推迟一个月,将其作为粟特新年的一部分予以庆祝,见 Y. Yoshida, "Buddhist Influence on the Bema Festival?" C. G. Cereti, M. Maggi & E. Provasi (eds.), *Religious Themes and Texts of Pre-Islamic Iran and Central Asia*, Wiesbaden, 2003, pp. 453 – 458.

③ *Corpus Scriptorum Ecclesiasticorum Latinorum*, V25/1, pp. 202 – 203, Vienna, 1891 – 1892. 转引自 I. Gardner & S. N. C. Lieu (eds.), *Manichaean Texts from the Roman Empire*, Cambridge University Press, 2004, p. 237. 这是奥古斯丁在探询摩尼教会中选民与听者的不同地位和待遇时记录下来的。

④ Geo Widengren, *Mani and Manichaeism*, p. 104; Iain Gardner, *The Kephalaia of the Teacher*, E. J. Brill, 1995, p. xxxvi.

⑤ 此说见于 C. R. C. Allberry & H. Ibscher (ed.), *A Manichaean Psalm-Book II* (Manichaean Manuscripts in the Chester Beatty II), Stuttgart, 1938. 博伊斯表示赞同,M. Boyce, *A Reader in Manichaean Middle Persian and Parthian*, p. 12;这一观点后来逐渐被多数学者所认同,见 J. Ries, "La fête de Bêma dans l' Église de Mani", *Revue des études Augustiniennes XXII*, Paris, 1976, p. 220; H. -Ch. Puech, *Sur le manichéisme et autres essais*, Paris, 1979, p. 391; H. -J. Klimkeit, *Gnosis on the Silk Road: Gnostic Parables, Hymns & Prayers from Central Asia*, New York, 1993, p. 145; Iain Gardner, *The Kephalaia of the Teacher*, p. xxxvi; W. Sundermann, "Manichaeism meets Buddhism: The Problem of Buddhist Influence on Manichaeism," P. Kieffer-Pülz & J. -U. Hartmann (eds.), *Bauddhavidyāsudhākarah. Studies in Honour of Heinz Bechert on the Occasion of His 65th Birthday*, Swisttal-Odendorf, 1997, p. 655.

⑥ Lodewijk Josephus Rudolf Ort, *Mani. A Religio-Historical Description of His Personality*, pp. 252 – 255.

⑦ 鉴于上述两种观点的分歧就在于对 drawings 的理解不同(前者认为它指的是摩尼的肖像,后者认为是摩尼亲手绘制的图画),此处笔者暂以"图画"这一笼统名词进行汉译。

……看啊,另一簇光明分子

将在那时被挑选出来。

数以千万的即将降临,并被召唤。

从那时起,庇麻将光芒四射……

在所有市镇。伟大的图画……

福音和书……

通过新一代的口口相传,将熠熠生辉,

即将到来并降生于世间。

许多(人)将坐在他的图画前;

其他将……他的庇麻……①

他,已揭示了……

他的是这庇麻;他坐在上面……

他的是这被赞颂的庇麻;他的脸庞是……

(图画)。他的是这图画……

……他挑选了他的选民……

……他的是这智慧,这庇麻和……②

其实,研究者们借此为据的同时,便已承认庇麻与摩尼图画一起出现在上下文中的例子实属罕见,③摩尼教经文中没有何种仪式里需膜拜圣典的记载,且上文内容并不完整。但,既然庇麻是摩尼以末日审判者身份降临人间而坐的圣座,那么,与一本画册相比,放上纪念对象——摩尼的肖像似乎更合情合理一些。但无论如何,相比于庇麻座的确实存在,学者们对其上还放有画像或圣典的猜测均无法得到证实。即便当时的庇麻座上果然置有摩尼画像,可科普特摩尼教会的活动时期太早,我们不能无视后期东西方教会在传播过程中出现的变异,并断言高昌教会的庇麻座上也有画像。况且,在摩尼教会中生活长达九年的奥古斯丁,于前引记载中也并未言及画像之事。用古代科普特语经文来证明后来庇麻节仪式,尤其是吐鲁番地区的实际情况,难以令人折服。

高昌城 α 寺遗址出土的一幅细画,即 **III 4979 b**④ 背面(图一)为我们真实描绘了庇麻节的场景。画面顶部有一个台子,上覆红布,现仅存其下端。它是整幅画的重点所在,一般认为此台即为庇麻宝座。画面偏左的三分之一处,紧挨着宝座坐着一人,身穿摩尼教白袍,有华丽的金色花纹镶边。他左手前臂抬

---

① H. J. Polotsky (ed.), *Manichäische Homilien. Manichäische Handschriften der Sammlung A. Chester Beatty* I., Stuttgart, 1934, p. 27, L16 - 25.

② H. J. Polotsky (ed.), *Manichäische Homilien. Manichäische Handschriften der Sammlung A. Chester Beatty* I., p. 33, L17 - 22.

③ Lodewijk Josephus Rudolf Ort, *Mani. A Religio-Historical Description of His Personality*, p. 254.

④ 见克里木凯特著,林悟殊译《古代摩尼教艺术》图版 21,台北:淑馨出版社,1995 年,释文见第 63 ~ 65 页;Z. Gulácsi, *Manichaean Art in Berlin Collection*, Brepols, 2001, p. 71. 该残片编号原为 MIK III 4979 b,MIK 即柏林印度艺术博物馆(Museum für Indische Kunst)的首字母缩写,表明残片现在的收藏地点。但因印度艺术博物馆和东亚艺术博物馆(Museum of East Asian Art)已于 2006 年 12 月合并为新的柏林亚洲艺术博物馆(Museum für Asiatische Kunst, Staatliche Museen zu Berlin),新馆藏品的编号不再使用以前的 MIK 标识,下文所涉之其他原藏于印度艺术博物馆的摩尼教绘画残片亦如此。

起,手掌摊开,两腿趺坐在一个饰以红布的大垫子上。头部虽已残缺,仅余一边脸颊、白发和长胡须,但仍可看出有头光环绕。他极有可能是当时高昌教会中的最高领袖——慕阇。他的左边跪坐着三个人。偏外侧两人的形象已残损,暂不讨论。另一人面目可辨,头有光环。在台子另一边还有一白衣人,似乎一手举起。在他的右边隔了一些距离处,跪坐一人。有光环和举手者都位于画面上端,靠近庇麻宝座和慕阇,他们的形象与别不同,身份恐高于一般选民。画面正中绘有一金属质三足器,满满地盛放着瓜和葡萄。其下方的一个红桌子上有一堆扁平状、边缘雕花的圆面包。桌子脚的左边有一镀金水罐,右边是一个装着某种食物的带足镀金盘。画面中部偏右跪坐着三个白衣选民,手中拿着镶金的书本,头仰起朝着慕阇的方向。最上面的一个选民将一本翻开的书举至下巴处,其余两人则把书笼于胸前。画面下部三分之二处为三排选民和听者。他们紧密地跪坐在一起,均着白衣白帽,有的选民胸襟前写有本人的名字。

与此画类似的覆有红布的台子,在另外三幅摩尼教绘画中也有出现。同为 α 寺遗址出土的被称为"布道(说法)图"的细画(编号 III 8259,图二)。[①]画面似可分为三个层次:最下方是六位听者,三男三女各分两侧跪坐。他们的上方绘有向左右延伸的枝叶,分别承托着两个莲花座,座上有两位白衣选民。选民的上方中央另有一莲花座,放了一个"X"形金色支架,其上用红布遮盖着一个物体,似呈"凸"字形。勒柯克认为是庇麻,上置摩尼画像。[②]而克里木凯特认为可能是一本书。[③]从"凸"形物的位置来看,它显然是画中最为尊贵重要的,是听者与选民共同礼敬的东西;再综观其被覆盖的状态、盖布的颜色,可见其功用当与 III 4979 b 中的庇麻座相似。高昌城(具体地点不详)出土的 III 6265 & III 4966c 正面(图三)[④]也绘有一相同的"凸"形物。画面最下方有一小水塘,枝叶从水中长出,上托一莲花座,"凸"形物便放在座上。其右有一白衣选民,手式与 III 8259 相同。莲座左边人物已失,仅余其身下垫毯的一角,但应该也是一位选民。该画的构图方式、人物姿势、花叶饰纹与 III 8259 几乎完全一样,只是残损更为严重而已。我们认为这里的"凸"形物应该也是庇麻座。

此外,木头沟出土的 III 8260 正面(图四),[⑤]也有一红布遮盖住的"凸"形物。该画为一菩提书式样的摩尼教忏悔文扉页。画面分为两层:下层左右两边跪坐着两个选民,中间有一状似香炉的东西。上层占了整个画面的三分之二。两颗花树下跪着一位选民,闭着双眼(或垂视下方),两手紧握于腹前,低着头,身体稍微往左,倾向一个用红布盖住的"凸"形物。其白冠则挂在身后右边的树枝上。脱冠的选民形象非常罕见,吐鲁番出土摩尼教艺术品中的选民,不论男女,均白衣白冠、穿戴严谨。因此,画中脱冠选民的形象定然不是画者随手为之,而是有所寓意。头冠在摩尼教中是获得拯救的象征,[⑥]没有头冠即代表无法得到拯救,而究其原因则是犯有罪孽。其实,从画中选民低头和垂下眼睑的神态、脸部表情、微俯的姿势以及手式来看,似在做忏悔。此画为摩尼教突厥语菩提书的一幅插图,书中除了摩尼赞美诗外,也包

---

①　Z. Gulácsi, *Manichaean Art in Berlin Collection*, pp. 56–61;克里木凯特则认为这是"忏悔图",见氏著,林悟殊译:《古代摩尼教艺术》图版 27,释文见第 70~71 页。

②　A. Von Le Coq, *Die buddhistische Spätantike Mittelasiens*, II. *Die Manichäischen Miniaturen*, Berlin: D. Reimer, 1923, p. 48.

③　克里木凯特著,林悟殊译《古代摩尼教艺术》,第 70 页。克里木凯特虽未明言是摩尼画册,但其观点当与 L. J. Rudolf Ort 相同。

④　Z. Gulácsi, *Manichaean Art in Berlin Collection*, pp. 62–65.

⑤　克里木凯特将该画名为"跪着的宗教人士或圣徒",见氏著,林悟殊译《古代摩尼教艺术》图版 29,释文见第 72 页;Z. Gulácsi 对其意义及性质未做判断,见 *Manichaean Art in Berlin Collection*, pp. 152–154.

⑥　H. -J. Klimkeit, "Temporal and Spiritual Power in Central Asian Manichaeism", M. Heuser & H. -J. Klimkeit, *Studies in Manichaean Literature and Art*, p. 230. 关于摩尼教中"冠"的含义,下文即有详述,此处不赘。

括忏悔文,此图或许正为配合内容而作。① 画中"凸"形物的位置虽异于前述三幅图,但形状确实相同。因此,笔者将之归于一类加以考量。

另有一幅细画 III 6257,②出土于高昌城 K 寺遗址。其背面(图五)左边绘有两个选民,仅残存头部。选民旁边至少放着两个容器,一个盛着石榴和葡萄,另一个堆满了与 III 4979 b 中相同的扁平状、边缘雕花的圆面包。容器上方还残留一红色台状物的下部。这一场景,包括物体的位置和颜色,都让我们想到了庇麻节图。③ 那么,台状物已缺的上半部分可能也放着一个红布覆盖的庇麻座。

上述四幅吐鲁番出土的摩尼教细画不仅涉及庇麻节,还包括了布道、忏悔等仪式,而这些仪式中都出现了庇麻座。此座用红布盖着,是否仍如奥古斯丁所言有五层阶,不得而知。但时空相差甚远,即便有所不同也在情理之中。新疆曾出土大量佛座(或称王座),分垫座型和莲花型。其中,有正面带双层垫及长菱形图案的方形高垫座,有平面呈椭圆形、正视图为"X"形佛座,还有楼梯状的台座。④ 众所周知,摩尼教借用了许多佛教的艺术表现符号:莲花座、树和宝珠等,⑤那么,佛陀的宝座是否对摩尼的庇麻座也有些许借鉴意义,或可作进一步的推敲。

"凸"形物用红布覆盖,其上并不见有画像。若定要用前辈学者所试图论证的"庇麻座上放有摩尼画像"这一观点来硬套高昌的模式,那么,唯一的解释就是画像和宝座一起被遮在了布下,可这种解释是无法说通的。覆盖画像使其不为徒众所见,抹杀了神像本应具有的沟通人神的宗教职能。制造圣像的目的,就是要人们领会神灵世界,对彼岸世界产生真实的感受。⑥ 一个不能被看到的圣像怎能使信众领悟到其中的玄奥,生出真实而热忱的宗教情感,这显然不是圣像制作者的初衷。而一幅不能被看到的画像,也同时失去了在其面前进行礼拜的意义。更有,带摩尼画像的庇麻座屡屡出现,反映了它在高昌教会的仪式中占有相当重要的地位,并表明教会不仅在一年一度纪念摩尼的庇麻节上要膜拜教主画像,而且,在日常的布道、忏悔等仪式中也要在信徒面前奉上摩尼画像。若真是如此,那这一宗教实践有悖于高昌摩尼教经典中的戒律,与严厉驳斥偶像崇拜者的说教自相矛盾,僧侣们在抄录经文或宣讲教义时,又如何能自圆其说。因此,在高昌的摩尼教会中,红布覆盖着的可能只是一个庇麻座,并无摩尼画像。空着的圣座象征末日审判或审判者,在仪式中出现或许只是警示信徒,必须虔诚地祈祷、忏悔、静思,获得"灵知",谨守戒律,以期在末日来临时顺利通过审判,升入光明王国。正如汉文《下部赞》所云:"戒行威仪恒坚固,持斋礼拜及赞诵。身口意业恒清净,歌呗法王无间歇。"⑦

高昌摩尼教会的庇麻节上,教徒虽举行礼拜仪式,但他们所礼拜的对象只是一个象征末日拯救的摩尼宝座,并非摩尼的画像。显然,这种有崇拜而无圣像的形式不能被视为圣像崇拜。

---

① 勒柯克认为该画属于摩尼教晚期作品,具有中国风格的影响。画面色彩暗淡,且无摩尼教常见的天青色背景。克拉克(L. V. Clark)则认为,该画是保存至今的少数几幅佛教细画之一,只是很蹩脚地模仿了摩尼教的原型。见 L. V. Clark, "The Manichaean Turkic Pothi-Book", *Altorientalische Forschungen* IX, Berlin, 1982, p.149.

② Z. Gulácsi, *Manichaean Art in Berlin Collection*, p.77.

③ J. D. BeDuhn, *The Manichaean Body*, Baltimore: The Johns Hopkins University Press, 2000, p.257; Z. Gulácsi, *Manichaean Art in Berlin Collection*, p.76.

④ 查娅·帕塔卡娅(Chhaya Bhattacharya)著,许建英译《中亚艺术(附丝路北道木器参考)》,《中亚佛教艺术》,乌鲁木齐:新疆美术摄影出版社,1992 年,第 144、149、233 页。

⑤ H. -J. Klimkeit,"Adaptations to Buddhism in East Iranian and Central Asian Manichaeism"; idem, "Indian Motivs in Manichaean Art", M. Heuser & H. -J. Klimkeit, *Studies in Manichaean Literature and Art*, pp. 237 - 253, pp. 291 - 299.

⑥ 蒋卓述:《宗教艺术论》,广州:暨南大学出版社,1998 年,第 205 页。

⑦ 《下部赞》释文,林悟殊:《摩尼教及其东渐》,台北:淑馨出版社,1997 年,第 305 页。

三、壁画中的摩尼形象

尽管供人礼敬的庇麻圣座上没有摩尼的画像,但高昌教会中确实存在摩尼的形象。对此,我们从高昌城 K 寺遗址出土的一块大型壁画上可得一见。

现存的高昌古城遗址由外城、内城和"可汗堡"(即回鹘王国的宫城)三大部分组成。内城除了"可汗堡"外,现存遗址绝大部分都是寺院。① 其中著名的、已确认的摩尼教遗址是城西南部的 α 寺和位于城中心、处在连接东西城门的大道之上的 K 寺。

K 寺是由勒柯克(A. von Le Coq)领导的第二次吐鲁番探险重点发掘的对象。它几乎在高昌城正中心,与北部中央位置上的回鹘王宫相对。城中有一条南北向大道横穿而过,它正是沿着"可汗堡"的城墙一直到达 K 寺。该遗址约 75 米见方,②但这只是该建筑群的北部和西部,整个遗址群范围很广,往东应该还有很大的一片建筑,但已基本被毁坏,③仅存有一组被勒柯克称之为"藏书室"的建筑。在这一"藏书室"及其走廊中出土很多摩尼教遗物。沿着 K 的北边有一建筑,在其中的一个穹顶屋里发现了被残酷杀害的佛僧干尸。该建筑的西面有一个桶状拱顶的小房间,也出土了大量的摩尼教丝织物和写本残片。④

在这次发掘中,该遗址所出摩尼教残片数量最多,⑤据博伊斯的《柏林藏吐鲁番出土摩尼教文献目录》,这些残片内容相当丰富,包括用中古波斯文、帕提亚文、粟特文和回鹘文书写的各种诗歌,如摩尼赞美诗、夷数赞美诗、第三使赞美诗、庇麻节赞美诗、涅槃赞美诗、祈愿诗、主教赞美诗、主教就职赞美诗等,还有《克弗来亚》、《阿达罕》释文、摩尼写给阿莫的书信(此系中亚教徒伪造)、忏悔仪式文、故事、术语表、布道文和咒语文书等非诗歌类文献,以及壁画、细画、旗幡、丝画等艺术品。此外,由于很多摩尼教文书的编号不够明晰,使得其真正的出土地无法确定。可能出土于 K 的还有创世论文书、传教史文书、譬喻经等。以上内容几乎囊括了宗教文献的各个方面,因此,当时的 K 寺藏书室里一定收藏了大量且内容完备、齐全的各种宗教书籍。K 寺是内城中除王宫外最重要的建筑遗迹,从其所在位置、占地面积和规模,以及所拥有的精美宗教壁画大厅,还有收藏了大量宗教经卷的藏书室来看,它应该是摩尼教在回鹘时期的王家寺院。⑥

遗址中心有三个主大厅,呈南北向一字排开。⑦ 南厅最大,北厅最小。⑧绘有摩尼形象的大型壁画(编号 III 6918,画面 168.5×88 cm,图六)就在中厅西墙上。他后方是按一定等级次序排列的众多选民和听

---

① 孟凡人:《高昌城形制初探》,《中亚学刊》第 5 辑,1996 年,第 37、49 页。

② [法] 莫尼克·玛雅尔著,耿昇译《古代高昌王国物质文明史》,北京:中华书局,1995 年,第 89、105 页;勒柯克著,陈海涛译:《新疆的地下文化宝藏》,乌鲁木齐:新疆人民出版社,1999 年,第 45 页。

③ 勒柯克著,赵崇民译《高昌——吐鲁番古代艺术珍品》,乌鲁木齐:新疆人民出版社,1998 年,第 15 页。

④ A. von Le Coq, *Die buddhistische Spätantike Mittelasiens*, II. *Die Manichäischen Miniaturen*, pp. 25 – 27.

⑤ M. Boyce, *Catalogue*, p. XV.

⑥ 孟凡人:《高昌城形制初探》,第 41 页。

⑦ A. von Le Coq, "A Short Account of the Origin, Journey, and Results of the First Royal Prussian (Second German) Expedition to Turfan in Chinese Turkistan", *JRAS*, 1909, pp. 304 – 305; idem, *Chotscho: Facsimile-Wiedergaben der Wichtigeren Funde der ersten königlich preussischen Expedition nach Turfan in Ost-Turkestan*, Berlin, 1913, p. 7.

⑧ 勒柯克著,赵崇民译《高昌——吐鲁番古代艺术珍品》,第 18 页。

者,均身穿白衣。① 按常理,无论是在西方抑或东方教会中,作为创教者的摩尼都应享有现实中的至高地位,因此,画中选民和听者所拱绕的对象应该是他。作为中心人物,若按佛教绘画的手法,他的尺寸应该是整幅画中最大的,且为正面朝前的姿势。这种规则其实也适用于摩尼教:高昌教会中的作画者同样以次要人物的身体语言来突出真正的中心人物。如前面讨论的 **III 4979 b**,画面上部中间的庇麻宝座是整幅画的中心,其左右两边的各级选民也都注视着中间。在寺院旗幡残片 **III 6286**(图七)一面的顶端正中绘有一位女神,正面朝前,拱卫于她两侧的是两个比例较小的选民,②该旗幡另一面的顶部也绘着类似的场景。

但是,**III 6918** 的构图却不是这样。画中所有的人(包括摩尼在内),眼睛均注视着他们的右边,仿佛还另有一位比摩尼更值得景仰膜拜的"大人物"存在。根据勒柯克当时的记载,事实正是如此。

勒柯克进入该遗址时,中厅西墙上保存有部分壁画,中部有一个人物形象,但被严重破坏,几乎辨认不出。此人身着红色和绿色的衣服,端坐在红色莲花宝座上,有黑色的头发和胡子。③ **III 6918** 上包括摩尼在内的所有人注视着的正是他。这位能接受摩尼礼拜的人物应该是一位教中大神,但无法断言具体为谁。就在西墙边的废墟中,发现了一小块壁画残片(**III 6917**,画面 21 × 30 cm,图八):一层褶皱很多的白袍上有一个圆形像章似的东西,"像章"中绘有一位女性拯救神。从绘有白袍的这一小块残画来看,此人的原始尺寸很大,可能与 **III 6918** 中的摩尼相当,④且是一位摩尼教选民,而不属于上述未知大神的一部分。既然尺寸与摩尼相当,其地位应该较高,绝非一般选民。也许有人会认为这一块白袍残画或许是摩尼身上的一部分。但我们注意到在摩尼的左上臂,接近肩头的位置上有一方形"像章"的残迹,内中也画着一个人物形象。Jorinde Ebert 在仔细研究了此类"像章"之后认为,在摩尼教会中,只有一位带圆形"像章"的慕阇,其他都是带方形"像章"的拂多诞。这和基督教传统一样,后者就只有最高者才佩带圆形徽章,第二级别多带方形。⑤ 虽然此观点与上述壁画的实情不一,因为这里带方形"像章"的是摩尼本人,而不是拂多诞。但是,它肯定了圆形与方形像章之间存在着差异。作为地位象征的像章在吐鲁番出土的摩尼教绘画作品中并不多见,它们显然各有寓意,但都代表着佩带者的卓越等级和身份。摩尼既然已经带了一个方形像章,那么,圆形像章就应该属于另一个人物。

据勒柯克的记载,在后来的第四次考古发掘中,他们发现在中部神像的另一侧还画了一个和摩尼类似的高级僧侣。⑥ 笔者以为,**III 6917** 可能就是此人形象的一部分。他和摩尼一样分列于神像的两侧,表明他也应该是一个现实教会中的人物,而非神灵。这和 **III 6917** 中着白衣的形象正好相符。他与摩尼大小尺寸相当,且同为现实教会中的人物,由他们分列于大神的两侧也符合构图原则。因此,圆形像章的佩带者可能就是这位和摩尼一同礼拜大神的人物。可惜的是,他的身份不甚清楚。

对此,克里木凯特猜测他可能是被摩尼派来东方传教的弟子阿莫(Mār Ammō)。⑦ 此说是。整个摩

① 克里木凯特著,林悟殊译《古代摩尼教艺术》,第 56~57 页;Z. Gulácsi, *Manichaean Art in Berlin Collection*, p. 198.

② Z. Gulácsi, *Manichaean Art in Berlin Collection*, p. 178.

③ 勒柯克著,赵崇民译《高昌——吐鲁番古代艺术珍品》,第 18 页。

④ 克里木凯特著,林悟殊译《古代摩尼教艺术》,第 58~59 页;Z. Gulácsi, *Manichaean Art in Berlin Collection*, p. 205.

⑤ Jorinde Ebert, "Segmentum and Clavus in Manichaean Garments of the Turfan Oasis", Durkin-Meisterernst, D., S. -Ch. Raschmann, J. Wilkens, M. Yaldiz, P. Zieme (eds.), *Turfan Revisited — The First Century of Research into the Arts and Culture of the Silk Road*, Berlin, 2004, pp. 72 – 83.

⑥ 勒柯克著,赵崇民译《高昌——吐鲁番古代艺术珍品》,第 18 页。

⑦ 克里木凯特著,林悟殊译《古代摩尼教艺术》,第 48 页。

尼教会之中,摩尼的地位无疑是最高的。但从 6 世纪后半 ~ 8 世纪早期,该教的中亚教会独立而成电那勿派,统管着向更东方的地区传教的事业。它实际上已成为"东方"教会的总部,与原美索不达米亚总教廷没有多少关联了。东方教会力图将其渊源追溯至阿莫传教中亚的时期,把他看作本教会的创始人。[①]在高昌教徒的眼中,阿莫的地位仅次于摩尼,几乎同样具有开宗立教的伟大形象。因此,和摩尼一起分侍大神两边的高等级选民很可能就是阿莫。

若按照佛教绘画的特点,不易证实这一推测。因为在佛教图像中,环绕于中心人物两边、大小相仿的次要人物,其地位是相当的。阿莫虽然是东方摩尼教会的创始人,可他毕竟是摩尼的门徒,似乎不可能和摩尼拥有完全平等的身份和地位。但既是入华摩尼教,我们就应从中国的礼法观念来加以考量。中国自古以来的左右尊尚问题,历朝并不一致:秦汉尚右,唐宋尚左,元代尚右,明代尚右,后改尚左,清朝尚左。[②]因此,当以尚左为主。老子云:"君子居则贵左,用兵则贵右","吉事尚左,凶事尚右"。[③]《淮南子》载:"凡高者贵其左,故下之于上曰左之,臣辞也。下者贵其右,故上之于下曰右之,君让也。"[④]所谓左右,自天子南向而坐的布局定格后,古人多以此为基点,东为左,西为右。《周礼》记:"建国之神位,右社稷而左宗庙。"[⑤]以出门方向计,右,在路门外之西。左,路门外之东也。[⑥]又,天子行朝时,臣属所站之方位也按其品位高低有严格的规定:"正朝仪之位,辨其贵贱之等。王南乡(向),三公北面东上,孤东面北上,卿大夫西面北上。"[⑦]除君王与三公的南北向之外,处于东面,亦即君王左侧的诸侯之位明显高于西边(右侧)的卿大夫。这种贵东的观念在中国的祭祀礼中也有体现。《礼记》云:"祭日于坛,祭月于坎,以别幽明,以制上下;祭日于东,祭月于西,以别外内,以端其位。"[⑧]在祭祀中以日为百神之主,配之以月,[⑨]东向祭日,西向祭月。日月与阴阳相对,"阳贵而阴贱,天之制也",[⑩]可以说,这种尚阳日之法与尚东(左)之礼正相印证。因此,从中国的传统礼法而言,以身份至高者为基点,大多认为位于其左侧的人要比右侧的更显尊贵。

此外,中国北方游牧民族自古以来也有尚左(东)的传统。《史记》载:匈奴"诸左方王将居东方,直上谷以往者,东接秽貉、朝鲜;右方王将居西方,直上郡以西,接月氏、氐、羌;而单于之庭直代、云中:各有分地,逐水草移徙。"[⑪]而其中,以"左贤王最贵重,唯太子得居之。"[⑫]即以单于驻地为基点,地位略高的左王,

① I. Colditz, "Shād-Ohrmezd and the Early History of the Manichaean Dīnāwarīya-Community", *Bamgerger Zentralasienstudien. Konferenzakten ESCAS IV Bamberg 8. - 12. Oktober 1991*, Berlin, 1994, pp. 229 - 234; H.-J. Klimkeit, "Manichaeism and Nestorian Christianity", *History of Civilizations of Central Asia* IV, Paris: UNESCO Publishing, 2000, p.69. 事实上,早期帕提亚教团的建立确应归功于阿莫,与摩尼本人几乎没有什么关系。见 W. Sundermann, "The Manichaean Texts in Languages and Scripts of Central Asia", S. Akiner & N. Sims-Williams (ed.), *Languages and Scripts of Central Asia*, School of Oriental and African Studies University of London, 1997, p.39; D. Durkin-Meisterernst, "The Parthian *mwqr'nyg b'š'h* (Turfan Collection, Berlin, M4aI V 3 - 16)", *ARAM, Mandaeans and Manichaeans*, V. 16, 2004, pp. 95 - 107.
② 吴桂就:《方位观念与中国文化》,南宁:广西教育出版社,2000 年,第 258 ~ 262 页。
③ 《老子校释》第三十一章,北京:中华书局,1984 年,第 125、127 页。
④ 《淮南鸿烈集解》卷一〇"缪称训",北京:中华书局,1989 年,第 331 页。又,"凡高者贵其左"后有小字注云:"天道左旋。"
⑤ 《周礼注疏》卷一七"小宗伯",《十三经注疏》,北京:中华书局,1980 年,第 766 页。
⑥ [清]孙希旦:《礼记集解》卷四六,北京:中华书局,1989 年,第 1235 页。
⑦ 《周礼注疏》卷三一"司士",《十三经注疏》,第 849 页。
⑧ 《礼记正义》卷四七,《十三经注疏》,第 1594 ~ 1595 页。
⑨ [清]朱彬:《礼记训纂》卷二四,北京:中华书局,1996 年,第 708 页。
⑩ 《春秋繁露》卷一一"天辨人在第四十六",北京:中华书局,1975 年,第 413 页。
⑪ 《史记》卷一一〇《匈奴列传》,北京:中华书局,1982 年,第 2891 页。
⑫ 《晋书》卷九七《匈奴传》,北京:中华书局,1974 年,第 2550 页。

方位居东,在单于庭的左边。此后,匈奴别种之突厥亦"尚东",突厥可汗"恒处于都斤山,牙帐东开,盖敬日之所出也。"①回纥可汗之下也有左右官职之设。龙朔中,其首领比粟毒犯边,高宗命郑仁泰讨平。比粟毒败走以铁勒本部为天山县,其后继任者为酋长,"皆受都督号以统蕃州,左杀右杀分管诸部。"②回鹘的相关史料中虽未明言左右之贵贱,但作为匈奴苗裔,其风俗又与突厥大抵相同,照常理推测,回鹘可能也有尚左(东)之习俗。这样,就能理解为什么高昌回鹘的画者会把摩尼画在大神的左边,而仅次于他的阿莫则画在右边了。该幅壁画显然没有完全套用佛教绘画的格式,而是更加贴合于中国及回鹘尚左的礼俗。摩尼与阿莫并立大神两侧,但左右分明,既突出了阿莫在高昌教徒心目中的地位,又反映了他与摩尼在身份上高低有序。③

当然,由于勒柯克亲眼见到的已经是几乎无法辨认的壁画残块,更令人扼腕的是,连上述两件残留壁画也已遗失,这里对壁画人物的讨论也只能是无法证实的猜测。对该幅壁画我们可作如下诠释:画面中部是一位摩尼教大神,而世间教会的教徒,包括各等级主教、选民和听者则以摩尼和阿莫为首,环绕于大神两侧,供奉或礼拜着他。由此,便形成了一幅上至神界下至人间的整体性宗教图景。但这样一幅壁画却没有按常理绘在最为醒目重要的地方,即三个主厅中面积最大的南厅内。不过,念及常理的同时,我们还必须考虑到勒柯克在中、北厅都发现了绘有摩尼传教士的精美壁画,④可在南厅几乎没什么收获;并且摩尼教教义认为南方是黑暗王国之所在,因此,在无确凿证据之前,不能妄断南厅就理所应当是这幅摩尼壁画最佳的绘制点。谨慎起见,我们暂不将南厅考虑在内。其实,它之所以被绘于大厅的西壁上,似与前述可汗牙帐东开敬日有异曲同工之感。回鹘可汗是世俗中的最高统治者,而壁画中的三位尊者则在宗教世界中占极高的地位,两者身份相当,朝向相同,或许共同反映着回鹘尚东敬日的习俗。摩尼教徒曾在一篇祈祷文中向于都斤山神致意:"当于都斤山神屈尊赐予我们力量,当我们获得了渴望已久的幸福,哦,我们的陛下,我们带着对您的万分热爱,(在加冕仪式上)表达愉悦之情","愿于都斤山神,明智的先王和列祖列宗的神明,以及尊贵宝座的神明赐福于我们神圣的王子,亦都护。"⑤然后,才呼唤本教的神灵:"愿七神和十二神给予他力量和支援,愿赐予我们勇敢、善良、崇高而伟大的国王陛下最美妙、最向往、最优美的光明。[愿]他的整个汗国和朝廷……"于都斤山(Ötükän)是突厥人心目中的圣山,占有它就意味着掌握了草原的统治权。⑥该文书不仅说明了回鹘人一直保持着对于都斤山的崇拜,也体现出摩尼教对回鹘原始信仰与崇拜的融汇与妥协。既如此,摩尼教依旧遵从回鹘敬拜太阳的传统也在情理之中,且不与本教崇拜日月的教义相违背。这里,需特别注意的是,该幅壁画中虽有摩尼形象,却只是一幅宗教宣传画,并不具备圣像崇拜的功能。

---

① 《周书》卷五〇《突厥传》,北京:中华书局,1971年,第910页。

② 《旧唐书》卷一九五《回纥传》,北京:中华书局,1975年,第5195、5197~5198页。

③ 有研究者在探讨山西太原虞弘墓出土的石椁壁刻时提出,在中亚有所谓"右为上,左为下"(这里的右和左是从观赏者的角度来说的)的图像布局。见毕波:《虞弘墓所谓"夫妇宴饮图"辨析》,《故宫博物院院刊》2006年第1期,第66~83页。若此种规律确实存在的话,或可为传自中亚的摩尼教之所以在壁画中做如此布局提供另一旁证。

④ A. von Le Coq, *Chotscho: Facsimile-Wiedergaben der Wichtigeren Funde der ersten königlich preussischen Expedition nach Turfan in Ost-Turkestan*, p.9.

⑤ 此处译文在勒柯克德译本的基础上,参考了克里木凯特的英译。见 A. von Le Coq, *Türkische Manichaica aus Chotscho III Nebst einem christlichen Bruchstück aus Bulayïq*, (APAW II, 1922), Berlin, 1922, pp.34, 35; H.-J. Klimkeit, *Gnosis on the Silk Road: Gnostic Parables, Hymns & Prayers from Central Asia*, p.357.

⑥ 岑仲勉:《外蒙于都斤山考》,《突厥集史》(下),北京:中华书局,2004年重印本,第1076~1090页;耿世民:《突厥汗国》,《新疆文史论集》,北京:中央民族大学出版社,第254页。

壁画,从美术学层面来讲,是指装饰壁面的画,包括用绘制、雕塑及其他造型或工艺手段,在天然或人工壁面上制作的画。它是建筑物的附饰部分,具有建筑的装饰与美化功能。[①] 在考古学家的眼中,壁画指的是壁面的笔绘彩色图像,包括各种形式的壁面装饰,如石线刻、砖雕、模印砖和彩绘画像等。[②] 本文所讨论的壁画自属后者。

中国古代寺院中的壁画历来是由当时驰名的画家来完成。唐代,在两京寺观壁面上作画的名家主要有吴道子、"善良画外国及佛像"的尉迟乙僧、"善佛事神鬼寺壁"的尹琳、杨庭光、李昭道、王维等。[③] 不惟京城,外州寺院中也存有历朝历代画家的壁画作品。李德裕镇守浙西时,创立甘露寺。曾"取管内诸寺画壁置于寺内",这些壁画出自晋顾恺之、戴安道,宋谢灵运、陆探微,梁张僧繇,隋展子虔,唐韩干等之手,[④]无一不是当时名家。而寺院邀请这些画家所付之代价亦是不菲。吴道子,传其画"风云将逼人,鬼神如脱壁"。长安平康坊菩萨寺"会觉上人以施利起宅十余亩,工毕,酿酒百石,列瓶瓮于雨庑下,引吴道玄观之,因谓曰:'檀越为我画,以是赏之。'吴生嗜酒,且利其多,欣然而许。"[⑤]甚而有皇帝亲自出面,一再请求才肯应召的周昉:"德宗建章明寺,召皓(昉之兄——笔者注)云:'闻卿弟善画,欲使之画章明寺壁。卿特为言之。'又经数月,再召之,昉乃就事。"[⑥]由此可见,不论是寺中僧人还是寺外信徒,都希望能请来声望高绝的名家为自己的寺观画壁。张大千先生也曾指出,"唐宋画家必画壁",而由于当时画佛风气盛行,仕宦商贾均争聘高手作壁画。[⑦] 同样,不论壁画的作者抑或是观者,其所注重的显然都是画法技法,而非宗教意义,不然,就不会出现中国艺术史上的唐长安光明寺内杨契丹、田僧亮、郑法士的"三绝",[⑧]以及北宋汴京相国寺"十绝"[⑨]之说,亦不会出现从南朝隋唐之际至9世纪中叶一直有以文人画壁的极盛潮流。[⑩]

另一宗教艺术圣地之敦煌,其寺窟壁画中的佛陀形象也不是用来让人顶礼膜拜的。敦煌壁画"始于宗教而终于审美",是以"动人心志"的创作手法和传神艺术来宣扬佛教文化,并展示以敦煌本土文化为特征的绘画性壁画。[⑪] 即便是摩尼教东传路途中所经过的索格底亚那地区的壁画,也以揭示城市社会中非贵族人群的情感观念为主。它作为一种基本媒介,对自己本土,乃至从锡尔河直到兴都库什和伊朗高原的广袤领土上的早期叙事性艺术的历史进行了理论重建。片治肯特寺院壁画虽不同于一般,没有逻辑连贯的史诗性长卷,但也主要是与粟特仪式和神话有关的叙事性题材。[⑫] 这种叙事性题材的壁画显然不是供人膜拜的。总之,不论从何种角度,壁画主要具有建筑性和装饰性的特点,[⑬]自来鲜有圣像崇拜的功

① 《中国大百科全书》美术卷 I"壁画"条(李化吉撰),北京:中国大百科全书出版社,2004 年,第 81 页。
② 郑岩:《魏晋南北朝壁画墓研究》,北京:文物出版社,2002 年,第 14 ~ 16 页。
③ 《历代名画记》卷三"记两京外州寺观画壁"、卷九"唐朝上",丛书集成初编 1646 册,北京:中华书局,1985 年,第 109 ~ 144、278、295 页。
④ 《历代名画记》卷三,第 142 ~ 144 页;又见《图画见闻志》卷五"故事拾遗",丛书集成初编 1648 册,第 212 ~ 213 页。
⑤ 段成式:《酉阳杂俎》续集卷五"寺塔记上",北京:中华书局,1981 年,第 249、252 页。
⑥ 《图画见闻志》卷五"周昉"条,第 206 页。
⑦ 李永翘编《张大千画语录》,海口:海南摄影美术出版社,1992 年,第 222、225 页。
⑧ 《历代名画记》卷八,第 262 页。
⑨ 《图画见闻志》卷五"相蓝十绝"条,第 201 ~ 203 页。
⑩ 姜伯勤:《敦煌艺术宗教与礼乐文明》,北京:中国社会科学出版社,1996 年,第 51 页。
⑪ 段文杰:《敦煌早期壁画的风格特点和艺术成就》、《试论敦煌壁画的传神艺术》,《段文杰敦煌艺术论文集》,兰州:甘肃人民出版社,1994 年,第 86 ~ 87、106 页;易存国:《敦煌艺术美学——以壁画艺术为中心》,上海人民出版社,2005 年,第 106、169 页。
⑫ Boris Marshak, *Legends, Tales, and Fables in the Art of Sogdiana*, New York: Bibliotheca Persica Press, 2002, pp. 22, 156, 162.
⑬ 祝重寿:《中国壁画史纲》,北京:文物出版社,1995 年,第 1 页;同作者《东方壁画史纲》,北京:文物出版社,2005 年,第 1 页。

能,其艺术价值应高于宗教价值。而相反的,膜拜艺术则是在艺术因素从属于宗教因素的基础上产生和发展起来的。[①] 且较之立体塑像更为真实的触觉感知性,平面壁画的视觉感知性在激发信众的宗教情感方面,始终略输一筹。

综合上情,我们认为,曾为回鹘王家寺院 K 寺中的这幅巨型壁画上虽保留有摩尼的形象,但它并不用于信众的崇拜仪式。而这种有画像无崇拜的形式,也不属于圣像崇拜。事实上,高昌摩尼教会仍遵守着不拜圣像的原始教义,其崇拜对象不是教中神灵的实体形象,而多为一些具有象征意义的宗教符号,如代表拯救的庇麻宝座。此外,值得注意的另一个重要象征物就是摩尼的头冠。

四、摩尼头冠的象征意义

上述大型人物壁画中,在细节上引人注目的除了摩尼白衣上的徽章外,就是他的头冠。头冠主体部分类似扇形,与后排选民的帽子形状一样,不同的是虽然它底色为白色,但其上绘有暗红色花纹,可能正是为了突显其身份不同且略高于身后的选民。更引人注意的是,围着头冠下端接近头发的地方,画有一圈黑色粗线,且有两条尖状物向上伸展。黑线在帽子左边呈弧度状,向帽后弯绕,似暗示帽子后面还有一根尖状物。这三条尖状物貌似突兀,毫无来由,实则在高昌回鹘供养人的冠饰上,或可寻得蛛丝马迹。

回鹘贵族除了戴一种被称为"古波斯王冠"的高筒形帽子之外,还有一种常见的三尖形无缘帽。[②] 帽子底部似三角形或圆形,上端竖有三个尖状物,与摩尼帽子上的有些类似,两个在前,一个在后,一条短纱巾从后边垂下。"可汗宫"绘画中大部分人物都戴这种帽子,在柏孜克里克壁画的供养人图像中也有出现。[③] 在宗教艺术中,人们往往会仿照世俗王者贵族的衣冠佩饰来塑造神灵的形象。古代南亚次大陆的神,是贵族统治者在天上的投影化身。[④] 雏形期的佛陀形象就是仿照世俗的王侯贵族而成,具有本地化倾向。[⑤] 在犍陀罗艺术中,菩萨的形象更是以印度当时衣着华丽的贵族为原型,其宝冠和王室人员的王冠大体相同,包括一个大圆雕饰,其上带着一个逐渐变细的凸榫和盘中间的一个中心宝珠。圆盘两侧各有一个雕刻精致的半圆形图案。[⑥] 贵霜时期的白沙瓦地区,这种仿自王族的型式,还被用来表现婆罗门教的帝释天和梵天。[⑦] 在中国的佛教艺术中,菩萨形象也大多是戴着宝冠。与玄奘所亲见的天竺君臣一样,"服玩良异,花鬘宝冠,以为首饰;环钏璎珞,而作身佩"。[⑧] 萨珊波斯王者的日月冠在北

---

① 乌格里诺维奇著,王先睿、李鹏译《艺术与宗教》,北京:三联书店,1987 年,第 125 页。

② 冯佳班(A. V. Gabain,其汉译名通常为"葛玛丽"——笔者注)著,邹如山译《高昌回鹘王国的生活》,吐鲁番地方志编辑室出版,1989 年,第 84 页。

③ [法] 莫尼克·玛雅尔著,耿昇译《古代高昌王国物质文明史》,第 150 页。

④ 白化文:《汉化佛教法器服侍略说》,北京:商务出版社,1998 年,第 178 页。

⑤ 高田修:《佛像の誕生》,东京,岩波书店,1987 年,第 113~121 页;更为详细的考证可参见田边胜美:《ガングーラかろ正倉院へ》,京都:同朋舍,1988 年;村田靖子著,金申译:《佛像の系谱:从犍陀罗到日本——相貌表现与华丽的悬裳座的历史》,上海辞书出版社,2002 年。

⑥ B. N. 普里著,许建英、何汉民译《中亚佛教(节选"中亚艺术"一章)》;查娅·帕塔卡娅著,许建英译:《中亚艺术(附丝路北道木器参考)》,《中亚佛教艺术》,第 385、121 页。有观点认为,早期佛陀类型从药叉形象演变而来,大多数佛陀和药叉一样戴一条大头巾,到了晚期才有时为一顶王冠所代替。但即便是这种头巾,也仿自印度贵族,是典型的尊贵的标志。见 J. E. 范·洛惠泽恩-德·黎乌著,许建英、贾连飞译《斯基泰时期——一种对公元前 1 世纪到公元 3 世纪印度北部的历史、艺术、铭文及古文字学的研究》,昆明:云南人民出版社,2002 年,第 147 页。

⑦ 雷奈·格鲁塞(René Grousset)著,常任侠、袁音译《印度的文明》,北京:商务印书馆,1965 年。

⑧ [唐] 玄奘、辩机著,季羡林等校注《大唐西域记校注》卷二"衣饰",北京:中华书局,2000 年,第 177 页。

魏之后传入中国，并成为菩萨的流行冠饰。进入唐代，菩萨也遍插珠翠，璎珞华贵富丽，宛若宫廷贵妇人。①即使在道教中，玉皇大帝也如人间帝王一般，头戴旒冕。宗教之所以会借用世俗王者的头冠来修饰教中的高级神祇，可能是因为前者是至高无上的身份与地位的象征。由此，摩尼教中教主摩尼的帽子或许也是出于这种考虑，从回鹘贵族的头冠上撷取到了灵感。

况且，摩尼教极重王权，其教义神话与"君王"这一身份有密切关联。摩尼将光明世界比作宫廷，由光明国王统治着。在希腊文书中，清净、光明、大力、智慧被简单地称为明父的"四面尊严"，而在吐鲁番出土摩尼教文书中，则被称为"天堂的四位君王"、"四位君王一般的神"或"四位光明王族的神"。三位拯救神——夷数、惠明使和大智甲也常被称为"王族"，而大智甲则被称为"教法之王"。② 摩尼本人作为波斯王室后裔，更是被冠以无数的"国王"称号，在教徒口中传诵。此类词句不胜枚举，如：

　　啊，他降临了，心灵的导师，光明分子的国王，他照亮了黑暗！
　　啊，他降临了，起死回生的神医，治疗百病……
　　啊，他降临了，勇敢无畏、仁慈神圣的舵手，他行驶船儿涉越重洋！
　　［缺五节］
　　啊，他降临了，智慧的光明国王，他撒播美妙的天赐！
　　啊，他降临了，折辱、摧毁和消灭我们仇敌的人！
　　我们的教父，摩尼教主，您值得被赞颂，被颂扬！
　　从光明众神和光明分子……③

在庇麻节赞美诗中，也有"哦，我主摩尼，众王之子，光明国王，我们赞美您！哦，我主摩尼，光明国王，您值得被赞颂！"④因而，在高昌摩尼教经典中，除了光明诸神被喻作国君之外，摩尼与君王的身份更是密不可分。有学者认为，摩尼教之所以吸引回鹘可汗的原因之一，可能就在于摩尼的王族血统。回鹘可汗作为摩尼的精神之子，承认了神——摩尼——可汗这一特殊的精神链，并由此找到了与高贵而悠久的波斯王室之间的一种精神联系。⑤ 显然，出身波斯王室的摩尼与回鹘可汗也有着密切的关联，那么，在摩尼教特有的白色头冠基础上添加具有回鹘王室特征的三根尖状物，既保持摩尼教原味，又体现了君王的尊贵，这无疑是将上述理念在宗教艺术上做了最好的调和与诠释。

葛玛丽在猜测摩尼头冠与回鹘贵族服饰有关的同时，认为头冠上尖状物的绘画技法蹩脚，可能是后

① 赵声良：《敦煌石窟北朝菩萨的头冠》，《敦煌研究》2005年第3期，第14~15页；李敏：《莫高窟唐代前期艺术中的菩萨头冠》，《敦煌研究》2004年第6期，第42~50页。

② H.-J. Klimkeit, "Manichaean Kingship: Gnosis at Home in the World", M. Heuser & H.-J. Klimkeit, *Studies in Manichaean Literature and Art*, p.212.

③ M. Boyce, *A Reader in Manichaean Middle Persian and Parthian*, text. cl; H.-J. Klimkeit, *Gnosis on the Silk Road: Gnostic Parables, Hymns & Prayers from Central Asia*, pp.84-85.

④ W. B. Henning, *Ein manichäisches Bet- und Beichtbuch* [Abhandlungen der (Königlich) Preussischen Akademie der Wissenschaften, Philosophisch-Historische Kl. X], Berlin, 1937, p.20; H.-J. Klimkeit, *Gnosis on the Silk Road: Gnostic Parables, Hymns & Prayers from Central Asia*, p.134.

⑤ A. V. Tongerloo, "Manichaean Religion and the Concept of Sovereignty among the Uighurs", Barbara Kellner-Heinkele (ed.), *Altaica Berolinensia. The Concept of Sovereignty in the Altaic World. Permanent International Altaistic Conference 34th Meeting. Berlin 21-26 July, 1991*, Wiesbaden, 1993, p.280.

来某位热心的回鹘摩尼教徒补画上去的。[①] 此说有待商榷。壁画作为建筑的附加装饰物,不仅画面的规格、大小早已预先设定好,恐怕其主题、设计也不可能是临时发挥。而且,无论何时何地,宫殿寺观壁画都代表了那个时代壁画的最高水准。[②] K 寺作为回鹘的王家寺院,其尊贵地位可想而知。能在王家寺院壁面上作画的画家,不但应该技法超群,其名望地位也应为同辈中之翘楚。正如前文所述,唐代两京大小寺观中的壁画不仅多出自名家,且有不少是由几位鼎盛一时的画家联袂而作,[③]包括敦煌石窟中的壁画,可能也非一般工匠所为。[④] 有学者认为,摩尼教书画的绘制主要是在皇宫进行的艺术。[⑤] 当然,我们不能妄测这幅壁画与回鹘的宫廷画师有关,但此画作者之技艺声望在当时也应属上流。如此,K 寺壁画应该是在回鹘画家的精心准备下绘制而成的,画中关键人物的设计、造型更应心中有数,不会草率下笔。更有,王家寺院中的教主形象,毕竟是十分神圣的,教徒恐不敢随意改动。

摩尼的这顶头冠还出现在另两幅画中。其一见高昌城出土的摩尼教轴卷式细画 III 4614。[⑥] 画面中央是一根柱子,两旁各侧立着一位站在莲花座上的神灵,其衣服褶皱的画法类似于佛教的守护神。[⑦] 柱子顶部放着一顶白色头冠,也呈扇形,但无暗红色花纹。头冠下端有一圈羽毛状黑色饰物,仅有一根粗长羽毛向上方伸出,这与壁画上的三尖状物不同。另一幅见 1981 年吐鲁番柏孜克里克 65 号窟出土的粟特文摩尼教书信(81TB65∶1)插画,年代约在 10 世纪。[⑧] 尽管其结构布局与 III 4614 十分相似,画面左右两边也有立于莲花座上的胁侍神灵,但他们中间没有柱子,而是一直行金字,意译为"致慕阇的辉煌伟大的荣光"。[⑨] 字的上方有一个用红色飘带围成的倒三角形空白区,[⑩]飘带在三角形上端两角处扎结后向上空翻飞,带上饰有摩尼教细画中常见的金色圆圈。在倒三角形的正上方,有一个金色托盘,盘上是一顶洁白头冠,但形状却不是扇形而似矩形,与前引庇麻节图、说法图中的选民帽样式一致。从头冠下端伸起三根黑色尖状物,与壁画同。

粗看之下,这三个头冠外表几乎一致,但细察之后便会发现它们各有差别:III 4614 与壁画的帽子主体部分一样,黑色饰物却不同;81TB65∶1 与壁画的黑色饰物相同,但主体部分又不一致。虽然 III 4614 和壁画的时间都被笼统定于 8~9 世纪,[⑪]但头冠的大同小异之处,却可说明前者罕见的羽毛类冠饰可能流行于壁画绘成之前。如上所述,K 寺曾为王家寺院,其壁画中的摩尼面貌定然不是随手画成的,即使它不是高昌教会艺术中摩尼形象的范本,也应该具有较高的权威性。那么,壁画中摩尼所戴的头冠样式既已定型,经书插画的作者又岂会随意设计更改。因此,很可能羽毛扇形冠出现于前,后来逐渐演变成三尖扇形冠,待 K 寺落成,画家自然将变化定型之后的新头冠画于寺壁之上。而正是由于在壁画绘制之前就已有插画显示了头冠在教徒心目中的非凡意义,且冠上已附有黑色羽毛饰物,那么,壁画作者在处理摩尼的头冠,尤其是冠上饰物时,更会谨慎小心。即便作画时三尖尚未出现,他也会将原有的羽毛画出,不可

① 冯佳班著,邹如山译《高昌回鹘王国的生活》,第 86 页。
② 王朝闻总主编《中国美术史》(隋唐卷),齐鲁书社、明天出版社,2000 年,第 76 页。
③ 《历代名画记》卷三,第 109~144 页。
④ 李永翘编《张大千画语录》,第 224 页。
⑤ Geo Widengren, *Mani and Manichaeism*, p. 111.
⑥ 克里木凯特著,林悟殊译《古代摩尼教艺术》,第 83 页;Z. Gulácsi, *Manichaean Art in Berlin Collection*, pp. 144–146.
⑦ Z. Gulácsi, *Manichaean Art in Berlin Collection*, p. 146.
⑧ 新疆吐鲁番地区文物局编《吐鲁番新出摩尼教文献研究》,北京:文物出版社,2000 年,第 1、5 页,图版见书前第 1 页"书信 A"。
⑨ Sims-Williams 教授读作"(这是)慕阇伟大的辉煌的荣光",同上,第 23、45 页。
⑩ Sims-Williams 教授认为这一空白是慕阇的形象,之所以留白可能是因为画家没见过慕阇的实际相貌,同上,第 45 页。
⑪ 克里木凯特著,林悟殊译《古代摩尼教艺术》,第 56、83 页。

能留下空白待后世教徒去添加。第三幅成于10世纪的81TB65∶1,更进一步显示了此头冠的演变进程,它仍延续了壁画中的三尖状饰物,但帽子主体部分变成了矩形。其实,在吐鲁番出土的摩尼教艺术品中,选民几乎都戴矩形帽,扇形帽并不常见。显然,前者在高昌摩尼教徒中远比后者流行。因此,最后教徒们也将摩尼的头冠定型为三尖矩形冠。

Ⅲ 4614和81TB65∶1的画面布局一致,说明它们想要表现的宗教寓意相同,画面的重点以及两位守护神所尊崇拱卫的对象并不是实体的人,而是具有象征性的代替物——头冠。这种象征性的表现手法在宗教艺术中颇为常见。在佛教艺术中,佛像的制作约始于公元1~2世纪的迦腻色伽时代。[①] 在佛陀以人形被塑绘之前,其存在都是通过不同的象征物来表现,如大象意味着佛陀诞生,马象征着年轻的佛陀离开王宫,菩提树代表悟道,法轮象征其初次说法,一双足迹是转轮圣王的吉祥标志,悬空的伞盖象征佛陀的神圣存在,窣堵波则代表了佛陀的涅槃等等。[②] 显然,摩尼教中的头冠也具有象征意义。前面已经提到,81TB65∶1上,两位胁侍神中间的文字里提到了"慕阇"。Ⅲ 4614的柱子中间也有一直行粟特文字,漫漶不清。J. D. BeDuhn教授将之释读为"光明……之主"。[③] 吉田丰先生则认为是"作为神的我们的主人、慕阇的荣光"。[④] 如后一释读更准确的话,那这两幅细画的重点以及头冠所象征的都是"慕阇",并非摩尼本人。但实际上,在吐鲁番出土的摩尼教赞美诗中,夷数有时也被称为"伟大的拯救者,我的慕阇(Teacher)",[⑤]头冠下所写的"慕阇"也可能代表夷数,进而暗指摩尼。因摩尼曾宣称自己是继佛陀、琐罗亚斯德和耶稣之后的第四位先知。且在摩尼教理念中,夷数和摩尼都是带来真知的拯救者,身份相同,几乎可以完全代换。当然,头冠还有另一层含义,可到摩尼教经典中去寻找。

在摩尼教教义中,人逝去之后,灵魂得到拯救的标志通常是光明外衣、宝座和王冠。早在北非摩尼教会的经文中,便提到了"光明王冠",也有将"你的胜利,你的工冠"联系在一起的说法。[⑥] 这里的"胜利"显然是被拯救之意。而王冠代表获得拯救,这一象征更是频繁出现于吐鲁番出土的各种体裁的摩尼教文书之中。[⑦] 在缅怀摩尼的第一代传法弟子扎库(Zaku)的赞美诗中,教徒们称颂他:"强大有力且善良的人,您和所有的先知、菩萨、神一样已获得了王冠。"[⑧]教徒们为教会及其主教祈福:"愿奥尔姆兹神,光明天堂的明父最终赐予你头冠、花环和王冠,愿你在那儿得到快乐,在喜悦中欢欣舞蹈,直到永远。"[⑨]在庇麻节仪式文中,教徒们认为"众神开启了富足天堂的大门。花环、花冠和王冠[已赐给

---

① 也有许多学者认为其起源可提早到贵霜以前。相关成果的述评详见宫治昭撰,李静杰译:《近年来关于佛像起源问题的研究状况》,《敦煌研究》2000年第2期,第74~82页。

② 《中亚文明史》第二卷,北京:中国对外翻译出版公司,2001年,第384~385页;罗伊. C. 克雷文著,王镛、方广羊、陈聿东译《印度艺术简史》,北京:中国人民大学出版社,2004年,第145页。

③ Z. Gulácsi, *Manichaean Art in Berlin Collection*, Appendix I, p. 239.

④ 新疆吐鲁番地区文物局编《吐鲁番新出摩尼教文献研究》,第45页。

⑤ M. Boyce, *A Reader in Manichaean Middle Persian and Parthian*, p. 101; H.-J. Klimkeit, *Gnosis on the Silk Road: Gnostic Parables, Hymns & Prayers from Central Asia*, p. 39.

⑥ Iain Gardner, "A Manichaean Liturgical Codex Found at Kellis", *Orientalia*, Vol. 62, 1993, p. 41.

⑦ V. Arnold-Döben, *Die Bildersprache des Manichaismu*, Cologne, 1978, pp. 149－155; H.-J. Klimkeit, *Gnosis on the Silk Road: Gnostic Parables, Hymns & Prayers from Central Asia*, p. 61, n. 28; idem, "Temporal and Spiritual Power in Central Asian Manichaeism", *Studies in Manichaean Literature and Art*, p. 230.

⑧ 帕提亚语文书(编号M6), M. Boyce, *A Reader in Manichaean Middle Persian and Parthian*, p. 140; H.-J. Klimkeit, *Gnosis on the Silk Road: Gnostic Parables, Hymns & Prayers from Central Asia*, p. 88.

⑨ 中古波斯语文书(编号M729), M. Boyce, *A Reader in Manichaean Middle Persian and Parthian*, p. 150; H.-J. Klimkeit, *Gnosis on the Silk Road: Gnostic Parables, Hymns & Prayers from Central Asia*, p. 96.

了]我们……"。①《胡威达曼》在讲述拯救神将灵魂带入光明王国的情景时,有详细的描写:

我会带(你)进入亘古和平的国土,

我会带(你)觐见众神,那是我自身的神圣[体]。

你会在欢乐中,在这被赞颂的地方感受到喜悦;

你将不再悲伤并……忘记所有的痛苦。

你将披上光明的外衣并被光明围绕;

我会给你戴上君主的王冠。

……

他(初人——笔者注)将王冠戴在所有朋友的头上,

并在他们身上披上欢乐的外衣。

所有的信徒和虔诚的选民

他都会赐予赞美之衣并为他们戴上王冠。②

　　前面已经提到,壁画中摩尼的头冠既表明了其宗教领袖的地位,也彰显出世俗王者的尊贵,那么,将这顶头冠作为获得拯救的象征让教徒礼敬,无疑是最佳的选择。因此,从某种意义上来讲,在高昌摩尼教会中,王冠与庇麻座一样象征着被拯救,意味着灵魂在死后升入光明王国。另一方面,细画中这顶摩尼的头冠放在中间,由神灵侍卫两侧,显示出一种被供奉崇拜的模式,而这种供奉当与摩尼有关,只是它通过对宗教象征符号的礼敬来体现,并非直面摩尼的人像,这也旁证了高昌教会尚未出现圣像崇拜。

　　在东西方教会中目前已知的共通点之一:庇麻是摩尼的宝座,象征着拯救。教徒需在庇麻前跪拜,并举行仪式。而吐鲁番细画又提示我们,在高昌,教徒们还有另一种形式的供奉,即将摩尼头冠也作为拯救的象征符号来礼拜。也许,这种膜拜形式仅停留在信众的宗教心理层面上,并未将之付诸于宗教实践,即高昌教会并没有举行某种特定的宗教仪式来礼拜头冠。但是,在崇拜性宗教典礼中,神圣象征主义、神话和仪式都可帮助人们领悟拯救的奥秘。③ 总之,在高昌摩尼教会中,庇麻与头冠均为末日拯救的象征性宗教符号,成为被教徒供奉崇拜的对象,也都暗含了对摩尼的礼敬,只是两者受重视的程度不一,毕竟为庇麻而举行的节日才是教会中一年一度最盛大隆重的。

五、余　论

　　高昌摩尼教会中应该还没有实体的摩尼圣像用于崇拜仪式,而目前唯一得到大多数学者认同的被绘于壁画上的摩尼形象,恐仍属宗教宣传的范畴。但,具有象征意义的宗教符号如庇麻、头冠确实存在,它

① W. B. Henning, *Ein manichäisches Bet- und Beichtbuch* [Abhandlungen der (Königlich) Preussischen Akademie der Wissenschaften, Philosophisch-Historische Kl. X], 1937, p. 20; H.-J. Klimkeit, *Gnosis on the Silk Road: Gnostic Parables, Hymns & Prayers from Central Asia*, p. 134.

② H.-J. Klimkeit, *Gnosis on the Silk Road: Gnostic Parables, Hymns & Prayers from Central Asia*, New York, 1993, pp. 105 - 106.

③ *The Encyclopedia of Religion* Vol. 7, p. 81.

们由于和摩尼息息相关受到了选民与听者的供奉礼拜。

高昌教会中用于崇拜的多是一种象征性宗教符号,与泉州草庵中的摩尼塑像有质的区别。由此,我们推测,中国摩尼教逐渐出现圣像崇拜的这一演变过程更有可能发生在中原。因为在中国民众的宗教生活中,主导民众意识的是这种信仰所具有的道德和神圣的功能,而并非宗教信仰境界的描述。功能化倾向的宗教观将对宗教认知的疑问放到了次要的位置。① 在这种意识的驱动下,人们显然更乐于接受可以被真切感知到的神像及由其所赐予的福祉。那些缥缈空泛的文字形容和象征符号远远不能满足人们的宗教情感寄托。关于这一点,入华后的佛教、本土的道教以及众多纷杂的民间信仰均可佐证,它们无一不热衷于完善自己的神灵谱系,并积极地将大大小小的各级神灵一一塑造成像;同时,中国的供养人更以造像作为累积功德的可靠途径,反过来也大大促进了偶像制造的风潮,使偶像崇拜成为更灵验的宗教实践模式。有学者认为,在中国,雕塑不是艺术,只是无名的偶像制造者们举行敬神祭礼的事物。② 此观点虽有失偏颇,但也或多或少地指出了人们制作偶像的功利性,而恰恰是这种功利性在中国民众的普遍宗教观中占据着较为重要的位置。

任何宗教的基础都是相信在超自然物和自然物之间存在联系,宗教膜拜正是借以实现这种虚幻联系的中介形式。③ 由是,为了适应中国民众并更好地融入周遭的宗教氛围,素来在传教策略上极具灵活性的摩尼教进入中原之后,也渐渐经历了一个由不拜圣像到圣像崇拜的演化过程。其实,作为摩尼教最后的消亡地,泉州建起一尊“佛身道貌”的摩尼塑像,出现圣像崇拜,当是该教在中国的必然走向。

---

① 杨庆堃著,范丽珠等译《中国社会中的宗教:宗教的现代社会功能与其历史因素之研究》,上海人民出版社,2007 年,第 39 页。
② 雷奈·格鲁塞(René Grousset)著,常任侠、袁音译《东方的文明》(下),北京:中华书局,1999 年,第 513 页。
③ 乌格里诺维奇著,王先睿、李鹏译《艺术与宗教》,第 115 页。

车师(姑师)的语源、语义及源流考辨

李树辉

新疆社会科学院民族研究所

关于"车师"一词的读音,学术界或按现代读音作 chēshī,或按近古读音作 jūshī;欧洲学者将其发音构拟为 quz;①岑仲勉先生构拟为 quṣi,认为该词与《阙特勤碑》中的 qošu/qušu 及于阗文中的 quyša"实同一语";②维吾尔族学者又将该词译为 quʃ bɛglik(鸟国)。表面看来仅仅是读音不同,实际上却直接涉及其人种、语言系属乃至许多重大的历史问题。关于其语源、语义,学者们至今也未能达成共识。另一方面,多将其作为"古代民族"看待,以"车师族"相称,而又无法解释该"族"何以自6世纪以后便不见于记载的原因,也无法解释自5世纪末开始同一地区出现的"高车族"的"源"与"流"以及车师与突厥、回鹘乃至现代维吾尔族的关系。本文拟结合其分布区域、活动历史,考订其语音、语义和语源,并对其人种、语言系属和源流试加探讨。

一、车师(姑师)的语源和语义

车师之名最早见于《汉书》,其前的《史记·大宛列传》作姑师,称"楼兰、姑师邑有城郭,临盐泽","楼兰、姑师小国耳"。姑师、车师实为同一名称的不同音译,③后分裂为数"国",《汉书》为加以区别而使用了车师这一别译形式,且与姑师之名并出:姑师指称部族,为其总称;车师指称部落,为其分称。有的学者认为"史、汉二书……元封三年前均称'姑师',元封四年后均称'车师'",④似不确。《汉书·西域传》:"至宣帝时,遣卫司马使护鄯善以西数国。及破姑师,未尽殄,分以为车师前后王及山北六国。"车师一词也常用于指称车师前国,同传:"地节二年,汉遣侍郎郑吉、校尉司马憙将免刑罪人田渠黎,积谷,欲以攻车师,至秋收谷,吉、憙发城郭诸国兵万余人,自与所将田士千五百人共击车师,攻交河城,破之。"同书《郑吉传》:"至宣帝时,吉以侍郎田渠黎,积谷,因以发诸国兵攻破车师,迁卫司马,使护鄯善以西南道。"所言车师皆指车师前国。《魏书·西域传》更是明言"车师国,一名前部"。

姑师先民在先秦史籍中被称作"戎"或"西戎",散居在陇山以西至东部天山地区的广大区域里。月氏徙居河西走廊后,诸戎部落或融于月氏,或向西方、北方迁徙。《左传·昭公九年》所记居于瓜州的"允姓之奸"当即是后来乌孙集团之一部。《水经注》卷四〇:"《春秋传》曰:允姓之奸居于瓜州……杜林

---

① 参见岑仲勉著《汉书西域传地里校释》,北京:中华书局1981年版,第482页。
② 参见岑仲勉著《汉书西域传地里校释》,第482页;《西突厥史料补阙及考证》,北京:中华书局1958年版,第177页。
③ 学术界也多持这一观点。参见嶋崎昌著《隋唐時代の東トゥルキスタン研究——高昌史研究を中心として》,东京:东京大学出版会1977年版,第3页。
④ 王素:《高昌史稿》,北京:文物出版社1989年版,第68页。

曰：……瓜州之戎，并于月氏者也。"就史乘所见，月氏西走前所并之国唯有乌孙。《通典》卷一七四"沙州"条注称："戎子名驹支也。""北庭府"条云："庭州在流沙之西北，前汉乌孙之旧壤，后汉车师后王之地。"《史记正义》云：乌孙、呼揭"二国皆在瓜州西北，乌孙战国时居瓜州"。可见，杜佑、张守节亦信乌孙即"允姓之戎"，即"驹支"。故而，藤田丰八断定"驹支为姑师、车师的同音异字"，姑师、车师为其被逐后的称谓，即认为：瓜州之戎＝允姓之奸＝乌孙＝姑师、车师。①

岑仲勉亦谓此说"自成一解"，但又称："唯依《传·序》则后王之地，姑师强盛之时已有之，东汉后王之地域，与西汉无异，其西部虽邻接乌孙，而《通典》旧壤之辞，于史无本，岂杜氏涉车延恶师而误笔耶？抑因庭州之西属乌孙，遂混指其全部耶？"②其实，将"瓜州之戎"视为乌孙集团之一部，则一切疑点均迎刃而解了。该部早在战国末年便受月氏所迫，退居东部天山地区。至于《通典》所说的"驹支"，就指的是姑师、车师。《太平寰宇记》卷一五六亦称，庭州"前汉为乌孙旧壤，地方五十里……州东界有山，其人并山居，讯其风俗，是乌孙遗类"。

今人将"车师"读为 chēshī 或 jūshī，皆误。"车"的读音实与"姑"同，二字皆读为 gu。《说文》释"姑"字读音为"古胡切"；至于"车"字的读音，[明]陈第：《毛诗古音考》卷一释之甚详：

> 车，音"姑"，后转韵"歌"。程晓诗："平生三伏日，道路无行车。闭门闭暑卧，出入不相过。"再转而韵"麻"，韵"鱼"，后世音也。
>
> 本证：
> 《何彼秾矣》："何彼秾矣，唐棣之华。曷不肃雝，王姬之车。"
> 《北风》："莫赤匪狐，莫黑匪乌。惠而好我，携手同车。"
> 《采薇》："彼尔维何，维常之华。彼路斯何，君子之车。"
>
> 旁证：
> 《易·暌·上九》："暌，孤见豕负涂，载鬼一车。先张之弧，后说之弧。"
> 《汉小麦谣》："丈夫何在西击胡，吏买马，君具车，请为诸君鼓咙胡。"
> 杨雄《酒箴》："尽日盛酒，人复借酤。常为国器，託于属车。"
> 曹植《应诏诗》："肃承明诏，应会皇都。星陈凤驾，秣马脂车。"

其实，"车"字韵"鱼"也并非是"后世音"，先秦便有用例。如《战国策·冯谖客孟尝君》中便以"乎"、"鱼"、"车"、"家"、"母"等字押韵：

> 有顷，(冯谖)倚柱弹其剑歌曰："长铗归来乎！食无鱼。"左右以告。孟尝君曰："食之比门下之客。"居有顷，复弹其铗歌曰："长铗归来乎！出无车。"左右皆笑之，以告。孟尝君曰："为之驾，比门下之车客。"于是，乘其车，揭其剑，过其友曰："孟尝君客我。"后有顷，复弹其剑铗歌曰："长铗归来乎！无以为家。"左右皆恶之，以为贪而不知足。孟尝君问："冯公有亲乎？"对曰："有老母。"孟尝君

① [日]藤田丰八：《东西交涉史の研究·西域篇》，东京：冈书院昭和八年版，第62~64页。
② 岑仲勉：《汉书西域传地里校释》，第360页。

使人给其食用,无使乏。于是,冯谖不复歌。

上引《毛诗古音考》之"旁证"诸例表明,汉晋时"涂"、"车"、"弧"、"胡"、"酤"、"都"仍同韵。清儒钱大昕指出:

> 《释名》:"古者言行曰'车',声如'居',所以居人也,今曰'车',声近'舍'。"韦昭辨之云:"古皆音尺奢反,从汉以来始有'居'音。"二说正相反。韦氏误也。韦特见《诗》"王姬之车"、"君子之车"皆与"华"韵,而不知读"华"为呼瓜切亦非古音也。古读"华"为"敷",《诗》"有女同车"与"华"、"琚"、"都"为韵,"携手同车"与"狐"、"乌"为韵,"车"之读"居"又何疑焉?宏嗣生于汉季,稍染俗学,故于古音不甚了了。①

又曰:

> 《史记·淳于髡传》:"瓯窭满篝,污邪满车,五谷蕃熟,穰穰满家"四句,不独"车"与"家"韵也,"瓯"、"窭"与"篝"韵,"污"、"邪"与"车"韵,"谷"与"熟"韵,"蕃"与"满"韵,"穰穰"重文,亦韵,"五"与"车"、"家"亦韵,盖无一字虚设矣。②

至今,"车"字在韩语(朝鲜语)中仍读为 ge 音。如"自转车"(自行车)的读音为 ʤaʤunge,"车马"的读音为 gema。

"师"字的读音,《说文》作"疎夷切",约读为 şi。汉语西北方音 ş、s 不分,故 ş 与 s 通。又,s 与 z 均为舌尖前擦音,发音部位相同,唯有清浊之别,故而 s 亦与 z 通。如此,则姑师、车师的汉代读音当为 gūsī/gūzī。姑师、车师也便是 oʁuz(乌护,乌古斯)的音译。汉语中没有 ʁ 音位,且为音节文字,将 aʁu-/oʁu-音译为"姑"或"车",将-z 音译为与之读音 zi/si 对应的"师"字乃极其正常之事。如 qïrʁïz(柯尔克孜)中的-z 音便译作"斯"(黠戛斯、纥扢斯、吉尔吉斯),此类译例不胜枚举。

oʁuz 或作 aʁuz、aʁuʒ,本意指"牛羊生产后的新乳"。③ oʁuz 部族的形成与得名,始于公元前 2 世纪上半叶,位于东部天山南北地区的乌孙国为其源头。该词用作部族名称及该部族狼图腾文化的形成,与汉代乌孙首领猎骄靡婴幼时为狼所哺养的神奇经历密切相关。④ 乌古斯部族是部落及人口最多的一个突厥语部族,共有 24 个部落(M I.77,M III.567),也是构成前突厥汗国和回鹘汗国的主体部族。⑤

从历史及地域上看,将姑师(车师)视为 oʁuz 的不同音译,也正相吻合。乌古斯是 6 世纪崛起于"金

---

① [清]钱大昕著,陈文和、孙显军校点《十驾斋养新录》卷五,《古今音》,南京:江苏古籍出版社 2000 年版,第 99 页。
② [清]钱大昕著,陈文和、孙显军校点《十驾斋养新录》卷一六,《古人声韵之密》,第 337 页。
③ [喀喇汗王朝] Mɛhmut Qɛʃqɛri:《Tyrki Tïllar Dïwanï》(《突厥语大词典》,后文简称《词典》)卷一,乌鲁木齐:新疆人民出版社 1980 年版,第 77 页。后文简称"M I"。因此,卷二、卷三(乌鲁木齐:新疆人民出版社 1983 年、1984 年版)简称"M II"、"M III",并与页码一同括注于文后。
④ 李树辉:《突厥狼图腾文化研究》,刊于《西北民族研究》1992 年第 1 期。
⑤ 李树辉:《乌古斯与突厥、回鹘、突厥蛮关系考——乌古斯和回鹘研究系列之六》,刊于《喀什师范学院学报》2001 年第 4 期,2002 年第 1、4 期。

山之阳"的前突厥汗国的主体部族,发祥地恰在东部天山地区。学术界一直将此"金山"误解为阿尔泰山,实指"高昌国之北山"即天山。① 《西州图经》称高昌县北山为"乌骨山"(《辽史·太祖本纪》作"乌孤山"或"胡母思山");称由高昌横贯天山通往庭州的通道为"乌骨道"(两《唐书》简称为"乌骨"),正与《周书·突厥传》等所载"高昌国之北山"相合。"乌骨"正是 oʁuz 的另一音译形式。② 交河为车师前国的居地,高昌则是车师后王姑句③的居地。据《汉书·西域传》记载,元始(1~5)中,姑句便是"驰突出高昌壁,入匈奴"的,可证其居于高昌城。④ 《后汉书·耿秉传》更是明言"车师有后王、前王,前王即后王之子"。《汉书·匈奴传》载:

> 其明年(地节三年,前67年),西域城郭共击匈奴,取车师国,得其王及人众而去。单于复以车师王昆弟兜莫为车师王,收其余民东徙,不敢居故地,而汉益遣屯士分田车师地以实之。

汉文史籍及突厥语碑铭所载游牧于色楞格河、鄂尔浑河及土拉河一带的乌古斯部落,当即是自这一时期开始,辗转东徙至该地的。其时,分布于东部天山地区的乌古斯居民受汉文化的影响而取其部族名的略音便译形式"滑"(音 gu)为姓。敦煌市马圈湾(玉门关西)出土第282号汉简对此有载。其文曰:

> 郡仓居摄三年正月癸卯转两
>
> 入　　　　√居摄三年四月壬辰大煎
>
> 粟小石卅一石六斗六升大
>
> 都步昌候史尹钦隧长张博受就人敦煌高昌里滑护字君房⑤

简文大意为:敦煌郡仓于居摄三年(8)正月癸卯(农历正月二十五日),陆续运来粮食。至四月壬辰(四月十六日)入大煎都候官(玉门都尉府辖下的候官,在今小方盘城西南42公里)。由大煎都候官之步昌候史(步昌燧为大煎都候官所辖烽燧之一)尹钦及隧长张博从运粮夫滑护手中接收。滑护字君房,敦煌高昌里百姓。此简值得注意者有二:(一)撰写于"居摄三年",表明公元8年时敦煌已有高昌里;(二)滑姓出自车师,高昌里民滑护应为车师国移民后裔。此人除姓名外又有字曰"君房",表明其家族在敦煌居住有年,汉化已深。史称,征和四年(前89)"开陵侯将兵别围车师,尽得其王民众而还"。⑥ 疑

---

① 李树辉:《突厥原居地"金山"考辨》,待刊。

② 学术界也多持这一观点。参见小野川秀美:《鐵勒の一考察》,《東洋史研究》五卷二号,1940年,第8~9页;安部健夫著:《西ウィグル國史の研究》,京都:中村印刷株式会社出版部昭和三十年(1955年)版,"序章"第7~8页,第13~14页;羽田亨:《九姓回鶻とToquz Oyuz との關係を論ず》,《田亨博士史學論文集》上卷,《歷史篇》,东洋史研究会1957年版,第385~386页;岑仲勉:《突厥集史》,北京:中华书局1958年版,第666页;嶋崎昌著:《隋唐時代の東トゥルキスタン研究——高昌史研究を中心として》,第199页。

③ "姑句"为突厥语 køk 的音译,字面意思为"天"、"蓝",也可用于指称"东"、"东方"。据《乌古斯可汗的传说》、《史集》、《突厥世系》及《伊米德史》等书记载,乌古斯可汗娶有二妻,二妻各生三子。这六子又各有四子,分别为乌古斯部族24个部落的始祖。这一数目也恰与《词典》所载乌古斯部族的部落数目相吻合。与此相应,《汉书·西域传》中有猎骄靡娶有细君公主和匈奴妻的记载,《周书》等载有"别感异气,能征召风雨"的伊质泥师都"娶二妻,云是夏神、冬神之女也"的传说,段成式:《酉阳杂俎·毛篇》亦称:"北虏之先索国有泥师都,二妻生四子。"此"姑句"应就是诸书所载乌古斯可汗次妻所生三子中的长子 køk。

④ 史籍中常将高昌城称为"高昌壁",今人难辨其意。突厥语称高昌城为 qotʃu balïq,"壁"(包括北方地区地名中的"铺"、"堡"等)实为 balïq(城)的音译。

⑤ 吴礽骧、李永良、马建华释校《敦煌汉简释文》,兰州:甘肃人民出版社1991年版,第28页。

⑥ 此据《汉书·匈奴传上》。同书《西域传》"车师后城长国"条明载其时间为征和四年(前89)。

其民众被移徙至敦煌,并置高昌里予以安置。

永元三年(91),分布于东部天山地区的乌古斯部落,以"八部"之名见于《后汉书·耿夔传》、《后汉书·南匈奴传》等。此后直到2世纪初,仍以"滑"、"八滑"或"滑国"等名见于史籍。所谓"八滑",也便是《汉书·西域传》所载"车师前、后王及山北六国"。"八滑"曾出兵随班勇北击匈奴。《后汉书·西域传》载:

> 顺帝永建元年(126),勇率后王农奇子加特奴及八滑等,发精兵击北虏呼衍王,破之。勇于是上立加特奴为后王,八滑为后部亲汉侯。阳嘉三年(134)夏,车师后部司马率加特奴等千五百人,掩击北匈奴于闾吾陆谷,坏其庐落,斩数百级,获单于母、季母及妇女数百人,牛、羊十余万头,车千余两(辆),兵器什物甚众。

长期以来,学术界一直将"八滑"视为人名。参考史籍中有关"滑国"的记载可断定,此句应有脱漏。车师后部一直是东部天山地区乌古斯诸部落的领导部落,故封后王农奇之子加特奴为"王"而封其余诸部落首领为"亲汉侯"。"王"、"侯"皆为授予人的封号,不可能用于部落或"国"。此外,今人也一直将"滑"、"八滑"或"滑国"与嚈哒相等同。① 其实,嚈哒属印欧人种,操用印欧语;②"滑"属蒙古人种,③操用突厥语。二者所处的地理方位也不相同。嚈哒在据有塔里木盆地,东境达于焉耆后,才与"八滑"搭界。此外,从生产方式上也同样可看出二者的不同。《汉书·西域传》有"车师田者惊去"之语,《后汉书·西域传》称车师之蒲类国"颇知田作",东且弥国"颇田作",皆可证其有农业;《梁书·西北诸戎传》亦称滑国"有五谷"。然而,诸史记载却都表明"嚈哒是典型的行国"。④

4世纪末,附属于拓跋鲜卑的柔然渐趋强大,到402年时已统一了漠北草原。柔然的居地本在东部天山北麓。《魏书·西域传》:"车师国,一名前部……其地北接蠕蠕。"社仑任首领时,兼并诸部,称雄北方。《魏书·蠕蠕传》述其疆界:"其西则焉耆之地(按,这是就其天山南麓的西界而言,同传称大月氏国"北与蠕蠕接"),东则朝鲜之地,北则渡沙漠,穷瀚海,南则临大碛。其常所会庭则敦煌、张掖之北。"乌古斯其他诸部落此时又为柔然的属部。这期间,车师前部的居民还曾以"车"姓见于史籍,如车师前部王名车伊洛,⑤子名车歇、车波利。车歇、车波利与车伊洛分别于541年和542年入朝北魏,定居洛阳,有"车师前部王车伯生息郡月光墓铭"⑥为证;而其部民仍留居在高昌境内,仅见于《吐鲁番出土文书》中的车姓便

---

① 其中最具代表性的是谭其骧主编《中国历史地图集》,该书第4册(北京:中国地图出版社1982年版,第19～20、21～22、58～59页)在葱岭西的"嚈哒"下便直接括注为"滑国"。日本学者亦是如此,参见内田吟风:《北アジア史研究——鲜卑柔然突厥篇》,京都:同朋舍1975年版,第435页。

② 《通典》卷193,《边防》称其为"大月氏之种类也……先时国乱,突厥遣通设字诘强领其国。俗同吐火罗"(《太平寰宇记·嚈哒国》所记相同)。

③ 关于车师的人种问题,学术界一直有存在着"印欧人种"和"蒙古人种"两说。持前说者往往以吐鲁番盆地出土的印欧人种头骨为据,然而当地也曾出土大量的蒙古人种头骨和具有混合人种特征的头骨。考古人类学只能确定头骨的人种属性,却无法判定哪种头骨属于车师人,因此也就不能为确定车师人的人种特征提供佐证。史籍中常以"胡"指称"深目高鼻"的印欧人种居民。《梁书·西北诸戎传》称滑国"无文字,以木为契。与旁国通,则使旁国胡为胡书"。众所周知,回鹘文正是由粟特文演变而来的。此段史料可证"滑"不属于胡人,即不属于印欧人种。另据《梁职贡图》残卷所绘滑国使者图像也可断定,滑国人属于蒙古利亚人种。

④ 余太山著《两汉魏晋南北朝正史西域传研究》,北京:中华书局2003年版,第352页。

⑤ 《魏书·车伊洛传》。《北史·车师传》作"车夷落"。

⑥ 冯承钧:《西域南海史地考证论著汇辑》,北京:中华书局1957年版,第42页注释13,第62～63页注释20。

有 14 次之多。

十六国时,"八滑"为嚈哒属部。其王曾受北魏册封,受北魏节制,鲜与江南地区交往。故而,其贡使初到江南地区时,南朝统治者竟连其国名都闻所未闻。《梁书·裴子野传》曰:

> 是时西北徼外有白题及滑国,遣使由岷山道入贡。此二国历代弗宾,莫知所出。子野曰:"汉颍阴侯斩胡白题将一人。服虔注云:'白题,胡名也。'又汉定远侯击虏,八滑从之,此其后乎。"时人服其博识。敕仍使撰《方国使图》,广述怀来之盛,自要服至于海表,凡二十国。

以上记载亦见于《南史·裴子野传》。滑国于梁武帝天监十五年(516)始遣使向南朝贡献方物。此后,有关滑国的记载方见于《梁书·西北诸戎传》及《南史·夷貊列传》等史籍以及南京故宫博物院藏《梁职贡图》残卷滑国使者右侧的题记。前书称:

> 滑国者,车师之别种也。汉永建元年(126),八滑从班勇击北虏有功,勇上八滑为后部亲汉侯。自魏、晋以来,不通中国。至天监十五年(516),其王厌带夷栗陁始遣使献方物。普通元年,又遣使献黄师子、白貂裘、波斯锦等物。七年(526),又奉表贡献。

"车师之别种"是说滑国不受同属乌古斯部族的柔然①的控制而依附嚈哒;而称"其王厌带夷栗陁始遣使献方物",则是因为滑国当时受厌带(嚈哒)统治,正与《洛阳伽蓝记》卷五有关嚈哒(嚈哒)"受诸国贡献,南至牒罗,北尽勅懃,东被于阗,西及波斯,四十余国皆来朝贺"的记载相合。此后崛起的突厥的辖境为"东自辽海以西,西至西海万里,南至沙漠以北,北至北海五六千里";②《梁书·西北诸戎传》亦称滑国"后稍强大,征其旁国波斯、盘盘、罽宾、焉耆、龟兹、疏勒、姑墨、于阗、句盘等国,开地千余里"。关于突厥立国的时间,通常认为在西魏大统十一年(545)左右。开皇五年(585)七月,隋文帝击败突厥后与其立约,沙钵略可汗上表曰:"突厥自天置以来,五十余载。"③据此推测,其立国的时间当在北魏建明元年(梁中大通二年,530 年)前后;④而就在这同一时期(即 521 年前后),《魏书·袁翻传》中亦有"高车所住金山"的记载。《周书·突厥传》称突厥"居金山之阳",《北史·突厥传》更称其"世居金山之阳"。或正因此,内田吟风推测:"当时突厥曾与高车同居于金山,或只不过是高车中的一个部族。"⑤无论从崛起时间、居地还是所拓地域来看,滑国和突厥都不可能同时并存,二者只能是同一个政权。撰写于建昌元年(555)十二月廿三日的《宁朔将军魏斌造寺碑》阳面铭文有"其后,属突厥雄强,威震朔方,治兵练卒(卒),侵我北鄙"之谓,高昌之"北鄙"正与该部的栖息地毗邻。"八滑"之名,直到 8 世纪时还见于《磨延啜碑》,作 sɛkiz oʁuz(八姓乌古斯)。

① 李树辉:《尉犁地名和柔然源流考》,刊于《新疆大学学报》2007 年第 2 期。又收入中国中外关系史学会、暨南大学文学院主编:《丝绸之路与文明的对话》(《中外关系史论丛》第 11 辑),乌鲁木齐:新疆人民出版社 2007 年版。

② 《周书·突厥传》。

③ 《隋书·突厥传》。

④ 内田吟风:《北アジア史研究——鲜卑柔然突厥篇》(京都:同朋舍 1975 年版)第 431 页推测,突厥立国的时间在 533 年前后。

⑤ 内田吟风:《北アジア史研究——鲜卑柔然突厥篇》,第 482 页。

北魏时,滑国之徙居内地者还有人受赐官号作"高车滑骨"。① 另据敦煌文献 S.113《西凉建初十二年(416)敦煌郡敦煌县西宕乡高昌里籍》可知,敦煌县高昌里至西凉时仍存。莫高窟第 285 窟西魏大统四年和五年(538、539)的榜题中也有"滑□安"、"滑黑奴"、"(滑)昔海"、"滑一"等滑姓供养人题名,知西魏时敦煌仍有车师国滑姓遗民。滑姓男供养人画像的衣饰都具有乌古斯突厥人的特征:身着小口袖圆领褶服装,头戴卷沿帽,腰带上系有打火石、针筒、刀子、磨刀石、解结锥、绳等"鞊鞢七事"。正与广布于天山、阿尔泰山地区的突厥石人及《梁职贡图》中滑国使者的画像相同。可见,乌古斯诸部落以"滑"(车)为国名和姓氏,都源于其部族之名。

二、车师(姑师)的源与流

东部天山南北地区,早在秦汉时便是乌古斯人的栖息之地。5 世纪末,嚈哒沿天山南麓向乌古斯人(史籍称之为"高车")发动进攻,②杀死其首领穷奇,并掳去穷奇子弥俄突等。乌古斯"部众分散",或往附柔然,或投归北魏。魏遣宣威将军、羽林监孟威抚纳降人,置于高平镇。对嚈哒作战的失败,加剧了其统治集团内部的矛盾并导致内乱。阿伏至罗长子企图弑父自立而被杀。接着,阿伏至罗又被部众所杀,另立跋利延为首领。507 年左右,嚈哒再次出兵,企图立弥俄突为王。高车部众杀跋利延,迎纳弥俄突。弥俄突后在北庭附近挫败柔然军队,击杀了柔然首领伏图。熙平元年(516),柔然可汗丑奴再度发动攻势,一举擒杀弥俄突,尽复被高车国占去的土地,势力复振。③ 高车国遂处于"主丧民离"的境地,"其部众悉入嚈哒"。④

几年后,弥俄突弟伊匐在嚈哒的支持下率众还居故地,重建高车国,⑤并于神龟元年(518)遣使至北魏。⑥ 北魏也于当年遣敦煌僧人宋云及惠生等出使西域。⑦ 520 年,柔然内乱,阿那瑰被族兄示发所逼,投归北魏。其从父兄婆罗门击走示发,立为可汗。次年,伊匐乘机发动进攻,婆罗门战败,率 10 部落在凉州降北魏。522 年,伊匐向北魏遣使朝贡,被封为"镇西将军、西海郡开国公、高车王"。⑧ 523 年左右,阿那瑰重返故土,势力复振,一举击败伊匐。伊匐败归后又为其弟越居所杀。越居自称高车王。接着,越居又为柔然击败,伊匐子比适复杀越居而自立。541 年,比适又为蠕蠕所破,越居子去宾自蠕蠕投魏,封为"高车王",拜"安北将军、肆州刺史"。⑨ 此后不久,生活于这一地区的乌古斯诸部渐趋强大。及至后期,随着其"西破嚈哒,东走契丹,北并契骨"等一系列征伐战争的胜利,最终成为"威服塞外诸国"的强大草原帝国,对整个东亚、中亚、西亚乃至东欧的历史都产生了重大的影响——这恐怕是其举事者当初也不曾料想到的壮举。乌古斯部族亦因此进一步向周边扩散。《梁书·西北诸戎传》称:

---

① 《魏书·王宝兴传》。
② 松田寿男认为:"嚈哒对高车的最早出兵,是在太和十四年以后至同二十一年之间的某一年,即从公元490年至497年之间的某一时期发生的事件。"([日]松田寿男著,陈俊谋译《古代天山历史地理学研究》,北京:中央民族学院出版社 1987 年版,第 253 页)
③ 《梁书·西北诸戎传》称柔然"天监中,始破丁零,复其旧土"即指此事。
④ 《魏书·高车传》。
⑤ 《资治通鉴·梁纪》卷五。
⑥ 《魏书·肃宗纪》。
⑦ 《洛阳伽蓝记》卷五。《资治通鉴·梁纪》卷五记此事为梁普通三年,即 522 年。
⑧ 《魏书·肃宗纪》。
⑨ 《魏书·高车传》。

（滑国）元魏之居桑乾也，滑犹为小国，属芮芮。后稍强大，征其旁国波斯、盘盘、厨宾、焉耆、龟兹、疏勒、姑墨、于阗、句盘等国，开地千余里。土地温暖，多山川树木，有五谷。国人以麨及羊肉为粮。其兽有师子、两脚骆驼，野驴有角。人皆善射，着小袖长身袍，用金玉为带。女人被裘，头上刻木为角，长六尺，以金银饰之。少女子，兄弟共妻。无城郭，毡屋为居，东向开户。其王坐金床，随太岁转，与妻并坐接客。无文字，以木为契。与旁国通，则使旁国胡为胡书，羊皮为纸。无职官。事天神、火神，每日则出户祀神而后食。其跪一拜而止。葬以木为椁。父母死，其子截一耳，葬讫即吉。其言语待河南人译然后通。

以上记载亦见于《南史·夷貊列传》、《通志·西戎下》、《太平寰宇记·西戎四》及《册府元龟·外臣部·交侵》等而文字略有差异。将上文与史籍有关突厥的记载相比照，可知滑国（高车国）也便是前突厥汗国，二者所处的时代、地域及所征服的周边诸国乃至其习俗均相吻合。《周书·突厥传》等称突厥原"臣于茹茹，居金山之阳"；《太平御览》卷七九六称"其源出于塞北，自金山至后魏，文帝时已八九十年矣"（按，《魏书·高车传》称，世祖时"高车诸部望军而降者数十万落……皆徙置漠南千里之地"）。上文称滑国元魏时"犹为小国，属芮芮。后稍强大……开地千余里"，当时控有这一广大地区的也唯有突厥。突厥之乌古斯人属蒙古人种；据莫高窟第285窟所绘滑姓男供养人画像以及《梁职贡图》残卷所绘滑国使者图像可知，滑国人也属蒙古人种。《周书·突厥传》称突厥首领"土门遂自号伊利可汗，犹古之单于也。号其妻为贺敦，亦犹古之阏氏也……大官有叶护，次没（设），次特勒（勤），次俟利发，次吐屯发，及余小官凡二十八等"；滑国亦称王为"可汗"，称王妻为"可敦"，同样有"叶护"、"特勤"等官职。[1] "可汗"为 qaʁan（≤χaqan≤χa:n≤χan）的音译，"贺敦"、"可敦"为突厥语 qatun（≤χatun）的音译，"特勤"为突厥语 tɛgin 的音译，都是地道的突厥语词。至于"叶护"则是 jabʁu/jafʁu 的音译，虽源于粟特语，很早便为突厥语族群所借用。[2] 上文称"其言语待河南人译然后通"，"河南人"指操用突厥语的吐谷浑人。其人能译滑国语言，也可证滑国人操用的是突厥语。

前突厥汗国及回鹘汗国均为乌古斯部族所建。《新唐书·回鹘传》称回鹘"俗多乘高轮车元魏时亦号高车部"；如前所述，"高车"也便是滑国。《周书·突厥传》等称突厥可汗"牙帐东开，盖敬日之所出也"；上文称滑国"毡屋为居，东向开户"；《洛阳伽蓝记》卷五，《宋云行纪》称其"王张大毡帐，方四十步，周回以氍毹为壁"。《旧唐书·回鹘传》等称回鹘"署官号皆如突厥故事"，其可敦"金饰冠如角前指"；上文称滑国女人"头上刻木为角，长六尺，[3]以金银饰之"；库木吐喇79窟门壁右侧上方所绘回鹘女供养人像以及高昌故城出土壁画中回鹘女供养人群像的头饰也均为"如角前指"；《宋云行纪》称其王妃"头戴一角，长八尺，奇长三尺，以玫瑰五色装饰其上。王妃出则舆之，入坐金床，以六牙白象四狮子为床。自余大

---

① 参见余太山撰《两汉魏晋南北朝正史西域传要注》，北京：中华书局2005年版，第406～407页。

② 《词典》卷三称该词为"授予出身平民的比可汗低两级的人的称号"（M III.41）。

③ 南京故宫博物院藏《梁职贡图》残卷滑国使者右侧的题记、《梁书·西北诸戎传》以及《南史·夷貊列传》皆作"六尺"。《梁职贡图》题记及《梁书·西北诸戎传》取材于裴子野《方国使图》（余太山著：《两汉魏晋南北朝正史西域传研究》，第62页），如此看来，《南史·夷貊列传》亦当同样取材于裴子野《方国使图》。南朝一尺约25.8 cm，"六尺"合154.8 cm，显然过长，当为"六寸"（约15.48 cm）之误。《通典·西戎五》、《太平寰宇记·西戎四》、《通志·西戎下》及《册府元龟·外臣部·交侵》皆作"长六寸"。另有库木吐喇79窟门壁右侧上方所绘回鹘女供养人像的头饰及高昌故城出土壁画中回鹘女供养人群像的头饰（见于吐鲁番地区文物中心编辑《高昌壁画辑佚》，乌鲁木齐：新疆人民出版社1995年版）可参证。至于《洛阳伽蓝记》卷五，《宋云行纪》中"长八尺"之谓也明显有误。

臣妻皆随伞，头亦似有角，团圆下垂，状似宝盖"。上文称滑国男子"着小袖长身袍，用金玉为带"，也正与库木吐喇79窟壁画及柏孜克里克千佛洞第32窟壁画所绘诸回鹘男子的服饰相同。希腊文史料称突厥可汗所坐的"黄金王座"是"一个由四只孔雀承负的王座，全部是用大块黄金做成的"；[1]《宋云行纪》称其王"坐金床，以四金凤皇为床脚"；上文称"其王坐金床"。《周书·突厥传》等称突厥"其征发兵马、科税杂畜，辄刻木为数，并一金镞箭蜡封印之，以为信契"，"其书字类胡"；上文称滑国"无文字，以木为契。与旁国通，则使旁国胡为胡书"；《梁职贡图》残卷"滑国使臣图题记"作"刻之约物数"。《周书·突厥传》等称突厥"拜祭天神"；《魏书·高车传》称"五部高车合聚祭天，众至数万"；上文称滑国人"事天神、火神"。阿拉沟、鱼儿沟和交河沟北台地的车师墓葬以及希伯巨石冢多为竖穴木椁墓；上文称其"葬以木为椁"。突厥、回鹘但凡有亲人死去皆截耳、劓面；上文称滑国人"父母死，其子截一耳"。

此前治突厥史者，鲜有人注意到此条史料，也不曾有人将滑国与前突厥汗国相联系。上文有关习俗的记载弥足珍贵，正可与诸史《突厥传》及《大慈恩寺三藏法师传》等相参补。尤其是有关文字的记载表明：回鹘文源于粟特文，且早于如尼文。

隋唐时，滑国以突厥之名为人所熟知，故而转以突厥之名见于史籍，滑国之名随湮没不彰。由于滑国曾依附嚈哒，受嚈哒统治，至唐代时已将滑国与嚈哒混为一谈。《通典》卷一九三，《边防》"嚈哒"条云：

> 嚈哒国，或云高车之别种，或云大月氏之种类……按刘璠《梁典》，滑国姓嚈哒。后裔以姓为国号，转讹。又谓之挹怛焉。其本源，或云车师之种，或云高车之种，或云大月氏之种。又，韦节《西蕃记》云：亲问其国人，并自称挹阗。又按《汉书》，陈汤征郅支，康居副王挹阗抄其后。重此，或康居之种类。然传自远国，夷语讹舛。年代绵邈，莫知根实，不可得而辨也。今考其风俗、物产及诸家所说而编之。

关于其本源，杜佑因"年代绵邈，莫知根实"而只能以"或云……或云……或云"的形式，"考其风俗、物产及诸家所说而编之"。书中甚至将滑国、高车并列，各列有专传，而内容则是对《后汉书》、《梁书》、《南史》等史籍的摘抄。至宋人的著作，如《太平寰宇记》、《通志》将车师、滑国并列，《文献通考》将滑国、高车并列，《太平御览》将车师、滑国、高车并列。《通志·都邑略》中甚至还出现了"滑国与车师邻接，车师之别种也"的说法，而其内容更是对包括《通典》在内的诸史的摘抄。不成想，连唐人都"不可得而辩"的这一问题，竟因其著作的流传和诸史的抄袭而渐成定论，贻误至今。将滑国和前突厥汗国早期的历史、所处的地域及所征服的周边诸国乃至其习俗相比较，可发现二者完全相同。这也正是《梁书》、《南史》等记滑国不记突厥，《周书》等记突厥而不记滑国的原因所在。

从构成上看，这一时期的突厥已与其崛起之初完全不同，而是除乌古斯部族外，尚包括有众多无血缘关系的游牧部落以及操用印欧语诸城邦国在内的汗国（ɛl）。《隋书·铁勒传》等称其辖境有"诸姓八千余"。突厥汗国以及其后的后突厥汗国和回鹘汗国的统治，更加速了印欧语族群和突厥语族群在人种、语言及文化等方面的融合。

古代印欧语族群被称作"塔特"（tat）。由于突厥人中混有许多九姓胡人，以至于出现了 tatsïz tyrk

---

① ［法］阿里·玛扎海里著，耿昇译《丝绸之路——中国-波斯文化交流史》，乌鲁木齐：新疆人民出版社2006年版，第367页。

bolmas baʃsïz børk bolmas(没有"塔特"就不会有突厥;没有头颅就不会有帽子)的谚语,意为就像没有头就没有帽子一样,没有波斯人也就不会有突厥(M II.409);"也没有与波斯人隔绝的突厥人"(M I.455)。语言方面的融合表现为,无论是突厥语还是波斯语都从对方吸收了许多词汇乃至语法成分,就连突厥语的"n方言"和"h方言"也是在波斯语的影响下形成的语言变体。[①] 从文化方面来看,狼是乌古斯人的图腾,而牛是印欧语族群的图腾。[②] 考古学者就曾在土库曼斯坦南部阿尔登-捷别村落遗址一处祭台上发现一个高1.5 cm的金狼头和一个高7.5 cm的金牛头。[③] 二者共现于同一处祭台的情况,正是其文化融合现象的体现。

三、结　语

综上所论,"车师"二字的读音,直接涉及其人种、语言系属及诸多重大历史问题。"车师"、"姑师"二名是汉文史籍对突厥语 oʁuz(乌护,乌古斯)一词的不同汉译,应读作 gūsī/gūzī,而不应读作 chēshī 或 jūshī。欧洲学者将其发音构拟为 quz,维吾尔语将其译为 quʃ bɛglik(鸟国)无任何依据,应回译为 oʁuz(乌古斯)或 oʁuz qɛbilisi(乌古斯部族)。"车师前国"、"车师前部"应回译为 oʁuz qɛbilisiniŋ alqa bølyk uruʁï(乌古斯部族的阿尔喀·毕律克部落),"车师后国"、"车师后部"应回译为 oʁuz qɛbilisiniŋ qara bølyk uruʁï(乌古斯部族的卡拉·毕律克部落)。该词在史籍中均称为"国",故今人也不应称其为"族"。oʁuz 的本意为"初乳",乌孙国为其源头。该部族的得名及其狼图腾文化的形成,与汉代乌孙首领猎骄靡婴幼时为狼所哺养的神奇经历密切相关。其后,进而演变为包含有24个部落的部族名称,并以"滑"、"八滑"、"滑国"、"八部"或"高车国"等名见诸于史籍,其民众则以部族名称 oʁuz 的略音便译形式"滑"或"车"为姓。乌古斯是部落及人口最多的一个突厥语部族,也是构成前突厥汗国和回鹘汗国的主体部族。

---

① 李树辉:《古代突厥语方言研究——乌古斯和回鹘研究系列之七》,刊于《喀什师范学院学报》2002年第5期,2003年第1、2、4期,2004年第1期。

② 李树辉:《古代亚洲印欧语族群牛图腾崇拜研究》,待刊。

③ [乌兹别克斯坦] И.札巴罗夫、Г.德列斯维扬斯卡娅著,高永久、张宏莉译《中亚宗教概述》,兰州大学出版社2002年版,第28页。

Uigur Manuscripts Related to the Monks Sivšidu and Yaqšidu at "Abita-Cave Temple" of Toyoq

Dai Matsui

Faculty of Humanities, Hirosaki University, Hirosaki, Japan

The Sivšidu-Yaqšidu-manuscripts in the St. Petersburg collection

The St. Petersburg Branch of the Institute of Oriental Studies of the Russian Academy of Science (hereafter SPF), preserves one of the biggest and richest collections of the Central Asian manuscripts in the world. [1] Several years ago the Toyo Bunko (Oriental Library) of Japan obtained the microfilm of the Central Asian manuscripts collection under contract with SPF, and they has released the microfilm to academic circle since 2002. [2]

I have been researching the Old Uigur secular texts in the SPF collection through the microfilm brought to the Toyo Bunko, and noticed that a group of the Uigur personal names appear in many fragments. In most cases the Uigur texts were written on the verso side or the margin of the scroll of Chinese Buddhist sutra, whose Chinese texts enable us to joint the fragments. **Table** on the next page displays the result of jointing the sixty-eight fragments into fifty-five texts and the Uigur personal names as seen there.

In the table, we find most frequently the Uigur names Sivšidu (< Chin. 修士奴 *Xiu-shi-nu*) and Yaqšidu (< 药师奴 *Yao-shi-nu*): The former appears in twenty-six of the texts, the latter in twenty-nine, and they appear together in twelve. Besides, we can pick up other Uigur names appearing in common together with Sivšidu and Yaqšidu, as follow. [3]

Kimqadu < 金华奴 *Jin-hua-nu*: 9, 44, 45

Kinšidu < 贤师奴 *Xian-shi-nu*: 9, 16, 28, 39, 48

Kintso < 贤藏 *Xian-zang*: 11, 3, 17, 23, 28, 30, 38, 41, 42

Kuyšidu < 惠师奴 *Hui-shi-nu*: 2, 5, 9, 16, 21, 40, 44

Pusardu < 菩萨奴 *Pu-sa-nu*: 2, 3, 10, 12, 21, 28, 31, 33, 37, 39, 41, 42, 43, 44, 46

---

[1] The Central Asian texts in SPF have signatures beginning with SI (= Ser-India), though in this paper I mention to the texts with those signatures for sub categories (Kr, 2Kr, 3Kr, 4bKr, O, Dx, etc.) under SI.

[2] Ts. Sato, in *Tōyō Gakuhō* 83-4 (2002), p.085; Umemura 2002, p.203. Moreover, the International Dunhuang Project of the British Library (http://idp.bl.uk) has undertaken digitization of the SPF collection since 2004. Some of the Chinese Buddhist scrolls have been available on their website and whole of the collection is expected to follow.

[3] Text number corresponds to the Table; *Italic* stands for the text carrying neither Sivšidu nor Yaqšidu.

Qayimdu ＜ 华严奴 *Hua-yan-nu*：4，52

Sambodu ＜ 三宝奴 *San-bao-nu*：9，10，22，25，34，49

Tayšingdu ～ 大僧奴 ＜ 大乘奴 *Da-sheng-nu*：6，13，40

Vapqadu ＜ 法华奴 *Fa-hua-nu*：28，41

Kök-Taz：23，41

Qara：30，39

Sarïγ：12，18

Sävinč：9，37，53

Taz：3，12，20，29，37，46

Tiginä：4，15，26，31，44

The first nine of the personal names mentioned above, from Kimqadu to Vapqadu, have the Buddhist names derived from Chinese as well as Sivšidu and Yaqšidu. [1] Still more, whole of them are attested frequently with Buddhist title, such as *tutung* (＜ Chin. 都统 *du-tong*) "headpriest" or its abbreviation *tu*, [2] *šäli* (＜ Chin. 阇梨 *she-li* ＜ Skt. *ācārya*), [3] *šilavanti* [＜ Skt. *śīlava(n)t*] or its abbreviation *šila*, and *toyïn* "monk". These titles may well suggest that they were Buddhist monks. Summing up, they should be contemporaries each other and belong to one and the same Uigur Buddhist monastery, so that we may well give the appellation as the "Sivšidu-Yaqšidu-manuscripts" to the fifty-five texts.

Some texts of the Sivšidu-Yaqšidu-manuscripts are inscriptions written by Sivšidu, Yaqšidu and their colleagues in memory of their pilgrimage and meditation at the Buddhist caves, or their reading Chinese sutras. Others are drafts of contract and correspondence, or scribbles by inexperienced scribes. Most of these writings show the date simply with the twelve animal-year cycle, which does not allow us the definite dating. However, we can safely date them to the 13th- 14th centuries or the Mongol era, since most of the texts were written in the cursive or semi-cursive script. [4] Moreover, on No. 25 (4bKr 15), Sivšidu wrote down the date as *küskü yïl žụn čxšapt ay yiti ygrmikä* "On the seventeenth (day), the leap (*žụn* ＜ 闰 *run*) twelfth month, the year of Mouse". Consulting the Sino-Mongolian calendar of the 13th- 14th centuries, "the year of Mouse" with "the leap twelfth month" should be indentified with 庚子 *geng-zi* of 1240 AD. Therefore, the Sivšidu-Yaqšidu-manuscripts as the whole may well be dated in the mid-13th century. [5]

---

① See Zieme 1994, for the Uigur names composed of Chinese Buddhist term and *-tu* / *-du* (＜ Chin. 奴 *nu*)；For Uigur transcription of Chinese, see Shogaito 1987；Shogaito 2003, pp. 126 – 136.

② Oda 1987.

③ Hamilton 1984, pp. 425 – 431；Zieme 1981, pp. 251 – 252；Oda 1987, n. 108.

④ For the scripts as the criteria for dating, see Moriyasu 2004b, pp. 228, 232 – 233.

⑤ It may be noted that the date by Yaqšidu in No. 15 (3Kr 5 – 22), *ud yïl žụn aram ay säkiz ygrmikä* "On the eighteenth (day), the leap first month, the year of Ox", might correspond to 乙丑 *yi-chou* of the 3rd year of 泰定 *Tai-ding*, 1325 AD, much later than No. 25 of 1240 AD. However, I regard that the inscription on No. 15 should be a scribble and its date is not actual.

Table: The Sivšidu-Yaqšidu-Manuscripts

No.	Signature	Sivšidu	Yaqšidu	Other Personal Names	Chinese Sutra		Taisho Identification		Edition or Photo Reproduction
1	Kr IV 250 + Дх 3652	Sivšidu		Qatïγ ayaγ-qa tägimlig	大般涅槃经	12	375	682c26 – 683a14	Matsui 2004, p. 62; DhSPB 11
2	Kr IV 252 + Дх 12145 + Дх 3650		Yaqšidu	Čïntso, Atay, Qumaγ, Kuyšidu, Pusardu-šäli	道神足无极变化经	17	816	813b26 – 813c03	Matsui 2005a, (5)
3	Kr IV 253 + 3Kr 5 – 21	Sivšidu	Yaqšidu	Pusardu-šäli, Taz-tutung, Balïčoγ-tutung, Kintso-šäli	灌顶随愿往生十方净土经	21	1331	531b28 – 532a02	
4	Kr IV 255		Yaqšidu	Tiginä-šäli, Qayïmdu-tutung, Buyana-tu	合部金光明经	16	664	380b16 – 380c08	
5	Kr IV 258 + 4bKr 34	[Si] všidu	Yaqšidu	Kuyšidu-tutung, Vapsïndu-tu(tung)	大般若波罗蜜多经	7	220	313b28 – 313c24	
6	Kr IV 262			Tayšïngdu-tutung	观药王药上二菩萨经	20	1161	665c07 – 665c17	Matsui 2004, No. 5
7	Kr IV 265		Yaqšidu	Buyana-tutung	妙法莲华经	9	262	038b08 – 038c11	Matsui 2004, No. 6
8	Kr IV 272		Yaqšidu		大般若波罗蜜多经	7	220	314a09 – 314b01	
9	Kr IV 284		Yaqšidu	Qan-Kimqadu-šilavanti, Kuyšidu-tutung, Kinšidu-tutung, šinšidu-tutung, Sambodu-šäli, Sävinč-tutung	妙法莲华经	9	262	033b01 – 033b14	
10	Kr IV 367 + Kr IV 395			Singdu-toyïn, Pïnguy, Šïnmi-šäli, Toqo-šäli, Sambodu-šäli, Pusardu-Qya, Ötüš-šäli, Čiti	(Uigur Buddhist sutra)				
11	Kr IV 616			Kintso-šäli	(No Chinese text)				
12	3Kr 3 – 15 + 4bKr 33		Yaqšidu	Yinä-Toγrïl, Sarïγ-toyïn, Atay, Pusardu, Taz-tu, Ödi-Toγrïl	大般涅槃经	12	374	564b15 – 564b21	
13	3Kr 3 – 16			大僧双尸罗, Liguy-šïl[a]	妙法莲华经	9	262	060b20 – 060b24	

续 表

No.	Signature	Sivšidu	Yaqšidu	Other Personal Names	Chinese Sutra	Taisho		Taisho Identification	Edition or Photo Reproduction
14	3Kr 4 – 20	Sivšidu			放光般若经	8	221	053a08 – 053a17	
15	3Kr 5 – 22		Yaqšitu	Ărük, Tiginä	No Chinese text				
16	3Kr 7 – 25 + Дх 3224	Sivšidu	Yaq[šidu?]	Kuyšidu, Kinšidu, Tayso, Buyan-Qulï	妙法莲华经	9	262	060b02 – 060b29	Matsui 2005a, (1) + (2)
17	3Kr 8 – 27	Sivšidu	Yaqšidu	Kintso-šäli	Chinese Commentary				
18	3Kr 33b	Sivšidu		Šinsun-šäli, Özmiš-Toγrïl, Arqaγur-ïnal, Sarïγ-toyïn, Öküz-Toγrïl, Känt-Qaya, Atay-ïnal	No Chinese text(?)				SUK Lo10 (with modifications)
19	4bKr 2	Sivšidu	Yaqšidu	Buyana-tu(tung), Toyïn-Qulï	添品妙法莲华经	9	264	164b05 – 164b23	
20	4bKr 3	Sivšidu		Taz	摩诃般若波罗蜜经	8	223	223c17 – 223c26	
21	4bKr 8	Sivšidu	Yaqšidu	Kuyšidu-tutung, Pusardu-šäli, Tolu-kyä	大般涅槃经	12	374	447a24 – 447b10	
22	4bKr 11		Yaqšidu	Idsüin-tutung, Taqïčoγ-tutung, Sambodu-tutung	菩萨璎珞本业经	24	1485	1014b12 – 1014c01	
23	4bKr 12	Sivšidu	Yaqšidu	Miguy-tutung, Tayšitu-tutung, Kintso, Kök-Taz, Vapdu	大智度论	25	1509	645a07 – 645b03	
24	4bKr 13	Sivšidu		Äsän	菩萨璎珞本业经	24	1485	1010b27 – 1010c23	
25	4bKr 15	Sivšidu		Sambodu-šäli	妙法莲华经	9	262	041c15 – 042a26	
26	4bKr 16a		Yaqšidu	Tiginä-tutung	大智度论	25	1509	161c15 – 162b07	
27	4bKr 18		Yaqšidu	Buyana-tutung	妙法莲华经	9	262	011b09 – 011b28	

续 表

No.	Signature	Sivšidu	Yaqšidu	Other Personal Names	Chinese Sutra	Taisho Identification			Edition or Photo Reproduction
28	4bKr 20	Sivšidu	Yaqšidu	Kinšidu, Kintso, Pusardu, Pusardu-šäli, Pusardu-Taz, Vapqadu, Vapšidu	大般涅槃经	12	374	452c09 – 452c17	Tugusheva 1996, No. 6; Zieme 1998; Matsui 2004, No. 1
29	4bKr 22	Sivšidu		Taz-tu	大般涅槃经	12	374	452b20 – 452c08	
30	4bKr 24			Kintso-šäli, Qara-tutung, Činšidu	大般涅槃经	12	374	452c21 – 453a03	
31	4bKr 25 + 4bKr 31	Sivšidu	Yaqši[du]	Pusardu-šäli, Tigin Oyul-Qaya, Tigüči-tutung	大般涅槃经	12	374	452b20 – 452c17	
32	4bKr 36	Sivšidu	Yaqšidu		放光般若经	8	221	081c05 – 081c07	
33	4bKr 38a		Yaqšidu	Pusardu-šäli	大般涅槃经	12	375	810c29 – 811a08	
34	4bKr 42			Sambodu	合部金光明经	16	664	361a10 – 361a 18	Matsui 2004, No. 7
35	4bKr 48 + Дх 12106		Yaqšidu	Buyana-tutung	大般涅槃经	12	374	562a24 – 562b03	DhSPB 16 (Дх 12106)
36	4bKr 49	Sivšidu			大般涅槃经	12	374	452c05 – 452c11	
37	4bKr 71			Qačuq, Tanguta(-šäli), Pusardu(-Taz), Sävinč-Qaya, Käd-Tonga, Äsäna, Täsik, Taz-tu, Tsompa-bikäči, Sävinč	妙法莲华经卷十 (Title only)	9	262		Umemura 2002; Matsui 2004, No. 4
38	4bKr 142 + Дх 12163		Yaqšidu	Kintso-šäli	维摩诘所说经	14	475	538b22 – 538c11	DhSPB 16 (Дх 12163)
39	4bKr 186		Yaqšidu	Pusardu-šäli, 智奴尊者, Kinšidu, Qara	合部金光明经	16	664	360c06 – 360c26	
40	4bKr 187a	Sivšidu		Kuyšitu, 惠师奴都通, 大乘奴都, 戒乘都通	妙法莲华经	9	262	025c17 – 026a06	
41	4bKr 218	Sivšidu	Yaqšidu	Vapqadu, Kintso, Pusardu, Kök-Taz	(No Chinese text)				

续 表

No.	Signature	Sivšidu	Yaqšidu	Other Personal Names	Chinese Sutra		Taisho Identification		Edition or Photo Reproduction
42	4bKr 236		Yaqšidu	Pusardu(-Taz), Kintso, Titso	维摩诘所说经	14	475	538c20 – 538c25	Tugusheva 1996, No. 5; Zieme 1998; Matsui 2004, No. 2
43	Дх 3225			Pusardu-*tutung*	妙法莲华经	9	262	048b17 – 048b29	Matsui 2005a, (3)
44	Дх 3226 + Дх 9535 + Дх 9536	Sivšidu	Yaqšidu	Kuyši-du, Pusardu(-qul)-*šäli*, Tiginä, Kimqatu	放光般若经	8	221	081c09 – 081c23	Matsui 2005a, (4)
45	Дх 3654		Yaqšidu	Äsän-čim, Tükälä, Tuɣmiša, Bärinč-Qiz, Kimqatuf-*šilavanti*, Šinvapdu-*šilavanti* = 善法 奴尸罗	放光般若经	8	221	025a23 – 025a30	Matsui 2005a, (7)
46	Дх 9548	Sivšidu		Pusardu, Qumaɣ, Taz	弘明集 (Title only)	52	2102		DhSPB 14
47	Дх 9553	Sivšidu			金刚般若波罗蜜经	25	1510	779c23 – 779c28	DhSPB 14
48	Дх 9560	Sivšidu		Kinšidu, Kušidu (= Kuyšidu?)	大般涅槃经	12	374	514b27 – 514c03	DhSPB 14
49	Дх 9569			[Sam]bodu, Qïtay-Toyrïl, Pin(tso?)	大智度论	25	1509	084b01 – 084b13	Matsui 2004, No. 8
50	Дх 9571	Sivšidu			妙法莲华经	9	262	060b06 – 060b16	DhSPB 14
51	Дх 12109		Yaqšidu	Qayïmtu-*tutung*, Atay-Tonguz, Atay, Šintso	道神足无极变化经	17	816	813c19 – 813c22	DhSPB 16
52	Дх 12234				妙法莲华经	9	262	060c13 – 061a11	DhSPB 16
53	Дх 12243			Sävinč	添品妙法莲华经	9	264	184c21 – 185a10	DhSPB 16
54	O 83	Sivšidu			金刚般若波罗蜜经	8	235	749b20 – 749c04	
55	津艺 014	Sivšidu	Yaqšidu		合部金光明经	16	664	373c06 – 373c21	Zieme / Niu 1996; Matsui 2004, No. 3

The Sivšidu-Yaqšidu-manuscripts and Toyoq

Though there is no declaration concerning the archaeological sites where the Sivšidu-Yaqšidu-manuscripts were originally discovered, we may suppose that they come from any of oases or sites in the Turfan depression, because forty-two of the manuscripts bore any signature of Kr, 3Kr and 4bKr, which stand for that they were obtained by N. I. Krotkov, the Russian Consulate General at Urumuqi (1898 – 1918). Consequently, the remaining texts, Nos. 43 – 55, which have been regarded as from Dunhuang, also must come from the Turfan area.[①]

Further we can identify the life sphere of Sivšidu, Yaqšidu and the other Uigur monks closely to the Toyoq Caves, according to the Uigur inscription written by Sivšidu himself on No. 24 (4bKr 13): $_2$[kü](s)kü yïl bišinč ay on yangïqa män $_3$(t)ïyoq qïzïl-lïγ sivšidu tutung qy-a bu $_4$ïduq tavγač kün-tä "On the tenth (day), the fifth month, the year of Mouse, I, Sivšidu-tutung of the Tïyoq valley [wrote] on this sacred Chinese scroll". It clearly displays that Sivšidu was "of the Tïyoq valley (tïyoq qïsïl-lïγ)". He also wrote another inscription as (t)ïyoq qïzïl tisär nägü bolur ärki tip qulutï sivšidu čïztï(m) "How is being the Tïyoq valley? Thus saying, I, the (Buddha's) servant Sivšidu, drew (= wrote) [this inscription]" on No. 1 (Kr IV 250). Still more, the scribe of the inscription on the recto side of No. 37 (4bKr 71), named Sävinč, was also "of Tïyoq (tïyoqluγ)".[②] The Uigur place name Tïyoq is a transcription of Chin. 丁谷 Ding-yu and identified to the modern 吐峪 Toyoq. As well known, Toyoq is a famous Buddhist sanctuary site with the cave temples on the both sides of the Toyoq valley.

Also we may note that Yaqšidu, one of Sivšidu's colleagues, stated himself as lükčüng-lüg "of Lükčüng (modern 鲁克沁 Lukchun < Uig. < Chin. 柳中 Liu-zhong)" in No. 23 (4bKr 12). However, I suppose that he was originated from (or born at) Lukchun but lived at Toyoq. Toyoq was materially supported by the population in Lukchun, as suggested by the Tudum-šäli inscription of the West Uigur period (ca. 10th-12th cc.), which memorized that Tudum-šäli donated the cultivated land in Lukchun (lükčüng) to the Buddhist monastery at the Toyoq valley (tïyoq qïsïl) and that the monastery by themselves controlled it.[③] Consequently it is the most plausible that the monks as seen in the Sivšidu-Yaqšidu-manuscripts should have put basement of their lives and Buddhist activities at the Toyoq Caves, and, in other words, that the Sivšidu-Yaqšidu-manuscripts were originally discovered there.

Most of the Toyoq Caves were opened during the reign of the 高昌 Gaochang Kingdom, alive throughout

---

① The considerable number of the Turfan texts in the SPF collection have been mistaken as from Dunhuang and given the Dx (= Dunhuang) signatures, such as Nos. 43 – 53 here. See, e. g. , DhSPB 17, postscript: 3; Rong 1996, p. 122; Sekio 2001. No. 54 was brought by S. F. Oldenburg, who researched not only at Dunhuang in 1914 – 1915 but also at Turfan in 1909 – 1910. No. 55 belongs to the "Dunhuang collection" of Tianjin, which had been purchased at the market and supposedly might include the Turfan materials.

② See Umemura 2002, though his reading män tïyoqluγ inčgä ärti should be corrected into män tïyoqluγ sävinčirik[ip] "I, Sävinč of Tïyoq, [wrote this inscription] disgustedly". See Matsui 2004, p. 53.

③ Geng 1981 = Geng 2003b, pp. 426 – 427; Moriyasu 1985, p. 35.

the Tang period, and renovated under the West Uigur Kingdom.[1] That is suggested not only by the Tudum-*šäli* inscription mentioned above, but also by an Uigur correspondence, 4bKr 222, which is written in semi-square script and certainly dated to the West Uigur Kingdom: It is addressed to *tïyoqluγ liu sič̌u* "the Temple-manager (Uig. *sič̌u* < 寺主 *si-zhu*) [named] Liu of Toyoq" from the Great-*tutung* (*uluγ tutung*) and referring to "a new temple (*yangï vrxar*)".[2] The Sivšidu-Yaqšidu-manuscripts prove that the Toyoq Caves were prosperous even in the Mongol times. That is also witnessed by the Mongolian fragments of the Buddhist sutra and by the temple banners, which were excavated at Toyoq by the German expeditions.[3] The Mongolian fragments seem to have been printed in China proper, indicating that the cultural and commercial network of the Uigur Buddhists at Toyoq reached at the further east in the Mongol times.

Abita qur "Abita-Cave" in Toyoq

Another noteworthy fact is that six of the Sivšidu-Yaqšidu-manuscripts mention to *abita qur* as the place for their worshipping and religious activities: No. 2, [14]*abita (qu)r atlγ varxar* "temple named *Abita-qur*"; No. 6, [2]*abita qu(r) sängräm* "*Abita-qur* Monastery"; No. 7, [11]*abi-ta qur-ta bošγut* [12]*alγalï* "to take instruction in *Abita-qur*"; No. 10, [2]*män pusarudu qy-a* [3]*bu abita qur-ta* [4]*iki ay qy-a turup* [5]*birü tägindim ärti* "[2]I, Pusardu-Qya, [4-5]certainly have been staying humbly for about two months [3]in this *Abita-qur*"; No. 34, [1]*abita qur-ta* "in *Abita-qur*"; No. 49, [2]*bu abita qur vaxar* "This *Abita-qur*-Temple".

Uig. *abita* (~ *abi-ta* ~ *amita*) is a loanword from Chin. 阿弥陀 *a-mi-tuo* (< Skt. *amita* ~ *amitābha* ~ *amitāyus*),[4] and *qur* is a transcription of Chin. 窟 *ku* (**k'uət*) "cave, grotte". Consequently *abita qur* means "Abita-Cave", and *abita qur sängräm* or *abita qur va(r)xar* may well be regarded as one and the same monastery (*sängräm* < Skt. *saṃghārāma*) or temple (*va(r)xar* < Sogd. *βrx'r* < Skt. *vihāra*). Its name is supposed to be the translation of Chin. 阿弥陀窟寺 "Abita-Cave Temple", even though not yet attested in the Chinese historical sources nor in the Turfan Chinese texts.[5]

Taking into account that the Sivšidu-Yaqšidu-manuscripts may well come from the Toyoq Caves, we can proceed to the conclusion that this "Abita-Cave Temple/Monastery" should be also located at the Toyoq Caves. The Uigur phrase *aγdïnïp* < *aγtïn*- "to climb up" attested in No. 2 and No. 6 (see below) would lend support to me, indicating that "the Abita-Cave Temple" would have been built on the high cliff of the valley just like the Toyoq valley.

---

[1] Miyaji 1995/1996.

[2] Tugusheva 1996, No. 7, though her reading *bučung* for *tutung*, *tavušlug* for *tïyoqluγ* and *šič̌i* for *sič̌u* should be corrected. For the correspondence between Uig. *sič̌u* and Chin. *si-zhu*, see Ht VII, p. 304.

[3] BTT XVI, Nrn. 22, 45; CATB, Nos. 24, 203, 204.

[4] Cf. UW, p. 37.

[5] For the Buddhist temples as seen in the Turfan Chinese texts, see Machida 1990. Noteworhty are those named = 窟寺 "XX-Cave-Temple", e. g., 外窟寺 *Wai-ku-si*, 西窟寺 *Xi-ku-si*, 宁戎窟寺 *Ning-rong-ku-si*, and 仙窟寺 *Xian-ku-si*. According to Prof. Kōgi Kudara, the latter two seem to belong to the Bezeklik cave temples. See Kudara 1992, pp. 2–4.

Among the Toyoq Caves, the Cave Stein IV-Vii and Cave 20 have the wall paintings which visualized the Pure Land of *A-mi-tuo* according to the essential triad of the Chinese sutras on the Pure Land Buddhism: 无量寿经 *Wu-liang-shou jing* (Taisho No. 360: Larger *Sukhāvatīvyūha-Sūtra*), 阿弥陀经 *A-mi-tuo jing* (Taisho No. 366: Smaller *Sukhāvatīvyūha-Sūtra*), and 观无量寿经 *Guan wu-liang-shou jing* (Taisho No. 365: **Amitāyur-dhyāna Sūtra*). [1] From the early 7th century on, possibly influenced by the Chinese Buddhism in China Proper, the cult of Pure Land spread widely among the inhabitants in the whole of the Turfan area under the direct domination of the Tang Dynasty. [2]

After the fall of the Tang domination, the Pure Land Buddhism of the Chinese in the Turfan area have influenced even on the Uigurs, their new ruler. [3] Especially the cult of Amitābha "the Buddha of Infinite Light" seems to have been rather effective in the course of the Uigur conversion into Buddhism from Manichaean, which was also the cult of light, during the later half of the 10th century. [4] As confirmed by the scholars, the Uigurs had the translations of the essential triads of Pure Land Buddhism sutras, [5] as well as of another literature entitled *Baγ-lin-ši-ki* (< 白莲社经 *Bai-lian-she jing*) with the contents concerning Amitābha. [6] The wish to be reborn in the Land of *Abita Burxan* "Abita Buddha" is often expressed in the Uigur Buddhist colophons [7] and even in a religious contract (SUK Mi09) among the four persons named Öz-Toγrïl, [...]-Toγrïl, ČYXWSY and Antso (< Chin. 安藏 *An-zang*). [8] However, those Uigur texts related to the Pure Land Buddhism mostly come from Sengim, Murtuq, the Ruined City 交河 Jiaohe (Yarkhoto), and Temples α and μ in the Ruined City 高昌 Gaochang (Qočo), while thus far no one has been identified as from Toyoq. [9] From this viewpoint, the Sivšidu-Yaqšidu-manuscripts and the "Abita-Cave Temple" attested in them could be important, since they reveal that one of the bases of the Uigur Pure Land Buddhism did exist also in the Toyoq Caves.

Conclusive remarks

A considerable number of the Chinese — Uigur bilingual manuscripts of secular and religious texts in the SPF collection apparently look similar to the Sivšidu-Yaqšidu-manuscripts. We may expect that they should be related or jointed with those mentioned here, by identifying the Chinese texts on the reverse side or by the

---

[1] Miyaji 1995/1996. Miyaji relates also Cave 42 to those Chinese sutras of the Pure Land cult, though Nobuyoshi Yamabe refuted his opinion. See Yamabe 1999; Yamabe 2002; Yamabe 2004.

[2] Arakawa 2000; Arakawa 2004a; Arakawa 2004b.

[3] Zieme 1992, esp. pp. 86 – 88; Zieme 2005, p. 36.

[4] Kudara 1995, pp. 13 – 14. Also see Moriyasu 2004a, pp. 174 – 192, for the Uigur conversion to Buddhism.

[5] Zieme/Kudara 1985, pp. 11 – 15; Zieme 1985; Kudara 1995, pp. 1 – 2; Elverskog 1997, pp. 50 – 51, 63 – 65; Kudara/Zieme 1997.

[6] Zieme/Kudara 1985, pp. 23 – 24; Elverskog 1997, pp. 86 – 87; Geng 2003a = Geng 2003b, pp. 312 – 321; Geng 2004; Geng 2008.

[7] BT XXVI, Nrn. 3, 12, 40, 42, 128, 135, 144, 149.

[8] See Matsui 2005b, p. 48, for restoration of the personal names crossed off on the original contract.

[9] For the original site number of the Berlin fragments, see Elverskog 1997, op. cit.; BT XXVI, op. cit. The two fragments, published by Kudara/Zieme 1997, come from Yarkhoto. Not certain is the excavation site of the manuscript in the Beijing National Library newly edited by Geng 2003a (= Geng 2003b, pp. 312 – 321; Geng 2004). SUK Mi09 has no site signature.

examination on the original paper. Such works will provide us with materials for further historical reconstruction of the Uigur Buddhism in Toyoq and the Turfan area.

Edition of the Sivšidu-Yaqšidu-manuscripts
with attestations of *abita qur* [①]

No. 2   Kr IV 252 + Дх 3650 + Дх 12145 verso (= Matsui 2005a, 5)

Дх 12145	1	道神足变化经
	2	bu tavγač kün-tä män pusardu šäli bitiyü [tägintim]
	3	čïn'ol äžük ärmäz ol küskü
Kr IV 252	4	küskü yïl bišinč bu tavγač kün-tä
	5	[t]avγač kün-tä bitimäk tamuluq bolγu qïlïnč ol tip
	6	saqïnïp män čintso atay qumaγ bitidim čïn'ol äžük ärmäz
	7	küskü yïl törtünč ay altï otuz-qa qulutï kuyšïṭu tutung
	8	bu tavγač kün-tä män yaqšidu tutung qy-a bitiyük män
	9	küskü yïl bišinč ay biš yangï uluγ yangï kün-tä qulut
	10	küskü yïl bišinč ay altï ygrmikä bu tavγač k[ün]-(tä)(…)
Дх 3650	11	män y[aqšid]u tut[ung] (qy-a)[ ]
	12	y-a qutluγ bolzun kim-ning ög qar(ï)n-ta ünmä(k)
	13	[t]uγmaq-lïγ üč yirtinčü-nüng uluγ
	14	abita (qu)r atlγ varxar-ta · amru aγ(ḍ)ïnïp yükünsär ·
	15	ažunïn tuγum-ïn sämritip aγḍïnïp tuγγa(l)ï tužit-ta ·
	16	(ï)duq tavγač kün-tä qulutï qul kiši yaqši(ṭ)u tutung
	17	iki käzig ödig qïltïm ödig ol
	18	küskü yïl bišinč ay bir Y[ ](…)[ ]
	19	[tavγa]č kün ü(z)ä (b)[iti](d)[im]

₁道神足变化经 *Dao-shen-zu bian-hua-jing*

₂On this Chinese scroll, I, Pusardu-*šäli* humbly wrote [this incription].

₃It is true. There is no false. [The year of] Rat

₄The year of Rat, the Fifth [month]. On this Chinese scroll

₅ "Writing on the Chinese scroll is a behavior to be reborn in Hell", ₆thus thinking, I, Čintso, and Atay and Qumaγ wrote [this]. It is true. There is no false.

₇The year of Rat, the Fourth month, on the Twenty-sixth. I, Kuyšïṭu-*tutung*

---

① Here I postponed the edition of No. 10 (Kr IV 367 + Kr IV 395), which will be studied in the future by Prof. Abdurishid Yakup (Berlin).

₈on this Chinese scroll, I, Yaqšidu-*tutung* wrote [this]. I

₉The year of Rat, the Fifth month, on the Fifth, which is the great new day. I

₁₀The year of Rat, the Fifth month, on the Sixteenth [day]. On this Chinese scroll

₁₁I, Y[aqšid]u-*tut*[*ung*, wrote this(?)]

₁₂₋₁₃Oh, may it be fortunate [as for] those who are born from mothers' womb. ₁₃The *Tri-sahasra-mahā-sahasra-loka-dhātu*

₁₄Since [I] usually clime to the temple named Abita-Cave and worship [there], ₁₅[I] would fatten (i. e. make rich) [my?] life and ascend to *Tušita*-Heaven to be reborn [there]. ₁₆[Thus saying?] on the sacred Chinese scroll, I, the (Buddha's) servant Yaqšidu-*tutung*, ₁₇made (= wrote) two lines of memory. This is memory.

₁₈The year of Rat, the Fifth month, on the F[irst or Eleventh day] . . .

₁₉On [the Chine]se scroll I [wrote].

Notes

2v1: This Chinese is seemingly an abbreviation for 道神足无极变化经 *Dao-shen-zu wu-ji bian-hua-jing*, the title of the Chinese Buddhist sutra on the verso side.

2v3, äžük ärmäz: "There is no false". My former reading *ažun* "life" should be corrected into *äžük* "false". ①

2v7: This line is written upside down.

2v9, uluγ yangï kün: This "great new day" is May 5ᵗʰ, known as 重五节 *Chong-wu-jie* or 端午节 *Duan-wu-jie*, one of the seasonal festivals in the Chinese calendar. This passage may well show that the Uigur Buddhist monks also regarded May 5ᵗʰ as an important fest, then calling "great new day". Similar festival days are seen in the Uigur Buddhist colophons: U 1919: *qutluγ qoyn yïl törtünc ay biš yägirmi aγïr uluγ posat kün* "Gesegnetes Schaf-Jahr, vierter Monat, am Fünfzehnten, dem sehr großen Fasten-Tag"; U 4709: *kui šipqanlïγ ud yïl altïnc ay bir yangï aγïr uluγ posad bačaq kün* "(im) Rind-Jahr, (das) dem 癸 *gui* der 十干 *shi-gan* (-Reihe) entspricht, (im) sechsten Monat, am Ersten, dem sehr großen Fasten-Tag"; U 4707: *qutluγ king šipqan-lïγ yunt yïl säkizinč ay bir yangï aγïr uluγ posat bač*[*a*]*γ kün üzä* "im glücklichen Pferde-Jahr, das dem 庚 *geng* der 十干 *shi-gan* (entspricht), im achten Monat, am Ersten, dem heiligen, großen Fasten-Tag". ②

2v12, ög qarïn: Hendiadys corresponding to Chin. 胞胎 *bao-tai* "mother's womb". ③

2v13, üč yirtinčü uluγ: Seemingly a mistake for *üč ming uluγ üč yirtinčü* ~ Chin. 三千大千世界 < Skt. *Tri-sahasra-mahā-sahasra-loka-dhātu*.

2v14 - 15: These two lines compose an alliterative verse: *abita qur atlγ varxar-ta: amru aγḍïnïp yu̱künsär: ažunïn tuγum-ïn sämritip: aγḍïnïp tuγγalï tužit-ta*. The last stanza is inverted to alliterate.

---

① Matsui 2004, p. 66; Matsui 2005, p. 148. I am grateful to Prof. Peter Zieme for correcting my mistake.

② BT XXIII, p. 148; BT XXVI, p. 136; Matsui 2008c, p. 26.

③ Uigurica II, p. 44.

2v15, ažunïn tuɣum-ïn: The hendiadys *ažun tuɣum* ~ *tuɣum ažun* corresponds to Chin. 生趣 *sheng-qu* "birth and reincarnation". ①

2v17, qulutï qul: Uig. *qulutï* < *qulut* is itself derived from *qul* "servant, slave". ② Here the scribe used them together to emphasize modesty.

2v18, bir Y[　]: To be restored as either *bir y*[*angï-qa*] "on the first (day)" or *bir y*[*grmikä*] "on the twentieth day."

No. 6　Kr IV 262 verso (= Matsui 2004, No. 5)

1　tonguz yïl čaxšapt ay bir yangï-qa · qulutï tayšingdu
2　tutung · abita qu(r) sängräm-kä yükünäyin
3　saqïnayïn aɣdïnïp yük(ü)nüp inč tägintim ödig
4　bolup ür ky-ä turzun tip ödiglätim čïn'ol
5　ážük ymä ärmäz ol saqïnïp bitidim yamu

[The rest is omitted]

₁On the first (day), the twelfth month, the year of Boar. I, the (Buddha's) servant Tayšingdu-₂*tutung*, ₂₋₃climbing up to the Abita-Cave Monastery to worship and meditate, and 3(I) worshipped and obtained the peace (in mind). ₃₋₄"[This writing] shall be memory and ₄stay [here] so long!" thus saying, I recorded [it]. It is true [and] ₅there is no false. Thus meditating, I did write.

Notes

6v1, yangï-qa: Inserted in the left side of the line.

6v1, tayšingdu: The final -*W* is drawn out for space filler.

6v4, turzun: The final -*WN* is written as like -*T*'.

6v5, ážük ymä ärmäz: See the note **2v3**.

No. 7　Kr IV 265 verso (= Matsui 2004, No. 6)

[Missing]

1　bu tavɣač kün [　　　　　　　　　]
2　kiši　　　　bit(i)[　　　　　　　　]
3　yana ymä [　　　　　　　　　　　]
4　män yaqšidu tutung bitidim (č)[ïn ol　　]
5　yana ymä bu nomtïn (…)maz [　　　　]
6　täginürbiz kim tavɣač　　　[　　　　]
7　　ayïtu biri (…)　　　qïz [　　　　]
8　　　ayïtu yïɣ(…)[　](.)[　　　　]
9　tonguz yïl säkizinč üč ygrmikä bu tavɣač[　　]

---

① ED, p.470; UW, p.333; DKPAM, p.236, 277.
② BT III, pp.57−58.

10 bu tavɣač kün-tä män buyan(a)

11 tutung abi-ta qur-ta bošɣut

12 alɣalï kälip bošɣut bošɣu

13 čim

14 (…) (…) (…) bu bu tavɣač

15   bu tavɣač-ta

₁[On] this Chinese scroll ₂Person Write ₃Again now ₄I, Yaqšidu-tutung wrote [this. It is] t[rue].
₅Again now, from this sutra … ₆I humbly [wrote?] Someone [sees? this] Chinese [scroll?]
₇Reporting … Girl ₈Reporting and collect(?) …

₉The year of Boar, the Eighth [month], on the thirteenth [day]. [On] this Chinese [scroll] …

₁₀On this Chinese scroll, I, Buyana-₁₁tutung, ₁₁₋₁₂coming to take the instruction in the Abita-Cave and
[taking?] the instruction, [wrote this(?)]

Notes

7v1 – 3, 5 – 8: Scribbles of uncertain context.

7v9, säkizinč üč ygrmikä: *ay* "month" should be supplemented between *säkizinč* and *üč*.

7v10, tavɣač kün: Written as like *T"VX'Č' KWY'N*.

7v11, qur: The final -*R* is drawn out as like -*K*.

7v13 – 15: Scribbles. ₁₅*bu tavɣač-ta* is a mistake for *bu tavɣač kün-tä*.

No. 34 4bKr 42 verso (= Matsui 2004, No. 7)

1 [šilav]anti sambodu ky-ä birlä abita qur-ta

2 [bitid]imz · kinki körgü bolɣay mu tip bitidim

3 [   ] qïlïnč bolɣuẓ-ïn bilip ög köngül

[Missing]

₁[We, …]-[*šilav*]*anti* and Sambodu, [came?] together to the Abita-Cave … ₂[we wrote?]. "Will
[this writing] be to see in future?" thus saying, I wrote. ₃… [I] knew that [it] is to be … behaviour,
[my?] mind …

Notes

34v2, [bitid]imz: Temporarily I restored as "we wrote". As well possible is to restore as [*bitiyü
tägint*]*imz* "we humbly wrote", [*yükünt*]*imz* ~ [*yükünü tägint*]*imz* "we (humbly) worshiped", or alike.

34v3, ög köngül: Hendiadys meaning corresponds to Chin. 意识 *yi-shi* "conscious mind,
consciousness".① My former reading *ök* for *ög* should be corrected.

No. 49 Dx 9569 verso (= Matsui 2004, No. 8)

1 [sam]bodu qïtay toɣrïl pin(tso)

2 [   ](.)-lar bu abita qur vaxar

---

① ED, p. 99; DKPAM, p. 172.

3　　[　biti]dimz sadu ädgü yamu

₁[Sam]bodu, Qïtay-Toγrïl and Pintso（?）… ₂[we came to?] this Amita-Cave Temple [and] …
₃We [wrote]. It is nice and good.

Notes

49v1, [sam]bodu：The initial *S'M-* is missing. I restored it in comparison with No. 341, yet it might
be replaced with any other personal name, e. g., [*Tay*]*podu* < Chin. 大宝奴 *Da-bao-nu*.

49v1, pin(tso)： < Chin. 斌藏 *Bin-zang*.

49v3, [　　biti]dimz： Cf. note 34v2.

Abbreviations and bibliography

Arakawa, M. 荒川正晴 2000：ヤールホト古墓群新出の墓表・墓誌をめぐって[On the Newly Discovered Tomb Epitaphs
　　from the Cemetery of Yarkhoto]. シルクロード學研究 *Silk Roadology* 10, pp. 160 – 170.

Arakawa, M. 荒川正晴 2004a：トゥルファン漢人の冥界觀と佛教信仰[Passport to the Other World：Transformations of
　　Buddhist Briefs among the Chinese People Resident in Turfan during the 4th to 8th Centuries]. In：T. Moriyasu (ed.), 中
　　央アジア出土文物論叢 *Papers on the Pre-Islamic Documents and Other Materials Unearthed from Central Asia*, Kyoto,
　　pp. 111 – 126.

Arakawa, M. 2004b：Passports to the Other World：Transformations of Religious Briefs among the Chinese in Turfan (4th to 8th
　　Centuries). In：D. Durkin-Meisterermst et al. (eds.), *Turfan Revisited*, Berlin, pp. 19 – 21.

BTT III：S. Tezcan, *Das uigurische Insadi-Sūtra*. Berlin, 1974.

BT XVI：D. Cerensodnom/M. Taube, *Die Mongolica der Berliner Turfansammlung*. Berlin, 1993.

BT XXIII：P. Zieme, *Magische Texte des Uigurischen Buddhismus*. Turnhout (Belgium), 2005.

BT XXVI：笠井幸代 Y. Kasai, *Die Uigurischen Buddhistischen Kolophonen*. Turnhout (Belgium), 2008.

CATB：Ch. Bhattacharya-Haesner, *Central Asian Temple Banners in the Turfan Collection of the Museum für Indische Kunst*,
　　Berlin. Berlin, 2003.

DhSPB：俄羅斯科學院東方研究所聖彼得堡分所藏敦煌文獻 *Dunhuang Manuscripts Collected in the St. Petersburg Institute
　　of Oriental Studies of the Academy of Sciences of Russia*, 17 vols. Shanghai, 1992 – 2001.

DKPAM：庄垣内正弘 M. Shogaito/L. Tugusheva/藤代節 S. Fujishiro, 古代ウイグル文 Daśakarmapathāvadānamālāの研究
　　The Daśakarmapathāvadānamālāin Uighur. Kyoto, 2000.

ED：G. Clauson, *An Etymological Dictionary of Pre-Thirteenth Century Turkish*. Oxford, 1972.

Elverskog, J. 1997：*Uygur Buddhist Literature*. Turnhout.

Geng, Shimin 耿世民 1981：回鶻文土都木薩里修寺碑考釋[Study on the Uigur Inscription about Temple-Repair by Tudum
　　Sali]. 世界宗教研究 *Shijie zongjiao yanjiu* 1981 – 1, pp. 77 – 83.

Geng, Shimin 耿世民 2003a：回鶻文"大白蓮社經"殘卷(二葉)研究[Study of Two Folios of the Uigur Text Abitaki]. 民族
　　語文 *Minzu yuwen* 2003 – 5, pp. 1 – 5.

Geng, Shimin 耿世民 2003b：維吾爾古代文獻研究 *Researches in Old Uighur Literature*. Beijing.

Geng, Shimin 耿世民 2004：Study of Two Folios of the Uigur Text "Abitaki". *Acta Orientalia Academiae Scientiarum
　　Hungaricae* 57 – 1, p. 105.

Geng, Shimin 耿世民 2008: Study on the Uighur Text Abitaki (3). In: P. Zieme (ed.), *Aspects of Research into Central Asian Buddhism: In Memoriam Kōgi Kudara*, Turnhout (Belgium), pp. 27 – 31.

Hamilton, J. R. 1984: Les titres *šäli* et *tutung* en ouïgour. *Journal Asiatique* 272, pp. 425 – 437.

Ht VII: K. Röhrborn, *Die alttürkische Xuanzang-Biographie VII*. Wiesbaden 1991.

Jia, Yingyi 賈應逸 1989: トユク石窟考[Study on the Toyuk Caves]. Tr. by H. Sudo. 佛教藝術 *Bukkyō geijutsu* 186, pp. 62 – 81.

Kudara, K. 百濟康義 1992: ベゼクリク壁畫から見た西域北道佛教の一形態[On the Trail of a Central Asian Monk: A Bezeklik Portrait Identified]. In: N. Fujisawa (ed.), キジルを中心とする西域佛教美術の諸問題 *Studies on the Buddhist Art of Central Asia*, Tokyo, pp. 1 – 6, +2 pls.

Kudara, K. 百濟康義 1995: 敦煌第 17 窟出土ウイグル譯"無量壽經"斷片[A Uigur Fragment of the Larger Sukhāvatīvyūha-Sūtra from the Dunhuang Cave 17]. 龍谷紀要 *Ryukoku kiyo* 17 – 1, pp. 1 – 15.

Kudara, K. 百濟康義/P. Zieme 1997: Two New Fragments of the Larger *Sukhāvatīvyūhasūtra* in Uigur. SIAL 12, pp. 73 – 82, +pls. VII – X.

Machida, T. 町田隆吉 1990: トゥルファン出土文書に見える佛教寺院名について[On the Names of the Buddhist Temples as Seen in the Turfan Chinese Texts]. 東京學藝大學附屬高校大泉校舍研究紀要 *Memoirs of Tokyo Gakugei University Senior High School Oizumi Campus* 15, pp. 27 – 42.

Matsui, D. 松井太 2004: シヴシドゥ・ヤクシドゥ關係文書とトヨク石窟の佛教教團[Notes on the Uigur Secular Documents Housed at St. Petersburg: Buddhist Monastery at Toyoq Caves and Monks Sivšidu and Yaqšidu]. In: T. Moriyasu (ed.), 中央アジア出土文物論叢 *Papers on the Pre-Islamic Documents and Other Materials Unearthed from Central Asia*, Kyoto, pp. 41 – 70.

Matsui, D. 松井太 2005a: ウイグル文シヴシドゥ・ヤクシドゥ關係文書補遺[Supplement to the Uigur Documents Related to Monks Sivšidu and Yaqšidu]. 人文社會論叢 *Studies in the Humanities* (*Cultural Science Volume*) 13, pp. 139 – 155.

Matsui, D. 松井太 2005b: ウイグル文契約文書研究補説四題[Four Remarks on the Uigur Contract Documents]. SIAL 20, pp. 27 – 64.

Matsui, D. 松井太 2008: Revising the Uigur Inscriptions of the Yulin Caves. SIAL 23, pp. 17 – 33.

Miyaji, A. 宮治昭 1995/1996: トゥルファン・トヨク石窟の禪觀窟壁畫について[On the Wall Paintings in Changuanku Cave of Tuyok Cave Temple at Turfan](1). 佛教藝術 *Bukkyō geijutsu* 221, 1995, pp. 15 – 41; (2) Bukkyō geijutsu 223, 1995, pp. 15 – 36; (3) Bukkyō geijutsu 226, 1996, pp. 38 – 83.

Moriyasu, T. 森安孝夫 1985: チベット文字で書かれたウィグル文佛教教理問答(P. t. 1292)の研究[Études sur un catéchisme bouddhique ouigour en écriture tibétaine (P. t. 1292)]. 大阪大學文學部紀要 *Memoirs of the Faculty of Letters, Osaka University* 25, pp. 1 – 85, +1 pl.

Moriyasu, T. 森安孝夫 1988: 敦煌出土元代ウイグル文書中のキンサイ緞子[Damask (Silk) Appearing from Kinsai as Seen in the Yüan Period Uighur Documents Unearthed in Tun-huang]. In: 榎博士頌壽記念東洋史論叢 *Studies in Asian History Dedicated to Prof. Dr. Kazuo Enoki on His Seventieth Birthday*, Tokyo, pp. 417 – 441.

Moriyasu, T. 森安孝夫 2004a: *Die Geschichte des uigurischen Manichäismus an der Seidenstraße*. Wiesbaden.

Moriyasu, T. 森安孝夫 2004b: From Silk, Cotton and Copper Coin to Silver: Transition of the Currency Used by the Uighurs during the Period from the 8th to the 14th Centuries. In: D. Durkin-Meisterernst et al. (eds.), *Turfan Revisited*, Berlin, pp. 228 – 239.

Oda, J. 小田壽典 1987: ウィグルの称号トゥトゥングとその周辺[On the Title *Tutung* in Uigur]. 東洋史研究 *Tōyōshi kenkyū* 46 - 1, pp. 57 - 86.

Rong, Xinjiang 榮新江 1996：海外敦煌吐魯番文獻知見録 *Dunhuang and Turfan Texts Preserved out of China*. Nanchang.

Sekio, Sh. 關尾史郎 2001：ロシア・サンクト＝ペテルブルク所藏敦煌文獻中のトゥルファン文獻について［On the Turfan Texts among the "Dunhuang Texts" Housed at St. Petersburg, Russia］. 敦煌文獻の總合的・學際的研究 *Comprehensive and Interdisciplinary Study on the Dunhuang Texts*, Niigata University, pp. 40 - 50.

Shogaito, M. 庄垣内正弘 1987：ウイグル文獻に導入された漢語に關する研究［Chinese in Uigur Script］. SIAL 2 (1986), pp. 17 - 156.

Shogaito, M. 庄垣内正弘 2003：ロシア所藏ウイグル語文獻の研究 *Uighur manuscripts in St. Petersburg*. Kyoto.

SIAL：内陸アジア言語の研究 *Studies on the Inner Asian Languages*.

SUK：山田信夫 N. Yamada, ウイグル文契約文書集成 *Sammlung uigurischer Kontrakte*, 3 vols. Ed. by J. Oda/P. Zieme/H. Umemura/T. Moriyasu. Suita (Osaka), 1993.

Taisho：大正新修大藏經 *Taishō shinshū Daizōkyō*.

Tugusheva, L. Ju. 1996：Neskol'ko ujgurskikh dokumentov iz rukopisnogo sobranija Sankt-Peterburgskogo filiala IV RAN. *Peterburgskoe Vostokovedenie* 8, pp. 215 - 238.

Uigurica II. By F. W. K. Müller. *Abhandlungen der Preußischen Akademie der Wissenschaften (Phil.-Hist. Klasse)* 1910 - 3.

Umemura, H. 梅村坦 2002：ペテルブルグ所藏ウイグル文書 SI 4bKr. 71 の一解釋［A Study of SI 4bKr. 71：An Uyghur Document Concerning the Sale of a Slave and the Loan of Silver］. SIAL 17, pp. 203 - 221, +pls. III, IV.

UW：K. Röhrborn, *Uigurisches Wörterbuch*, vols. 1 - 6 +. 1977 - 1998 +.

Yamabe, N. 山部能宜 1999：An Examination of the Mural Paintings of Toyok Cave 20 in Conjunction with the Origin of the Amitayus Visualization Sutra. *Orientations* 30 - 4, pp. 38 - 44.

Yamabe, N. 山部能宜 2002：Practice of Visualization and the Visualization Sûtra：An Examination of Mural Paintings at Toyok, Turfan. *Pacific World* 3 - 4, pp. 123 - 152.

Yamabe, N. 山部能宜 2004：An Examination of the Mural Paintings of Visualizing Monks in Toyok Cave 42. In：D. Durkin-Meisterernst et al. (eds.), *Turfan Revisited*, Berlin, pp. 401 - 407.

Zieme, P. 1981：Uigurische Steuerbefreiungsurkunden für buddhistische Klöster. *Altorientalische Forschungen* 8, pp. 237 - 263, +Taf. XIX - XXII.

Zieme, P. 1985：Uigurische *Sukhāvatīvyūha*-Fragmente. *Altorientalische Forschungen* 12 - 1, pp. 129 - 149, +pls. I - VIII.

Zieme, P. 1992：*Religion und Gesellschaft im Uigurischen Königreich von Qočo*. Opladen.

Zieme, P. 1994：Samboqdu et alii. Einige alttürkische Personennamen im Wandel der Zeiten. *Journal of Turkology* 2 - 1, pp. 119 - 133.

Zieme, P. 1998：Turkic Fragments in 'Phags-pa Script. SIAL 13, pp. 63 - 69, +2 pls.

Zieme, P. 2005：Religions of the Turks in the Pre-Isalmic Period. In：D. J. Roxburgh (ed.), *Turks: A Journey of a Thousand Years, 600 - 1600*, London, pp. 32 - 37.

Zieme, P./K. Kudara 百濟康義 1985：ウイグル語の觀無量壽經 *Guanwuliangshoujing in Uigur*. Kyoto.

Zieme, P./Niu Ruji 牛汝極 1996：The Buddhist Refuge Formula. An Uigur Manuscript from Dunhuang. *Türk Dilleri Araştırmaları* 6, pp. 41 - 56.

P. S. This English paper is based on my previous Japanese articles (Matsui 2004 & Matsui 2005a) with modifications and revisions.

Plates

Дх 12145   Kr IV 250   Дх 3650

Text No. 2 （after Matsui 2005, plate III）

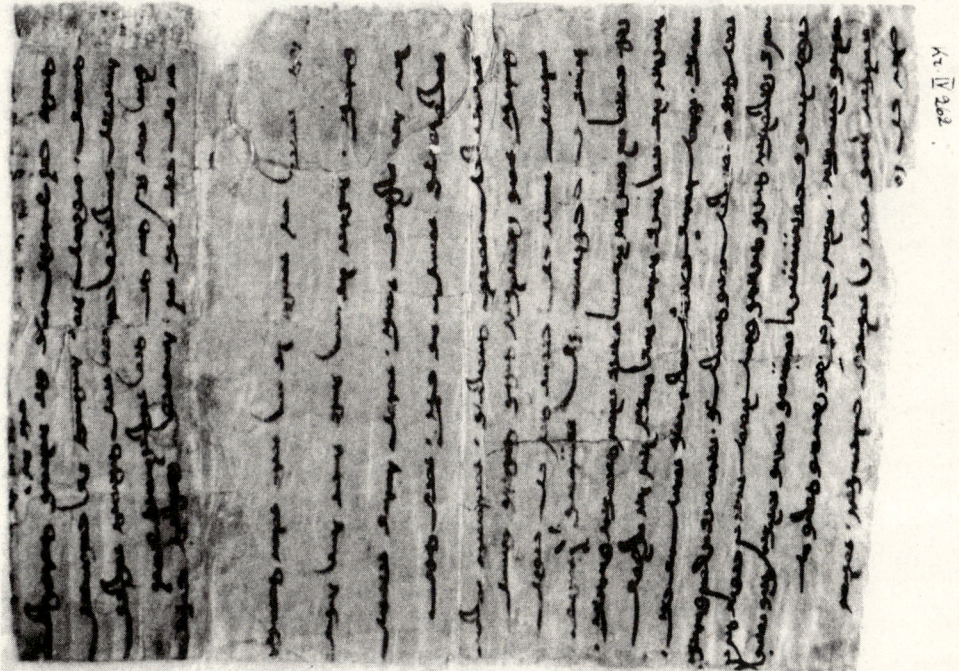

Text No. 6   Kr IV 262 verso（after Matsui 2004, p. 64）

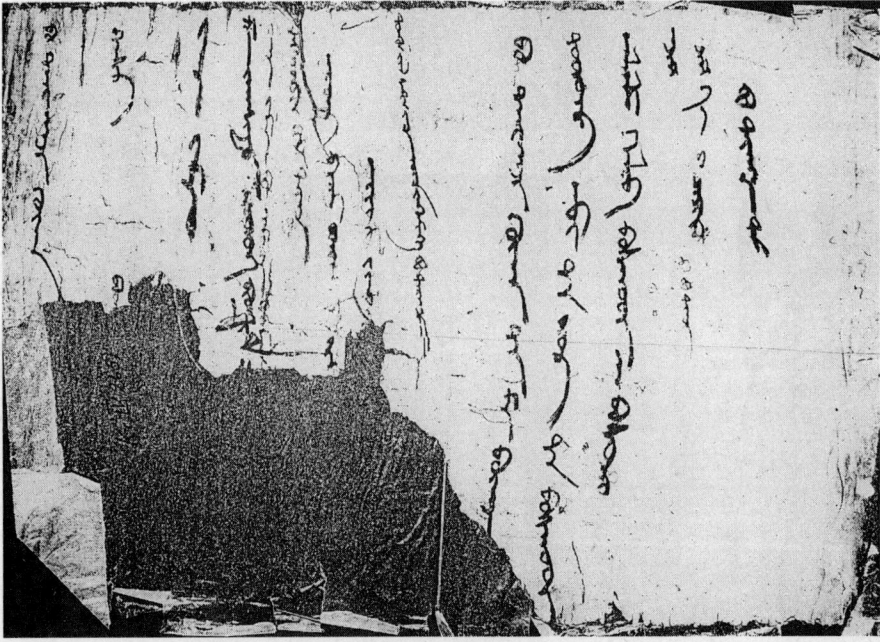

Text No. 7　Kr IV 265 verso（after Matsui 2004，p. 64）

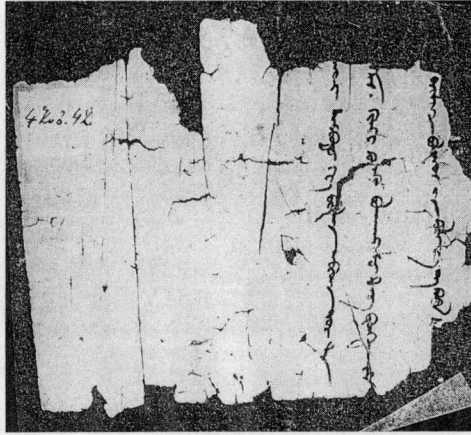

Text No. 34　4bKr 42（after Matsui 2004，p. 65）

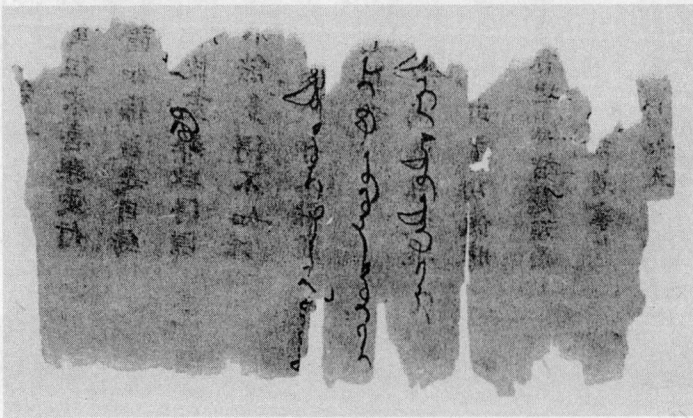

Text No. 49　4bKr 42（after Matsui 2004，p. 65）

The Christian Library at Turfan:
the Syriac-script manuscripts from Bulayïq

Erica C. D. Hunter

Department for the Study of Religions, School of Oriental and
African Studies (SOAS) University of London, England

The *Arts and Humanities Research Council*, the foremost research funding body in the United Kingdom, awarded in January 2008 a *Major Research Grant* for the project, "The Christian Library at Turfan". The project is lead by Dr. Erica Hunter (SOAS), who is joined by Prof. Nicholas Sims-Willliams (SOAS) and Prof. Peter Zieme (*Berlin-Brandenburgische Akademie der Wissenschaften* [BBAW]), as well as Dr. Mark Dickens (SOAS). The strength of the project derives from its participants, each of whom is an established expert in their own language field.

Research Context

The *German Turfan Expedition* conducted four campaigns at the Turfan Oasis between 1902 and 1914. During the 2nd and 3rd seasons (1904–1907), a library was unearthed at the monastery site of Shüipang near Bulayïq yielding ca. 945 manuscripts and manuscript fragments written in Syriac and Christian Sogdian, the latter largely using the Syriac script. Some 52 manuscripts in Christian Turkic as well as several fragments in New Persian and a Middle Persian (Pahlavi) Psalter were also found. In addition, a few Christian texts in Syriac, Sogdian, Turkish and Persian were discovered at other sites in the Turfan oasis (Astana, Qocho, Qurutqa and Toyoq). This material provides a unique snapshot of Christianity in Central Asia, and specifically at Turfan, in the early mediaeval period (mainly 9th–12th centuries, from which most of the manuscripts appear to date).

The manuscripts encompass a variety of genres. Many of the Syriac texts are liturgical (from the *Hudra*) or biblical (from the Old and New Testament *Peshitta*), however hagiographies, such as the life of St George, are also represented. Other texts include a dialogue between a Jew and a Christian, a history of the city of Nisibis and a pharmacopaeic text. Many of the Christian Sogdian manuscripts are also biblical, again translations from the *Peshitta*. Hymns and psalms abound, some having Syriac marginalia; one even carries a Greek superscription and shows the influence of the Septuagint. There are Psalter fragments in New Persian and Middle Persian (Pahlavi); the former being a bi-lingual text (with Syriac). Translations from Evagrius

Ponticus, the *Apophthegmata Patrum* and the East Syrian spiritual writings into Sogdian reflect an active interest in the ascetical life. The lives of John of Dailam and Serapion are also found, as is the legend of Barshabba who brought Christianity from the Sassanid empire to Marv. Likewise the Christian Turkic texts cover various genres: prayer-books, a story about the magi, an omen book, the hagiography of St George and some economical documents.

This wealth of material was brought to Berlin now over a century ago. Preserved under glass plates, the manuscripts are still largely in an excellent physical condition. Today, as part of the *German Turfan Collection*, they are housed in various locations in Berlin. The 550 Christian Sogdian and 52 Christian Turkic manuscripts are held by the *Turfanforschung* in the *Berlin-Brandenburgische Akademie der Wissenschaften* (BBAW) and can be viewed on the official website http://www. bbaw. de/forschung/turfanforschung/dta. html. The *Turfanforschung* is the repository for the New Persian fragments and the Middle Persian (Pahlavi) Psalter, that was already published in 1933 and is now available on-line http://www. bbaw. de/forschung/turfanforschung/dta/ps/dta_ps_index. html. The majority of the 395 Syriac manuscripts are housed in the Oriental Dept. of the *Staatsbibliothek*, Potsdamer Strasse, Berlin, although some are in the *Museum für Asiatische Kunst* at Dahlem, Berlin. This is also the repository for several Christian Sogdian manuscripts.

Research Questions

The research project aims to produce catalogues for the manuscripts from Turfan that are written in Syriac script. Two volumes are planned. One will be devoted to Syriac manuscripts, the other to Christian materials in Iranian languages, the majority being Christian Sogdian manuscripts written in Syriac script, but also the handful of New Persian manuscripts. The quantities of material (395 Syriac, 500 Christian Sogdian manuscripts in Syriac script) dictate that separate catalogues be produced. The cataloguing of this material is a *desideratum*, bringing significant collections of medieval Christian manuscripts from a secure Central Asian provenance into the mainstream scholarly repertoire. Both catalogues will be included in the *Union Catalogue of Oriental Manuscripts in German Collections* (Katalogisierung der Orientalischen Handschriften in Deutschland [KOHD]), a national project of the Academy of Sciences in Göttingen directed by Dr. H. -O. Feistel.

The Syriac and Christian Iranian catalogues will complete the on-going programme of cataloguing the Turfan material that is at present being undertaken by the KOHD in Berlin under the aegis of the *Berlin-Brandenburgische Akademie der Wissenschaften* (BBAW). The minority of Christian Sogdian manuscripts in the native Sogdian script (ca. 50 items) and the Christian manuscripts in Uygur Turkic (also ca. 50) will be included in catalogues currently being prepared by Dr. Christiane Reck and Dr. Simone Raschmann for inclusion in the KOHD. The Syriac and Christian Iranian catalogues will complement the on-going digitising programme of the Turfan material that has received the financial support of the *German Research Foundation* (DFG) in 1997 and again in 2005. The Christian Sogdian and Uygur Turkic manuscripts have already been digitized. The digitising of the Syriac manuscripts is scheduled to commence in February 2009. The synchronization of the catalogue preparation and the digitizing of the manuscripts will give scholars maximum access to an archive whose significance for Christian studies in Central Asia is unparalleled and will throw much light onto the religious, ethnic and cultural environment of medieval Turfan.

Research Methods:

The programme is planned in two major stages:

I. Cataloguing the Syriac, Christian Iranian and Christian Turkic manuscripts

This stage assembles the material for the catalogues that will be compiled under the direction of the respective language specialist:

- Christian Sogdian (500), New Persian manuscripts: Prof. Nicholas Sims-Williams
- Syriac (395 manuscripts): Dr. Erica C. D. Hunter and Dr. Mark Dickens
- Christian Turkic (52 manuscripts): Prof. Peter Zieme

The Christian Sogdian manuscripts have been extensively studied by Prof. Nicholas Sims-Williams. He has already laid the foundations for the proposed catalogue by compiling an inventory of the Christian Sogdian manuscripts written in Syriac script and has recorded the data for the New Persian manuscripts.

The Syriac manuscripts have remained almost completely unresearched, except for a handful of articles[1]. The initial thrust of the project will be directed towards sorting and classifying these manuscripts. Several old Handlists are held at the *Turfanforschung*, but these contain many discrepancies. Individual records for each of the manuscripts are being compiled, to fit with the scheme devised for the Christian Sogdian entries and the other catalogues. As part of this process, each individual Syriac fragment is physically examined and its entry compiled. The final entries will accord with the conventions established for the other catalogues in the KOHD series.

Prof. Peter Zieme has spent many years researching and publishing the Old Turkic manuscripts and is currently preparing their individual descriptive entries. These will be made available to Dr. Simone Raschmann, who is working cataloguing the Uygur Turkic material.

II. Editing and translation of select Syriac, Christian Sogdian and Christian Turkic manuscripts

This stage focuses on the edition and translation of selected Syriac, Christian Sogdian and Christian

---

[1] H. -J. Polotsky, edition of Syriac Barshabba fragments in Müller-Lentz, *Soghdische Text II* (Berlin: 1934) 522, 559 – 564; H. Engberding, "Fünf Blätter eines alten ostsyrischen Bitt- und Bussgottesdienstes aus Innerasien", *Ostkirchliche Studien* 14 (1965) 121 – 148; M. Maróth, "Ein fragment eines syrischen pharmzeutischen Rezeptbuches", *Altorientalische Forschungen* 11 (1984) 115 – 125; M. Maróth, "Ein Brief aus Turfan", *Altorientalische Forschungen* 18 (1985) 283 – 287; M. Maróth, "Ein Unbekannte Version der Georgios-Legende aus Turfan", *Altorientalische Forschungen* 18 (1991) 86 – 108; M. Maróth, "Die syrischen handschriften in der Turfan-Sammlung" in H. Klengel & W. Sunderman, *Ägypten, Vorderasien, Turfan* (Berlin: 1991) 126 – 128; N. Pigoulewsky, "Manuscripts syriaques et syro-turcs de Hara-hoto et de Turfan", *Revue de l'Orient Chrétien* X (1935 – 1936) 3 – 46; E. Sachau, "Litteratur-Bruchstücke aus Chinesisch-Turkistan", *Sitzungsberichte der Königlich Preussischen Akademie der Wissenschaften* [*SPAW*] (Sitzung der philosophisch-historischen Classe von 23 November) (1905) 964 – 978.

Turkic texts to address three areas relating to the Mesopotamian heritage of the monastery at Bulayïq.

I. The transmission of texts from Mesopotamia to Central Asia

Many texts at Turfan were transmitted from Mesopotamia to Central Asia. The lives of Serapion and John of Dailam were translated from Syriac into Sogdian (manuscript "C3", consisting of fragments of ca. 60 folios). Several Syriac counterparts exist to the Sogdian manuscript including a West Syrian prose life (Harvard syr. 38 ff. 175a – 186b)[①] and an East Syriac panegyric (Cambridge Add. 2020). Cambridge Add. 2020 has numerous episodes that are absent from the Harvard manuscript. Nicholas Sims-Williams is preparing an edition of Cambridge Add. 2020 and Harvard syr. 38 in comparison with the C3 fragments to reconstruct their transmission history as well as investigating the question of a "lost source".

II. The relationship of the monastery at Turfan with northern Mesopotamia

Prof. Miklós Maróth identified a long, but damaged, Syriac manuscript of the history of Nisibis.[②] Nisibis was, of course, a city with a renowned reputation in the Church of the East and nearby Mt. Izla was the *locus* of east Syrian monasticism. This unique text demonstrates western links of Turfan with the Mesopotamian homeland of Syriac Christianity. In combination with other textual material, such as the Syriac and Sogdian "Barshabba" legend, and with the archaeological data published by Albert von le Coq, the larger question can be addressed: of Bulayïq's place in the monastic network of the Church of the East that stretched to Central Asia and China during the 9th and 10th centuries. We can ask, "in what ways was the monastery at Turfan a regional outpost of an international network that stretched from Baghdad to Xian?"

III. The "Christianities" of Turfan

Syriac was primarily conveyed to Central Asia via Iran through the proselytising activities of the Syriac-speaking churches (Church of the East, Syrian Orthodox and Melkite). Syriac assumed primarily a liturgical role, but Psalter fragments include that translations were made into the vernacular languages of Iran and the Turfan oasis: Sogdian, Old Turkic, New Persian and Middle Persian. Most of the Psalter fragments were translated from the *Peshitta*. Recent identifications include passages from Psalms 22 – 26 in a four-folio booklet [HT (Turfan Handschrift) Syr 71]. The vitality of translation processes is shown by the Middle Persian Psalter (the only extant Christian manuscript in Middle Persian) which preserves readings that agree with the Hebrew original or Greek versions against the *Peshitta*. The Syriac-New Persian bilingual fragment and the Sogdian Psalm fragment with superscription in Greek also comment on the transmission of biblical texts in Central Asia and, concomitantly, the identities of the churches that used these texts. The Christian communities at Turfan were diverse.

Dissemination of Research Results:

The project aims to disseminate its research via several trajectories:

---

① S. Brock, "A Syriac life of John of Dailam", *Parole de l'Orient* 10 (1981 – 1982) 123 – 189.

② Maróth in Klengel, *op. cit.*, (Berlin: Akademie Verlag, 1991) 127.

● *Catalogues:*

Two hard-copy catalogues will be produced: (1) *Syriac manuscripts* and (2) *Iranian manuscripts in Syriac script* as part of the *Union Catalogue of Oriental Manuscripts in German Collections* (Katalogisierung der Orientalischen Handschriften in Deutschland [KOHD]) which is a national project of the Academy of Sciences in Göttingen. (Director, Dr. H.-O. Feistel, Staatsbibliothek, Berlin).

● *Monographs:*

Various monographs are planned, including Nicholas Sims-Williams' edition and translation of the Christian Sogdian C3 manuscript (approximately 60 folios) on the lives of Serapion and John of Dailam. Informal agreement has been reached to publish this monograph in the *Berliner Turfantexte* series.

● *Major scholarly articles:*

A number of scholarly articles are envisaged including:

— translation of the unpublished Syriac history of Nisibis [Erica Hunter]

— comparative study of Psalters [Nicholas Sims-Williams, Mark Dickens and Erica Hunter]

— comparative study of the Syriac and Christian Sogdian "John of Dailam" manuscripts [Nicholas Sims-Williams and Erica Hunter]

— comparative study of the Syriac and Christian Sogdian "Barshabba" manuscripts [Nicholas Sims-Williams and Erica Hunter]

— edition and translation of selected Christian Turkic texts [Peter Zieme]

The publications of the project will be of particular interest for scholars and students researching a variety of areas:

● Christianity in medieval Central Asia

● The relationship of mediaeval Central Asia and Mesopotamia

● the roles Syriac, Christian Sogdian and other languages played in mediaeval Central Asia

● Transmission of biblical texts, especially the Psalter and the dialogue between languages in medieval Central Asia

唐诗中所见葡萄(酒)文化景观

海 滨

昌吉学院

在空前开放的唐代社会格局中,西域民俗文化景观强烈的地方色彩和民族风情格外引人注目。元稹《法曲》描述西域胡俗时说:"自从胡骑起烟尘,毛毳腥膻满咸洛。女为胡妇学胡妆,伎进胡音务胡乐。《火凤》声沉多咽绝,《春莺啭》罢长萧索。胡音胡骑与胡妆,五十年来竞纷泊",[①]这当然是安史之乱后的情形。之前呢? 向达先生很全面地概括道:"李氏起自西陲,历事周隋,不唯政制多袭前代之旧,一切文物亦复不间华夷,兼收并蓄。第七世纪以降之长安,几乎为一国际的都会,各种人民,各种宗教,无不可于长安得之。太宗雄才大略,固不囿于琐微,而波罗球之盛行唐代,太宗即与有力焉。开元、天宝之际,天下升平,而玄宗以声色犬马为羁縻诸王之策,重以蕃将大盛,异族入居长安者多,于是长安胡化盛极一时,此种胡化大率为西域风之好尚:服饰、饮食、宫室、乐舞、绘画,竞事纷泊;其极社会各方面,隐约皆有所化,好之者盖不仅帝王及一二贵戚达官已也。"[②]

将元稹之诗歌和向达之论述互相补充印证,我们可以推想唐代西域民俗盛行的总体风貌:从宫廷王室、达官贵族到民间市井,西域民俗都受到欢迎和追捧;从饮食、宫室等物质民俗到节庆、娱乐等行为民俗以至于审美性比较强烈的服饰妆扮民俗等,几乎各种西域民俗的文化景观都有其流行的天地。我们选择其中有代表性的、影响较大的西域民俗文化景观饮食、服饰、时妆、居处和节庆等略事考察。关于历史记载中这几类西域民俗景观的具体内容和盛行状况,学者们的讨论已经比较丰富而详尽,兹不再展开,这里主要考察这些具体的西域民俗文化景观在诗歌中的反映和表现。

西域饮食文化景观。胡食以肉酪为主,见于诗歌者有牛、羊、驼、酏酥等食物。岑参《酒泉太守席上醉后作》写道了炙牛和烹驼:"浑炙犁牛烹野驼,交河美酒金叵罗",[③]岑参《玉门关盖将军歌》则写道乳制品酏酥:"灯前侍婢泻玉壶,金铛乱点野酏酥。"[④]流行于中原的西域面食的代表——胡饼蜚声京城内外,但反映在诗歌中的却只有白居易《寄胡饼与杨万州》和皮日休《初夏即事寄鲁望》这两首。白诗中的胡饼系烤出:"胡麻饼样学京都,面脆油香新出炉。寄与饥馋杨大使,尝看得似辅兴无",[⑤]皮诗中的胡饼系蒸出:"胡饼蒸甚熟,貊盘举尤轻。茗脆不禁炙,酒肥或难倾。"[⑥]此外,唐诗很少有涉及胡食者。

西域服饰文化景观。胡服以氍毹为主,诗歌中略有反映,如岑参写道:"将军纵博场场胜,赌得单于貂

---

① 元稹:《法曲》,冀勤点校《元稹集》,中华书局,1982年,第282页。
② 向达:《唐代长安与西域文明》,河北教育出版社,2001年,第42页。
③ 岑参:《酒泉太守席上醉后作》,廖立笺注《岑嘉州诗笺注》,中华书局,2004年,第427页。
④ 岑参:《玉门关盖将军歌》,同上,第378页。
⑤ 白居易:《寄胡饼与杨万州》,顾学颉校点《白居易集》,中华书局,1979年,第382页。
⑥ 皮日休:《初夏即事寄鲁望》,《全唐诗(增订本)》,中华书局,1999年,第7083页。

鼠袍",①"黑姓蕃王貂鼠裘,葡萄宫锦醉缠头";②刘商写道:"水头宿兮草头坐,风吹汉地衣裳破。羊脂沐发长不梳,羔子皮裘领仍左。狐襟貉袖腥复膻,昼披行兮夜披卧";③耿湋写道:"毡裘牧马胡雏小,日暮蕃歌三两声";④张籍写道:"去年中国养子孙,今著毡裘学胡语。"⑤西域服饰多华丽繁富,尤其以乐舞表演者为代表,这类诗歌为数不少,但其服饰主要作为乐舞文化景观的一个附属部分而反映在诗歌中。集中描写西域服饰的有这样一首小宫词曰:"明朝腊日官家出,随驾先须点内人。回鹘衣装回鹘马,就中偏称小腰身",⑥这倒是着意刻写了西域回鹘衣装的特点,但遗憾的是这类作品数目寥寥。

西域妆饰文化景观。胡妆的流行被元白所诟病、痛斥,但恰恰是白居易的讽喻诗《时世妆》保留了些许记载:"时世妆,时世妆,出自城中传四方。时世流行无远近,腮不施朱面无粉。乌膏注唇唇似泥,双眉画作八字低。妍媸黑白失本态,妆成尽似含悲啼。圆鬟无鬓堆髻样,斜红不晕赭面状。昔闻被发伊川中,辛有见之知有戎。元和妆梳君记取,髻堆面赭非华风。"⑦除此之外,详细反映胡妆的诗歌也很少。

西域宫室文化景观。胡人之居处多为穹庐毡帐,岑参、王昌龄等人的边塞诗提及过毡墙毳幕但较简略,如岑参写道:"雨拂毡墙湿,风摇毳幕膻";⑧王昌龄写道:"碧毛毡帐河曲游,橐驼五万部落稠,敕赐飞凤金兜鍪";⑨而白居易以《青毡帐二十韵》为代表的十余首毡帐诗则具体而微地介绍了毡帐之由来、形制以及自己在毡帐中待客饮宴、生活起居的细节,很有意思也很有意味,如《青毡帐二十韵》曰:"合聚千羊毳,施张百子卷。骨盘边柳健,色染塞蓝鲜。……王家夸旧物,未及此青毡"。⑩但遗憾的是,这类毡帐诗仅以白居易为代表,缺乏普遍性。已有学者全面深入地讨论了这个话题,⑪此处不赘述。

西域之宫室居处的另一个典型是来自拂林的自雨亭子,根据《唐语林》和两《唐书》的描述,其略似于清代圆明园之水木明瑟之类,是皇室豪门夏天避暑纳凉的绝佳盛境。也许以其绝少之故,大约只有刘禹锡《刘驸马水亭避暑》略有反映。⑫

西域之节庆娱乐文化景观。这方面以带有狂欢性质的泼寒胡戏为代表,历史记载很丰富,群臣谏止此戏的讨论也不少。但反映在诗歌中,除了张说的《苏摩遮》五首外,⑬也很寥寥。

在历史文献和考古文物所展现的世界里,在民俗学和文化学的研究著作中,西域饮食文化景观、西域服饰文化景观、西域妆饰文化景观、西域宫室文化景观、西域之节庆娱乐文化景观等民俗文化景观的命题不仅是成立的、成熟的,而且是丰富的、饱满的,甚至是令人叹为观止的。但是,与诗歌反映的情况两相对照,则是严重不对称的。历史材料建构的民俗文化的绝胜景观在诗歌的世界里几乎找不到对应的文学反映,只有寥落的几个民俗事象的景点或个案而已。

---

① 岑参:《赵将军歌》,廖立笺注《岑嘉州诗笺注》,中华书局,2004年,第774页。
② 岑参:《胡歌》,廖立笺注《岑嘉州诗笺注》,中华书局,2004年,第784页。
③ 刘商:《胡笳十八拍·第五拍》,《全唐诗(增订本)》,中华书局,1999年,第3449页。
④ 耿湋:《凉州词》,同上,第2994页。
⑤ 张籍:《陇头行》,同上,第4296页。
⑥ 花蕊夫人:《宫词》,同上,第9071页。
⑦ 白居易:《时世妆》,顾学颉校点《白居易集》,中华书局,1979年,第82页。
⑧ 岑参:《首秋轮台》,廖立笺注《岑嘉州诗笺注》,中华书局,2004年,第486页。
⑨ 王昌龄:《箜篌引》,《全唐诗(增订本)》,中华书局,1999年,第1436页。
⑩ 白居易:《青毡帐二十韵》,顾学颉校点《白居易集》,中华书局,1979年,第703~704页。
⑪ 吴玉贵:《白居易"毡帐诗"与唐朝社会的胡风》,《唐研究》第五卷。
⑫ 刘禹锡:《刘驸马水亭避暑》,卞孝萱校订《刘禹锡集》,中华书局,1990年,第319页。
⑬ 张说:《苏摩遮》,《全唐诗(增订本)》,中华书局,1999年,第977页。

唯一的例外者就是西域的葡萄(酒)文化。历史文献的记载和考古文物的实证都显示出,唐代葡萄(酒)文化是相当成熟和发达的,而唐诗中关于葡萄(酒)的诗歌则数量众多且内容丰富。这两个方面是相称的。

葡萄(酒)文化景观在唐诗中大体呈现出三个层面的意义:因为葡萄是一种遍及西域广袤的地理空间、延续数千年而依然生机勃勃的风物,所以在文史典故和诗歌传统中,葡萄(酒)有时就成为西域的代称符号;因为葡萄(酒)在西州、凉州、并州的广泛生产,唐朝诗人有了更多地接触、了解和描摹的机会,葡萄(酒)有时就成为诗人笔下曼妙的歌咏对象;在西域,葡萄(酒)是社会生活中比较常见的风物;在中原,尽管有两次大规模引进的契机,但葡萄(酒)仍然被置于很高的地位,常常作为高贵、珍稀的奢侈物品出现在诗歌中。

一、西域的代称符号

法国国家科研中心学者童丕(Eric Trombert)在《中国北方的粟特遗存——山西的葡萄种植业》一文中以大量的文献史料和出土资料论证了山西栽培葡萄和酿造葡萄酒与粟特人的关系后,得出这样的结语:

> 在历史演进过程中,太原酒的进贡在同样的情况下两次被皇帝下令废除:唐统治时期,837年元月;以及明初,太祖统治时期。……两个皇室反对在山西生产葡萄酒的决定证实了中国文人学士意识中的某种关联,即葡萄栽培与"西方蛮族"之间的关系。作为"胡"文化的因素——广义上是粟特、突厥、畏兀儿以及蒙古的混合文化的因素——葡萄酒的使用被汉人所禁止。这一认识同对山西葡萄种植业起源所作的假设观察相吻合:它可以被视为所有胡人的共同成果,伊朗人对草原民族早期影响的见证。[①]

童丕所指的第一次废除令是在唐文宗开成年间,《册府元龟》卷一六八《帝王部·却贡献》记载了当年河东蒲萄酒和西川春酒的进贡同时被叫停,[②]这是发生在会昌灭佛前不久的事实,其思想背景是儒家道统的恢复和民族主义的抬头。明太祖发布禁令的背景很复杂,但民族主义也是不可忽视的因素。与两次叫停葡萄酒进贡形成鲜明对比的,是中国历史进程中的两次影响很大的葡萄和葡萄酒的引进。那两次,分别是汉武帝经营西域期间和唐太宗征服高昌之后。汉武帝经营西域所获的标志性物种就是葡萄、苜蓿、汗血马,《史记·大宛列传》载:"宛左右以蒲陶为酒,富人藏酒至万余石,久者数十岁不败。俗嗜酒,马嗜苜蓿。汉使取其实来,于是天子始种苜蓿、蒲陶肥饶地。及天马多,外国使来众,则离宫别观旁尽种蒲萄、苜蓿极望。"[③]汉武帝取乌孙国的西极马和大宛国的天马是基于交通和军事装备的实际需要的,种植葡萄则更多地体现炫耀的意味。汉唐帝王遥相呼应,唐太宗则更胜汉武帝,在军事政治行动上,他灭高昌而且置西州,将唐王朝的州县行政管理推行到了西域;在引进西域风物的标志性事件上,太宗收葡

---

① 童丕:《中国北方的粟特遗存——山西的葡萄种植业》,见《粟特人在中国》,中华书局,2005年,第215页。
② 《册府元龟》第二册卷一六八"帝王部"之"却贡献",中华书局,第2028页。
③ 《史记》卷一二三,中华书局,1959年,第3174页。

萄、得酒法并且亲自损益造酒，把西域的葡萄美酒创造性地推广到了长安。《南部新书》记载："太宗破高昌，收马乳蒲桃种于苑，并得酒法，仍自损益之，造酒成绿色，芳香酷烈，味兼醍醐，长安始识其味也。"①《唐会要》与《太平御览》所载略同。这两次引进行为的背后恰恰是开放的社会政治格局和兼容并包的思想背景。将这历史进程中对比鲜明的引进与却贡事件综合考察，主导统治者行动的思想意识中至少有一个方面——就是童丕所提出的中国文人学士中的"葡萄栽培与西方蛮族"乃至胡文化之间的关联。这种关联使得纯为自然物水果的葡萄和生活之饮品的葡萄酒变成了中原帝国征服西域的一个象征符号，被赋予了一种政治色彩。反映在唐诗中，就是如下的一系列表达：

绝域阳关道，胡沙与塞尘。三春时有雁，万里少行人。苜蓿随天马，葡萄逐汉臣。当令外国惧，不敢觅和亲。（王维《送刘司直赴安西》）②

汉家兵马乘北风，鼓行而西破犬戎。尔随汉将出门去，剪虏若草收奇功。君王按剑望边色，旄头已落胡天空。匈奴系颈数应尽，明年应入蒲桃宫。（李白《送族弟绾从军安西》）③

白日登山望烽火，黄昏饮马傍交河。行人刁斗风沙暗，公主琵琶幽怨多。野云万里无城郭，雨雪纷纷连大漠。胡雁哀鸣夜夜飞，胡儿眼泪双双落。闻道玉门犹被遮，应将性命逐轻车。年年战骨埋荒外，空见蒲桃入汉家。（李颀《古从军行》）④

卢橘为秦树，蒲萄出汉宫。烟花宜落日，丝管醉春风。笛奏龙吟水，箫鸣凤下空。君王多乐事，还与万方同。（李白《宫中行乐词八首》）⑤

中兴诸将收山东，捷书日报清昼同。河广传闻一苇过，胡危命在破竹中。祗残邺城不日得，独任朔方无限功。京师皆骑汗血马，回纥喂肉葡萄宫。已喜皇威清海岱，常思仙仗过崆峒。三年笛里关山月，万国兵前草木风。（杜甫《洗兵马》）⑥

汉家海内承平久，万国戎王皆稽首。天马常衔苜蓿花，胡人岁献葡萄酒。五月荔枝初破颜，朝离象郡夕函关。雁飞不到桂阳岭，马走先过林邑山。甘泉御果垂仙阁，日暮无人香自落。远物皆重近皆轻，鸡虽有德不如鹤。（鲍防《杂感》）⑦

这些作品，有的为赠别从军西域的亲友而写，充满了斗志昂扬的乐观精神，如王维和李白的两首赠别诗；有的是关注边塞战争的苦难，悲悯胡人和汉兵的凄惨命运，表达对于穷兵黩武的朝廷边策的不满，如李颀诗；有的装点盛世升平，尽情表达宫中行乐的欢娱气氛，如李白诗；有的则忠实记录了回鹘借兵援助唐朝收复长安的史实，如杜甫诗；鲍防的诗虽然旨在讽喻帝王，但其中天马、胡人两句则在客观上显示了一个泱泱王朝的强大权威和气势。无论诗歌的内容如何，都无一例外地运用了前引《史记·大宛列传》

① 唐宋史料笔记丛刊《南部新书》丙卷，中华书局，2002年，第32页。
② 王维：《送刘司直赴安西》，陈铁民校注《王维集校注》，中华书局，1997年，第405～406页。
③ 李白：《送族弟绾从军安西》，安旗主编《李白全集编年注释》，巴蜀书社，2000年，第451页。
④ 李颀：《古从军行》，《全唐诗（增订本）》，中华书局，1999年，第1348页。
⑤ 李白：《宫中行乐词八首》其三，安旗主编《新版李白全集编年注释》，巴蜀书社，2000年，第406页。
⑥ 杜甫：《洗兵马（收京后作）》，[清]仇兆鳌：《杜诗详注》，中华书局，1979年，第514页。
⑦ 鲍防：《杂感》，《全唐诗（增订本）》，中华书局，1999年，第3484～3485页；朱玉麒：《道藏所见李白资料汇辑考辨》"天马常衔苜蓿花"与"胡人岁献葡萄酒"分别见于《道藏》所收《图经衍义本草》之卷四〇、卷三五，皆曰李白所作诗句。

的典故,无论诗歌褒贬倾向如何,暗含着一个潜在的命题:葡萄(酒)是中原王朝征服西域的象征符号。

　　这样的命题无疑是有一定缘故的。从客观的历史事实出发,假如要寻找一种遍及西域广袤的地理空间、延续数千年而依然生机勃勃的风物作为西域的典型代表或者象征物,葡萄(酒)应该是最佳的选择。

　　历史文献和考古发现都证明了这一点。

　　葡萄,植物学名为 Vitis vinifera。西方学者认为,"葡萄"一词在汉代时的发音相当于希腊文 batrus 或者波斯语 budawa 的译音。"葡萄"在我国史籍中又写作"蒲陶"、"蒲萄"、"蒲桃"、"葡桃"等,葡萄酒则相应地叫做"蒲陶酒"或以"葡萄"径称。根据考古资料,小亚细亚里海和黑海之间及其南岸地区是世界上最早栽培葡萄的地区。大约在七千年以前,南高加索、中亚细亚、叙利亚、伊拉克等地区也开始了葡萄的栽培。波斯(即今日伊朗)和古埃及是最早栽培葡萄和用葡萄酿酒的两个古国。欧洲最早开始种植葡萄并进行葡萄酒酿造的国家是希腊。罗马人从希腊人那里学会葡萄栽培和葡萄酒酿造技术,并传遍欧洲。这些地域则被广义的西域所涵盖。

　　历史文献中关于西域葡萄(酒)产地的记载大致情况是:

　　《史记·大宛列传》中记载出产葡萄(酒)的地方有安息、大宛及大宛周边地区。

　　安息在大月氏西可数千里。其俗土著,耕田,田稻麦,蒲陶酒。[1]

　　大宛在匈奴西南,在汉正西,去汉可万里。其俗土著,耕田,田稻麦。有蒲陶酒。多善马,马汗血,其先天马子也。[2]

　　宛左右以蒲陶为酒,富人藏酒至万余石,久者数十岁不败。俗嗜酒,马嗜苜蓿。[3]

首部正史首涉西域、首叙葡萄(酒)就提及了世界上最早种植葡萄的古国之一——波斯(安息),而处于汉武经营西域之关键位置的费尔干纳盆地的大宛国又影响着周边国家的风物民俗。从史记的记载可以看出,这两个地区不仅有着发达的农业,葡萄种植和葡萄酒的酿造也已达到了成熟的程度。

　　随着汉王朝与西域交往的日渐频繁与深入,更多的葡萄(酒)产地进入了人们的视野。《汉书·西域传》记载的葡萄(酒)产地除了安息、大宛之外,又增加了且末国、难兜国、罽宾国、乌弋山离国、大月氏国等:

　　安息国,王治番兜城,去长安万一千六百里。不属都护。北与康居、东与乌弋山离、西与条支接。土地风气,物类所有,民俗与乌弋、罽宾同。[4]

　　大月氏国,治监氏城,去长安万一千六百里。不属都护。……东至都护治所四千七百四十里,西至安息四十九日行,南与罽宾接。土地风气,物类所有,民俗钱货,与安息同。[5]

　　(大宛)土地风气物类民俗与大月氏、安息同。大宛左右以蒲陶为酒,富人藏酒至万余石,久者至数十岁不败。俗嗜酒,马嗜苜蓿。[6]

---

① 《史记》卷一二三,中华书局,1959 年,第 3162 页。
② 同上,第 3160 页。
③ 同上,第 3174 页。
④ 《汉书》卷九六,中华书局,1962 年,第 3889 页。
⑤ 同上,第 3890 页。
⑥ 同上,第 3894~3895 页。

且末国,王治且末城,去长安八百二十里。户二百三十,口千六百一十,胜兵三百二十人。……西北至都护治所二千二百五十八里,北接尉犁,南至小宛,可行三日。有蒲陶诸果。①

罽宾国,王治循鲜城,去长安万二千二百里。不属都护。户口胜兵多,大国也。……罽宾地平,温和,有目宿,杂草奇木,檀、槐、梓、竹、漆。种五谷、蒲陶诸果。②

难兜国,王治去长安万一百五十里。户五千,口三万一千,胜兵八千人。东北至都护治所二千八百五十里,西至无雷三百四十里,西南至罽宾三百三十里,南与若羌、北与休循、西与大月氏接。种五谷、蒲陶诸果。③

(乌弋山离国)地暑热莽平,其草木、畜产、五谷、果菜、食饮、宫室、市列、钱货、兵器、金珠之属皆与罽宾同。④

其中,大月氏居阿姆河流域,且末国在今新疆且末县附近,罽宾国在今克什米尔地区,难兜国在罽宾东北,乌弋山离国在罽宾西北。诸国之道里距离有远近,但风土、出产、草木、果蔬与饮食则相类。

《后汉书·西域传》记载的葡萄(酒)产地又增加了今新疆哈密附近的伊吾和今泽拉夫善河流域的粟戈国。伊吾的出现意味着葡萄(酒)的产地已经到了西域的最东面门户,再向东向南就入玉门关了。

伊吾地宜五谷、桑麻、蒲陶。其北又有柳中,皆膏腴之地。⑤

粟戈国属康居。出名马牛羊、蒲萄众果,其土水美,故蒲萄酒特有名焉。⑥

《晋书·西戎传》除了继续保留了大宛之外,新增加的葡萄(酒)产地有锡尔河北岸的康居,而《晋书·吕光传》则出现了塔里木绿洲的一个重要国家龟兹:

大宛国,去洛阳万三千三百五十里,南至大月氏,北接康居,大小七十余城。土宜稻麦,有蒲陶酒,多善马,马汗血。⑦

康居国在大宛西北可二千里,与粟弋、伊列邻接。其王居苏薤城。风俗及人貌、衣服略同大宛。地和暖,饶桐柳蒲陶,多牛羊,出好马。⑧

(吕)光入其城(龟兹)……胡人奢侈,厚于养生,家有蒲桃酒,或至千斛,经十年不败。⑨

《梁书·诸夷传》记载的葡萄(酒)产地有塔里木盆地南缘的重要国家于阗国和吐鲁番盆地的高昌国:

---

① 《汉书》卷九六,中华书局,1962 年,第 3879 页。
② 同上,第 3884 ~ 3885 页。
③ 同上,第 3884 页。
④ 同上,第 3889 页。
⑤ 《后汉书》卷八六,中华书局,1965 年,第 2914 页。
⑥ 同上,第 2922 页。
⑦ 《晋书》卷九七,中华书局,1974 年,第 2542 页。
⑧ 同上,第 2544 页。
⑨ 《晋书》卷一二二,中华书局,1974 年,第 3055 页。

（于阗），其地多水潦沙石，气温，宜稻、麦、蒲桃。①

（高昌国），其国盖车师之故地也。南接河南，东连燉煌，西次龟兹，北邻敕勒。置四十六镇，交河、田地、高宁、临川、横截、柳婆、洿林、新兴、由宁、始昌、笃进、白力等，皆其镇名。……国人言语与中国略同。有《五经》、历代史、诸子集。面貌类高骊，辫发垂之于背，著长身小袖袍、缦裆袴。女子头发辫而不垂，著锦缬缨珞环钏。姻有六礼。其地高燥，筑土为城，架木为屋，土覆其上。寒暑与益州相似。备植九谷，人多啖麦及羊牛肉。出良马、蒲陶酒、石盐。多草木，草实如茧，茧中丝如细纩，名为白叠子，国人多取织以为布。布甚软白，交市用焉。有朝乌者，旦旦集王殿前，为行列，不畏人，日出然后散去。大同中，子坚遣使献鸣盐枕、蒲陶、良马、氍毹等物。②

《魏书·高昌传》也提及了高昌的葡萄酒。

（高昌）地多石碛，气候温暖，厥土良沃，谷麦一岁再熟。宜蚕，多五果，又饶漆，有草名羊刺，其上生蜜而味甚佳。引水溉田，出赤盐，其味甚美，复有白盐，其形如玉，高昌人取以为枕，贡之中国。多蒲萄酒。③

世界著名的葡萄（酒）产地吐鲁番终于进入了我们的视野，自此开始，吐鲁番葡萄（酒）的丰富种类和优秀品质始终成为历代史家笔下的话题。交河、田地、高宁、洿林等高昌辖镇是正史和笔记小说中著名的葡萄（酒）产地。直到元代，忽思慧的《饮膳正要》仍然把吐鲁番的葡萄酒列为最佳："（葡萄酒）益气调中，耐气强志。酒有数等，有西番者，有哈剌火者，有平阳、太原者，其味都不及哈剌火者、田地酒最佳。"④其中的哈剌火者大约在今天的吐鲁番市二堡乡，田地大约位于今吐鲁番地区鄯善县西南鲁克沁镇西的柳中故城。此二地至今盛产优质的葡萄。

《魏书·西域传》记载的葡萄（酒）产地除了龟兹国，又增加了焉耆国、副货国、南天竺国、拔豆国、康国。

焉耆国，在车师南，都员渠城，白山南七十里，汉时旧国也。……气候寒，土地良沃，谷有稻粟菽麦，畜有骆驼。养蚕不以为丝，为充绵纩。俗尚葡萄酒，兼爱音乐。⑤

（龟兹国），物产与焉耆略同，唯气候少温为异。⑥

（副货国），国中有副货城，周匝七十里。宜五谷、萄桃，唯有马、驼、骡。⑦

（南天竺国），有拔赖城，城中出黄金、白真檀、石蜜、蒲陶。土宜五谷。⑧

（拔豆）国中出金、银、杂宝、白象、水牛、牦牛、蒲萄、五果。土宜五谷。⑨

① 《梁书》卷四八，中华书局，1973 年，第 814 页。
② 同上，第 811 页。
③ 《魏书》卷一〇一，中华书局，1974 年，第 2243 页。
④ （元）忽思慧：《饮膳正要》，中国书店，1993 年，第 58 页。
⑤ 《魏书》卷一〇二，中华书局，1974 年，第 2265 页。
⑥ 同上，第 2266 页。
⑦ 同上，第 2278 页。
⑧ 同上，第 2278 页。
⑨ 同上，第 2278 页。

(康国)气候温,宜五谷,勤修园蔬,树木滋茂。出马、驼、驴、犎牛、黄金、硇沙、(贝甘)香、阿薛那香、瑟瑟、麖皮、氍毹、锦、叠。多蒲萄酒,富家或致十石,连年不败。①

在这些产地中,拔豆国地望待考,焉者是天山南麓农业化程度很高的重镇,副货国大约位于今布哈拉或白沙瓦,南天竺国似即南印度,康国则是阿姆河和锡尔河之间的河中地区九姓胡诸国的代表。

《周书·异域传》、《隋书·西域传》、《南史·西域诸国传》、《北史·西域传》等史书中关于葡萄(酒)产地的记载大率沿袭辗转前人旧记,涉及的西域诸国有高昌国、康国、于阗国、焉耆国、龟兹国、副货国、南天竺国、拔豆国、康国,具体内容则与前引文字略同,兹不赘述。

唐以前西域的葡萄(酒)产地已经遍及葱岭内外,唐代亦然。关于唐朝西域葡萄(酒)的产地,历史文献记载详细而丰富。

《旧唐书·西戎传》记载的葡萄(酒)产地有高昌、焉耆、龟兹、康国等:

> 高昌者,汉车师前王之庭,后汉戊己校尉之故地。……厥土良沃,谷麦岁再熟;有蒲萄酒,宜五果。②
>
> 焉者国,在京师西四千三百里,东接高昌,西邻龟兹,即汉时故地。……其地良沃,多蒲萄,颇有鱼盐之利。③
>
> 龟兹国,即汉西域旧地也。在京师西七千五百里。……有良马、封牛。饶蒲萄酒,富室至数百石。④
>
> 康国……人多嗜酒,好歌舞于道路。⑤

《新唐书·西域传》记载的葡萄(酒)产地除了焉者、龟兹、康国外,又增加了笈赤建国、乌茶国、商弥、大食等地:

> 焉者国直京师西七千里而赢,横六百里,纵四百里。东高昌,西龟兹,南尉犁,北乌孙。逗渠溉田,土宜黍、蒲陶,有鱼盐利。⑥
>
> 龟兹,一曰丘兹,一曰屈兹,东距京师七千里而赢,自焉者西南步二百里,度小山,经大河二,又步七百里乃至。横千里,纵六百里。土宜麻、麦、秔稻、蒲陶,出黄金。俗善歌乐。⑦
>
> 有笈赤建国,广千里,地沃宜稼,多蒲陶。⑧
>
> 康者……人嗜酒,好歌舞于道。⑨
>
> 乌茶者,一曰乌伏那,亦曰乌苌,直天竺南,地广五千里,东距勃律六百里,西属宾四百里。山谷

---

① 《魏书》卷一〇二,中华书局,1974 年,第 2281 页。
② 《旧唐书》卷一四八,中华书局,1975 年,第 5293 ~ 5294 页。
③ 同上,第 5301 页。
④ 同上,第 5303 页。
⑤ 同上,第 5310 页。
⑥ 《新唐书》卷二二一上,中华书局,1975 年,第 6228 页。
⑦ 同上,第 6230 页。
⑧ 同上,第 6233 页。
⑨ 《新唐书》卷二二一下,中华书局,1975 年,第 6243 页。

相属,产金、铁、蒲陶、郁金。①

有商弥,地大二千里而赢,多蒲陶。②

俱位,或曰商弥。……地寒,有五谷、蒲陶、若榴。③

大食,本波斯地。……蒲陶大者如鸡卵。④

其中的筊赤建国大约位于今塔什干地区的汗阿巴德,乌荼国北接葱岭南连天竺,商弥(俱位)国位于克什米尔地区,大食则指据有了波斯旧地的阿拉伯帝国。

唐书的《西域传》外,汉文的文献还有不少值得注意。

《大唐西域记》记载的玄奘取经沿途种植葡萄或酿造葡萄酒的地方有阿耆尼国、屈支国、素叶水城、筊赤建国、乌仗那国、斫句迦国等:

阿耆尼国东西六百余里,南北四百余里。……泉流交带,引水为田。土宜糜、黍、宿麦、香枣、蒲萄、梨、柰诸果。⑤

屈支国,东西千余里,南北六百余里。国大都城周十七八里,宜糜、麦,有粳稻,出蒲萄、石榴,多梨、柰、桃、杏。⑥

清池西北行五百余里,至素叶水城。城周六七里,诸国商胡杂居也。土宜糜、麦、蒲萄,林树稀疏。气序风寒,人衣毡褐。⑦

筊赤建国,周千余里。地沃壤,备稼穑。草木郁茂,华果繁盛,多蒲萄,亦所贵也。⑧

乌仗那国周五千余里,山谷相属,川泽连原。谷稼虽播,地利不滋,多葡萄,少甘蔗。⑨

斫句迦国周千余里。国大都城周十余里,坚峻险固,编户殷盛。山阜连属,砾石弥漫。临带两河,颇以耕植。蒲萄、梨、柰其果寔繁。⑩

阿耆尼国即焉耆,屈支国即龟兹,素叶水城即碎叶,筊赤建国大约位于今塔什干地区的汗阿巴德,乌仗那国北接葱岭南连天竺,斫句迦国位于今叶城。尤其值得重视的是在"印度总述"部分,玄奘详细记载了印度的物产,其中葡萄和葡萄酒是其大宗:

至于枣、栗、椑、柿,印度无闻;梨、柰、桃、杏、蒲萄等果,迦湿弥罗国已来,往往间植;石榴、甘橘,诸国皆树。⑪

---

① 《新唐书》卷二二一上,中华书局,1975 年,第 6239 ~ 6240 页。
② 《新唐书》卷二二一下,中华书局,1975 年,第 6249 页。
③ 同上,第 6249 页。
④ 同上,第 6262 页。
⑤ 《大唐西域记校注》卷一,中华书局,2000 年,第 48 页。
⑥ 同上,第 54 页。
⑦ 同上,第 71 页。
⑧ 同上,第 81 页。
⑨ 《大唐西域记校注》卷三,中华书局,2000 年,第 270 页。
⑩ 《大唐西域记校注》卷一二,中华书局,2000 年,第 998 页。
⑪ 《大唐西域记校注》卷二,中华书局,2000 年,第 211 页。

若其酒醴之差，滋味流别。蒲萄、甘蔗，刹帝利饮也；曲蘖醇醪，吠奢等饮也；沙门、婆罗门饮蒲萄、甘蔗浆，非酒醴之谓也。杂姓卑族，无所流别。①

　　唐代吐鲁番地区出产葡萄（酒）的情况在地上地下文献中都有充分反映，在《吐鲁番出土文书》中，涉及葡萄的文书出自 39 个墓，58 件。② 这些文书显示，吐鲁番地区的葡萄种植很普遍，葡萄酒酿造很发达，葡萄园的管理、葡萄（酒）的交易等是这些文书的主题。正因为如此，吐鲁番地区才能源源不断向中原的朝廷进贡葡萄（酒）。官方贡赋方面的记载中提到的西州地区（今吐鲁番）主要贡物就是葡萄（酒），《新唐书·地理志四》载："西州交河郡，中都督府。贞观十四年平高昌，以其地置。开元中曰金山都督府。天宝元年为郡。土贡：丝、氎布、毡、刺蜜、蒲萄五物酒浆煎皱乾。"③《元和郡县图志·陇右道》记载的西州贡赋有："开元贡：氎毛，刺蜜，乾蒲萄。"④这与出土文献的记载可以互相印证。

　　位于西域东大门的伊州（今哈密地区）作为葡萄（酒）产地曾经在《后汉书》中出现，唐代的沙州传马坊账册里也有类似记录。伯三七一四背《唐总章二年八、九月沙州传马坊传马驴使用文书残卷》中载伊州种有葡萄，产葡萄酒。⑤

　　《通志·四夷西戎》提及了遥远的地方奄蔡，奄蔡约位于咸海、里海北部："（奄蔡）出名马、牛、羊、蒲萄众果。其土水美，故蒲萄酒特有名焉。"⑥

　　《册府元龟》记载了西突厥叶护曾贡献马乳葡萄："（贞观二十一年）三月，帝以远夷各贡方物珍果咸至，其草木杂物有异于常者，诏曰使详录焉。叶护献马乳蒲桃一房，长二丈余，子亦稍大，其色紫。"⑦西突厥可汗曾设牙帐于碎叶城，《大唐西域记》述及碎叶城时说那里出产葡萄，《大慈恩寺三藏法师传》记载玄奘取经途次碎叶城，西突厥统叶护可汗以葡萄浆相待，可见西突厥领地是有葡萄出产的——也许不是很普遍，或者西突厥的西域附庸国是有葡萄出产的。

　　非汉文文献中记载西域葡萄（酒）比较丰富的要数精绝国佉卢文木牍。精绝国是两汉文献中的西域三十六国之一，故址即今新疆尼雅古城。民丰县尼雅遗址先后出土公元三至四世纪的精绝国佉卢文木牍残卷七百二十余件，涉及农业经济方面的文书约一百五十余件，占文书总数的百分之二十一。与畜牧有关的文书约八十余件，占出土文书总数的九分之一，与葡萄种植和酒业管理有关的文书近二十余件，占整个农业经济文书的约八分之一。文书主要涉及了精绝国的葡萄种植与葡萄园土地所有制之形式、精绝国的嗜酒之风及精绝国的酒业管理等问题。⑧

　　文物考古资料方面，伊朗北部扎格罗斯山脉新石器时代晚期聚落遗址罐子中残余的葡萄酒，古埃及第一、二王朝的陵墓中曾发现有"王家葡萄园印章"和酒具，土库曼国境内之尼萨古城宫殿遗址内发掘出

---

① 《大唐西域记校注》卷二，中华书局，2000 年，第 215 页。
② 陈习刚：《唐代葡萄和葡萄酒考述》，湖北大学硕士学位论文，2000 年，第 8 页。
③ 《新唐书》卷四〇，中华书局，1975 年，第 1046 页。
④ 《元和郡县图志》卷四〇，中华书局，1983 年，第 1030 页。
⑤ 李锦绣：《唐代财政史稿》上卷第三分册，北京大学出版社，1995 年，第 1041～1042 页。
⑥ 《通志》卷一九六，中华书局，1987 年，第 3151 页。
⑦ 《册府元龟》第十二册卷九七〇"外臣部"之"朝贡三"，中华书局，1960 年，第 11400 页。
⑧ 卫斯：《西域农业考古资料索引·第六编农业文书·三、佉卢文农业文书（一）畜牧》，《农业考古》2003 年 3 期～2006 年 3 期。文书可参看林梅村《秦汉魏晋出土文献 沙海古卷 中国所出佉卢文书（初集）》，文物出版社，1998 年版；T·贝罗著、王广智译《新疆出土佉卢文残卷译文集》（T. Burrow: A Translation of the kharoshi Documents from Chinese Tur kestan）1940 年由伦敦英国皇家野洲协会出版。刊《尼雅考古资料》（内部刊物），乌鲁木齐，1988 年版。

的帕提雅王国时期象牙"来通"（Rhyton）口缘处雕刻有葡萄藤蔓等是考证研究葡萄和葡萄酒最常用的资料案例,此处不赘述。这些资料都显示了在广义的西域地理空间里的实存物质完全可以印证文献资料的实录性和准确性。

二十世纪以来,在新疆的乌鲁木齐、特克斯、民丰、库车等地,曾陆续出土葡萄实物、葡萄坠金耳环、大型贮酒器、酿酒工具等。当然最典型的还是吐鲁番地区的出土文物,最具代表性的有约两千五百年前的葡萄标本、一千七百年前的"庄园主生活图"壁画以及大量的从麹氏高昌王国到西州时期的葡萄实物遗存。

据《光明日报》报道,在2003年进行的新疆吐鲁番鄯善县洋海墓地的考古发掘中,考古人员从约二千五百年前的一座墓穴中发掘出一株葡萄标本。新疆考古所专家认定它属于圆果紫葡萄的植株。其实物为葡萄藤,全长1.15米、每节长11 cm、扁宽2.3 cm。这是新疆考古中发现最早的葡萄种植的实物标本。①

吐鲁番地区文物局局长李肖2004年8月6日宣布,一幅"庄园主生活图"壁画近期在吐鲁番地区阿斯塔那古墓被发现,这幅壁画展现了一千七百年前葡萄种植及酿酒业的概貌,表明那时葡萄种植及酿酒业已经成为吐鲁番地区农庄生活的主要部分。"庄园主生活图"壁画发现于阿斯塔那古墓一个9平方米墓室的正面壁室,长2.5米,宽约0.6米。在壁画的下角画有一块葡萄地,画面上还再现了葡萄酿酒从榨汁到蒸馏等的全过程。此次发现将成为研究中国葡萄历史的重要史料。②

1960年在吐鲁番阿斯塔那320号墓,1969年在吐鲁番哈拉和卓52号墓,1972年在吐鲁番阿斯塔那169号墓、198号墓,1973年在吐鲁番阿斯塔那527号墓中均发现葡萄。这五座墓均属麹氏高昌王国时期。1966年在吐鲁番阿斯塔那69号墓出土一串葡萄干,此墓属麹氏高昌王国至唐西州时期。1960年在吐鲁番阿斯塔那318号墓,1966年在61号墓、44号墓,1969年在150号墓,1972年在186号墓、192号墓,1973年在213号墓,1975年在吐鲁番哈拉和卓104号墓均出土葡萄。此八座墓均属唐西州时期。③

综合上述文献和出土文物资料,我们可以大致描绘从早期葡萄种植以来尤其是从中国汉朝以来到隋唐时期在整个西域地区的葡萄（酒）出产地分布情况。以葱岭和天山为界来划分,葱岭以西的产地有费尔干纳盆地、锡尔河与阿姆河之间的河中地区、伊朗以及更遥远的地中海沿岸诸国、咸海里海以北地区;葱岭以南的产地则有克什米尔地区和印度;昆仑山以北,天山以南的塔里木盆地周边的绿洲和天山东段南坡的吐鲁番盆地、哈密盆地都是重要的葡萄（酒）出产地;从碎叶城出产葡萄（酒）及西突厥叶护向太宗贡献葡萄的记载来看,天山以北也有葡萄（酒）生产,只是不及西域其他地区丰富罢了。

在西域如此巨大的地理空间跨度和汉唐如此漫长的历史时间跨度中,诸多的民族从兴盛走向了衰亡,诸多的政权在战争中颠覆,诸多的风物化为灰烬或者被永远尘封,只有东来的丝绸、西来的葡萄（酒）的地位始终不变、魅力依然强大。在西域诸国人的眼里,丝绸可以作为中国这个强盛而富足的帝国的象征,丝绸贸易不仅为他们带来令人艳羡的财富,拥有丝绸这样的奢侈品也吸引了别人艳羡的目光;在汉唐中原人尤其是文人的眼中,葡萄（酒）也完全可以成为西域的代称,因此诗人们把葡萄入汉家、岁献葡萄酒作为汉唐帝国征服西域、令四方来朝的最具代表性的象征符号,那也是很正常的了。我们通过下面几首诗进一步考察:

① 《光明日报》,2004年4月8日,第一版。
② http://travel.soxj.com/news/show.asp? ArticleID=2276。
③ 王炳华:《新疆农业考古概述》附"吐鲁番地区晋——唐时期出土农作物统计表",《农业考古》1983年1期,第118~121页。

芳郊绿野散春晴,复道离宫烟雾生。杨柳千条花欲绽,蒲萄百丈蔓初萦。林香酒气元相入,鸟啭歌声各自成。定是风光牵宿醉,来晨复得幸昆明。(沈佺期《奉和春日幸望春宫应制》)①

识子十年何不遇,只爱欢游两京路。朝吟左氏娇女篇,夜诵相如美人赋。长安春物旧相宜,小苑蒲萄花满枝。柳色偏浓九华殿,莺声醉杀五陵儿。曳裾此日从何所,中贵由来尽相许。白夹春衫仙吏赠,乌皮隐几台郎与。新诗乐府唱堪愁,御妓应传鸤鹊楼。西上虽因长公主,终须一见曲陵侯。(李颀《送康洽入京进乐府歌》)②

洛阳三月梨花飞,秦地行人春忆归。扬鞭走马城南陌,朝逢驿使秦川客。驿使前日发章台,传道长安春早来。棠梨宫中燕初至,葡萄馆里花正开。念此使人归更早,三月便达长安道。长安道上春可怜,摇风荡日曲江边。万户楼台临渭水,五陵花柳满秦川。秦川寒食盛繁华,游子春来不见家。(崔颢《渭城少年行》)③

明主重文谏,才臣出江东。束书辞东山,改服临北风。万里望皇邑,九重当曙空。天开芙蓉阙,日上蒲桃宫。天子初未起,金闺籍先通。身逢轩辕世,名贵鸳鸾中。故人荣此别,何用悲丝桐。(皎然《送梁拾遗肃归朝》)④

沈佺期的应制诗,写杨柳条、葡萄藤,固然可能是眼前所见的自然景致,但应制之作要突出皇家瑞气,其中的"离宫"应该暗含着《史记·大宛列传》"离宫别观旁尽种蒲萄、苜蓿极望"的典故并与昆明池(汉武帝为征伐昆明操练水军而开凿昆明池)典故等呼应。李颀赠别康洽诗,述及长安春物,第一项就是"小苑蒲萄花满枝",而且把这美景与九华殿和五陵等相并列,联系到康洽的粟特九姓胡身份,李颀在这首诗的创作过程中潜意识里无疑也化用了《史记·大宛列传》的典故。崔颢诗径称旧典"葡萄馆",并以"念此使人归更早,三月便达长安道"牢牢将葡萄馆与长安城的微妙关系锁定。皎然送梁肃归京,想到的依然是"葡萄宫"。可见诗人们往往有意无意地把葡萄宫(苑、馆)与长安、帝都相联系。究其就里,在汉唐相沿袭的文史传统和诗人的理念中,葡萄(酒)已超越了一般的地理、风物的意义,而包含着一定的政治象征意味。

二、曼妙的歌咏对象

当然,对于"杨柳千条花欲绽,蒲萄百丈蔓初萦"、"长安春物旧相宜,小苑蒲萄花满枝"的理解仅仅停留在描摹美好春天充满勃勃生机的自然景物的层面,也无不可。毕竟,并非所有的唐代诗人都把葡萄(酒)视为西域的代称符号,有大量的唐诗恰恰就是唐代社会葡萄(酒)生产、传播和流行的实录,葡萄(酒)就是诗人们喜爱的一种歌咏对象。

从历史文献和诗文记载来看,自从葡萄和葡萄酒再次被引进中原后,唐王朝行政辖区内的葡萄种植和葡萄酒酿造还是比较普遍的,除了长安外,最负盛名的要数西州、凉州和并州。

① 沈佺期:《奉和春日幸望春宫应制》,《全唐诗(增订本)》,中华书局,1999 年,第 1036 页。
② 李颀:《送康洽入京进乐府歌》,同上,第 1351 页。
③ 崔颢:《渭城少年行》,《全唐诗(增订本)》,中华书局,1999 年,第 1324 页。
④ 皎然:《送梁拾遗肃归朝》,同上,第 9296 页。

西州

岑参《与独孤渐道别长句兼呈严八侍御》和《酒泉太守席上醉后作》二诗真实记录了唐西州的特产浐林葡萄、武城刺蜜和交河葡萄酒:"轮台客舍春草满,颍阳归客肠堪断。……桂林蒲萄新吐蔓,武城刺蜜未可餐";[①]"琵琶长笛曲相和,羌儿胡雏齐唱歌。浑炙犁牛烹野驼,交河美酒金叵罗。"[②]

唐西州,即今吐鲁番地区。今日之交河故城是汉代车师国故地,汉帝国曾与匈奴五争车师于交河,麹氏高昌国时期为其辖镇,唐西州时期为交河县。交河产葡萄及酒。《太平广记·神十一》记载汝阴人的故事曰:"房中施云母屏风,芙蓉翠帐,以鹿瑞锦障暎四壁。大设珍殽,多诸异果,甘美鲜香,非人间者。食器有七子螺、九枝盘、红螺杯、蘡叶碗,皆黄金隐起,错以瑰碧,有玉罍,贮车师葡萄酒,芬馨酷烈。"[③]玉罍所盛之车师葡萄酒就是交河葡萄酒;李白《对酒》诗曰:"蒲萄酒,金叵罗,吴姬十五细马驮",[④]金叵罗所盛即葡萄美酒;岑参诗"交河美酒金叵罗"中所谓的交河美酒应该就是交河葡萄酒。

从麹氏高昌国时期到唐西州时期,除了交河,吐鲁番地区的葡萄产地还有高昌、田地、柳中、浐林、高宁、武城、崇化等;除了葡萄和葡萄酒,此地特产尚有良马、刺蜜、石盐、棉花等。岑参《与独孤渐道别长句兼呈严八侍御》所谓的武城刺蜜是理所当然的吐鲁番特产,那么桂林葡萄如何理解呢? 遍查相关的历史、地理书,吐鲁番及周边西域地区无桂林之地名,南方之桂林似与此桂林无涉,而前引《梁书·诸夷传》载高昌国有辖镇浐林产葡萄,《太平御览》与《太平广记》也都有浐林葡萄的记载,吐鲁番文书中也出现过浐林的葡萄和葡萄酒名簿等,那么岑诗中的桂林葡萄很可能是浐林葡萄。

关于浐林葡萄,还可从笔记小说中找到旁证。《太平广记·异人一》记载了梁天监中武帝身边杰公等四个异人的超人见识,其记载杰公最详:

> 高昌国遣使贡盐二颗,颗如斗大,状白似玉,干蒲桃、刺蜜、冻酒、白麦面。王公士庶皆不之识。帝以其自万里绝域而来献,数年方达,文字言语,与梁国略同,经三日,朝廷无祇对者,帝命杰公迓之。谓其使曰:"盐,一颗是南烧羊山月望收之者,一是北烧羊山非月望收之者。蒲桃,七是浐林,三是无半。冻酒,非八风谷所冻者,又以高宁酒和之。刺蜜,是盐城所产,非南平城者。白麦面是宕昌者,非昌垒真物。"使者具陈实情:"麦为经年色败,至宕昌贸易填之。其年风灾,蒲桃刺蜜不熟,故驳杂。盐及冻酒,奉王命急,故非时耳。"因又问紫盐医珀,云自中路,遭北凉所夺,不敢言之。帝问杰公群物之异,对曰:"南烧羊山盐文理粗,北烧羊山文理密,月望收之者,明澈如冰,以毡橐煮之可验。蒲桃,浐林者,皮薄味美;无半者,皮厚味苦。酒,是八风谷冻成者,终年不坏;今臭其气酸,浐林酒滑而色浅,故云然。南平城羊刺无叶,其蜜色明白而味甘;盐城羊刺叶大,其蜜色青而味薄,昌垒白麦面,烹之将熟,洁白如新,今面如泥且烂,由是知蜜麦之伪耳。交河之间平碛中,掘深数尺,有末盐,如红如紫,色鲜味甘,食之止痛。更深一丈,下有医珀,黑逾纯漆,或大如车轮,末而服之,攻妇人小肠症瘕诸疾。彼国珍异,必当致贡,是以知之。"[⑤]

① 岑参:《与独孤渐道别长句兼呈严八侍御》,廖立笺注《岑嘉州诗笺注》,中华书局,2004年,第346~347页。
② 岑参:《酒泉太守席上醉后作》,同上,第427页。
③ 《太平广记》卷三〇一,中华书局,1961年,第2387页。
④ 李白:《对酒》,安旗主编《新版李白全集编年注释》,巴蜀书社,2000年,第65页。
⑤ 《太平广记》卷八一,中华书局,1961年,第519页。

《太平御览》引《梁四公记》的记载与此略同而简括：

> 高昌遣使献干葡萄冻酒。帝命杰公迓之，谓其使曰："蒲桃，七是洿林，三是无半。冻酒非八风谷所冻者，又无高宁酒和之。"使者曰："其年风灾，蒲桃不熟，故驳杂。冻酒，奉王急命，故非时耳。"帝问杰公群物之异，对曰："蒲桃，洿林者，皮薄味美；无半者，皮厚味苦。酒是八风谷冻成者，终年不坏。今臭其气酸，洿林酒滑而色浅，故云然。"①

综合这两段文献，我们可以形成这样几个认识：

其一，梁武帝天监年间，麹氏高昌国遣使贡献之物有石盐、干葡萄、刺蜜、冻酒、白麦面、紫盐、医珀等，其中的紫盐、医珀途经北凉时被夺去，剩下的贡品中，白麦面以次充好，葡萄刺蜜成色驳杂，而石盐和冻酒则因为王命迫急而没有按照时间和程序来收取和生产。多闻而广识的杰公准确而犀利地把一切解释得清清楚楚。

其二，高昌国的葡萄质量与产地有关。洿林的葡萄是上品，皮薄味美；无半的葡萄质量较次，皮厚味苦。因为风灾，葡萄减产，洿林的葡萄不够贡献，所以夹杂了无半的葡萄。从现有文献看，在吐鲁番各地出产的葡萄中，洿林的葡萄属于上品。

其三，高昌国的葡萄酒有一种特殊的品种曰冻酒。唐代葡萄酒的酿制大体分为两类，第一种是自然发酵法，绞压葡萄成浆，自然发酵后而成，西域诸国主要适用这种酿造方法。葡萄浆若保留果皮、果渣等混合发酵，可酿得红葡萄酒；葡萄浆若及时与果皮果渣等分离，纯果汁发酵，可酿得白葡萄酒。第二种是加曲酿造法，类似中原地区以粮食酿酒之法，在酿制过程中加入麹蘖，进行酿造。采用曲种的不同、曲量的大小会决定葡萄酒的口味各异。太宗破高昌得酒法，亲自损益酿造八种风格的葡萄酒。除了运用西域自然发酵法得若干种之外，其余的品种很可能就是通过加曲酿制而得的。王绩《题酒店楼壁绝句八首》其二曰："竹叶连糟翠，蒲萄带麹红。相逢不令尽，别后为谁空"，②李白《襄阳歌》曰："遥看汉水鸭头绿，恰似葡萄初酦醅。此江若变作春酒，垒麹便筑糟丘台"，③描写葡萄酒时都提到了糟麹，很明显，他们描述的正是葡萄酒的后一种酿造法。冻酒是葡萄酒酿制完成后的一道重要的陈化程序，并非一般意义上的冰镇或冰贮。一般的葡萄酒酿制在自然的温度下完成陈化达到成熟稳定的阶段，大约需要两到三年的时间。冻酒则是将当年的新酦酒或者幼龄酒在北方寒冷冬季进行冷冻处理，加速葡萄酒的陈化，改善葡萄酒的质量、口感和纯度。从文献来看，高昌国的八风谷是最好的冻酒场所。可见，冻酒程序对葡萄酒的新鲜程度、冷冻时间和地点都有着特别高的要求，《四公记》里杰公敏感地发现冻酒非八风谷冻者，而且还和入了高宁酒，使者解释说："冻酒，奉王急命，故非时耳。"正是因为风灾和王命急，无法保证冻酒条件，所以只能敷衍了事。

既然武城的刺蜜、洿林的葡萄、八风谷的冻酒都是吐鲁番贡品中的上品，远在江南的梁王朝也有高人通晓其事，那么亲赴西域、频频往返于轮台和高昌之间的岑参自然会非常熟悉这里的特产，他在诗中写道了武城刺蜜，又以桂林葡萄对举，我们将这个桂林葡萄推测为洿林葡萄还是比较合理的。岑参的安西北

① 《太平御览》卷八四五，《饮食部三·酒下》，中华书局，1960年，第3778页。
② 王绩：《题酒店楼壁绝句八首》其二，韩理洲校点《王无功文集》，上海古籍出版社，1987年，第98～100页。
③ 李白：《襄阳歌》，安旗主编《新版李白全集编年注释》，巴蜀书社，2000年，第245～246页。

庭诸作在描写景致时确有夸张成分,但涉及地名基本都是写实的,这首诗也不例外。岑参的这首赠别诗从天山北麓的轮台写起,中间写到吐鲁番风物,轮台与西州的关系又有交叉重叠,[①]这里的刺蜜、葡萄自然是岑参的写实之笔,刺蜜、葡萄的出产地同样也应该是写实的,联系到唐西州地区特产种类和具体产地的历史文献和出土文书记载,目前只有浒林比较符合。岑参的诗歌的确从一个侧面反映了唐代西州葡萄(酒)出产的实际情况。

凉州

凉州是陇右河西最重要的都会。陇右河西作为丝绸之路的必经之地,华戎杂处,东西交汇,成为西域向中原过渡的缓冲区域。《隋书·裴矩传》记载:"及(炀)帝西巡,次焉支山,高昌王、伊吾设等,及西蕃胡二十七国,谒于道左。皆令佩金玉,被锦罽,焚香奏乐,歌舞喧噪;复令武威、张掖士女盛饰纵观,骑乘填咽,周亘数十里,以示中国之盛。"[②]《资治通鉴》唐纪三十二载,天宝年间,"自安远门西尽唐境万二千里,闾阎相望,桑麻翳野。天下称富庶者无如陇右"。[③]这里既是东西方的交通要道,也是物质文化交流的重要通道,当然也是葡萄(酒)东传的必经之地。《本草纲目》引陶弘景《名医别录》就明确指出:"蒲萄生陇西、五原、敦煌山谷。"[④]在这条通道的西头,沙州境内有葡萄种植和葡萄酒生产,敦煌遗书伯5034号《沙州地志》曰:"艳典种蒲桃于城中";[⑤]"从石城至播仙八百五十里,有水草。从新城西南向蒲桃城二百四十里,中间三处有水草,每所相去七十余里,从蒲桃城西北去播仙镇四百余里,并碛,路不通"。[⑥]敦煌遗书斯367号《沙州伊州地志》载:"蒲桃城,南去石城镇四里,康艳典所筑,种蒲桃此城中,因号蒲桃城。"[⑦]蒲桃城是沙州辖城,为粟特人康艳典所筑并广种葡萄,与陶弘景《名医别录》的记载恰可互证,敦煌一带的确是葡萄(酒)产地。在这条通道的东头,秦州也出产葡萄,杜甫在秦州时作《寓目》诗曰:"一县蒲萄熟,秋山苜蓿多",[⑧]堪为证据。

当然,西头的沙州和东头的秦州是无法和凉州这个古老而又富庶的城市相比肩的。凉州在这条通道上占据着独特的重要地位,玄奘西行途经此地,看到这里是"河西都会,襟带西蕃、葱右诸国,商旅往来,无有停绝"。[⑨]岑参在《凉州馆中与诸判官夜集》说:"弯弯月出挂城头,城头月出照凉州。凉州七里十万家,胡人半解弹琵琶。"[⑩]美国学者谢弗在研究唐代外来文明时感叹:"凉州是一座地地道道的熔炉,正如夏威夷对于二十世纪的美国一样,对于内地的唐人,凉州本身就是外来奇异事物的亲切象征。"[⑪]这样一个拥有农业文明基础又拥有商业贸易,聚集了大量移民又吸纳着新奇风物的凉州,无疑是葡萄(酒)生产和流行的温床,因为胡人在内的民众强烈地渴望它,农业和酿造业可以生产它,或者通过商业可以购买它。吕光曾经攻陷了西域著名的葡萄(酒)大国龟兹并从那里掠夺了无数珍宝,"(吕)光入其城(龟兹)……胡

---

① 参见薛天纬师《岑参诗与唐轮台》,《文学遗产》,2005年第五期,第39~46页。
② 《隋书》卷六七,中华书局,1973年,第1581页。
③ 《资治通鉴》卷二一六,中华书局,1956年,第6919页。
④ 李经纬主编《本草纲目校注》,辽海出版社,2001年,第1146页。
⑤ 郑炳林:《敦煌地理文书汇辑校注》,甘肃教育出版社,1989年,第47页。
⑥ 同上,第48页。
⑦ 同上,第66页。
⑧ 杜甫:《寓目》,[清]仇兆鳌:《杜诗详注》,中华书局,1979年,第602页。
⑨ 中外交通史籍丛刊:《大慈恩寺三藏法师传》,中华书局,2000年,第11页。
⑩ 岑参:《凉州馆中与诸判官夜集》,廖立笺注《岑嘉州诗笺注》,中华书局,2004年,第424页。
⑪ [美]谢弗:《唐代的外来文明》,中国社会科学出版社,1995年,第38页。

人奢侈,厚于养生,家有蒲桃酒,或至千斛,经十年不败"。① "光以驼二千余头,致外国珍宝及奇伎、异戏、殊禽、怪兽千有余品,骏马万余匹而还。"②回到姑藏(凉州)时,适逢符坚被姚苌杀害,吕光旋建立后凉,定都姑藏(凉州)。史书没有明确地开列吕光战利品的详单,但葡萄(酒)在其中应该是理所当然的。到了唐朝,士大夫文人已经把葡萄酒作为凉州的一个重要象征了,张说《元仁惠石柱铭》:"寻加朝散大夫,守凉州都督府长史。分乘两蕃,人康颂作。化澄巴濮,无侵橘柚之园;教溢河湟,不饮蒲萄之酒。离歌就具,岁暮临辰。命踬修途,荣惭厚德。"③张说赞美元仁惠德行高重,其中重要的一条原因就是身为凉州都督府长史居然能够做到"不饮蒲萄之酒",高风亮节令人钦佩之余,也从一个侧面证明了葡萄酒的确是凉州的重要特产。

大臣可以自坚操守,不饮凉州葡萄之酒,皇帝后妃则无妨尽享特贡,妙饮醇美的凉州春醪:

> 开元中,李龟年遽以李太白(白)所作词进,上命梨园子弟约略调抚丝竹,遂促龟年以歌。太真妃持玻璃七宝杯,酌西凉州蒲萄酒,笑领意甚厚。上因调玉笛以倚曲,每曲遍将换,则迟其声以媚之。太真饮罢,饰绣巾重拜,上意龟年常话于五王,独忆以歌,得自胜者,无出于此,抑亦一时之极致耳。④
> 李白进清平乐词,太真以玻璃七宝杯酌西凉葡萄酒饮白。⑤
> 穆宗临芳殿赏樱桃,进西凉州葡萄酒。帝曰:"饮此顿觉四体融和,真太平君子也。"⑥

杨贵妃赏音乐,以玻璃七宝杯酌西凉葡萄酒;穆宗赏樱桃,进西凉州葡萄酒。如此的赏心乐事都一再证明凉州与葡萄(酒)的关系。反映在诗歌中,元稹《西凉伎》写得最典型:

> 吾闻昔日西凉州,人烟扑地桑柘稠。蒲萄酒熟恣行乐,红艳青旗朱粉楼。楼下当垆称卓女,楼头伴客名莫愁。乡人不识离别苦,更卒多为沉滞游。⑦

既然是葡萄酒熟,那说明此地的葡萄酒不限于商业贸易所得,的确是当地酿造的。

并州

前面讨论的西州、凉州均为确指。此处之并州,则既有确指,又有泛指。何以言之?唐代河东道产葡萄(酒),尤其以太原府为盛。唐代天下贡赋的记载中,葡萄(与)太原府息息相关。《新唐书·地理志三》载:"太原府太原郡,本并州,开元十一年为府。土贡:铜镜、铁镜、马鞍、梨、蒲萄酒及煎玉粉屑、龙骨、柏实人、黄石钫、甘草、人参、礜石、礬石。"⑧《元和郡县图志》记载河东道太原府的贡赋情况:"开元贡:人参,黄石钫,柏子仁,蒲萄,甘草,龙骨,特生草,铜镜。"⑨《通典·食货》载:"太原府,贡铜镜两面,甘草三十一斤,

① 《晋书·吕光传》,《晋书》卷一二二,中华书局,1974 年,第 3055 页。
② 《魏书·吕光传》,《魏书》卷九五,中华书局,1974 年,第 2085 页。
③ 《文苑英华》第五册卷七九〇,中华书局,1966 年,第 4175 页。
④ 李浚:《松窗杂录》,四库全书本,第 3 页。
⑤ 《白孔六帖》卷一五。
⑥ 《清异录》卷下。
⑦ 元稹:《西凉伎》,冀勤点校《元稹集》,中华书局,1982 年,第 281 页。
⑧ 《新唐书》卷三九,中华书局,1975 年,第 1003 页。
⑨ 《元和郡县图志》卷一三,中华书局,1983 年,第 362 页。

礜石三十斤,龙骨三十斤,蒲萄粉屑,柏子仁。"①太原本并州,并州产葡萄(酒),此为确指。然而,李肇《国史补》又载:"酒则有郢州之富水,乌程之若下,荥阳之土窟春,富平之石冻春,剑南之烧春,河东之干和蒲萄,岭南之灵溪、博罗,宜城之九酝,浔阳之湓水,京城之西市腔、虾蟆陵郎官清、阿婆清。又有三勒浆类酒,法出波斯;三勒者,谓庵摩勒、毗梨勒、诃梨勒。"②《本草纲目》引苏颂《图经本草》又曰:"今河东及近汾州郡皆有之。……盖北果之最珍者,今太原尚作此酒寄远也。"③可见,葡萄是包括并州在内的河东道的特产,但以并州为代表,这里姑且以并州泛指河东。

唐诗中涉及并州葡萄(酒)的很多:

珍果出西域,移根到北方。昔年随汉使,今日寄梁王。……(刘禹锡《和令狐相公谢太原李侍中寄蒲桃》)④

汾云晴漠漠,朔吹冷飔飔。豹尾交牙戟,虬须捧佩刀。通天白犀带,照地紫麟袍。羌管吹杨柳,燕姬酌蒲萄。(蒲萄酒出太原)银含凿落盏,金屑琵琶槽。遥想从军乐,应忘报国劳。(白居易《司徒令公分守东洛,移镇北都,一心勤王,三月成政,形容盛德,实在歌诗,况辱知音,敢不先唱?辄奉五言四十韵寄献,以抒下情》)⑤

野田生蒲桃,缠绕一枝高。移来碧墀下,张王日日高。……有客汾阴至,临堂瞪双目。自言我晋人,种此如种玉。酿之成美酒,令人饮不足。(刘禹锡《蒲桃歌》)⑥

筐封紫葡萄,筒卷白茸毛。卧暖身应健,含消齿免劳。衾衣疏不称,梨栗鄙难高。晚起题诗报,寒澌满笔毫。(姚合《谢汾州田大夫寄茸毡葡萄》)⑦

竹叶连糟翠,蒲萄带麹红。相逢不令尽,别后为谁空。(王绩《题酒店楼壁绝句八首》其二)⑧

刘禹锡第一首诗题名为《和令狐相公谢太原李侍中寄蒲桃》,既指出葡萄寄自太原,又点明这是首和诗,类似的作品应该不少。白居易诗句"燕姬酌蒲萄"自注曰:"蒲萄酒出太原。"刘禹锡《蒲桃歌》所写非河东葡萄,但他种植葡萄的成就令汾阴的晋人瞪目,可见汾阴人也是善种葡萄的。姚合诗题即点明田大夫自汾州寄来了葡萄。王绩《题酒店楼壁绝句八首》系作于晚年归隐故乡后,其故乡正在绛州龙门。五首作品均为河东出产葡萄(酒)的客观实录。

除此之外,李白诗《将游衡岳,过汉阳双松亭,留别族弟浮屠谈皓》写道:"忆我初来时,蒲萄开景风。今兹大火落,秋叶黄梧桐。"⑨可见汉阳是有葡萄的。武元衡诗《送寇侍御司马之明州》写道:"地穷沧海阔,云入剡山长。莲唱蒲萄熟,人烟橘柚香。"⑩可见明州一带也有葡萄种植。韩愈诗《燕河南府秀才得生

① 《通典》卷六,中华书局,1988年,第113页。
② 李肇:《国史补》卷下,《四库全书》本,第15~16页。
③ 李经纬主编《本草纲目校注》,辽海出版社,2001年,第1146页。
④ 刘禹锡:《和令狐相公谢太原李侍中寄蒲桃》,卞孝萱校订《刘禹锡集》,中华书局,1990年,第460页。
⑤ 白居易:《司徒令公分守东洛,移镇北都,一心勤王,三月成政,形容盛德,实在歌诗,况辱知音,敢不先唱?辄奉五言四十韵寄献,以抒下情》,顾学颉校点《白居易集》,中华书局,1979年,第764页。
⑥ 刘禹锡:《蒲桃歌》,卞孝萱校订《刘禹锡集》,中华书局,1990年,第354页。
⑦ 姚合:《谢汾州田大夫寄茸毡葡萄》,《全唐诗》(增订本),中华书局,1999年,第5742页。
⑧ 王绩:《题酒店楼壁绝句八首》其二,韩理洲校点《王无功文集》,上海古籍出版社,1987年,第98~100页。
⑨ 李白:《将游衡岳,过汉阳双松亭,留别族弟浮屠谈皓》,安旗主编《李白全集编年注释》,巴蜀书社,2000年,第1333~1334页。
⑩ 武元衡:《送寇侍御司马之明州》,《全唐诗》(增订本),中华书局,1999年,第3555页。

字》写道:"还家敕妻儿,具此煎炰烹。柿红蒲萄紫,肴果相扶櫜。芳茶出蜀门,好酒浓且清。何能充欢燕,庶以露厥诚。"①可见,河南也有葡萄生产,苏颂《图经本草》所谓"近汴州郡皆有之"的话是有依据的。另外,姚合有一首谐趣横生的绕口令式的《蒲萄架》诗,现仅存残句:"萄藤洞庭头,引叶漾盈摇。皎洁钩高挂,玲珑影落寮。阴烟压幽屋,濛密梦冥苗。清秋青且翠,冬到冻都凋。"②可见,洞庭湖也是有葡萄的。

与葡萄的传播流行相伴,葡萄纹也是汉唐之间常见的纹饰,《西京杂记》载:"汉霍光妻遗淳于衍蒲桃锦二十四匹,散花绫二十五匹。"③"尉佗献高祖鲛鱼、荔枝,高祖报以蒲桃锦四匹。"④林梅村结合考古发现认为"长安城不仅种植葡萄,而且以穿戴葡萄纹锦缎为时尚"。⑤另,《邺中记》也记载:"织锦署在中尚方,锦有大登高、小登高、大明光、小明光、大博山、小博山、大茱萸、小茱萸、大交龙、小交龙、蒲桃文锦、斑文锦……"⑥这种情形在南朝赋作中有反映——江淹《丽色就赋》曰:"帐必蓝田之宝,席必蒲桃之文,馆图明月,室画浮云。"⑦

进入唐朝,葡萄纹饰依然十分流行。新疆民丰出土有唐代的葡萄动物纹锦,日本奈良正仓院藏有盛唐时期的葡萄纹饰丝织品,当然最著名的葡萄纹饰要数唐代铜镜的代表——"瑞兽葡萄纹铜镜"。诗歌中关于葡萄纹饰的描写主要是锦带等。岑参诗中有"黑姓蕃王貂鼠裘,葡萄宫锦醉缠头",⑧上官仪诗中有"罗荐已擘鸳鸯被,绮衣复有蒲萄带",⑨白居易诗中有"裙腰银线压,梳掌金筐蹙。带襵紫蒲萄,袴花红石竹",⑩施肩吾诗中有"夜裁鸳鸯绮,朝织蒲桃绫。欲试一寸心,待缝三尺冰",⑪曹松诗中有"蒲桃锦是潇湘底,曾得王孙价倍酬",⑫阎德隐诗中有"楚王宫里能服饰,顾盼倾城复倾国。合欢锦带蒲萄花,连理香裙石榴色"⑬等,都是明证。

这些诗歌记录甚至补充了以西州、凉州和并州为代表的唐代社会葡萄(酒)生产、传播和流行状况,具有无可替代的史料价值。诗歌可以见证历史,但诗歌毕竟不是历史。历史要还原真的事实,而诗歌要表达诗人对美的追慕。因此,有的唐诗在实录之外还着力传摹葡萄(酒)的审美情韵,有的唐诗则整篇歌咏葡萄(酒)。这样的诗歌以刘禹锡和唐彦谦的咏葡萄诗为代表,刘唐二人的下列四首诗几乎为葡萄作了栩栩如生而又典雅高华的写真与小传。

野田生蒲桃,缠绕一枝高。移来碧墀下,张王日日高。分岐浩繁缛,修蔓蟠诘曲。扬翘向庭柯,意思如有属。为之立长架,布濩当轩绿。米液溉其根,理疏看渗漉。繁葩组绶结,悬实珠玑礧。马乳带轻霜,龙鳞跃初旭。有客汾阴至,临堂睊双目。自言我晋人,种此如种玉。酿之成美酒,令人饮不

① 韩愈:《燕河南府秀才得生字》,《全唐诗》(增订本),中华书局,1999年,第3811页。
② 姚合:《蒲萄架》,同上,第5756~5757页。
③ 《西京杂记》卷一,中华书局,1985年,第4页。
④ 《西京杂记》卷三,同上,第19页。
⑤ 林梅村:《古道西风——考古新发现所见中西文化交流》,三联书店,2000年,第189页。
⑥ 《邺中记》,丛书集成初编,第3804册,第8页。
⑦ 《江文通集汇注》,中华书局,1999年,第77页。
⑧ 岑参:《胡歌》,廖立笺注《岑嘉州诗笺注》,中华书局,2004年,第784页。
⑨ 上官仪:《八咏应制二首》其一,《全唐诗》(增订本),中华书局,1999年,第510页。
⑩ 白居易:《和梦游春诗一百韵》,顾学颉校点《白居易集》,中华书局,1979年,第292~293页。
⑪ 施肩吾:《杂古词五首》其三,《全唐诗》(增订本),中华书局,1999年,第5630页。
⑫ 曹松:《白角簟》,同上,第8328页。
⑬ 阎德隐:《薛王花烛行》,同上,第8852页。

足。为君持一斗,往取凉州牧。(刘禹锡《蒲桃歌》)①

珍果出西域,移根到北方。昔年随汉使,今日寄梁王。上相芳缄至,行台绮席张。鱼鳞含宿润,马乳带残霜。染指铅粉腻,满喉甘露香。酝成千日酒,味敌五云浆。咀嚼停金羧,称嗟响画堂。惭非末至客,不得一枝尝。(刘禹锡《和令狐相公谢太原李侍中寄蒲桃》)②

西园晚霁浮嫩凉,开尊漫摘葡萄尝。满架高撑紫络索,一枝斜嚲金琅玕。天风飕飕叶栩栩,蝴蝶声干作晴雨。神蛟清夜蛰寒潭,万片湿云飞不起。石家美人金谷游,罗帏翠幕珊瑚钩。玉盘新荐入华屋,珠帐高悬夜不收。胜游记得当年景,清气逼人毛骨冷。笑呼明镜上遥天,醉倚银床弄秋影。(唐彦谦《咏葡萄》)③

金谷风露凉,绿珠醉初醒。珠帐夜不收,月明堕清影。(唐彦谦《葡萄》)④

葡萄之异于其他果木的一大特点就是藤蔓的绵长扶疏,刘、唐诗中写道:"分岐浩繁缛,修蔓蟠诘曲。扬翘向庭柯,意思如有属。为之立长架,布濩当轩绿。""满架高撑紫络索,一枝斜嚲金琅玕。天风飕飕叶栩栩,蝴蝶声干作晴雨。"这个特点也为很多诗人注意,李峤《藤》就以葡萄为例:"色映蒲萄架,花分竹叶杯";⑤杜甫《解闷十二首》其十一就写道:"翠瓜碧李沈玉甃,赤梨葡萄寒露成。可怜先不异枝蔓,此物娟娟长远生";⑥韩愈《题张十一旅舍三咏·蒲萄》写道:"新茎未遍半犹枯,高架支离倒复扶。若欲满盘堆马乳,莫辞添竹引龙须",⑦语气虽然是在批评旅舍主人的疏懒,但诗笔却充分展示了被张十一敷衍凑合的葡萄藤蔓。因为蔷薇枝蔓也酷似葡萄树这一特点,所以唐人也喜欢在蔷薇诗中以葡萄作譬,如储光羲《蔷薇》曰:"高处红须欲就手,低边绿刺已牵衣。蒲萄架上朝光满,杨柳园中暝鸟飞",⑧孟郊《和蔷薇花歌》曰:"终当一使移花根,还比蒲桃天上植。"⑨这些诗句都围绕葡萄树枝蔓蜿蜒、蒙络摇坠的特性来写,为我们展开了一幅幅接荫连架、垂索扶疏、绿意盎然的美景。张谓《延平门高斋亭子应岐王教》写道:"昨夜蒲萄初上架,今朝杨柳半垂堤。片片仙云来渡水,双双燕子共衔泥",⑩这正是典型的春天美景。

葡萄的另一大特点就在于其果实。其形状则子实逼侧、星编珠聚,其口感则甜润多汁、入口自消,刘禹锡写道:"繁葩组绶结,悬实珠玑纍。马乳带轻霜,龙鳞跃初旭","鱼鳞含宿润,马乳带残霜。染指铅粉腻,满喉甘露香";以至于品尝葡萄的人们不但"咀嚼停金羧,称嗟响画堂",而且晚来一步的客人竟然"不得一枝尝"。正因为其形如"绿珠",才有资格伴随石崇的金谷园之游:"金谷风露凉,绿珠醉初醒。珠帐夜不收,月明堕清影","石家美人金谷游,罗帏翠幕珊瑚钩。玉盘新荐入华屋,珠帐高悬夜不收"。

葡萄的第三大特点就是酿成美酒带来的无穷滋味。葡萄美酒的滋味已为很多文人所赞誉,《艺文类聚·果部下》记录了曹丕的一篇诏书,他赞美了葡萄之后盛赞葡萄酒:"魏文帝诏群臣曰:且说蒲萄,醉酒

① 刘禹锡:《蒲桃歌》,卞孝萱校订《刘禹锡集》,中华书局,1990年,第354页。
② 刘禹锡:《和令狐相公谢太原李侍中寄蒲桃》,卞孝萱校订《刘禹锡集》,中华书局,1990年,第460页。
③ 唐彦谦:《咏葡萄》,《全唐诗》(增订本),中华书局,1999年,第7742页。
④ 唐彦谦:《葡萄》,同上,第7727页。
⑤ 李峤:《藤》,同上,第714页。
⑥ 杜甫:《解闷十二首》其十一,[清]仇兆鳌:《杜诗详注》,中华书局,1979年,第1518页。
⑦ 韩愈:《题张十一旅舍三咏·蒲萄》,《全唐诗》(增订本),中华书局,1999年,第3851页。
⑧ 储光羲:《蔷薇》,同上,第1407～1408页。
⑨ 孟郊:《和蔷薇花歌》,同上,第4272～4273页。
⑩ 张谓:《延平门高斋亭子应岐王教》,同上,第1131页。

宿醒,掩露而食,甘而不饴,脆而不酸,冷而(不)寒,味长汁多,除烦解。又酿以为酒,甘于麴米,善醉而易醒,道之固以流涎咽唾,况亲食之耶!他方之果,宁有匹之者!"①陆机在《饮酒乐》感叹道:"蒲萄四时劳醇,琉璃千钟旧宾。夜饮舞迟销烛,朝醒弦促催人。春风秋月桓好,欢醉日月言新。"②庾信《燕歌行》也陶醉于葡萄酒:"蒲桃一杯千日醉,无事九转学神仙。定取金丹作几服,能令华表得千年。"③所以刘禹锡说:"酝成千日酒,味敌五云浆""酿之成美酒,令人饮不足",也就不奇怪了。

三、珍稀的奢侈物品

前引刘禹锡《蒲桃歌》的结尾试图借用一个典故强化葡萄酒之美味,而正是这个典故,又使得我们反观葡萄(酒)进入中原后的情状并引发出葡萄(酒)的一个极其重要的特性。这个典故就是孟佗斛酒换取凉州牧。

《三国志·魏书·明帝纪》裴松之注引(汉)赵岐撰《三辅决录》曰:

> 伯郎,凉州人,名不令休。其注曰:伯郎姓孟,名他(佗),扶风人。灵帝时,中常侍张让专朝政,让监奴典护家事。他仕不遂,乃尽以家财赂监奴,与共结亲,积年家业为之破尽,众奴皆惭,问他所欲,他曰:"欲得卿曹拜耳。"奴被恩久,皆许诺。时宾客求见让者,门下车常数百乘,或累日不得通。他最后到,众奴伺其至,皆迎车而拜,径将他车独入。众人悉惊,谓他与让善,争以珍物遗他。他得之,尽以赂让,让喜。他又以蒲桃酒一斛遗让,即拜凉州刺史。④

为了谋求官位,孟佗(他)千方百计贿赂专擅朝政的张让而不得,最后以一斛葡萄酒获得了凉州刺史。可见汉灵帝时,葡萄酒是多么珍贵!刘禹锡的诗中把一斛换作了一斗,分量缩小了十分之一,意思是来自汾州的晋人看到自己移种的葡萄特别好,便推测他日收获酿成好酒,一斗就可以换取当年孟佗一斛贿得的职位。刘禹锡不免有些自夸,但他使用这个典故还是隐约透露出葡萄酒在当日也依然难以轻易求得的信息。

我们在考察汉唐间西域葡萄(酒)的产地情况时,"饶葡萄"、"多葡萄酒"、"千斛、千石"这样的表达很频繁,抛开夸张的成分,葡萄(酒)仍然是西域社会生活中比较常见的风物。但是在中原,尽管有两次大规模引进,葡萄(酒)似乎仍是难得的奢侈品。

现存汉文文献中首次出现葡萄是在司马相如《上林赋》:"于是乎卢橘夏熟,黄甘橙楱,枇杷橪柿,亭奈厚朴,楟枣杨梅,樱桃蒲陶,隐夫薁棣,荅遝离支,罗乎后宫,列乎北园。"⑤葡萄在中原地区第一次出现是在汉朝皇帝的上林苑里,这就为葡萄赋予了一种珍稀、华贵乃至奢侈的特性。

汉武经营西域,引进葡萄(酒)后,情况似乎并无太大改观。东汉时斛酒换刺史就是明证。《汉武内

① 《艺文类聚》卷八七,上海古籍出版社,1982年,第1495页。
② 《乐府诗集》卷七四,中华书局,1979年,第1049页。
③ 《乐府诗集》卷三二,同上,第473页。
④ 《三国志》卷三,中华书局,1971年,第92页。
⑤ 费振纲:《全汉赋》,北京大学出版社,1993年,第64页。

传》曰："武帝时,西王母下,帝为设蒲萄酒。"①《汉武内传》虽然后出,但武帝为迎接西王母而设葡萄酒,很明显是把葡萄酒作为极其难得的奢侈品来看待的,至少在作者的观念中是如此。

魏晋南北朝情况似乎也没有改观。前引曹丕的诏书说诸果难匹葡萄,除了葡萄品质的确是好的内在原因,物以稀为贵恐怕也是主要缘由。据前引《梁四公记》,如果不是杰公多闻广识,梁朝王公士庶居然无人认识高昌国的那些贡品(包括葡萄和酒)。吕光攻陷了西域著名的葡萄(酒)大国龟兹后"士卒沦没酒藏者相继矣",②说明当时距离西域不远的河西地区也匮乏葡萄酒。

杨衒之《洛阳伽蓝记·白马寺》载:

> 浮图前,奈林、蒲萄,异于余处,枝叶繁衍,子实甚大。奈林实重七斤,蒲萄实伟于枣,味并殊美,冠于中京。帝至熟时,常诣取之,或复赐宫人。宫人得之,转饷亲戚,以为奇味。得者不敢辄食,乃历数家。京师语曰:"白马甜榴,一实直牛。"③

洛阳城中自有葡萄,不过白马寺前的葡萄异于其他地方,所以宫人得之,尚以为奇味,往往转赠数户人家才被吃掉。葡萄虽有,好葡萄依然珍贵无比。

[唐]段成式《酉阳杂俎》记载了一场南北朝人之间的有趣对话:

> 蒲萄,俗言蒲萄蔓好引于西南。庾信谓魏使尉瑾曰:"我在邺,遂大得蒲萄,奇有滋味。"陈昭曰:"作何形状?"徐君房曰:"有类软枣。"信曰:"君殊不体物,可得言似生荔枝。"魏肇师曰:"魏武有言,末夏涉秋,尚有余暑。酒醉宿醒,掩露而食。甘而不饴,酸而不酢。道之固以流味称奇,况亲食之者。"瑾曰:"此物实出于大宛,张骞所致。有黄、白、黑三种,成熟之时,子实逼侧,星编珠聚,西域多酿以为酒,每来岁贡。在汉西京,似亦不少。杜陵田五十亩,中有蒲萄百树。今在京兆,非直止禁林也。"信曰:"乃园种户植,接荫连架。"昭曰:"其味何如橘柚?"信曰:"津液奇胜,芬芳减之。"瑾曰:"金衣素裹,见苞作贡。向齿自消,良应不及。"④

庾信出使东魏时曾目睹了葡萄园种户植的场面,并饱餐过葡萄。当魏使尉瑾南来时,就有了这场对话。对话中,庾信对葡萄的追忆留恋与没有北上经历的陈昭对葡萄的陌生形成了鲜明对比,也再次印证了前引《梁四公记》里的场面。

但即使在北朝,葡萄也并非总是寻常物。《北齐书·李元忠传》载:

> (李元忠)曾贡世宗蒲桃一盘。世宗报以百练缣,遗其书曰:"仪同位亚台铉,识怀贞素,出藩入侍,备经要重。而犹家无担石,室若悬磬,岂轻财重义,奉时爱己故也。久相嘉尚,嗟咏无极,恒思标

---

① 《汉武内传》,载[明]陶宗仪等编《说郛三种》卷七"诸传摘玄",上海古籍出版社,1988年,第134~135页。
② 《晋书·吕光传》,《晋书》卷一二二,中华书局,1974年,第3055页。
③ 杨衒之:《洛阳伽蓝记》卷四,山东友谊出版社,2001年,第142页。
④ [唐]段成式:《酉阳杂俎》卷一八,历代笔记小说选刊《酉阳杂俎》,学苑出版社,2001年,第239页。

赏,有意无由。忽辱蒲桃,良深佩带。聊用绢百匹,以酬清德也。"其见重如此。[1]

臣子贡一盘葡萄,君王回赠百练缣并作书嘉许,葡萄之贵重,亦可见一斑。

唐朝情况如何呢?我们先看高祖时的情况:

> 尝赐食于御前,(陈叔达)得蒲萄,执而不食。高祖问其故,对曰:"臣母患口干,求之不能致,欲归以遗母。"高祖喟然流涕曰:"卿有母遗乎!"因赐物百段。[2]

> 尝赐食,(陈叔达)得蒲萄,不举,帝问之,对曰:"臣母病渴,求不能致,愿归奉之。"帝流涕曰:"卿有母遗乎?"因赐之,又赉物百段。[3]

这近乎颍考叔纯孝般的感人故事发生在寻常百姓身上倒也罢了,陈叔达系陈宣帝之子,历仕隋唐,为高祖掌枢密,军书文诰,多出其手,其母患口干,欲求葡萄而不得。唐朝立国之初,葡萄难得,或可想见。

太宗平高昌,引进了葡萄和酒法,有条件的地方陆续引种了葡萄,甚至还出现了前文所述的凉州、并州这样的葡萄(酒)的主产地,来自高昌和西域其他的葡萄(酒)也不断输入中原,葡萄(酒)不再像前代那样珍稀,但毕竟非寻常之物。唐代段成式《寺塔记·光宅坊光宅寺》载:"普贤堂,本天后梳洗堂,蒲萄垂实则幸此堂。"[4]武后将临幸普贤堂的时间选在每年葡萄垂实的季节,原因也许很复杂,但至少说明葡萄垂实是个特殊的时节。《太平御览》卷九七二引《唐景隆文馆记》曰:"四月上巳日,上幸司农少卿王光辅庄,驾返顿后,中书侍郎南阳岑羲设茗饮蒲萄浆,与学士等讨论经史。""大学士李峤入东都祔庙,学士等祖送城东。上令中官赐御馔及蒲萄酒。"[5]葡萄酒仍然是皇帝赏赐重臣的主要礼物。

终唐一代,葡萄(酒)始终被置于很高的地位,无论是西州、并州进贡的葡萄(酒),还是杨贵妃、唐穆宗手中的西凉州葡萄酒,都是高贵、珍稀、奢华的象征。李德裕写诗述梦,他在梦中回到曾经工作过的内署:"赋命诚非薄,良时幸已遭。君当尧舜日,官接凤凰曹。目睇烟霄阔,心惊羽翼高。椅梧连鹤禁,璧坦接龙韬。我后怜词客,吾僚并隽髦。著书同陆贾,待诏比王褒。重价连悬璧,英词淬宝刀。泉流初落涧,露滴更濡毫。赤豹欣来献,彤弓喜暂櫜。非烟含瑞气,驯雉洁霜毛。静室便幽独,虚楼散郁陶。花光晨艳艳,松韵晚骚骚。画壁看飞鹤,仙图见巨鳌。倚檐阴药树,落格蔓蒲桃。"[6]他在"落格蔓蒲桃"后自注道:"此八句悉是内署物色,惟尝游者,依然可想也",其自矜之情,跃跃于诗句间。足以使他自矜自傲的理由之一就是葡萄这样的内署物色外人很难见到,只有尝游者,才有可能去追忆。

从汉到唐,虽然葡萄(酒)被两度引进,并在唐朝比较广泛地得以传播,但葡萄(酒)始终以其珍稀难得而成为奢侈和富贵的象征。如果我们再反观前引诸葡萄(酒)诗,就会发现其中或隐或显地流露出一种向往、一种渴望。那些以葡萄(酒)为政治象征的诗篇和诗句在张扬帝国声威、讽喻黩武政策的同时并未掩饰对这种难得的奢侈品的向往,"天马常衔苜蓿花,胡人岁献葡萄酒",开放的国门,强盛的国势,这

---

① 《北齐书》卷二二,中华书局,1972年,第315页。
② 《旧唐书·陈叔达传》卷六一,中华书局,1975年,第2363页。
③ 《新唐书·陈叔达传》卷一〇〇,中华书局,1975年,第3925页。
④ [唐]段成式:《寺塔记》,人民美术出版社,1964年,第19页。
⑤ 《太平御览》卷九七二,中华书局,1960年,第4308~4309页。
⑥ 李德裕:《述梦诗四十韵》,《全唐诗》(增订本),中华书局,1999年,第5426~5427页。

个王朝理应享受这种华夷如一、万方来贡的荣耀;"长安春物旧相宜,小苑蒲萄花满枝",威仪的天子之居,富庶繁华的帝都,这个美丽城市的绝胜春景中不能没有葡萄花的芬芳。那些描摹赞誉葡萄(酒)的诗篇诗句更是充满了对这种奢侈品的无比艳羡和拥有之后的充分满足感,刘禹锡得意洋洋地自夸:自己移植的葡萄长势那么好,竟然让精通此道的晋人瞠目,等这葡萄酿成了美酒,定会比当年孟佗行贿的葡萄酒优秀十倍,区区一个刺史如探囊取物也! 天真的自矜自夸中充满了乐观和自信。即使一个捧剑仆,写起葡萄来也是那么洒脱俊逸,取象高华而富贵:"青鸟衔葡萄,飞上金井栏。美人恐惊去,不敢卷帘看。"①即使是那些实录性的诗句也并非呆板凝滞的文字堆砌,而是充满了对这种难得的奢侈品的欣赏和褒扬。元稹追忆西凉州的葡萄酒时,诗句中洋溢着兴奋和恣意的快感:"吾闻昔日西凉州,人烟扑地桑柘稠。蒲萄酒熟恣行乐,红艳青旗朱粉楼!"白居易在回顾太原的葡萄酒时,又不忘记那精美的酒盏、动人的音乐和美丽的燕姬:"羌管吹杨柳,燕姬酌蒲萄。(蒲萄酒出太原)银含凿落盏,金屑琵琶槽",一切是那么灵动,那么美妙!

---

① 捧剑仆:《诗》,《全唐诗》(增订本),中华书局,1999 年,第 8459 页。

Criminal Law Practices in Turfan Uigurs According to Civil Documents

A. Melek ÖZYETGİN

Ankara University, Faculty of Letters, The Department of The Turkish
Language and The Literature, Sıhhiye/Ankara, Turkey

Introduction

We have very limited information about the history of Turkic laws before Islam. Particularly, the written rules regulating law in ancient Turkic eras, and rule books are not available at the present day. Most of the information we have comes from indirect resources. Today, one of the major resources about the ancient Turkic law system is the Uigur civil documents. The civil documents date back to a period between the 10th century and 13th century. The documents from the most eminent representative of the culture of the settled Turkic tribes during the middle period, namely Turfan-Uigurs, show us legal processes not only between people, but also between people and the government.

In this paper, I will discuss criminal law practices in Uigur civil documents. The reason why I have chosen this topic is that criminal law is the oldest law branch and a field in close relations with social culture. In a sense, criminal law is a kind of expression of social culture. It is appropriate to say that, in terms of resources and practices, more comprehensive future research should cover this topic, which is now to be dealt with on the Turfan-Uigur State basis. We have already stated that the written rules or rule books on which the Uigur criminal law is based are not available at the present day. From the Hun period, the origins of the Turkic-Uigur law certainly lie in the ancient Turkic official and customary rules. On the other hand, in the civil documents, it is possible to see clues about the understanding of law of the Chinese, who lived together with the Uigurs for centuries. Similarly, the effect of the Mongolians should be under consideration.

Generally in the Uigur contract tradition, it is agreed that Chinese contracts were taken as models and that a lot of Chinese origin words were used in the Uigur documents. Formalistic and content similarities between the Uigur civil documents and the ancient Chinese contracts are remarkable. Masao Mori

(1961: 113), [1] a Japanese Uigurist, recognizes the Chinese effect in that sense, but states that the Uigurs created their correspondence tradition based on their own culture mixed with some Chinese factors in Turkic style. In other words, it is not wrong to say that the Uigurs had their own customs and habits which became perfectly authentic and peculiar to their own language with inspiration of Chinese practices. On the other hand, we should not forget that the Uigurs and the Chinese may have developed similar law viewpoints as they lived together for centuries within Asian culture, while considering the Chinese effect on the Uigur-Turkic understanding of law (Ayiter 1952: 418).

When the Uigur documents about criminal law practices are examined in terms of content, it is seen that they are composed of land contracts, slavery sale contracts, adoption contracts, emancipation of slave contracts, and loan contracts and of personal and family declarations which are fundamental to wills and censuses. In those contracts including agreements on certain topics between people or between people and the government, there are some penalty clauses as dissuasive precautions against unjustifiable protests and they are to protect legality by securities. Similarities between these penalty clauses in most of the contracts show us that the Uigur society had an understanding of systematic criminal law.

It is possible to find some clues about official rules criminal law based on, although the rules of the system are not available today: For instance; the following statement in a document of tax payments no. Mi04 is noteworthy: *"yasa-takı kıyın-ka tägir-män."* *män oz-mış togrıl* (7) *kin öŋdün basa togrıl-ka* (8) *kim-niŋ kayu-nıŋ küçin* (9) *tutup çam çarım kılsar-män* (10) *yasa-takı kıyın-ka tägir-* (11) *-män:* "I, Ozmış Togrıl, am consent to penalty if I am to raise a subsequent objection against Basa Togrıl, relying on someone else's power."

A similar use is observed in adoption contract no. Ad01: *män çintso ayag-qa tägimlig-ning inim içim oglum qam qadaşım ilmäzün tartmazun apam birök ilgli tartıglı saqınsar savları yorumazun yasa-taqı qın-qa tägsünlär* "I, respectable Çintso, let not my brother, my uncle, my son and relatives interfere, not take by force; if so, let not their word acceptable and demand they be punished by law". Here, it is clear that penalty applies on a certain basis of rules. The rules on which law is based in contracts are called *yasa*, a word of Mongolian origin. At the same time, the term *yosun*, [2] another Mongolian origin word, is used in contracts.

There are two sources which impositions of penalties in the Uigur civil documents are based on. The first one is official rules by the state authorities. These specify imposition of a penalty for crime against the state and about various property rights between people. The second one is customary rules. As it is known, customary rules consist of accepted practices in traditions which regulate social life. In Uigurs, penalties in

---

[1] Also see. Masao Mori, "A Study on Uygur Documents of Loans for Consumption," *Memoirs of the Research Department of the Toyo Bunko*, Vol. 20, 1961; Masao Mori "The Clause of Warrant in the Uigur Documents of Sale and Purchase," *Toyo Gakuho*, Vol. 44, No. 2, Tokyo 1961, 1－23.

[2] ED 975b *yosun* "manner, custom", Mo. *yosun* "habit, accepted practice, system, social order" (Kovalevskiy III, 238). Also see TMEN IV 408, *yosun* "habit, accepted practice". RSl. III, 441, *yosun* "rule, method". The word is available today: Yak. *çoşun*, Soy. *yozu*, Kzk. *çozuk* "habit, custom, accepted practice", Şor. *çozak* "trust, faith, religion, rule", Tat. *yusuk* "eligible, proper" (VEWT 202). The word is frequently used in the Golden Horde yarlıqs (Özyetgin 1996: 169)

contracts on interpersonal dealings, leasing and loans are mostly based on customary rules. Such an understanding of law where both official rules and customary rules are found together is the most considerable factor that organizes the Uigur social and economic life.

In Uigur contracts, penalty clauses specified according to customary rules are stated using the following phrase: *il yangınça* or "according to provincial rules". Thus, in a sense, the term *İl yaŋınça* corresponds to customary rules. For example, it is seen that a penalty clause in a loan contract is specified *il yanıngça* or according to customary law:

1. *Yılan yıl üçünç ay (iki yangıq-a) manga* 2. *qıryaquz-qa böz kärgäk bolup* 3. *vaptu-dın iki [iki] bag* 4. *böz aldım yangıd-a iki şıg* 5. *tang birürmän birmädin käçür [sär]* 6. *-sär- män **il yangınça** tüşi bilä* 7. *köni birürmän* "I, Qıryaquz, needed böz on the 2nd of the 3rd month of the snake year, and bought two bunches of böz from Vaptu. First, I will give two 2 şıg of corn. If time is overdue, I will give the complete amount back with interest according to provincial rules". (Yamada Lo15 TM 212 U5257 US p. 29, Clark 13)

In another document, a statement in **Pl02**, which is a pledging contract, is remarkable: *män samboqdu tutung birtke ... bolmışqa ton ätük adaq baş birmäz-män äv täg yogun iş işlätsär män il-ning tutug y(a)ngınça birürmän qalmış turuşı yangı tutug y(a)ngınça bolzun* "I, Samboqdu, will not give Bolmış clothes or shoes as Tutung birt (the tax). If I make him work busily at home, I will give according to provincial (country) pledging rule. Let the rest of his life be according to the new hypothrcation rule". The phrase ***ilniŋ tutug yangınça*** in this contract shows us that there were special rules about pledging specified by customary law.

yaŋ in the phrase *İl yangınça* is of Chinese origin and it basically means "a pattern, model" and abstractly "kind, sort, manner" (Giles 12, 854) see (ED940b). The word appeared in Uigur language as well as the literature of post-Islam period: DLT *yaŋ* "center or pattern of something" (III, 361). KB *yaŋ* "custom, habit, style", Kİ *yoŋ* (< *yaŋ*) "customary law", Çag. *yaŋla* "alike". Ottoman *yaŋ* "shape, form, kind" (Caferoğlu: 17). The concept used with the word İl was used to mean "customary law" in Uigur society. Similarly, the phrase *İl yangınça* is found in DLT and KB.

Reşit Rahmeti Arat, a great Turkologist and Uigurist, substiantially divides impositions of penalites in the Uigur civil documents into five (1964: 49 – 51):

1. Death penalty
2. Corporal punishment
3. Financial penalty-property penalty
4. Law penalty
5. Penalties by accepted practices and judgements

In this paper, I will discuss every penalty according to documents and based on Reşit Rahmeti Arat's classification. In the study, I will examine commitment of crime that leads to a penalty, persons that a penalty directly relates, powers (state, society etc.) with penal sanctions, different impositions of penalty in various law procedures and the role and the power of the state as lawmaker.

Death penalty, the most severe sentence, comes at the top of the list of such penalties. In the civil documents, we come across death penalty only in the personal declarations which served as a basis for censuses. In the past, censuses were fundamental to organize personal responsibilities towards the government, so it was essential that censuses should be recorded properly. When the role of the declarations in regulating social, economic, and military structure of the state is taken into account, the state had to introduce dissuasive penalties in order to ensure that such declarations would be right and to prevent false representations:

[Iduk] kut t(ä)ngrikäni[m(i)zkä] ülcäy *tümen ilçi begler-ke* tümän ilçi beg[lärkä] *m(e)n yıgmış bitig birürmen ulug depter-te bititmiş negü kimimtin taş negü m-e yok bar tip ayıg ünüp sözi (ayak ürüp sözi) çın bolsar öz başım ölürm(e)n* "May, his the royal highness, Iduk-Kut, be blissful! I, Yıgmış, give Tümen ilçi rulers written certification. If there is rumour that there is someone else apart from the ones recorded in *Ulug depter* and if it is proved to be true I am consent to my own death" [USp. 40 T. I. T. M. 224 (101/016/R. 40)]

In these documents, it is striking that people are consent to death penalty in case of false representation. This case shows us that population reports[1] and birth records were seriously and meticulously kept. There is no death penalty record caused by a committed crime among the current examined documents. As far as it is known, in Uigurs, death penalty applied only when there was crime against the national security and economy etc.

There are documents in which we find examples of the second: *corporal punishment*. Also, we come across corporal punishment[2] in a detailed declaration (entry made in the register) by a Uigur family. In the declaration, names and ages of a person called Yölek and his family members are listed. In the same section, two people called Yoluga and Çerig, who were probably acquaintances or neighbors, bear witness for confirmation of the information. If there is false representation, they will be consent to "57 whipping" as well as financial penalty. Then it is sealed by Yölek:

---

① As it is stated before, we have a limited number of documents about Turkic census. The four documents (121/R41, 101/R40, 140a/055, 215/67) mentioned by Reşit Rahmeti Arat in his notable extensive article entitled "In the Ancient Turkic Law Documents" are the only ones we currently have. The two documents no. 121/R41, 101/R40 in Arat appeared in Radloff's *Uigurische Sprach-denkmäler* (1928: 57-59). The texts of the two other documents whose top parts are missing were first completed and published by Osman Fikri Sertkaya: Osman Fikri Sertkaya, "Eski Uygur Türklerinden Hukuk Belgeleri Örnekleri," *Türklerde İnsanî Değerler ve İnsan Hakları* (*Başlangıcından Osmanlı Dönemine Kadar*), Türk Kültürüne Hizmet Vakfı Yay., İstanbul 1992, pp. 131-148.

② The first publication of the document whose top part is missing (TM 111, U5298; (R (153/4)) was by Peter Zieme: P. Zieme, "Ein Uigurischen Familienregister aus Turfan," *Altorientalische Forschungen*, IX (1982), pp. 263-267. Zieme put a date on the declaration as 1275.

... [al]tı k[işi ärür] [m(ä)n] yöläk beš al [tmıš yašar] · [k]işim aŋa-a otuz yašar · [q]ızım b [aq]šal üç γ(i)g(i)rmi yašar · ... oglum [qut]lug sı[ŋgur] on yaš[ar] ...än oglum buyan sıŋgur [sä]kiz yaš[ar] ...n o[glu]m barak sıŋgur beš yašar · [munça] kişi-lär-im-niŋ barı çın · munça yaš-lıg ärür-i çın · bu (9) [kişi]-lär-im-ni yolug-a · çärig ekägü bilir bu sözlär çın äzük [bo]lup ayıg ünsär 'älig yeti kamçı yip maŋa tägir yastuk -tın kurug kalır-m(ä)n. "... includes six people. I, Yölek, am 55. My wife, Arıga, is 30. My daughter, Bakşal, is 13... My son, Kutlug Sıŋgur, is 10 ... my son, Buyan Sıŋgur, is 8... my son, Barak Sıŋgur, is 5. I certify that they are my family and their ages are right. Both Yoluga (and) Çerig know them. My words are all true, if there is wrong information I will be punished by 57 whipping and not get my yastuq. "

In the second part of the document, Yoluga and Çerig testify that all the information Yölek mentiones above is right and say they are consent to a penalty that Yölek would be given if the information is proved to be wrong. Similar impositions of penalties are found in censuses in the Chinese tradition. For example, Sangha (Sang-ko), a Tibetan Buddhist monk, held a census in 1289 in South China, which was under the control of the Yuan Empire. All the residents in South China were asked to go to a suitable local governmental office and register themselves and all the recorded families were given sealed certificates (hu-t'ieh). The registered ones were responsible for controlling their neighbors in order to avoid any kind of mistakes and false representation. According to the command, those who did not get registered were sentenced to death, whereas those who knew that their neighbor had made a false representation were beaten with a stick for 107 times, and those who made a false representation concerning their income were whipped for 77 times. [1]

Another whipping penalty is seen in **WP04**. The document is a will which divides someone's wealth between their children and stipulates that everyone equally profits from possessions for joint use. Generally, penalties in Uigur wills were paid to the government as possessions or money. However, in this document (WP04), the one to object to the will was mentioned and it was asked that this person should not to take an interest in the will and be whipped:

... bu bitig-ni qayu-sı taplamadın çatış-//////γ-lar ////////////// -nı yontmamış yazuk-ka tgip ülüş almadın kişi-si /////////////////////// yiti kamçı berge yip yitzün. "If there is a conflict over this will without confirmation ... let it not be valid (let them not be influential). Regarding the crime they commit by preventing something from being valid, let them not take an interest and his wife ... be whipped for seven times" (WP04$_{31-34}$).

---

[1] Uematsu Tadashi, "The Control of Chiang-nan in the Early Yuan," *Acta Asiatica*, 45, Tokyo 1983, p. 61. Also see Ikeda On, "T'ang Household Registers and Related Documents," Ed. Arthur F. Wright, Dennis Twitchett, *Perspectives on the T'ang*, New Haven-London 1973, pp. 121 – 150.

The third type of penalty in the Uigur civil documents is *financial penalty and property penalty*. These penalties as dissuasive penalties in order to prevent any contract breakings always applied as a financial compensation. The history of financial penalties goes back to ancient times. In such impositions, financial compensation means fixation and payment the amount of money and possessions as blood money in return for the committed crime. This compensation was given to the aggrieved because of the crime or his relatives. However, the state took a certain part of the pay in different law systems (Arık 1996: 20 – 21; Arsal 1947: 207).

In Uigurs, we see that financial penalties and property penalties are paid to the government concerning land contracts, slavery sale contracts, adoption contracts, emancipation of slave contracts, wills and miscellaneous contracts that show certain legal procedures. Yet, in the Uigur documents, it is striking that there are different practices in terms of the creditor of the financial or property penalty. In Uigur contracts that have the same content but made at different dates, we see different impositions of penalties. For example; for a sale contract, if there is a contract breaking, it is common to punish the person who has broken the contract with double pay of the item for sale to the buyer and the government takes no interest in the penalty. In other sale contracts probably made at a later time, the amount specified as the penalty is paid not to the aggrieved but to the government as cash or property.

In the Uigur civil documents we examined, it is observed that financial penalties and property penalties are paid in two ways according to the type of the contract. The first one is the institution of compromise which has played an important role in the history of criminal law. The institution is based on an agreement between the offender and the aggrieved. In Uigurs, particularly in land sale contracts, there was a guarantee that the offender would provide the aggrieved with the goods of the same kind in the proportion of one to one or generally two to one. In most of the land sale contracts examined, penalty pays ate based on such compromise. The second method in some of the documents examined is that the state institution is more closely involved with impositions of penalties and that financial or property penalties are directly paid to the government.

A. Financial and property penalties in sale contracts

a. Impositions of penalties in land sale contracts:

In Uigurs, penalties are clearly stated in contracts in order to guarantee clauses of land sale contracts and to ensure their dissuasive and enforcer nature against protests. Impositions of penalties as a guarantee by the seller to prevent the buyer from any damage or unfair practices caused by the third person's intervention are found in the documents.

We clearly see that there are various penalties available for those who are to object to clauses of land sale contracts and those who are to bring suits. On the contrary of the modern law procedures, in Uigurs, quiet enjoyment (a case where others cannot claim any rights over property) is different. In today's sale contracts, the seller is liable to this debt. That is; the seller is held responsible for a third person divesting the buyer of his property by assertation of a right or preventing the buyer from using his property (Zevkliler 2007: 123).

Moreover, the seller is liable to compensate any damages of the buyer caused by this case. In Uigur contracts, although the seller verbally reassures the buyer for sale rights, we see that the protesting third person is liable to the payment of quiet enjoyment debt, not the seller, and that again the third person is held responsible for any damages. In the contracts, it is observed that the seller is not directly responsible for the compensation of the buyer's loss and that there are warnings against possible third persons to break the contract. In sale contracts, the sections where these impositions of penalties are mentioned are generally alike :

Sa04

15. män şabi-nıng 16. ogulum qızım içim inim qam qatşım ygänim 17. tagayım aytmazun istmäzün aytglı istgli sqınsr 18. savları yorımazun taqı birök ärklig bäg işi küç- 19. -in tutup alayın yulayın tisär-lär bu oq ögän 20. üzä suvaq-lıg iki tançu yir yaratu birip yulup 21. alzun yultaçı kişi qor-lug bolzun basmıl qor-suz 22. bolzun "I am Şabi; let my son, my daughter, my elder brother, my younger brother, my relatives, my nephew and my uncle not tell (anything) or want anything (let them not protest)! If they intend to tell or want (protest), let their words not be influential (and) even if the powerful ruler and his wife use their influence and take it back, they are to buy two pieces of watering land in this carrier. Let the buyer end up a loser! Let Basmıl not be damaged".

Sa08

15. biz 16. ikägü-ning inimiz içimiz qamız qadaş- 17. -ımız çamlamazun kim ärklig bäg 18. işi küçün tuḍup çamlasar bu oq 19. yir tänglig iki yir birip alšun- 20. -lar yulšun-lar yulguçı qorlug bolzun 21. toyınçog qorsuz bolzun "We both; let our younger brother, our elder brother and relatives not protest. Whoever uses the influence of powerful ruler (and) (his) wife and protests, he is to buy two pieces of land equal to this one! Let the buyer end up a loser. Let Toyınçoq not be damaged".

Sa15

8. män sinsidu-nung aqam inim on-luqum ... 9. qılmašun-lar 'ärklig bäg işi küçin tutup ... 10. yir birip sözlär-i yorımašun yuldaçı ... 11. kök buqa qorsuz bolzun "I am Sinsidu; let my elder brother, my brother, onluk (arbat)... not protest! The powerful ruler and his wife use their influence ... let their words not be influential. The seller ... let Kök Buqa not be damaged".

In the documents, for those who protest the terms *yultaçı* (Sa04、Sa15、Sa06、Sa07、Sa09), *yulguçı* (Sa08) and *çamlaguçı* "protester" (Sa16) are used. These people are to be given the penalty fixed by contract because of their intervention and be losers. On the other hand, the buyer is mentioned and prevented from any damages. Here, the person who is referred to with the terms *yultaçı*, *yulguçı* and *çamlaguçı* is the one responsible for the payment of the quiet enjoyment in case of contract breakings.

In the sale contracts we have, there are two observed ways for the compensation of damages caused by third person's intervention in the favor of the buyer. The first and the common one is that the person who breaks the contract doubles the payment and gives the buyer two pieces of lands or vineyards etc. for sale. Therefore, the penalty clause requires the proportion of one to two. Only in Sa01 and Sa02, it is conspicuous that protesters give only one land equal to the one for sale for the compensation of the buyer's loss. Except for this, in the land sale contracts no: Sa03、Sa04、Sa05、Sa06、Sa07、Sa08、Sa09、Sa10、Sa13、Sa15 and Sa16, the protester is responsible providing the aggrieved with two pieces of land in return for the one for sale as a penalty.

As well as land sale contracts, in a land exchange contract, it is seen that if the clauses of the contract are violated, the aggrieved is provided with a compensation of the one to two proportion as this is the case in some of the same land contracts. In Ex01, some of whose parts are missing, it is stated that two people who have exchanged a land with a vineyard will give the aggrieved two pieces of land of the same kind as a penalty, in case of protests by their relatives and elder or younger brothers.

In Uigur land sale contracts, another imposition of a penalty for the compensation of losses is penalty payment which is called by different names is given to the top authorities of the government. In the land sale contracts no: Sa11 and Sa12, it is striking that contract breakers pay the penalty directly to the top governmental authorities:

Sa11

13. bu borluq yolınta män tärbiş-14. -ning aqam inim yigenim tagayım kim kim m-ä bolup 15. çam çarım qılmazun-lar apam birök ärklig bäg 16. işi yat yalavaç küçin tuđup çam çarım 17. qılsar-lar 18. ulug sụü-kä bir altun yasđuq içgär-i agılıq- 19. -qa bir bir kümüş yastuq bägät-lär-kä birär 20. ädär-kä yaraşu at qızğut birip söz-21. -lär-i yorımazun "I, Terbiş, concerning this vineyard, let my elder brother, my younger brother, my nephew and my uncle or others not protest. But they use the powerful ruler and (his) wife's influence or that of strangers and protest, let them pay the Great Majesty (Great Khan) one golden yastuk, the royal treasury one silver yastuk, give rulers fine horses as a penalty (payment) and let their words not be influential!"

Sa12

8. bu kün-tin mınça tapmış-nıng aqa-sı ini-si yigän-i tagay-ı 9. kim kim m-ä çam çarım qılmazun-lar apam birök ärklig bäg 10. iş-i küçin tutup çam çarım qılsar-lar 11. ulug sụü-kä bir altun yastuq basıp il bäg-lär-ingä ädär-kä 12. yaragu at birip sözlär-i yorımazun 15. çamlaguçı kişi qoor-lug bolzun vapso tu qoor-suz bolzun "From now on, let Tapmış's elder brother, younger brother, his nephew, his uncle or anyone else not protest! If they protest, using the influence of the powerful ruler and his wife let them pay the Great Majesty (Great Khan) one golden yastuk, and give the provincial rulers fine horses. Let their words not be influential! Let the protester end up a loser. Let Vapsotu not be damaged".

These documents are significant in that they show penalties were under the monopoly of the state at that time. In both of the documents, there is a clause stipulating that *ulug süü*[1] (the Great Majesty) shall be given is one golden *yastuk* as a penalty. Besides the penalty pay, only in Sa11, it is demanded that one silver *yastuk* be paid to *içgärü agılıq* or "the royal treasury". Apart from that, in both of the documents, it is

---

[1] Reşit R. Arat suggests that the word *süü* (Chinese *dz'uo tsu*, Mo. *su ~ sü*, Kalmuk sü) corresponds to Turkic word "kut" and points out that the word means "happiness and majesty". See Reşit Rahmeti Arat, *Eski Türk Şiiri*, Ankara: Türk Tarih Kurumu Yayınları, 1991, p. 389; L. V. Clark, *Introduction to the Uyghur Civil Documents of Xinjing (13 - 14th cc.)*, Dissertation of Indiana University (Bloomington), Ph. D. , 1975, p. 14.

required that provincial rulers be given fine horses. Also, in the contract, protesters are wished to be heavily fined by paying the specified amounts by contract and their words would not be influential. The reason why the penalty is paid not to the aggrieved, but to the state authorities is that penalties as dissuasive factors are socially accepted and they reveal the power, the control and the lawmaking function of the government. Money and properties which are submitted to important people in the hierarchy of the state, starting at the top, are also revenues or gains for the government as penalty pays. We can consider the case in Uigurs in the same way.

In Sa03, another land sale contract, a different penalty pay is found:

Sa03

11. män yrp yanga-nıng ädgününg 12. içimiz inimz qamız qaṭaşımız ogulumız qızımz ayıtmaz- 13. -un istämäzün ayıtglı istägli saqınsar-lar savları 14. yorımazun-lar birök "ärklig bäg işi küçin tutup 15. alayın yulayın tisär-lär bu" oq ögän-tä bu yir tngin-16. -çä iki yir birip alzunlar 24. bu sav-ta qayu-sı agısar-biz üçär yüz bişär otuz qu(a)npu 25. içrä quvpar birüşür-biz "We are Yrp Yanga and Edgü; let our elder brother, younger brother, our relatives, sons and daughters not tell (anything) or want anything (or protest)! If they intend to tell (something) or want something (or protest) let their words not be influential. If they tend to take it back, using the influence of the powerful ruler and (his) wife, they are to buy two pieces of land in this carrier equal to this land. Whoever goes back on his words, he will pay 325 quanpu to the palace as a penalty".

In this contract, it is seen that the protester pays penalties both to the buyer and the government. In the contract, it is stated that if the protester or the seller with a joint responsibility goes back on his words, he will pay 325 quanpu to the palace or the official authorities as a penalty, as well as providing the buyer with two pieces of land financially equal to the land he has bought. In case of no compensation for losses caused by contract violation, third persons as protesters get the financial penalty in order to prevent the buyer from being aggrieved. The document is crucial in that it indicates the control and enforcement of the official institutions in impositions of penalties. However, we unfortunately have no other documents to compare.

In the contract, the following statement takes place: *bu sav-ta qayu-sı agısar-biz üçär yüz bişär otuz qu(a)npu 25. içrä quvpar birüşür-biz*. The word **quvpar ~ quvar** is of Chinese origin: "Whoever goes back on his words, he will pay 325 quanpu (25) to the palace as a penalty." "Penalty pay means punishment" (Bussgeld, Bestrafung) (Yamada 1993 – II: 278). The word is found in a land sale contract and a slavery trade contract: Ad02 *qayusı bu sav-tın agış-sar-biz birer yasduq quvar birüşürbiz* "Whoever goes back on his words, he will pay one yastuq as a penalty". This word must be a technical term which means "official financial penalty" in sale contracts. It is noteworthy that the Turkic originated word **qızgut**[1] corresponds to

---

① *Qızgut* < Turkic *qız-* "get annoyed, get angry" (?). As well as the civil documents, it is seen in U. II 26, 14 as *kın kızgut* (ED681b). In DLT, the word can be traced: *qızgut* "penalty; torture, penalty or torture before others for making an example of one" (I, 451). *kızgut* (Erdal I, 313), which means "penalty" is given in U II 20, 1 and 26,14, U III 56, 7, BT II 1095, Maitr 81v2 together with the word *kıyın*. Erdal suggests *kızgut* is about the verb *kızgur-* "to inflict exemplary punishment" (II, 749). If we try to explain the word with the verb root *kız-*, Erdal says *-g* is not inexplicable, yet relates the word with *bışgur-*, *bışgut*, *yapgur- yapgut* in terms of word formation.

the Chinese word *quvpar* used in the Uigur civil documents. The word *qızgut* in Sa11 might be compared to *quvpar* ~ *quvar* in Sa03. In the Uigur civil documents, *Qızgut* is used in Mi01 ve Em01, which means "financial penalty, penalty" (Yamada 1993 - II: 276).

b. Penalty clauses in slavery trade documents

Slavery trade documents are similar to land sale documents. In some of the contracts we examined, it is understood that an agreement of compromise is made in the event of a case which demands a penalty. For example; in the contracts no: **Sa21、Sa22、Sa23、Sa24、Sa26、Sa28 and Sa29**, which are all about slavery trade, there are statements stipulating that protesters will give the aggrieved two slaves, instead of one, who are equal to the referred slave:

Sa22

... bu qarabaş yolınta män yrp togrıl ... içim inim tugmışım qadaşım yigänim tagayım kim qayu çam çarım qılmazunlar apam birök çam çarım qılsarlar bu qarabaş tänginçä iki qarabaş yaratu birip yulup alzun "About this slave; I am Yrp Togrıl ... let my elder brother, younger brother, my relatives, my nephew, my uncle or anyone else not protest, if they do so let them prepare and give two slaves equal to this one".

Sa24

Män atay tutungnung içim inim tugmışım qadaşım ygänim tgayım kim kim mä ärsär çam çarım qılmazunlar apam birök ärklig bäg işi yat yalavaç küçin tutup yulayın alayın saqınsarlar bu qrabaş tänginçä iki qrabaş birip yulup alzunlar "I am Atay Tutung, let my elder brother, younger brother, my relatives, my nephew, my uncle or anyone else not protest, if they intend to buy and sell using the influence of the powerful ruler and his wife, let them trade two slaves equal to this one".

It is clear that the method of compromise is not applied to the imposition of penaly in slavery trade document no: **Sa27** and protesters pay the penalty to the government and the top authorities: *... kim kim mä bolup çam çarım qılsar ulug süükä aq yastuq bäglärkä ädärkä yaragu at birip sözleri yorımazun* "... Whoever protests, let him pay the Great Majesty one aq (silver) yastuk, and give provincial rulers fine horses and let their words not be influential!"

B. Impositions of penalties in emancipation of slave contracts

In the contract no: Em01, which shows a slave is set free by his master, it is stated that protesters, especially the master and his relatives, will pay a penalty to the government and those in the state hiererachy:

Bu bitigtäki söztin öngi bolsar biz ulug suuqa bir altun yastuq aqa ini tägitlär birär kümüş yastuq ıduqqutqa bir yastuq şazın ayguçıqa bir at qızgut ötünüp sözläri yonmazun "In case of any contradicting situation with the words here, let them pay ulug süü one golden yastuq, princes and princelings one silver yastuq each, and İdikut (the Uigur emperor) one yastuq, şazın ayguçı (counsellors) one at qızgut (penalty pay) and let their words not be influential".

Particularly this document gives us more clues than other penalty documents about penalties paid to the government. The document shows there is a more systematic imposition of a penalty available, which is not seen in other official financial-property penalty contracts. In other words, it is remarkable that the penalties in the document are more advanced and comprehensive. We should certainly consider the fact that the dates of the documents where we see the official financial-property penalties might be different. This document is probably one from the period when the government took a larger interest in penalties. It is seen that as well as the Great Khan (Ulug Süü), the Uigur Khan İdikut, under the control of the Great Khan, is paid penalties. Given the hierarachical order here, penalties are paid as one golden yastuq to the Great Khan, who is in the centre, one silver yastuq each to princes as his successors and then one yastuq to the Uigur khan (İdikut) and one horse each to the official counselors. In another contract, Mi01, we see that the official penalty is paid to İdikut (see below).

C. Impositions of penalties in adoption documents

Two of the three adoption contracts we examined include the official penalties paid to the government, whereas in one contract (Ad03), unlike the others, penalty is demanded to be paid according to accepted practices.

We see that in the adoption contracts no. Ad01 and Ad02, penal sanctions are of the government initiative. Among the documents we examined, in Ad01, which might be considered as one of the oldest documents, it is stated that a penalty can be applied within the framework of the rules the government introduces:

Ad01

män çintso ayag-qa tägimlig-ning inim içim oglum qam qadaşım ilmäzün tartmazun apam birök ilgli tartıglı saqınsar savları yorumazun yasa-taqı qın-qa tägsünlär "I, respectable Çintso, let my brother, my uncle, my son and my relatives not intervene, or juggle me out of what is mine, if they do so, let their words not be influential and they be punished by law".

In this adoption contract, the following penalties will be paid according to the above mentioned law against protesters among the relatives of the adopted:

Ögödäy süüsingä iki yürüng atan ötünüp ambı balıq tarugalarınga ädärkä yaraşu at birip Çintso ayagqa tägimligkä birkä iki birip agır qınqa tägirbiz "We are consent to pay our majesty Ögödey two white camels, give the darugas of Ambı Balıq fine horses and respectable Çintso two (adoptees) instead of one, so we will be heavily punished".

It is understood that the document was arranged during the Great Khan Ögödey period. In this document, it is seen that the official penalty is not paid in cash but as properties. It is demanded that Ögödey, as the representative of the state, be paid two white camels, and darugas, as the administrative representatives of the state in provinces and governors, one horse each.

Here, another striking point is that in case of violation of the contract, the loss of the aggrieved is compensated in the proportion of two to one. This statement is not found in the documents where other official penalties are paid to the government.

In another adoption document no: Ad02, although the state high officials are not directly mentioned, it is stated those who protest for the *quvar* (~ *quvpar*), which is the official penalty paid to the government, will pay one yastuq each:

Qayusı bu savtın agışsarbiz birär yastuq quvar birüşürbiz "Whoever goes back on his words, he will pay (the government) one yastuq as a penalty".

D. Impositions of penalties in wills

It is understood that impositions of penalties concerning family law matters are the official penalties paid to the government.

In Uigurs, the specified penalties are clearly stated in wills in order to guarantee clauses in wills and to ensure their dissuasive and enforcer nature against possible protests. Impositions of penalties in case of protests and personal statements of the inheritor are presented in documents in order to prevent particulary successors from any damages or unfair practices because of clauses of will. It is possible to see that there are financial penalties, property penalties and corporal punishments available for those who protest against clauses of will and bring suits.

In a will no. **WP01**, the following impositions of penalties are mentioned in case that sons of the family can protest against the house which the family man vests his wife with as an inheritance:

oglum qoşang 'äsän qay-a olar ögäy anamız biz-kä tgir alır-biz tip almazun qatıl-mazun-lar apam birök alır-biz tip çamlasar-lar ulug süü-kä bir altun yastuq oglan tigit-lärkä birär kümüş yastuq içgärü agılıg-qa bir yastuq içgärü agılıg-qa bir at birip agır qıyn-qa tgip sözläri yorımazun "Let my sons Koşan, Esen Kaya not intervene, claiming that this belongs to them and she is their step mother. If they bring a suit to take it back, let them pay the Great Majesty one golden yastuk, and princes one silver yastuk each, the royal treasury one yastuk, and a horse. Let them be heavily punished. Let their words not be influential" (WP01$_{7-17}$).

In another will (**WP02**), similar impositions of penalties for those who could protest against the person the inheritor grants an emancipation document:

äv-täki qatınlarım mning tugmış-larım kim ymä çmlamazun-lar çmlasar-lar içgärü agılıg-qa bir altun yastuq qoço bägingä bir at balıg bägingä bir ud birip agır qıyn-qa tägzün "Let my wifes and my relatives or anyone else not protest. If they do (or bring a suit), let them pay the royal treasury one golden yastuk, the Koço ruler a horse and the provincial ruler a cattle. Let them be heavily punished" (WP02$_{11-16}$).

It is striking in wills that the institutions to which penalties are paid are directly top state institutions. In the documents, there is a stipulation that *ulug süü*[1] "the Great Majesty" (the Great Khan) one golden *yastuk*. In addition to this penalty pay, it is demanded that princes be paid one silver yastuk each, *içgerü agılık* or "the royal treasury" one *yastuk* and a horse. Also, it is wished that they will be heavily punished by paying these amounts and their words won't be influential. In another will, protesters are heavily punished by paying the treasury one golden yastuk and the Koço rulers a horse and cattle each.

Apart from financial and property penalties, in the document no. **WP04**, the protester of the will is mentioned and is demanded to take no interest in the will and be whipped. (See the above mentioned corporal punishment)

E. Impositions of penalties in miscellaneous contracts

Among the civil documents, we see financial and property penalties paid to the government in securities that we call miscalleneous contracts in terms of content. For example; in a security no. **Mi01** a girl is given as security for a loan and then she is taken back. After that, it is demanded that there should be no protests for the girl's clothes and personal belongings. In case of protests, the protester will give the Great Majesty five golden yastuq, shahzadahs one golden yastuq each, İdik-Kut one golden yastuq and the counselor of Koçu province one silver yastuq. The imposition here in this document is noteworthy. When it is compared to the penalty proportions paid to the government in other documents, the proportion in this document is much higher and heavier:

Kim qayu kişi inäçikä çam ... qılmazunlar apam çam çanm qılsarlar ulug süükä biş altun yastuq aqa ini tigitlärkä birär altun yastuq qızgut ötünüp iduqqutqa bir altun yastuq kögürüp qoço balıq ayguçıqa bir kümüş yastuq birip agır qıynqa tägzünlär "Let no one protest against İnäçi ... If they do, let them pay the Great Majesty five golden yastuq, princes and princelings one golden yastuq each, İdikut (the Uigur emperor) one golden yastuq, and the counselor of Koço one silver yastuq. Let them be heavily punished". (Mi01)

This document must have been arranged later than the others. In another miscalleneous contract (**Mi03**), a slave disappears. Someone finds the dead body of the slave and takes his clothes for himself. Because of them, there is a bargain between the master of the slave and the borrower of the clothes. As a result of the bargain, it is decided that if the master protests he will pay the Great Majesty two yastuk, the miŋ ruler one yastuq, the daruga of Lükçüŋ a half yastuk:

... ulug süükä 2 yastuq ötünüp ming bägikä 1 yastuq lükçüng targuınga yarım yastuq birip agır qın tgirmän "... I will pay the Great Majesty two yastuq, the ruler of the troop one yastuq, and the daruga of Lükçüŋ province a half yastuq. I will be heavily punished" (Mi03).

---

① See footnote 5 for the word *Ulug süü*.

Penalties according to accepted practices and judgements

In Uigur contracts, there are penalties according to accepted practices and judgements based on customary rules, as well as the official penalties. In case of any damage of personal interests, such penalties require the compensation of the financial loss. Penalties according to accepted practices and judgements are rather seen in loan documents, pledging documents and exchange documents. In these contracts where there is *İl yanıŋça* statement, penalty rate is given according to accepted practices in a certain province. In such impositions, it is seen that the government does not take any interest in the penalty. Although penalties in loan contracts, pledging contracts and exchange contracts are generally similar, there are some exceptions. For example; in one of the adoption documents which generally include the official impoisitions of penalties, it is demanded that the penalty be according to accepted practices. In the contract no. Ad03, there is the following: let those who protest against adoption: *törü yargu yosunı birle ata yazmış yazukka tegsün* "be punished according to accepted practices and judgements inherited from ancestors":

Penal practices and sources may vary according to the type of the contract. For example: interests are striking as an imposition of a penalty in loan contracts concerning special borrowings.

a. Loan contracts

Among the Uigur civil documents, loan contracts have the highest number. In almost all of the thirty loan contracts we examined, it is seen that penalties are imposed according to provincial rules and accepted practices. There are impositions in this contract as dissuasive precautions to prevent the lender from being damaged in case of no return of borrowed things. In the loan contracts we examined, there are interesting penalty pays including various interest rates over the same kind of goods or different products according to customary rules:

Luu yıl ekin丨i ay beş o丨uz-ka maŋa torçı-[k]a süç[üg]-kä böz [kär]gäk bolup k(a)yımtu-tın bir y(a)rım böz aldım küz y(a)ŋı-ta o丨uzar tänbin süçüg-ni bir kap berürmän bermädin käçür-sär-män il yaŋınç-a asıgı bilä köni berürmän "I, Torçı, needed cotton cloth in return for wine on the 25th of the second month of the dragon year and bought one and a half roll of cotton cloth from Kayımtu. In autumn, I will give thirty *tenbin* of wine as a bowl. If time is overdue, I will give it back directly with an interest according to the provincial rules".

In the contracts, it is seen that interest rates are high in case of return of borrowed things. There is no clear statement about penalty interests in the contracts. These probably vary according to the related provincial rules concerning the contract:

Document no:	Borrowed unit	Back payment and imposition of penalties
Lo06	Sheep mat	For every sheep mat, 6 böz, for every month the interest is 1 böz
Lo07	6 stır kümüş	Every month, for the interest a half baqır kümüş
*Lo13	3 halves of böz	Will give 7 bowls of böz. In case of no payment, the amount will be given at an interest İl yanınça
*Lo20	4 küri yür	8 küri yür. In case of no payment, the amount will be given at an interest İl yanınça
Lo27	12 batır künçit	22 batır künçit. In case of no payment, the amount will be given at an interest İl yanınça
*Lo28	1 küri künçit	2 küri künçit. In case of no payment, the amount will be given at an interest İl yanınça
*Lo29	4 teng kepez	7 teng kepez. In case of no payment, the amount will be given at an interest İl yanınça

b. Pledging documents

It is understood that impositions of penalties are arranged according to customary rules in pledging documents as well. In the document no. **Pl01**, interest pay is demanded as a penalty. In another pledging document (**Pl02**), the interesting point is that there is a special law on pledging:

män samboqdu tutung birtke … bolmışqa ton ätük adaq baş birmäz-män äv täg yogun iş işlätsär män ilning tutug y(a)ngınça birürmän qalmış turuşı yangı tutug y(a)ngınça bolzun "I, Samboqdu, will not give Bolmış clothes or shoes as Tutung birt (tax). If I make him work busily at home, I will give according to provincial (country) pledging rule. Let the rest of his life be according to the new pledging rule".

Result

Generally, impositions of penalties in the Uigur civil documents are encountered as the compensation of the financial loss with an interest or special compensations paid to the government in case of personal interests are damaged. Heavier penalties like death penalty and corporal punishments are given when there is an offense against the government. We understand that at first customary law practices applied concerning personal property rights and then impositions of penalties under the monopoly of the state were introduced. In a sense, different practices in contracts show us the developmental history of the Uigur penal law.

When it is considered in terms of penal law, it is seen that financial indemnifications are generally made through a process of compromise between people. As well as the one to two proportional values, there are back payments at various interest rates in Uigur contracts. In these contracts, the payer is a third person who would like to break the contract. Such penalties in the contracts directly have preventive and dissuasive functions, so the responsible party gives a guarantee to the other party.

Before Islam, the government was the only authority in Turkic states in terms of penal law. However, we see that unwritten customary rules formed by people have a functional role in the penal law system. It is noteworthy when contracts between people are broken, the process of compromise is effective and penal indemnifications are presented not to the government, but to the aggrieved.

In some of the Uigur documents, it is seen that penalties are paid not to the aggrieved, but to governmental institutions. The state must have had a source of revenues in this way. Given the fact that the contracts we obtained belong to different political periods and have different dates, it is possible to see various impositions of penalties for the same situaiton. In other words, penalties paid to the aggrieved at first were later paid to the government.

The state interest in penalties in Uigurs must have been after the Chinggis reign. As it is well known, Uigurs underwent the control of the Chinggis Empire in 1209. The Chinggis developed states over the region they extended and became stronger. Then they gave the power of impositions of penalties to the state monopoly. The Great Khan (ulug süü) in the centre was the first to be paid official penalties. In several documents, the Great Khan and his rulers are followed by the Uigur emperor İdikut in terms of penalty pays. We see that the Great Khanate had a source of revenues thanks to penalty pays. Accordingly, we can suggest impositions of penalties in Uigurs changed after the Chinggis reign.

We have stated that the origins of the Uigur law system including penalties is a topic to be studied in future research. It is not wrong to think there was an influential common law system including all Asian people (Chinese, Indians, and Mongols) as well as Turkic customary rules which shaped this understanding of law and the official rules introduced by state authorities. No matter the source is, the related documents clearly show us that Uigurs as a settled civilized society applied their law system successfully in social life.

吐鲁番所出土地租佃契多是民间的互助互惠契

乜小红

武汉大学历史系

在中国古代经济史的研究中,围绕着土地经营研究的分量不小,而涉及到土地租佃问题时,传统观点认为:"租佃关系是以土地私有制为基础的一种剥削关系。"[1]简单地说,凡属发生租佃关系者,必存在着剥削。然而,对吐鲁番出土的大批土地租佃契进行研究,使人感到此说并不完全符合历史的实际。

对于封建社会内的土地经营状况,传统的观点是:地主阶级拥有大量的土地等生产资料,而农民占有极少,或甚至没有土地等生产资料。农民要进行生产,必须向地主租用土地佃种,然后向地主交租,地主对农民的剥削从而完成——这是对封建社会所作的一种公式性的理解,而在实际生活中,并非只有地主与贫农这两极的存在,在这两极中间,还存在着相当数量的自耕农民。特别是在中国中世纪,在封建国家直接支配土地经营的情况下,个体小农按户按口耕种一定数量的土地才是一种合法的存在。

吐鲁番出土文书所涉及的高昌国时代,推行的是占田制度,规定百姓可以小额占有一定量的土地进行营种。[2] 唐灭高昌国建立西州后,又在西州推行了均田制,基本上按"一丁合得常田四亩、部田二亩"[3]的标准,给百姓授田经营,据此标准每年对百姓进行土地的还授。如此一来,吐鲁番文书所涉及的高昌国及唐西州时期的土地占有状况,主要是个体自耕农经营占着主体的地位。

既然整个社会的土地主要由自耕农民来经营,租佃关系也就不会发达。然而恰恰相反,其租佃关系却是特别发达。何以会出现这样一种特殊现象?这是首先需要弄清楚的。

一、高昌——西州租佃关系发达的原因

从高昌王国到唐西州租佃关系的发达,并不是由于土地大量集中于地主手中,无地、缺地的农民需要耕种而发生租佃,而是由于国家推行土地还授的均田制度所使然。高昌国由于没有找到民间的户籍簿不便于细论,从唐代户籍中,可以具体看到均田农民拥有份地的情况。在阿斯塔那35号墓所出的《武周载初元年(690)西州高昌县宁和才等户手实》中,列出了身居高昌县某乡的诸户拥有田土状况,兹转引几户如下:

    户主宁和才:合受常部田:

---

① 张传玺:《契约史买地券研究》之《上编:契约史研究》第六章《论中国封建社会土地所有权的法律观念》,中华书局,2008 年。
② 陈国灿:《高昌国的占田制度》,《魏晋南北朝隋唐史资料》第 11 期 (唐长孺教授八旬寿诞纪念论文集)1991 年 7 月。
③ 吐鲁番阿斯塔那 103 号墓所出《唐侯菜园子等户佃田簿》中,在列写每户土地盈欠状况时,均写有"壹丁合得常田肆亩,部田贰亩"的标准。见《吐鲁番出土文书》(录文本)第 4 册,第 239~240 页。

一段二亩　常田　城北廿里新兴

一段一亩　部田三易　城西七里沙堰渠

一段一亩　部田三易　城南五里马堆渠

一段一亩　部田三易　城西五里胡麻井渠①

据《手实》所载,户主宁和才年 14 岁,还有一妹年 13 岁,母赵氏 52 岁,属于无丁壮的缺劳动力的人户,然而此户拥有的两亩常田,即较好的地,却在高昌县城北 20 里处。另外 3 亩三易的部田,一在城西 7 里;一在城西 5 里;一在城南 5 里。这种份地状况的分布,对于缺劳力的宁和才户来说,是无法耕种的。不过,为了活命,不能让土地抛荒,唯一的办法,就是将远处的土地出租给人佃种,到收获时,能收得一些租粮来维持生活。下面再看一户王隆海的情况:

户主王隆海:合受常部田:

一段半亩　常田　城南一里杜渠

一段一亩半　常田　城西卌里交河县

一段二亩　常田　城北廿里新兴叠底渠

一段二亩　常田　城南二里王渠

一段二亩　常田　城南二里杜渠

一段四亩　部田　城东五里胡道渠

一段一亩　部田　城西十里南路坞

一段四亩　部田　城西五里屯头渠

一段一亩　部田　城西五里马堆渠

一段一亩　部田　城东五里左部渠

一段一亩　部田　城东五里胡道渠②

王隆海户,据《手实》有二丁,一是王隆海本人 51 岁,有笃疾;一是其弟王隆住 41 岁,另还有弟妻翟 35 岁。这三口之家,虽然其兄笃疾,丧失劳动力,但仍属有丁壮劳力的人户。有常田 8 亩,部田 12 亩,可是,田地在高昌城的东、西、南、北都有,最远的一块常田在城西 40 里交河县,另一块在城北 20 里,距离都太远。唯有城南 1~2 里的三块常田较近,可自行耕种。如要维持生产,势必要将在城西 40 里交河县的一亩半常田和城北 20 里新兴的二亩常田出租给当地附近的农民佃种,然后再就近佃种一些土地,才能维持一种常态的生产。下面再看一户老寡户,即:

户主大女曹多富,年柒拾捌岁　合受常部田

---

① 《吐鲁番出土文书》(录文本)第 7 册,文物出版社,1986 年,第 415 页。

② 同上,第 416~418 页。

　　一段二亩　常田　城西十里武城渠

　　一段卅步居住园宅①

　　这位 78 岁的孤寡老人唯一的一块土地就在城西十里的武城渠,现不知此二亩常田距居住园宅是远还是近。即使离得很近,由于自己年老,也无法自己耕种,为了维持生活,只有出租或是雇人代种,才能获取一部分收获物。

　　以上三户的状况,代表了三种类别:即丁壮劳力户型(王隆海户)、劳力缺乏户型(宁和才户)、丧失劳力户型(曹多富户)。不论哪一种户型,都无法用自己的劳力耕种自己的全部土地,原因是:每户的多块份地许多都距本户住地太远,而且非常分散。何以会出现这类情况? 这直接源于施行均田制度时的土地还授办法及规定,根据旧、新《唐书·食货志》的记载,有如下几项规定:

　　一、授田之制,丁及男年十八以上者,人一顷,其八十亩为口分,二十亩为永业。②

　　二、世业之田,身死则承户者便授之;口分则收入官,更以给人。③

　　三、凡收授皆以岁十月,授田先贫及有课役者。④

依照上述唐令精神,凡百姓中满十八岁的男子,都要授田,全国的标准是人丁一顷,唐西州为狭乡,丁男授田只有"一丁合得常田四亩、部田二亩",⑤均田民身死,其口分田由官府收回,好分配给人。唐西州由于土地少,均田民身死后,其土地全部官收,以便及时重新分配给待授者。即使如此,土地常不够分配,这从吐鲁番文书中"欠田簿"的出现即可看出,如日本所藏从吐鲁番所获"大谷文书"1912 号载:

　　宁昌乡

　　合当乡第九第八户欠田丁中总一百人

　　八 十 七 人 第 九 户

　　康大智二丁欠常田二亩部田四亩刘盛感二丁欠常田二亩部田三亩申屠嗣嘉丁欠常田二亩部田□⑥

　　紧接此片之后是大谷 2886 号、2891 号,列的全部是第九等户各户的欠田数。因此,只要那里退出一块地来,官府就立即将此地分配给待分配者,并在当年十月待受田者姓名下登录"充分",出土文书中大量的"退田簿"及"授田簿"就是极生动的说明,如大谷 2604 号中所列康蛇子死退常部田另行分配给人情况:

　　康蛇子死退一段贰亩常田城东廿里高宁　东申德　西李秋　南安僧俶北竹乌□

　　　　给史尚宾　充

　　一段壹亩部田城东五里左部渠　东至荒　西安守相　南至渠　北至□

　　① 《吐鲁番出土文书》(录文本)第 7 册,文物出版社,1986 年,第 423 页。

　　② 《新唐书》卷五一《食货一》,北京:中华书局,1975 年,第 1342 页。

　　③ 《旧唐书》卷四八《食货上》,北京:中华书局,1975 年,第 2088 页。

　　④ 《新唐书》卷五一《食货一》,北京:中华书局,1975 年,第 1343 页。

　　⑤ 吐鲁番阿斯塔那 103 号墓文书《唐侯菜园子等户佃簿》中,在每户名下均要重申"壹丁合得常田肆亩,部田贰亩",反映了唐西州均田制下每丁授田的标准。见《吐鲁番出土文书》(录文本)第 4 册,文物出版社,1983 年,第 239 页。

　　⑥ 小田义久主编《大谷文书集成》第一卷,京都法藏馆 1984 年,第 134~135 页。

给史尚宾　充

一段贰亩部田城西七里白渠　东麹明堆　西贾海仁　南至荒　北 ☐☐☐☐

给康忠☐　充

如此一来,待分配者所得土地,就必然会出现东面廿里一块、五里一块,西边七里一块的插花现象。每年的土地还授地块不一,使得越到后来,每户的份地插花愈益严重,甚至插到邻县去,除前列王隆海有一亩半常田在"城西卌里交河县"外,还有高昌县的翟急生户有一段二亩常田,就在"城西六十里交河县";① 高昌县的户主史苟仁有二亩常田和一亩部田在"城东廿五里柳中县";另还有一亩部田在"城东卌里柳中县"。② 农户的份地距离如此遥远,很不利于耕作,要想进行正常的生产,只有与当地的农户进行换种,而换种最好的方式是平等的、临时性的租佃,大谷2847号《武周如意元年(692)王渠成家堰堰头文书》所载即是最好的说明:

1. 成家堰王渠　堰头竹辰住
2. 竹达子一亩　竹辰住佃　东吴德师　南竹住　西渠　　北丁尉
3. 竹辰住二亩　自佃　　　东康海善　西渠　　南道　　北竹达子
4. 康海善四亩　自佃　　　东索僧奴　西竹住　南张汉姜　北马才仕
5. 张汉姜二亩　竹住佃　　东索僧奴　西渠　　南街　　北康善
6. 索僧奴二亩　佃人竹辰住 ☐☐☐☐③

（后缺）

上列五户名旁均标有"昌"字,推测应是宁昌乡的简称,或许成家堰地段的土地正在此乡。竹辰住在此充当堰头,表明他就是家居于此的当乡人。竹辰住的份地可能分配在他渠他乡,耕种不便,于是他便在自己已有二亩份地的周边,又佃种了北边竹达子一亩;南边的张汉姜二亩;东边的索僧奴二亩。当然这种租佃都要靠订立租佃契约来实现的,这样,实际的耕作区连成了一片,很有利于农耕生产的进行,这也正好说明唐西州土地租佃契约特别流行的原因。

租佃解决了均田制施行过程中农民对所得份地不便耕种的问题,所以租佃起了巩固均田制的作用。租佃对于高昌国时期施行的占田制同样也起着一种补充作用,高昌的占田制,据所出文书记载的"人得部麦田伍亩"④看,也是一种人丁限占田地的标准。如占不到,可以用买卖方式补入,也可以用租佃方式补入。这也就是高昌王国时期既流行土地买卖契约,又流行土地租佃契的原因。

---

① 《吐鲁番出土文书》(录文本)第7册,文物出版社,1986年,第421页。
② 同上,第419页。
③ 小田义久主编《大谷文书集成》第一卷,京都法藏馆,1984年,第104页,图版第83页。
④ 阿斯塔那140号墓出有《高昌重光某年条例得部麦田、口丁头数文书》,其中提到"……捌人,人得部麦田伍亩……,……部麦田肆拾亩",其后又有"占依官限占足"等语,反映出了高昌国占田的标准。载《吐鲁番出土文书》(录文本)第5册,文物出版社,1983年,第51页。

二、农户间为方便耕种而出现的互换租佃

国家给农民"充分"的土地既然如此分散,均田农民为了生产,当然要想一些办法来改变这种状况:一种是对口互换土地耕种;另一种是远处出租近处佃种。对于互换土地耕种,如《唐张小承与某人互佃田地契》,共存 11 行,此处摘录其前 7 行契文如下:

1. □□承匡渠西奇口分常田五亩　　东王令玮　　南□□　　西官田　北苏祀奴
2. ＝＝＝＝ 年十一月廿四日□逐隐便将上件地
3. ＝＝＝＝ 酒泉城口分检渠常田一段五
4. ＝＝＝＝ 家各十年佃□,如以后两家
5. ＝＝＝＝ 种,各自收本地。如营田以后,
6. ＝＝＝＝ 役,各自祗承,不得遮护,两
7. 共平章,恐人无信,故立此契为记。①

从此契知张小承将自己在高昌匡渠的五亩常田,与某人在酒泉城的五亩常田换种,各自承担土地的赋役。此契约定换地十年,肯定是能给双方带来便利的结果。

以上是土地数额条件完全对等的换地,还有一种不对等的换种,如《唐天宝七载(748)杨雅俗与某寺互佃土地契》,录其契文前 9 行如下:

1. ＝＝＝＝ 渠口分常田一段肆亩 东　西　南　北
2. ＝＝＝＝ 平城南地一段参□ 东　西　南　北
3. □□七载十二月十三日杨俗寄住
4. 南平,要前件寺地营种,今将郡
5. 城樊渠口分地彼此逐□□种,缘
6. 田地税及有杂科税,仰□□□□
7. 各自知当。如已后不硕佃地者,
8. 彼此收本地,契有两本,各执一
9. 本为记②

这是寄住在南平城的杨雅俗,愿将自己在高昌城樊渠的四亩常田,与马寺在南平城南的一段三亩地交换佃种,并各自承担换地后的各自税役差科。这是一种不等额的交换,或许是由于南平城南的三亩是质地优良的菜地的缘故。

---

① 《吐鲁番出土文书》(录文本)第 10 册,文物出版社,1991 年,第 303 页。
② 同上,第 275～276 页。

换地耕种是为了方便就近劳作,不过,有时也难以找到条件完全相等的合适地段来交换,于是,在更多的情况下,还是各自按需要来租佃。

吐鲁番出土阿斯塔郡 10 号墓中,有多件高昌县武城乡人傅阿欢从贞观二十三年(649)到永徽四年(653)的"夏田契",[①]契中呈现的特点是:(一) 所夏佃的每次都以孔进渠的二亩常田居多,表明傅阿欢家住武城乡的孔进渠附近,每年都要就近租入土地佃种,如此做肯定是由于他原有的份地距家太远;(二) 每次都是佃前预付银钱,有时甚至提前近一年便给付租金,如永徽四年四月十三日就向支醜囗交了银钱陆文,夏永徽五年左部渠的两亩麦田,这显然是为了保证到时有田种采取的措施。

同墓所出的《唐龙朔元年(661)孙沙弥子夏田契》中写有:"龙朔元年十一月廿六日,武城乡人孙沙弥子于顺义乡人李虎祐边夏龙朔叁年中石宕渠口分常田贰亩,……"[②]石宕渠的走向,据孙晓林的研究,[③]是由高昌城北三里至二里再流向城东一里至五里,武城乡境在高昌城西至城北,孙沙弥子住地可能距此渠常田不远,故愿花大力气在一年多以前就预订了龙朔三年(663)中的租佃。他如此提前预订租佃是一贯的,如在此年之前的显庆五年(660)就订契约从"(宁)昌乡人董尾柱边,夏石宕渠口分常田贰亩,要迳六年壹年佃种,田壹亩,即日交与夏价银钱拾伍文",[④]由此也反映出顺义乡人李虎祐的住地和(宁)昌乡人董尾柱的住地,距石宕渠均较远,故才出租,反映出了民间的择便佃种意愿。

择便佃种的契约,有时一订就是好几年,如《唐永徽二年(651)孙客仁夏田契》中写的是:"永徽二年十月一日,孙客仁于赵欢相(边夏囗囗)渠常田肆亩,要迳六年佃,年田壹亩与夏价囗囗斛……",对赵欢相的四亩常田,孙客仁一租就是六年,其每年租价文缺,想必也是较优厚的。

由上看到,作为佃田户一方的傅阿欢、孙沙弥子、孙客仁等,从其预租预付等行为看,都不是贫困的农民,而是有经营土地能力的农户。而这种能力也缘于他们在另地有相等数额的常田在出租的缘故,如同前节所列的王隆海,只有将城西 40 里交河县的一亩半常田和城北 20 里新兴的二亩常田出租出去,才有条件就近佃进土地。如此,我们不难看出,唐代的西州,几乎每家每户都存在着既有土地出租、又须土地佃入的情形,而这种互换佃种的租佃关系中,并不存在谁剥削谁的问题,而这一类的租佃契在租佃关系中所占的比例最大。

三、互助互惠式的租佃

按照正常的历史理论逻辑,土地出租者通常是不劳动的地主,是他们用收取租金来剥削佃种者。然而,在高昌国及唐西州,这类现象不是很多,所以,陈国灿先生在研究《唐代的租佃契与租佃关系》一文中说:"在吐鲁番出土的租佃契中,大部分都是均田农民之间进行土地出租和佃种时订立的。"[⑤]由此,他将这种出租区分为三种类型:一是小土地出租型;二是富户赁租型;三是换地佃种型。[⑥] 在这三种类型中,实际上第二类只是少数,唯有小土地出租型和换地佃种型居多,而在这种小土地所有者中,有许多贫困的

① 《吐鲁番出土文书》(录文本)第 5 册,文物出版社,1983 年,第 76～88 页。
② 同上,第 87 页。
③ 孙晓林:《唐西州高昌县的水渠及其使用、管理》,《敦煌吐鲁番文书初探》,武汉大学出版社,1983 年,第 524 页。
④ 《吐鲁番出土文书》(录文本)第 5 册,文物出版社,1983 年,第 85～86 页。
⑤ 陈国灿:《唐代的经济社会》第四章《唐代的租佃契与租佃关系》,台北:文津出版社,1999 年,第 110 页。
⑥ 同上,第 110～117 页。

土地出租者,颇引人注意。在阿斯塔那42号墓中,出有《唐永徽元年(650)严慈仁牒为转租田亩请给公文事》,现将牒文转录于下:

1.　　　　常田四亩　东渠
2. 牒　慈仁家贫,先来乏短,一身独立,
3. 更无弟兄,唯租上件田,得子已供喉命,
4. 今春三月,粮食交无,遂将此田租与安横
5. 延。立券六年,作练八匹,田既出赁,前人从
6. 索公文,既无力自耕,不可停田受饿。谨以
7. 牒陈,请裁,谨□
8.　　　　永徽元年九月廿　日云骑尉严慈仁①

严慈仁勋为"云骑尉",可比正七品。他的四亩常田,或许也是朝廷所赐,由于他"先来乏短,一身独立",属于单贫人户,到了春三月已经断炊无粮,"既无力自耕,不可停田受饿",所以被饥饿所迫而将四亩常田出租,这是典型的贫困土地出租者。

另有一件阿斯塔那363号墓中所出的《唐仪凤年间(676~679)西州蒲昌县竹住海佃田契》,转引契文如下:

1. ▭年拾月壹日,高昌县宁昌乡人卜老
2. ▭年柒月拾□,蒲昌县人竹住海於高昌县
3. ▬▬▬▬▬▬▬▬年,年别与租价
　　（中缺）
4. ▭取秋麦 ▬依高平元斛 ▬
5. ▭如不净好,听向风常取。若过麦月不 ▬
6. ▭法生利,到种田之日,竹不得田佃者,准前
7. ▭付。其竹取田之日,得南头佃种。租殊
8. 佰役仰田主,渠破水谪仰佃人,其田要迳仪凤□②
　　（后缺）

本件契文从全文文意看,知第1行属于误将出租田亩人前列的误写,实是第3行应写的内容,由此明白这是蒲昌县人竹住海向高昌县宁昌乡人卜老师租种田亩的契约。这是隔县佃种,有可能卜老师有一块份地在蒲昌县境内。与本契同出的还有三件经济文书,能说明土地出租者卜老师的状况:一件是卜老师"诉男及男妻不养赡"的呈辞,同时提到他"两眼俱盲";另两件是他借钱的"举钱契",其中一件很可能就是卜老

---

① 《吐鲁番出土文书》(录文本)第6册,文物出版社,1986年,第223页。
② 《吐鲁番出土文书》(录文本)第7册,文物出版社,1986年,第530页。

师于仪风二年九月五日向"竹住海边举取银钱捌文"的契约,反映出了卜老师自身丧失劳动能力和经济上的窘迫的状况,同时也说明了佃田人竹住海的富裕。

像这类有小块份地又丧失劳动能力的农户相当多,前揭的宁和才户属缺乏劳动力的人户,其在城北二十里新兴的二亩常田及城西、城南的部田,都只有靠出租来解决生产问题。又前揭的大女曹多富户,虽然仅有一段二亩常田在城西十里的武城渠,但对作为七十八岁的她来说,是完全无能为力的,她属于丧失劳动力的人户,只有靠出租收取租粮来维持生活。类似状况者并不少见,如阿斯塔那 518 号墓中所出《唐阿麹辞稿为除租佃名事》,其中主体内容写的是:

> 县司:阿麹上件地,去春家无手力营佃,即租与宁
>
> 大乡人张感通佃种讫,望请附感佃名,除阿麹名,
>
> 谨辞。①

阿麹的土地由于"家无手力营佃",故出租给宁大乡人张感通佃种,请求县府在土地簿上附上张感通佃人名,以便向张征地子麦。

这些都是贫困的土地出租者,他们与佃种者的关系是一种求助性的帮扶关系,根本谈不上地租剥削的问题。

在互助互惠式的租佃中,还有一种"舍佃"式的佃种:即两家合种一块地,由一家出地,另一家出种子、耕牛、劳力合种;秋收后,两家对收获物平分。如《唐龙朔三年(663)西州高昌县张海隆夏田契》,全 13行,兹录前 7 行如下:

> 1. 龙朔三年九月十二日武城乡人张海隆於
>
> 2. 同乡人赵阿欢仁边夏取肆年中、
>
> 3. 五年、六年中,武城北渠口分常田贰亩,海
>
> 4. 隆、阿欢仁二人舍佃食。其耒牛、麦子、
>
> 5. 仰海隆边出,其秋麦,二人庭分,若海隆
>
> 6. 肆年、五年、六年中不得田佃食,别钱伍拾文
>
> 7. 入张;若到头不佃田者,别钱伍拾文入赵。②

此舍佃契一订即为三年,意味着一种长期性的合作。类似的二人合作舍佃亭分的事例,又见于阿斯塔那 15 号墓文书《唐权僧奴佃田契》。③ 田主有常田一分,薄田一分;"田中耕牛、人力、麦子、粟子仰权僧奴承了",而且"田中粪堛土",即施肥,也"仰权僧奴使足",秋收后也是"贰人场上亭分",作为佃作者权僧奴的负担,比之上例中张海隆的负担要重一点。从这两例看,田主方是既无种子、耕牛,又无劳力的人户,属于弱势的均田民。而佃方则拥有种子、耕牛、劳力,相对处于强势。这样一种弱强联合舍佃,也是一

---

① 《吐鲁番出土文书》(录文本)第 7 册,文物出版社,1986 年,第 358 页。
② 《吐鲁番出土文书》(录文本)第 5 册,文物出版社,1983 年,第 117 页。
③ 《吐鲁番出土文书》(录文本)第 4 册,文物出版社,1983 年,第 59 页。

种互通有无的合作租佃,带有一定的互助性质,其结果达到一种互惠的效果。

四、剥削性租佃的存在

在大量互助互惠租佃关系存在的同时,也存在着一定数量带剥削性的租佃,一种是官田或官僚地主的土地出租,阿斯塔那365号墓所出《高昌延昌二十八年王幼谦夏镇家麦田券》就是一种官田出租的契券,该券前3行写有:

1. 延昌二十八年戊申岁十二月廿二日,王幼谦从主簿孟儁边
2. 夏镇家细中部麦田贰拾伍亩,亩与夏价麦贰斛柒
3. 斗,租在夏价中。[①]

这是高昌王国时期的官僚、即镇家田出租,每亩租价二斛七斗麦,按高昌国规定,凡民种官田每亩都要给官府纳租三斛,[②]"租在夏价中"是指此种租赋已包括在夏官田价中了,不另交租赋之意。相比较而言,镇家田所收租额略低于官田租。类似的夏镇家麦田契还有一些,如阿斯塔那364号墓所出《高昌延昌二十六年某人从□□崇边夏镇家菜园券》,[③]以及同墓所出《高昌某人夏镇家麦田券》。[④]

唐代的西州,官田也主要靠出租经营,日本大谷探险队曾在吐鲁番获得一批武周天授二年(691)高昌县诸渠堰头所申当堰佃种田地牒,即通常称之为"堰头文书"者,其中记录了分布在各堰地段内的官田及官僚所有田的亩数及佃种人姓名情况,现据《大谷文书集成》第一卷所公布文书图版,[⑤]将其列表如下:

大谷文书号	地 点	田 主 名	亩 数	佃人姓名	备 注
1213	索渠第四堰	县公廨	17	梁 端	
1217	匡 渠	县公廨	7+3	氾嘉祚	
1217	匡 渠	牛参军	6	索定刚	
2367		仓曹职官田	7	朱贞行	
2369	匡 渠	州公廨地	6	张习礼	
2369	匡 渠	司 马	12	范增护	
2372	索渠第一堰	□□职田	8.5	焦智通	种粟
2372	索渠第一堰	都督职田	11.5	宋居仁	种粟

---

① 《吐鲁番出土文书》(录文本)第2册,文物出版社,1981年,第359页。
② 阿斯塔那88号墓所出《高昌高乾秀等按亩入供账》中,高文邕一亩六十步地,入供粮三斛七升半;将罗子下二亩地,入供粮合六斛。据此,知每亩纳租三斛。见《吐鲁番出土文书》(录文本)第2册,文物出版社,1981年,第183页。
③ 《吐鲁番出土文书》(录文本)第3册,文物出版社,1983年,第187页。
④ 同上,第191页。
⑤ 小田义久主编《大谷文书集成》第一卷,京都法藏馆,1984年,图版第72~86页。

大谷文书号	地　点	田主名	亩　数	佃人姓名	备　注
2372	索渠第一堰	县公廨	7亩100步	唐智宗	种粟
2372	索渠第一堰	张少府	1	康善隆	
2373		明　府	2	周苟尾	种粟
2845		县公廨佐史	10	汜义感	
2845		县令田	2	奴集聚	

由上表看到,绝大部分的官田及官僚所有田,都是靠出租来佃种的,而且其数量都较大,所占的地段都较好,由此推想其所收租额也较高,其存在着剥削则是肯定的。至于这些官田或官僚田是否还像高昌国时期那样用契约形式将出租固定下来,由于尚未见到这类契约,尚难定断。

对于唐代官僚土地的出租,见于阿斯塔郡230号墓中所出的一批案卷,这是武周天授二年(691)天山县主簿高元祯的职田受到西州都督府调查的案卷,[①]其中有一件被调查的"知田人"郭文智供称:

主簿南平职田总有五十五亩八十步,出租已外,见佃廿五亩八十步。[②]

据上载,主簿在南平的职田有三十亩是出租的,主簿高元祯出租的三十亩地是否订有租佃契约? 由于未见实物,也不得而知。

关于官僚职田的租额,在《唐开元二十二年(734)杨景璿牒为父赤亭镇将杨嘉麟职田出租请给公验事》中载有:

赤亭镇将杨嘉麟职田地七十六亩亩别粟六斗,计卅五石六斗,草一百五十二围。[③]

据此,职田每亩收租粟六斗,草二围,租额倒不是很高,但具有剥削性。

另一种剥削性的租佃存在于寺院,《唐贞观十四年张某夏田契》[④]是一件残缺的租佃契,从残存文字推知是张某从弘宝寺都维那边夏该寺在匡渠的"常田拾柒亩",所收租有糜、粟、麦,从残存的"种糜,与伍斛"看,这是早期小量制的租额,只相当于中唐前后量制的1/3,即使如此,每亩的租价也并不低。

阿斯塔那506号墓所出《唐大历六年某寺田园出租及租粮破用账》,列有该寺亩出租及租粮状况,兹将账中第3~9行内容转引如下:

---

① 《吐鲁番出土文书》(录文本)第8册,文物出版社,1987年,第145~165页。

② 阿斯塔那230号墓所出72TAM230:68号文书与日本大谷4940+4937号相拼接文书《武周天授二年郭文智辩辞》,见陈国灿《对唐西州都督府勘检天山县主簿高元祯职田案卷的考察》,《敦煌吐鲁番文书初探》,武汉大学出版社,1983年,第471页。

③ 《吐鲁番出土文书》(录文本)第9册,文物出版社,1990年,第101页。

④ 《吐鲁番出土文书》(录文本)第4册,文物出版社,1983年,第40~41页。

壹 拾 捌 亩 陆 拾 步 出 租 并 常 田

樊渠地六亩_{亩别麦粟各六斗。王居随}　计柒硕贰斗_{麦粟各半}

杜渠菜园一亩八十步,得麦粟肆硕_{麦粟各半傅元相}

张渠地半亩,麦粟陆斗。各半王德实

樊渠四亩_{亩别四斗}　计粟壹斛陆斗。　王居遂

石宕渠一亩一百步,得糜壹硕壹斗。　崇福寺

酒泉城地五亩,租得粟伍硕。　　刘客①

根据同墓所出文书推断,此账是高昌城内马寺的收支账,此寺总有常部田陆拾亩陆拾步,除了上述壹拾捌亩陆拾步常田出租外,其余的均"空荒不种"。从租额数看,马寺所收似乎少了很多,其实这是量制的差别,中唐前后的量制比之高昌国时期及初唐的量制约要大三倍,亩获租麦、粟各陆斗,相当于旧制的叁斛陆斗,也不算少了。这完全都是佃户们劳作所生产出来的成果,当它被当作地租交给马寺时,也意味着马寺对佃户地租剥削的完成。

综上分析,我们从吐鲁番出土的众多租佃契看到,从高昌国到唐西州的农业生产中,租佃关系特别发达,这是由于国家掌控着所有的土地,对农民随时调剂分配土地,特别是唐代年年实行土地还授的均田制度的结果。这就必然会出现农民份地东五里一块、西十里一块的现象,农户们为了解决份地插花、不便耕作的困难,开展了换地佃种、互租互佃的形式来维持生产,于是便有大量租佃契的流行。此外,还有一种互通有无、相互帮扶的租佃关系,这也是既有利于农业生产进行,又有助于解决一些农户困难的措施。在整个农业租佃关系中,以民间的互租互佃契和相互帮扶契为主体,而这两类契约均具有农户间互助互惠的性质,不存在剥削问题。而带剥削性的租佃契,则存在于官僚所有土地和寺院占有的土地上,比之于整个租佃契约关系来说,所占比例不是很大。这就是吐鲁番出土土地租佃契反映出的一些特点。

---

① 《吐鲁番出土文书》(录文本)第10册,文物出版社,1991年,第296页。

新疆出土宗教文物及宗教文化

伊斯拉菲尔·玉苏甫　　安尼瓦尔·哈斯木

新疆维吾尔自治区博物馆

新疆不仅是我国很早就出现人类活动踪迹的地区之一,而且自古就是一个多民族聚居的地区,各民族在不同的历史时期曾经信奉过多种宗教,因而长期以来多种宗教在这里流传和并存,文献记载与考古发现也在不断地证实这一点。据考古发现来看,这里也存在着原始宗教,它的主要表现为自然崇拜、祖先崇拜和图腾崇拜等。

从2002年和2004~2005年新疆文物考古研究所在罗布泊地区孔雀河下游的小河墓地发掘资料看,在距今约四千年的这一文化遗存发现生殖崇拜现象,如男性墓上方均立有表示女性生殖器的桨形立木,而女性墓上方则为圆形或多棱形立木,此外墓葬中还出土有随葬的木祖。[①] 这种生殖崇拜在哈密焉布拉克墓地[②]和呼图壁县康家石门子岩画中也有充分的体现。对太阳的崇拜在古代新疆也广泛存在,其中,公元前1000年初,跟今约三千八百多年之孔雀河古墓沟墓地发现的地表井然有序地立着的七圈木桩,及环圈外呈放射状展开的木桩,犹如光芒四射的太阳,[③]最具代表性。随着社会的发展,以及以自然崇拜等为重要标志之原始宗教进入晚期阶段,人们的信仰开始从多神向一神过渡,萨满教就是这一时期的产物。由于萨满教曾广泛流行于我国北方古代各民族中,因而在新疆出现的也比较早。虽然有关萨满教在文献中多有记述,但考古发现极为有限。如:2003年3~5月,新疆文物考古研究所与吐鲁番地区文物局在鄯善县洋海墓地进行的发掘中,从一号墓地21号墓出土一具40岁左右男尸。其头部前方立一根木棍,木棍上套一副马镳头。头向南,足向北,下肢向右侧屈,身穿毛织的衣裤,足穿皮靴,皮靴上有铜扣装饰,头戴一圈用贝壳装饰的彩色毛缘,脖子上带着一串项链,质地有玛瑙、绿松石等,戴单圈的圆形耳环,右边的金质,左边的铜质。右手握木柄铜斧,一个木钵,腰身下有两个皮套,分别装有弧背铜刀和铜锥;左手握着法器,为缠绕铜片的木棍,脚下有一副羊头骨。[④] 依据其装束与萨满巫师非常相似之特点,故目前被许多人认为有可能是当时的萨满巫师。出现这种情况,很显然与新疆所具有的历史及地理特点是有着密切联系的。新疆地处丝绸之路要冲,是东方文化与西方文化交流与荟萃的地带。历史上民族的迁徙与经济文化的交流是频繁的。因而在与国外、国内各民族的相互交往中,宗教的传播便成为非常自然的事情。所以生活在这里之人们所信奉过的宗教,既有自国外传入的,也有从我国内地传入的。正由于这一缘故,也

---

① 新疆考古研究所:《2002年小河墓地调查与发掘报告》,《新疆文物》2003年第2期;《罗布泊地区小河流域的考古调查》,《新疆文物》2007年第2期。

② 哈密焉布拉克墓地出土有两件雕刻有男性生殖器和女性生殖器的木俑,实物现收藏于新疆文物考古研究所。

③ 新疆社会科学院考古研究所:《孔雀河古墓沟墓地发掘及其初步研究》,《新疆文物考古新收获》,新疆人民出版社,1995年。

④ 新疆考古研究所、吐鲁番地区文物局:《鄯善县洋海一号墓地发掘简报》,《新疆文物》2004年第1期;干尸现存于吐鲁番地区博物馆,依据装束,虽然被许多人认为可能是当时的萨满巫师,但由于对其进一步研究工作正在进行之中,故未能最终确定,因而目前认为可能为萨满巫师。

遗留下来大量与宗教文化有关的古代文化遗产,这为我们进一步认识与了解古代新疆历史与多元文化,从另一个侧面提供了许多有益的线索。故而在论及当地文化时,应对该地区的宗教文化发展脉络有一基本的了解。鉴于此目的,在此,就新疆的宗教文化作一综述。

一、祆　教

祆教原名琐罗亚斯德教,源于波斯。由于其教徒不仅崇拜日月星辰,而且也崇拜火,因此,我国史籍称其为火祆教、拜火教、波斯教等。对此,我国学者陈垣先生有"西历纪元前五六百年,波斯国有圣人,曰苏鲁阿士德(Zoroaster);因波斯过拜火旧俗,特倡善恶二原之说,谓善神清净而光明,恶魔污浊而黑暗;人宜弃恶就善,弃黑暗而趋光明;以火以光表至善之神,崇拜之,故名拜火教;因拜光又拜日月星辰,中国人以为其拜天,故名之曰火祆。……西历226年,波斯国萨珊王朝兴,定火祆为国教,一时盛行于中央亚细亚"[1]之精辟论述。

祆教是最早传入新疆的宗教,从考古发现来看大约在公元前4世纪就传入了新疆,这一点已有考古发现所证实。譬如:1976～1978年,在天山东部阿拉沟发掘的竖穴木椁墓除获得大量珍贵文物外,还发现了祆教祭祀用的高足承双兽方铜盘,[2]经碳14测定,时代在战国至汉。至魏晋南北朝时期,随着粟特商人们在丝绸之路上的频繁往来,以及在丝路沿线建立定居点,他们所信仰的祆教开始盛行于塔里木盆地。据《魏书》记载"高昌国俗事天神","焉耆国俗事天神","疏勒国俗事祆神","于阗国好事天神";《旧唐书》卷一九八:"(于阗国)好事祆神";到五代时,祆教仍在于阗流行,《旧五代史·外国传》有:于阗"其俗好事祆神"之记载。这说明,当时祆教在新疆地区已具有相当大的影响力。另外,吐鲁番出土文书也表明,在麴氏高昌时期,吐鲁番地区不仅有多座祆教寺院,而且还曾设有专门负责祆教事务的官员"萨薄",[3]譬如:《高昌永平二年(550)十二月三十日祀部班示为知人名及谪罚事》中有关祆教官员"萨薄"及其人名的记录。由于祆教在西域人以及由西域移居内地的人们当中有很大的影响,在北齐与隋时就开始设官进行管理了,据《隋书·百官志》载:北齐有"萨甫",隋有"萨保",都应该是"萨薄"的同音异译。据《通典》卷四十《职官典》记唐"萨宝府"的各级官吏为萨宝、率府、府史、祆正、祆祝等几种。[4] 在于阗文中spāta(萨波)这一官称很可能来自粟特文srtpw,"萨簿"实际上是由商队首领发展而来的胡人聚落首领的意思。[5] 另外,史料还涉及高昌祆教的祭祀问题,如吐鲁番出土文书所载《高昌章和五年(535)取牛羊供祀账》[6]就反映了祆教祭祀问题,同时需要注意的是,吐鲁番文书中用牛羊祭祀祆教天神,可谓祆教中国化的一种表现。除了文书,在出土其他实物中也有与祆教有关的文物,譬如:吐鲁番地区文管所于1981年在吐峪沟发现了一座麴氏高昌国时期的粟特祆教徒墓葬,发现两个盛放骨殖的陶棺,一个为圆桶状,另一个为长方形;另外,20世纪初,德国人勒克柯在吐鲁番地区进行探险活动期间,在吐鲁番胜金口两座寺

① 吴泽主编《陈垣史学论著选》,上海人民出版社,1981年,第109页。
② 穆舜英、王明哲、王炳华:《建国三十年新疆考古的主要收获》,《新疆考古三十年》,新疆人民出版社,1983年。
③ 余太山主编《西域文化史》,中国友谊出版公司,1996年,第102页。
④ 高永久:《西域古代民族宗教综论》,高等教育出版社,1997年,第64页。
⑤ 荣新江:《萨保与萨薄:北朝隋唐胡人聚落首领的争论与辨析》;叶奕良:《伊朗学在中国论文集》,北京大学出版社,2003年,第128～143页。
⑥ 实物现收藏于新疆维吾尔自治区博物馆。

庙遗址中发现两尊袄教天神阿胡拉·玛兹达的泥塑头像和两尊女神泥塑像,无论从制作工艺还是艺术造型上看,当系袄教女神——娜娜的艺术形象。[①] 其中一尊头像高 20 cm,宽 17.5 cm。长有三眼,面部为浅蓝色,头发、眉毛和上翘的胡子皆作红色,眼球虽为红色,瞳孔为黑色,但眼眶却为红色,整个头部充满"火"色;[②]另一尊高约 7 cm,目前收藏在柏林印度艺术博物馆。此外,在和田丹丹乌里克发现的粟特袄教神祇图像[③]和从吐鲁番阿斯塔那——哈拉和卓墓葬出土和乌恰县发现的波斯萨珊朝银币(正面为诸王头像,背面为拜火坛)[④]等,都是袄教在新疆流行的很好例证。

唐代以后,袄教的影响在新疆有所衰退,自伊斯兰教在新疆得以广泛传播开始,袄教才逐渐消失,但其遗风仍存在于世居新疆的各少数民族风俗习惯之中。

二、佛 教

公元前 3 世纪,是印度历史上宗教文化最辉煌的时期,而佛教就是这一文化辉煌时期的代表。经过几个世纪的完善与发展,佛教开始东渐。在古代印度佛教东渐过程中,西域起着至关重要的作用。就新疆而言,由于塔里木盆地的古代居民在历史上就与中亚及南亚的许多民族在文化、经济上保持着密切的联系,因而塔里木盆地周边的佛教文化自然成为该地区古代民族文化的一个重要组成部分。虽然目前认为于阗是佛教传入我国的第一站,然关于其传入时间,目前说法不一,存在几种不同的观点。但我们依据于位于和田市以南玉龙喀什河西岸,距和田市 25 公里处之买力克阿瓦提遗址中发现的公元前 1 世纪前后的佛教遗址和佛教艺术品,其中有小立像、残座佛像、小佛头和残缺的佛身[⑤]等受到犍陀罗佛教艺术影响的文物和文献资料,认为"公元前后"之说,较符合新疆的历史实际。

佛教传入新疆后,由于得到当地统治阶层的支持,很快就取代原有的萨满教和袄教,成为当地居民信仰的第一宗教,同时也成为民族文化的重要组成部分,而且还形成了于阗、疏勒、龟兹、焉耆和高昌等佛教中心。佛教传入新疆后,其宗教思想经历了从小乘到大乘的转变过程。大约从公元 3 世纪开始,大乘佛教已在新疆不少地方流布,[⑥]并出现了于阗和高昌这两个中心。在于阗和高昌之间,则主要为小乘佛教流行的地区,龟兹与焉耆是其中的代表。

由于佛教在新疆的影响力非常大,因而除文献记载之外,遗留在地上和地下的佛教文物及艺术品也非常丰富,种类有佛教典籍、各类佛像、石窟、佛寺、壁画、佛塔、舍利盒等。譬如:19 世纪 90 年代,俄国驻喀什领事彼德罗夫(N·P·Peterovski)、法国的德兰(J·L·Dutreui de Rhins)等人先后在和田购得佉卢文犍陀罗语《法句经》残页,这是目前所知最早的于阗佛教经典。[⑦] 在于阗地区及敦煌发现的于阗语佛教

① 林梅村:《丝绸之路考古十五讲》,北京大学出版社,2006 年,第 295 页。

② 林梅村:《高昌火袄教遗迹考》,《文物》2006 年第 7 期。

③ 荣新江:《粟特袄教美术东传过程中的转化——从粟特到中国》,载巫鸿编《汉唐之间文化艺术的互动与交融》,文物出版社,2001 年,第 58 页。

④ 新疆发现的波斯萨珊朝银币有一千余枚,目前除少量收藏在吐鲁番博物馆、新疆金融研究所及钱币部分收藏者手中,980 余枚收藏在新疆博物馆。

⑤ 陈慧生:《佛教文化的东传》,《新疆宗教研究资料》第十七集,新疆社会科学院宗教研究所,1989 年。

⑥ 李泰遇主编《新疆宗教》,新疆人民出版社,1989 年,第 37、127 页。

⑦ 林梅村:《犍陀罗〈法句经〉的部派问题》,《新疆文献研究续集》,文物出版社,1989 年。

文献为数甚多,而且这里还发现有相当数量的梵文佛典残卷。① 另外,早期拜城克孜尔石窟,从形式、风格与壁画内容看,有可能在东汉晚期就已开始开凿。可认为,这是佛教在新疆盛兴时期的开始。从魏晋南北朝一直到唐代,是新疆佛教乃至佛教文化得以发展的黄金时期,因而反映这一时期佛教文化的遗物亦极为丰富。石窟寺、寺院和佛塔几乎遍布了天山以南地区,其中著名的有龟兹地区的克孜尔、库木吐拉、克孜尔尕哈、森姆塞木石窟、阿艾石窟与苏巴什佛寺遗址;喀什地区的脱库孜沙来佛寺和莫尔佛塔;于阗地区的热瓦克、买利克阿瓦提、丹丹乌里克、安迪尔、喀拉墩和达麻沟等佛寺;焉耆地区的七个星佛寺;吐鲁番地区的柏孜克里克、胜金口和吐峪沟石窟,及位于交河故城内的西北小寺等大量的地面佛教建筑;昌吉地区的北庭西大寺。同时出土的各类文物也很丰富,譬如:1959 年,自脱库孜沙来佛寺遗址出土有婆罗迷文和梵文佛经残片、泥塑大佛头;②20 世纪 90 年代还出土有浮雕说法图和陶制佛头;③在柯坪县发现了三件陶制彩绘舍利盒;④20 世纪初,在库车苏巴什佛寺遗址也发现过两件彩绘舍利盒,一件由法国人伯希和带走,另一件为木制,盒盖上绘有翼童子四人,分别执箜篌、琵琶、笛等乐器,现收藏在日本;1959 年,在焉耆七个星佛寺遗址发现一批公元 6 ~ 7 世纪的具有浓郁犍陀罗风格的泥塑供养人和菩萨像;⑤1959 年,在哈密脱米尔底佛寺遗址发现了"回鹘文《弥勒会见记剧本》"和回鹘文《十业道譬喻鬘经》;⑥1975 年,从焉耆七个星佛寺遗址还发现了"焉耆语《弥勒会见记剧本》"这一我国目前最早的佛教文学剧本;⑦在民丰尼雅 A35 建筑遗址发现 4 件木雕菩萨像;⑧从于阗县喀拉墩佛寺遗址出土一批以如来像、如来坐像、有翼天使为内容的壁画和如来坐像范;⑨和田地区皮山县杜瓦遗址出土有如来头部型范,在策勒县丹丹乌里克佛寺遗址发现与佛教有关的壁画和雕塑,洛浦县热瓦克佛寺发现了泥塑和彩绘菩萨雕像,策勒县老达麻沟发现如来铜坐像等。⑩

而吐鲁番地区既是丝绸之路的必经之地,同时也是西域佛教的另一个中心。北凉占领高昌,尤其是沮渠安周统治高昌时期,在这里大兴佛教,广建佛寺,为麴氏高昌时期(499 ~ 640)这里佛教势力的大盛奠定了基础。公元 5 世纪高昌国建立后,佛教信仰愈盛并达到一个高峰。他们广建佛寺,著名的吐峪沟、柏孜克里克千佛洞就是此时开凿的,并在唐西州时期在这里建造了"宁戎寺"。除此,在吐鲁番出土文书中的佛寺名称还有很多,主要有魏寺、史寺、冯寺、王寺、张寺等 40 余种。值得注意的是还有许多以少数民族姓氏命名的佛寺,譬如:有粟特人、龟兹人、鄯善人、天竺人和车师人的寺院。虽然,当时这里已开始转化为汉传佛教,从阿斯塔那-哈拉和卓晋唐墓葬、胜金口佛寺和安乐故城等地出土的佛经主要为汉文佛经,种类有《妙法莲华经》、《金光明经》、《大般涅槃经》、《法华经》等。⑪从所发现的遗物看,吐鲁番地区最早的佛教典籍,当属 20 世纪初日本大谷探险队自吐峪沟石窟获得的一批佛教文物,其中一件是支法护译的《诸佛要集经》抄本残页。该抄本题跋明确,此经由敦煌月支菩萨法护所译,且由其大弟子竺法于东晋元康六年(296)三月所抄。⑫而现存最早的遗迹为德国吐鲁番考察队在高昌古城发现的一座八面体基座

① 杨富学:《回鹘之佛教》,新疆人民出版社,1998 年,第 11 ~ 12 页。
②⑥⑦⑪ 实物现收藏在新疆维吾尔自治区博物馆。
③ 实物现收藏在喀什地区博物馆。
④ 坷坪县发现的陶舍利盒目前收藏在新疆维吾尔自治区博物馆,而木质舍利盒现收藏于日本东京国立博物馆。
⑤ 黄文弼:《新疆考古的发现》,《考古》1959 年第 2 期。
⑧⑨ 《シルクロード一絹と黄金の道》,2002 年,日本东京:实物现收藏在新疆文物考古研究所。
⑩ 实物现收藏在和田地区博物馆。
⑫ 贾应逸、祁小山:《印度到中国的佛教艺术》,甘肃人民出版社,2002 年。

的北凉石佛塔(现藏德国柏林印度艺术博物馆)。① 此外,吐鲁番地区还出土有回鹘文等其他文字的佛典以及相关的文物。

当然在上述地区发现的佛教文物并不仅仅是这些,还有许多于19世纪末20世纪初外国探险家在新疆进行的一系列探险活动中,从天山以南的各佛教遗址所获得的佛教文物,目前还流失在海外。譬如:德国探险队在新疆地区进行的四次考察活动中,从吐鲁番地区的高昌、交河故城遗址、胜金口、木头沟、吐峪沟佛寺遗址以及库鲁克塔格遗址、焉耆硕尔楚克、库木吐拉与森姆塞木石窟、苏巴什佛寺遗址和图木休克等处获得大量各类文物,其中就包括许多佛教文献。从已刊布的资料粗略统计,在德国国家图书馆所藏吐鲁番文书中,汉文佛典大约有4 414个号,主要有《大般涅槃经》、《妙法莲华经》、《佛顶尊胜陀罗尼经》、《大智度论》、《大般若波罗蜜多经》、《金光明经》、《金刚般若波罗蜜经》、《佛说观无量寿佛经》、《金光明最胜王经》、《大方广佛华严经》和《增一阿含经》等;回鹘语佛教文献大约有1 921个号,主要有《金光明最胜王经》、《维摩诘所说经》、《法华经》、《佛说十王经》、《地藏菩萨本愿经》、《慈悲道场忏法》、《十业道譬喻鬘经》、《大慈恩寺三藏法师传》、《观无量寿经》、《佛说天地八阳神咒经》、《阿烂弥王本生故事》和《阿弥陀经》等;汉文回鹘文双语佛经大约有2 224个号,主要有《妙法莲华经》、《大方广佛华严经》、《大般涅槃经》、《大乘起信论》、《佛说长阿含经》、《道行般若经》、《摩诃般若波罗蜜多经》、《法句经》、《大智度论》、《金光明最胜王经》、《大宝积经》、《贤劫经》和《中阿含经等》。德国国家图书馆所藏吐鲁番文书中原藏于Mainz科学院部分大约有汉文佛经39个号,主要为《大般涅槃经》、《妙法莲华经》、《文殊师利所说摩诃般若波罗蜜多经》、《中阿含经》、《佛说七俱胝佛母准提大明陀罗尼经》和《阿毗答摩俱舍论》等;回鹘文佛教文献大约498个号,主要为《金光明最胜王经》、《慈悲道场忏法》、《十业道譬喻鬘经》、《维摩诘所说经》、《佛陀传》、《佛本生故事》、《菩萨赞颂》、《阿烂弥王本生故事》、《妙法莲华经》、《药师琉璃光如来本愿功德经》和《佛说圣妙吉祥真实名经》等;婆罗迷文梵语和回鹘语佛经45个号,主要有《长阿含经》等;婆罗迷文回鹘语佛经18个号,主要为《瑜伽舍勒》和《舌头谏譬喻》等;粟特文佛经3个号,主要为《妙法莲华经》;吐蕃文回鹘语佛经6个号,主要为《佛说北斗七星延命经》和《佛说天地八阳神咒》等。德国国家图书馆所藏吐蕃语文献中有藏语佛经99个号,主要为《千手千眼观世音菩萨广大圆满无碍大悲心陀罗尼经》、《佛说出生一切如来法眼遍照大力明王经》和大乘佛经、佛教涅槃经典等;藏语汉语双语佛经6个号,主要为《大般涅槃经》和《妙法莲华经》。德国国家图书馆藏吐鲁番文献蒙文编号部分中存有回鹘文蒙经佛教文献大约52个号,主要为《普贤菩萨行愿赞》、《文殊所说最胜名义经》、《般若波罗碧多心经》、《正法华经》、《佛名经》和《妙法莲华经》等。德国印度艺术博物馆所藏吐鲁番文献中,汉语佛教文献大约有80个号,主要为《佛说摩诃般若波罗蜜经》、《佛说宝雨经》、《金刚般若波罗蜜多经》和《阎罗王授记四众预修生七往生净土经》等;回鹘文佛经大约有70个号,主要为《十王生七经》、《羚羊本生》等;汉语回鹘语双语佛教文献1个号,为《阿含经》难语解;汉文婆罗迷文佛经1个号,为《观自在菩萨如意轮念诵仪轨》;婆罗迷文回鹘语佛教文献约16个号;粟特语佛教文献7个号,主要为《阿烂弥王本生故事》等;西夏文佛典3个号,为版刻佛画残片和曼陀罗;藏语佛经1个号。现不知所在的德藏吐鲁番文献中存有汉文佛经2个号,为《大方广佛华严经》等;回鹘文佛经约存74个号,主要为《佛说天地八阳神咒经》、《具注历日》、《大乘无量寿经》、《大乘大般涅槃经》、《弥勒会见记》、《观无量寿经》、《十业道譬

---

① 林梅村:《丝绸之路考古十五讲》,北京大学出版社,2006年,第287页。

喻鬘经》、《维摩诘所说经》、《佛顶心大陀罗尼》和《妙法莲华经·观世音菩萨普门品》等;西夏文佛经 1 个号,为《瑜伽长者问经》。①

斯坦因在其第三次中亚考察时,在吐鲁番地区不仅发掘了阿斯塔那古墓,揭取了柏孜克里克石窟壁画,而且在大阿萨、小阿萨遗址、高昌古城、交河故城、木头沟、吐峪沟和丫头沟遗址均有许多收获,其中佛教文献占重要位置。据已刊布的资料看,从这些地方发现的汉文佛经大约有 312 个号,主要为《妙法莲华经》、《大般涅槃经》、《摩诃般若波罗蜜多经》、《大般若波罗蜜多经》、《大智度论》、《金刚般若波罗蜜经》、《灌顶经》、《四分比丘尼戒本》、《仁王经》和《悲华经》等;回鹘文佛经 3 个号;粟特文佛典 2 个号和藏语佛典 1 个号。②

在中亚探险与考察方面,俄国早在西方列强来华之前就已开始,并收集了许多文物和文献,而且多数收藏品来自吐鲁番地区。尤其是克列门兹、奥登堡和马洛夫等不仅在吐鲁番的高昌故城、交河故城、柏孜克里克、胜金口等遗址进行了发掘,而且还在焉耆七格星和库车的苏巴什、森木塞姆、克孜尔尕哈、库木吐拉等遗址进行了考察,获得了大量的文物和佛教文献。从已刊布的资料看,在俄罗斯圣彼得堡东方学研究所藏吐鲁番文献中大约有汉文佛教文献 458 个号,主要为《大方等无想大云经》、《大般涅槃经》、《妙法莲华经》、《耆婆五藏论》、《添品妙法莲华经》、《别译杂阿含经》、《大方广佛华严经》、《佛说如来不思议秘密大乘经》、《六度集经》和《金光明最胜王经》等;回鹘文佛经约 54 个号,主要有《佛说圣妙吉祥真实名经》、《佛说天地八阳神咒经》、《金光明最胜王经》、《佛说十力经》和《缘起圣道经》等,另外还有汉语回鹘语双语佛经约 64 个号。③此外,在土耳其伊斯坦布尔图书馆藏吐鲁番文书中存汉文佛经 39 个号,回鹘文佛经 26 个号,梵文佛经 11 个号;美国普林斯顿大学葛斯德图书馆藏吐鲁番文献中也有 1 个号的佛教文献。④

日本的大谷探险队先后三次来到新疆,不仅在吐鲁番等地进行了一系列的考察,而且还对阿斯塔那古墓葬进行了首次大规模的发掘,获得了大量各类文物和文献。从已刊布的资料粗略统计,譬如:在京都龙谷大学大宫图书馆藏大谷文书中有汉文佛教文献约 1 190 个号,主要有《俱舍论颂疏论本》、《解深密经》、《维摩义记》、《御注金刚般若波罗蜜经宣演》、《大方便佛报恩经》、《杂宝藏经》、《盂兰盆经赞述》、《灌顶经》、《无垢净光大陀罗尼经》和《佛说弥勒下生成佛经》等;回鹘文佛经约 93 个号,主要有《天地八阳神咒经》、《别译杂阿含经》、《阿弥陀经》、《维摩诘所说经》、《文殊师利成就法》、《功德赞》、《大乘无量寿经》、《阿毗达磨俱舍论》和《普贤行愿赞》等;粟特文佛典约 79 个号,主要有《大般涅槃经》、《法王经》和《金刚般若经》等;粟特文音译汉文佛典有 8 个号;吐蕃文梵语佛典 1 个号,为《法身舍利偈》;蒙文佛典为 2 个号。在京都龙谷大学橘瑞超藏书中有汉文佛经 6 个号,为《观无量寿经》、《菩萨梦经》、《金光明经》、《妙法莲华经》、《佛说佛名经》和《大般若经》;梵文佛典 2 个号,均为《白伞盖陀罗尼经》;西夏文佛经 1 个号,为《六祖坛经》;《流沙残阙》所收吐鲁番文书中存汉文佛经 2 个号,为《阿弥陀经》和《妙法莲华经》;回鹘文佛经 1 个号,为《须达拏本生话》;吐蕃文佛教文献残片 1 个号和吐蕃文梵语《法身舍利偈》;《西域考古图谱》所刊未收入大谷藏吐鲁番文书中约有汉文佛经 60 个号,主要为《道行般若经》、《鞞婆沙论》、《维摩诘经》、六朝写《正法华经》、六朝写《佛说咒神经》、六朝写《大智度论》、六朝写《四分律》、六朝

---

①②③④ 荣新江主编《吐鲁番文书总目》(欧美收藏卷),武汉大学出版社,2007 年。由于涉及的佛教文献较多,这里因篇幅所限,仅列举了其中一小部分,对此感兴趣者可参阅该书。

写《悲华经》、六朝写《大乘方便经》、《阿毗答磨大毗婆沙论》和《百喻经》等;回鹘文佛经约四十个号,主要为《天地八阳神咒经》等;西夏文佛典有 3 个号以及蒙古文佛典 1 个号,另有梵文佛典 1 个号。京都国立博物馆藏吐鲁番文书中存有 1 个号的佛教文献,为《优塞戒经》。京都大学文学部藏题"中村不折氏旧藏"回鹘文文书照片中 6 个号的回鹘文佛经,为《佛说天地八阳神咒经》、《父母恩重经》、《白伞盖陀罗尼经》和《慈悲道场忏法》等。东京书道博物馆藏吐鲁番文书中大约一百五十二个号的汉文佛经,主要为《弥勒上生经》、《妙法莲华经》、《摩诃般若波罗蜜经》、《譬喻经》、《维摩经义经》、《金光明经》、《佛说菩萨藏经》、《佛说欢普贤经》、《佛说老女人经》、《般若部论》和《法华经》等;回鹘文佛经 1 个号。东京静嘉堂文库藏吐鲁番文书中有汉文佛经大约六百一十个号,主要为《佛说大乘入诸佛境智光明庄严经》、《十住经》、《大般涅槃经》、《正法华经》、《佛说首楞严三味经》和《金刚仙论》等;回鹘文佛经有 6 个号,主要为回鹘文佛经残片。奈良天理大学图书馆藏吐鲁番文书中有 1 件《维摩诘经》卷下残片。大阪四天王寺出口常顺藏吐鲁番文书中有汉文佛经 120 个号,主要为《正法华经》、《菩萨善戒经》、《妙法莲华经》、《金光明经》、《十诵律》、《悲华经》、《道行般若经》、《首楞严三味经》、《阿毗昙八犍度论》、《佛说决罪福经》和《放光般若经》等;另有 1 个号的回鹘文佛经题记和粟特文佛典残片。三井八郎右卫门藏吐鲁番文书中有 1 件《华严经》残片。日本散见的吐鲁番文书中有 4 个号的回鹘文佛经,主要为《妙法莲华经·普门品》、《华严经》和《观无量寿经》断片。此外,在京都藤井有邻馆藏文书中也有 5 个号的汉文佛经,主要为《劝善经》、《佛顶尊胜陀罗尼经》、《受八开斋戒文》和《式叉摩那尼六法书》等。①

另外,旅顺博物馆在整理大谷文书时,整理出 24 132 片写经残片,其中 13 930 片在《大正藏》中查到了具体经文内容。经过整理研究初步确定这些佛经残片的内容是分别出自 502 部佛教经典。② 与此同时,2000～2005 年,吐鲁番地区文物局组织专业人员,对 1980 年 10 月～1981 年 7 月出土于吐鲁番柏孜克里克千佛洞的五百余件汉文佛经残片进行了定名。所出佛经就其内容而言,包括佛经的经、律、论、密等部分,其中既有大乘通论之宝积部,又有达成别祥道果之般若部、华严部、涅槃部,还有小乘共依之阿含部。有写本和印本,写本多属宋代以前,更早的有十六国以来的写本,较古老的写本,多集中于小乘经典的抄写;高昌王国以后,则多数是对大乘经典的传抄、供养,其中特别突出的是对《妙法莲华经》的传抄,多至百件以上。③ 经具体划分,在所发现的佛经中《法华经》为 120 片,其 117 片属《妙法莲华经》、《正法华经》2 片,《添品妙法莲华经》1 片。④

正如上文所论,在已刊布的资料中,有关佛教方面的文献非常丰富,所包含的文字种类与覆盖的地域都很广。据统计情况看,虽然有相当数量的佛教文献发现于吐鲁番地区的各古代文化遗存中,但自其他地区所获与佛教有关之文化遗存、文物和文献,亦表明了佛教乃至佛教文化在新疆地区的传播和影响程度。

可以说,佛教从公元前后传入新疆大地后,经过几个世纪的传布,在公元 3～9 世纪得到空前的发展

---

① 参阅陈国灿、刘安志主编《吐鲁番文书总目》(日本收藏卷),武汉大学出版社,2005 年。

② 刘广堂:《旅顺博物馆藏新疆出土汉文佛经写本综述》,收录于旅顺博物馆、龙谷大学共编《旅顺博物馆藏新疆出土佛经研究论集》,2006 年,第 1～28 页。

③ 新疆维吾尔自治区吐鲁番学研究院、武汉大学中国 3 至 9 世纪研究所编著《吐鲁番柏孜克里克石窟出土汉文佛教典籍》序言第 2 页,文物出版社,2007 年。

④ 汤士华:《浅谈吐鲁番地区新出土佛经中〈正法华经〉残片及整理情况》,收录于旅顺博物馆、龙谷大学共编《旅顺博物馆藏新疆出土佛经研究论集》第 263～269 页,2006 年。

和繁荣,并在天山以南各地一度创造了极为绚丽多彩的佛教文化,留下许多精美的文化艺术产品。以后因种种原因开始走向衰退,尤其是当伊斯兰教传入以后,佛教在新疆地区最终衰落,使得伊斯兰教在传统的佛教地区内兴盛起来。

三、道 教

道教是以"道"为最高信仰的中国古代特有的宗教,产生于东汉顺帝年间,即公元2世纪初。至迟到公元5世纪就传入了新疆,并进而传播到西方世界。虽然对于道教从什么时候开始正式传入新疆,因所获资料有限尚无法确定,但有一点是可以明确的,即:肯定是由于丝绸古道的开通与畅通,屯戍官兵与内地人民的到来是有着直接关系的。

依据现有的资料,在东晋末年,在高昌地区已有道教流传,这在吐鲁番出土文书中均有表现。譬如:1963年在吐鲁番阿斯塔那1号墓(63TAM1:11)出土的"西凉建初十四年(418)韩渠妻随葬衣物疏"中有:"时见,左清(青)龙,右白虎。书物数:前朱雀,后玄武,……要。急急如律令";①1975年从哈拉和卓墓地96号墓(75TKM96:17)出土的"北凉真兴七年(425)宋泮妻隗仪容随葬衣物疏"有:"辛关津河梁,不得留难,如律令"。②青龙、白虎、朱雀、玄武在我国出现很早,最初是用做方位,后来成为道教的护卫神祇。东晋葛洪《抱朴子》一书对此有较详尽的记述。而上述"随葬衣物疏"的发现,说明5世纪初道教确实在吐鲁番地区已开始传播。此外,在吐鲁番地区还出土过一些符咒残片、桃人木牌及各类祭神鬼的文书等。这些文书除内容颇具价值外,其文字还是珍贵的西域道教书法艺术品。除了吐鲁番,当时道教在和田地区也有传布。据《魏书·西域传》可知:"于阗西五百里云比摩寺,是老子化胡成佛之所",这里把一座寺院直接认为属道教圣地。这种传说的产生,至少说明道教在于阗地区是有影响力的。

南北朝以后是新疆道教的发展时期,因而属于这一时期的文物也极为丰富。譬如:1963年在吐鲁番阿斯塔那2号墓(63TAM2:1)出土的"北凉缘禾六年翟万年随葬衣物疏"中有"时见左清(青龙),右白虎,前朱雀,后玄武"③之记载。特别是1959年,在阿斯塔那303号墓(59TAM303:1/1)出土一件"高昌和平元年(551)符箓"。该符箓黄纸朱书,上端有一人像,其左手持刀,右手持叉,下端书符咒,开头为"天帝四神",结尾为"急急如律令"。④ 道教在早期曾盛行过授符制度,即对入道教者授以符箓。这件符箓的发现则表明此习俗也曾一度在高昌地区盛行。另外,20世纪90年代末,在和田布扎克墓地出土了一口彩绘青龙、白虎、朱雀、玄武图案的木棺,这则说明直到五代时期道教仍然在新疆南部存在着。

在新疆地区除发现大量与道教有关的文书等文物之外,还发现大量反映西域道教的绘画艺术品,尤以吐鲁番阿斯塔那—哈拉和卓墓地出土最多,其中最著名者为东晋时期的"墓主人生活图"和唐代的绢本与麻本"伏羲女娲图"。

有关道教的文献在流失海外的吐鲁番文书中也存有许多,且主要出土于高昌故城、交河故城、吐峪沟、木头沟。譬如:在德国国家图书馆藏吐鲁番文献中存有约二十三个号,主要为《道经》、《占死丧法》、

---

① ② 《吐鲁番出土文书》第一册第15、61页,文物出版社,1981年。
③ 《吐鲁番出土文书》第一册,文物出版社,1981年,第175页。
④ 《吐鲁番出土文书》第一册,文物出版社,1981年,第33页。

《解梦书》、《太上洞玄灵宝无量度人上品妙经》、《占卜书》、《周易》、《李老君周易十二钱卜法》、《易卦占》、《符咒》、《御注孝经疏·五刑章》和道教讲经文等文献。德国印度艺术博物馆藏吐鲁番文书中存 3 个号,为占卜书。现不知所在的德藏吐鲁番文书中有 1 个号,为回鹘语道教符箓。英国图书馆藏吐鲁番文献中存 3 个号的道家书。美国普林斯顿大学葛斯德图书馆吐鲁番文献有 7 个号,为随葬衣物疏和《孝经》。[①]京都龙谷大学大宫图书馆藏大谷文书中有大约四十七个号的道教文献,主要为《符箓》、《禄命书》、《推人游年八卦法》、《易占书》、《御注孝经》、《镇宅禳解符咒》、《辟邪论》、《道教符印》、《占卜书》、《太玄真一本际经》、《太上洞玄灵宝昇玄内教经》、《洞玄灵宝天尊说十戒经》、《孝经注》、《阴阳书》、《太上洞玄灵宝真文度人本行妙经》、《洞渊神咒经》、《太上洞玄灵宝自然九天生神章经》、《道德经序诀》和《老子·河上公本谦德》第六十一章残片等文献。东京书道博物馆藏吐鲁番文书有 1 件《道德经》残片。大阪四天王寺出口常顺藏吐鲁番文书中存 2 个号的道教文献,均为《占星书》。此外,京都藤井有邻馆藏文书中也有 1 件道教文书。[②]

　　唐以后新疆地区的道教势力虽然时有消长,但总体上趋于衰落。不论怎么讲,作为我国土生土长的一种宗教,从产生之时起就表现出宗教"杂家"的面貌,其中融会了许多其他宗教的文化成分,体现自身的包容性特点。

　　可以看出,道教在古代新疆的传播,由于是在一个比较特殊的地理、民族宗教和文化背景下展开的,因而"既没有中原道教那种独成一体、博大深远的道教文化,也没有形成如同西域佛教那种丰富多彩、富有民族地方特色的佛教文化"体系。[③]尽管如此,但从发现的大量道教文献看,新疆古代道教在中国宗教文化史中仍然具有十分重要的位置。

四、景　教

　　景教又称波斯经教、秦教和景教等,是我国唐代对基督教聂思脱利教派的称呼。此教约形成于公元 5 世纪上半叶,是由叙利亚人、时任君士坦丁堡大主教聂思脱利(Nestorius)创立。由于其学说遭到反对,本人被流放,信徒流亡到波斯。公元 6 世纪开始,势力在波斯得以扩大的聂思脱利教,开始传至中亚、印度和我国新疆地区。

　　虽然唐宋时期新疆的景教文化曾一度十分兴盛,但据考古发现物来看,其影响主要局限于吐鲁番地区。因而在高昌故城、葡萄沟废弃的寺址墙壁上和小桃沟(Qurutqa)均发现过许多有关景教的壁画,以及用叙利亚文、粟特文乃至回鹘文书写的景教文献。遗憾的是,这些珍贵的资料在 19 世纪末 20 世纪初,通过外国探险队已基本流失国外。

　　据已刊布的资料看,在德国国家图书馆藏吐鲁番文献中存有约十五个号的回鹘文景教文献,主要为《圣乔治受难记》等。德国印度艺术博物馆藏吐鲁番文献中存有 4 个号,为福音体文字基督教文献、叙利亚文基督教文献、粟特语景教文献和回鹘语《圣乔治受难记》。现不知所在的德藏吐鲁番文献中有 2 个号

---

① 参阅荣新江主编《吐鲁番文书总目》(欧美收藏卷),武汉大学出版社,2007 年。
② 参阅陈国灿、刘安志主编《吐鲁番文书总目》(日本收藏卷),武汉大学出版社,2005 年。
③ 李进新:《新疆宗教演变史》,新疆人民出版社,2003 年,第 171 页。

的回鹘语景教文献。俄罗斯圣彼得堡东方学研究所藏吐鲁番文献中有1个号的叙利亚景教文献。[1] 京都龙谷大学大宫图书馆藏大谷文书中有1个号的粟特文基督教文献残片。[2] 除了文献,20世纪初,德国吐鲁番考察队在高昌古城附近发现一所基督教寺院遗址,从中发掘出许多壁画和文书残片,其中除《基督进耶路撒冷》这幅名画外,还有一幅较完整的壁画残片描绘了一位正在向基督忏悔的青年女子形象。这些壁画形象生动地再现了1 000多年前基督教在高昌流行的历史风貌。这些艺术品全被运往德国,现存柏林印度艺术博物馆。[3]

唐代以后,景教在北方草原地区开始广为传播,其中在新疆伊犁地区就存在着景教的影响。据考古发掘资料来看,1960年,在位于霍城县东北10公里左右的阿力麻里故城采集到三块(其中两块现藏于新疆维吾尔自治区博物馆;D. 168号者完整、D. 169号者残缺),刻有十字架及叙利亚文的景教徒墓碑。[4]另外,伊犁州博物馆藏一块,霍城县博物馆现藏有1984、1989年发现的两块。[5] 这说明在14世纪中叶,有景教徒存在并在这里从事着传教活动。

虽然关于景教的考古发现非常有限,发现的地域主要以吐鲁番的葡萄沟景教寺院遗址、霍城县的阿力麻里故城遗址和部分文献为主,但依据现有的这些资料,我们仍然可以窥视该宗教在当地的传布情况,以及所产生的一些影响。尤其是发现的景教文献,无疑是研究我国新疆乃至亚洲地区景教历史不可多得的宝贵资料。

五、摩 尼 教

摩尼教在我国文献典籍中称之为明教、明尊教、明门或摩尼教。是公元3世纪中叶由波斯人摩尼(Mani)所创立,其教义的核心是明暗二元论。曾经是历史上一个世界性宗教,流行于中世纪一千余年间,后经丝绸之路传入我国新疆等地,使得塔里木盆地周边地区的摩尼教文化不仅成为中国摩尼教文化的一个有机组成部分,而且它还在整个摩尼教文化中占有了重要地位。从文献记载和考古发现来看,塔里木盆地周边地区摩尼教文化的产生与中亚粟特人有着密切的关联,可以认为粟特人在摩尼教文化的东传上,起到了极其重要的作用。当时粟特人主要是经丝绸之路的南道及中道到达天山以南地区的,因而除了楼兰地区以外,摩尼教还传入了于阗和高昌。以吐鲁番地区而言,要远早于回鹘人的到来,这与大批粟特人的到来是有关的。而到了以高昌为中心的西州回鹘王国时期,即公元10世纪时,由于摩尼教文化得以发展,故而这里曾一度盛行摩尼教。

摩尼教与其他宗教不同,并没有流传到现在,因而在世界范围内也没有摩尼教信徒,但这不表示这一在中世纪颇有影响之宗教的不存在。而探险活动和考古发现则揭开了这个面纱,开始让世人重新认识和了解该宗教。

摩尼教寺院遗址和文献资料的再发现,是20世纪初的事情。德国探险队在新疆考察之际,在吐鲁番

① 参阅荣新江主编《吐鲁番文书总目》(欧美收藏卷),武汉大学出版社,2007年。
② 参阅陈国灿、刘安志主编《吐鲁番文书总目》(日本收藏卷),武汉大学出版社,2005年。
③ 林梅村:《丝绸之路考古十五讲》,北京大学出版社,2006年,第297~298页。
④ 黄文弼:《新疆考古发现》,《考古》1959年第2期。
⑤ 王林山主编《伊犁哈萨克自治州文物古迹之旅·草原 天马 游牧人》图11(从新博调拨),伊犁人民出版社,2008年,第121页(图8者藏于新疆维吾尔自治区博物馆,登记号为D. 168)。

的高昌故城、柏孜克里克千佛洞等遗址中,首先发现了摩尼教寺院、洞窟和壁画。尤其是 V. 勒克柯发掘高昌 K 寺,判定其为摩尼教高昌回鹘王室寺院,内见大量摩尼教经典、一幅大型壁画。画面中如真人大小、身着摩尼教祭祀服饰的长者为男女信徒环绕,信徒前胸都用粟特文写出各自的波斯语名。勒克柯认为长者为摩尼本人的图像。其他还有绢画、摩尼教女选民麻布画及精美之摩尼教经典插图。插图说明文字为回鹘文、粟特文,标明一些图像为回鹘王、王妃像。另外"a"遗址,也发现摩尼教选民壁画、男女选民绢画,一幅回鹘王及王室祈祷的文字。除了这些,德国探险队在吐鲁番获取的摩尼教文献残片达数千件之多,其中有摩尼教的忏悔文、赞美诗以及摩尼的重要著作《沙卜拉干》等,从而开始了摩尼教研究的新纪元。1960 年,英国伦敦大学的玛丽·博伊斯教授出版了她所编辑的《德国收藏的吐鲁番伊朗文摩尼教手抄文献目录》,公布了德国吐鲁番摩尼教文献收藏概况。[①]

在新疆地区也随着考古发掘与调查工作的不断深入,与摩尼教有关的壁画、洞窟和文献也在陆续被发现。其中,柏孜克里克千佛洞 38 号窟是高昌地区现存内容最为丰富、保存最完好的一个摩尼教洞窟。[②] 1980 年,在柏孜克里克千佛洞发现回鹘文摩尼教《三王子故事》,编号为 80T. B. I—1、2、3、4、5)和粟特文摩尼教写经;[③]而 1981 年,自柏孜克里克千佛洞 65 号窟(当时编为 21 号窟)发现了 8 件摩尼教文献,其中三件是用粟特文写的,[④]另外五件为回鹘文。编号为 81TB65:1 的粟特文摩尼教写经,是由九张纸粘连而成的长卷,高 26 cm、长 268 cm,村墨书粟特文 135 行,在接缝处和低行书写的地方钤有朱色印鉴;中间是一幅工笔重彩的彩绘插图,有一行金字标题。[⑤] 这是一件摩尼教信徒来往信札,是研究摩尼教的重要资料之一。

虽然新中国成立后,随着文物考古工作的不断深入,在新疆的吐鲁番等地在陆续发现着与摩尼教有关的文化遗存和文献资料,但由于大批摩尼教文献在早年已流失海外,故有必要给予说明。从已刊布的资料来看,在德国收藏的摩尼教文献比较多,这些文献基本出土于吐鲁番地区的柏孜克里克、吐峪沟、高昌故城、交河故城、木头沟、胜金口等遗址。譬如:德国国家图书馆藏吐鲁番文献中汉语回鹘语文献中存 5 个号,主要为摩尼教发愿文、赞美诗和《惠明布道书》;回鹘语汉语摩尼教文献约 27 个号,主要为回鹘语《摩尼教君主赞颂文》、《摩尼教徒忏悔词》、《赞美诗》、《摩尼教天体学说文献》、《为国王慕阇祈祷文》、《摩尼教书信》、《惠明布道书》、《致摩尼教主书信草稿》、《摩尼教归国王颂词》、《新年为王家祈祷文》、《新年祈祷文》、《君主赞美诗》、《戒律文献》、《摩尼教教史文献》和回鹘语摩尼教发愿文等;汉语粟特语摩尼教文献为 11 个号,主要为粟特语摩尼教叙事文献、神祇名录、譬喻文书和《惠明布道书》等;回鹘语摩尼教文献约 204 个号,主要为摩尼教历史文献、传说故事、《摩尼教忏悔词》、《月神赞美诗》、天体学说文献、《新年为牟羽可汗祈祷文》、《摩尼教赞美诗》、末世学说文献、《二宗经》、早期传教史文献、《惠明布道书》、摩尼教《佛陀传》、布道书、《光明王国布道书》、《圣餐赞美诗》、《为选民施舍赞美诗》、《国王与术士》、《胡威达曼》、《牟羽可汗入教记》、《巨人传》和《沙卜拉干》等;粟特语摩尼教文献存 1 个号;突厥卢尼文摩尼教文献有 2 个号;突厥卢尼文回鹘语摩尼教文献 9 个号,为摩尼教故事与文献;摩尼文摩尼教文

① 柳洪亮主编《吐鲁番新出摩尼教文献研究》前言,文物出版社,2000 年,第 2 页。
② 柳洪亮主编《吐鲁番新出摩尼教文献研究》前言,文物出版社,2000 年,第 238 页。
③ 实物现存吐鲁番地区博物馆。
④ 吐鲁番地区文管所:《柏孜克里克千佛洞遗址清理简记》,《文物》1985 年第 8 期。
⑤ 柳洪亮主编《吐鲁番新出摩尼教文献研究》前言,文物出版社,2000 年。

献约 100 个号,主要为《回鹘王(? Bügü Bilge Khan)颂词》、《摩尼教忏悔词》、赞美诗、天体学说、《为王家与听者祈祷文》、《为王国与寺院祈祷文》和《二宗经》等;粟特回鹘语摩尼教文献为 1 个号;婆罗迷文回鹘语和龟兹语摩尼教文献 9 个号;回鹘文帕提亚语摩尼教文献 1 个号,为《初声赞夷数文》。部分原藏于 Mainz 科学院的德国国家图书馆藏吐鲁番文献中约有三十九个号的回鹘语摩尼教文献,主要为布道书、赞美诗、《盗贼寓言》、《巨人传》、天体学说、忏悔词、杂写、题记、故事、历史文献和回鹘王颂词等;突厥卢尼文回鹘语摩尼教文献约 15 个号,为摩尼教故事和文献等;突厥卢尼文中古波斯语与回鹘语摩尼教文献为 2 个号;中古波斯语摩尼教占卜书 1 个号。德国印度艺术博物馆藏吐鲁番文献中亦存有一批摩尼教文献,其中突厥卢尼文—摩尼文回鹘语摩尼教文献 1 个号,为摩尼教词汇对照表;突厥卢尼文中古波斯语与回鹘语摩尼教文献 1 个号,为赞美诗;摩尼文中古波斯语摩尼教文献 14 个号,主要为《为回鹘王家祈愿文》等;中古波斯语—帕提亚语摩尼教文献 2 个号;粟特文摩尼教文献 11 个号,主要为《胡威达曼》和赞美诗等;帕提亚语摩尼教文献 3 个号;摩尼文帕提亚语摩尼教文献 2 个号;摩尼文回鹘语摩尼教文献 5 个号,主要为《摩尼大赞美诗》和《摩尼教徒忏悔词》等;回鹘语摩尼教文献 9 个号,主要为雨石文书等;摩尼文摩尼教文献 3 个号,为供养人题记等;摩尼文粟特语摩尼教文献为 2 个号;摩尼文中古伊朗语摩尼教文献 2 个号,为《为回鹘王家祈愿文》等;摩尼文帕提亚语与中古波斯语摩尼教文献为 1 个号;粟特文回鹘语摩尼教文献为 1 个号;中古伊朗语摩尼教文献 2 个号;摩尼文帕提亚语与回鹘语摩尼教文献为 1 个号;此外,还有摩尼教壁画与题记。在现不知所在的德藏吐鲁番文书中有约 45 个号的回鹘语摩尼教文献,主要为《为国王慕阇祈祷文》、《具注历目》、《就职赞美诗》、《二宗经》、布道书、天体学说和譬喻文书等;摩尼文回鹘语摩尼教文献约 15 个号,主要为布道、《为回鹘国王祈愿文》、传说故事、天体学说和赞美诗等;粟特语摩尼教文献 1 个号,为譬喻文书;突厥卢尼文回鹘语摩尼教文献 3 个号;摩尼文摩尼教文献为 1 个号。在英国图书馆藏吐鲁番文书中有 2 个号的突厥卢尼文摩尼教文献和 1 个号的摩尼文摩尼教文献。[①]京都龙谷大学大宫图书馆藏大谷文书有约 94 个号的粟特文摩尼教文献,主要为《光明智慧布道书》、赞美诗、忏悔文、书信、文献题记、摩尼教徒字母起首词汇表、教会史、《巨人书》、摩尼教徒使用的国名表残片、故事和摩尼教徒使用的词汇表等;摩尼文帕提亚语文献约 64 个号,主要为赞美诗等;粟特语转写帕提亚语摩尼教文献 3 个号;摩尼文摩尼教文献约 6 个号;古突厥语摩尼教文献 1 个号;摩尼文中古波斯语摩尼教文献约 27 个号,主要为赞美诗等;摩尼文粟特语文献 14 个号;粟特文音译中古波斯语摩尼教文献 1 个号;粟特语音译西伊朗语摩尼教文献 1 个号;此外,还有 1 个号为摩尼文中古波斯语与帕提亚语摩尼教文献。另外,在京都龙谷大学橘瑞超藏书中有 2 个号的摩尼教文献,京都大学文学部藏吐鲁番文书中有 1 个号为回鹘文摩尼教文献。[②]

　　总之,自摩尼教寺院、洞窟、壁画和文献在吐鲁番陆续发现以来,这里作为东方摩尼教团活动的中心,受到学者们的极大关注。同时,对摩尼教遗迹的寻觅以及整理研究,也引起了学术界的普遍重视。目前虽然有许多问题还未能得以解决,但种种迹象表明,佛教的衰落为摩尼教在高昌地区的兴起提供了良好的时机,因而摩尼教在新疆乃至吐鲁番盆地的发展期当在高昌回鹘前期,即 9 ~ 10 世纪。

---

① 参阅荣新江主编《吐鲁番文书总目》(欧美收藏卷),武汉大学出版社,2007 年。
② 参阅陈国灿、刘安志主编《吐鲁番文书总目》(日本收藏卷),武汉大学出版社,2005 年。

六、伊 斯 兰 教

伊斯兰教起源于阿拉伯半岛,是穆罕默德于公元7世纪初创立的一种宗教。在我国史籍中有"大食法"、"大食教"、"天方教"、"穆罕默德教"、"回教"、"回回教"、"清真教"等许多种称谓。伊斯兰教产生后不久,就由海路首先传入我国内地。9世纪末至10世纪初,又由陆路经中亚传入我国新疆地区。①

由于喀拉汗朝的统治者萨图克·布格拉汗首先改宗伊斯兰教,并强行在汗国境内推行,故使传布范围扩大。虽然喀拉汗朝统治者以武力进行了推行,但遭到佛教徒强烈反对,一度与信奉佛教的高昌回鹘王国和于阗王国形成对峙。因而伊斯兰教传入新疆后,在三百多年时间里,基本局限于且末和拜城以西,即喀什与阿图什周围地区,直到13世纪才传入天山以北地区。在新疆地区得到大力推广则在察合台汗国时期,尤其从秃黑鲁·帖木尔开始,不仅使16万蒙古人皈依了伊斯兰教,而且他还向各地派出传教士进行推广。其继任者黑的儿火者更是一位狂热的伊斯兰教推行者,他执政后通过一系列征战,到15世纪末,使具有悠久历史和灿烂佛教文化的吐鲁番地区也伊斯兰化了。哈密是新疆信仰伊斯兰教最晚的地区,虽然15世纪以前,伊斯兰教已传入这里,但直到16世纪初才取得优势。可以说,伊斯兰教自公元10世纪初传入喀什,经过六个多世纪的发展,终于在全疆取代佛教,成为在新疆占统治地位的宗教,而且直到目前,生活在这里的维吾尔、哈萨克、回、柯尔克孜、塔吉克、乌兹别克、塔塔尔等民族仍在信奉。

就喀拉汗朝而言,随着伊斯兰教被奉为国教,伊斯兰文化完全取代佛教文化,广泛地渗透到了人们的精神生活和社会生活之中。使得当地居民在语言文字、文化艺术、工艺美术与建筑风格等方面均发生了巨大的变化,因而也遗留下来许多具有浓郁伊斯兰风格的文化遗产,譬如:建筑有萨图克·布格拉汗麻扎、马赫穆德·喀什噶尔麻扎、玉素甫·哈斯哈吉甫麻扎、莎车县的阿勒通麻扎、库车大寺、额敏和卓纪功塔(亦称苏公塔)、哈密回王陵、秃黑鲁·帖木尔麻扎、苏里坦·歪思汗麻扎、阿帕克和卓麻扎和艾提尕尔清真寺等等。当然,还有许多生活器皿与工艺美术品以及文学作品等,譬如:有《突厥语大词典》、《福乐智慧》等。

出土和传世的各类文物、古籍中有许多亦带有很深的伊斯兰文化风格与特色。因为伊斯兰教传入新疆后,生活在新疆地区的维吾尔等民族在接受伊斯兰教的同时,也一度接受并使用阿拉伯语及其文字,来书写了自己的历史与文化。因而,截至目前所发现的喀拉汗王朝时期的公函、文件、信札、契约等中就有以阿拉伯语、回鹘文突厥语或用阿拉伯文拼写突厥语完成的文献。譬如:1959年,从巴楚县脱库孜沙来故城遗址出土了一批阿拉伯文文书和一件哈卡尼亚文《请伯克赐财物书》。② 当然,属于这一时期的文献有很多,其中英国驻喀什总领事马继业从和田获得的阿拉伯文与回鹘文文书及20世纪初在莎车县郊外某花园树下发现的,以阿拉伯文阿拉伯语书写的文书及来自阿拉伯文的哈卡尼亚文文献,均流散国外。③ 除了在文字上对操突厥语民族产生巨大影响之外,工艺美术等方面的影响也很大。除了文献,从出土与传世的钱币、铜器、玉器等看,此时的风格与特点同先前的已迥然不同,可以说完全表现了另一种文化风

---

① 李泰遇:《新疆宗教》,新疆人民出版社,1989年,第127页。

② 实物现收藏在新疆维吾尔自治区博物馆。

③ 关于哈卡尼亚文(喀拉汗朝文献)的具体情况,请参阅伊斯拉菲尔·玉素甫、安尼瓦尔·哈斯木《新疆发现的古文字》,《新疆丝路考古珍品》,上海译文出版社,1998年,第21~30页。

格,其最大的特点是：不论是发现量最大的钱币,还是铜器与玉器,上面除铭刻有铸造者或制造者的名号、回历纪年外,基本都铭刻或錾刻有"经文",这应该说是伊斯兰文化的最大影响之一。

总之,步入伊斯兰化时代以后,新疆地区操突厥语的诸民族在许多方面均有很大的变化,其中在意识形态与文字、文化艺术等方面的变化为最大。而且这种影响直到目前仍然在维吾尔等信仰伊斯兰教的民族的精神生活中,占据着主要的位置。

概而言之,新疆自古以来就是一个多民族聚居的地区,而且现在仍然是一个多民族聚居的地区。历史上生活在新疆的各民族曾经信奉过多种宗教,现在的各民族仍然信奉着多种宗教。其中,除上述的这些宗教之外,还有藏传佛教(喇嘛教)、天主教、东正教等,有关这些宗教的文化遗产保留的也不少。正由于新疆地区这种得天独厚的地理优势和自然条件,导致各个民族、各种文化,尤其是各种宗教文化在这里交融荟萃,构筑了丰富多彩的新疆宗教文化,使其成为西域历史文化的重要组成部分,而且通过自身的特点演绎着西域古老文明的无穷魅力。

再探石窟用途

山部能宜

日本东京农业大学

一、吐峪沟和敦煌石窟

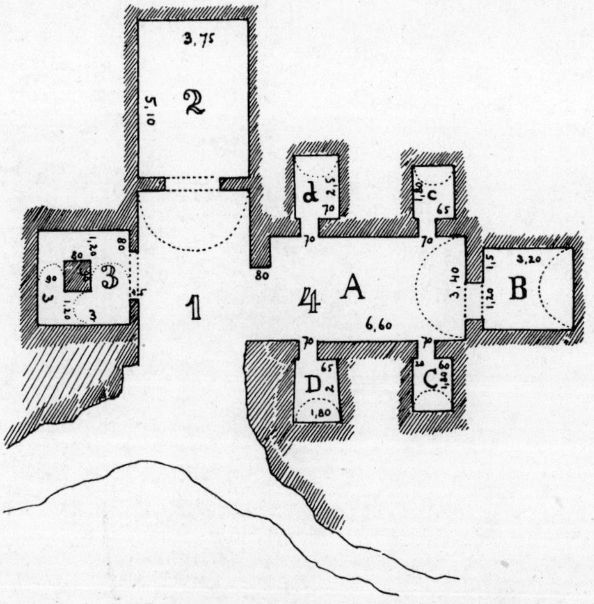

图一 "苦修者洞"（吐峪沟第 41 ~ 42 窟）。Albert Grünwedel, *Altbuddhistische Kultstätten in Chinesisch-Turkistan*, Berlin: Georg Reimer, 1912, p. 327, Fig. 658.

在中亚的佛教石窟遗址里,有一些带有几个小侧室的石窟。石窟学者们一般认为其为"禅窟"。① 图一显示吐峪沟第 42 窟（右侧;公元 6 世纪?）。② 根据禅观僧的壁画和石窟的结构,我曾在几篇论文中论证了这个石窟和观想有密切的关系。③ 我现在仍相信我的这种主张是正确的。

敦煌也有类似的石窟,所以在这篇论文中首先考察这些石窟。图二是莫高窟现存最古的石窟之一第 268 窟（5 世纪）的平面图。左右的甬道是后代的,现在被塞住了。虽然莫高第 268 窟比吐峪沟第 42 窟小得多,但基本的结构很相像。④ 然而,对莫高第 268 窟我有以下一些疑问。

第一,侧室的面积。吐峪沟第 42 窟侧室的面积大约是 1.8 × 2 m,因而这些侧室为了一个人的

---

① 马世长:《新疆石窟中的汉风洞窟和壁画》,《中国美术全集绘画编 16 新疆石窟壁画》,文物出版社,1989 年,第 47 页;贾应逸、祁小山:《印度到中国新疆的佛教艺术》,甘肃教育出版社,2002 年,第 418 ~ 419 页。

② 根据霍旭初交给的碳 14 测定的资料,宁强说吐峪沟第 20 窟的年代是公元 585 年。Ning Qiang, Visualization Practice and the Function of the Western Paradise Images in Turfan and Dunhuang in the Sixth to Seventh Centuries, *Journal of Inner Asian Art and Archaeology*, 2, 2007, 134 + n. 8. 也见《印度到中国新疆的佛教艺术》,第 433 ~ 434 页。

③ Nobuyoshi Yamabe, An Examination of the Mural Paintings of Toyok Cave 20 in Conjunction with the Origin of the *Amitayus Visualization Sutra*, *Orientations* 30(4), 1999, pp. 38 – 44; Practice of Visualization and the *Visualization Sūtra*: An Examination of Mural Paintings at Toyok, Turfan, *Pacific World: Journal of the Institute of Buddhist Studies* 3rd ser., 4, 2002, pp. 123 – 152; An Examination of the Mural Paintings of Visualizing Monks in Toyok Cave 42: In Conjunction with the Origin of Some Chinese Texts on Meditation, in *Turfan Revisited: The First Century of Research into the Arts and Cultures of the Silk Road*, ed. Desmond Durkin-Meisterernst, et al., Berlin: Dietrich Reimer, 2004, pp. 401 – 407.

④ 在吐峪沟第 42 窟和莫高第 268 窟内有相似的夜叉和飞天。所以,这两个洞窟似乎有关系。

· 784 ·

修行是够大的。然而,莫高第268窟的侧
室面积仅仅是1×1 m。我参观这个石窟
的时候,感到这些侧室为了长期的修行则
显得太小。

第二,侧室的门楣。在这个石窟里,
主尊的龛有火焰状的龛楣。这里没有问
题,问题是侧室的入口也有类似的门楣
(图三)。让我们想想看,当时的比丘们
会在佛龛一样的侧室里修行吗?虽然不
能说这是完全不可能的,可是却有一些不
自然,因为我在中国和日本看过很多朴素
的禅堂。

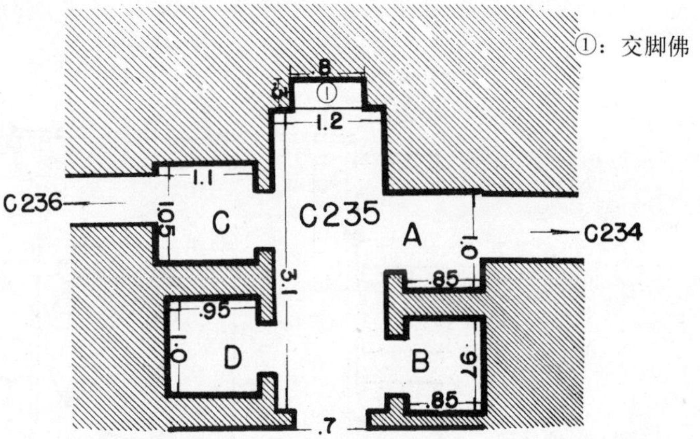

①:交脚佛

图二　莫高第268窟平面图。石璋如:《莫高窟形(二)窟图暨
附录》,中研院历史语言研究所,1996年,第152页,图
196(部分)。

莫高第285窟(6世纪)也有类似的结构,所以学者们一般认为这个石窟也是禅窟(图四)。正壁有三
个龛:一个有佛像,两个有禅定僧像。左右的侧壁一共有八个侧室(图五)。①

这里的侧室也比较小,所以不敢肯定这些侧室是为了禅定实用的。更重要的是佛龛(图六)、禅定僧
龛(图七)和侧室(图八)都有类似的楣。这两个禅定僧有圆光,可能是阿罗汉。也许他们是佛的大
弟子。

图三　莫高第268窟内景。敦煌研究院:《敦煌石窟全集22石窟建筑卷》,商务印书馆,2003年,第46页,图21。

---

① 这里也有夜叉,在此观察莫高第285窟和吐峪沟第42窟的关系。

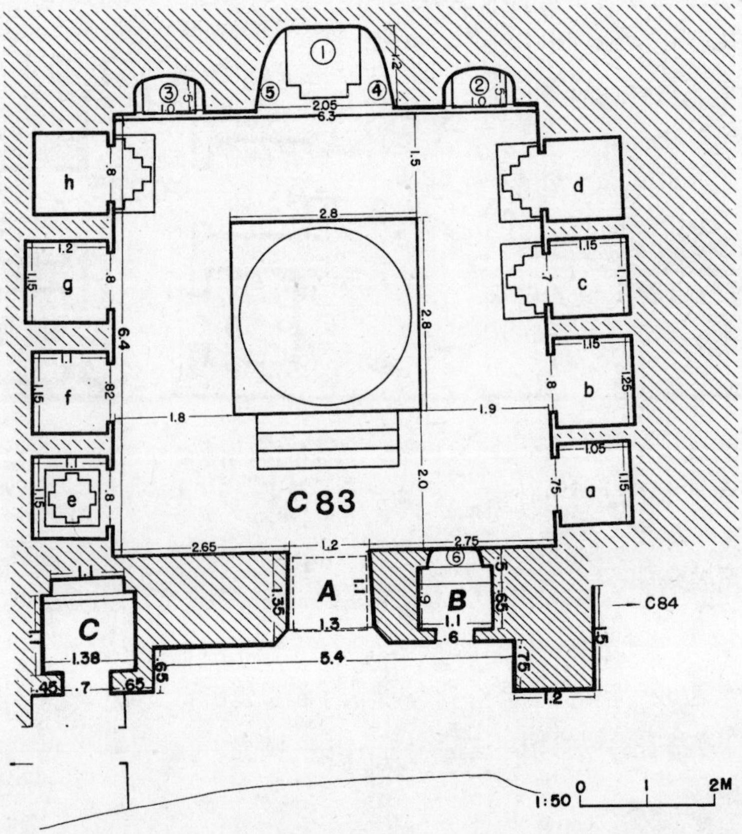

图四　莫高第 285 窟平面图。《莫高窟形 (二)》,第 71 页,图 70 (部分)。

图五　莫高第 285 窟内景。《石窟建筑卷》,第 47 页,图 22。

如果这样的话，他们的龛有与佛龛类似的楣是不奇怪的。令人惊讶的是比丘们应该为修行而用的侧室也有类似的楣。佛龛的楣是最讲究的，禅定僧龛的简朴一些，侧室的最简单。所以，好像有一种等级。然而，一般的比丘们在这种地方日常修行则是不自然的。如果这些侧室事实上是为了禅定用，那应该只是高位的和尚们在某种仪式上使用。在莫高第259窟（5世纪）①里，佛像在侧壁上的龛内坐着（图九）。要是比丘们实际上在第285窟的侧室里坐禅，那就是他们替这些佛坐。

另外一个问题是这个石窟太华丽，好像不适合禅定修行（图五）。执行仪式的地方有华丽的装饰是很自然的，②但如果修行的地方有太多的装饰，那对集中自己内心则没有帮助。还有值得注意的一点是，禅经说观察佛像以后，修行者应回他自己的地方去修禅观。《坐禅三昧经》

图六　莫高第285窟佛龛。《石窟建筑卷》，第49页，图24（部分）。

图七　莫高第285窟禅定僧龛。《石窟建筑卷》，第48页，图23。

图八　莫高第285窟侧龛。敦煌文物研究所：《中国石窟敦煌莫高窟一》，平凡社，1980年，图130（部分）。

———————————

① 樊锦诗、马世长、关友惠：《敦煌莫高窟北朝洞窟的分期》，《中国石窟：敦煌莫高窟》，文物出版社，1982年，第188～191页。

② 在莫高第285窟主室的中央有一个坛。东山健吾说这个可能是戒坛（《敦煌三大石窟》，讲谈社，1996年，第83页）。对这个主张他没有提出具体的理由，所以不能判断其是否正确。可是，我认为这个石窟很可能是为了某种仪式用的。

图九　莫高第 259 窟内景。《石窟建筑卷》,第 70 页,图 42。

说:"若初习行人,将至佛像所,或教令自往谛观佛像相好。相相明了。一心取持还至静处,心眼观佛像。"①《五门禅经要用法》说:"若观佛时当至心观佛相好。了了分明谛了已。然后闭目忆念在心。若不明了者。还开目视极心明了。然后还坐正身正意系念在前。如对真佛明了无异。即从座起跪白师言。我房中系念见佛无异。师言。汝还本坐。"②所以佛像不必在禅窟里。

更令人产生疑问的是,敦煌莫高窟北区也有好几个有类似结构的窟。北区一般被认为是比丘们住的地方。图十是此种石窟的一例(B132)。③ 这里没有装饰,禁欲的气氛对修行很合适(图十一)。这些侧室的面积大约是 2.4×2.4 m,④为了方便睡觉。所以,这个石床可能是为就寝用的。⑤ 在日本,禅僧们睡觉的床也用来修禅定。所以,在这侧室里的床上坐禅是完全可能的。我推测他们可能在南区的礼拜窟里观察佛像,然后回到在北区自己的禅房里观想。⑥

还必须注意到,在北区这种石窟很多,可是在南区的只有三个窟⑦(第 268,285,487⑧)。而在莫高窟应该有许多比丘,⑨为了普通的比丘们的日常修行,只有三个石窟应该是完全不够的。

---

① 大正藏 15:276a9 - 12。

② 大正藏 15:325c18 - 23。

③ "仅据现有资料无法直接判断石窟的开凿年代。据窟形分析,这种多室窟的年代应较早,可早到北朝。"敦煌研究院:《敦煌莫高窟北区石窟二》,文物出版社,2004 年,第 211 页。

④ 同上,第 202 ~ 211 页。

⑤ 甬道连接 B132 窟和 B133 - 136 窟。B133 窟前室有烟道。这些石窟确实是生活的地方。同上,第 212 页 + 图 86。

⑥ 北区也有几个有壁画的窟。在这些窟里观想也是可能的。见敦煌研究院《敦煌石窟全集 22 石窟建筑卷》,商务印书馆,2003 年,第 44 页。

⑦ 赵声良:《敦煌北朝石窟形制诸问题》,《敦煌研究》2006(5),第 2 页。

⑧ 第 487 窟是北魏代的。壁画、塑像都没有了。中央有方形低坛。见《敦煌三大石窟》,第 83 页;《敦煌北朝石窟形制诸问题》,第 2 页;茂木计一郎:《窟構造について》,《敦煌石窟学术调查(第一次)报告书》,东京艺术大学美术学部敦煌学术调查团,1985 年,第 10 页。

⑨ 根据藤枝晃的研究,菊池英夫认为 9 ~ 10 世纪敦煌所有的僧尼总数大概一千人左右。见菊池英夫《唐代敦煌社会的外貌》,《講座敦煌と敦煌の社会》,大东出版社,1980 年,第 104 页。

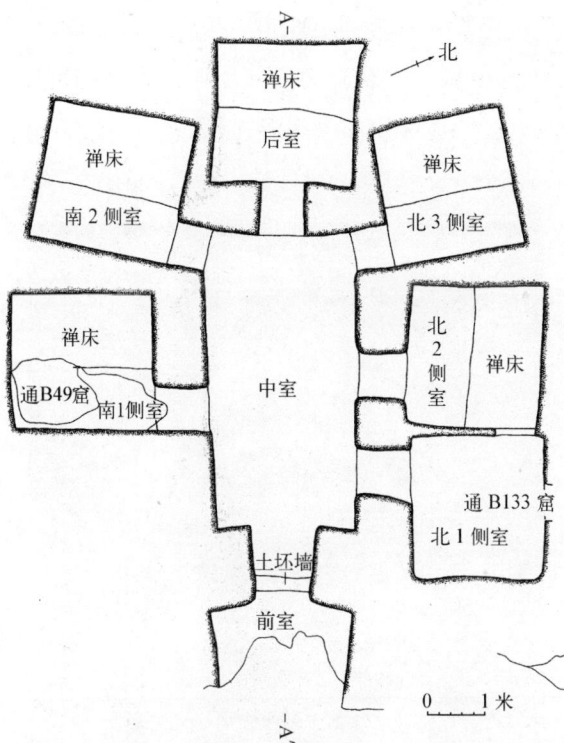

图十　莫高窟北区 B132 窟平面图。敦煌研究院：《敦煌莫高窟北区石窟二》，文物出版社，2004年，第199页，图106（部分）。

图十一　莫高窟北区 B132 窟南1侧室南壁。《敦煌莫高窟北区石窟二》，图版100（C）1。

这些问题让人怀疑莫高第 268 窟和第 285 窟是否是为了禅观用的。冲本克已指出莫高第 285 窟的侧室很像北区叫做"坐亡窟"或"坐化窟"的小窟和南区的"供养窟"。所以，他主张南区第 285 窟的侧室也是坐亡窟或供养去世高僧的窟。[①] 赵声良认为这些侧室是象征性或是仪式性的禅室，[②] 因为"在中亚和敦煌石窟中，除了夏天较短的时间外，一年中倒有相当长的时间处于寒冷时期，在这样的条件下，在仅能容身的矮小禅室中修行，真正是一种苦修"。[③] 他们的意见值得认真考虑。

二、印度的僧房窟

学者们一般认为中亚的禅窟渊源于印度的僧房窟。[④] 印度的石窟寺院一般有两种石窟：塔庙窟和僧房窟。塔庙窟是深处有塔的比较大的石窟，这种石窟是为了礼拜用的；僧房窟一般是由中央的大厅和周围的几个小房构成的。小房里一般有一个或两个石床，显然是比丘们住的地方。

值得注意的是，印度最初期的石窟一般是模仿木制结构。图十二是在巴拉巴尔（Barābar）山，邪命外道（Ājīvika）的洛玛斯·里希（Lomas Ṛṣi）窟正面（印度现存最古的石窟之一；公元前 3 世纪）。门口上的

① 冲本克已：《敦煌莫高窟北区石窟之课题》，《2004 年石窟研究国际学术会议论文集》，上海古籍出版社，2006 年，第 433 页。
② 《敦煌北朝石窟形制诸问题》，第 2 页。
③ 同上，第 5 页。
④ 萧默：《敦煌建筑研究》，文物出版社，1989 年，第 42 页；《石窟建筑卷》，第 43～45 页；《敦煌北朝石窟形制诸问题》，第 2 页；《窟构造について》，第 11 页。

装饰有仿木椽头，如实模仿木造堂的正面。① 这种仿木结构的门楣在佛教的石窟也是很一般的装饰。图十三是巴伽（Bhājā）第 12 窟的正面（公元前 2 世纪～公元 1 世纪）。这石窟的顶部现在还有木制结构。外部的石椽头模仿内部的木椽头是明确的。图十四是纳西克（Nāsik）第 18 窟的正面（公元 1 世纪）。这个塔庙窟的门口和明窗都有大马蹄样的楣。

图十二　洛玛斯、里希窟正面。《世界美术大全集インド（1）》，小学馆，2000 年，图版 179。

图十三　巴伽第 12 窟正面。《世界美术大全集》，图版 180（部分）。

图十四　纳西克第 18 窟正面。《世界美术大全集》，图版 195（部分）。

在僧房窟，这种楣在各个小房的入口处很常见。例如，图十五是阿旃陀（Ajantā）第 12 窟的内部（公元前 1 世纪）。② 莫高窟的龛楣明显源于这些仿木的门楣。③

另外一个需要注意的是，早期（公元前 2 世纪～公元 2 世纪）僧房窟的结构很简单，中央大厅的周围有几个小房（图十六）。没有大规模的佛龛，装饰少，适合比丘们的生活和修行。印度早期的僧房窟有朴素和禁欲的气氛，有一点像莫高窟北区的僧房窟。仪式应该在旁边的塔庙窟内举行。后期（公元 5 世纪～8 世纪）的僧房窟与早期的差别很大。正壁中央的小房变成了佛龛。在此石窟里，佛龛的左右还有侧龛（图十七）。这一时期的僧房窟

---

① 高田修：《佛教美术史论考》，中央公论美术出版社，1969 年，第 92～93 页；平冈三保子、西インドの石窟寺院：《世界美術大全集インド（1）》，小学馆，2000 年，第 258～259 页；李崇峰：《中印佛教石窟寺比较研究》，北京大学出版社，2003 年，第 3 页。
② 这种楣也许表示这些小房渊源于在野外开掘的独立石窟。
③ 王洁、赵声良：《敦煌北朝石窟佛龛形式初探》，《敦煌研究》2006 年第 5 期，第 25 页。

图十五　阿旃陀第 12 窟内景。Étienne Lamotte, *History of Indian Buddhism*, Sara Webb-Boin, trans., Louvain: Peeters Press, 1988, 图版 25。

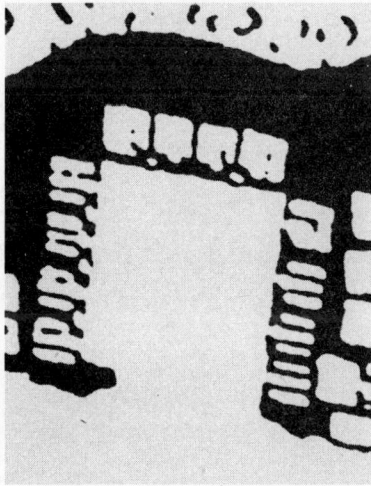

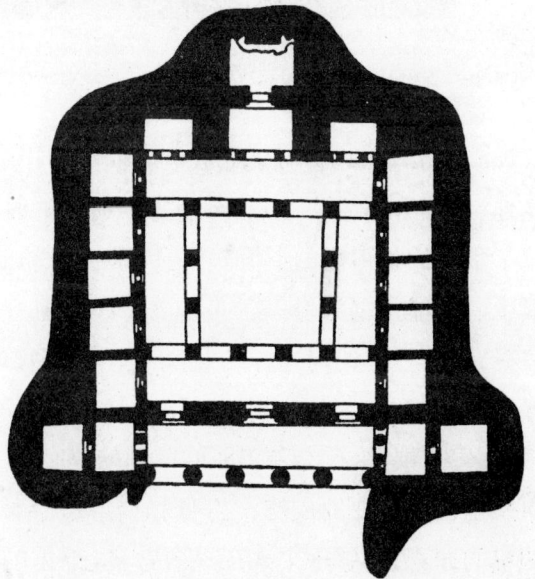

图十六　阿旃陀第 12 窟平面图。Dieter Schlingloff, *Guide to the Ajanta Paintings*, vol. 1, Narrative Wall Paintings, New Delhi: Munshiram Manoharlal Publishers, 1999, 封地(部分)。

图十七　阿旃陀第 2 窟平面图。Benoy K. Behl, *The Ajanta Caves*, London: Thames and Hudson, 1998, p. 235.

也有很多的壁画和雕塑(图十八)。阿旃陀有名的壁画大部分是在这一时期的僧房窟。

关于这种佛龛,葛瑞高利、绍本(Gregory Schopen)指出这是《根本说一切有部律》①和铭文说的"香

① 例如：Raniero Gnoli ed., *The Gilgit Manuscript of the Śayanāsanavastu and the Adhikaraṇavastu*, Roma: Istituto Italiano per il Medio de Estremo Oriente, 1978, pp. 10.32 – 11.5.

图十八　阿旃陀第 2 窟内景。立川武藏、大村次乡《アジャンタとエローラ》,集英社,2000,第 16~17 页(部分)。

室"(*gandhakuṭī*)。① 香室是存放信徒们为佛捐献的贵重财物的地方。香室里的财物是为了装饰佛的住处(佛塔和香室)的。香室里集中财物的时期,僧伽所接受的供品也应该不少。这些供品似乎促成了华丽的僧房窟的形成。不过,那么华丽的僧房窟是否适合修行则是一个问题。这时期塔庙窟很少。可能是因为僧房窟变成了礼拜的地方,他们便不需要塔庙窟了。比丘们应该还住在那些小房里,管理香室的财物,②举行仪式。可是,我认为,这一时期想修禅的比丘必须去僧房窟以外的地方修行。③

总之,有佛龛、侧龛和美丽的壁画的莫高第 285 窟应该受了印度后期的僧房窟的影响。要是佛龛原来是僧房改变而成的,④佛龛和僧房有类似的楣也许不会那么奇怪。因为中亚所谓的"禅窟"的侧室的面积,不够一个人在里面就寝,不可能是生活的地方。所以,学者们一般认为那应该是修行的地方。不过,要是印度的原形的窟已经不适合修行的话,莫高第 285 窟里比丘们实际修行的可能性则也很小。

---

① Gregory Schopen, The Buddha as an Owner of Property and Permanent Resident in Medieval Indian Monasteries, in *Bones, Stones, and Buddhist Monks*, Honolulu: University of Hawai, i Press, 1997, p.263ff; Gregory Schopen, 小谷信千代译《大乘仏教兴起时代インドの僧院生活》,春秋社,2000 年,第 131~146 页。

② 管理香室的比丘叫 *gandhakuṭī-vārika*. The Buddha as an Owner of Property, p.268. 也见: Jonathan A. Silk, *Managing Monks: Administrators and Administrative Roles in Indian Buddhist Monasticism*, Oxford: Oxford University Press, 2008, pp.120 - 121.

③ 他们可能在野外修头陀行或在近旁的小窟里坐禅。

④《大乘仏教兴起时代インドの僧院生活》,第 137 页。

三、现在的禅堂

在此比较一下中国和日本现在的禅堂。图十九是香积寺(西安)的禅堂,这个禅堂叫念佛堂,所以有佛像(图二十)和为了礼拜用的坐垫。然而墙壁是单调白颜色的,堂里装饰很少。比丘们在这个朴素的禅堂的床上坐禅。

图十九　香积寺念佛堂禅床。笔者摄影。

图二十　香积寺念佛堂佛坛。笔者摄影。

图二十一是佛光山台北分院的禅堂。除了长老的座位,坐禅的地方是朴素的床。睡觉的小房和石窟有一点像(图二十二)。这里的堂也没有很多装饰,很朴素。

图二十三是日本曹洞宗的僧堂的一例(圣护寺,熊本)。禅堂里也没有装饰,很简朴。在日本的禅院,僧堂是坐禅和生活的地方。所以,禅堂里放有被褥、袈裟、钵等私用东西的地方。临济宗的僧堂的结构也差不多。

图二十一　佛光山台北分院禅堂。笔者摄影。

图二十二　佛光山台北分院禅堂。笔者摄影。

图二十三　圣护寺僧堂。笔者摄影。

四、吐鲁番的石窟

　　现在我们回到中亚。在交河西边的雅尔湖第 4 窟有所谓"禅窟"的结构（图二十四）。图二十五是窟的内部。雅尔湖一共有 7 个洞窟，第 4 窟是中窟，主室的规模相当大，有美丽的壁画。后室里有低坛，可能是安置佛像的地方。除了此窟和第 7 窟以外，这些石窟没有壁画，应该是僧房窟。中央的第 4 窟很可能是住在这些僧房窟里的比丘们举行礼拜和仪式的地方。然而，入口的顶部有放光的坐禅比丘画（图二十六）。[①] 这是禅经描述的禅观中的体验。《禅秘要法经》说："尔时复当自然见身上，有一明相……光光七宝色，从胸而出，入于明中。此相现时，遂大欢喜，自然悦乐，心极安稳，无物可譬。"[②]《五门禅经要用法》说："教谛观身，若言我自见身光出绕身四边，其明转盛。便自以手推此光明远至四方。有无量人寻光来至。"[③]因此，雅尔湖第 4 窟应该和禅观思想有关系。值得注意的是，第 4 窟的两个侧室内部入口上有两个小孔（图二十七）。[④] 我认为这里原来有搁板。日

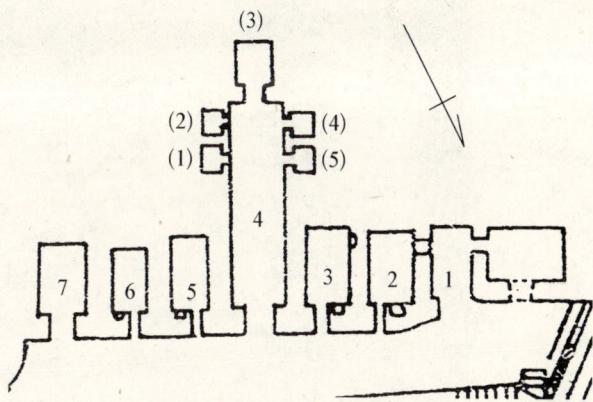

图二十四　雅尔湖石窟平面图。柳洪亮，《雅尔湖千佛洞考察随笔》，《敦煌研究》1988 年第 4 期，第 45 页，图1（部分）。第 4 窟侧室和后室的号码是笔者添写的。

　[①]　这个比丘和拜锡哈第 3 窟的放光禅观僧壁画有一点相似。

　[②]　大正藏 15：257a4 – 23。

　[③]　大正藏 15：330c29 – 31a2。

　[④]　侧室 1 和 4 有这样的小孔。

本的禅堂有放个人东西的地方。要是比丘长期居留在这个侧室里,当然要保管袈裟和钵等。所以,搁板的存在暗示这侧室是实用的。

图二十五　雅尔湖第4窟内景。笔者摄影。

图二十六　雅尔湖第4窟入口顶,禅定比丘。笔者摄影。

图二十七　雅尔湖第 4 窟侧室 1 内部。笔者摄影。

柏孜克里克第 10 窟也有好几个侧室（图二十八）。虽然现在已经看不清楚，晁华山的论文里说这个石窟的主室以前有"行者观想"图。① 侧室 3 的内部入口上有一个小龛（图二十九），②根据它的形状判断不可能是佛龛。雅尔湖的僧房窟（第 1 窟侧室）也有一样的龛（图三十）。其实，现在维吾尔族的房子里还用类似的龛（图三十一）。这种龛一定是放东西的地方。因此，柏孜克里克第 10 窟的侧室应该是实用的。

令人惊奇的是，柏孜克里克第 10 窟侧室 3 的后边有一个竖坑（图三十二）。因为此竖坑并没有煤烟的痕迹，不可能是烟道。而且内部有梯子（图三十三），所以这也许是为吐鲁番应对不安定状况所做的紧急出口。③

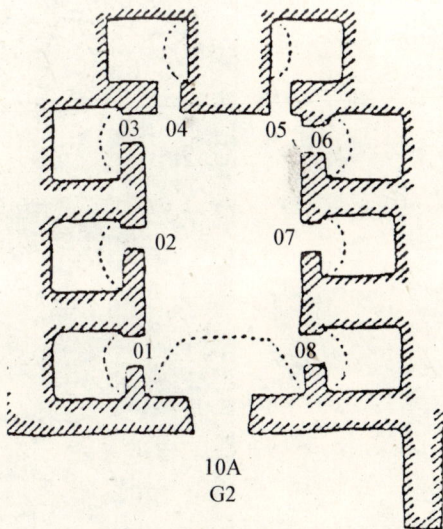

图二十八　柏孜克里克第 10 窟平面图。晁华山，《寻觅湮没千年的东方摩尼寺》，《中国文化》8，1993：图 2（部分）。

---

① 晁华山：《寻觅湮没千年的东方摩尼寺》，《中国文化》1993 年第 8 期，第 2 页。
② 侧室 2 和 3 有这种小龛。
③ 也见阿尔伯特·格伦威德尔（Albert Grünwedel）《新疆古佛寺》，中国人民大学出版社，2007 年，第 421 页。

图二十九　柏孜克里克第 10 窟侧室 3 内部。笔者摄影。

图三十　雅尔湖第 1 窟侧室内景。笔者摄影。

图三十一　现代维吾尔族的房子入口内部。笔者摄影。

图三十二　柏孜克里克第 10 窟侧室 3 竖坑。笔者摄影。

图三十三　柏孜克里克第 10 窟侧室 3 竖坑内部的梯子。笔者摄影。

五、苏巴什石窟

　　苏巴什石窟有更多的问题。[①] 苏巴什是库车北部很著名的大寺庙的遗址。

　　图三十四是苏巴什第 5 窟。这个石窟十分大,有一个后室,十个侧室,还有几个小室,所以结构比较复杂。后室有穹隆,应该是安置佛像的地方。图三十五是主室的内部,各个小室都有楣,侧室的面积大概是 1.5 m×1 m。主室的顶部有树下禅定比丘的壁画(图三十六)。这说明石窟和禅定思想有关系。我认为这个石窟用于禅定是可能的。

　　图三十七是苏巴什第 3 窟。这个窟也十分大,可是只有一个后室,两个侧室,另外两个小房。这里的

①　关于苏巴什石窟,见黄文弼:《塔里木盆地考古记》,科学出版社,1958 年,第 28～30 页；Louis Hambis, ed. , *Douldour-âqour et Soubachi: Planches*, Paris: Librairie Adrien-Maisonneuve, 1967, pl. 66, Fig. 132; Madeleine Hallade, Simone Gaulier, Liliane Courtois, *Douldour-âqour et Soubachi: Texte*, Paris: Éditions Recherche sur les civilisations, 1982, pp. 56－58; Chao Huashan, Simone Gaulier, Monique Maillard, Georges Pinault, *Sites divers de la région de Koutcha: Épigraphie koutchéenne*, Paris: Centre de recherche sur l'Asie centrale et la Haute Asie, Collège de France, 1987, pp. 134－158；李丽:《新疆龟兹地区中小型石窟调查》,《汉唐之间的宗教艺术与考古》,文物出版社,2000 年,第 166～170 页。这些石窟的年代不详,可是伯希和说一个石窟里胡乱涂写着"开元十三年三月十二日"字样。见: Paul Pelliot, *Carnets de route 1906－1908*, Paris: Les Indes savantes, 2008, p.143. 根据侧室门和门楣的样式,萧默认为这些石窟"至迟也应该是北朝的产物"(《敦煌建筑研究》,第 42 页)。

小室也都有楣(图三十八)。问题是这些小室很窄,大概只有0.8 m宽。一个人仅仅能在内坐禅,且长时间坐禅不舒适。不可思议的是,大石窟的侧室却很少。这个石窟里也有禅定僧的壁画(图三十九),和禅定思想一定有关系。然而,根据上述的理由,我认为比丘们在这个石窟里实际修行的可能性不大。如果比丘们在这些小室里坐禅的话,那应该是短时间的,具有某种象征性或仪式性的目的。

图四十是苏巴什第1窟。图(四十一)是此窟的平面图。[1]中窟的内部有7个小室,一些小室有楣。这里的小室大约只有0.6 m宽,坐禅用则太窄。一些小室的后壁有小孔,可能是保持佛像的支柱的痕迹。这些小室应该是为了安置佛像的龛,[2]不是坐禅的地方。

黄文弼也言及另外一个值得注意的窟(石窟C)。[3] 他说的石窟C和现在的编号的对应不详。根据黄的说法,石窟里有两具尸骨:一男一女。所以在苏巴什,一部分石窟为了墓葬用,[4]这个问题还需要进一步研讨。

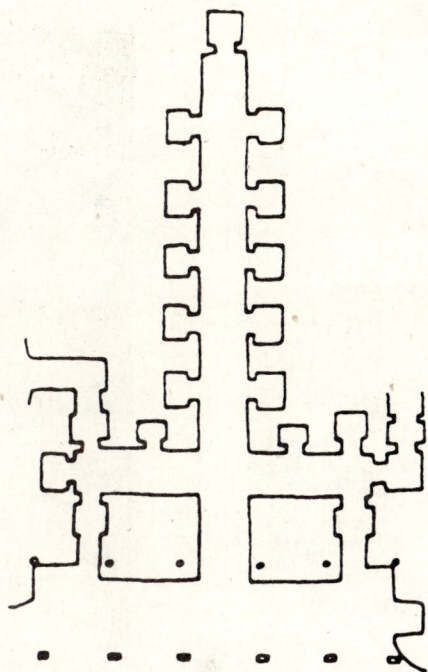

图三十四　苏巴什第5窟平面图。霍旭初、祁小山:《丝绸之路、新疆佛教艺术》,新疆大学出版社,2006年,第100页,图2。

图三十五　苏巴什第5窟内景。同上,100页,图1。

---

① 也见阿尔伯特·冯·勒柯克(Albert von Le Coq)《中国新疆的土地和人民》,中华书局,2008年,第60页,图14。
② 勒柯克也有同样的意见。同上,第61页。
③ 《塔里木盆地考古记》,第29页。
④ 原来其他用途的石窟也可能后来转用坟墓,可是也要考虑苏巴什中部佛塔中发现过东晋时代的墓葬。见《印度到中国新疆的佛教艺术》,第381页。

图三十六　苏巴什第5窟顶，禅定比丘。Angela F. Howard, Miracles and Visions among the Monastic Communities of Kucha, Xinjiang, *Journal of Inner Asian Art and Archaeology* 2, 2007, p. 84, Fig. 7.

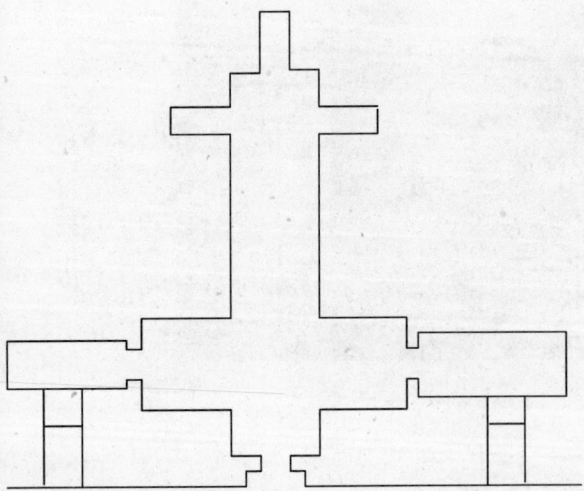

图三十七　苏巴什第3窟平面图。笔者作图。

图三十八　苏巴什第3窟内景。《新疆文物古迹大观》，新疆美术摄影出版社，1999年，第207页，图554。

图三十九　苏巴什第 3 窟顶，禅定比丘。笔者速写。

图四十　苏巴什第 1 窟外景。笔者摄影。

图四十一　苏巴什第 1 窟平面图。李丽，《新疆龟兹地区中小型石窟调查》，《汉唐之间的宗教艺术与考古》，文物出版社，2000 年，第 167 页，图 7。

六、胜 金 口

为了探讨小侧室的用途,一个重要的窟是克雷门茨(Klementz)编号的胜金口第 2 寺庙的第 2 窟(图四十二)。① 这窟的顶部现在崩塌了(图四十三,左侧),可是根据阿尔伯特·格伦威德尔(Albert Grünwedel)的文章,该窟以前有一个后龛和两个侧龛。侧龛大约宽 0.6 m,深 0.46 m,②因此这些龛为了坐禅不够大。重要的是格伦威德尔提到后龛的后壁上画了佛,侧龛的后壁上画了讲法的和尚们。

图四十四是窟的左侧壁。龛内有坐在椅子上讲法的和尚们的画像。各个龛有楣。格伦威德尔还提到从这些和尚们的口出的云上站有狮子。他认为这是狮子吼（siṃhanāda）的象征。按照《根本说一切有部毗奈耶杂事》的记述"于讲堂处画老宿苾刍宣扬法要",③该窟好像是讲堂。然而事实上,其作为讲堂则不够大(宽 2.42 米,深 3.50 米,高 2.80 米)。④ 我认为该窟更可能是为了纪念高僧们而建的影堂。⑤

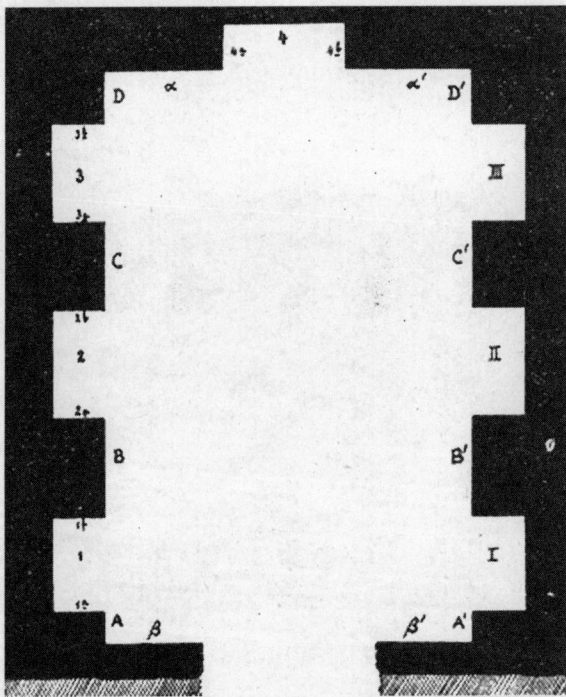

图四十二　胜金口第 2 寺庙第 2 窟(克雷门茨编号)。Albert Grünwedel, *Bericht über archäologische Arbeiten in Idikutschari und Umgebung im Winter 1902－1903*, München：Königlich Bayerischen Akademie der Wissenschaften, 1906, p.122, Fig.114. 财团法人东洋文库所藏。

---

① Albert Grünwedel, *Bericht über archäologische Arbeiten in Idikutschari und Umgebung im Winter 1902－1903*, München：Königlich Bayerischen Akademie der Wissenschaften, 1906, pp.121－131.
② Ibid.,p.121.
③ 大正藏24：283b5。
④ *Bericht*, p.121.
⑤ 其外,胜金口北寺第 4 窟有"禅窟"的结构。关于这石窟,见：*Bericht*, pp.158－159；C.M.杜丁：《中国新疆的建筑遗址》,中华书局,2006 年,第62~64 页；《寻觅湮没千年的东方摩尼寺》,第3~6 页；柳洪亮：《吐鲁番胜金口北区寺院是摩尼寺吗》,《吐鲁番学新论》,新疆人民出版社,2006 年,第829~836 页。柳认为胜金口第 4 窟是佛教高僧的影窟。

图四十三　胜金口第 2 寺庙第 1 窟(右侧)、2 窟(左侧)。笔者摄影。

图四十四　胜金口第 2 寺庙第 2 窟,左侧壁。Monique Maillard, *Grottes et monuments d'Asie centrale*, Paris：Adrien Maisonneuve, 1983, Fig. 44. a.

七、锡格沁石窟

　　焉耆的佛教遗址锡格沁也有"禅窟"。因为没去过那里,在此的意见仅依据以前的文章和照片。在图四十五里,我们再看侧室门口的楣。该石窟好像对应格伦威德尔的平面图(图四十六)。[①] 窟的结构和

──────────
① 《新疆古佛寺》,第 347 ~ 349 页。

面积,与莫高第 268 窟的有一些相似。格伦威德尔的文章说主室的侧壁有从肩放火的阿罗汉的壁画。侧室的后壁也有比丘的壁画。据贾应逸知,侧室后壁的壁画是比丘观想图。① 所以,这窟也可能和禅定有关系。然而,这里侧室很小,令人怀疑其实用性。这个石窟的用途还要慎重地探讨。

图四十五　锡格沁"禅窟"。*Grottes et monuments*, pl. 116.

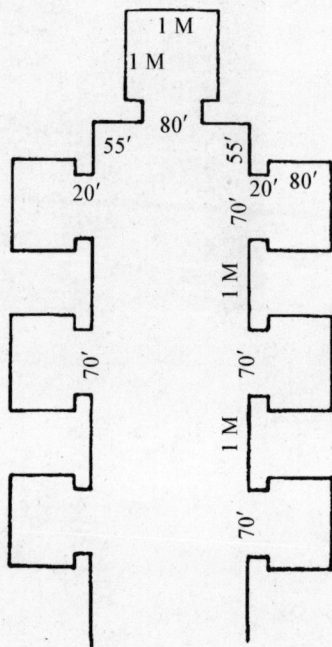

图四十六　*Altbuddhistische Kultstätten*, p. 194, Fig. 440.

结　论

本文探讨了中亚的几个有侧室的石窟。其中的一些石窟有一定实用性,用于禅定是很可能的。有一些石窟则似乎没有实用性。由此必须联想到在印度(阿旃陀)后期的僧房窟已经不是为修行用,而好像是举行仪式的地方。中亚所谓的"禅窟"②应该受了那些印度后期的僧房窟的影响。

然而,这些看起来不似禅窟的中亚石窟的用途到底是什么? 很遗憾我还不能得出确实的结论。禅定石窟的用途不是简单的问题。也许这些石窟的用途不是单一的。一些石窟可能是为了礼拜或举行仪式用的,一些可能是为了纪念高僧们用的,还有一些可能是墓。所以,我们必须把这种石窟一个一个地进行探讨。在探讨中,还必须注意到,侧室的存在并不能证明这些石窟是为了禅定用的。

① 《印度到新疆的佛教艺术》,第 398 页。
② 敦煌以东带有小侧室的"禅窟"是少见的,值得注意的是酒泉文殊山石窟。见暨远志《酒泉地区早期石窟分期试论》,《敦煌研究》1996 年第 1 期。

柏孜克里克石窟方形窟誓愿画配置状况的比较

——以图像构图与主题的演变为中心

承哉熹(韩国)

中国社会科学院研究生院

考古系博士生

誓愿画作为柏孜克里克石窟中最具代表性的题材,主要见于中心柱窟的第18窟中心柱左右两侧壁上,中心殿堂窟的第15、20窟回廊中,方形窟的第22、24、31、33、37、38、42、47、48、50窟左右两侧壁上等。

由于其中第20窟的一系列誓愿画构图与样式风格极为出色,而且画面上部保存有梵文题记,以往对誓愿画的研究主要以第20窟为重点,侧重于揭示誓愿画的宗教含义,尤其是依据佛经和由此衍生的誓愿画名称问题。然而,要从整体上了解柏孜克里克石窟誓愿画,对主要存在于方形窟内的誓愿画的研究必不可少。方形窟的誓愿画无论在画面数量、画面装饰纹样,还是个别图像特征和主题之间的组合上,都显示出了明显的变化。

本文基于格伦威德尔的报告书[1]与实地调查,按照各窟誓愿画的画面数量对誓愿画进行分类分析,以此探讨誓愿画主题组合的特征以及各个主题配置的演变,为今后进而讨论分期创造条件。

在方形窟中誓愿画绘制于左右两侧壁上,画面幅数最多的第31窟共有14幅誓愿画,两侧壁上各7幅;第33窟的誓愿画是12幅画面,两侧壁上各6幅。将画面幅数较多的此两座窟归为A组。第22、37、42窟有8幅画面,第24、38窟有6幅画面,将这些窟归为B组。画面幅数较少的窟为第47、48、50窟,它们各有4幅画面,将画面幅数最少的这些窟归为C组(本文略)。

一、方形窟第31、33窟的誓愿画

(一)第31窟誓愿画主题组合与配置特征

在方形窟的一系列誓愿画中,画的幅数最多的第31窟的誓愿画主题和第20窟(中心殿堂窟)誓愿画的15个主题(最为典型)基本相同。但是因洞窟形制的不同,誓愿画在石窟内的配置也有所变化。下面看第31窟誓愿画在该窟内的配置情况。

① Grünwedel, Albert: *Altbuddhistische kultstätten in Chinesisch-Turkistan*; Berlin: G. Reimer, 1912.(赵崇民、巫新华译《新疆古佛寺: 1905～1907年考察成果》,北京:中国人民大学出版社,2007年。)

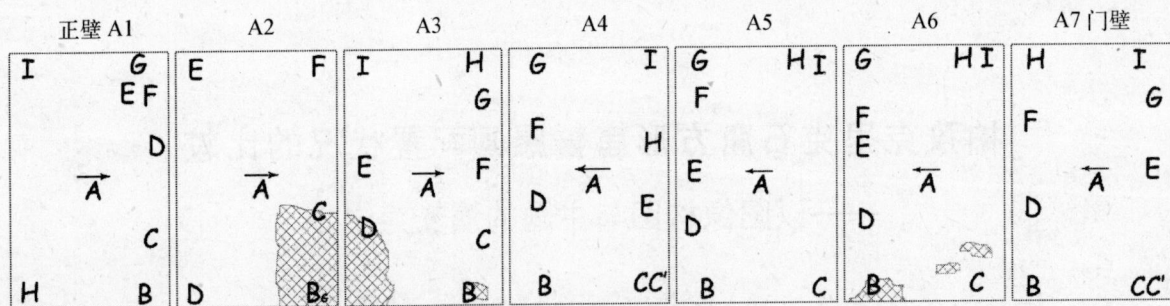

图一　第31窟右侧壁誓愿画示意图

示意图说明：

1）英文大写指示各个图像。英文大写后边加小型"G"所指示的图像，现在已经不存在，但是在格伦威德尔的1905～1907年调查报告 Altbuddhistische kultstätten in Chinesisch-Turkistan 中能确认。在以下图像说明中会把小型"G"省略。（以下图相同）

2）在示意图中""指已不存在的画面。（以下图相同）

3）第31窟每一幅誓愿画不算边饰高2.65米、宽1.69米，此图与愿画比例为1：70。

4）A1～A7的图像构图如下：

A1：A为大型立佛；B为跪着供奉一颗宝珠的王；C、D为两位菩萨；E、F为两位比丘；G为一座寺庙；H为一位合十比丘；I为一位比丘。此画面是王（前生的释迦）供养宝珠的场面，与第20窟第8主题类似。[①]

A2：A为大型立佛；B为一跪姿身披铠甲的王，手举一个冒烟的灯；D为跪姿僧人，手举一个冒烟的灯；C为一位菩萨；E为菩萨（?）；F为一位比丘。此画面是王（前生的释迦）供养灯的场面，与第20窟第9主题类似，不过冒烟的表现很独特。

A3：A为大型立佛；B为一位王，C为一位比丘给国王剃度；D、E为两位菩萨；F为一位合十的比丘；G为一位菩萨；H为一位金刚；I为一位人物（?）。此画面是一位比丘给国王（前生的释迦）剃度的场面。在主题上与第20窟的第3、12主题类似，但是按剃度国王的姿势（骑坐），与第20窟第12主题更接近。

A4：A为大型立佛；B为一个身披铠甲的跪姿国王，他在向后指着他的宝座；C与C′为王与王后，他们手捧盛有点心的盘子；D为金刚；E、F与H为合十的菩萨；G为一座寺庙；I为一位人物（?）。此画面是王（前生的释迦）招请佛（过去佛）的场面，与第20窟第4主题类似。

A5：A为大型立佛；B为跪姿祈祷的佛；C为一手捧盘子的王后；D为金刚（?）；E与F为菩萨；H为一座寺庙；I为合十的比丘；G为云（可能燃灯佛授记的善慧）。此画面由燃灯佛授记与佛（前生的释迦）祈祷的主题（第20窟第10主题）结合，与第20窟第7主题类似。

A6：A为大型立佛；B为跪姿合十的国王；C为立姿的国王（?）；D为一位举华盖菩萨；E与F为菩萨（?）；H与I为两位合十的比丘；G为一座寺庙。此画面是祈祷的国王（前生的释迦）与伞盖供养，与第20窟第2、5主题类似。

A7：A为大型立佛；B为双手指着后边的跪姿婆罗门（?）；D与F为两位人物（?），尚不能确定；H为云，里面有身光的跪姿人物（可能前生的释迦：善慧）；C与C′为王与王后，手捧供养品；E与G为两位比丘；I为一座寺庙。此画面是燃灯佛授记的内容，与第20窟的第7主题类似。

在第20窟回廊后壁中的三个主题（供养宝珠的王和王后、供养灯的王和比丘、祈祷的佛）和回廊右侧内壁的一个主题（乘船过江的佛）在第31窟中分别绘制于正壁前面的A1、A2以及a1、a2；在第20窟回廊左右侧的主题（招请佛的王和婆罗门、剃度的王、祈祷的王与伞盖供养、供养袈裟的婆罗门）在第31窟中绘制于门壁前面的A3、A4、A6、a3、a4、a5；第20窟回廊后壁中央的燃灯佛授记，在第31窟中绘制于离门壁近的A5、A7。从第31窟这样的配置上可以看出，除了燃灯佛授记以外，中心殿堂窟回廊后壁的誓愿画主题转移到方形窟的正壁前边两侧壁，而回廊左右侧的誓愿画主题转移到方形窟门壁前边两侧壁。

（二）第33窟誓愿画主题组合与配置特征

除了第33窟誓愿画A2、a1画面以外，第31窟一系列誓愿画的主题与配置都跟第33窟基本一致，格伦威德尔甚至认为第33窟的誓愿画是第31窟的仿造品。[②] 下面看第33窟誓愿画在石窟内的配置。

---

① 关于第20窟回廊誓愿画的主题配置，参考 Le Cop, A. von, Chotscho, Berlin, 1913（Reprint Graz 1979）（赵崇民译《高昌—吐鲁番古代艺术珍品》，新疆人民出版社，1998年）。

② 格伦威德尔在报告中记载了第33窟誓愿画共有16幅画面，但是实地调查发现第33窟总共有12幅画面。第31、33窟的先后关系从石窟形式（规模）、誓愿画各个主题的图像构图与样式风格着手，需要仔细地分析。

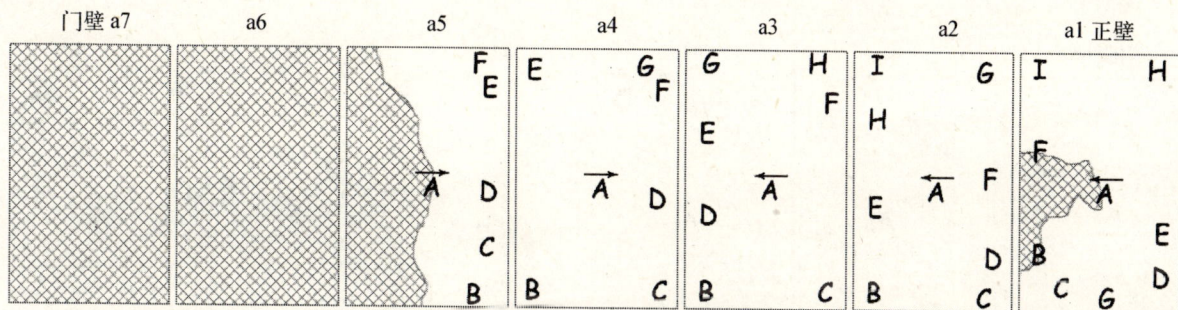

图二　第31窟左侧壁誓愿画示意图

示意图说明：

1）第31窟每一幅誓愿画不算边饰高2.65米、宽1.69米，此图与愿画比例为1：70。

2）a1～a7的图像构图如下：

a1：此画被英国斯坦因窃走，A为大型立佛；G为一艘船，佛（A）站在船上；B为戴帽子的男子牵着驮着东西的骆驼和骡子；C为一个老头正回首向后看；D为戴着帽子的商人手捧供品；E为一个戴白色小帽的男子；F为祈祷的菩萨；I为金刚；H为比丘。此画面是商人（前生的释迦）用船将过去佛渡江的场面，与第20窟第14主题类似。

a2：此画也被英国斯坦因窃走，A为大型立佛；B为跪姿祈祷佛；C为手捧一盘供养品的童子；D为一位祈祷菩萨；E为一位菩萨；F为一位祈祷比丘；G为散花天神；H为一位合十的比丘；I为一座寺庙。此画面是佛（前生的释迦）祈祷的场面，与第20窟第10主题类似。

a3：A为大型立佛；B为跪姿祈祷国王；C为手捧进供点心的王后；D为一位菩萨；E为举华盖的菩萨；G为一位菩萨；H为一座寺院；F为比丘，此画面是国王祈祷的场面。在第20窟祈祷王的主题中，跪姿祈祷国王跟伞盖（第2主题）、旗（第5主题）供养人一起，但这画面却跟供养点心的王后一起。

a4：A为大型立佛；B为立姿的婆罗门，供养袈裟；C为在草庐前面的婆罗门，供养袈裟；D为立姿合十的菩萨；E为合十的比丘；F为一位人物（？）；G为一位菩萨。此画面是婆罗门（前生的释迦）供养袈裟的场面，与第20窟第13主题类似。

a5：A为大型立佛；B为国王；C为比丘给国王剃度；D为一位比丘；E为一位金刚；F为一座寺庙；左边全都破坏。此画面是国王剃度的场面，与第20窟的第3、12主题类似。

a6与a7的画面都被破坏。

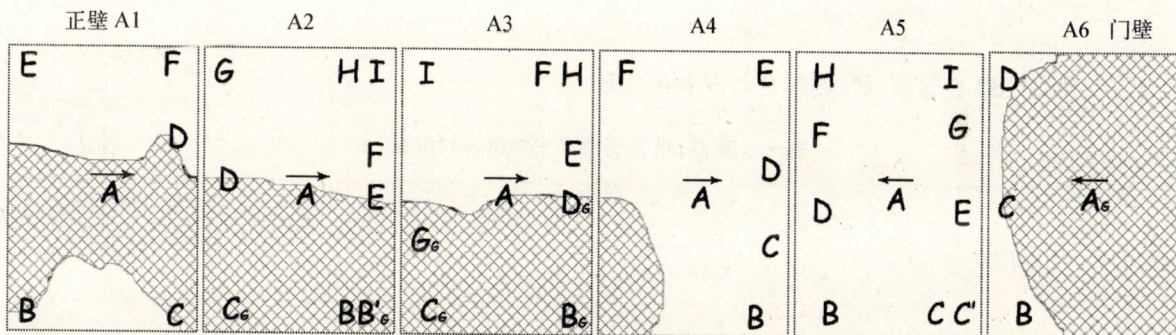

图三　第33窟右侧壁誓愿画示意图

示意图说明：

1）第33窟每一幅誓愿画不算边饰高2.15米、宽1.45米，此图与愿画比例为1：60。

2）A1～A6的图像构图如下：

A1：A为大型立佛；B为立姿的王后；C为跪姿的国王；D与E为两位菩萨；F为一座寺庙。由于只有画面上部和下部的一部分留存，不能确认此画面的主题。（可是据C的一部分画面来推测，可能是国王供养宝珠的场面）

A2：A为大型立佛；C为有胡子的祈祷男子，他旁边有驮着东西的骆驼、马与驴；B为两个有胡子的跪姿男子，每个人捧着一盘供品；D为金刚；E与F为两位菩萨；H与I为二比丘；G为合十的菩萨。此画面是商人（前生的释迦）供养过去佛的场面，与第20窟第6主题类似。

A3：A为大型立佛；B为身披铠甲的王，手持燃着的灯；C为手持灯的比丘；D与E为两位菩萨；F与H为两位祈祷比丘；G为一位比丘；I为合十的比丘。此画面是王（前生的释迦）供养灯的场面，与第20窟第9主题类似。

A4：A为大型立佛；B为一位婆罗门（菩萨）；C为比丘给婆罗门（菩萨）剃度；D为合十的比丘；E为金刚；F为合十的比丘；画面左下侧已破坏。此画面是婆罗门（菩萨）剃度的场面，与第20窟的第3、12主题类似。

A5：A为大型立佛；B为一位身披铠甲的跪姿王，他在向后指着他的宝座；C与C'为王与王后，他们手捧盛有点心的盘子；D为金刚；F为菩萨；H为一座寺庙；E与G为两位菩萨；I为散花的天神。此画面是国王（前生的释迦）招请佛（过去佛）的场面，与第20窟第4主题类似。

A6：B为祈祷的佛；C为金刚；D为云，里面的形象很模糊，其余部分都被损坏。虽然图像"D"的画面很模糊，可是无疑表现燃灯佛授记的内容与第20窟的第7主题类似。

门壁 a6   a5   a4   a3   a2   a1 正壁

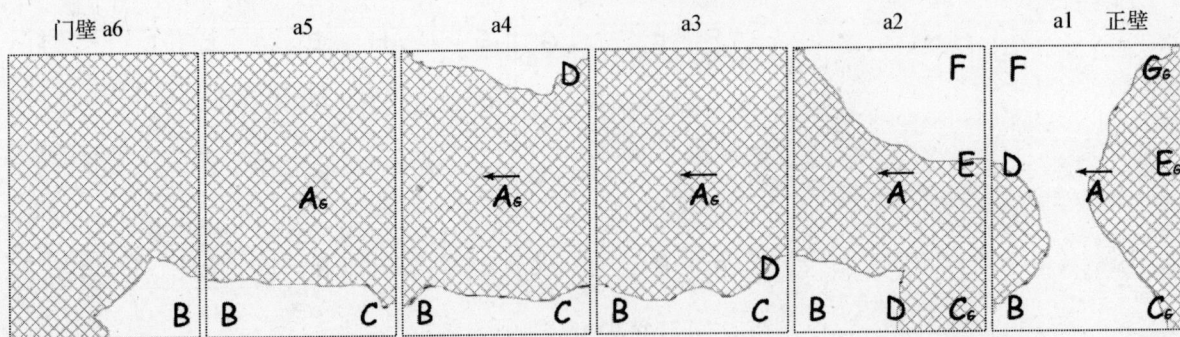

图四　第33窟左侧壁誓愿画示意图

示意图说明:

1) 第33窟每一幅誓愿画不算边饰高2.15米、宽1.45米, 此图与愿画比例为1:60。

2) A1～A6的图像构图如下:

a1: A 为大型立佛; B 为跪姿婆罗门, 指着他的宝座; C 为手捧盘子的菩萨; D 与 E 为两位比丘; F 为一位祈祷菩萨; G 为一位金刚。此画面是婆罗门(前生的释迦)招请过去佛的场面, 与第20窟第1、15主题类似。

a2: A 为大型立佛; D 为一船, 上面有佛(A); B 为跪姿男子, 头戴帽子, 手捧一盘供养品; C 为跪姿男子, 他前边有骆驼与骡子; E 为一位比丘; F 为一位菩萨; 左侧上部遭破坏。此画面是商人(前生的释迦)用船将过去佛渡江的场面, 与第20窟第14主题类似。

a3: A 为大型立佛; B 为祈祷的跪姿佛; C 为手捧供养品的童女; D 为手捧供养品的菩萨; 其余部分都被毁掉。此画面是佛(前生的释迦)祈祷的场面, 与第20窟第10主题类似。

a4: A 为大型立佛; B 为跪姿合十的国王; C 为手持华盖的王后; D 为一位比丘, 其余部分都被毁掉。此画面是祈祷的国王(前生的释迦)与伞盖供养, 与第20窟第2、5主题类似。

a5: A 为大型立佛; B 为披铠甲立姿的国王, 手捧供养品; C 为跪姿的菩萨, 手持供养品(袈裟?)。此画面可能是国王和菩萨(前生的释迦)供养袈裟的场面, 与第20窟第11、13主题类似。

a6: B 为跪姿合十的国王; 其余部分都被毁坏。

(三) 第31、33窟誓愿画主题组合与配置的比较

表一　第31、33窟誓愿画主题组合与配置

布局 窟号	左侧壁						右侧壁						
	门壁		正壁				正壁					门壁	
	a7	a6	A5	a4	A3	a2	a1	A1	A2	A3	A4	A5	A6	A7
第31窟	毁损	毁损	剃度的王	供养袈裟的婆罗门	祈祷的王(与手捧供品的王后)	祈祷的佛	过江的佛(过去佛)	供养宝珠的王	供养灯的王	剃度的王	招请佛的王	祈祷的佛与燃灯佛授记	祈祷的王与伞盖供养	燃灯佛授记
	a6	A5	a4	a3	a2	a1	A1	A2	A3	A4	A5	A6		
第33窟	毁损	供养袈裟(?)的菩萨	祈祷的王与伞盖供养	祈祷的佛	过江的佛(过去佛)	招请佛的婆罗门(?)	不知道内容供养宝珠的王(?)	供养财宝的商人	供养灯的王	剃度的婆罗门(菩萨)	招请佛的王	燃灯佛授记		

从表一可见,第31、33窟誓愿画主题配置大体相同,跟第31窟一样,第33窟正壁前边的主题在第20窟中位于回廊的后壁,第33窟门壁前边的誓愿画主题在第20窟中位于回廊的左右侧壁。

但与第31窟相比,第33窟的誓愿画减少了两幅画面,并且在正壁前边的画面中增加了主题,即A2的供养财宝的商人和a1的主题(因画面损坏而不能确定)。在第31窟誓愿画主题中,剃度的王与燃灯佛授记的场面被两次绘制(燃灯佛授记画在第31窟的A5和A7位置;剃度的干画在第31窟的A3和a5位置),但是在第33窟中没出现这种现象。因此可以看出,第33窟的誓愿画模仿了第31窟,但不像中心殿堂的第15、20窟那样仿造得一模一样。遗憾的是,由于这两座石窟左侧壁离门壁最近的位置破坏得很严重,不能准确地分析这些主题组合的规律。

二、方形窟第22、37、42窟的誓愿画

(一)第22窟誓愿画主题组合与配置特征

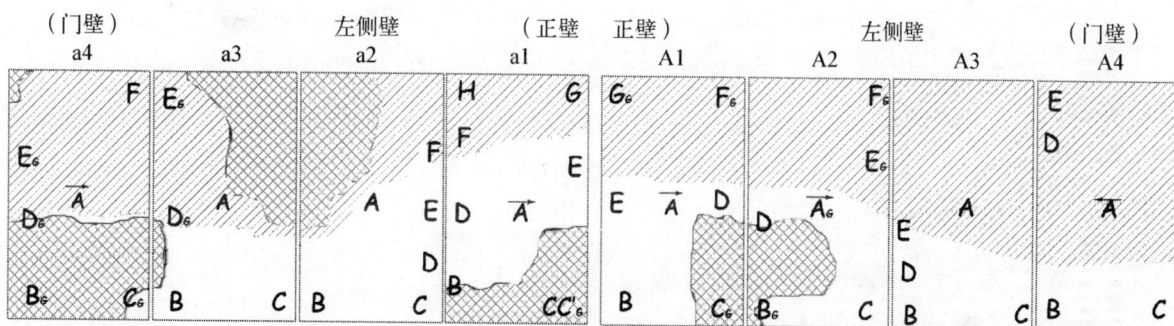

图五 第22窟誓愿画示意图

示意图说明:

1) 在示意图中" "是虽然保留画面但特别模糊的部分。

2) 第22窟每一幅誓愿画不算边饰高3.05米、宽1.76米,此图与愿画比例为1∶80。

3) A1～A4、a1～a4的图像构图如下:

A1:A为大型立佛;C为婆罗门,坐在庐草前,身穿金丝长衬;B为跪姿的婆罗门,身穿金丝长衬;D为双手合十的菩萨;E、F为两位菩萨;G为一座寺庙。此画面是在芦草前的婆罗门(前生的释迦)招请过去佛的场面,与第20窟第1、15主题类似。

A2:A为大型立佛;C为立姿合十的菩萨;B为跪姿祈祷的国王;E为正在闻一朵花的菩萨;F为金刚;其余部分不能确认。此画面现存状况不是很好,画面几乎掉落。此画面不能确定内容,可是按格伦威德尔的报告认为此画面则是一位比丘给国王(前生的释迦)剃度的场面,与第20窟的第3、12主题类似。

A3:A为大型立佛;B为祈祷的国王;D为一位合十的菩萨;E为一位举伞盖的菩萨;C为举伞盖的国王。此画面是祈祷的国王与华盖供养的场面,与第20窟第2、5主题类似。

A4:A为大型立佛,面朝正壁;C为王后,手捧大盘,盘子里有东西;E为云,里面跪姿人物(前生的释迦);B为菩萨(或者婆罗门);D为合十的菩萨;此画面是燃灯佛授记的场面,与第20窟的第7主题类似。

a1:A为大型立佛;B为一位立姿的婆罗门(前生的释迦),双手拿虎皮的袈裟(?);C与C′为王与王后,每个人都手捧一个金盘子,盘内有扁平的饼;D与E为两位菩萨;F与G为两位菩萨;H为一座寺庙。此画面也是婆罗门供养袈裟的场面,与第15窟的第13主题类似,然而就第15窟而言,在画面中与跪姿婆罗门的对称处被绘制立姿的婆罗门,可在此却绘有立姿的王与王后。

a2:A为大型立佛;B为合十祈祷的国王;C为跪姿国王(前生的释迦);D为比丘给国王剃度;E为一位菩萨;F为金刚。此画面是一位比丘给国王(前生的释迦)剃度的场面,与第20窟的第3、12主题类似。

a3:A为大型立佛;B为身披铠甲的举伞盖王;C为身披铠甲的跪姿国王;D与E为两位菩萨;其余的画面都损坏。此画面是祈祷的国王与伞盖供养的场面,与第20窟第2、5主题类似。

a4:A为大型立佛;C为手捧盛有鲜花盘子的仙女;B为手执花环的菩萨;D与E为两位菩萨,双手合十;F为云,里面画着一跪姿俯身的人物。此画面是燃灯佛授记的场面,与第20窟的第7主题类似。

（二）第 37 窟誓愿画主题组合与配置特征

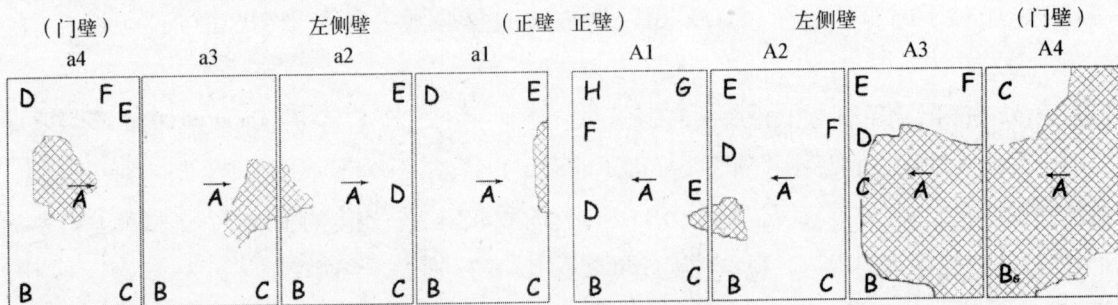

图六　第 37 窟誓愿画示意图

示意图说明：

1）第 37 窟每一幅誓愿画不算边饰高 1.85 米、宽 1.1 米，此图将原画面缩小到 1/50。

2）A1~A4、a1~a4 的图像构图如下：

A1：A 为大型立佛；B 为一身披铠甲的跪姿国王，他在向后指着他的宝座；C 与 E 为王与王后，他们手捧盛有点心的盘子；D 为金刚；F 为比丘；H 为一座寺庙；G 为散花天神。此画面是国王（前生的释迦）招请佛（过去佛）的场面，与第 20 窟第 4 主题类似。

A2：A 为大型立佛；B 为跪姿祈祷的佛；D 为一位菩萨；E 为云，圆形的云里面有一个小型深鞠躬的人；C 为一位王后，手捧供养盘子；F 为合十的菩萨。此画面是燃灯佛授记的内容，与第 20 窟的第 7 主题、第 22 窟 A4、a4 的主题与第 31 窟 A5（?）、A7 的主题、第 33 窟 A6 主题类似。

A3：A 为大型立佛；B 为跪姿合十的国王；C 为一位人物，可能不确定此图像；D 为举伞盖的菩萨；E 为一座寺院；F 为合十的比丘。此画面可能是祈祷的国王（前生的释迦）与伞盖供养。

A4：此画面也是燃灯佛授记的内容。B 为跪于佛陀前面的菩萨，并披散其发；C 为云，里面有一个小型深鞠躬人。与第 20 窟的第 7 主题、第 22 窟 A4、a4 的主题及第 31 窟 A5（?）、A7 的主题、第 33 窟 A6 主题类似。

a1：A 为大型立佛；B 为国王，手捧盛有点心的盘子；C 为一位婆罗门，跪在草庐前，双手拿袈裟；D 与 E 为菩萨。此画面是婆罗门（前生的释迦）供养袈裟的场面。

a2：A 为大型立佛；B 为剃度的国王，上边的比丘已破坏；C 为祈祷的国王；D 与 E 为两位菩萨。此画面是一位比丘给国王（前生的释迦）剃度的场面。

a3：A 为大型立佛；B 为举伞盖的国王；C 为祈祷的国王；其余画面已破坏。此画面是祈祷的国王与旗供养的场面。

a4：A 为大型立佛；B 与 C 的画面特别模糊不能确认；D 与 E 为比丘；F 为一座寺庙。

（三）第 42 窟誓愿画主题组合与配置特征

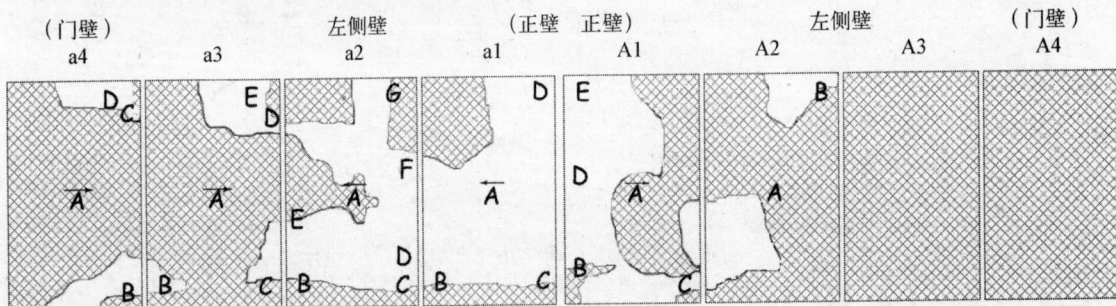

图七　第 42 窟誓愿画示意图

示意图说明：

1）第 42 窟每一幅誓愿画不算边饰高 2.55 米、宽 1.53 米，此图将原画面缩小到 1/70。

2）A1~A4、a1~a4 的图像构图如下：

A1：A 为大型立佛；C 为一个身披铠甲的跪姿国王，他指着身后的宝座；B 与 D 为王与王后，他们手捧盛有点心的盘子；E 为散花天神；其余画面已破坏。此画面是国王（前生的释迦）招请佛（过去佛）的场面，与第 20 窟第 4 主题类似。

A2：除了画面右侧上部与左侧下部以外，都已毁损，然而"B"的一部分留存。B 为云，里面有一位深鞠躬的人。由此，此画面是燃灯佛授记的内容，与第 20 窟的第 7 主题类似。

A3、A4 已被毁损。

a1：A 为大型立佛；B 为婆罗门，在草庐前面，双手拿虎皮的袈裟（?）；C 为立姿的国王；D 为比丘。此画面特别模糊，不能确认其内容，可能是婆罗门（前生的释迦）供养袈裟的场面，与第 20 窟第 11、13 主题类似。

a2：A 为大型立佛；C 为国王；D 为给国王剃度的比丘；B 为合十的国王；E 为王后；F 与 G 为两位菩萨。此画面是国王剃度的场面，与第 20 窟的第 3、12 主题类似。

a3：A 画面大部分都损坏，只有 B、C、D、E 的一部分保存；C 为跪姿祈祷的国王；B 可能为举伞盖人，但很模糊；D 为比丘；E 为一座寺庙。此画面是一位国王祈祷与华盖供养的场面，与第 20 窟第 2 主题类似。

a4：A 画面大部分都损坏，只有 B、C、D 的一部分保存；B 为婆罗门，在草庐前面，双手指着后边；C 为比丘；D 为一座寺庙。此画面是婆罗门（前生的释迦）招请过去佛的场面，与第 20 窟第 1、15 主题类似。

（四）第22、37、42窟与第31、33窟誓愿画状况的比较

表二 第22、37、42窟誓愿画主题组合

布局 石窟	门壁	左侧壁			正壁	门壁		右侧壁
	正壁							
	a4	a3	a2	a1	A1	A2	A3	A4
第22窟	燃灯佛授记	祈祷的王与华盖供养	剃度的王	供养袈裟的婆罗门	招请佛的婆罗门	剃度的王(?)	祈祷的王与华盖供养	燃灯佛授记
第37窟	不知道内容，可是不是燃灯佛授记	祈祷的王与华盖供养	剃度的王	供养袈裟的婆罗门	招请佛的王	燃灯佛授记与祈祷的佛	祈祷的王与华盖供养	燃灯佛授记
第42窟	招请佛的婆罗门(?)	祈祷的王与伞盖供养	剃度的王	供养袈裟的婆罗门	招请佛的王	燃灯佛授记	毁损	毁损

这些洞窟誓愿画的画面幅数跟第33、31窟相比，减少了一半。在主题组合上的变化也很明显，在这些洞窟中，原来见于第20窟回廊后部的主题，也就是第33、31窟的正壁前边侧壁上的主题已消失，只有第33、31窟的门壁前边的五个主题（招请佛的婆罗门[王]、供养袈裟的婆罗门、剃度的王、祈祷的王与伞盖[旗]供养、燃灯佛授记）被继承下来。就第22、37、42窟而言，共有8幅画面中有些主题被两次反复使用，并且其他中小型誓愿画也是这5个主题被反复或者省略。

综上所述，可看出誓愿画主题组合的两个倾向，在22、37、42窟中，第37、42窟的誓愿画的配置很相似。右侧壁是从正壁开始，由里向外的顺序依次为：招请佛的王、燃灯佛授记、祈祷的王与伞盖（或者旗）供养、燃灯佛授记；左侧壁从正壁开始，顺序为供养袈裟的婆罗门、剃度的王、祈祷的王与伞盖（旗）供养、招请佛的婆罗门，在右侧壁中燃灯佛授记两次出现。然而就第22窟而言，与上述的两座窟有所区别，两侧边誓愿画的主题相互对应，从正壁开始由里向外都是按照招请佛的婆罗门（和袈裟供养的婆罗门）、剃度的王、祈祷的王与旗供养、燃灯佛授记的顺序排列。

小 结

上面按照画面幅数，先把10个方形窟的誓愿画归为3组，分析了方形窟誓愿画主题结合的特征以及在石窟内誓愿画配置的演变。上述分析表明第31、33窟誓愿画在整个方形窟誓愿画中具有一定的意义，它们可能是誓愿画从中心殿堂窟向方形窟转变过程中的典型模式，B组和C组（本文略）誓愿画则是A组誓愿画组合的简化形式。

此外，还要说明的是，在绪论中提起过方形窟誓愿画装饰纹样的变化，指的是誓愿画上下部和画面之间的边饰的变化。在此因资料的不足不能论证，可是本人认为按照画面上部的装饰帐幕和题记框是否存在、画面之间的装饰带和画面下部装饰纹样的变化特点，并结合誓愿画构图的差异来进行分析，可能会揭示分为3组的整个10个方形窟誓愿画的先后关系，此问题拟另文论述。

Comparative Study of the Stupas of Bamiyan and Rawak in the Light of Recent French Excavations

Eléonore Buffler

Postgraduate student at the Strasbourg University (UMR 7044), France

Introduction

In the course of the French archaeological excavations directed by Prof. Z. Tarzi on the site of the "Eastern Monastery" of Bāmiyān, Afghanistan, since 2002, I have been able to establish that the "Great Stupa", for whose excavation I was responsible, had been built to a cruciform plan.

This type of stupa appears to have been relatively widespread in Asia, since it is found not only in Afghanistan but also in Pakistan, India, Kashmir, Central Asia and as far as South-East Asia.

The study of this very distinctive plan prompted us to consider questions about its origin, development and diffusion in different regions of Asia, particularly in Xinjiang — a diffusion in which Bāmiyān may have played an important role.

Origin and development of the cruciform stupa

The cruciform stupa, according to the study by G. Tucci,[1] forms part of the group of eight stupa believed to commemorate the eight great events in the life of the Buddha.

Each stupa is distinctive in its shape, derived from the Indian prototype built in each of the cities which, according to the Buddhist texts, are associated with the life or teachings of the Buddha. Thus are commemorated eight events in his life: his Birth, his Enlightenment, the Great Miracle of Sravasti, his First Sin, the submission of the elephant, the Descent from Tushita Heaven, the monkey's gift of honey at Vaishali, and the Mahaparinirvana.[2]

In the course of his work, G. Tucci identified the stupa "Descent from Tushita Heaven" (Fig. 1) as being a monument in cruciform plan with four staircases, one on each façade.

It is on this occasion[3] that the Buddha ascends to the Heaven of the Thirty-three Gods, where dwells his

---

① G. TUCCI, *Stupa. Art, Architectonics and Symbolism*, New Dehli, 1988, p. 13.

② *Ibid.*, p. 21.

③ A. FOUCHER, *La Vie du Buddha, d'après les textes et les monuments de l'Inde*, Paris, 1993, p. 274.

reborn mother Maya, to teach the Law. He thus disappears from the Earth, only reappearing three months later near the city of Sankasya. His "Descension" is made with great ceremony, the Buddha descending on a triple staircase specially fashioned by the gods in precious metals, accompanied by Brahma on his right and Indra on his left. This "Descension" takes place beneath a heaven filled with divinities throwing flowers and singing his praises. At the foot of the staircase, Buddha is welcomed by a crowd of the faithful and by his disciples. The site of this miracle is said to have been marked at Sankasya by King Ashoka, and its vestiges were apparently still visible to Chinese pilgrims who came to visit in the 7th and 8th centuries.

All iconographic representations accord the utmost importance to this triple staircase, which is found on each of the sides of the cruciform stupa whose form is even described in Buddhist texts, notably in the *Kriyasamgraha*[①] ("Manual of Buddhist Rituals"), a later Nepalese text written by

Fig. 1　Buddha's Descent from the Tushita Heaven, second half of 3rd century India, Andhra Pradesh, Nagarjunakonda. Limestone; 121. 9 × 75. 6 cm. Rogers Fund, 1928 (28. 31).
© Metropolitan Museum of Art de New York.

Kuladatta. This text provides us with details of the stupa and its base. Thus it is stated that the platform of the stupa can have twenty angles — which, according to Mireille Bénisti, may correspond to a platform with twenty "sawtooth" redents, fashioned in the shape of a square platform with a projection on each of its four sides (Fig. 2) — and here again we find our cruciform plan.

Monique Maillard[②] associates this type of stupa with "the diffusion of new currents of Great Vehicle Buddhism" in which "Vajrayana would play an increasing role" and, in particular, with the dissemination of Tantric texts by certain Buddhist monasteries such as Khotan. Although I am not an expert on this matter, I would nevertheless question the validity of this hypothesis in view of the fact that here in Bāmiyān we are in the presence of a Small Vehicle sect, namely the Lokottaravadin, as was stated by Xuanzang[③] on his visit in the 7th century.

On the basis of the various studies already done on the evolution of the stupa, we can attempt to establish an outline of evolution in which we can place the cruciform stupa.

①　M. BENISTI, "Etude sur le stupa dans l'Inde ancienne," *BEFEO*, L. 1 (1960), p. 89.
②　M. MAILLARD, *Grottes et monuments d'Asie Centrale*, Paris, 1983, p. 170.
③　Z. TARZI, *L'architecture et le décor rupestre des grottes de Bāmiyān*, vol. 1, Texte, Paris, 1977, p. 180.

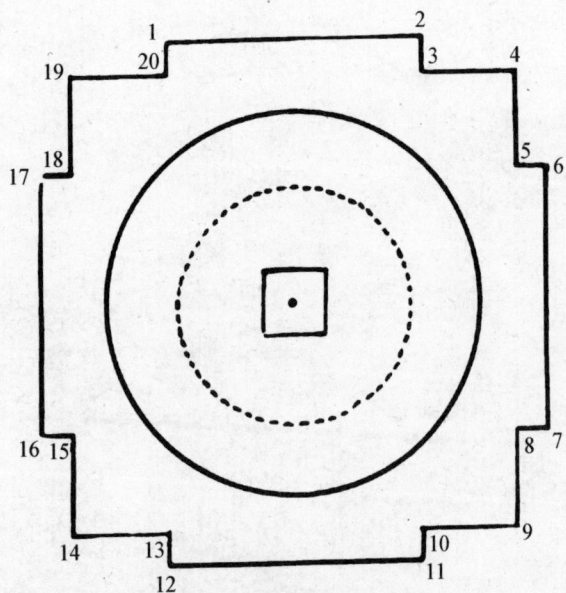

Fig. 2　Sketch of the twenty angles stupa according to M. Bénisti, "Etude sur le Stupa dans l'Inde ancienne," *BEFEO*, L. 1 (1960), p. 96.

The stupa of Indian type, built on a circular plan, sees its base modified over time and passing from a circular to a square form, to which are later added one, then two, and finally four staircases.[①]

Within this model of cruciform stupa, T. Fitzsimmons[②] distinguishes two categories with, on the one hand, the cruciform stupa of Afghanistan and Pakistan in which the square plan of the base is still visible, and on the other hand the stupa of Central Asia (Xinjiang and Tajikistan) and Kashmir in which the size of the staircases is so great that it effectively disguises the square shape of the structure. In this second group the staircases are completely integrated into the structure of the stupa itself and, from this point on, no longer appear simply as architectural elements added on to allow access to the main body of the stupa.

This distinction, although of great importance, does not appear to us sufficient in itself to explain the evolution that took place in this type of stupa in Asia. The increasing complexity of the base plan of the cruciform stupa — in addition to the integration of the staircases and the increase in their size — is in fact accompanied by an increase in the number of redents, thus giving birth to the star-shaped stupa.

The shape therefore progresses from a simple modification of the square base, with the addition of a staircase on each façade, to an increasingly elaborate cruciform plan which gradually takes on the appearance of a star.

The introduction of this type of stupa in Buddhist architecture appears to go back to quite a distant date, as is shown by this representation on a bas-relief (Fig. 3) from northern Pakistan, dated to the 2nd to 3rd centuries AD, and also by this terracotta plaque (Fig. 4) found at

Fig. 3　Cruciform stupa from Northern Pakistan, 2nd–3rd Centuries A. D. after J. EBERT, "Niches, Columns and Figures in Some Petroglyphic Stupa Depictions of the Karakorum Highway," *AAS*, LIV. 3 – 4 (1994), Pl. 10.

①　T. FITZSIMMONS, *Stupa Designs at Taxila*, Kyoto, 2001, pp. 20 – 27.

②　*Ibid.*, p. 91.

Harwan① (Kashmir), in our opinion dating from the 5ᵗʰ century AD.

Fig. 4   Terracotta from Harwan (Kashemir). 5ᵗʰ Century A. D. after R. C. KAK,
Ancient Monuments of Kashmir, London, 1933, Pl. XVIII.

The evolution of the cruciform stupa can be divided into three phases: a first phase which is characterised by the addition of a staircase on each of the four façades of the monument, with the stupa now adopting a cruciform plan but with its square base still visible; a second phase which sees the elongation of the projection and of the staircase which it supports; and finally a third and last stage during which the stupa, initially cruciform in plan, becomes increasingly elaborate, its shape now resembling more that of a star than of a cross, and with the square base of the monument no longer visible but hidden within this form with multiple redents.

We will now study these three phases of evolution in turn, beginning with the earliest.

Among the oldest examples of the cruciform stupa some, in particular the stupa of Ahin Posh and Tahkal Bala, have been dated on the basis of the coin deposits found within the monument. These appear to represent foundation deposits, contemporaneous with the building of the stupa rather than with the later alterations leading up to the adoption of the cruciform shape. In any case this appears to be confirmed by the research carried out by Shoshin Kuwayama on the stupa of Shah-ji-ki-Dheri, which resulted in the dating of the cruciform plan of the monument to the years 560 – 630. ②

Thus the stupa of Ahin Posh③ (Figs. 5 and 6), situated in the region of Jalalabad, and stupa B at Tahkal Bala④ (Fig. 7), in the region of Peshawar, were both built in the 2ⁿᵈ century AD but were probably altered at a later time.

---

① P. PAL (Ed.), *Art and Architecture of Ancient Kashmir*, Bombay, 1989, p. 18 and S. L. SHALI, "Klosterbauten der alten Siedlung in Harwan (Kashmir)," *Das Altertum*, XXX. 1 (1984), pp. 49 – 53.

② Sh. KUWAYAMA, *The Main Stupa of Shāh-jī-kī Ḍherī. A Chronological Outlook*, Kyoto, 1997, p. 61.

③ A. FOUCHER, *La vieille Route de l'Inde de Bactres à Taxila*, vol. 1, Paris (MDAFA, I), 1942, p. 152.

④ E. ERRINGTON, "Tahkāl: the Nineteenth-century Recorded Two Lost Gandhāra Sites," *BSOAS*, L. 2 (1987), p. 311.

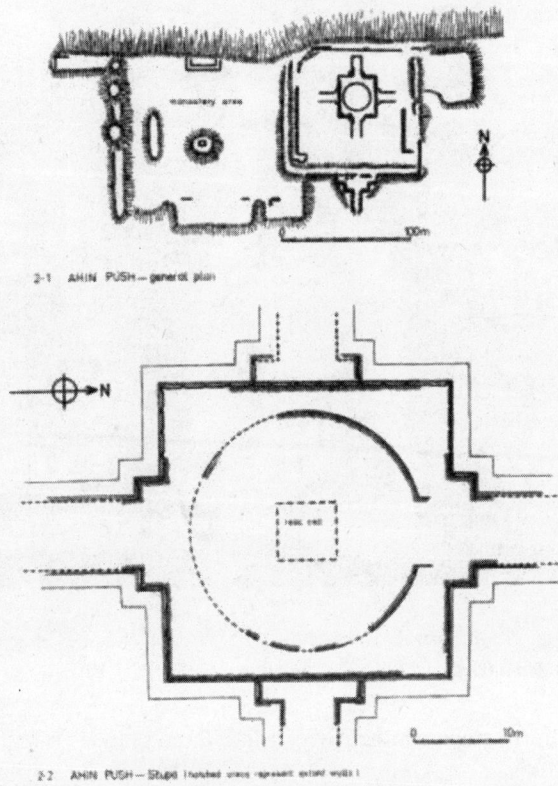

2-1 AHIN PUSH—general plan

2-2 AHIN PUSH—Stupa (hatched areas represent extant walls)

Fig. 5　Plan of the stupa of Ahin Posh（Afghanistan）after W. BALL, J.‒Cl. GARDIN, *Archaeological Gazetteer of Afghanistan. Catalogue des sites archéologiques d'Afghanistan*, Vol. 2, Paris, 1982, p. 418.

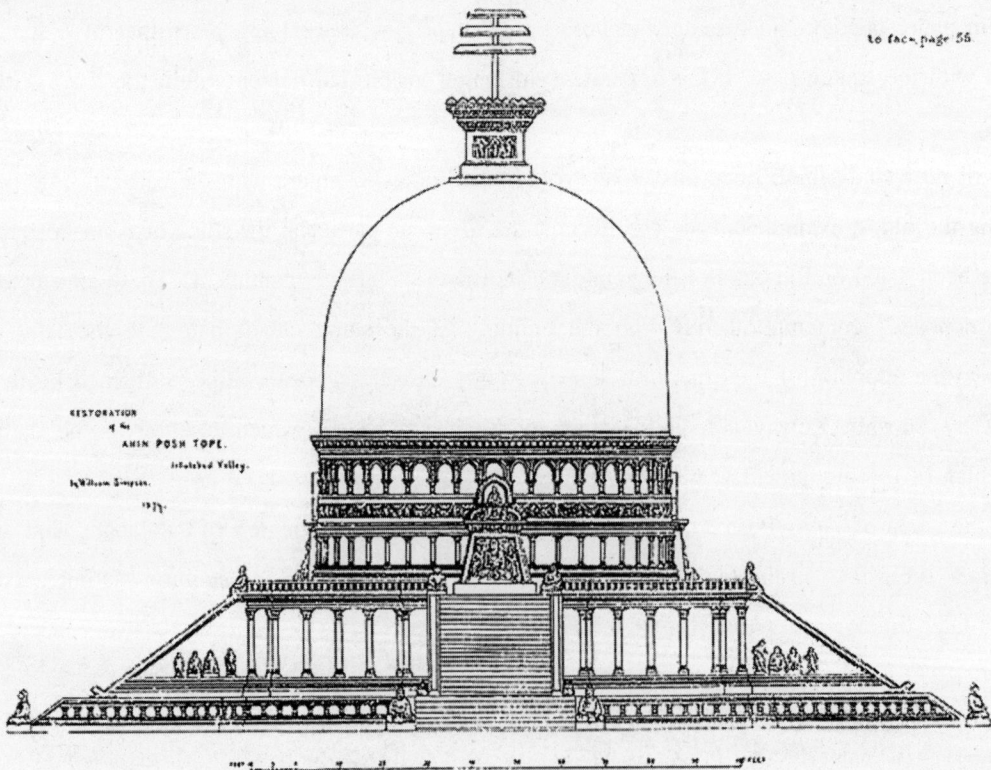

Fig. 6　Restitution of the stupa of Ahin Posh after W. SIMPSON, "Buddhist Architecture in the Jellalabad Valley," *Tr. R. I. B. A.*, 1879‒1880.

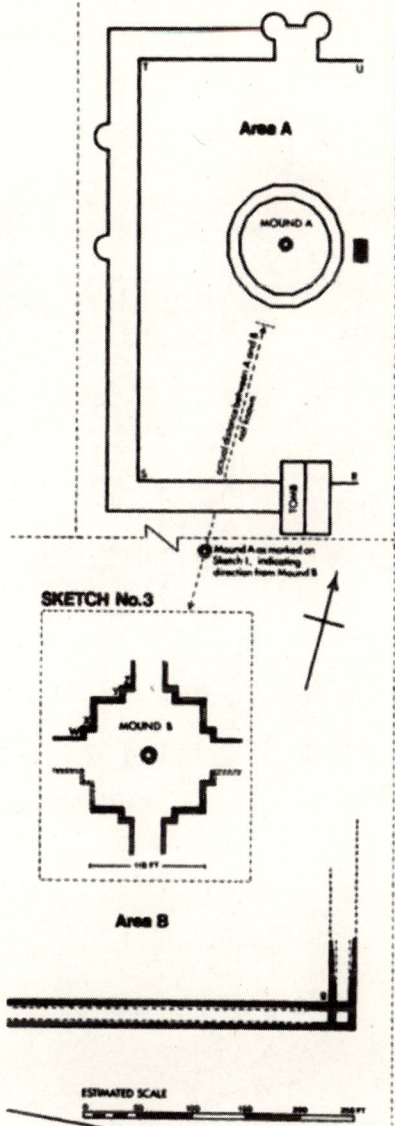

Fig. 7   Plan of Tahkāl Bālā after E. ERRINGTON, "Tahkāl: the Nineteenth-Century Recorded Two Lost Gandhāra Sites," *BSOAS*, L. 2 (1987), p. 309.

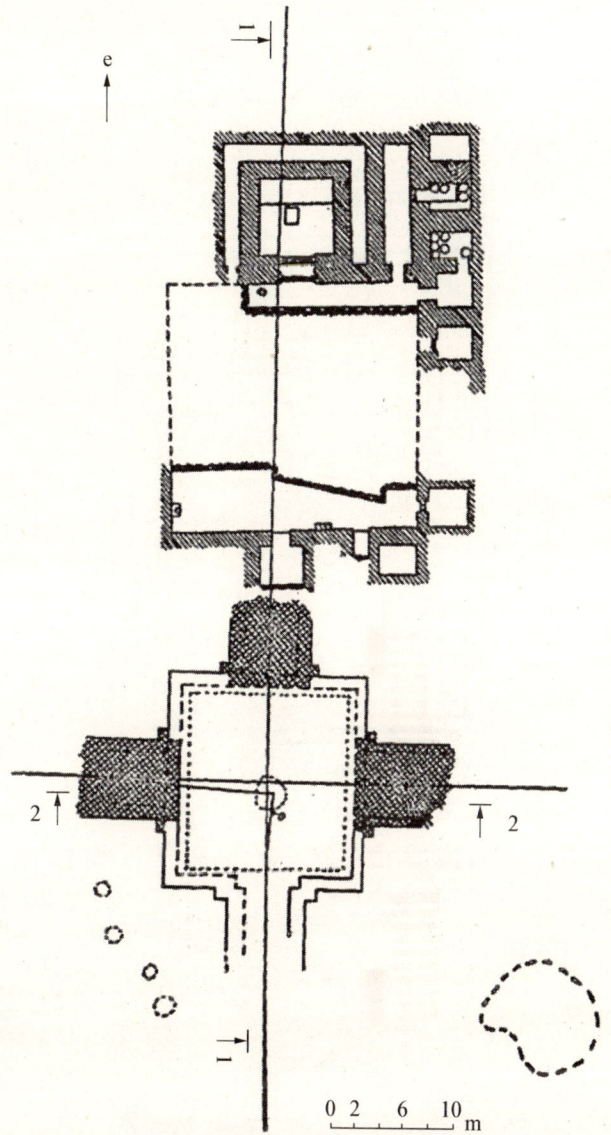

Fig. 8   Plan of Ushtur Mullo after T. ZEJMAL, "Buddhiiskii kompleks Ushtur Mullo," *Archeologiceskie raboty v Tadzikistane*, XIX (1979), p. 189.

Among other examples of the old cruciform stupas we also find the monuments of Ushtur Mullo[1] (Fig. 8), built in the 2nd to 3rd centuries and partially rebuilt after the 5th century, and Bhamala[2] (Figs. 9 and 10), situated in the region of Taxila and dated to the 5th to 8th centuries AD, as well as those of Top-i-Rustam[3] at Balkh, where the stupa (Figs. 11 and 12) was built near the end of the 2nd century and restored around the middle of the 6th century.

---

[1]   N. LAPIERRE, *Le bouddhisme en Sogdiane d'après les données de l'archéologie (IV-IXe siècles)*, Paris, 1998, p. 29.

[2]   K. A. BEHRENDT, *The Buddhist Architecture of Gandhāra*, Leyde, p. 267.

[3]   A. FOUCHER, *La vieille Route de l'Inde de Bactres à Taxila*, vol. 1, Paris (MDAFA, I), 1942, pp. 94–96.

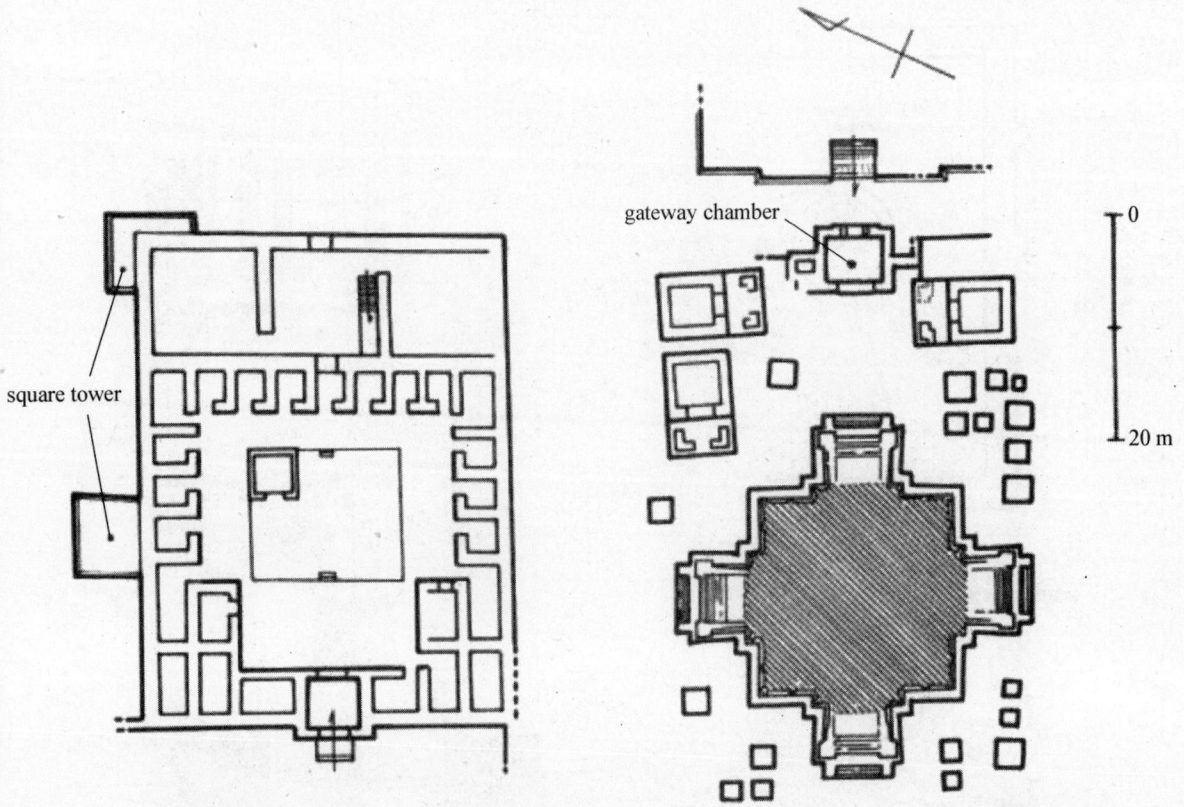

Fig. 9　Plan of Bhamāla after Sh. KUWAYAMA, *The Main Stupa of Shāh-jī-kī Ḍherī. A Chronological Outlook*, Kyoto, 1997, Fig. 17.

Fig. 10　recent view of the stupa of Bhamāla

Fig. 11   Reconstitution of the elevation of the stupa of Tope Rustam, Balkh, after A. FOUCHER, *La vieille route de l'Inde de Bactres à Taxila*, Paris (MDAFA I), 1942, Fig. 25, p. 95.

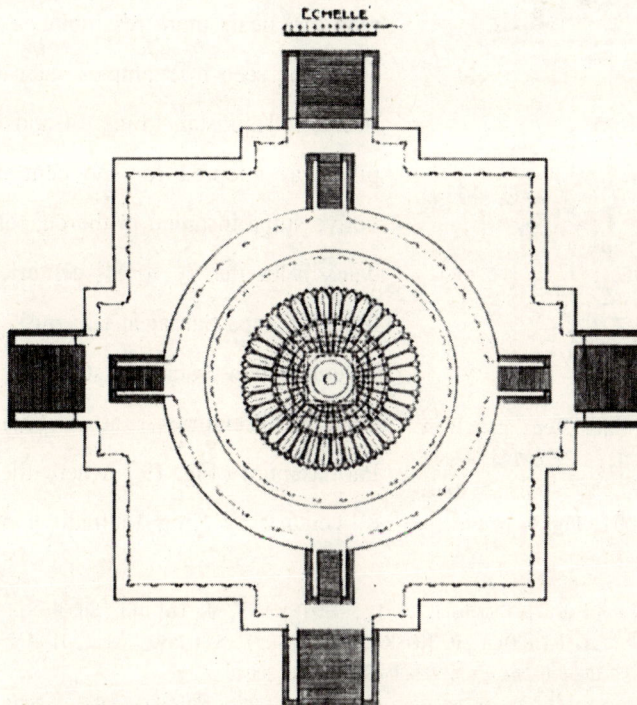

Fig. 12   Reconstitution of the plan of the stupa of Tope Rustam, Balkh, after A. FOUCHER, *La vieille route de l'Inde de Bactres à Taxila*, Paris (MDAFA I), 1942, Fig. 23, p. 90.

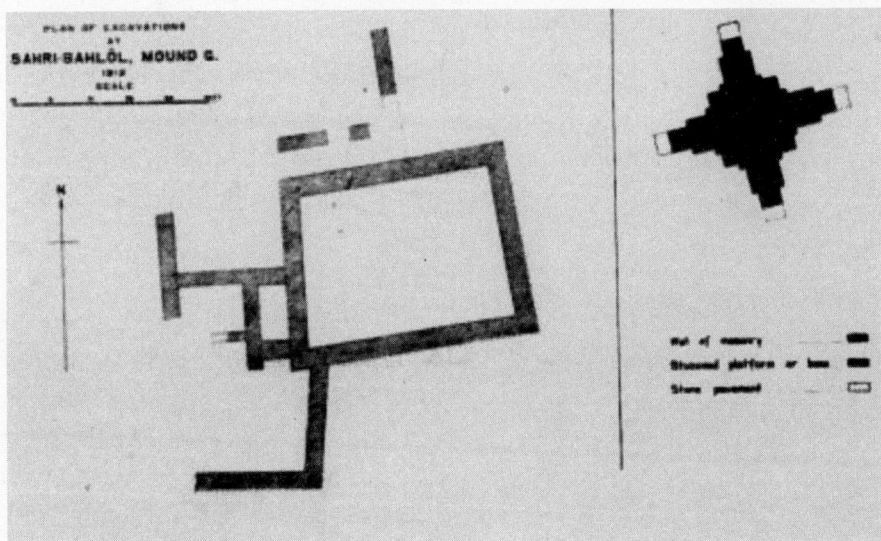

Fig. 13   Plan of the site G of Sahrī-Bāhlol after M. A. STEIN, "Excavations at Sahri-Bahlol," *ASIAR 1911 – 1912*, Calcutta, 1915, Pl. XXXV.

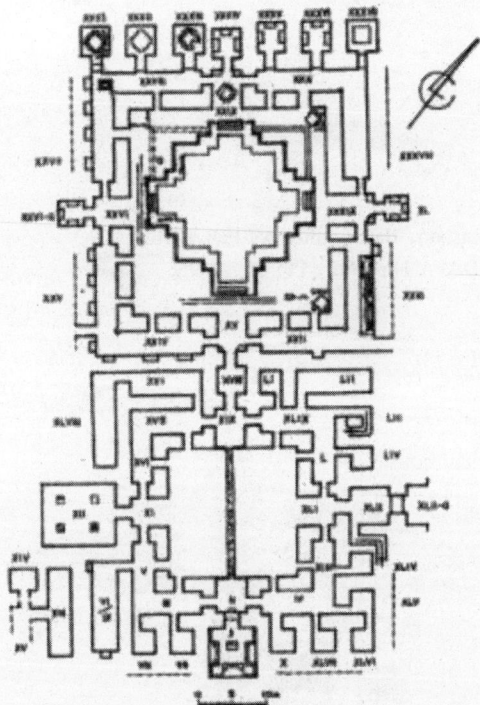

Fig. 14   Plan of monastery of Ajina Tepa after B. A. LITVINSKIJ, T. I. ZEYMAL, *The Buddhist Monastery of Ajina Tepa, Tajikistan*, Rome, 2004, Fig. 3, p. 20.

Stupa G at the Sahrī-Bāhlol[1] site (Fig. 13), dating from the 5th to 8th centuries,[2] may mark an intermediate phase in the development of this cruciform plan; in fact it is noticeable that the projection supporting the staircase becomes broader, and also apparently longer.

In its latest phase, the cruciform stupa is built to a plan that bears more resemblance to a star than to a cross, as can be seen in examples such as those of Ajina Tepa,[3] southern Tajikistan (Figs. 14 and 15), where the cruciform plan was adopted for the central stupa but also for the votive stupa installed in the chapels; this monastic complex dates from the 7th to 8th centuries. Further examples are found at Tapa Sardar at Ghazni[4] (Figs. 16 and 17) where several votive cruciform stupas date from the 7th to 8th and even 9th centuries, at Ushkur[5] (Fig. 18) and at Parihasapura (Fig. 19) where the stupas were built in the 8th century by King Lalitaditya of the Karkota dynasty,[6]

① F. TISSOT, "The Site of Sahrī-Bāhlol in Gandhāra," in J. SCHOTSMANS, M. TADDEI (Ed.), *SAA 1983*, Naples, 1985, p. 611 et F. TISSOT, "Sahrī-Bāhlol (Part IV)," in A. PARPOLA, P. KOSKIKALLIO (Ed.), *SAA 1993*, vol. 2, Helsinki, pp. 733 – 744.

② K. A. BEHRENDT, *The Buddhist Architecture of Gandhāra*, Leyde, 2004, p. 267.

③ B. A. LITVINSKIJ, T. I. ZEYMAL, *The Buddhist Monastery of Ajina Tepa, Tajikistan*, Rome, 2004, p. 11.

④ M. TADDEI, G. VERARDI, "Clay Stupas and Thrones at Tapa Sardār Ghazni (Afghanistan)," *Zinbun*, Kyoto, XX (1985), p. 19.

⑤ P. PAL (Ed.), *Art and Architecture of Ancient Kashmir*, Bombay, 1989, p. 24.

⑥ J. NAUDOU, *Les Bouddhistes Kashmiriens au Moyen Age*, Paris, 1968, pp. 50 – 51.

and finally at Paharpur (Figs. 19 and 20) where the stupa dates from the end of the 8th and beginning of the 9th centuries — as well as in India [Antichak, dating from the 9th century (Fig. 22) and in South-East Asia but, since the writer is not a specialist in these regions, we will leave these examples aside].

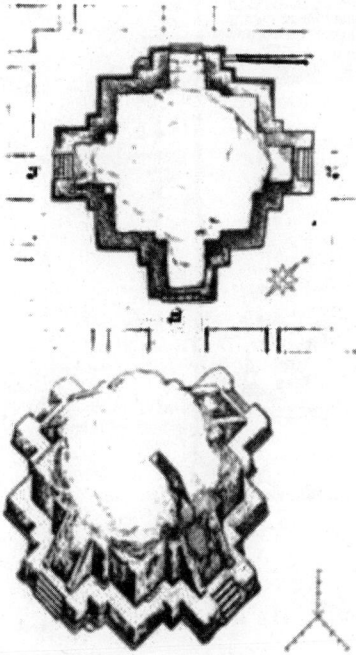

Fig. 15 Plan and axonometry of the principal stupa of Ajina Tepa after B. A. LITVINSKIJ, T. I. ZEYMAL, *The Buddhist Monastery of Ajina Tepa, Tajikistan*, Rome, 2004, Fig. 17, p. 36.

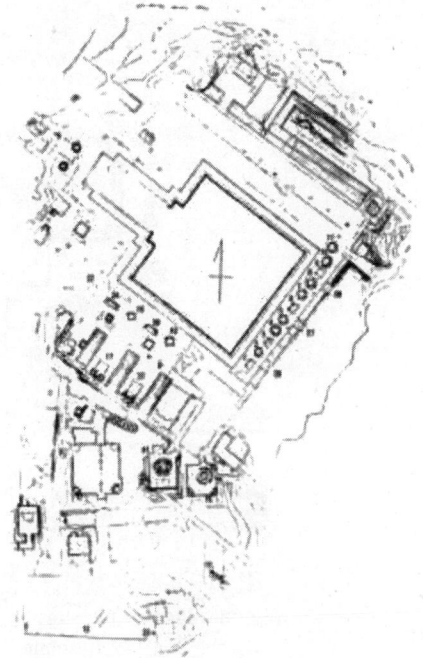

Fig. 16 General plan of Tapa Sardar after M. TADDEI, G. VERARDI, "Clay Stupas and Thrones at Tapa Sardar, Ghazni (Afghanistan)," *Zinbun*, *Kyoto*, XX (1985), Fig. 1, p. 18.

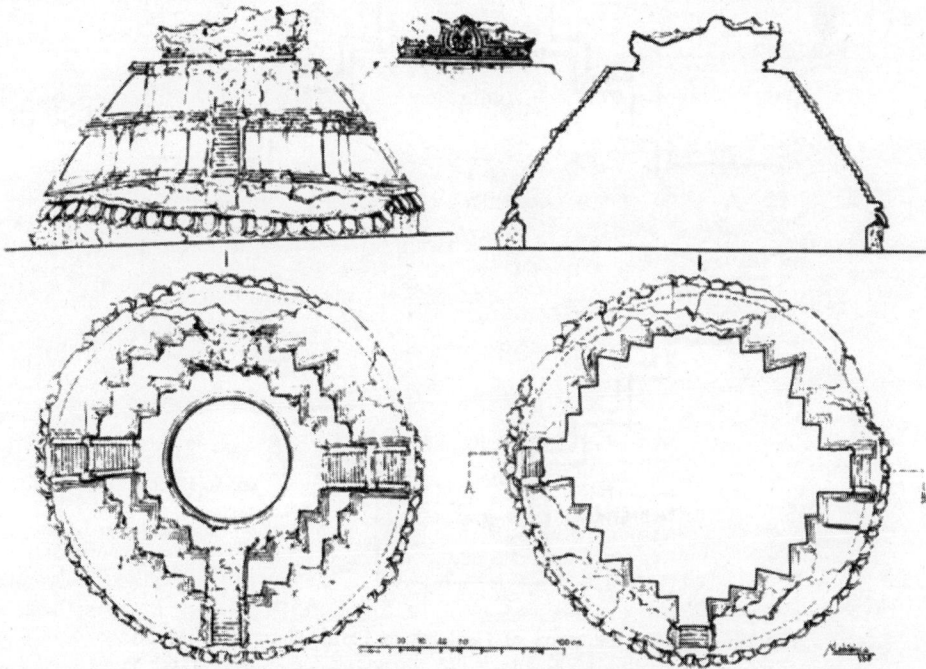

Fig. 17 Side view, vertical section, horizontal and zenithal point of view of stupa n°8 after M. TADDEI, G. VERARDI, "Clay Stupas and Thrones at Tapa Sardar, Ghazni (Afghanistan)," *Zinbun*, *Kyoto*, XX (1985), Fig. 2, p. 22.

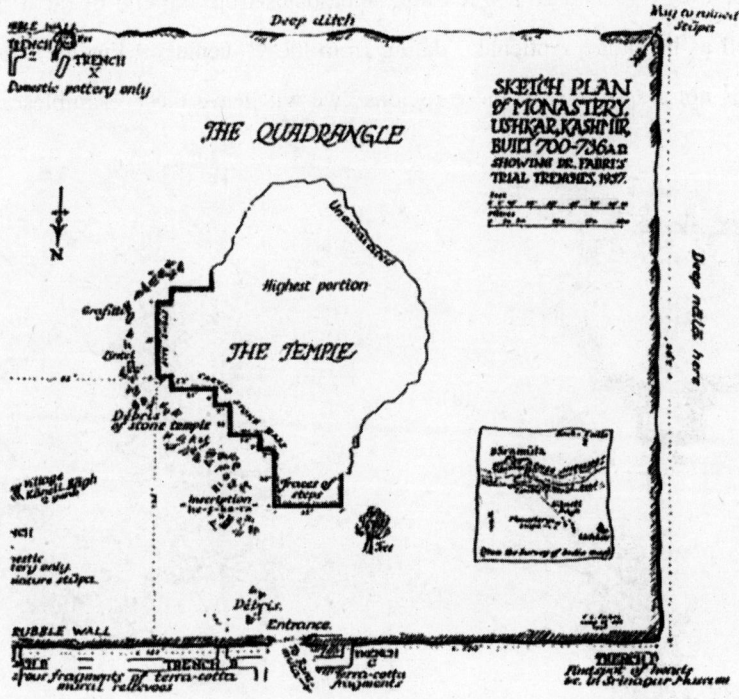

Fig. 18 Plan of the stupa of Ushkur after Ch. FABRI, "The Road to Central Asia. 3. Kashmir," *Marg*, IX. 2 (1956), pp. 57 – 59.

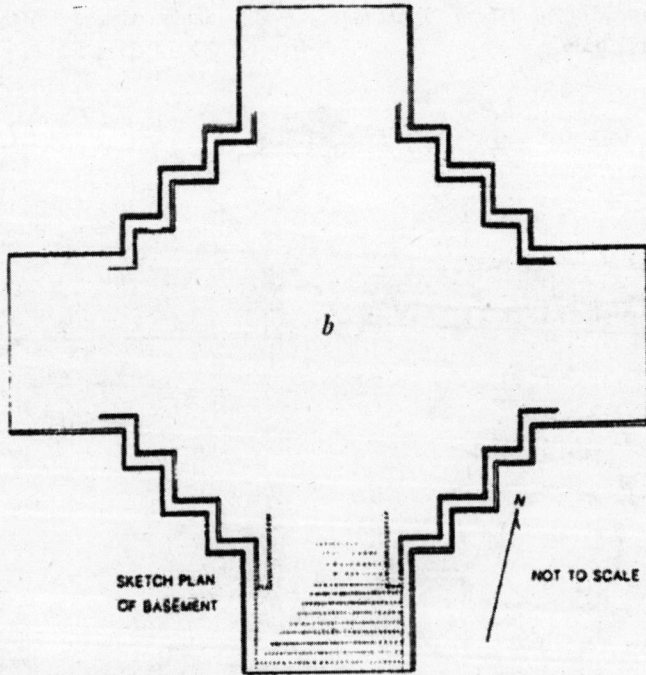

Fig. 19 Plan of the stupa of Cankuna at Parihasapura after M. M. RHIE, *Early Buddhist Art of China and Central Asia*, I, Leiden, 1999, Fig. 4. 24 a et b.

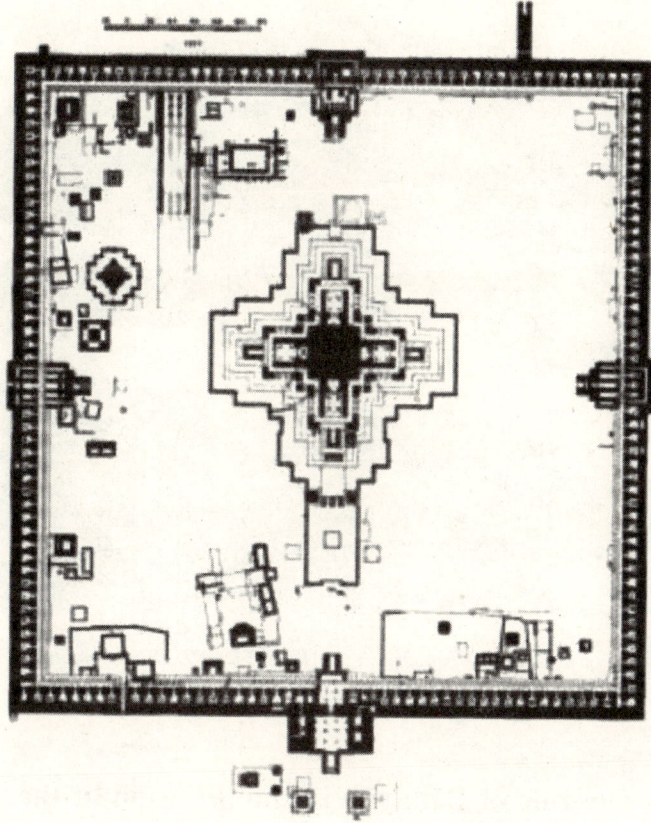

Fig. 20   General plan of the monastery of Pāhārpur after H. G. FRANZ, *Von Gandhara bis Pagan*, Graz, 1979, Fig. 130, p. 91.

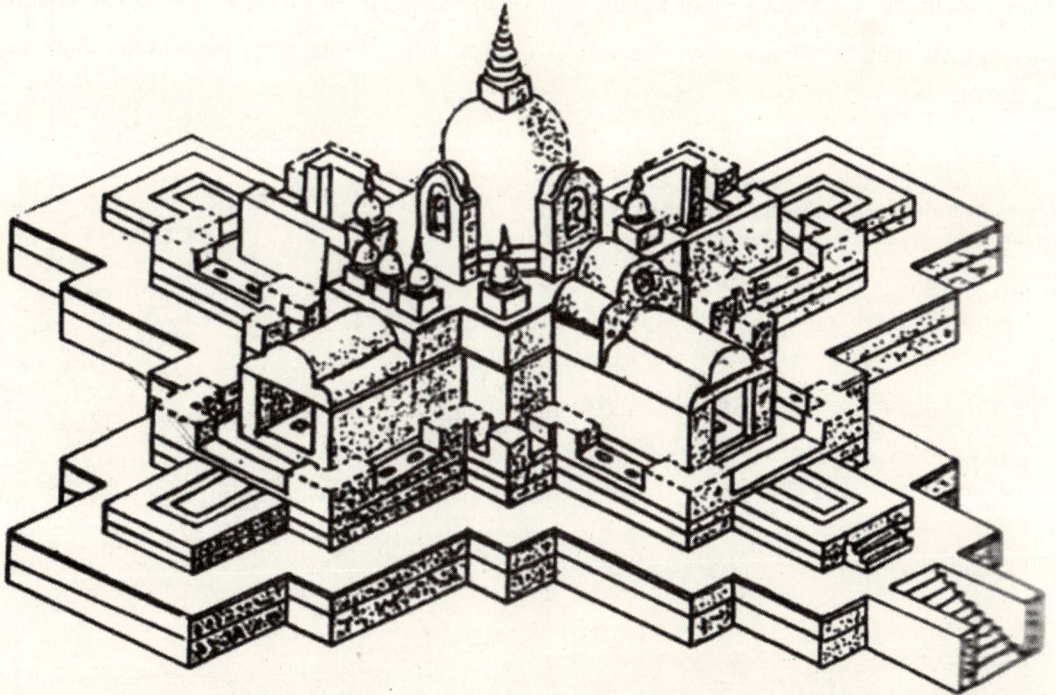

Fig. 21   Reconstitution of the elevation of the stupa of Pāhārpur after H. KOTTKAMP, *Der Stupa als Repräsentation der Buddhistischen Heilsweges: Untersuchen und Entwicklung architektonischer Symbolik*, Wiesbaden, 1992, Fig. 117.

Fig. 22　View of the stupa of Antichak after H. G. FRANZ, *Von Gandhara bis Pagan*, Graz, 1979, Pl. XXV, Fig. 51.

The role of Bāmiyān in the diffusion of the
cruciform model in Chinese Central Asia

Situated about 250 km north-west of Kabul, in a valley in the Hindu Kush, Bāmiyān was at a crossroads of the ancient trade routes linking Afghanistan with Asia, with China to the east, India to the south and Persia to the west (Fig. 23).

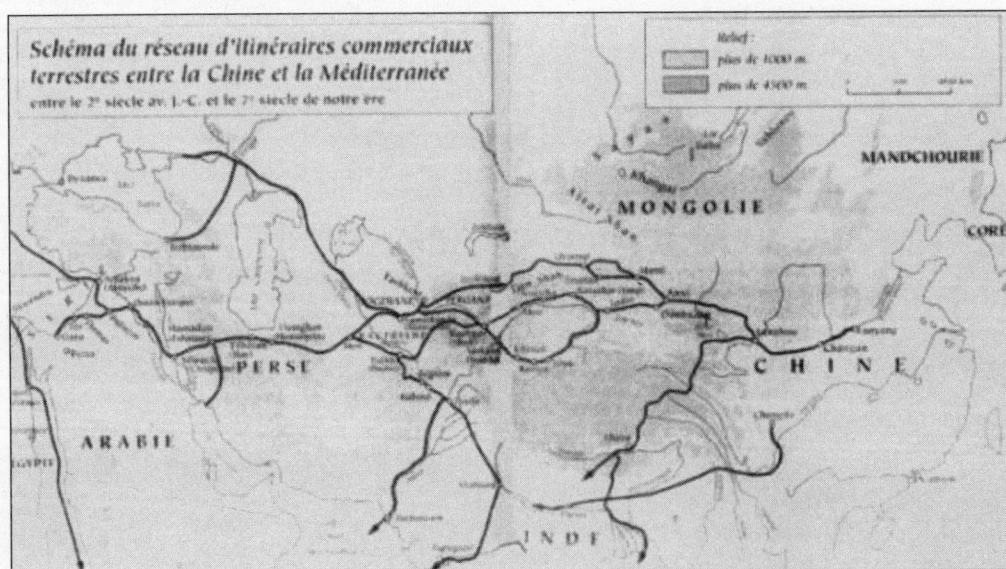

Fig. 23　Map of the Silk Road (3th B. C. - 7th A. D.) after L. BOULNOIS, *La Route de la Soie. Dieux, guerriers et marchands*, Olizane, 2001[3].

With around 750 caves, the Bāmiyān site is clearly the largest Buddhist complex in Afghanistan. These caves were carved out of the cliff which dominates the valley to the north, stretching for more than 1. 3 km and rising in places to a height of 150 m. [1]

The site is mentioned in the stories of numerous pilgrims and travellers, especially in the 19th century, including W. Moorcroft and G. Trebeck, Sir Alexander Burnes and Dr. J. Gerard, C. Masson and others. However, it was only from the 1930s onwards that it became the subject of proper research under the direction of French archaeologists, thanks to an archaeological agreement signed in 1922 between the French Republic and the Kingdom of Afghanistan, which would lead to the creation of the French Archaeological Delegation in Afghanistan (Délégation Archéologique Française en Afghanistan — DAFA). These first archaeological studies were initiated by André Godard[2] and Joseph Hackin[3] and continued under the leadership of the latter and of his architect Jean Carl.

After the Second World War, Benjamin Rowland[4] was the first to resume study of the site, followed in the 1970s by Zémaryalaï Tarzi[5] whose work was the subject of a publication in 1977, and by various Japanese teams: one from the University of Kyoto led by Prof. S. Mizuno,[6] and others from the Universities of Nagoya,[7] Seijo[8] and finally Kyoto with Prof. T. Higuchi[9] from 1970 to 1978.

Notable also in the same period was the presence of a team from the Archaeological Survey of India, who were allotted the task of restoring the two great Buddhas as well as the mural paintings in several recesses. In addition, this Indian team undertook a complete inventory of the surviving paintings.

The work of P. H. Baker and F. R. Allchin[10] on the Shahri Zohak must also be noted, as well as that of Marc Le Berre[11] who studied the architecture of the Bāmiyān region, especially the ruins of the fortified monuments. In the process he visited more than a hundred "castles" or forts in a radius of 50 km around Bāmiyān, while Jean-Claude Gardin and Bertille Lyonnet studied the shards collected by Le Berre and devoted a section in his work to these.

It was not until 2002, one year after the fall of the Taliban, that archaeological study of the Buddhist

① T. HIGUCHI, G. BARNES, "Bāmiyān: Buddhist Cave Temples in Afghanistan," *World Archaeology*, XXVII. 2 (Oct. 1995), p. 282 and 287.

② A. GODARD, Y. GODARD, J. HACKIN, *Les antiquités bouddhiques de Bāmiyān*, Paris, MDAFA, II, 1928.

③ J. HACKIN, J. CARL, *Nouvelles recherches archéologiques à Bāmiyān 1930*, Paris, MDAFA, III, 1933 et J. HACKIN, "Recherches archéologiques à Bāmiyān en 1933," in *Diverses recherches archéologiques en Afghanistan 1933–1940*, Paris, MDAFA, VIII, 1959, pp. 1–6.

④ B. ROWLAND, "The Colossal Buddhas at Bāmiyān," *Journal of the Indian Society of the Oriental Art*, XV (1947), pp. 62–73; *Ancient Art from Afghanistan*, New York, 1966; "The Wall Painting of Bāmiyān," *Marg*, XXIV. 2 (1971), pp. 25–43.

⑤ Z. TARZI, *L'architecture et le décor rupestre des grottes de Bāmiyān*, 2 vols, Paris, 1977.

⑥ S. MIZUNO, "Buddhist Sites of the Hindukush, North and South," *Bunmei no Jujiro*, Tokyo, 1962, pp. 106–143.

⑦ S. KASHIWAGI, "The Iconographic Plan of the 35 meter Buddha at Bāmiyān," *Nagoya University Faculty of Letters Research Paper*, XLII (1966), pp. 59–75 et "Discovery of the N-cave at Bāmiyān," *Nagoya University of Letters Research Papers*, XLV (1967), pp. 93–120.

⑧ S. TAKADA, "Investigations of Mural Paintings in the Great Buddha Niche," *Bukkyo Geijutsu*, CXVII (1978), pp. 41–44.

⑨ T. HIGUCHI, *Japan-Afghanistan Joint Archaeological Survey in 1974*, Kyoto, 1976; *Japan-Afghanistan Joint Archaeological Survey in 1976*, Kyoto, 1978; *Japan-Afghanistan Joint Archaeological Survey in 1978*, Kyoto, 1980 et *Bāmiyān*, 4 vols, Kyoto, 2001².

⑩ P. H. BAKER, F. R. ALLCHIN, *Shahr-I Zohaq and the History of the Bāmiyān Valley, Afghanistan*, Oxford (Ancient Iran and India Trust, Série 1), 1991.

⑪ M. LE BERRE, *Monuments préislamiques de la région de l'Hindukush central*, MDAFA, XIV (1987).

monuments of Bāmiyān was resumed by Prof. Tarzi. On the basis of past investigations and of the accounts of Xuanzang, the famous Chinese pilgrim who visited Bāmiyān between 629 and 632 AD, Prof. Tarzi set up an archaeological expedition with the aim of finding the "eastern monastery" and the statue of the sleeping Buddha which it was supposed to contain. Situated to the south-east of the 38 metre Buddha, this "eastern monastery" was believed to be somewhere around the foot of the cliff, to the east, and in the vicinity of the only sizeable stupa in the valley. The excavations of 2002[①] were cut short, but those of 2003 resulted in the opening of several trenches and the discovery of the "eastern monastery" whose principal architectural features (stupa 2, caitya I, stupa 4, gallery A9, etc.) were uncovered only in the course of the seasons of 2005, 2006 and 2007. It was also during these seasons that the north and east façades of stupa 1 — or the "Great Stupa" (GS) — were uncovered, thus revealing its cruciform plan (Fig. 24).

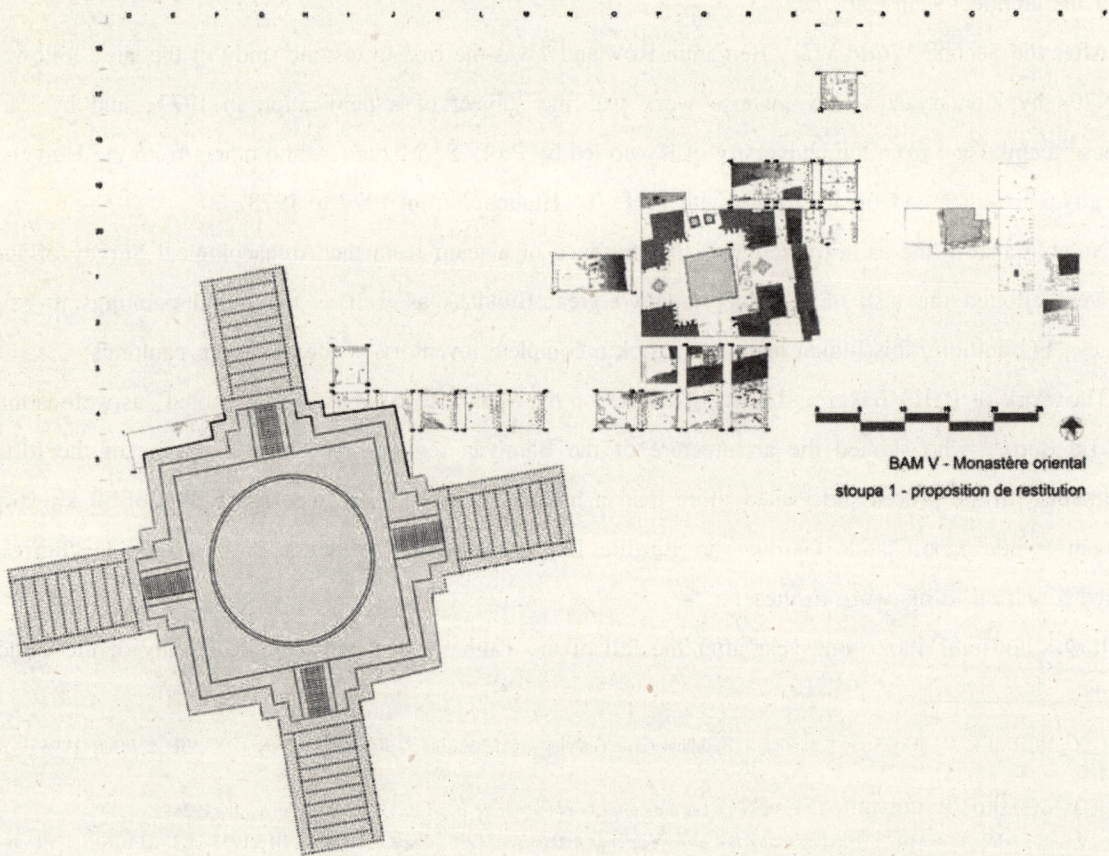

BAM V - Monastère oriental
stoupa 1 - proposition de restitution

Fig. 24   General plan of the "Eastern Monastery" (Plan of © Ph. BODO)

The "Great Stupa" measures 29 m across and still rises to several metres in height in spite of its poor state of preservation (Fig. 25). Since the whole structure was virtually destroyed, the surface of the monument was no longer visible except for its base.

The whole of the structure excavated was entirely covered by a thick coating of ashes (Fig. 26)

---

① Z. TARZI, "Bāmiyān Pr. Tarzi's Survey and Excavation Archaeological Mission, 2003," *The Silk Road*, I. 2 (Winter 2003), pp. 37 - 39.

Fig. 25　View of the "Great Stupa (GS)" of the "Eastern Monastery" (Photo © Z. TARZI)

Fig. 26　View of the Northern section of the Great Stupa's excavations (Photo © Z. TARZI)

consisting not only of pieces of charred wood, some of which were clearly from beams, but also of fragments of iron and bronze as well as numerous clay fragments. This layer clearly demonstrates the size and intensity of the fire which ravaged the monument; as for the different elements it contained, they could indicate the existence of a *vedika* or *pado-vedika*[①] or else of a crown or cover.

---

① Z. TARZI, "Bāmiyān 2006: The Fifth Excavation Campaign of Pr. Tarzi's Mission," *The Silk Road*, IV. 2 (Winter 2006–2007), pp. 19–20.

Another important point, in this case relating to the form of the monument itself, is the discovery in 2006 of a staircase built onto the north façade (Fig. 27). The presence of this staircase has led us to believe that this stupa may have been built on a cruciform plan.

From the study of our findings, both architectural and material, Prof. Tarzi[1] has concluded that this "eastern monastery" underwent two phases of construction and development:

— a first phase, probably contemporaneous with the construction of the Small Buddha, dating from the Kushan era and lasting from the 3rd or even 2nd century to the 5th century AD. This first period comes to an end with the destruction of the site by the Sasanians or the Hephtalites.

— a second phase, in this case contemporaneous with the restoration of the Small Buddha and the building of the Great Buddha, and which goes back to the 6th century and lasts until the 9th century, namely until the destruction of Bāmiyān by Ya'qub Ben Laith as-Saffari in 871. This second period corresponds to an extension phase of the "eastern monastery" site with the construction of the Great Stupa, but also to a phase of restoration and development of some parts of the site.

While the Great Stupa is unfortunately not very well preserved in elevation, it is nevertheless possible to gain some idea of its original appearance thanks to the votive stupas 3 and 5, built in Caitya I and contemporaneous with the construction of the Great Stupa.

These two votive stupas in clay are preserved on two vertical levels, thus allowing us to envisage what their painted decoration may have been, with regularly spaced columns and modillions (Figs. 28, 29 and 30).

Here we find the same plan as that which was used for the Great Stupa, namely a square — or almost square — plan, to which a staircase was added on each façade. Each one measures 1. 96 m from north to south, and 1. 99 m from east to west.

The Great Stupa of Bāmiyān would appear to represent the "missing link" between the oldest Afghan, Pakistani and Central Asian forms (Ahin Posh, Tahkal Bala, Ushtur Mullo, Bhamala, Top-i-Rustam at Balkh) and the Central Asian forms of Xinjiang.

In fact several examples of this type of stupa are known in Xinjiang, two of which are situated on the southern Silk Road: the Rawak Stupa[2] and Stupa F. VI at Farhad-Beg-Yailaki.

On the northern route, however, the known examples are later — we refer in particular to Temple Z at Qocho, the two stupas at Kichik-Hassar (Constructions I and II), and to the stupas built around the site of

---

[1] Z. TARZI, "Bāmiyān 2006: The Fifth Excavation Campaign of Pr. Tarzi's Mission," *The Silk Road*, IV. 2 (Winter 2006 – 2007), pp. 20 – 21.

[2] M. A. STEIN, *Ancient Khotan*, vol. 1, Oxford, 1907, pp. 484 – 486.

Fig. 27 View of the Northern face of the "Great Stupa (GS)" (Photo © Z. TARZI)

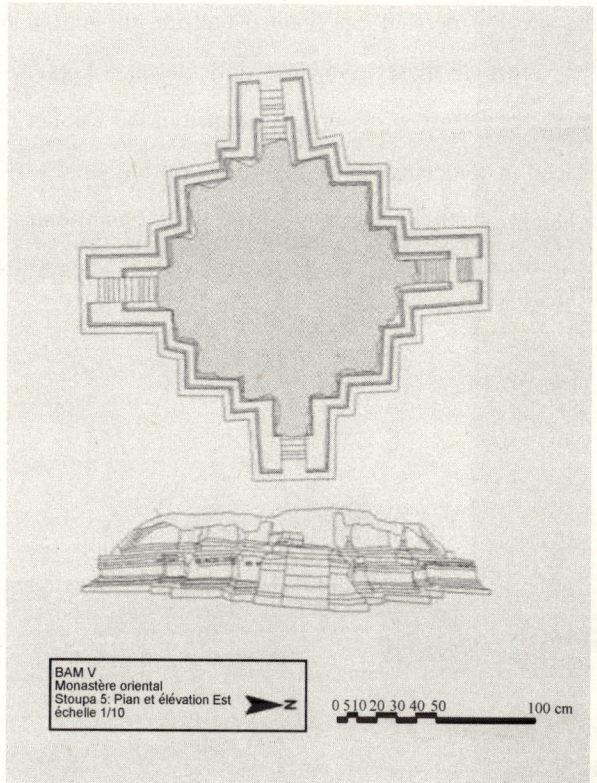

Fig. 28 Plan of the Votive stupa n°5 (Plan of © Ph. BODO)

Fig. 29 View of the votive stupa n°5 (Photo © Ph. BODO)

Fig. 30 View of votive stupa n°5 before restoration (Photo © Z. TARZI)

Sangym-aghyz of which the best preserved example is situated close to Temple 9. All these monuments are generally dated to the Uyghur era[1] (end of 9th to end of 13th centuries); they could be compared with our present study but they appear to show a strong Chinese influence, very different from that which is visible on the sites of the southern route,[2] and for this reason we will set them aside.

From all these examples, only Rawak (Figs. 31 and 32) shows a strong similarity in its plan with the stupas of Bāmiyān. Rawak is situated in the Khotan region, on the southern part of the Silk Road. Its stupa is placed in a rectangular courtyard measuring 49.69 by 42.98 m; it is preserved up to the base of the dome at a height of 10 m, and it is 23.8 wide. This monument shows a strong similarity in plan with the stupas of Bāmiyān. It is generally dated to the 6th–7th centuries.

Fig. 31   Recent view of the stupa of Rawak

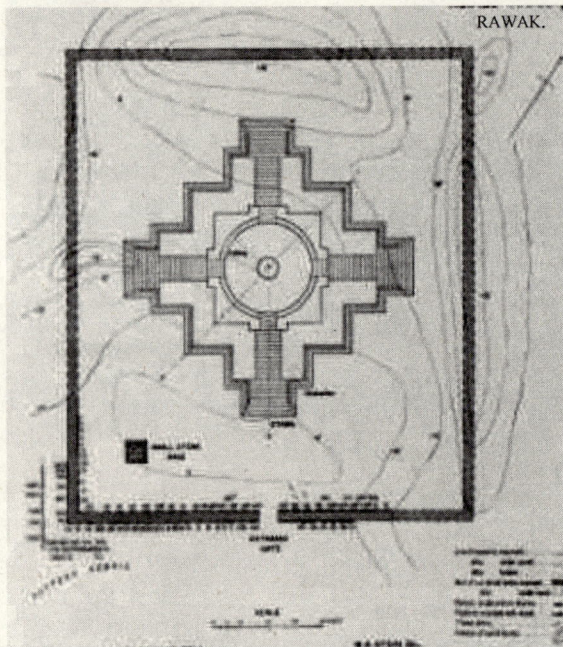

Fig. 32   Plan of the stupa of Rawak after M. A. STEIN, *Ancient Khotan*, I, Oxford, 1907, Pl. XXXIX.

The cruciform plan of the Bāmiyān stupas appears subsequently to have undergone a wide diffusion outside its own area, as witnessed in the numerous ex-voto found in Afghanistan (Figs. 33–35), in Xinjiang and in Gansu (Figs. 37–40). These ex-voto may represent an intermediate development phase between the typical Bāmiyān plan and that of Farhād Beg Yailakī.

Both their construction and their consecration are governed by ritual.[3] They are generally placed either on or next to the stupa, or even within the structure. Certain writers, such as M. Taddei,[4] thought that they

---

① M. MAILLARD, *Grottes et monuments d'Asie Centrale*, Paris, 1983, p. 170.

② M. MAILLARD, *Op. Cit.*, p. 171.

③ G. TUCCI, *Stupa. Art, Architectonics and Symbolism*, New Dehli, 1988², pp. 57–59.

④ M. TADDEI, "Inscribed Clay Tablets and Miniature stūpa from Ghazni," *Afghanistan*, XXVI. 2 (1973), p. 30.

Fig. 33 Miniature Stupa (model C) after M. TADDEI, "Inscribed Clay Tablets and Miniature Stupas from Ghazni," *Afghanistan*, XXVI. 2 (1973), p. 23.

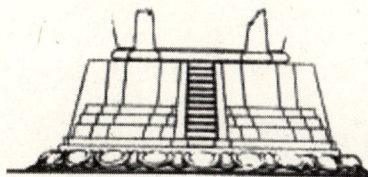

Fig. 34 Miniature Stupa (model D) after M. TADDEI, "Inscribed Clay Tablets and Miniature Stupas from Ghazni," *Afghanistan*, XXVI. 2 (1973), p. 23.

Fig. 35 Miniature Stupa (model E) after M. TADDEI, "Inscribed Clay Tablets and Miniature Stupas from Ghazni," *Afghanistan*, XXVI. 2 (1973), p. 23.

were made by the monks and sold to pilgrims as souvenirs of their pilgrimage.[1] Xuanzang[2] tells us that in India this type of ex-voto is made under the name of "Dharma-sarira" and that, once a considerable number of them has been assembled, a large stupa is built to receive them.

These stupas were consecrated by the addition of a phrase carved onto their surface, or else by a tablet inserted into the interior of the ex-voto.

Several examples of ex-votos have been found in Afghanistan on the site of Gudul-i Ahangaran in the Ghazni region (Figs. 33, 34 and 35), these small stupas being somewhat reminiscent of those at Tapa Sardar, similarly placed on a lotus; other examples are found in the Gilgit region (Fig. 36).

Miniature stupas of the same type have been found in Xinjiang (Fig. 38) at the sites of Khadalik and in the Sangym valley, and also in Gansu (Figs. 39 and 40) and in Mongolia (Fig. 37).

Fig. 36 Miniature Stupa discovered at Gilgit (?) after H. G. FRANZ, "Der Buddhistische Stupa in Afghanistan — Ursprünge und Entwicklung (Teil 2)," *Afghanistan Journal*, V. 1 (1978), Fig. 38, p. 35.

The plans of these votive stupas are characterised by a double projection at the level of the staircase. This cruciform plan appears to be elaborated further in Stupa F. VI at Farhad-Beg-Yailaki (Figs. 41 and 42), situated near Domoko in the Khotan region and dated to the 6th century.[3]

---

[1] M. TADDEI, "Inscribed Clay Tablets and Miniature stūpa from Ghazni," *Afghanistan*, XXVI. 2 (1973), p. 40.

[2] *Ibid.*

[3] M. A. STEIN, *Serindia*, vol. I, Oxford, 1921, pp. 1250–1254.

Fig. 37　Miniature stupa discovered at Karakhoto after M. A. STEIN, *Innermost Asia*, vol. III, Oxford, 1928, Pl. LIII, K. K. I. 0225.

Fig. 38　Miniature stupa discovered at Sangym-aghyz after A. Von LE COQ, *Chotscho*, Berlin, 1913, Pl. 59, b.

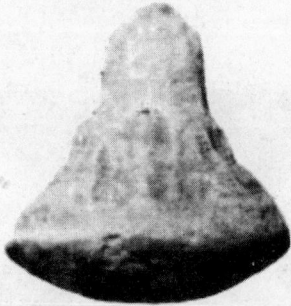

Fig. 39　Miniature stupa discovered in Gansu after M. A. STEIN, *Serindia*, vol. IV, Oxford, 1921, Pl. CXXXIX, So. a. 006 (Hight and diameter of the base: 7,62 cm).

Fig. 40　Miniature stupa discovered in Gansu after M. A. STEIN, *Serindia*, vol. IV, Oxford, 1921, Pl. CXXXIX, So. a. 009.

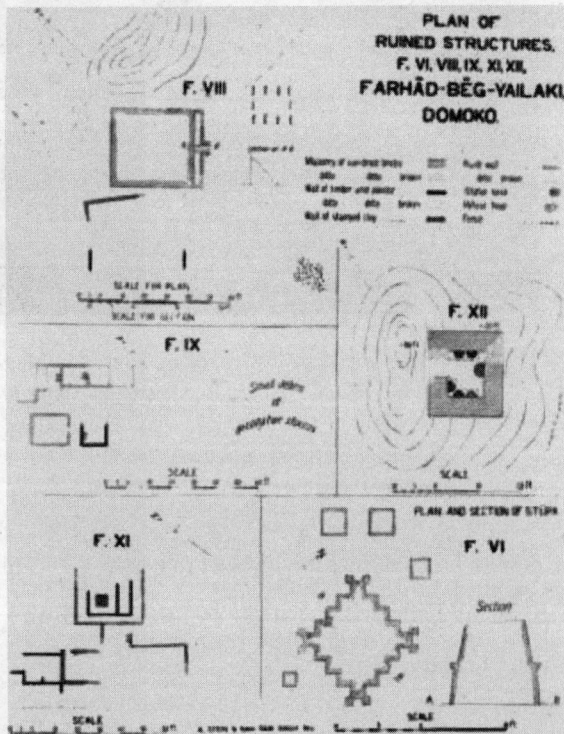

Fig. 41　Plan of the stupa of Farhād Beg Yailakī after M. A. STEIN, *Serindia*, vol. I, 1921, Pl. 58.

Fig. 42　View of the stupa of Farhād Beg Yailakī after M. A. STEIN, *Serindia*, vol. I, Oxford, 1921, Fig. 311, p. 1250.

We hope that in this study we have demonstrated the role played by Bāmiyān in the diffusion of the cruciform type of stupa in Asia and especially in Xinjiang. In fact it appears to have been adopted there and then adapted over the course of time.

Although we have not had access to all the elements necessary for an overall understanding of this process of diffusion, we can nevertheless assume that the Silk Road played a very important role between Afghanistan and China. It is partly thanks to it that a religious dialogue was made possible at certain times, as is witnessed through the various texts found at Bāmiyān among which were some in the Khotan language. [1] In addition to this linguistic evidence, we therefore have a fresh example of these religious exchanges which are here expressed in the dissemination of an architectural form.

ABBREVIATED TITLES

AAs   Artibus Asiae

ASIAR   Archaeological Survey of India. Annual Report

BEFEO   Bulletin de l'Ecole Française d'Extrême-Orient

BSOAS   Bulletin of the School of Oriental and African Studies

MDAFA   Mémoires de la Délégation Archéologique Française en Afghanistan

SAA   South Asian Archaeology

Tr. R. I. B. A.   Royal Institute of British Architects Transactions

BIBLIOGRAPHY

P. H. BAKER, F. R. ALLCHIN, *Shahr-I Zohaq and the History of the Bāmiyān Valley, Afghanistan*, Oxford (Ancient Iran and India Trust, Série 1), 1991.

K. A. BEHRENDT, *The Buddhist Architecture of Gandhāra*, Leiden: Brill (Handbook of Oriental Studies, section 2, vol. 17), 2004.

M. BENISTI, "Etude sur le stupa en Inde ancienne," *BEFEO*, L. 1 (1960 - 1962), pp. 40 - 108.

E. ERRINGTON, "Tahkāl: the Nineteenth-Century Recorded Two Lost Gandhāra Sites," *BSOAS*, L. 2 (1987), pp. 301 - 324.

T. FITZSIMMONS, *Stupa Designs at Taxila*, Kyoto: Institute for Research in Humanities, Kyoto University, 2001.

A. FOUCHER, *La vie du Bouddha, d'après les textes et les monuments de l'Inde*, Paris: Maisonneuve, 1993.

A. FOUCHER, *La vieille Route de l'Inde de Bactres à Taxila*, vol. 1, Paris, MDAFA, I, 1942.

A. GODARD, Y. GODARD, J. HACKIN, *Les Antiquités bouddhiques de Bāmiyān*, Paris, MDAFA, II (1928).

J. HACKIN, J. CARL, *Nouvelles recherches archéologiques à Bāmiyān 1930*, Paris, MDAFA, III (1933).

J. HACKIN, "Recherches archéologiques à Bāmiyān en 1933," in *Diverses Recherches archéologiques en Afghanistan 1933 -*

---

[1]   D. KLIMBURG-SALTER, *The Kingdom of Bāmiyān. Buddhist Art and Culture of the Hindukush*, Rome, 1989, p. 58.

1940, Paris, MDAFA, VIII (1959), pp. 1 - 6.

T. HIGUCHI, *Japan-Afghanistan Joint Archaeological Survey in 1974*, Kyoto: Kyoto University, 1976.

T. HIGUCHI, *Japan-Afghanistan Joint Archaeological Survey in 1976*, Kyoto: Kyoto University, 1978.

T. HIGUCHI, *Japan-Afghanistan Joint Archaeological Survey in 1978*, Kyoto: Kyoto University, 1980.

T. HIGUCHI, G. BARNES, "Bāmiyān: Buddhist Cave Temples in Afghanistan," *World Archaeology*, XXVII. 2 (Oct. 1995), pp. 282 - 302.

T. HIGUCHI, *Bāmiyān: Afuganisutan ni okeru Bukkyo sekkutsu jiin no bijutsu kokogakuteki chosa*, 1970 - 1978, 4 vols, Kyoto: The Kyoto University Archaeological Mission to Central Asia, 2001².

S. KASHIWAGI, "The Iconographic Plan of the 35 meter Buddha at Bāmiyān," Nagoya University Faculty of Letters Research Paper, XLII (1966), pp. 59 - 75.

S. KASHIWAGI, "Discovery of the N-cave at Bāmiyān," Nagoya University of Letters Research Papers, XLV (1967), pp. 93 - 120.

D. KLIMBURG-SALTER, *The Kingdom of Bāmiyān. Buddhist Art and Culture of the Hindukush*, Rome: IsMEO, 1989.

Sh. KUWAYAMA, *The Main Stupa of Shāh-jī-kī Ḍherī. A Chronological Outlook*, Kyoto: Institute for Research in Humanities, Kyoto University, 1997.

N. LAPIERRE, *Le bouddhisme en Sogdiane d'après les données de l'archéologie* (IV-IXᵉ siècles), Thèse, Paris, 1998.

M. LE BERRE, *Monuments préislamiques de la région de l'Hindukush central*, MDAFA, XIV (1987).

B. A. LITVINSKIJ, T. I. ZEYMAL, *The Buddhist Monastery of Ajina Tepa, Tajikistan*, Rome: IsIAO, 2004.

M. MAILLARD, *Grottes et monuments d'Asie Centrale*, Paris: Maisonneuve, 1983.

S. MIZUNO, "Buddhist Sites of the Hindukush, North and South," *Bunmei no Jujiro*, Tokyo, 1962, pp. 106 - 143.

J. NAUDOU, *Les Bouddhistes Kaśmīriens au Moyen Age*, Paris: PUF, 1968.

P. PAL (Ed.), *Art and Architecture of Ancient Kashmir*, Bombay: Marg Publications, 1989.

B. ROWLAND, "The Colossal Buddhas at Bāmiyān," *Journal of the Indian Society of the Oriental Art*, XV (1947), pp. 62 - 73.

B. ROWLAND, *Ancient Art from Afghanistan*, New York, 1966.

B. ROWLAND, "The Wall Painting of Bāmiyān," *Marg*, XXIV. 2 (1971), pp. 25 - 43.

S. L. SHALI, "Klosterbauten der alten Siedlung in Harwan (Kashmir)," *Das Altertum*, XXX. 1 (1984), pp. 49 - 53.

M. A. STEIN, *Ancient Khotan*, vol. 1, Oxford: The Clarendon Press, 1907.

M. A. STEIN, *Serindia*, vol. I, Oxford: Clarendon Press, 1921.

M. TADDEI, "Inscribed Clay Tablets and Miniature Stupas from Ghazni," *Afghanistan*, XXVI. 2 (1973), pp. 21 - 49.

M. TADDEI, G. VERARDI, "Clay Stupas and Thrones at Tapa Sardār Ghazni (Afghanistan)," *Zinbun*, Kyoto, XX (1985), pp. 17 - 32.

S. TAKADA, "Investigations of Mural Paintings in the Great Buddha Niche," *Bukkyo Geijutsu*, CXVII (1978), pp. 41 - 44.

Z. TARZI, *L'architecture et le décor rupestre des grottes de Bāmiyān*, 2 vols, Paris: Imprimerie nationale, 1977.

Z. TARZI, "Bāmiyān Pr. Tarzi's Survey and Excavation Archaeological Mission, 2003," *The Silk Road*, I. 2 (Décembre 2003), pp. 37 - 39.

Z. TARZI, "Bāmiyān 2006: The Fifth Excavation Campaign of Pr. Tarzi's Mission," *The Silk Road*, IV. 2 (Hiver 2006 - 2007), pp. 10 - 26.

F. TISSOT, "The Site of Sahrí-Bāhlol in Gandhāra," in J. SCHOTSMANS, M. TADDEI (Ed.), *South Asian Archaeology 1983*, Naples: Istituto Universitario Orientale Dipartimento Di Studi Asiatici, 1985, pp. 567-614.

F. TISSOT, "Sahrí-Bāhlol (Part IV)," in A. PARPOLA, P. KOSKIKALLIO (Ed.), *South Asian Archaeology 1993*, vol. 2, Helsinki: Suomalaien Tiedeakatemia, 1994, pp. 733-744.

G. TUCCI, *Stupa. Art, Architectonics and Symbolism*, New Dehli, 1982.

柏孜克里克第 17 窟《观无量寿经变》琐议

霍旭初

新疆龟兹石窟研究所

柏孜克里克石窟第 17 窟窟顶南披后部,存有一幅《观无量寿经变》(以下简称《观经变》)壁画。这是高昌地区为数不多而有特色的一幅《观经变》。

该《观经变》壁画与各地习见的《观经变》形式与内容有较大差异,故有学者对此壁画定为《观经变》有许多异议。有的认为这幅壁画是《无量寿经变》,有的说是《阿弥陀经变》。认为是《观经变》的最重要的理由,是此壁画中有"上品上生"、"上品中生"……至"下品下生"汉文墨书榜题,这是无可争议的《观无量寿经》的证据,完全可以确定此壁画的内容。但是,在对此《观经变》的争议中,涉及净土信仰的诸多方面的问题,以及与敦煌同类壁画的比较、唐代西州地方佛教等问题。因此,深入讨论柏孜克里克第 17 窟《观经变》,对认识唐西州时期佛教信仰和佛教艺术特点是有益处的。这里,对上述一些问题进行粗浅的讨论。

一

《观无量寿经》系南朝宋畺良耶舍所译,是"阿弥陀净土"信仰有代表性的三部经典之一,另两部即三国曹魏康僧铠译的《无量寿经》和十六国姚秦鸠摩罗什译的《阿弥陀经》。《观无量寿经》是三部净土经中翻译最晚,但也是后来居上、影响巨大的一部。《观无量寿经》的显著特点是强调通过"观想"的手段和途径,到达往生极乐世界的目的。《观无量寿经》以"未生怨"故事为引子,大力宣扬西方极乐世界净土的美妙。"未生怨"故事是讲阿阇世王弑父禁母后,其母韦希提夫人求阿弥陀佛为其指引解脱秽土苦难之路。阿弥陀佛首先向韦希提夫人描述佛国净土——西方极乐世界的景象,然后仔细讲述进入西方净土的修行方法:主要内容有"修三福"和"十六观"。"修三福"是:世福,如孝养父母、奉事师长、慈心不杀、修十善业等;戒福,如受持三归、具足众戒、不犯威仪;行福,如发菩提心、深信因果、读诵大乘、劝进行者。如此三事,被称为"净业"。信徒们通过"修三福"才能具备死后进入"极乐世界"的资格。"十六观"是《观经》的中心内容。"十六观"的一至十三观是观想西方净土的殊胜美妙,后三观集中讲述"九品往生"。"九品往生"又称"三辈生想"。"九品往生"将往生西方极乐净土的人,分成"三辈九品",即"上品上生"、"上品中生"、"上品下生"、"中品上生"、"中品中生"、"中品下生"、"下品上生"、"下品中生"、"下品下生"。历代净土高僧对"九品往生"有多种不同解释,内容十分繁杂。每品中的三类都有复杂而不同的修行要求和往生程序。从敦煌莫高窟等中国石窟中的《观经变》壁画看,各地"九品往生"的造型,大多是用象征性的莲花和莲花童子来表示往生。在净土七宝莲花池中,绘出全开、半开、含苞的莲花,上面坐有僧人和善男信女。还有的仅是花蕾或莲籽,用化生的快慢变化表现"九品往生"的等级和次序。

在中国佛教艺术中,敦煌是《观经变》壁画的集大成者。从隋代开始至盛唐、中唐,《观经变》是诸净土经变画中数量最多的一种。敦煌唐代规范化的《观经变》的形式是:图中央为"阿弥陀净土",净土中心是阿弥陀佛和观音菩萨、大势至菩萨和众胁侍菩萨以及西方净土的种种美景妙象。两侧是"未生怨"和"十六观"。敦煌莫高窟唐代的《观经变》壁画标准样式,代表了中国内地《观经变》的规范形式,成为判定和绘制《观经变》的圭臬。柏孜克里克第 17 窟仅有"九品往生"内容,而无《观经变》最有标志性的"未生怨"和"十六观",因而成为怀疑该图是否为《观经变》的最重要的理由之一。但这是一种"以偏概全"的误解,这种观点忽略了《观经变》发展演变的历史过程和不同地区有不同佛教艺术形式的区别。

二

《观无量寿经》首先完整出现"未生怨"、"十六观"和"九品往生"的内容。"往生"概念是净土思想的核心之一,三部净土经典对"往生"都有不同程度的阐述。最早的《无量寿经》中,仅提出了"三辈往生",指出往生"西方净土"有上辈、中辈和下辈三个等级,但三辈里没有九品之分。《阿弥陀经》没有提出往生的等级问题,只是要求"若一日、若二日、若三日、若四日、若五日、若六日、若七日,一心不乱。其人临命终时,阿弥陀佛与诸圣众现在其前。是人终时,心不颠倒,即得往生阿弥陀佛极乐国土",①也无九品的区别。只有《观无量寿经》提出了"三辈九品"往生的要求和途径,"往生"的条件和途径也极大丰富起来。这样就给我们一个清晰的时间界定:凡有"九品往生"内容的佛教造型艺术,应该都是在《观无量寿经》译成之后出现的。

隋代与唐代初期,《观无量寿经》在中原进入了普及发展的新阶段。此时期,敦煌莫高窟已出现根据《观无量寿经》绘制的《观经变》,但是内容上还不全面,艺术模式上还不规范,特别是还没有出现以"净土世界"为中心,"未生怨"和"十六观"用两侧条幅形式来表现的新《观经变》形式,故一般将其定为《阿弥陀经变》。这样就造成了以有否"未生怨"、"十六观"来判断是否为《观经变》的标准偏差。从而出现了《观经变》产生的时代错觉,故《观经变》产生的实际时代被大大地推后。

三

《观经变》发展成有"未生怨"、"十六观",尤其是"九品往生"的突出内容,与唐初净土信仰大师的倡导弘扬有直接关系。特别是经过道绰、善导对《观无量寿经》理论的论述阐发,给《观无量寿经》注入新的理论活力,极大地推动了《观无量寿经》的发展。尤其是经过善导大师创造性地对《观无量寿经》的阐述,将净土信仰推向了崭新的发展阶段。善导原宗学"三论宗",后偶读《观无量寿经》受到启发,顿悟《观无量寿经》的真谛,认为《观无量寿经》是最易超脱之法门。他说:"修余行业,迂僻难成,唯此观门,定超生死。"②善导研读《观无量寿经》后,著有《观无量寿经疏》四卷(又称《观经四帖疏》)、《往生礼赞》、《净土法事赞》、《般舟赞》、《观念法门》等。《观无量寿经疏》是他最重要、最有影响的纲领性著作。《观无量寿

---

① 《阿弥陀经》,《大正藏》第 12 册,第 347b 页。
② 《往生西方净土瑞应传·善导禅师第十二》,《大正藏》第 51 册,第 106b 页。

经疏》极大地推动《观无量寿经》新净土思想的发展,善导也就成了中国佛教净土宗的实际创始人。

善导最重要的贡献是根据唐代佛教"末法"思潮的流行,观察社会一般民众的愿望,发展了"他力本愿"、"往生"和"念佛"思想。"他力本愿"是因民众"根机"不高,"成佛"的素质比较低劣,需要借助阿弥陀佛的"愿力"而往生西方净土。所以,"他力本愿"思想,给广大信徒极大的希冀与动力。"往生"就是脱离苦难"秽土",达到"净土"目标的途径。善导首先提出的是"凡夫"命题,认为一切善恶众生都是"凡夫",善导认为:"上品三人是遇大凡夫,中品三人是遇小凡夫,下品三人是遇恶凡夫。以恶业故临终藉善,乘佛愿力,乃得往生,到彼华开方始发心。何得言是始学大乘人也。若作此见,自失误他,为害兹甚。今以一一出文显证,欲使今时善恶凡夫同沾九品。生信无疑,乘佛愿力悉得生也。"①善导"凡夫"论,解决了众生地位平等的问题,其中关于"韦希提夫人亦是凡夫"的论点,特别具有突破性。以往净土大师都说韦希提夫人本是菩萨,才因见到众生受苦受难,才假托韦希提夫人凡身,请佛说法。善导反对这种说法,他公然宣称韦希提夫人也是"凡夫",韦希提夫人是靠佛力才能见到西方净土。"(韦希提)夫人是凡非圣,由非圣故仰惟圣力冥加。"②善导首先从打破韦希提夫人"圣人"身份地位开始,然后将所有一切众生一概列入"凡夫"。虽然"凡夫"还有"三辈九品"的等级差别,但善导将一切众生都以"凡夫"看待,实际上是赋予任何人都有进入"极乐世界"的资格。这就为广大众生往生进入"西方净土"打破了樊篱,敞开了净土大门,降低了进入"极乐世界"的门槛。"念佛"是善导对"往生"者的最基本要求,前面有"他力本愿"的外力帮助和取得"凡夫"的"往生"资格与途径,然而往生者还要努力一心"念佛"修炼自己,前往"西方极乐世界"的愿望才能实现。在善导提倡的新思想理论的倡导和影响下,突出表现"未生怨"、"十六观"内容的新《观经变》形式便应运而生。

四

柏孜克里克第17窟《观经变》主体部分,即阿弥陀佛居中央,两侧为观音菩萨和大势至菩萨,组成"西方极乐世界"的主体——"西方三圣"。在"西方三圣"和众菩萨下方较大的空间里,绘出"九品往生"的情景。中央是用栏楯围起的"西方三圣"莲座的根茎部分,其两侧有从"七宝池"中涌出的十余株莲花。一部分莲花上有各类人物,一部分莲花为莲蕾状,尚未绽开。这些都是表示往生者修行程度的不同、悟道的迟早。一些人物状态各异,有跪在莲花上的,有站立莲花上的,有结跏而坐的,有的携带琵琶乐器,还有的身后有坐佛在指引,有的前面有幡幢,表示有菩萨接引前往净土。这些均表现了往生者在佛的愿力协助下,前往"极乐世界"的场面。

柏孜克里克第17窟《观经变》,可以看作是善导的新理论之前的《观经》形式,一方面还没有"未生怨"和"十六观"的内容出现,一方面又突出"九品往生"内容,这些完全符合善导注疏之前《观无量寿经》的原经内容。唐代初期,敦煌莫高窟就出现了有"未生怨"、"十六观"内容的壁画,但没有采用"中唐配条幅"的形式。后来出现了大型"净土变"壁画,也是没有突出"未生怨"、"十六观"而定为《阿弥陀经变》。敦煌这些壁画所以没有被定为《观经变》,主要就是因为没有出现或没有突出"未生怨"和"十六观"内容。

---

① 《观无量寿经疏》卷一《玄义分》,《大正藏》第37册,第248b页。
② 《观无量寿经疏》卷二《序分义》,《大正藏》第37册,第260b页。

这种鉴别标准,在敦煌莫高窟一度长期被使用,"约定俗成"成为定论。这种论点对早期《观无量寿经变》的认识产生了极大的影响。这也影响了对柏孜克里克第 17 窟同类壁画的识别。其实柏孜克里克与敦煌初期《观经变》一样,壁画艺术表现上和对《观无量寿经》的诠释上,有所取舍,有所着重。近年有敦煌学者对敦煌"西方净土变"进行图像学的研究,经过细致的考察与排比,认为敦煌隋代与唐代初期一些"净土变"壁画,实际上都是《观经变》,①纠正了长期《观经变》在敦煌出现较晚的时间概念。这对考察《观经变》的发展演变,以及对唐代"净土信仰"的变化都有重要的启发和借鉴意义。该文根据敦煌三部"净土经变"的特点,归纳出"净土变"绘画上的一些特征,对鉴别《观经变》大有裨益。兹转录于下:

	说法场所	观音、大势至菩萨	一化佛、二化菩萨	弟 子	往生化生
无量寿经	楼阁说法	有名,无形象	无	有	三辈往生
阿弥陀经	楼阁说法	无	无	有	无
观无量寿经	树下说法	化佛冠、宝瓶冠	有无数	1~13 观中无	九品往生

(引自王惠民《敦煌隋至唐前期净土图像考察——以观无量寿经变为中心》)

从以上敦煌壁画的特点看,柏孜克里克第 17 窟与上述区别内容有一定的关联。特别是具备树下说法、观音、大势至菩萨戴宝冠、九品往生的特点。尤其是榜题中明确写出"九品往生"。柏孜克里克第 17 窟《观经变》,不仅从敦煌壁画中得到研究的参考依据,也为研究敦煌同类壁画提供了一个直接的参考证据。

五

佛教净土信仰起源较早,可以追溯到印度吠陀时代。《梨俱吠陀》中就有"于彼处所,我获不死(Amita)"的境界。Amita 即阿弥陀,其词源是 Amitayus,汉译为"无量光",这正是净土教主无量寿佛一词的来源,梵文音译即阿弥陀佛。西方净土思想的成熟与发展是在贵霜朝时期,即公元 2 世纪上半叶,地方是在印度北部。佛经中有关于净土信仰产生的记载:鸠摩罗什译《妙法莲华经·药王菩萨本事品》曰:"……若如来灭后,后五百岁中,若有女人闻是经典,如说修行。于此命终,即往安乐世界,阿弥陀佛、大菩萨众,围绕住处,生莲华中,宝座之上,不复为贪欲所恼,亦复不为瞋恚愚痴所恼,亦复不为憍慢嫉妒诸垢所恼,得菩萨神通、无生法忍。"②佛灭后五百年正相当于公元后贵霜王朝时期。这段不多的文字,也正是"西方极乐世界"的雏形描述。

净土信仰在北印度形成后,迅速沿"北传佛教"路线向东传播。公元 2 世纪中国内地就有净土经典陆续译出,最早是东汉安世高译出《无量寿经》二卷(今已失);不久,支娄迦谶译出《无量清净平等觉经》四卷;三国吴支谦译《阿弥陀经》二卷;曹魏康僧铠译《无量寿经》二卷;曹魏帛延译《无量清净平等觉经》二卷(今已失);西晋竺法护译《无量寿经》(今已失);东晋竺法力译《无量寿至真等正觉经》(今已失);东晋

① 王惠民:《敦煌隋至唐前期净土图像考察——以观无量寿经变为中心》,《唐代佛教与佛教艺术》,台湾觉风佛教艺术文化基金会,2006 年 6 月,第 183~209 页。
② 《妙法莲华经》,《大正藏》第 9 册,第 054b 页。

佛陀跋陀罗译《新无量寿经》(今已失);十六国姚秦鸠摩罗什译《阿弥陀经》;南北朝刘宋宝云译《新无量寿经》(今已失);昙摩蜜多译《新无量寿经》(今已失)等等。近代有学者对上述译本进行研究,认为有些译本为重复或讹伪之作,实际只有五种译本可信。不管怎样,在这段历史中,比较密集地译出净土经典,足以说明当时中原"净土信仰"的盛行。

高昌地区何时传入佛经,目前尚无准确的结论。按佛教传入中国内地主要先经西域的共识,高昌应该在公元2世纪就出现佛教的传播。现知高昌地区有确切纪年的文书例证,是20世纪初在吐峪沟石窟发现的《诸佛要集经》,该经跋文记载此经系竺法护于(元)康二年(292)翻译,写成于元康六年(296)。当然此经跋文没有直接证明高昌地区佛教流行的情况,但根据西域其他地区佛教的流布情况,高昌已是西域佛教的中心地之一,恐无怀疑。

"净土信仰"传入高昌地区的时间,是个难以考证的课题,目前出土的资料还不能明确证明此问题。日本大谷考察队获得的佛教文献比较多,但他们的断代十分笼统。龙谷大学和静嘉堂藏有《观无量寿经》残片,都定为"六朝写本",没有明确的朝代,更无具体年代。不过,从出土文书写体和净土经内容看,高昌地区至唐代初期,"净土信仰"已经相当流行。《观无量寿经》在"净土信仰"中,也占有重要地位,这是高昌《观经变》绘制的基础。

高昌地区早于柏孜克里克第17窟的"净土变"图像,有吐峪沟第1、42、20窟。第1、42窟主要描绘了"净土世界"的"七重宝树"及"化生童子"的美妙景象。用图案化的艺术手法,突出描绘《阿弥陀经》"极乐国土,七重栏楯,七重罗网,七重行树,皆是四宝周匝围绕,是故彼国名曰极乐"的内涵。吐峪沟20窟是重要的净土内容的洞窟。其左窟壁上保存有著名的"净土观想图",其中尚存有:"花座观"、"树观"、"琉璃观"、"水观"、"宝楼观"、"普想观"等。以上各观想图都有榜题,榜题中写有"行者观想……"。"行者"即"观行者",系指一切佛道的修行者。《观无量寿经》"十六观"中,"行者"之名多有出现,是观想的主体称谓。这证明吐峪沟20窟"净土观想图"是依据《观无量寿经》而绘制。但又不是敦煌莫高窟的模式,也与柏孜克里克第17窟差异很大。这表示了不同地区、不同时期存在多式多样的《观经变》。根据中外学者的研究,吐峪沟第1、20、42号窟,年代约在公元6世纪。①

六

柏孜克里克第16、17窟是两个毗邻的大型洞窟,两窟有共同的窟前建筑,应是同时期所建。17窟窟门前内壁存有男供养人画像。据学者研究,根据人物造型、服饰装束,供养者为突厥人,故第17窟应该是唐西州时期"突厥部落贵族们修建的"洞窟。②柏孜克里克第16、17窟壁画,总体风格属于中原佛教艺术体系,但壁画构图、布局、图案、装饰还是有不同的特色。第17窟的《观经变》绘在长条窟顶部,为中原洞窟所罕见。阿弥陀佛现十方佛令韦希提夫人观想的内容,也与中原壁画有很大区别。"九品往生"中各种"凡夫"的姿态、服饰、物品也都有自己的特点。因而,柏孜克里克第17窟的《观经变》与习见的敦煌莫高窟等地的《观经变》相比,独具特色。它应该是高昌地方传统文化与中原大乘佛教理念相结合的产物,

① 贾应逸、祁小山:《印度到中国新疆的佛教艺术》,甘肃教育出版社,2002年,第434页。
② 柳洪亮:《高昌石窟概述》,载《中国美术分类全集·新疆壁画全集》6吐峪沟、柏孜克里克,辽宁美术出版社、新疆美术摄影出版社,1995年,第10页。

在中国佛教艺术中独树一帜，可以看成是西域汉文化圈中一种特有的艺术形式。从这点说，这个罕有的艺术遗存，其价值之高不言而喻。

至于新的《观经变》形式为何没有在高昌地区发现，当与安西都护府移治于龟兹，西州的政治、军事地位发生变化有关。[①]安西都护府移至龟兹后，升格为安西大都护府，而西州降为都督府。这一变化影响中原移民西进与文化输入的规模与进度，也使中原佛教回馈西州的力度大大降低。比较明显的是，代表中原佛教艺术高峰的敦煌佛教造型艺术，对西州的影响逐渐减弱。隋代与唐初敦煌出现的以一部经为一幅图的大型"经变画"，在西州没有形成主流。与西州相比，龟兹倒是紧跟中原佛教艺术发展的风头，在龟兹汉风洞窟里，很快出现了与敦煌莫高窟"模式"完全相同的"经变画"。有的很可能就是敦煌画师亲自来到龟兹直接的绘画"移植"。龟兹石窟中目前能够看到的"净土"壁画，有库木吐喇石窟的《观经变》和《东方药师变》以及阿艾石窟的《观经变》等。库木吐喇与阿艾石窟的《观经变》均采用中原"中堂加条幅"的敦煌标准形式，即两侧有"未生怨"和"十六观"的内容。如前所述，这是新的《观经变》形式。据学者研究，龟兹这批汉风洞窟的年代，属于安西大都护府时期是无疑的，具体有"观经变"的洞窟当在盛唐期间，与敦煌石窟新《观经变》的大量绘制，几乎是同步进行的。

安西与中原年代如此一致发展，除了国家的统一、中央实行有效的行政管理外，还由于唐代对佛教实行统一管理的制度起到重要的作用。据在库木吐喇石窟发现的汉文题记，中央政权在安西四镇设有"都统"职官，管理整个安西的佛教事物。"都统"是僧都统的略称。一般都是由中央政府直接委任，甚至是由皇帝任命。安西有"都统"掌管佛教事物，使安西佛教纳入国家统一的管理轨道。因此，安西佛教进入发展的黄金时期。据文献记载，安西地区与中原地区一样，修建众多佛教寺院。武则天时敕令全国修建"大云寺"、"龙兴寺"，安西很快就实施修建。这些都表明，凡有政权资源支撑的地方，任何宗教都可以蓬勃发展。正是如此，西州地方在安西都护府迁离后，各方面都受到制约，由于"边缘化"而造成西州佛教与其东面(敦煌)和西面(龟兹)不能同步发展的特殊历史现象。

也正是这样的特殊情况，西州时期留下的佛教艺术，保留了地方的、民族的别具一格的佛教艺术特色，成为十分宝贵的、风格迥异的艺术遗产，不仅对研究佛教艺术有很高价值，也是认识唐代边塞佛教信仰难得的资料。

---

① 霍旭初：《善导与唐西州阿弥陀净土信仰》，载《吐鲁番学研究》2008 年第 1 期。

西域幻术的流播以及对中土小说的影响

王 青

南京师范大学文学院

所谓幻术,亦即我们现在通常所说的魔术,它是通过有意识地制造人们的视听错觉,从而营造超经验、超自然的幻象的一种技艺。现代的幻术主要是一种表演艺术,魔术师和观众有一种心照不宣的默契,即大家所看到的是魔术师的表演,并非真实存在的事物。不过,最早的幻术,大致应该是从巫术演变而来,在很多场合,观众都相信幻术所造成的幻象是真实存在的,因此,古代幻术的功能与影响远大于作为表演艺术而存在的现代幻术。它是宣传宗教信仰的有力武器,同时又是神奇志怪小说的重要题材内容;它改变了人们对自然规律的认识,从而引发了丰富的想象。

一、大秦幻术的传入

幻术具有地域性,不同地区的幻术创造者根据当地的文化、技术和物质材料创造出不同的幻术;但同时又具有普遍性,时至今日,世界各国幻术的手法、原理大同小异,同样的幻术在各地都有表演。这是因为,相对于一些以语言为载体的表演艺术,幻术以形体表演和物像展示为主,因此不受语言的限制,能够在世界范围内较为顺畅地传播。西域地区是数大文明辐辏之地,自古以来就是交通要道,来自各地的幻术均通过此处流播到中土。

上古幻术有两个中心区域,第一是在埃及,第二就是印度,西北丝绸之路是两地幻术传入中土的重要途径之一。据《列子·周穆王》载:"周穆王时,西极之国有化人来,入水火,贯金石;反山川,移城邑;乘虚不坠,触实不硋。千变万化,不可穷极。既已变物之形,又且易人之虑。穆王敬之若神,事之若君。"而所谓"西极之国",《北堂书钞》卷一二九、《太平御览》卷一七三、卷六二六引此条时均作"西域";《艺文类聚》卷六二则引作"西胡"。①可见,这个化人亦即魔术师来自西域。不过,《列子》这本书不大靠得住,很有可能是魏晋时人的伪作,其中的记载并不足以说明西域幻术远在周穆王时即已传播中土。但到西汉时,中东地区的职业幻术表演者通过西域已经来到中土却是肯定的。

《史记》卷一二三《大宛列传》云:"条枝在安息西数千里,临西海……国善眩。"《正义》引颜师古云:"今吞刀吐火、殖瓜种树、屠人截马之术皆是也。"《汉书》卷六一《张骞传》云:"而大宛诸国发使随汉使来,观汉广大,以大鸟卵及黎轩眩人献于汉。"颜师古注曰:"眩,读与幻同。即今吞刀吐火,植瓜种树,屠人截马之术皆是也。本从西域来。"东汉永宁元年(120),又有大秦幻人被掸国国王进献给汉朝廷。《后汉书》卷五一《陈禅传》载:

---

① 见杨伯峻集释《列子集释》,北京:中华书局,1979年,第90页。

西南夷掸国王献乐及幻人,能吐火,自支解,易牛马头。明年元会,作之于庭,安帝与群臣共观,大奇之……尚书陈忠劾奏禅曰:"古者合欢之乐舞于堂,四夷之乐陈于门……今掸国越流沙,逾县度,万里贡献,非郑卫之声,佞人之比……"①

此事又见于《后汉书》卷八六《西南夷传》:

掸国王雍由调复遣使者诣阙朝贺,献乐及幻人,能变化吐火,自支解,易牛马头。又善跳丸,数乃至千。自言我海西人。海西即大秦也,掸国西南通大秦。②

掸国即今之缅甸。以上材料涉及的国家有条枝、黎轩、大秦、海西,这些国家的具体所指众说纷纭,争议颇多。③我比较赞同白鸟库吉、伯希和(Paul Pelliot)的观点,即黎轩指托勒密治下的埃及亚历山大城,Alexander 一名省去 A 与 X 等音后,即成(A)lek(s)an(dria),译成中文就是"黎轩"。④ 除了白鸟库吉、伯希和提出的许多证据之外,我想补充一点:在埃及,幻术极其发达。在 1823 年发现的韦斯特卡尔纸草(Westcar papyrus)中,有一篇形成于古王国时代(约公元前 3000~2200 年),写定时代则有可能是在十二王朝(约公元前 2000~1783 年)时期的、被后人命名为《魔术师的故事》的小说。此篇小说记载了很多古埃及的魔法。如乌巴阿奈尔的妻子与国王的侍童通奸,乌巴阿奈尔用蜡做了一条七指长的鳄鱼,等着侍童去河里洗澡时,将这条蜡做的鳄鱼扔进水里,将其变成了一条七肘长的大鳄鱼,捉住了侍童;如一群美女在河中划船,其中的一位将头上所戴的孔雀宝石掉进了水里,采采莽克赫能把池子里的一部分水连底放到另一部分上去,捡起宝石后,又将池水搬回原处;又如魔术师代敌则能让一只切掉了头的鸭子搧动翅膀,继续行走,并使其身首重合。然后,他又在鹅和公牛身上重现了这个魔法。⑤ 代敌所行的魔术就是颜师古所说的截马之术,也就是大秦魔术师所表演的"易牛马头"。

永宁元年来到中土的魔术师自称是海西人,又说即大秦人,与黎轩实指一地。《后汉书》卷八八《西域传》:"大秦国一名犁鞬,以在海西,亦云海西国。"所以,黎轩(鞬)为城名;大秦为国名,指的是罗马东部的地区(Roman Orient),或者说是罗马帝国在亚洲的领土;而海西则是指方位而言。此地幻术发达似乎为中土人士所熟知,《三国志》卷三〇《东夷传》裴注引《魏略·西戎传》曰:"大秦国一号犁轩,在安息、条支西大海之西……俗多奇幻,口中出火,自缚自解,跳十二丸巧妙。"《新唐书》卷二二一下《西域传下》"拂菻"条也称:"古大秦也,居西海上,一曰海西国……俗喜酒,嗜干饼。多幻人,能发火于颜,手为江湖,口幡眊举,足堕珠玉。有善医能开脑出虫以愈目眚。"

从以上材料我们也可以看出,埃及的魔术师在当时被当作珍奇物品在各国宫廷之间互相转赠。他们不仅被送到中西亚之条枝、大宛,还从海路被送到缅甸,然后又分别进入中土。从陈忠的弹劾之辞中我们

---

① [南朝宋]范晔撰《后汉书》,北京:中华书局,1965 年,第 1685 页。
② 同上注,第 2851 页。所谓跳丸,就是快速地抛接多球。球数越多,难度越高,目前世界最高水平是能抛接 8~9 个球。"数乃至千",应该是观众眼花缭乱的一种错觉。
③ 综合性的评述可参见龚缨晏撰《20 世纪黎轩、条支和大秦研究评述》,《中国史研究动态》2002 年第 8 期,第 19~27 页。
④ 两位学者的观点,分别见白鸟库吉撰、王古鲁译《大秦国与拂菻国考》,《塞外史地论文译丛》第一辑,北京:商务印书馆,1939 年,第 17~18 页;伯希和撰、冯承钧译《犁轩为埃及亚历山大城说》,《西域南海史地考证译丛》第七编,北京:商务印书馆,1995 年,第 34~35 页。
⑤ 以上参见[英]派特力(Flinders W. M. Petrie)编译、倪罗译《埃及古代故事》,北京:作家出版社,1957 年,第 1~18 页。

可以看出,他对掸国之地理方位极其陌生,掸国为西南夷,即今之缅甸,来中土并不需要"越流沙,逾县度",然而陈忠一看是异国幻人,表演的又是变化吐火、自支解等幻技,便会想到"越流沙,涉县度",①可见此前来中土表演的大部分是来自西域的幻师。

实际上,东汉中期,幻术在民间市集的表演已经习见。张衡《西京赋》在描绘西汉时长安广场表演的各种术艺时提及的杂技有角抵、扛鼎、寻橦(爬杆)、冲狭、燕濯、跳丸、走索、曼延,以及各种动物表演,当然也有各种幻术——"奇幻儵忽,易貌分形。吞刀吐火,云雾杳冥。画地成川,流渭通泾。东海黄公,赤刀粤祝"。现存于南阳汉画馆的"幻人吐火"画像石上画着这样的图像:一个头戴尖顶冠(尖端前倾)、长胡子、高鼻梁的人,服装与汉服不同,显然是"洋人"。他手中拿的不知何物,脸部前面有一道白光,像是从嘴里吐出来的,吴曾德认为这是幻术(或称眩术)中的吐火表演,②可见吐火乃是胡人的绝技。不过,在东汉时已为中土艺人掌握。迄今发现"吐火"的汉代石刻已近十幅,徐州铜山洪楼的东汉大型百戏乐舞图中均有吐火,可见"吐火"幻术为百戏所必备。③掸国所来的海西幻人之所以受到重视,原因并不在于所表现的幻技,而在于他们是掸国政府的朝贡,能够满足汉天子万国来朝的虚荣心。

东汉以后,西域地区还是不断将幻人作为当地特产进贡给中原政府。《太平御览》卷七三七"方术部"、《法苑珠林》卷六一引崔鸿《十六国春秋·北凉录》曰:"玄始十四年(426)七月,西域贡吞刀吐火秘幻奇伎。"《魏书》卷一〇二《西域传》载:西域悦般国于真君九年(448),"遣使朝献;并送幻人,称能割人喉脉令断,击人头令骨陷,皆血出或数升或盈斗,以草药内其口中,令嚼咽之,须臾血止,养疮一月复常,又无痕瘢。世祖疑其虚,乃取死罪囚试之,皆验"。这里的幻人表演的似乎不是幻术,而是医术。

二、印度的幻术及其传入

除了埃及之外,印度也是一个幻术历史非常悠久、幻术技艺非常发达的国家。从佛经材料中可以看出,魔术表演者称之为"幻师",是古印度一个非常常见的职业,他们经常在十字路口作公共表演。佛经中常用幻师以及幻法设喻,以说明人生的幻化虚无。《佛本行集经》卷一四《空声劝厌品》云:"如影亦如山谷响,亦如戏场众幻师。"④《杂阿含经》卷一〇云:"譬如幻师若幻师弟子,于四衢道头,幻作象兵、马兵、车兵、步兵。有智明目士夫,谛观思惟分别,谛观思惟分别,时无所有、无牢、无实、无有坚固。所以者何?以彼幻无坚实故。"⑤《五阴譬喻经》亦云:"譬如比丘幻师与幻弟子于四衢道大人众中,现若干幻化,作群象、群马、车乘、步从。目士见之,观视省察,即知不有,虚无不实,无形化尽。所以者何?幻无强故。"⑥

印度的幻术有很多是大型表演,应该利用了很多的机关布景。《大般若波罗蜜多经》卷四九《初分大乘铠品》云:"如巧幻师或彼弟子,于四衢道在大众前,幻作地狱、傍生、鬼界无量有情各受众苦,亦复放光变动大地……如巧幻师或彼弟子,于四衢道在大众前,幻作种种贫穷孤露、根支残缺、疾病有情,随其所

---

① 据《汉书·西域传》记载,县度山在乌秅城之西,大致在今塔什库尔干西南四百公里,山有栈道,要有悬绳索才能渡过去,故名县渡。

② 吴曾德撰《汉代画像石》,北京:文物出版社,1984年,第99页。

③ 傅起凤、傅腾龙撰《中国杂技史》,上海:上海人民出版社,2004年,第62页。

④ 《大正藏》第3册,第717页,c。

⑤ 《大正藏》第2册,第69页,a。

⑥ 《大正藏》第2册,第501页,b。

须,皆幻施与。"①而同书卷三八六《初分诸法平等品》云:

> 如巧幻师,或彼弟子,执持少物,于众人前幻作种种异类色相。谓或幻作男女、大小象马牛羊驼驴鸡等种种禽兽;或复幻作城邑、聚落、园林、池沼,种种庄严,甚可爱乐;或复幻作衣服、饮食、房舍、卧具、香花、璎珞、种种珍宝;或复幻作无量种类伎乐俳优,令无量人欢娱受乐;或复幻作种种形相,令行布施、或令持戒、或令修忍、或令精进、或令修定、或令修慧、或复现生刹帝利大族、或复现生婆罗门大族、或复现生长者大族、或复现生居士大族;或复幻作诸山大海、妙高山、王轮围山等;或复现生四大王众天、三十三天、夜摩天、睹史多天、乐变化天、他化自在天……或复现作预流、一来、不还、阿罗汉、独觉;或复现作菩萨摩诃萨,从初发心、修行、布施、净戒、安忍、精进、静虑、般若、波罗蜜多。②

由此可见,印度的幻术与戏剧表演密切结合,由演员利用面具、布景、服装等幻化出种种人物,并利用机关布景幻化出自然景物、珍珠宝物和家常用品。佛教则充分利用了这种表演艺术来宣传教理教义。《大宝积经》卷八五《授幻师跋陀罗记会》记载了"天帝释助如来与幻师斗法"一事,撩开了其中神话的面纱,从中我们也可以看出一些古印度大型魔术表演的端倪:

> 于彼城中有一幻师,名跋陀罗……时彼幻师即于其夜,诣王舍城于最下劣秽恶之处,化作道场,宽广平正,缯彩幡盖,种种庄严,散诸花香,覆以宝帐;复现八千诸宝行树,其宝树下一一皆有师子之座,无量敷具悉皆严好。为欲供养诸比丘故,而复化为百味饮食,并现五百给侍之人,服以白衣,饰以严具。作是化已……四王即便变现无量殊妙庄严之具,倍于幻师幻化之事……幻师尔时见斯事已,嗟叹惊悔,欲摄所化,尽其咒术,幻化之事宛然如故。便自思念:"此为甚奇,我从昔来于所变化隐现从心,而于今时不能隐没,必由为彼如来故然。"时天帝释知彼心念,告幻师言:"汝于今者为如来故,庄严道场无能隐没。"③

魔术师在短时间能够变就宝帐、幡盖、宝树、狮子座、敷具以及各种人物等,并能随心所欲让其隐没,这大致应该是早就设计好的机关布景。所变出来的种种人物有一些可能是幻师弟子所表演,更多的可能是由木偶承当。《道行般若经》卷一《摩诃般若波罗蜜道行品》设喻曰:"譬如幻师于旷大处化作二大城,作化人满其中,悉断化人头。于须菩提意云何,宁有所中伤死者无?"④这种化人很可能是机关木人。古印度制造机关木人的技术能够达到以假乱真的地步。《大庄严论经》卷五载:

> 我昔曾闻,有一幻师……幻尸陀罗木作一女人,端正奇特。于大众前抱捉此女,而鸣唼之,共为欲事。时诸比丘见此事已,咸皆嫌忿,而作是言:"此无惭人,所为鄙亵。知其如是,不受其供!"时彼

---

① 《大正藏》第5册,第277页,b-c。
② 《大正藏》第6册,第995页,a-b。
③ 《大正藏》第11册,第486页,c-487页,c。
④ 《大正藏》第8册,第427页,c。

幻师既行欲已,闻诸比丘讥呵嫌责,即便以刀斫刺是女,分解支节,挑目截鼻,种种苦毒而杀此女。①

在《列子·汤问》篇中记载周穆王西巡狩时在国外提到一位工人名偃师,所造之倡者也与真人一般无二。在佛典中经常提及机关木人,②它最初乃是幻术中的重要道具,后来发展为一种专门的表演艺术,即木偶戏。

在佛经中,我们也可以看到一些我们所熟知的古典魔术,如"自断其身"。《央掘魔罗经》卷四载:"譬如幻师于大众中自断身份以悦众人,而实于身无所伤损。诸佛世尊亦复如是,如彼幻师种种变现以度众生。"③又如"巧变珠宝",《大乘理趣六波罗蜜多经》卷一〇云:"如世幻师幻作金银珍宝真珠璎珞,求其实体了不可得。"④这些都是印度传统幻术。《拾遗记》卷二载:

> 南陲之南,有扶娄之国。其人善能机巧变化,易形改服,大则兴云起雾,小则入于纤毫之中。缀金玉毛羽为衣裳。能吐云喷火,鼓腹则如雷霆之声。或化为犀、象、狮子、龙、蛇、犬、马之状。或变为虎、兕,口中生人,备百戏之乐,宛转屈曲于指掌间。人形或长数分,或复数寸,神怪歘忽,衒丽于时。乐府皆传此伎,至末代犹学焉,得粗亡精,代代不绝,故俗谓之婆侯伎,则扶娄之音,讹替至今。⑤

杂技专家认为,上文所叙的"易貌"、"兴云"、"大小赢缩"、"吐火"、"鼓腹成雷"、"乔妆巨象狮子"、"人变虎兕"及"手中傀儡"等节目,均真实可信。⑥ 唐朝时,王玄策曾西行印度,来到婆栗阇国,其地在今印度比哈尔邦北部的达尔彭加(Darbhanga),正如同中土帝王常以百戏招待客人,印度国王同样以杂技表演招待王玄策,使他亲见印度高超的杂技、幻术技艺。《法苑珠林》卷四引王玄策《西国行传》云:

> 王使显庆四年(659)至婆栗阇国,王为汉人设五女戏。其五女传弄三刀,加至十刀。又作绳伎,腾虚绳上,著履而掷,手弄三仗、刀楯枪等。种种关伎、杂诸幻术、截舌抽肠等,不可具述。⑦

同书卷七六《绮语部·感应缘》又载:

> 大唐贞观二十年(646),西国有五婆罗门来到京师,善能音乐、祝术、杂戏,截舌、抽肠、走绳、续断。又至显庆已来,王玄策等数有使人向五印度。西国天王为汉使设乐,或有腾空走索,履展绳行,男女相避,歌戏如常。或有女人手弄三仗、刀稍枪等,掷空手接,绳走不落。或有截舌自缚,解伏依旧,不劳人功。如是幻戏种种难述。⑧

---

① 《大正藏》第4册,第285页,a。
② 有关机关文人的佛教文献可参见季羡林撰:《列子与佛典》、《比较与民间文学》,北京:北京大学出版社,1991年,第83~86页;钱钟书撰《管锥编》第2册,北京:中华书局,1979年,第704页。
③ 《大正藏》第2册,第540页,b。
④ 《大正藏》第8册,第913页,a。
⑤ [晋]王嘉撰、齐治平校注《拾遗记》,北京:中华书局,1981年,第53页。
⑥ 傅起凤、傅腾龙撰:《中国杂技史》,上海:上海人民出版社,2004年,第152页。
⑦ 《大正藏》第53册,第296页,a。
⑧ 同上注,第859页,c。

我怀疑所谓扶娄之国,或即是婆栗阇国。古无轻唇音,"扶"与"婆"音近,这从"扶娄"讹作"婆侯"即可得知;而"栗阇"的快读与"娄"亦很接近。《拾遗记》卷四又载燕昭王七年(前305):

> 沐胥之国来朝,则申毒国之一名也。有道术人名尸罗……善衔惑之术。于其指端出浮屠十层,高三尺,及诸天神仙,巧丽特绝。人皆长五六分,列幢盖,鼓舞,绕塔而行,歌唱之音,如真人矣。尸罗喷水为雾雾,暗数里间。俄而复吹为疾风,雾雾皆止。又吹指上浮屠,渐入云里。又于左耳出青龙,右耳出白虎。始出之时,才一二寸,稍至八九尺。俄而风至云起,即以一手挥之,即龙虎皆入耳中……①

指端涌出浮屠的幻术,可能是印度僧人的常技,直到清代康熙年间,《聊斋志异》卷三所记之"番僧"尚有此幻技。

> 释体空言:在青州见二番僧,像貌奇古,耳缀双环,被黄布,须发鬈如。自言从西域来……或问:"西域多异人,罗汉得毋有奇术否?"其一蓦然笑,出手于袖,掌中托小塔,高裁盈尺,玲珑可爱。壁上最高处,有小龛,僧掷塔其中,矗然端立,无少偏倚。视塔上有舍利放光,照耀一室。少间以手招之,仍落掌中。其一僧乃袒臂,伸左肱,长可六七尺,而右肱缩无有矣;转伸右肱亦如左状。②

这应该是幻术中的藏挟之术,利用服装和其他机关藏挟物品,再突然变出,让人产生无中生有、凭空生成的错觉。袖中之塔是折叠起来的,到时可以拉长。

印度幻术进入中土大致依靠三条途径,第一是官方进贡。与西域诸国一样,天竺诸国也将幻人作为贡品进献给中土。《旧唐书》卷二九《音乐二》载:

> 大抵散乐杂戏多幻术,幻术皆出西域,天竺尤甚。汉武帝通西域,始以善幻人至中国。安帝时,天竺献伎,能自断手足,刳剔肠胃,自是历代有之。我高宗恶其惊俗,敕西域关令不令入中国。③

第二是民间艺人的流动表演。西晋时期,就有印度的魔术师千里跋涉,通过西域来到中土表演幻术,《搜神记》卷二就记载了一位天竺幻师的幻术表演:

> 晋永嘉中,有天竺胡人,来渡江南,言语译道而后通。其人有数术,能断舌续断,吐火变化,所在士女聚共观试。其将断舌,先吐以示宾客,然后刀截,流血覆地。乃取置器中,传以示人。视之,舌头半舌,观其口内,唯半舌在。既而还取含之,坐有顷,吐已示人,坐人见舌还如故,不知其实断不也。其续断,取绢布与人,各执一头,对剪一断之。已而取两断,合视祝之,则复还连,绢与旧无异,故一体也。时人多疑以为幻作,乃阴而试之,犹是所续故绢也。其吐火者,先有药在器中,取一片,与黍(食

---

① 《拾遗记》,第94页。
② 〔清〕蒲松龄撰《铸雪斋抄本聊斋志异》,上海:上海古籍出版社,1979年,第184页。
③ 〔后晋〕刘昫等撰《旧唐书》,北京:中华书局,1975年,第1073页。

唐)含之,再三吹吁,已而张口,火满口中,因就爇取取以爨之,则便火炽也。又取书纸及绳缕之属投火中,众详共视,见其烧然,消糜了尽。乃拨灰中,举而出之,故是向物。①

这位天竺幻师的表演包含了四个幻术,这些幻术至今为止仍有表演。第一个幻术为断舌复续。此一幻术在后世有着两种演法:其一是"钢针刺舌",把一枝粗大而锐长的钢针,从舌头中心穿过,一会儿拔去针后,舌上泯然无迹。另一种是"利刃划舌",用锋利的刀把舌头划破数处,鲜血直流,少顷就恢复原状。这两种幻术,清代还有人演,从源流上看,可能从"断舌复续"演变而来;第二个幻术是剪带还原。这种幻术在东方信仰佛教的国家,缅甸、锡兰、日本都有流传,方法各有不同。但在中国幻术中尤其著名,已成为国际幻术界公认为中国幻术代表之一。拿一条绸布当中剪断,顷刻接连的节目,内行叫做"接大绦"。亦可用带子、绳子等代替绸布。此一幻术的"门子"在于剪断的带子与展示的带子并不是同一条;第三个幻术是吐火之术,上文所引材料已经表明,此一幻术在西域来华幻师中极其常见,在中土也已经普遍流传;第四个幻术是烧物不伤,这也是一个流传至今的传统幻术,现在仍然有"烧纸还原""双烧带绳"等魔术节目。②

据荀氏《灵鬼志》载:"太元十二年(387),有道人外国,能吞刀吐火,吐珠玉金银;自说其所受术,即白衣,非沙门也。"③然后,又表演了入居小笼、吞吐人物等幻技。此人也应该是一个进行流动表演的职业魔术师。

印度幻术流播中土的第三个途径是佛教僧侣的神技展示。来华僧人中的一部分或多或少地掌握一些幻术,用以制造神迹,培养信仰,吸引信徒。一些以神异著称的僧人实际上就是魔术师,如佛图澄,他所展现的神技中,至少有以下两项属于现在尚在表演的魔术。《高僧传》卷九《神异上·佛图澄传》载:

> 澄知勒不达深理,正可以道术为征。因而言曰:"至道虽远,亦可以近事为证。"即取应器盛水,烧香咒之。须臾生青莲花,光色曜目。勒由此信服。④

这实际上就是幻术"钵内生莲",在后世一直在表演传续。早期是从盆里或小缸里变出莲花,有灌水的或不灌水的;以后又发展为"火里生金莲"的节目,即在一盆火里变出金色的莲花。这两种形式,都久已失传,到了清代只保留下一种"茶内生莲"的表演——用茶杯倒上滚热的茶,把一粒莲子投下去,一会儿就舒叶展瓣,开出小小的花朵。形式的大小虽有不同;衍变的痕迹,还是可以推寻的。⑤ 同传又载:

> 澄左乳傍有一孔,围四五寸,通彻腹内。有时肠从中出,或以絮塞孔。夜欲读书,辄拔絮,则一室洞明。又斋日辄至水边,引肠洗之,还复内中。⑥

---

① [晋]干宝撰、李剑国辑校《新辑搜神记》,北京:中华书局,2007 年,第 58~59 页。
② 以上参见傅文正《佛教对中国幻术的影响初探》,张曼涛主编:《现代佛教学术丛刊》18《佛教与中国文化》,台北:大乘文化出版社,1978 年,第 241~242 页。
③ [晋]荀氏撰《灵鬼志》,鲁迅辑《古小说钩沉》,《鲁迅辑录古籍丛编》,北京:人民文学出版社,1999 年,第 151 页。
④ [梁]慧皎撰、汤用彤校注《高僧传》,北京:中华书局,1992 年,第 346 页。
⑤ 同注①,第 243 页。
⑥ 《高僧传》,第 356 页。

这个与西域商胡中流行的利刃刺腹有异曲同工之处,同样是一个幻术。据张鹭《朝野佥载》卷三载:

> 河南府立德坊及南市西坊皆有胡祆神庙。每岁商胡祈福,烹猪羊,琵琶鼓笛,酣歌醉舞。酹神之后,募一僧为祆主,看者施钱并与之。其祆主取一横刀,利同霜雪,吹毛不过,以刀刺腹,刃出于背,仍乱扰肠肚流血。食顷,喷水咒之,平复如故。此盖西域之幻法也。①

除了佛图澄之外,鸠摩罗什虽以译经而著称,但也拥有一些简单的幻术。《出三藏记集》卷一四《鸠摩罗什传》载:

> 光中书监张资……寝疾困笃。光博营救疗。有外国道人罗叉,云能差资病。光喜,给赐甚丰。罗什知叉诳诈,告资曰:"叉不能为益,徒烦费耳。冥运虽隐,可以事试也。"乃以五色丝作绳结之,烧为灰末,投水中。灰若出水还成绳者,病不可愈。须臾,灰聚浮出,复绳本形。既而叉治无效,少日资亡。②

《高僧传》卷三《鸠摩罗什传》与此同。这实际上是烧物不伤幻术的变异,与现代魔术节目中的"双烧带绳"大同小异。据《晋书》卷九五《艺术·鸠摩罗什传》载,姚兴逼迫罗什纳妓后:

> 尔后不住僧坊,别立解舍,诸僧多效之。什乃聚针盈钵,引诸僧谓之曰:"若能见效食此者,乃可畜室耳。"因举匕进针,与常食不别,诸僧愧服乃止。③

此一情节不见于《出三藏记集》与《高僧传》,不知《晋书》何据。不过,吞针似是印度传统幻术。《旧杂譬喻经》有如下寓言,说是"天神化作一人下凡,于市中卖之":

> 臣问:"此名何等?"答曰:"祸母。"曰:"卖几钱?"曰:"千万。"臣便顾之,问曰:"此何等食?"曰:"日食一升针。"臣便家家发求针。如是人民两两三三相逢求针,使至诸郡县扰乱在所,患毒无憀。④

吞针幻术与后世表演的吞刀片应该是类似的。在众多刀片中,只有亮给观众看的一把是真刀片,其余的都是钝的,表演者利用喝水的工夫将刀片吐在杯中。表演吞针时,绝大部分针是特意伪造的道具,是可以吞食的。此一幻术后来在中土也一直有人表演。综上所述,佛教僧人同样是幻术传播的重要力量。

三、中土小说中的幻术表演

大秦、印度以及西域本地的幻术自汉朝后通过不同途径传入中土,经常在宫廷、市集以及寺院内表

---

① [唐]刘餗、张鹭撰,程毅中点校《隋唐嘉话　朝野佥载》,北京:中华书局,1979 年,第 64～65 页。
② [梁]释僧佑撰,苏晋仁、萧炼之点校《出三藏记集》,北京:中华书局,1995 年,第 533 页。
③ [唐]房玄龄等撰《晋书》,北京:中华书局,1974 年,第 2502 页。
④ 《大正藏》第 4 册,第 514 页,c。

演,大大促进了中土幻术的发展。由于幻术本身神变莫测、新鲜奇异,具有极高的审美价值,所以在中国小说中屡有记载。最著名的幻术描述莫过于蒲松龄《聊斋志异》卷一中的"偷桃"与"种梨",两者都是传统的外国幻术,通过西域流播到中土。清代的偷桃之术,其表演形式如下:

> 有官人命术士取桃,术士言惟王母园中有之,欲上天窃之……乃启笥,出绳一团,约数十丈,理其端,望空中掷去;绳即悬立空际,若有物以挂之。未几,愈掷愈高,渺入云中,手中绳亦尽。乃呼子曰:"儿来!余老惫,体重拙,不能行,得汝一往。"遂以绳授子,曰:"持此可登。"……子乃持索,盘旋而上,手移足随,如蛛趁丝,渐入云霄,不可复见。久之,坠一桃,如碗大……忽而绳落地上,术人惊曰:"殆矣!上有人断吾绳,儿将焉托!"移时,一物坠。视之,其子首也。捧而泣曰:"是必偷桃,为监者所觉。吾儿休矣!"又移时,一足落;无何,肢体纷坠,无复存者。术人大悲,一一拾置笥中而阖之……坐官骇诧,各有赐金。术人受而缠诸腰,乃扣笥而呼曰:"八八儿,不出谢赏,将何待?"忽一蓬头童首抵笥盖而出,望北稽首,则其子也。[①]

此一幻术实际上分两部分:第一是通天而上的绳技,第二是自我肢解。前半部分最早见载于《太平广记》卷一九三引《原化记》:

> 唐开元年(713～742)中……狱中有一囚笑谓所由曰:"某有拙技,限在拘系,不得略呈其事。"吏惊曰:"汝何所能?"囚曰:"吾解绳技。"……官曰:"绳技人常也,又何足异乎?"囚曰:"某所为者,与人稍殊……众人绳技,各系两头,然后其上行立周旋。某只须一条绳,粗细如指,五十尺,不用系著,抛向空中,腾踯翻覆,则无所不为。"官大惊悦,且令收录。明日,吏领至戏场,诸戏既作,次唤此人,令效绳技,遂捧一团绳,计百余尺,置诸地,将一头,手掷于空中,劲如笔。初抛三二丈,次四五丈,仰直如人牵之,众大惊异。后乃抛高二十余丈,仰空不见端绪。此人随绳手寻,身足离地。抛绳虚空,其势如鸟,旁飞远飏,望空而去,脱身行狴,在此日焉。[②]

在摩洛哥旅行家依宾拔都(Ibn Batuteh)所撰:《游记》中,我们可以看到此幻术的全貌:

> 此夕有一幻术士来,其人乃大汗之奴隶也……其人持一木球,球面有数孔,每孔皆有绳贯之。术士将球掷上空中,球渐高不见……术士手中,尚有绳断数根而已。彼令其徒,执紧绳乘空,俄顷不见。术士呼之三次,其徒不应。术士持刀,似大怒者,自亦系身于绳而上。转瞬,彼亦不见。片时,彼由空中,掷下童子之一手于地,次又掷一脚,次又掷一手、一脚,次又掷一躯干,再次掷下一头。彼乃喘息而下,衣满溅血。跪伏总督前,唇接地,用中国语,求总督命令。总督与之谈数语。彼将童子四肢,连接成架。复用力踢之。所杀之童子,忽立起,来至吾辈之前。吾详观其,毫无损伤。余乃大惊,心悸

---

① 《铸雪斋抄本聊斋志异》,第13页。
② [宋]李昉等编《太平广记》,北京:中华书局,1961年,第1449页。

不可言状。①

依宾拔都（Ibn Batuteh）所见幻术乃是在元至正八年（1348）。经过数百年的发展，已将绳技和自我肢解之术结合，创造了一个全新的魔术。1613 年，明朝人钱希言在其《狯园杂志》卷二中又记载了这一魔术，题名为《偷桃小儿》。1670 年，荷兰人梅尔敦（Edward Melton）在巴达维亚（Batavia，爪哇岛之首府）看到华人表演此幻术，并绘一图，以形容所见。② 钱钟书说：在德国故事中，也有术士掷绳高空，绳引小驹，术士攀马蹄，妻牵夫足，婢牵妇衣，鱼贯入云而逝，见之于《格林童话》。同样，爱尔兰故事言有精绳技者抛丝线挂浮云上，使一兔、一犬、一童缘而登天，继遣一少女去善视兔，良久不下，绳师心疑，遂收其线，则女方与童狎而兔为犬，怒斩童首，观者责其忍，乃复安头颈上，以面背向，童即活。③

我原先以为，此一幻术乃中土首创，最近才发现，此一幻术在国际魔术界极其著名，其名为"印度神仙索"（Indian Rope Trick）。《吠檀多经文》和著名古印度诗人迦梨陀娑（Kālidāsa）都提到过这套魔术。但他们提及的只是此幻术的前半部分：魔术师将绳抛向天上，绳子挂在天上垂下，一小童便沿绳爬上，并在上端作平衡表演，随后又消失，并出现在人群中。19 世纪时，一些西方名人如毕伯、高尔基等，都亲眼看到过印度绳技。但目前此套魔术的完整版本似已失传，现在的魔术师只能在舞台上表演前半部分。曾经有人悬赏能够在有观众围观的空地表演这一魔术的魔术师，但至今仍未有人领走悬赏。有专家对其中的门子有详细的揭秘：在此幻术中，魔术师使用的是一种特殊的绳子，绳头有铁钩，这种钩子是由很多向下的钩子组成的。表演前，由于绳子是卷着的，钩子藏在里面看不见。在表演场地的上方，魔术师预先拴好了一根很细的横着的绳子，绳的一头可以系在树上，另一头可以固定在墙上或其他建筑物上，高度大约在二十呎左右。魔术师选择日落前表演，以使观众眼睛受阳光的强烈刺激，或用明亮的火把照亮场地，或用篝火制造出浓浓的烟雾，其目的都是使观众看不见那根横着的细绳子。魔术师在表演时将系有钩子的绳子往上抛，挂在横着的细绳子上，小童跟着爬了上去，然后顺着横着的细绳滑到树上去。观众在耀眼的眩光中，觉得小孩子一下失去身影，而此时魔术师将绳子向上一抖，钩子因而脱离横着的绳子而坠落地面。抛下断肢这一部分人们所知不多，据分析是孩子将被杀猴子的肢体碎块藏在衣服里，然后在与魔术师争论时朝下扔。④ 从中国对此一幻术的记载来看，都是在室内表演的，因此相对来说较为容易。但《聊斋志异》中的幻术表演则将西域技法与中国古有的神话传说天衣无缝地结合在一起，设计了精巧但极其合理的情节，成为一个完整的小型戏剧。它具备了戏剧一些最重要的元素，有开端，有发展，有悬疑，当达成一个惊心魄的高潮后，又急转直下，制造一个圆满的皆大欢喜的结局。艺术上成功的结果之一就是同时带来了商业上的成功，这从"坐官骇诧，各有赐金"即可看出。

《聊斋志异》中记载的另一个幻术是"种梨"：首先是有一道士故意与卖梨人讨梨，卖梨人执意不肯，旁观的佣保看不下去，遂付与道士钱一枚让他买得一梨。道士啖梨且尽：

① 转引自张星烺编《中西交通史料汇编》第 2 册，北京：中华书局，2003 年，第 651～652 页；另可参见马金鹏译《伊本·白图泰游记》，银川：宁夏人民出版社，1985 年，第 559～560 页。

② 《中西交通史料汇编》第 2 册，第 652 页。

③ Vivian Mercier, The Irish Comic Tradition, 24，见钱钟书撰《管锥编》第 2 册，北京：中华书局，1979 年，第 704 页。

④ 参见维基百科"印度神仙索"（Indian Rope Trick）条，以及威廉·庞德斯通（William Poundstone）撰、张大川等译《更大秘密》"印度绳技是真的吗"一节，上海：上海科技教育出版社，2006 年，第 207～215 页。

把核于手,解肩上镵,坎地深数寸,纳之而覆以土。向市人索汤沃灌。好事者于临路店索得沸沈,道士接浸坎上。万目攒视,见有勾萌出,渐大;俄成树,枝叶扶苏;倏而花,倏而实,硕大芳馥,累累满树。道士乃即树头摘赐观者,顷刻向尽。已,乃以镵伐树,丁丁良久方断。带叶荷肩头,从容徐步而去。

初,道士作法时,乡人亦杂立众中,引领注目,竟忘其业。道士既去,始顾车中,则梨已空矣,方悟适所俵散,皆己物也。又细视车上一靶亡,是新凿断者。心大愤恨。急迹之,转过墙隅,则断靶弃垣下,始知所伐梨本,即是物也。道士不知所在。一市粲然。①

很显然,这是一个幻术表演,实即颜师古所说的"植瓜种树"之术。此术除黎轩幻人在中土表演过之外,佛经中也曾提及。《贤愚经》卷一〇《须达起精舍品》载:"六师众中有一弟子名劳度差,善知幻术,于大众前咒作一树,自然长大,荫覆众会,枝叶郁茂,花果各异。众人咸言。此变乃是劳度差作。"②据《搜神记》卷一载,三国时,中土术士徐光已经掌握了此一幻技:

> 吴时有徐光,常行幻术于市里。从人乞瓜,其主勿与,便从索瓣,杖地而种之。俄而瓜生蔓延,生花成实,乃取食之,因赐观者。鬻者反视所出卖,皆亡耗矣。③

《太平御览》卷七三七、《法苑珠林》卷六一引孔伟《七引》也提到此幻术:"弄幻之时,因时而作,殖瓜种菜,立起寻尺,投芳送臭,卖黄售白。"时至唐朝,此术为一些道士炫耀神术时所搬演。《酉阳杂俎》前集卷五《诡异》云:"元和中,江淮术士王琼,尝在段君秀家……取花含默对于密器中,一夕开花。"④据蒋防《幻戏志》载:晚唐时,泾川节度周宝曾向道士殷天祥"求种瓜钓鱼,若葛仙翁也"。"(马湘)乃于席上以瓦器盛土种瓜,须臾引蔓生花,结实取食,众宾皆称香美异于常瓜。"⑤《幻戏志》显然是伪作。蒋防自大和二年(828)春以后的行迹不见记载,其文集则编定于开成二年(837),其人肯定卒于此年之前。《幻戏志》说,马自然与马植结识于马植罢相任常州刺史之时。马植罢相是在大中四年(850)二月以后,蒋防肯定无缘得知此事。而此书所记殷七七事迹,据《太平广记》卷五二引《续仙传》所载,应在薛朗、刘浩之乱(光启三年,887)的二十年之前,亦即867年左右,此时蒋防已死三十年了。不过,书虽伪,其事迹却有所本。此书殷七七、马自然事迹出自《续仙传》,陈复休事出自《仙传拾遗》,叶法善事出自《集异记》与《仙传拾遗》。伪作者合此四人为《幻戏志》一书,是因为此四人均以变幻之术著称,与其说是道士,不如说是魔术师。除种瓜之术外,殷七七还能开非时之花,变栗为石,缀于鼻,掣拽不落。"酌水为酒,削木为脯,使人退行,指船即驻,呼鸟自坠,唾鱼即活。撮土画地,状山川形势,折茅聚蚁,变成城市。人有曾经行处,见之历历皆似,但少狭耳。"马自然"于遍身及袜上摸钱,所出钱不知多少,掷之皆青铜钱,撒投井中,呼之一一飞出。人有收取,顷之复失……命延叟取纸画一白鹭,以水噀之,飞入菜畦中啄菜。其主赶起,又飞下再三。

---

① 《铸雪斋抄本聊斋志异》,第14页。
② 《大正藏》第4册,第420页,b。
③ 《新辑搜神记》,第54页。
④ [唐]段成式撰、方南生点校《酉阳杂俎》,北京:中华书局,1981年,第53页。
⑤ [唐]蒋防撰《幻戏志》,影印龙威秘书本,《丛书集成新编》第82册,台北:台湾新文丰公司,1986年,第109页。

湘又画一猧子，走赶捉白鹭，共践其菜，一时碎尽”。① 陈复休则有地下掘金、砂中藏器，叶法善与明皇游月宫等，均属于幻术。

《聊斋志异》所载，其形态非常接近于徐光所演。事实上，那乡人、佣保很可能都是魔术师的助手，他们与道士担任各自的角色，合作演出了一场小型戏剧，骗过了包括蒲松龄在内的所有观众。魔术表演的本意在于谋取利益，但此一表演也宣传了不吝施舍、哀悯穷苦的社会道德，具有一定的教育意义。

四、神奇情节的幻术背景

由于绝大部分人对于幻术的“门子”一无所知，所以常常信以为真，作为神异之事记录下来；中土小说中的很多神奇传说实际上是一些简单的幻术技巧。《酉阳杂俎》前集卷五记有“噀壁成画”之绝技，其云：

> 大历中，荆州有术士从南来，止于陟圮寺。好酒，少有醒时。因寺中大斋会，人众数千，术士忽曰：“余有一技，可代抃瓦(厂＋盍)珠之欢也。”乃合彩色于一器中，驔步抓目，徐祝数十言，方饮水再三噀壁上。成“维摩问疾”变相，五色相宜如新写。逮半日余，色渐薄，至暮都灭。惟金粟纶巾鹙子衣上一花，经两日犹在。②

后来的魔术表演中有“口吐字画”、“壁现龙舟”等，其“门子”在于预先用五倍子水、碱水、白笈水等画壁，等到干时，不露痕迹。然后用皂矾、姜黄水喷上去，马上就会现出五色图案。此一绝技最早也是由西域传入。据《拾遗记》卷四载：“始皇元年（前246），骞霄国献刻玉善画工名裔。使含丹青以漱地，即成魑魅及诡怪群物之像。”③

魏晋以后，西域方士屡屡在中土表演咒龙祈雨之术，如《高僧传》载佛图澄祈水，其法是：“澄坐绳床，烧安息香，咒愿数百言，如此三日，水泫然微流。有一小龙长五六寸许，随水来出……有顷，水大至，隍堑皆满。”同书卷一〇《神异下・涉公传》载：“涉公者，西域人也……能以秘咒，咒下神龙。每旱，(苻)坚常请之咒龙，俄而龙下钵中，天辄大雨。”但均对咒龙祈雨的细节语焉不详。《太平广记》卷四一八引《抱朴子》“甘宗”条有较为详细的描述：

> 秦使者甘宗所奏西域事云：外国方士能神咒者，临川禹步吹气，龙即浮出。初出，乃长数十丈。方士吹之，一吹则龙辄一缩。至长数寸。乃取置壶中，以少水养之。外国常苦旱灾。于是方士闻有旱处，便赍龙往，出卖之。一龙直金数十觔。举国会敛以顾之。直毕，乃发壶出龙。置渊中。复禹步吹之。长数十丈。须臾雨四集矣。④

---

① ［唐］蒋防撰《幻戏志》，影印龙威秘书本，《丛书集成新编》第82册，台北：新文丰公司，1986年，第109页。又见于《太平广记》卷三三、五二引《续仙传》。

② 《酉阳杂俎》，第54页。

③ 《太平广记》卷二一〇引《王子年拾遗记》作：“秦有烈裔者，骞霄国人。秦皇帝时，本国进之。口含丹墨，噀壁以成龙兽。”

④ 《太平广记》，第3402页。

与中土传统巫术相比,这种方技便捷而具有观赏性,能让人立竿见影地看到龙的变化,因此,很快战胜了中土巫术取得压倒性的优势地位。来到中土的方士充分利用了这一方术技巧来争取信仰。《太平广记》卷四二一引《宣室志》载萧昕为京兆尹时亲见天竺僧不空三藏祈雨:

> 取华木皮,仅尺余,缵小龙于其上,而以炉瓯香水置于前。三藏转咒,震舌呼祝,咒者食倾,即以缵龙授昕曰:"可投此于曲江中。"投讫亟还,无冒风雨。昕如言投之,旋有白龙才尺余,摇鬣振麟自水出。俄而身长数丈,状如曳素,倏忽巨天……云物晦凝,暴雨骤降。①

这种祈雨方术的场面与效果无疑给中土人士留下了深刻的印象,成为一种亲眼目睹的神异事迹而被广泛传播。在不断传播的过程中,作为祈雨方术的念咒情节与其他仪式性场面渐渐开始淡化,而印象最突出的龙在水中瞬间由小变大之情状则被反复强化,最后演变为龙的自然变化,成为彻头彻尾的神异故事。这类故事在唐朝小说中多次出现,如《太平广记》卷四二二引《宣室志》载:

> 故唐太守卢元裕未仕时,尝以中元设幡幢像,置盂兰于其间。俄闻盆中有唧唧之音。元裕视,见一小龙才寸许,逸状奇姿,婉然可爱。于是以水沃之,其龙伸足振鬣,已长数尺矣……有白云自盆中而起,其龙亦逐云而去。②

然而,揭开方士们自神其术的种种表演,这一咒术实际上是一幻术。其来源非常古老,我们上文提及埃及的魔术师乌巴阿奈尔用蜡做了一条七指长的鳄鱼,扔进水里后,鳄鱼在瞬间之内马上变成了七肘长,其法与咒龙祈雨术有异曲同工之处。后世的中国魔术中有鲤鱼变龙,其"门子"在于龙的身子是由篾丝盘曲而成,可以伸缩;变化时,放开约束篾丝的机关,篾丝伸展开来就变成了一条巨龙。

以上所述,基本上是对幻术技法信以为真的叙述,也就是说,它是在幻术表演的可能范围之内的。而在另一些小说中,则是在幻术表演的基础上糅合了作者的想象,踵事增华,从而异中见异,奇中出奇。这些变幻应该是幻术也做不到的,从而成为真正的传奇。我们以吴均《续齐谐记》中的《阳羡书生》为例来加以说明。此篇小说中有口中吐人之神异情节,其云:

> 书生乃出笼,谓彦曰:"欲为君薄设。"彦曰:"善。"乃口中吐出一铜奁子,奁子中具诸饰馔,珍羞方丈……酒数行……又于口中吐一女子,年可十五六,衣服绮丽,容貌殊绝。共坐宴。俄而书生醉卧,此女谓彦曰:"虽与书生结妻,而实怀怨。向亦窃得一男子同行,书生既眠,暂唤之,君幸勿言。"彦曰:"善。"女子于口中吐出一男子,年可二十三四,亦颖悟可爱,乃与彦叙寒温。书生卧欲觉,女子口吐一锦行障遮书生。书生乃留女子共卧。男子谓彦曰:"此女子虽有心,情亦不甚,向复窃得一女人同行。今欲暂见之,愿君勿洩。"彦曰:"善。"男子又于口中吐一妇人,年可二十许,共酌,戏谈甚

---

① 《太平广记》,第3426页。

② 同上注,第3438页。同卷引《纪闻》载:"唐安太守卢元裕子翰言,太守少时,尝结友读书终南山。日晚溪行,崖中得一圆石,莹白如鉴,方执玩,忽次,堕地而折,中有白鱼约长寸余,随石宛转落涧中,渐盈尺,俄长丈余,鼓鬐掉尾,云雷暴兴,风雨大至。"显然,这是同一故事的传闻异辞。

久。闻书生动声，男子曰："二人眠已觉。"因取所吐女人，还纳口中。须臾，书生处女乃出，谓彦曰："书生欲起。"乃吞向男子，独对彦坐。然后书生起，谓彦曰："暂眠遂久，君独坐，当悒悒邪？日又晚，当与君别。"遂吞其女子，诸器皿悉纳口中。留大铜盘，可二尺广，与彦别曰："无以藉君，与君相忆也。"①

此故事的前身是晋人荀氏的《灵鬼志》中的相关记载，不少学者已经指出这一故事固非中土所有，经过了一个漫长的本土化过程。段成式《酉阳杂俎·续集·贬误篇》首先指出它出自佛教经籍《旧杂譬喻经》卷上，其云：

梵志独行来入水池浴，出饭食。作术吐出一壶，壶中有女人，与于屏处作家室。梵志遂得卧，女人则复作术，吐出一壶，壶中有年少男子复与共卧。已便吞壶，须臾梵志起，复内妇着壶中，吞之已，作杖而去。②

口中吞人似乎是印度传统幻术。《佛说遗日摩尼宝经》中有"譬如幻师化作人，还自取幻师啖"③的说法。在《佛说摩诃衍宝严经》云："譬如幻师化作幻人，而食幻师，无有真实。"④幻师变出幻人，幻人反过来将幻师吞食，此幻术的详细情形现已不得而知。《拾遗记》卷二的记载能够让我们窥见一些端倪。据说，扶娄国人能够"口中生人，备百戏之乐，宛转屈曲于指掌间。人形或长数分，或复数寸"。而卷四说道人尸罗能够"张口向日，则见人乘羽盖，驾螭、鹄，直入于口内。复以手抑胸上，而闻怀袖之中，轰轰雷声。更张口，则向见羽盖、螭、鹄相随从口中而出"。⑤ 由此我们可知道，所吞吐之人实为幻人，其形不过数分，最多数寸。《旧杂譬喻经》中表现的幻术较为复杂一些，吐出之人还能吐物，肯定是使用了某种幻术手法。此经虽已不复明言梵志所吐之人为偶人，不过还说是梵志作术，隐约表明其幻术背景。但到了中土文献中，幻术的背景被完全取消，口中所吞吐之偶人变成了真实人物，因此显得奇幻不可思议。

同样，《太平广记》卷二八六引《原化记》"胡媚儿"条所记幻术与此有些类似：

唐贞元中，扬州坊市间，忽有一妓术丐乞者，不知所从来，自称姓胡，名媚儿，所为颇甚怪异。……一旦怀中出一琉璃瓶子，可受半升，表里烘明，如不隔物，遂置于席上。初谓观者曰："有人施与满此瓶子，则足矣。"瓶口刚如苇管大，有人与之百钱，投之，铮然有声，只见瓶间大如粟粒，众皆异之。……俄有好事人，与之十万二十万，皆如之。或有以马驴入之瓶中，见人马皆如蝇大，动行如故。有度支两税纲，自扬子院，部轻货数十车至，驻观之，以其一时入，或终不能致将他物往，且谓官物不足疑者，乃谓媚儿曰："尔能令诸车皆入此中乎？"媚儿曰："许之则可。"纲曰："且试之。"媚儿乃微侧瓶口，大喝，诸车辘辘相继，悉入瓶，瓶中历历如行蚁然。有顷，渐不见。媚儿即跳身瓶中，纲乃

① ［梁］吴均撰《续齐谐记》，影印古今逸史本，《丛书集成新编》第82册，台北：新文丰公司，1986年，第43～44页。
② 《大正藏》第4册，第514页，a。
③ 《大正藏》第12册，第191页，a。
④ 同上注，第196页，c。
⑤ 《拾遗记》，第94页。

大惊,遽取扑破,求之一无所有。①

前文明言入瓶之马驴"皆如蝇大",显见是一幻术表演,然后面描述数十辆真实之大车辘辘入瓶,媚儿自身亦跳入瓶中,就基本上属于建立在幻术基础上的想象了。

幻术对中国宗教、文学的巨大影响,更重要也更关键的一点在于:它改变了人们对于世界、万物存在的基本观念,改变人们对于自然规律的看法,它使人们相信有超自然、超规律,甚至是反自然、反规律的事物的存在。颜之推的看法很有代表性,他说:"世有祝师及诸幻术,犹能履火蹈刃,种瓜移井,倏忽之间,十变五化。人力所为,尚能如此;何况神通感应,不可思量,千里宝幢,百由旬座,化成净土,踊出妙塔乎?"②这种"一切皆有可能"的信心,对于宗教来说,能够引发对神灵实有的信仰,对文学创作来说,则能激发、调动丰富的想象力。中国小说中的丰富多彩的神通描写,或多或少受到幻术的影响,对此,还有待于深入的研究。

---

① 《太平广记》,第2278页。
② [北齐]颜之推撰、王利器集解《颜氏家训集解》卷五《归心》,北京:中华书局,1993年,第383页。

大谷收集品中新发现的带有景教符号的地藏麻布画初探

——兼论回鹘高昌时期景教与其他宗教的关系

王振芬　孙惠珍

　　所谓"大谷收集品",是指上世纪初日本西本愿寺第二十二代门主大谷光瑞组织的"中亚探险队"在我国新疆、中亚等地所获古代艺术品和资料的总称,这些文物是研究古代丝绸之路民族、历史、文化的珍贵资料,历来为学界所重视。旅顺博物馆收藏了大谷收集品中的一部分,本文介绍的地藏菩萨麻布画就是其中的一件。在现已公之于世的有关大谷收集品的诸出版物中均不见关于它的任何记录,从这一意义上讲,本文是首次将其公布于学术界。更重要的是该画与一般意义上的地藏菩萨图像有所不同,其中带有景教十字符号的景教神像使其具有特殊的价值,是研究回鹘高昌时期佛教与三夷教关系的珍贵资料。同时,也因为现在已知被确定与景教艺术品的相关联的文物大都收藏在国外,从而使旅顺博物馆的这件藏品具有不同寻常的意义。

　　该麻布画残损较重,现存的麻布面上有大部分颜料剥落。该画1910年至1911年在日本西本愿寺别邸二乐庄与其他大谷收集品曾经有过初步的整理,现还保存有当时整理时留下的原始登记号码,分别为各麻画残片的原始编号:"2181"、"2182"、"2183"、"2184",和由各残片组成的大幅画帖的登记编号:"麻三○四G"、"纸四"、"第一○八"。从这些编号得知,整幅麻画由四块大小不一的残片组成。在这四个残片中只有"2183"和"2184"图案比较清晰,"2184"是用黑色线条描绘的一只红色的武士长靴,而"2183"是此件麻画的主体。最初整理时有部分拼接错误,现将其重新拼对如图一所示。

图一

众所周知，大谷收集品的收集者是几个并无考古学常识的僧侣，因此而造成的出土品原始档案资料的缺失，是我们今天研究这批文物的难点之一。所以，我们无法找到关于其出土地的确切记录，但从大谷收集品的整体来源情况和该画的艺术风格分析，应该是回鹘高昌时期吐鲁番地区的出土品。从绘画的艺术手法来看，该画体现了回鹘高昌时期佛教绘画的艺术特色，画面整体用鲜艳的赭色敷底，花纹、头光、衣服等也以红色为主，局部使用明亮的绿色和黄色，脸部是用白色铺底，用墨色线条勾出五官，唇和其中一尊女像眉间、双颊的花钿则用红色点染。整幅画线条感十分突出，粗细有致，生动自然，这些都充分体现了回鹘民族对热烈色彩的特别喜好。① 位于吐鲁番附近木头沟的伯孜克里克石窟，公元九至十世纪时是回鹘高昌王家贵族寺院，在定名为愿度图的石窟壁画中很容易找到与之相类的艺术风格。特别是画面左侧的锷装武士，着武士服饰，虽然由于残损看不清具体装束，但腰带部露出的半圆形腹护却清晰可见，外披红色披风，梳齐肩长发，头顶花瓣形冠，留唇髭，颔下蓄须，俨然是一位回鹘王者形象。在其前侧为一头梳双髻的贵族妇女，身穿宽袖红色长袍。在二者之上有三朵莲花，花朵呈伞盖形，这些均体现出回鹘高昌的艺术风格。

地藏菩萨为绘画主尊，披帽状，呈坐姿，现仅存右手，腹前托起，手中应持宝珠。单就被帽地藏图像本身来看，最早出现于晚唐，所以判定该麻画的时代并不是件困难的事，它应该属于公元九至十世纪回鹘高昌时期。

探讨该画的难点是其在艺术表象下的思想内容，这也是本文论述的重点。

地藏是释迦灭度后至弥勒成佛之间的"救世主"，是无佛时代的"准佛"，这一点在实叉难陀译的《地藏菩萨本愿经》中有明确的表述，释迦曾嘱咐地藏"汝当忆念吾在忉利天宫殷勤付嘱：令娑婆世界至弥勒出世已来众生，悉使解脱，永离诸苦，遇佛授记"。同出于唐代的两部有关地藏的经典为实叉难陀译《地藏菩萨本愿经》和玄奘《地藏十轮经》，都宣扬了地藏的种种救度誓愿。但真正体现地藏个性的是晚唐、五代出现的《道明和尚还魂记》和《阎罗王受记经》。前者现存只在敦煌写本中发现，后者又称为《十王经》，不仅见于敦煌写本，而且目前发现了回鹘、西夏等多种，但二者都是由中国僧人编写的所谓"伪经"，正是这两部"伪经"成为晚唐、五代以来地藏信仰的重要经典。表现在图像上是代表地狱观念的地藏、十王审判、六道轮回组合图像的出现和流行。这种组合图像的一个显著特征是地藏像较以前增大，"被帽像多为主尊，坐像，如同佛的说法图，俨然成为释迦涅槃之后、弥勒成佛之前这一阶段的救世主，地藏身份大大得到提升"。②

概括地说，地藏与十王、六道组合的图像一般为：主尊地藏多呈被帽状，半跏趺坐于莲台上，双手持锡杖、宝珠，前侧左右分别配列戴冠执的十王，他们是负责地狱审判的冥王，在地藏头光两侧有六道云气纹，分别代表天、人、阿修罗、畜生、饿鬼、地狱六道。有的图像还在十王前置比丘形象的道明和尚和狮子，也有的图像是在主尊地藏前左右分列善、恶二童子形象。

现在我们看到的这件旅顺博物馆收藏的地藏麻画，与过去所见到的地藏组合像都有所不同，因为画面中并不见典型意义上的十王。站立在地藏左侧的是两个更呈世俗形象的王者和贵族。另外还有一个残损严重的武士形象（图二），与地藏组合像中的诸王形象不同。

---

① 贾应逸、祁小山著《印度到中国新疆的佛教艺术》，甘肃教育出版社，2000 年，第 503 页。
② 王惠民：《中唐以后敦煌地藏图像考察》，《敦煌研究》2007 年第 1 期。

但从该画的构图方式上看，整体画面表现有主有次，突出了地藏的主尊地位，也应该是属于地藏与十王组合像范畴。但究竟是组合像中的哪一种，由于残损严重，我们只能从现残存的画面上做出一个推测，初步认为应是地藏与六道组合的构图。判定这一点的主要依据是：在地藏像左上方有一带状云气纹，残存的画面上还能看清描绘的是动物，这在地藏图像中一般表示六道之一：畜生道。但在一般地藏十王像中主尊地藏前方两侧都有协助其掌管冥间审判事务的十冥王、判官，他们都着现实社会中汉族官员服饰，手持笏板。而在这幅麻画中在十王位置上现存两身画像，如前所述，一位是锷装王者的形象，另一位是汉装的妇女。

最不同的是二者均有头光。画中地藏兼具头光和身光，表现的是其正面形象，地藏左侧残存的锷装王者和世俗妇女两个形象，稍侧向于主尊，也具有头光，从这种构图方式来看，说明他们的身份应该是主尊地藏的胁侍或眷属。这与我们过去所见到的地藏十王像有所不

图二

同，一般的地藏十王像中的十王都是现实社会中的王者形象，不具头光，在这里为其明确地表现出头光，实际上是把二者作为佛教世界的角色，因为头光是佛教绘画中确定其佛格身份的标志。所以从这一点上它与一般意义上的地藏十王像就有了实质的不同，显然是与一般意义上的十王从地位上有所提高。实际上，不论地藏身侧的这两身像具体身份如何，有一点是可以确定的，他们都是协助地藏完成其救度六道得脱地狱弘愿的。该地藏麻画中另一个值得关注的特别之处是在锷装王者像头光上有一个十字符号（图三），由于画面残损，无法看清其原貌，但就已经发现的同类图像来说，这个十字应该是其手中所持之物。关于这个十字形符号，学术界已经公认为是唐至元代在中国境内多有存在的景教的标志，手持十字的画像应该就是表示其景教徒的身份。所以画中立侍于地藏旁边的锷装回鹘王者是一位皈依了景教的景教徒。基督教，唐代称景教，实际上是对叙利亚人聂斯托里为首的基督教聂斯托里派（Nestorian Christianity）的称谓。唐代以前，景教仅在中国民间传播，直到唐高宗时才得到中国官方认可。太平兴国七年（982），北宋使者王延德访问高昌回鹘王国（今新疆吐鲁番），他见到当地"复有摩尼寺、波斯僧，各持其法，佛经所谓外道者也"。[①] 唐代景教称"波斯教"，所以唐代来华的景净和阿罗本又称"波斯僧"。太平兴国"九年（984）五月三日，西州回鹘与波斯外道来朝贡"[②]。所谓"波斯僧"和"波斯外道"皆指高昌回鹘王国的波斯景教徒而言。近一个世纪以来，在包括敦煌在内的古代西域多有关于景教文物被发现，最著名的是1907年，英人斯坦因在敦煌千佛洞考察时，攫走的包括《大秦景教三威蒙度赞》（附有景教经典目录三十种）等唐代景教译经和一幅残破的基督像绢画（图四）。还有德国吐鲁番考察队在高昌古城郊外

---

① 《宋史·高昌传》。
② 《宋史·天竺传》。

发现的一所景教废寺中发现的两幅景教残画(图五、六),这两幅画现藏柏林印度艺术博物馆。

图三

图四

图五

据京都大学羽田亨教授考证,"敦煌出土的应为基督画像的绢画断片……大概为敦煌地方唐代画家接受景教司祭或教徒的订货,按其意旨或其他参考材料画成。在整个写实画法中,佛教被采入为基调。仅凭这些资料,是不能论述该地基督教美术性质的。高昌的壁画与其教义传播应一起来自波斯或粟特,其间尚无什么特殊的变化。而敦煌之基督画像(?)已见有唐代佛像画样式的影响了"[①]。他还在这幅画的文字说明中介绍说:"基督(?)画像,斯坦因氏在敦煌获得的绢本设色画残片,现藏大英博物馆。头饰及有波斯式翼的王冠上带有十字章,面貌等都具有写实风格。"朱谦之先生认为:"敦煌基督画像的发现,无疑反映在敦煌石室封闭前正在东西各地流行的基督画像崇拜,因而推定为来中国的景教徒,即自称朵利架司(Catholicos)派的景教徒所携带之景教尊弥施诃即基督之画像,是最合

——————————
① [日]羽田亨著、耿世民译《西域文化史》,收入《西域文明史概论(外一种)》,中华书局,2005年,第158~159页。

理不过的了。"①不论是唐代画家制作的还是景教徒携带来的画像，它的一个显著特点是画像所表现出的西方影响。伦敦大学艺术史系韦陀教授将其定性为"景教人物图"，时代断在公元八至九世纪。而德国人获得的两幅景教绘画作品，日本学者佐伯好郎考证为第5世纪以来在东方诸国所传棕榈祭日的壁画，表现基督于耶路撒冷入城的情景，右边一人左手持香盒，右手持盛圣水的碗或者是钵，对面三人各执杨柳小枝。棕榈祭日起源于《新约全书·约翰传》第十二章第十二、十三节，是原始景教的内容，只不过叙利亚的景教会使用红柳代替棕榈。有的学者进一步考证右边一人为基督耶稣，其对面三人依次为彼得、约翰和抹大拿的玛丽亚。②

　　同样是由德国考察队发现的绘制于同一景教寺院东侧一室的另外一幅壁画，是一位骑在马上的肖像人物（图七），同样是肩荷着有十字架徽章的旗杆，与斯坦因的敦煌发现品有异曲同工之处。关于景教画像，建中二年立的《大秦景教流行中国碑》说："秦国大德阿罗本，远将经像，来献上京"，说明景教在传播中国时，不仅带来了经典，还同时带来了画像。不难推测，这些画像应该就是纯粹的基督圣像，而"藏经洞所出波斯艺术风格的基督残画，完全可能是以阿罗本从波斯带到长安的圣像为底本而摹绘的"。

图六

图七

　　与这些已知的景教艺术作品相比，旅顺博物馆藏的这件地藏麻画中的景教人物表现了与众不同的气质，从绘画风格上，它是一幅完全回鹘化的作品，如果不是有一个景教符号，看不出它与景教艺术之间的任何联系。

　　首先，需要明确的一点是，该麻画是一幅以表现地藏菩萨为主要内容的佛教绘画，而不是景教作品。但它与景教内容相关连，表现了一尊作为地藏胁侍的景教神祇，这在以往发现的有关景教的艺术品中是仅见的构图。释读这件作品涉及外来宗教与本土宗教之间的关系问题，正如有的学者所说的那样："从中国宗教史上来看，凡是外来宗教在中国扎根传播，都面临着一个中国化的问题"，特别是景教原本就是一个在本土受到排挤的异端，所以在其向外传播过程中迫切需要得到当地文化的认同和强有力的势力的支持，景教一方面通过各种手段获得政治上层势力的支持，另一方面竭力迎合占主流地位的宗教信

①　朱谦之：《中国景教》，东方出版社，1993年，第195页。
②　[日]羽田亨氏著作《西域文化史》，第19~20页。

仰的思想,也就是说在宣传其本教教义时要注意到不与这些宗教的教义相冲突,所以,正如许多学者注意到的一样,在新疆和敦煌发现的诸景教经典中有许多佛教或者是道教的术语和教义,因为公元一世纪就已经传入的佛教与发源于中国本土的道教是隋唐时期两大主流宗教,尤其是佛教,据唐长庆年间(821~824)舒元舆所撰《鄂州永兴县重严寺碑铭》记载:"故十族之乡,百家之间,必有浮图为其粉黛。国朝沿近古而加焉,亦容杂夷而来者,有摩尼焉,大秦焉,祆神焉,合天下三寺,不足当吾释寺一小邑之数也。"①形象反映了当时佛教与三夷教即摩尼教、景教、祆教之间势力对比。同时,也进一步说明如此势力微小的景教若想在中国立住脚跟,不借于佛教势力的支持和庇护是不可能的。

　　旅顺博物馆藏的这件带有景教符号的地藏麻画实际上所反映的就是景教对佛教的依附,正如我们在上面所讲到的那样,画中表现的是一个有景教徒身份的神邸充当了地藏菩萨胁侍的角色。从教义上讲,"强调耶稣的复活,强调受到东部教堂崇敬的殉难者和圣徒的复活,最后还强调每一个信徒的复活,这是我们在丝绸之路上所发现的叙利亚景教文献的主导题材"②。复活的观念源于东方基督教派聂斯脱利的理论中对耶稣人的天性的关注,所以"复活后的基督,在丝绸之路上也是景教派基督徒信仰的核心",③这一点正体现在对景教所强调的十字上,"凡是有景教徒留下足迹的地方,我们都会见到这一标志,特别是在七河流域、塔里木盆地、中国,甚至在拉达克"。景教碑中说"判十字以定四方,鼓元风而生二气,暗空易而天地开,日月运而昼夜作,匠成万物,然立初人","印持十字,融四炤以合无拘",把十字与创世联系起来。德国人克林凯特认为:"景教的十字——受推崇人物的十字,也启示人们想到那个复活的人。"基督教徒潘绅在其《景教碑文注释》中专门对此做出了解释:"按十字架本为刑具,此罗马之极刑,以纵横二木,合为十字,钉人之手足,竖而举之,使悬木而迟迟以死。吾主被难,实惨死于十字架,以成救世之功,后人追念其救赎大恩而重视此十字架焉。"所以景教的十字表达的是一种救赎和复活的观念。

　　这一观念与地藏菩萨的地狱救度观念有殊途同归之处。就地藏救赎苦难的性格而言,与观世音菩萨类似,但在佛教发展过程中地藏侧重于地狱救度,而观音主要是救度现实苦难,正如在《瑜伽集要焰口施食仪》中地藏发出"众生度尽方证菩提,地狱未空誓不成佛"的弘愿。景教经典《序听迷诗所经》中谈道:"何因众生在于罪中?自于(得)见天尊。天尊不同人身,复谁能(得)见?众生无人敢见近尊。善福善缘众生,始得见天尊。世间元不见天尊,若为得识,众生自不得见天(尊)。为(若)自(得)修福,然不坠恶道地狱,即得天(道)。得(者)如有恶业众,堕落恶道,不见明果,亦不得天道,众生等好自思量。"④二者以共同的善恶宗教伦理道德观为理论基础,以追求宗教终极解脱为目的。这种教义原理上的一致性使地藏和景教徒聚合在地藏十王图中有了可能性和可行性。

　　但是,在这幅麻画中带有景教十字标志的锷装王者的实际身份应该令人关注,由于残损的关系,我们无法确定画像头冠上是否也有十字,按照现在所见到的资料,其冠上也应该有,这种形象以往学者都把它直接认定为耶稣基督。另外一个重要的关注点就是其体现出的回鹘王者形象,二者结合,顺理成章将其认定为一位皈依了景教的回鹘王者并不过分。史籍中并无任何回鹘王改信景教的记录,但据德国学者

---

① 《唐文粹》卷六五,浙江人民出版社(影印本),第2册,1986年。
② [德]克林凯特著、赵崇民译《丝绸古道上的文化》,新疆美术摄影出版社,第82页。
③ 朱谦之:《中国景教》,第349页。
④ 大正新修大藏经第五十四册。《事汇部类·外教部》。

克林凯特的论述:"大约在公元 8 世纪之后,在撒马尔罕也出现了一个大主教区。当时可能已经是提摩休什一世的领导时期,他在一封信中谈到了基督教教徒'在印度人和中国人那里的情况,在吐蕃人和突厥人那里的情况,以及在所有由这个教长领导的教区内的情况',并且强调说'突厥人的一个国王'也皈依了。"①

唐武宗会昌五年禁断佛教时,景教也遭禁断,但景教徒和景教艺术在其后一直至元代仍然存在,这些景教遗物有一个共同的特点,就是以十字为标志,典型的构图是一朵佛教的象征物——莲花,上托十字。但这些十字大都直接放置于佛座上(图八),从构图方式上看,十字俨然成为佛的替代物,实际上也是景教借助于佛教表现手法的一种证明。

图八

与旅顺博物馆收藏的这件地藏麻画相类似的是一件由德国人勒科克发现于高昌古城的一件摩尼教绘画绢画(图九),据其记载,此画具体出土地为 K 遗址一座摩尼教建筑中的"藏书室长廊",与其同时发现的还有"大量摩尼教写本残卷、绢画残片以及碎布片",勒科克对这幅画进行了较为详细的描述:"这是一幅大型绢画的右侧周边,旁边还有一片原为紫色的丝绸残片。这片丝绸上有白色图案,看来是用蜡染法染成的。

此绢画的底色为美丽的绀青蓝色,画着两个坐着的菩萨,身旁还有童子的形象。画面已残破不全,两个菩萨一个在上,一个在下,他们下边是供养人。

靠上的那个菩萨坐在一朵莲花上,莲花瓣为粉红色,又以暗红色加以晕染。为表示出花托部分,画面上用金粉勾出了边线。菩萨衣服为白色,用鲜红色勾边。项光用金粉绘出;第二个菩萨坐在桔黄色莲花宝座上,衣服也是白色勾鲜红边,在项光与大腿之间还可看到深红色罩衫的一部分。

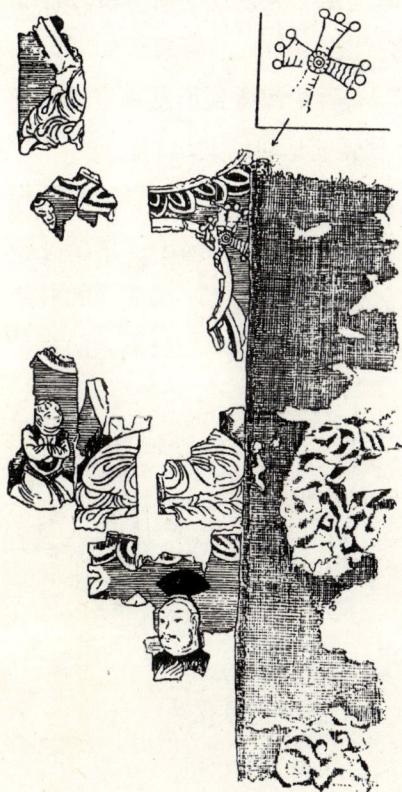

图九

这幅画的最重要部分,是头光右侧上方的十字,装了金并以鲜红线条勾边,用黑线条装饰。这个十字的竖轴上端、横轴的左右两端,各绘有三颗白色的珠子,红色勾边。"②

由于该画中也有十字标志,很容易让人把它与景教联系起来,勒科克也注意到了这个问题,他在介绍上文提到的那幅高昌发现的骑马景教壁画时说:"骑士右肩上扛着一个旗杆,旗杆尖端为十字架。我们认为这是一幅基督教绘画。虽然后来在一幅破坏严重的摩尼教壁画上,也出现了同样的十字架,使这种看

---

① [德]克林凯特著《丝绸古道上的文化》,新疆美术摄影出版社,1994 年 9 月,第 83 页。
② [德]勒科克著、赵宝民译《高昌——吐鲁番古代艺术珍品》,新疆人民出版社,1998 年,第 23 页。

法有所动摇,但由于此画面上没有出现摩尼教那种白色的法衣,从而使这种看法具有存在的可能性。"① 勒科克在文中提到的是"壁画",但就我们对其发现品的了解,应该是指这件绢画。绢画上带有的景教十字符号让勒科克心生困惑。实际上这是一幅摩尼教绘画作品,绀蓝色的背景、白色袍服都是典型的摩尼教艺术特征。

就勒科克发现的这件摩尼教绢画来讲,其性质与旅博收藏的佛教的地藏菩萨麻画相同,都是其中加进了一个有明显景教标志的景教神。而该画的重要意义在于表明了景教在其东传过程中曾经一度依附于同样为"三夷教"之一的摩尼教,有的学者认为它体现了摩尼教艺术的"景教化和佛教化",②摩尼教在传入过程中"佛教化"应该是不难理解的事实,但其"景教化"似乎与事实相背,因为景教在唐代时期的势力远不如摩尼教。据史料记载,公元763年之后不久,回纥牟尼可汗皈依摩尼教,并确立摩尼教为国教,以及其后回纥高昌王国时期摩尼教的全盛发展。

最后还有一点是值得强调的。旅博收藏的带有景教神邸的地藏麻画与德国人发现的带有景教神邸的摩尼教绢画,充分说明了回纥高昌王国时期的回纥文化表现出一种多元文化混合的特质,正如羽田亨曾经指出的那样:"新转入定居生活的所谓回纥文化的处女地上播下的所有种子都得到了发育生长。在这些不同文化之间,随着时间的推移,自然产生了混合之势。这种融合混成就是回纥文化的特征。"③合成文化并不等于说各种宗教及其文化合而为一,没有了自身的特点,而是说在这种相互交叉影响的过程中,各种文化发生融合现象,形成富有回纥文化特征的多元文化。产生这种融合主要归因于:"伊斯兰教征服之前,中亚地区长期不存在中央集权,而是分布着众多的城邦国家。在这一带没有一统天下的占绝对统治地位的宗教,而是汇合混杂地流行着各种各样的信仰,既有地方固有的崇拜,也有四方流入的多种宗教。"④

但是我们也应该看到,由于各种宗教文化传入时间先后、宗教势力强弱不同,以及传教方式差异等因素的影响,在多元文化中其角色也会不同,表现出主与次、强与弱、主流与依从等区别。

---

① [德]勒科克著、赵宝民译《高昌——吐鲁番古代艺术珍品》,新疆人民出版社,1998年,第57页。
② 李进新:《新疆宗教演变史》,新疆人民出版社,2003年,第240页。
③ [日]羽田亨著、耿世民译《西域文化史》,第65页。
④ [德]克林凯特著、赵崇民译《丝绸古道上的文化》,第120页。

摩尼教与冥府系图像

赵诚金

韩国东国大学校美术史学科

一、序　　言

　　大约在 3 世纪萨珊王朝波斯统治下的美索不达米亚地区,有一位名叫"摩尼"(216～274/276/277)的人,摩尼是摩尼教的创始人物。摩尼教习合伊朗的拜火教、西亚的基督教、希腊的灵知哲学、印度的佛教等,构成以善与恶、光明与黑暗的永恒对立为基础的彻底的二元论教理。摩尼教在新的传教地区收纳当地宗教的优点,通过这样的宗教习合谋求教势的扩张,并积极推进翻译成当地语言的进程,从而使之迅速蔓延。

　　回鹘的第 3 代牟羽可汗(759～780)开宗后,在围绕争霸东部天山地区的问题与吐鲁番展开北庭争夺战(789～792)时非常活跃的怀信可汗时期,正式成为国教。

　　公元 840 年,受到十库系民族吉尔吉斯的袭击,回鹘国的部分人到河西回廊的甘州驱逐西藏势力,成立回鹘王国(甘州回鹘)。还有一部分人在东部天山落脚,于公元 850 年为止成立以焉耆为首都的天山回鹘王国(西回鹘王国)。于公元 9 世纪末～10 世纪初,设北庭别失巴里为夏季首都,设其南侧的高昌(现在的吐鲁番)为冬季首都,领土扩张到西域北道的龟兹流域。

　　吐鲁番回鹘王国从迁移初期至约公元 10 世纪前半叶以摩尼教为国教,但进入公元 10 世纪中叶以后开始信奉佛教,在柏孜克里克石窟的鼎盛时期开凿和重修很多石窟。在此过程中,摩尼教与佛教美术相互影响的关系留存到吐鲁番美术中。

　　本论文将通过现存吐鲁番冥府系图像,察看唐末以后在敦煌与中原地区流行的佛教冥府系图像,吐鲁番回鹘王国与摩尼教光明二元论相遇,从而更加形象地表现善恶概念。

二、轮回思想与地狱图

　　古代印度有轮回转生思想,认为所有众生死后会根据生前积业获得新生——即六道,这六道包括天上道-人间道-阿修罗道-畜生道-恶鬼道-地狱道。用画或雕刻等表现这种轮回转生的,就是生死轮回图。

　　佛教的生死轮回图(Bhavacakra)是表现众生在六道或五道中生死的形象,也叫生死轮图、五趣生死轮图或六道轮回图。据《根本说一切有部毗那耶杂事》记载,释迦牟尼在世时,这已成为古代印度寺院壁画的主题,可见这是最古老的佛教绘画形态。事实上,阿旃陀 17 窟入口左侧壁上还留有 Gupta 时期的五趣生死轮图证明这些。初期的生死轮回图普遍把众生五道(或六道)转生形象绘于轮子里,而公元5世纪以后西域和敦煌等地的卢舍那佛(图一)则在人体里描绘六道世界。拜火教(祆教,Mazdaism)对摩尼教的善与恶、光明与黑暗的二元论教理的影响要比基督教多一些,拜火教的经典《Avesta》,明显呈现善与恶的对立。据拜火教的终末论,死者的灵魂会过名叫činwad puhl 的"审判之桥"。生前积德的人能够顺利通过桥,但恶性昭著的人过桥时桥会变成刀刃,过桥者掉进地域。象征生前善行的美丽姑娘引领善人的灵魂进入既是光明之神又是善神的阿胡拉·玛兹达(Ahura Mazdāh)的世界。2003年发掘的北周时期史君墓东壁浮雕就很真实地再现此场面。

史君墓浮雕右下方画有为了守护死者灵魂,在表明阴阳境界的 činwad puhl 入口处祭火坛前生火的拜火教师徒,上面画有守护此桥的狗,桥上有为了接受审判领着很多动物过 činwad puhl 的人。左侧画面生动描绘夫妻在演奏乐器的6个飞天的引领下,飞向天国的场面。中间画面的中上部,描绘的是在飞天的引领下带着坟主到天国的两匹带翅膀的天马。右侧画面的上方描绘的是圆圈里的阿胡拉·玛兹达与在下面被天使所包围的坟主夫妇(图二)。

图一　卢舍那佛,克孜尔壁画

图二　北周大象2年(580)

从上述画中可以感受到彻底分成天堂与地狱的拜火教来世观,可见自从摩尼教吸收佛教的生死轮回思想后,二元论思想表现得更加强烈。

摩尼僧道明翻译的摩尼教《下部赞》中有关地狱的故事。

摩尼教《下部赞》:一切地狱之门户,一切轮回之道路,徒摇常住涅磐王,竟被焚烧囚永狱,今还与我作留难,枷锁禁缚镇相萦。

三、吐鲁番地狱图

高昌城 α 寺出土的摩尼教经典断片(图三)是摩尼教最后审判之画,死者在接受关于生前积业的审判。身穿绿色长袖,上面披着半袖长衫的人物,右肩上扛着白色细棍,向画面右侧的人物指手画脚地说着什么。本来脸上有浓浓的胡须痕迹,但如今已被剥落。中间人物脖颈上挂着水牛头,两手放到身后,面向左侧人物站着,穿的是白色裤衩,光着脚。右侧人物身穿和中间人物一样的裤衩,但脖颈上没有挂任何东西,两手耷拉着。两个人物头上均缠绕白带,头发是卷发,身体的轮廓用朱红线描绘。两个人物之间放有看似绿色谷物捆的东西,下面画一双朝天的脚。画面左端有另外一个人物的左肩与

图三　纸本着色,8.2×11 cm,8～9 世纪,MIK Ⅲ 4959

一点发丝,还反复使用深浅色,立体地描绘衣服上的皱褶。这幅画暗示,正在接受审判的死者来生会投胎水牛,可见这幅画无疑是受到佛教生死轮回图的影响。

柏孜克里克 18 窟北壁上的六道轮回图(图四,100 cm×175 cm,公元 9 世纪中叶～12 世纪初)画于回鹘高昌国前朝。上方集中画有天上道-人间道-阿修罗道-畜生道-恶鬼道,下方分成 6 个区,画有地狱道的多个情形。地狱道占有整个壁画的一半面积,所占比重非常大。按照顺时针方向看,第一个场面是,牛头狱卒正要把死者放入冒火焰的锅里。第二场面是,一个死者被倒着放入大锅里。第三场面是一个死者躺在床上,狱卒们准备把另一个死者也放到床上,这个死者合掌求饶。第四场面是,狱卒们从冒火焰的容器中舀出水强行灌入死者的嘴里。第五场面是极热地狱。第六场面是狱卒抓住死者的头用臼春人。此壁画的左右侧,画有《根本说一切有部毗那耶杂事》中象征怒火冲天的蛇。第五场面画有象征贪欲的鸽子,没有象征愚蠢的猪,但呈现初期生死轮的样像。六个场面用红、白、黑背景色,左右对称,画得非常有计划。人间道的人物均穿戴回鹘人的服饰,但地狱图的死者与恶鬼狱卒均穿着印度裤衩。

如上所述,吐鲁番地区共存摩尼教的地狱图与佛教的地狱图,故事梗概有些类似。

图四　柏孜克里克18窟　六道轮回图

在佛教冥界审判死者罪业的十位王中,有在死后百天审判罪业的平等王,而平等王在摩尼教中也以审判官的身份出现。

　　摩尼教《下部赞》:忆念战栗命终时,平等王前莫屈理。

　　根基在吐火罗(Tokhara)的摩尼教道全面进军中亚地区时,摩尼教之所以使自身教理佛教化,是为了更好地宣教,他们把佛教尊名应用到摩尼教教理中。

　　交河古城出土的十王断片(图五)与回鹘时期新开凿的木头沟3区出土的壁画(图六),也是说明地狱图当时在此地区盛行的很好的例证。尤其是十王断片中有头戴写有"王"字的远游冠,前方摊开名簿卷的十王,而这与Stein收集的敦煌十王经图(图七)形成很好的对比。

图五　十王断片,纸本彩色,18×26.8 cm,
　　　公元8~9世纪,MIK Ⅲ 6327

图六　木头沟3区,格伦威德尔临摹本

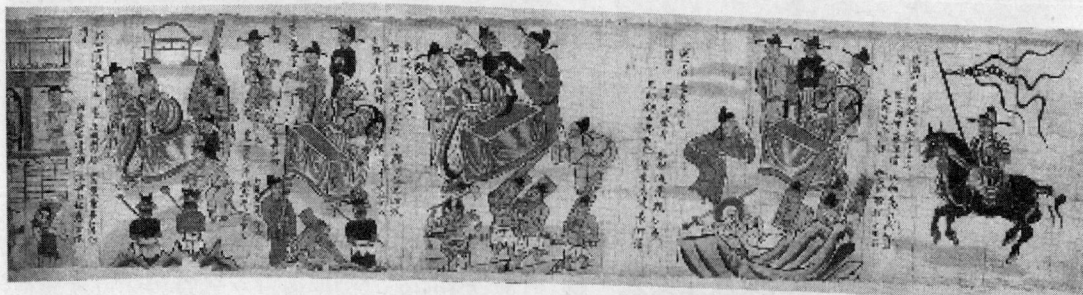

图七　敦煌《十王经》,10世纪,29×491 cm,S3961

龟兹地区库木吐拉79窟(图八,9世纪及以后)于高昌回鹘占领期形成,有79个窟的地狱图画面由两个部分所组成。第一部分描绘的是以魔王为中心的人像,以及被绑住双手等待审判的恶鬼;第二部分描绘地域的各种刑法。能清楚地看到单膝跪在魔王前面的侍者与把名簿放在膝盖上的判官。前壁画有回鹘供养像(图九)与回鹘文,可推测地狱也是由回鹘供养者所画。

图八　库木吐拉79窟　地狱图

吐鲁番的地狱图可以得到这般发展并盛行的原因如下。

第一,吐鲁番盆地是附属于天山回鹘王国的王室寺院,信奉摩尼教与佛教,而且是祈愿从事队商贸易的队商安危与死后永生的宗教圣地,这营造了多种宗教共存的环境。

第二,摩尼教习合伊朗的拜火教、西亚的基督教、希腊的灵知哲学、印度的佛教等,构成以善与恶、光明与黑暗的永恒对立为基础的彻底的二元论教理,因此其理念与地狱图不谋而合。

第三,摩尼教与拜火教不同,在新的传教地区收纳当地宗教的优点,通过这样的宗教习合谋求教势的扩张,并积极推进翻译成当地语言的进程,从而得以迅速蔓延。

图九　库木吐拉79窟　回鹘供养人

四、结　语

摩尼教曾为回鹘高昌王国的国教,摩尼教以善与恶、黑暗与光明为基本教理,从很久以前就开始收纳已在吐鲁番地区立足的佛教思想,并吸收符合摩尼教思想的地狱图,进一步强化和发展。从吐鲁番发展的地狱图,后来传到中国大陆的敦煌与其他地方,并对邻近的韩国与日本也产生很大影响,其中有摩尼教,而吐鲁番回鹘王国的信徒们成为很好的手足。

参 考 文 献

1）闵丙勋："天山回鹘王国与柏孜克里克石窟"，《流域》，松出版社，2007 年春·夏号，pp. 251～252。

　Ninian Smart 著/윤원철译，《世界的宗教》，艺敬，2004，pp. 303～306。

　Michel Tardieu, *LE MANICHEISME*, Universitaires de France, 1981.

2）丁载勋：《回鹘摩尼教的收容与其性格》，《历史学报》第 168 辑，2000。

　『위구르 유목제국사 744～840』，문학과 지성，2005.

3）中国的多个地区都陆续挖掘出粟特人墓，1982 年在甘肃省天水发现粟特人石棺之后，于 1999 年在山西省太原挖掘出隋开皇 12 年（592）死亡的虞弘之墓。2000 年以后由西安市文物保护考古所同时期挖掘出 3 基粟特人墓与位于西安市城墙外测东北数公里的墓志，通过这个墓志推测到这是北周（556～581）时代粟特人"安伽"、"史君"、"康业"的墓。这些粟特人墓均为房子形态，中间放有安置尸体的尸床。在中国定居的粟特人，按照中亚粟特地区的出生地赋予安（布卡拉）、史（喀什）、康（撒马尔罕）等姓氏。

4）摩尼教《下部赞》：一切地狱之门户，一切轮回之道路，徒摇常住涅磐王，竟被焚烧囚永狱，今还与我作留难，枷锁禁缚镇相萦。

5）摩尼教《下部赞》：忆念战栗命终时，平等王前莫屈理。

6）《摩尼光佛教法仪略》。

7）Hans-Joachim Klimkeit, *MANICHAEAN ART AND CALLIGRAPHY*, Leiden E. J. Brill 1982.

8）Ninian Smart 著/윤원철译《世界的宗教》，艺敬，2004，pp. 303～306。

9）Michel Tardieu, *LE MANICHEISME*, Universitaires de France, 1981.

　Susan Whitfield, *The Silk Road Trade*, *Travel*, *War and Faith*, The British Library, 2004.

　— *Aurel Stein On The Silk Road*, The British Museum Press, 2004.

10）林悟殊：《摩尼教及其东渐》，中华书局，1985。

11）森安孝夫：《ウイグル＝マニ教史の研究》，大阪大学，1991。

　《シルクロードと世界史》，大阪大学，2002·2003 学年度报告书。

12）Central Asian Art from the Museum of Indian Art Berlin, SMPK, 东京国立博物馆，1991。

Between West and East — The Central Eurasian Nomads in the Forest-Steppe Belt of Eastern Europe (Ⅵ-Ⅶ A. D.) Problem of the Human and Animal representations

Bartłomiej Sz. Szmoniewski

Institute of Archaeology and Ethnology

Polish Academy of Sciences, Cracow, Poland

Introduction

The representations of human and animals (predators) in the form of metal mounts and figurines from initial phases of early middle Ages in the area of Eastern European Forest-Steppe Belt are a specific cultural phenomenon. They can be considered from various research perspectives which interlink and make a whole.

The symbolic meaning of the representations is inseparably bound to the socio-economic background of the area where the objects have been found. While analysing them one has to consider the complex cultural and historical processes, whose influence is undeniable in creating some images, mostly the religious ones. [1]

The following article mentions only some of the research problems posed by a complex analysis of metals human and animals figure (applications, belt elements, dies). The main subject will be the reconstruction of their symbolic significance in the reconstructed meaning systems, as well their cultural belonging — ethnic attribution.

Anthropomorphic representations

Based on stylistically analysis we can distinguished four variety of human representations as fallow: a) Martynivka, b) Pregradnaja-Trebujeni and c) Moshenka.

The first *Martynivka variety* includes 4 representations of humans mounts found in the hoard from Martynivka (near Cherkasy, Ukraine), together with five mounts in the shape of animals also classifieds as Martynivka variety of the animal representation and one from an unknown location in the region of Cherkasy,

---

[1] E. Bugaj, *Motywy figuralne na ceramice germańskiego kręgu kulturowego* (Poznań 1999), p. 217.

which is, however, a much cruder and somewhat schematic representation. [1]

The Martynivka variety of human shaped mounts stand out among other items in that hoard collection by means of their realistic representation of the body, in sharp contrast to the highly stylized and disproportionate representation of the head. The legs are slightly bent and spread outwards, with some kind of shoes on every foot. The hands are equally bent, with hands resting on the hips. Thickened engravings at the wrists may designate bracelets. The much distorted cylindrical head has only outline mouth and nose, with delicately marked eyebrows and eye sockets. There are two types of headband representation, either a simple band, or one with radial decoration. Along the chest and down to the waist, there is a separate rectangle decorated with a series of diagonal, overlapping cuts. [2] Judging by the published illustration, the Martynivka human-shaped mounts seem to have been partially gilded.

The body posture on the Cherkasy figurine is similar: bent arms with hands resting on the hips, but because of the schematic representation it is difficult to determine whether the position of the legs is the same. Moreover, the head is round with holes for eye sockets and exaggerated eyebrows. However, much like in one of the Martynivka figurines, the headband is represented as radial engravings around the face. There is also a tongue-like protrusion with vertical grooves above the overhead.

The second *Pregradnaia-Trebujeni* variety of human — shaped mounts — it is the group of figurines, we could add similar mounts from two sites in the Caucasus region (Peregradnaia stanica, Karachayevo-Cherkesiia region, Russia) and the Republic of Moldova (Trebujeni, Orhei district), respectively. [3] The Peregradnaia mount was found together with an animal-shaped figurine of the Felnac-Komunta variety. [4] The representation of the human in the Peregradnaia stanitsa mount is equally schematic, with body posture and head composition in clear parallel to the Martynivka mounts: bent legs spreading outwards, bent arms with hands resting on the waist, oval head with large eyesockets and outlined nose and mouth. The hair is rendered by a number of vertical grooves above the forehead. Unlike the Martynivka mounts, it is possible to identify the dress of the Pregradnaia stanitsa figurine as a short caftan reaching down to the knees, with a wide collar, and girdled at the waist.

The third is *Moschenka* variety. There is even less resemblance between the Martynivka mounts and the Trebujeni figurine, except the clearly similar body posture, with bent arms and legs, and the equally comparable, disproportionate representation of the head. Somewhat related are the figurines from Moshchenka

① M. Lebada, *Piznij rims'kij rannij vizantijskij časi* in: Platar. Koleksia predmetiv starovini rodin Platonovih ta Tarut (Kiїv 2004), p. 215, no. 24.

② For detailed pictures, see L. V. Pekarskaja, D. Kidd, *Der Silberschatz von Martynovka (Ukraine) aus dem 6. und 7. Jahrhundert*, Monographien zur Frühgeschichte und Mittelalterarchäologie, Falko Daim (ed.) (Innsbruck 1994), p. 118, 119 with Figs. 25 and 26.

③ T. M. Minaeva, *Nakhodki bliz st. Pregradnoj na r. Urupe*, in *KSIIMK*, 68, 1957, p. 133, Fig. 52/1.; G. D. Smirnov and J. A. Rafalovich *Ranneslavianskie nakhodki VI–VII vv. Iz Starogo Orkheia*, Izvestiia Akademii Nauk Moldavskoi SSR 12, 1965, Fig. 1.

④ B. Sz. Szmoniewski, *Cultural Contacts in Central and Eastern Europe: What do Metal Beasts Images Speak about?* In Ethnic Contacts and Cultural Exchanges North and West of the Black Sea from the Greek Colonization to the Ottoman Conquest, ed. V. Cocojaru, Iasi, 2005, p. 429. I leave aside a number figurines only vaguely resembling the Martynivka mounts, such as those from the Kubrat hoard or from the collection of the Dobrich Museum (R. Rashev, Prabalgarite prez V–VII vek, Velike Tarnovo, 2000, 77 Fig. 83.8 – 15).

(Chernihiv region, Ukraine), as well from unknown locations in the Carpathian Basin and in the Lower Dnieper region of the Cataracts, respectively. ① The bent legs spreading outwards, the bent arms with hands on the hips are clearly marked on the two figurines from Ukraine. Morevoer, the human on the Moshchenka figurine had a round head with hair represented as radially distributed grooves. Similarly, the figurine from the Carpathian Basin has grooves spreading radially from the forehead, as well as clearly marked eyes, nose, moustache, and mouth. It is possible that all three mounts were produced by means of the same die.

Zoomorphic representations

Basing on the analysis of available material including ready-made objects such as metal applications, belt elements and dies to produce applications, we can perceive three stylistic varieties: a) Martynivka (Martynovka), b) Velestínon, c) Felnac and d) Malaja Pereshchepina② I will deal mainly with the Martynivka variety because of its stylistic richness and its finding site located in the zone of early Slavonic settlement.

The Martynivka variety. The Martynivka variety includes mainly animal applications from treasure finds in Martynivka, near Cherkassy, ③ Ukraine, Cherkassy area (oblast')④ Ukraine, Trubchëvsk, near Bryansk, Russia, ⑤ Penkovka culture settlement — Mytkovska isle near Skibintsy village, near Vinnytsya, Ukraine, ⑥ and the die from the Velestínon treasure, nomos Magnísia, Thessaly, Greece. ⑦ The list includes also a zoomorphic application from Nydam, Sønderjyllands Amt, Jutland in Denmark, ⑧ however, this find may be the model one because of its earlier origin — which is mentioned below.

The most frequently mentioned stylistic variety is represented by the Martynivka treasure, after which it

---

① I. O. Gavritukhin, *Srednedneprovskie ingumtsi vtoroi poloviny V –Ⅵ v.* In Kul'turnye transformatsii I vzaimovliianiia v dneprovskom regione na uskhode rimskogo vremeni I v rannem srednevekov'e, eds. V. M. Goriunova, O. A. Shcheglova, St. Petersburg, 2004, 210, 218 Fig. 75. 2; O. M. Prikhodniuk, Pienkovskajia kultura, Voronezh, 1998, 143 Fig. 75. 8; A. Kiss, *Archäologische Angaben zur Geschichte der Stättel des Frühmittelalters*, Alba Regia 21, 1984, 198 Fig. 20.

② In this text I do not discuss the finds of dies with animal and fantasy images are known from the treasure from Biskupija near Knin, Croatia, among others a horse/pegasus from an unknown place in the western part of the Balkan Peninsula (see Z. Vinski, *Kasnoantički starosjedioci u salonitanskoj regiji prema arheološkoj ostavštini predslavenskog supstrata*, in Vjesnik za Arheologiju i Historiju Dalmatinsku 69 (1967), pp. 16 – 21, tab. XI, XII, XIII/1 – 3). Two embossed images of winged horses come from Zaraysk, oblast Moscow, Russia (see Cs. Bálint, *Die Archäologie der Steppe. Steppenvölker zwischen Volga und Donau vom 6. bis zum 10. Jahrhundert* [Vienna-Köln 1989], p. 41, 42, Fig. 17/2).

③ L. V. Pekarskaja, D. Kidd, *Der Silberschatz von Martynovka (Ukraine) aus dem 6. und 7. Jahrhundert*, Monographien zur Frühgeschichte und Mittelalterarchäologie, Falko Daim (ed.) (Innsbruck 1994).

④ M. Levada, *Piznij rims'kij rannij vizantijskij časi* in: Platar. Koleksia predmetiv starovini rodin Platonovih ta Tarut (Kiïv 2004), p. 215, n. 43, 44.

⑤ O. M. Prikhodnjuk, V. A. Padin, N. G. Tikhonov, *Trubachevskij klad antichnogo vremeni*, in: I. Erdely, O. M. Prikhodnjuk, Materialy I tys. n. e. po arkheologii i sitorii Ukrainy i Vengrii (Kiev 1996), pp. 79 – 102.

⑥ P. I. Khavljuk, *Ranneslavjanskie poselenija Semenki i Samchintsy v srednem techenii Juzhnogo Buga*, in MIA 108 (1963), p. 321, Fig. 2.

⑦ J. Werner, *Slawische Bronzefiguren aus Nordgriechenland*, Abhandlungen der Deutschen Akademie der Wissenschaften zu Berlin, Klasse für Gesellschaftswissenschaften, Jahrgang 1952, Nr. 2 (Berlin 1953), pp. 3 – 8, pl. 1 – 6.

⑧ F. Rieck, *Nydam-rige fund i farligt miljø*, Marinarkoeologisk Nyhedsbrev fra Roskilde (Roskilde 1996), pp. 5 – 6.

was named. The find consisted of 5 zoomorphic and 4 anthropomorphic[1] representations which didn't belong to one homogenous stylistic group. As W. Szymański[2] justly remarked, they could be divided into two types considering their physical properties. The first group included slim-shaped images, seemingly caught in movement with open mouths and protruding tongues and fangs. The limbs ended in a roughly marked claw. The other group, according to the same scientist, contained specimens of massive proportions, less dynamic with slightly bent limbs ending in a kind of hoof. The mouth was gaping with peg-like teeth.

The closest stylistic resemblance to the above mentioned applications, but of a dynamic variety, is visible in the representations from the treasure found in the Cherkassy area. At first sight they seem almost identical, but a closer analysis reveals differences. Firstly, their silhouettes are plumper, and the position of legs is less dynamic. A different shape and ornamentation are characteristic for the shield which is interpreted as a mane. The greatest similarity is shown in the limbs which end with talons. Fanciful flowing tails, ending in a small shield are an interesting decorative element. The mouth is open with peg-like teeth resembling fangs.

One of the 21 bronze dies found at Velestínon nomos Magnísia, in Thessaly, Greece shows a general stylistic similarity to the above mentioned variety. The artefact possesses — like the applications described above — a shield of limbs joined together and ending with roughly marked claws. Arching back makes one think about an animal crouched before leaping. The mouth is differently shaped, on the outside limited by a vertical strip, while on the inside it is widening with a protruding tongue. The tail is short and raised.

The next animal representation comes from a Penkovka culture settlement on Mytkovska isle near Skibintsy village in Ukraine. Apart from the general similarity shown in the shape of the body and the limbs, the other elements are different. There is a remarkable presentation of the head en face with precisely marked rears, eye sockets and a grooved mane.

This plane with the mouth en face is a clear reference to the anthropomorphic representations of the Martynivka and Cherkassy treasures, in which the faces are presented in the same way.

Under the mouth, in the centre of the body there is a surface which could be a kind of shield but is devoid of any ornamentation.

Equally remarkable are three outlined applications from the Trubchëvsk treasure. The first possesses a characteristic ornamented shield, at the body decorated with three and at the mouth with two grooves. The slim body has one preserved slightly bent hind leg with grooves resembling claws. The mouth pattern resembles that of the Velestínon die, open-work, with fangs, nearby an eye socket in the form of a hole. The

[1] According to B. A. Rybakov there should be 12 applications including 4 anthropomorphic and 8 zoomorphic, see B. A. Rybakov, *Drevnie rusy* (*K voprosu ob obrazovanii jadra drevnorusskoj narodnosti v svete trudov I. V. Stalina*) in *SA* 1953 (XVII), p. 88.

[2] W. Szymański, rewiev, L. V. Pekarskaja, D. Kidd, *Der Silberschatz von Martynovka* (*Ukraine*) *aus dem 6. und 7. Jahrhundert*, Monographien zur Frühgeschichte und Mittelalterarchäologie, Falko Daim (ed.) (Innsbruck 1994), in *Archeologia Polski* 41 (1996) 1 - 2, pp. 198 - 199; W. Szymański, *Wokół skarbu z Martynowki*, in H. Kóčka-Krenz, W. Łosiński (eds), *Kraje słowiańskie w wiekach średnich. Profanum i sacrum* (Poznań 1998), p. 359.

next application also has a slim body and smooth surface with a marked hump which may be the remnants of a shield. The mouth is open with a peg-like tooth (two joined teeth). The third artefact is only an outline devoid of any ornamentation, and its form is similar to the static group of animal figurines from Martynivka but of smaller size.

Finally, we have to mention the last but the most beautiful lion application from the swamp site in Nydam in Denmark. [1] The artefact was made by casting, partially gilded. It is an artistic representation of a predator with a short, oval head and open mouth with two sharp teeth and a convex eye. On the neck there is a surface ornamented with fish scale (overlapping, semicircular, engraved dents). On one side the decoration ends with a strip ornamented with alternately engraved incisions, separated in the middle by one groove decorated with a fishbone ornament. In the place where the upper part of the foreleg should begin there is a damaged ornament with three circular dents. The other preserved limb is characteristic for predators, with the claw specific for the majority of representations described here.

The Velestínon variety. The other stylistic group named Velestínon for the purpose of this article consists of zoomorphic representations from the find in Velestínon. [2] The find contained 21 dies made of bronze or copper alloys, 8 of which are animal representations. One of the dies was recognised as belonging to the Martynivka variety. Within the presented variety two subtypes can be seen. The first is represented by three samples of predators, which because of their physical features can be identified as felines. Each of them is presented in different position: two are static, with their heads in profile and en face one dynamic with the head en face. The other subgroup containing 4 specimens can be interpreted as images of canines (wolves). Two of the representations are compositions made of a predator and a human figure, and a predator with a cub in his mouth. The remaining two highly stylised specimens show many stylistic features common to all predator representations.

The Felnac — Kamunta variety. The variety known as Felnac — Kamunta is represented by five artefacts, three of which are dies used for producing applications. Two die were found in the Felnac deposit, jud. Arad, Romania[3] one comes from Kamunta, respublika North Ossetia in Caucasus,[4] and two last applications were found in the northern part of Caucasus in Pregradnaja stanica, respublika Karachay-Cherkessia[5] and Kugul' kray Stavropol'. [6] This variety is stylistically the most homogenous.

The Malaja Perescepina variety. This least variety is represented by two, embossed appliqué, found in

---

[1] I got acquainted with the Nydam application during my visit to Nationalmuseet in Copenhagen while on a scholarship from Kazimierz Salewicz Fundation. Here I would like to thank dr. L. Jørgensen from Nationalmuseet for his invaluable help.

[2] J. Werner, *op. cit.* see also D. Kidd, *The Velestínon (Thessaly) Hoard — A Footnote*, in Falko Daim (ed.), *Awarenforschungen*, Archaeologia Austriaca Monographien, vol. I (Vienna 1992), pp. 509 – 515.

[3] E. Garam, *Funde byzantinischer Herkunft in der Awarenzeit vom Ende des 6. bis zum Ende des 7. Jahrhunders*, Monumenta Avarorum Archaeologica (Budapest 2001), pl. 137.

[4] E. Chantre, *Recherches anthropologiques dans la Caucase, tome III*, (Paris-Lyon 1887), p. 94, pl. XIX/2, J. Werner, *op. cit.* (see fn. 8), pl. 1/1 – 5, 2/1 – 8, 3/1 – 8, idem, *Der Grabfund von Malaja Pereščepina und Kuvrat, Kagan der Bulgaren*, Bayerische Akademie der Wissenschaften Philosophish-Historische Klasse Abhandlungen, H. 91 (München 1984), fn. 114.

[5] T. M. Minaeva, *Nakhodki bliz st. Pregradnoj na r. Urupe*, in *KSIIMK*, 68 1957, p. 133, Fig. 52/2.

[6] A. K. Ambroz, *Khronologija drevnostej severnogo Kavkaza V – Ⅶ vv.* (Moscow 1989), p. 80, Fig. 24/14.

the burial in Malaja Perescepina. ① Those two appliqués have stylistic difference from the figurines presented above.

The three first mentioned specimens show a striking stylistic resemblance. Two dies from Felnac depict predators probably from the canine family (wolves) in a dynamic stance, slim with straight forepaws and the hind legs slightly bent. The mouths are elongated, open, without characteristic fangs. On the neck there is the characteristic surface with the ornament of vertical and diagonal grooves representing the animal's mane.

In the case of the Kamunta, die the general pattern is almost identical, the only difference being the mouth with changed proportions and so resembling more a lion's head.

The application from Pregradnaja Stanica has a similar form, with a surface where the body meets the mouth with a series of vertical and slightly curved cuts. The decoration ends towards the mouth with a series of circular dents. The mouth is wide open with a circular drilled-through eye socket. The last one, application from cemetery Kugul' is broken.

Zoomorphic Phaleras

The phalera is molted or embossed disk made of bronze, silver or gold. Very interesting phaleras which have connection with central Asia are found in the Avars cemeteries. Bronze discs are known from graves from present day Slovakia and Hungary. According to central European researchers those phaleras are examples of the contacts between the Avars societies and Sogdians. Analogical objects are known also from Eurasian steps. ②

Symbolism of presentations

The interpretation of the symbolic meaning of the presented zoomorphic representations is a complex and difficult task. Therefore clarification of the role of symbols in old cultures seems indispensable here.

Symbols and their meanings are specific for concrete cultural traditions. ③ They can be individual, made only to serve a concrete task, but the most important are those which have become known to everybody, which makes them property of the whole culture. Creating symbols is a result of the need of notional organisation and ordering of reality. The last element is extremely significant for creating various symbolic systems in various communities. ④ It is used mainly to present and define human attitude towards the other world, the supernatural or transcendental world. It must be remembered, however, that our interpretation can

---

① J. Werner, *Der Grabfund von Malaja Peresčepina und Kuvrat. Kagan der Bulgaren*, Bayerische Akademie der Wissenschaften Philosophish-Historische Klasse Abhandlungen, H. 91 [München, 1984] because of their stylistic difference from the figurines presented here.

② B. Kavánová, *Bronzová zoomorfnífaléra z Mikulčic a jejízařazenive stratigrafii sídliště na předhradi*, Pravek Nř7, 1997, pp. 373 –388; B. Kavánová, *K puvodu a funkci zoomorfni falery z Mikulčic*, Zbornik na pocest Dariny Bialekovej, ed. G. Fusek, Nitra, 2004, pp. 175 –178.

③ C. Renfrew, P. Bahn, *Archeologia. Teorie, metody, praktyka* (Warszawa 2002), p.369.

④ A. Szyjewski, *Etnologia religii* (Kraków 2001), p.76, 91.

vary from the one of its maker who gave symbolic meaning to the representations basing on his knowledge of the surrounding world. [1]

There have been a few attempts at the reconstruction of their position, but the most interesting suggestion was put forward by W. Szymański. He divided the objects in question from the Martynivka treasure into four group compositions consisting of one anthropomorphic and two zoomorphic images, pointing out the recurring numbers. The composition group was reconstructed as a pyramid pattern, the base of which are two zoomorphic images (a lion, a hippo) with their heads facing each other which represents the light and the dark. [2] The pattern is completed by a human figurine, which is interpreted as the image of the tribe leader, the incarnation of god on earth[3] or more likely, considering the symbolic meaning, sun — god sitting on the throne. [4] A similar pattern can be used to reconstruct the composition of the set of applications from Cherkassy area, though it has to be mentioned that only lions appear there. Therefore, another pyramid pattern is possible but with the lions facing outwards, which changes the symbolic meaning of the representation. As mentioned above, such a pattern represents the eastern and western horizons with the sun, symbolised by an anthropomorphic figure, travelling between them.

W. Szymański in his plastic version of the composition of applications from Martynivka, assumed that they could have been spaced individually on four surfaces making a unified whole. [5] The surfaces could have been on the front and back part of a priest's or a shaman's robe. Therefore a few words must be added concerning the symbolic meaning of the shaman robe, which is the reflection of cosmos shown through a complicated pictorial and numerical system. According to A. Szyjewski, the shaman robe differed from the attire of other members of the community, and was the shaman's attribute and distinguishing feature. [6]

The essential aspect is its division into four parts reflecting four supernatural powers again reflecting the four points of the compass. It is worth noticing that it was divided into right and left side and red and black colours, which were associated with the other and the netherworld as well as with the solar and lunar power. [7] The applications in the above mentioned composition may be elements of the attire of high-ranking individual performing specific functions in the local community, including the ritual ones. [8] The remaining individual finds of applications or belt elements could be parts of bigger sets not preserved till our times. The possibility of using them as objects with magical and apotropaic properties has also to be considered. [9]

It is worth having a closer look at some aspects of the religion of the Bulgarians, here. The sun had immense significance there, as well as the eastern horizon as the adoration of the rising sun; it is supposed

---

[1] Renfrew, Bahn, *op. cit.*, p.370.

[2] *Ibidem*, p.362.

[3] L. V. Pekarskaja, D. Kidd, *op. cit.*, p.28, 29.

[4] W. Szymański, *op. cit.*, 1998, p.362.

[5] *Ibidem*.

[6] A. Szyjewski, *op. cit.*, p.369.

[7] *Ibidem*.

[8] W. Szymański, *op. cit.*, 1998, p.363.

[9] J. Werner, *op. cit.*, 114.

that there existed a cult of the moon, too. So, as I mentioned above, we would deal here with the light and the dark side. The central character here is khagan, the messenger and representative of god, and consequently the great priest. [1] The symbolism of animal representations described briefly above focuses on adoration of the sun and the dark. So, according to the division, we would have the sun represented by a human figurine and two horizons or the sun and night.

In the case of the set of zoomorphic figurines we are discussing, there is no uniform interpretation in literature of the subject. Most attention was paid to the Martynivka treasure. According to B. A. Rybakov, whose concept was indiscriminately accepted by Russian researchers, those artefacts were images of horses. [2] A different opinion was expressed by Joachim Werner, [3] who interpreted them as predators — lions. A few years ago it was suggested that the figurines should be divided into two types of images of lions and hippopotamuses, it was however unfounded. [4] It was W. Szymański [5] who discussed the anthropo- and zoomorphic representations most thoroughly. Basing on a detailed analysis, this researcher justified the division of the animal representations into two groups: a) the felines — a lion, b) the hoofed (ungulate) — a hippopotamus.

Selected dies from the Velestínon treasure are also interpreted as images of lions, including a sea lion, a tiger and other predators. [6] Interpreting one of the representations as a sea lion seems highly unlikely. In my opinion it is a stylised representation of a recumbent predator from a feline family, with an outstretched hind leg. Similar representations, differing only in the position of the head, are known from Lombard burial sites ex. in Castel Trosino. [7] Two more dies can be identified as stylised images of lions, while all the others seem more likely to represent predators from the canine family, which is suggested by their physical features. The same applies to the dies from Felnac and applications from Caucasus, which seem to resemble wolves. But the Kamunta die shows numerous features of predators from the feline family.

Concluding the debate on the species of particular representations, I would like to devote a few lines to discussing their symbolism. Lion is the most frequently represented animal, since because of its strength it is ascribed both good and evil features. [8]

First of all, it symbolizes the sun, as killer-lions were sun-heroes, however because of its dualism it can be regarded both as *lumineux* and *obscur*. The composition consisting of two lions with their heads directed

① E. Tryjarski, *op. cit.*, p. 221, 222.

② B. A. Rybakov, *op. cit.*, p. 76, 87, 88, Fig. 21, "v izobrazhenii konja chuvstvuetsja sochetanie dvukh protivorechivykh maner: s odnoj storony realism perekhodjashchij v naturalism (zuby, vysunutyj jazyk), a s drugoj sil'naja stilizatsija i geometrizatsija".

③ J. Werner, *op. cit.*, p. 5, and idem, *Slawische Bügelfibeln des 7. Jarhunderts*, in: G. Behrens, J. Werner, *Reinecke Festschrift* (Mainz 1950), p. 169.

④ O. M. Prikhodnjuk, A. M. Shovkopljas, S. Ja. Ol'govskaja, T. A. Struina, *Martynovskij klad*, in *MAIET* 2 (1991), p. 82, 88.

⑤ W. Szymański, *op cit.*, 1996, p. 198, 199.

⑥ J. Werner, *op. cit.*, p. 4.

⑦ H. Dannheimer, *Ostmediterrane Prunksättel des frühen Mittelalters*, in *Bayerische Vorgeschichtsblätter* 65 (2000), pl. 28.

⑧ L. Réau, *Iconographie de l'art Chrétien*, vol. I (Paris 1955), p. 92.

outside is the symbol of the two opposite horizons — eastern and western — and so the daily journey of the sun in the sky. [1]

Hippopotamus is a symbol of great energy and brutality; it is associated with evil forces. Only in one case it is perceived as having positive meaning — when it is an image of a female — the symbol of fertility. [2]

The wolf symbolises, on the one hand, the night and night killing, and the sun which brings death with its rays and causes draughts. For Turkish tribes the wolf was an allegory of war. In this context, we should mention the dog, which like the wolf, is a symbol of chthonic gods of darkness, death and the moon. It is also a symbol of fidelity, courage and wariness, the guardian of the netherworld. [3] The dog was a valuable animal — god for Turkish peoples. [4]

While discussing the basic symbolic meanings of zoomorphic representations, one should mention the horse, since a group of slim animals from Martynivka shows certain features of horse anatomy. The horse is a symbol of sunlight and moonlight, day and night. A set of two horses represents the morning and the evening star, which accompany the sun. [5] Like the dog, the horse was an important animal in the pantheon of Turkish gods. [6]

Besides the symbolism of the representations, the number of images and their place in the composition played an important role. This raises the question of the function of these representations. In the literature of the subject there has been an ongoing discussion of the issue, limited mainly to interpreting these applications as elements of clothing (jacket), [7] harness, [8] saddlebow ornaments [9] or decorative elements of a chest or another container serving a special purpose. [10]

Ethnic attribution

The meaning attached to images of humans and animals goes back to antiquity, as illustrated in many media, such as mosaic, pottery painting, or metalwork. [11][12] Early medieval human-shaped clasps or pendants

[1] A. de Vries, Dictionary of Symbols and Imaginery (Amsterdam — London 1974), p. 300, 301; J. Chevalier et Alain Gheerbrant, Dictionnaire de symbols, Mythes, reves, coutumes, gestes, formes, figures, couleurs, nombres (Paris 1982), p. 463.

[2] A. de Vries, op. cit., p. 253; J. Chevalier et Alain Gheerbrant, op. cit., p. 406.

[3] W. Kopaliński, Słownik symboli (Warszawa 1990), pp. 463-465.

[4] E. Tryjarski, Protobułgarzy, in K. Dąbrowski, T. Najgrodzka-Majchrzyk, E. Tryjarski, Hunowie Europejscy, Protobułgarzy, Chazarowie, Pieczyngowie (Wrocław—Warszawa—Kraków—Gdańsk 1975), p. 224.

[5] W. Kopaliński, op cit., p. 157.

[6] E. Tryjarski, op. cit., p. 223.

[7] W. Szymański, op. cit., 1998, p. 362.

[8] L. V. Pekarskaja, D. Kidd, op. cit., p. 28, 31.

[9] Gy. László, Études archéologiques sur l'histoire de la société des Avares, in Archaeologica Hungarica 34 (1955), pp. 276-278, Fig. 81-82; A. Kiss, Archäologische Angaben zur Geschichte der Stättel des Frühmittelalters, in Alba Regia 21 (1984), p. 191, 197, Fig. 16, 17.

[10] W. Szymański, op. cit., 1998, p. 362, 363.

[11] D. Kidd, op. cit., 1992, p. 511.

[12] D. Kidd, op. cit., ; Drandaki ΥΓΙΕΝΩΝ ΧΡΩ ΚΥΡΙ(E) A late Roman brass bucket with a hunting scene, ΜΟΥΣΕΙΟ ΜΠΕΝΑΚΗ 2 2002, pp. 37-53.

are known from several burial sites in northern Italy, the northern Black Sea coast, the Caucasus region, and the Volga-Ural area. [1][2] Animal-shaped mounts have been found in Dalmatia, [3] on the northern Black Sea coast, in Greece, [4] northern Italy, and the northern Caucasus region. [5] Besides zoomorphic figurines, images of lions may be found in the Byzantine[6] and Sassanian art, [7] while peacocks from anthropozoomprphic brooches are frequently represented in the art of early Byzantium, as well as in that of western Asia and of China. [8]

The geography of occurrence of the human — shaped and animal — shaped mounts representations is not limited to one area. It has been noticed that they occur most frequently in the area of the forest-steppe of the present day Ukraine and in northern Caucasus.

The findings from the boundary area between forest and steppe were included in the complex known in the literature of the subject as "the Ant antiquities". In one case a metal fitting was found in the Penkovka culture settlement on Mytkowska isle near Skibintsy village. The treasures, which the anthropo and zoomorphic representations come from, have very complex internal structure. It is worth noticing, that they are accompanied by anthrop-zoomorphic, whose surfaces are decorated with many interesting symbolic images. [9] The issue of treasures in itself is a complex one and should be analysed from various research perspectives. [10]

Defining the ethnic attribution of the representations described here is rather complicated. The area of the forest-steppe zone occupied by the Penkovka culture settlement was, in the earlier phases of the middle Ages, the area where various cultural influences clashed. Therefore, it is an arduous task to define the ethnic component of this culture basing on archaeological data. Some researchers tend to define the Penkovka culture as a polyethnic structure, [11] while others regard it as homogenous. [12] O. M. Prikhodnjuk emphasizes strong

① O. v. Hessen, *Secondo contributo alla archeologia Longobarda in Toscana. Reperti isolati e di provenienzia incerta*, Accademia Toscana di Scienze e Lettere La Colombara, Studi XLI (Firenze 1975), p. 36, pl. 6/1, 3; H. Dannheimer, *op. cit.*, pl. 28, pl. 31/4.

② O. v. Hessen, op. cit., 108 Fig. 6. 2; V. B. Kovalevskaia *Khronologija drevnostej severokavkazkikh Alan*, in V. Ch. Tmenov, *Alany. Istorija i kul'tura — Alantä: istori ämä kul'turä* (Vladikavkaz 1995), 1995, 141 – 145; Gavritukhin op. cit (2004), p. 210.

③ Z. Vinski, *Kasnoantički starosjedioci u salonitanskoj regiji prema arheološkoj ostaŭtini predslavenskog supstrata*, in *Vjesnik za Arheologiju i Historiju Dalmatinsku*, 69 (1967), pp. 16 – 21, pl. XI, XII, XIII/1 – 3.

④ G. R. Davidson, *The minor objects*, Corinth XII (1952), Fig. 68/934.

⑤ M. Kazanski, *Les plaques-boucles mediterraneennes des Ve- Vie siecles*, *Archeologie Medievale 24*, 1994, p. 190, Fig. 17. 2 and 3; Dannheimer, *op. cit.*, 2000, pls. 28 and 31. 4.

⑥ Ch. Diehl, *Manuel d'art byzantin*, vol. I (Paris 1925), Fig. 130, 132, 134.

⑦ D. Collon, *Ancient Near Eastern art* (London 1995), p. 206, Fig. 172.

⑧ M. Buzov, *Prikaz jeena na ranošcanskim mozaicima prema srednjovjekovnoj umjestnosti*, Starohrvatska prosvjeta 3, 21/1991, 59, 66 Figs. 2 and 4; B. Darling, *Silk Road Cross-cultural Design Motifs on Shôsô-in Treasures: The Peacock*, Silk Roadology 18, 2003, pp. 71 – 90.

⑨ B. Sz. Szmoniewski, *Anthropozoomorphic brooches of the Dnepr type in initial phases of the Early Middle Ages. The Migration of a style-idea-object*, in S. Moździoch (eds), *Spotkania Bytomskie V* (Bytom Odrzański 2004), pp. 301 – 312.

⑩ S. Matthews, *Material culture and context as composition: Substances and incorporation in Bronze Age hoards*, paper presented to the session "Hoards from the Neolithic to the Metal Ages in Europe: technical and codified practices" at eleventh Annual Meeting of the European Association of Archaeologists, 5 – 11 September 2005, Cork. I wish to thank Steven Matthews who has sent me his unpublished paper.

⑪ W. Szymański, *Słowiańszczyzna wschodnia. Kultura Europy wczesnośredniowiecznej*, vol. I (Wrocław 1973), pp. 31 – 34; I. O. Gavritukhin, A. M. Oblomskij, *Gaponovskij klad i ego kul'turno-istoricheskij kontekst*, in *Ranneslavjanskij Mir* (Moscow) 3 (1996), pp. 121 – 124, 141 – 144.

⑫ M. B. Ljubichev, *Pen'kivs'ka kul'tura: shche raz pro teritoriju ta etnichnu prinadlezhnost'*, in R. V. Terpilovskij, *Etnokul'turni protsesi v Pivdenno-Skhidniy Evropi v I tisjacholitti n. e.* (Kiev—L'vov 1999), pp. 123 – 131.

bonds between the Penkovka culture people and Turkish tribes. [1]

Various tribes settled also in the areas of northern Caucasus. In mid sixth century Kutrigur-Bulgarians had settlements in the steppes located on the west from Don River, Onogur — Bulgarians had their dwellings on the Kuban, while the steppes stretching between the Don and the Kuban belonged to Utigur — Bulgarians. [2] The present day Ossetia was inhabited by Iranian tribes, the Alans among others. After the ca. 550 and until the end of 580s or 590s, the lands of both groups were incorporated into the rising Turkic qaganate encompassing an enormous stretch of the Eurasian continent, from Korea to the Black Sea. [3] During the civil war of 581 to 593, the qaganate split into an eastern and a western "wing," the latter under the leadership of the Bulgar Dulo clan. [4] Under Kubrat, the emerging "Great Bulgaria" occupied the lands between the Ergeni Upland, Volga and Don rivers to the east; the Sea of Azov and the Dnieper river to the East; and the Kuban river to the south. The northern neighbors of Great Bulgaria must have been the descendents of the Antes. [5] Kubrat himself may have been buried on the northern frontier of his polity, if the Malo Pereshchepyne assemblage is indeed his grave. In any case, the assemblage contained luxuries of undoubtedly Byzantine origin. [6] After Kubrat's death of ca. 650, his polity disintegrated and Great Bulgaria was occupied by the Khazars. [7] The Khazar qaganate ruled for three centuries over the steppe lands of Eastern Europe, away from the developments taking place in Central Asia, within the Eastern Turkic qaganate. [8]

The situation was also rather complex in southern Europe, particularly in the Balkans where large numbers of Slavs, Avars, and Bulgars have moved during the seventh century. [9] The fact that the Balkan region produced analogies for at least some of the artefacts found in hoards of bronze and silver strongly suggests connections with the social and political phenomena at work in the forest-steppe zone. Such phenomena may in turn be associated with the rapid changes taking place in the steppe lands. Shcheglova's first group of hoards may be related to the rise of the Turkic qaganate and turbulence created in the steppe by the advance of the Turkic armies to the west. While the Turkic hegemony may have triggered a greater military and political presence of Byzantium on the northern shore of the Black Sea, it also made possible

[1] O. M. Prikhodnjuk, *Voenno-politicheskiy sojuz antov i tjurskiy mir po dannymi istoricheskikh i arkheologicheskikh istochnikov*, in *MAIET* 7 (2000), pp. 134 – 167.

[2] E. Tryjarski, *op. cit.*, p. 164.

[3] E. Tryjarski op. cit., 1975, p. 172. For the Turkic qaganate, see L. Gumilev, Dzieje dawnych Turków, Warszawa, 1972, 56; B. Gafurow, Dzieje I kultura ludów Azji Centralnej. Prehistoria, starożytność, średniowiecze, Warszawa, 1978, 229; Sinor and Klyashtorny 1996, 327 – 347 and Talgatovich 2006, 11 – 16.

[4] E. Tryjarski, *op. cit.*, 1975, p. 172. For the civil war, see L. Gumilev, op. cit., 1972, pp. 98 – 111; B. Gafurow, op. cit., 1978, pp. 229 – 230.

[5] D. Angelov, Obrazuvane na bagarskata narodnost, Sofia, 1971, 191 – 192; E. Tryjarski, op. cit., 1975, p. 174.

[6] J. Werner, op. cit., 1984; A. Avenarius, Die byzantishe Kultur und die Slawen, Vienna-Munich, 2000, pp. 22 – 23 and Figs. 1 – 3.

[7] E. Tryjarski, op. cit., 1975, 175; T. Nagrodzka-Majchrzyk, Chazarowie, in K. Dąbrowski, T. Najgrodzka-Majchrzyk, E. Tryjarski, *Hunowie Europejscy, Protobułgarzy, Chazarowie, Pieczyngowie* (Wrocław — Warszawa — Kraków — Gdańsk 1975), p. 397.

[8] L. Gumilev, op. cit. 1972, pp. 140 – 142.

[9] K. M. Setton, *The Bulgars in the Balkans and the occupation of Corinth in the seventh century*, Speculum 25, 1950, 502 – 543; N. Fettich, op. cit., 1972; E. Tryjarski, op. cit. 1975, pp. 246 – 247; F. Curta, *The Making of the Slavs: History and Archaeology of the Lower Danube Region ca 500 – 700 A. D.*, Cambridge, 2001.

stronger ties with Central Asia and its rich silver and lead resources.

During his 568 embassy to Sizabul, the qagan of the Turks, the Byzantine envoy Zemarchus saw a dwelling, "in which there were gilded wooden pillars and a couch of beaten gold, which was supported buy four golden peacocks. In front of this dwelling were drawn up over a wide area wagons containing many silver objects, dishes and bowls, and a large number of statues of animals also of silver and in no way inferior to those which we make, so wealthy is the ruler of the Turks. "[1]

Neither is it possible, at the present stage of research, to answer the question asked by W. Szymański: with which ideological system can we associate the symbolic meanings and the function of zoomorphic and anthropomorphic images? I fully agree with the answer he gave, namely that he connected the trends of various origins, with a significant role of Iranian and Byzantine, relict Germanic, and maybe Turkish motifs. [2] However, I would pay greater attention to analysing the motifs connected with the latter tribes.

---

[1] Menander the Guardsman, in Blockley 1985, p. 121.

[2] W. Szymański, *op. cit.* , 1998, p. 363.

从（偈颂体的）《弥勒下生成佛经》漫谈中印文化交流

刘 震

德国慕尼黑大学印度学系

在佛教历史中，Maitreyavyākaraṇa——《弥勒下生成佛经》是一种流传非常深远的经文。[1] 它讲述了今世佛——释迦牟尼佛授记其弟子舍利弗（亦有文本作阿难），未来世将有佛弥勒出世；并讲述其生活环境、诞生、出家、成道和转法轮的故事。

目前存世的 Maitreyavyākaraṇa 就有五部经。[2] 前四部经只存有汉文本，并为散文体；第五部，即其汉文本为义净所译的 T 455《佛说弥勒下生成佛经》，是基于前经编写成偈颂体的一部经，[3]而且删去了弥勒拜谒大迦叶这一情节，依照佛诞的标准描写[4]，扩展了弥勒诞生的情节。和前四部不同，这部经平行地具有一个以上的异文，而且以不同的语言——梵语、藏语、汉语、波斯语作载体。从现存的各个版本来看，这部经除开篇或者结尾为散文体，其余部分由大约一百颂诗歌组成。这在印度文学中也叫做 Śataka——"一百颂"。

这部经最初当然由梵语写就。目前发现的梵本有四个：三个较为完整、字迹易于辨识的写本和一份仅有几句偈颂的残片。在本文中分别标识为 A ~ D。

四个梵本的概览[5]如下：

写本的标识	A	B	C	D
所知的发现地	印度东部	瑙坡（Naupur，巴基斯坦吉尔吉特附近）	尼泊尔	阿富汗（?）
发现年份	1917	1931 ~ 1938	?	?
可考的书写年代	公元十世纪下半叶[6]	公元七至八世纪	公元 1621 年	公元六至七世纪
现存偈颂数[7]	25cd ~ 102	31 ~ 108	1 ~ 100	四个偈颂的残本
字体	库里拉（Kuṭila）[8]	吉尔吉特/巴米扬 II	尼瓦里（Nevārī）	吉尔吉特/巴米扬 I
公布者	列维（Sylvain Lévi）	马仲达（Prabhas Chandra Majumder）	石上善应	哈特曼（Jens-Uwe Hartmann）
编订年份	1932	1959	1981	2004

---

① 之所以称之为"一种经文"而不是"一部经"，是因为现存就有五部经归于 Maitreyavyākaraṇa 名下（参见《法宝义林（别册）》，s. v.），除了本文所要讨论的这部经，其余皆为散文体；另外，经文之间的内容也各不相同。所以说与其如《开元录》等经录的传统说法——"同经异译"，不如说它们同属于一种文体。以文体名作经题为多部经共用的现象，在佛教文献中屡见不鲜，类似的还有《药师经》、《出家经》（汉译中以《本起经》为题）等。

② 即 T 453 ~ 457 及其在其他语言中的异文。另外，据 T 455、428b 所引《开元录》，有"三存三失"之说。

③ 参见 LIU 2005：13。

④ 同上：9。

⑤ 表格数据根据 HARTMANN 2004：1。

⑥ 依据 A 本的题记暂作推定。

⑦ 偈颂的编号根据各个编订者而定。

⑧ LÉVI 1932：355。

经书流传的时间和地域属于(根本)说一切有部大行其道的时间和地域。吉尔吉特地区同时也发现了该部派的律,另外还有大量经论,一部分属于大乘。直面原典,就可以看到,原诗的格律为随颂体(Anuṣtubh),也叫室路迦(Śloka)。即每颂四句,每句八个音节。

从内容上来看,D 本因为过于残缺,无从比较,A、C 二本比较接近,B 本与余本的差异最大。那么现存的三个语言的译本分别译自哪个梵本? 或者更贴切地说,分别和哪个梵本亲缘关系最近?

其三个译本为:

语言	译 者	译文名及收录处	译出年代
汉	义净	佛说弥勒下生成佛经(T 455, 426a ~ 428b)	701
藏	胜友(Jinamitra)、吉祥积护(dPal-brtsegs-rakṣita)	('Phags pa) byams pa lung bstan pa (Q 1001, Mdo, Hu 312a ~ 316a)	九世纪初
波斯	拉失德丁(Rashīd al-Dīn)、春吉祥(Kāmalashrī)	Jāmi' al-tavārīkh(《印度史》)中	1305/06

从以上七个文本的概览可以看出:这部经流传的时间何其之长,地域跨度何其之大。究其原因,不外乎:1. 影响深远的弥勒信仰;2. 篇幅短小的诗歌体形式;3. 为广大佛教徒耳熟能详的文本素材。下面的陈述中将逐一体现这些因素的作用。

本经的波斯译本,为拉失德丁的《印度史》中"佛陀生平和教法"部分的第17章。该史集为这位波斯史学名家应一位在迦什弥尔的皈依了伊斯兰教的蒙古王公的要求,与当地的一位僧人合作的。所谓的"佛陀教法"就是收录的一些当时当地流行的佛经的波斯译文,本经也是在入选之列。不过译文为散文,而且教义已经伊斯兰化,一些信息,诸如人名,反而采自其他弥勒文学。因为译者的演绎成分太多,很难断定其与哪个梵本最为接近。

本经的藏译本译自藏传佛教的前宏期。大部分经录将其归入"经部(Mdo)",意为一般的非大乘经典;只有根本说一切有部的非大乘经典才允许译成藏文,本经也属于此列。但也有经录将其划入"大乘经典([theg pa] chen po'i mdo)"。[①] 藏文根据自己的诗歌格律特色,将梵语的每句八个音节改成了藏语的七个。在梵文 B 本所特有的变异,大部分只能在藏译中找到对应。经偈颂的逐句统计,其与前三个梵本的亲缘关系依次为:A、B 和 C。

最后再看汉译。汉译的首尾皆是散文。中间为数目正好的一百颂。每颂四句,每句五言。这是汉译者所偏好的体例,以此翻译随颂体的梵诗。[②] 对于这恰到好处的一百颂,有可能是义净有意将一个情节——弥勒成佛之后,诸天的赞颂中的几颂略去的缘故。

与藏译比较,汉译常被认为失之忠实。但事实上一个好的汉译首先以汉地读者的理解为己任,其翻译规则见《宋高僧传·译经篇》之论。[③]

比如经文的最后一颂,梵文(A102,B108,C100)为:

---

① LIU 2005:7 起。
② "五言四句"见《高僧传》,T 2059, 415b。
③ T 2061, 722c - 723b。

tasmād ihātmakāmena māhātmyam abhikāmkṣatā /

saddharmo gurukartavyaḥ smaratāṃ buddhaśāsanam //

c：saddharmā gurukarttavya B；gurukartavyaḥ ］gurukattavyaḥ C；

d：-śāsanam ］-śāsanam B.

笔者给出的参考译文为："是以，在此欲善自我、追求大我者，应敬重正法、念佛教法。"

藏文为：

/ de phyir 'dir na bdag nyid che /

/ 'dod cing bdag la legs 'dod pas /

/ sang rgyas bstan pa dran bzhin tu /

/ dam pa'i chos la gus par bya /

可说是字字对应的直译。而汉译为：

若求解脱人　希遇龙花会

常供养三宝　当勤莫放逸

可以想见，义净或许认为词经日常念诵的作用大于思辨作用，没有必要在此解释何谓"大我"；而且最后两句，供养三宝和勤修佛法，比梵文中的更加模式化的诗句似乎也更加容易为中国人记诵。

汉译与梵本的亲缘关系依次为：A、C和B。

汉译较藏译与吉尔吉特地区的写本关系相对疏远，这在同样由义净汉译的《根本说一切有部毗奈耶》的版本比较中也得到了印证。[①] 可见，以吉尔吉特地区为代表的西北印度的佛教文献与藏区的关系比较密切，而对汉传的文献影响不大。义净所取的经文应该并非来自该地区，或者说并非来自该文本传承系统。

义净为取经从海陆登陆印度东南部，转而北行，并在东北部的那烂陀寺盘桓数年。不过对于他是否到过比那烂陀寺更远的地方却找不到文献的直接记载。王邦维认为他不可能向西北——即包括玄奘在内的很多求法高僧进入印度的地方继续前行。通过义净所翻译的母本的来源推测，义净到过西北印的可能性不大。

此外，如前所述，吉尔吉特地区所发现的梵文写本也是迄今为止数量最丰的归入（根本）说一切有部名下的佛教藏书。这些文献兼有经律两藏、大小两乘。但是和义净所翻的经目重合的不到一半。[②] 如果两地藏书各自代表了两地所奉持的经典，那么即便义净所处之地与（根本）说一切有部有很深的渊源，它

① MELZER 2006：109；LIU 2008：11。
② 参见 V. Hinüber 1979：339～353 及王邦维 1995：26～33。

们的教法也是有相当差别的。假使义净去过西北印度,则其所翻译的经文种类或许与吉尔吉特的经目会有很多的重合。

从《西域记》和《南海寄归内法传》可知,当时印度寺院里大小乘并存的现象很普遍。① 这从吉尔吉特和义净译经的经目中亦可得到证实。还有一个很好的明证,就是这部《弥勒下生成佛经》本身。

Schopen(1982:225~235)罗列了本经中引经据典的地方,发现全部来自四部或四阿含之类非大乘的经典,并以此认为,此经为非大乘经。但是我们应该看到,像《大智度论》、《瑜伽师地论》等论著也是引用的非大乘经典。最主要的原因就是它们已经成为各部各派佛教徒共同承认的经典并且耳熟能详。编写《弥勒下生成佛经》的目的不是像其他大乘经典一样,去宣扬一种新的思想,而只是服务于弥勒信仰,方便信徒记忆和诵读;再者,这部经的主题是未来佛的传记,其写作模式只能在现有的佛陀传里寻找,而佛传的起源和主要文献都在非大乘的经典里;最后,不可忽视的是,这部经的藏译在赤松德赞(Khri-srong-lde-btsan)统治时期(也就是胜友和吉祥积护二人翻译我们这一部经时候)的经录——lDan kar ma中,就归入了"theg pa chen po'i mdo sde rgya las bsgyur"(译自汉文的大乘经集)。② 可见经文种类的划分在现实中有很大的随意性,如同佛教徒本身对自己的部派的划分一样。

以上是通过文本分析找出现存梵本和译本的联系,从而为中印文化交流的记载添加一些旁证。而下面提到的将是一个直接的证据,那便是梵本 A 的题跋:

Maitreyavyākaraṇam samāptam || ye dharmā hetuprabhavā hetu teṣān tathāgato hy avadat | teṣām ca yo nirodha evamvādī mahāśramaṇaḥ ||śubham astu || cīnadeśīvinirgataḥ bhikṣu puṇyakīrtir | yad atra puṇyam tad bhavatv ācāryopādhyāyamātāpitṛpūrvaṇgamamkṛtvā sakalasattvarāśer anuttarajñānaphalāptaya iti || śrīmad gopāladevarājyasam vat 17 phālgunadine 9 Ghosalīgrāme likhati | om hārītī mahāyakṣiṇī hara hara mama sarvapāpāni svāhā ||

译文为:

《弥勒下生成佛经》(Maitreyavyākaraṇa)竟。那些由因缘而生的法,如来已解释了它们的因缘,而大沙门教授了它们的熄灭。愿清净!在中国出生的比丘福称(Puṇyakīrti)。在此为功德的,但愿能有助于达到无上智慧之果,为了整个众生的群体,以轨范师、亲教师、母亲【和】父亲为首的!【他】抄写于吉祥神圣的瞿波罗王(Gopāla)十七年颇勒具那(Phālguna)月的第九天,拘舍离(Ghosalī)村内。吽!鬼子母(Hārītī)!大母夜叉!夺走,夺走,我所有的罪过!娑婆诃!

这段题跋里面最令我们感兴趣的无疑是那个来自中国的僧人福称。"福称"只是他在印度使用的梵文名字,如同玄奘在印度被称作"大乘天"或者"解脱天"一样,③其梵文名与汉文的法名并无联系,从而无

---

① 季羡林 2000:67~87;王邦维 1995:88~108。
② 参见 LALOU 1953:325。是否真的存在一部由汉译译出的藏文本,或者当时藏地已经知道了义净的汉译,而将自己的译本误作汉文的再译,这里无法作定论。
③ T 2053,248a。

从推断此为何人。不过题跋所记的年号为瞿波罗王十七年。我们只能尝试是否能够通过这个时间记录找到和中国历史记载的交集。

所谓瞿波罗王即为波罗王朝的一位统治者。波罗王朝为公元八到十二世纪统治东北天竺,今印度比哈尔邦和孟加拉国的一个朝代。因其国王名字皆以波罗(pāla)作为结尾,故称"波罗王朝"。对波罗王朝的纪年和断代的研究,主要靠出土文物及其铭文、写本的题记,辅以印度本土和印度之外的历史文献。因其材料相对丰富,所以这段历史相较于印度其他部分的历史来说,还算是清晰的。①

随着碑铭、造像、写本等材料的不断发现,印度本土学者对波罗王朝的纪年研究也在不断发展和修正。根据笔者所掌握的最近的、由印度碑铭学家 Sircar 在七十年代中期给出的王统年表,这个瞿波罗王为整个王朝中三个瞿波罗王中的第二个,大约在公元 957~977 年在位。② 由此所推的《弥勒下生成佛经》的梵本 A 的抄写年代为公元 973 年。

此外,有一个 Vāgīsvarī 的造像出土自那烂陀,一个造像的底座发现自菩提迦耶(Bodh Gayā),都被断代为波罗二世年间的物品。③ 以上两个地方则是中国赴印朝圣者必到之处。很有可能梵本 A 写成之地也不外乎这两个佛教圣地。最后,在菩提迦耶还发现了五块宋代僧人赴印朝拜留下的汉文碑。④

再看中国方面的历史记载。五代末期至北宋晚期是历史上中印文化大规模交流的最后一次高潮,交流的形式当然还是以取经和译经为主,还有大批的赴印朝圣团体,政府参与甚至组织了这些活动;从印度来华的僧人也得到了政府的分封和安置。

冉云华(Jan 1966:144~159)根据《宋史》、《宋会要》、《佛祖统纪》和《祥符法宝录》等文献梳理出了一条该时期的中印文化交流的线索,罗列了这一百多年间的两个民族交往的一系列事件。因前述汉僧福称的活动时间不会晚于公元一千年,在此仅摘出至此为止的汉僧朝圣活动如下:

人名	赴印时间	归国时间	团队人数	是否为官方组织	在印期间主要活动	携回物品及同返之人
继业⑤	964	976	300	是	求舍利及贝多叶书,游西域及印度北部诸国	同左
道圆	936~943	965	未详	未详	游五天竺往反十八年,十二年在途,六年在印度	于阗使者、佛舍利贝叶梵经
行勤	966	未详	157	是	往西竺⑥求法,历焉耆、龟兹、迦弥罗等国	未详
建盛	未详	971	未详	否(?)	游历西竺	进贝叶梵,同梵僧曼殊室利(中天竺王子)偕来
继从	未详	978	未详	未详	游历西天	梵经佛舍利塔菩提树叶孔雀尾拂

---

① HUNTINGTON 1984:29。

② 同上:37。但当时 SIRCAR 尚未见一造像,其铭文可使瞿波罗二世父亲的在位时间再后推五年,是以其在位时间理应顺延,本文改 SIRCAR 表中给出的断代 952~972 为 957~977。

③ 同上:54~55。

④ 详见下文。

⑤ 此据 T 2089,981c 的《游方记抄·继业西域行程》,为范成大所作。但冉云华(JAN 1966:144,注98)疑为仿行勤及他人游记,继业本人更似属于行勤团队的成员。

⑥ "西竺"为西域及印度(天竺),抑或西北印度(西天竺)? 冉云华认为指前者(JAN 1966:145)。

人名	赴印时间	归国时间	团队人数	是否为官方组织	在印期间主要活动	携回物品及同返之人
光远	未详	982	未详	是(?)	同上	进西天竺王子表、佛顶印、贝多叶、菩提树叶
法遇	未详	983	未详	未详	未详	佛顶舍利、贝叶梵经
法遇	983 之后	未详	未详	是	造龙宝盖金襕袈裟,将再往中天竺金刚座所供养	未详
辞澣	未详	984~987	未详	未详	自西域还	与胡僧密坦罗奉北印度王及金刚坐王那烂陀书来
重达	980~981①	991	未详	否(?)②	自西天还,往反十年	佛舍利贝叶梵经

从前面推算的时间来看,既然福称在印度的时间为 973 年,那么他可能加入了行勤、继从、光远和法遇的首次入印活动。但行勤似乎没有从西天竺更向东行,可以排除福称参与的可能性。所以,如果波罗王朝的纪年可信的话,《弥勒下生成佛经》的梵本 A 就写成于史载继从至法遇的这三次朝圣中。还有,梵文 kīrti 亦有"光(芒)"的意思,Puṇyakīrti 是否为光远的梵文名字,亦未可知。

这些记载除了明确提到中天竺及那烂陀等具体地名,所提及的拜谒佛陀成道处的金刚座(vajrāsana)和取回菩提树叶(即贝多叶)则说明了朝圣者到过菩提迦耶。这不由令人再次想起前面所提的五块那里出土的汉文碑(以下称碑铭 1~5)。第一块的落款中有"重达"之名,所以可以断定,这就是重达那次西行所留的碑铭。③ 另外四块碑则为十一世纪初的天禧、明道年间所立。中文的史料并没有详述西行僧人的具体活动。唯一能讲述中印最后一次大规模文化交流的具体活动内容的只有这五块碑。汉地的僧人到了菩提迦耶,自然地,主要是朝觐释迦牟尼佛证道之地。④ 但是这些朝圣者却多表达了对弥勒的崇敬。

碑铭 1:"大汉国僧志义,先发愿劝三十万人修上生行,施三十万卷上生经,自颂三十万卷:如上功德,回向同生内陀。……并愿亲奉弥勒慈尊。"

碑铭 2:"大雄慈氏,悲物留真,……"

碑铭 3:"回斯福善。愿值龙华。"

由此可见弥勒信仰在当时之流行。碑铭 1 所指的"上生经"应该就是 T 452,《佛说观弥勒菩萨上生兜率天经》。既然此经曾被广为布施,那《弥勒下生成佛经》以梵本的形式以一位汉地僧人的名义被抄写也是在情理之中的。和前面提到的一样,《上生经》也唯有小乘元素,而曾被判定为非大乘经,但是中国的佛教徒还是想办法将它改判为大乘经典。⑤ 这类经产生于小乘的环境里,但之后在印度本土已经界限混淆不清了,到了汉藏两地更是只有服务于大乘的用途。可以想象,如果这类经始终贴着"小乘"标签的话,中国的佛教徒是不会有那么大的热情抄写、传播它们的。

---

① 师觉月(P. C. Bagchi)认为重达西行当在公元 980~981 年间。见周达甫 1957:80。

② 重达一行中的僧人志义在碑铭中自称"大汉国僧";和另外四块碑不同的是,整个碑铭只字未提国名、帝号、年号,可见此行并非是以国家名义进行的。参见同上:79~82。

③ 据碑铭 1,西行之为首者并非重达,而是志义,而修行活动则以归宝为首。同上:79。可能归国觐见皇帝的是重达,因而被记载。

④ 据碑铭 1~5,供养金刚座的方式为写《赞佛身座记》、披挂金襕袈裟与造塔。史载法遇的第二次赴印所携之物亦是金襕袈裟。

⑤ T 1773《弥勒上生经宗要》,299b1 起。

缩 略 语

ed. = editor. 编辑。

Q = 北京藏文大藏经甘珠尔(大谷大学版)。Blockdruck des tibetischen bKa''gyur aus Peking (Ōtani-Edition)。

s. v. = sub verbo, sub voce, 在……词下。

T = Taishō Shinshū Daizōkyō (《大正新修大藏经》), 100 vols. , Tokyo 1924 起。

vol. = volume. 卷。

参 考 文 献

中文资料

季羡林:《大唐西域记校注(上下)》(中外交通史籍丛刊6),北京:中华书局,2000。

王邦维:《南海寄归内法传校注》(中外交通史籍丛刊8),北京:中华书局,1995。

周达甫:《改正法国汉学家沙畹对印度出土汉文碑的误释》,《历史研究》(第六期),1957,第79~82页。

西文资料

法宝义林(别册) = Hôbôgirin, Rép

1978 Répertoire du canon bouddhique sino-japonais, Édition de Taishō (Taishō Shinshū Daizokyō), Compilé par Paul Demieville, Hubert Durt, Anna Seidel (Fascicule annexe du Hôbôgirin), Tokyo, Paris.

Hartmann, Jens-Uwe

2004 Maitreyavyākaraṇa. Ed. Jens Braarvig, Manuscripts in the Schøyen Collection, vol. IV. Oslo. (尚未出版)

VON Hinüber, Oskar

1979 Die Erforschung der Gilgit-Handschriften (Funde buddhistischer Sanskrit-Handschriften I). Nachrichten der Akademie der Wissenschaften in Göttingen I. Philogisch-Historische Klasse 12: 329~359.

Huntington, Susan L.

1984 The "Pāla-Sena" Schools of Sculpture. Leiden.

Ishigami, Zenno (石上善应)

1967 On the "Maitreya-vyākaraṇa". Memoirs of Taisho University No. 52, The Departments of Literature and Buddhism. Tokyo: 41~52.

JAHN, Karl

1965 Rashīd al-Dīn's History of India. The Hague.

JAN, Yünhua

1966 Buddhist Relations between India and Sung China. History of Religions, Vol. 6. Chicago: 24~42 & 135~168.

LALOU, Marelle

1933 Les Textes Bouddhiques — Au Temps du Roi Khri-sroṇ-lde-bcan. Journal Asiatique, 211: 313~353.

LÉVI, Sylvain

1932 Maitreya le consolateur. Études d'orientalisme publiées par le Musée Guimet a la mémoire de Raymonde Linossier, Librairie Ernest Leroux, Paris: 355~402.

Liu, Zhen（刘震）

2005 *Das Maitreyavyākaraṇa. Ein Vergleich der verschiedenen Fassungen mit einer Übersetzung des Sanskrit-Textes*. Ludwig-Maximilians Universität München（未出版的硕士论文）.

Majumder, Prabhas Chandra

1959 Ārya Maitreya-vyākaraṇa. Ed. Nalinaksha Dutt, *Gilgit Manuscripts*, vol. IV, Calcutta：187～215.

Melzer, Gudrun

2006 *Ein Abschnitt aus dem Dīrghāgama*. Ludwig-Maximilians-Universität München（未出版的博士论文）.

Schopen, Gregory

1982 Hīnayāna Texts in a 14ᵗʰ Century Persian Chronicle：Notes on some of Rashīd al-Dīn's Sources. *Central Asiatic Journal* 26：225～235.

The Wall Paintings of Kizil Cave 118 — The Story of King Māndhātar and the Early Buddhism of Kucha

Satomi Hiyama

Graduate School of Arts and Sciences of Tokyo University, Japan

1. Description and Previous Interpretation of Kizil Cave 118 (Hippocampenhöhle)

Kizil Cave 118 is located in the inner cliff of the Kizil Grottoes. It has rectangular chamber and a vault ceiling arched perpendicularly to the entrance (Fig. 1), and originally had an antechamber in front of the main chamber, which already disappeared when found by German expedition. [1]

The murals of Cave 118 are painted mainly with warm colors. The ornaments and hair style of figures have similarity with other First style paintings, especially with Kizil Cave 77 (Höhle der Statuen, Fig. 2), 207 (Mallerhöhle), Kumtura Cave GK20, 21, 22 and Subashi, which have the other incidences of the pendant with double-hanged beads. German expedition classified this cave as First Style and gave its date as

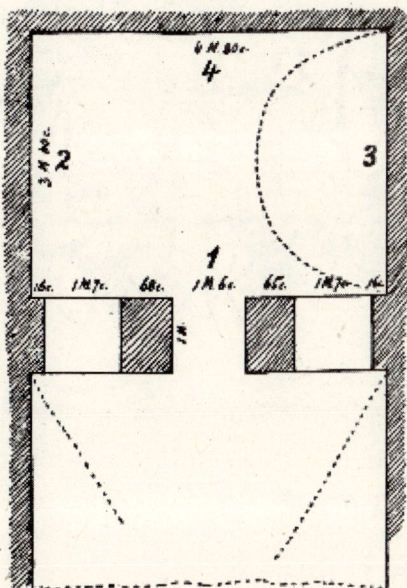

Fig. 1 (*Kultstätten*, Fig. 227a)

Fig. 2 (*Chūgoku sekkutu Kijiru sekkutu*, Vol. II. p. 18)

---

[1] Grünwedel, von Albert. *Altbuddhistische Kultstätten in Chinesisch-Turkistan*. Berlin: herausgegeben mit Unterstutzung der Baessler-instituts, 1912. p. 102.

the first half of 5th century,[1] but the Radiocarbon Dating executed by Chinese team dated it from the end of 3th century to the midst of 4th century.[2] It is common point to either that Cave 118 is regarded as one of the oldest caves among the Kizil.

The wall paintings of Cave 118 are painted on the main wall, upper parts of both side wall and vault ceiling. There was large painting looking like palace scene rimmed by ten friezes in the main wall (Fig. 3). In the center of it, a man looking like a king is sitting surrounded by many people. The mural of the both side walls are separated into upper and lower parts. In the upper part of right side wall, a man whose clothing is same as that of the king-like man of main wall is sitting surrounded by Devaputras (Fig. 4). In lower part the same man is lying on the bed with Devaputras to the right and women without halos on the left gazing on him sorrowfully. The left side wall is exhibited in Asian Museum of Berlin today, and the caption introduces it as "Palace scene"[3] (Fig. 5). In the upper part of left side, the man with brown skin and acute ears is sitting in the center surrounded by ten Devaputras. The background of this scene is like a palace; we can find similar background in "Maitreya in the Tuṣita heaven", the Second Style mural often painted above the entrance of Central Pillar cave. The lower part of left side wall describes Mount Sumeru with "X" shape, its center coiled by two Nāgas with sun and moon above. Sea surrounds Mount Sumeru and directly links to "Sea Frieze" below the vault (Fig. 6-a, b). In the central spine of the vault ceiling celestial figures are depicted. Around it, a scene of mountainous landscape spread in the vault (Fig. 7), in which Devaputras, a hunter,

Fig. 3 (*Kultstätten*, Fig. 228)

① Le Coq, Albert von. *Die Buddhistische Spätantike in Mittelasien v. 4: Atlas zu den Wandmalereien*. Berlin: D. Reimer, 1924. pp. 5–6.

② 霍旭初、王建林:《丹青斑驳千秋壮观·克孜尔石窟壁画艺术及分期概述》,见《龟兹佛教文化论集》,新疆龟兹石窟研究所便,乌鲁木齐:新疆美术摄影出版社,1993 年,第 201～228 页。

③ Marianne Yaldiz. et. al. *Magische Götterwelten: Werke aus dem Museum für Indische Kunst, Berlin*. Berlin: Museum für Indische Kunst, 2000. p. 201.

Fig. 4　(*Kultstätten*, Fig. 244)

Fig. 5　(*Kultstätten*, Fig. 243)

monks, Brāhmaṇas and various animals are depicted. Below the both side of vault, there are friezes called as "Sea Frieze", in which many kinds of strange sea animals are depicted. Some laymen, a monk and a painter appear on both sides of the big mural in the main wall.

By these mysterious and quite interesting figures, Cave 118 has fascinated many scholars. A. Grünwedel[1] and A. Miyaji[2] consider the murals of both side walls as "Śakamuni in the Tuśita heaven", but

---

①　*Kultstätten*. p. 112.

②　Miyaji Akira(宮治昭). *Nehan to Miroku no zuzogaku*. Tokyo: Yoshikawakobunkan, 1992. p. 420.

Fig. 6 （*Kultstätten*, Fig. 237b, 238b）

Fig. 7 （*Kultstätten*, Fig. 237a, 238b）

it is incomprehensible why Śakamuni was described without a halo. The mural of the main wall is regarded as the scene of "Śakamuni in his palace" by many Chinese and Japanese scholars,[1] however we cannot explain

---

[1] Shinkyō Uiguru Jichiku Bunbutsu Kanri Iinkai and Haijōken Kijiru Senbutsudō Bunbutsu Hokanjo eds. *Chūgoku sekkutu Kijiru sekkutu.* vol. 3. Tokyo: Heibonsya, 1985. p. 175. 苏北海:《龟兹石窟壁画裸体艺术探源》(《新疆艺术》1989 年第 6 期)。霍旭初:《克孜儿石窟前期壁画芸术》(《中国壁画全集 8　克孜尔》,天津人民美术出版社·新疆美术摄影出版社,(1992 年) pp. 27－28. Inoue Masaru. (井上豪) "*Hekiga shudai kara mita Kijiru dai118kutsu no seikaku*" Akita kōritsu bijutu kōgei tanki daigaku kiyō. vol. 11. Akita: Akita kōritsu bijutu kōgei tanki daigaku, 2006, p. 49.

the existence of three Brāhma□as with the gesture of a surrender in Śakamuni's Palace.

2. The Identification of Murals

（a）The story of King Māndhātar

In Cave 118 we can find same man three times in the center of main wall and right side wall, thus he must be a main character of the whole murals. He is sitting in the earthly and heavenly palace, and lying on the bed — only the story of King Māndhātar can explain all of these scenes.

The King Māndhātar first appeared in Indian myth.[1] In *Mahābhārata*, he is described as a son of the Yuvanāśva and grew up by suckling milk spilled from the finger of Indra（Sakka）, becoming the ideal king of the entire world. In contrast with his character as an ideal king in Indian myth, Buddhist canons portray him as a greedy king.[2] According to the Buddhist version, he was born from a forehead of King Upośada, and with his power as Cakravartirājan conquered all the continents on the earth. Not satisfied in his desire, he went up to Mount Sumeru and invaded the Trayaśtimsa heaven. Indra, the king of heaven, gave him a half of his throne and ruled the world together. When Māndhātar had a desire to kill Indra and rule the world alone, however, he immediately got sick and lost his power, fell into the earth and died.

Māndhātar story can be seen in many reliefs of Amarāvati-school,[3] particularly in Nāgārjunakonda.[4]

---

① Zin, Monica. "The Identification of the Bagh Paintings," *EAST AND WEST* vol. 51. Roma: IsIAO, 2001, pp. 307 – 309.

② *Jātaka*, no. 258. （ed. M. V. Fausböll. vol. 2. London: 1879）pp. 311 – 14., *Dīghanikāyaṭṭhakathā*, Part II （ed. by Stede, W., London: 1971）p. 481f., *Majjhimanikāyaṭṭhakathā*, Vol. 1. （ed. Woods, J. H. and Kosambi, D. London 1922）, p. 225f., *Dhammapadaṭṭhakathā* （ed. by Norman. H.C. vol. 3. London: Published for the Pali Text Society by Oxford University Press, 1912, p. 240）, *Gilgit Manuscripts*, 2nd ed. vol. III – I（ed. N. Dutt., Delhi: Sri Satguru, 1984）pp. 92. 16 – 97. 8, *Mūlasarvāstivāda-Vinaya Bhaisajyavastu* （ed. by Matsumura, H., in: *Four Avadānas from The Gilgit Manuscripts*. Ph. D. Diss., Canberra 1980）, pp. 349 – 354. *The Gilgit Manuscpipt of Sa ṇ ghabhedavastu, Being the 17th and last Section of the Vinaya of the Mūlasarvāstivādin*. Part 1. （ed. by Raniero Gnoli with the Assistance of T. Venkatacharya. Roma: Istituto Italiano per il medio ed estremo oriente, 1977.）p. 16, *Sanskrithandschriften aus den Turfanfunden*, Vol. 4, M 152. （ed. Waldschmidt, E. Wiesbaden 1980.）pp. 244 – 246. S607. （*ibid.* Vol. 3. 1971.）243f., *Divyāvadāna* XVII （eds. Cowell, E. B. and Neil, R. A. Cambridge 1886, pp. 210 – 28）, Bodhisattvāvadānakalpalatā. （ed. Vaidya, P. L., 1 – 2, Durbhanga 1959.）No. 4, pp. 38 – 45. transl. Rothenberg, B. L., Ph. D. Diss. University of Wisconsin 1990, pp. 210 – 228, 东晋瞿昙僧伽提婆译《中阿含经》卷十一《王相应品四洲经第三》(T1. No. 26. 494b9 – 496a13), 西晋法炬译《佛说顶生王故事经》(T1. No. 39. 822b11 – 824a16), 北凉昙无谶译《佛说文陀竭王经》(T1. No. 40. 824a19 – 825a15), 东晋瞿昙僧伽提婆译《增一阿含经》卷第八(T2. No. 125. 583b15 – 584c10), 吴康僧会译《六度集经》第四十《顶生圣王经》(T3. No. 152. 21c8 – 22b15), 宋施护等译《顶生王因缘经六卷》(T3. No. 165. 393a11 – 406b22), 元魏慧觉等译《贤愚经》六十四《顶生王品》(T4. No. 202. 439b25 – 440c15), 姚秦竺佛念译《出曜经》卷第四(T4. No. 212. 630a1 – a19), 唐义净译《根本说一切有部毗奈耶药事》卷十二(T24. No. 1448. 56b4 – 57a15), 唐义净译《根本说一切有部毗奈耶破僧事》卷一(T24. No. 1450. 100c18 – 101a01), 西晋法立共法炬译《大楼炭经》卷第六(T24. No. 1450. 100c18 – 101a01), 隋阇那崛多等译《起世经》卷第十(T1. No. 24. 363a13 – 18), 隋达摩笈多译《起世因本经》卷第十(T1. No. 25. 418a19), 发合思巴造元沙罗巴译《彰所知论》卷一(T32. No. 1645. 231a14), 'Dul-bagź, sMan-gyigźi（trans. Schiefner, F. Anton von and Ralston and W. R. S. *Tibetan tales derived from Indian sources: translated from the Tibetan of the Kah Gyur*. 2nd ed. Delhi: Sri Satguru Publications, 1988）pp. 1 – 20, Dzaṅs blun'zes bya ba'i mdo No. 45 （ed. and trans. Schmidt, I. J. Der Weise und der Thor, 1 – 2. St. Petersburg and Leipzig: 1843）ed. No. 1, pp. 294 – 301. trans. No. 2, pp. 369 – 376.

③ Zin, Monica. 2001. pp. 299 – 322. Miyaji Akira(宫治昭). "Minami Indo no Tenrinjōō no zuzō—Māndhātar ō setsuwazu wo chūshin ni" *Yoritomi Motohiro Hakase kanreki kinen ronbunshu*. Kyoto: Hōzōkan, 2005, pp. 163 – 184.

④ Ramachandran, T. N. *Nāgārjunakonda, 1938*. Delhi: Manager of Publications, 1953, pp. 32 – 34. Pls. XXXVII, XXXVIII., A. H. Longhurst, A. H. *The Buddhist antiquities of Nāgārjunakonda*, *Madras Presidency*. Delhi: Swati Publications, 1991, pp. 47 – 48. Pls. XXX, XXXI, XXXIX, XXXVIII, XLIII.

Fig. 8 （*Chūgoku sekkutu Kijiru sekkutu*, Vol. I. pl. 35.）

The one relief of Nāgārjunakonda has similar composition to the right side wall of Cave 118 （Fig. 8），[1] its upper part represents Māndhātar and Indra sharing one throne, but in the case of Cave 118 they are depicted separately on opposite side walls. This similarity of composition suggests a relationship between the Buddhist arts of Southern India and of Kucha.

The main wall（Fig. 3）depicts Māndhātar's reign on earth. At that time he had strong power, being depicted with a halo. The naked woman sitting beside him stands for the episode of his birth. When Māndhātar was born all of the women in the palace of king Uposada spilled breast milk and said "mām dhātu（Let him suck me）", therefore people named the baby "Māndhātar".[2] The women playing various instruments behind her represent his harem.

Three Brāhmanas are depicted in the left of main wall, one of them with a gesture of surrender, describing the story of Rsis who were exiled by Māndhātar because of killing birds cruelly.[3]

The upper parts of both side walls（Fig. 4, 5）depict the scene of Indra and Māndhātar sharing the throne in Sdarśana palace. They sit on the throne at equal height. The warrior sitting by Māndhātar is Yakśa Divaukasa, who is an adviser of Māndhātar.[4] Not only Divaukasa but also the episodes of breast milk and Rsis can be found in Sanskrit and Chinese texts only.

The lower right wall（Fig. 4）depicts Māndhātar falling to earth. He is about to die because of his bad desire.

But the description of the lower left wall and vault are beyond the story of Māndhātar. It is natural to regard them as a scene of Mount Sumeru and Trayastimsa heaven, because texts describe Māndhātar going up to Sumeru and meeting Indra living at the top, seeing there the beautiful landscape of Trayastimsa heaven.

---

① Longhurst, A. H. *ibid.* pl. XLIII.

② *Bhaisajyavastu*（ed. by Matsumura, 349 − [1]），*Sanghabhedavastu*（ed. 16），*Divyāvadāna*（XVII, ed. 210），*Bodhisattvāvadānakalpalatā*（IV, 15. trans. p. 212），《顶生王因缘经》卷一（T3. No. 165. 393b1 −4），《药事》（T24. No. 1448. 56b8 −12），《破僧事》（T24. No. 1450. 100c22 −25），'Dul-bagź, sMan-gyigźi（trans. p. 1）.

③ *Bhaisajyavastu*（ed. by Matsumura, 350 −[4]），*Divyāvadāna*（XVII, 211 −212），*Bodhisattvāvadānakalpalatā*（IV, 25 −45, trans. pp. 214 −217），《顶生王因缘经》（T3. No. 165. 393c7 −20），《药事》（T24. No. 1448. 56b16 −21），'Dul-bagź, sMan-gyigźi（trans. pp. 3 −4）.

④ *Bhaisajyavastu*（ed. by Matsumura, 351. [12]），Divyāvadāna（ed. p. 211），Bodhisattvāvadānakalpalatā（IV, 18, trans. p. 213），《因缘经》（T. 3. No. 165. 393b24），《药事》（T. 24. No. 1448. 56b25），'Dul-bagź, sMan-gyigźi（trans. p. 3），《贤愚经》（T. 4. No. 202. 440a21），*Dzańs blun'zes bya ba'i mdo*（trans. p. 373）.

The descriptions of these murals, however, have another source from the cosmology of Āgama and Abhidharma.

(b) The Source of Two Nāgas Coiling around the Sumeru

Below the scene of Indra's palace, there is the Mt. Sumeru coiled with two Nāgas (Fig. 5). The motif of two Nāgarājas appearing from the sea is common in India and Gandhāra, but what does the coiling Nāgas mean?

Some texts say that when Māndhātar climbed up to the Sumeru, guardian Nāgas tried to stop his invasion.[①] Some reliefs of Amarāvati and Nāgarjunikonda depict a scene in which Nāgas are trodden underfoot by Māndhātar. *Mūlasarvāstivāda-Vinaya Bhaisajyavastu* and *its Chinese version*, however, only have descriptions like; "At that time, two Nāgarājas, Nanda and Upananda saw the King Māndhātar and his armies, thought them as Asuras."[②] Texts give us no more information about Nāgas, but some canons of Āgama give us a hint to interpret these figures. In a scene of war between Devas and Asuras, Āgama texts have such a description; "At that time, two Nāgarājas, Nanda and Upananda coiled themselves around Mount Sumeru sevenfold and shook the mountain, then it started raining. They hit the ocean and the sea level rose up to the top of Sumeru. By these unusual events, Devas noticed the invasion of Asuras."[③] This story is common in Āgama texts. We must pay attention the fact that the Buddhism of Kucha made much of Āgama, because there are a large number of early Sanskrit manuscripts of Āgama and Abhidharma found in Xinjiang. Besides, Fotushemi (佛图舌弥), "the scholar of Āgama" was a leader of five big temples of Kucha in 4th century, who taught Kumārajīva to *Abhidharma Sutra*.[④] The position of sun and moon is also explained by the texts of Āgama and Abhidharma.[⑤]

(c) The Mural of Vault

The mural of vault (Fig. 7) is quite chaotic. Not small number of scholars thought this mural as reflecting Central Asia's trend of the contemplation, but too less information about contemplation was given in this cave. This paradisiacal landscape should be regarded as a scene of heaven influenced by the motif of "Indraśailaguhā" in Gandhāran reliefs, because this vault located just between two heavenly palace scenes of Indra and Māndhātar. However it is inexplicable why there are five types of human, that is, six Dēvaputras

---

① *Bhaisajyavastu*(ed. by Matsumura. 351[14 −21]), *Divyāvadāna* (ed. 218), *Bodhisattvāvadānakalpalatā* (trans. p. 221),《因缘经》(T3. No. 165. 398a16 −398b22),《药事》(T24. No. 1448. 56c7 −11), *Dzaṅs blun'zes bya ba'i mdo*. (trans. pp. 11 −12)

② "tathā nandopanando nāgarājo māndhātṛbalam dṛṣṭvā, asurā hy eta iti caturangena balakāyena pratyudgatah." (ed. by Matsumura, 351 −[14 −21])"时难陀邬波难陀龙王。见彼大王。及诸军众。意作是念。此是阿修罗。即集四兵众来见是曼陀多王"(《药事》卷十二, T24. No. 1448. 56c7 −8)。

③ 后秦佛陀耶舍共竺佛念译《长阿含经》卷第二十一《世记经战斗品第十》(T1. No. 1. 143a26 −b1),《大楼炭经》卷第五《战斗品第十》(T1. No. 23. 301b12 −b14),《起世经》卷第八《斗战品第九》(T1. No. 24. 352b16 −b20),《起世因本经》卷第八《斗战品第九》(T1. No. 25. 407b20 −b24), 梁宝唱撰《经律异相》卷第四十六 (T53. No. 2121. 239a5 −a20), 唐道世撰《法苑珠林》卷第五 (T53. No. 2122. 309c20 −c22)。

④ [梁]释僧祐:《出三藏记集》,苏晋仁、萧铼子点校,北京:中华书局,1995,410 −411。

⑤ 《长阿含经》卷第二十二(T1. No. 1. 145b7 −13),《大楼炭经》卷第六(T1. No. 23. 305b21 −b24),《起世经》卷第九(T1. No. 24. 358c4 −7),《起世因本经》卷第九(T1. No. 25. 413c5 −10),《增一阿含经》卷第三十四(T2. No. 125. 736a6 −8),《阿毗达磨俱舍论》卷第十一(T29. No. 1558. 59a17 −27),《立世阿毗昙论》卷第五(T32. No. 1644. 195a10 −11)等。

with halo, a Dēvaputra without halo, a hunter, two Brāhmanas and five monks. Two types of Dēvaputras and the hunter wear the same pendant, and the Dēvaputra without halo is not flying but standing on earth. These figures can be also explained by *Āgama* and *Abhidharma*; in the beginning of the world, original humans were as beautiful as Dēvaputras and emitted the light from their bodies, could fly in the sky and ate only "delight". However they started to become corrupted when their desires, especially appetite had grown. They lost their ability of flight, their beauty and light. [1] After the corruption of all the people on earth, the first king appeared and gave people morality. Following the arrival of king the Brāhmanas, and then the monks appeared. It is possible that the paintings of vault reflect these five stages of the change of human because we can find this myth not only in the *Āgama* and *Abhidharma* texts but also in two Sarvāstivāda-texts, *Mūlasarvāstivāda-Vinaya* and *Mūlasarvāstivāda-Vinaya Sanghabhedavastu*, and some manuscripts written in Sanskrit and Tokharian-A found in Xinjiang. It is noticeable that this myth can be linked to Māndhātar story only in the beginning of *Sanghabhedavastu* and *its Chinese version*, because according to these texts, after the story of corruption of people, Māndhātar is introduced as the fifth king, in his rule people got morality and started to enlighten themselves for the first time. [2]

Fig. 9 (Zin, Monica 2001, Fig. 9)

One of the sea animals in "Sea frieze" can be also explained by *Sarvāstivāda-Vinaya* (Fig. 6). These friezes have two quite strange fishes, one of them with the head of human and another with heads of human, monkey and horse. The same fish appears in the vault of Kizil Cave 8 (Fig. 9). It can depict the special Makara fish only described in this text. [3] According to this story, one day huge strange fish with eighteen kinds of animal heads was caught by fishermen. Buddha came to enlighten him and explained the reason of being born as such an ugly fish, i. e. in a past life he spoke evil of Kaśyapa

---

① *Aggañña-sutta* 27、*Sanghabhedavastu* (ed. p. 16),《长阿含经》第六《小缘经》(T1. No. 1. 37b28 – 39a20)卷第二十二《世记经世本缘品》(145a20 – b8),《大楼炭经》(T1. No. 23. 305b3 – 309c9),《起世经》(T1. No. 24. 358b4 – 365a6),《起世因本经》(T1. No. 25. 413b1 – 419c24),《有部毗奈耶》(T23. No. 1442. 635a15 – c22),《破僧事》(T24. No. 1450. 99b11 – 102a12),《阿毗达磨俱舍论》卷第十二(T29. No. 1558. 65b15 – c19),《立世阿毗昙论》(T32. No. 1644. 225b23 – 226a6),《彰所知论》(T32. No. 1645. 230c20 – 231a12),国王五人经(季羡林:《敦煌吐鲁番吐火罗语研究导论》,台北: 新文丰出版公司,1993 年,第 200 页)。

② "vasmin samaye Māndhātā rājā rājyam kārayati tasmin samaye manuṣyāh cintakā *abhūvan tulakā* upaparīkṣakāh / te cintayitvā tulayitvā upaparīkṣya prthakchilpasthānakarmasthānāni māpayantīti teṣām manujā manujā iti samjñodapādi" (*Sanghabhedavastu*),"即立为王彼时有情咸皆思惟。互相谙议分别好恶。各习一艺。时彼有情审思量故"(《破僧事》)。

③ 《有部毗奈耶》(*The Chinese version of Mūlasarvāstivāda-Vinaya*. T23. No. 1442. 668c19 – 675a3)。

Buddha. This Makara fish suggests to us the murals of Cave 118 have close relationship with the traditions of Sarvāstivāda-school.

3. The Conclusion

The wall paintings of Cave 118 depicted mainly the story of King Māndhātar, which based on Sarvāstivāda-version. The description of this story, however, also visualizes the cosmology of *Āgama* and *Abhidharma*. The main stream of the Buddhism of Kucha was Sarvāstivādin, but they placed *Āgama* and *Abhidharma* into quite important position and indeed a large number of early Sanskrit manuscripts belong to *Āgama* and *Abhidharma*,[1] thus Cave 118 reflects the circumstance of early Buddhism of Kucha. People entering in Cave 118 were able not only to understand the story of Māndhātar, but also locate themselves in Buddhist universe and context. It is noted that the Cave 118 is one of the oldest caves in Kucha — which may suggest that people in ancient Kucha Kingdom accepted the Buddhism with the interest in the cosmology and geography brought by it.

---

[1] Sander, Lore. "Early Prakrit and Sanskrit Manuscripts from Xinjiang (second to fifth/sixth centuries C. E.): Paleography, Literary Evidence, and Their Relation to Buddhist Schools," *Collection of Essays 1993: Buddhism Across Boundaries — Chinese Buddhism and The Western Regions*. ed. by Erik Zürcher, Lore Sander and others. (Taipei: Foguang Cultural Enterprise, 1999)

雅尔湖石窟 4 号窟千佛图像研究

汤士华　　陈玉珍

新疆吐鲁番学研究院　西北民族大学历史文化学院

一、序　说

雅尔湖石窟(图一)位于吐鲁番市西约10公里交河故城西南河谷南崖壁上。下距河谷底约20米,窟区东西长40余米。现存洞窟自西向东依次编号7个窟。[①] 窟前有宽约4.5米的平台,从崖前残留痕迹看,应有廊檐等木构建筑物与洞窟结合为一个整体。平台两端尚存阶梯通道与谷底连接。1号窟西15米内是塌毁的僧房废墟,阶道入口处西侧露出两条烟道,上部合一,显然是两灶合用一烟囱。7号窟东10米内,有两处坍塌的洞窟遗迹,也发现灶台的痕迹,南壁还残存一个小龛。若包括两侧塌毁的僧房残迹,东西长约65米。

图一

1至7号窟(图二[②])主室均为长方形纵券顶窟。1号窟窟门部分坍塌,西壁南端有一门洞与侧室相

---

①　根据20世纪10年代俄国奥登堡考察队成员杜丁的记述,雅尔湖石窟应分为上下两排,下面的一排洞窟遭到破坏。我们今天看到的是上面的一排洞窟。参见[俄] C. M. 杜丁著,何文津、方久忠译:《中国新疆的建筑遗址》,北京:中华书局,2006年,第47页。

②　此平面图采自陈世良《雅尔湖石窟调查报告》,文载解耀华主编:《交河故城保护与研究》,乌鲁木齐:新疆人民出版社,1999年,第286页。

连通,侧室为横券顶,侧室北壁大部分坍塌,仅存窗户残迹。窟内无壁画,仅在主室后壁有一条红色边框线和红色汉文题记,字迹难以辨认。2号窟窟门偏东,窟门西侧凿一放置物品的小龛。窟内无壁画,后壁和窟门西侧壁残存零散红色汉文题记。西壁有尖硬物刻画的竖行回鹘文,西侧壁南端有一矮洞与1号窟主室联通,似是后来挖通的。3号窟窟门偏东,窟门西侧凿一放置物品的小龛,西侧壁南端亦凿有一方形小龛。窟内东西侧壁有零散的红色汉文题记,西侧壁还有尖硬物刻画的汉文文字。5号窟窟门偏西,窟门东壁内壁凿一放置物品的小龛。窟内无壁画,西侧壁中部、窟门东侧有红色汉文题记,窟内西侧中部有尖硬物刻画出来的突厥文题记数行,东侧壁有刻画出的汉文题记,窟内西侧北部靠近窟门处,有刻画的一只羊,形态与岩画中的相近。6号窟窟门偏西窟门东侧内壁凿出放置物品的小龛,窟内无壁画,窟门两侧壁上有零散的红色汉文题记,均难以识别。7号窟四壁及顶部均绘有壁画,正壁与两侧壁的中间会有一幅较大的一佛二菩萨像。其余部分均为千佛。窟顶中央有三行莲花图案,有莲蕾、莲叶、鹤、鸭、树、鸟及化生童子等。

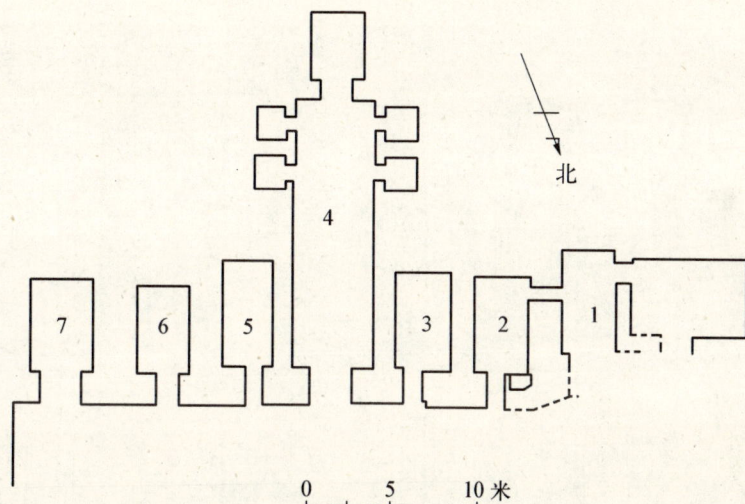

图二

　　4号窟是一个高大的长方形纵券顶窟,于主室正端壁上又凿出后室,主室两侧后部相对凿出四个小禅窟。主室长14.7米、宽4.3米、高4.2米,后室长3.8米、宽2.9米、高3米。4号窟主、后室均绘有壁画,总面积约110平方米。

　　主室壁画:东西两壁为大型"佛说法图"。每壁上下两层,每层并列11幅,下层大部分已模糊不清,上层除去被盗割的几幅外,其余保存较好。"佛说法图"构图是佛居中央,坐仰莲、伏莲双瓣莲花座,左右两面围绕6位闻法菩萨与佛弟子。佛的华盖、头光与身光图案各不相同,华丽繁复。每幅"佛说法图"之间有绘制精美的卷草纹装饰,侧壁与券顶连接处绘一条垂帐纹图案,券顶绘左右相向而对8排千佛,每排57身。主室窟门西侧内壁存供养比丘6身,身着百衲衣;主室窟门顶绘坐禅比丘一身,条幅式的身光似太阳光芒四射,形象独特;主室正壁所绘壁画,模糊不可辨。

　　后室壁画:西壁上部绘"龙王礼佛图",下部前端绘击连鼓的雷公与霹电;东壁残留菩萨像。门道西内侧绘一男供养人像,门道东内侧绘女供养人像,券顶绘千佛。由于后室不见阳光,颜色较主室鲜艳,除去被盗割与脱落部分,图像清晰,特别是西壁人物冠饰细微可辨,有多处榜题被割,东壁尚残留回鹘文榜题两则。令人瞩目的是,在主室券顶及后室顶部均绘有千佛图像(图三、图四),特别是主室券顶部分的千佛图像,尚存汉文千佛榜题(图五),引起笔者的极大兴趣。本文试作初步探讨,希请方家指正。

图三

图四

图五

二、千佛图像分析

1. 微观分析

千佛图像由六大部分组成：佛体、台座、背光、华盖、榜题、边框，这六大部分可兼而有之，也可仅有其中几个。总体上可以认为，前三大部分为基本特征，不可或缺；而后三大部分属选择性特征，可有可无。4号窟千佛图像无华盖与边框，现结合其色彩构成与排列组合略作分析。

1）底色白灰色，直接在抹好的白灰上绘制千佛图像与榜题，无底稿，上下不能对齐。

2）头顶肉髻，眉间有白毫；佛结禅定印，手不外露；佛着双领下垂式袈裟，内服僧祇支，袈裟与莲花座为红色，头光与身光内亦有部分使用红色。

3）坐姿为结跏趺坐，台座为俯莲座，花瓣 14 至 20 个不等。

4）头光与身光为圆形，头光叠压在身光上，成交叠状，且均为两身一组，绿白相间，光光相接。

5）榜题框为白底墨书，边框为红色，亦有少量无边框，直接书写在泥墙上。

2. 宏观分析

1）图像内分析

千佛图像在视觉上总是呈现大面积的集中排列，这是大多数千佛图像最明显的特征之一。千佛的排列一般非常规整，上下左右从各个方向来看都成整齐的行列，加上颜色的配置，在视觉上不但产生了层次感，而且也产生了动感。梁晓鹏先生依据敦煌莫高窟千佛图像在视觉上排列组合以及与经文对照特征，将其归纳为线性、对称性、衔接性、交替性、动态性与互文性等六大特征。① 所谓线性，即指千佛图像大小基本一致，上下、左右皆成直线排列，从各个角度看都能排成一个行列，且整齐有序。雅尔湖千佛洞 4 号窟由于没有底稿，线性特征不是很完美，其对成性体现在东西各四排，佛头相向而对。千佛图像千面一孔，为了不使观想者陷于乏味之中，画师们总是要通过色彩上的变化，来实现"光光相接"的视觉效果，可为交替性的一种体现。4 号窟千佛图像，以醒目的绿色来调节佛徒们视觉疲劳，从而进入到亦幻亦真的佛国世界。

2）图像外分析

《佛说千佛因缘经》中提到，有八万四千菩萨异口同声地问释迦牟尼佛："世尊与贤劫千佛，过去世时，种何功德，修何道行"，因此能够"常生一处，共同一家"②。这既说明佛的出现总是伴随着千佛，也暗示着千佛的出现所伴随的是佛。所以在大多数千佛图中总是有佛说法图，或一佛，或二佛并坐，或一佛二菩萨等。千佛题材的雕塑绘画在石窟中的表现是多种多样的，诸如：以观释迦牟尼像而表现化佛；以观三世十方诸佛像而表现十方诸佛；以观释迦多宝并坐而表现十方化佛；以观弥勒佛而表现贤劫千佛与星宿千佛；以观维摩、文殊辩法而表现贤劫千佛；以观七佛而表现化佛；依据《佛名经》观千佛而表现十方诸佛等等。③

雅尔湖 4 号窟主室所绘壁画可分两大部分，东西侧壁共 44 幅大型说法图，券顶部分为 8 排有榜题的千佛图像。这种构图布局，在柏孜克里克千佛洞中是很常见的，以大型立佛为中心的佛本行经变，在高昌回鹘时期石窟壁画中最富有代表性，④而券顶部分所绘千佛又是这一时期的主流程式。这种布局充分展现了千佛图像与佛说法图在石窟中的普遍共生性，也体现了大乘禅学依据《佛名经》来指导禅僧观想的实际需要。

三、千佛榜题释录

1. 榜题格式

遵循左图右史原则，榜题书写在佛像右上方处，为"南无……佛"。"无"字常写作"无"，有时亦写作

---

① 梁晓鹏：《敦煌莫高窟千佛图像研究》，北京：民族出版社，2006 年，第 94～104 页。

② 《大正藏》卷一四《经集部一》，No. 426，第 661a 页。

③ 林梅：《北方石窟千佛问题探讨》，《炳灵寺石窟学术研讨会论文集》，第 230 页。

④ 贾应逸：《高昌回鹘壁画艺术特色》，《新疆艺术》1989 年第 1 期，第 43～48 页。

"無"。"无"字笔画简,书手写作方便,这很好解释。而"佛"字常写作"佛",个别情况下亦写作"仏"。为什么会出现这种情况呢?这需要从壁画制作技法说起。千佛画的制作过程大致可分为7个步骤,①其中,最基础的算是确定位置坐标,用土红粉线弹出直线确定千佛画的总体外框,并将千佛画的平面划分为大致相等的若干小方块,即确定每一单幅画面的位置和大小。我们通过仔细观察,发现制作此幅壁画的画师们只是确定了千佛画的总体外框和每排千佛图像的界限,并没有每个小千佛的具体位置确定下来,微观而察,是比较粗糙的,上下千佛并不能整齐相对。千佛图像画好之后,才开始画榜题边框,由于千佛名号长短不一,字数较少的自然能够写下,字数较多的千佛名号受榜题边框长度限制,留下书写空间狭窄,"佛"比"仏"占的空间大,故写作"仏";另有,限于千佛画像限制,题榜较短,故亦写作"仏"。

2. 对应之佛经

据日本学者井口泰淳研究,佛典中属于佛名经类的佛经共有48种61部,其中收入《大藏经》,并且现在能够看到的佛名经有14种17部。② 在众多佛名经中,雅尔湖4号窟千佛名号所依何经,通过对榜题的逐一释录,可以看到,与"阙译人名今附梁录"版本之《现在贤劫千佛名经》(以下简称《贤劫经》)大致相符。

榜题中出现的千佛名号,绝大部分都能在《贤劫经》中找到,且多数集中在千五百佛名中。最为瞩目的是,榜题之千佛名号有相当部分排列顺序可与《贤劫经》中的连续对应。以上两点,使我们有理由相信,"阙译本"之《贤劫经》,很可能就是雅尔湖4号窟千佛画榜题的直接佛经依据。当然,《贤劫经》与榜题中的千佛名号还是有一些出入的。

四、雅尔湖4号窟之功用及开凿年代

南北朝时期,南朝偏重宗教义理,北朝偏重宗教修行。北方许多著名高僧,远离闹市,"凿仙窟以居禅"。③ 创建莫高窟的乐僔,以及继乐僔以后的法良,皆为禅师;炳灵寺第169窟供养人像列中有题名"□国大禅师昙摩毗之像";玄高在麦积山"专精禅律";昙曜早年是北凉的著名禅师,后来到达平城,主持创建云冈石窟;东魏武定四年(546)创建大流圣窟(今河南安阳灵泉寺东侧)的道凭,"入夏既登,遂行禅境"……大量资料证明,北方诸石窟,大多与著名禅师有极其密切的联系。④

雅尔湖石窟距交河故城不远,但谷深幽静,前有河水流淌,很适宜僧人禅修,吐峪沟石窟之环境亦然。吐峪沟第20窟壁画,左壁的中下部,绘制有净土观想图,表现的是禅观僧们观想的种种净土内容。⑤ 其中有几处汉文题记均有"行者观"字样,此"行者"当为壁画中的禅僧无疑,印度新德里国立博物馆藏有斯坦因从邻近第20窟的Ⅳ~Ⅶ窟窃取壁画,两处榜题有"禅师观"字样。吐峪沟石窟从形制上分,有中心柱、方形窟和纵券顶长方形窟之别。其中第1、20、42号窟为长方形纵券顶窟,主室后壁凿一小屋,第1和42

① 宁强、胡同庆:《敦煌莫高窟第254窟千佛画研究》,《敦煌研究》1986年第4期,第35~36页。
② 井口泰淳:《敦煌本〈仏名經〉の諸体系》,《东方学报》第35号,1964年,第397~437页。
③ [唐]道宣:《广弘明集》卷二九,《大正藏》卷五二《史传部四》,No. 2103,第339b页。
④ 刘慧达:《北魏石窟与禅》,《考古学报》1978年第3期,第337~352页;贺世哲:《莫高窟北朝石窟与禅观》,《敦煌学辑刊》第1集,1980年,第41~52页。
⑤ Nobuyoshi Yamabe, Practice of Visualization and the Visualization Sūtra: An Examination of Mural Paintings at Toyok, Turpan, *Pacific World: Journal of the Institute of Buddhist Studies*, Third Series Number 4, 2002, pp. 123-152.

号窟主室两侧壁各凿两个小屋,是为禅室。根据贾应逸先生研究,这三个窟壁画描绘的是比丘禅定观想的情景。依据的经典主要有《禅法要解》、《禅秘要法经》、《思维略要法》和《坐禅三昧经》等。这种主室后壁凿小屋,侧壁各凿两个小室的纵券顶长方形石窟,与雅尔湖 4 号窟的形制完全相同。主室窟门顶所绘坐禅比丘(图六)找不出二次绘画痕迹,当为开凿后所绘,又《禅秘要法经》载:"尔时复当自然见身上,有一明相……光光七宝色,从胸而出,入于明中。此相现时,遂大欢喜,自然悦乐,心极安稳,无物可譬。"①《五门禅经要用法》亦载:"教谛观身。若言我自见身光出绕身四边,其明转盛。便自以手推此光明远至四方。有无量人寻光来至。"②于是,我们推断雅尔湖 4 号窟在早期曾是一个禅窟。

图六

　　阎文儒先生指出雅尔湖石窟的开凿年代,"从壁画的画风来看,最早的应在晋设高昌郡时期(公元 327～450)";③柳洪亮先生认为应在"车师前部晚期,约 5 世纪初",④并将之与柏孜克里克石窟相比较。在笔者看来,确定雅尔湖石窟开凿的年代应更多地与吐峪沟石窟相比照,雅尔湖 7 号窟的千佛绘制工整,大量使用冷色调,这与吐峪沟石窟中的千佛有异曲同工之妙,同时,雅尔湖 4 号窟的洞窟形制很容易让我们联想起吐峪沟第 1 和 42 号窟,⑤这三个洞窟均为长方形纵券顶形制,东西侧壁各有两个小侧室,主室后壁有后室。贾应逸先生将 42 号窟定于北凉时期,我们深信此说。⑥吾人故知,443 年,北凉王沮渠无讳占据高昌,自称高昌王,但并未据有交河;450 年,其弟沮渠安周破车师,至 460 年一直领有交河。由此,可

　　① 《大正藏》卷一五《经集部二》,No. 613,第 257a 页。
　　② 《大正藏》卷一五《经集部二》,No. 619,第 330c 页。
　　③ 阎文儒:《新疆天山以南的石窟》,《文物》1962 年 7～8 期。
　　④ 柳洪亮:《雅尔湖千佛洞考察随笔》,《敦煌研究》1988 年第 4 期,第 49 页。
　　⑤ Nobuyoshi Yamabe, An Examination of Visualizing Monks in Toyok Cave 42: In Conjunction with the Origin of Some Chinese Texts on Medition, *Turfan Revisited-The First Century of Research into the Arts and Cultures of the Silk Road*, Berlin: Dietrich Reimer Verlag, 2004, pp. 401－407.
　　⑥ 贾应逸:《新疆吐峪沟石窟佛教壁画泛论》,《佛学研究》第 4 期,1995 年,第 240～249 页。

以推定,雅尔湖石窟的开凿与绘制壁画当在北凉残部沮渠安周占据交河之时。

五、高昌回鹘时期的千佛信仰

高昌回鹘王国时期,佛教信仰兴盛。雅尔湖4号窟为双层壁画,其中外层即绘于高昌回鹘时期。柏孜克里克千佛洞为高昌回鹘时期的王家寺院,其中回鹘时期的壁画一个显著的特点是大量使用暖色,尤其是红色来绘制,雅尔湖4号窟亦然,这一点我们可从后室壁画中清楚地看到。高昌回鹘时期的壁画最富有代表性的是以大型立佛为中心的佛本行经变,雅尔湖4号窟东西两侧壁共有44幅说法图,规模宏大,气势磅礴。最为直接的证据是后室东侧壁有两行回鹘文榜题,后室门两侧绘有回鹘供养人像,"结合洞窟形制分析,显然是回鹘高昌王室成员"[1]。

前文提及券顶部分绘千佛是高昌回鹘时期壁画的主流程式,由此我们就很有必要探讨一下其成因。

千佛图像用来表达佛经内容,包括千佛名经(如三世三千佛、贤劫千佛和十方诸佛等)和其他佛经(如《法华经》等)。表现千佛名经时,千佛为图像的主题,因而往往具有榜题说明所属;或者大量的表现千佛形象。表现其他佛经时,千佛作为其经中的重要角色,起着供养对象和行为见证的作用,因此弱化了千佛本身的具体特点,表现为无佛名榜题,甚至无榜题。雅尔湖4号窟券顶部分,不但有千佛,且皆有榜题。绘制此千佛图像,显然是为表述《现在贤劫千佛名经》。

对于出家僧人,念佛可以入禅定,由禅定得智慧,由智慧达解脱。《现在贤劫千佛名经》载:"若持诵此千佛名者,则灭无量阿僧祇劫所集众罪,必得诸佛三昧神通,无碍智慧,及诸法门、诸陀罗尼,一切经书种种智慧,随宜说法,皆当从是三昧中,求修习此三昧。当行净命,勿生欺诳,离于名利,勿怀嫉妒,行六和敬,如是行者,疾得三昧法也。"[2]当然,在昏暗的洞窟中,禅定僧难以看清具体的佛名,因此这是一种无声的念佛。

千佛图像是劝谕信众和修行者的观想对象。《五门禅经要用法》之《观十方诸佛法》载:

> 念十方佛者,坐观东方廓然大光,无诸山河石壁,唯见一佛结加趺坐举手说法。心明观察光明相好画然明了,系心在佛不令他缘,心若余念摄之令还,如是见者便增十佛。既见之后复增百佛千佛乃至无边身,近者则使转远转广,但见诸佛光光相接。心明观察得如是者,回想东南复如上观,既得成已西北方四维上下亦复如是。既向方方皆见诸佛已,当复一时并观十方诸佛,一念所缘周遍得见,定心成就者,于定中见十方诸佛皆为说法。疑网悉除得无生忍,若有宿罪因缘,不见诸佛者,当一日一夜六时忏悔劝请随喜,渐自得见,纵使劝请不为说法,是人心快乐身体安无患也。[3]

对于禅修的人来说,具体的佛形象是帮助其入定的好方法,比文字所描述的抽象的佛名要生动得多,尤其是画家通过色彩的调配在千佛图中实现的光光相接的效果,当是修行者看后便难以忘怀、历历在目的画面。千佛图像的绘制还是功德表现。《过去庄严劫千佛名经》载:

---

① 柳洪亮:《雅尔湖千佛洞考察随笔》,《敦煌研究》1988年第4期,第48页。
② 《大正藏》卷一《经集部》,No.447,第383a页。
③ 《大正藏》卷一《经集部》,No.619,第327c页。

若有善男子善女人,闻是三世三劫诸佛名号,欢喜信乐持讽读诵而不诽谤,或能书写为他人说,或能画作立佛形象,或能供养香花伎乐,叹佛功德至心作礼者,胜用十方诸佛国土满中珍宝纯摩尼珠,积至梵天,百千劫中布施者。是善男子、善女人等,已曾供养是诸佛已,后生之处历侍诸佛,至于作佛而无穷尽,皆当为三世三劫中佛而所授决,所生之处常遇三宝,得生诸佛刹土,六情完具,不堕八难,当得诸佛三十二相、八十种好,具足庄严。①

千佛图像无论对于修行者还是信仰者,都有着非常重要的意义,所以历经数代,千佛图像仍是石窟壁画不可或缺的组成部分。高昌回鹘时期的石窟亦如此,然而,独有雅尔湖 4 号窟中的千佛图像有如此完整的榜题,则值得深思。莫高窟 246 窟,始建于北魏,西夏重修。窟型是北魏盛行的人字坡顶和中心塔柱相结合的形式。中心柱东向面录顶帐形龛内有西夏重修的释迦、多宝佛及胁侍菩萨、供养菩萨各二身。窟内壁画均为西夏重绘,四壁画千佛,有榜题。该窟东壁门南上端明确表明所绘千佛为贤劫千佛,其四壁所书千佛名号也多与《现在贤劫千佛名经》(阙译本)相合。②

吐鲁番地区古称高昌,曾是高昌回鹘王国(866～1283)所在地,自古为中西交通的咽喉、丝绸之路的重地。20 世纪初以来,吐鲁番共出土了汉、梵、佉卢、粟特、突厥、于阗、龟兹、波斯、叙利亚、吐蕃、回鹘、西夏、蒙古等二十多个文种的文献。这些文献大部分是佛经写卷和刊本,这自然与吐鲁番作为佛教东传的中枢密切相关。据出土文献推测,至迟在西晋元康年间(291～299),佛教已传到高昌,而后逐渐繁盛。③ 11 世纪早期,西夏频频举兵,攻打觊觎已久的瓜、沙、肃三州,灭归义军政权。是后,西夏势力被沙州回鹘逐出,敦煌为沙州回鹘所有。④ 至 11 世纪后期,河西终入西夏版图,高昌回鹘成为西夏的近邻。

西夏建国于 1038 年,但在此前,其佛教已相当兴盛。西夏统治者延请回鹘高僧讲经说法,主持西夏文《大藏经》的翻译。国家图书馆藏西夏文《现在贤劫千佛名经》前面有一幅木刻版译经图,图的正中间有一高僧像,像上西夏文款识义为"都译勾管作者安全国师白智光",据考证此人即回鹘人。⑤ 当然,回鹘与西夏的交往并非单向的,西夏文佛经残片在吐鲁番出土,即证明了西夏佛经也曾经输入高昌。吐鲁番出土的西夏文文献计有 4 件,其一为 20 世纪初"德国吐鲁番考察队"于吐鲁番所发现,编号为 T M 109,为经折装印本残片的两个折页,共存文字 12 行,内容为曹魏康僧铠译《郁伽长者问经》之西夏文转译本。另外 3 件则是 1980 年考古人员在清理吐鲁番柏孜克里克石窟积沙时发现的,均系佛经印刷品残卷。这些西夏文残卷均为 12～13 世纪的遗物。从其字行排列不整齐、字体大小不均且墨色浓淡有别等因素看,它们很可能是泥活字印本。这些既是西夏人入居高昌的佐证,同时也是回鹘-西夏文化交流的结果。⑥ 既然西夏与高昌回鹘有如此密切的佛教往来,那么莫高窟 246 窟和雅尔湖 4 号窟中的千佛图像,在不同地域的同一时期出现,是否能成为又一佐证,亦未可知。

① 《大正藏》卷一《经集部》,No. 446,第 365a 页。
② 梁晓鹏:《敦煌莫高窟千佛图像研究》,北京:民族出版社,2006 年,第 18 页。
③ 西晋元康六年(296)竺法护译《诸佛要集经》,是目前吐鲁番出土最早的一件写经。
④ 杨富学:《西夏与回鹘势力在敦煌的兴替》,《西夏研究》第 3 辑(第二届西夏学国际学术研讨会论文集),北京:中国社会科学出版社,2006 年,第 137～143 页。
⑤ 史金波:《西夏佛教史略》,宁夏:人民出版社,1988 年,第 78 页;杨富学:《回鹘文献与回鹘文化》,民族出版社,2003 年,第 480～481 页。
⑥ 杨富学:《论回鹘文化对西夏的影响》,《宋史研究论丛》第 5 辑,保定:河北大学出版社,2003 年,第 179～194 页。

附表：4号窟千佛榜题释录（排序：由东向西自里向外）

	1	2	3	4	5	6	7	8	9	10	11	12	13	14	15	16	17	18	19
第1排	缺	被割	被割	南谟迦叶如来佛	被割	被割	被割	被割	被割	南无妙花如来佛	被割	被割	南（被割）	南无大□佛	南天大力佛	南无（缺）	被割	被割	被割
第2排	缺	南无大明佛	南无炎肩佛	南无照曜佛	南无日藏佛	缺	缺	南无善明佛	南无无忧佛	南无提沙佛	南无明曜佛	南无提□佛（贤劫无功无）	南无功德明佛	南无兴成佛	南无灯曜佛	南无示义佛	被割	被割	被割
第3排	（南无）□□佛	（南无）坚□□仏	南无福威德佛	南无不可坏佛	南无德相佛	南无多睺佛	南无众主佛	南无梵声佛	南无坚际佛	南无不高佛	南无作明佛	南无善思议佛	南无宝积佛	南无德敬佛	南无花目佛	南无众首佛	南无无世光佛	南无得义伽佛	南无多德佛
第4排	脱落	脱落	（南无）坚精进佛	南无明赞佛	南无师子德佛	南无□□佛	南无德赞佛	南无□□佛	南无极高行佛	南无众明佛	南无金刚相佛	南无金刚佛	南無金众佛	南无畏佛	南无安乐佛	南（无）弗沙佛	南无边威德仏	南无义意佛	南乐无王佛
第5排	脱落	脱落	南无□□佛	南无…（佛）	南无□藏佛	南无师子相佛	掉色	（南无）珠角佛	南无宝藏佛	南无琢相佛	南无求利佛	南无乐说聚佛	南无法自在佛	南无华天佛	南无梵德佛	南无□□佛	南无连花佛	南无威德首佛	南无供敬佛
第6排	脱落	（脱落）仏	南无电明仏	南无见有边佛	南无违蓝王佛	南无日明佛	南无多天佛	南无离闇佛	南无游戏佛	南无宝相佛	南无吉祥佛	南无坚戒佛	南无光明佛	南无多智佛	南无妙色佛	南无无量意佛	南无莺伽陀佛	南无电相佛	南无须曼（色佛）
第7排	南无安住佛	南无慧聚佛	南无藏释佛	南无德树佛	南无（脱落）	南无威（脱落）	南无珠髻（佛）	南无大名佛	南无月相佛	南无离垢佛	南无善思佛	南无云音佛	南无善意佛	南无观视佛	南无妙象佛	南无德臂佛	南无爱作佛	脱落	脱落
第8排	南无花光佛	南无仁爱佛	脱落	脱落	脱落	脱落	脱落	脱落	南无精进德佛	南无善守佛	南无欢喜佛	南无不退佛	南无师子相佛	脱落	脱落	脱落	脱落	脱落	脱落

续 表

	20	21	22	23	24	25	26	27	28	29	30	31	32	33	34	35	36	37	38
第 1 排	被割	被割	被割	被割	被割	被割	被割	被割	被割	被割	被割	被割	被割	被割	被割	南无调御佛	南无喜口(佛)	南无灭已佛	南无宝口佛
第 2 排	被割	被割	被割	被割	被割	被割	被割	被割	被割	被割	被割	被割	南无无量形佛	南无照明佛	南无宝相佛	南无离畏佛	南无宝藏佛	南无月面佛	南无口名佛
第 3 排	南无不住佛	南无不口佛	南无妙乐佛	南无无量持佛	南无善寂灭佛	南无功德敬佛	南无福德佛	南无开花佛	南无无边行佛	南无口口佛	南无违蓝佛	南无月面佛	南无德净佛	南无去名佛	南无善众仏	南无口口意佛	南无焰肩佛	南无安(洋)行佛	南无梵牟尼佛
第 4 排	南无断恶佛	(南无)口热佛	南无善调佛	南无名德佛	南无花德佛	南无勇德佛	南无金刚军佛	南无大德如来佛	南无寂灭意佛	南无明意佛	南无富足佛	南无勇口佛	南无见一切义佛	南无(净)垢佛	南无口大副花仏(贤劫无)	南无大威德仏	掉色	南无天口佛	南无口口佛
第 5 排	南无治怨贼佛	南无离娇佛	南无常乐佛	南无见有边佛	南无基良佛	南无宝月佛	南无乐禅佛	南无德宝佛	南无应名称佛	南无大音声佛	南无金刚珠佛	南无无量寿佛	南无宝众佛	掉色	南无(脱落)	南无庄严(俗体)佛	南无宝上仏	南无利慧佛	南无虚空佛
第 6 排	南无上利佛	南无沙国佛	南无那罗达佛	南无天名佛	南无多功德佛	南无师子相佛	南无游戏佛	南无花身佛	南无辩才口佛	南无大王佛	南无珠庄(俗体)严佛	南无施愿佛	南无山顶佛	南无珠明佛	南无善见(贤劫无)佛	南无花德仏	南无炎炽佛	南无上善佛	掉色
第 7 排	南无连花佛	南无智日佛	南无宝语仏	南无日积(佛)(贤劫无)	南无善行意佛	南无花首佛	南无天力佛	南无(脱落)	南无花山(佛)	南无乐(脱落)	南无无极高德佛	南无上尊(佛)	南无(脱落)	南无名相佛	南无(脱落)	南无(脱落)	南无(脱落)	南无光明(佛)	南无利(脱落)
第 8 排	脱落	脱落	脱落	脱落	脱落	脱落	脱落	脱落	脱落	脱落	(脱落)佛	脱落	脱落	脱落	脱落	脱落	脱落	脱落	脱落

续表

	39	40	41	42	43	44	45	46	47	48	49	50	51	52	53	54	55	56	57
第1排	掉色	掉色	掉色	掉色	掉色	南无宝口佛	南无极高行佛	掉色	南无宝口口佛	南无口声佛	南无香济佛	南无香象佛	掉色	被割	被割	脱落	掉色	掉色	掉色
第2排	掉色	南无爱相佛	南无口口佛	掉色	南无无忧佛	(南无)口众佛	南无师子象佛	南无善意佛	掉色	南无德口佛	南无觉相佛(贤劫无)	南无梵自在佛	南无口口佛	南无珠口宝佛	南无珠口(佛)	南无(无)德口仏	掉色	掉色	掉色
第3排	南无无口佛	南(无)…佛	掉色	掉色	(南无)月明佛	南无口口佛	南无口口佛	南无口口佛	南无(师)子意德	南无无口佛	南无风行佛	无字	南无香王佛(贤劫无)	掉色	南无众口口佛	南无众清净仏	掉色	掉色	掉色
第4排	南无善口佛	南无口口佛	南(无)口天佛	南无一切天佛	南无梵(寿)佛	掉色	南无口口佛	南无口口佛	掉色	南无口意佛	南无口口佛	南无金口口佛	南无口口佛	南无口口佛	南无口名佛	脱落	掉色	掉色	
第5排	南无高出佛	掉色	南无大口口佛	南无大口名佛	南无口光佛	(南无)口藏佛	南无大威德佛	掉色	(掉色)仏	南无师子口仏	南无金刚牢仏	南无口口仏	南无满愿仏	南无大车佛	南无势力行佛	南无众妙佛	掉色		掉色
第6排	南无口王佛	南无德法佛	南无不动佛	南无善寂行佛	南无无损佛	南无分威别仏(仏)	南无大光明佛	南无日光耀佛	掉色(仏)	掉色	掉色	掉色	南无口仏	南无(掉色)	(南无)善口(仏)	南无须色佛	南无大口爱佛	掉色	掉色
第7排	掉色	南无破(脱落)	南无善众佛	南无宝口(脱落)	南无(脱落)	南无施明佛	掉色	南无口口佛	南无世(脱落)	南无…佛	南无宝发佛	南无宝施佛	南无宝王佛	南无妙慧佛	南无妙香花佛	掉色	南无口比方佛	南无宝口名佛	南无月观佛
第8排	脱落	脱落	脱落	脱落	脱落	脱落	脱落	南无口论佛	南无吉手佛	南无…佛	南无口德佛	南无口自在仏	掉色	南无天香花佛	南无天王佛	脱落	脱落	脱落	南无师口口佛

Musical culture of the Golden Horde nomads
(based on the burial of a warrior with a kobyz)

Alexander V. Yevglevsky

Faculty of History, Donetsk National University, Ukraine

My report is devoted to a bowed musical instrument, so I have to touch upon the problem of the state of art in musical archaeology as a part of culture heritage of the Golden Horde nomads and even broader, — of the Turkic Eurasian culture sphere. I am not a music expert, and I flattered myself thinking that I would be able to considerably expand our knowledge of the music culture of the nomads having examined many finds of musical instruments used by them. But I am very disappointed. Now it is safe to say that a common level of our knowledge of music culture not only of the Golden Horde nomads but also of medieval Eurasian nomads is far lower than that of any other kind of creative work of bygone centuries. In this connection, a find of a bowed string instrument of a kobyz type in a barrow nomadic interment of the 13th century in Ukraine is of great importance.

A burial with this musical instrument was found in 1984 at the Ingulets river (the right tributary of the Dnieper river) near Kirovo village. In 1991 there was a short commentary about it in a local newspaper and after that not only the musical instrument but also the whole complex were completely forgotten.

The Monument Description

The inlet burial under discussion was found almost in the barrow center at a depth of 2. 6 meters from its top. A grave pit soil was firmly rammed which favoured very good preservation of things. At the pit bottom a complex double-decked wooden latticework was placed. A field reconstruction revealed that it was a sleigh (see Fig. 1) of unusual construction. It could slide neither over a snow nor grass. Therefore, the sleigh was intentionally made for funeral rite purposes.

A westwardly oriented stretched mature man was laid on his back over the transverse planking of the lower deck (see Fig. 2).

The funeral inventory comprises an iron buckle, a wooden dish, a wooden dipper, a quiver, a bow, a knife, a fire-steel and 10 arrows. Between the quiver and the sleigh side there was a wooden musical instrument over which a long wooden fiddlestick was placed. The inventory permits to date the burial back to the 2nd half of the 13th century.

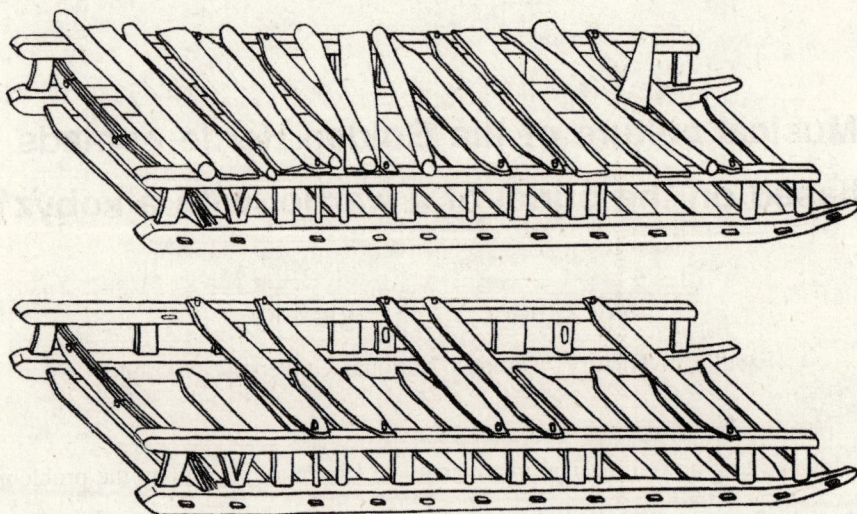

Fig. 1

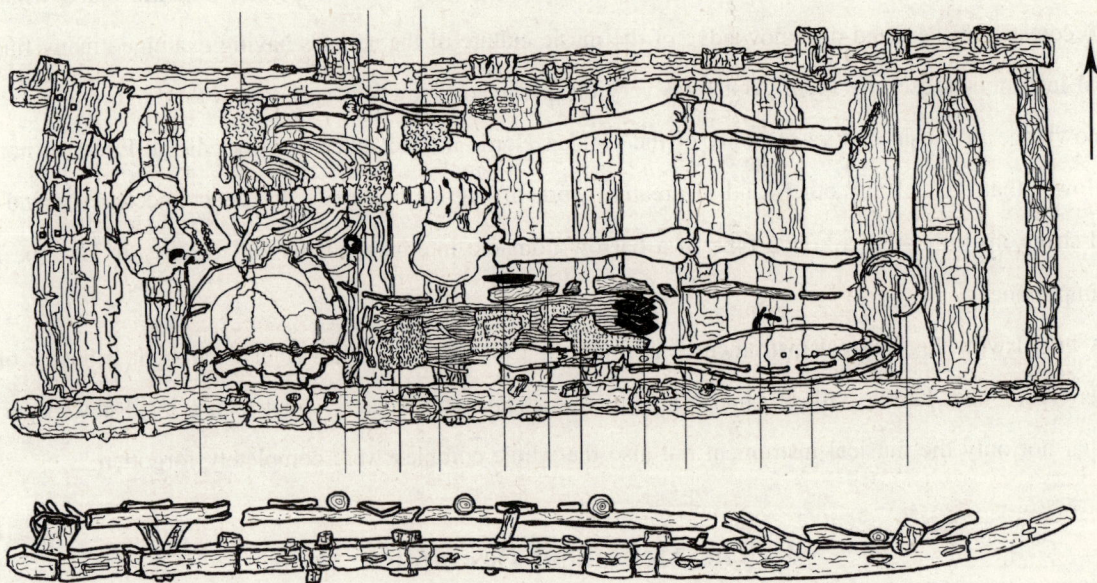

Fig. 2

The Instrument Construction

Let's examine the musical instrument construction. The instrument appeared to be broken near its neck, some little components were lacking but in spite of this its condition may be considered as quite satisfactory. Judging by the preserved parts the instrument was quite long — from 87 to 92 centimeters (see Fig. 3). The instrument consists of 2 parts: a boatshaped body (see Fig. 4) and a head with three pins (see Fig. 4) attached to the neck with the help of a peculiar adapter. The body and the neck were hollowed out of one piece of wood (the pine family) and the head — of another one (ash). One very little part, namely a yoke-shaped rest for the strings (see Fig. 4), was preserved especially well. Three cuts for the strings are clearly visible in the upper arched part (see Fig. 4).

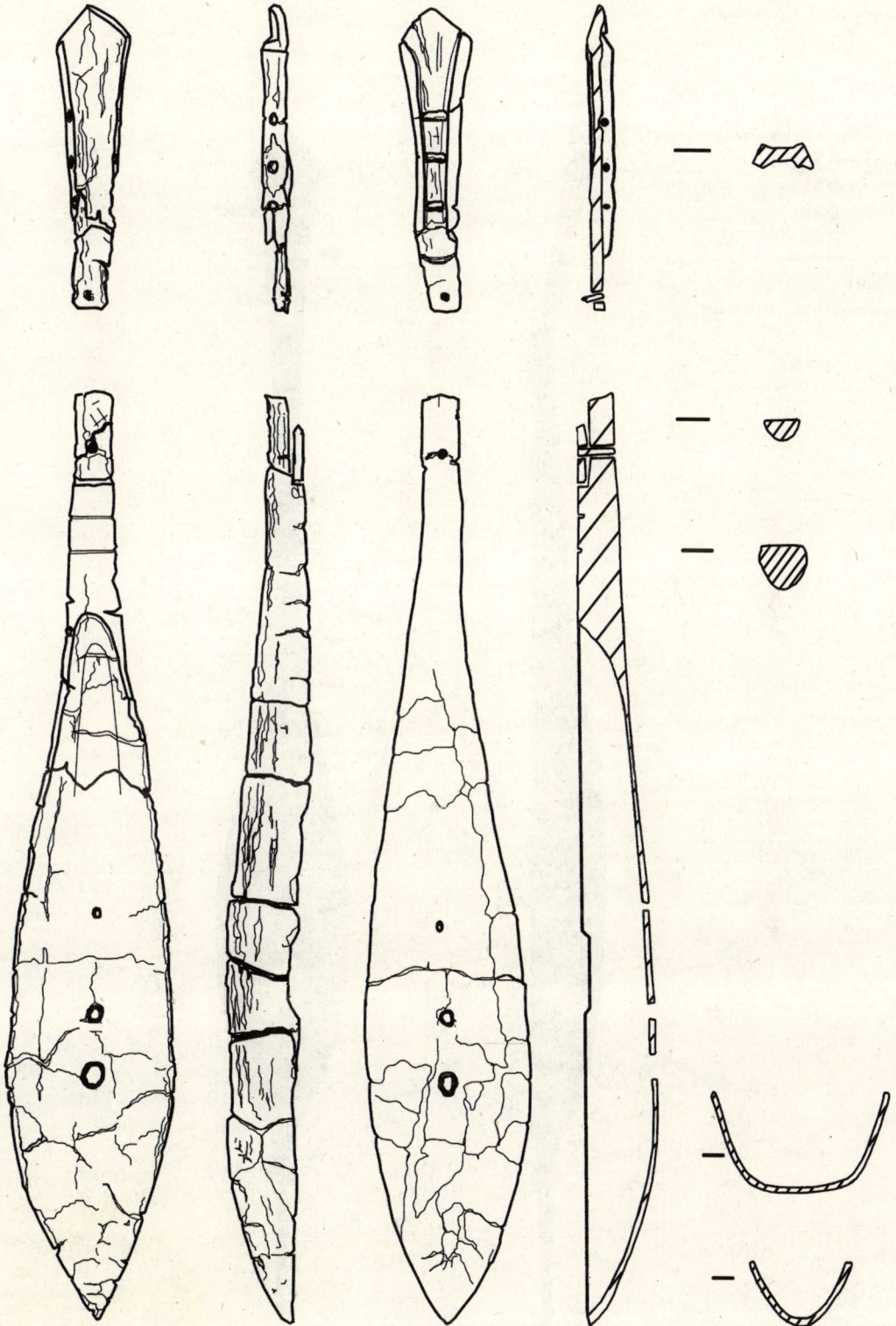

Fig. 3

1. Головка грифа
2. Колки
3. Отверстие для выхода струн
4. Лад
5. Гриф
6. Струны
7. Корнус
8. Верхняя дека (кожаная мембрана)
9. Деревянная вставка
10. Подставка (порожек) под струны
11. Нижняя дека
12. Резонаторные отверстия
13. Струнодержатель
14. Отверстие для стержня
15. Подставка под инструмент

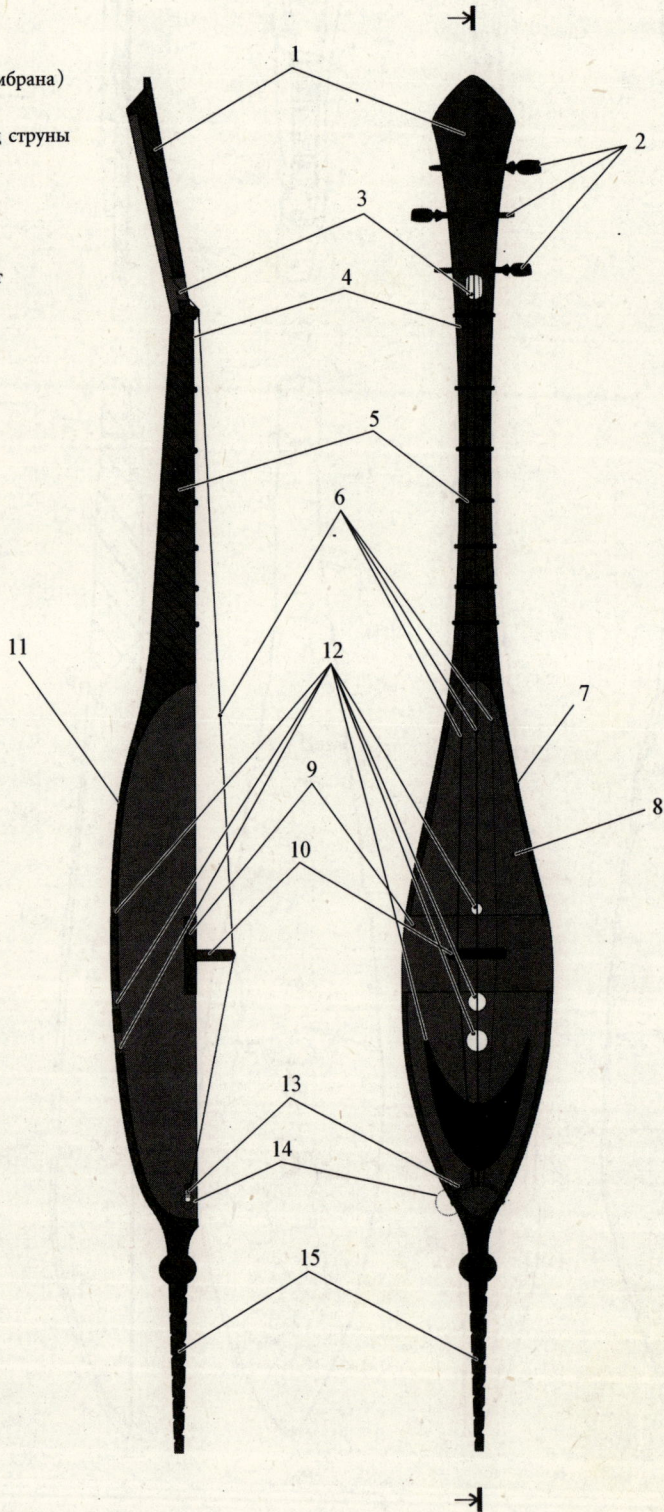

Fig. 4

Shallow cuts with the right angles were made in the sides of the central part of the body (see Fig. 4). Apparently, those were the grooves for a wooden insertion intended to be a holder for the string rest.

The string pins were placed in such a way that the strings had to pass through a hole or three holes to t rear side of a fingerboard somewhere in its missing part (see Fig. 4). The head with the pins were apparent placed at a small angle to the fingerboard plane to prevent the strings from touching each other.

The stops were separated on the fingerboard with the help of cuts and probably tendons or horseha inserted into them. There were 5 or 6 stops including the missing part of the fingerboard (see Fig. 4).

The question of an upper sounding board presence is still unresolved. When the instrument was foun there were no traces of that in the grave. But at least a leather board had to be there. Otherwise, the thre resonator holes in the rear side of the instrument are useless.

An interesting part of the instrument is a twisted wooden rod with a broken edged little cup (see Fig. 4) This object lay under the dish apart from the kobyz but both of them were obviously connected. Apparently it was an instrument rest which had to be leant against the ground to provide the instrument with: 1 necessary steadiness; 2) the vertical position; and 3) to prevent the instrument from injury while contactin the earth.

Kobyz from Ust-Kurdium

An instrument allied with our kobyz, which also comes from the Golden Horde nomadic interment, is kept in a museum somewhere upon the Volga (see Fig. 5). Its condition is worse than that of the instrument from Kirovo so we cannot describe the construction of that instrument in detail.

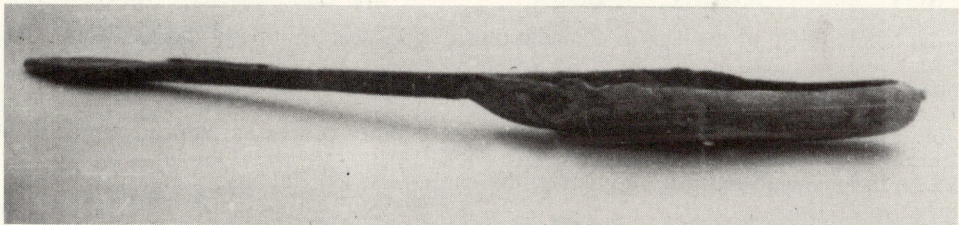

Fig. 5

That is all that we know about the finds of bowed instruments so far. No other kinds of musical instruments have been found in medieval nomadic burials.

Peculiarities of the Instrument Sound

Taking into consideration the design philosophy of the instrument from Kirovo it may be defined as the first tenor kobyz close to an Altaic instrument ikili (the first tenor). The pitch of the instrument from Kirovo was probably the fourth because it was the pitch that corresponded to the tonal system of the nomadic Turkic and Mongol bowed string instruments.

The first tenor kobyz must have got a pleasant muffled chest sound. When playing a songful melody a ...or sounds harmoniously with a distinctive twang overtone. If the Kirovo kobyz (the first tenor) played in ...modern orchestra it would fill the middle and the low registers favouring a sonorous and rich harmony.

It is most convenient to play an instrument like the kobyz when sitting on a small eminence with the legs ...ossed. It enhances the steadiness of the instrument while playing. Therefore, playing the kobyz was like ...aying a modern double bass when a bow moves virtually perpendicular to the kobyz which is positioned ...rtically or slightly inclined to the left.

Peculiarities of the Golden Horde Nomads' Culture

Resting upon the historical ethnography data we may conclude.

1. Apparently, the main musical instrument of medieval Turks was a kobyz which probably existed in ...vo forms: a bowed string instrument and a plucked string instrument. Both kinds had a common name for a ...ng time. Therefore, it is often difficult to distinguish one from another in written and graphic sources.

2. Nomadic musicians-travellers were not only players of well-known folk (tribal and kin) songs but ...lso improvisers on the given or their own themes.

3. Similar to all folk musical cultures of pentatonic pitch, the music of Turkic nomads of the Golden ...lorde has its own distinctive characteristics.

4. Melodies of the East European nomads of the 13th— the 14th centuries are of narrow range and rarely ...xceed an octave interval. In fact, the nature of the folk songs was not very diverse. Mostly they were ...houghtful, pensive, lyrical songs. A harmonic accompaniment to singing with the kobyz usually consists of ...he consonances of the fourth, the fifth and sometimes the big sixth and the little seventh. This may be ...xplained by the tonal system of the Turkic nomadic music of Eastern Europe of the 13th— the 14th centuries.

5. A missionary role of the World religions (whether it was Islam, Christianity or Buddhism), ...levelopment of urban tendencies, sedentarization and some other processes induced by civilization had a ...negative effect on the nomadic musical tradition at the end of the 19th century. Largely, because of this we ...have almost lost musical culture heritage of medieval nomads.

There is no evidence of this in written sources either. Neither book miniatures nor wall painting of ...temples and palaces contain images of a kobyz or similar instruments. However, kobyzes are mentioned in ...numerous heroic epic poems. For example, a kobyz is mentioned in a "My Grandfather Korkut's Book" — ...the ancient Turkic epos comprising ancient folk legends of the 10th— the 15th centuries — which tells us about ...Korkut — the inventor of song and kobyz playing. According to the legend, he had lived for over 200 years ...until his kobyz stopped playing.

Conclusion

A composition of musical instruments, their construction and sound abilities are interwoven with peculiarities of styles and genres of music. Therefore, careful consideration of musical instruments will perr to shed light not only upon the special features of nomadic folklore but also upon many other cultural a historic problems involved, and to point out the peculiarities of medieval nomads' mentality.

The kobyzes under discussion as well as different written and graphic sources indicate the oriental roots bowed string instruments like the violin.

Forgotten Images and Living Symbols:
in Search of Symbolic Tradition in Central Asian Rock art

Andrzej Rozwadowski

Institute of Eastern Studies

Adam Mickiewicz University

Poznan, Poland

Rock art in Central Asia has been created for thousands of years and is related to rich mosaic of diverse ethnic, religious and economic traditions which provided dynamic interactions throughout the history of this region: starting with the Indo-Iranian (Bronze Age), through Early Nomadic peoples (Iron Age) till Arabs' conquest (Rozwadowski 2004). Each of these cultural traditions had its distinctive features influencing the art on rocks allowing us to make attempts to decode the symbolic content of rock art of a given period. Any culture, however, at least potentially, is a dynamic system open for adopting new symbols into its old background. Assuming that it concerns also Central Asia, and there are plenty of examples of such circumstances, it can be suggested that also symbols expressed in rock art imagery can be analyzed from this point of view. Originally created in a given cultural context they could function in different symbolic situations being faced to processes of reinterpretations.

The majority of rock art in Central Asian is believed to be of prehistoric age, dating from the Mesolithic, through Neolithic, Bronze and Iron ages. Some images come also from recent times, but this recent historical-ethnographic rock art has rarely captured the interest of scholars — with exception of a handful of recent publications (e. g. Ranov 2002; Samashev 2002) — for two significant reasons. First, rock art studies traditionally have been the exclusive domain of archaeology and archaeologists have only recently started to look beyond strictly prehistoric and early historic phenomena; that is, to archaeological remains dating after the adoption of writing in a given region. Second, the subject matter of some of the more recent images (e. g. graffiti hearts crossed with an arrow accompanied by phrases like 'X loves Y') may suggest that this art is 'accidental' and is devoid of deeper meaning connected with local beliefs. In fact, examples of recent graffiti are not particularly common, especially when compared to motifs that are indisputably either prehistoric or early historic in age.

Historical-ethnographic rock art, however, warrants meticulous study. Recent rock art research in many parts of the world has revealed the existence of previously unrecognised ethnographic information, dating from the turn of the 19th century, and this has resulted in a radical improvement of our understanding of the art.

Significant examples of this come from South Africa (e. g. Lewis-Williams 1981) and North America (e. g. Whitley 2000), where analyses of information recorded by pioneer ethnographers have demonstrated the great value of this information for understanding both recent and ancient forms of rock art.

A detailed analysis of Central Asian ethnography reveals an important symbolic context relating to rock art, and it also sheds new light on the problem of rock art chronology. In particular, this concerns the feast of the New Year, commonly known as Navruz. It is celebrated during the Vernal Equinox (20, 21 or 22 of March) and marks the beginning of spring farming activities.

Navruz is culturally derived from Iranian tradition and initially widespread among the Iranian peoples of Central Asia. Its ultimate antiquity is difficult to determine unequivocally; however, if one considers that it is based on a universal and archaic calendrical system which divides the year into two halves (centred on the Vernal and Autumnal Equinoxes), then it seems plausible that it may extend back even to Indo-Iranian times (Eliade 1958: 49 – 92). With respect to astronomical phenomena, the Indo-Iranian year was divided into two seasons (a conclusion supported by analogous binary divisions in the Iranian and Indian traditions). The first season for Indo-Aryans was the time of 'spring, summer and rain', defined as *devayana*, the 'season (literally 'way') of gods.' Their second season correlates with our autumn and winter, and was the time of darkness and death known as *pitryana*, 'the season of fathers' (Krasnowolska 1998: 50). We do not know whether during Indo-Iranian times the onset of spring alone marked the beginning of the year. We do know, however, that this was the situation by the time of Zarathustra (if one accepts the calculation that he lived circa 6th century BCE). It is possible that Zarathustra himself named this festival *No Roz*, 'the New Day,' in middle Persian (Boyce 1975: 175). This custom has eventually disseminated into the celebrations of contemporary Central Asian nations. Among the Kazakhs, for example, *Nauryz* (Kazakh) was conjoined with the special day of *ulus* becoming 'The Day of the Nation,' *Ulys kun* (Karmisheva 1986: 50 – 51).

A significant element of the Navruz ritual festival is the ethnographically documented tradition of painting the outside and inside of house walls amongst the Tadjiks (see e. g. Kisliakov, Pisarchik 1970: Figs 32 and 61). Information about their three-day festivities was collected from them and other inhabitants of the mountainous regions of the Pamirs by, among others, Ivanov (1947). Their first day of celebrations was called 'the day of cleaning.' The second was 'the day of preparing a *bodja*' (a wheat cereal and meat dish), while the third was 'the day of greetings.' The activities conducted on the first day were especially significant. On this day women were the only ones who stayed inside the house. The men took all of the home furnishings outside and cleaned them, while the women started preparing *kumoch* breads. The women then took off their clothes and cleaned the inside of the house. Once finished, they washed themselves, put on clean clothes and began painting the walls. The designs included animals (goats, camels, horses, oxen), humans (horse riders, shepherds with sheep herds), plants, palm prints, solar-lunar symbols and geometric patterns (circles, rhombs, crosses, rosettes, wavy lines and others) (Fig. 1). When the paintings were completed the women took the bread from the fire and everyone was invited into the 'new' house.

House wall paintings were mainly within the women's domain, but in some villages men and children

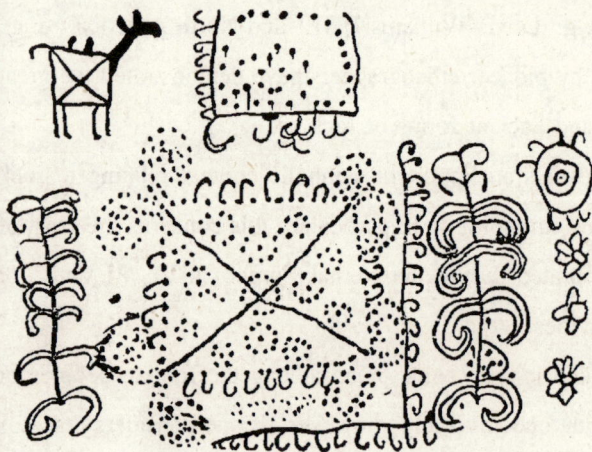

Fig. 1   Paintings of house wall in the village Sokhcharv
(after Andreev 1928).

(Jasiewicz, Rozwadowski 1998: 290, 2001).

also painted them (Ivanov 1947: 82). Men usually decorated the front walls of houses, while the main room containing the hearth was the women's task. Some of Ivanov's informants claimed that women specialised in plant and ornamental motifs while the men made animal images. Other informants claimed that all of the motifs inside the house were the work of women alone, with the exception of goat paintings. The most interesting fact, however, is that, as the women were busy decorating the house walls, the men sometimes visited sacred spots away from the house where they painted pictures on rocks

This is particularly valuable information since there is one other known source that connects the Navruz wall painting tradition with rock art: a photograph taken at the end of the 19th century by Leon Barszczewski (Fig. 2; see also Bero 1983; Jasiewicz 1994). It shows a group of Tadjiks standing in front of a house, with an oval painting (horizontally divided and filled with dots) visible on the house wall. Although there is no known commentary on this photograph by Barszczewski, it is highly possible that it is an example of Navruz paintings. What emphasises its great importance, however, is the fact that the Zaraut-Kamar grotto, located in this same region, contains a strikingly similar rock painting (Fig. 3). The great similarity between the two paintings suggests that they may date even to the same approximate time of around the end of the 19th century.

Formozov (1965, 1969) was the first to point out the analogy between the Zaraut-Kamar rock painting and the Tadjik wall paintings, although, basing on some parallels between the wall paintings and a small number of archaeological finds dating from the middle of the first millennium BCE, he suggested (Formozov 1969: 78) that part of Zaraut-Kamar paintings were relics of the Iron Age.

Fig. 2   Painted oval motif on the house wall as photographed by Leon Barszczewski in the late XIX century. The contour of the painting was digitally enhanced.

The fact that Tadjiks have inhabited southern Uzbekistan throughout historical times favours the hypothesis that the Zaraut-Kamar paintings were created in connection with Navruz. Equally important, Arabic inscriptions are painted on the same rock surface in the grotto: as Ivanov (1947: 82) noted, poems or fragments of prayers were painted on house walls along with the Navruz designs. Furthermore, there are more painted Arabic inscriptions in another small rock shelter in the Zaraut Valley which confirms the paintings were made in this region during historical times. All these painted areas emphasise the sacred character of the Zaraut-Sai valley, which may have been a local *mazar* (Arabic, 'place of reverence, homage' — Sukhareva 1975: 87).

There are also ancient bull paintings at Zaraut-Kamar (see Fig. 4). This raises the possibility that the oval painting in the niche may have symbolic connections with these bulls. During the Navruz rite the bull is identified with general concepts of welfare and fertility. In Uzbekistan people believe in 'the holy bull,' a harbinger of good luck. After the sunset on the last day of the year, families go to the nearby hills expecting the holy bull to appear. Accordin to some beliefs its body consists of cosmic light, his horns are golden and legs silver, and it draws a ca holding the moon. He only appears, however, very briefly and visually spotting him is quite difficult to d (Berezikov 1991: 236). Another Navruz rite worth noting involves the bringing of oxen to the house. The are fed with ritual foods, adorned, and led in a procession which precedes the ploughing (Antonova, Chv

10 cm

Fig. 3 Painting (red colour) in the Zaraut-Kamar rock shelter situated below composition of humans and animals shown in Fig. 4. Traced by author.

Fig. 4 Main composition in Zaraut-Kamar (paintings in red). Traced by author.

1983：28；Krasnowolska 1998：72). Ox symbolism is also rooted in archaic aspects of power and fertility：the animal is strongly associated with the mythological figure of Boboi Dhekon, and is treated as an ancestor and guardian of farmers (Krasnowolska 1998：121). The relationship of the bull to fertility in the large sense of the term — from the procreation of people, through the creation of plants and animals, to the creation of the world — extends back to Indo-Iranian times (Rozwadowski 2003). Perhaps, it is for this reason that the ancient Zaraut-Kamar bull paintings may have been influential in the selection of this rock shelter for the painting of contemporary Navruz oval motifs. Moreover, the analysis of the Navruz ritual suggests that this motif as well as a number of other paintings executed at this time had a magical significance related to breeding and fertility magic (Jasiewicz, Rozwadowski 2001).

Given the numerous unresolved questions about the chronology of putative Stone Age rock paintings (Rozwadowski, Huzanazarov 1999), it is then possible to consider that some of the Zaraut-Kamar painted motifs are not very old. The recognition of a possible connection between the Zaraut Valley rock art and the Navruz rituals suggests there must be a re-evaluation of Central Asian rock art chronology. The hitherto predominant belief that the paintings are the oldest manifestations of Central Asian rock art clearly must be independently verified. To cite one example, rock paintings found in 1980 in the Sangi-Djiumon and the Aksakal-Atasai valleys (Nuratau, central Uzbekistan) are considered by some scholars to date to the Neolithic and the Bronze Age (Hudjanazarov 1992：154；Shirinov, Khujanasarov 1998：54). This conclusion is based on similarities between geometric ceramic decorations from dated archaeological sites, and the geometric rock paintings, mainly triangular in form (Fig. 5). The paintings in these valleys, however, may also be connected to recent Navruz rituals：a major component of the Navruz wall paintings are geometric designs. Ivanov (1947：82) describes "circles, circles with a cross inside, rosettes, 'brackets,' rhombs and other geometric patterns." Some Sangi-Djiumon paintings, for example, consist of 'concentric' triangles (Fig. 5) and these are similar to Navruz motifs. Notably, this same triangular imagery is also common on *tumor* talismans, which are popular in

Fig. 5 Paintings in Sangi-Djiumon. Traced by author.

Central Asia and are thought to protect against evil forces. The *tumor* is often triangular in shape and triangles are sewn onto it. Equally interesting is the fact that these talismans are left as offerings at sacred places or *mazars* (Abramzon 1978：50), and the Sangi-Djiumon valley is certainly such a place.

Moreover, the colour of the Sangi-Djiumon paintings are still relatively intense and not faded. This, therefore, supports the contention that they are of a relatively recent origin, particularly when we take into account its constant exposure to the environment. Additionally, the composition as a whole appears to have been created using a pattern. The ethnographic literature again indicates that patterns were used for wall paintings during the Navruz.

Rock paintings apparently related to Navruz are also found in the nearby Aksakal-Atasai Valley where a spiral (Fig. 6) and human handprints are represented in a rockshelter. Leaving painted handprints on house walls was a common Navruz custom. According to an inhabitant of Vir village, leaving palm prints at this holy time was necessary to avoid the risk of death in the coming year.

Fig. 6   Stone with painted spiral (red) partly covered by contemporary paintings (white). Photo by author.

The study of Zaraut-Kamar rock paintings through the prism of the Navruz ritual as presented in this paper was limited to territory of south and central Uzbekistan. Navruz rites, however, were known on much wider territory. It cannot be excluded that the ideas put here can appear of significance for rock art studies also in other parts of Central Asia.

References

Abramzon, S. M. 1978. Predmety kulta kazakhov, kirgizov i karakalpakov. In S. M. Abramzon and L. I. Lavrov (eds), *Materialnaya kultura i khoziaystvo narodov Kavkaza, Srednei Azii i Kazakhstana* ("Sbornik Muzeia Antropologii i Etnografii", vol. 34), 44 – 67. Leningrad: Nauka.

Andreev, M. S. 1928. *Ornament gornykh tadzhikov i kirgizov Pamira*. Tashkent.

Antonova, J. V. and Chvir, L. A. 1983. Tadzhikske viesennie igry i obriady i indoiranskaya mifologiya. In R. S. Lipets (ed.), *Folklor i istoricheskaya etnografiya*, 21 – 44. Moskva: Nauka.

Berezikov, E. 1991. *Legendy i tainy Uzbekistana*. Tashkent: Izdatelstvo Literatury i Iskusstva imeni Gafura Gulyama.

Bero, M. 1983. Obraz kultury Azji Środkowej w materiałach Leona Barszczewskiego. In Z. Jasiewicz (ed.), *Kultura i życie społeczne Azji Środkowej*, 23 – 43. Poznań: Wydawnictwo Uniwersytetu im. Adama Mickiewicza.

Boyce, M. 1975. *A History of Zoroastrianism. Volume one: the Early Period.* Leiden-Köln: E. J. Brill.

Eliade, M. 1958. *Patterns in comparative religion.* London, New York.

Formozov, A. A. 1965. The rock paintings of Zaraut-Kamar, Uzbekistan. *Rivista di Scienze Preistroiche* 20: 63 - 83.

Formozov, A. A. 1969. *Ocherki po pervobytnomu iskusstvu. Naskalnye izobrazheniya i kamennie izvayaniya epokhi kamnia i bronzy na territorii SSSR.* Moskwa: Nauka.

Hudjanazarov, M. 1992. Naskalnye risunki Sangidjumonsaya. In *Mezhdunarodnaya konferentsiya "Sredniaia Aziya i mirovaya tsivilizatsiya"* (tezisy dokladov), 153 - 154. Tashkent.

Ivanov, S. V. 1947. K voprosu ob izuchenii stennykh rospisei gornykh tadzhikov. *Kratkie Soobshcheniya Instituta Etnografii AN SSSR* 2: 80 - 84.

Jasiewicz, Z. 1994. Leon Barszczewski's collection of photographs from Russian Turkestan and the Bukharan Emirate as a historical and etnographical source. In I. Baldauf and M. Friedrich (eds), *Bamberger Zentralasienstudien. Konferenzakten WSCAS IV*, 361 - 368. Berlin: Klaus Schwratz Verlag.

Jasiewicz, Z., Rozwadowski, A. 1998. Malowidło naskalne z groty Zaraut-Kamar a malowidło na ścianie domu z końca XIX wieku. *Lud* 82: 279 - 297.

Jasiewicz, Z., Rozwadowski, A. 2001. Rock paintings — wall paintings: new light on art tradition in Central Asia. *Rock Art Research* 18 (1): 3 - 14.

Karmisheva, B. Kh. 1986. Statsionarnoe zhilishche uzbekov-lokaitsev (seredina 1940 - nachalo 1950 godov). In V. A. Litvinskii (ed.), *Etnografiya Tadjikistana*, 11 - 28. Dushanbe: Donish.

Kisliakov, N. A. and Pisarchik, A. K. 1970 (eds), *Tadjiki Karategina i Darvaza*, vol. 2. Dushanbe: Donish.

Krasnowolska, A. 1998. Some key figures of Iranian calendar mythology. Winter and Spring. Kraków: Universitas.

Lewis-Williams, J. D. 1981. *Believing and seeing: symbolic meanings in southern San rock paintings*, Academic Press, London-San Francisco.

Ranov, V. A. 2002. Gora rubobov v Lyangare (Badakhshan). In V. V. Bobrov (ed.), *Pervobitnaya arkheologiya: chelovek i iskusstvo*, 63 - 68. Novosibirsk: Kemerovskii Gosudarstvenniy Universitet, Institut Arkheologii i etnografii CO RAN.

Rozwadowski, A. 2003. *Indoirańczycy — sztuka i mitologia. Petroglify Azji Środkowej.* Poznań: Wydawnictwo Naukowe UAM.

Rozwadowski, A. 2004. *Symbols through time: interpreting the rock art of Central Asia*, Institute of Eastern Studies, Adam Mickiewicz University, Poznań.

Rozwadowski, A. and Huzanazarov (Khujanazarov), M. 1999. The earliest rock art of Uzbekistan in its Central Asian context: some dilemmas with chronological estimations in Central Asian rock art studies. In M. Strecker and P. Bahn (eds), *Dating and the earliest known rock art*, 79 - 82. Oxford: Oxbow Books.

Samashev, Z. 2002. Shamanic motifs in the petroglyphs of Eastern Kazakhstan. In A. Rozwadowski with M. M. Kośko (eds), *Spirits and Stones: Shamanism and rock art in Central Asia and Siberia*, 33 - 48. Poznań: Instytut Wschodni UAM.

Shirinov, T. Sh. and Khujanasarov (Hudjanazarov), M. 1998. The rock pictures of Uzbekistan. *Bulletin of SCST of the Republic of Uzbekistan* 2: 51 - 63.

Sukhareva, O. A. 1975. Perezhitki demonologii i shamanstva u ravninnykh Tadjikov. In G. P. Snesraev and V. N. Basilov (eds), *Domusulmanskie verovaniya i obriady v Srednei Azii*, 5 - 93. Moskva: Nauka.

Whitley, D. 2000. *The art of the shaman: rock art of California.* Salt Lake City: University of Utah Press.

图书在版编目（ＣＩＰ）数据

    吐鲁番学研究 ：第三届吐鲁番学暨欧亚游牧民族的
起源与迁徙国际学术研论会论文集 / 新疆吐鲁番学研究院
编. -- 上海 ：上海古籍出版社，2010.5
    ISBN 978-7-5325-5536-9

    Ⅰ. ①吐… Ⅱ. ①新… Ⅲ. ①游牧－民族历史－吐鲁
番地区－国际学术会议－文集 Ⅳ. ①K284.5-53

    中国版本图书馆CIP数据核字(2010)第035538号

吐鲁番学研究

第三届吐鲁番学暨欧亚游牧民族的起源与迁徙
国际学术研讨会论文集

新疆吐鲁番学研究院　编

上海世纪出版股份有限公司
上 海 古 籍 出 版 社　出版、发行

（上海瑞金二路272号　邮政编码200020）

    （1）网址：www.guji.com.cn
    （2）E-mail: gujil@guji.com.cn
    （3）易文网网址：www.ewen.cc

新华书店上海发行所发行经销　上海惠顿实业公司印刷

开本889x1194 1/16　印张58.5　插页5　字数1,420,000
2010 年 5 月第 1 版　2010 年 5 月第 1 次印刷
印数：1-1,500

ISBN978-7-5325-5536-9
K·1275　定价：258.00元

事上都具有重要地位。《魏略·西戎传》记载"从玉门关西出,发都护井,回三陇沙北头,经居卢仓,从沙西井转西北,过龙堆,到故楼兰,转西诣龟兹,至葱领"。记有泰始四年(268)留屯高昌之部兵逃亡簿籍的楼兰文书反映出当时高昌处于楼兰西域长史的管辖之下,则楼兰与高昌有密切的往来,两地之间的交通应是经由墨山国直接翻越库鲁克塔格山。[①] 楼兰绿洲为当时中原控扼西域的咽喉之地。楼兰古城外至今依稀可辨的古河道,纵横交错,[②]连同出土的汉简文书反映了楼兰绿洲驻军屯田的状况,繁盛一时。现所见楼兰文书最后的时间是前凉建兴十八年(330),目前国内学界主要据此认为楼兰绿洲废弃于 4 世纪中叶,成为荒无人烟之地,并对其原因进行了深入探讨。[③] 孟凡人先生则提出楼兰绿洲的最后废弃或在 5 世纪左右,楼兰绿洲的废弃并不等于完全没有人在此活动,很有可能尚有少部分土著居民在这一带游牧。[④] 另有学者认为直到唐代,焉耆王请求唐朝重开"大碛路"也反映出楼兰绿洲并未彻底消失。[⑤] 但重开此路,焉耆需要求助于唐朝,说明从焉耆经由楼兰至玉门关沿途险恶,没有强大势力对该路线的维护,则难以通行。这反映出楼兰绿洲生态环境较以前恶化,人口流散。

位于楼兰绿洲之北、库鲁克塔格山中的绿洲墨山国,虽然不如楼兰绿洲环境变迁之剧烈,但应同样经历了人口流散的问题。[⑥] 与楼兰绿洲同样成为萧条之地。

在此需说明的是,罗新先生所谓的"墨山国之路"并未就此消失。[⑦] 因为依傍孔雀河的营盘一直是孔雀河东西、南北交通的重镇。斯文·赫定在营盘考察时,曾提到:

> 在路上我们遇到了由 4 个商人组成的一个商队,他们刚刚从吐鲁番来到营盘一带。从他们嘴里,我们得到了如下情况:他们是车尔臣的居民,一个多月以前从这条路前往吐鲁番,他们到那儿是为了买汉人的银器、毛驴、骡子、瓷器和其他中国商品,并打算在车尔臣出售这些东西。他们预计还得再走 25 天才能到家。他们是 10 天前离开吐鲁番上路的,沿途曾经在布得审图,阿齐克布拉克,阿尔皮姆,辛格尔,一个叫不出名字的泉边,阿斯干布拉克,托克拉克布拉克和营盘宿营。……再向南,据说有狭长的沙包,到铁干里克的路穿过那里。[⑧]

由铁干里克可直接到达鄯善和且末的统治中心。所以即使楼兰绿洲在当时消失,从高昌仍能经营盘至鄯善都城。这比绕道库尔勒和焉耆要近,但绕道焉耆,沿途能保证行路者及其牲畜的补给。这也反映出翻

---

① 参见罗新:《墨山国之路》,《国学研究》第五卷,北京大学出版社,1998 年,第 501~503 页。

② 陈汝国:《楼兰古城历史地理若干问题探讨》,《新疆大学学报》1984 年第 3 期,第 55 页。

③ 黄文房:《楼兰王国的兴衰及其原因的探讨》,《罗布泊科学考察与研究》,科学出版社,1987 年,第 315~318 页;张莉:《楼兰古绿洲的河道变迁及其原因探讨》,《中国历史地理论丛》2001 年第 1 期;王炳华:《沧桑楼兰》,浙江文艺出版社,2002 年,第 125~129 页;另外,罗新先生曾提出孔雀河于北朝以后改道,楼兰绿洲消失,从而导致经由楼兰的交通路线发生变化。(罗新:《墨山国之路》,《国学研究》第五卷,北京大学出版社,1998 年,第 503 页。)但未见具体论证。

④ 孟凡人:《楼兰新史》,光明日报出版社,1990 年,第 271 页。另,孟凡人先生根据《水经注》成书于 5 世纪末 6 世纪初,已将楼兰称为故城,所以认为楼兰城最后废弃或在公元 5 世纪左右。楼兰城一带最终荒无人烟可能在入唐以后,见孟凡人:《楼兰新史》,光明日报出版社,1990 年,第 269~271 页。

⑤ 具体论证参见郑炳林:《试论唐贞观年间所开大碛路——兼评西域史地研究论稿》,《敦煌学辑刊》1985 年第 1 期;王素:《高昌史稿——交通编》,第 143~146 页,第 146 页注②。

⑥ 参见罗新:《墨山国之路》,第 505 页。

⑦ 罗新先生认为 442 年沮渠无讳从焉耆东北趣高昌反映出当时从鄯善至高昌不再经由墨山国之路了。见《墨山国之路》,第 505 页。

⑧ 斯文·赫定著,王安洪、崔延虎译:《罗布泊探秘》,新疆人民出版社,1997 年,第 33 页。

越库鲁克塔格山脉的艰难,库鲁克塔格山与较为荒凉的楼兰地区成为高昌、焉耆与鄯善地区的生态划界。继阚氏、北凉余绪之后,柔然、高车等先后据有高昌,而吐谷浑据有鄯善正是这种生态环境阻隔的反映。

上述系 5 世纪前,塔里木盆地南部与东部绿洲普遭废弃,这与当地极其严酷的自然环境密切相关。南部和东部为盆地中最干旱地区,降水量小,蒸发量大,生态环境极其脆弱。[①] 文书中有关水资源缺乏、借用及对树木的保护都是对此种状况的反映。[②] 5 世纪时,这些地区荒凉至极,甚或沦为沙漠,成为地区间的自然分界,这也是后来柔然等控制下的高昌麹氏政权"南接河南",[③]吐谷浑"西邻于阗,北接高昌",[④]嚈哒"北尽敕勒,东被于阗",[⑤]在西域形成三足鼎立之势的自然环境的原因。

综上,公元 5 世纪,塔里木盆地诸绿洲国的存在状况主要是政治形势变动不居、经济总体上有所发展、生态环境较以前恶化。政治形势的变化使各游牧势力在西域的角逐出现阶段性的变化。5 世纪初期,在塔里木盆地诸绿洲国无强大外力统治的情况下,柔然在西域的扩张甚为顺利;中期时,塔里木盆地由北魏与北凉残余势力经营,柔然在西域的势力一度受阻;随着两支力量的退出或消失,柔然独霸西域;5 世纪末期,塔里木盆地再次陷入动乱无强首的境地,除高车、柔然外,嚈哒、吐谷浑也趁机在西域扩张势力,塔里木盆地最终成为各方力量的汇聚中心。此间,各绿洲国为角逐于此的游牧势力提供经济上的补充,使各游牧势力在西域的角逐更为激烈。而塔里木盆地绿洲国生态环境的状况,深刻影响着各游牧势力在西域的角逐扩张,最终使柔然、嚈哒及高车、吐谷浑等游牧势力在西域形成鼎立的格局。

---

① 参见中国科学院塔克拉玛干沙漠综合科学考察队《塔克拉玛干沙漠地区水资源评价与利用》,科学出版社,1993 年,第 4 ~ 11 页;中国科学院新疆综合考察队、中国科学院地理研究所编:《新疆水文地理》,科学出版社,1966 年。
② 佉卢文 347、368、482、502、604 号,见林梅村:《沙海古卷——中国所出佉卢文书(初集)》,第 96、103 ~ 104、125、121 ~ 122、165 ~ 166 页;林梅村:《新疆尼雅发现的佉卢文契约》,载《西域文明——考古、民族、语言和宗教新论》,东方出版社,1995 年,第 164 ~ 188 页;楼兰文书 190 号,见林梅村《楼兰尼雅出土文书》,文物出版社,1985 年,第 51 页。
③ 《梁书·西北诸戎传》。
④ 《梁书·河南传》。
⑤ 《洛阳伽蓝记》卷五。

大蒙古国时期商贸政策的演变

——兼论草原之路对蒙古文明进程的影响

刘中玉

中国社会科学院历史研究所

13 世纪初,大蒙古国的建立不仅仅意味着蒙古高原内部的统一,同时也可视为高原与其他各文明区域的联系与交往进入一个崭新的时期。其特点是以强劲的武力征服作后盾,利用军队来开辟天险,重新贯通草原之路,从而使游牧经济与农耕地区的经济发生密切的联系,使刚刚脱胎于部落的大蒙古国在文化、经济、行政管理等方面都获得了较大的提升,在一定程度上对维持相对松散的游牧帝国和推动蒙古社会的文明进程起到了重要作用,但客观上也成为加速帝国分裂的原因之一。在此,本文拟先从草原贸易的必要性谈起,针对蒙古国时期商贸政策演进的具体情况以及相关背景展开论述,同时兼论草原之路的贯通对蒙古文明进程的影响问题。

一、草原贸易的必要性

"草原虽然没有内部贸易的经济需求,但却有对外贸易的社会必要",[1]这是由游牧经济的单一性特点所决定的。由于草原自然环境的限制,生活于斯地的游牧民,不仅时受饥馑之虞,而且经常面临着被其他部族或国家吞并灭亡的危险。因此要在弱肉强食的世界中赢得生存权或维持强权,必须通过与周边定居文明的交流和交换来获得经济上、文化上的提升,来增强自己在军事上、政治上的实力和地位。而在游牧国家成立后,由于游牧经济本身的薄弱,不足以维持广大的国家组织,可汗要想巩固国家的经济基础和他以及统治氏族的权力基础,除了进行掠夺和发展贸易外别无他途,否则国家便会分崩离析,或回归到原有部族林立的状态,或以另一氏族为核心而形成一个新的政权组织。[2] 所以,和战相续一直是游牧民族与定居民族交往的主要特点,这是史学界的普遍共识。[3] 不过,相对于掠夺和战争来说,贸易互市是主流。刚刚崛起的蒙古便同样面临着这种情况。蒙古高原虽然统一了,但其内部资源有限,原有的生产体系不足以应

---

① Owen Lattimore, *Inner Asian Frontiers of China*, p. 69, Beacon press, 1962.

② 田村实造:《中国王朝の研究》(上),第35~56页,东洋史研究会1964年;护雅夫:《游牧民族史上における征服王朝の意义》,《岩波讲座世界历史》(九),1970年,第12~17页。

③ 如格列科夫、雅库博夫斯基认为,"在封建时代,凡是农业社会与游牧社会毗邻而处的地方,为掠取战利品的军事侵袭总是与和平贸易关系相交替。"(参见余大钧译:《金帐汗国兴衰史》,第22页,商务印书馆,1985年。)萧启庆在综诸家之说的基础上对北亚游牧民族南侵各种原因进行归纳,认为游牧民族南侵的经济因素在于:"深深植根于他们的经济体系之中。游牧经济有对自然变化的脆弱性、对农耕社会的倚存性和工艺文明的迟进性。对农耕社会的贸易与掠夺,是游牧民族解决经济问题的两个变换手段。从表面看来,无论为解决因气候变化所造成的经济困难或为取得游牧社会所不生产的奢侈品,掠夺都不失为一便捷的手段。……和平的朝贡与贸易,则是游牧民解决对农耕社会经济依存问题的另一方式。这种贸易的发展,往往有赖于武力为后盾,要求贸易不遂,常迫使游牧民族发动战争。但贸易不遂不是造成游牧民族南侵的唯一原因,而游牧民族在武力上的优势,也未必是与农耕国家建立贸易关系的唯一要件。"(萧启庆:《北亚民族南侵各种原因的检讨》,《元代史新探》,新文丰出版公司,1983年,第303~322页。)

对庞大的国家机器的运转,而掠夺和战争只能解一时之困,要想维持内部稳定,发展商贸才是长久之策。

成吉思汗对此有着清醒的认识,他在答复花拉子模沙的国书中便明确讲到双方通商的重要性,甚至认为这"关系到世界福利",只有当双方共同承担建设商路、开展商贸的义务,则"就没有(人)动(坏)念头了,也没有(人)支持纷争和叛乱了"。① 为此他采取了一系列的措施,如设置岗哨、优待商人等。其后大蒙古国的后嗣之君窝阔台、贵由、蒙哥亦非常重视商贸,并在成吉思汗的基础上,进一步完善了大蒙古国时期的商贸政策,确立了有效的管理秩序。

二、大蒙古国时期商贸政策的演变

大蒙古国时期商贸政策的演变是与蒙古同周边地区交流的日益密切、受东西方文明影响的日趋加深分不开的,它经历了一个由粗放到秩序化的过程。具体体现在道路开辟、驿站设立、城市建设、商人和市场管理等几个方面。

商路的开辟和驿站之设的目的主要有二:军事和商用。成吉思汗充分认识到商贸的紧迫性,他不仅在商路上设置了岗哨,而且颁布札撒,"凡进入他的国土内的商人,应一律发给凭照,而值得汗受纳的货物,应连同物主一起遣送给汗",以保证商人的旅行。对于到来的商人,则在纯白色的毡帐里接待他们,以示尊敬。② 同时,他对开辟新商路也十分用心。草原统一后,西逃的乃蛮部王子屈出律攫取了哈喇契丹的政权,控制了当时的天山以南地区,阻断了通向中国内地的商路。而成吉思汗此时的势力已扩及七河以北,有能力开辟新的商路。③ 前文已述,成吉思汗与他西方的邻居花拉子模缔结亲睦关系的目的很明确,就是通商。所以在接待了从花拉子模忽毡(Khojend)前来的三个兼具使节身份的商人后,先后向对方派出了使节和商队(1218 年成吉思汗派遣一个 450 人的伊斯兰商队去花拉子模),希望从控制着七河以南商业通道的花拉子模那里打开缺口,获得伊斯兰世界的物质用品(后因花拉子模沙的轻率,杀死商队并扣留财物,导致双方关系迅速恶化,升级为战争)。

但是,当时的岗哨是不固定的,管理也很混乱,一些使臣不仅经常延迟,而且沿途对百姓随意盘剥,使百姓不堪其苦,疲惫之甚,因此反抗不断。1238 年不花剌的塔剌必起义,除开蒙古统治者缺少管理经验以及包税商人的苛剥外,驿路之害也是一个主因。窝阔台亦认识到这一点,"我们使臣往来,使百姓也沿途(跟着)奔驰,往来的使臣其行程也要迟延,百姓人民也遭受痛苦"。为了革除这些弊端,窝阔台决定将岗哨固定,并征求宗王那颜尤其是察合台的意见,《蒙古秘史》载:"现在我们一律使它有一定的位置,由各处的千户,派出站户、马夫,在各个处所设置驿站。使臣无紧要事,不得沿着百姓(骚扰),要按照驿站奔驰。这些事情,是察乃、孛勒合答儿两个人想起来,向我们提议的。我想似乎可行。请察阿歹(察合台)哥哥裁断。这些所说的事体,如属当行,并且赞同的话,察阿歹哥哥(你)就作主吧。"察合台对此表示赞同,认为"在所有的(事体)之中,设置驿站(一)事,是最对的",并提议"我从这里迎着,把驿站接起来。再从这里派使臣到巴秃(拔都)那里,教巴秃也把他的驿站,迎着连接起来"。④ 于是在 1229 年 8 月,窝阔

---

① 《史集》第 1 卷第 2 分册,第 259 页。
② 《世界征服者史》(上),第 90 页。《史集》第 1 卷第 2 分册,第 258 页。
③ 巴托尔德著,耿世民译:《中亚简史》,中华书局,2005 年,第 40 页。
④ 《蒙古秘史》第 279 节,第 444 页。今参见《元史》卷 49,《兵志四》站"赤"条。